S0-BDL-457

THE LABOR RELATIONS PROCESS

Sixth Edition

William H. Holley, Jr.
Auburn University

Kenneth M. Jennings
University of North Florida

The Dryden Press
Harcourt Brace College Publishers
Fort Worth Philadelphia San Diego New York Orlando Austin San Antonio
Toronto Montreal London Sydney Tokyo

Acquisitions Editor	John Weimeister
Developmental Editor	Tracy Morse
Project Editor	Michele Tomiak
Art Director	Lora Knox
Production Manager	Jessica Wyatt
Picture and Rights Editor	Adele Krause
Executive Product Manager	Lisé Johnson
Copy Editor	Joan Harlan
Proofreader	Elizabeth Hallmark
Compositor	Graphic World
Text Type	10/12 New Caledonia

Portions of this work were published in previous editions.

Address for Editorial Correspondence
The Dryden Press, 301 Commerce Street, Suite 3700, Fort Worth, Texas 76102

Address for Orders
The Dryden Press, 6277 Sea Harbor Drive, Orlando, Florida 32887-6777
1-800-782-4479, or 1-800-433-0001 (in Florida)

ISBN: 0-03-018009-0
Library of Congress Catalog Card Number: 96-83790

Printed in the United States of America
9 0 1 2 3 4 5 039 9 8 7 6

The Dryden Press
Harcourt Brace College Publishers

To Betty, Jackie, Allison and Bret,
who hopefully have received at least
a portion of what they have given

The Dryden Press Series in Management

Anthony, Perrewé, and Kacmar
Strategic Human Resource Management
Second Edition

Bereman and Lengnick-Hall, Mark
Compensation Decision Making: A Computer-Based Approach

Bourgeois
Strategic Management: From Concept to Implementation

Bracker, Montanari, and Morgan
Cases in Strategic Management

Brechner
Contemporary Mathematics for Business and Consumers

Calvasina and Barton
Chopstick Company: A Business Simulation

Costin
Classic Readings in Strategy

Costin
Readings in Total Quality Management

Costin
Managing in the Global Economy: The European Union

Costin
Managing in the Global Economy: Latin America

Costin
Management Development and Training: A TQM Approach

Czinkota, Ronkainen, and Moffett
International Business
Fourth Edition

Czinkota, Ronkainen, Moffett, and Moynihan
Global Business

Daft
Management
Fourth Edition

Daft
Understanding Management

Dessler
Managing Organizations in an Era of Change

Foegen
Business Plan Guidebook
Revised Edition

Gatewood and Feild
Human Resource Selection
Third Edition

Gold
Exploring Organizational Behavior: Readings, Cases, Experiences

Greenhaus and Callanan
Career Management
Second Edition

Harris, Michael
Human Resource Management: A Practical Approach

Harris and DeSimone
Human Resource Development

Higgins and Vincze
Strategic Management: Text and Cases
Fifth Edition

Hills, Bergmann, and Scarpello
Compensation Decision Making
Second Edition

Hodgetts
Modern Human Relations at Work
Sixth Edition

Hodgetts and Kroeck
Personnel and Human Resource Management

Hodgetts and Kuratko
Effective Small Business Management
Fifth Edition

Holley and Jennings
The Labor Relations Process
Sixth Edition

Jauch and Coltrin
The Managerial Experience: Cases and Exercises
Sixth Edition

Kindler and Ginsburg
Strategic & Interpersonal Skill Building

Kirkpatrick and Lewis
Effective Supervision: Preparing for the 21st Century

Kuratko and Hodgetts
Entrepreneurship: A Contemporary Approach
Third Edition

Kuratko and Welsch
Entrepreneurial Strategy: Text and Cases

Lengnick-Hall, Cynthia, and Hartman
Experiencing Quality

Lewis
Io Enterprises Simulation

Long and Arnold
The Power of Environmental Partnerships

Morgan
Managing for Success

Ryan, Eckert, and Ray
Small Business: An Entrepreneur's Plan
Fourth Edition

Sandburg
Career Design Software

Vecchio
Organizational Behavior
Third Edition

Walton
Corporate Encounters: Law, Ethics, and the Business Environment

Zikmund
Business Research Methods
Fifth Edition

The Harcourt Brace College Outline Series

Pentico
Management Science

Pierson
Introduction to Business Information Systems

Sigband
Business Communication

Preface

The sixth edition of *The Labor Relations Process* reflects our original objective in writing the book: to provide students with a textbook that will generate an understanding of and appreciation for union-management relationships. We have attempted to involve the student with the subject matter and to create an interest in related issues that will continue after the student completes the course. A model of the labor relations process (Exhibit 1.2) is presented in the first chapter and expanded in subsequent chapters through extensive references to academics and practitioners that focus on real-world situations and concerns. This provides a balance between concepts and applications for the reader.

As with the first edition and all subsequent editions, the sixth edition of *The Labor Relations Process* continues to be the most comprehensive text on the market.

Features of the Sixth Edition

The sixth edition approaches our student involvement objective by enhancing our commitment to application, an emphasis that is unmatched by other textbooks in this area. We contend that application generates student interest in the subject matter while enabling students to demonstrate their understanding of concepts and principles and apply this information to real-world situations. These opportunities and related efforts should sharpen readers' communication skills, a desirable skill for any student, regardless of his or her academic major or intended occupation.

Application has been enhanced through new "Labor Relations in Action" features, National Labor Relations Board cases concerning potential unfair labor practices committed during the three phases of the labor relations process, and new arbitration cases. There are also two extensive application experiences at the end of the book (Bridgestone-Firestone labor dispute and the corporate organizing campaign at Food Lion), including an updated, computerized collective bargaining case. Also featured are in-depth treatments of labor-management conflict at the *New York Daily News* and an overtime grievance, both of which are recommended for advanced and/or graduate student analysis. The book has also maintained many of the previous edition's features: a focus on currency, ethics, international issues, and the "Labor Relations in Action" boxes:

- Currency. This edition offers many opportunities for readers to become involved with the current applications of the labor relations process. For example, recent collective bargaining occurred with management and union officials at American Airlines, Caterpillar, Major League Baseball, and General Motors.
- Ethics. Ethical issues and situations are integrated throughout the book and highlighted with marginal logos. Issues such as ethical considerations in bargaining behavior, union organizing, and termination of union advocates are discussed.
- International Labor. Chapter 15, the chapter that deals with international issues, has been updated and expanded to include changes in Canada, Mexico, and Germany as well as the effects of the North American Free-Trade Agreement.
- Labor Relations in Action. The "Labor Relations in Action" boxes integrate current events in labor relations and have been updated with several new applications, discussed next.

Key Chapter-by-Chapter Changes in the Sixth Edition

Each chapter has been extensively updated in terms of sources, laws and judicial decisions, studies, and statistics. Additional attention has been given to explaining the labor relations process and influences in Chapter 1 and indicating how this process operates in subsequent chapters. Following are some of the key changes to the sixth edition:

- Chapter 1. "Getting Online with Labor Relations Research" (introducing students to computerized search possibilities on current labor relations topics).
- Chapter 2. "NAFTA's Legislative Passage over Organized Labor's Opposition."
- Chapter 3. Updated assessment of the National Labor Relations Board with comments from its new chairperson, William B. Gould IV.
- Chapter 4. Updates on union membership and mergers and coverage of John Sweeney's election to the presidency of the AFL-CIO.
- Chapter 5. Union goals and courses of action and new union organizing strategies.
- Chapter 6. "Bargaining Cost Complexities from Five Negotiation Situations" and "Negotiations in Professional Basketball: Too Many Participants."

- Chapter 7. Trends in strikes and hiring striker replacements, proposed Workplace Fairness Act and Team Act, and President Clinton's Executive Order regarding striker replacements.
- Chapter 8. "Tough Contract Administration Questions."
- Chapter 9. "How Employer Promulgated Arbitration Differs from Arbitration Found in Labor Agreements."
- Chapter 10. "Arbitrators and Employee Theft: Proof and Penalty."
- Chapter 11. Updated trends in union security provisions and the relationships between unions and female and minority employees.
- Chapter 12. Strikes involving outsourcing (General Motors and Boeing) and "Bell South-Communications Workers of America Partnership."
- Chapter 13. "United Airlines' ESOP."
- Chapter 14. "Privatization of the Public Sector."
- Chapter 15. Updated union density and compensation costs in major countries.
- Chapter 16. New chapter: "The Labor Relations Process: Synthesis and Possibilities."

Supplementary Materials

The new *Instructor's Manual* includes chapter outlines, answers to end-of-chapter discussion questions, case notes, suggested student readings and term projects, and both instructors' and students' instructions for the Collective Bargaining Negotiations Exercise (available on disk). The *Test Bank* has been revised, updated, and expanded. The number of transparency masters has been increased.

A Computerized Test Bank, in IBM, Macintosh, or Windows format, is also available free to adopters. The Computerized Test Bank enables instructors to select, edit, and add test items and print tests for classroom use.

Five videos on two cassettes are available, showing workplace issues for union employees and managers on topics ranging from violence at work to the Americans with Disabilities Act and strikes. Also included is a special CBS report on the state of unions.

Harcourt Brace College Publishers may provide complimentary instructional aids and supplements or supplement packages to those adopters qualified under our adoption policy. Please contact your sales representative for more information. If as an adopter or potential user you receive supplements you do not need, please return them to your sales representative or send them to:

Attn: Returns Department
Troy Warehouse
465 South Lincoln Drive
Troy, MO 63379

Acknowledgments

We are especially grateful to the following professors for their reviews and suggestions on this revision: Todd Baker, Salt Lake Community College; Dr. Dennis W. Gibson, Troy State University; Zeinrab A. Karake, The Catholic University of America; Dr. Thomas W. Lloyd, Westmoreland County Community College; and Peter A. Veglahn, James Madison University.

We also extend our appreciation to those who made valuable suggestions for previous editions: John C. Bird, Mollie Bowers, James F. Byers, Joseph M. Cambridge, Anthony Campagna, William Chase, Boyd Childress, Milton Derber, Satish P. Deshpande, James B. Dworkin, Geraldine Ellerbrock, Paul Gerhart, Carol L. Gilmore, Thomas P. Gilroy, David Gray, Charles R. Greer, Marvin Hill, Jr., Wayne Hochwarter, Janis Holden, Denise Tanguay Hoyer, H. Roy Kaplan, Katherine Karl, Philip Kienast, Kenneth A. Kovach, Charles Krider, Howard T. Ludlow, Douglas McCabe, Karl O. Magnusen, Marick Masters, William Maloney, Pamela Marett, Jonathan Monat, Roy Moore, William L. Moore, Thomas Noble, Dane M. Partridge, Robert Penfield, Alex Pomnichowski, Roy R. Reynolds, Robert Rodgers, Richard L. Rowan, Peter Sherer, David Shulenberger, Herman A. Theeke, Suzanne M. Vest, William Werther, Elizabeth Wesman, Carolyn Wiley, and Roger S. Wolters.

We would like to thank James H. Browne of the University of Southern Colorado and Paul A. Dorsey of Milliken University for preparing the computerized version of the Collective Bargaining Negotiations Exercise and testing it in actual class situations. We are also grateful to William H. Ross of the University of Wisconsin-La Crosse for once again providing an extensive and up-to-date list of suggested student readings and term projects for the *Instructor's Manual.*

We also wish to thank those individuals who have either directly or indirectly aided in the preparation of this book: Betty Geitz, Brenda Ryan, and Margie Wright.

Finally, we would like to thank The Dryden Press for its fine work on this book. We are grateful to our acquisitions editor, John Weimeister, as well as Lisé Johnson, Lora Knox, Adele Krause, Tracy Morse, Michele Tomiak, and Jessica Wyatt.

William H. Holley, Jr.
Auburn University

Kenneth M. Jennings
University of North Florida

May 1996

About the Authors

William H. Holley, Jr., is a Regions Bank Professor at Auburn University, where he teaches labor relations, collective bargaining and arbitration, and human resource management. He received his B.S. and M.B.A. from Mississippi State University and his Ph.D. from the University of Alabama. He has been active in the Southern Management Association, a division of the Academy of Management, where he has served as Secretary and President, and on the editorial board of the *Journal of Management* for three terms. He is a coauthor of *Personnel/Human Resource Management* with Ken Jennings and of *Labor Relations: An Experiential and Case Approach* with Roger Wolters. His research has been published in a wide range of journals, such as the *Academy of Management Journal, Labor Law Journal, Personnel Psychology,* and others. He is presently Executive Secretary Treasurer of the National Academy of Arbitrators. He also serves on the editorial boards of the *Journal of Collective Negotiations in the Public Sector* and *Employee Rights and Responsibilities Journal.*

Kenneth M. Jennings, Jr., is Richard de Raismes Professor of Industrial Relations at the University of North Florida, where he teaches undergraduate and graduate courses in labor relations and human resource management. After receiving his B.S. from Knox College and M.S. from the University of Illinois, he spent four years with Union Carbide in various industrial relations assignments. He then received a Ph.D. from the University of Illinois, and he has been at the University of North Florida for 20 years. He has written numerous books (*Balls and Strikes: The Money Game in Professional Baseball* and *Labor Relations at the New York Daily News* being the latest) and articles in journals such as *Industrial and Labor Relations Review, Industrial Management, Personnel Journal, Employee Relations Law Journal,* and *Transportation Journal.* A Chicago Cubs fan and collector of jazz recordings and baseball cards, he lives with his wife, Jackie.

Contents in Brief

Contents

PART ONE

Part 1 introduces the labor relations process that will be discussed throughout the book, placing it in historical and legal perspectives. It also examines differences in union and management organization and labor relations strategies.

RECOGNIZING RIGHTS AND RESPONSIBILITIES OF UNIONS AND MANAGEMENT

Union-Management Relationships in Perspective

1

This chapter first defines the three phases of the labor relations process, then places this process into an analytical perspective. It introduces the activities, focal point, participants, and influences of the labor relations process, which will be discussed in detail in subsequent chapters.

Phases in the Labor Relations Process

The **labor relations process** occurs when management and the exclusive bargaining agent for the employees (the union) jointly determine and administer work rules. It is neither automatically nor uniformly applied across public and private sector organizations in the United States. The labor relations process includes the following three phases:

1. **Recognition of the legitimate rights and responsibilities of union and management representatives.** This phase includes the legal right of employees to join unions (see Chapter 3), union organizing drives (see Chapter 5), and the rights of management and union officials, as well as their responsibilities to abide by related laws and labor agreement provisions.
2. **Negotiation of the labor agreement, including appropriate strategies and tactics and impasse-resolution techniques.** Strikes and mediation are examples of the latter (discussed in Chapter 7). This phase is usually the most publicized by the media, even though phases 1 and 3 are equally essential.
3. **Administration of the negotiated labor agreement—applying and enforcing the terms of the agreement on a daily basis.** This phase of the process (discussed in detail in Chapters 8 and 9) accounts for the most time and energy spent by union and management officials and usually involves a larger number of these officials than the preceding phases.

Clearly, the sequence of the labor relations process is cumulative. Formal negotiations seldom occur if the parties have not first recognized each other's legitimate rights and responsibilities. Similarly, the first two phases are necessary for the existence of the third phase—administration of the labor agreement. This sequence is applied to an increasingly significant topic, employee drug testing, in the "Labor Relations in Action" box.

Of course, not all labor-management relationships have focused on these three phases. Indeed, employees and their representative unions at some public and private sector facilities are still striving to accomplish the first phase of the process.[1]

The phases of the labor relations process are subject to qualitative variation as well. In the first phase, for example, organizations vary in the amount of respect union and management officials have for each other's goals. In the second phase, negotiations are carried out with different levels of intelligence, preparation, and sincere desire to achieve results. The third phase may vary as to how well the negotiated labor agreement is understood and effectively administered in good faith by both parties. There are probably as many different relationships as there are union and management officials negotiating labor agreements.

Elements in the Labor Relations Process

Exhibit 1.2 provides a framework for the labor relations process. The elements shown can be applied to the labor relations activities at a single manufacturing facility, at some or all of the facilities owned by a single company, or in an entire industry. The exhibit cites three major categories: (1) the focal point of labor relations, which is the work rules; (2) the participants in the process, which are the union and management organizations, employees, third-party neutrals, and the government; and (3) constraints or influences affecting the parties in their negotiation and administration of the work rules.

These categories are interrelated (as is shown by Case 4.2, about the *New York Daily News*). They will be discussed separately, however, to reflect their unique dimensions and considerations.

Focal Point of Labor Relations: Work Rules

Any academic discipline needs a focal point so that research, investigation, and commentary can generate applicable insights. "Labor" or "industrial" relations can become a very broad topic including many academic concerns. Sociologists have examined employee alienation, psychologists have investigated causes of job satisfaction, economists have studied wage determination, and political scientists have assessed the structural relationships of the internal union organization and its members and leaders.

Drug Testing and the Labor Relations Process

Drug testing has been called the "Jar Wars" of the 1980s and 1990s. A nationwide concern over drug use and its accompanying problems has resulted in many businesses taking measures against drug use. In 1982, only 3 percent of Fortune 500 companies were involved in employee drug testing. Ten years later, a 1992 American Medical Association survey found 75 percent of the responding firms testing for employee drug use.

Whether for altruistic reasons—social responsibility or concern for employee welfare—or for monetary advantages—lower insurance rates, increased productivity, or reduction of property damage—concern has been translated into controversy, which illustrates the three phases of the labor relations process.

Recognition of the Legitimate Rights of Union and Employer Organizations The desire for a drug-free workplace appears to be a legitimate one, which would attract opposition only from drug users, pushers, or radical subversives. Yet organized labor is one of the most formidable opponents of the current drug testing movement, contending that random or mandatory testing assumes its members are guilty and must prove their innocence.

The government has partially resolved the first phase. Unions have contended in various legal suits that management's unilateral imposition of employee drug testing ignores the legal rights of their members and organizations and violates the Fourth Amendment prohibitions against suspicionless search and seizure.

The Supreme Court has not held private sector employers accountable to constitutional restraints.[a] However, government agencies have formulated guidelines that can apply to both private and public sector employees. A recent Supreme Court decision, *Skinner* v. *Railway Labor Executives' Association*, ruled that post-accident drug and alcohol testing required by the Federal Railroad Administration did not violate rail employees' Fourth Amendment rights even though the regulations did not "individualize" suspicion of drug or alcohol use prior to testing.[b] The court contended that the government's compelling public safety interest in ensuring that rail workers are not impaired on the job outweighed the "minimal" employee rights intrusion.

Another Supreme Court decision, *National Treasury Employees Union* v. *Von Raab*, upheld the U.S. Custom Service's policy of testing applicants for promotion for illegal drug use. The majority contended, "Employees involved in drug interdiction reasonably should expect effective inquiry into their fitness and probity."

Negotiation of the Labor Agreement Unions want to subject drug testing to the second phase of the labor relations process although related efforts in the railroad and airline industries do not come under the National Labor Relations Act (NLRA, discussed more in

(continued)

Drug Testing and the Labor Relations Process—cont'd

Chapter 3). The Supreme Court in *Consolidated Rail Corp.* v. *Railway Labor Executives' Association* indicated that companies in these industries may add drug screening to periodic physical examinations without having to bargain with unions over this practice.

This situation is not the case for most unionized, private sector companies that are covered by the NLRA and the National Labor Relations Board (NLRB, also discussed more in Chapter 3), a government agency charged with overseeing this labor legislation. The NLRB has made it clear that employee drug testing is a mandatory bargaining issue (discussed more in Chapter 6) where the details of such a program should be negotiated with the union until agreement or impasse. In the case of impasse, an employer may proceed with implementation of the program unless limited by other contract language.

The past practice of "for-cause" drug testing, also, does not give management the go-ahead to implement a change in the existing program such as a switch to random testing or testing as an addition to routine physicals. Unions must protest at the outset of such a program, however, or their lack of immediate response may be interpreted as a waiver of their rights. Even when a current program for routine physicals includes urinalysis, any change in the use of the samples should be an immediate matter of union interest.

Management also cannot assume that an agreement in principle with the union on drug testing constitutes any waiver of the union's right to be included in outlining the specifics of the actual program.

Unions might seek to bargain over who will be tested and under what conditions; the type of test (hair follicles versus urinalysis, for example); and what procedures will be used to ensure accurate results (possibly including retests). In their negotiations, unions will question the existence of any hard evidence that employees who occasionally use marijuana have higher accident rates and litigation claims.

Two unions, the United Auto Workers and the American Federation of State, County, and Municipal Employees (AFSCME) have negotiated labor agreement language that stresses that management should emphasize prevention, education, and rehabilitation through counseling as the major aspects of any drug screening program. The first drug testing program approved under a UAW labor agreement stressed that testing will be solely on a for-cause basis determined by a supervisor and confirmed by a medical professional. No random drug testing is allowed except for employees in safety-sensitive jobs such as commercial drivers, large crane operators, and top-security personnel. The employee would not receive discipline for failing the test on two occasions; however, he or she would presumably be discharged for the third occasion of failing the test established for one of nine drugs. AFSCME, moreover, stresses in its contract negotiations and labor-agreement language that drug tests should not be required without clear evidence that the affected employee is "impaired by the use of alcohol or controlled substances."

Administering the Labor Agreement on a Daily Basis Unions might protest management's administration of employee drug testing through grievances, and possibly arbitration,[c] (discussed in Chapters 8 and 9) for two general reasons:

1. The labor agreement did not specify drug testing; therefore, a unilaterally established management policy on the subject is a possible invasion of employee privacy rights[d]) and/or unmeasurable unless a demonstrated employee drug problem and/or related evidence (e.g., product damage or accidents) exists.
2. Management did not administer related labor agreement provisions correctly (e.g., did not ensure that the evidence belonged to the accused employee, misinterpreted the drug tests, etc. See Exhibit 1.1 for related procedures involving flight attendants).

Currently, the drug testing controversy shows no signs of letting up. This issue, with its accompanying questions and problems, will continue to be an important one in labor-management relations.

a. "Supreme Court Declines to Review Legality of Private-Sector Drug Tests," Bureau of National Affairs, Inc., *Daily Labor Report,* No. 218 (November 10, 1992), pp. A-4 & A-5.
b. For related and additional considerations, see Thomas H. Christopher, "Employee Drug Testing: A Constitutional Perspective," *Employee Responsibilities and Rights Journal* 4, no. 1 (1991), pp. 311–328, and Barbara Noble, "The New Deal on Drug Testing," *New York Times,* January 8, 1995, which discuss the Omnibus Transportation Employee Testing Act of 1991.
c. Charles L. Redel and Augustus Abbey, "Arbitration of Drug Use and Testing in the Work Place," *Arbitration Journal* 48 (March 1993), pp. 80–85; and Steven M. Crow and Lillian Y. Fok, "Drug Testing at a Labor Arbitration," *Dispute Resolution Journal,* January 1995, pp. 37–43.
d. John M. Norwood, "Drug Testing in the Private Sector and Its Impact on Employees' Right to Privacy," *Labor Law Journal* 45 (December 1994), pp. 731–748. For possible evidential problems in drug testing see "Hair, Saliva Testing Under Consideration to Replace Urinalysis, Ease Alcohol Tests," Bureau of National Affairs, Inc., *Daily Labor Report,* No. 126 (July 5, 1994), pp. C-1–C-4.

Exhibit 1.1 Rights and Responsibilities of Flight Attendants in Two Drug and Alcohol Testing Situations

RANDOM DRUG AND ALCOHOL TESTING

GUIDELINES

1. You cannot refuse to take a random drug or alcohol test.
2. You must comply with the requests of the Breath Alcohol Technician during alcohol testing and the Collection Site Person during drug testing.
3. You must sign or initial the forms when asked to do so.
4. ***For drug testing,*** make sure to observe your sample until it is sealed and labeled; the numbers on the sample and the form should match. If the lab reports your test as positive, you have only 72 hours from the time you are notified to request a retest (at your expense).
5. ***For alcohol testing,*** make sure you get a clean mouthpiece for the confirmatory test; the machine registers 0.00 on an air blank before and after the test; and that the printed test result matches the result displayed on the machine.

DRUG AND ALCOHOL TESTING
Reasonable Cause/Reasonable Suspicion Test

GUIDELINES

1. Get a witness to hear reason(s) for test request.
2. Get reason(s) in WRITING, signed by you, witness and supervisors, if possible.
3. Get the name of supervisor(s) requesting the test. There must be two for drug testing and one for alcohol testing.
4. Follow random test procedures on reverse side.
5. Call your Grievance Representative immediately after the test.

Grievance Representatives ______________________________ (__)______

______________________________ (__)______

SOURCE: Association of Flight Attendants AFL-CIO.

Exhibit 1.2 Elements in the Labor Relations Process

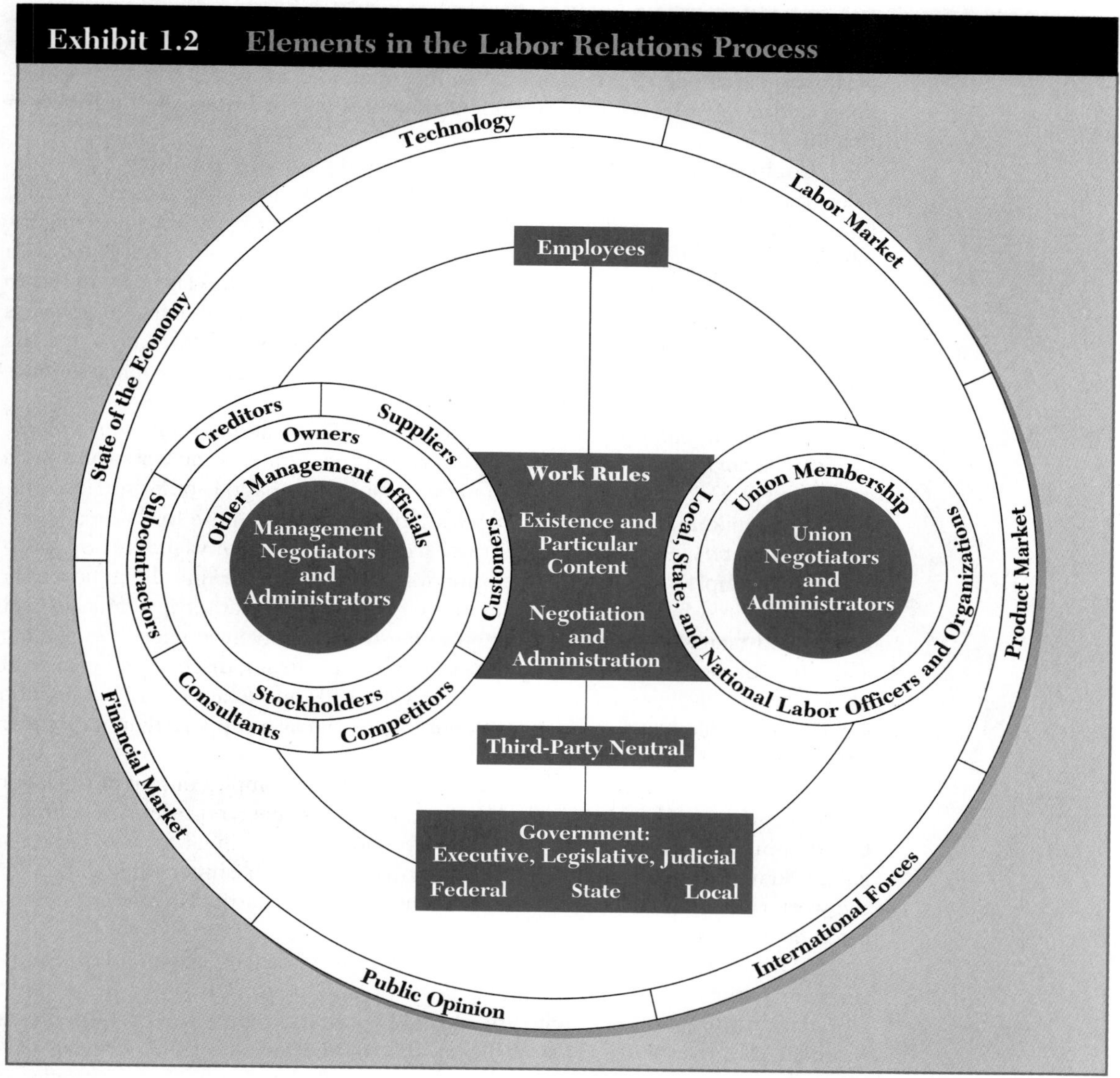

In 1958 John Dunlop's book *Industrial Relations Systems* provided a useful focal point for the diverse academic approaches. Dunlop suggested that the center of attention in labor relations should be the work rules negotiated between management and union officials. It is important to understand the influences determining whether a work rule exists and, if so, its particular content.[2] **Work rules** can be placed in two general categories: (1) rules governing compensation in all its forms—overtime payments, vacations, holidays, shift premiums, and so on, and

(2) rules specifying the employees' and employers' job rights and obligations, such as no employee strike or employer lockout during the term of the labor agreement, performance standards, promotion qualifications and procedures, job specifications, and layoff procedures. Additional examples of work rules are furnished in Exhibit 1.3.

Compensation work rules such as negotiated wages are often publicized because they are easily understood by the public. Union and management officials, however, can attach equal or greater significance to the second work rule category, job rights and obligations. Managers, for example, might be most concerned with obtaining a contract provision whereby production employees can be required to perform "minor repairs," instead of requiring higher-paid maintenance employees to do them. Many unions have sought work rules that would give members the rights to refuse overtime or even to work less than 40 hours a week while maintaining the original wages and benefits.[3]

Work rules can vary in three characteristics: They can be *common or unique*, they can be *vague or specific*, and they can *change over time*. Some work rules, such as the first one in Exhibit 1.3, are common to many occupations or industries. Others may be unique to a particular job classification, such as those for baseball players and cemetery employees. Work rules likewise may vary in vagueness or specificity: for example, consider the provision for "Clerical and Technical Employees at a College" cited in Exhibit 1.3. This rule at first appears rather insignificant; yet unions and management could easily become heatedly involved over the meaning and intent of the word *democracy*. For example, a professor, discharged because of poor teaching evaluations, might contend this decision violated the "democratic ideal" cited in the labor agreement because he or she also supported an unpopular political cause.

An analysis of work rules helps us understand the complex output of the labor relations process. The formal labor agreement in this sense represents a compilation of jointly negotiated work rules. However, as discussed in Chapter 8, labor relations activities are not limited to those involving the establishment and content of the work rule; it is also appropriate to examine how the particular rule is administered between union and management officials.

Work rules also change over time as a response to changing workplace conditions and societal values. For example, the contemporary work rules for airline flight attendants would most certainly differ from the following three work requirements formulated in the 1930s: (1) swat flies in the cabin after takeoff, (2) prevent passengers from throwing lighted cigar butts out the windows, and (3) carry a railroad timetable in case of plane trouble. Drug testing has been previously discussed; in addition, several other issues have recently emerged that have immediate relevance to a large number of unions.

Acquired Immune Deficiency Syndrome, or AIDS AIDS represents a relatively new working condition that has commanded employer and union concern and shaped work rules. Almost 99 percent of hospitals recently surveyed by the Occupational Safety and Health Administration have written policies regarding occupational exposure to blood-borne infectious diseases such as AIDS. One nurses' union recently negotiated a contract containing "precedent-setting" health and safety provisions aimed at protecting members from occupational exposure to the virus that causes AIDS.[4]

Smoking "No-smoking" rules have also been relatively recent in their formulation and application. In 1908, a Columbia University professor insisted that "the deleterious effects of tobacco are greatly exaggerated," a belief that prevailed for the next

Exhibit 1.3 Examples of Work Rules

JOB OR INDUSTRY CLASSIFICATION	WORK RULE
Government Installation	The Employer agrees to furnish adequate protective clothing for employees required to work outside during rain, sleet, snow, hail, or other atmospheric conditions detrimental to health or safety, provided the employee subjected to such assignments normally and historically performs the majority of his work assignment indoors. Employees who normally perform a majority of their work outdoors shall furnish their own protective clothing. . . .
Professional Baseball	The Player and the Club recognize and agree that the Player's participation in certain other sports may impair or destroy his ability and skill as a baseball player. Accordingly, the Player agrees that he will not engage in professional boxing or wrestling; and that, except with the written consent of the club, he will not engage in skiing, auto racing, motorcycle racing, sky diving, or in any game or exhibition of football, soccer, professional league basketball, ice hockey, or other sport involving a substantial risk of personal injury.
Television	The latest version of the script will be made accessible to the Player in the casting office twenty-four hours in advance of a scheduled reading or immediately after the scheduling of the interview, whichever last occurs.
Steel Industry	An employee reporting to work on his regularly-scheduled shift, unless he is notified by the Company not to report at least sixteen (16) hours prior to the scheduled starting time, shall be given work which is available, but in the event he is not permitted to start work, or works less than one hour, he shall be given four (4) hours' pay. In the event that an employee works more than one hour of his regular shift before being sent home because of lack of work, he will receive eight (8) hours' pay. This provision shall not apply in the event that an employee refused available work which he is physically able to perform or in the event that catastrophes, failures of utilities, or acts of a public enemy interfere with work being provided.
Clerical and Technical Employees at a College	The Board and the Union recognize and agree that while democratic principles should prevail in every American school system, urban colleges in a city as diverse in population as is Chicago must be exemplary in their expression and practice of the democratic ideal.
Cemeteries	In all cases where a grave is dug straight down, a second man shall be assigned to assist the digger after a depth of five feet is reached.

70 years.[5] Now, union and management officials and possibly arbitrators at thousands of facilities jointly determine whether the issuance of a no-smoking policy is reasonable and whether an employee was properly disciplined or discharged for violating the rule.

Workplace Violence A recent report indicated that nearly 1 million employees each year are injured on the job, and the second-leading cause of workplace deaths is homicide. Fifteen unions have formed the Inter-Union Workplace Assault Coalition to combat this problem, discussed in more detail in Chapter 12.[6]

Electronic Monitoring Electronic monitoring of employee work performance has become a recent and widespread issue affecting factory and an estimated 6 million office employees, particularly in the service industries. New technology such as computers, bar code scanners, and pressure sensitive plates has enabled management to monitor employee performance in various ways such as counting the number of keystrokes made on computer keyboards and listening to employees' telephone conversations with customers.

The U.S. Postal Service has adopted one of the more recent forms of electronic monitoring in its nationwide installation of a computer chip in a mail collection box that, when activated by a letter carrier at a mail pickup, will record the time and location. This work issue is not opposed by the union as one official contends customer allegations about poor service will be resolved efficiently.

Participants in the Labor Relations Process

Management Officials Through the corporate structure, managers represent the stockholders. The negotiated and administered work rules involve managers at several organizational levels and functions. Labor relations managers and representatives are typically found at corporate, divisional, and plant levels. Related objectives are developed at the upper levels and coordinated at the corporate and divisional levels to ensure that a particular work rule at one location, such as a wage rate for a particular job classification, does not adversely alter precedents or conditions at another production facility.

Plant level labor relations representatives implement these directives, but they must also deal with other managers at the location, particularly production and maintenance managers and first-line supervisors, who direct the daily work activities of hourly employees. As will be further discussed in Chapter 8, management's first-line supervisors typically hear and attempt to resolve employees' grievances on the production floor. In some cases, they are surprised to learn that higher-level management officials have overturned their decisions. Alert union leaders may use dissension among management officials to influence labor relations activities and the company's position toward unions.

Management consultants' activities in the labor relations process are varied, ranging from restructuring personnel practices in nonunion firms (without any organizing campaign) to designing and presenting the employer's response throughout the campaign and representation election. Controversy occurs over the consultants' effectiveness and ethics. One union estimate found that consultants were involved in more than 90 percent of the representational elections lost by unions.[7] However, another research effort found that the impact of consultants on union victories in representation elections was not very great.[8]

Management must be conscious of its competitors, who may challenge the company's product in quality, price, and/or service. A company must consider its competitors when negotiating terms of the labor agreement. In some cases (the airline industry, for example) a strike can result in customers and revenues being transferred to competitors.

An advertisement of Ford Motor Products stressed that its particular labor-management relationship gives it a competitive edge. The advertisement was titled, "A Breakthrough in Labor Relations Has Helped Create the Highest Quality Vehicles Made in America." It referred to a new era of commitment and mutual respect between union and management. Another example of blurred organizational distinctions between management and union officials is reflected in the United Airlines buyout, discussed in Chapter 13.

Union Officials Union leaders, usually elected by the members, represent the membership, but they, like their management counterparts, do not necessarily represent a consensual group because unions experience internal differences of view. Members and officers do not completely agree on priorities; sometimes conflict occurs over specific tactics to be used in accomplishing commonly shared bargaining objectives. (See the Chapter 6 "Labor Relations in Action" box pertaining to professional basketball, for example.)

Union and management officials are subjected to their own pressures, which can either brighten labor relations differences or blur their organizational distinctions when joint problem resolution is sought and obtained. Many times the sociodemographic (age, race, and sex, for example) composition of a union's membership can raise certain labor relations issues/tensions. For example, a recent proposed labor agreement between United Auto Workers and Navistar contained the following provisions: (1) cash payments of $1,400 to each retiree ($700 to spouses of deceased retirees); and (2) management's right to hire new members at 70 percent of the UAW scale and increase that rate to 100 percent of scale over the next 2 1/2 years. However, the 15,000 current members rejected this proposed labor agreement because they wanted the monies given to them in either a cash payment or increased pension payments when they retired.[9]

The influx of immigrant populations into the clothing and textile industries has prompted the Amalgamated Clothing and Textile Workers' Union and the International Ladies Garment Workers' Union (UNITE) to offer bilingual education and an English-as-a-second-language course to new union members.

In another situation, the top officer of the Houston Police Officers Association and a male objected to female union members posing scantily clad in a charity calendar: "It makes policewomen look like bimbos and sex objects."[10]

Employees Perhaps the most significant participant category is employees, because they often determine whether a union is even present in an organization (representation elections and union organizing drives are discussed in Chapter 5); whether a negotiated labor agreement is accepted or rejected; and the extent to which a threatened strike is actually carried out (Chapter 7).

Employees are treated here as a separate category because they may have loyalties to both management and union organizations.[11] This situation is found in both the private and public sectors: for example, public employees such as fire fighters, police, and teachers may feel torn between the critical or professional nature of their jobs and the strategic advantages of a strike. Employees want their organizations to thrive and prosper; at the same time, they want to share in the rewards of success. Because their desires may shape the existence and content of particular work rules, employees can be considered the third participant in the labor relations process.

The Government The government participates through three branches: executive, legislative, and judicial, occurring at federal, state, and local levels. In the public sector, government officials also serve as management officials in the labor relations process.

In the private sector the federal government has traditionally played an indirect role at the bargaining table. A mediator from the Federal Mediation and Conciliation Service can assist union and management officials in reaching an agreement. The mediator's advice, however, can be refused; this individual can also be asked by one or both parties to leave the negotiations. The federal government's "hands off" approach in most private-sector bargaining situations is based on the belief that most management and union officials are better equipped than their government counterparts to assess their needs and limitations and reach a mutually acceptable labor agreement.

Although the federal government does not dictate the terms of a negotiated labor agreement, laws, judicial decisions, and administrative agencies can influence or restrict work rules. For example, union and management officials cannot negotiate a mandatory retirement age of 60 years because this would conflict with the Age Discrimination in Employment Act. Or, although coal miners have long believed that if females worked in the mines, bad luck would result, union and management officials would be violating sexual discrimination aspects of the Equal Employment Opportunity Act if they negotiated a provision prohibiting female employees from working in the mines. Perhaps more widespread is the controversy over negotiated seniority provisions that are used for administration decisions, such as promotions and layoffs, and affirmative action programs monitored by the government. (This will be discussed in Chapter 12.)

Third Party Neutrals Differences between union and management officials that arise in negotiating the labor agreement or administering its provisions are often resolved by third-party neutrals. **Mediators** (discussed in Chapters 7 and 14) are the most frequently used third-party neutrals in contract negotiations. The mediator assists the union and management officials in resolving their differences themselves.

He or she only offers advice and does not have binding decision-making authority.

An **arbitrator** is a third-party neutral hired by union and management officials to make a final and binding decision on a disputed issue. This participant sometimes becomes involved in the second phase of the labor relations process, resolving a negotiations impasse, but is far less used in this capacity than a mediator. The arbitrator's most frequent efforts pertain to the third phase of the labor relations process, resolving a grievance, which is further discussed in Chapter 9.

Influences Affecting Participants' Negotiation and Administration of Work Rules

The labor relations participants who affect the development of work rules are in turn influenced by external variables or constraints in their labor relations activities (see the outer circle of Exhibit 1.2). These influences can sometimes affect one another and may relate to the particular firm, the local community, or society in general. The following discussion furnishes a few illustrations of how these influences can affect the existence and content of work rules.

Technology Perhaps the most immediate and persistent influence on work rules is the technology of the particular workplace. **Technology** has four dimensions: (1) equipment used in the operation; (2) the pace and scheduling of work; (3) characteristics of the work environment and tasks to be performed; and (4) information exchange. Consider, for example, the major equipment found at a steel mill, blast furnaces, which require very high temperatures for operation. These furnaces cannot be simply turned on and off like a household oven. Often several days are required for either reaching these high temperatures or for cooling the furnaces for repairs. This equipment characteristic affects the facility's work rules. In essence, steel mills must be operated 24 hours a day, 7 days a week—a situation prompting related work rules such as wage premiums for working the night shift, weekends, and holidays.

In some cases the introduction of equipment reduces or eliminates employees in a particular job classification.[12] This situation occurs when industrial robots handle tasks formerly performed by employees. A rather common application occurs in the auto industry, where mechanically joined arms perform spot welding, spraying, machine unloading, and assembly. Unions faced with having membership replaced by robots have increased related bargaining demands (such as more paid time off and the 4-day week) for their members' job security.

However, unions might not face as strong a challenge from robotics as was initially anticipated. Orders for American-made robots have been falling since their peak of $504 million in 1984. A current estimate suggests that fewer than 5 percent of American companies have installed even one robot and that the total number of robots in the United States (37,000) is far less than that found in Japan (270,000). Managers have found that robots are expensive to make and often shut down, requiring human attention.[13]

Even less managerial enthusiasm for automation has been generated by the U.S. Postal Service experience, where a $5 billion automation program featuring bar coding has fallen short of its projected work force reduction of 87,000 full-time employees by 1995. The program has also not significantly reduced expenses because of higher costs and operating inefficiencies.

There is, however, a possibility in some organizations that highly automated equipment can threaten union members' job security, a situation that can affect their bargaining goals and behavior. In the supermarket industry electronic scanners are used to change item prices, record customer purchases, and maintain products' inventory counts. These activities result in fewer stockhands and reduced skills and compensation of cashiers.

This situation has also occurred in recent negotiations between American Telephone and Telegraph and two unions. Management wanted to replace some human operators with voice-recognition computers. Negotiations continued for 30 days past the deadline; however, agreement was reached when AT&T raised its proposed wage hike to 11.8 percent from 8 percent, agreed to cut back on nonunion temporary workers, and gave union members the right to work in nonunion subsidiaries. This agreement was not attributed to union militance; indeed, Morton Bahr, president of the Communications Workers of America, indicated that serious bargaining rather than a strike was necessary because a somewhat automated telephone company could operate without unionized employees for at least a month without customers noticing any differences. AT&T has sharply reduced the number of telephone operators from 250,000 in 1956 to 60,000, and the number of employees in this classification is still dwindling. An even more dramatic reduction of employees/union members in public service utilities might occur when the nation's 35,000 meter readers are replaced by tiny electrical devices that indicate the amount and location of power use.[14]

The pace and scheduling of the workday also affect the work rules of certain occupations. For example, bus companies optimizing their productivity and revenue would concentrate on rush hour traffic (6:00–9:00 A.M., 3:00–7:00 P.M.) when buses would be likely to be filled with passengers. But problems would remain in scheduling work because many bus drivers might have a daily work schedule of 3 hours on, 3 hours off, 1 hour on, 2 hours off, 4 hours on. Because of the nature of the work, most labor agreements in related industries have provisions pertaining to the permissible number, length, and possible compensation of intervals (times off) between daily work assignments.

The work environment and tasks to be performed can also influence work rules: for example, particular safety equipment is required on certain jobs in the manufacturing and construction industries. A more specific example and related labor relations controversy pertains to police officers, who prefer the Glock Semiautomatic 9-millimeter pistol over the .38-caliber six-shot revolver. The Glock now used by 250,000 police in 4,500 of the nation's 13,000 departments holds nearly three times more bullets, reloads faster, and is more accurate than the .38-caliber. Many officers contend the pistol is needed to offset the sophisticated weapons used by drug dealers and street thugs. However, some police and city officials resist implementing the Glock, contending that its lighter trigger and repetitive firing could increase the chances of an innocent bystander being harmed or even killed.[15]

Computer operations can help both union and management officials in their daily labor relations activities. Union officers can use computer applications to maintain membership and dues records as well as word processing for communication to the membership. Union and management officials can also use computer applications in the areas of contract negotiations (costing the various proposals) and administration (maintenance and research of grievances and arbitration decisions).[16]

The AFL-CIO has introduced two computer information networks, LaborNET (for members only) and Labor-WEB (public access), the organization's new "home page" on the Internet's World Wide Web that will enable practitioners and students of industrial relations to become well informed on current developments.[17] One AFL-CIO official contends that labor's message will be communicated to more people since some 35 percent of American families have computers at home and since computer access at the work site is growing.[18] Many students needing to research a current labor relations topic for a class assignment must find sources other than somewhat dated and possibly unresponsive academic journals. The following "Labor Relations in Action" box should help students who are researching labor relations topics, as will Appendix B, "Internet Possibilities for the Labor Relations Process."

Labor Market The skills and wage levels of employees in the local **labor market** can affect negotiated work rules. Management is often concerned with the skill level of employees in the particular community. For example, a firm needing skilled employees from a relatively unskilled labor market would probably wish to negotiate work rules regarding apprenticeship programs. Management would also consider negotiating a 90-day probationary period within which it could terminate the employment of an unskilled or nonproductive employee, and the union could not protest the action through the grievance procedure.

Both management and union representatives are also interested in the compensation rates for comparably skilled employees in the labor market. Certainly, the wages paid by other companies in the local area affect negotiated wage rates. In some cases, particularly in the construction trades, some unions have had to reduce their wages to counter nonunion competition.

A recent major shift of skills involves some 20 million members of the Baby Boom generation who mostly work in service jobs that are neither blue-collar nor white-collar. These "new-collar" employees include insurance agents, keypunch operators, loan officers, and salespeople, particularly those in telemarketing.[19] They typically do not have a full college education, and they use their heads on the job but probably are seldom asked to take much intellectual initiative. Unions are interested in organizing new-collar employees and are emphasizing skill-related concerns such as career development, professional autonomy, dealing with technological change, and stress management.

Sometimes the labor market occupies a broader geographical area than management or union officials anticipated, a situation that offers advantages to management, particularly if a strike occurs. During the recent Caterpillar strike,

LABOR RELATIONS IN ACTION

GETTING ONLINE WITH LABOR RELATIONS RESEARCH[a]

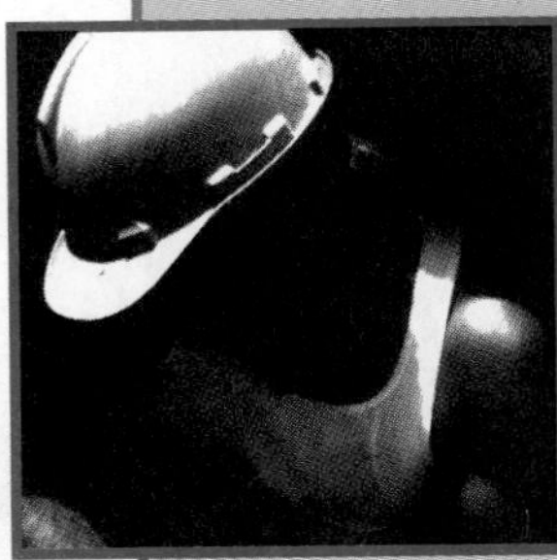

The number of electronic sources for locating information on collective bargaining and labor relations is constantly increasing. The most efficient method for finding reports in journals, magazines, newspapers, and other periodical literature is through the use of indexes, which are found in most university and college libraries in both print and electronic form. You will choose your sources depending on the time period you want to cover, the amount of information you need, the availability of resources in your area, and your interest in free versus fee-based information.

Computer databases have several advantages, such as currency, the ability to print in a variety of formats, and the ability to combine terms and other qualifiers (for example, date, language, and publication title) to broaden or narrow a search. They can, however, be costly and require time to become skilled in their use. Be aware that the coverage of electronic indexes may overlap. To decrease the chance of redundancy and unnecessary cost, retrieve as many periodicals as possible from databases that you can search without charge, and then eliminate those periodicals from your search in electronic databases.

Subscriptions to several thousand online databases are being sold by vendors such as Knight-Ridder, Inc., BRS Search Service (now CDP Online), Mead Data Central, Inc. (LEXIS/NEXIS), DataTimes, H.W. Wilson, and OCLC (Online Computer Library Center). Vendors typically charge a connection fee for the time spent online, a fee for each record displayed or requested, and a telecommunications charge. For those databases discussed here, costs range from $1.60 per connect-minute and $.50 per type to $2.20 per connect-minute and $1.40 per type.

Some end-user services for online systems eliminate the need for librarian search mediators. Knight-Ridder offers *Knowledge Index*, a subsystem of the larger collection of databases, at night and on weekends to individual users through CompuServe at reduced rates. *FirstSearch*, produced by OCLC, is a collection of databases that provides several business indexes and is often offered free of charge to students.

General business indexes are extremely useful in locating articles on collective bargaining. *Business Periodicals Index*, published by the H.W. Wilson Company, covers approximately 350 journals in business and economics and is found in libraries of all types. In fact, it may be the only business index in a small library. The index is available in print, online, and on CD-ROM.

Business Index, produced by Information Access Corporation, indexes more publications than *Business Periodicals Index*. Coverage includes *The Wall Street Journal*, the business section of *The New York Times*, regional publications, and trade journals. Trade journals, such as *Automotive News, Supermarket News, Editor & Publisher* and *Modern Healthcare* can provide related insights into labor issues and unions such as UAW, UFCW, Newspaper Guild, and ANA, respectively.

ABI/INFORM, produced by University Microfilms International (UMI), is an index to the scholarly literature of business but is not limited to scholarly titles. Coverage also includes general business magazines and trade periodicals. *ABI/INFORM* may be searched online and through CD-ROM.

Business Newsbank Plus, published by Newsbank, Inc., is a full-text CD-ROM database of articles from newspapers, wire services, and regional business journals. This is a good one-stop place, usually free to students, for articles about a particular event published in newspapers from the city or region where the event took place, often providing a different perspective from that of a national newspaper. For example, articles retrieved from *Business Newsbank Plus* on the Bridgestone/Firestone strike, which lasted from July 1, 1994, through May 30, 1995, were published in regional newspapers such as the *Des Moines Register,* the *Akron Beacon Journal,* the *Daily Oklahoman,* and the *Indianapolis Star.*

Newspapers are an excellent source of business information because of the detailed analysis of events not often found in other periodical literature. Because they are published daily, they offer the latest news of labor negotiations. Citations to articles in leading newspapers may be found in print indexes, while a rapidly increasing number of electronic indexes provides the complete text and indexing of national and regional newspapers.

UMI offers a bibliographic online database, *Newspaper & Periodicals Abstracts* and the complete text of several major newspapers on CD-ROM through ProQuest. Knight-Ridder publishes a large number of full-text newspaper databases, provided by individual newspaper publishers, in its PAPERS collection. Other systems offering the complete text of newspaper articles include NEXIS, Dow Jones, IAC, DataTimes, and Newsbank.

Consider a search through electronic databases for articles on the Bridgestone/Firestone strike. The following search was used to retrieve citations from several databases:

bridgestone and (labor or union) and strike and py=1994-1995

The databases searched and the number of citations found are *ABI/INFORM,* 7; *Business Newsbank Plus,* 16; *Business Index,* 22; *Business Periodicals,* 4; *Newspaper and Periodicals Abstracts,* 16; and *Trade & Industry Index,* 34.

The Bureau of National Affairs *Daily Labor Report* (hard copy or from the online complete-text database available through Knight-Ridder's *BNA Daily News*) is also useful in researching labor relations topics. Coverage includes legislation pending in Congress, discussion of court cases, bargaining settlements, statistical information, and other items relating to labor.

a. Thanks to Sarah Philips, Associate Librarian and Head, Reference Department, University of North Florida, for presenting this information.

Exhibit 1.4 Union Response to a Changed Labor Market Consideration

The New York State Nurses Association and the RNs of Mt. Sinai Medical Center

You have the right to know who's caring for you when you're in the hospital.

Of the many changes in our health care system today, one pernicious and rarely mentioned change is the "downskilling" of hospital services. In an effort to save money, hospitals all over the country are replacing highly skilled registered nurses with minimally trained unlicensed personnel, and asking them to provide care for patients with complex health problems. These unlicensed "technicians" or "aides" walk in off the street and receive a few weeks of training and low wages.

Registered nurses receive years of intensive education and must pass a rigorous statewide exam to join the profession. They are independent practitioners who are held accountable for their practice, and must maintain high standards or lose their license. Replacing them with marginally skilled "techs" is a grave disservice to the public.

Imagine this scenario: A patient in the coronary care unit is sweating and thirsty and appears listless. She asks the unlicensed tech for a glass of water, which he promptly brings. But a registered nurse knows that these are classic symptoms of a heart attack, and immediately assesses the patient's pulse, blood pressure, and skin color, and if necessary, begins treatment. Having an RN at the bedside could have been the difference between life and death.

In fact, volumes of research demonstrate that hospitals employing more RNs deliver better care. A 1994 study at the University of Pennsylvania found that hospitals with more RNs per patient had a mortality rate 50% lower than similar hospitals caring for similar patients but with fewer RNs. A 1991 study found that patients recover more slowly when they receive care in hospitals employing fewer professional RNs.

Just because a hospital is prestigious or well-endowed does not guarantee quality care. Mt. Sinai Medical Center has already replaced RNs in its clinics and operating rooms with unlicensed personnel. Because "technicians" in the OR receive so little training, most of them have been unable to perform satisfactorily. Most have left their positions within just a few months.

The New York State Nurses Association has asked Mt. Sinai to guarantee not to replace any more RNs. This would be a guarantee to the citizens of New York as well as its nurses not to diminish the quality of care it delivers. But Mt. Sinai has refused, and has talked instead about the possibility of replacing as much as 40% of the RN workforce.

Our members want to protect the three most important things in their professional lives: their patients, their jobs, and their practice. That is why we are alerting the public to this health care menace. Every patient deserves a registered nurse. When you're in the hosppital, ask for an RN. Ask for a *real* nurse.

120 Wall Street, New York, NY 10005 Phone: 212-785-0157

SOURCE: *New Tork Times*, February 7, 1996.

management wanted the 12,600 striking employees to return to work. According to a company spokesperson, only some 400 of these individuals complied with management's request. However, non-employees in the community and from distant locations expressed interest in management's offer of work at the rate of some 30,000 telephone calls an hour. This response prompted the strikers' return to work. Exhibit 1.4 reflects an example of a union trying to restrict the labor market to its members.

Product Market The labor relations process can be affected by the **product market,** where the company either sells its product or purchases key elements for manufacture of its product. Management would be more vulnerable if a strike occurred at a time when major customer sales were anticipated. For example, management at a brewery would prefer to avoid a labor agreement expiring, possibly leading to a strike, during the summer months. Indeed, one major brewery has been successful in changing the contract expiration date from June 1 to March 1.

A recent dispute between the *New York Daily News* and nine unions (discussed in more detail in Case 4.2) focused on newsstand dealers since 85 percent of the newspapers were sold by these individuals. The unions were successful in preventing copies of the *News* from reaching the newsstands. Moreover, the dealers were unconcerned about the absence of these newspapers because they made up losses by selling more copies of *The New York Times* and the *New York Post.*

The second dimension of the product market, the source of key elements for product manufacture, is illustrated by the UAW's deep concern over the facts that many of the parts for U.S. automobiles are being manufactured in other countries and that it is often difficult to determine which parts on "American" cars are foreign made.[20]

International Forces The Persian Gulf crisis and "Operation Desert Storm," which involved United States troops in the Middle East, affected thousands of unionized employees, particularly in the automobile industry. General Motors, for example, announced that it was sharply cutting back its production during this time because it maintained that many potential customers would wait until the hostilities were over before making a major purchase decision. The United Auto Workers had negotiated guaranteed income security provisions with GM before the announcement was made, thereby making the possibility of employee layoffs slight. The company, however, did press the unions for some work rule concessions such as the reduction of work shifts, overtime hours, and speed of production.

More recently, unions have been concerned about competitive labor costs generated by the North American Free-Trade Agreement (NAFTA, discussed more in Chapter 2), which involves the United States, Canada, and Mexico and some $6 trillion worth of goods and services a year. Whether NAFTA will increase or decrease jobs in the long run is unknown. However, NAFTA will have a significant impact on work rules.[21] It would, for example, make it possible for a Mexican trucker earning 7 dollars a day to drive an 18-wheeler loaded with auto parts from Mexico to Detroit. Before the agreement, that driver would have to stop at the Rio Grande, where the goods would be loaded onto an American truck.

Public Opinion The two general dimensions of **public opinion** are (1) influential individuals and organizations within the community and (2) attitudes and traditions held by community residents. The mass media represent an important influence within the community, serving as both generator and conduit of community opinion. The media are profit-making businesses, and at least one prominent union official contends that this orientation biases the reporting of labor relations activities:

> The media tend to cover collective bargaining as if it were a pier six brawl. The intricate moves and tradeoffs that really make up bargaining aren't as newsy as impassioned rhetoric or a picket line confrontation.
>
> Reporters are given little training in covering collective bargaining. They are told to look for the "news"—the fist fight, the walkout, the heated exchange—and, as a result, frequently miss the "story," which is the settlement. . . .
>
> Every union proposal is a "demand," every management proposal is an "offer."[22]

A recent study analyzing 40 years of *The New York Times* columns concerning labor unions agreed with the preceding quotation as it found that the newspaper has become increasingly concentrated on strike activities and has exaggerated the frequency of strikes.[23]

Exhibit 1.5 suggests that, according to the Gallup Poll and irrespective of the media's contribution, not a great deal of current public confidence is placed in unions/organized labor (26 percent in 1993), and this confidence level has dropped for the past 20 years at a rate similar to that of big business. Unions' only solace regarding public opinion statistics is that a majority of the public currently has confidence in only four out of 13 various American institutions (e.g., the military, organized religion, the Supreme Court, and the police), and organized labor currently fares better than big business and Congress.

The attitudes and traditions dimension of public opinion can pertain to the local municipality or to a broader geographical region. It can even be extended to include societal differences in labor relations patterns, such as those affecting U.S. trade with Japan, the European Community, and Eastern Europe (covered in Chapter 15). Consider, for example, the goals of a prominent Japanese union leader whose standard of living goals for his members include:

- The square footage of a member's apartment (for example, 154 square feet for a union member in his or her twenties).
- The age (36) at which a member first owns golf clubs and a piano.
- The formal education of the member's children—a private university for the son and a junior college for the daughter.

These values would not likely be imported into the U.S. labor movement. However, Japanese managerial philosophies have affected the labor relations process in the United States, as Japanese auto makers have built eight wholly owned or joint venture factories here, three of them represented by the United Auto Workers.

Public opinion, like the other external influences, can affect one or more phases of the labor relations process as well as the content of negotiated work rules.

Exhibit 1.5 **Summary of Public Opinion Responses Indicating Confidence in Various American Institutions**

"Year" = Year the following question was asked: "How much confidence do you yourself have (in the following institutions in American society): A great deal, quite a lot, some, or very little?"
Numbers = Percentage of those respondents indicating "a great deal" or "quite a lot." Corresponding response percentages for other institutions in 1993 that do not have years for same national trend given below are: police, 52%; television news, 46%; U.S. Supreme Court, 53%; medical system, 34%; and newspapers, 31%.

INSTITUTION	YEAR									
	1975	**1977**	**1979**	**1981**	**1983**	**1985**	**1987**	**1989**	**1991**	**1993**
Military	58	57	54	50	53	61	61	63	69	76
Church and Organized Religion	68	64	65	64	62	66	61	52	56	63
Public Schools	NA	54	53	42	39	48	50	43	35	39
Banks	NA	NA	60	46	51	51	51	42	30	38
Newspapers	NA	NA	51	35	38	35	31	NA	32	31
Congress	40	40	34	29	28	39	NA	32	18	19
Organized Labor	38	39	36	28	26	28	26	NA	22	26
Big Business	40	40	34	29	28	39	NA	32	18	23

Notes: NA = not available.

SOURCE: The Gallup Poll: Public Opinion 1993 (Wilmington, Delaware: Scholarly Resources, Inc., 1994), pp. 55-67.

This influence can affect the first phase of the labor relations process—determining whether employers locate in a community and/or accept unions at their facilities. After experiencing a bitter, well-publicized strike between Caterpillar and the UAW, the mayor of Peoria, Illinois, feared employers would not locate in his community:

> We had worked so hard to make this a city with the image of having a cohesive relationship between labor and management, a place that people should think about expanding their businesses or opening new ones. Now comes this strike, which is going to damage our reputation.[24]

However, in some cases, communities stress the nonexistence of unions and/or their populations' anti-union attitudes as a benefit for organizations during expansion or relocation. For example, the Economic Development Council of Richmond, Virginia, recently placed a full-page ad in *The Wall Street Journal* that urged firms to relocate and join Richmond's 14 corporate headquarters. Among the sales points: "There isn't a single office union in the Richmond area. In fact, there haven't been any attempts to organize one."[25]

Community opposition to unions might be based on moral values. Union officials attempt to counter this obstacle when attempting to organize employees who contend that their religious beliefs prevent them from joining a union. For example, the Communications Workers of America has published a pamphlet, "The Church Believes in Unions," which features the endorsements of prominent representatives of the Catholic, Jewish, and Protestant religions. The AFL-CIO has similarly reported in its national publication, *AFL-CIO News,* Pope John Paul II's endorsement of unions as playing a "decisive role" in negotiating minimum wages as well as in helping employees to "share in a fully human way" in determining other workplace conditions.

Public opinion can also affect the second phase of the labor relations process, negotiating the labor agreement and work rules. For example, teachers desiring limits on the number of students allowed in a classroom might stress to the community that increased class size would lower educational quality. Educational administrators, on the other hand, would probably indicate to the community that a teachers' strike over this issue would place educational funding in jeopardy.

The possibility and extent of a strike to obtain certain working conditions can also be influenced by public opinion. For example, unionized employees at Alliant Techsystems Inc. ended a week-long strike by an overwhelming vote (937 to 116) during Operation Desert Storm. They worked at one of two companies that manufactured 25-millimeter shells for armored vehicles used by the Army and Marine Corps. Many of the employees felt the wrath of their neighbors, who strongly supported the war effort, a situation that no doubt influenced their return-to-work decision. Unions representing employees such as U.S. Air Express pilots and National Hockey League players have inserted full-page newspaper advertisements indicating their bargaining position in strikes/lockouts.

Perhaps the most vivid example of public opinion affecting the third phase of the labor relations process, administering the labor agreement, occurred in Milwaukee, Wisconsin. The Milwaukee Police Association (MPA) called for Police Chief Philip Arreola's resignation because he suspended and subsequently dismissed two of its members, who allowed a Laotian youth to return to a serial killer's apartment, where he was eventually murdered. The MPA claimed that Arreola was pressured by the public to take disciplinary action against the officers, who had fine work records, and urged the chief to step down because 98 percent of the MPA's 1,570 members believed he mishandled the discipline, and 93.6 percent of the members indicated they had no confidence in the chief. Arreola then informed a cheering rally led by Jesse Jackson that he would not step down. Arreola remained in his position, and a subsequent vote by the civilian Milwaukee Fire and Police Commission upheld the dismissals of the two police officers.

Union officials are aware of the significant influence that public opinion can have on the three phases of the labor relations process. Albert Shanker, president of the American Federation of Teachers, indicated why he wrote the first of 1,000 columns entitled "Where We Stand" some 20 years ago. After strikes were conducted by his union in 1967 and 1968, Shanker reflected,

> I became one of the best-known figures in New York City, but people saw me only as a militant union leader—urging teachers to strike, refusing to settle, going to jail. In late 1968, I became convinced that I had been dead wrong in believing that the public's opinion of me didn't matter. Public schools depend on public support. And the public was not likely to support the schools for long if they thought teachers were led by a powerful madman. . . .
>
> I decided to devote some time and energy to letting the public know that the union's president was someone who read books and had ideals and ideas about how to fix the schools.[26]

Union officials seek to enhance public opinion in three general ways: *monitoring and reacting to negative comments made in the media; getting organized labor's positive message out to the community;* and *cultivating relationships with various groups in the community.* An example of monitoring and reacting to media comments occurred when officials of the Association of Flight Attendants criticized NBC and a comedienne on the "Tonight Show" for labeling flight attendants "high-altitude hookers" and "humorously" portraying a flight attendant who drinks and steals on the job.[27]

Another reaction to a comment made in the media involved some members of Local 44 of the International Association of Theatrical Stage Employees, who booed and spilled water on Bruce Willis when he visited the movie set of *Hook.* This event occurred a few months after Willis stated in an interview, "Unions are the number one cost in making films." A union official, aware that Willis's salary for *The Last Boy Scout* approximated $14 million, justified his organization's protest by saying, "After what [Willis] has taken out of the industry, he's an idiot to make statements like that."[28]

Some 30 labor groups, including the AFL-CIO Labor Institute of Public Affairs (LIPA), have recently used public access and cable television channels to indicate union perspectives and accomplishments. LIPA has produced many programs for public access television, including "Working in America," which won an Emmy Award.[29] Exhibit 1.6 reflects an advertising effort by public sector unions concerning the public and members' response to the Oklahoma City bombing disaster. It also reflects the first way to enhance public opinion and approaches to the third related tactic by cultivating relationships with the entire local community; community subgroups such as civil rights groups, feminist organizations, and church alliances; or community action groups. They can appeal on the basis of common goals, a sense of fair play, or reciprocity (where the union has previously built up a reservoir of goodwill and credibility). Citizens may be asked to help the union by supporting boycotts of a product, providing direct assistance to strikers (such as support of local merchants or local welfare), pressuring local government agencies to censure or control the employer's actions, supporting a corporate campaign, or backing the union in an organizing drive.[30]

Exhibit 1.6 Unions' Advertisement to Mobilize Public Opinion

The Call Of Duty

The United States of America is a government of, by and for the people.

The people who work in government service are the faces of America. Serving all of us. In times of crisis. And every day. We honor them.

Today, we grieve for those who died.

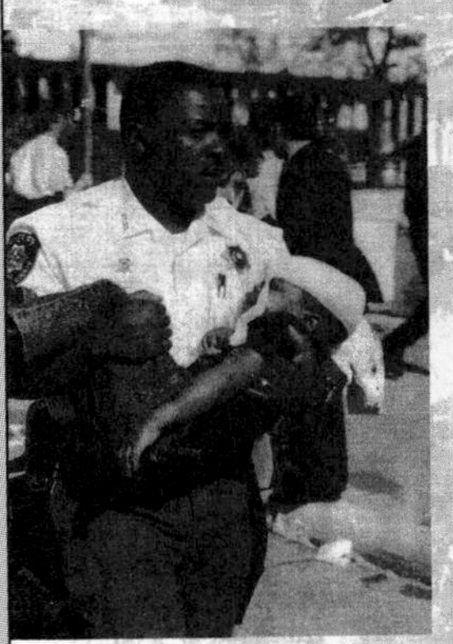

Friends. Neighbors. Little league coaches and Sunday school teachers. Children, parents, aunts, and uncles. Public employees. That's who died in the Oklahoma City tragedy.

And that's who came to the victims' aid—other public employees. 911 operators. Special disaster teams. Crowd control experts. Search and rescue units. Counselors. Police, fire and medical staffs. And those working day and night to apprehend the terrorists who committed this vile act.

Public servants, ordinary citizens, heroes all. Responding to the call of duty.

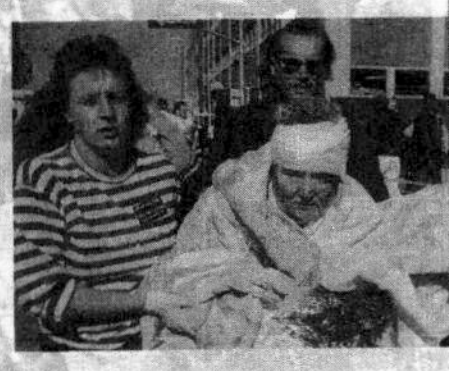

Isn't it time to end the constant attacks on the people who serve us? Who knows what the twisted mind of a terrorist might think? ***Or do.***

Next time you hear someone viciously attack our government, and the Americans who work for it, tell them— STOP IT. THIS IS OUR GOVERNMENT.

AFSCME®
in the public service
1625 L Street NW, Washington, DC 20036

SOURCE: *New York Times,* April 27, 1995, p. A-9.

Labor unions should also consider cultivating high-school students to influence union membership in the future. A recent study confirmed that high-school students, while lacking a basic knowledge of labor history and collective bargaining, share relatively little anti-labor bias and appear more receptive than adults to advantages of unionization.[31]

Financial Market An element of important consideration in the labor relations process is the **financial market,** the arena in which the employers (and unions) seek to borrow funds to develop their investment strategies. Companies also consider exchange rates between countries to determine plant location for producing and trading. When a company wants to expand its plant capacity and increase jobs, it frequently has to borrow money in the financial markets at the same time as it may request wage concessions from the union (see Chapter 13) and/or request elimination of work rule restrictions to productivity (see Chapter 12). A union must also enter the financial markets in order to support an employee stock option plan (ESOP) (See Chapter 13) while it agrees to wage concessions to support the stock purchase. For example, when 80,000 employees of United Airlines, through their major unions, gained control of 55 percent of the company stock for $4.8 billion, employees agreed to wage cuts for five years and work rule changes to improve productivity (see the "Labor Relations in Action" box in Chapter 13).

Exchange rates between countries (see Chapter 15) can alter companies' investment strategies because exchange rates affect the comparative wage rates and, consequently, the comparative labor costs of production. As an example, when the peso in Mexico was devalued by as much as 50 percent of the U.S. dollar, the labor costs of production in Mexico declined dramatically and made producing goods in Mexico more attractive and economical for multinational corporations. Thus, products were made in Mexico at lower wage rates and shipped to the United States and elsewhere at comparatively lower prices. As well, in 1995, when the German mark was strong in comparison with the U.S. dollar and wage rates in Germany were higher (over 50 percent—see Chapter 15), firms such as Mercedes-Benz determined that producing automobiles in the United States was more attractive and located a plant in the United States. Later in the same year, Mercedes-Benz announced plans to build a plant in mainland China, where wage rates were among the lowest in the world and where most developed countries experienced highly favorable currency exchange rates. As exchange rates vary between countries and over time, the investment strategies and, consequently, employment will shift, and labor-management relationships will be affected either directly or indirectly through these changes.

State of the Economy: National, Industrial, and Firm-Specific Indicators The state of the **economy** is usually referred to by indicating movement among such quantitative indicators as inflation, unemployment, and productivity. During the late 1960s and through the 1970s, the United States witnessed a rising inflation rate, which influenced the negotiation of work rules—notably, union insistence that a labor agreement include provisions to increase wages if increases occur in the cost of living (see Chapter 13).

Conversely, the Labor Department recently indicated that the average negotiated labor agreement duration (35.8 months) is the longest since figures started being kept in 1972. Currently, many unions and employers find that steady, low inflation makes it easier to commit to long-term contracts because company labor costs and employee living expenses become more predictable.

Two other economic indicators that can affect work rules are interest and unemployment rates. An increase in interest rates could retard home and industrial construction projects. Under these circumstances, work rules might be negotiated to ensure that construction workers are not laid off and/or that they receive some compensation for the reduced work load.

The unemployment rate affects work rules providing job protection. Chapter 6 discusses ways in which the unemployment rate can affect the bargaining power of union and management officials. If this and other economic measures pertaining to the Gross National Product, productivity, cost of living, compensation at all employee levels, and exports and imports are unfavorable, unions will be more likely to accept bargaining concessions.

Summary

While unique to the particular labor-management activities, attitudes, and relationships at each organization (discussed more in Chapter 4), the labor relations process includes the following three phases: recognition of the legitimate rights and responsibilities of union and management representatives, negotiation of the labor agreement, and administration of the terms of the negotiated labor agreement on a daily basis.

The labor relations process focuses on jointly negotiated and administered work rules that pertain to compensation and employees' and employers' job rights and obligations. These rules can vary to the extent that they are unique to a particular job classification or industry and are vague or specific. They can also reflect the dynamic nature of labor relations by changing over time.

Union and management officials represent two participant categories in the labor relations process. Neither grouping is consensual, however, because different perspectives occur between and within organizations. Employees represent perhaps the most significant participant category because they can have loyalties to both union and management officials and because they determine whether a union receives representation at an organization and whether a strike is taken and successfully completed. Other participants are third-party neutrals (mediators and arbitrators) and the government, with its executive decisions, legislative action, and judicial decisions.

These participants are influenced in their rule-making efforts by several variables such as technology (equipment, pace and scheduling of work, the work environment and tasks to be performed, and information exchange); labor and product markets; international forces such as the North American Free Trade Agreement (NAFTA); public opinion; financial market; and the state of the economy.

Key Terms

labor relations process
work rules
mediator
arbitrator
technology
labor market
product market
public opinion
financial market
economy

Discussion Questions

1. Exhibit 1.2 illustrates the focal point of the labor relations process and many variables that affect the process. Select an academic discipline such as political science, economics, or sociology, and indicate three specific ways the discipline could add insights into the labor relations process.
2. Discuss the different dimensions of technology, indicating how this variable might contribute to two unique and specific work rules for unionized employees at a grocery store. Also indicate with examples how two other external constraints or influences (see the outer circle of Exhibit 1.2) could affect the work rules at a grocery store.
3. "The 'Labor Relations in Action' concerning employee drug testing illustrates the focal point but not the phases of the labor relations process." Is this statement true or false? Explain your answer.

References

1. See, for example, William N. Cooke, "The Failure to Negotiate First Contracts: Determinants and Policy Implications," *Industrial and Labor Relations Review* 38 (January 1985), pp. 162–178.

2. John Dunlop, *Industrial Relations Systems,* rev. ed. (Boston: Harvard Business School Press, 1993), pp. 13–16.

3. Peter T. Kilborn, "Labor Wants Shorter Hours to Make Up for Job Losses," *New York Times,* October 11, 1993, p. A-7.

4. Bureau of National Affairs Inc., *Daily Labor Report,* September 10, 1992, p. A-12.

5. Mollie H. Bowers, "What Labor and Management Need to Know about Workplace Smoking Cases," *Labor Law Journal,* January 1992, pp. 40–49.

6. Sharolyn A. Rosier, "Assaults at the Workplace," *AFL-CIO News,* December 12, 1994, p. 5.

7. Bureau of National Affairs Inc., *Daily Labor Report,* no. 37 (February 25, 1985), p. F-1; Jules Bernstein, "The Evolution of the Use of Management Consultants in Labor Relations: A Labor Perspective," *Labor Law Journal* 36 (May 1985), p. 296.

8. John J. Lawler, "The Influence of Management Consultants on the Outcome of Union Certification Elections," *Industrial and Labor Relations Review* 38 (October 1984), pp. 38–51. See also Bureau of National Affairs Inc., Special Report, *Labor Relations Consultants: Issues, Trends, and Controversies* (Washington, D.C.: Bureau of National Affairs Inc., 1985); and Terry A. Berthel, "Profiting from Unfair Labor Practices: A Proposal to Regulate Management Representatives," *Northwestern University Law Review* 79 (1984), pp. 506–565.

9. Robert L. Rose, "Navistar UAW Members Reject Trading Wage Concession for Retiree Payments," *The Wall Street Journal,* June 2, 1994, p. A-2.

10. *Newsweek,* June 20, 1994, p. 6.

11. For an early study of employee dual loyalty, see Theodore V. Purcell, *Blue Collar Man: Patterns of Dual Allegiance in Industry* (Cambridge: Harvard University Press, 1960). See also Michael E. Gordon and Robert T. Ladd, "Dual Allegiance: Renewal, Reconsideration, and Recantation," *Personnel Psychology* 43 (1990); Julian Barling, Bill Wade, and Clive Fullagar, "Predicting Employee Commitment to Company and Union: Divergent Models," *Journal of Occupational Psychology* 63 (1990), pp. 49–61; and Clive J.A. Fullagar, Daniel G. Gallagher, Michael E. Gordon, and Paul F. Clark, "Impact of Early Socialization on Union Commitment and Participation: A Longitudinal Study," *Journal of Applied Psychology* 80 (February 1995), pp. 147–157.

12. See, for example, Paul Osterman, "The Impact of Computers on the Employment of Clerks and Managers," *Industrial and Labor Relations Review* 39 (January 1986), pp. 175–186. See also Michael Wallace and Arne L. Kallenberg, "Industrial Transformation and the Decline of Craft: The Decomposition of Skill in the Printing Industry, 1931–1978," *American Sociological Review* 47 (June 1982), pp. 307–324; David Gann and Peter Senker, "Construction Robotics: Technological Change and Work Organization," *New Technology, Work and Employment* 8 (March 1993), pp. 3–9; and Lorraine Giordano, *Beyond Taylorism: Computerization and the New Industrial Relations* (New York: St. Martin's, 1992).

13. Andrew Tanzer and Ruth Simon, "Why Japan Loves Robots and We Don't," *Forbes,* April 16, 1990, p. 152.

14. Pascal Zachary, "Worried Workers: Service Productivity is Rising Fast—And So Is the Fear of Lost Jobs," *The Wall Street Journal,* June 8, 1995, p. A-1.

15. Jane Fritsch, "Gun of Choice for the New York Police Runs Into Fierce Opposition," *New York Times,* May 31, 1992, p. 23.

16. Neil De Clereq, Alec Meiklejohn, and Ken Mericle, "The Use of Microcomputers in Local Union Administration," *Labor Studies Journal* 10 (Spring 1985), pp. 3–45.

17. For related considerations, see "AFL-CIO Goes On-Line with New Labor NET, *AFL-CIO News,* July 26, 1993, p. 6; "Labor Unions Are Getting Off to a Slow Start in Cyberspace," *The Wall Street Journal,* May 30, 1995, p. A-1; and Montieth M. Illingworth, "Workers on the Net, Unite!" *Information Week,* August 22, 1994, pp. 27–36.

18. "AFL-CIO Information Now Available on Internet," Bureau of National Affairs, Inc., *Daily Labor Report,* no. 107 (June 5, 1995), p. A-16.

19. Dana Milbank, "New Collar Work: Telephone Sales Reps Do Unrewarding Jobs That Few Can Abide," *The Wall Street Journal,* September 9, 1993, p. A-1.

20. James R. Healey, "Tangled Web of Rules Obscures Autos' Origins," *USA Today,* March 2, 1992, pp. 1 and 3B.

21. For a somewhat detailed account of this situation at one company see Ron Suskind, "Tough Vote: Threat of Cheap Labor Abroad Complicates Decisions to Unionize," *The Wall Street Journal,* July 28, 1992, pp. A-1, A-8.

22. Lane Kirkland, "Labor and the Press," *American Federationist* 82 (December 1975), p. 3. See also John A. Grimes, "Are the Media Short Changing Organized Labor?" *Monthly Labor Review* 110 (August 1987), pp. 53–54.

23. Diane E. Schmidt, "Public Opinion and Media Coverage of Labor Unions," *Journal of Labor Research* 13 (Summer 1992), pp. 151–165. See also William J. Puette, *Through Jaundiced Eyes: How the Media View Organized Labor* (Ithaca, NY: ILR Press, 1992); and Paul Jarley and Sarosh Kuruvilla, "American Trade Unions and Public Approval: Can Unions Please People All of the Time," *Journal of Labor Research* 15 (Spring 1994), pp. 97–117.

24. Jonathan P. Hicks, "Dreams and City

Image Put at Stake in Strike," *New York Times,* April 10, 1992, p. A-31.
25. *The Wall Street Journal,* October 18, 1988, p. A-13.
26. Albert Shanker, "Where We Stand," *New York Times,* December 16, 1990, p. 7.
27. "AFA Not Amused by Joan Rivers' Portrayal of Flight Attendants," *Flight Log,* May–June 1993, p. 7.
28. "Bad Feelings by Movie Unions toward Willis Could Die Hard," *Florida Times-Union,* July 13, 1991, p. D-5.
29. Candice Johnson, "TV Window Opened to Get Labor's Message Out," *AFL-CIO News,* July 11, 1994, p. 12.
30. James Craft, "The Community as a Source of Union Power," *Journal of Labor Research,* 11 (Spring 1990), p. 149. This article discusses several examples of working with the community. For a detailed account of a community effort involving religious institutions in an attempt to restore closed steel mills as a community and employee owned enterprise, see Thomas G. Fuechtmann, *Steeples and Stacks: Religion and Steel Crisis in Youngstown* (New York: Cambridge University Press, 1989).
31. Tom Juravich, "Anti-Union or Unaware? Work and Labor as Understood by High School Students," *Labor Studies Journal* 16 (Fall 1991), pp. 16–32.

2 Evolution of Labor-Management Relationships

The American labor movement as we know it has adjusted to changing social events, employers' attitudes and actions, and employee preferences for more than 100 years. A historical perspective is necessary to better understand current union behavior and helps us predict how most unions might react to sudden and dramatic change.

There is no best way to obtain this perspective.[1] Insights from many academic disciplines (sociology, economics, political science, and so forth) have to be considered, and many focal points can be assessed. Our discussion focuses on what has worked and not worked for organized labor through two interrelated historical dimensions: (1) relationships between labor and management organizations; and (2) organizational characteristics of labor organizations.

This second dimension is important to labor relations students and practitioners because the current American Federation of Labor-Congress of Industrial Organizations (AFL-CIO, which represents 89 national and international unions and 14 million affiliated union members) has been historically affected by four major labor organizations: the Knights of Labor (KOL), the Industrial Workers of the World (IWW), the American Federation of Labor (AFL), and the Congress of Industrial Organizations (CIO).

The strength of any labor organization depends on four criteria:

- *Its structural and financial stability.*
- *Its ability to work within established political and economic systems, particularly the wage system.*
- *Supportive or disruptive features of the broader social environment such as legislation, media, and public opinion.*
- *The ability of union leaders to identify and satisfy members' goals and interests.*

Readers can use these criteria to assess why some labor organizations failed in the past and to predict the likelihood of current unions posing a strong challenge to management.

The historical dimensions are organized into three time periods: 1869 to World War I; World War I to World War II; and World War II to the present.

• • •

1869 to World War I

Unions as we know them today did not exist before 1800. There were small guilds, joint associations of employers and craftspeople, that pressed for professional standards and restriction of outside competition.[2] These guilds pressed concerns that typically benefited employees and employers alike. By 1820 there had been only a few scattered strikes, usually over wages, since only two industries, shoemaking and printing, had even the semblance of collective bargaining. There was also no general labor philosophy or labor movement in the United States at this time,[3] as the unions were limited to local geographical regions.

The 1850s and 1860s saw development of the U.S. factory system, improved transportation, and product mobility, factors that extended a company's (and potential unionized employees') organization beyond the local community. For example, an employer could produce shoes at lower wages in Baltimore and ship them to Boston, where they could be sold at a lower price. Labor needed to take wages out of competition; thus, it needed a national organization.

The Civil War (1861 to 1865) refined and encouraged mass-production techniques, concentrating large numbers of semiskilled and unskilled employees under one factory roof—a situation that attracted organized labor.

The period of 1869 to World War I saw the formation of three national labor organizations: the Knights of Labor (Knights or KOL), the American Federation of Labor (AFL) under Samuel Gompers, and the Industrial Workers of the World (IWW). Each of these organizations will be discussed in terms of its orientations and goals, organizational structure, and strategies and tactics. Reasons suggested for the demise of the KOL and the IWW and other issues discussed illustrate the previously mentioned criteria for a labor organization's strength. Three prominent labor episodes of this period are also discussed: the drive for an 8-hour workday (including the Haymarket Riot of 1886), the Homestead strike (1892), and the Pullman strike (1894).

These three events and other union-management confrontations through the 1930s reflect a degree of unbridled violence that has been unmatched in contemporary times. The "Labor Relations in Action" box gives brief examples of steps companies would take to keep out unions and what employees were willing to do to force management to recognize their working concerns and unions. One way to gauge this historical difference is to imagine how these events would be covered on a national evening news program today.

LABOR RELATIONS IN ACTION

Labor, Violence, and Media Coverage

Bitter, bloody violence has beset the American labor movement since its beginnings. Compared to nineteenth century and pre–World War II events, company and union actions are polite and well-mannered today, far removed from the death and slaughter perpetrated by both parties in earlier times. While corporate management did whatever it could to destroy unions and disrupt strikes (hiring "goon" squads and replacements, for example), usually with the support of local, state, and federal authorities, employees had no compunction about fighting back as viciously as they could and used particular venom against strikebreakers. Following the breakup of the Molly Maguires in the coal fields of Pennsylvania in 1877 and the great railroad strikes of the same year, labor unrest continued and increased into the next century. Listed below is a chronology of some of the worst incidents of violence, with excerpts from the *New York Times*.

July 1892 Coeur d'Alene, Idaho—The Bunker Hill & Sullivan Company's determination to keep the mines open with strikebreakers precipitated violence from the striking miners. "Western Miners at War . . . [they] load 750 pounds of giant powder . . . sent it down the track toward the Frisco Mine." The resulting explosion killed one guard and injured 20. (*New York Times,* July 12, 1892, p. 1.) Idaho Attorney General George Roberts stated, "The mob must be crushed by overwhelming force. We can't retreat now." (*New York Times,* July 14, 1892, p. 1.) Continuing the battlefield imagery, the paper reported the next day, "Union Miners of the Coeur d'Alene District Disperse . . . State Authorities, Aided by the Federal Troops, in Full Possession of the Field." (*New York Times,* July 15, 1892, p. 3.)

February 24, 1912 Textile workers' strike, Lawrence, Mass.—Because of their poor living conditions during the strike, which had begun the previous month, the employees began to send their children to other cities. The police intervened because the mill owners complained that sending these children away would engender sympathy for the strikers in other cities. "Police Clubs Keep Lawrence Waifs In . . . Head Broken Over an Order to Prevent Strikers Shipping Their Children Away." The police prevented about 40 children from boarding a train for Philadelphia and took them to the police headquarters. "Fifty arrests were made, many of them women who had fought the police savagely and several heads were broken by the clubs of officers . . . four companies of infantry and a squad of cavalry surrounded the railroad station." As the police led the children from the police station to waiting cabs to transport them to the municipal home for neglected children, "a crowd of 500 foreigners [assembled] and a riotous scene followed . . . such a stubborn fight was made by the excited crowd . . . [that] a squad of militia was called. . . ." (*New York Times,* February 25, 1912, p. 2.)

April 20, 1914 Ludlow Massacre—When the Colorado Fuel and Iron Company refused to recognize a miners' union, the miners struck. The United Mine Workers Union established a tent colony for the miners and their families at Ludlow. Frequent clashes between the miners and the mine guards caused the Colorado governor to call out the National Guard, which attacked the tent camp and set fire to the tents, burning 11 children and 2 women. The "war" lasted 10 days and resulted in at least 46 deaths, and in the midst of the Mexican invasion President Wilson had to send in federal troops to stop the bloodshed. "The bodies of eleven children and two women have been recovered at Ludlow . . . union officials said . . . that the troops surrounding Ludlow had used dynamite in the ruins of the colony for destruction of the bodies of the dead . . . in an attempt to hide evidence of how many had died." (*New York Times,* April 23, 1914, p. 22.)

June 22, 1922 Herrin Massacre—When John L. Lewis, leader of the United Mine Workers, called a coal strike, the Illinois Coal Company in Herrin hired strikebreakers, which enraged the union miners. "5,000 Strikers from Illinois Mine . . . 14 Reported Killed, Score Wounded . . . Passing Train Crew Saw Heap of Bodies Lying in a Pit on a Hillside." (*New York Times,* June 22, 1922, p. 1.). The next day the paper reported "29 to 40 Killed by Miner Strikers . . . Massacred While Bound . . . Eyewitnesses of Both Factions Describe Slaughter by Crazed Strikers . . . 15 Bodies Thrown in Pond . . . Some Hanged to Roadside Trees . . ." (*New York Times,* June 23, 1922, p. 1.)

May 26, 1937 Battle of the Overpass—Richard T. Frankensteen and Walter Reuther attempted to organize the Ford Motor Company in Dearborn, Michigan, for the United Auto Workers. Company agents reacted immediately. "An outburst of violence, in which union organizers were beaten, kicked and driven away, marked the first attempt to organize the employees of the Ford Motor Company." The *New York Times* quoted Frankensteen, "They bounced us down the concrete steps of the overpass. . . . Then they would knock us down, stand us up, and knock us down again." (*New York Times,* May 27, 1937, p. 1.)

May 30, 1937 Memorial Day Massacre—During a strike at the Republic Steel Plant, strikers marched on the plant. "4 Killed, 84 Hurt as Strikers Fight Police in Chicago . . . Crowd Uses Guns and Rocks, Policy Employ Clubs, Tear Gas, and Bullets." (*New York Times,* May 31, 1937, p. 1.)

SOURCE: We are grateful to Kathy Cohen, Assistant Director, Libraries, University of North Florida, for preparing this discussion. The Haymarket Riot and Homestead Incident are described in some detail in the text and are therefore not covered here.

The Knights of Labor (KOL)

Goals and Organizations of the KOL Founded by Uriah S. Stephens as a secret society in 1869, the Knights of Labor (KOL) maintained secrecy until 1882 so that the members would not be discharged by their employers for participating in a labor organization.

There are two major reasons for discussing the KOL. First, it was a union national in scope, larger than any previous union in American history. In the early 1880s, it had a steady growth, reaching a membership of more than 100,000 in 1885. Between 1885 and 1886, the organization's membership increased sharply, to 700,000. The KOL achieved more power, prestige, and notoriety than any other previous labor organization.[4] However, its goals and strategies also contributed to its demise as an effective organization. So the Knights served as an important negative lesson to the American Federation of Labor and more contemporary labor organizations in establishing and achieving their objectives.

The Knights strongly objected to the method of industrial organization and operation that began during the Civil War. This view led them to establish two major interrelated goals:

1. Change the existing labor-management relationship so that the depersonalized and specialized aspects of mass production can be avoided.
2. Attain moral betterment for employees and society.

The KOL's goals can best be grasped through the views of Terence V. Powderly, its leader and chief spokesman from 1879 to 1883. Powderly felt that mass production reduced the employees' feelings of pride and personal accomplishment.[5] In previous times, employees could be satisfied with their craftsmanship, a sense of skilled accomplishment in fashioning high-quality products from beginning to end. Mass production created several specialized employee classifications, each contributing to the completed product. Powderly placed this situation in perspective by considering the shoemakers' situation:

> The man who was called a shoemaker thirty years ago made shoes; the man who claims to be a shoemaker today makes only part of a shoe. What was once a trade in itself is a multiplicity of trades. Once there were shoemakers, now we have Beaters, Binders, Bottomers, Buffers, Burnishers, Channellers, Crimpers, Cutters, Dressers, Edge Setters . . . and several other workers at the shoe trade, and they all consider themselves shoemakers.[6]

Employees working in these specialized classifications could not obtain meaning or satisfaction from their fragmented work tasks, according to Powderly. He also felt that bankers and owners of gold were the villains of industrial society, causing higher taxes for employees and the creation of monopolies that further depersonalized the individual employee.[7]

The Knights believed that changing the existing industrial and societal system would help accomplish their second goal, moral betterment and increased dignity for their members. Powderly claimed that members must place their concerns on a "higher" ground than material working conditions, as these physical effects were but stepping stones to "a higher cause, of a nobler nature . . . the more exalted and divine nature of man, his high and noble capabilities for good."[8] The leadership of the KOL was continually concerned that its members would devote too much attention to improving working conditions and ignore the goal of moral betterment—to make every man his own master.[9]

The moralistic overtones of the Knights guided their membership policies, organizational structure, and strategies and tactics. Since moral betterment affected all members of society, the Knights encouraged people of all callings to join their organization except professional gamblers, stockbrokers, lawyers, bankers, and those who lived in whole or in part by the sale or manufacture of intoxicating liquors.[10] Employers were also encouraged to join the KOL, the rationale being that they along with employees were being duped by financiers and lawyers and once educated to this fact would join hands with the employees in improving society.

Thus the *local assembly*, the basic unit in the KOL, could consist of employers and employees from several trades. There were 1,100 KOL local assemblies in 1886; the purpose of these organizations was to educate members on KOL principles. However, the authority and power of the Knights was centralized, resting with the General Executive Board headed by Powderly.[11] As will be seen later in this section, the structure of the KOL differed dramatically from that of the AFL.

Strategies to Accomplish the KOL's Goals The Knights used at least four strategies to accomplish their goals. First, political action was viewed as important, particularly since the Knights felt that previous legislation had led society down the wrong road. The Knights believed that politicians were motivated by self-interest and therefore required careful watching. However, the Knights believed in operating through the existing party. They also actively lobbied against importation of foreign labor and for appropriations to public school systems.

A second strategy was the encouragement of producer and consumer cooperatives. Unlike the socialists, the Knights did not want the cooperatives to be owned by the state. Instead, they wanted current employees to save enough from their wages to either purchase the operation or establish a new cooperative. Since factories would then be owned by the employees, conflict between labor and capital would cease.[12] Cooperatives would also enable the employees to become their own masters; they would have a voice in decision making, including the determination of a fair distribution of profits.

The Knights' leadership believed cooperatives would affect the established wage-profit system most directly; yet they made little attempt to establish a cooperative or to financially aid approximately 100 cooperatives established at the local or district level during the mid-1880s. Most of the cooperatives failed because of "inefficient managers, squabbles among shareholders, lack of capital, and injudicious borrowing of money at high rates of interest."[13]

The KOL pursued a third strategy when it actively avoided the use of strikes to obtain its goals. Indeed, the leadership often actively discouraged strikes and, in some cases, demoralized strikers with their statements.[14] Some leaders viewed strikes as a last resort, feeling they would distract members from the major goal of moral betterment and lessen the common interests of employers and employees. The General Executive Board set up a complicated procedure that local assemblies had to follow before they could obtain strike funds.[15] Powderly believed that no employees should be able to enter a strike that would result in other employees losing their jobs; therefore, a procedure was needed to ensure that every employee possibly affected by a strike would have a voice in the strike decision.[16] Yet the red tape involved in obtaining strike funds caused great dissension between the KOL leaders and members. Local assemblies that conducted strikes were left on their own financially, and the members bitterly resented the lack of support from the board.[17] It became common for local assemblies to conduct strikes without support from the Executive Board—in 1886, at least 538 local assemblies participated in either a strike or a boycott of an uncooperative employer's products.

The Knights' leadership preferred a fourth strategy to the strike: namely, the education of the members and citizens as to the perceived evils of the existing industrial system as well as the Knights' goals for societal improvement. Usually the leaders would meet with members of local assemblies in private sessions to inform them of the organization's goals and objectives. The emphasis on education instead of job action efforts (strikes and boycotts) is further discussed in the next section.

Reasons for the KOL's Failure and Demise Despite tremendous growth, the KOL experienced a sudden demise. One reason for its growth must be the successful strike taken by the local assemblies against Jay Gould's railroads in 1885, in which the Knights showed the public that an aggressive, well-disciplined group could take on one of the most powerful financiers and win. Yet the effect of this strike may have been limited because neither the Knights nor the newspapers publicized the events. Another reason for the KOL's growth was its identification with the 8-hour workday, an issue that was important to the nation's work force.[18] However, as discussed in the next section, the KOL's endorsement of the 8-hour workday was rather weak.

Faulty assumptions in the KOL's orientation The Knights were reform oriented, interested in changing existing aspects of society. The advantages of hindsight make clear that the KOL erred in assuming that technological advancement could be halted and possibly reversed. The KOL also overestimated the extent to which employers and employees shared common interests. While some common ground is shared, each group is motivated by self-interest. Employers are concerned about increased efficiency and profitability of the operation, while employees are concerned about job security and improvement of working conditions.

The organization's third faulty assumption was that all categories of employees would have identical interests. The KOL was ahead of its time in its attempt to organize unskilled employees—a goal eventually accomplished by unions within the Congress of Industrial Organizations (CIO) in the late 1930s. However, as further discussed in Chapter 11, employees do not all have the same interests, particularly if they have different skills and work classifications. The "one big union" approach (enrolling nearly anyone who expressed an interest in the Knights) was further complicated by many immigrant members whose differences in race, language, and religion presented barriers.[19]

A lack of legislation protecting the rights of employees to join unions and engage in collective bargaining This point is further discussed in the next chapter. Suffice it to say that the Knights, as well as other labor organizations before 1935, did not have the full force of the law on their side.

Inability of the KOL's leadership (particularly Powderly) to identify with members' goals The Knights insisted upon adopting a middle-class program for the American labor force, which they refused to contemplate in industrial, working-class terms. Many of the members showed little, if any, interest in the Knights after they joined. Almost all local assembly meetings required the members to dress up after a day's work to engage in intellectual discourse. In essence, the members had nothing to do except "ceremonialize, play politics, and study."[20] Powderly felt his position was above the membership. Instead of understanding members' needs, he imposed his goals, on his terms:

> I will talk at no picnics. . . . When I speak on the labor question I want the individual attention of my hearers and I want the attention for at least two hours and in that two hours I can only epitomize. At a picnic where . . . the girls as well as the boys swill beer I cannot talk at all.[21]

The preference for intellectual deliberation over immediate, gut-level response is perhaps best viewed through Powderly's approach to the 8-hour workday movement.

The 8-Hour Workday Movement and the Haymarket Riot One of the more important reforms desired by many employees in the late 1800s was reducing the prevalent 10-hour workday to 8 hours. Samuel Gompers, who was a Knights member and an official of other labor organizations (Federation of Organized Trades and Labor Unions and the Cigar Makers' Union), pressed Powderly to support a nationwide general strike on May 1, 1886, for the 8-hour workday. Powderly was receptive to the 8-hour day, as it would give employees more leisure time to pursue intellectual activities. However, he did not join with Gompers because he did not believe the length of the workday was the major problem: "To talk of reducing the hours of labor without reducing the power of machinery is a waste of energy."[22]

Supporters of the 8-hour workday believed that, if instituted, it would result in more people working, thereby reducing the unemployment problem. On May 3, 1886, some workers striking over this issue in Chicago become involved in a skirmish with the police, and at least four strikers were killed. A leader of this dispute published an inflammatory circular urging "Revenge!" and "Workingmen to Arms!" The circular also indicated that a mass rally would be held the next day at Haymarket Square in Chicago. The stage was set for an event (known later as the **Haymarket Riot**) that virtually eliminated the KOL's effectiveness.

On May 4, 1886, approximately 3,000 people attended the scheduled meeting, which began peacefully. Police who monitored the meeting were ordered by their

A mass rally by strikers supporting the 8-hour workday movement began peacefully but ended in violence and death in Chicago's Haymarket Square.

chief to return to the station. However, Police Captain Bonfield, whom the governor of Illinois later charged as being responsible for the incident, ordered them back to the meeting. During a speech a bomb was thrown into the gathering of police, killing 7 and wounding 60. What happened next is uncertain. The *Chicago Tribune* reported that "anarchists and rioters poured in a shower of bullets before the first action of the police was taken."[23] Yet another report in the same article stated that the police opened fire on the crowd immediately after the bomb exploded. Regardless of the order of events, the police did shoot into the crowd, killing several and wounding 200.

Eight individuals allegedly responsible for the incident were arrested. Four of the eight were hanged, one committed suicide in prison, and three were eventually pardoned by the governor of Illinois after serving some of their sentences. Their trial was at best shoddy: for example, the hand-picked jury included a relative of one of the bombing victims.[24] The trial never did establish who threw the bomb; however, the accused were judged guilty by the *Chicago Tribune* before the trial took place. More specifically, the paper stressed that the "mob" was led by "two wirey whiskered foreigners,"[25] who were "Nihilistic Agitators."[26]

The Knights were not directly labeled in the immediate press accounts of the strike nor in the subsequent series of unsuccessful strikes over the 8-hour workday, which involved nearly 340,000 employees. However, the strikes contributed to the organization's demise for at least two paradoxical reasons. A substantial body of public opinion labeled the Knights as being involved in the strikes. Yet many of the Knights' members criticized the leadership for not participating enough in the events during and after Haymarket.[27] Indeed, Powderly strongly discouraged strikes over the 8-hour workday, believing instead that members should write essays on the subject. Thus, the Haymarket Riot dramatically reflected the split between the KOL and the newly formed American Federation of Labor, under Gompers, an organization that was to flourish and endure.

The American Federation of Labor (AFL)

Origin and Goals of the AFL An outgrowth of the Federation of Organized Trades and Labor Unions of the United States and Canada, the **American Federation of Labor (AFL)** was formed in 1886 after some of its member national unions (most notably the Cigar Makers) were expelled from the Knights.[28] As previously mentioned, Samuel Gompers, a major founder of the AFL, was a member of the Knights but became disenchanted with the leadership's long-range social reform philosophy. Gompers was also upset about KOL activities involving the cigar makers—in particular, the KOL's raiding of its members and supplying of strikebreakers when the cigar makers struck firms.

He met with the Knights in December 1886 to discuss these problems, but the meeting did not resolve the situation. Indeed, Gompers became incensed when a pamphlet was circulated among KOL representatives that attacked Gompers personally by indicating "the General Executive Board has never had the pleasure of seeing Mr. Gompers sober."[29] Also, in retrospect, KOL leaders blundered when they concentrated on influencing craft employees, a move that resulted in bitter reactions from the trade unions. The Knights would have been better off (and still consistent with their goals) if they had devoted more attention to the unskilled employees, where the trades did not have any argument.[30]

Unlike the KOL, the AFL was not established as one big union. (This is discussed more fully in Chapter 4.) It represented a federation or organization that many national unions could join while each national union maintained its separate union status. Craft unions, such as the Cigar Makers, dominated the early stages of the AFL. The AFL influenced its member unions through its services, particularly organizing activities, philosophies, and strategies.

It is impossible to discuss the AFL apart from Gompers since "in the early years, the A.F. of L. existed only in the person of Gompers and in the annual conventions."[31] With the exception of 1895, Gompers was president of the AFL from its founding in 1886 until his death in 1924. Therefore, much of the discussion of the goals, strategies, and organization of the AFL is from the perspective of Gompers, a point of view that relates strongly to the current thinking of organized labor; relatively little change has occurred in orientation, strategies, and organization since the time of Gompers.

Gompers placed little emphasis on intellectual betterment, and he scorned other union leaders' pretensions to show labor union members the course of action they should pursue.[32] He criticized the KOL as representing "a hodgepodge with no basis for solidarity with the exception of a comparatively few trade assemblies."[33] Gompers believed that the goals and organization of unions should flow directly and naturally from the members' needs, not from the pronouncements of top leaders who structured unions based on their views of what should have been, rather than what was.

Gompers particularly scorned those union leaders who tried to change the existing social system through revolutionary means.[34] Although he was a socialist in his early years, he grew to despise this philosophy, contending that it was economically unsound, socially wrong, and impossible to apply in an industrial setting.[35] He also believed that union members should work for equitable treatment within industrial society rather than revolt against it.[36]

Thus, the AFL's major, if not sole, goal was to improve the material conditions of members through the existing capitalistic system. This goal was attacked by the critics of the AFL as representing pure and simple unionism. Gompers embraced this intended insult; indeed, he seemed to devote most of his attention to ensuring that the AFL's "pure and simple" approach to collective bargaining successfully differentiated it from other labor organizations.

"Pure and simple unionism" had two major objectives. The primary objective was economic betterment of the organization's members; Gompers believed the "truth," or essence, of labor unions should be measured in terms of their economic accomplishments:

> Economic betterment—today, tomorrow, in home and shop, was the foundation upon which trade unions have been built. Economic power is the base upon which may be developed power in other fields. It is the foundation of organized society. Whoever or whatever controls economic power directs and shapes development for the group or the nation.[37]

Thus, the AFL's notion of "employee dignity" equated with measured economic gains. This view differed from the KOL's contention that employee dignity is attained by participation as equals in meaningful work and in other societal concerns.[38]

Gompers also stressed a second objective of pure and simple unionism—the enhancement of the capitalistic system, which could benefit both employees and employers. Workers could obtain more only if capitalism continued to flourish. Without capitalism, neither employees nor employers would receive revenues. The AFL therefore believed labor and management shared some similar interests. However, Gompers did not agree with Powderly that this situation would lead to complete employer-employee agreement on all issues. He realized that major differences of opinion would occur over the distribution of revenues and that employees would probably have to pressure employers in order to receive their fair share.

Strategies and Tactics of the AFL This realization prompted the AFL to rely on one of its three major tactics—the strike. Unlike the Knights, Gompers believed the strike was a viable collective bargaining alternative:

> A workman must convince his employer that he is entitled to an advance in wages. . . . Why should the wage-earner work for less than living wages, which he would have to do if he could not strike? The worker is expected to continue to work at whatever wages his employer is willing to give in order to save the public from inconvenience.[39]

A second AFL tactic (particularly when its headquarters moved to Washington, D.C.) was that of involvement in the political arena. Gompers, an aggressive lobbyist, attempted to translate election votes of AFL members into "rewards" for political friends of labor and "punishments" for political enemies of labor. However, political efforts during Gompers's leadership were neither intense nor widespread throughout the AFL.[40]

AFL political efforts were directed at influencing the existing two-party system instead of forming a third political party. Gompers felt that establishing a third party would divert too much time from fundamental collective bargaining efforts. He also felt that any new political party would fall into the socialists' control.[41]

The third AFL tactic was to secure increased status for organized labor and collective bargaining. Gompers devoted much attention to the National Civic Foundation, formed in 1899 to promote industrial peace through collective bargaining. This organization, composed of prominent labor, management, and political officials, attempted to guide public opinion toward the positive aspects of collective bargaining. However, at least one observer of industrial relations has questioned the success of this tactic, believing that "its rhetoric surpassed its performance."[42]

Organization of the AFL The AFL's organizational structure was based on two related principles: exclusive jurisdiction and decentralized authority. The AFL avoided the concept of "one big union"—which proved ineffective for the KOL—and insisted on the principle of exclusive jurisdiction. This principle rested on the twofold observation that (1) each craft or trade had unique working conditions and job interests and (2) combining members of different trades into one organization would jeopardize those interests and cause unnecessary dissension. The AFL believed in one union representing a particular craft; for example, separate unions would represent carpenters, painters, and cigar makers.

Gompers also strongly believed the AFL was a voluntary organization held together by the mutual self-interests of members. Unlike Powderly, who believed that centralized authority was necessary to achieve the Knights' objectives, Gompers viewed the central AFL as a "rope of sand," dependent entirely on the acceptance of its members. Thus, the real authority rested with various national unions and their member locals. As is further discussed in Chapter 4, these principles continue to influence contemporary union organizations.

The organization activity as well as the organizational structure of the AFL must be considered. Gompers was a most active union organizer; he claimed to have helped in organizing 28 unions representing different crafts such as painters, paper makers, firefighters, and post office clerks.[43] Much of this effort was due to Gompers's view of himself as "one of the boys"—he took pride in his ability to socialize with the members on their own terms.

In spite of Gompers's efforts, the AFL's early growth was not spectacular. Its original membership of 150,000 had increased to only 250,000 six years later. The initial slow growth was due to the counterattack of industry (discussed in the section on World War I to World War II), the generally repressive attitude of the government and the courts, and the difficulties raised by the depression of 1893. Yet

Gompers could view these modest membership gains as a tribute to the AFL's powers of "stability and permanency."[44]

From its formation until World War I, the AFL was directly or indirectly involved in three prominent events: the Homestead and Pullman incidents and the formation and demise of the Industrial Workers of the World (IWW).

The Homestead Incident

The Carnegie Steel Works, located in Homestead, Pennsylvania, was ironically the scene of one of the more violent episodes in labor history. The founder of the works, Andrew Carnegie, was a renowned philanthropist who gave every indication of being receptive to organized labor. In one article, written before the Homestead Incident, he stated that a strike or a lockout was a "ridiculous affair" as it represented only a test of strength instead of determining what was "fair and just."[45] Carnegie also believed that labor-management problems would occur in large firms run by salaried managers instead of owners, because the former group had no permanent interest in the desires of the workmen.

Carnegie's remarks proved prophetic in the **Homestead Incident** of July 6, 1892. Although many have labeled the incident a strike, one labor historian has noted that no strike vote was ever taken by the membership[46] and that the employer prohibited the employees from working. During negotiation between the mill and the Amalgamated Association of Iron, Steel, and Tin Workers (an affiliate of the AFL), a 15-foot-high solid board fence, topped with barbed wire, was constructed around the building. Andrew Carnegie was vacationing in Scotland during negotia-

The bloody confrontation between Pinkerton agents and employees of the Carnegie Steel Works in Homestead, Pennsylvania, in 1892 was one of the most violent in labor history and actually set back the cause of unions in the steel industry.

tions and had delegated these duties to a management official named Henry Clay Frick. The union labeled the structure around the steel mill "Fort Frick." Members were also undoubtedly aware that Frick was negotiating with Pinkerton detectives while labor-management negotiations were being conducted. Frick intended to use Pinkerton detectives inside the facility to protect the company's property and as strikebreakers.

On June 30, 1892, the company made its last offer, which represented a substantial reduction of previous wages,[47] and locked out its 4,000 employees. Workmen then began an around-the-clock surveillance of the plant. One newspaper account indicated, "The line of pickets covers the river, roads, and railways so tightly that no stranger can enter the town without being known to the strikers."[48] On the morning of July 5, 300 Pinkertons gathered at Ashtabula, Ohio, and proceeded by rail to Youngstown, Ohio. They then traveled up the Monongahela River by barge. On July 6, word had reached the townspeople that the Pinkertons would be entering the plant from the river. Six thousand people lined the river banks at 2:00 A.M., and employees prepared two small cannons, one on each side of the river, to be used on the Pinkertons.[49]

The Pinkertons attempted to land by the company's beach at 5:00 A.M.; shots were exchanged, and three Pinkertons were killed. Shooting by both sides continued for 12 hours, with an additional seven townspeople killed and 50 wounded. The Pinkertons surrendered to the townspeople and were forced to run a bloody gauntlet before being locked up for their protection. The townspeople had taken the weapons from the Pinkertons, a situation that resulted in 8,700 National Guard militiamen being sent to secure the town. There were few further attempts by Pinkertons or strikebreakers.[50] The incident ended for all purposes some five months later (November 20, 1892) when the Amalgamated lifted its prohibition against returning to work.

Homestead has been labeled the Waterloo of unions in the steel industry. National membership in the Amalgamated dropped from 24,000 in 1892 to 8,000 in 1894. On the local level, only 800 of the original Homestead employees were reinstated. Carnegie's mills showed a dramatic increase in profits when the union was eliminated,[51] a message that must have encouraged other employers to take an anti-union stance.

While Homestead represented a victory for management, the AFL and organized labor did benefit to some extent from the situation. First, Gompers demonstrated to existing and potential union members his very real concern about the Homestead situation.[52] The funds contributed by the AFL to help defray the employees' legal expenses also demonstrated that the AFL was interested in helping its member unions in a material sense.[53] Finally, the Homestead situation received more sympathetic newspaper accounts than did the Haymarket Riot. The press charged Carnegie with provoking the situation. For example, the *Chicago Tribune* strongly criticized the company's use of Pinkertons and contended that Carnegie's company as well as any large industrial organization "has duties and obligations toward society which it must not forget, and not the least of them is to do all in its power, and make all of the concessions it can, to preserve civil and industrial peace."[54] At a minimum, the press could not continually criticize the involved union or employees in this incident, especially since no individual was found guilty of participating in the incident.

The Pullman Strike

Strikes were common in the railroad industry; for example, the Great Upheaval of 1877 involved independent railroad employee associations protesting wage cuts. It was a bitter and violent confrontation in which more than 100 employees were killed and several hundred were badly wounded.[55]

Yet the **Pullman Strike** of 1894 assumes significance because of the principal personalities involved (Eugene Debs and George Pullman) and an organization (the American Railway Union, or ARU) that had the potential to challenge the AFL for union members. It also approached being the only revolutionary strike in the United States; it became a nationwide strike in one industry and came near to involving all industries.[56]

As a result of the 1893 depression, the Pullman Company laid off 3,000 of its 5,800 employees and cut wages 25 to 40 percent. Both actions were important since they occurred in the milieu of George Pullman's company town. This town represented a social, paternalistic experiment by the owner of the Pullman Palace Car Company. The company owned all the houses, buildings, and services in the town; employees were not allowed to own their own homes.[57] Pullman did not correspondingly reduce rents and charges for other services when it reduced wages; thus, the wage cuts resulted in some employees having a net two-week pay of $1 to $6 during the winter of 1893 to 1894.

This situation generated much hostility among employees, many of whom were members of the American Railway Union (ARU), formed in 1893. The ARU was completely independent from the AFL; indeed, it competed for members with the AFL-affiliated railway brotherhoods. The ARU accepted any white employee, regardless of specific job classification, so that railroad employees could present a unified front to the railroad companies.[58] It was attractive to many employees because employers previously had been able to create dissension among the different craft unions by playing off one against the other in wage negotiations.

The ARU's local unions had sole authority to call a strike, and the Pullman strike began on May 11, 1894. Debs, the union leader, informed the strikers that the strike should represent a protest against philosophical issues instead of mere material betterment: "The paternalism of Pullman is the same as the interest of a slave holder in his human chattels. You are striking to avert slavery and degradation."[59]

At first the strikers followed Debs's orders not to damage railroad property. The ARU instead adopted a strategy of not operating any train that included a Pullman sleeping car—the common practice was to cut these cars from the train and move them to the side tracks. If any employee was discharged for this action, then the entire crew would quit, leaving the train immobilized. This tactic, employed in 27 states and territories, was intended to make railroad carriers put pressure on Pullman to agree with the ARU's bargaining position.

However, the railroad employers rallied behind Pullman and countered the union's strategy by hiring strikebreakers. They also decided to include federal mail on nearly every train and were able to obtain an injunction on July 2, 1894 (subsequently upheld by the Supreme Court), to prevent any employee from interfering with the delivery of the mail. Employees could no longer engage in their strike strategy of rendering the trains inoperative. Some 16,000 troops, dispatched by President Cleveland to enforce the injunction, either delivered the mail and operated the trains or protected strikebreakers so that food and other perishable items could be delivered throughout the country.

The strike then took a particularly ugly turn; employees burned at least 700 railroad cars in Chicago on July 7, 1894. Interestingly, management was also criticized for this incident, at the least for failing to take minimum security measures such as guarding or locking the railroad cars. At a maximum, some management officials may have provoked the incident to receive additional support from the government. This possibility is suggested because all the burnt cars were old (the more expensive Pullman cars were not on the property), and very few of the cars were loaded with any product.[60]

The resulting negative public opinion and increased action by the federal troops forced Debs to seek Gompers's cooperation. Debs wanted Gompers to call a national strike to enforce Debs's last offer, which was simply management's reinstatement of the striking employees. Gompers refused to support Debs, contending that he did not have authority to call a general strike. Gompers also believed that the proposed settlement would, in effect, admit to the public that the ARU had failed to win material benefits for its members. Much of Gompers's reluctance was based on his view of Debs as being "a leader of irregular movements and lost causes."[61] However, Gompers's inaction might also have been due to his desire to eliminate a potential rival to the AFL and bolster his reputation in the business community.

Debs was eventually convicted and sentenced under the Sherman Antitrust Act of 1890; and the ARU, which had grown to 150,000 members in one year, quickly faded from existence. Organized labor did learn an important lesson from this strike: it would be difficult to alter the existing system against the wishes of a persistent, if not exceptionally stubborn, owner (Pullman), the federal government (troops, injunctions, legislation), the AFL (which supported this system), and negative public opinion (fueled by exaggerated and dramatic newspaper articles).

The Industrial Workers of the World (IWW)

The **Industrial Workers of the World (IWW)** was formed as an alternative to the AFL on June 27, 1905. "Big Bill" Haywood, initial organizer of the IWW, originated the organization's goals in calling the convention of 209 delegates to order with the following remarks:

> Fellow Workers. . . We are here to confederate the workers of this country into a working class movement that shall have for its purpose the emancipation of the working class from the slave bondage of Capitalism. . . . The aims and objects of this organization should be

> to put the working class in possession of the economic power, the means of life, in control of the machinery of production and distribution without regard to capitalist masters.[62]

The initial goal of the IWW was to overthrow the existing capitalistic system by any means, since it felt the employers and employees had nothing in common. The IWW and the Knights agreed on one point: the existing wage and profit system had to be changed. The Knights, however, stressed that employees and employers had common interests and that change must be peaceful and gradual. The IWW, on the other hand, had no reservations about using any method that would result in the quick destruction of capitalism.

The IWW also wanted to remove any societal aspect or group that supported capitalism. This approach placed the IWW in direct opposition to the AFL. The IWW regarded the AFL as an "extension of the capitalist class"[63] because it advocated "pure and simple unionism," which was dependent on capitalism. Haywood believed that Gompers had sold out the ARU when he had not supported Debs in the Pullman strike, and he viewed Gompers as an arrogant, power-hungry leader.[64] Thus, the IWW appeared to have two general enemies: capitalism and the AFL, which did not recognize a working-class movement of hourly employees as being a class-conscious group apart from the rest of society. An analysis of the IWW reveals that establishing goals can be an easier task than accomplishing them.

The IWW never did establish an effective organization; in fact, its leaders never made up their minds about precisely what kind of organizational structure it should adopt.[65] Most of the IWW officials agreed with Haywood's objective of organizing "every man that earns his livelihood either by his brain or his muscle."[66] But major differences arose over how to organize one big union into an effective organization. Some members felt that the IWW should work slowly, for example, infiltrate the established AFL unions and gradually persuade members that the IWW cause was best. Others felt that this temporary acceptance of collective bargaining with the capitalists only made employees "better paid slaves" and would hinder the quick and necessary overthrow of the capitalistic system.[67]

In addition to organizational differences, there were at least four reasons for the demise of the IWW, reasons that served as negative lessons for contemporary organized labor.

1. **Lack of permanent membership and financial base.** A large proportion of the IWW consisted of itinerants—individuals who either were unemployed or traveled from job to job, particularly in the agriculture, mining, and lumber industries. This contributed to an unstable financial base. Many IWW leaders thought the members' dues should not be mandatory; instead, they should be paid out of a voluntary "inner conviction"; for example, in 1907 only 10,000 members out of the total 31,000 members paid any dues. The lack of revenues resulted in meager strike funds, and by 1909 the organization was deeply in debt.
2. **Inability of the IWW to appeal to members' interests.** The IWW did not consider the short-run material interests of its members. Its major emphasis on long-term philosophical goals and its concern with propa-

ganda as a means to achieve these goals failed to demonstrate tangible signs of success on a continuous basis.[68] The average trade unionist, inside or outside the IWW, had no desire to help the underdog. Indeed, it was all he could do to look out for himself.[69]

3. **Identification of the IWW with sabotage and violence.** The relationship between the IWW and sabotage and violence was ambiguous. The IWW in 1914 became the only labor organization to ever officially endorse sabotage at its convention. Yet no local, state, or federal authority could ever establish legal proof of any IWW-instigated violence. A strike in 1917 closed the logging camps and sawmills of the Pacific Northwest but did not record any violent acts of sabotage by the IWW.[70] The IWW often stated that sabotage does not equal destruction of equipment. For example, employees could "sabotage" the company by "malicious obedience" (following the work rules to the letter, thereby creating a slowdown) and by informing customers that the company's product was of inferior quality. However, at least one article in the IWW's paper, the *Industrial Worker,* indicated how emery dust and ground-up glass could cause the destruction of machinery.

   Evidence suggests that the IWW's leadership denounced any type of physical violence.[71] Yet, there are also some accounts of incidents in which the IWW members and leaders pledged a "life for a life" or "an eye for an eye."[72] At a minimum, it appears that the IWW did not actively discourage its link with violence.

4. **Alienation of the news media and government officials.** The newspapers enhanced the IWW's reputation for violence by labeling members as "desperate villains who set fire to wheat fields, drove spikes into sawmill-bound logs, derailed trains, destroyed industrial machinery, and killed policemen."[73] Part of this negative image was enhanced by leaders of IWW factions who would damn one another in the press. The IWW also engaged in several "free speech fights"—soap box speeches in local communities. This strategy, which has since been copied by various protest groups, including students, relied on there being more participants than there were available jail spaces. City officials, faced with such a situation, typically allowed the "unlawful" demonstration to continue.[74] In many of these speeches, the IWW would shout antisocial comments such as "there is no God."[75]

   The press, never enthusiastic about unions in general, reserved a special hatred for the IWW. One editorial against the IWW stated:

   > They would be much better dead, for they are absolutely useless in the human economy; they are the waste material of creation and should be drained off into the sewer of oblivion there to rot in cold obstruction like any other excrement.[76]

   The IWW also remained alienated from the government. It did not actively use the existing political system because many of its transient members could not meet voter registration requirements. It also incurred the wrath of the federal government when it refused to support involvement in World War I, proclaiming instead that the war represented a capitalistic plot. The government responded to the IWW's antiwar stance by arresting more than 100 leaders and sentencing most of them to prison terms ranging from 5 to 20 years. In effect, the IWW went out of existence in 1918, even though the organization remains today with a handful of members.

The onset of World War I found the AFL on unfirm ground. It had been the first nationally organized labor movement to withstand a severe economic depression, a hostile press, reluctant or hostile employers, and three rival labor organizations (KOL, ARU, and IWW). Yet the AFL had internal pressures from at least three sources: (1) socialists and other related political groups that advocated independent political action and the organization of unskilled industrial employees; (2) pacifist members who wanted the AFL to remain neutral or take a stand against the war;[77] and (3) member unions that became involved in jurisdictional problems caused by increased specialization and technological change (for example, the plumber was no longer responsible for the complete installation of the water and heating system for a building). Perhaps the most lingering concern of the AFL was that the largest proportion of the organizable labor force, the unskilled industrial employees, remained essentially outside the ranks of organized labor.[78] This concern and its eventual resolution are discussed more in the following section.

World War I to World War II

The period from World War I to World War II witnessed several important phenomena:

1. The inability of unions, particularly the AFL, to make substantial membership gains in the 1920s.
2. The development of employer strategies to retard union growth.
3. Increased union concern over organizing the unskilled industrial employees, which led to a bitter rivalry between the AFL and CIO (Congress of Industrial Organizations).

Some union organizing drives in various industries will be cited briefly to give a further indication of the problems and prospects facing organized labor in this period.

Union Organizing after World War I: Problems and Prospects

The AFL overcame its initial reluctance toward participating in World War I and eventually pledged its cooperation when the United States became directly involved in the war. The government, aware of the necessity of uninterrupted production during wartime, responded by attempting to meet labor's concerns. Government agreements with the AFL provided for the enforcement of trade union standards in all government contracts; labor representatives were appointed to all government agencies, including the War Labor Board; and Gompers was made a member of the Advisory Commission of the National Council of Defense. In short, organized labor was elevated to a more prominent status than had heretofore been seen. Accordingly, the AFL had a sizable growth in membership during this period (an increase from 2,370,000 members in 1917 to 3,260,000 members in 1919). Legislative interests were also met; a long-time AFL goal of severely restricting immigrants, a strongly competitive labor source, was accomplished.

The rather sharp increase in the cost of living that followed World War I, coupled with the newly recognized status of labor, resulted in an unprecedented number of strikes. For example, the Seattle General Strike occurred in 1919, along with other strikes by actors, New York waterfront employees, and coal miners. The most widespread strike occurred in 1919 in the steel industry, where some 367,000 employees walked off the job in 70 major cities.

This strike actually resulted in a setback to organized labor in the steel industry. Many possible factors contributed to the setback. Some were notably similar to those found in the Homestead and Pullman incidents, while others reflected a typical situation unions faced in the 1920s and early 1930s. Of crucial importance were internal union difficulties: an organizing campaign conducted by 24 unions instead of one common industrial union, improvised leadership rather than a consistent union approach to the issue, and poor financial resources. U.S. Steel was also successful in withstanding the strike by using strikebreakers and maintaining strong ties with other companies and social institutions such as the press and the pulpit. Thus, the strike was terminated without a labor agreement, and another 15 years would elapse before organized labor would make inroads into the steel industry.[79]

Although the steel industry did not reflect all industrial reactions to collective bargaining, apparently many other unions were similarly powerless to organize companies that, like U.S. Steel, firmly believed unions were not in the firm's best interests. For example, another 1919 strike almost paralyzed the coal industry when no miners returned to work until President Wilson persuaded them to accept a temporary wage increase and submit all other issues to a newly appointed Bituminous Coal Commission. In 1920 the commission awarded increases ranging from 20 to 30 percent; but this was the last victory for mine employees for several years.

In spite of increased status and militancy, something went wrong for organized labor in the 1920s; the "Golden Twenties" for the majority in the United States was a dreary decade for labor—both for hourly employees in terms of real income[80] and for labor unions in terms of membership. Between 1920 and 1924, total union membership declined from 5,110,000 to 3,600,000; membership in AFL unions dropped from 4,078,000 to 2,866,000. By 1930 total union membership dropped to 3,400,000, and AFL membership dropped to 2,700,000.[81] This decline was caused by at least two major factors: (1) aggressive counteractions by employers and (2) organized labor's inability to overcome anti-union sentiment among potential union members.[82]

Counteractions by Employers Concerned with the increased status given labor during the war, employers actively engaged in efforts to roll back gains in union membership, beginning in the 1920s and continuing through the 1930s. These tactics took the form of either (1) aggressive opposition toward labor unions or (2) formation of an acceptable alternative to unions.

Employers actively opposed unions throughout the *open-shop movement,* which is discussed in more detail in Chapter 11. The alleged purpose of this movement was to ensure that employees had the freedom to determine whether they would choose to join a union. Rationale for this movement was found in its companion name, the **American Plan**—employers felt that employees should adhere to the traditional American value of "rugged individualism" instead of the "foreign," "subversive," and "corrupt" principles of labor unions.

Many employers equated the open shop—the right to join or not to join unions—with no unionized employees. Steps were taken to prevent employees from joining a union. For example, some employers would hire industrial spies to determine which employees had pro-union sentiments.[83] These employees would then be discharged and possibly *blacklisted,* meaning that their names would be given to other employers, who would refuse to hire them. Employer violence against participants in union organizing drives was also a potential strategy to counter unions during this period.[84]

A variation of the open shop, or American Plan, occurred in the 1930s, with the development of the Mohawk Valley Formula. This approach was used when a union attempted to organize or strike a facility in the community. The Mohawk Valley Formula would be implemented with the following steps:

> Form a citizens' committee in the community, label the union leaders as outside agitators, stir up violence or the fear of violence, have a "state of emergency" declared, organize a back-to-work movement, and finally have the back-to-work employees march into the plant protected by armed police.[85]

Employers also countered unions by providing an alternative model to unionism. The 1920s saw widespread employer *paternalism,* which assured that the employer had a superior wisdom and knew what was best for the employees. Paternalistic practices included free lunches, baseball fields, vacations, pensions, and employee counseling.[86] Employers felt that employees receiving these benefits would be indebted to the employer and realize that unions would be unnecessary since they could not bargain for what the employees already had.

Employee Representation Plans Company-established unions represented another substitute model for unions. Called **Employee Representation Plans** (ERPs), they included as many as 1.5 million employees and appeared superficially similar to unions in that selected employee representatives would discuss working conditions with management officials. But ERPs differed from unions in two major respects. First, unions had more autonomy than ERPs. Employers could strongly influence the selection of ERP officers and could also veto any decision made by the joint labor-management committee. Second, ERPs were usually limited to a single facility, and employees under ERPs could neither press for work rules that would remove unfair competition from other facilities nor push for legislation at the local, state, or federal level.[87]

Labor's Inability to Overcome Antiunion Sentiment The lack of organizing gains during the 1920s also has to be attributed to the antiunion sentiment of potential union members and the activities and attitudes of organized labor. Part of this problem may have been due to the relatively good economic conditions that prevailed:

> While job insecurity may have deterred some employees from joining unions in the face of employer opposition, many of them apparently felt that unions were no longer as necessary as they had formerly believed them to be. What profit strikes or other agitation for collective bargaining when the pay envelope was automatically growing fatter and a more abundant life seemed to be assured with our rapid approach to the final triumph over poverty?[88]

Many potential members also believed that much of organized labor was corrupt and subject to control by the socialists and communists. Racketeering had become a feature of some local union-employer relationships. For example, in one incident a union official signed a two-paragraph agreement with three major employers guaranteeing no wage increase for three years and requiring all employees to join the union or be discharged. None of the employees had ever solicited the union, nor did they ever see a union official during the life of the contract. This "sweetheart" arrangement or contract was often coupled with financial kickbacks to the union official, meaning the employer paid the union official a portion of the wage savings.[89]

Some labor unions had also been accused of harboring communists and other political radicals. Many prominent union leaders would occasionally accept help from almost any group that would devote time and effort in organizing employees, believing that they could control these political elements once the local union had been established. However, they overestimated their controlling ability in some instances. One former president of the Steelworkers Union recalled how communists could dominate local union meetings by using the *V technique,* where the leader would find a seat in the center of the auditorium in about the second or third row. Then the following would ensue:

> A few rows back, two of his associates would locate about ten seats apart, and this same pattern would be followed all the way to the rear of the hall. When the chief spokesman opened debate, his line would then be parroted all the way through the V behind him, giving an illusion of widespread strength. They would also wait until other union members, tired and bored, had gone home before trying to push through their own proposals.[90]

Thus, labor, particularly the AFL, devoted much of its attention during the 1920s to overcoming its negative public image.[91] These efforts detracted from active organizing efforts, particularly since Gompers had lost much of his former physical enthusiasm for this activity. In 1924 Gompers died, and his successor, William Green, did not revive any major organizing activities, as he had to maintain the AFL's existing organization in an adverse atmosphere.[92] This situation eventually led to the formation of the Congress of Industrial Organizations (CIO).

Rise of the CIO and Industrial Unionism

Major disagreement occurred within the AFL over organizing the large ranks of unskilled and semiskilled employees. Tremendous technological shifts occurring during and after World War I reduced the demand for highly skilled employees; hence, an increasing percentage of the labor force consisted of production workers. In 1926, for example, 85 percent of the hourly employees at Ford Motor Company required less than two weeks of training.[93] Since craft employees no longer dominated the industrial scene, the AFL needed to organize production employees as well.

Many of the AFL unions did not want to enroll production employees. Some AFL leaders believed these employees were inferior to craft employees and possessed less bargaining power, while others thought their inclusion would confuse and distort the AFL's organization. William Green himself did not view industrial employees as being compatible with the AFL's organizational principle of exclusive jurisdiction.

Some leaders thought that a separate union would be needed for each company's or industry's products. Thus, if General Electric had 50 different products, then 50 different AFL unions (each having exclusive jurisdiction over its members' interests) would be needed for effective collective bargaining. In other words, at least 50 separate collective bargaining agreements could be negotiated by GE and its unions. Other leaders believed that industrial unionism would at least weaken the AFL's concept of organized labor. The president of one AFL union urged his members to stamp out "the awful serpent of industrial trade unionism that would destroy this International and weaken the entire structure of the Labor Movement."[94]

The issue came to a head in 1935 under the direction of John L. Lewis, president of the AFL's United Mine Workers Union. The AFL rejected the concept of industrial unionism through three separate votes at its 1935 convention.[95] On November 9, 1935, the Committee for Industrial Organizations (CIO) was formed. Its purpose was allegedly "educational and advisory;" in reality, it was intended to promote organizing the unorganized, particularly those in the mass-production industries.[96]

In January 1936, AFL leaders were shocked to find that the Committee for Industrial Organizations had been formed among AFL unions. They had thought the industrial unionism issue had been buried once and for all at the 1935 convention. The Committee not only discussed the industrial union concept but also requested the immediate granting of industrial union charters to a number of industries such as the rubber workers and the auto workers. The Committee further insisted that an organizing campaign be started at once in the steel industry.

The AFL, confronted with the most serious challenge in its history, ordered the Committee to disband or get out. Personalities intensified the issue. John L. Lewis, a powerful man in voice and action, sought and obtained power and publicity in his union activities.[97] Lewis managed to provoke AFL leaders into a confrontation while at the same time whipping his United Mine Workers members into a "lather of rage" against the AFL.[98] The split over the industrial unionism issue resulted in seven unions with almost a million members forming a rival and completely independent labor federation, the **Congress of Industrial Organizations (CIO),** in 1938.[99]

The development of the CIO coincided with a significant upsurge in union membership. By November 1937, the CIO's affiliated unions had organized 75 percent of the steel industry, 70 percent of the automobile industry, 65 percent of the rubber industry, and about one-third of the maritime and textile industries.[100] The AFL also saw rapid growth in membership during the late 1930s and the 1940s. It organized the mass-production employees into local labor unions and national councils assigned to various craft unions. The steady growth of the AFL during the late 1930s was also aided by employers' preference to deal with the more conservative organization instead of taking their chances with the new, unpredictable, and more politically radical CIO.[101]

Why did union membership increase dramatically in the 1930s and 1940s? This question is particularly important since the CIO, like the unsuccessful Knights and IWW before it, organized employees of different crafts into one union for each industry. At least five factors seem to account for the growth in unionism during this period: the strong CIO leadership, the CIO's realistic goals, the CIO's effective use of sit-down strikes, passage of the Wagner Act, and changes in employees' attitudes.

Strong CIO Leadership The aggressive and effective CIO leaders (John L. Lewis, Sidney Hillman, and David Dubinsky, among others) infused new life into a movement previously content with resting on its laurels. Most of the CIO union leaders had extensive organizing experience and prided themselves on keeping in touch with their membership.[102] Union leaders' accomplishments should not be overstated, however, since organizing drives involved the tireless efforts of many individuals who typed up circulars, contacted prospective members, and provided routine services that assured union election victories. In fact, one biographer of John L. Lewis indicated his lack of involvement in the many organizing chores by noting that he preferred "arriving only in time for the triumphant finale."[103]

Much organization effort in the steel, mining, automobile, and other industries was effectively directed toward second-generation immigrants. Some 30 percent of the CIO leadership came from a "new immigrant" background. One historian notes, "The success of the CIO was based on the mobilization of ethnic workers and on their willingness to join unions."[104]

Realistic Goals The CIO shared only a superficial similarity with the KOL in respect to grouping employees with different job interests, believing that organizing along industrial lines would still consider the common interests of employees. More importantly, the CIO dramatically differed from the Knights and the IWW in its goals—short-run gains instead of long-range reform—which paralleled the AFL's "pure and simple unionism" approach, including support of the established economic order, as illustrated in Lewis's remarks:

> I think most people have come to realize, that we cannot progress industrially without real cooperation between workers and management, and that this can only be brought

> about by equality in strength and bargaining power of labor and management. Labor is sincere in its desire to help. It looks forward to an industrial procedure which will increase productive efficiency and lower prices to the consumer.[105]

The Effective Use of Sit-Down Strikes The CIO also developed a most successful tactic for heightening employer recognition of its unions—the *sit-down strike,* in which employees stayed inside the plant instead of picketing outside. This technique was very successful since employers were reluctant to physically remove the employees from the plant for fear that their equipment could be damaged in the confrontation.

The tactic was initially applied by the IWW at a General Electric facility in 1906, but the most famous of these strikes occurred in December 1936 at a General Motors facility in Flint, Michigan. At one time, 26,000 General Motors employees had belonged to a union; in early 1936, there were only 122 union members, many of whom were management spies.[106] A local grassroots organization was secretly established to build up the union at Flint. The sit-down strike was locally planned; Lewis and the CIO preferred to organize the steel industry before attempting major organizing drives in the automobile industry. The CIO, however, did lend its active support once the strike was under way.

The sit-down strike at Flint lasted 44 days and received widespread community support while hindering GM's efforts to reverse its negative profit situation of previous years.[107] The strike resulted in employer recognition of the union, a fact that was noticed by many employees in other trades. Between September 1936 and June 1937, some 500,000 employees in the rubber, glass, and textile industries put the technique to use. Although effective, the sit-down strike was short-lived because public opinion eventually frowned on this tactic, and a subsequent decision by the Supreme Court declared such strikes illegal.

Passage of the Wagner Act Another (and perhaps the most significant) reason for the increased number of union members was the passage of the Wagner Act in 1935 (discussed more in Chapter 3). The federal government indicated through this law that collective bargaining was in the national interest. More important were the provisions establishing the National Labor Relations Board to administer union representation elections, define employer unfair labor practices, and enforce the legal rights of employees to join unions.

Changes in Employees' Attitudes Many employees' previously negative attitudes toward organized labor changed dramatically. They had experienced the Great Depression of the 1930s and realized that job security could not be achieved solely through hard work and loyalty to the employer. These employees now viewed unions as a mechanism to promote job security as well as provide other material benefits.

By the onset of World War II, organized labor had reversed its membership decline of the 1920s, rising to almost 9 million members in 1940. Yet the rivalry between the CIO and the AFL was intense and violent as AFL and CIO organizers often physically clashed over the right to represent factory employees. James Hoffa, a former president of the International Brotherhood of Teamsters (then an AFL union), recalled violent organizing drives of 1941 between the CIO and his union:

> Through it all the members wore two pins, putting on a Teamsters button when we were around and switching to a CIO button when those guys showed up. They were waiting to see which union was going to win the battle. You couldn't really blame them. They were scared out of their britches because they didn't want to get caught in the bloody middle.[108]

The CIO-AFL rivalry existed in almost every industry[109] and extended to the local level, where it was common for an employer to have both AFL and CIO unions representing the same employees. Even employers with the best intentions could not build an effective labor-management relationship in this environment.

World War II to the Present

The AFL at first did not want the United States to become involved in World War II; however, this attitude changed after the bombing of Pearl Harbor. Concern over the nation's defense prompted union-management cooperation. For example, both union and management officials participated on War Production Board subcommittees. Such panels weighed employee suggestions, which saved 31 million man-hours and $44 million during World War II.[110]

The cooperative spirit was not total, particularly from the standpoint of strikes taken during wartime. In February 1943 organized labor complained to President Roosevelt that the cost of living during wartime had increased far beyond wage increases permitted by the government under the 1942 "Little Steel Formula."[111] The United Mine Workers conducted a series of strikes to obtain wage increases of $2 a day in 1943. These actions resulted in President Roosevelt's seizing the mines, but eventually a compromise wage settlement was obtained.

The public viewed these and other strikes with anger and alarm, considering them violations of the no-strike pledge announced by organized labor in 1941. Negative public sentiment increased when labor strikes continued and, after 1942, increased every year of the war. The number of employee days lost to strikes was estimated to be the equivalent of no more than one day per year per worker for the four war years.[112] Yet the mere act of participating in a strike was viewed by some as unpatriotic.

Labor's collective bargaining concerns shifted at the end of the war to the issues of full employment and further wage increases in order to sustain national purchasing power and thereby create an expanding market for industrial goods. Labor, remembering the reconversion period of World War I, was also concerned about employer policies aimed at restricting union growth and wage gains.

Unions backed their postwar concerns with strikes. "During no period in the history of the United States did the scope and intensity of labor-management conflicts match those recorded in the year following VJ Day, August 14, 1945."[113] In this 1-year period, more than 4,600 strikes, involving 5 million employees and resulting in almost 120 million man-days of idleness, affected almost every major industry. They were basically nonviolent, representing essentially economic tests of strength and endurance. Generally, both labor and management wanted to be free to resolve their differences at the bargaining table without the government interference and wage restrictions that were present during World War II.

Developments in Organized Labor Since World War II

Three major developments have occurred in organized labor since World War II: increased concern over new collective bargaining issues, organizing drives aimed at white-collar and public-sector employees, and the merger of the AFL and CIO.

New Collective Bargaining Issues The return to peacetime after World War II and, particularly, the Korean War saw increased efforts to extend the provisions of the labor agreement to include all aspects of the collective bargaining relationship. In the late 1950s and early 1960s, the relative scarcity of jobs coincided with the need for price stability to ease the deficit in international payments.

Unions directed their collective bargaining efforts toward guaranteeing members job security in the face of possible technological advances and wages that would compensate for inflation. Organized labor's response toward technological change (discussed in more detail in Chapter 12) brought notable results during this period, including the Automation Fund Agreement between Armour and Company and the Packinghouse Workers and Meat Cutters' unions (1959), the Mechanization and Modernization Agreement in the Pacific Coast longshore industry (1960), and the Long-Range Sharing Plan negotiated between Kaiser Steel and the United Steelworkers (1962).

Employee benefits represented a second new bargaining area. Before World War II, labor cost was overwhelmingly straight-time pay for time actually worked.[114] Subsequent bargaining efforts by labor unions (and personnel policies of nonunion firms) have resulted in a substantial increase in employee benefits (pensions, insurance plans, and so forth), which are currently estimated at 38 percent of payroll costs.[115]

The trend in multiyear labor agreements after World War II put pressure on union leaders to safeguard wage increases against the possibilities of inflation. In 1948 General Motors and the United Auto Workers negotiated a long-term agreement with a cost-of-living provision that adjusted wages for inflationary changes during the life of the contract. This contract provision spread to other labor-management negotiations. In 1952 almost 3 million employees (approximately 20 percent of the employees covered by labor agreements) had cost-of-living provisions in their contracts.[116]

Recent competition from foreign companies and nonunion organizations in the United States has resulted in **concession bargaining,** in which management seeks to obtain from the union work-rule modifications and flexible or reduced wages.

Work-rule modifications include scheduling changes, fewer rest breaks, and combining job classifications to give management more flexibility in employee work assignments.

Wage concessions represent the most significant organized labor development since World War II. Audrey Freedman of the Conference Board notes that, "wages, even under union bargaining pressures, are far more responsive to economic conditions at the industry and firm level and even the product level. . . ."[117] Examples of wage flexibility include:

- "Two-tiered wage plans," where employees hired after the negotiated labor agreement have a lower hourly pay rate than their counterparts.
- "Lump sum" wage increases usually associated with a firm's economic performance for a given time period. This wage payment does not continue, as the employee's wage rate remains the same after the bonus is given.

Organization of Public-Sector Employees The second major development in organized labor since World War II involves the organization of different types of employees. More specifically, public (government) employees (discussed in Chapter 14) have received increased attention from union organizers and are now the most heavily organized group of employees.

Merger of the AFL and CIO Perhaps the most dramatic postwar development in organized labor was the merger of the AFL and CIO. The intense rivalry between them did not end after World War II. However, the presence of three influences during the 1950s resulted in the eventual merger of these organizations in 1955.[118]

First was the change in the presidents of the AFL and CIO. Phillip Murray became president of the CIO when Lewis resigned in 1940 and continued the verbal feud against the AFL and its president, William Green. In November 1952, however, both Green and Murray died. Their successors (Walter Reuther of the CIO and George Meany of the AFL) had no particular fondness for each other; but unlike Green and Murray, they had not previously gone on record against each other. Therefore, a merger could occur without either president's losing face.

Another influence contributing to the **AFL-CIO** merger was the recognized ineffectiveness of union raiding. The two labor organizations investigated employee representations elections in which the AFL tried to organize employees affiliated with CIO unions, and vice versa. During a two-year period (1951 to 1952), 1,245 such elections involved some 366,740 employees, with only 62,000 employees changing union affiliation. This figure overestimates the number affected because it does not consider the offsetting nature of elections. An AFL union could organize a CIO-represented factory of 1,000 employees only to have a CIO union organize an AFL factory of 1,000 employees—the net change would be zero. In fact, the extensive raiding during 1951 and 1952 resulted in a net gain for the AFL of only 8,000 members, or only 2 percent of the total number of employees involved.[119]

Both the AFL and the CIO finally realized that organized labor would benefit if the energies devoted to raiding each other were spent on organizing nonunion employees. Accordingly, many of the AFL and the CIO unions signed a no-raiding agreement in 1954. Instead of concentrating on differences emphasized in raiding activities, the two major federations could now look at similar goals that might be more easily attained by a merger.

One similar goal was the desire of both organizations to reward their political friends and punish political enemies.[120] In many instances, the independent organizations failed to achieve this goal. For example, they were unable to defeat Senator Taft (one of the authors of the Taft-Hartley Act, who was perceived as being antilabor) and failed to elect Adlai Stevenson (supporter of organized labor) over Dwight D. Eisenhower. Both organizations felt that a merger might increase their effectiveness in the political arena.

The AFL-CIO merger on December 12, 1955, involved 15,550,000 members, making the new organization the largest trade union center in the world. The president of the AFL-CIO, George Meany, believed this merger would lead to more employees becoming unionized and to a greater political influence for labor within the American two-party system.[121]

The merger resulted in the continued reduction of union raiding. It also reduced the influence of union locals within the national unions, since they could no longer threaten to affiliate with the rival national organization.[122] However, as will be further discussed in the next section, the AFL-CIO merger has not resulted in a tremendous increase in union membership or political influence. It did reduce the former divisiveness within organized labor, but it cannot be concluded that the merger was a significant impetus for growth and change.

Aspects of Organized Labor Unchanged Since World War II

Organized labor as it existed at the end of World War II compared with its present state appears to have more similarities than differences:[123]

- Exclusive representation, in which one union is given a job territory selected by a majority of employees who vote.
- Collective bargaining agreements that embody a sharp distinction between negotiation and interpretation of contract provisions. Once the contract is negotiated, the no-strike, no-lockout, and grievance procedures assure that the parties will use an arbitrator instead of job action to resolve any disputes over the labor agreement's meaning.
- The government's role has been basically passive in industrial relations, with most of its attention focused on procedural aspects of the process.

Three major labor relations similarities from World War II to the present are organized labor's political ineffectiveness, difficulty in achieving consensus among unions and union members, and emphasis on short-run bargaining goals.

1. Limited Effectiveness in Political Efforts Organized labor has remained a minority movement since World War II, and union membership has never exceeded

28 percent of eligible workers. It has seldom, if ever, mobilized its members into a unified public voice. Union influence in American politics has unfortunately received little systematic empirical research,[124] although some observations can be made from available nonquantitative accounts.

Since World War II, the relationship between organized labor and the Democratic and Republican political parties has been largely unpredictable.[125] In 1976 organized labor helped President Carter win key political victories in New York and Ohio. However, subsequent disappointment with the Carter administration translated into insufficient union votes in Carter's reelection bid against President Reagan in 1980. Organized labor was also unsuccessful in the 1980 and 1984 elections, backing Democratic candidates Walter Mondale and Michael Dukakis, who lost to Republicans Ronald Reagan and George Bush.

The AFL-CIO's member Executive Council could not agree on endorsing a candidate in the 1992 presidential election; therefore, it could claim neither victory nor defeat over Mr. Clinton's selection. The "Labor Relations in Action" box reflects organized labor's inability to defeat the North American Free Trade Agreement as NAFTA passed over strong union opposition.

Two general barriers block organized labor's political efforts. First, elected candidates must consider a wide range of programs, some of which might ignore or even contradict union goals. Active political support does not ensure complete cooperation from the elected government official. Perhaps the most dramatic example of this barrier is found with the Professional Air Traffic Controllers Organization (PATCO), whose president endorsed Reagan in the 1980 election, believing that Carter was not sympathetic to union members' concerns. Reagan informed the PATCO president that he would devote attention to the air controllers. A subsequent nationwide strike by air traffic controllers prompted his administration to fire nearly 12,000 controllers and decertify PATCO.[126]

Second, union voters are not solely concerned about issues pertaining to organized labor. Labor's political strength depends on persuading its members that their self-interest is at stake and that they should act to defend it.[127] However, union members have preferences that extend beyond the work situation. Even former AFL-CIO president George Meany viewed one such issue, support of the Vietnam War, as being significant enough to withhold political support of the Democratic presidential candidate (George McGovern) in 1972. It would be difficult to predict whether a union member who was strongly against abortion would vote for a pro-labor political candidate who was also pro-choice.[128] Additional problems in mobilizing political support are discussed in the following second similarity.

2. Difficulty in Achieving Consensus among Unions and among Members Understandably, agreement among the diverse national unions within the AFL-CIO federation and members within national and local unions is rare. This problem occurs in any large organization, particularly one that grants a large amount of autonomy to its members. The AFL-CIO is always subject to national unions withdrawing from it. The federation also realizes that many national unions can get along

NAFTA's Legislative Passage over Organized Labor's Opposition

NAFTA and the 1992 Election Results Organized labor did not help Bill Clinton win the 1992 presidential election as much as it helped George Bush lose. In 1992, 24 percent of members of union households voted for Bush, compared with 42 percent in 1988; however, only 55 percent voted for Clinton in 1992, compared with a 57 percent vote for Dukakis in 1988 (21 percent of the voters from union households voted for Ross Perot in 1992). These statistics reflected the presidential candidates' positions on NAFTA—Bush clearly supported the agreement, Perot clearly opposed the arrangement, and Clinton waffled as he approved of Bush negotiating NAFTA but indicated he would not support it ". . . 'til I read all the fine print, cross every 't' and dot every 'i'. . . . "[a]

On August 12, 1992, President Bush announced that the negotiation of NAFTA among Canada, Mexico, and the United States was successfully completed. He also predicted that this "historic" agreement would sweep aside trade barriers, thereby generating jobs and economic growth in all three countries.

Union officials roundly condemned Bush's announcement, contending the agreement would favor U.S. investors and corporations, who would move plants to Mexico to take advantage of cheap wages and poor working conditions in producing goods for export to the U.S. market. In early September, the AFL-CIO endorsed Clinton, and then AFL-CIO president Lane Kirkland indicated that his organization would not press the Arkansas governor for specifics on NAFTA until after the election.

Many union leaders hoped that President-elect Clinton would place NAFTA on the back burner, particularly since the 1992 elections brought 110 new members, many of whom opposed the agreement, into the House of Representatives. Moreover, the AFL-CIO had endorsed 248 winning House candidates in these elections. However, organized labor's rather passive approach regarding Mr. Clinton and NAFTA changed dramatically when President Bush signed the treaty on December 17, 1992.

Organized Labor, President Clinton, and NAFTA's Consideration AFL-CIO officials continued to meet with Mr. Clinton during the first three months of his presidency to push for specific labor standards, such as a minimum wage, to be included in a parallel agreement to the treaty. They also implemented a radio and billboard media effort to communicate that NAFTA meant lost jobs and urged the public to pressure legislators returning to their districts during the April 1993 recess.

Unions' concern toward NAFTA increased when the completed side agreements were announced on August 13, 1993. Labor officials maintained that these supplements failed to fulfill

President Clinton's promise of an acceptable NAFTA because they pertained to a participating country's existing laws and did not require, or even strongly encourage, a participating country to alter laws in order to improve the situation of employees and/or union organizations. They also objected to a lack of enforcement procedures and related penalties should a company ignore or violate related labor legislation. NAFTA opposition was reinforced at many Labor Day rallies. Kirkland echoed the vows of other union officials when he stressed, "We believe NAFTA is a sell-out of working Americans [and] the labor movement is going to fight this issue with everything we've got.[b]

However, Kirkland and other union leaders differentiated NAFTA from the Clinton administration, particularly since Clinton appointed at least 10 union representatives to key positions in his administration and recommended William Gould IV, a strong collective bargaining advocate, as chairman of the National Labor Relations Board. The President also supported a national health-care program that represented a very high priority with unions, since with its passage, they could remove this often difficult issue from the bargaining table and concentrate on other issues such as wages and job security.

Clinton, aware of this goodwill or cover, visited the AFL-CIO's annual convention in October 1993, where he stressed his accomplishments (the family and medical leave law, for example), urged labor's support for health-care reform, and defended NAFTA as increasing U.S. exports and related jobs. Some 1,000 delegates gave the President a standing ovation when the speech was over, a reaction in large part attributed to Lane Kirkland, who had indicated before the president's appearance that Mr. Clinton was "a proven friend of labor" and that NAFTA was a "lethal poison pill" drafted by former President George Bush, a Republican.

Dimensions of Political Cover Given by the Clinton Administration Both Clinton and union officials shifted attention to legislators as the NAFTA vote in the House of Representatives was scheduled for November 17th. Three sources of presidential cover (enabling legislators to more successfully defend their position against hostile voters) were given to legislators who wanted to vote for NAFTA:

Providing Legislators with Additional Rationales. Clinton indicated that the Japanese would step into a trade agreement with Mexico if NAFTA were defeated. He also arranged the House vote on NAFTA to occur just before he left for an important international conference (Asia-Pacific Economic Cooperation). Vice-President Gore and others stressed that the President's reputation and effectiveness at this meeting could be weakened if NAFTA were defeated.

(continued)

LABOR RELATIONS IN ACTION

NAFTA's Legislative Passage over Organized Labor's Opposition—cont'd

These and other arguments were enhanced by President Clinton's lobbying efforts that included 18 public events, meetings with more than 150 wavering House members in October, selectively timed endorsements, extensive telephone work, and the assignment of Cabinet members and senior officials to persuade undecided House members. All the living former Presidents and secretaries of state were mobilized to convince legislators; also, 15 governors were involved in last-minute lobbying the day before NAFTA's vote.

Benefits to Legislators. For example, one legislator received support for two additional C-17 cargo planes to be built in her district, while Missouri Republicans were offered up to $150 million to rebuild some Midwest levees damaged by the summer floods that didn't qualify for aid under other government programs. Additional parallel arrangements bene-fitting Florida's tomato, citrus, and vegetable growers were likely associated with some 15 of the 23 legislators' eventual NAFTA support.

Direct Challenges against Those Who Opposed NAFTA. President Clinton directly challenged organized labor's anti-NAFTA tactics on a "Meet the Press" interview:

> The vociferous, organized opposition of most of the unions telling these [House] members in private they'll never give them any money again, they'll get them opponents in the primary, you know, the real roughshod muscle-bound tactics.[c]

Lane Kirkland regarded the comments as a "Hail Mary" pass at a time when the administration knew that NAFTA would be defeated, while Ron Carey, president of the Teamsters, wanted Mr. Clinton to apologize for his remarks as,

> [the] President's use of the words "muscle-bound" and "roughshod" were an insult to every working man and woman in America. If he had used similar code words to attack civil rights groups, women's groups, or environmental organizations who oppose NAFTA, he would be strongly condemned by every member of Congress.[d]

Vice-President Gore represented the Clinton administration when he seemingly trounced anti-NAFTA spokes-

quite well without its support. For example, the expulsion of the Teamsters and the United Auto Workers from the federation did not hinder these organizations' ability to increase their membership, grow in influence, and engage in collective bargaining. (Both the Teamsters and the UAW have since returned to the AFL-CIO.)

Lack of consensus is also found at the local union level, especially when younger employees become members. Most labor unions have a long tradition of struggle and sacrifice; their leaders have risked physical hardships merely to gain

person, Ross Perot, in a televised debate. President Clinton regarded the debate as a turning point and maintained that NAFTA would now pass through Congress. House Minority Leader Newt Gingrich also realized the political cover generated by the debate. "Suddenly, it became respectable—members could look at that day and say, 'Look, if Gore can win that decisively, then I'm in a position that I can vote yes and go home and I can defend myself.'"[e]

House members' voting flexibility on NAFTA was further enhanced by public opinion polls that indicated a nearly even split over the agreement and an increased belief that NAFTA would create more jobs in the long run.[f] Some legislators further realized that labor's power in their union-dominated districts had been diminished by related job losses prior to considering NAFTA and were influenced by their current constituents' ambivalent or positive attitudes regarding the Agreement.[g] NAFTA was eventually approved in the House by a 234–200 margin and, predictably, passed in the Senate by a 61–38 vote.

SOURCE: Adapted from Ken Jennings and Jeffrey Steagall, "Unions and NAFTA's Legislative Passage: Confrontation and Cover," *Labor Studies Journal,* forthcoming.

[a]Ronald Brownstein, "Clinton May Oppose Bush on Trade Pact," *Los Angeles Times,* August 1, 1992, p. A-17.

[b]"Labor Day is 'No NAFTA' Holiday," *AFL-CIO News,* September 20, 1993, p. 6.

[c]James Gerstenzag and Melissa Healy, "Clinton Hits Labor on NAFTA Tactics," *Los Angeles Times,* November 8, 1993, p. A-15.

[d]"Labor Reacts to Criticism by Clinton on NAFTA Efforts," Bureau of National Affairs, Inc., *Daily Labor Report,* Number 215 (November 9, 1993), p. A-11.

[e]Adam Nagourney, "At White House, A 'Code Blue,'" *USA Today,* November 19, 1993, p. 10-A.

[f]Gwen Ifill, "Americans Are Split on Trade Accord, Poll Finds," *New York Times,* November 16, 1993; and, Gerald F. Seib, "Voters' Tide Turns Toward Support of NAFTA, as Debater Gore Helps the Pact, and Vice Versa," *The Wall Street Journal,* November 17, 1993, p. A-24.

[g]Gerald F. Seib, "NAFTA Vignette: Lowey Displays a Gutsy Profile," *The Wall Street Journal,* November 11, 1993, p. A-24; and Michael Wines, "From Rust Belt, Voting Yes on Trade Pact is Folly, No?," *New York Times,* November 17, 1993, pp. A-1, A-10.

employer recognition of their union. However, many of the younger members are now asking the leaders, "What have you done for me lately?"

3. Pursuit of Short-Range Material Goals Instead of Long-Range Reform The Knights of Labor likely taught organized labor a permanent lesson—that goals should relate to members' needs instead of being abstract attempts to change the existing societal system. The period since World War II has witnessed tremendous economic growth and technological change; therefore, union leaders believe these issues deserve more attention than other societal concerns.

Even when unions make bargaining concessions, as they sometimes might, due to recessionary economic conditions, the concessions are viewed as short-term and material—lower wages in exchange for job security, for example.

Summary

In obtaining a contemporary perspective of organized labor, one must be aware of the evolution of labor-management relationships as well as of various labor organizations that have attempted to influence those relationships. Current labor organizations have learned important lessons from their historical counterparts. Criteria for comparing the effectiveness of various labor organizations are their structural and financial stability; their ability to work within established political and economic systems; and supportive or disruptive features of the social environment such as mass media, legislation, and the ability of union leaders to identify and satisfy members' goals and interests. Organized labor did not exert much influence before 1869, although employees became increasingly concerned with working and market conditions associated with mass production. The active years of organized labor can be grouped into three time periods: 1869 to World War I, World War I to World War II, and World War II to the present.

Three major labor organizations developed in the period from 1869 to World War I: the Knights of Labor (KOL), the American Federation of Labor (AFL) under Gompers, and the Industrial Workers of the World (IWW). These organizations had different goals, strategies, and organizational characteristics, which in part furnished reasons for the demise of the KOL and IWW. The Haymarket Riot, the Homestead Incident, and the Pullman Strike hurt organized labor, although Gompers managed to derive some benefit from each of these events.

The period immediately following World War I saw limited growth in union membership. Factors contributing to this situation included several strategies used by employers to counter union organizing campaigns. Internal differences occurred within the AFL regarding the advantages of organizing the heretofore nonunion unskilled and semiskilled employees working in the nation's factories. This disagreement led to the formation of a rival union organization, the Congress of Industrial Organizations (CIO), whose major objective was to organize industrial employees. The CIO achieved substantial membership gains in the late 1930s and 1940s.

Three major developments have occurred in organized labor since World War II. Concern has increased over new collective bargaining issues; organizing drives have been aimed at public employees; and the AFL and CIO have merged. Although several influences prompted the AFL-CIO merger, the impact of this event on contemporary union-management relationships is difficult to assess. More similarities than differences are apparent when the state of organized labor at the end of World War II is compared with its present state. Organized labor remains a minority, yet influential, movement in our society. It has continued to have a minimal effectiveness in the political community, possibly because of the difficulty of mobilizing younger union members. Also, the short-range, material collective bargaining goals have remained basically unchanged since World War II.

Key Terms

- Haymarket Riot
- American Federation of Labor (AFL)
- Homestead Incident
- Pullman Strike
- Industrial Workers of the World (IWW)
- American Plan
- Employee Representation Plans
- Congress of Industrial Organizations (CIO)
- concession bargaining
- AFL-CIO

Discussion Questions

1. "Strive for the better day" was stated by Gompers (AFL); however, the remark could have just as easily been stated by Powderly (KOL) or Haywood (IWW)—but with entirely different meanings. Explain.
2. Considering the criteria for labor organization strength mentioned on page 34, why did the AFL survive and the IWW fade into obscurity?
3. Briefly explain how the Haymarket, Homestead, and Pullman incidents helped as well as hurt the AFL.
4. Discuss the various employer tactics used to thwart union growth in the 1920s and 1930s.
5. Why was the CIO successful in organizing members in the late 1930s when it had the same "one big union" approach that proved unsuccessful for the KOL in the 1880s?
6. What were several reasons behind the merger of the AFL and the CIO? To what extent will these or other factors continue this merger into the near future—say, the next 10 years?
7. Discuss two similarities of organized labor as it existed at the end of World War II and as it does in the present. Speculate as to how these similarities might be modified in the near future.
8. Organized labor's political strength was clearly demonstrated in NAFTA's legislative passage. True? False? Why?

References

For an early update on historical aspects of organized labor, see "Annual Bibliography on American Labor History" in *Labor History*.

1. Robert Ozanne, "Trends in American Labor History," *Labor History* (Fall 1980), p. 521. See also Barry Goldberg, "A New Look at Labor History," *Social Policy* 12 (Winter 1982), pp. 54–63; and Robert H. Zieger, "Industrial Relations and Labor History in the Eighties," *Industrial Relations* 22 (Winter 1983), pp. 58–70.

2. Henry Pelling, *American Labor* (Chicago: University of Chicago Press, 1960), pp. 12–13.
3. Edward B. Mittelman, "Trade Unionism 1833–1839," in John R. Commons et al., eds. *History of Labor in the United States* (1918; reprint ed. New York: Augustus M. Kelly, Publishers, 1966), vol. 1, p. 430.
4. William C. Birdsall, "The Problems of Structure in the Knights of Labor," *Industrial and Labor Relations Review* 6 (July 1953), p. 546.
5. For a discussion of how the expansion of the markets affected unionization among the shoemakers, see John R. Commons, *Labor and Administration* (New York: Macmillan, 1913), pp. 210–264.
6. T. V. Powderly, *Thirty Years of Labor: 1859–1889* (Columbus, Ohio: Excelsior Publishing House, 1889), p. 21.
7. Ibid., pp. 58–59.
8. Ibid., p. 163.
9. Philip Taft, *Organized Labor in American History* (New York: Harper and Row, 1964), p. 90.
10. Gerald N. Grob, *Workers and Utopia* (Evanston, Ill.: Northwestern University Press, 1961), p. 35. Powderly was most concerned about the evils of drinking; for example, he spent almost 50 pages of his autobiography, *Thirty Years of Labor*, discussing this issue.
11. Birdsall, "The Problems of Structure," p. 533.
12. Melton Alonza McLaurin, *The Knights of Labor in the South* (Westport, Conn.: Greenwood Press, 1978), p. 39.
13. Joseph G. Rayback, *A History of American Labor* (New York: Macmillan, 1968), p. 174.
14. Joseph R. Buchanan, *The Story of a Labor Agitator* (1903; reprint ed. Westport, Conn.: Greenwood Press, 1970), pp. 318–323.
15. For details of these procedures, see Taft, *Organized Labor*, p. 91.
16. Powderly, *Thirty Years of Labor*, pp. 151–157.
17. It should be noted that local assemblies were somewhat responsible for this situation as they contributed only $600 to the General Assembly's strike funds in 1885–1886 (McLaurin, *The Knights of Labor*, p. 54). For more details of KOL strike activities, see Normal J. Ware, *The Labor Movement in the United States, 1860–1895* (1929; reprint ed. Gloucester, Mass.: Peter Smith, 1959), pp. 117–154. It should be further noted that the Knights made more effective use of boycotts than any previous union. However, as was true with strikes, the boycotts were instigated by the local assemblies and forced on the Knights' national leaders (Grob, *Workers and Utopia*, p. 61).
18. Donald L. Kemmerer and Edward D. Wickersham, "Reasons for the Growth of the Knights of Labor in 1885–1886," *Industrial and Labor Relations Review* 3 (January 1950), pp. 213–220.
19. Foster Rhea Dulles, *Labor in America: A History*, 3d ed. (New York: Thomas Y. Crowell, 1966), p. 127.
20. Ware, *The Labor Movement*, p. 96.
21. Dulles, *Labor in America*, p. 135.
22. Powderly, *Thirty Years of Labor*, p. 514. It should also be noted that Powderly believed Gompers misled employees by advocating the 8-hour workday without telling them that their wages would be proportionately reduced. Most workers thought they would receive 10 hours payment for 8 hours of work.
23. "A Hellish Deed!" *Chicago Tribune*, May 5, 1886, p. 1.
24. For additional details of the rigged nature of the trial, see Samuel Yellen, *American Labor Struggles* (1936; reprint ed. New York: Arno Press, 1969), pp. 60–65.
25. "A Hellish Deed!"
26. "Their Records," *Chicago Tribune*, May 5, 1886, p. 1. See also Paul Avrich, *The Haymarket Tragedy* (New Jersey: Princeton University Press, 1984).
27. Sidney Lens, *The Labor Wars: From the Molly Maguires to the Sitdowns* (Garden City, N.Y.: Doubleday, 1973), p. 67.

28. The origination of the AFL was changed to 1881 in 1889 to include activities under the Federation of Organized Trade and Labor Unions. At least one historian has claimed that the revised date is regrettable since the parent organization (Federation of Organized Trades and Labor Unions) had little similarity to the AFL in terms of effective organization and broad-based support (Ware, *The Labor Movement*, p. 251). See also Glen A. Gildemeister, "The Founding of the American Federation of Labor," *Labor History* 22 (Spring 1981); and Harold C. Livesay, *Samuel Gompers and Organized Labor in America* (Boston: Little, Brown and Company, 1978), pp. 75–86.
29. Samuel Gompers, *Seventy Years of Life and Labor* (New York: E. P. Dutton, 1925), p. 266.
30. Ware, *The Labor Movement*, pp. 70–71.
31. Normal J. Ware, *Labor in Modern Industrial Society* (1935: reprint ed. New York: Russell and Russell, 1968), p. 262.
32. Dulles, *Labor in America*, p. 155.
33. Gompers, *Seventy Years of Life and Labor*, p. 245.
34. Samuel Gompers, *Labor and the Employer* (1920; reprint ed. New York: Arno Press, 1971), pp. 33–34.
35. Stuart Bruce Kaufman, *Samuel Gompers and the Origins of the American Federation of Labor: 1848–1896* (Westport, Conn.: Greenwood Press, 1973), p. 173. For details of this relationship, see Gompers, *Seventy Years of Life and Labor*, pp. 381–427.
36. Louis Reed, *The Labor Philosophy of Samuel Gompers* (1930; reprint ed. Port Washington, N.Y.: Kennikat Press, 1966), p. 20. See also an editorial by Gompers in the *American Federationist*, June 1924, p. 481; and Sarah Lyon Watts, *Order Against Chaos: Business Culture and Labor Ideology in America 1880–1915* (New York: Greenwood Press, 1991), pp. 9–10.
37. Gompers, *Seventy Years of Life and Labor*, pp. 286–287, 381–427.
38. Alice Kessler-Harris, "Trade Unions Mirror Society in Conflict between Collectivism and Individualism," *Monthly Labor Review* 110 (August 1987), p. 33.
39. Gompers, *Labor and the Employer*, p. 202.
40. Marc Karson, *American Labor Unions and Politics: 1900–1918* (Carbondale, Ill.: Southern Illinois University Press, 1968), p. 29; and Julia Green, "Strike at the Ballot Box: The American Federation of Labor's Entrance into Election Politics, 1906–1909," *Labor History* 32 (Spring 1991), pp. 165–192.
41. Reed, *The Labor Philosophy of Samuel Gompers*, pp. 106–110.
42. Milton Derber, *The American Idea of Industrial Democracy: 1865–1965* (Urbana, Ill.: University of Illinois Press, 1970), p. 117.
43. Gompers, *Seventy Years of Life and Labor*, p. 342. For additional details regarding early AFL organizing, see Philip Taft, *The AF of L in the Time of Gompers* (1957; reprint ed. New York: Octagon Books, 1970), pp. 95–122.
44. Dulles, *Labor in America*, pp. 163–164.
45. Andrew Carnegie, "An Employer's View of the Labor Question," in *Labor: Its Rights and Wrongs* (1886; reprint ed. Westport Conn.: Hyperion Press, 1975), pp. 91, 95. For a recent collection and analysis of material pertaining to the situation, see David P. Demarest Jr., ed. *The River Ran Red* (Pittsburgh: University of Pittsburgh Press, 1992).
46. Yellen, *American Labor Struggles*, p. 81.
47. For details of the wage package, see Ibid., pp. 77–80. See also E. W. Bemis, "The Homestead Strike," *Journal of Political Economy* 2 (1894), pp. 369–396; and Linda Schneider, "The Citizen Striker: Workers' Ideology in the Homestead Strike of 1892," *Labor History* 23 (Winter 1982), pp. 47–66. For some additional insights into Frick's background, see Carol Aymowitz, "Frick's Homey Mansion," *The Wall Street Journal*, September 24, 1990, p. A-12.

48. "Surrounded by Pickets," *New York Times,* July 4, 1892, p. 1.
49. "Mob Law at Homestead," *New York Times,* July 7, 1892, p. 1.
50. "Leader O'Donnell Is Glad," *New York Times,* July 12, 1892, p. 2; and "Bayonet Rule in Force," *New York Times,* July 13, 1892, p. 1.
51. Lens, *The Labor Wars,* p. 77.
52. "A Talk with Gompers," *New York Times,* July 7, 1892, p. 2; and "Provoked by Carnegie," *New York Times,* July 7, 1892, pp. 2, 5.
53. Taft, *The AF of L in the Time of Gompers,* p. 136.
54. "Arbitrate the Homestead Strike," *Chicago Tribune,* July 8, 1892, p. 4. See also "The Origin of the Trouble," *New York Times,* July 8, 1892, p. 2.
55. Yellen, *American Labor Struggles,* p. 3.
56. Lens, *The Labor Wars,* p. 81. See also Susan Kay Morrison's unpublished paper, "Eugene V. Debs: His Ride on the Pullman," 1981.
57. For additional details about the town, see Almont Lindsay, *The Pullman Strike* (Chicago: University of Chicago Press, 1967), pp. 38–60.
58. For more details regarding ARU's organization, see Philip S. Foner, *History of the Labor Movement in the United States,* vol. II (New York: International Publishers, 1955), p. 256.
59. Lindsay, *The Pullman Strike,* p. 124.
60. Ibid., p. 215.
61. Gompers, *Seventy Years of Life and Labor,* p. 403.
62. *Proceedings of the First Convention of the Industrial Workers of the World* (New York: Labor News Company, 1905), p. 1.
63. Ibid., p. 143.
64. Bill Haywood, *Bill Haywood's Book: The Autobiography of William D. Haywood* (New York: International Publishers, 1929), p. 73.
65. Melvyn Dubofsky, *We Shall Be All: A History of the Industrial Workers of the World* (Chicago: Quadrangle Books, 1969), p. 481.
66. Haywood, *Bill Haywood's Book,* p. 181.
67. For additional details pertaining to these differences, see Dubofsky, *We Shall Be All,* pp. 105–119; Joseph Robert Conlin, *Bread and Roses Too* (Westport, Conn.: Greenwood Publishing, 1969), pp. 97–117; and Lens, *The Labor Wars,* pp. 154–155.
68. David J. Saposs, *Left-Wing Unionism* (1926; reprint ed. New York: Russell and Russell, 1967), p. 148.
69. Louis Adamic, *Dynamite: The Story of Class Violence in America* (1934; reprint ed. Gloucester, Mass.: Peter Smith, 1963), p. 174.
70. Robert E. Ficken, "The Wobbly Horrors, Pacific Northwest Lumbermen, and the Industrial Workers of the World, 1917–1918," *Labor History* 24 (Summer 1983), p. 329.
71. Conlin, *Bread and Roses Too,* pp. 97–117. See also Fred Thompson, *The IWW: Its First Fifty Years* (Chicago: Industrial Workers of the World, 1955), pp. 80–87.
72. Adamic, *Dynamite,* pp. 163–164.
73. Conlin, *Bread and Roses Too,* p. 96.
74. Philip S. Foner, ed., *Fellow Workers and Friends: I. W. W. Free Speech Fights as Told by Participants* (Westport, Conn.: Greenwood Press, 1981), p. 15.
75. Foner, *History of the Labor Movement,* vol. III, p. 465.
76. Conlin, *Bread and Roses Too,* p. 68.
77. For additional details, see Frank L. Grubbs, Jr., *The Struggle for Labor Loyalty: Gompers, the AFL, and the Pacifists, 1917–1920* (Durham, N.C.: Duke University Press, 1968).
78. James O. Morris, *Conflict within the AFL: A Study of Craft versus Industrial Unionism, 1901–1938* (1958; reprint ed. Westport, Conn.: Greenwood Press, 1974), pp. 9–10.
79. Taft, *Organized Labor,* pp. 355–358; and Francis Fox Piven and Richard A. Cloward, *Poor People's Movements* (New York: Pantheon Books, 1977), p. 104. For details of this strike, see Lens, *The Labor Wars,* pp. 196–219.
80. Frank Stricker, "Affluence for Whom?

Another Look at Prosperity and the Working Classes in the 1920s," *Labor History* 24 (Winter 1983), pp. 5–34.

81. Lens, *The Labor Wars,* pp. 222, 296, 312.

82. Derber, *The American Idea,* p. 246. For an application of these reasons to a specific industrial situation during this time period, see Stephen L. Shapiro, "The Growth of the Cotton Textile Industry in South Carolina: 1919–1930" (Ph.D., diss., University of South Carolina, 1971), pp. 168–171.

83. For additional details regarding this tactic, see Clinch Calkins, *Spy Overhead: The Story of Industrial Espionage* (1937; reprint ed. New York: Arno Press, 1971).

84. Violence was limited neither to this time period nor to the employer. One of the more publicized episodes of employer violence was the Ludlow Massacre of 1914. The mining camps in Colorado were involved in a strike for union recognition when, on April 20, militiamen opened fire on a tent colony, killing two strikers and one boy. They then set fire to the tents, killing two women and eleven children. For more details of this event, see Leon Stein, ed., *Massacre at Ludlow: Four Reports* (reprint ed.; New York: Arno Press, 1971). Perhaps one of the more vivid examples of union violence occurred in Herrin, Illinois (1922), where miners tortured and killed at least 26 management officials and strikebreakers. For details of this episode, see Saul Alinsky, *John L. Lewis: An Unauthorized Biography* (New York: Vintage Books, 1970), pp. 43–50.

85. Richard C. Wilcock, "Industrial Management's Policies toward Unionism," in Milton Derber and Edwin Young, eds., *Labor and the New Deal* (Madison: University of Wisconsin Press, 1957), p. 293.

86. For a case study of paternalism, see "Welfare Work in Company Towns," *Monthly Labor Review* 25 (August 1927), pp. 314–321. For a more thorough discussion of employer counteractions during this time period, see Larry J. Griffin, Michael E. Wallace, and Beth A. Rubin, "Capitalist Resistance to the Organization of Labor Before the New Deal: Why? How? Success?" *American Sociological Review* (April 1986), pp. 147–167.

87. Derber, *The American Idea,* pp. 220–221; and Morris, *Conflict within the AFL,* pp. 40–41. For more details on ERPs, see Ware, *Labor in Modern Industrial Society,* pp. 414–435. For a contemporary assessment of the problems and prospects facing the single-firm, independent union, see Arthur B. Shostak, *America's Forgotten Labor Organization* (Princeton: Industrial Relations Section, Department of Economics, Princeton University, 1962).

88. Dulles, *Labor in America,* p. 245.

89. This example was drawn from a more detailed account of racketeering during this period found in Sidney Lens, *Left, Right, and Center: Conflicting Forces in American Labor* (Hinsdale, Ill.: Henry Regnery, 1949), pp. 86–108.

90. David J. McDonald, *Union Man* (New York: E. P. Dutton, 1969), p. 185. See also Max Gordan, "The Communists and the Drive to Organize Steel, 1936," *Labor History* 23 (Spring 1982), pp. 226–245. For further historical insights into the relationship between organized labor and communism, see Harvey A. Levenstein, *Communism, Anticommunism and the CIO* (Westport, Conn.: Greenwood Press, 1981).

91. James O. Morris, "The AFL in the 1920s: A Strategy of Defense," *Industrial and Labor Relations Review* 11 (July 1958), pp. 572–590.

92. See, for example, "William Green: Guardian of the Middle Years," *American Federationist* 88 (February 1981), pp. 24–25.

93. Bruce Minton and John Stuart, *Men Who Lead Labor* (New York: Modern Age Books, 1937), pp. 14–15.

94. Morris, *Conflict within the AFL,* p. 216.

95. For additional details pertaining to the background of this historic convention, see Herbert Harris, *Labor's Civil War* (1940; reprint ed. New York: Greenwood Press.

96. Lens, *The Labor Wars,* p. 284.
97. Cecil Carnes, *John L. Lewis: Leader of Labor* (New York: Robert Speller Publishing, 1936), p. 299.
98. David Dubinsky and A. H. Raskin, *David Dubinsky: A Life with Labor* (New York: Simon and Schuster, 1977), p. 226.
99. The seven unions were the United Mine Workers; the Amalgamated Clothing Workers; the International Ladies Garment Workers Union; United Hatters; Cap and Millinery Workers; Oil Field, Gas Well and Refinery Workers; and the International Union of Mine, Mill, and Smelter Workers.
100. Benjamin Stolberg, *The Story of the CIO* (1938; reprint ed. New York: Arno Press, 1971), p. 28.
101. Milton Derber, "Growth and Expansion," in Derber and Young, *Labor and the New Deal,* p. 13; and Steve Rosswurm, ed., *The CIO's Left-Led Unions* (New Brunswick, N.J.: Rutgers University Press, 1992).
102. See, for example, John Hutchinson, "John L. Lewis: To the Presidency of the UMWA," *Labor History* 19 (Spring 1978), pp. 185–203; and Steven Fraser, *Sidney Hillman and the Rise of American Labor* (New York: The Free Press, 1991).
103. James Arthur Wechsler, *Labor Baron: A Portrait of John L. Lewis* (New York: William Morrow, 1944), p. 71; and Robert H. Zieger, "Leadership and Bureaucracy in the Late CIO," *Labor History* 31, no. 3 (1990), pp. 253–270.
104. Thomas Gobel, "Becoming American: Ethnic Workers and the Rise of the CIO," *Labor History* 29 (Spring 1988), p. 174.
105. S. J. Woolf, "John L. Lewis and His Plan," in Melvyn Dubofsky, ed., *American Labor since the New Deal* (Chicago: Quadrangle Books, 1971), pp. 110–111.
106. Lens, *The Labor Wars,* p. 295.
107. Sidney Fine, *Sit-Down: The General Motors Strike of 1936–1937* (Ann Arbor: The University of Michigan Press, 1969), pp. 156–177. For another perspective of the sit-down strike, see Daniel Nelson, "Origins of the Sit-Down Era: Worker Militancy and Innovation in the Rubber Industry, 1934–1938," *Labor History* 23 (Winter 1982), pp. 198–225.
108. James R. Hoffa and Oscar Fraley, *Hoffa: The Real Story* (New York: Stein and Day Publishers, 1975), p. 65.
109. For a detailed account of the AFL-CIO rivalries in several industries, see Walter Galenson, *The CIO Challenge to the AFL* (Cambridge, Mass.: Harvard University Press, 1960).
110. Richard B. Morris, ed., *The U. S. Department of Labor Bicentennial History of the American Worker* (Washington, D.C.: U.S. Government Printing Office, 1976), p. 236.
111. For details of this formula and the extent that cost-of-living estimates exceeded this formula, see Taft, *Organized Labor in American History,* pp. 549–553 and 557–559.
112. Dulles, *Labor in America: A History,* p. 334.
113. Arthur F. McClure, *The Truman Administration and the Problems of Postwar Labor, 1945–1948* (Cranburry, N.J.: Associated University Press, 1969), p. 45.
114. George H. Hildebrand, *American Unionism: An Historical and Analytical Survey* (Reading: Addison-Wesley, 1979), pp. 36–37.
115. *Policies and Practices, Personnel Management* 267 (January 1982), p. 188. Copyright 1982 by Bureau of National Affairs Inc., Washington, D.C.
116. Robert M. MacDonald, "Collective Bargaining in the Postwar Period," *Industrial and Labor Relations Review* 20 (July 1967), p. 568.
117. Audrey Freedman, "How the 1980's Have Changed Industrial Relations," *Monthly Labor Review* (May 1988), p. 37.
118. For a more detailed discussion of historical attempts at the merger of the AFL and CIO, see Joel Seidman, "Efforts toward Merger 1935–1955," *Industrial and Labor Relations Review* 9 (April 1956), pp. 353–370.

119. "Document: AFL-CIO No-Raiding Agreement," *Industrial and Labor Relations Review* 8 (October 1954), p. 103.
120. "A Short History of American Labor," *American Federationist* 88 (March 1981), p. 14.
121. George Meany, "Merger and the National Welfare," *Industrial and Labor Relations Review* 9 (April 1956), p. 349.
122. Richard A. Lester, *As Unions Mature* (Princeton, N.J.: Princeton University Press, 1958), p. 25.
123. John T. Dunlop, "Have the 1980s Changed Industrial Relations?" *Monthly Labor Review* 111 (May 1988), pp. 29–33.
124. For problems and prospects associated with this research, see Matrick F. Masters and John Thomas Delaney, "Union Political Activities: A Review of the Empirical Literature," *Industrial and Labor Relations Review* 40 (April 1987), pp. 336–353.
125. Max M. Kempelman, "Labor in Politics," in George W. Brooks, et al., eds., *Interpreting the Labor Movement* (Ann Arbor, Mich.: Industrial Relations Research Association, 1967), p. 188; and Dick Bruner, "Labor Should Get Out of Politics," in Charles M. Rehmus and Doris B. McLaughlin, eds., *Labor and American Politics: A Book of Readings* (Ann Arbor: University of Michigan Press, 1967), p. 430. For an assessment of organized labor's limited effectiveness in the political arena since the 1930s, see Piven and Cloward, *Poor People's Movements,* pp. 161–172; Graham K. Wilson, *Unions in American National Politics* (New York: St. Martin's Press, 1979), p. 36; David Montgomery, *Workers' Control in America: Studies in the History of Work, Technology, and Labor Struggles* (New York: Cambridge University Press, 1979), p. 170; David Brody, *Workers in Industrial America* (New York: Oxford University Press, 1980), p. 243; and Marick F. Masters and John Thomas Delaney, "The AFL-CIO's Political Record, 1974–1980," in Barbara D. Dennis, ed., *Proceedings of the 34th Annual Meeting of the Industrial Relations Research Association* (Madison, Wisc.: Industrial Relations Research Association, 1982), pp. 351–359.
126. For contrary evidence supporting unions' political sophistication, see John Thomas Delaney, Marick F. Masters, and Susan Schwochau, "Union Membership and Voting for COPE-Endorsed Candidates," *Industrial and Labor Relations Review* 43 (July 1990), pp. 621–635.
127. Patricia Cayo Sexton and Brendan Sexton, *Blue Collars and Hard Hats: The Working Class and the Nature of American Politics* (New York: Random House, 1971), p. 307. See also David Halle, *America's Working Man* (Chicago: University of Chicago Press, 1984), pp. 190–191. For related insights, see Michael H. LeRoy, "The 1988 Elections: Re-emergence of the Labor Bloc Vote?," *Labor Studies Journal* 15 (Spring 1990), pp. 5–32; Tom Juravich, "Beyond the Myths of '84: Union Members and the Presidential Election," *Labor Studies Journal* 11 (Fall 1986), pp. 135–148; "How AFL-CIO Members Voted in the 1984 Election," *The AFL-CIO American Federationist* 91 (December 1, 1984), pp. 5–8; and James W. Endersby and Michael C. Munger, "The Impact of Legislation Attributes on Union PAC Campaign Contributions," *Journal of Labor Research* 13 (Winter 1992), pp. 79–97.
128. See, for example, "How the Abortion Issue is Shaking the House of Labor," *Business Week,* August 6, 1990, p. 39.

3 Legal Influences

Labor relations law serves as the framework for most of our labor relations activities. This chapter establishes the legal foundation for the major phases of the labor relations process: organizing unions, negotiating labor agreements, and assuring employee rights in contract administration. It is essential today not only to know the law but to understand and appreciate the interrelationships between the law and the labor relations process.

This chapter logically follows the one on historical development of unions in the United States because labor relations law and union development go hand in hand. Law as it pertains to labor is traced from the first major court case involving union activities, through the development of common law and the use of antitrust legislation that inhibited the growth of unions, to the laws that pertain to most private firms today: the Norris–La Guardia, Wagner, Taft-Hartley, and Landrum-Griffin Acts. Because these acts cover the major portion of U.S. industries and businesses, a substantial amount of space is devoted to their content. The Railway Labor Act, which principally covers railroads and airlines, is also explained and assessed. A final section briefly considers several other laws that can affect the labor relations process.

Origin of Labor Relations Law

Labor relations law in the United States is derived from statutory law, judicial decisions and interpretations, constitutional rights, and administrative decisions by agencies of the executive branch. Likewise, at the state and local government levels, law is developed and established by analogous documents and actions.

Statutory law can be created and amended by legislative enactment at the federal, state, or local levels of government. Congress has enacted numerous labor relations laws in the interest of employees and employers, public welfare, and interstate commerce. Three major ones—the Norris–La Guardia Act, the National

Labor Relations Act, as amended, and the Railway Labor Act—are discussed at length later in the chapter. State legislatures may pass laws and local municipalities pass ordinances to fill voids in the federal laws or to cover issues not covered by federal laws, such as the right of city employees to engage in collective bargaining.

The judicial branch of government, with its accompanying court system at the federal, state, and local levels, functions to determine a law's constitutionality and conformity to legal standards, to assess the accuracy of interpretations by administrative agencies, and to issue injunctions that restrict or require certain activities. In addition, the courts must decide issues not covered by laws and make rulings under the general guides of "equity." These decisions and rulings constitute *case,* or *common law,* which has developed over the years, setting precedents and providing guidance for future decisions.

One notable example of common law doctrine that has created much controversy in recent years is the **employment-at-will** doctrine. This doctrine simply means that an employer may terminate an employee for any reason, good or bad, or for no reason. While the doctrine has been modified in many state courts, it remains intact in many others. (This doctrine is more thoroughly discussed in Chapter 10.)

Several provisions of the U.S. Constitution have been interpreted as applying to labor relations activities. For example, Article I, Section 8, which authorizes Congress to regulate commerce, has been used to determine the constitutionality of several statutory enactments. The First Amendment, which assures the rights of peaceful assembly, freedom of association, and free speech, usually has been interpreted as allowing employees to form and join unions and has provided the justification for union picketing (to communicate information to possible union members and union supporters). The Fifth and Fourteenth Amendments contain due process provisions, and the Fourteenth Amendment provides equal protection under law. These amendments have been used for employment protection in discharge decisions, refusal-to-hire cases, and discrimination cases regarding equal employment opportunity where either state or federal employees are involved.

The executive branch includes the administrative agencies responsible for administration of applicable laws. These government agencies establish policies and make rules to guide the administration of these laws. They make decisions within the framework of the statutes or laws that are legal and binding, although they are subject to appeal to the courts. As long as the decisions are within the authority of the administrative agency and are accurate interpretations of its delegated authority, they have the same effect as law.

Some of the more important administrative agencies mentioned include:

- **National Labor Relations Board (NLRB):** Administers the National Labor Relations Act as amended by the Taft-Hartley and Landrum-Griffin acts, conducts union representation elections, and adjudicates unfair labor practice charges.
- **Federal Mediation and Conciliation Service (FMCS):** Provides mediation services to unions and management in collective bargaining and assists these parties in selecting arbitrators in grievance administration.

- **U.S. Department of Labor (DOL):** Performs many employment-related services, such as research and data-collecting functions; administers federal wage and safety laws; and enforces federal contract compliance under equal employment opportunity requirements. In addition, its secretary serves as the president's cabinet member responsible for employment-related matters.
- **National Mediation Board:** Handles union representation issues under the Railway Labor Act, provides mediation services to parties in negotiations, assists in disputes over contract interpretation, and, in cases involving emergency disputes, proposes arbitration and certifies the dispute to the president as an emergency.
- **National Railroad Adjustment Board:** Hears and attempts to resolve railroad labor disputes growing out of grievances and interpretation or application of labor agreements.
- **State and local administrative agencies:** Are responsible for the enforcement and administration of state laws and local ordinances involving labor relations topics.

Early Legal Interpretations Involving Labor-Management Relationships (1806–1931)

As the previous chapter demonstrated, in earlier times labor unions in the United States had to struggle for their existence. With the absence of legislative direction, the judiciary system not only controlled the relationships between labor unions and employers but also played a key role in limiting union organizing for many years, especially from the early 1800s to the 1930s.

Criminal Conspiracy

The first major labor relations case in the United States, known as the "Cordwainers case," occurred in 1806, when a group of journeymen shoemakers in Philadelphia were indicted, convicted, and fined $8 each for forming an illegal criminal conspiracy. The shoemakers had joined together in an attempt to raise their wages and refused to work with nonmembers or at a wage rate less than they demanded. Twelve jurors (all businessmen) found the shoemakers guilty of forming an illegal coalition for the purpose of raising their own wages while injuring those who did not join the coalition.[1]

The prosecutor in the trial stated:

> Our position is that no man is at liberty to combine, conspire, confederate and unlawfully agree to regulate the whole body of workmen in the city. The defendants are not indicted for regulating their own individual wages but for undertaking by a combination, to regulate the price of labour of others as well as their own.

> It must be known to you, every society of people are affected by such confederacies; they are injurious to the public good and against the public interest.[2]

The application of the criminal conspiracy doctrine to attempts by employees to organize unions aroused much public protest, not only from employees but also from factory owners who feared the closing of their factories if their employees' feelings grew too strong. These feelings were undoubtedly considered in 1842 when the Supreme Judicial Court of Massachusetts (*Commonwealth* v *Hunt*) set aside the conviction for criminal conspiracy of seven members of the Journeymen Bootmakers Society who refused to work in shops where nonmembers were employed at less than their scheduled rate of $2 per pair of boots. While not rejecting the criminal conspiracy doctrine, Justice Shaw cut the heart from it by insisting that the purpose of the concerted activity must be considered, not just the fact that the activity occurred. His decision stated that an association of workers could be established for "useful and honorable purposes" as well as for purposes of "oppression and injustice"; however, the means of achieving these purposes could also be legal or illegal. Therefore, to determine its legality, an investigation must be made of the objectives of the particular labor union involved and of the means used to achieve its objectives.[3]

Justice Shaw wrote:

> We think, therefore, that associations may be entered into, the object of which is to adopt measures that may have a tendency to impoverish another, that is, to diminish his gains and profits, and yet so far from being criminal or unlawful, the object may be highly meritorious and public spirited. The legality of such an association will therefore depend upon the means to be used for its accomplishment. If it is to be carried into effect by fair or honorable and lawful means, it is, to say the least, innocent; if by falsehood or force, it may be stamped with the character of conspiracy. It follows as a necessary consequence, that if criminal and indictable, it is so by reason of the criminal means intended to be employed for its accomplishment; and as a further legal consequence, that as the criminality will depend on the means, those means must be stated in the indictment.

Civil Conspiracy

The *Commonwealth* v *Hunt* decision virtually ended the use of the criminal conspiracy doctrine in labor relations. However, the courts developed the civil conspiracy doctrine, while holds that a group involved in concerted activities can inflict harm on other parties even though it is pursuing a valid objective in its own interest.[5] In the *Vegelahn* v *Gunter* case, an injunction was issued against a union that was picketing for higher wages and shorter hours. While the court agreed that the purposes were legitimate, it concluded that the picketing and a refusal to work would lead to more serious trouble and that employers could seek injunctive relief.[6]

Breach of Contract (Contractual Interference)

Breach of contract, a common-law rule, was used by employers in restricting union membership and union-organizing activities. For example, an employer would require its employees to sign a **yellow-dog contract**—an agreement stating that they would neither join a union nor assist in organizing one. Because this contract would be a condition of continued employment, any violation would allow the company to discharge the employee. More importantly, if any union organizers who were employees not of the company, but of the national union, attempted to solicit union members among those who had signed yellow-dog contracts, they would be interfering with a legal contractual relationship between the employer and its employees. Thus, the employer could go to court and secure an injunction against the union organizers and any union-related activities. Union organizers who violated the court order then could be charged with contempt of court and possibly fined and imprisoned.[7] As a result, the employer could use the yellow-dog contract in two ways: (1) directly with the employee and (2) as a basis for obtaining an injunction against union organizers. Both ways were strong instruments by which employers were able to restrict union-organizing activities.

Application of Antitrust Legislation to Labor Unions

In the late 1800s an attempt was made to guard against increasing business monopolies, concentration of ownership, and business combinations that eliminated competition. One such attempt was the passage of the Sherman Antitrust Act of 1890, whose coverage neither included nor excluded labor unions. Section I of this act states that "every contract, combination in the form of trust or otherwise, or conspiracy, in restraint of trade or commerce among the several states . . . is hereby declared to be illegal."[8] Such wording made it debatable whether Congress had intended labor unions to be covered.

The answer was not given until 1908 in the landmark decision, *Loewe* v *Lawlor* (better known as the Danbury Hatters case). The United Hatters of America, having organized 70 of 82 firms in the industry, wanted to organize Loewe and Company, a nonunion employer located in Danbury, Connecticut. They sought to have their union recognized, gain the union wage scale, and have only union members employed (a closed shop). When the company refused, the union struck. However, strikers were replaced, and operations were continued. Recognizing the strike failure, the United Hatters, who numbered 9,000, organized a nationwide boycott assisted by the American Federation of Labor, which had 1.4 million members, and directed toward all retailers, wholesalers, and customers. The boycott was successful; the employer thereupon went to court and eventually appealed to the Supreme Court. The high court ruled that unions were covered under the Sherman Act. The end result was that the union owed the company $250,000 (treble damages), and the membership was responsible for payment.[9]

Once the *Loewe* decision was publicized, organized labor concluded that it must seek changes in the act. An aggressive campaign led to the enactment of the Clayton Act of 1914. Included among its provisions were the following:

> [The] labor of a human being is not a commodity or article of commerce. Nothing contained in the antitrust laws shall be construed to forbid the existence and operations of

> labor [unions] . . . nor shall such organizations . . . be held or construed to be illegal combinations or conspiracies in restraint of trade.
>
> No restraining order or injunction shall be granted . . . in any case between an employer and employees . . . growing out of a dispute concerning terms or conditions of employment, unless necessary to prevent irreparable injury to property. . . .
>
> No such restraining order . . . shall prohibit any person or persons . . . from ceasing to perform work . . . recommending, advising, or persuading others by peaceful means so to do . . . peacefully persuading any person to work or abstain from working . . . peacefully assembling in a lawful manner, and for lawful purposes.[10]

When Samuel Gompers, president of the American Federation of Labor, read the provision of the act, he proclaimed it U.S. labor's Magna Carta. Gompers's joy, however, was short-lived; a series of Supreme Court decisions in the 1920s left no doubt that the Clayton Act was not labor's Magna Carta. In fact, the Clayton Act hurt union growth and development more than it helped because under the act, employers could now seek injunctions on their own, whereas only the U.S. district attorneys could seek injunctions under the Sherman Act.

The first major case occurred in 1921 and involved the printing press industry. The machinists union had been successful in organizing all four major manufacturers of printing presses except Duplex Printing Press. While the three unionized companies operated under an 8-hour day and union wage scale, Duplex continued a 10-hour day and paid below the union scale. Failing to unionize Duplex, the union organized a strike, which was also unsuccessful. Because Duplex was operating at a lower cost than the other companies and posed an economic threat to them, the machinists union formed a boycott, refusing to install or handle Duplex products and warning users against operating Duplex equipment. The company petitioned for an injunction under the Clayton Act. The case was appealed to the Supreme Court, which ruled that unions were not exempt from antitrust legislation when they departed from normal and legitimate union activities. Further, the Clayton Act restricted injunctions only when a boycott involved an employer and its own employees. Since many of the boycott activities were conducted by sympathetic union members, not employees of Duplex, the issuance of the injunction was legal.[11]

Another Supreme Court decision in the same year defined "peaceful persuading" as a single representative at each employer entrance announcing that a strike was occurring and trying to peacefully persuade employees and others to support the strike.[12] With only one person on the picket line, the unions would obviously be unable to demonstrate their strength and unity in the strike.

With injunctions easier to obtain, a series of devastating Supreme Court decisions, absence of favorable labor legislation, use of antiunion tactics such as "goon squads," blackmail, and blacklisting, and the U.S. economy beginning a period of economic prosperity in the 1920s, the labor movement entered a comparatively static period. Although the Railway Labor Act (covered later in this chapter) was passed in 1926, this was primarily a time of regrouping, self-analysis, and establishment of new strategies.

The Norris–La Guardia Act

In the early 1930s, with the beginning of the country's most severe economic depression, political pressure on Congress mounted, and general dissatisfaction was expressed with judicial restrictions in labor relations. In 1932 Congress passed the Norris–La Guardia Act (also called the Federal Anti-Injunction Act). Marking a change in U.S. policy in labor relations, the act allowed employees "full freedom of association, self-organization, and designation of representatives of [their] own choosing, negotiation of terms and conditions of . . . employment" and "freedom from employer interference, restraint, or coercion." Further, it recognized employees' right to freedom from employer interference in their efforts of "self-organization and other concerted activities for the purpose of collective bargaining or other mutual aid or protection."[13]

Before 1932, the judiciary was particularly abusive in issuing labor injunctions (restraining orders). Judges could issue injunctions against individuals and/or groups; these injunctions had to be obeyed immediately or the offenders would be held in contempt of court, thereby subjecting them to imprisonment, fines, or both. The same judge who issued the injunction would enforce it against violators. Judges also had a wide array of alternatives, such as issuing a temporary or permanent injunction without a hearing and without the union being represented, and issuing a blanket "broad application" injunction to stop a union-organizing campaign or a more narrow injunction against an individual union organizer to keep him from contacting employees about union membership.[14]

The act restricted the role of the federal courts in labor disputes. Foremost was the restriction of issuance of any injunction, temporary or permanent, in any case involving or growing out of a labor dispute,[15] except where the employer, in open court and under cross-examination, could prove the following conditions:

1. Unlawful acts had been threatened or committed.
2. Substantial and irreparable injury to the employer's property would follow.
3. Greater injury would be inflicted upon the employer by denial of an injunction than upon the union by granting an injunction.
4. The employer had no adequate remedy at law.
5. Public officers were unable or unwilling to furnish adequate protection.
6. The employer had made every effort to settle the dispute through collective bargaining (including the offer of mediation, voluntary arbitration, and so on) before going to court.

If an injunction was issued, it had to be directed toward stopping specific acts; thereby the general, all-encompassing injunctions that had become customary were prohibited. In addition, individuals held in contempt of court (usually labor leaders who violated a court injunction) would be provided a trial by jury.

The Norris–La Guardia Act also declared that the yellow-dog contract was unenforceable in federal courts.[16] This provision allowed union organizers more freedom in contacting employees about joining unions with less fear of a breach of contract violation, a tactic that had been used successfully against them. However, many companies continued to discharge employees for union activities.

Although the passage of the Norris–La Guardia Act signalled a change in U.S. policy in labor relations, the act did not establish an administrative agency to enforce this policy or the act's provisions. This meant that organized labor had to pursue enforcement through the judicial system, which had not been responsive to labor's interests and needs. Another deficiency of the Norris–La Guardia Act was that no specific employer unfair labor practices were prohibited. These deficiencies were not resolved until three years later.

Historical Development of the National Labor Relations Act and Its Amendments

In addition to the Norris–La Guardia Act, 1932 witnessed a new president, Franklin Roosevelt, who was backed strongly by labor unions, and a new Congress receptive to labor legislation as a means of ending a long depression. One of the first acts of this new administration was to encourage Congress to pass the National Industrial Recovery Act—a law designed to stabilize economic activity by allowing businesses to form associations to draw up codes of fair competition to standardize marketing, pricing, financial, and other practices. Upon approval of the codes by the National Recovery Administration, firms could display the "Blue Eagle" symbol that supposedly signified compliance and identified firms from which customers should purchase their goods and services. Section 7 of the act required the codes to guarantee employees the right to unionize without employer interference, and a National Labor Board was later established to help settle disputes and to determine violations under Section 7.

Because the act did not require employers to deal with unions, and because the National Labor Board could not enforce its orders effectively, many employers chose to create their own company unions. Prompted by the board's failure, increasing employer resistance, and growing strike activity, in 1934 Congress issued a joint resolution calling for the president to establish a National Labor Relations Board to investigate violations under Section 7 and to hold elections to determine whether the employees would choose a union to represent them.[17] This board, created like its predecessor by executive order of the president, had trouble enforcing its orders and determining employee organizational units for conducting elections. Then, in 1935, the Supreme Court ruled the codes of fair competition unconstitutional, invalidating the National Labor Relations Board.

Senator Robert Wagner, chairman of the National Labor Relations Board and an active participant in labor law matters, in 1935 steered through Congress a separate labor relations law—the *Wagner Act,* or National Labor Relations Act (NLRA). It established a new national policy that encouraged collective bargaining, guaranteed certain employee rights, detailed specific employer unfair labor practices, and established the National Labor Relations Board to enforce its provisions. The board would adjudicate unfair labor practices and conduct representation elections (other provisions are covered later in the chapter).

For the next two years, significant employer resistance to the act mounted because most employers believed it would be ruled unconstitutional like the National Industry Recovery Act.[18] However, in 1937 the Supreme Court decided five labor relations cases—the most publicized, *NLRB* v. *Jones & Laughlin Steel Corporation* [301 U.S. 1 (1937)]—and declared the Wagner Act constitutional.

With Supreme Court recognition of the Wagner Act and the improvement of economic conditions in the United States, unions experienced tremendous growth and power.[19] In fact, for the next 10 years, union activities caused many to believe that the labor relations pendulum had swung too far toward unions. Examples that precipitated much public antagonism were strikes over union representation rights between CIO and AFL unions, boycotts that hurt innocent bystanders, union walkouts over bargaining issues, refusal to negotiate in good faith with employers, and pressure on job applicants to become members of unions in order to qualify for employment.

As a reaction to organized labor's actions, in 1947 Congress amended the National Labor Relations Act by enacting the *Taft-Hartley Act*, or Labor Management Relations Act. Calling it a "slave labor act," labor groups immediately mounted a successful campaign to have President Truman veto the bill; however, Congress easily overrode Truman's veto. Regaining greater balance in labor relations legislation, the act reorganized the NLRB and included union unfair labor practices covering such topics as union membership, bargaining requirements, boycotts by unions not involved in the dispute, and strikes over work assignments.

In the late 1950s, a special Senate committee headed by John McClellan vigorously pursued the abuses of power and corruption by union leaders, particularly those of the Teamsters and specifically of Dave Beck and James Hoffa.[20] Exposing shocking examples of union corruption and abuses of power, Congress reacted in 1959 by passing the Landrum-Griffin Act, also called the Labor-Management Reporting and Disclosure Act. Its first six titles pertain mostly to union internal affairs and government (covered in Chapter 4), and Title VII further amends the National Labor Relations Act. Since 1959, there have been two successful legislative attempts to enact major modifications in the NLRA. The NLRA was first extended to cover the U.S. Postal Service in 1970 (see Chapter 15) and then to cover the private health-care industry in 1974 (see Chapter 16).

The National Labor Relations Act: The Wagner Act of 1935 as Amended by the Taft-Hartley Act in 1947 and the Landrum-Griffin Act in 1959

The National Labor Relations Act is discussed here primarily from a contemporary perspective. The origins of each specific provision are only briefly discussed where appropriate to avoid confusion.

Statement of Public Policy

The United States was in the midst of its most severe economic depression when the Wagner Act was passed. The act

- established a new U.S. labor relations policy of encouraging collective bargaining and gave some indication of the federal government's more active role in national economics,
- recognized that employer denials of the employees' rights to organize and employer refusal to accept collective bargaining had previously led to strikes and industrial conflict,
- acknowledged that inequality of bargaining power between employees and employers affected the flow of commerce and aggravated recurring economic depressions by depressing wages and purchasing power and thereby prevented the stability of wages and working conditions, and
- recognized that protection by law of the right of employees to organize and bargain collectively would promote the flow of commerce, restore equality of bargaining power, and encourage friendly adjustment of industrial disputes.[21]

The Taft-Hartley amendments added that industrial strife could be minimized if employees and labor unions, as well as employers, recognized one another's rights and declared that no party had the right to engage in activities or practices that jeopardized the national health or safety.

Rights of Employees (Section 7)

Under Section 7 of the NLRA (see Exhibit 3.1) employees were assured certain rights: (1) to form and organize their own labor organizations, (2) to become members of labor unions or to refuse to join (unless there is a valid contractual

Exhibit 3.1 Rights of Employees

Sec. 7. Employees shall have the right to self-organization, to form, join, or assist labor organizations, to bargain collectively through representatives of their own choosing, and to engage in other concerted activities for the purpose of collective bargaining or other mutual aid protection, and shall also have the right to refrain from any or all of such activities except to the extent that such right may be affected by an agreement requiring membership in a labor organization as a condition of employment as authorized in section 8(a)(3).

SOURCE: Labor-Management Relations Act, 1947, as amended.

requirement to join), (3) to bargain collectively through representatives of their own choosing, and (4) to engage in other concerted activities for the purpose of collective bargaining or other forms of mutual aid or protection, such as strikes, picketing, and boycotts.

These rights are not unlimited; they can be restricted. For example, the right to strike can be limited by a strike's objective, its timing, and the conduct of the strikers. If a strike's purpose is to achieve a contract provision forcing the hiring of only union members, its purpose is illegal; therefore, the strike is illegal. If a strike occurs in violation of a no-strike provision in the contract, the timing of the strike is inappropriate, and all striking employees may be disciplined. Further, strikers do not have the right to threaten or engage in acts of violence. For example, neither sit-down strikes nor refusals to leave the plant are protected strike activities. Strikers also exceed their rights when they physically block persons from entering a struck plant or when threats of violence are made against employees not on strike. Picketing and boycott activities are likewise limited. (These activities are further explained in Chapter 7.)

Collective Bargaining and Representation of Employees

The NLRA specifies important elements of collective bargaining. (Because representational procedures and elections are nearly always prerequisites to collective bargaining, they are explained in detail in Chapter 5.) Collective bargaining requires both the employer and the representative of the employees to meet at reasonable times and confer in good faith with respect to wages, hours, and other terms and conditions of employment. While the act does not compel either party to agree to a proposal from the other party or to make a concession, it does require the good faith negotiation of an agreement. If an agreement is reached, it must be reduced to writing and executed in good faith.

Other procedural requirements cover those times when either party may desire to change an existing contract. First, the party requesting a change, usually the union, must notify the other party in writing 60 days before the expiration date of the existing agreement of a desire to change it. Upon receipt of the request, the other party, usually management, must offer to meet and negotiate a new contract. Within 30 days after notifying the other party, the initiating party must notify the Federal Mediation and Conciliation Service if no agreement has been reached on the proposed change. Both parties are required to continue to negotiate without a strike or lockout until 60 days after the first notice or until the contract expires, whichever is later. Only when the contract expires and other procedural obligations have been fulfilled is the union allowed to strike or the company to lock out.

Unfair Labor Practices

While unfair labor practices of employers were included in Section 8 of the Wagner Act of 1935 to protect employees from employer abuse, unfair labor practices of labor organizations were added in 1947 and 1959 for employer, employee, and union member protection.

Unfair Labor Practices: Employer First, the employer is forbidden to interfere with, restrain, or coerce employees in the exercise of the rights in Section 7. Violations include employer threats to fire employees if they join a union, threats to close the plant if the union is organized—especially when other plants owned by the employer are located in the same area—or questioning employees about their union activities. If such violation does occur, the employee or the union may file an unfair labor practice charge with the NLRB, which then initiates its enforcement procedure (covered later in the chapter). Employees are also protected in pursuing their joint working condition concerns even if they do not belong to a labor organization. [8(a)(1)]

The NLRB at first was excessively restrictive in its rulings on employer expressions about unionism and ruled that most employer speeches to employees about unionism were unlawful interference with union activities. However, in 1947 restrictions were eased. Employers were given the right to explain their labor policies, present the advantages and disadvantages of unions, and communicate orally and in writing their arguments and opinions as long as they contained no threats or promises of benefits. (Current application and interpretation of this provision as it pertains to union election campaigns is covered in Chapter 5.)

Attempting to dominate, interfering with the formation of, and financing and supporting a labor union are all prohibited employer activities. For instance, the existence of a **company union,** one that receives financial help from the company, is illegal. Nor are companies allowed to pressure employees into joining a particular union, to take an active part in organizing a union, to promote one union over a rival union during a representation election campaign, or to otherwise engage in "sweetheart" arrangements with union officials. [8(a)(2)] Recent developments in labor-management cooperation programs and employee involvement efforts in proposed legislation called the "Team Act" are addressed more fully in Chapter 7.

Employer discrimination against employees in terms of hiring, tenure of employment, or terms and conditions of employment for the purpose of encouraging or discouraging union membership constitutes an unfair labor practice. However, if the labor agreement requires union membership as a condition of employment and the employee does not pay (or offer to pay) the required union initiation fees and membership dues in accordance with the agreement, the employee may be discharged (see Chapter 11). [8(a)(3)]

Another unfair labor practice pertains to discharge of or discrimination against an employee because he or she had filed charges or given testimony in an NLRB investigation, hearing, or court case under the act. Employers may not refuse reinstatement to, demote, or lay off employees because they have filed charges with the NLRB or testified at NLRB hearings. [8(a)(4)]

Employers may not refuse to bargain in good faith about wages, hours, and terms and conditions of employment with the representative chosen by the employees. Employer obligations include the duty to supply relevant economic information, to refrain from unilateral action, and to negotiate with employees after purchasing a unionized plant. (For a more thorough discussion, see Chapter 6.) Refusing to meet with the union for purposes of negotiation, refusing a union request for cost data concerning an insurance plan, and announcing a wage increase without consulting the union are unfair labor practices. [8(a)(5)]

Unfair Labor Practices: Labor Union Unfair labor practices committed by unions were included in both major amendments in 1947 [Section 8(b)] and 1959. The first forbids a union or its agents to restrain or coerce employees in the exercise of their rights guaranteed under the act. Examples include mass picketing that prevents entrance to the plant by nonstriking employees, threats to employees for not supporting the union, refusal to process a grievance because the employee has criticized the union officers, and refusal to refer an employee to a job based on such considerations as race or lack of union activities. [8(b)(1)]

A second union unfair labor practice pertains to actions that cause an employer to discriminate against an employee with regard to wages, hours, and conditions of employment or for the purpose of encouraging or discouraging union membership. For example, the company may be forced to assign better jobs to union members. Or, when two unions compete to represent the same workers, the company may be forced to side with the more aggressive union by assigning better jobs to its members. Such prohibited practices include causing an employer to discharge employees who circulate a petition challenging a union practice or who make speeches against a contract proposal. [8(b)(2)]

A third provision imposes on unions the same duty as employers to bargain in good faith. Refusing to negotiate with the employer's attorney, refusing to process a grievance of a bargaining unit employee, and striking a company to compel it to leave a multi-employer bargaining unit are some activities illegal under the amended act. [8(b)(3)]

The fourth unfair labor practice includes four prohibited activities. The union may not:

- Force an employer or self-employed person to enter into a hot-cargo agreement (a signed agreement stating that union members will not be required to handle "hot cargo"—goods made by nonunion labor and workers at a struck plant except in the garment industry). (See Chapter 7 also.)
- Restrict any person from using, selling, handling, and transporting goods of a producer, processor, or manufacturer that is directly involved in a labor dispute (secondary boycott—covered in more detail in Chapter 7).
- Force any employer to recognize or bargain with a particular labor organization if another labor organization has already been certified by the NLRB.
- Cause any employer to assign certain work to employees in a particular labor union, trade, or craft rather than another. [8(b)(4)]

Unions are prohibited from charging excessive or discriminatory membership fees. Any discrepancy would be investigated by the NLRB in accordance with the practices and customs of other unions in the particular industry and wages paid to the affected employees. For example, if a union raises its initiation fee from $75.00

to $250.00, an amount equal to four weeks' pay, when other unions charge only $12.50, the practice would be declared illegal. Also prohibited is charging black or female employees higher fees so as to discourage their membership. Labor unions are also forbidden to cause or attempt to cause an employer to pay for services that are not performed or not to be performed; this practice, known as *featherbedding*, is discussed further in Chapter 12. [8(b)(5)][8(b)(6)] Another union unfair labor practice covers organizational and recognition picketing [8(b)(7)], which is discussed in Chapter 5.

Other legal issues affecting labor relations are addressed in later chapters:

- Chapter 4: Rights and obligations of unions and employers.
- Chapter 5: Representation elections, picketing during union organizing campaigns, prehire agreements, composition of bargaining units, and the decertification process.
- Chapter 6: Bargaining in good faith.
- Chapter 7: Strikes, boycotts, and pickets; national emergency work stoppages.
- Chapter 8: Duty of fair representation.
- Chapter 9: Legal aspects of arbitration.
- Chapter 10: Employee right to representation.
- Chapter 11: "Right to work" and union security; rights of minorities.
- Chapter 12: Jurisdictional work disputes and safety issues.
- Chapter 13: Pay discrimination, wage-price controls, and ERISA.

Enforcement of the Act

National Labor Relations Board Because the rights of employees provided by the act are not self-enforcing, and because guaranteeing the rights through the court system would be cumbersome and time-consuming, an independent federal agency, the National Labor Relations Board, was established to administer the act.

The organization of the National Labor Relations Board (NLRB) includes a five-member board that is recommended by the president and confirmed by the U.S. Senate; the Office of the General Counsel; and 50 regional and field offices. The general counsel has final authority to investigate unfair labor practice (ULP) charges and issue complaints and general supervisory responsibilities over the regional field offices, and the board establishes policy, supervises administrative law judges, and decides final appeals within the NLRB structure. In ULP charges, the general counsel's role is like that of a prosecutor, and the board's like that of a judge. Enforcement of NLRB cease and desist orders and remedial actions is through the U.S. Courts of Appeals. For example, the general counsel must seek enforcement of its orders from the Court of Appeals. This provides for yet another hearing.

The NLRB has two major functions: (1) supervising and conducting representation elections (covered in Chapter 5) and (2) adjudicating employer and union unfair labor practices. The NLRB processes are set in motion only when requested in writing and filed with the proper NLRB office. Such requests are called petitions in the case of elections and charges in the case of unfair labor practices.

While the NLRB has authority to administer the acts in all cases involving interstate commerce, it has exercised its discretion and established jurisdictional standards for those cases it will accept, which are those it believes have a substantial effect on commerce. For example, a gas station, hotel, retail store, or apartment complex must gross $500,000 in annual volume before the NLRB will accept its petition or charge, whereas gross annual receipts of private colleges and universities must reach $1 million.

NLRB Procedure Regarding Unfair Labor Practices The procedure for an unfair labor practice complaint (see Exhibit 3.2) starts when an employee, employer, labor union, or individual files a charge with an NLRB office. The party that is charged is then notified that an investigation of the alleged violation will be conducted, and the charge is investigated by the NLRB representative from a nearby regional or field office. Interviews are conducted, documents studied, and other necessary steps taken. At each step the charge may be settled or withdrawn, or the NLRB may dismiss the case due to lack of evidence. (In cases of an unlawful boycott or strike, the NLRB may request a federal district court to issue a temporary restraining order.) If the investigation confirms the charge, the regional director of the NLRB issues a complaint and provides notice of a hearing. The charged party must then respond within 10 days to the complaint.

In many cases, the parties themselves may agree to a resolution before the investigation, and no further steps are needed. However, if there is not resolution between the parties and a formal complaint is issued, an unfair labor practice hearing is conducted before an administrative law judge, who presents findings and recommendations to the board based on the evidence presented at the hearing. All parties are authorized to appeal the administrative law judge's decision directly to the board. The board considers the evidence, and if it believes an unfair labor practice has occurred, it issues an order to cease and desist such practices and to take appropriate affirmative action. On the other hand, if the board believes that the evidence does not support the complaint and no unfair labor practice has been committed, it will dismiss the complaint. Parties may appeal the board's decision as shown in Exhibit 3.2.

Cease and desist orders simply direct the violators to stop whichever activities were deemed unfair labor practices. The board exercises some discretion in determining **appropriate affirmative action,** and typical orders to employers include those to

- Disestablish an employer-dominated company union.
- Offer employees immediate and full reinstatement to their former positions, and pay them back wages plus interest.

Exhibit 3.2 Basic Procedures in Cases Involving Charges of Unfair Labor Practices

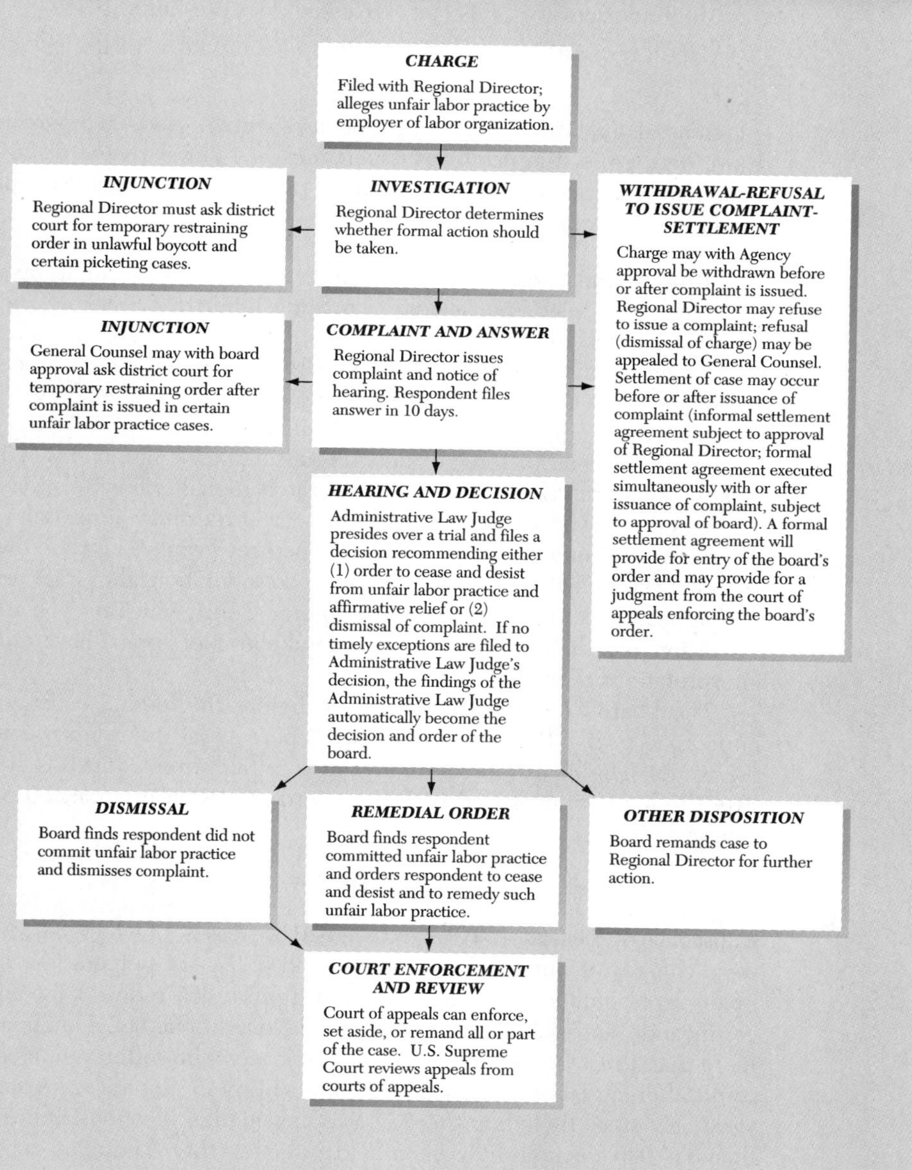

CHARGE
Filed with Regional Director; alleges unfair labor practice by employer of labor organization.
INJUNCTION
Regional Director must ask district court for temporary restraining order in unlawful boycott and certain picketing cases.
INVESTIGATION
Regional Director determines whether formal action should be taken.
WITHDRAWAL-REFUSAL TO ISSUE COMPLAINT-SETTLEMENT
Charge may with Agency approval be withdrawn before or after complaint is issued. Regional Director may refuse to issue a complaint; refusal (dismissal of charge) may be appealed to General Counsel. Settlement of case may occur before or after issuance of complaint (informal settlement agreement subject to approval of Regional Director; formal settlement agreement executed simultaneously with or after issuance of complaint, subject to approval of board). A formal settlement agreement will provide for entry of the board's order and may provide for a judgment from the court of appeals enforcing the board's order.
INJUNCTION
General Counsel may with board approval ask district court for temporary restraining order after complaint is issued in certain unfair labor practice cases.
COMPLAINT AND ANSWER
Regional Director issues complaint and notice of hearing. Respondent files answer in 10 days.
HEARING AND DECISION
Administrative Law Judge presides over a trial and files a decision recommending either (1) order to cease and desist from unfair labor practice and affirmative relief or (2) dismissal of complaint. If no timely exceptions are filed to Administrative Law Judge's decision, the findings of the Administrative Law Judge automatically become the decision and order of the board.
DISMISSAL
Board finds respondent did not commit unfair labor practice and dismisses complaint.
REMEDIAL ORDER
Board finds respondent committed unfair labor practice and orders respondent to cease and desist and to remedy such unfair labor practice.
OTHER DISPOSITION
Board remands case to Regional Director for further action.
COURT ENFORCEMENT AND REVIEW
Court of appeals can enforce, set aside, or remand all or part of the case. U.S. Supreme Court reviews appeals from courts of appeals.

SOURCE: National Labor Relations Board.

- Upon request, bargain collectively with the exclusive bargaining representative of the employees.

Orders to unions include those to

- Refund excessive or illegally collected dues plus interest.
- Upon request, bargain collectively in good faith with the prescribed employer.

In fiscal year 1993, 31.2 percent of cases were settled, 29.8 percent were withdrawn before the complaint was issued, and 34.4 percent were dismissed before a complaint was issued. Just over 2 percent of the cases reached the board in Washington for a hearing and decision.[22]

The Role of the Judiciary The courts under the enforcement provisions of the act serve three major purposes: (1) provide injunctive relief where appropriate, (2) review appealed decisions and orders of the NLRB, and (3) enforce orders after a request is made by the NLRB. As part of the enforcement procedure, the act authorizes the NLRB to petition for an injunction in connection with unfair labor practices where either an employer or a union fails to comply with a board order. In 1994, the board authorized the general counsel to seek injunctions in 57 cases—the highest number in the 60-year history of the National Labor Relations Act.[23] It also provides that any person aggrieved by a board order may appeal directly to an appropriate court of appeals for a review. Upon reviewing the order, the court of appeals may enforce the order, return it for reconsideration, alter it, or set it aside. The final appeal, of course, is to the U.S. Supreme Court, which may be asked to review a decision, especially where several federal courts of appeal have differed in their interpretations of the law.

The board's record of enforcement before the federal courts of appeal was impressive in the 1980s, when about 80 percent of its orders were enforced by the courts. The board's record with the U.S. Supreme Court was equally impressive; the high court agreed with the board's decision in about 80 percent of the cases.[24]

Assessment of the Administration of the NLRB

In fiscal year 1994, the NLRB received 40,861 cases, of which 34,782 (85 percent) were charges of unfair labor practices and 5,724 (14 percent) were petitions for union representation elections. There were also 355 requests for amendments to certification and bargaining unit classification. About $82.2 million ($28 million more than in 1993) was recovered for employees who suffered monetary losses as a result of unfair labor practices; 4,165 offers of reinstatement were made, and 3,722 were accepted. Including the 5,724 representation elections held in 1995, more than 350,000 elections have been held and more than 35 million votes cast.[25]

The National Labor Relations Act and its administration have critics in the academic community. Professor James Gross, an authority on the National Labor Relations Act, has stated that "The current national labor policy favors and protects the powerful at the expense of the powerless. In the essential moral sense, therefore, the current national labor policy is a failure."[26]

Professor Janice Bellace has suggested that most labor commentators find the current application of labor laws has actually discouraged unionism. She stated:

> Current labor law tolerates long delays in getting to an election and in having the election results certified. Labor supporters will also point out that even when there is a union at a workplace, labor law permits the threatened and actual replacement of strikers from the first day of the strike. They will decry this, particularly because rules on the labor contract do not maintain the status quo when the contract expires, thus enabling employers demanding concessions to take back in a flash those contract items gained by the union over the years. Finally, labor supporters deride a statute with remedies so weak they do not deserve the label "remedy."[27]

The NLRB has its critics among labor and management officials. But, since the bulk of the work of the NLRB is done at the regional office level, the actual quality of work of the NLRB can be measured only by the fairness of the regional offices,

Exhibit 3.3 Median Time to Decide Contested Cases (1960–1989)

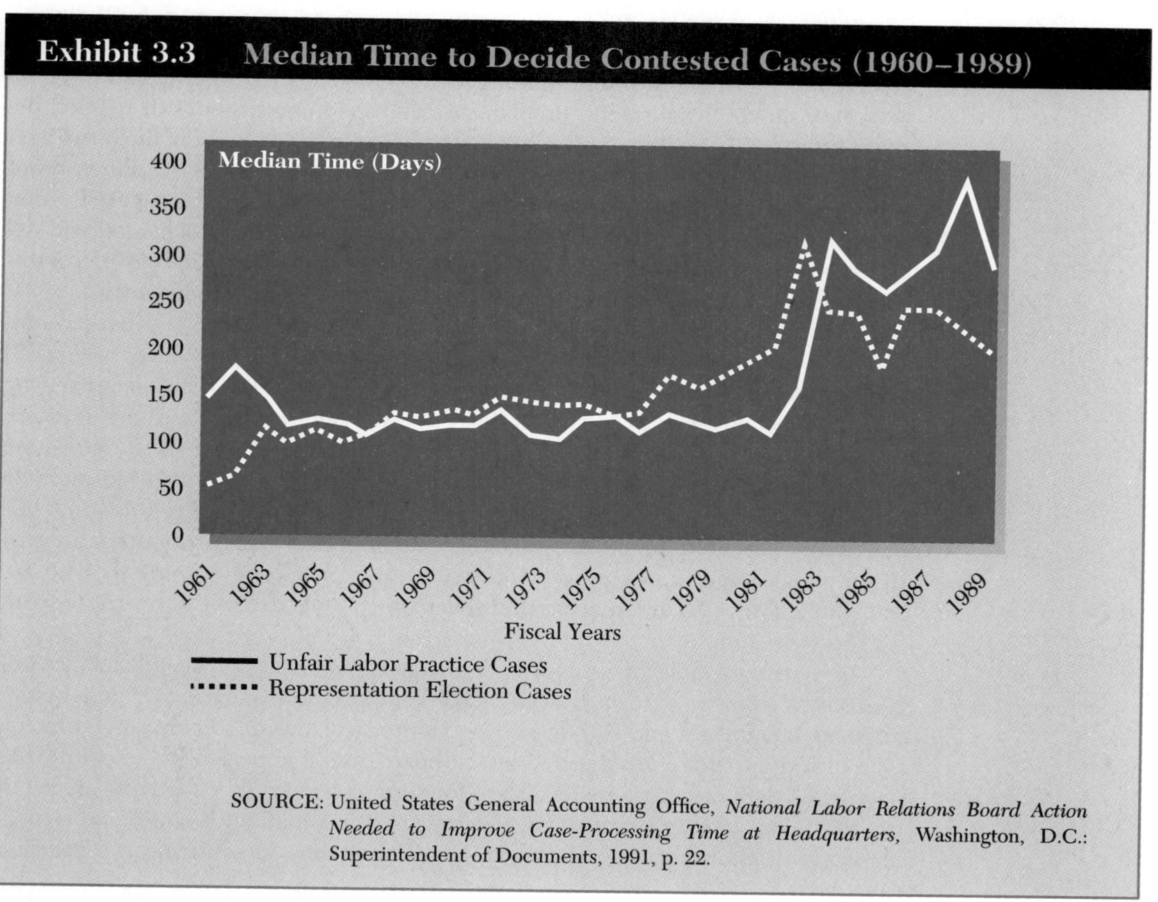

SOURCE: United States General Accounting Office, *National Labor Relations Board Action Needed to Improve Case-Processing Time at Headquarters,* Washington, D.C.: Superintendent of Documents, 1991, p. 22.

the competence of their staffs, and their commitment to the policies of the National Labor Relations Act.[28]

The General Accounting Office (GAO) released a damaging report to Congress entitled *Action Needed to Improve Case-Processing Time at Headquarters.* This report revealed that between 1984 and 1989 only about 67 percent of the 5,000 cases appealed to the board in Washington were decided within one year. Ten percent of the cases took from three to more than seven years to decide. Such time delays existed even though the number of cases assigned was only 874, compared with 1,875 in 1980. Between 1984 and 1989, the medians for processing unfair labor practice cases ranged from a low of 273 days to a high of 395 days—two to three times higher than medians during the 1970s. For representation cases, the medians ranged from 190 to 256 days, higher than the medians during the 1970s. (See Exhibit 3.3, which shows the steady increase in the median time to decide unfair labor practice and representation cases from 1960 to 1989.) The GAO report identified several reasons for the excessive delays: (1) lack of standards and procedures for preventing excessive delays, (2) lack of timely decisions on leading cases, and (3) board member turnover and vacancies (the highest in history during the 1980s).[29]

While the board has continually faced new problems, such as union officers' failure to carry out the duty of representing their members fairly, deferral to arbitration of certain statutory rights, and preplanned and repetitive violations of the act, the subject that has caused the most criticism has been the inadequacy of the board's remedial powers. At present, it has no constitutional penal powers; it cannot award damages; and it cannot impose severe penalties even when the violations are flagrant and repetitive. For individuals who have been discriminatorily discharged and deprived of employment for improper reasons, reinstatement with back pay plus interest rarely covers the real costs that accompany the period of unemployment.[30]

The board's record of obtaining reinstatement for unfairly discharged employees has not been impressive either. Approximately 95 percent of all 8(a)(3) violations entail some form of employment loss; about 90 percent occur during organizing drives, just prior to elections, and during first-contract negotiations. In determining the merits of the complaints, the board attempts to determine the employer's motive in the treatment of an employee. Criteria used include: (1) whether the employer acted in a coercive manner, (2) whether the employee had a poor work record, and (3) whether the employer had an economic necessity for displacing the employee. Most illegally discharged employees who are reinstated by the NLRB receive their back pay but choose not to return to work for the same employer.

In past years, delay in employee discharge cases involving alleged violations of 8(a)(3) was a problem. It took the NLRB 50 days to settle an 8(a)(3) charge before it issued a complaint and 240 days to settle after issuance of a complaint. It took a total of 551 days for cases decided by the board, and if appealed to the courts, the number of days increased to 860. Therefore, employers could effectively prevail in use of the law, and union activists, if terminated in violation of 8(a)(3), were permanently displaced or not reinstated in sufficient time to assist in an organizing campaign.[31]

LABOR RELATIONS IN ACTION

Justice Delayed

At the Lundy Packing Co. in Clinton, North Carolina, two employees were terminated during a 1974 union organizing drive and 44 employees struck in protest. The employees unconditionally offered to return to work, but the company refused to reinstate them. The union filed an unfair labor practice charge, and the NLRB ordered the company to reinstate the employees with back pay in 1976. The company appealed the decision and the Fourth Circuit Court of Appeals upheld the NLRB decision. The company appealed to the U.S. Supreme Court, which refused to review the case.

A six-month hearing was held before an administrative law judge (ALJ) of the NLRB in 1979 to resolve the back pay award. A decision was issued in September 1981, and the company appealed the decision to the board. Not until September 1987 did the board make its decision to uphold the ALJ's decision. Then the company appealed this NLRB decision to the Fourth Circuit Court. On September 7, 1988, the appeals court upheld the NLRB order.

On February 6, 1989, individual checks, ranging from $11,000 to $57,000 and totaling $1.7 million, were mailed to the affected employees. These payments came nearly 15 years after the union had initiated the organizing campaign.

During the interim years, the union was never able to win union representation rights but represented the affected employees throughout the nearly 15 years of legal proceedings. A union spokesperson revealed that the union received no money for its legal work, although its costs were substantial.

SOURCE: "Discharged Lundy Packing Workers Share $1.7 Million Backpay Award," *Daily Labor Report*, February 24, 1989, pp A-4 to A-5.

An example of the use (or misuse) of the legal procedure is highlighted in the 15-year case involving the discharge of employees in an organizing campaign, which was finally concluded in 1989 (see "Labor Relations in Action"). This atypical case highlights not only illegal and expensive behavior by an employer, but more importantly, it raises the ethical question of why the U.S. Congress continues to tolerate such an imbalance between an employer's potential use of legal procedure under current law and those rights provided to employees.

The commitment of unfair labor practices, litigation costs, and potential remedial decisions of the NLRB have become considerable influences in the strategic choices of labor and management. For example, an employer may knowingly commit an unfair labor practice and incur the litigation and remedial costs in the anticipation that these costs will be less than those of compliance with the law. Likewise, the incentive for either the union or management to commit an unfair labor practice that will cause the other party to file a charge depends on the expected costs and gains in terms of the litigation and remedial costs and the probability of a favorable NLRB ruling.[32]

The General Accounting Office reported in 1995 major NLRB violations among federal government contractors. Highlights of the GAO findings are displayed in Exhibit 3.4.

Nonpartisan analysts have agreed that the board's remedies for serious unfair labor practices regarding refusal to bargain in good faith in the initial contract have been woefully deficient. Several attempts have been made to broaden the NLRB's authority, but none have succeeded thus far.[33] For example, when the NLRB attempted to assert itself by imposing a checkoff provision on an employer who had not bargained in good faith[34] and requiring the company to compensate its employees for monetary losses incurred as a result of the company's unlawful refusal to bargain with the certified union, the courts overruled the NLRB, stating that it had gone beyond its statutory authority.[35]

It is even debatable whether stricter, harsher, and costlier remedies would reduce the number of unfair labor practice charges filed or deter illegal behavior. Although several unions, former board members, and at least one circuit court of appeals have endorsed financial reparations to employees in specific refusal to bargain cases, it is important to recognize that the intent of the act is not to reduce the intake of cases but to promote collective bargaining as a method for management officials and union representatives to jointly determine their working conditions.[36] Some have suggested that the board should press more vigorously to fully realize its present enforcement authority in the courts.

Orders of the NLRB are not self-enforcing; the NLRB must apply to the appropriate court of appeals for enforcement. If the NLRB order is enforced by the

Exhibit 3.4 GAO Findings of Federal Contractors and Violations of Labor Law in 1993

- Eighty firms received over $23 billion in federal contracts.
- Six violators received almost 90 percent of the more than $23 billion in contracts.
- Fifteen of the firms were involved in serious violations, i.e., were ordered to reinstate or restore more than 20 employees or had been issued a broad cease and desist order.
- Remedies affected nearly 1,000 individual employees as well as thousands of additional represented employees.
- Most of the contracts awarded came from the Department of Defense and went to firms primarily engaged in manufacturing.

SOURCE: United States General Accounting Office, *Worker Protection: Federal Contractors and Violations of Labor Law*, Washington, D. C.: Superintendant of Documents, 1995.

court, it becomes a lawful decree of that court, requiring compliance and backed with civil contempt sanctions. If court-enforced orders are violated, the violator can be held in contempt of court and subject to more serious penalties. On the other hand, contempt of court actions were not effective in the strike of Pittston Coal company when the mineworker's union was fined nearly $50 million (the fine was subsequently abolished by the Supreme Court) and several union leaders were jailed.[37]

Not to be overlooked is the fact that the members of the NLRB are presidential appointees. The appointment process has a substantial influence on the philosophy and direction of the NLRB and its decisions. "Interpretations of the facts and law governing union-management relations is . . . dependent in part on the makeup of the board."[38] During the 1980s, for example, the board appointed by President Reagan overturned many decisions that had existed for as long as 20 years. Similarly, during their tenure in office, members of the board appointed by Presidents Kennedy and Johnson had reversed 31 previous decisions. Some of these recent reversals, shown in the "Labor Relations in Action," demonstrate the importance of presidential appointments to the board and courts.

Because members of the NLRB are appointed by the president and approved by the Senate, appointments usually reflect the president's political philosophy and attitudes. The Senate's confirmation of the present NLRB Chair, William B. Gould IV, took several months. Thus, a question frequently asked is whether decision making is influenced by pro-union or pro-employer preferences of board members and the appointing president. Recent research has found such influence in roughly 20 percent of the decisions, in which it may appear that the board decisions "flip-flop" through the course of different presidential administrations. However, the remaining 80 percent are not influenced by political bias or pro-union/pro-employer preferences because the board generally adopts the decisions of the regional offices and the Administrative Law Judges, full-time professionals who are not political appointees. Evidence shows that board members are primarily influenced by their accountability to the public and that they weigh the potential impact of their decisions on both labor and business.[39]

Since March 1994, when William Gould assumed the position of Chair of the National Labor Relations Board, the NLRB has initiated several actions to improve its efficiency. First, Gould established an NLRB advisory panel, which consists of 25 leading union attorneys and 25 leading management attorneys, to make recommendations for improving the NLRB functions. Second, a procedure was devised for assigning settlement judges who have authority to conciliate or mediate between the opposing parties. Third, the Administrative Law Judges were given authority to ask for oral arguments in lieu of written briefs and to issue a bench decision within 72 hours of the close of a hearing, instead of submitting a written decision. (Full hearings with written briefs and decisions average 235 days.) Fourth, the board is currently exploring additional rule-making opportunities that could avoid or reduce costly litigation and eliminate unnecessary delays in representational elections. Finally, the board has increased the use of injunctions to stop violations of the National Labor Relations Act that, if allowed to continue, would cause irreparable harm.[40] Chairman Gould has not been reluctant to

LABOR RELATIONS IN ACTION

Controversial Reversals in Labor Relations Rulings by the NLRB and the Courts during the Reagan and Bush Administrations

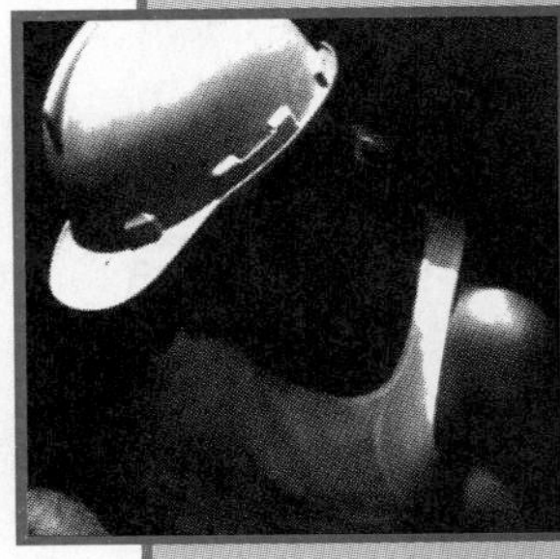

Meyer Industries[a]

Previous rulings: An individual employee is protected from discipline for participating in a concerted activity of concern to other employees.

New ruling: For an individual employee to be protected for participating in a concerted activity, he/she must have authority of other employees to act on their behalf.

Milwaukee Springs[b]

Previous ruling: Relocation of unit work for labor costs not only required bargaining but because it occurred during the term of a contract, required the union's consent before relocation.

New ruling: Union consent is required only when there is language in the contract specifically prohibiting the employer from relocating the work.

Indianapolis Power & Light Company[c]

Previous ruling: Despite a no-strike clause, employees may honor another union's picket line.

New ruling: A broad no-strike clause in the contract waives the employee's right to engage in a sympathy strike, thus permitting employers to discipline sympathy strikers.

Sears Roebuck & Co.[d]

Previous ruling: Employees who are not represented by unions have the right to representation during an interview that they believe could lead to discipline.

New ruling: Employees who are not represented by a union have no right to have a representative at an investigatory interview.

Olin Corp.[e]

Previous ruling: An arbitrator's decision can be overturned if it is not consistent with the key concepts of the NLRA as interpreted by the Board.

New ruling: An arbitrator's decision will not be overturned if the arbitrator had decided essentially the same issue a party tries to present to the NLRB, assuming that the arbitrator was presented essentially the same facts that would be relevant to resolving the case if the board were to consider it again.

Rossmore House[f]

Previous ruling: Virtually all interrogation of employees who are union supporters is prohibited.

New Ruling: Employers may, in certain circumstances, interrogate union supporters without committing an unfair labor practice.

Otis Elevator Division of United Technologies[g]

Previous ruling: The company must bargain with the union before it can transfer work normally performed by bargaining unit employees to another facility.

New ruling: The union does not have the right to bargain over an employer's decision to transfer production work from one facility to another where such management's decision is based on considerations other than labor cost, which might be amenable to resolution through the negotiation process.

Lechmere[h]

Previous ruling: Companies were allowed to ban nonemployee union organizers from company premises when circumstances were such that organizers could contact employees through the "usual channels" of communication. The NLRB had concluded that the "usual channels" did not include newspapers, radio, or television and that organizers must have some other means to contact workers directly.

New ruling: The Supreme Court ruled that the union generally lacks reasonable alternatives to access to employees only when the employees live on the company's premises.

SOURCE: "Remarks on Recent Developments in NLRB Case Law by William Kocol, Deputy Regional Attorney for NLRB Region 13," *Daily Labor Report,* March 18, 1985, pp. E-1–E-4, "Remarks of Former NLRB Chariman Edward B. Miller on Recent Board Cases," *Daily Labor Report,* June 4, 1984, p. E-1; and Peter Walther, "The NLRB Today," *Labor Law Journal* 36 (November 1985), pp. 803–816.

[a]268 NLRB 73 (1984); 281 NLRB 118 (1986)

[b]268 NLRB 87 (1984)

[c]273 NLRB 211 (1985)

[d]274 NLRB 55 (1985)

[e]268 NLRB 86 (1984)

[f]269 NLRB 198 (1984)

[g]269 NLRB 891 (1984)

[h]*Lechmere* v. *NLRB,* 60 USLW 4145 (January 28, 1992)

share his views on U.S. labor law. Samples are included in the "Labor Relations in Action" on page 101.

Transportation-Related Labor Relations Laws (Railway and Airlines)

Rail and air transportation labor relations are covered by the Railway Labor Act, and deregulation legislation has had dramatic effects on them. Although the Railway Labor Act was passed in 1926 to apply only to the railway industry, it was actually the first comprehensive labor relations law. Like other labor laws, the Railway Labor Act did not develop overnight; it resulted from years of union activity and attempts to pass laws accommodating railway labor relations.[41] The act relies almost entirely on collective bargaining for settling labor disputes, but it has established mandatory mediation by the National Mediation Board (NMB).

Under the Railway Labor Act, if the two parties are unable to resolve their differences over negotiating their agreement (major dispute), the dispute is subject to mandatory mediation through the National Mediation Board. If mediation does not succeed, the parties have the option of proceeding to arbitration. If either party rejects arbitration, there is a 30-day status quo period during which the president may appoint an emergency board. This has occurred 224 times over the past 67 years (191 times in the railway industry and 33 times in the airline industry). Also, Congress has intervened 17 times to either extend the status quo, impose a settlement, or provide for final and binding arbitration in the railway industry.[42]

The first major amendment to the Railway Labor Act occurred in 1934. It provided assistance to unions by barring employers from attempting to influence employees in selecting their bargaining representatives. Further, employers were directed to bargain collectively with certified labor representatives, and company-dominated unions and yellow-dog contracts were forbidden. The National Railroad Adjustment Board (NRAB), a bipartisan group of 18 union and 18 management representatives, was established to assist in resolving grievances and interpreting provisions of the labor agreements. Where the board could not agree to a settlement, the amendment provided that the grievance be settled by an arbitrator selected by the parties. The National Mediation Board was empowered to conduct representation elections and to help resolve conflicts in negotiating new labor agreements. In 1936, the act was amended again, and coverage was extended to a new and developing industry—air transportation—although the airlines continued their local system boards for grievance resolution.[43]

There are several differences between the Railway Labor Act (RLA) and the National Labor Relations Act (NLRA):

(a) The RLA covers the railway and airline industries, whereas the NLRA covers all private industries with few exceptions.

(b) Union representation under the RLA is based on the majority of all employees eligible to vote through mail-in ballots, whereas union representation under the NLRA is based on the majority vote of those who vote, usually in secret ballot elections held at the work site.

Statements by William B. Gould IV, Chairman of the National Labor Relations Board, on a Broad Number of Labor Law Issues Including His Approach to His Office

Before the Senate Labor Committee for His Confirmation Hearings, October 1993

Prior to moving from the role of private practitioner to the academic arena, I began to arbitrate and mediate a wide variety of labor-management disputes in both the private and public sector. I have been an arbitrator, mediator and factfinder in more than 200 labor disputes since 1965 and I have written opinions and awards in approximately 140 cases. I have ruled in favor of management in approximately 59% of the cases where the award was clearly in favor of one side or the other and in approximately 54% of the cases *in toto*.

Address to the Washington State Labor Council, August 1994, on Improving the Efficiency of the NLRB

Prompt and effective resolution of unfair labor practice charges is critical to our credibility—particularly in campaigns involving organizational activity where employees who are not protected by a labor organization may lose faith or hope in our process if a considerable length of time elapses before adjudication.

Even subsequent to the time that is involved in both the investigation and the issuance of a complaint by the General Counsel—a process which takes 51 days on average—it takes an additional 5 to 6 months on average for the Administrative Law Judge to issue a ruling subsequent to the close of hearing and, after that, the case can be appealed to both the Board in Washington and then on to the federal judiciary.

My belief is that there are two obvious avenues through which we can attack aspects of the delay problem under our statute. The first relates to an area where we need, and have had these past five months, coordination and cooperation with the General Counsel, Fred Feinstein. Here I have reference to the authority to obtain injunctive relief against employer unfair labor practices in federal district court without necessarily proceeding in the first instance to a hearing before an Administrative Law Judge.

Remarks to The Employers Group, Los Angeles, September 1994, on His Vision of the Industrial Relations Environment

I favor an industrial relations environment in which investment opportunities and fair-profit margins and fair-employment policies are promoted and encouraged. Only through such policies can we have jobs in our globally competitive economy. And only through the creation of jobs can we begin to address the often perplexing and difficult questions of industrial relations and labor law policy bound up with that.

(continued)

Statements by William B. Gould IV, Chairman of the National Labor Relations Board, on a Broad Number of Labor Law Issues Including His Approach to His Office—cont'd

Statement to the Commission on the Future of Worker-Management Relations, Popularly Known as the Dunlop Commission, September 1994

Employees ought to be able to know the economic facts of life which affect them and their job and financial security. Unless the data sought is confidential in the sense that its disclosure would injure the employer's competitive position, the union should have automatic access to all information which might arguably affect the employer's capability to offer wages and conditions of employment at the bargaining table.

. . . the statute should resolve all ambiguities by allowing employers to provide unions with access to plant facilities, desks, secretarial help, xeroxing, office space and the like without fear of offending the statutory prohibition against unlawful assistance and support.

. . . the statute permits relationships between consenting employers and unions on a "members only" basis where the union does not represent a majority of employees. There is no reason why a duty to consult and notify cannot be imposed where it is on a limited number of issues such as discharge or discipline, health and safety, where a significant number of employees, e.g., 20 to 30 percent in the establishment, desire such representation.

Remarks to the Atlanta Bar Association, December 1994, on the Encouragement of Informal Resolution and Promotion of Cooperation

One new procedure will provide for the use of settlement judges—who do not have the power to adjudicate—to resolve conflicts arising out of unfair labor practice allegations. Another new procedure will expedite our procedures through the use of bench decisions by Administrative Law Judges within 72 hours of oral summation.

Statements Before the House Committee on Economic and Educational Opportunities, July 1995, on His Goals for the National Labor Relations Board

. . . the Board is concerned with establishing the appropriate procedures for both employee free choice and the collective bargaining process. Under the statutory philosophy, the determination of substantive conditions of employment is for the parties themselves.

As Chairman of the NLRB, my goals have been to eliminate unnecessary and wasteful litigation between the parties, devise new settlement procedures, eliminate delays in our processes, increase the effectiveness of our enforcement of the Act, and strengthen the Agency's reputation for impartiality and efficiency.

SOURCE: Statements taken from published speeches in the *Daily Labor Report,* October 3, 1993 to July 13, 1995.

(c) A significantly higher percentage of employees in the railway and airline industries are organized by unions under the RLA.

(d) Under the RLA, the union cannot strike and the employer cannot lock out until they have exhausted the impasse resolution procedures required by the National Mediation Board; under the NLRA, the parties can engage in self-help actions if they have followed the required notices.

(e) Under the RLA, arbitration of minor disputes (grievances) in the railway industry is mandatory, and the government bears the expense of arbitration; under the NLRA, grievance arbitration procedures are negotiated by the parties, and the parties pay for the arbitration (airline grievance arbitration is similar to arbitration under the NLRA).[44]

Assessment of the Railway Labor Act

Faced with such problems as changing markets for freight transportation, severe competition, government regulation, and public interest in uninterrupted railroad service, labor relations in the railway industry are unique. Complicating the situation further are the chronic financial instability of the numerous independent railroads, the presence of strong, competing craft unions, and tradition-bound work rules. These factors affect labor relations in the following ways: (1) Because the public depends on railroad transportation for many essential goods, much effort has been made to avoid strikes (five interventions by Congress). (2) With the "fractionated" craft unions, the labor relations process takes much time and creates many opportunities for disputes. (3) The tradition-bound work rules of the operating crafts strictly control not only how a particular job will be performed, but also which craft will be assigned the job. These work rules postpone the introduction of new technology and magnify the problems of a declining industry.[45] Any assessment of the Railway Labor Act must be kept in proper perspective. There are over 7,000 labor agreements in the railroad and airline industries, and about 1,000 railroad and 200 airline agreements (mostly local) are in negotiations during any given year.[46] Further, any measure of the act's effectiveness must be made with reference to its objectives—to promote free collective bargaining and protect the public from interrupted flows of commerce.[47]

Regarding negotiations, mediation has been the most important method of intervention under the act; however, few nationwide railroad wage cases have been settled by mediation since 1936. Its greatest success has been in settling minor controversies after the major issues have been resolved. This does not mean that mediation is unimportant—minor disputes left unresolved could easily lead to major strikes in future negotiations.

Since its inception, the NMB has successfully resolved 5,500 representation issues, largely without incident or challenge. The mediation staff has handled nearly 12,000 negotiations with only 350 (or 3 percent) unsuccessful—a record unmatched by almost any other major industry. Only 17 emergency boards have been appointed over the past 10 years, well below the 4-per-year average of earlier decades. Also, compared with the 1930s and 1940s, when about 80 percent of all railroad grievances were resolved by the NRAB, now over 90 percent of the 1,000 each year are resolved by neutral referees. Congress was forced to intervene in labor disputes under the Railway Labor Act in 1962, 1966, 1967, 1971, and 1972; however, from 1972 to 1992 the parties were able to resolve their differences through the procedures of the RLA.[48]

In June 1992, however, Congress had to intervene again to end a two-day work stoppage by the Machinists Union that had shut down a major portion of the U.S. railway traffic. The legislation ordered the railroad employees back to work, and the four-year-old dispute became subject to mediation-arbitration procedures, including the "last, best offer" procedure. The union and company negotiators were able to concur on a 42-month collective bargaining agreement. Union officials believed that the agreement reached through negotiations was better than that which would have been imposed by an arbitration board, even though the agreement included work-rule concessions and did not maintain the same level of real wages for the membership.[49]

Deregulation Legislation

The Airline Deregulation Act of 1978 ended government controls of fares and routes, and the Motor Carrier Act of 1980 reduced the amount of economic regulation of the industry by the Interstate Commerce Commission. The Staggers Rail Act of 1980 gave railroads more flexibility in setting rates and service levels.

Since the enactment of these laws, employment has remained relatively unchanged in the airline and trucking industries but has continued to decline in the railroads. Relative wages have remained constant in airlines while declining in trucking and rising in railroads. Labor costs have increased at a slower pace in airlines and trucking while they have declined in railroads.[50]

Since the Railway Labor Act did not restrict subjects for mandatory bargaining as did the National Labor Relations Act, the airline unions were able to restrict some of management's strategies, such as establishing double-breasted firms (the same firm owning both a union and a competing nonunion airline) and transferring company assets to another firm owned by the same airline.[51]

Airline deregulation prompted the introduction of 128 nonunion carriers; by 1987, only 37 had survived. Their introduction sparked a wave of mergers by the major airlines, ticketing agreements between major carriers and regional and commuter airlines, hub-and-spoke airports, and frequent flier programs to promote airline allegiance.[52] Deregulation also brought about the benefits of price competition, with 90 percent of passengers traveling at discount prices averaging 60 percent below the coach price. During the same time accident rates have not increased, and service to small communities has not deteriorated; however, there have been increased congestion at airports and in the airways, delays in departures and arrivals, threats to safety, and a general decline in the quality of air service.[53]

The past several years in the industries covered under the Railway Labor Act have been interesting. The airline industry has suffered record losses, $3.9 billion in

1990; $1.94 billion in 1991; and $4.03 billion in 1992. Eastern Airlines has ceased operations; America West, Continental, Midway, USAir, and others have operated under bankruptcy protection. The continuing losses and shifting business strategies have increased the difficulties of achieving new labor agreements in the industry. In the railway industry, the nation's largest carriers and major rail unions successfully concluded their negotiations, but only after exhausting all dispute resolution procedures available under the Railway Labor Act, including presidential emergency boards and Congressional intervention.[54]

Promising Developments Regarding the Railway Labor Act

Despite problems, several recent events and developments provide the basis for some optimism:

- The most recent national railroad agreements have included a fixed term, a no-strike clause, and common expiration dates.
- Recent negotiations have also been characterized by union-management cooperation, which has resulted in fewer conflicts and outside interventions.
- Emergency board procedures have been drastically improved, and the ritualism and legalism so prevalent in the 1960s have been reduced.
- Encouraging progress has been made on some long-standing manning and work-rule issues, such as the fireman on diesel trains, combined road and yard service, and interdivisional runs.
- New leadership has had a positive influence on both management and unions, and neutrals and government officials have provided capable assistance in the bargaining and dispute-resolution processes.

Critical issues remain to be resolved, including secondary picketing, bargaining stalemates, restrictive work rules in some agreements, intercraft wage structure problems, and crew size disputes.[55] But there is still reason to be optimistic if the recent trend can be sustained. As one authority has said:

> No labor law can ensure peaceful and constructive labor relations. Although specific amendments to the Railway Labor Act may be desirable—notably, in connection with representational questions—we should be careful about casting into oblivion a law that both parties, on balance, seemingly want to retain.[56]

Other Laws That Affect Labor Relations

Other statutes and executive orders, more narrow in scope, influence labor relations either directly or indirectly. The following section highlights only their major provisions; however, practitioners find that detailed knowledge of them is essential to most business operations. (Related legislation is summarized here, but its specific implications for labor relations activities and unions are discussed in the appropriate chapters.)

The Americans with Disabilities Act of 1990 (ADA)

The Americans with Disabilities Act of 1990 (ADA), which covers an estimated 40 million disabled Americans, went into effect in January 1992. Considered a "Bill of Rights" for Americans with a wide variety of disabilities, the act applies to employment, public accommodations, transportation, and telecommunications. The employment provisions cover virtually every aspect of the employment process. The act prohibits discrimination in advancement, discharge, compensation, training, and other terms and conditions of employment that are usually included in collective bargaining agreements. The act requires employers to make reasonable accommodations for disabled employees, except when doing so would subject the employer to undue hardship. (This subject will be addressed more fully in Chapter 12.)

Bankruptcy Act

Bankruptcy legislation enacted in 1984 includes standards for the rejection of collective bargaining agreements by companies for obtaining modifications in labor agreements. It requires companies to provide relevant information to unions and good faith efforts to reach an agreement. In cases where no agreement can be reached, the act specifies the requirements for terminating or altering provisions of the agreement. (See Chapter 6 for more details.)

Worker Adjustment and Retraining Notification Act

Triggered by major plant closings without notification, The Worker Adjustment and Retraining Notification Act (WARN) was passed in 1988. WARN requires employers with 100 or more employees to give 60 days advance notice to employees (excluding those employed less than 20 hours per week) who will be affected by a plant closing or major layoff. Also, the union, the chief elected local government official, and the state government must be notified. The law also allows the union and companies to negotiate a clause in their collective bargaining agreement that could require more than 60 days of advance notice.

The situations covered include

- "plant closing" resulting in an employment loss for 50 or more workers at one site within a 30-day period.
- "mass layoff" of at least 33 percent of the workforce (minimum of 50 employees) within any 30-day period.
- "mass layoff" involving at least 500 employees within any 30-day period.

Remedies to affected employees for employer violations include back pay and benefits for up to 60 days and payments (maximum of $500 per day) to local communities for a period of up to 60 days. Enforcement will be via a lawsuit in a federal district court by aggrieved employees, the union, or the local government.

WARN ties in closely with the Job Training Partnership Act (JTPA), which provides funds to state and local governments for training and retraining. In cases of plant closing and mass layoff, state "rapid response" teams are available to work with labor and management officials to set up retraining and re-employment programs for the affected workers. (See Chapter 12 for increased coverage.)

Racketeering Influenced and Corrupt Organizations Act (RICO)

RICO, part of the Organized Crime Control Act, forbids anyone involved in racketeering from investing in or controlling through racketeering activity any enterprise (businesses or labor unions) engaged in interstate commerce. The law provides for penalties of up to $25,000, 20 years of imprisonment, and forfeiture of all relevant property. If found guilty, the convicted person may be required to divest himself of all interests in the organization and restricted from any future activities in that or related organizations. In addition, any persons who suffered damages from the prohibited activities are entitled to threefold recovery of damages. In 1988 and 1989, the Justice Department used RICO against the International Brotherhood of Teamsters, and the Teamsters were placed under a court-appointed trustee.

Employment Discrimination Laws and Executive Orders

The Civil Rights Act of 1991 prohibits any form of employment discrimination by companies, labor unions, and employment agencies on the basis of race, color, religion, sex, or national origin. By creating the Equal Employment Opportunity Commission, the act provided an enforcement procedure that includes investigations, attempts at conciliation, and suits filed on behalf of the complainant.

The **Age Discrimination in Employment Act of 1967,** as amended in 1978, 1984, and 1986, prohibits employment discrimination against those over the age of 40, permits compulsory retirement for executives who are entitled to pensions of $44,000 per year or more, and authorizes jury trials in covered cases.

Executive Order 11246, as amended by Executive Order 11375, prohibits employment discrimination in the federal government and by federal government contractors and subcontractors receiving $50,000 or more. Those having contracts of $50,000 or more and employing 50 people or more are required to establish affirmative action plans that prescribe specific goals and procedures for increasing the percentage of minority employees. Firms that fail to comply could lose part or all of their contracts. (See Chapter 11 for related coverage.)

The **Vocational Rehabilitation Act of 1973** (Section 503) requires holders of federal government contracts in excess of $2,500 to take affirmative action to employ and advance in employment qualified physically and mentally disabled individuals. Further, if any disabled individual believes that a federal contractor has failed or refused to comply with the act, he or she may file a complaint with the Department of Labor, which will investigate the complaint and take any warranted action. In addition, Section 504 extends coverage to organizations receiving federal financial assistance and is enforced by the Department of Health and Human Services.

Related Labor Relations Laws

The **Military Selection Act of 1967** requires employers to restore veterans whose military service time does not exceed four years to the positions they held before entering the armed services or to similar positions of like seniority, status, and pay.

Also, the **Vietnam Era Veteran Readjustment Assistance Act** requires employers with government contracts of $10,000 or more to take affirmative action to employ and advance disabled veterans and qualified veterans of the Vietnam War.

The **Social Security Act of 1935,** as amended, established two national systems of social security for protection against loss of income due to unemployment, old age, disability, and death: (1) retirement, survivors, and disability insurance, and health insurance for persons over age 65; and (2) unemployment insurance, which operates under a state-administered, federal-state plan whose operating costs are paid by the federal government.

Other important laws include the Wage Laws and Employee Retirement and Income Security Act of 1974 (covered in Chapter 13), the Occupational Safety and Health Act (covered in Chapter 12), the Family and Medical Leave Act (covered in Chapter 13), and federal and state laws and local ordinances that pertain to public-sector labor relations and equal employment opportunity.

Summary

This chapter has presented the major provisions of federal labor relations laws in the United States. These legal influences must be understood in order to fully appreciate the remaining chapters in this book because nearly all issues in labor relations are either directly or indirectly influenced by labor relations law.

While many think of law in terms of statutes passed by the U.S. Congress or state legislatures, labor relations and other types of law proceed not only from statutes but also from the U.S. Constitution, judicial decisions, and administrative decisions of government agencies. Similar laws and decisions develop at the state and local government levels.

Developing the legal influences historically, this chapter began with the early struggles of labor unions to exist as they faced an unsympathetic judiciary and lack of any permissive legislation. Several hurdles included the criminal conspiracy and civil conspiracy doctrines as well as the breach-of-contract rulings. Then the Sherman Act, passed primarily to control business monopolies, was applied to labor unions also. With support of labor, the Sherman Act was amended by the Clayton Act; however, this act also proved unfavorable to unions.

While the 1920s did bring passage of the Railway Labor Act, little legislative action occurred in other sectors. However, the 1930s, with the country's most severe economic depression, brought about major changes. The enactment of the Norris–La Guardia Act changed the public policy toward labor relations. Not only did it recognize employees' rights to various freedoms, such as freedom of association and self-organization, it also restricted the role of the federal courts in labor disputes.

Recognizing several deficiencies in the Norris–La Guardia Act, Congress passed the National Labor Relations Act in 1935. This act dealt with employer unfair labor practices, established an administrative agency, the NLRB, and guaranteed a number of employee rights, such as the right to form and join unions and to participate in concerted actions. Then, in 1947 and again in 1959, Congress amended the National Labor Relations Act with passage of the Taft-Hartley Act and the Landrum-Griffin Act, respectively. The 1947 amendments added union unfair labor practices and restrictions on union security clauses, and the 1959 act added regulations of government and internal operations of unions and amended regulations on strike, picketing, and boycott activities.

Starting in 1863, union activity in the railroad industry played a key role in the legislative arena. The Railway Labor Act of 1926, whose major purpose is to provide for stable and effective labor relations without major interruptions in commerce, established procedures for resolving labor disputes and created the National Mediation Board and National Railroad Adjustment Board to accomplish the act's purposes. While the assessment of these measures may seem less than optimistic, several recent developments give some evidence of success: acceptance of negotiations and responsibilities by the parties, recent no-strike clauses, improved employer-union cooperation on important issues, new leadership in both unions and management, and improved emergency board procedures.

Other laws that relate to unions, management, and employment are highlighted throughout the chapter.

Key Terms

employment at will
yellow-dog contract
company union
cease and desist order
appropriate affirmative action

Discussion Questions

1. How have the major labor relations laws helped or hindered the development of unions?
2. How were yellow-dog contracts used to limit activities of union organizers? How were they used to slow union growth?
3. Why did the 1914 Clayton Act, called U.S. labor's Magna Carta by AFL president Samuel Gompers, prove to be less than a benefit to unions?
4. What was missing in the Norris–La Guardia Act (regarding administration of the law) that was present in the National Labor Relations Act? Why was its absence important?
5. Although the National Labor Relations Act gives employees certain rights, these rights are not unlimited. Discuss.

6. The NLRB has been criticized for its lack of success in the reinstatement and continued employment of discharged employees under the NLRA. What could be changed in the NLRA or its administration that would improve its record on reinstatement?
7. Why is there still a separate labor relations law for the railway and airline industries?
8. Project the effects of the bankruptcy and deregulation laws on labor relations, and then on society in general.

References

1. J. R. Commons and E. A. Gilmore, *A Documentary History of American Industrial Society* (Cleveland, Ohio: A. H. Clark, 1910), p. 68.
2. Quoted by John Fanning in "The Balance of Labor-Management Economic Power under Taft-Hartley," *Proceedings of the 40th Annual Meeting of the Industrial Relations Research Association,* ed. Barbara D. Dennis (Madison, Wis.: IRRA, 1988), p. 70.
3. *Commonwealth* v. *Hunt,* 45 Mass. 4 (1842).
4. Reported in Walter E. Oberer, Kurt L. Hanslowe, and Jerry R. Andersen, *Labor Law,* 2d ed. (St. Paul, Minn.: West Publishing Co., 1979) pp. 20–21.
5. E. E. Herman and G. S. Skinner, *Labor Law* (New York: Random House, 1972), p. 21.
6. *Vegelahn* v. *Guntner,* 44 N.E. 1077 (1896). See Herbert L. Sherman, Jr., and William P. Murphy, *Unionization and Collective Bargaining,* 3d ed. (Washington, D.C.: Bureau of National Affairs Inc., 1975), p. 3.
7. *Hitchman Coal & Coke Company* v. *Mitchell,* 245 U.S. 229 (1917).
8. 26 Stat. 209 (1890).
9. *Loewe* v. *Lawlor,* 208 U.S. 274 (1908).
10. 38 Stat. 731 (1914).
11. *Duplex Printing Press Co.* v. *Deering,* 254 U.S. 443 (1921).
12. *Truax* v. *Corrigan,* 257 U.S. 312 (1921).
13. 47 Stat.70 (1932).
14. Benjamin Taylor and Fred Witney, *Labor Relations Law* (Englewood Cliffs, N.J.: Prentice-Hall: 1992), pp. 6–8.
15. A labor dispute was defined as "any controversy concerning terms or conditions of employment, or concerning the association or representation of persons in negotiating, fixing, maintaining, changing, or seeking to arrange terms or conditions of employment regardless of whether or not the disputants stand in the proximate relation of employer and employee." 47 Stat. 70 (1932).
16. Ibid.
17. Alvin L. Goldman, *The Supreme Court and Labor-Management Relations Law* (Lexington, Mass.: D.C. Heath, 1976), pp. 26–28; and Sherman and Murphy, *Unionization and Collective Bargaining,* pp. 7–9.
18. Goldman, *The Supreme Court,* pp. 28–31.
19. Sherman and Murphy, *Unionization and Collective Bargaining,* p. 9.
20. Goldman, *The Supreme Court,* pp. 31–39.
21. This section was taken from the Wagner Act, 49 Stat. 449 (1935); Labor Management Relations Act, 61 Stat. 136 (1947); Landrum-Griffin Act, 73 Stat. 519 (1959); Office of General Counsel, National Labor Relations Board, *A Guide to Basic Law and Procedures under the National Labor Relations Act* (Washington, D.C.: Government Printing Office, 1976), unless otherwise noted.
22. *Fifty-Eighth Annual Report of the National Labor Relations Board for Fiscal*

Year Ended September 30, 1993 (Washington, D.C.: U.S. Government Printing Office, 1994), pp. 1–5.
23. *Daily Labor Report,* September 13, 1994, p. D-2.
24. *Fifty-Eighth Annual Report of the National Labor Relations Board for Fiscal Year Ended September 30, 1993* (Washington, D.C.: U.S. Government Printing Office, 1994), pp. 1–5.
25. *Fifty-Eighth Annual Report of the National Labor Relations Board for Fiscal Year Ended September 30, 1993* (Washington, D.C.: U.S. Government Printing Office, 1994), pp. 1–5; updated by *Daily Labor Report,* July 13, 1995, p. E-4.
26. James A. Gross, "The Demise of the National Labor Policy: A Question of Social Justice," in *Restoring the Promise of American Labor Law,* ed. Sheldon Friedman et al. (Ithaca, N.Y.: ILR Press, 1994), pp. 57–58.
27. Janice R. Bellace, "Labor Law Reform for the Post Industrial Workplace," *Labor Law Journal* 45 (August 1994), p. 460.
28. Karen Boroff, "Factors Influencing Unfair Labor Practice Charges," *Labor Law Journal* 43 (November 1992), pp. 709–714.
29. United States General Accounting Office, *National Labor Relations Board: Action Needed to Improve Case-Processing Time at Headquarters* (Washington, D.C.: Superintendent of Documents, 1991), pp. 1–7.
30. John H. Fanning, "We are Forty—Where Do We Go?" *Labor Law Journal* 27 (January 1976), pp. 5–6.
31. William N. Cooke, "The Rising Toll of Discrimination against Union Activists," *Industrial Relations* 24 (Fall 1985), p. 438.
32. Robert J. Flanagan, "Remedial Policy and Compliance with the NLRA," *Proceedings of the 39th Annual Meeting of the Industrial Relations Research Association,* ed. Barbara D. Dennis (Madison, Wis.: IRRA, 1987), pp. 21–27.
33. Frank W. McCulloch and Tim Bornstein, *The National Labor Relations Board* (New York: Praeger Publishers, 1974), p. 180.
34. *H.K. Porter Co.* v. *NLRB,* 73 LRRM 2561 (1970).
35. *Auto Workers* v. *NLRB,* 76 LRRM 2573 (1971); *Ex-Cell-O Corp.* v. *NLRB,* 77 LRRM 2547 (1971).
36. Bernard Samoff, "The Case of the Burgeoning Load of the NLRB," *Labor Law Journal* 22 (October 1971), pp. 264–265.
37. Douglas S. McDowell and Kenneth Huhn, *NLRB Remedies for Unfair Labor Practices* (Philadelphia: Industrial Research Unit, University of Pennsylvania, 1976), pp. 245–246.
38. William N. Cooke and Frederick H. Gautschi III, "Political Bias in NLRB Unfair Labor Practice Decisions," *Industrial and Labor Relations Review* 35 (July 1982), p. 549.
39. William N. Cooke, Aneil K. Mishra, Gretchen M. Spreitzer, and Mary Tschirhart, "The Determinants of NLRB Decision-Making Revisited," *Industrial and Labor Relations Review* 48 (January 1995), pp. 254–256.
40. "Selected Statements on NLRB Before House Oversight Hearing," *Daily Labor Report,* July 13, 1995, pp. E-1–E-3.
41. Charles M. Rehmus, "Evolution of Legislation Affecting Collective Bargaining in the Railroad and Airline Industries," in Charles M. Rehmus, ed., *The Railway Labor Act at Fifty* (Washington, D.C.: U.S. Government Printing Office, 1977), p. 4.
42. *Fact Finding Report, Commission on the Future of Worker-Management Relations* (Washington, D.C., U.S. Departments of Labor and Commerce, May 1994), p. 99.
43. Rehmus, "Collective Bargaining," pp. 14–15. The remaining amendments were comparatively minor.
44. *Fact Finding Report, Commission on the Future of Worker-Management Relations* (Washington, D.C.: U.S. Departments of Labor and Commerce, May 1994), pp. 99–100.

45. Douglas M. McCabe, "The Railroad Industry's Labor Relations Environment: Implications for Railroad Managers," *ICC Practitioners' Journal* 49 (September-October 1982), pp. 592–602.
46. Charles M. Rehmus, "The First Fifty Years—And Then," in Rehmus, ed., *Railway Labor Act at Fifty,* p. 246.
47. Beatrice M. Burgoon, "Mediation under the Railway Labor Act," in Rehmus, ed., *Railway Labor Act at Fifty,* p. 23.
48. Charles M. Rehmus, *The National Mediation Board at Fifty* (Ithaca, N.Y.: Cornell University, 1984), pp. 1–20.
49. "Amtrak, Conrail Pacts," *Monthly Labor Review* 115 (October 1992), p. 38.
50. "Deregulation in Three Transport Industries Has Produced Widely Diverse Labor Market Results," *Daily Labor Report,* May 13, 1986, p. A-13.
51. Clifford B. Donn and Pamela C. Marett, "Deregulation and the Future of Transportation Trade Unionism in the United States," *Labor Law Journal* 41 (August 1990), p. 493.
52. Mark Kahn, "Introduction," *Cleared for Takeoff: Airline Labor Relations Since Deregulation,* ed. Jean T. McKelvey (Ithaca, N.Y.: ILR Press, 1988), p. 3.
53. Alfred Kahn, "In Defense of Deregulation," *Cleared for Takeoff: Airline Labor Relations Since Deregulation,* ed. Jean T. McKelvey (Ithaca, N.Y.: ILR Press, 1988), pp. 344–345. For a legal analysis, see Beth Adler, "Comment: Deregulation in the Airline Industry: Toward a New Judicial Interpretation of the Railway Labor Act," *Northwestern University Law Journal* 80 (Winter 1986), pp. 1003–1006.
54. *57th and 58th Annual Report of the National Mediation Board* (Washington, D.C.: National Mediation Board, 1994), pp. 2–5.
55. Cullen, "Emergency Boards," pp. 176–183. Also see "The Railroads Lose Their Bargaining Unity," *Business Week,* April 10, 1978, pp. 31–32.
56. Mark L. Kahn, "Labor-Management Relations in the Airline Industry," in Rehmus, ed., *Railway Labor Act at Fifty,* p. 128.

Unions and Management: Key Participants in the Labor Relations Process

4

As noted in Chapter 1, two key participants in the labor relations process are the union, which as the exclusive bargaining agent represents employees in the bargaining units, and management, which represents the owners or stockholders of the company. This chapter first provides a general explanation of the goals, strategies, and organizational structure of the company and the union for labor relations purposes. Because companies and unions are organized differently to meet different purposes, basic goals, strategies and organizational structures will be presented that may be adjusted to meet respective differences. The second part of the chapter focuses on union governance and structure by describing the characteristics of unions, government at the various levels, organizational structure, and problems with corruption and misuse of power within a few unions.

Goals and Strategies: Management and Unions

Unions and management of companies have goals that are similar and goals that may at times conflict. Their goals provide direction and serve as the basis for their organization's strategies, plans, and organizational structure. Exhibit 4.1 displays some major goals for both companies and unions, which in several cases are similar and consistent and in others have potential for conflict. The areas of potential conflict create possibilities for an adversarial relationship, and the areas of agreement create possibilities for cooperation and labor peace. As will be noted, most of the time unions and management are able to settle their differences without resorting to a work stoppage (less than 1 percent of total man-days are lost to work stoppages). The collective bargaining process itself is a mechanism designed by the parties and confirmed by the U.S. Congress as the preferred method for resolving differences between unions and management.

Both the company and the union want the company to survive and remain competitive. Union agreement with this goal is logical because the employees would

Exhibit 4.1 Goals of the Company and the Union

THE COMPANY WANTS:	THE UNION WANTS:
To survive and remain competitive	The company to survive and remain competitive as well as for the union to survive and remain secure
To grow and prosper	The company to grow and prosper as well as the union
To achieve a favorable return on its investment	The company to achieve a favorable return on its investment and return "fair" wages to employees
To effectively use human resources	The company to effectively use human resources within the rules and policies of the agreement and to achieve job security and employment opportunities for members
To attract, retain, and motivate employees	The company to attract, retain, and motivate employees within the rules and policies of the agreement
To protect management's rights to make decisions and retain flexibility	To protect union and employee rights that were negotiated and included in the labor agreement
To obtain a commitment from the union that there will be no strike for the duration of the agreement	To obtain a commitment from the company that there will be no lockout for the duration of the agreement

lose their jobs and the union would not survive without the company. Likewise, the union wants to survive as the representative of the employees of the company and will take steps to retain this designation. When a company wishes to remain nonunion or to have the union decertified, an inevitable conflict occurs.

The company wants to grow and prosper—a sign of success of its management. The union agrees with this goal and supports it because it creates more opportunities and benefits for employees, adds union members, allows more funds for union activities, and strengthens the union as an institution. Likewise, both company and union want the company to achieve a favorable return on their investment. While they may disagree on what is meant by "favorable," both parties understand the mechanics of the financial side of the business. However, the union also wants to achieve a favorable or "fair" return for the employees' efforts, input, and contribution. Here, there may be a disagreement over what is a favorable return to the investors and a "fair" return to the employees.

Two related goals of the company are to achieve the effective utilization of its human resources and to attract, retain, and motivate employees. The union accepts these goals for the company as long as the company abides by the provisions that were negotiated and included in the collective bargaining agreement. For example, the company may wish to have the most productive employee work on an overtime assignment to be able to ship a rush order; however, the agreement may require that overtime assignments be made on a rotating basis. The presence of the union does not prevent making overtime assignments to the most productive employee; however, the overtime provision is a negotiable subject, and the parties must live by the provisions that they agree on.

The company wants to protect its rights to make decisions and retain the flexibility to operate the business. The union accepts the philosophy that some decisions are best made by management, including the type of products, the price of the products, financial policies, customer relations, advertising and promotion decisions, product design, and plant layout. At the same time, the union represents the interests of employees and attempts to provide protection and guarantee job opportunities for them by negotiating provisions in the labor agreement such as contracting out work, use of seniority, and promotions and transfers to provide for these rights.[1]

The company wants a union commitment to have no work stoppage for a specified period of time; this guarantees a stable work force and allows the company to make production promises to customers. This commitment comes in the form of a "no-strike" clause in the labor agreement. The union may want a commitment from the company that employees have the right to have their grievances heard by management and may appeal them to a third-party neutral (arbitrator) when necessary to resolve differences.

Once the union and the company decide on their respective goals, they determine the appropriate strategies to reach these goals. Companies have been involved in strategic planning much longer than unions, and their strategic plans are usually more detailed and sophisticated. Only in recent times have unions started to think and operate in terms of strategic planning.

Company Strategic Planning

A company's strategy in labor relations is determined by its managerial philosophy, the ethics of its management, its economic condition, the composition of the work force, competition in the industry, the time in the life of the company, and the capabilities of management. Management has choices about its strategy. It may believe that the company is better off remaining nonunion and devote much time and effort to assuring positive human resources management. Some employers resist unions bitterly to ward off the large wage gap between union and nonunion employees (weekly earnings averaged $602 for union members versus $447 for nonunion workers in 1995, according to the Bureau of Labor Statistics). Management members who are in a highly competitive industry may be willing to do almost anything to keep unions out. Management at other companies may choose to change from a hard-bargaining approach to one of labor-management cooperation after it finally accepts the philosophy that both parties would gain more by cooperating than by conflicting. Exhibit 4.2 shows the range of company strategies in labor relations, from union suppression to labor-management cooperation.

Nonunion Companies' Strategies Some authorities believe that labor relations underwent profound changes in the 1980s, brought on by forces external to

Exhibit 4.2 Company Strategies in Labor Relations

UNION SUPPRESSION	UNION AVOIDANCE	UNION SUBSTITUTION	CODIFIED, BUSINESSLIKE	ACCOMMODATION OR LABOR-MANAGEMENT COOPERATION
Union busting Illegal acts Refusal to bargain Decertification Filing for bankruptcy Encouraging strikes	Positive human resources management Double-breasting	Company paternalism Company-sponsored employee organizations Forms of employee participation and employee involvement	Neutral in union campaign Straightforward approach	Gain-sharing Union involvement Employee empowerment ESOPs

union-management relationships. These forces include competition from abroad, deregulation, and competition from nonunion companies. More and more companies are finding that their labor relations strategies are driven by economic choices and their need to adapt to new, more competitive business conditions. Because union suppression, union avoidance, and union substitution strategies have existed in different forms since the Industrial Revolution, a company may choose to attempt to maintain its nonunion status by preventing or supplanting unions. Another company may choose one of the nonunion strategies as a legitimate response that has been forced on it to cut costs, innovate, enter new markets, and devise flexible labor force strategies. This latter approach focuses on costs and productivity of human resources and the management of human resources.[2]

A company may use a more aggressive approach, called the union suppression strategy, to maintain its nonunion status or to destroy the union. The 1980s and 1990s have seen several highly visible examples of the union suppression strategy. One example is Greyhound, which was reorganized in 1987 through a leveraged buy-out, thereby incurring high debt. Although the company was profitable in 1989, the new owners went into contract negotiations determined to reduce their labor costs. No agreement was reached, and the union went on strike. The company announced that it was prepared to replace striking employees and had accumulated over $54 million in its strike preparation fund to defeat the union. By March 1990, the company had to borrow $25 million and suffered a first-quarter loss of $56 million. A few months later, Greyhound filed for reorganization in bankruptcy court. In 1993, with numerous unfair labor practice charges against the company and with back pay claims in excess of $125 million, Greyhound began operating as a nonunion interstate bus line.[3] Then, in April 1993, the parties reached an agreement after a three-year strike.

Other extreme tactics used by some companies to avoid unionization include the following:

- Developing a spy network (tattletales) to identify union supporters.
- Refusing to hire former employees of unionized companies (but giving the applicant a reason other than prior union affiliation for employment denial).
- Establishing a case for discharge (including documentation) of known union advocates.
- Seeking to determine prospective employees' attitudes toward unions from interviews, references, and so on, then refusing to hire them (again giving another reason) if they are pro-union.
- Giving psychological tests (job-interest questionnaires) to determine the likelihood that an applicant will be interested in a union.
- Locating new plants in areas where union membership is low and expanding the company's nonunion plants.
- Using a standard application of a State Employment Service that asks applicants whether they have been a member of a union and using the application as part of the pre-employment inquiry.[4]

Some employers facing union-organizing campaigns have committed unfair labor practices deliberately, with the expectation of economic returns to them.[5] One study of employers led to this disappointing conclusion:

> [I]n the past, the compliance system [of the National Labor Relations Act] has been inadequate to the extent that some employers have found it profitable to commit unfair labor practices in order to forestall unionization. Those employers obeying the law because "it's the law" have faced a greater probability of incurring costs of unionization and may have been at a competitive disadvantage to employers who violated the law. Such inequities do not encourage compliance with the law and provide evidence of the need for labor law reform.[6]

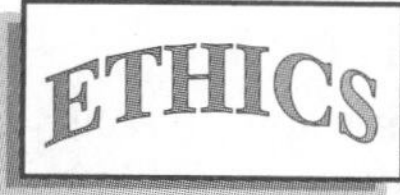

When illegal practices yield economic returns to the violators, ethical questions are raised as to the fairness of the law and its application. Some companies that select the *union avoidance* strategy take a strong stance against union representation, even in facilities where unions already exist. They open nonunion facilities and attempt to keep them nonunion. They shift their capital investments away from the unionized facilities and make plant improvements in the nonunion plants. Where the union represents the employees, they attempt to reduce the labor costs by lowering wages and benefits, modifying traditional work practices, and encouraging decertification to the point of committing illegal actions. In these situations, the labor relations environment is highly adversarial, and union-management collaboration is not considered an option.[7]

One company, Ingersoll-Rand Company, was reported as initiating an anti-union corporate strategy in the 1970s. Its strategy included the following: (a) concentrate building or buying new U.S. plants in open shop states, and acquire other firms whose plants are partly or wholly nonunion, (b) relocate production from union plants to nonunion plants, and (3) use labor and community relations techniques that bypass local union officers, encourage union decertification, and oppose union organizing efforts. By 1990, union representation had declined from 100 percent to 25 percent of Ingersoll-Rand's eligible work force. Top company officials were reported as saying that the company wanted to remain "union-free," to listen to employees as individuals, not through a third-party union, and to stop unions from forcing the company to take actions with which it disagreed.[8]

Some companies adopting the union avoidance strategy practice *positive human resources management* or operate *double-breasted.* Company officials who adopt positive human resources management recognize the importance and necessity of maximizing "employee voice." Moreover, they implement the claim that people are the most important asset of the organization. Such organizations involve their employees in the decision-making processes of their organizations. These efforts are included under the general umbrella of "participative management," "total quality management," and "total quality control" programs.[9] In unionized organizations, the union is sometimes involved; those efforts are covered in Chapter 7.

Companies such as IBM, Texas Instruments, Eastman Kodak, and Delta Airlines have essentially adopted this strategy. Positive human resources management programs include the following elements:

- The absence of symbols of rank and status such as parking spaces, company cars, or country club memberships for managers.
- Carefully considered surroundings—locating where high-quality schools and universities are near and keeping individual facilities small.
- Overall corporate strength—high profits, fast growth, high technology, or dominant market position.
- Programs to promote employment security, such as work sharing or overall reduction in pay to avoid layoffs in hard times.
- Promotion from within—job posting, career development, and training and education programs.
- Influential human resources management programs, for example, having the human resources manager report directly to top management.
- Competitive pay and benefits, especially having compensation that is equitable externally and internally and comparable to the pay at unionized companies.
- Management that listens—using systematic approaches such as attitude surveys, open-door policies, and appeal procedures.
- Careful grooming of managers—focusing on long-term results, using assessment centers, and appraising in terms of competence and employee relationships.[10]

Double-breasting exists when one company has two or more subsidiaries, one unionized and the others nonunion or open shop. These arrangements take several forms: (1) a holding company has financial control of one or more operating subsidiaries, (2) a unionized company buys a nonunion subsidiary and continues to operate it nonunion, and (3) a nonunion company buys a unionized subsidiary and continues to operate it unionized. At present, the law requires the open shop and unionized units of a holding company to be separately managed and operated as distinct entities. The NLRB determines whether two seemingly separate companies should be treated as one by considering the following guidelines: interrelation of operations, centralization of control of labor relations, common management, and common ownership or financial control.[11] The board stated:

> No one of these factors has been held to be controlling, but the Board opinions have stressed the first three factors, which go to show "operational integration," particularly centralized control of labor relations. The Board has declined in several cases to find integration merely upon the basis of common ownership or financial control.[12]

A third company strategy to maintain nonunion status is the *union substitution* strategy. This strategy originated in the company paternalism and company unions common in the 1920s but still exists today in the form of employee committees and other forms of employee participation. Although the NLRA has outlawed company unions and unlawful assistance to unions affiliated with national organizations, some companies have organized and supported employee committees for the purpose of discussing and resolving grievances.[13] Even though these committees differ from traditional unions because they do not negotiate labor agreements, they could subsequently come under the provisions of the National Labor Relations Act if their discussions over wages and employment conditions are interpreted as negotiations by the NLRB. Further, the employer could be directed to disband the committee or recognize and bargain with committee members as a labor union.[14]

Many nonunion companies have initiated employee-involvement programs to restore the sense of working in a small business, to gain employee commitment to the enterprise, to dissuade union organizing, and to provide feedback to enhance motivation and productivity. Over 85 percent of companies in a Conference Board survey have a system for giving nonunion employees information about the competitive conditions or economic circumstances of their company. The majority have employee participation programs such as quality circles and small-group discussions of production and quality of work and have provided formal complaint and grievance systems.[15]

During recent years nonunion companies have become more concerned about employee terminations, which are estimated to be about three million each year in the United States. At least half these terminations occur without the employee being protected by either law or contract. In other words, the employee is terminated under the *employment-at-will doctrine* that states that either the employer or the employee is free to terminate the employment relationship "at will" (at any time, for any reason or no reason). Laws exist that prohibit discrimination on the basis of race, sex, color, religion, age, national origin, and union activities, and a collective bargaining agreement usually protects employees against termination without "just cause" (see Chapter 10).

Some nonunion companies provide for arbitration as a fair method of resolving employee grievances, and some companies establish grievance procedures with arbitration as the last step. A pronounced increase in the number of employment arbitration cases in the nonunion sector is predicted due to legislative encouragement of mediation and arbitration in the Americans with Disabilities Act and the U.S. Supreme Court's suggestion that pre-dispute agreements to arbitrate will be upheld by the courts.[16] (More discussion on this topic is provided in Chapter 9.)

The most common system for resolving employee grievances is the "open door" policy, wherein employees may present their grievances to management representatives. The success of this system depends on how conscientious managers at all levels are in fulfilling this policy and whether employees fear that presenting their grievances to managers above their immediate supervisor will have undesirable consequences.

Other forms of nonunion grievance procedures include grievance appeal boards, appeal steps up to top management, and peer review committees.[17] The grievance appeal board allows employees to present their grievances to a board for a final decision. In this system, three management members and two employees might hear the grievance and decide the outcome. Although the system is sometimes called a "jury of one's peers," management representation is usually greater than that of employees and can outvote employee board members if necessary.[18]

Unionized Companies' Strategies The labor relations function in unionized companies differs from that in nonunion companies in several ways. First, in the unionized setting, two parties, the union and management, are involved. Instead of decisions being made by management alone, many decisions, such as wages, hours, promotion, layoffs, and other terms and conditions of employment, are made bilaterally through negotiations. Second, the presence of the union formalizes the employee-representation activities because employees may file a grievance if they believe that the company has violated terms of the negotiated agreement. Third, the negotiated rules and policies that govern the employment relationship for those employees covered under the collective bargaining agreement essentially become company policy because both parties have to abide by the terms that they have negotiated.[19]

One strategy adopted by unionized companies is the *businesslike, codified* strategy. These companies accept unions as the legitimate representative of the employees and conclude that if the employees want a union, they will deal with it. They do not attempt to have the union decertified, do not commit flagrant unfair labor practices, and do not try to substitute participative groups for unions. Company managers respect and trust their union counterparts and expect the same in return. For the relationship to last, both parties must realize that respect and trust are fundamental to both their futures. The approach of these companies is to deal directly and bargain with the union over wages, hours, and terms and conditions of employment at the appropriate times. When the labor agreement negotiations are complete, managers of these companies administer the agreement as they interpret it. In other words, they "go by the book." Although General Electric was known in the 1950s for its "take-it-or-leave-it" approach to labor negotiations, its strategy today can be categorized as a businesslike approach. The remaining chapters explain this approach to labor relations. Also, as noted previously, strategies of companies and unions change during their lifetimes and with economic conditions, changes in leadership, and personalities of participants.

The fifth strategy shown in Exhibit 4.2 is one of *accommodation and labor-management cooperation.* This strategy entails the union cooperating with management, rather than the parties having an adversarial relationship. Management and unions actively work together to create an organizational climate and a way of operating that will allow employees to participate directly in decisions in their work areas as members of task teams and as members of problem-solving groups. Unions represent their members in decision making as well as in collective bargaining.[20]

Unions can contribute to companies' strategic planning and implementation activities. For example, a union can provide input from a clearly defined group of employees, as well as transfer information about corporate plans and direction to those represented employees. The union leaders can help the rank and file employees better understand the business plan and lend credibility to the plan. While these contributions are clearly positive, union involvement in strategic planning takes more time because the union leadership must meet with the membership to explain planned actions. Also, in order to retain a competitive edge, upper management often does not want to reveal new directions and planned actions. As a result, unions typically have a greater opportunity to have a role in strategy implementation than in strategy formulation. For example, if a company is facing increasing losses due to foreign competition, the company may enlist the assistance of the union in finding ways to reduce costs. Alternatives include cooperative approaches to job design or developing a new reward system, such as gain-sharing, to encourage labor-management cooperation. Another possibility is the introduction of new technology to improve productivity, which may include restructuring existing jobs.[21] (This topic is discussed further in Chapter 12.)

> For organizations and unions to achieve a more collaborative relationship, managers, unions, and employees must overcome their resistance to change. Managers must develop a more open, less authoritarian managerial style; unions must abolish their traditional "us versus them" approach and adopt the team concept; and employees must accept a greater worker commitment and more involvement in determining how to get the job done and how to get it done right.[22]

Employee empowerment is reflected in employee involvement and participation programs, which include quality circles, quality-of-work-life efforts, labor-management participation teams, and autonomous work units. These efforts address such issues as product quality, work-unit performance, new technology, safety and health, and supervision. Here, union leaders and members accept responsibility for success of the organization. Unions demonstrate their capacity to confer value to their members and create wealth for all of the organization's stakeholders.[23]

This relationship ensures that unions and management focus on common goals, which include the health of the business in a changing economic environment, and new issues, such as adopting new technology to assure competitiveness and business survival. Management accepts unions as stakeholders in an ongoing complex, multi-stakeholder organization designed to ensure survival and provide an equitable return for all involved in the process. Several companies and unions have already proceeded in this direction. General Motors and the United Auto Workers have included cooperation, gain-sharing, and teamwork in the new GM Saturn plant. The Amalgamated Clothing and Textile Workers (now UNITE) and Xerox have organized Horizon Study Teams to investigate and make recommendations on a wide range of strategic business decisions. (Other examples are discussed in Chapter 7.)

To achieve this new union role, management and union leaders must develop different skills. Union leaders need business decision-making skills; they must understand the business and the problem-solving process. At the same time, they must maintain contact with the membership to better represent members' interests. Management must take steps to reorient its views from seeing unions and labor agreements as constraints to recognizing a more cooperative union-management relationship. Management must provide the union and its leadership with a secure position as the legitimate, permanent representative of the bargaining unit employees. This means abandoning efforts to decertify the union or to reduce the union's importance at the workplace. It means developing a mutual trust between parties at every level of the organization.[24]

Companies may choose a mixed strategy, which can encompass union avoidance, union substitution, or labor-management cooperation, at various sites in a multi-plant operation. For example, a company may operate double-breasted and strongly oppose the union at one of its nonunion plants while at the same time engaging in labor-management cooperation at another plant. Such strategic choices are made at the highest levels of the organization, and the advantages and disadvantages of each strategy are seriously debated and deliberated before any strategy is adopted by the company.

Upper management considers the market pressures, operational and financial factors, and collective bargaining relationships in its deliberations. If market pressures are intense due to import penetration, management may be inclined to choose union avoidance in the nonunion sector. However, if a high proportion of the plants are unionized, management may choose the labor-management cooperation strategy. Researchers continue to examine which factors lead to certain strategies.[25]

Union Strategic Planning

Labor unions, like other organizations, define their operational goals, determine their organizational strategies and plans, develop policies and procedures, and manage their resources to reach their goals and maximize their performance. Unions also are involved in long-range planning, establishing procedures for budgeting, attracting able staff members, communicating with members to provide information and to obtain reliable feedback, and establishing controls for financial accountability.[26]

Labor unions in the United States have been involved in strategic planning for only a short time. For years, unions as a rule reacted to managerial decisions with little concern for long-range implications. Today, more and more unions are finding it essential to become involved in strategic planning. Several unions, such as the Communications Workers, the Auto Workers, and the Steelworkers, have recognized the need for long-range strategic planning and created strategic planning committees. To survive, all unions must develop such plans. A typical union's strategic plan includes: (1) a mission statement, (2) analysis of the external environment, (3) internal analysis of the union's strengths and weaknesses, (4) long-term and short-term objectives, and (5) strategy development. A survey of AFL-CIO unions found:

1. Typical mission statements are: to organize workers for the purpose of collective bargaining; to foster legislation of interest to the working class; and to disseminate economic, social, and political information affecting workers' lives and welfare.
2. The analysis of the external environment includes an examination of the changing demographics of the work force (toward more worker diversity), appraisal of current and future political and legislative concerns, consideration of labor's image, and analysis of employer practices and industry trends.
3. The internal analysis includes an examination of the union's internal functioning, such as union governance, openness for discussion of diverse opinions, and appraisal of the professional staff whose jobs are to provide service to the members.
4. Organizational objectives are set for short-term and long-term activities. Short-term objectives may include meeting membership needs through collective bargaining, reducing substance abuse, improving pensions, and enhancing job security. The most common long-term objective is simply the survival of the labor organization.
5. Further work is needed to define strategies for addressing labor unions' long-term concerns for continual survival and growth as institutions.[27]

Some unions, like the United Auto Workers, have established internal commissions to participate in strategy planning. The report of the Commission on the Future of the UAW, entitled "A Strong Union in a Changing World," addressed the union's major economic concern about the erosion of the nation's industrial base and related problems of corporate flight and disinvestment. It also urged more effective use of the media in presenting the union's public positions on tax policy and fairness; dislocated employees; the changing work force; issues of sexism and racism; and rapid change in technology and methods of work. The AFL-CIO Executive Council established the Committee on the Evolution of Work to review and evaluate changes that are occurring within unions and in the labor force, occupations, industries, and technology. This committee produced a report entitled *The Changing Situation of Workers and Their Unions,* which provides strategic plans in several areas of union activities. Exhibit 4.3 outlines these plans.

Exhibit 4.3 Recommendations of the AFL-CIO Committee on the Evolution of Work

1. New methods of advancing the interests of workers, which include associate union membership, expanded use of the electronic media, and corporate campaigns to secure neutrality of employers in organizing efforts.
2. Increasing members' participation in their unions, which includes increased interaction between local union members and national union leaders, orientation of new members, and greater resources devoted to training officers, stewards, and members.
3. Improving the labor movement's communications, training for union spokespersons in media techniques, efforts to better inform reporters about unions and trade unionism, and advertising to improve the public's understanding of labor.
4. Improving organizing activity by carefully choosing and training organizers, better use of modern technology, greater involvement of union members in organizing campaigns, experimenting with new organizing techniques, and attracting workers who are covered under contracts but who have not joined unions (estimated to be 2 million employees).
5. Structural changes to enhance the labor movement's overall effectiveness by adopting guidelines and providing assistance for union mergers, resolving organizing disputes among unions, modern budgeting, program analysis, and planning techniques to improve the administration of unions.

SOURCE: *The Changing Situation of Workers and Their Unions* (Washington, D.C.: AFL-CIO, 1985).

Between 1987 and 1993, several international unions, such as the Air Line Pilots Association, Steelworkers, Service Employees International Union, American Federation of Teachers, and the Bakery, Confectionery, and Tobacco Workers have undertaken strategic planning efforts. These international unions have added new terms to their operational language, such as strategy development, organizational assessment and planning, and implementation. They have used surveys, interviews, and focus groups for building participation and consensus. The results have been mission statements, goals and priorities, assignment of responsibilities, funding activities and budget allocations, dues split between the local and international unions, and measures for evaluating success.[28]

While strategic planning is still a rare event in local unions, it will become more common as international unions provide leadership and assistance to these efforts. Efforts to date include the rebuilding of the steward system, new budget and management information systems, new internal and external organizing programs, and restructuring of the board and staff organization.[29]

Unions have made labor concessions as a quid pro quo for debt restructuring. They have increased the frequency of union representation on corporate boards of directors, usually in exchange for wage concessions (in the automobile, airline, trucking, and food processing industries). Unions have obtained direct ownership in corporations through employee stock ownership plans (ESOPs, covered in more detail in Chapter 13) and have attempted direct buyouts of several companies. These forms of union involvement have come about not by virtue of the union's statutory rights, but by virtue of the union's accumulation of market and financial power.[30]

Company Organization for Labor Relations Activities

There are many organizational structures for labor relations activities in U.S. companies. The following discussion introduces some of the basic organizational considerations, although different company characteristics will alter these designs.[31]

In larger corporations, the labor relations function is usually highly centralized, with policy, strategic planning, and bargaining decisions made at the corporate level. In fact, the final economic decisions are usually made by the chief operating executive with the advice of corporate-level labor relations managers. In smaller companies with only one or a few facilities, these decisions are made at the plant level and shared by plant management with the plant labor relations manager, who offers advice.

In larger companies, at the operations or plant level, the plant manager and plant labor relations manager play the key roles in certain labor relations activities such as contract administration, grievance handling, and monitoring labor relations activities. In smaller companies, activities at the plant level also include bargaining, strategic planning, and policy formulation.[32]

The duties and responsibilities of all labor relations managers and specialists are determined in large part by the organizational structure and its degree of centralization or decentralization of authority. The duties typically include corporatewide responsibility for policies, procedures, and programs ranging from union organizing drives at nonunion facilities to negotiations with the union at others.

Exhibit 4.4 shows the organizational chart for the labor relations function in a large, complex company. As shown in the organizational chart, the vice-president of personnel and industrial relations reports directly to the president and has the director of labor relations reporting to him or her. Each of the company's six product lines has its own labor relations organization.

A large, diversified company having several divisions or product lines will typically have a vice-president of industrial relations, which includes human resources and labor relations activities, who reports directly to the president and has the director of labor relations reporting to him or her.

Industrial relations managers at the plant level also typically have responsibilities for both human resources and labor relations activities. They help implement related corporate and divisional policies, participate in contract negotiations, and resolve employee grievances over daily labor agreement administration. They

Exhibit 4.4 Labor Relations Organization: Dotted-Line Relationships

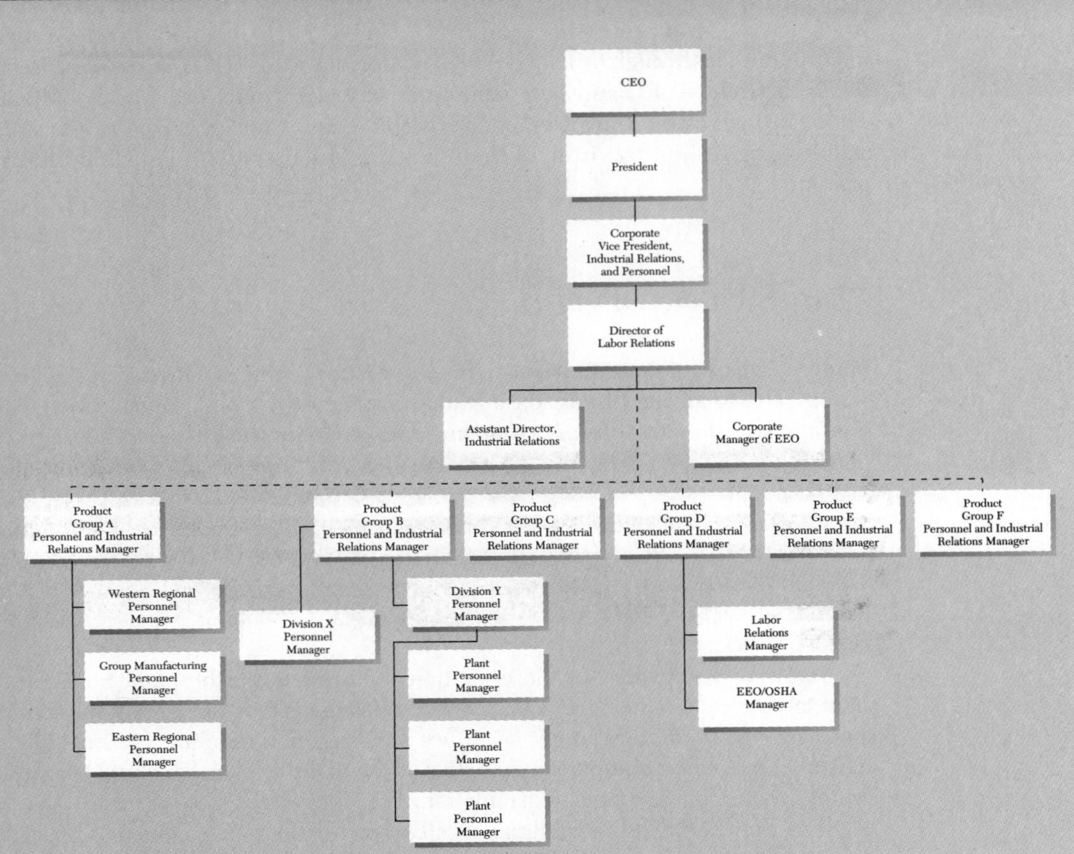

Note: Each respective Group Personnel and Industrial Relations Manager has a direct reporting relationship to his or her respective group management while maintaining a "dotted-line" relationship to the corporate staff, which has the responsibility for formulation of corporatewide labor relations policies and procedures.

As each group is dependent upon the corporate function as the formulator of this policy, the lines of communication and working relationships are strong, and the level of communication very high.

Their function is to administer corporate policies and procedures as formulated by the Vice President of Personnel and Industrial Relations and his or her staff.

SOURCE: Audrey Freedman, *Managing Labor Relations* (New York: The Conference Board, 1979), p. 28.

Exhibit 4.5 Management Organization at the Plant Level (Approximately 1,100 Hourly Employees)

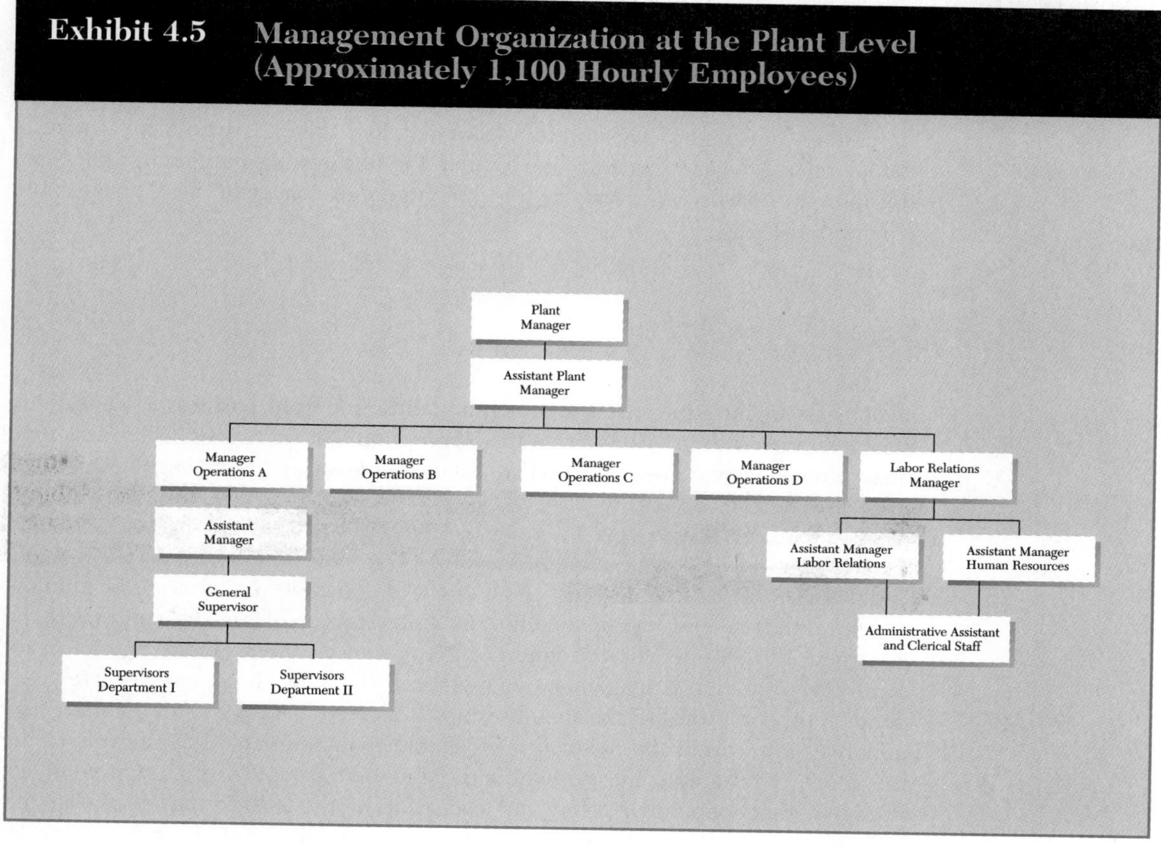

typically are accountable both to the plant manager for daily labor relations activities and to divisional or corporate industrial relations officials for approval of negotiated labor agreements.

Exhibit 4.5 suggests relationships between labor relations managers and other managers at the plant level (operations B, C, D, and E are not delineated in detail for the sake of brevity). The facility's operations can be grouped in one or more of the following ways: by location (furnace room one versus furnace room two at a steel mill, for example); by product (manufactured valves versus gaskets, for example); by function (such as maintenance); or by technology (electroplated and chemical plated processes, for example).

The labor relations manager is on the same level as managers of the operations, but neither individual has authority over the other. Instead, plant labor relations managers have *line-staff* relationships with other managers. Line-staff relationships occur when two or more organizational members from different lines of authority work together on a particular policy (a no-smoking policy, for example) or activity (such as grievances). Neither has authority over the other; therefore, resolution or output of this relationship is often determined by past perceived benefits each has derived from the other.

Relationships between labor relations managers and other management officials at the plant level can be tension laden. Consider, for example, the attitude a shift supervisor might have toward a labor relations manager who has awarded to the union a grievance against him or her for performing bargaining unit work (Chapter 8) or who has overturned a discharge decision made by the supervisor (Chapter 10).

Union Governance and Structure

Unions as organizations are fundamentally different from business organizations. Business organizations are built on the assumption that power, authority, and legitimacy flow downward from the owner or stockholders through management. Union organizations, on the other hand, have mechanisms such as a written constitution and bylaws that ensure an opportunity for members to participate in the governance of the organization—hold office, attend meetings, vote in elections, or express dissatisfaction with the leadership. Thus, in the democratic organization of a union, power, authority, and legitimacy ultimately flow upward from the consent of the governed. If the leadership of a union wishes to move in a new direction, such as toward greater union-management cooperation, the new direction ultimately depends on the approval of the membership. If elected leaders do not consider new initiatives in terms of the political realities, they will be rejected by the vote of the members. For example, in cases where the members do not trust management's actions in a joint cooperative effort, the leadership must put forth the appropriate effort to build a trusting relationship before developing the joint effort.[33]

Over 100 different international and national unions and over 60,000 local unions exist in the United States; their governance is discussed in this chapter following a brief description of their organizational structure. As with companies, unions' organizational structures reflect their activities. Exhibit 4.6 shows the organizational structure of an international union, which includes the various officers, operational departments and staff, regions, and local unions. In this case, the basic functions include financial activities handled by the secretary-treasurer, research, administration, education, organizing, political action, and international affairs. These activities are usually carried out at the union's national headquarters, with some headquarters staff members possibly working in the field. The regional offices are headed by a vice-president, who has an advisory relationship with the local unions in the region. Regional offices are established to better serve the needs of the local unions and to represent the national office in the region.

At the local union level, the organizational structure is fairly simple. Exhibit 4.7 shows the officers and the shop stewards. In small unions, these are all part-time positions; only in the larger unions does the financial support allow full-time union leaders. Most local unions have at least one vice-president, a secretary, and a treasurer. The addition of any other officer, such as the sergeant-at-arms in Exhibit 4.7, depends on the needs of the union. Shop stewards are usually elected to represent the membership in their respective departments. The following section explains how unions are governed at the different levels and presents some of the major problems in the governing process.

To understand union governance, one can compare the union with a unit of state or federal government. The executive, legislative, and judicial activities occur at various levels. The local union meetings and national conventions are the legislative bodies; the officers and executive boards comprise the executive bodies; and the various appeal procedures serve the judicial function. A union can also be compared to a private organization because it is a specialized institution having a primary purpose of improving the economic conditions of its members.

Unions claim the democratic ideal, but realistically they must rely on a representative form of government. On the whole they seem to be as democratic as local, state, and federal governments. In fact, the union membership has more of a say in the way the union operates than most citizens have in their governments or most stockholders in their corporations.[34]

Exhibit 4.6 Organizational Chart of an International Union

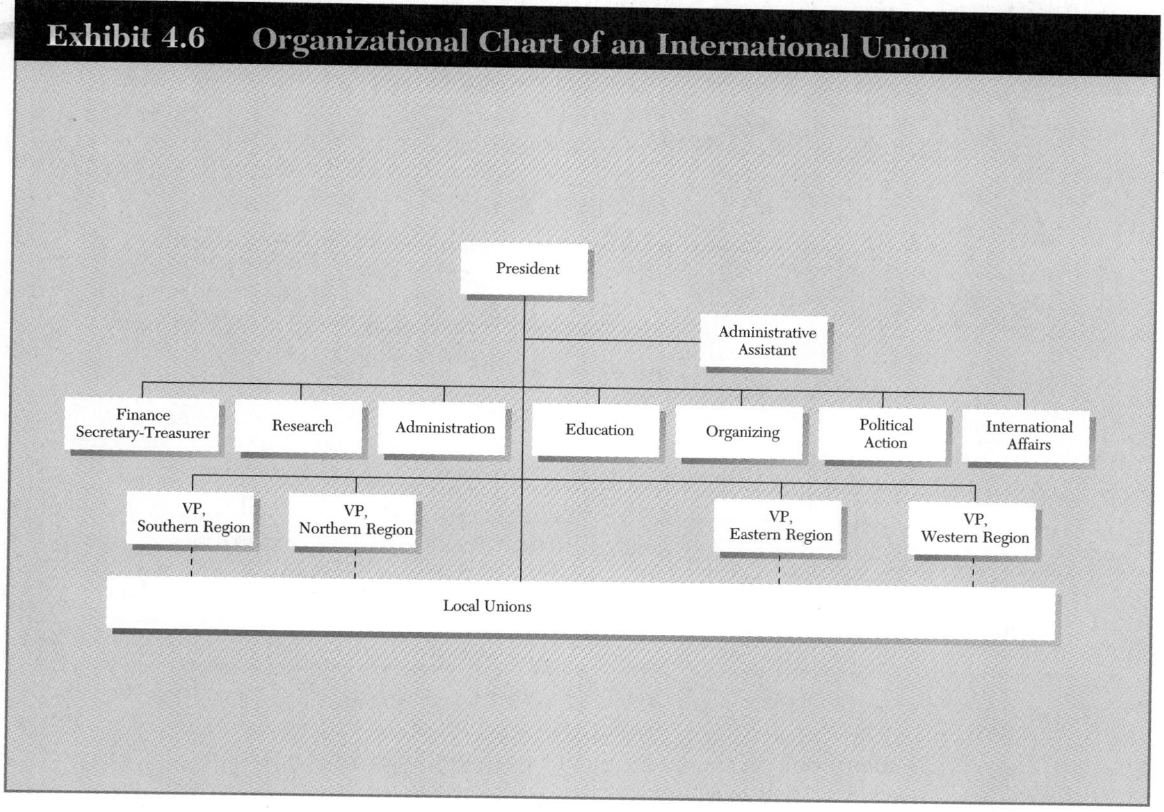

To appreciate unions as organizations, one must recognize their wide diversity, the organizational relationships of the various levels, the functions of the officers, and the varying degrees of control. The next section explores the characteristics of craft and industrial unions, the functions of local union officers, and the government and operations of local unions. The national or international union, which is composed of the local unions within a craft or industry, is explained in a similar framework. Not to be overlooked are the various intermediate levels of union organizations that provide specific functions for their affiliated unions. A fourth level for many union organizations is the federation, or the AFL-CIO, whose organizational structure, functions, and officer responsibilities are also discussed.

The Local Union

Although there are generally four levels of unions—local, national (or international), intermediate, and the federation of unions—the local union is the main

Exhibit 4.7 Organizational Chart for a Local Union

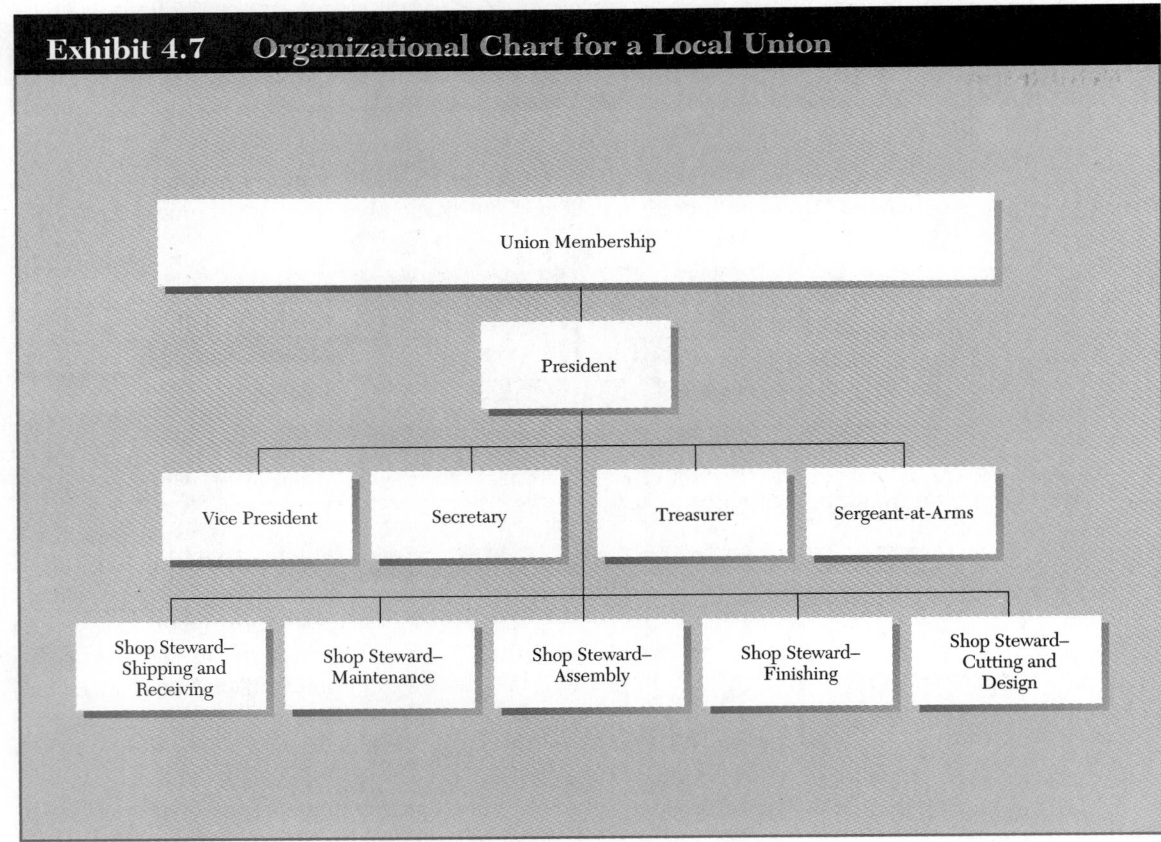

point of contact for the individual employee. The typical union member often identifies more closely with the local union than with the other union levels. He or she attends and sees local officers at the local meetings and workplace. When the union member has a grievance, the local union officers are the first to assist. When a strike occurs, the local union officers are the ones who make continuous contact with the strikers on the picket line. Although the national union may negotiate the master labor agreement under which the local union member works, and the AFL-CIO may deal with the president and Congress on certain issues facing the nation, the local union serves as the vital link between the individual union member and the national union, which in turn might link with the AFL-CIO.

Organizationally, the local union is a branch of the national union. It receives its charter from the national union and operates under the national union's constitution, bylaws, and rules. The constitution of the national union prescribes the number and types of officers, their duties and responsibilities, and the limits of their authority. Although union constitutions vary in length and content, they often mandate certain financial reports and require that a certain number of meetings be held, that the local labor agreement conform to the master labor agreement negotiated by the national union if there is companywide bargaining, and that approval to call a strike be obtained by the local union. With the trend toward greater centralization of authority by the national union, the local union over the years has lost much of its operational flexibility.

Differences Between Local Craft and Industrial Unions The operation of the local union in large part depends on the type of employees making up its membership. Although there is not a clear-cut division between them, unions can be divided generally into two groups: craft and industrial.

Differing union organizations The **craft unions** are composed of members who have been organized in accordance with their craft or skill, for example, bricklayers, electricians, carpenters, or ironworkers. **Industrial unions** have been organized on an industry basis, for example the Steelworkers, Auto Workers, Rubber Workers, Mine Workers, Textile Workers, and so on. This, of course, does not mean that there are no skilled employees in the steel, auto, rubber, or textile industries; but it does mean the electricians in a steel plant would likely be members of the Steelworkers.

Differing scope of the labor agreement The craft and industrial unions differ in other ways that have an effect on their operations. First, the craft unions, which frequently represent the building trades, usually negotiate short labor agreements (supplemented by detailed agreements on special topics, such as apprenticeship programs and safety) that cover a small geographic region, and each has considerable independence from the national union compared with industrial unions. Because of the nature of their work, craft union members may work on several job sites for several employers in a given year under the same labor agreement. The labor agreement covers the construction companies and a number of building trades' unions in the particular geographic area.

The industrial union, on the other hand, may be covered by a national labor agreement negotiated between the company and the national union, which covers all of the company's unionized plants. For example, General Motors plants in Atlanta, Detroit, and Los Angeles are covered by the same master agreement. Well over 100 pages long, it explains in detail the wage plan, transfers, pensions, layoffs, and so on. A separate local agreement is negotiated to cover matters of concern to the specific local plant and its employees, which must be consistent with the master agreement. In plants having no national labor agreement, a plant-wide agreement covering production and maintenance employees is typically negotiated.

Differing skills Types of skills help demonstrate another difference in local union operations. The craft members are highly skilled artisans who have completed formal training, usually in a formal apprenticeship program. Many industrial employees, on the other hand, do not require much prior job training. Therefore, the craft union members often feel that they have higher status than their industrial counterparts. The training programs available for the industrial union members are usually offered by the company, whereas the training received by members of craft unions is jointly controlled and operated by the unions. So craft unions select those who will be offered the apprenticeship training, while companies alone select the trainees in the plants. Such an arrangement has allowed the craft unions to limit the numbers in the craft, sometimes to only their families and friends. In addition, the administration of these apprenticeship programs may adversely affect minority group members, a situation discussed in Chapters 11 and 12.

Differing job characteristics The nature of their work creates a unique opportunity for craft unions to operate under conditions that approximate a closed shop. Since many of the work assignments last only a short period, the craft members, such as electricians on a building project, return to the union hiring hall for their next assignment after their part of a project is completed. Upon receiving the assignment, the union members could report to another job site and work, possibly for another company. Usually, these arrangements are worked out in advance by the business agent of the craft union and the companies who agree to operate under the existing labor agreement. In other words, the union hiring hall serves as a clearinghouse or placement office for the construction companies as well as the union members. Since the hiring hall must be operated in a nondiscriminatory manner, nonunion employees may also use its services; however, use by nonunion employees is still quite rare. In comparison, the typical member of the industrial union is hired by the company and will work for the same employer—usually at the same facility—until employment is terminated.

Differing leadership roles Another difference between craft and industrial unions pertains to the roles of the business agent and shop stewards of the craft union and the local union officials of the industrial unions. The **business agent,** the full-time administrator of the local craft union, provides many of the same services as the local union president of a large industrial union. Both are considered the key administrative officials of their respective local union halls, and they lead the local union negotiations and play a key role in grievance administration. However, the business agent has additional duties, such as administering the union hiring hall, serving as the chief "watchdog" over the agreement at the various work sites, and appointing an employee on each job site to serve as the shop steward. The **shop steward,** who may be the first person on the job or a senior employee, handles employee grievances, represents the business agent on the job, and contacts the business agent if anything goes wrong.

The shop steward is the personification of the union to the members; the impressions of the steward greatly influence the members' perceptions of the union. Where impressions of the steward are positive, members also have positive views of grievance procedures and have greater union commitment. Stewards spend about 12 hours per week on labor relations matters; between 50 and 80 percent of this time is spent on grievance handling. Therefore, training of shop stewards in grievance handling is important because it results in less time required to process grievances, an increased likelihood that the shop steward will seek re-election, and the ability of the steward to devote more time to improving relations between the union and management.[35]

In local industrial unions, the president may or may not serve full-time. If the position is full-time, the salary comes from union dues. If the position is part-time, the president is compensated from the union treasury only for the time taken off the company job (at the regular rate of pay). Presidential duties include participating in local negotiations, maintaining the local union office, assisting in grievance administration, and assuring that management abides by the agreement. On many occasions, a staff member of the international union (usually the international union representative) assists local officers in negotiations and in administering the labor agreement and ensures that the local's activities conform to the national constitution and directives. The shop steward, the elected representative in each department in the plant or facility, represents the members at local union meetings, handles grievances at the shop level, and collects dues, if necessary.[36] Union officers may be granted preference in shift assignment and protected from layoffs; however, they must be involved in the day-to-day administration of the collective bargaining agreement.

Many unions today are neither pure craft unions nor pure industrial unions in nature. They are likely still concentrated in their traditional sector (that is, the core of the United Auto Workers is the automobile industry and the United Steelworkers, the steel industry, for example). Many unions are more appropriately described as "general unions" because of their multijurisdictional organizations. As an example, only 66.2 percent of the UAW organizing effort between 1986 and 1988 occurred in manufacturing with 15.3 percent in the service industry and 12.3 percent in wholesale and retail trades. During the same period, 64.4 percent of the Steelworkers organizing effort was in manufacturing, 16.3 percent was in the service industry, and 7.8 percent was in wholesale and retail trades.[37]

Government and Operation of the Local Union There are several common ways for union members to participate in union activities: holding office, participating in meetings, attending conventions, voting (elections, ratification, and strike vote), and helping with the monthly newsletter.

Union members whose growth needs are not fulfilled on their job are usually more willing to become involved in union administration. Also, individuals are usually more willing to participate in union administration when their values are closely aligned with their role in the union.[38]

Participation in meetings Attendance at local union meetings often varies between 5 and 10 percent of the membership; attendance is higher, however, among union members who perceive a potential payoff for participation.[39] When the union is confronted with important business or a crisis, such as during union elections, taking a strike vote, negotiations, or ratifying the negotiated agreement, attendance also rises. Unions and their members have been criticized for their lack of attendance, but formal attendance cannot be taken as the real measure of membership participation. Much membership participation takes place on an informal basis at the plant level among employees, among friends during lunch, or between shop stewards and members during rest breaks. Concerns are channeled to the union leadership through these stewards, who regularly attend local meetings. The influence of these information channels over union policies and actions should not be underestimated. Local unions are learning to use survey methods and interviewing techniques to gather information about such issues as safety and healthy, contract provisions, promotional opportunities, job stress, perception of the union, recruitment of new members, and so on not only to prepare for negotiations, but to improve the operations of the union and assess membership attitudes.[40]

The union leaders almost always attend local union meetings, as do departmental representatives, "hard-core" members, pressure groups, social groups, and aspirants to union leadership positions. Union stewards are expected to attend local union meetings and represent the interests of those in their unit. Although direct votes occur only in major issues, the union steward can usually reflect the membership views.[41]

Locals have tried a number of techniques to increase attendance of regular members, such as providing beer, sandwiches, movies, and door prizes, fining members who miss a specified number of meetings, or refusing to let them seek an elected office. While some gimmicks may increase the attendance in the short run, many members still feel the meetings are "long, boring, and frustrating affairs."[42]

Local meetings are held at a time that meets with the approval of the majority. While they often start late and last too long, the average length is about two hours. The content inspires little attendance because much of the time is devoted to reading reports from the treasurer, project leaders, and committee chairpersons. Opportunities are provided for members to discuss these reports, but this procedure itself takes time, especially when a grievance involving someone in attendance is presented or when a controversial issue is raised before the meeting as a whole. Parliamentary procedure is used at times to excess by quasi-parliamentary experts who may want to tie up the meeting. Although the meeting may stray from the ideal, generally the business of the local is accomplished.

Functions of the meeting While the local union meeting may seem boring and not well attended, it serves several vital functions in the local union government. First, the meeting is the union's single most important governmental activity, and all authority at the local level is derived from it. Second, the meeting provides an opportunity for members to communicate with union leaders, express gripes directly, and call attention to their concerns. Likewise, it is an opportunity for leaders to give information to members, present results of activities, seek union support, and give direction to the membership. Last, the meeting is the supreme legislative body; this is where decisions are made on such items as disposition of grievances, approval of expenses and constitutional changes, election of officers, and ratification of the contract.[43]

The National or International Union

The national or international (these terms are used interchangeably in this chapter) union in the United States occupies the "kingpin" position in organized labor "because of its influence in collective bargaining—the core function of American unions."[44] Size alone (see Exhibit 4.8) indicates the magnitude of the influence of national unions—millions of members work under labor agreements that are directly or indirectly the result of national union actions. The local union operates under its constitution and directives, and the federation (AFL-CIO) derives its influence, prestige, and power from the affiliated national unions.

The national union operates under a **constitution** adopted in a convention by representatives from locals. These constitutions have evolved over time through three stages: first, the locals were initially careful to restrict the power of the national union; second, as national unions became more active in collective bargaining, political action, and so on, the locals became subordinate bodies; and third and currently, the constitution includes provisions that not only authorize the major national union functions but also protect individual rights and rights of locals in relation to the national union.[45]

The Convention The supreme governing body of the national union is its **convention,** which is usually held annually or biennially.[46] It serves the national union in many ways: as the constitutional assembly, the legislature of the national union, the final court for union decisions, and the means for nominating officers (and the election in many cases). The convention provides the time and place for national officers to report to the members their accomplishments and failures. It provides the agenda for policy formulation, program planning, and rule making. It represents the time in which the voice of the membership holds leaders accountable for their actions. However, not all activities are official; the convention provides a reward for drudgery work at the local, an opportunity for politicking and public relations, and a time and place for the members to "let their hair down."

The convention makes use of the *delegate system,* in which the number of delegates allowed depends on the number of members in the local. Since even the smallest union is allowed one delegate, the number of delegates is not in direct proportion to the size of the local, although larger locals usually have more delegates. The convention conducts its business similarly to Congress and various state legislatures in that much committee work (including the possible holding of hearings) is performed prior to debate and vote on the convention floor. However, much discussion also takes place in the convention hotel bars and in smoke-filled rooms.[47]

Although many subjects may go before the convention, several continue to emerge year after year.

- Internal government: dues; financial matters; authority of the president, executive board, and locals.
- Collective bargaining: problems with current agreements, membership requests for future negotiations, establishment of bargaining priorities, determination of strategy for next negotiations.

Exhibit 4.8 International Unions

ORGANIZATION	MEMBERS (IN THOUSANDS)
National Education Association (NEA) (Ind).	2,100
Teamsters (IBT)	1,316
State, County (AFSCME)	1,167
Food and Commercial (UFCW)	997
Service Employees (SEIU)	919
Auto Workers (UAW)	771
Electrical (IBEW)	710
Teachers (AFT)	574
Machinists (IAM)	474
Carpenters (CJA)	408
Communications Workers (CWA)	472
Steelworkers (USW)	421
Laborers (LIUNA)	408
Operating Engineers (IUOE)	305
United Needle Trades, Industrial, and Textile Employees Union (UNITE)	276
Hotel and Restaurant (HERE)	258
Postal Workers (APWU)	249
Plumbers (PPF)	220
Paper Workers (UPIU)	188
Government Workers (AFGE)	149

SOURCE: Courtney D. Gifford, *Directory of U.S. Labor Organizations, 1994–95 Edition* (Washington, D.C.: Bureau of National Affairs, Inc., 1995), pp. 67–69.

- Resolutions in support of or against domestic and international public policies: labor law reform, inflation, interest rates, unemployment, international balance of payments, loss of jobs to foreign countries.[48]

Leadership and Democracy Between conventions, the national union is led by its executive board, whose members are elected by the membership. In some cases, executive board members are elected on a regional basis, and they are responsible for regional intermediate organizations that maintain contact between the locals in the region and the national. The relationship between the executive board and the national union president is usually specified in the constitution. For example, some national union presidents primarily carry out the policies of the executive board; others direct the affairs of the national union, subject to the approval of the board. However, the largest group of presidents has virtually unrestricted authority to appoint staff, regulate locals, and direct the activities of the national union. The rationale for allowing such great authority to be vested in the chief executive is that the union frequently finds itself in struggles with employers or in other situations where it must act decisively and quickly. Thus, a strong executive is needed and a single spokesperson for the union is required. However, the concentration of power creates opportunities for misuse of power, and an internal system of checks and balances must be devised to assure democracy and adequate representation. Experiences that brought on the passage of Titles I to VI of the Landrum-Griffin Act (covered later in this chapter) have shown that internal control often does not work effectively, however, and that government regulation is essential. Members' rights to participate in union elections and governance include the right to nominate candidates in elections, vote in elections, attend membership meetings, participate in the deliberations, and vote on the business at these meetings such as setting dues and assessments.[49]

Democracy within the union can improve its overall efficiency and effectiveness. Union leaders will better represent the members because they will know what the members want. Democracy will make it easier to eliminate corrupt and ineffective officers who do not represent the members' interests. Further, paid union officials cannot do all the tasks needed within a union and have to rely on the efforts of unpaid leaders. These volunteer leaders will have a greater commitment to the union if they are involved in it democratically. Not all union leaders share this positive view of democracy, however. On the opposite side are those who believe that unions need discipline and unity to be effective and that democracy means factionalization within the union, which makes it less effective.[50] A general conclusion about union democracy was well stated by George Strauss:

> Union democracy is desirable, not because democracy is good in itself (as it is) but because *on balance* democracy increases union effectiveness in representing members' interests and in mobilizing these members to support its collective bargaining objectives. Town meeting democracy, in which large numbers of members participate personally is feasible only in small locals and occasionally on the shop floor. The best we can hope for generally is responsive leadership. But insuring continued responsive leadership requires that members be able to oppose their leaders' policies and to

> change their leaders if they become irresponsive—and to do this without great personal cost. Thus a reasonable requirement of democracy is that it allows low-cost opposition.[51]

One slight sign of democracy and active participation by members has been the turnover rates of national union presidents. Some former international union leaders maintained their positions for extended periods of time (Dan Tobin, Teamsters, 45 years; John L. Lewis, Mine Workers, 39 years). In the 1950s and 1960s, the turnover rate for union presidents was about 20 percent, rising to 25 percent in the 1970s. Then, in the late 1980s, the turnover rate reversed to 10 percent. While turnover is not the necessary prerequisite for union democracy, the general rule is that the union leader must be responsive to the membership and satisfy the membership's objectives to remain in office.[52] The president's tenure in office tends to be longer in larger unions, with formalized communication networks, centralized bargaining, and heterogeneous rank-and-file members.[53]

Profile of Labor Leaders Most labor leaders come from working class families; 62.1 percent of their fathers were hourly employees. They have an average of 14.1 years of formal education. Over 70 percent have some college experience; 17 percent have postgraudate education; and another 27 percent are college graduates. They first joined a union for the same reasons most union members do today; 40 percent joined because it was a condition of employment; 33 percent joined because they believed in the goals of organized labor; and 25 percent wanted better pay and working conditions. Their reasons for pursuing union leadership positions included the following (80 percent or more responded positively to these survey items): challenging work; interesting work; extended my range of abilities; opportunity to learn new things; achieve something I personally valued; believed in the goals of the union; and opportunity to improve working conditions of fellow employees.[54]

Administration The operational departments of international unions vary in kind and number, but the typical international union will have at least the following departments: (1) executive and administration; (2) financial and auditing; (3) organizing and servicing; and (4) technical staff, which includes research, education, economics, law, publications, and public relations.

Likewise, the international unions create operating departments to serve various special interests among their membership. For example, in 1989 the United Auto Workers established the Transnational and Joint Ventures Department for the 8,000 UAW members who were employed by three Japanese-managed vehicle makers at U.S. sites: the Toyota-General Motors, Ford-Mazda, and Chrysler-Mitsubishi joint ventures (Nissan remains nonunion).

The executive and administrative group includes the president, vice-president(s), secretary-treasurer, and their assistants. This group is chiefly responsible for the activities of the overall union. In some cases the vice-president may concentrate on organizing or collective bargaining, whereas the secretary-treasurer will focus on financial matters.

Salaries of international union presidents vary widely, from about $5,200 per year for Caesar Chavez, late of the United Farm Workers, to $572,000 for the International Brotherhood of Teamsters in 1987 (Ron Carey, current president, has drastically reduced the salary). Generally, union presidents' salaries are comparable to those of executives in government and universities and typically range from $80,000 to $150,000, with an average of $123,000 for larger unions.

Professional Staff Members Unions have two kinds of professional staffs. The first group is either appointed or elected and holds such titles as international union representative, staff representative, business agent, or organizer. These staff members work away from the international union headquarters and assist local unions in bargaining, contract administration, and organizing. The second group performs more technical, specialized functions at the union headquarters. This group includes such professionals as industrial hygienists, physicians, economists, attorneys, accountants, computer operators, and specialists in education, media, public relations, and so forth. Interestingly, the staff members have formed staff unions, mostly to promote their job security and equitable salary schedules. Most of these unions are independent, but 13 of the 40 bargaining units have affiliated with a national labor union, such as the Communications Workers of America, the Steelworkers, and the Newspaper Guild. In addition, an association of these unions, called the International Congress of Staff Unions (ICSU), was formed in 1988 to share information and provide mutual support and assistance.

National unions have traditionally selected their staff through political processes by rewarding demonstrated leadership and loyalty at the local level. Union officers traditionally have been suspicious of college-educated persons and have believed that the staff should work its way up the ranks. More recently, national unions are using personnel practices used by business and government. With the election of more college-educated persons to national offices, much of the resistance to college education has declined. For example, Richard Trumka, newly elected secretary-treasurer of the AFL-CIO, is an attorney. Another attorney, Jack Sheinkman, is president of UNITE.

In the past there has been no recognized sequence of professional training for union officials, and experience and performance have been stressed in appointments and elected office. However, training has increased significantly over the last several years. Most national unions provide in-house training for their professional staff. Numerous universities have labor education programs that offer professional development for union members. The George Meany Center for Labor Studies in Silver Springs, Maryland, had an enrollment of 6,417 in the 1989–1990 school year, up from only 236 in 1969–1970. The Center, in cooperation with Antioch College, sponsors a college degree program designed for union staff, and 159 union officials have graduated from this program.[55]

Services to and Control of Locals As indicated earlier, the locals are constitutionally subordinated to the national union, but the degree of subordination varies with the union. The national union provides services to the local union in several ways while at the same time controlling local union leaders. For example, where a national product market exists, a **master labor agreement** with one firm might be negotiated to cover all its facilities (such agreements have been negotiated in the steel, auto, rubber, aircraft, and electrical appliance industries). Also, a union such as the United Auto Workers may negotiate an agreement with a company like General Motors at the national level, and this agreement may establish a pattern for negotiating with other auto companies such as Ford and Chrysler. Following the negotiations of the master agreement between the national and each company, the local union will negotiate a local agreement with officials at each plant, covering local rules, policies, and benefits. Deviations from the master agreement must be okayed by the national union. (See Chapter 6 for further coverage.)

The national union assists locals in collective bargaining, grievance administration, strike activities, and internal financial administration. These services also provide an opportunity for national union staff members to ensure that the local unions are conforming to national policies.

The international union representative, in addition to organizing new unions, also helps the local unions in grievance administration and labor arbitration. The national supports the local in strike situations, but the local must get approval in order to qualify for strike benefits. The national union provides counseling and consultation for internal financial administration (bookkeeping, dues collection, purchases, financing union lodges, and so on), but trusteeship (receivership) procedures are available whereby the national union can set aside the local for abuses such as malfeasance, corruption, and misuse of funds in favor of a trustee under national direction.

Dues, Fees, and Distribution of Funds Although all union members pay dues or fees to their national unions, the amount and form vary considerably. Such dues are the chief source of revenue for unions. Typically, the monthly dues are about $20, and the initiation fee is about $40. Some unions set a single rate, but most allow the local some flexibility in making the final determination. Frequently, dues are collected via a dues checkoff system (discussed in more detail in Chapter 11). The member agrees to a payroll deduction of union dues, which are collected by the employer and paid directly to the union.

Several specialized unions with small memberships, such as the Director's Guild, Football Players, Mine Workers, and Iron Workers, charge over $100 for an initiation fee, and the Radio Association charges $2,000. Usually when dues are higher than average, the payments include premiums for insurance, pension payments, and other benefits.

The local unions forward a portion of the monthly dues for each member to the national union. The nationals use these funds for various purposes beneficial to the membership. While the largest percentage of funds goes to the general fund, which covers administrative and operational costs and salary expenses, allocations are also made to accounts such as a strike fund, a convention fund, union publications, educational activities, and a retirement fund.[56]

Use of union dues and fees for political purposes and non-collective bargaining activities has come under fire in the last few years. Union members who disagree with the manner in which their unions contribute or use their funds have challenged their unions. Recent court decisions have caused several unions, such as the Machinists, Auto Workers, Communications Workers, and American Federation of State, County, and Municipal Employees, to adopt dues rebate plans. These plans allow a rebate of a portion of member dues spent on political activities if the member requests it in advance (usually annually).

The U.S. Supreme Court has ruled that if a union uses dues and fees of protesting employees for non-collective bargaining activities and purposes, it breaches its fiduciary duty of fair representation. In addition, a district court judge listed 12 activities, including political ones, that were considered non-collective bargaining activities.[57] While unions can continue to solicit volunteer contributions through such units as the AFL-CIO Committee on Political Education (COPE), the UAW's Community Action Program (CAP), and the UMW's Coal Miners' Political Committee (COMPAC), collections may be more difficult.

While union membership has not increased over the past two decades, unions have been prosperous financially, and their influence has increased in recent years. The level of unions' assets and income has enhanced their ability to finance strikes and other union activities. As an example, in 1960, private sector union membership was 14.6 million and its receipts were $1.4 billion. In 1987, union membership was 10.9 million and its receipts were $11.8 billion. This is a drop in membership of more than 25 percent and an increase in receipts of more than 700 percent. Taking inflation into account, receipts increased 220 percent. On a per-member basis, the receipts in real dollars were more than doubled.[58]

Mergers of National Unions Encouraged by the AFL-CIO merger, but mostly spurred by rising costs, the need for stronger bargaining positions, expensive jurisdictional disputes, decline for some U.S. industries, economies of scale, avoidance of external controls, and the need for self-preservation, mergers of national unions have occurred at a quickening pace.

Since 1955, the AFL-CIO has emphasized cooperation, and there have been 133 mergers. By 1965, 48 mergers occurred, while 45 occurred in the following decade. Between 1986 and 1994, the pace slowed to 40. Then, in 1995, the Clothing and Textile Workers merged with the Garment Workers Union to form the United Needle Trades, Industrial, and Textile Employees Union (UNITE), and the Rubber Workers united with the Steelworkers. Also in 1995, the presidents of the Auto Workers, Machinists, and Steelworkers announced a merger of their three unions that would take place by the year 2000 and create the largest union in the United States.[59]

Mergers occur through **amalgamation,** which is the joining together of two or more unions, or through **absorption,** which occurs when a large union takes over a smaller union. Mergers do not always produce a complete fusion or a total submergence of the absorbed unions. Occasionally there is a strong membership resistance to the merger, and the larger union may establish a division within its union to allow members of the former union to have a separate voice in the policy of the larger union after the merger. Other causes of resistance stem from members' interest in preserving their craft identity, desire to carry on their union's historical traditions, and membership identity with a small geographic region.[60]

Typically, mergers have not succeeded immediately in welding together functions, organizational units, and staff members. They have required the time, patience, and good will of all parties as officers and staff members who have different personalities and modes of operation are meshed. The local unions must be accommodated as well as the employers and the collective bargaining relationships. Mergers have been particularly difficult when one of the unions feels a loss of its autonomy and when the merger occurs between unions whose prior dealings have been characterized by intense rivalry. Often members' pride is hurt, and fear surfaces when they find out that their union may be submerged by another.

In a more positive vein, the resulting larger unions gain more clout with industrial giants and can negotiate more as equals. The greater size generates resources to provide better training in collective bargaining, grievance administration, and steward leadership; to offer greater strike benefits; to lobby more effectively for legislation; and to maintain a staff to combat unfair labor practices. Moreover, successful mergers reduce the risks to smaller unions from technological change, economic recessions, declines in membership, unemployment, and financial strains.[61]

Most officers of unions with 50,000 or fewer members (includes more than half of AFL-CIO affiliates) believe that mergers have the best prospects of providing and maintaining member services. The benefits include more effective lobbying, increased bargaining power, expertise, economies of scale, and more effective strikes. The trade-offs are reduction in membership participation and less attention to needs of special interest groups. The potential advantages of a merger coupled with the risks of not merging suggest that mergers of national unions will be continued in the future.[62]

Intermediate Organizational Units

Structurally, between national headquarters and the locals lie the intermediate organizational units—regional or district offices, trade conferences, conference boards, and joint councils. These units usually operate under the guidance of their various national units, but their activities are important to the union members and employers in their areas.

The regional, or district, offices house the regional or district officers, the staff, and the international union representatives for the geographic area served. For example, Michigan has a number of Auto Workers' district offices; the Steelworkers have district offices in Pittsburgh, Birmingham, and elsewhere. The offices are established for national unions to better serve their respective locals.

Trade conferences are set up within national unions to represent a variety of industrial groups. For example, the Teamsters has established 11 trade conferences for such groups as freight, laundry, airlines, and moving and storage. These groups meet to discuss various mutual problems and topics of interest.

Conference boards are organized within national unions in accordance with the company affiliation to discuss issues that pertain to the union and the particular company. For instance, each of the national unions within the steel, auto, rubber, and electric industries has established conference boards that meet to discuss negotiations and related problems. Delegates are chosen from the local unions to represent the interests of their constituents at meetings, to plan the next negotiations, and then to relay these plans to the local union members.

Joint councils involve groupings of local unions that have common goals, employers, and interests. Examples are the building trades councils established in most metropolitan areas in the United States. They negotiate with the association of construction employers in the area, coordinate their activities, and assist in resolving jurisdictional disputes between unions.

Independent Unions There were 41 independent unions (not affiliated with the AFL-CIO) in 1991. These unions represent mostly service and health-care providers. The largest union in the United States, the National Education Association (2,100,000 members), is among these independent unions. Other independent unions include the American Nurses Association (149,000 members), American Physicians and Dentists (1,690 members), Life Insurance Agents (1,150 members), National Labor Relations Board Union (1,370 members), Professional Engineering Association (510 members), and United Plant Guard Workers of America (26,000 members).[63] There are also approximately 1,500 independent local unions that have nearly half a million members. Independent local unions are found in a few large organizations such as DuPont, Texaco, Exxon, AT&T, and Procter & Gamble; in several medium-sized firms such as Dow-Jones, Weirton Steel, and Zenith; and in numerous small companies in a variety of industries.[64]

Employee Associations Unions are supporting new employee associations that provide a wide range of services to their members. In Cleveland, 9 to 5: The Association for Working Women, a 15,000-member affiliate of the Service Employees International Union, provides a toll-free hotline, offers courses on sexual harassment and VDT injuries, and lobbies on workplace issues. In New York, AIM (Associate ILGWU Members), a 2,500-member affiliate of the International Ladies Garment Workers Union (now part of UNITE), provides English classes for its members, graduate-equivalency diploma classes, skills training, and legal assistance with immigration, minimum wage, safety and health, sexual harassment, disability, and pensions laws. In Montana, the 1,400-member Montana Family Union, sponsored by the AFL-CIO and made up of government employees, small business owners, and even priests, offers its members major medical benefits at less than 50 percent of their individual rates. While critics refer to these employee associations as "watered-down unions," they are serving important social functions, and their membership has grown to 500,000 nationally while total membership in unions has declined to approximately 16 percent of the labor force.[65]

The American Federation of Labor and Congress of Industrial Organizations (AFL-CIO)

The American Federation of Labor and Congress of Industrial Organizations (AFL-CIO), while not including all U.S. labor unions, is composed of 73 national and international unions that have 60,000 local unions and about 14 million members. In addition, there are 32 directly affiliated local unions. Members represent a diversity of occupations, such as actors, construction workers, barbers and hairdressers, steelworkers, bus drivers, railroad workers, telephone operators, newspaper reporters, sales clerks, garment workers, engineers, schoolteachers, and police. These AFL-CIO affiliates maintain day-to-day relationships with several thousands of employers and administer about 160,000 labor agreements. Most (over 99 percent) of these agreements are negotiated without strikes or other forms of conflict and serve as the basis of employment conditions under which many work.

Established in 1955 when the American Federation of Labor and the Congress of Industrial Organizations merged, the AFL-CIO recognized the principle that both craft and industrial unions are appropriate, equal, and necessary parts of U.S. organized labor. The federation accepts the principle of *autonomy*—each affiliated union conducts its own affairs; has its own headquarters, offices, and staff; decides its own economic policies; sets its own dues; carries out its own contract negotiations; and provides its own services to members.

No national union is required to affiliate with the AFL-CIO. About 41 unions remain outside the AFL-CIO. Member unions are free to withdraw at any time; however, their voluntary participation plays an essential role that advances the interest of every union. National unions continue their membership because they believe that a federation of unions serves purposes their own individual unions cannot serve as well.

Examples of AFL-CIO services include:

- Speaking for organized labor before Congress and other branches of government.
- Representing U.S. labor in world affairs, keeping in direct contact with labor unions throughout the free world.
- Coordinating activities such as community services, political education, lobbying, and voter registration with greater effectiveness.
- Helping to coordinate efforts to organize nonunion employees throughout the United States.

Another vital service enhances the integrity and prestige of AFL-CIO unions—they must operate under established ethical practice codes covering union democracy and financial integrity. The federation also assists in minimizing conflicts that cause work interruptions by mediating and resolving disputes between national unions, such as organizing disputes and conflicts over work assignments.[66]

Organizational Structure The AFL-CIO organizational structure, shown in Exhibit 4.9, illustrates the importance of the convention. Meeting every two years and at times of particular need, delegates decide on policies, programs, and direction for AFL-CIO activities. Each national or international union is authorized to send delegates to the convention. Each union's representation of delegates at the convention is determined by the number of dues-paying members. In addition, other affiliated organizations, such as state labor councils, are represented by one delegate each.

Between conventions, the governing body is the Executive Council, composed of the president, secretary-treasurer, and 33 vice-presidents (10 of which are established as "diversity set-asides" elected by majority vote at the convention). In 1995, there was a hotly contested election for the presidency, as revealed in the "Labor Relations in Action" on pages 147 and 148.

The other members of the Executive Council are likely to be current or previous presidents of international unions affiliated with the AFL-CIO. The Executive Council meets at least three times a year and handles operational duties involving legislative matters, union corruption, charters of new internationals, and judicial appeals from member unions.

The AFL-CIO has been criticized for the lack of minorities on its 51-member Executive Council. While it now has three black members, it has only three female members, even though women make up 34 percent of the unionized members and 44 percent of the total civilian labor force.[67]

Between meetings of the Executive Council, the president, who is the chief executive officer, has authority to supervise the affairs of the federation and to direct its staff, and the secretary-treasurer handles all financial matters. To assist his administration, the president has appointed 15 standing committees on various subjects, which, with the assistance of the AFL-CIO staff, provide related services to member unions. The staff, located at headquarters in Washington, D.C., corresponds closely to these standing committees in order to better serve the member unions. (See Exhibit 4.9 for a listing of standing committees and staff divisions.) The General Board, composed of the Executive Council and one officer from each member union, is available to act on matters referred to it by the Executive Council.

The AFL-CIO has established 50 state central bodies (plus one in Puerto Rico) to advance the statewide interests of labor through political, lobbying, and organizing activities, which involve attempts to elect friends of labor, to have favorable legislation passed, and to organize nonunion workers, respectively. Each local union of the AFL-CIO–affiliated unions in a particular state may join the state organization and participate in and support its activities. In addition, 625 *local central bodies* have been formed by local unions of the national affiliates to deal with civic and community problems and other matters of local concern.

To accommodate and serve the interests and needs of various trade and industrial unions, the AFL-CIO has established eight *trade and industrial departments.* The Industrial Union Department represents the interests of industrial unions,

Exhibit 4.9 Structural Organization of the American Federation of Labor and Congress of Industrial Organizations

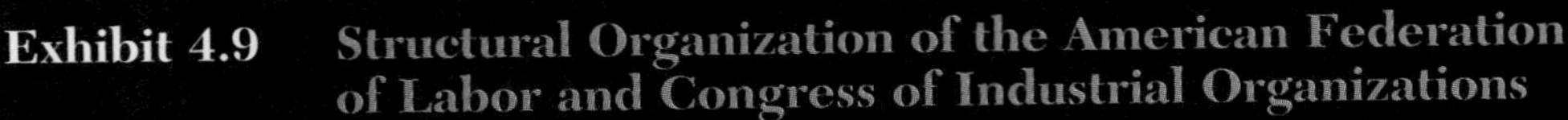

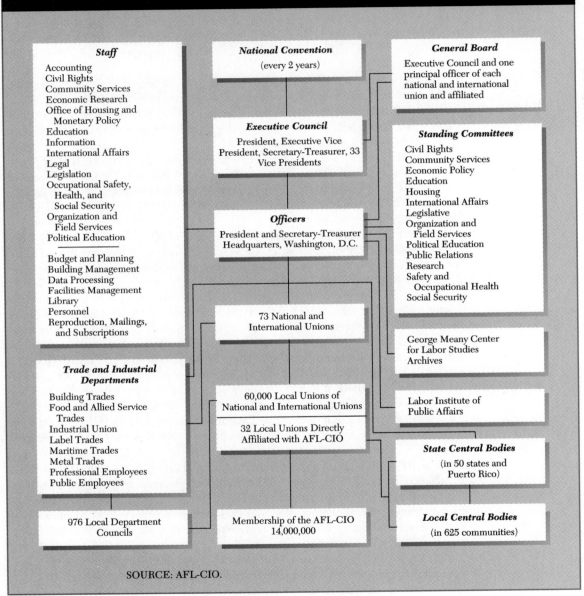

Staff
Accounting
Civil Rights
Community Services
Economic Research
Office of Housing and Monetary Policy
Education
Information
International Affairs
Legal
Legislation
Occupational Safety, Health, and Social Security
Organization and Field Services
Political Education

Budget and Planning
Building Management
Data Processing
Facilities Management
Library
Personnel
Reproduction, Mailings, and Subscriptions

Trade and Industrial Departments
Building Trades
Food and Allied Service Trades
Industrial Union
Label Trades
Maritime Trades
Metal Trades
Professional Employees
Public Employees

976 Local Department Councils

National Convention
(every 2 years)

Executive Council
President, Executive Vice President, Secretary-Treasurer, 33 Vice Presidents

Officers
President and Secretary-Treasurer
Headquarters, Washington, D.C.

73 National and International Unions

60,000 Local Unions of National and International Unions

32 Local Unions Directly Affiliated with AFL-CIO

Membership of the AFL-CIO
14,000,000

General Board
Executive Council and one principal officer of each national and international union and affiliated

Standing Committees
Civil Rights
Community Services
Economic Policy
Education
Housing
International Affairs
Legislative
Organization and Field Services
Political Education
Public Relations
Research
Safety and Occupational Health
Social Security

George Meany Center for Labor Studies
Archives

Labor Institute of Public Affairs

State Central Bodies
(in 50 states and Puerto Rico)

Local Central Bodies
(in 625 communities)

SOURCE: AFL-CIO.

Changes at the Top of AFL-CIO Lead to Combative Campaign

Sixteen years ago, when Lane Kirkland replaced George Meany, Kirkland became only the fourth person to hold the position of president of the AFL-CIO (including the AFL before). At that time, union membership represented 24.1 percent of the work force, compared with 15.8 percent in 1995. This low percentage exists at the same time as numerous surveys show that 40 percent of the work force would like to join a union. Kirkland was criticized for being more "intellectual than firebrand" that put him "out of touch with the workers." For example, one critic contended, "He spends an extraordinary amount of time dealing with Eastern Europe while we're going to hell in a handbasket."[a] Despite his supporters' claims that Kirkland has brought better relations with the White House, greater focus on organizing efforts, and a few more women and minorities in top union positions, some wanted fresh leadership, more emphasis on organizing, and less emphasis on international affairs.

On May 9, 1995, Thomas Donahue, secretary-treasurer during Kirkland's 16 years as president, announced his retirement. Next, Kirkland, then 73 years old, announced that he would seek reelection to his ninth term, despite the vow of 11 presidents of AFL-CIO-affiliated unions to campaign against him.

On June 11, 1995, with mounting leadership challenge and retirement pressures, Kirkland announced he would retire on August 1, 1995, and supported his long-time secretary-treasurer, Thomas Donahue, who decided to change his plans and not retire, for president.

The challengers were led by John Sweeney, president of the 1.1 million-member Service Employees International Union, a union that has prospered during the 1980s and 1990s, growing from 626,000 in 1980, when Sweeney became president, to 1 million in 1995. The SEIU spends about one-third of its $453 million budget on organizing, whereas most unions spend only 2 to 4 percent of their budgets. Also, Sweeney has relied on 1930s-style campaigns that turn membership drives into community issues involving churches and nonprofit groups. His "Justice for Janitors" campaign has signed up 35,000 members in 20 cities since 1985. In Washington, D.C., the SEIU held public rallies to protest a $32 million tax break the city was providing large developers, prompting them to sign union contracts.[b]

Interestingly, Sweeney was recruited by Donahue in 1960 to work in an SEIU local union in New York City and several months before had supported Donahue as a compromise candidate to replace Kirkland. Sweeney has had a life-time association with unions. Although his mother cleaned houses, his father was a unionized transportation worker. He told friends that the most important things in life are church, family, and the union: He has been quoted as saying: "Without the church, there's no redemption; without family, there's no love; and without the union, there's no food on the table."[c]

(continued)

CHANGES AT THE TOP OF AFL-CIO LEAD TO COMBATIVE CAMPAIGN—CONT'D

However, by mid-June, developments led to Sweeney heading a slate that included Richard Trumka, president of the United Mine Workers, for Secretary-Treasurer and Linda Chavez-Thompson, of the American Federation of State, County, and Municipal Employees and the granddaughter of an illegal immigrant from Mexico, for the newly created position of Executive Vice-President.

Sweeney and his supporters launched a campaign that included: (1) increasing the amount of money (up to $20 million) for organizing new employees, (2) organizing more minorities, women, and younger employees, (3) reconsidering the AFL-CIO's 60-year alliance with the Democratic party, and (4) changing organized labor's image by more aggressive marketing, possibly by ownership of radio or television stations.[d]

Thereafter, Donahue selected Barbara Easterling of the Communications Workers of America as his running mate for Secretary-Treasurer. Easterling, the first woman to hold a leadership position in the AFL-CIO, is the daughter of Polish immigrants who worked in the mines and tire factories of Ohio, and she began her employment as a telephone operator in Akron, Ohio.

At the Executive Council meeting on August 1, 1995, Kirkland officially retired, and Donahue and Easterling were voted in 21 to 12 as interim President and Secretary-Treasurer, respectively. Donahue announced that he wanted to train 1,500 new labor union organizers, develop a new ethical practice code for union leaders, and consolidate the AFL-CIO's four international institutes. Mr. Sweeney said he liked what he heard and responded: "It was a great speech, and I was happy to write the first draft in my (campaign) platform."[e] Although Sweeney claimed 60 percent of the votes needed to win at the AFL-CIO convention in October 1995 when allocating votes on the basis of the size of the unions, Donahue claimed the initial victory with his election by two-thirds vote of the Executive Council.

When the final votes were counted, John Sweeney was elected President with 58 percent of the votes, Richard Trumka was elected Secretary-Treasurer, and Linda Chavez-Thompson was elected to a new position of Executive Vice-President.

[a]Aaron Bernstein, "Why Lane Kirkland Looks Like a Lame Duck," *Business Week* (February 13, 1995), p. 44.
[b]Aaron Bernstein, "Can A New Leader Bring Labor Back to Life?" *Business Week* (July 3, 1995), p. 87.
[c]Robert Rose, "John Sweeney Plots a Revolution at AFL-CIO," *The Wall Street Journal* (June 14, 1995), p. B1.
[d]Richard Greer, "What Lane Kirkland's Challengers Hope to Accomplish," *The Atlanta Constitution* (June 11, 1995), p. K3.
[e]Richard Rose, "Donahue Succeeds Kirkland as Head of the AFL-CIO," *The Wall Street Journal* (August 2, 1995), p. A-8.

mostly members of the former CIO. Another department, the Union Label Department, promotes the purchase and sale of union-made goods and services. The remaining departments represent the interests of such union groups as the building trades, food and beverage trades, maritime employees, metal trades, public employees, and professional employees. In addition, throughout the United States where there is sufficient interest and support, 976 *local department councils* have been organized.[68]

The AFL-CIO established a no-raiding clause for its affiliated unions in 1962 to keep one affiliated union from attempting to draw members from another or seeking to represent a group of employees at a worksite where a union already exists. Then, in 1962, the AFL-CIO set up an Internal Dispute Plan to adjudicate conflicts among its affiliated unions. Because the Teamsters had been an independent union from 1955 to 1987, when it rejoined the AFL-CIO, and since it is noted for its aggressive organizing activities, it was only natural that the Teamsters were involved in about half of the 23 decisions under the Internal Dispute Plan.[69]

The AFL-CIO's operations are financed through regular member dues, called *per capita taxes,* which are paid by affiliated unions on behalf of their members. Currently, the per capita tax is $.42 month, or $5.04 per year, for each member. Thus, the AFL-CIO's operating budget is over $60 million, of which nearly all covers regular operating expenses. A major portion of the budget goes to the salaries of the staff. The detailed financial report of the AFL-CIO is submitted to the delegates at each convention.[70]

The AFL-CIO recently recognized the potential of maintaining contact with employees who are not members of unions by establishing an **associate membership program.** They include those who voted for the union in elections where the union did not win, employees in nonunion companies who would vote for the union if given a choice, and employees who are represented by the union but have not joined it. There were 300,000 associate union members by 1989, and the number continues to grow steadily. This program helps the AFL-CIO maintain contact with these employees and provides benefits for a nominal fee, including life insurance, prescription drug coverage, travel services, legal services, and a credit card program[71] (see Exhibit 4.10). In 1991, the AFL-CIO included as part of its Union Privilege Benefit Program for associate members a mortgage plan under which union members and their relatives who are first-time home buyers would be eligible for financing with a total down payment of 5 percent (3 percent in cash and 2 percent obtained through an unsecured loan).[72]

Other AFL-CIO activities are educational and informational, presenting the federation's stance on a variety of issues. For example, the AFL-CIO publishes a weekly *AFL-CIO News* that keeps members up to date on current events that pertain to them and presents various reports on problems and policies of organized labor. The AFL-CIO maintains the George Meany Center for Labor Studies, which offers short courses in union leadership development, and a Speaker's Bureau to provide labor speakers for high school and college classes, and makes educational films available to interested groups for a nominal fee.

In the political arena, the AFL-CIO receives much attention. As representative of organized labor, it serves as the focal point of political activities.

Not only does it lobby aggressively for favorable legislation, but it publishes the voting records of each senator and representative at both federal and state levels. It attempts to influence appointments, such as Supreme Court judges, the Secretary of Labor, and National Labor Relations Board members, who are important to organized labor. Its policy of "reward your friends, punish your enemies" has not changed much since Samuel Gompers's day. The AFL-CIO's Committee on Political Education (COPE) has a network in each state and in most large communities. COPE seeks voluntary contributions to provide funds for its activities, which include voter registration, "get-out-the-vote" campaigns, preparation of leaflets and posters, and research on behalf of its candidates.[73]

Although the Federal Election Campaign Act of 1971, amended in 1974, has restricted financial contributions to federal candidates, the AFL-CIO, COPE, and state and local bodies can still amass amazing support to help their candidates for office, especially when the candidate is clearly the choice of organized labor. Organized labor and corporations have become major players in the funding of political campaigns at the federal level, primarily through Political Action Committees.

While organized labor has played a major role in U.S. politics, it remains independent of a national political party. Over the years it has been more closely aligned with the Democratic party, both philosophically and politically. It has become perhaps the single most important political force that has supported government programs to help the socially and economically disadvantaged. It has supported consumer and environmental protection and safety and health legislation that has benefited all employees, union and nonunion alike.

Organized labor has accumulated much power and influence through its own established network and has also been instrumental in organizing other politically

Exhibit 4.10 Union Privilege Benefit Program

1. Life insurance: rates 25 percent lower than comparable plans, no medical exam required, guaranteed coverage for senior citizens (more than $1 billion in policies already issued).
2. Prescription drug coverage: pays 30 percent on prescriptions, toll-free hotline for questions, all family members eligible.
3. Travel services: 5 percent cash back on travel expenditures, short-notice vacation hotline, free travel insurance, guaranteed highest airline, hotel, and car rental discounts.
4. Legal services: free consultation by phone or in person for up to 30 minutes, free follow-up services, 30 percent discount on complex matters, over 650 participating offices of attorneys.
5. MasterCard program: no annual fee, lower rates, no check fees (over $150 million in interest and fees saved by participants by 1989).

SOURCE: *AFL-CIO News,* August 19, 1989.

active groups with socially oriented objectives, such as minorities and senior citizens. However, organized labor's overall political strength and effectiveness should not be exaggerated. In some states and municipalities, union membership is so negligible that its influence is inconsequential. In others, where union membership is high, its influence is significant, and political candidates must actively solicit its support.[74] The AFL-CIO does not control the membership's votes; however, members are an independent lot, and they have other reasons for voting for candidates.

Union Corruption and the Landrum-Griffin Act

Like some business executives, a few union officials have encountered problems with law enforcement officials. Unethical and illegal practices, including corruption, racketeering, and embezzlement, have been discovered in some local and national unions. Union abuses of power were exposed by the McClellan hearings of the late 1950s. Large amounts from Teamsters pension funds had been misused. Union officials have been indicted for conspiracy to bribe a U.S. senator and for embezzlement. Indictments have been rendered where "ghost workers" were maintained on payrolls even though no services were performed. While union corruption cannot be condoned, its magnitude is diminished by the savings and loan scandal in the United States in the late 1980s and early 1990s, in which 331 persons were convicted to serve an average sentence of $3^1/_2$ years and estimated cleanup costs were $500 billion, for an average cost of about $2,000 for each U.S. citizen.[75]

In 1989, the Teamsters and the federal government settled charges that the union was under the influence of organized crime. The settlement occurred just before the scheduled opening of a trial for alleged violations under the Racketeer Influenced and Corrupt Organizations Act (RICO). The settlement barred persons allegedly involved in organized crime from participating in union activity and provided for three persons, jointly selected by the parties and acting separately from one another, to temporarily oversee union activities and supervise secret-ballot elections of union officers.[76]

While the Teamsters in 1995 represented one of the most democratic international unions because of the federal government's intervention, several recent incidents of union problems with the law have occurred:

- $52 million fine against the Mine Workers during a 10-month strike against Pittston Coal Co. in 1989 for refusing to comply with court injunction (in 1994, the U.S. Supreme Court unanimously vacated the fine because it was imposed without a jury).
- USX Corporation executives and two United Steelworkers officials were convicted of illegally entering into a kickback scheme (giving pensions to otherwise ineligible union officials who were former employees of USX) to secure union concessions for reopening of an Alabama steel mill.

- Two unions, the Carpenters and Paperworkers, were fined $110,000 for interfering with a $600,000 contract between a contractor and a pulp and paper plant after the unions held a meeting with the plant officials and threatened to set picket lines. In addition, the contractor was awarded $20 million in punitive damages.

An accurate assessment of union corruption is reflected by the following conclusion:

> Union corruption stories are front-page news. They create images that tend to linger and are reinforced each time new allegations are raised. Certainly, Jimmy Hoffa's lasting notoriety is evidence of this phenomenon.
>
> In fact, the level of corruption among unions and union leaders is negligible. The Labor-Management Reporting and Disclosure Act . . . insures this. Very few institutions in American society are as closely regulated or as open to scrutiny as are American unions. . . . The evidence is clear that all but a minute fraction of American union leaders are honest and dedicated in the performance of their duties. Supporting this conclusion is an investigation by a former Attorney General that found serious problems of corruption in less than one-half of 1 percent of all local unions.[77]

The AFL-CIO established the **Ethical Practices Committee** in its efforts to control corrupt practices and racketeering of its member unions, and its Executive Council was given the authority to suspend any affiliated union with corrupt practices. Then, in 1959, the U.S. Congress showed its concern with union abuse and the potential misuse of union power by amending the National Labor Relations Act through passage of the **Landrum-Griffin Act** (the **Labor-Management Reporting and Disclosure Act**), which has several provisions governing union operations and government. For example, it governs the following:

- Disclosure by union officers and employees (and employers and their agents) about financial dealings, trusteeships, and any private arrangements made with any employees.
- Regulation of union trusteeships, including rules for their establishment and maintenance, and the protection of the rights of members of unions under trusteeship.
- Fiduciary responsibilities of union officers and representatives. It also disqualifies criminals and former communists from holding union offices, and it requires certain union officers to be bonded to assure the faithful discharge of their duties and responsibilities.
- Rights to participate in union elections and governance, such as the right to nominate candidates in elections, to vote in elections, to attend membership meetings, to participate in the deliberations, and to vote on the business, such as setting dues and assessments.

The law was intended to promote union democracy and financial integrity. Success in the administration of the law requires initiative on the part of union members and availability of necessary information to union members.

In 1984, the Comprehensive Crime Control Act, containing the Labor Racketeering Amendments, was passed. These amendments, backed by the AFL-CIO, closed the loopholes in the existing laws against labor malfeasance. Convicted labor officials cannot hold any union position for up to 13 years; previous law allowed for elongated appeals during which the officials might remain in office. Any convicted management official must be transferred outside the labor relations function and cannot serve as a consultant or advisor in labor relations.

Current Status of Labor Unions

Labor unions' status can be assessed from both statistical and general or philosophical standpoints. Unions have shown a steady decline in membership as a proportion of the total labor force since 1945, when union membership was about 36 percent of the labor force. Exhibit 4.11 shows that union density declined to 14.9 percent of the labor force in 1994. With an estimated work-force growth of about one million per year, unions will have to gain over 150,000 new members each year just to maintain about 15 percent.[78]

This reduction has three general explanations: structural changes in the labor force, organizational practices, and companies' use of current laws governing the workplace. Of these three explanations, research suggests that changes in the structure of the labor force is the most important.[79]

Employment has shifted from traditionally unionized industries (manufacturing, railroads, mining) to high-technology industries (computers, scientific instruments) that are difficult to organize. A shift has also occurred in the occupational mix toward more professional, technical, and service (white-collar) employees, who are also traditionally difficult to organize. Employment has also been growing faster in small businesses than in larger ones. Data show that 80 percent of new jobs have been created in firms with 100 or fewer employees, where fewer than 9 percent of the employees are members of unions.[80] There has also been a demographic shift of those who are employed. Many new entrants are female, better educated, and younger, employees who have traditionally been more difficult to organize.

The growth in part-time employment helps explain some of this decline. Since 1957, part-time employment has increased from 12.1 percent of the total labor force to 19 percent in 1995. Because union membership among part-time employees is only 7.5 percent, this lowers the overall union density percentage of the total labor force.[81] Many part-time employees are members of the so-called contingent work force, the fastest growing part of the labor force. The contingent work force includes not only part-time employees, but freelancers, subcontractors, independent professionals, and the self-employed. As U.S. companies attempt to become "leaner" and more efficient, a few analysts have predicted that as much as half the work force will be contingent employees by the year 2000. If these predictions are correct, unions will have difficulty maintaining their current 14.9 percent of the labor force.[82]

Exhibit 4.11 Union Membership Trends, 1960–1995

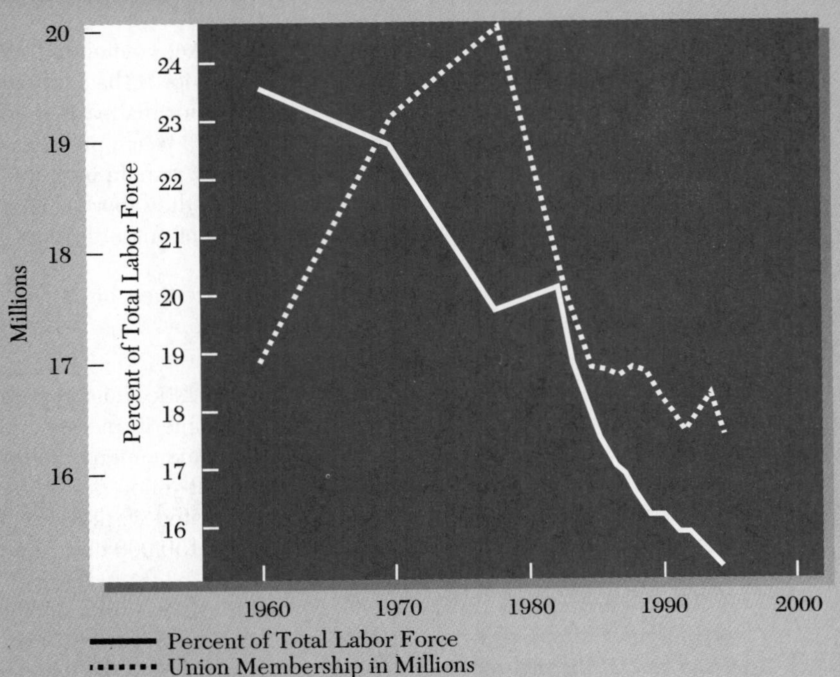

	Union Membership	Total Labor Force Number	Total Labor Force Percentage
1960	17,049,000	72,142,000	23.6%
1970	19,381,000	85,903,000	22.6
1978	20,238,000	102,537,000	19.7
1983	17,717,000	88,290,000	20.1
1984	17,340,000	92,194,000	18.8
1985	16,996,000	94,521,000	18.0
1986	16,975,000	96,903,000	17.5
1987	16,913,000	96,303,000	17.0
1988	17,002,000	101,407,000	16.8
1989	16,960,000	103,480,000	16.4
1990	16,740,000	103,905,000	16.1
1991	16,568,000	102,786,000	16.1
1992	16,390,000	103,688,000	15.8
1993	16,598,000	105,067,000	15.8
1994	16,748,000	107,989,000	15.5
1995	16,360,000	110,038,000	14.9

SOURCE: Updated from "Union Membership in 1995" (Washington, D.C.: Bureau of Labor Statistics, U.S. Department of Labor, updated annually). For more detailed data for earnings and union membership differences on a statewide and industrywide basis, see Barry T. Hirsch and David A. Macpherson, *Union Membership and Earnings: Data Book 1993* (Washington, D.C.: Bureau of National Affairs, Inc., 1994).

In addition, union membership declines during economic recessions through layoffs and permanent job loss. Individual unions may suffer more dramatically. For example, the United Steelworkers lost more than half its membership due to plant closings and cuts in the work force in the last 12 years. The Amalgamated Clothing and Textile Workers Union has lost 125,000 members, 45 percent of its total membership, since 1980. During this time the proportion of foreign-made apparel grew to about 60 percent of the total apparel consumption, and foreign-made shoes increased from 50 to 84 percent.[83]

More organizations are learning how to operate their businesses on a nonunion basis. Sometimes this entails moving some or all operations to less unionized sections of the United States (the west and south). Managers are also adopting human resource management practices, including antiunion campaigns (see Chapter 5), to keep their firms nonunion. They have become more sophisticated in understanding the reasons employees organize unions and more aggressive in presenting their firms' viewpoints to the employees.

Some union officials indicate that employers often use labor law loopholes to forestall or negate free employee union choices through secret-ballot elections. For example, pre-election time delays, contested elections, lengthy appeals, and stalled labor agreement negotiations are possible under the National Labor Relations Act (see Chapter 3).

Legal alterations that have expanded employees' legal rights through the Americans with Disabilities Act, Equal Employment Opportunity Act, Occupational Safety and Health Act, Employee Retirement and Income Security Act, and other legislation have helped make union organizing more difficult. These legal rights give employees a "free ride" in areas for which the union once was the primary protector and provider, and the increasing costs of these programs to employers have caused them to stiffen their resistance to unions, to be more cost conscious, and to increase their managerial sophistication in personnel practices.

Some would suggest that union membership decline or stagnation reflects a broader insight into organized labor's social significance. A related question is, "Have unions become obsolete?" David Lipsky, Dean of Cornell University's School of Industrial and Labor Relations, suggests that organized labor's "corpse is still moving," as no other American institution can claim such a membership following today.[84] Lane Kirkland contends labor organizations' success cannot be measured solely in membership statistics since unions are not economic institutions competing for market shares. This argument is strengthened when we realize that many parts of the labor force (managers, self-employed people, and the unemployed, for example) do not join unions.

Indeed, many unions appear to be committing more of their resources to serving the needs of their current members rather than to organizing new members. As unions mature and have organized a major portion of the workers within their jurisdictions, their expenditures, time, and efforts focus on representation services, such as negotiating contracts, research on wages and benefits, preparation for arbitration, processing grievances, and so on. In fact, organizing new employees may not be in the interests of the present union membership if these efforts would siphon funds earmarked for present members' services. Because unions are political organizations and the leaders are elected by the current membership, the incentive to organize new members is frequently less than the incentive to provide services to current members.[85]

Unions' social significance can also be assessed in general terms by considering what the consequences would be if unions were absent from our society. Some would argue that unions' previous bargaining gains, coupled with current legislation aimed at protecting employees' welfare, make unions obsolete. Others have suggested that unions must remain to ensure that employers do not reduce previously negotiated working conditions. This belief likens organized labor to the military in peacetime—a strong, countervailing power needed to preserve the existing situation.[86] In other words, unions are necessary to maintain some balance between employer and employee rights and responsibilities.

Summary

This chapter discussed two of the major participants in the labor relations process: unions and management. First, the goals of unions and management were presented, with emphasis on where the goals are the same and where they have potential for conflict. Companies' labor relations strategies, ranging from union suppression to labor-management cooperation, were explained.

Union strategic plans, which are at the embryonic stage in most unions, were discussed, and examples from the AFL-CIO were presented. Companies and unions are structured according to their goals; typical examples of company labor relations organizations and organizations at various levels of unions were displayed.

The last part of the chapter focused on union governance. First, general characteristics of craft and industrial unions were explained. Then, the government and organizational activities of the local union, the national or international union, the intermediate bodies, and the federation (the AFL-CIO) were discussed. Because unions, like businesses and government, have experienced corruption and misuse of power and authority, examples of these problems and of steps that have been taken to seek a resolution were provided.

The current status of labor unions can be assessed from both statistical and general standpoints. A nearly 30-year drop in the proportion of unionized employees has occurred in the United States. However, this change and related general explanations (employment shifts, organizational practices, and legal alterations) do not indicate that unions have lost their societal significance.

Key Terms

craft unions
industrial unions
business agent
shop steward
constitution
convention
master labor agreement
amalgamation
absorption
conference boards
joint councils
associate membership program
Ethical Practices Committee
Landrum-Griffin Act (Labor-Management Reporting and Disclosure Act)

Discussion Questions

1. Compare the steps companies may take to implement a positive human resources management program with principles of effective management.
2. What suggestions can you offer to emphasize common goals of companies and unions as opposed to conflicting goals?
3. Analyze the dilemma of nonunion companies in terms of employee termination under the employment-at-will doctrine.
4. Assess the strategic plans of the AFL-CIO and determine whether these plans provide direction for growth.
5. Locate a local union and/or a local plant and draw an organizational chart for each.
6. Select a craft union and an industrial union and point out differing characteristics of these two types of unions.
7. Compare the government of the local union with student governments and municipal governments, with special attention to participation by members.
8. Explain why and how national unions' presidents have been able to accumulate so much authority and power.
9. Differentiate among the business agent of a local union, a shop steward, and an international union representative. How do their roles differ?
10. Since the AFL-CIO does not negotiate labor agreements on behalf of national unions, how can it claim to be the "spokesperson for organized labor" in the United States?
11. Compare the requirements for union democracy to any student organization with which you are familiar.

References

1. Audey Freedman, "How the 1980's Have Changed Industrial Relations," *Monthly Labor Review* 111 (May 1988), pp. 35–39.
2. Martin M. Perline and David J. Poynter, "Union Orientation and Perception of Managerial Prerogatives," *Labor Law Journal* 40 (December 1989), p. 781.
3. Stephen R. Sleigh, Michael Kapsa, and Charis Hall, *The Costs of Aggression* (Washington, D.C.: Industrial Union Department (AFL-CIO), 1992), pp. 2–3.
4. Alan Balfour, "The Unenforceability of the UAW's 'Neutrality Pledge' from General Motors," paper presented at the Second Annual Meeting of the Southern Industrial Relations Association, 1981.
5. Charles R. Greer and Stanely A. Martin, "Calculative Strategy Decisions during Organization Campaigns," *Sloan Management Review* 19 (Winter 1978), p. 73.
6. Ibid.
7. William N. Cooke and David G. Meyer, "Structural and Market Predictors of Corporate Labor Relations Strategies," *Industrial and Labor Relations Review* 43 (January 1990), pp. 280–282.
8. Keith Knass and Michael Matuszak, "An Antiunion Corporate Culture and Quality Improvement Programs," *Labor Studies Journal* 19 (Fall 1994), pp. 21–39.
9. Douglas M. McCabe and David Lewin, "Employee Voice: A Human Resource Management Perspective," *California*

Management Review 34 (Spring 1992), pp. 112–114.
10. Fred K. Foulkes, "How Top Nonunion Companies Manage Employees," *Harvard Business Review* 59 (September–October 1981), pp. 121–125.
11. Herbert R. Northrup, "Construction Doublebreasted Operations and Pre-Hire Agreements: Assessing the Issues," *Journal of Labor Research* 10 (Spring 1989), pp. 219–227.
12. *Twenty-First Annual Report of the NLRB* (Washington, D.C.: U.S. Government Printing Office, 1956), pp. 14–15.
13. Herbert L. Sherman and William P. Murphy, *Unionization and Collective Bargaining* (Washington, D.C.: Bureau of National Affairs, 1975), p. 47.
14. *NLRB* v. *Cabot Carbon Co.,* 360 U.S. 203 (1959). The union challenged a General Foods job-enrichment program that divided employees into work groups for the purpose of working job assignments, scheduling overtime, and discussing job-related concerns with a consultant (with management representatives in attendance on occasion). While the NLRB ruled that no union existed, it could raise interesting issues in the future. *General Foods Corporation and American Federation of Grain Millers, AFL-CIO and Its Local* 70, 231 NLRB 122 (1977). Also see Donna Sockell, "The Legality of Employee-Participation Programs in Unionized Firms," *Industrial and Labor Relations Review* 37 (July 1984), pp. 541–556.
15. Audrey Freedman, *The New Look in Wage Policy and Employer Relations* (New York: The Conference Board, Inc., 1985), pp. 16–18.
16. Arthur Eliot Berkeley and E. Patrick McDermott, "The Second Golden Age of Employment Arbitration, *Labor Law Journal* 43 (December 1992), pp. 774–777.
17. Richard B. Peterson and Douglas M. McCabe, "The Nonunion Grievance System in High Performing Firms," *Proceedings of the 1994 Spring Meeting, Industrial Relations Research Association,* Paula B. Voos, ed. (Madison, Wis.: Industrial Relations Research Association, 1994), p. 529.
18. Douglas M. McCabe, "Corporate Nonunion Grievance Arbitration Systems: A Procedural Analysis," *Labor Law Journal* 40 (July 1989), pp. 432–438.
19. John E. Butler, Gerald Ferris, and Nancy K. Napier, *Strategy and Human Resources Management* (Cincinnati, Ohio: South-Western Publishing Co., 1991), pp. 147–158.
20. William N. Cooke and David G. Meyer, "Structural and Market Predictors," pp. 280–282.
21. Butler, Ferris, Napier, pp. 147–158.
22. Francis A. O'Connell, Jr. "The Changing Character of Industrial Relations: Comment," *Journal of Labor Research* 12 (Fall 1991), p. 323.
23. Robert T. Thompson, "The Changing Character of Employee Relations," *Journal of Labor Research* 12 (Fall 1991), pp. 316–317.
24. Edward E. Lawler, III and Susan A. Mohrman, "Unions and the New Management," *The Academy of Management Executive* 1 (no. 3, 1987), pp. 293–300.
25. William N. Cooke and David G. Meyer, "Structural and Market Predictors," pp. 292–294.
26. John T. Dunlop, *The Management of Labor Unions* (Lexington, Mass.: Lexington Books, 1989), pp. xii–7.
27. Christine L. Scheck and George W. Bohlander, "The Planning Practices of Labor Organizations: A National Study," *Labor Studies Journal* 15 (Winter 1990), pp. 69–84.
28. Tracy Fitzpatrick and Weezy Waldsteing, "Challenges to Strategic Planning in International Unions," *Proceedings of the 46th Annual Meeting of the Industrial Relations Research Association,* Paula B. Voos, ed. (Madison, Wis.: IRRA, 1994), pp. 73–84.
29. Susan J. Schurman and Hal Stack, "From Strategic Planning to Organizational Change in Local Unions," *Proceedings of the 46th Annual Meeting of the In-*

dustrial Relations Research Association, Paula B. Voos, ed. (Madison, Wis.: IRRA, 1994), pp. 85–94.

30. Katherine Van Wezel Stone, "Labor and the Corporate Structure: Challenging Conceptions and Emerging Possibilities." *The University of Chicago Law Review* 55 (Winter 1988), pp. 76–78.

31. John T. Dunlop, "Have the 1980's Changed U.S. Industrial Relations?" *Monthly Labor Review* 111 (May 1988), p. 33.

32. Audrey Freedman, *Managing Labor Relations* (New York: The Conference Board, Inc., 1979), pp. 7–33.

33. Bert Spector, "Transformational Leadership: The New Challenge for U.S. Unions," *Human Resource Management* 26 (Spring 1987), pp. 3–11.

34. Alice H. Cook, *Union Democracy: Practice and Ideal* (Ithaca, N.Y.: Cornell University, 1963), pp. 19–26.

35. James E. Martin, John Christopher, and John M. Magenau, "A Longitudinal Examination of Union Steward Behaviors and Behavioral Intentions," *Proceedings of the 46th Annual Meeting of the Industrial Relations Research Association,* Paula B. Voos, ed. (Madison, Wis.: IRRA, 1994), pp. 422–431; Paul F. Clark, Daniel G. Gallagher, and Thomas J. Pavlak, "Member Commitment in an American Union: The Role of the Grievance Procedure," *Industrial Relations Journal* 21 (1990), pp. 147–157.

36. Allan Nash, *The Union Steward: Duties, Rights, and Status* (Ithaca, N.Y.: New York State School of Industrial and Labor Relations, 1977), pp. 20–22.

37. Victor G. Devinatz, "From Industrial Unionism to General Unionism: A Historical Transformation?" *Labor Law Journal* 44 (April 1993), pp. 252–256.

38. Steven L. McShane, "A Path Analysis of Participation in Union Administration," *Industrial Relations* 25 (Winter 1986), pp. 72–78.

39. John C. Anderson, "Local Union Participation: A Reexamination," *Industrial Relations* 18 (Winter 1979), p. 30.

40. John Lund, "Using Surveys to Learn More about Membership Attitudes," *Labor Studies Forum* 4 (no. 4, 1991), pp. 1–4.

41. James E. Martin and John M. Magenau, "An Analysis of Factors Related to the Accuracy of Steward Predictions of Membership Views," *Labor Law Journal* 35 (August 1985), pp. 490–494.

42. Leonard R. Sayles and George Strauss, *The Local Union,* rev. ed. (New York: Harcourt, Brace & World, 1967), pp. 96–100.

43. Ibid, pp. 93–105.

44. Jack Barbash, *American Unions* (New York: Random House, 1967), p. 69.

45. Ibid, pp. 71–72.

46. The Landrum-Griffin Act requires a convention at least every five years, and some unions, such as the Teamsters, take the limit of five years.

47. George Strauss, "Union Government in the U.S.: Research Past and Future," *Industrial Relations* 16 (Winter 1977), p. 234.

48. Barbash, *American Unions,* pp. 76–80.

49. Marick F. Masters, Robert S. Atkin, and Gary W. Florkowski, "An Analysis of Union Reporting Requirements Under Title II of the Landrum-Griffin Act," *Labor Law Journal* 40 (November 1989), pp. 713–722.

50. George Strauss, "Union Democracy," in *The State of Unions,* eds. George Strauss, Daniel G. Gallagher, and Jack Fiorito (Madison, Wis.: Industrial Relations Research Association, 1992), pp. 203–205.

51. Ibid., p. 201.

52. Shulamit Kahn, Kevin Long, and Donna Kadev, "National Union Leader Performance and Turnover in Building Trades," *Industrial Relations* 25 (Fall 1986), pp. 276–289.

53. Lawrence French, David A. Gray, and Robert W. Brobst, *Political Structure and Presidential Tenure in International Unions: A Study of Union Democracy,* paper presented at the annual meeting of the Academy of Management, Detroit, 1980, p. 16.

54. Phillip L. Quaglieri, "The New People of Power: The Backgrounds and Careers of Top Labor Leaders," *Journal of Labor Research* 9 (Summer 1988), pp. 271–283.
55. Paul F. Clark and Lois S. Gray, "Union Administration," in *The State of Unions,* eds. George Strauss, Daniel G. Gallagher, and Jack Fiorito (Madison, Wis.: Industrial Relations Research Association, 1992), pp. 179–193.
56. Charles W. Hickman, "Labor Organizations, Fees and Dues," *Monthly Labor Review* 100 (May 1977), pp. 19–24.
57. Ibid., pp. 117–118. Examples include recreation, social and entertainment activities, organization and recruitment of new members, convention attendance, general news publications, support of pending legislation, and contributions to charity.
58. James T. Bennett, "Private Sector Unions: The Myth of Decline," *Journal of Labor Research* 12 (Winter 1991), pp. 1–5.
59. Lisa Williamson, "Union Mergers: 1985–94 Update," *Monthly Labor Review* 118 (February 1995), pp. 18–24.
60. Gary N. Chaison, "Union Mergers and Integration of Union Governing Structures," *Journal of Labor Research* 3 (Spring 1982), p. 139.
61. Charles J. Janus, "Union Mergers in the 1970s: A Look at the Reasons and Results," *Monthly Labor Review* 101 (October 1978), pp. 13–15.
62. "Officers of Small Unions Found Receptive to Concept of Merger," *Daily Labor Report,* February 13, 1986, pp. A-8–A-9. Also see Gary N. Chaison, "Union Merger Outcomes: The View from the Smaller Unions," unpublished paper, Clark University, pp. 1–26.
63. James W. Robinson, "Structural Characteristics of the Independent Union in America Revisited," *Labor Law Journal* 43 (September 1992), pp. 567–575.
64. Sanford M. Jacoby and Anil Verma, "Enterprise Unions in the United States," *Industrial Relations* 31 (Winter 1992), p. 140.
65. Dana Milbank, "Labor Broadens Its Appeal by Setting Up Associations to Lobby and Offer Services," *The Wall Street Journal,* January 13, 1993, pp. B-1, B-5.
66. *This is the AFL-CIO* (Washington, D.C.: American Federation of Labor and Congress of Industrial Organizations, 1992), pp. 1–10.
67. Cathy Trost, "To the Union Chiefs, It's Still a Brotherhood," *The Wall Street Journal,* November 20, 1985, p. 30.
68. U.S. Department of Labor, Bureau of Labor Statistics, *Directory of National Unions and Employee Associations, 1975* (Washington, D.C.: U.S. Government Printing Office, 1977), pp. 1–4.
69. Joseph Krislov, "The AFL-CIO Effort to Minimize Union Membership Conflicts: 1962–1987," *Labor Studies Journal* 16 (Summer 1991), pp. 3–5.
70. *This is the AFL-CIO,* pp. 8–10.
71. "Solidarity, New Initiatives by Unions Mark Labor Day 1989, Kirkland Says," *Daily Labor Report,* September 1, 1989, p. A-9.
72. "New AFL-CIO Mortgage Plan to Feature Low Down Payments," *Daily Labor Report,* June 19, 1991, pp. A-1–A-2.
73. *This is the AFL-CIO,* pp. 10–12.
74. David Greenstone, *Labor in American Politics* (Chicago: University of Chicago Press, 1977), pp. xiii–xxix.
75. "The S&L Felons," *Fortune,* November 5, 1990, p. 90.
76. George Ruben: "Developments in Industrial Relations," *Monthly Labor Review* 112 (May 1989), p. 58.
77. Paul F. Clark, "Union Image-Building at the Local Level," *Labor Studies Journal* 15 (Fall 1990), p. 55.
78. Charles McDonald, "U.S. Union Membership in Future Decades: A Trade Unionist's Perspective," *Industrial Relations* 31 (Winter 1992), p. 22.
79. C. Timothy Koeller, "Union Activity and the Decline in American Trade Union Membership," *Journal of Labor Research* 15 (Winter 1994), pp. 19–31.

80. *The State of Small Business* (Washington, D.C.: U.S. Government Printing Office, 1984), pp. xv, 9.
81. Arleen Hernandez, "The Impact of Part-time Employment on Union Density," *Journal of Labor Research* 16 (Fall 1995), pp. 485–491.
82. Jaclyn Fierman, "The Contingency Work Force," *Fortune,* January 24, 1994, pp. 30–36.
83. "Union Leaders Tie Recent Losses in Membership to Weak Economy," *Daily Labor Report,* August 13, 1992, p. A-9.
84. David B. Lipsky, "About the 'L' in ILR," *ILR Report* 26 (Spring 1989), p. 3.
85. Joseph B. Rose and Gary N. Chiason, "New Measures of Union Organizing Effectiveness," *Industrial Relations* 29 (Fall 1990), pp. 457–468.
86. Kenneth A. Kovach, "Do We Still Need Labor Unions?" *Personnel Journal* 58 (December 1979), p. 850.

5 WHY AND HOW UNIONS ARE ORGANIZED

This chapter focuses on the essential elements of unionization: why unions are formed, the procedures for organizing employees into unions, new union strategies for obtaining union recognition, and union decertification.

The chapter highlights employees' choices (1) whether to become involved in union formation where there is no union and (2) whether to vote for or against union representation if and when there is a representation election. Although an employee's choices to assist in the formation of a union, to vote for a union, and to join a union are highly interrelated, they are separate decisions. Employees may join unions voluntarily or be required to join. The circumstances in which an employee may be required to join a union are covered in Chapter 11. Employees who vote for union representation in an election in which the union loses are nevertheless left without union representation.

WHY UNIONS ARE FORMED

Unions are not present in every organization; in many instances, employees have chosen to remain nonunion. This section provides explanations of employees' collective behavior that cut across many organizations; the following section attempts to explain what propels employees at a particular facility to vote for a union.

Work and Job Conditions Explanation

Alienation Theory The **alienation theory** is based on the belief that employees might seek collective action to relieve their feelings of alienation, which have resulted from the extensive use of machinery in manufacturing operations. Employees became alienated from their work because[1]

- They lost contact with their own labor when the products they created were taken away from them, thereby reducing their spirit and status.

- They lost involvement in their work when the machine dominated, separating the work of the hand from the work of the brain.
- They became estranged from fellow employees when their work made them so tired and competitive that they were incapable of having authentic relationships.

As a result, employees might become aware of their common plight, and class consciousness could compel them to join together in a union or to engage in collective activities to improve their working situation. Unions can and do address a possible aspect of employee alienation, namely the employees' desire to speak their minds without fear of management reprisal. In other words, "intertwined with the motives for union membership is the almost universal desire to tell the boss to 'go to hell.'"[2] A union typically indicates to its potential members that the employees' rights to voice their opinions regarding a managerial action are protected by negotiated grievance procedures and disciplinary policies (see Chapters 8 and 10).

Employees might be dissatisfied with some aspect of their jobs while not being alienated from their work. Some research has shown that employees might join unions if they (1) are dissatisfied with physical characteristics of the workplace, low wages, or lack of benefits and (2) believe that a union will help them achieve the job-related conditions important to them.[3]

Scarcity Consciousness Theory—The Need for Job Security In his classic book, *A Theory of the Labor Movement,* Selig Perlman suggested that employees are attracted to unions on the assumption that unions will protect their jobs. Many employees, particularly manual workers, strongly believe they are living in a country of limited opportunity and become **scarcity conscious**—the employees collectively believe that jobs are difficult to obtain and retain. This belief is particularly true today for some industries, such as auto, steel, and coal. Thus, employees turn to unions for job protection.[4]

Unions therefore are attractive to the many employees concerned about job security, regardless of their skill or occupational level. Few employees, including white-collar employees and managers, are currently immune from the possibility of a layoff. And unions do offer several ways of strengthening employees' job security: They can negotiate work rules, which prescribe procedures for performing a job, thereby ensuring that a certain number of employees will be assigned work. They can negotiate apprenticeship programs, which ensure that qualified people are available for certain skilled jobs. They can negotiate seniority and layoff provisions, which require the company to lay off employees by their seniority and to recall the most senior ones first. They can negotiate grievance procedures, which include a final step of arbitration to protect them against unjust discharges, unfair treatment, and violations of the labor agreement. They can lobby for legislation protecting employees' job rights, in regard to such issues as plant closings and employment discrimination, which has been a viable alternative used by unions throughout the years. Here, unions attempt to strengthen job security by pressing for restrictions against cheap labor—foreign citizens, child labor, prison labor—quotas or restrictions against imported products such as steel, automobiles, and textiles, and adjustment assistance to employees who are displaced as a result of foreign competition.

Employees' Backgrounds and Needs

Employees' previous experiences with unions can strongly affect their attitudes toward unions and their decision to join one. Eighty-seven percent of those who have had experience with unions, usually as members, said they would vote for a union if given a choice; only 27 percent of those who have had no experience with unions would vote for the union if given the choice.[5]

Many might even be influenced by parental attitudes and family experiences regarding unions. One active union member stated, "I attended union meetings with my father before I was ever inside a church." Another commented, "My dad was a great union man and that's where I got it—if it wasn't union, it wasn't no good."[6] Of course, parental comments regarding unions may be unfavorable as well.

Unions, like all formal organizations, potentially satisfy the members' needs by providing a means of enhancing a sense of identity and maintaining self-esteem. Thus, unions can appeal to three interrelated social needs of members: the need for affiliation, or belonging; the need for status; and the need to belong to something purposeful, useful, and creative that is on a higher level than improved wages and working conditions.

The union's possible benefit of social affiliation is strengthened or weakened by the degree of prestige or self-esteem it offers its members. Some employees join a union for the same reason they would join any social organization, namely, to enjoy the responsibility and status associated with being a member of that organization. This feature can be particularly attractive to employees whose jobs are basically interchangeable and carry very few elements of prestige or room for advancement.

Employees who become union officers can often attain prestige or self-esteem in their dealings with management officials:

> As a shop steward or union officer or member of the grievance committee, a worker can become "a fellow your buddies look to." Such positions give him the opportunity to win other workers' approval by being "a fellow who stands up to the boss" with impunity. The role of "a fellow who stands up to the boss" is made more significant because the definition of the boss has been enlarged to include not merely the foreman but "the head office in Pittsburgh." He can win prestige as "a guy that gets results" in such matters as the distribution of work, assignment to jobs, seniority policy, and protection from discrimination.[7]

Chapter 8 discusses the notion that union officers and management officials are equals in their day-to-day administration of the labor agreement. However, as the preceding quotation suggests, the union steward can often emphatically disagree with a management official six levels above the steward on the organizational chart. This ability to challenge without fear of reprisal is not usually afforded nonunion employees or even management officials when they deal with their organizational superiors.

Studies of employee characteristics associated with employee votes have been mixed. Some have shown that employees' characteristics such as age, gender, and education are not closely associated with favorable union votes or attitudes.[8] Race appears to be the one exception—several studies have suggested that more black employees have positive attitudes toward potential union advantages than their white counterparts.[9] Other studies indicate that young people are more likely to support unions, and women are less likely to support unions.[10]

Procedures for Organizing Unions

In forming and joining a union, employees mainly consider whether the union will improve their personal situations in terms of wages and benefits, promotional opportunities, and job security. Can the employees expect to satisfy their job-related goals and needs by supporting a union? Will the union provide the means for achieving these goals? If employees perceive that a union will help them attain their goals, they will likely vote for it in an election and support its activities afterwards. If they are not convinced, they will not vote for the union and will not support its activities.

The union's campaign to secure employee support may contribute to a union vote, especially among those who are familiar with the union's positions and who attend union campaign meetings. Employees who are satisfied with working conditions are less likely to attend union campaign meetings, but if they attend, they often become more favorable toward the union.

The company's campaign can affect the vote because it affects employees' belief in the anticipated influence of the union. If the company campaigns hard, some employees will believe that the employer has "seen the light" and will now improve conditions without the union. A strong antiunion campaign may convince some employees that the employer is so antiunion that the union cannot improve working conditions.[11]

While there may be many reasons why a particular group of employees votes for or against the union in a specific election, several influences have been identified that affect union votes generally. Exhibit 5.1 shows the relationships among the general influences on employees.

Researchers have argued that social pressure influences employee votes. When employees know a number of union supporters within a work group, this knowledge helps to form a group cohesion. When this group of employees is regularly blocked by employer actions, they respond as a group and their actions can lead to union formation. As union supporters, they are better able to convince others that the union has the power to bring about changes in the workplace and are more convincing in influencing other employees' votes.

Employees who are not satisfied with their pay, supervision, and/or work may view the union as the instrument to satisfy their job needs. Some researchers have argued that job dissatisfaction is the beginning of employees' efforts to start a union formation campaign. They argue that job dissatisfaction sets in motion a search to

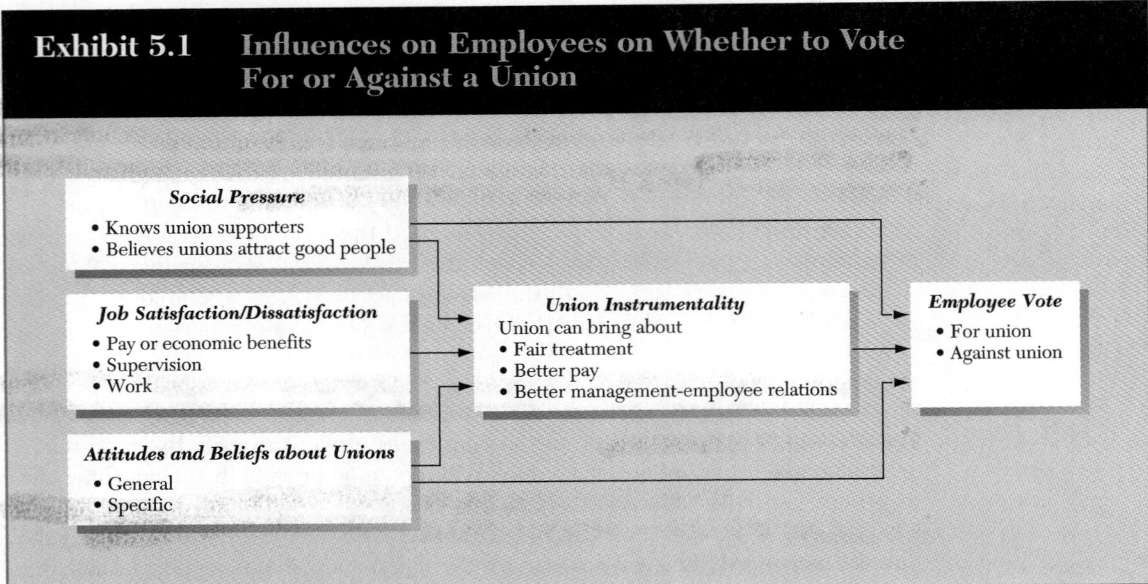

end the uncomfortable dissonance between what is desired (good pay, effective supervision, and so on) and what they are experiencing. Job dissatisfaction results in the formation of a coalition of employees designed to bring about changes in economic and working conditions.[12]

General beliefs about unions means that an employee believes, for example, that a union will improve wages, benefits, and working conditions, provide a return to the employee for the dues paid, and secure pro-employee legislation. These general beliefs include whether an employee believes unions are autocratic, increase the risks of a plant closing, stifle individual initiatives, or ignore the members in strike decisions. To influence employees' general beliefs about unions, union organizers should place more effort on national campaigns, such as the "Union Yes" campaign of the AFL-CIO.

Specific beliefs about unions are more related to an individual's job and workplace. To influence employees' specific beliefs about unions, union organizers should focus attention on communicating the union's unique characteristics and its impact at the workplace. Specific beliefs that can be focused on include[13] expectations about improvement in pay, benefits, and job security as a result of unionization. Other beliefs include expected improvement in recognition, job advancement, worker participation, treatment by supervisors, and reduction in sexual and racial discrimination on the job.

In an organizing campaign, unions need to show employees that significant positive results will occur at their workplace if they vote and join a union. Unions must promote the union's ability not only to improve wages and benefits, but to help make work more meaningful and increase employee participation. At the same time, the employer will attempt to show that it has acted reasonably toward employees and has been fair and sincere in dealings with employees.[14]

Social pressure, job dissatisfaction, and general and specific beliefs about unions interact with **union instrumentality**, which is the employees' perception of whether the union will be instrumental in attaining desired outcomes, such as higher wages, improved working conditions, job security, and protection from arbitrary treatment by management.[15] In general if these interactions are positive, the employee will vote for the union; if not, the employee will vote against it.[16] For the individual employee, any one of the influences may cause the employee to vote a certain way. For example, if an employee believes his or her supervisor is considerate and supportive, this belief may be enough to cause a vote against union representation.[17]

An individual's decision on whether to vote for union representation depends on his or her subjective assessment of the benefits to be obtained as weighed against the subjective assessment of the cost. If the expected benefits are higher than the cost, the employee will vote for the union. Otherwise, the vote will be against representation. If employees have a good chance of promotion, can expect a higher wage based on their present level of effort, and are pleased with their supervisor, they probably will not vote for representation.

The Union's Challenge of Organizing the Diverse Work Force

Unions recognize that some occupations, such as retail sales, registered nursing, janitorial services, and food services, are expected to expand in the 1990s. In addition, one-fourth of all workers in the United States are part-time employees; these employees are hired on a temporary basis (called by many "contingent workers"), are independent contractors, and are hired as subcontractors or leased workers. As noted earlier, minorities and skilled employees will also become a larger percentage of the work force. In fact, it is estimated that by the year 2000, one-fourth of the work force will be minorities and that the greatest increases will come from the Hispanic and Asian populations. Unions must design organizing strategies to attract these employees.[18]

Organizing campaigns may be structured around "women's issues," personal empowerment, and social justice in cases where the targeted work force is mostly female.[19] The potential of and considerations affecting minorities and female employees is discussed in more detail in Chapter 11.

Organizing Professional Employees

Professional employees provide a challenge to unions and an opportunity to increase union membership. While unions have made significant inroads in many professions, such as acting, professional sports, writing, music, nursing, and teaching, debate continues over the compatibility of unionism with professionalism. There are excellent arguments on both sides of the continuum, and the unions must successfully address these concerns before they will increase the memberships of professional employee unions. On one side is the argument that the selection of a union entails the rejection of key professional values, such as collegial participation in organizational decision making, professional independence, and a merit-based performance and reward system. On the other side is the argument that collective bargaining is often the most effective method of achieving and maintaining these same professional values.

Evidence drawn from a study of collective bargaining agreements covering professional employees reveals that the overwhelming majority of contract provisions include subjects quite similar to those traditionally in industrial sector agreements. These provisions include wages, fringe benefits, grievance-arbitration procedures, and so on. In addition to those traditional subjects, these agreements also address professional issues. These issues can be categorized into six groups: (1) professional standards, (2) mechanisms for professional participation in policy making, (3) regulation of professional work, (4) training and professional development, (5) commitment of organizational resources to professional goals, and (6) criteria for personnel decisions and the role of professionals in making these decisions. The conclusion was that, while there is variation in the collective bargaining agreements among professional employee unions, unionism and professionalism are not inherently incompatible. Moreover, professional values and interests can be incorporated into the bargaining process along with the economic and job security issues of professional employees. With concrete evidence of compatibility between professionalism and unionism, the opportunity is present for unions to promote their product and services.[20]

Role of the Union in Organizing Employees

Employees' initial interest in unionization is usually based on their present dissatisfaction with some work-related situation coupled with a belief that each of them acting alone cannot change his/her current situation. The union does not create this dissatisfaction with working conditions among employees; instead, it is in the union's interest to improve job satisfaction among employees by negotiating to improve working conditions. Therefore, during an organizing campaign, the union advertises the benefits that would flow from a negotiated collective bargaining agreement and successful handling of grievances.[21]

Most managers of nonunion companies incorrectly believe that labor unions initiate union organization drives; instead it is usually the employees themselves who begin the process by contacting the union. This contact with union organizers usually occurs after the employees believe that there is sufficient support for the union and that the union's expertise and representation will help them.[22]

Union organizers enter the campaign by playing three general roles that influence employees' decisions on whether to vote for unionization. First, organizers try to educate the workers on the benefits of the union, labor movement traditions, and protections afforded by union representation and the present laws. Next, union organizers attempt to persuade workers to vote for unionization and respond to statements and allegations made by management during the organizing campaign. Third, organizers try to support workers in their individual and collective actions.[23] In order to ensure that these roles are carried out capably, unions recruit and select union organizers with the appropriate education, competencies, and personality characteristics.

Unions, especially those in the service industries, are hiring union organizers who have different characteristics from the traditional union organizers in manufacturing. They are almost 15 years younger on average, ten times more likely to be female, average almost four more years of education, and have an average of about seven fewer years of union organizing experience. They are six times less likely to have held elected positions in local unions and are less than half as likely to have served in appointed positions in local or national unions. While nearly all of the union organizers in manufacturing were rank-and-file members early in their careers, only about half of the union organizers in the service industries were rank-and-file members.[24]

Union organizers must recognize that the work force has changed sharply and has become more complex. Employees do not typically have a homogeneous set of problems; they are widely diverse. As well, the growth industry sectors and occupations are different from those which have been traditional strongholds for unions, such as manufacturing, mining, trucking, shipping, railroads, and construction. As a result, the selection of staff members to work as union organizers has changed. Instead of appointing staff members as political rewards, unions are selecting union organizers not only from the rank-and-file members, but also from colleges, law schools, VISTA, and other sources. Unions are then investing funds in training union organizers at the AFL-CIO's George Meany Center and improving their organizing capability through training at the newly created Organizing Institute.[25]

The union organizer does not create job dissatisfaction but rather assists in transforming this employee dissatisfaction into collective action. The union organizer tailors the organizing approach to employee concerns and problems and focuses on the special needs of various groups, such as older workers, female or minority workers, or white-collar workers. The organizer tries to sell the idea that group action via the union provides the instrument through which employee concerns and dissatisfaction can be most effectively addressed.[26]

The influence of union organizers should never be underestimated by a company. The union organizers may be first seen distributing handbills to employees as they leave the company parking lots. They dress like the employees so that the employees will identify with them. While their dress may be misleading, management should realize that union organizers are professionals at what they do. Like their counterparts in management, contemporary union organizers must understand the psychology of the workplace and the labor relations climate in which employees work. The union organizers must be able to (1) sort out these complex factors for the employees on a group or individual basis and (2) communicate in the employees' language how the union can assist in fulfilling their needs in the specific work environment.

As an example, Exhibit 5.2 lists a number of work-related concerns and problems. To the right of each is a possible course of action the union could take to satisfy the concern to alleviate the problem. The union organizer would bring to the employees' attention outcomes that could result from such activities by the union on their behalf.

The union enters the organizing campaign knowing that it must convince the uncommitted employees that the union is composed not of outsiders but of concerned fellow employees, that the changes the union proposes are worth fighting for, that the union will be able to protect employees against reprisals, and that union officials can be trusted. The union realizes that its success depends on the development of a strong inside organizing committee to convey the message directly to employees who do not attend union meetings and the ability of the union organizer to convey his or her own personal commitment and concern, get to know the employees, listen to employees about their job concerns, and have employees themselves speak at public meetings to express their feelings and their commitment to the cause.

Exhibit 5.2 Union Strategy and Courses of Action to Achieve Employee Goals and Resolve Job-Related Concerns

EXAMPLES OF WORK-RELATED PROBLEMS AND EMPLOYEE CONCERNS	ACTIONS BY UNIONS TO ENCOURAGE EMPLOYEES TO JOIN UNION
Relations between employees and management are poor.	Union will represent the interests of employees to management.
Employees do not trust their employer's promises.	Union will negotiate a contract requiring management to abide by its agreements.
Employees prefer to deal with management as a group.	Union provides an opportunity for individual employees to deal as a group with the employer.
Employees want to have more influence in workplace decisions.	Union provides a mechanism for influence by collective bargaining and administering the agreement.
Employees feel that productivity improvement would be more effective if employees had more say in how programs are run.	Union provides a mechanism in which employees can provide input into those issues that affect the workplace.
Employees question the effectiveness of the company's system for resolving employee problems and grievances.	Unions typically negotiate a grievance procedure that provides for representation of employees at each step and for hearings before an outside, neutral arbitrator.

SOURCE: Richard B. Freeman and Joel Rogers, *Worker Representation and Participation Survey*, Princeton, N.J.: Princeton Survey Research Associates, 1994.

Unions have used many different organizing tactics to convince employees to vote for the union. Exhibit 5.3 shows union tactics that have been used where the union has won 50 percent or more of elections and where the union has lost a majority of elections. Successful tactics include house calls, small group meetings with employees, active and representative committees of employees, home visits, demonstrations of solidarity, and campaigns focused on work-related concerns. Less successful tactics include distribution of leaflets at the plant gate, mass mailings, phone calls, rallies, picketing, and corporate campaigns.[27]

Role of the Company in Union Organizing

The employer realizes that the keys to its success are whether it is able to sustain and increase employees' concern about how the union would perform if chosen and whether it can convince employees that the employer's past record shows that it deserves their support or at least a second chance. The employer enters the campaign with three advantages: (1) it has instant and prolonged access to the employees; (2) although it can make no promises during the election campaign, it informs employees of the possibility of improvement without cost and without the creation of a new bureaucracy; and (3) it can take advantage of the fact that most people find the thought of substantial change in their lives frightening.[28]

Exhibit 5.3 Effect of Union Tactics on Election Outcomes

UNION TACTIC	EFFECT ON ELECTION OUTCOME
House calls	Positive
Small group meetings	Positive
Active and representative committees of employees	Positive
Union organizer visits employees' homes before election	Positive
Rank-and-file members from other organized units make house calls	Positive
Demonstration of solidarity by wearing union buttons or T-shirts	Positive
Campaign focused on dignity in the workplace, fighting job discrimination, and product or service quality	Positive
Gate leafletting	Negative
Mass mailings	Negative
Phone calls	Negative
Rallies, picketing, and corporate pressure tactics	Negative

Positive effect: union wins 50 percent or more of elections.
Negative effect: union loses 50 percent or more of elections.

SOURCE: "Union Tactics Found Key Factor in Winning Organizing Elections" (Study by Kate Bronfenbrenner), *Daily Labor Report,* December 3, 1991, pp. A-7–A-10.

Employer campaign tactics attempt to avert an employee vote in favor of unionization. Usually more than one campaign activity must be used. The most frequently used employer tactics are hiring a labor lawyer, spreading rumors about loss of jobs, and spreading rumors about store or plant closings. In terms of making a difference in the outcome of the election, employees are more likely not to choose the union when the employer spreads rumors about a store or plant closing. However, employees are more likely to choose the union when the employer intentionally delays the election and when the unions work closely with community leaders to facilitate community acceptance of the union. Two employer tactics that have backfired and are associated with employees' vote for the union are shifting work and jobs to other facilities and testing applicants in order to identify union sympathizers.[29]

Exhibit 5.4 also lists certain employer practices and their effect on the election. For example, the employer has much influence on changing the election unit composition and the date of the election but only modest influence on the outcome of the election through such activities as publicizing the disadvantages of the union, displaying posters, and making campaign speeches. Companies must be cautious in election campaigns because they may overdo their resistance and cause a negative reaction from employees, especially when both attorneys and management consultants are used.[30] Thus, if employers overreact to a union's campaign with suppressive tactics, such overreaction may create a more favorable climate for unionization.[31]

The use of consultants in organizational campaigns has increased dramatically. One study reported that most elections studied were directed by consultants. In these campaigns, employer unfair labor practices were committed in over half of the elections, and companies actively resisted the union by making captive audience speeches and writing letters to employees in nearly all of the cases.[32] Use of consultants to advise employers how to persuade employees not to vote for a union requires reports to be filed with the Secretary of Labor, even though the consultants have no direct contact with employees.[33]

Attorneys who specialize in union-avoidance campaigns are frequently employed either to offer advice on questions of labor law or to devise strategy and conduct the union-avoidance campaign. Additionally, attorneys may offer legal advice, plan the week-to-week campaign strategy, interview supervisors to identify sources of employee discontent and ameliorate the discontent that led to the organizing campaign, raise the perceived costs of union representation by such tactics as publicizing major layoffs and closings at unionized plants, train supervisors in how to effectively present the employer's position to the employees, prepare and edit campaign literature and speeches for company officials, and build support and sympathy for the employer in the local community. An inexpensive campaign in a small to medium-sized firm with one attorney could cost up to $30,000 in legal fees. An "all-out" campaign with several attorneys using all of the latest campaign tools, such as slick videotapes, visits by prominent politicians and civil rights leaders, and so on, could easily exceed $100,000. The cost of a campaign in a large, multi-plant firm involving a dozen attorneys could exceed $1 million. These costs are incurred at the rate of $150 to $250 per hour for attorneys from specialized labor-law firms ($300 or more for "big name" attorneys).[34]

Illegal discharge and other forms of discrimination against union activists, used by employers to affect the outcome of the election, have increased dramatically in the past several years. Such discrimination reduces the probability of an organizing success by 17 percent and nearly cuts in half the likelihood of the first contracts being obtained. Nearly all these illegal activities occur during an organizing drive, just prior to an election, or during the first contract negotiations. Such violations generally occur when employers perceive the financial gains of keeping unions out are far greater than the cost of back-pay awards and reinstatement of union advocates. And such is often the case. One study reported that less than half of illegally discharged workers were offered reinstatement, and only 69 percent of those ever returned to work. Because it takes so long to settle a case, and reinstatement comes so long after the organizing drive, some employers have been able to frustrate the

Exhibit 5.4 Election Campaign Practices and Activities Used by Employer to Affect the Outcome of an Election

EMPLOYER PRACTICES	EFFECT ON ELECTION OUTCOME
Changing election unit composition	Fairly strong
Changing election date	Fairly strong
Publicizing disadvantages of unions (other than strikes)	Modest
Displaying posters on bulletin boards	Modest
Employing outside consultants	Some
Restricting employee solicitation	Some
Sending personal letters	Some
Holding small group meetings	Some
Giving handbills to employees	Some
Sending messages in payroll envelopes	Some
Showing movies	Some
Publicizing negative image of unions	Some
Publicizing employer good points	Some
Warning of results of potential strikes	Some

Fairly strong = Correlation with election outcome, .55 to .68.
Modest = Correlation with election outcome, .35 to .39.
Some = Correlation with election outcome, .23 to .30.
All correlations were statistically significant.

SOURCE: Kent F. Murrmann and Andrew A. Porter, "Employer Campaign Tactics and NLRB Outcomes: Some Preliminary Evidence," *Proceedings of the Thirty-fifth Annual Meeting, Industrial Relations Research Association*, ed. Barbara D. Dennis (Madison, Wis.: Industrial Relations Research Association, 1983). p. 67.

legal process and use it against the union and employees interested in the union.[35]

Some companies use as their guide the book *Winning Union Campaigns,* by Robert Pearlman, a former staff attorney with the NLRB. In the book, management is advised that the "consequences of illegal labor practices must be kept in perspective," and they must be "subordinated to the prime objective, which is remaining union free." Management is advised that the best bet is to "campaign aggressively" and avoid "playing the union's game" by allowing "fear of the NLRB to stifle communications." Pearlman advises that in the event the company loses the election after an aggressive campaign, the bargaining order won't be issued until two to four years after the election. By that time, employees will be too intimidated to support the union and the union not in a position to take employees out on strike if negotiations reach an impasse.[36]

How do employers reconcile their personal ethics when either they or their representatives knowingly commit illegal practices by discharging an employee or a group of employees for exercising their legal right to support a union? Moreover, why does the U.S. Congress continue to tolerate such an imbalance in the legal procedures governing the exercise of statutory rights that have existed in the United States since 1935?

Methods for Organizing Unions

There are three basic ways for organizing unions: (1) voluntary recognition, (2) NLRB directives, and (3) secret-ballot elections (see Exhibit 5.5).

By far the simplest and least confrontational path to union recognition is voluntary recognition. The most publicized example of voluntary recognition is General Motors' recognition of the United Auto Workers at its Spring Hill, Tennessee, Saturn plant (see Chapter 7). An innovative approach to voluntary union recognition occurred when the city of Minneapolis and the developer of Minneapolis Hilton and Towers entered into a lease agreement that provided for the union's right of access to employees during nonworking time, voluntary card checks, predefined bargaining unit, and employer neutrality during union organizing drives. In 31 days, Local 17 of the Hotel and Restaurant Employees International Union and Local 638 of the Teamsters had signed 80 percent of the employees, and both locals were certified as the representatives of different groups of Hilton employees. Thus, both the union and the company saved an enormous amount of time by avoiding a union campaign which could have taken several months (some campaigns take years in cases where legal appeals are fully used).[37]

In rare and very controversial cases, the NLRB may direct the employer to recognize and bargain with the union. While the NLRB considers secret-ballot elections superior, it has discretionary authority to use alternative means to determine the majority interests of employees. In the landmark *Gissel* case, the NLRB decided (and the Supreme Court agreed) that a company may be ordered to recognize and bargain with a union under the following conditions:

Exhibit 5.5 Basic Union Representation Procedure

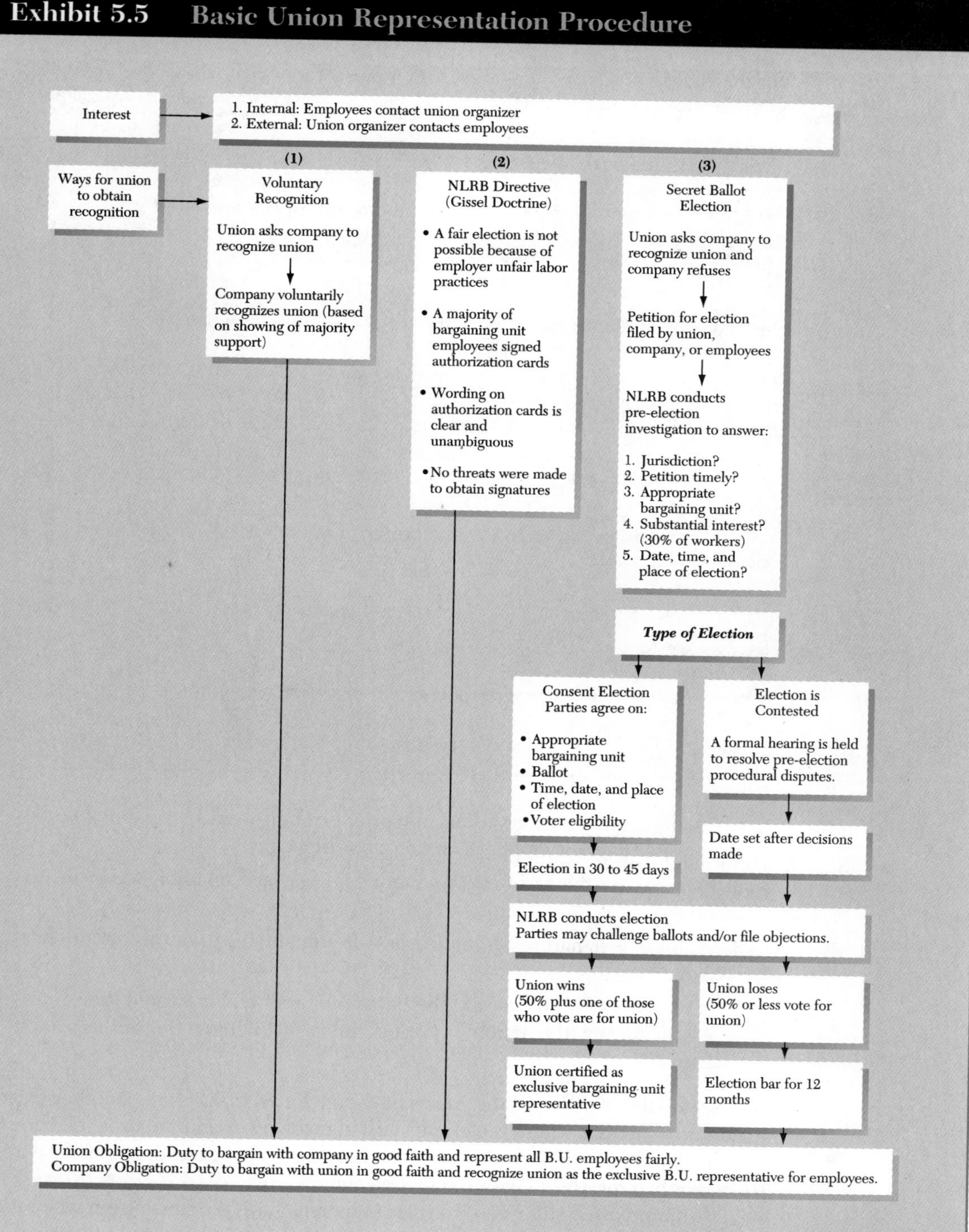

Interest
1. Internal: Employees contact union organizer
2. External: Union organizer contacts employees
Ways for union to obtain recognition
(1)
Voluntary Recognition
Union asks company to recognize union
Company voluntarily recognizes union (based on showing of majority support)
(2)
NLRB Directive (Gissel Doctrine)
• A fair election is not possible because of employer unfair labor practices
• A majority of bargaining unit employees signed authorization cards
• Wording on authorization cards is clear and unambiguous
• No threats were made to obtain signatures
(3)
Secret Ballot Election
Union asks company to recognize union and company refuses
Petition for election filed by union, company, or employees
NLRB conducts pre-election investigation to answer:
1. Jurisdiction?
2. Petition timely?
3. Appropriate bargaining unit?
4. Substantial interest? (30% of workers)
5. Date, time, and place of election?
Type of Election
Consent Election Parties agree on:
• Appropriate bargaining unit
• Ballot
• Time, date, and place of election
• Voter eligibility
Election is Contested
A formal hearing is held to resolve pre-election procedural disputes.
Election in 30 to 45 days
Date set after decisions made
NLRB conducts election
Parties may challenge ballots and/or file objections.
Union wins (50% plus one of those who vote are for union)
Union loses (50% or less vote for union)
Union certified as exclusive bargaining unit representative
Election bar for 12 months
Union Obligation: Duty to bargain with company in good faith and represent all B.U. employees fairly.
Company Obligation: Duty to bargain with union in good faith and recognize union as the exclusive B.U. representative for employees.

Exhibit 5.6 Example of a Union Authorization Card

United Food & Commercial Workers International Union
Affiliated with AFL-CIO-CLC
AUTHORIZATION FOR REPRESENTATION

I hereby authorize the United Food & Commercial Workers International Union, AFL-CIO-CLC, or its chartered Local Union(s) to represent me for the purpose of collective bargaining.

__________ (Print Name) __________ (Date)

__________ (Signature) __________ (Home Phone)

__________ (Home Address) (City) (State) (Zip)

__________ (Employer's Name) __________ (Address)

__________ (Hire Date) __________ (Type Work Performed) __________ (Department)

__________ (Hourly Rate) __________ (Day Off) Day Shift _____ Night Shift _____ Full Time _____ Part Time _____

Would you participate in an organizing committee? Yes ________ No ________

SOURCE: Courtesy of the United Food and Commercial Workers International Union.

1. Evidence reveals that a fair, impartial election would be impossible because of flagrant employer unfair labor practices.
2. Wording on the authorization cards[38] is clear and unambiguous (see Exhibit 5.6).
3. Employee signatures on the cards were obtained without threat or coercion.
4. A majority of employees in the bargaining unit had indicated their interest in having the union represent them by signing the authorization cards.[39]

In essence, the NLRB and the courts have concluded that holding another election in certain situations where the employer had made a fair and impartial election impossible would not be a realistic remedy because a rerun election would favor the party that had interfered with the first election.

Most employers still refuse to voluntarily recognize the union even when union organizers present signed authorization cards (Exhibit 5.6) from a majority of employees or 30 percent of the employees (a figure considered a sufficient showing of interest by the NLRB). Management might be concerned that these cards were obtained through inappropriate means (such as after drinking parties, under threats of violence, or through forgeries, for example). They also realize that authorization cards are not very accurate predictors of union success in representation elections. In a study conducted in northern Ohio, researchers found that unions won only 11.1 percent of elections when only the minimum number of employees (30 percent) signed authorization cards. However, in campaigns where between 80 and 89 percent of eligible employees signed cards, the union won 71.4 percent of the elections.[40]

Initiation of Campaigns for Organizing Unions

The union pre-election campaign is not simply a process of exchanging letters and handbills and then holding an election. The campaign usually goes through several stages:[41]

1. Contacting employees as a result of either employee requests for help or distribution of union literature (handbilling) at the workplace by the union.
2. Determining interest by calling meetings, visiting homes, and counting responses to handbills. (See "Labor Relations in Action" for an array of responses received by union organizers who were seeking support from employees.)
3. Setting up an organizing committee by identifying leaders and educating them about the benefits and procedures of the union, the law, and the issues likely to be raised by management.
4. Building interest by soliciting signatures on authorization cards (see Exhibit 5.6). (Most organizers will wait to announce that the union represents a majority until over 50 percent, and usually 60 to 80 percent, have signed cards.)

During this time the union discovers and highlights employees' problems, compares wages at their facility to wages at unionized facilities, and explains the role of the union in helping to satisfy their job-related needs. In other words, the union will attempt to convince the workers that they need a union and then that they should sign union authorization cards and should support the forthcoming organizing campaign by wearing union buttons, attending meetings, and signing up members. While various means are available to gain support, research indicates that one-to-one contact, peer contact and persuasion, and high-quality, professionally designed written communications are most effective.[42] Other efforts used by unions include television and radio advertising, "hotline" telephone numbers, group meetings, and handbilling.

Organizing new locals is costly. Evidence shows that the cost of each additional union member is about $600.[43] These costs include direct, out-of-pocket expenditures for such items as the printing and mailing of leaflets and other literature, rent for office space, salaries for staff hired, and legal fees. These efforts take time from the union staff that could be devoted to providing services to present union members (handling grievances, arbitration, and negotiation).

LABOR RELATIONS IN ACTION

Objections to Joining the Union

"Why should I join the union when I get exactly the same wages and benefits without joining?"

"I can't afford to join. I've got a family to support, and my check just isn't big enough [to cover union dues]."

"I don't believe in unions. They are too strong and powerful now to suit me."

"I don't need a union. My employer is fair and will take care of me. What could the union get for me that I wouldn't have gotten anyway?"

"My husband (or other relative) doesn't like unions."

"The union does not do anything for you [grievances are not settled satisfactorily]. I don't like the people who are running things in the union."

"I can handle my own affairs. I can take care of myself. I'll make my own decisions. I do not intend to stay on this job forever; I'm looking for a promotion."

"My religion doesn't permit me to belong to any outside organizations."

"My boss doesn't believe in unions. I've seen what happens to union members."

"I don't want anything to do with unions. They are all corrupt."

"I don't know enough about the local or the union movement."

"I'm not interested. I just don't want to join."

"I'll think about it. Maybe I'll join someday."

SOURCE: Organizing Committee, AFSCME Council 24, WSEU, 5 Odana Court, Madison, Wisconsin.

The costs of organizing new members must be compared to the returns:

- Extra compensation made possible by increased bargaining power.
- Additional dues and fees paid by new members.
- Enhanced political influence.
- Social benefits and satisfaction derived from extending membership to others.[44]

Companies often learn of union organizing attempts from supervisors or rank-and-file employees and through observing handbilling at the work site before they receive official notification (by letter or telegram) from the union demanding recognition. Some companies react vigorously, while others do little to acknowledge any union's attempt to organize the employees. Some employers tell their employees about their opposition and urge them not to sign union authorization cards. Because the cards may specifically state that the signee favors union representation, any employee signature assists the union in establishing itself in the company. See "Labor Relations in Action" for typical employer messages during a union campaign.

LABOR RELATIONS IN ACTION

Examples of Employer Messages during a Representation Election Campaign

- Tell employees that union contracts often contain wage cuts or give-backs.
- Mention that the union does not provide jobs and give examples of companies that have laid off employees who were union members.
- Explain that if the workers choose the union, the employer will be obligated to bargain with the union in good faith, but that the employer cannot be forced to agree to contract provisions that are not in its best interests.
- Tell employees that a company must remain competitive and has a right to make a profit. If its labor costs are so high that it cannot sell its product at a profit, it cannot remain in business.
- Advise employees that they can revoke the authorization card and explain the procedure to do so.
- Indicate that the union dues vary, but that typically dues are $50 per month or $600 per year.
- Tell employees that the employer has the legal right to hire permanent replacements for strikers.

SOURCE: Paul S. McDonough, "Maintain a Union-Free Status" *Personnel Journal* 69 (April 1990), pp. 108–114.

Filing a Petition for the Election Prior to 1935, in order to obtain recognition the union usually had to show its strength and employee interest in representation by such actions as strikes. The Wagner Act and the NLRB changed this situation by developing procedures and guidelines for peacefully determining the majority interest of employees through elections or some other comparable demonstration. The procedure is initiated when the potential bargaining representative for the employees files a petition for an election.

The NLRB is authorized to conduct an election only when a valid petition has been filed by an employee, group of employees, an individual or labor organization, or an employer. Usually the petition is filed by the union after it has requested union recognition from the employer and the request is denied. The petition must be supported by evidence (usually authorization cards) that a substantial interest in union representation (30 percent of the anticipated bargaining unit) exists. Further, it must show that the employer has declined a request by the union to be recognized as the exclusive bargaining agent. An employer cannot petition for an election until the union seeks recognition. If the employer could, it would petition at the time when the union's support was weakest. After receiving a petition, the NLRB will first determine whether it has jurisdiction and the petition is valid. If so, it will promptly notify the company and request a listing of employees. Companies are not required to submit this list but usually comply with the request as an act of good faith. Next, the NLRB will arrange a conference with the company and union to discuss the possibility of a consent election. Here, if both sides agree to the appropriate bargaining unit, voter eligibility, ballot, date, time, and place for the election, a consent election will be held. If either party refuses to agree on any of these items, a formal hearing to settle these matters will be conducted.

Election Investigation and Hearing If the union and management officials cannot agree to a consent election, the NLRB will investigate the petition, hold a hearing, and then direct an election if it finds that there is substantial interest in union representation. This investigation will secure answers to the following questions:

1. What is the anticipated appropriate bargaining unit?
2. Does substantial interest in representation (30 percent) exist among employees in the unit?
3. Are there any barriers to an election in the form of existing unions, prior elections, or present labor agreements?

Appropriate Bargaining Unit An appropriate bargaining unit is a grouping of jobs or positions in which two or more employees share common employment interests and conditions (community of interests) and which may reasonably be grouped together for collective bargaining purposes. Determination of an appropriate bargaining unit is left to the discretion of the NLRB, which decides in each representation case how employee rights can best be protected under the act. The board's decision has, however, been limited by law in several ways. The statute includes the following:

- Professional employees cannot be included in a unit composed of both professional and nonprofessional employees unless a majority of the professional employees vote to be included in a mixed unit.
- A proposed craft unit cannot be ruled inappropriate simply because a different unit has been previously approved by the NLRB unless a majority of employees in the proposed craft union vote against being represented separately.
- Plant guards cannot be included in any bargaining unit that has nonguard employees in the unit because of the potential conflict of interest, such as searching a fellow union member's locker for stolen property.
- Supervisors and managers are not considered employees covered under the act and may not be in any bargaining unit.
- Excluded are agricultural laborers, public employees (except postal employees), and independent contractors, although some of these may be covered in separate state statutes.
- Confidential employees and family members are excluded.

Thus, the NLRB's determination of the appropriate bargaining unit influences whether the union will win the election, who will vote in the election, whether one union will prevail in an interunion contest, whether craft employees will have their own union or be included in a plantwide unit, who the union must represent, who will be covered by the collective bargaining agreement, or whether the union will include key employees who could give direction and leadership for the bargaining unit employees.

Analysis of NLRB representation elections indicates that the success of a union campaign depends on the composition of the appropriate bargaining unit. When the appropriate bargaining unit is composed of similarly skilled groups, the union will likely succeed. This may be so because decisions within unions are made through a democratic process, and a degree of consensus is necessary to facilitate decision making and to win the support of the majority. However, when different skill groups comprise the bargaining unit, achieving consensus is more difficult, and majority support for the union likewise is harder to achieve and maintain. Thus, the NLRB's policy of including in a bargaining unit all "production and maintenance" employees within a plant (which would include a diversity of skills) may have contributed to the decline in union membership as a percentage of the total labor force. A more narrowly defined bargaining unit composed only of employees of similar skills (such as electricians) would favor the union winning the representation election and sustaining the continuation of the union.[45]

If the union wins, the appropriate bargaining unit may determine who will be required to join the union. Therefore, the composition of the bargaining unit is important to the employer, the union, and the public.

Some companies pay attention to these considerations and take preventive steps regarding management structure, employee interactions, and personnel policies and practices. For example, if the company prefers a large multi-unit bargaining unit, it will retain centralized control on management practices and decisions. If it prefers smaller, independent units, it will decentralize decision making in these independent units. Since the union has no control over management structure and the authority-responsibility relationship, it can try to convince the NLRB that the bargaining unit should be composed only of those employees who are supporting the union.[46]

Should a plant have several small bargaining units, the employer may face different unions in negotiating several times throughout the year, which could cause continuous instability in labor relations. Separate units concerned with similar jobs may cause disputes over rights to jobs, leading to strikes or slowdowns. Should a small bargaining unit be merged with a nationwide bargaining unit, any confrontation that resulted in a strike could cause a nationwide shutdown and complications for customers in need of the companies' products. Chapter 6 will cover the various bargaining structures and their implications.

The bargaining unit itself may cover employees in one plant or in two or more facilities of the same employer. The NLRB considers the "community of interests" in determining the composition of an appropriate bargaining unit. It evaluates the following factors:

- Interests of employees and employers.
- Commonality of wages, working conditions, training, and skill.
- History of collective bargaining either at the location in question or another facility owned by the company.
- Transfers of employees among various facilities.
- Geography and physical proximity of the workplaces.
- Employer's administrative or territorial divisions.
- Degree of separation (or distinctiveness) of work or integration (or interrelatedness) of work.[47]

Where the relevant factors do not give a clear indication for the composition of an appropriate bargaining unit, an election (commonly called a Globe election, from the original NLRB case) may be held to determine employee interests. For example, one group of electricians in a steel plant might wish to be represented by the International Brotherhood of Electrical Workers (IBEW) instead of the United Steelworkers of America (USA). The USA wants to include all electricians in a bargaining unit composed of all production and maintenance employees in the plant. Under such circumstances, the electricians' vote will determine whether they will be members of USA, a separate electricians' union (IBEW), or no union.

In 1989, the NLRB engaged in its first rule-making effort to determine appropriate bargaining units for private acute-care hospitals. Eight standard bargaining units were established for approximately 4,000 acute-care hospitals: (1) all registered nurses, (2) all physicians, (3) all professionals except registered nurses and physicians, (4) all technical employees, (5) all skilled maintenance employees, (6) all business office clericals, (7) all guards, and (8) all other nonprofessional employees. Such rule-making practices reduce the number of cases in which employers are able to contest the number and composition of the appropriate bargaining unit. Employers intentionally use this tactic to delay the election and thereby increase the chances that the union will not win representational rights.[48]

Eligibility of Voters Before an election is conducted, voter eligibility must be determined. The general rule is that employees on the payroll before the date of the election are eligible. An employee must be employed in the unit on the date of the election. However, employees who are on sick leave, vacation, temporary layoff, or temporary leave, such as military duty, may vote in the election. In addition, the NLRB will occasionally consider irregularity of employment, such as in the construction, food processing, and longshoring industries. Economic strikers who have been replaced by permanent employees are allowed to vote in any election within 12 months after the strike begins. This policy ensures that management does not provoke a strike and hire replacements who could vote out the union. Employees hired after the union files its petition but before the election may be challenged for their eligibility by the union.

Untimely Petitions Several rules make a petition for a representation election untimely. The first is a legal requirement that prohibits any NLRB representation election where one has been held in the last 12 months or where a petition for election covers a group of employees who are already covered by an existing contract and already members of a legally certified union.

The second rule and potential barrier to elections is an administrative determination that was made in the interest of stable and effective labor relations. The NLRB rule, called the **contract bar doctrine,** specifies that a valid, signed agreement for a fixed period of three years or less will bar any representation election for the life of the agreement (a longer contract is still limited to three years). Thus, the contract bar doctrine could extend the 12-month statutory limitation on elections to three years. To do otherwise would be unfair to union and management officials who have negotiated a multiyear labor agreement in good faith.

"Names and Addresses" (Excelsior Rule) Within seven days after the regional director of the NLRB has approved a consented election or after an election has been directed, the employer must file a list of names and addresses of all eligible voters with the regional director. This information is then made available to the union. Refusal to comply could be identified as a bad faith act on the part of the employer and cause the election to be set aside or the NLRB to seek the names and addresses by subpoena. The purpose of this disclosure rule is to give the unions the same access to employees that management already possesses.[49]

The Election The representation election, acclaimed as one of the great innovations of American labor law, is conducted by NLRB officials and held within 48 days (median) of the initial request. NLRB data show that 90 percent of the eligible voters in NLRB elections, as compared with about 50 percent in major political elections, choose to vote.

The high voter turnout in union representation elections might be due to the convenient voting procedure (usually carried out on company property) and the belief of many employees that their vote more directly affects their lives (at least their working conditions) than do political elections. Finally, both unions and management realize that an employee could express union preference to a union representative and an opposite preference to the management representative to avoid a confrontation during the election campaign. Neither side is sure of employee voting preferences when faced with a secret ballot; therefore, union and management officials work to get out the vote.

Voter participation tends to decline the longer it takes for the NLRB to conduct the election. Thus, some employers are motivated to refuse to consent to an election in hopes of increasing the chances of the union losing the election. Also, because most single-unit elections are close, the number of nonparticipants affects the outcome of many elections.[50] Also, a small number of votes greatly influences the outcome of the election; research shows that a switch of eight votes would have changed the outcomes of half the elections.[51] Furthermore, small increases in the time to process cases are important; a delay of ten days has proven to be a significant factor in differentiating employer wins from employer losses. The number of pre-election days has also been linked to union losses. During the first six months of delay, there is an average drop-off in union victories of 2.5 percent per month. Consent elections have the highest victory rate; however a decided downward trend has occurred in these types of elections.[52]

The size of the election unit has tended to be negatively related to union victories. The larger election unit is closely related to delay because it takes longer to process and is more likely to result in a hearing than in a voluntary settlement.[53] Recent research has also revealed that success in union organizing has been influenced positively by the size of the union and democracy within the union and negatively influenced by the union's propensity to strike and centralization of the union's decision making.[54]

A recent study of NLRB election data from 1980 to 1990 revealed that independent unions (those unions not affiliated with the AFL-CIO) have had a higher "union win" ratio than AFL-CIO affiliates. Thus, the AFL-CIO's "big labor" image may be a liability, and the AFL-CIO may need to encourage union autonomy, as did the AFL prior to the merger of the AFL and CIO in 1955, the year when union density reached 35 percent of the private work force.[55]

Using a ballot with the appropriate company and union designations (see Exhibit 5.7), a secret-ballot election is conducted under NLRB supervision, usually during working hours on payday at the employer's location. However, the NLRB has discretionary authority to conduct it by mail ballot if a regular election would not be fair and reasonable. For example, if it is physically impractical for eligible voters to cast their ballots at a centralized location for such reasons as widely scattered work, adverse weather conditions, or excessive travel required, the regional director of the NLRB may allow an election by mail.

The NLRB must determine whether the majority of the employees in an appropriate bargaining unit want to be represented by a union for collective bargaining purposes. It defines majority as the simple majority rule generally accepted in democratic elections, which means that those choosing not to vote in the election have decided to assent to the wishes of the majority who did vote. Therefore, a majority of the employees who vote (50 percent plus one of those voting) in the election must favor representation before a union will be certified by the NLRB.

If two or more choices are placed on the ballot, a runoff election may be necessary between the choices receiving the two highest numbers of votes in the initial election. If the majority votes "no union," no representation election can be held for 12 months. If a union receives the majority of the votes, the NLRB will certify it as the exclusive bargaining agent of the employees in the bargaining unit. Interestingly, where more than one union has vied for representation rights in the same election, unions have fared extremely well. Between 1977 and 1985, unions have won between 70 and 91 percent of such elections.[56] The major reason for this positive vote is that two unions would have to gain support from a sufficient number of the bargaining unit's employees to be placed on the ballot. Such support usually indicates that the employees have already decided to vote for the union; the election is conducted to determine which union will receive the majority vote.

Exhibit 5.7 Examples of Secret Ballots for Union Representation Elections

UNITED STATES OF AMERICA
National Labor Relations Board
OFFICIAL SECRET BALLOT
FOR CERTAIN EMPLOYEES OF
CONTAINER CORPORATION

Do you wish to be represented for purpose of collective bargaining by
METAL PRODUCTS MACHINERY AND RELATED
EQUIPMENT WORKERS OF AMERICA
AFL-CIO

MARK AN "X" IN THE SQUARE OF YOUR CHOICE

YES	NO
☐	☐

DO NOT SIGN THIS BALLOT. Fold and drop in ballot box.
If you spoil this ballot return it to the Board Agent for a new one.

UNITED STATES OF AMERICA
National Labor Relations Board
OFFICIAL SECRET BALLOT
FOR CERTAIN EMPLOYEES OF
CONTAINER CORPORATION

This ballot is to determine the collective bargaining representative, if any, for the unit in which you are employed.

MARK AN "X" IN THE SQUARE OF YOUR CHOICE

(Name of Union A)	NEITHER	(Name of Union B)
☐	☐	☐

DO NOT SIGN THIS BALLOT. Fold and drop in ballot box.
If you spoil this ballot return it to the Board Agent for a new one.

After the votes have been counted, either party has five days to file objections alleging misconduct or to challenge the ballots of voters whom one party believes should not have voted in the election. This part of the representation process receives considerable criticism because the delay in assessing the ballot challenges and objections concerning misconduct seem excessive.

In 1994, the NLRB conducted 3,572 representation elections involving 210,834 employees. In 1993, there were 3,586 elections involving 231,187 employees. In both years, 90 percent of the eligible voters cast ballots, far more than in a presidential election or for any other political election for that matter. The election is usually conducted on the employer's premises during working hours and involves a subject about which most employees are vitally interested—whether or not they will be represented by a union. In 1994, unions won 1,665 representation elections, or 46.6 percent, down from 1,706, or 47.6 percent, the previous year.[57]

After the Election As noted in Chapter 1, the first step of the labor relations process, the recognition of legitimate rights and responsibilities of unions and management representatives, includes more than the representation election. After unions win bargaining rights in a representation election, they attempt to negotiate a labor agreement; however, they fail to secure the first contract 25 to 30 percent of the time. Several factors increase the likelihood of reaching agreement: existence of relatively high wages already at the company, presence of other bargaining units within the company, large election victories, and active participation of international union representatives. Factors that reduce the chances of attaining the first contract include location in a southern state with right-to-work laws, the national union having to approve the local union contracts, presence of outside labor-management consultants hired by the company,[58] NLRB delays in resolving employer objections and challenges to election results, employer refusal to bargain in good faith, and discrimination against employees after the election.[59]

Delays associated with filing objections to campaign conduct have increased threefold over the last 20 years, and the median amount of delay time is now about 210 days. Then, employers fail or refuse to bargain in good faith 13 percent of the time. This unfair labor practice adds approximately 140 days. Additional delay can occur if appeals are made to the full board in Washington, D.C., or to the court of appeals or Supreme Court.

In addition to the delays, there has been a sixfold increase in the number of unfair labor practice charges for firing union supporters and an elevenfold increase in the number of back pay awards. Research has discovered that employers discharge union activists or union supporters for two main reasons: (1) to get the key union organizers out of the facility, and (2) to send a chilling message to the rest of the work force. With such trends in statistics, it does not appear that ethical considerations prevent all employers from breaking the law.

Duties of the Exclusive Bargaining Agent and Employer The exclusive bargaining representative (the union) chosen by the majority of the employees in the appropriate unit has the duty to represent equitably and fairly all employees in the unit regardless of their union membership and to bargain in good faith with the employer. The employer has a comparable obligation, that is, to bargain in good faith with the exclusive bargaining agent and to refuse to bargain with any other union seeking to represent the employees. Further, any negotiated labor agreement will cover the employees in the bargaining unit, regardless of their union membership status.

After Election Loss by Union After losing a representation election, typically the union reduces its activities because there can be only one election every 12 months. However, there are some creative ways in which the union can maintain contact with employees, particularly those who supported it during the campaign, and provide a representational service to those included in the bargaining unit. Exhibit 5.8 includes alternative activities that could increase the chances of success of any future unionization drive.

Conduct of the Representation Election Campaign

All elections are conducted according to NLRB standards, which are designed to assure that employees in the bargaining unit can indicate freely whether they want to be represented by a union for collective bargaining purposes. However, election campaigns differ substantially, and the strategies of individual unions and employers vary widely. For example, handbills similar to those in Exhibit 5.9 are frequently used in addition to speeches, informal talks, interviews, and films. Thus, the election campaign, one of the most interesting and controversial activities in labor relations, has led to a body of doctrines and rules. Due to changes in NLRB philosophy, those doctrines and rules are subject to change.

Campaign Doctrines and NLRB Policies

The **totality of conduct doctrine** guides the NLRB interpretations of unfair labor practice behavior. This doctrine essentially means that isolated incidents such as campaign speeches must be considered within the whole of the general circumstances of the campaign and with the possibility that other specific violations have occurred.

Employer statements to employees may seem harmless on the surface, but under the circumstances that exist at the time of the statements, they may carry implied threats. For example, if an employer stated that a third-party intervention could make it economically impossible for it to continue in business, it would be making an illegal statement during a union election campaign. However, if the employer made the same statement during an attempted leveraged buyout, there would be no legal violation.

In 1982, the NLRB concluded that it would no longer probe into the truth or falsity of the parties' campaign statements but would intervene in cases where a party had used forged documents that render voters unable to recognize propaganda for what it is. The board concluded that today's voters (employees) are more educated and sophisticated than their historical counterparts and can analyze materials more

Exhibit 5.8 Possible Activities for Unions After Losing a Representation Election

1. Maintain in-plant committees, designate employees as union stewards, identify them with steward buttons, and through them, maintain contact with member and nonmember employees.
2. Distribute employment-related union literature in the plant during non-working time and serve as the voice of employees on all matters of common employment-related matters of concern.
3. Union stewards can present employee grievances to management. If management refuses to meet with the union committee, employees may leave their work as a group to request a discussion of their employment-related problems directly with management. If the response is unsatisfactory, the union may engage in a work stoppage; however, striker replacement rules apply.
4. A nonmajority union can provide a shield of concerted activity for an individual employee who refuses to drive a faulty truck, reports OSHA violations, refuses to act in violation of personal ethics or morality, or sues for unpaid overtime.
5. Help employees know and enforce their individual employment rights concerning workers' compensation, third-party tort claims, wage and hour violations, and so on.
6. In-plant committees help employees know and receive their entitlements, such as medical benefits, sick leave, severance pay, pensions, unemployment compensation, disability pay, and social security.
7. Inform employees of rights under common law doctrines and exceptions to employment-at-will doctrine, including employee manuals, employment contracts, public policy exceptions, good faith exceptions, tort suits involving outrageous conduct, defamation, and invasion of privacy.
8. Reinforcing OSHA statutory procedures: (1) establish in-plant safety committees, (2) file complaints through the union, (3) serve as representative of employees to accompany compliance officer on plant "walk-around," discuss claims, and participate in conferences, (4) act as representative of employees in the proceedings before the OSHRC, (5) enforce the Hazard Communication Standard by filing complaints if employer fails to provide toxic training to employees and has not prepared a written communication program, and (6) petition for information contained on Material Safety Data Sheets.
9. Represent employees under plant closure laws, pregnancy leave acts, polygraph and privacy acts, and whistle-blowing statutes.
10. Represent employees under unjust discharge procedures modeled after labor arbitration.

SOURCE: Clyde W. Summers, "Unions Without Majorities: The Potentials of the NLRA," *Proceedings of the 43rd Meeting of the Industrial Relations Research Association* (Madison, Wis.: IRRA, 1991), pp. 154–162.

accurately. This assessment was influenced by a research study involving over 1,000 employees in 31 elections in five states. This study cast doubt on the previously held assumption that employees are unsophisticated about labor relations and are swayed easily by campaign propaganda. In fact, votes of 81 percent of the employees could have been predicted from their pre-campaign intent and their attitudes toward working conditions and unions in general. The study concluded that employees' votes appeared to be the product of attitudes that resulted from their everyday experiences in the industrial world and not from the campaign itself.[60]

Exhibit 5.9 Examples of Handbills Distributed During Representation Election Campaigns

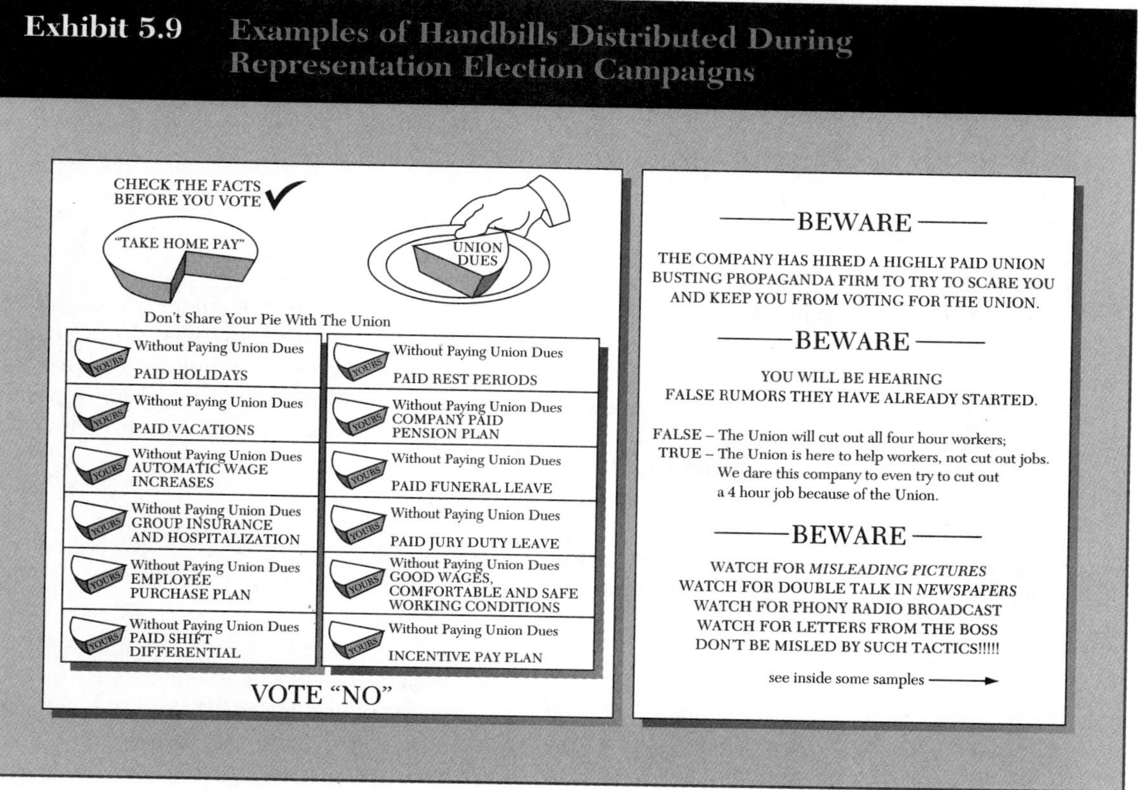

CHECK THE FACTS
BEFORE YOU VOTE
"TAKE HOME PAY"
UNION DUES
Don't Share Your Pie With The Union
YOURS Without Paying Union Dues PAID HOLIDAYS
YOURS Without Paying Union Dues PAID REST PERIODS
YOURS Without Paying Union Dues PAID VACATIONS
YOURS Without Paying Union Dues COMPANY PAID PENSION PLAN
YOURS Without Paying Union Dues AUTOMATIC WAGE INCREASES
YOURS Without Paying Union Dues PAID FUNERAL LEAVE
YOURS Without Paying Union Dues GROUP INSURANCE AND HOSPITALIZATION
YOURS Without Paying Union Dues PAID JURY DUTY LEAVE
YOURS Without Paying Union Dues EMPLOYEE PURCHASE PLAN
YOURS Without Paying Union Dues GOOD WAGES, COMFORTABLE AND SAFE WORKING CONDITIONS
YOURS Without Paying Union Dues PAID SHIFT DIFFERENTIAL
YOURS Without Paying Union Dues INCENTIVE PAY PLAN
VOTE "NO"
BEWARE
THE COMPANY HAS HIRED A HIGHLY PAID UNION BUSTING PROPAGANDA FIRM TO TRY TO SCARE YOU AND KEEP YOU FROM VOTING FOR THE UNION.
BEWARE
YOU WILL BE HEARING FALSE RUMORS THEY HAVE ALREADY STARTED.
FALSE – The Union will cut out all four hour workers;
TRUE – The Union is here to help workers, not cut out jobs. We dare this company to even try to cut out a 4 hour job because of the Union.
BEWARE
WATCH FOR MISLEADING PICTURES
WATCH FOR DOUBLE TALK IN NEWSPAPERS
WATCH FOR PHONY RADIO BROADCAST
WATCH FOR LETTERS FROM THE BOSS
DON'T BE MISLED BY SUCH TACTICS!!!!!
see inside some samples →

The data used in the study were later reanalyzed, and additional (some different) conclusions were made:[61]

- Employer predisposition favoring the union is a very important determinant of voting behavior.
- Written communications distributed later in the campaign and meetings held early in the campaign most probably have an effect.
- Threats and actions taken against union supporters are effective in discouraging support for the union.

Thus far, these later analyses have not influenced the board's position on election campaigns.

Captive Audience—24-Hour Rule

One legal approach used by employers to discourage union support includes presenting "captive audience" speeches, which are delivered to employees during working hours. The speeches, authorized by the Taft-Hartley amendments in 1947, must not be presented within 24 hours of an election, and the speech's content must not include threats of reprisal or promises of benefits. But if the union has no acceptable means of communicating with the employees, as in the lumber and logging industry, where employees live on company property, and if the employer's unfair labor practices have created a serious election campaign imbalance, the NLRB and the courts may grant the union access to plant bulletin boards, parking lots, and entrances so that it may communicate with the employees. Still, it is extremely difficult for the union to respond effectively by using its traditional means of contacting employees, such as plant employee solicitations, distribution of literature before or after work, house calls, and union meetings.[62]

Polling or Questioning Employees

Polling employees or asking questions about their interest in unions was considered unlawful interference with employee rights in early days. In 1984, the NLRB announced that it would no longer automatically consider an employer interrogation about an employee's union sentiment an unlawful inquiry in violation of section 8(a)(1). It announced that it would examine the totality of the circumstances surrounding such interrogations in light of:

1. The background of the interrogation.
2. The nature of the information sought.
3. The identity of the questioner.
4. The place and method of the interrogation.

Therefore, an employer's questioning of open and active union supporters and other employees about their union sentiments in the absence of threats or promises does not necessarily violate the law. However, NLRB decisions since 1984 reveal that employers are still at risk in these interrogations because it is necessary only to establish that the questions asked may reasonably be said to have a tendency to interfere with the free exercise of an employee's rights under the act.[63]

Distribution of Union Literature and Solicitation by Employees on Company Property

The NLRB and the courts have long held that except in special circumstances employees may not be prohibited from distributing union organizing materials or soliciting union support in nonworking areas during nonworking time[64] unless the employer can show that such activity would disrupt production, employee work, and plant discipline. For example, employees of restaurants and retail establishments cannot distribute union materials in customer areas, and employees of health-care institutions cannot distribute materials in areas designated strictly for patients.[65] However, distribution of materials by employees in such places as hospital cafeterias predominantly patronized by hospital employees cannot be prohibited.[66] In addition, the employer cannot prohibit distribution of union material if the basis for the prohibition is that part of its content includes political issues, such as right-to-work laws and minimum wages.[67] Nor can the employer prohibit employees from wearing buttons, hats, or T-shirts promoting the union.

Some employers publish *no solicitation rules* that prevent employees from discussing union organizing on working time. However, to be enforceable, these no solicitation rules must be posted in advance of the organizing drive, and these rules must prohibit all types of solicitation by employees except United Way.

The employer may limit the type of information distributed to employees by classifying company data as "confidential." The NLRB has upheld the discharge of five employees who distributed wage data comparing the company's wage scale with that of other plants in the area. The NLRB found that the company had declared this wage information to be confidential and that it had not been obtained in the normal course of employment.

For 35 years, the NLRB has traditionally weighed the union's right to access to employees in a unionizing campaign against the private property rights of an employer. In the 1992 *Lechmere* decision, the Supreme Court ruled (Justice Clarence Thomas wrote the court's opinion) that a company can ban a union organizer who is not an employee of the company from the property if the union has a reasonable alternative means of reaching individual employees with the union message, such as through newspaper advertising and home visits. The court would restrict exceptions to extraordinary situations in which the work site is isolated geographically and the union could not easily contact potential members except at the work site. Thus, the Supreme Court has made a distinction between employee and nonemployee access to individual employees during an organizing campaign and has made the union's efforts to communicate with employees more difficult as well as more costly.[68]

The *Lechmere* decision applied to a store's parking lot designated for customer and employee use, and the store had strictly enforced a "no solicitation" rule to parties. Since the *Lechmere* decision, the NLRB has been faced with the application of the Supreme Court's decision in similar situations. The NLRB has ruled that nonemployee handbillers have access rights to a neutral third party's property, specifically from the entrance of the store and not merely the entrance to the parking lot. The union was able to show that handbilling at the entrance of the parking lot was dangerous and that the use of media was cost-prohibitive.[69] Also, nonemployee union handbillers will be illegally prohibited from solicitation on company property when and if the employer has allowed church and school groups, fundraisers, Boy Scouts, Little League teams, and so on, to solicit on company property.[70]

Showing Films During Election Campaigns

Films presented to discourage workers from joining unions have taken on new dimensions, especially since the 1950s, when the movie *And Women Must Weep* was produced by the National Right-to-Work Committee. This movie portrays union violence, strikes, vandalism, phone threats, a house bombing, and even the shooting of a baby of a dissident union member. Frequent use of the film by employers prompted the International Association of Machinists to produce a rebuttal film, entitled *Anatomy of a Lie,* which claims no evidence exists of a connection between the shootings and other misconduct and the union's activities. On-site interviews with persons involved in the strike are shown to reveal an opposite view of the employer film, and the president of the union is filmed stating that nearly 99 percent of the union members voted to strike. The NLRB's position regarding the showing of these films has varied; its current position is that their showing alone does not constitute an unfair labor practice and is not sufficient cause to have the results of an election set aside.[71]

New Union Strategies

In response to employers' strategies to maintain nonunion status, unions have had to be creative in their actions. Some well-publicized strategies by unions include the following:

- Withholding union pension funds from investment in companies whose behavior is deemed antiunion and where organizing efforts are restricted.
- Pressuring the company's bank and creditors.
- Challenging company applications for industrial revenue bonds, zoning variances, and so forth.
- Embarrassing company directors and officers by picketing their homes, opposing management in proxy battles, and communicating daily with stockholders.
- Suing the company or officers for breach of fiduciary duty, fraud, or racketeering.
- Extending boycotts to health and life insurance, bank accounts, and stock purchasers.
- Offering concessions to one corporate buyer to favor a corporate takeover.
- Offering seminars to union members on the internal operations of banks and corporations.
- Attending stockholder meetings and making stockholders aware of managerial attitudes toward employees and unions in hopes that adverse publicity and embarrassment will change management's behavior.
- Using a taped telephone speech in which an employee may call a well-publicized number and receive the "union message" for the day or week during an organizing campaign. These messages range from benefits of joining unions and anticompany messages to personal testimony of popular, well-known plant employees. Some unions have also provided Internet communication abilities.

- Attempting to develop acceptance of unions in the community by allying with church groups or civil rights organizations as a way to address social, economic, and personal needs of the people.
- Coordinating organizing activities and combining resources of several groups in large metropolitan areas to promote unionization in that area.
- Negotiating a neutrality agreement that includes a clause stating that if the union seeks to organize employees in nonunion plants, management will remain neutral and a statement defining the limits of acceptable union organizing behavior. If management signs the agreement, the union will have to behave in a manner that neither demands nor ridicules the company or its management.[72]

Various unions have also formulated specifically tailored organizing campaigns aimed at a particular organization. For example,

- The United Food and Commercial Workers (UFCW) slipped into Smitty's Super Value stores in Phoenix, Arizona, and videotaped alleged safety and child labor law violations and gave the film to regulatory agencies and the press.
- The UFCW conducted a four-month review of the accident and injury reports of IBP Inc., a Nebraska-based meatpacking company, and filed a complaint with the OSHA. The company admitted to keeping two sets of injury records and was fined \$5.7 million (later reduced to \$975,000). The result was a strike settlement at one plant and a successful union organizing campaign at another with no company resistance.[73]
- The UFCW helped nonunion employees of Food Lion (a grocery chain) file complaints with the Department of Labor because they were required to work without receiving compensation. (See Case 4.1.)
- The Clothing and Textile Workers Union set up a "cost-o-meter" which monitored management's costs and payments to consultants during an election campaign. The union would report cost figures similar to those in Exhibit 5.10.[74]

Some unions have changed their organizing strategies: unions such as the Paperworkers have broadened their jurisdiction beyond employees in the pulp and paper industry, and the UAW has moved into clerical and professional groups. Other unions, such as the Operating Engineers, Office Employees International Union, and the Bakery, Confectionary, and Tobacco Workers, have narrowed their focus and concentrated on their traditional strengths.[75] In Cleveland, Ohio, a 9 to 5: The Association of Working Women chapter of 15,000 members has affiliated with the Service Employees International Union (SEIU), which provides a toll-free hotline, education, and lobbying for women's issues such as sexual harassment, pay equity, family leave, and computer-related injuries. In Washington, D.C., a group of janitors walked into the posh Old Ebbit Grill across from the White House, pulled out

Exhibit 5.10 Cost-O-Meter

Two lawyers, all day	$1,750
Prepare briefs	2,000
Management's lost time	750
Letters to homes of employees, including postage and printing	250
Supervisor's lost time for antiunion meetings	1,000
Consultant's fees	5,000
Total	$10,750

With this money, we could

1. give everyone a raise of $.10 an hour,
2. hire one more full-time worker, or
3. buy supplies for the patients.

Which one would you choose?

SOURCE: *Report on Union Busting, RUB Sheet* (Washington, D.C.: AFL-CIO, May/June 1990), pp. 1–2.

çola cans filled with ball bearings, shook them violently, and loudly chanted: "Justice for janitors." Although the restaurant did not employ janitors, the Old Ebbit Grill is a tenant in a building that used U.S. Services, Inc. (USSI) for its cleaning, and the SEIU was attempting to organize USSI.

In the construction industry, unions use "salting," a practice of having union organizers apply for vacant jobs with nonunion contractors and openly admitting that they are union members. If they are hired, they attempt to organize the employees. If the contractors do not hire them, they file unfair labor practice charges with the NLRB claiming discrimination against union members.[76] On November 28, 1995, the U.S. Supreme Court ruled that employers cannot discriminate against any paid union organizers who sought employment even though they were intending to try to organize a union within the company after they were hired and would have been paid by the union while they attempted to organize. While this case originated in the construction industry, it has application to other industries and provides an opportunity for unions to increase membership.

The AFL-CIO has also assisted in organizing efforts through its "Union Yes" and Associate Union Membership programs, covered in Chapters 1 and 4. It has also

- Published two manuals, *The Inside Game: Winning with Workplace Strategies* and *Developing New Tactics: Winning with Coordinated Corporate Campaigns,* which "help unions persuade employers to deal fairly and equitably with workers through the application of pressures beyond the workplace."

- Opened an office of Comprehensive Organizing Strategies and Tactics (COST) to train union leaders to conduct corporate campaigns to combat employer resistance to union organizing. Tactics include electronic media; pickets; direct mailing; pressure on banks, creditors, customers, and board members; and purchase of stock.[77]
- Launched a Union Privilege Benefit Program with a discount credit card and legal services to employees. This program is available for current members, retains ties with former members, and attracts new members.[78]
- Developed a nationwide computerized tracking system that will give union leaders comprehensive, up-to-date information on union organizing trends within major industries, corporations, and locations.
- Created a software package capable of providing information to union organizers about particular campaigns, antiunion tactics of employers, successful union responses, and themes used during organizing campaigns that appeal to employees.[79]
- Created the Organizing Institute in 1989 to recruit and train organizers from the rank-and-file membership, colleges, and VISTA and other service institutions. By 1994, some 270 organizers had graduated, and there was a waiting list of international unions wanting to hire institute graduates.

Decertification Procedure

Whenever employees believe that the union is not representing their interests, they may turn to a decertification procedure. In the last decade, decertification elections have nearly doubled, and researchers have identified a variety of reasons:

- Fair treatment of employees by employers.
- Poor job by unions (especially smaller unions) of providing services to members.
- Inability of unions to negotiate an effective first contract after winning bargaining rights.
- Striking employees having skills that can be readily replaced[80] so that when a strike occurs, the employer hires replacements.

Any employee, group of employees, or employee representative may file a petition for a decertification election 12 months after the union has been certified or upon expiration of the labor agreement (see "contract bar doctrine" discussed earlier). This petition must be supported by at least 30 percent of the bargaining-unit employees.

While employers cannot initiate the petition or assist in filing a petition for a decertification election, they can question the union's majority status and petition the NLRB for a representation election. This petition must be supported by objective evidence to show that the union no longer represents the majority of the bargaining-unit employees.[81] Examples of objective data include employee reductions, high employee turnover, changes in the composition of the bargaining unit, requests from employees to discontinue bargaining, statements from employees that they wish to discontinue union representation, and a downward trend in employees authorizing dues deductions. If the employees choose to decertify their union, another representation election cannot be held for 12 months.[82] However, after a valid petition is filed with the NLRB, but before the election, the employer must still bargain with the union until the question of union representation is resolved.

Although employers must be careful of their role in the decertification process, they have exhibited growing interest in it. For example, a one-day seminar, "The Process of Decertification" by Executive Enterprises, offered for $795 per person, is designed to teach management representatives about the entire process of decertficiation. Many employers have concluded that they should become more involved, especially since they are becoming aware that they do not necessarily have to play a passive role in the decertification process.

Employers may become active participants in the decertification efforts after the petition is filed; however, they should do so only after analyzing the costs and benefits of such a strategy. For example, if the company actively campaigns against the present union and the union wins the election and continues to represent employees, the long-term relationship with the union may be irreparably damaged. Moreover, if the company's relationship with the present union is reasonable and productive, it might be wiser to retain it than chance a later replacement by a more militant union.

If the employer chooses to become engaged in the decertification campaign, similar representation election rules and policies apply. For instance, after the petition is filed with the NLRB, the employer may communicate with employees and forcefully state its opposition to the present union, lawfully respond to employee questions, and inform them about the decertification election process. The employer may conduct captive audience speeches, send letters to employees, and conduct small group discussions during the decertification election campaign. Management may tell employees about the employer's perception of the disadvantages of the union, that the employer prefers to deal directly with individual employees instead of through a third party and wants to build a "trusting, team-oriented" relationship with employees, not an adversarial one. At the same time, employers must be careful not to plant the idea of decertification in the minds of employees by offering unsolicited advice, distributing booklets that explain how to decertify the union, or circulating a decertification petition. During the union decertification campaign, union officials will attempt to convince employees of the benefits of continued union representation.[83]

Decertification campaigns are conducted by unions and management in a manner similar to certification campaigns. Decertification elections are usually initiated by a group of employees who are not satisfied with the working conditions and economic provisions achieved by the union through collective bargaining. During the campaign period, the union officials prefer to use handbills, conduct personal visits, and make special pleas with members to refuse signing any decertification petition. Management prefers to rely on legal counsel and small group meetings with employees. Researchers have found both management and the unions have been successful in their campaigns when they emphasize personal contacts with employees and listen genuinely to their concerns, instead of mailing letters and giving out handbills.[84]

Employers must be aware of related unlawful activities, such as the following:

- Obtaining NLRB forms for employees who may be interested in union decertification.
- Providing services such as typing, assistance in phrasing the petition for decertification, and use of company stationery by employees who are interested in launching a decertification campaign.
- Initiating discussions on how or whether to decertify the union.
- Allowing supervisors or any other persons identified with management to promote the decertification process.[85]

Unions respond to any challenge to their existence as the certified representative of the bargaining unit employees. They attempt to convince the employees that there are reasons to continue their union membership and representation and not to seek decertification. They do this by improving the level of services to the employees and by attempting to gain improvements in benefits through negotiation.[86]

The number of decertification elections has increased fivefold since the 1950s. In 1994, 493 decertification elections were held, and unions lost 66 percent of them. However, the number of employees involved was quite small; only 11,022 employees chose not to continue union representation. That was only .00066 of the total union membership in the United States during 1994. Further, the size of the bargaining units where employees chose not to continue union representation was small—generally less than 34 employees.[87]

Recent research has identified several explanations for union decertification. First, the affiliation status of the local union involved in the union decertification election is important because affiliated unions have greater resources available to hold membership support and ultimately to retain union representation. In 440 of 492 decertification elections involving independent local unions, the union was decertified; whereas, in only 36 of 1,155 elections involving AFL-CIO affiliates was the union decertified.

A second factor affecting decertification is the availability of local employment and income opportunities. As employment opportunities increase, there is a decreased likelihood of support for the retention of the union. However, as income opportunities exceed the average, there is increased support to retain the union. Further, where employees face income and employment opportunities that are limited to part-time, low-wage employment, support for union retention is significantly lower. For those employees whose income from part-time employment is relatively small, the expense of continuing to support the union is reduced. These reasons may help to explain such corporate strategies as moving to small southern towns where alternative employment is relatively sparse and increasing the number of part-time employees.[88]

The employees, like the employer, must be aware of possible consequences of their activities attempting to decertify the union. Decertification advocates must be prepared for pressure from union officials and isolation from fellow employees who are pleased with the union. The NLRB has upheld the union's right to discipline union members who actively participate in the campaign to decertify the union, as long as the disciplinary action does not affect the employee's employment status.[89]

In addition to decertification elections, there are the "raid" elections or multi-union elections. These elections occur when a different union (a challenger) attempts to replace an incumbent union. The bargaining-unit employees are given a choice between (1) the incumbent union, (2) the challenger union, and (3) no union. Like other types of elections, the employer may campaign in an attempt to persuade employees to vote "no union," and the union in effect will be decertified. Between 1975 and 1989, there were 1,414 "raid" elections. The incumbent unions won 49.6 percent, the challenger unions won 40.9 percent, and 9.5 percent resulted in a no-union vote.

Companies have used several deunionization strategies in recent years. One strategy is the withdrawal of recognition of the incumbent union on the grounds that it no longer holds majority status. In these cases, the employer must be able to show through objective evidence that a majority interest in the union no longer exists. Employers have been able to do this by showing that only a few employees are having their dues deducted through a "check-off" system, a strike was called and few employees participated, and/or employees on their own signed a petition denouncing their union membership.[90]

Summary

This chapter provides insights into reasons unions are formed. It discusses the most important theories and explanations ranging from alienation and class consciousness to the employees' backgrounds and personal desires. The role of a union is to fulfill employees' perceived needs and answer job-related concerns. Unionization efforts progress from first contacts with employees to signing the authorization cards, petition for election, hearings, determination of the appropriate bargaining unit, and the eventual representation election. Within this framework numerous rules, regulations, and legal requirements govern the union certification process. The procedures by which employees can be formed into unions through voluntary recognition, NLRB directives, and secret ballot elections are explained.

In recent times, unions have launched new strategies to organize nonunion employees. The AFL-CIO has taken the lead with the introduction of several programs under its auspices. Finally, in those cases where the union is judged by employees as not representing their interests, a decertification procedure is available through the election process. Generally, only a few employees and only small bargaining units have been involved in decertification elections.

Key Terms

alienation theory
scarcity consciousness theory
union instrumentality
contract bar doctrine
totality of conduct doctrine

Discussion Questions

1. Refer to the reasons why employees become members of unions to assess the means used by union organizers to meet these needs.
2. Select an organization with which you are familiar, and determine the number of bargaining units that would be appropriate for its structure.
3. Explain the contract bar doctrine. How would it influence the negotiation of the first labor agreement?
4. Discuss the shifting position of the NLRB regarding representation election campaigning. Appraise each position.
5. Prescribe a "do" and "don't" list for supervisors involved in unionization campaigns so they will not commit any unfair labor practices.
6. Why do you believe employers are becoming more interested in decertification elections?
7. Explain the following statement: "It is not the union that organizes the employees; it is management."
8. What would be a good response from a union organizer for each statement in the "Labor Relations in Action" on page 178?
9. What new strategies have unions used to counter employer efforts to maintain nonunion status? Appraise the effectiveness of these strategies.

References

1. Kai Erikson, "On Work and Alienation," *American Sociological Review* 51 (February 1986), p. 2. For examples of this situation, see Michael Hanagan and Charles Stephenson, *Confrontation, Class Consciousness, and the Labor Process.* (New York: Greenwood Press, 1986).

2. Clinton S. Golden and Harold Ruttenberg, "Motives for Union Membership," in E. Wight Bakke, Clark Kerr, and Charles W. Anrod, eds., *Unions, Management, and the Public* (New York: Harcourt, Brace, 1948), p. 49.

3. M.D. Dunnette and W.K. Kirchner, *Psychology Applied to Industry* (New York: Appleton-Century-Crofts, 1965), pp. 199–200; and Henry S. Farber and Daniel H. Saks, "Why Workers Want Unions: The Role of Relative Wages and Job Characteristics" (Working Paper, Cambridge, Mass.: M.I.T., 1978), pp. 27–28. See also W. Clay Hamner and Frank J.

Smith, "Work Attitudes as Predictors of Unionization Activity," *Journal of Applied Psychology* 63 (1978), p. 415; William J. Bigoness, "Correlates of Faculty Attitudes Toward Collective Bargaining," *Journal of Applied Psychology* 63 (1978), pp. 228–233; Chester A. Schreisheim, "Job Satisfaction, Attitudes toward Unions, and Voting in a Union Representation Election," *Journal of Applied Psychology* 63 (1978), pp. 548–552; J. G. Getman, S. B. Goldberg, and J. B. Herman, *Union Representation Elections: Law and Reality* (New York: Russel Sage Foundation, 1976); Edward L. Harrison, "Employee Satisfaction and Voting Behavior in Union Representation Elections," In Dennis F. Ray and Thad B. Greene, eds. *Toward Renewal of Management Thought and Practices* (State College, Miss.: Southern Management Association, Mississippi State University, 1978), p. 169.

4. Selig Perlman, *A Theory of the Labor Movement* (1928; reprinted New York: Augustus M. Kelley, 1968), p. 242.

5. Hoyt N. Wheeler and John A. McClendon, "The Individual Decision to Unionize," in *The State of the Unions,* ed. George Strauss, Daniel G. Gallagher, and Jack Fiorito (Madison, Wis.: IRRA, 1991), pp. 65–67.

6. Joel Seidman, Jack London, and Bernard Karsh, "Why Workers Join Unions," *Annals of the American Academy of Political and Social Sciences* 274 (March 1951), pp. 775–784.

7. E. Wight Bakke, "Why Workers Join Unions," *Personnel* 22 (July 1947), p. 3.

8. J.G. Getman, S.B. Goldberg, and J.B. Herman, *Union Representation Elections: Law and Reality* (New York: Russel Sage Foundation, 1976). See also Henry S. Farber and Daniel H. Saks, "Why Workers Want Unions: The Role of Relative Wages and Job Characteristics," *Journal of Political Economy* 88 (April 1980), pp. 349–369; and Jack Fiorito and Charles R. Greer, "Gender Differences in Union Membership, Preferences and Beliefs," *Journal of Labor Research* (Spring 1986), pp. 145–164.

9. Farber, *Why Workers;* and Stephen M. Hills, "The Attitudes of Union and Nonunion Male Workers toward Union Representation," *Industrial and Labor Relations Review* (January 1985), pp. 179–194.

10. Hoyt N. Wheeler and John A. McClendon, "The Individual Decision to Unionize," pp. 64–67.

11. J.M. Brett and T.J. Hammer, "Organizational Behavior and Industrial Relations," in T.A. Kochan, et al., eds. *Industrial Relations Research in the 1970s: Review and Appraisal* (Madison, Wis.: Industrial Relations Research Association, 1982), pp. 245–251.

12. Jeanette A. Davy and Frank Shipper, "Voter Behavior in Union Certification Elections: A Longitudinal Study," *Academy of Management Journal* 36 (February 1993), pp. 187–199.

13. Satish P. Deshpande and Chockalingam Viswervaran, "Predictors of Unionization: The Role of Specific Beliefs, General Beliefs, and Normative Pressures," *Labor Studies Journal* 19 (Fall 1994), pp. 68–69.

14. Satish P. Deshpande and Jack Fiorito, "Specific and General Beliefs in Union Voting Models," *Academy of Management Journal* 32 (December 1989), pp. 883–895.

15. Thomas A. DeCottis and Jean-Yves Le Lovarn, "A Predictive Study of Voting Behavior in a Representation Election Using Union Instrumentality and Work Perceptions," *Organizational Behavior and Human Performance* 27 (February 1981), pp. 103–118. Also see Stuart A. Youngblood, Angelo S. Denisi, Julie L. Molleston, and William H. Mobley, "The Impact of Work Environment, Instrumentality Beliefs, Perceived Labor Union Image, and Subjectivity Norms on Union Voting Intentions," *Academy of Management Journal* 27 (December 1984), pp. 576–590.

Masoud Hemmasi and Lee A. Graf, "Determinants of Faculty Voting Behavior in Union Representation Elections: A Multivariate Model," *Journal of Management* 19 (Nov. 1, 1995), pp. 13–32.

16. Stuart A. Youngblood, William H. Mobley, and Angelo S. DeNisi, "Attitudes, Perceptions, and Intentions to Vote in a Union Certification Election: An Empirical Investigation," in B.D. Dennis, ed., *Proceedings of the Thirty-Fourth Annual Meeting: Industrial Relations Research Association* (Madison, Wis.: Industrial Relations Research Association, 1982), pp. 244–253; Tom Langford, "Involvement with Unions, Union Belief Perspectives, and Desires for Union Membership," *Journal of Labor Research* 15 (Summer 1994), pp. 257–270.

17. Edward L. Harrison, Douglas Johnson, and Frank M. Rachel, "The Role of the Supervisor in Representation Elections," *Personnel Administration* 26 (September 1981), pp. 69–70.

18. Dorothy Sue Cobble, "Union Strategies for Organizing and Representing the New Service Workforce," in *Proceedings of the 43rd Annual Meeting of the Industrial Relations Research Association* (Madison, Wis.: IRRA, 1991), p.76.

19. Marion Crain, "Gender and Union Organizing," *Industrial and Labor Relations Review* 47 (January 1994), p. 245.

20. David M. Rabban, "Is Unionism Compatible with Professionalism?" *Industrial and Labor Relations Review* 45 (October 1991), pp. 97–112.

21. Michael E. Gordon and Angelo S. Denisi, "A Re-examination of the Relationship Between Union Membership and Job Satisfaction," *Industrial and Labor Relations Review* 48 (January 1995), p. 234.

22. John J. Hoover, "Union Organization Attempts: Management's Response," *Personnel Journal* 61 (March 1982), pp. 214–215.

23. Thomas F. Reed, "Do Union Organizers Matter? Individual Differences, Campaign Practices, and Representation Election Outcomes," *Industrial and Labor Relations Review* 43 (October 1989), pp. 102–117.

24. Thomas F. Reed, "Profiles of Union Organizers from Manufacturing and Service Unions," *Journal of Labor Research* 11 (Winter 1990), pp. 73–80.

25. Charles McDonald, "U.S. Union Membership in Future Decades: A Trade Unionist's Perspective," *Industrial Relations* 31 (Winter 1992), pp. 19–21.

26. James A. Craft and Marian M. Extejt, "New Strategies in Union Organizing," *Working Paper Series* (Pittsburgh, Penn.: University of Pittsburgh, 1982), p. 304.

27. "Union Tactics Found Key Factor in Winning Organizing Elections" (Study by Kate Bronfenbrenner), *Daily Labor Report,* December 3, 1991, pp. A-7–A-10.

28. Julius G. Getman, "Ruminations on Union Organizing in the Private Sector," *The University of Chicago Law Review* 53 (Winter 1986), p. 59.

29. Richard B. Peterson, Thomas W. Lee, and Barbara Finnegan, "Strategies and Tactics in Union Organizing Campaigns," *Industrial Relations* 31 (Spring 1992), pp. 370–374.

30. John J. Lawler and Robin West, "Impact of Union-Avoidance Strategy in Representation Elections," *Industrial Relations* 24 (Fall 1985), pp. 406–420.

31. Satish P. Deshpande and Chockalingam Viswervaran, "Predictors of Unionization: The Role of Specific Beliefs, General Beliefs, and Normative Pressures," *Labor Studies Journal* 19 (Fall 1994), pp. 68–69.

32. Donna Sockell, "Contemporary Challenges of Labor Law," in Barbara D. Dennis, ed. *Proceedings of the Fortieth Annual Meeting of the Industrial Relations Research Association* (Madison, Wis.: Industrial Relations Research Association, 1988), pp. 85–90.

33. *United Autoworkers* v. *Secretary of Labor,* 678 F. Supp. 4 (D.C., 1988).

34. Bruce Kaufman and Paula E. Stephan, "The Role of Management Attorneys in Union Organizing Campaigns," *Journal of Labor Research* 16 (Fall 1995), pp. 439–454.

35. William N. Cooke, "The Rising Toll of Discrimination Against Union Activists," *Industrial Relations* 24 (Fall 1985), p. 437.

36. "Adherence to Labor Laws Not in Management's Interests, Says Ex-NLRB Staff Member," *Report on Union Busters, RUB Sheet* (Washington, D.C.: AFL-CIO, March/April, 1990), p. 1.

37. John W. Budd and Phil K. Heniz, "Union Representation Elections and Labor Law Reform: Lessons From the Minneapolis Hilton," Working Paper, Industrial Relations Center, Minneapolis, Minn., July 1994.

38. An authorization card signifies that the employee desires to be represented by the union in collective bargaining. The employee thereby authorizes the union to represent him with his employer. The signed card may be used later by the union as proof of majority representation, as support to demand recognition, and as evidence that there is "substantial interest" among the bargaining unit to support a petition to the NLRB for representation election. Schlossberg and Sherman, *Organizing and the Law,* p. 50.

39. *NLRB* v. *Gissel Packing Co.* 395 U.S. 575 (1969).

40. Harry E. Graham and Karen N. Neilsen, "Union Representation Elections: A View From the Heart of It All," *Labor Law Journal* 42 (July 1991), pp. 438–441.

41. William E. Fulmer, "Step by Step through a Union Campaign," *Harvard Business Review* 59 (July–August 1981), pp. 94–95. For a review of the research literature on union certification elections, see Herbert G. Heneman, III and Marcus H. Sandver, *Industrial and Labor Relations Review* 36 (July 1983), pp. 537–559.

42. David R. Stephens and Paul R. Timm. "A Comparison of Campaign Techniques in Contested Faculty Elections: An Analysis of the Florida Experience," *Journal of Collective Negotiations in the Public Sector* 7 (1978), pp. 167–177.

43. Paula B. Voos, "Does It Pay to Organize? The Cost to Unions," *Monthly Labor Review* 107 (June 1984), pp. 43–44.

44. Paula Voos, "Union Organizing: Costs and Benefits," *Industrial and Labor Relations Review* 36 (July 1983), pp. 576–580. Also see Paula Voos, "Trends in Union Organizing Expenditures, 1953–1977," *Industrial and Labor Relations Review* 38 (October 1984), pp. 52–66.

45. Rebecca S. Demsetz, "Voting Behavior in Union Representation Elections: The Influence of Skill Homogeneity and Skill," *Industrial and Labor Relations Review* 47 (October 1993), pp. 99–113.

46. Robert Sebris, Jr., and Robert D. McDonald, "Bargaining Unit Determination Case Trends of the NLRB," *Labor Law Journal* 37 (June 1986), pp. 378–382.

47. Robert J. Alberts, "The Appropriate Bargaining Unit, Geographic Proximity, and The 'Nearest Neighbor': An Alternative Analysis," *Labor Law Journal* 41 (July 1990), pp. 424–426.

48. Clyde Scott and Nicholas A. Beadles II, "Unit Placement Decisions in Acute-Care Hospitals," *Labor Law Journal* 44 (March 1993), pp. 143–152.

49. *Excelsior Underwear, Inc.*, 156 NLRB 1236 (1966).

50. Richard N. Block and Myron Roomkin, "Determinants of Voter Participation in Union Certification Elections," *Monthly Labor Review* 105 (April 1982), pp. 45–47.

51. Myron Roomkin and Richard N. Block, "Case Processing Time and the Outcome of Representation Elections: Some Empirical Evidence," *University of Illinois Law Review* 1981, reprinted in *Oversight Hearings on the Subject "Has Labor Law Failed?"* (Washington, D.C.: Committee on Education and Labor, 1984), pp. 844–845.

52. Marcus H. Sandver and Herbert G. Heneman III, "Union Growth through the Election Process," *Industrial Relations* 20 (Winter 1981), pp. 109–115.

53. William N. Cooke, "Determinants of the Outcomes of Union Certification Elections," *Industrial and Labor Relations Review* 36 (April 1983), pp. 402–414.

54. Cheryl L. Maranto and Jack Fiorito, "The Effect of Union Characteristics on the Outcome of the NLRB Elections," *Industrial and Labor Relations Review* 40 (January 1987), pp. 225–238.

55. Victor G. Devinatz and Daniel P. Rich, "Representation Type and Union Success in Certification Elections," *Journal of Labor Research* 15 (Winter 1995), pp. 85–92.

56. James B. Dworkin and James R. Fain, "Success in Multiple Union Elections: Exclusive Jurisdiction vs. Competition." *Journal of Labor Research* 10 (Winter 1989), pp. 91–100. For multiunion elections involving incumbent unions and raids from another union, see Charles Odewahn and Clyde Scott, "An Analysis of Multi-Union Elections Involving Incumbent Unions," *Journal of Labor Research* 10 (Spring 1989), pp 197–205; Clyde Scott and Charles Odewahn, "Multi-Union Elections Involving Incumbent: The Legal Environment," *Labor Law Journal* 40 (July 1989), pp. 403–410.

57. *Annual Reports of the National Labor Relations Board for Fiscal Year 1993–1994* (Washington, D.C.: U.S. Government Printing Office, 1994 and 1995), pp. 13–15.

58. "Study Calls for Labor Law Reform to Aid Unions Seeking First Contracts," *Daily Labor Report,* July 10, 1985, p. A-10.

59. William N. Cooke, "The Failure to Negotiate First Contracts: Determinants and Policy Implications," *Industrial and Labor Relations Review* 38 (January 1985), pp. 163–178.

60. *Shopping Kart Food Market,* 94 LRRM 1705 (1977); Julius G. Getman, Stephen B. Goldberg, and Jeanne B. Herman, *Union Representation Elections: Law and Reality* (New York: Russell Sage Foundation, 1976); and Neal Orkin and Mara Landberg, "Election Campaign Propaganda: Board Policy Then and Now," *Labor Law Journal* 46 (July 1995), pp. 440–446.

61. William T. Dickens, "The Effect of Company Campaigns on Certification Elections: *Law and Reality* Once Again," *Industrial and Labor Relations Review* 36 (July 1983), pp. 574–576.

62. Richard N. Block, Benjamin W. Wolkinson, and James W. Kuhn, "Some Are More Equal Than Others: The Relative Status of Employers, Unions and Employees in the Law of Union Organizing," *Industrial Relations Law Journal* 10 (no. 2, 1989), p. 220.

63. David P. Brenskelle, "Questioning Employees Concerning Union Sentiment Remains a Risky Proposition," *Employee Relations Law Journal* 13 (Summer 1987), pp. 141–147.

64. *Republican Aviation Corp.* v. *NLRB,* 324 U.S. 793 (1945).

65. "Justices Twice Back Right to Distribute Union Literature on Company Property," *The Wall Street Journal,* June 23, 1978, p. 6; Peter G. Kilgore, "No-Solicitation/No-Distribution Rules: The Word Battle of 'Time' Versus 'Hours' Continues." *Labor Law Journal* 35 (November 1984), pp. 671–672.

66. *Beth Israel* v. *NLRB,* 46 U.S.L.W. 4765 (June 22, 1978).

67. *Eastex, Inc.* v. *NLRB,* 46 U.S.L.W. 4783 (June 22, 1978).

68. "NLRB Member Oviatt Says *Lechmere* Creates Presumption Against Union Access," *Daily Labor Report,* February 3, 1992, p. A-5; "Employers and Union Foresee More Costly Organizing Tactics," *Daily Labor Report,* January 29, 1992, p. A-15; and "*Lechmere* Decision Makes Organizing More Difficult for Unions, NLRB Attorney Says," *Daily Labor Report,* June 5, 1992, p. A-1.

69. Karen E. Boroff, "Shopping for Access After *Lechmere,*" *Labor Law Journal* 46 (June 1995), pp. 366–370; Eileen P. Kelly, Owen Seaquest, Amy Oakes, and Lawrence S. Clark, *"NLRB v. Lechmere:* Union Quest for Access," *Journal of Labor Research* 15 (Spring 1994), pp. 155–167.

70. Kevin Conlon and Catherine Voight, "Distinguishing *Lechmere:* Union Organizers' Access to Employers' Property," *Labor Law Journal* 44 (August 1993), pp. 496–501.

71. Joseph A. Pichler and H. Gordon Fitch, "And Women Must Weep: The NLRB as Film Critic," *Industrial and Labor Relations Review* 28 (April 1975), pp. 395–410.

72. James A. Craft and Suhial Abboushi, "The Union Image: Concept, Programs, and Analysis," *Journal of Labor Research* 4 (Fall 1983), pp. 300–311; James A. Craft and Marian M. Extejt, "New Strategies in Union Organizing," *Working Paper Series* (Pittsburgh, Penn.: University of Pittsburgh, 1982), pp. 5–17; James A. Craft, "The Employer Neutrality Pledge: Issues, Implications, and Prospects," *Labor Law Journal* 31 (December 1980), pp. 753–754; Mark L. Adams, "Conflict of Interest or Bona Fide Employees: The Status of Paid Union Organizers," *Labor Law Journal* 46 (February 1995), pp. 98–105; Herbert R. Northrup, "Salting the Contractors' Labor Force: Construction Unions Organizing with NLRB Resistance," *Journal of Labor Research* 14 (Fall 1993), pp. 469–492; and Dinah Payne, Stephen M. Crow, and Sandra Hartman, "The Fate of Full-Time Paid Union Organizers as Employees: What Next from the Supreme Court?" *Labor Law Journal* 46 (June 1995), pp. 371–375.

73. Robert Tomsho, "Unions Search for Regulatory Violations to Pressure Firms and Win New Members," *The Wall Street Journal,* February 28, 1992, pp. B-1, B-5.

74. *Report on Union Busting, RUB Sheet* (Washington,D.C.: AFL-CIO, May/June 1990), pp. 1–2.

75. Victor B. Devinatz, "The Changing Scope of Union Organizing," *Labor Law Journal* 45 (February 1994), pp. 121–123.

76. Michael Ballot, "New Directions in Union Organizing," *Labor Law Journal* 45 (December 1994), pp. 779–784.

77. "AFL-CIO Soon to Open New Office to Develop Organizing Strategies," *Daily Labor Report,* April 3, 1986, p. A-1.

78. Gene Zack, "Credit Card Legal Services Plan Offered," *AFL-CIO News,* July 5, 1986, p. 1.

79. "Tracking System for Union Election Petitions Being Developed by AFL-CIO," *Daily Labor Report,* March 26, 1992, pp. A-7–A-8.

80. James B. Dworkin and Marian Extejt, "Why Workers Decertify Their Unions: A Preliminary Investigation," paper presented at the Annual Meeting of the Academy of Management, August 1979.

81. Lisa M. Lynch and Marcus H. Sandver, "Determinants of the Decertification Process Evidence from Employer-Initiated Elections," *Journal of Labor Research* 8 (Winter 1987), p. 87.

82. Kenneth C. McGuiness and Jeffrey A. Norris, *"How to Take a Case before the National Labor Relations Board,* 5th ed. (Washington, D.C.: Bureau of National Affairs, Inc., 1986), p. 66.

83. Clyde Scott, Kim Hester, and Edwin Arnold, "Decertification Elections: An Analysis of Recent Activity," *Labor Law Journal* 46 (February 1995), pp. 67–74.

84. David M. Savino and Nealia S. Bruning, "Decertification Strategies and Tactics: Management and Union Perspectives," *Labor Law Journal* 43 (April 1992), pp. 201–208.

85. William A. Krupman and Gregory I. Rasin, "Decertification: Removing the Shroud," *Labor Law Journal* 30 (April 1979), pp. 234–235.

86. Trevor Bain, Clyde Scott, and Edwin Arnold, "Deauthorization Elections: An Early Warning Signal to Decertification?" *Labor Law Journal* 39 (July 1988), pp. 432–436.

87. *Annual Report of the National Labor Relations Board for Fiscal Year 1994* (Washington, D.C.: U.S. Government Printing Office, 1994 and 1995), pp. 13–15.
88. David Meyer and Trevor Bain, "Union Decertification Election Outcomes: Bargaining-Unit Characteristics and Union Resources," *Journal of Labor Research* 15 (Spring 1994), pp. 117–136.
89. *Tawas Tube Production, Inc.* 151 NLRB 9 (1965).
90. Edwin Arnold, Clyde Scott, and John Rasp, "The Determinants of Incumbent Union Victory in Raid Elections," *Labor Law Journal* 43 (April 1992), pp. 221–228; Clyde Scott and Edwin Arnold, "Raid Elections: An Analysis of Employer Campaigns," *Labor Law Journal* 41 (September 1990), pp. 641–648. Also see Robert W. Schupp, "When Is a Union Not a Union? Good Faith Doubt by An Employer," *Labor Law Journal* 42 (June 1991), pp. 357–364.

CASES FOR PART ONE

Case 1.1 T-Shirt Offer: Election Interference

On the day before the union election, the union hosted a free picnic luncheon for employees during the first and second shifts' meal breaks in a parking lot adjacent to the Young Skin's plant. At the picnic, the union took 88 snap shots. During the luncheon, union representatives distributed "Union Yes" T-shirts carrying the slogan, "The Best Things in Life Are Negotiable. Union Yes." Between "Union" and "Yes" was a square containing a check mark. To receive a T-shirt, employees were required to sign a pro-union petition that was to be used as a handbill on election day, headed "We Are Voting Yes on August 2nd!" and stating that the undersigned employees agreed to openly support the union and asked their co-workers to join them.

The company contended that the T-shirts cost $4 to $5 and their free distribution was objectionable conduct, and that the union induced employees to sign the pro-union petition by requiring signing as a condition of receiving a T-shirt. The company compared the T-shirt offer to a union's offering to waive initiation fees contingent on employees' signing authorization cards. The Supreme Court had found such a fee waiver objectionable in a previous case because it "allow[ed] the union to buy endorsements and paint a false portrait of employee support during its election campaign." The company said the monetary value of the T-shirts was irrelevant, noting that the waived initiation fee was a "nominal" $10.

The union stated that it was clear to all concerned that the T-shirts were inexpensive and that their free distribution would not interfere with employee free choice. It is a considerable leap to conclude that the offer of these "Union Yes" T-shirts contingent on employees' signing a pro-union petition was an inducement tantamount to buying endorsements.

The Supreme Court in the previous case ruled that all employees, regardless of their views on unions, had an economic interest in obtaining the fee waiver that was offered as an inducement to sign union authorization cards. The inducement here—the "Union Yes" T-shirt—however, would reasonably be desirable only to employees who favored the union and wanted to proclaim their pro-union view. Thus, the union's requiring employees to sign a pro-union petition in order to obtain a pro-union T-shirt would not reasonably induce nonsupporters to sign the petition and thereby allow the union to paint a false portrait of employee support.

Even if the T-shirts might be desirable to nonsupporters, the union in that event had a justifiable interest in trying to assure that T-shirts were distributed only to employees who would wear them as campaign paraphernalia in support of the union. Requiring employees desiring T-shirts to sign a pro-union petition was a reasonable means for the union to try to accomplish this objective.

The company also contended that the union created an atmosphere of fear and coercion by photographing employees at the picnic luncheon. In many of the photographs, employees posed for the camera, sometimes displaying their union T-shirts. The photographs were for the purpose of memorializing the chicken meal and perhaps to publish in a union newspaper. Two employees later said they were "concerned" or "felt funny" about their pictures being taken.

The company contended that the employees who were photographed might well have felt that their responses to the union campaign activity were being recorded for the purpose of future retaliation. The union responded that while photographing some activities might suggest retaliatory purpose, the union photographing employees enjoying a voluntarily attended picnic does not reasonably suggest any such purpose. When the company's security guard, who attended the picnic, asked why a union representative was taking photographs, the union representative stated, "You are all going to make the front page of *USA Today*," and "we want to remember this fun-filled memory." Union representatives stated that the photographs were taken for submission to the union newspaper and copies were given to employees. Later, the union had, in fact, distributed photos to employees at a party celebrating the union's victory in the election (217 in favor of the union and 200 against it and 16 challenged ballots).

Questions

1. What are the general rules governing election interference?
2. Compare the present case to the following ones:
   - *NLRB* v. *Savair Mfg. Co.*, 414 U.S. 270 (1973); 84 LRRM 2929 (1973)
   - *Pepsi Cola Bottling Co.*, 289 NLRB 736 (1988); 128 LRRM 1275 (1988)
   - *Mike Yurosek & Sons, Inc.*, 292 NLRB 1074 (1989); 130 LRRM 1308 (1989)
3. Did the union interfere with the outcome of the election by offering the T-shirts? If so, why? If not, why not?
4. Did the union interfere with the outcome of the election by taking the photographs at the picnic? If so, why? If not, why not?

Case 1.2 Election Campaign Literature: Frozen Wages and Benefits

Montrose is a company engaged in the manufacture and distribution of shellac at its place of business in Athens, Washington. A representation petition was filed by the union on September 8, 1989. The union lost the election on October 19, 1989, in a unit of 67 of Montrose's employees. Out of the 67 eligible voters, 30 votes were cast for the union and 30 votes were cast against the union. The union filed objections and unfair labor practice charges, challenging the company's use of an antiunion campaign which ended with the mailing of a 19-page document entitled "The Decision Is Yours" to all unit employees one to two days prior to the election. The following language was contained on page 9 of the document:

> When bargaining for a first contract does begin, it can be a long, complicated and technical procedure which can go on for months, a year, . . . or longer.
>
> While bargaining goes on, wage and benefit programs typically remain *frozen* until changed, if at all, by a contract.
>
> If the Union wins, you take the risks. . . . You will have to "wait and see" if anything happens with wages and benefits. The Union, however, is free to begin collecting dues right away. [Emphasis in original.]

The Union alleged that the language amounted to a threat in violation of Section 8(a)(1) because the message communicated by the company to employees was that wage and benefit programs would remain frozen during the potentially long period of negotiations.

Montrose contended that, in the context of the circumstances, the language contained in the company's campaign literature did not constitute a threat within the purview of Section 8(a)(1).

The company's statement appeared in a 19-page document that was devoid of any other unlawful or objectionable statements. The statement appeared only in the 19-page document, even though the company had distributed several additional campaign materials to employees. During this entire time period, no other allegations of unfair labor practices were made or objectionable conduct committed by the company.

The company argued that it was important to note that it did not say that preexisting benefits would be lost if the union won the election. Its statement was that wage and benefit programs would be frozen; in other words, the statement implied only that they would not change. The company's conduct had been consistent because it had established a past practice of granting predetermined wage increases following probationary and training periods. Such practice continued during the election campaign. Moreover, the company had a practice of giving the employees Thanksgiving turkeys and a Christmas party, and this practice continued. Finally, the company had established a past practice of granting a Christmas bonus and annual merit increases in December.

During the election campaign, William Mischell, vice-president and general manager, told employees that the amounts of the Christmas bonus and merit increases would be subject to negotiation with the union if the union won the election, although the past practice of granting bonuses and merit increases would continue. However, the amount would be subject to negotiations.

The company stated that the word *frozen* was preceded by the word *typically,* which modified and limited its meaning. Thereby, this reduced the possibility that employees would reasonably perceive the statement to be a threat that their wage and benefit increases would be lost. In addition, the statement was made in a third-party context that further reduced the possibility of its perception by the employees as a threat.

Questions

1. What are typical actions prohibited in Section 8(a)(1)?
2. What would be the typical employee's reaction after reading the excerpts from page 9 of the election campaign literature?
3. What would be your interpretation of the company's intent in the wording of the excerpts from page 9?
4. Did the company violate Section 8(a)(1) of the NLRA? If so, why? If not, why not?

Case 1.3 Loudspeaker Messages Before and on Day of Election: Election Interference

Acoustical Enterprises manufactures commercial acoustic soundproofing material at a plant in Mocus Corner, South Dakota. On December 20, 1987, the union filed a petition with the NLRB seeking certification as the exclusive bargaining representative of Acoustical production and maintenance employees. An election was set for 2:00 P.M. on February 18, 1988.

As the election approached, the main issue became the wages and benefits received by the nonunion Mocus Corner employees versus those received by the unionized employees at a Bronx, New York, plant. Acoustical made widely divergent statements about the extent of any difference between the two plants, and the election rhetoric became quite heated. In particular, the union repeatedly made disparaging remarks about Acoustical's main spokesperson, Fran Orange.

On the day before the election and on election day, the union parked a car mounted with a loudspeaker system 25 to 30 yards from the Acoustical plant's main entrance. On both days, the union broadcast music and campaign messages focusing on the wages and benefits issue and on Orange from approximately 6:50 A.M. to 7:05 A.M., and from just before 12:00 noon to 12:35 P.M. Also, on February 17, the union broadcast from 3:25 P.M. to 3:40 P.M. and just before and after 5:30 P.M. These broadcasts were intentionally made to coincide with the beginning and ending of the day shift (7:00 A.M.–3:30 P.M.) and with lunch breaks (12:00–12:30 P.M.) at the plant. The February 17, 5:30 P.M. broadcast coincided with the end of an overtime day shift.

The loudspeaker system had a range of well over 100 yards, and the union's messages were clearly heard on the plant grounds. Because of industrial noise, however, the broadcasts were inaudible inside plant buildings when machinery was in use. However, at the lunch break, when no machinery was in use and when employees were outside the plant buildings, the broadcasts were more easily heard. Employees were not free to leave the plant area during their lunch break.

The election was held as scheduled, and the union won by an 81 to 71 vote. Acoustical filed election objections, including one over the union sound car broadcasts. The company contended that the broadcasts violated the longstanding rule of *Peerless Plywood Co.*, 107 NLRB 427 [33 LRRM 1151] (1953), which prohibits speeches by either the union or the employer to massed assemblies of employees, on company time, within 24 hours of an election.

On March 17, 1988, the union requested Acoustical to bargain. Acoustical refused. On April 11, 1988, the union filed an unfair labor practice charge under Section 8(a)(1), (5) of the National Labor Relations Act. Acoustical answered the charge, admitting its refusal to bargain but contending that the union had been improperly certified.

Questions

1. Review the captive-audience, 24-hour rule. Is it appropriate to apply this rule to both parties?
2. Which party has the advantage in presenting its position during a representation election? Why?
3. Did the union violate the NLRB's *Peerless Plywood* rule? Why? Why not?

Case 1.4 Cookout, Day Off with Pay: Election Interference

Two days before the election, A to Z Plastics offered all unit employees, with no strings attached, a day off with pay solely in connection with its admitted purpose to deliver the final message in its antiunion campaign. The union alleged that employees, including those who elected not to attend the cookout and listen to the company's speeches, received what was tantamount to a substantial bonus for no other reason than to influence the upcoming election. The union contended that employees could reasonably see that the company's conduct was intended to influence their votes in favor of the company's position. This granting of such benefit in these circumstances constitutes objectionable conduct sufficient to require that the election results be overturned.

The company asserted a business justification for its action, arguing that it had no other way to end its antiunion campaign except to hold a cookout and grant a paid day off. Attendance at the cookout was not required. The cookout was necessary as a means of gathering all three shifts of employees together to address them en masse at the end of its campaign. The company's decision to hold a cookout for its employees was consistent with past practice. Three times in the previous five years the company had held a cookout for its employees, given them the day off to enable them to attend, and paid them their regular pay. These occasions gave everyone an opportunity to "get together and talk."

The tally of ballots from the election showed 5 votes for the union and 44 votes against, with 1 challenged ballot.

Questions

1. Is the content of the company's message at issue in this case? If so, why? If not, why not?
2. Did the company's conduct affect the outcome of the election? Does the margin in the votes matter in this case?
3. Do you find the company's arguments persuasive? The union's?
4. What ruling should be made by the NLRB? Give your reasoning.

Case 1.5 Atlas Towers: Composition of Bargaining Unit

The Atlas Towers is a 30-story hotel in Atlantic City, New Jersey. The hotel derives approximately 83 percent of its gross revenues from its convention business. It has 1,250 rooms and employs about 832 regular full-time nonsupervisory employees. It has 4 restaurants, 3 cocktail lounges, a nightclub, recreational facilities, 52 meeting rooms, and an exhibition hall.

Because it is mainly a convention hotel, its facilities and organizational structure have been designed specifically for the purpose of serving convention business, and its operations are closely coordinated and functionally integrated. The conventions require each department to cooperate with the others to provide the promised services. Thus, the front office, sales, catering, reservations, food and beverage, and communications employees are involved in selling conventions to prospective customers and in an effort to ascertain customers' needs during their stay.

Atlas Towers has an extensive internal communications and record-keeping system. This consists of a MICOR computer system,[1] a pneumatic tube system linking the front desk and other parts of the facility, communications (PBX) and food and beverage outlets, a beeper paging system, and a walkie-talkie system.

The booking, planning, and execution of conventions require close coordination among all hotel areas. Preconvention meetings are held to review a convention résumé that outlines the convention functions and roles of each area. The convention résumé is circulated to approximately 40 different departments and contains instructions for each.

General Manager James Ussery sends numerous memoranda to the department heads, assistant department heads, and assistant area managers. These memoranda demonstrate Ussery's close involvement in minor details of the hotel's day-to-day operation and reflect management's highly centralized control.[2] Individual department heads oversee routine operations in their areas but do not establish basic work policies or have final control over department functions.

The hotel's human resources department establishes uniform personnel policies, including wages and benefits,[3] which apply to all hotel employees except property operations employees, whose terms and conditions of employment have been specified in a collective bargaining agreement. Human resources screens all applicants and refers qualified applicants to the department managers for interviews.[4] The director of human resources must approve all personnel decisions, including any discipline supervisors recommend. Hotel employees have an employee cafeteria, employee locker rooms, and a recreation program. There are employee training programs throughout the hotel in which employees of different departments participate. Some employees receive cross-training in other departments. For example, some communications employees received training to make them more aware of what goes on in the front office. There is also a "priority one" training program that covers any employee who has face-to-face contact with guests.

The hotel has a uniform transfer policy. The human resources department posts openings, and employees from any area may apply. The employee's current supervisor must sign a form, and the human resources department must approve the transfer. There have been numerous transfers among departments, including approximately 27 transfers in two years from housekeeping to other departments. There have also been transfers from the food and beverage and stewards area to housekeeping, and from communications to housekeeping, secretary, front office, and accounting. Other transfers have occurred from food and beverage to sales, front office, and accounting; from office to food and beverage; from

[1]The MICOR System is used by employees in accounting (cashiers), housekeeping, front desk, and communications. MICOR's information includes guest names, guest room locations, guest conventions, and room status.

[2]Some examples of the day-to-day issues with which Ussery has been involved include the policy regarding furnishing meals to police officers, cleaning guest elevator doors, availability of rollaway beds, the purchase of a knife for the dessert wagon, use of employee name tags, the maintenance and cost of shower curtains, approval of a front office clerk's vacation period, guest entrapment in elevators, and cleaning the lower ground floor area.

[3]A hotelwide wage and salary program sets pay rates for each job classification, including the hiring rates and frequency and amounts of pay increases. Individual supervisors and department heads do not determine when their employees receive a pay increase. Among other hotelwide personnel policies the human resources department formulates with Ussery's approval are work hours, disciplinary procedures, dress standards, holidays, night differential pay rates, benefit improvements, funeral leave, vacation policy, jury duty, overtime pay, and probation periods. All hotel employees except property operations employees receive the same fringe benefits.

[4]Each manager makes the final hiring decisions from among those human resources refers.

housekeeping to the front desk; from greeter to catering; from bellstand to food and beverage; from communications to accounting; from room service to secretary; from personnel to catering; from public facilities to security; and from stewards to bellstand.

Employees from different areas have frequent contact with each other. Contacts between accounting personnel and other employees include the following: front office cashiers issue keys to food and beverage employees, restaurant cashiers, housekeeping, engineering, and laundry employees. Shipping and receiving employees deal with engineering, food and beverage, laundry, and housekeeping employees in handling goods to be picked up by other departments or delivered. Night auditors have contact with restaurant employees when they pick up reports and read registers in the restaurant outlets. Accounts payable clerks obtain approvals for payments of invoices from every department.[5] Restaurant cashiers occasionally assist the hostesses or greeters in the dining rooms.

Laundry employees have contact with buspersons, banquet employees, kitchen employees, the storeroom clerk, shipping and receiving, communications, catering, room service, and the bellstand. Employees from other departments bring laundry to be cleaned and pick up clean laundry and uniforms.

Housekeeping employees maintain contact with the front desk cashiers through the MICOR system regarding all room status changes. The front desk provides house counts to housekeeping for budgeting and scheduling purposes. Housekeeping employees have contacts with food and beverage employees when they clean restaurant outlets and work with public facilities employees in cleaning areas around the meeting rooms.

Food and beverage employees keep contact with the front office or house count and the pay-in-advance guest list. They have contact with restaurant cashiers and night auditors and work closely with the inventory control office. The convention services department advises food and beverage as to the services each convention requires. Food and beverage employees work with housekeeping employees in setting up VIP rooms.

Communications employees assist cashiers regarding guest telephone charges (using the pneumatic tube system). Operators take restaurant reservations when food and beverage receptionists are not available. Restaurant cashiers call operators to verify guest room numbers, and operators call outlets to locate guests and give out information regarding the hours of the food and beverage outlets. Housekeeping employees call operators if a message light is left on in a vacant room or if a telephone is missing or damaged. Public facilities employees notify operators when a telephone needs to be removed from a meeting room. All departments notify communications when repairs are necessary.

Some interchange of employees between departments goes on, mainly in emergency situations. Accounting employees have worked as bartenders, and credit employees as hostesses. During an ice storm, accounting employees assisted housekeeping. Catering, sales, and accounting employees have been used as bar cashiers. Housekeeping employees sometimes fill in at the laundry and uniform room. A housekeeping employee fills in for the restroom attendant. Housekeeping employees have filled in as waitresses or buspersons, and they help in shipping and receiving when a large order arrives. They also occasionally substitute for lobby porters (bellstand).

The union had proposed that the appropriate bargaining unit should consist of all full-time and regular part-time housekeeping, laundry, public facility, and exhibit employees, as follows:

> All full-time and regular part-time housekeeping, laundry and public facility and exhibit employees employed by the Employer at its

[5]Generally, rank-and-file employees in other departments are not involved with this function unless there is a question about receipt of merchandise.

Atlantic City facility, including aides, on-call aides, turn-down aides, attendants, the payroll clerk, dispatchers, night cleaners, stock-room attendant, locker room attendant, drapery attendant, washman, chuteman, laundry attendant, linen runner, seamstress, uniform room attendant, meeting room attendant, banquet houseman and assistant team leaders, excluding office clerical employees, secretaries, property operations employees, front office employees, food and beverage employees, steward employees, room service employees, communication employees, the hostesses, guest greeters, purchasing employees, human resources employees, the tower clerk, marketing and sales employees, accounting employees, security employees, guards and supervisors as defined in the Act.

The employer proposed a unit consisting of all employees employed at the facility, excluding only property operations department employees, confidential employees, security officers, guards/watchmen and supervisors as defined in the NLRA.

The regional director of the NLRB had determined the unit to be all full-time and regular part-time food and beverage employees. This unit would include the following:

All full-time and regular part-time food and beverage employees, steward employees, room service employees, guest services employees, bellmen, cashiers, and stockroom attendant; *excluding* office clerical employees, secretaries, property operations employees, communication employees, housekeeping, laundry and public facility and exhibit employees, human resources employees, purchasing employees, the Tower clerk, marketing and sales employees, accounting employees, security employees, guards and supervisors as defined by the Act.

The decision of the regional director has now been appealed to the board in Washington for a decision.

Questions

1. Explain the importance of the union's and employer's position regarding the composition of the appropriate bargaining unit.
2. What are the criteria that should be used in this determination?
3. Considering the views of the employer and the union and the decision of the regional director, what should the NLRB decide to be the appropriate unit?
4. Justify this decision.

References

Arlington Hotel Co., 126 NLRB 400 (1960).
77 Operating Co., 160 NLRB 927 (1966).
Regency Hyatt Hotel, 171 NLRB 1347 (1968).
Holiday Inn, Alton, 270 NLRB 199 (1984).
Holiday Inn, Southwest, 202 NLRB 781 (1973).
Holiday Inn, 214 NLRB 651 (1974).
Days Inn of America, 210 NLRB 1035 (1974).
Ramada Inn v. NLRB, 487 F.2d 1334 (1973).
Westward-Ho Hotel, 437 F.2d 110 (1971).

Case 1.6 Closing a Plant After a Successful Union Election

Mid-South Packing Company was formed in 1982 as a holding company by the leveraged buyout of several packing and distribution centers in Arkansas, Mississippi, Louisiana, and Tennessee. In all, Mid-South operates over 20 units in four states, including the Clarksdale, Mississippi, plant. In 1986, Mid-South transferred the Clarksdale, Mississippi, plant from its Tennessee division to its new Mississippi-Arkansas division and considered making substantial repairs to the 60-year-old plant, which was in poor condition.

On January 17, 1986, Mid-South was informed that a sufficient number of employees at the Clarksdale plant had signed authorization cards with the International Union of Electronic Workers (IUE) to require a representation election. During the union organizing campaign, Mid-South threatened to close the plant should the union emerge victorious in the election, among other antiunion tactics.

The union won the election and the company filed objections. The union responded to the objections and filed several unfair labor practice charges as well. During negotiations initiated by the company, the union agreed to drop the charges in exchange for the company's promise to recognize the union and bargain in good faith. The company agreed to withdraw its objection to the election, and the IUE was certified as the bargaining representative for the Clarksdale plant employees on April 28, 1986.

On May 5, 1986, the company informed the union that it was shutting down the Clarksdale, Mississippi, plant and actually shut the doors four days later. The union filed a new set of unfair labor practice charges with the NLRB alleging that the company had violated the National Labor Relations Act by shutting down the plant and by refusing to bargain with the union about the plant closure.

Mid-South claimed that the Clarksdale plant was not a profitable operation despite its showing a net profit in 1986 and the second-highest production level among the six plants in the Mississippi-Arkansas division. The company claimed reopening this plant would not only impose an undue or unfair burden on the company but would threaten the continued viability of its entire operation. Company officials concluded that the plant would require $150,000 in repairs merely to reopen, and that the plant would have closed regardless of how the employees had voted in the representation election.

The union charged that the reason for the shutdown was the successful union election campaign. The union was certified as the legal bargaining agent for the Clarksdale plant employees, and the company had agreed to bargain in good faith with the union. Instead, the company shut down the plant and did not bargain in good faith. The union also claimed that among the unfair practices committed by the company during the organizing campaign, the company had threatened to close the plant, and then after the union won the election, the company did, in fact, close the plant.

Questions

1. Does the NLRB have authority to require a company to reopen a plant?
2. Did the company commit an unfair labor practice?
3. Should the NLRB consider the cost of $150,000 to reopen the plant?
4. What should be the NLRB's decision? Justify your answer.

Case 1.7 Inflammatory Conduct?

Issue

Did the employer interfere by creating literature of leaflets that contained negative and threatening racial or ethnic references, including the reproduction of a Nazi swastika, and by discussing that literature in "captive audience" meetings with employees and asserting that the literature had been produced by the union and sent to the employer's management officials?

Background

A representation election was conducted on December 19, 1992, with a unit of nonprofessional employees. The results were 286 for and 301 against the union, with 10 challenged ballots, an insufficient number to affect the results.

Dwight Kane, the employer's president and chief executive officer, had held several meetings with employees during the critical period prior to the election. These meetings were "captive audience" meetings that employees were required to attend. Kane discussed his view of the drawbacks and potential liabilities if the employees selected the union as their bargaining representative. After discussing the subjects of collective bargaining, strikes, and arbitration, Kane mentioned that employees had complained to him about harassment by other employees during the campaign. Kane stated that he also had been harassed, and he held up a letter and said, "[T]his is what I've received, and I'm angry over it." Kane then circulated among the employees an anonymous letter that he said he had received. The letter read as follows:

> You will get it sooner or later. It's only a matter of time you. . . . We know where you live.

The letter also contained a reproduction of a swastika and a photograph of David Duke.

Kane told the employees that he was not saying, nor did he have any proof, that the union was responsible for the letter. Instead, Kane said that the "environment that created animosity between employees was what might generate" such a letter.

The Union

The union argued that Kane's presentation of the letter during the critical period in the context of antiunion meetings was an attempt to inflame and incite religious or racial tensions during the campaign. The introduction of the document during Kane's campaign speeches required more than the weak disclaimer expressed by Kane, that is, "I am not saying that this letter was sent by the union." The union claimed that the employees were, at the least, provoked to contemplate the union's responsibility for and involvement in the preparation and mailing of the letter. The union stated that Kane's presentation of the letter could not be characterized as merely casual remarks but was a deliberate attempt by the employer in numerous formal campaign meetings to overstress and exacerbate racial or religious feelings by irrelevant, inflammatory appeals during the critical period. Further, Kane's conduct interfered with the employees' free choice in the election, and the election should be set aside.

The Company

The company responded that the question to be answered is whether the statements at issue appeal to racial or religious prejudice against a particular group and are inflammatory and irrelevant. While Kane's conduct was objectionable, his remarks did not deliberately seek to overstress and exacerbate racial feelings by irrelevant, inflammatory appeals.

The company claimed that numerous NLRB decisions supported the company. The NLRB has consistently reiterated that it would overturn the results of an election in those circumstances where it is determined that the "appeals or arguments can have no purpose except to inflame the racial feelings of voters in the election."

Kane's conduct here did not rise to the level of a sustained appeal to racial prejudice of the type condemned. Kane's remarks did not appeal to feelings of racial and religious bias, nor did they seek to pit race against race. Rather, they denounced such feelings. Although Kane repeated his discussion of the letter in several meetings, it certainly was not a centerpiece of the employer's campaign. The record does not show that race was a significant aspect of the campaign in this case. No evidence was found that the employer created the letter in question, and Kane did not attribute it to the union.

The company claimed that the NLRB's decision in *Beatrice Grocery Products,* 287 NLRB 302 (1987), was particularly instructive and applicable here. In *Beatrice,* the NLRB found that a union representative's statement involving an alleged racial appeal to employees did not warrant setting the election aside. In so finding, the NLRB stated that "[b]ecause the statement represented an effort to denounce racial prejudice in another (the employer), rather than to incite prejudice against a particular racial or religious group . . . it does not constitute the kind of gratuitous appeal to racial prejudice that *Sewell* brands as objectionable conduct" (287 NLRB at 303).

Kane's remarks did not attack a particular racial, ethnic, or religious group, nor did they constitute a bigoted attack on any individual. Kane's comments could not have been reasonably intended to interfere with the election by destroying the atmosphere necessary to the exercise of free choice.

Questions

1. What is the captive-audience rule? Does it apply in this case?
2. What are the rules that govern employer speeches prior to a representation election?
3. What should be the NLRB's principle here in deciding whether to set aside the election?
4. Must there be proof that the employer created the literature in order to blame Mr. Kane for his actions?
5. What should be the NLRB's decision? Why?

Case 1.8 Wearing Antiunion Hats

Issue

Did the employer commit an unfair labor practice when a representation election was conducted on December 22, 1993; the tally of ballots showed 78 for and 90 against the union, with 2 void and 8 nondeterminative challenged ballots; and at least three of the employer's supervisors directly distributed antiunion hats to employees a week before a representation election?

Background

About a week before the representation election, three of the employer's supervisors distributed hats to bargaining-unit employees. These hats included the following message on the front: "What Part of uNiOn Don't They Understand," with the *N* and *O* in *union* printed in a contrasting color. Bindery shift supervisor Sam Novak handed a hat to everyone in his area with the explanation, "Here's a free hat." When an employee asked about what he could do if he didn't want a hat, Novak responded that he could throw it away. Night shift supervisor Linda Jacks presented the hats to her employees by explaining that they could have one if they wanted one. Press supervisor Steve Jones handed out a hat to every employee. He told them: "Here's another hat." No one kept a list of who did or did not take the proffered hats.

The Union

The union argued that an employer may make antiunion paraphernalia available to employees at a central location unaccompanied by any coercive conduct. Here, however, the employer did more than make the hats available; rather, various supervisors personally distributed the hats, presumably to a large number of bargaining-unit employees, a week before the election. When supervisors approached individual employees and solicited them to wear antiunion or pro-employer paraphernalia, in effect, employees were forced to make an observable choice that demonstrated their support for or rejection of the union.

The union stated that its conduct here is analogous to that found in *Gonzales Packing Co.*, 304 NLRB 805, 815 (1991), where a supervisor approached 10 voters at their workstations the day before the election and, in the presence of a large number of bargaining-unit employees, asked them whether they wanted "VOTE NO" stickers. In *Gonzales Packing*, the NLRB found that it was not aware of any case in which the company was found legally innocent where a supervisor directly approached a substantial number of employees and invited those employees on-the-spot to choose whether or not to display an antiunion slogan. Here, however, supervisors personally offered antiunion hats to bargaining unit employees.

The Company

The company argued that no list was made of which employees accepted or rejected the anti-union hats proffered by the employer's supervisors. The supervisors' direct distribution of anti-union paraphernalia does not amount to objectionable conduct sufficient to set aside the results of an election. Rather, in determining whether alleged preelection misconduct warrants setting aside the election results, the NLRB must consider the "totality of the circumstances." Consideration should be given not only to the timing of the alleged misconduct but also to the number of potential voters affected and the closeness of the election. Attention should also be given to whether the conduct, when viewed in context, could reasonably be found to have a coercive effect.

Supervisors distributed the hats in an indifferent manner. Numerous statements by union witnesses revealed that throughout the election campaign, union supporters openly displayed their sentiments by wearing buttons and hats favoring the union.

There is no reason to find that the supervisors' distribution of the hats warrants setting aside the election. To the extent that such distribution can be analyzed as a form of interrogation of employees' union sentiments, the appropriate approach is the "totality of the circumstances" analysis. As such, the union has failed to make any showing that the distribution of the antiunion hats was coercive. The company argued that the situation in this case contrasts starkly with the situation in *Gonzales Packing Co.*, where a supervisor of 50 to 60 employees singled out 10 employees the day before the election to ask whether they wanted a "VOTE NO" sticker like those worn by antiunion employees. In that case, the NLRB affirmed an 8(a)(1) violation and correspondingly found such conduct warranted ordering a new election. Employees whom the supervisor approached with the stickers had already indicated that they were unwilling to be identified with the "VOTE NO" movement and that the supervisor's approach would therefore reasonably have been viewed by them as pressure from management to become active in the antiunion campaign.

Lastly, no independent evidence could be found of coercive behavior, and the record establishes that the employer's antiunion campaign was free from any unfair labor practices. The company urged the NLRB to rule for the company and certify the results of the election.

Questions

1. What is the "totality of circumstances" analysis?
2. What instructions should a company give supervisors to guide their actions during an election campaign?
3. How should the NLRB rule? Give your reasoning.

PART TWO

Part 2 pertains to key activities in the labor relations process: the negotiation and administration of the work rules. These topics are approached from the vantage point of legal and quasi-legal (labor agreement) proscriptions on related behavior as well as with an eye to the practical realities forged out of the relationships between union and management officials.

NEGOTIATING AND ADMINISTERING THE LABOR AGREEMENT

6 Negotiating the Labor Agreement

Negotiation, or collective bargaining, is a common feature of everyday life. While this chapter covers negotiations between union and management officials over conditions of employment, many aspects of negotiations have broader applications to other bargaining activities in our society.

This chapter first defines collective bargaining and explains initial influences affecting this activity. Subsequent sections consider prenegotiation activities such as bargaining team selection, proposal formulation and assessment, and collective behavior (situations, tactics, and communication style). The next section places these diverse collective bargaining considerations in perspective by describing the "bargaining power model," a likely resolution framework. Ethical and legal considerations affecting collective bargaining conclude this chapter.

Collective Bargaining: Definition and Structure

Collective bargaining is an activity whereby union and management officials attempt to resolve conflict by exchanging commitments in a manner that will sustain and possibly enrich their continuing relationship. Negotiation or collective bargaining is characterized by the following:[1]

- *Interdependence*—union and management officials need each other to complete a labor agreement or contract.
- *Alteration of the other group's perceptions* to obtain a favorable settlement.
- *Subjectivity*—Imprecise bargaining procedures and values that each group assigns to bargaining issues and outcomes.

Attitudes of union and management officials toward collective bargaining and the negotiated settlement influence their relationships during the length of the labor agreement. A successful collective bargaining settlement occurs when both parties can claim victory—both believe they have gained something, even if that gain is simply maintaining the status quo. A successful settlement also reinforces a labor-management relationship whereby the parties, while not always agreeing, nonetheless trust each other to be honest and straightforward in their positions without trying to unnecessarily damage the other side.[2]

Meaning and Dimensions

Bargaining structure has two general dimensions: (1) employee groupings that can affect the collective bargaining outcome and (2) the employees and employers who are subject to the provisions of the negotiated labor agreement.

Unions are responsive to several groups within and outside their organizations. Every organization has *informal work groups* (the night-shift crew or the company bowling team, for example) that have unique preferences and place pressures on union officers to achieve their preferences in collective bargaining.

In some cases union and management officials are influenced by other collective bargaining settlements. For example, a labor settlement between city government and the police might influence subsequent negotiations between the city and the firefighters. In the private sector, the United Rubber Workers' union has on occasion struck for cost-of-living labor agreement provisions similar to those obtained previously by the United Auto Workers' union.

A related concept is **pattern bargaining,** whereby union and/or management negotiators informally attempt to extend a negotiated settlement from one formal structure to another. Pattern bargaining occurs among very similar companies; for example, a labor agreement negotiated at Ford Motors might be applied to General Motors (see "Labor Relations in Action"). It might also occur if union or management negotiators attempt to apply a settlement obtained for one segment of the industry (automobile manufacturing) to another company that produces tires or headlights. For example, management and union negotiators might prefer pattern bargaining as a way to take wages out of competition from company to company. The objective of standardizing wages through pattern bargaining is beneficial for management because it will not need to worry about competitors receiving a labor cost advantage; it is also beneficial to union negotiators (who are usually at the national level) because they realize local union leaders and their memberships might vote them out of office if a labor settlement in one company is perceived as less than a settlement in a similar company—a pattern bargaining approach might remedy this potential problem.[3]

Sometimes management negotiators actively resist pattern bargaining, particularly if they think that a settlement would jeopardize their competitive capabilities. (Refer to the "Labor Relations in Action" involving General Motors, for example.)

The Negotiating Unit The second dimension of the bargaining structure, the **negotiating unit,** refers to the employees and employers who will be bound by the negotiated labor agreement. There are four major negotiating units:

LABOR RELATIONS IN ACTION

How Pattern Bargaining Affected General Motors in Recent Contract Negotiations

General Motors (GM) appeared much more concerned than Ford and Chrysler about two collective bargaining issues as the automobile manufacturers approached labor agreement expiration dates in 1993. GM's fully funded health insurance costs were twice as much as those of its competitors, and management wanted its unionized employees to absorb some of these costs, which salaried employees had done a year before.

Management at GM also stressed that it could not match Ford or Chrysler's package if it included extensive job-security benefits. The company had thousands of employees on layoffs during the previous three-year agreement at a cost of $3.5 billion to $4 billion. Moreover, GM, unlike Ford or Chrysler, expected to lay off some 65,000 employees during the next three years.[a]

Both Ford management and the UAW wanted Ford's labor agreement to be settled first and then replicated at the other automobile manufacturers. One Ford spokesperson indicated the company did not want its competitors establishing the pattern. UAW negotiators realized that Ford gave them the most maneuvering space because the company's labor costs were sometimes $5 an hour less than the others. However, GM issued a statement indicating, "[W]hen our time comes, we will seek an agreement that addresses concerns and issues that are unique to General Motors."[b]

After union and management negotiators at Ford agreed to a three-year settlement three days after the previous contract expired, pressure was placed on GM. Ford's full payment of health insurance continued, and nearly full wages would be given to laid-off employees (a not-very-costly item because Ford, unlike GM, neither had nor expected many employees with this status).

Chrysler reached a similar agreement with the UAW shortly after the Ford settlement. Attention then shifted to GM in view of the UAW's bargaining leverage; its president, Owen Bieber, observed at this time:

> All of the analysts and the media pumping up the idea that somehow General Motors can't afford this contract, and that we're in deep trouble with General Motors, is absolutely ridiculous . . . This contract is not a company-buster by any stretch of the imagination.[c]

GM's chairman, John F. Smith, still wanted union concessions on health insurance and payments to laid-off employees; however, he thought these concessions would only be granted after a 90-day strike, a situation he maintained would permanently reduce GM's presence in the domestic auto market.[d]

GM quickly settled for an agreement that was most similar to the pattern (for example, health insurance fully paid by the employer). However, GM did receive more ways to avoid paying laid-off

(continued)

LABOR RELATIONS IN ACTION

How Pattern Bargaining Affected General Motors in Recent Contract Negotiations—cont'd

employees. Under the previous agreement, employees at closed plants drew full pay from GM and could refuse transfers to GM plants farther than 50 miles away. Now, the company pays employees at closed plants 95 percent of take-home wages or 70 percent of pretax wages. Also, at several factories, the 50-mile transfer limit has been expanded to 75 miles or more, so GM can require employees to transfer to a specific plant or have their benefits reduced. GM has also increased moving benefits.[e]

GM experienced a significant drop in its stock price right after the settlement; however, its per share price increased about 40 percent in the next 15 weeks before the fourth-quarter results were published. Even though the company posted a $2.47 billion profit for the year of the labor settlement (versus substantial losses in the previous year), its stock dropped in heavy trading. This situation was most likely caused by overly high investor expectations (and helped by Chrysler's record fourth-quarter earnings posted a week earlier).[f]

[a]Joseph B. White, "GM's Smith Faces Crucial Test Today on Whether to Take UAW Pattern Deal," *The Wall Street Journal,* October 4, 1993, p. 1-A.
[b]Robert L. Simison and Neal Templin, "Ford to Lead Round of UAW Contracts; GM Loses Effort to Set Industry Pattern," *The Wall Street Journal,* August 31, 1993, p. A-3.
[c]James Bennet, "UAW Sights Now Set on Chrysler Bargaining," *The New York Times,* September 21, 1993, p. C-8 (article also furnishes terms of Ford agreement).
[d]"Ford Pact May Be Too Expensive for GM," Bureau of National Affairs, Inc., *Daily Labor Report,* no. 195 (October 12, 1993), pp. A-3, A-4.
[e]Joseph B. White and Neal Templin, "GM, UAW Agree to Tentative Contract That Offers Company Savings in Layoffs," *The Wall Street Journal,* October 25, 1993, p. A-3.
[f]James Bennet, "GM Posts $2.47 Billion Profit for '93," *The New York Times,* February 11, 1994, p. C-1.

- The negotiating unit may be the same as the *appropriate bargaining unit* (ABU) determined by the NLRB for representation election purposes and is the *minimal* collective bargaining component. (See the first example in Exhibit 6.1.)
- The negotiation unit may represent more than one ABU. This is called **centralized bargaining** (see the remaining examples in Exhibit 6.1), of which there are two major types. *Single employer—multi-plant bargaining* may be used when one company has several separate facilities, each having a separate ABU. The employer and union representatives at these facilities

Exhibit 6.1 Possible Structures for Collective Bargaining

STRUCTURE	EXAMPLE
1. Single Employer—Single Union	
Single location	ABC Manufacturing Co.—UNITE
Multiple locations	General Motors—UAW
2. Single Employer—Several Unions	
Single location	Johnson Metal, Buffalo, New York—all crafts and industrial unions
Multiple locations	General Electric—IBEW and IAM
3. Multiple Employers—Single Union	Trucking Management Incorporated—Teamsters
4. Multiple Employers—Several Unions	Association of General Contractors of North Alabama—Birmingham Trade Council

might combine into one negotiating unit for collective bargaining purposes.

- In *multi-employer bargaining*, more than one employer and the corresponding union or unions form one negotiating unit each at the bargaining table. This type of centralized bargaining is common in the trucking, construction, longshore, and newspaper industries.
- The negotiating unit may be a combination of the preceding arrangements. ABUs might be combined for certain issues (pension plans, for example) that are equally applied to employees throughout the industry, whereas working conditions specific to the individual ABU are resolved at the local facility. In many cases the local negotiations can run counter to centralized bargaining.

Centralized Bargaining One or both parties might consider centralized bargaining because of product interdependence, market factors, or legal considerations. For example, a company may have three manufacturing facilities, each having a separate ABU. If the products at the facilities are interdependent (Facility A's product is needed for Facility B, whose product is in turn completed with products at Facility C), then management would probably prefer centralized bargaining—a common expiration date and one possible strike at all facilities—instead of three different contract expiration dates and possible separate strikes at each of the facilities. Separate bargaining could shut down manufacturing operations three times compared to one shutdown under centralized bargaining.

If the three facilities are independent of each other—each facility can produce a completed product without parts and products from other facilities (for example, three steel mills, each completing a similar product, or three facilities having unrelated products such as baseball gloves, cereal, and marbles), management would probably prefer to negotiate separately with each facility's ABU. Separate negotiations would probably result in different contract expiration dates for the three facilities. If one facility went out on strike, the others could still continue production, and in the case of facilities that produce similar products, management could transfer some of the orders from the struck facility to the other two facilities where the contracts had not expired.

Some believe that conglomerate companies with a wide range of products have too much bargaining power over unions. One sample of nine conglomerates revealed 846 different manufacturing products sold. A union threatening a strike to shut down one of these manufacturing facilities or even an entire product line will not be able to put sufficient pressure on a conglomerate to reach a bargaining settlement.[4] The union therefore prefers centralized bargaining in this situation, realizing that a strike could effectively shut down the company's entire operations, thereby increasing union bargaining strength.

Market factors also influence the degree of centralization of the bargaining unit. In a highly competitive market, a multi-employer (centralized) negotiating unit would be desirable to employers who fear being placed at a competitive disadvantage if other employers subsequently negotiate lower wage rates. Combining with other employers into a multi-employer negotiating unit alleviates this fear while minimizing another problem—the loss of customers to competitors during a strike.

Unions are also concerned about market problems in some industries (construction, coal, trucking, ladies' garment, longshore, and others) and attempt to extend the negotiating unit to include the entire geographic area in which the product is competitively produced. This is to prevent a few employers from separately negotiating lower wages, which would allow production at lower costs, thereby attracting customers from the other firms and resulting in employee layoffs. In essence, the unions are attempting to standardize wages, hours, and other terms of employment in order to exclude them as competitive factors and force the employers to compete instead on the basis of factors such as product design, service, marketing, and so on.

Multi-employer bargaining also has other advantages and disadvantages. A union engaged in multi-employer bargaining has a powerful advantage over rival unions because the NLRB holds that while a multi-employer negotiating unit is intact it is the only appropriate bargaining election unit. Thus, the NLRB will dismiss a rival union's petition for an election in a single firm as long as the incumbent union and the firm are engaged in multi-employer negotiations or are parties to a multi-employer agreement. "The rival union can only obtain an election that covers all the employees in the multi-employer unit."[5]

Both labor and management can pool their respective negotiation expenses by hiring a few experts to negotiate an agreement covering several firms. Yet a corresponding disadvantage of centralized bargaining is that the hired negotiators usually do not have extensive knowledge of the parties' attitudes and strategies. Centralized bargaining tends to become more formal and less flexible in terms of meeting employee and employer concerns at the individual workplace. Finally, multi-employer bargaining can create tensions among the member employers, as evidenced in a recent coal negotiation—an employer might pull out of the association if it feels it can get a better deal negotiating separately with the union.

The decision to engage in centralized bargaining can also be affected by legal guidelines. Currently, the union can have representatives from other unions (desiring a centralized negotiating unit) at the bargaining table as negotiating team members. If the employer wishes to negotiate only with the single union, however, that union cannot delegate its authority to accept or reject the employer's settlement to the representatives of the other unions. The courts have also ruled unlawful a "lock-in" agreement between unions, which deprives individual unions of the right to sign a contract until all other unions have agreed to sign.

In *Charles D. Bonanno Linen Service Inc.* v. *NLRB*, the Supreme Court ruled that an employer who withdraws from a previously agreed-upon multi-employer bargaining arrangement without the union's consent during a bargaining impasse commits an unfair labor practice. The employer withdrawal was not allowed, and the employer was bound to any subsequent agreement reached by the union and the multi-employer bargaining group.[6]

PRE-NEGOTIATION ACTIVITIES

Selection of the Negotiating Team and Related Bargaining Responsibilities

Union and management negotiators seek bargaining team members who can keep their emotions and opinions in check. An indiscreet negotiating team member can unintentionally reveal confidential settlement points and strategies to the other team.

The individual's experience and background are also considered in the selection process. Management wants at least one line manager who supervises bargaining unit employees on its team to either interpret or answer related negotiating issues. Unions also prefer to select team members from a variety of operating departments to ensure membership representation and the discussion of working concerns that might be uniquely related to a particular department.

Political or organizational considerations are also involved in the selection of negotiating team members. The union negotiating team is elected by the members, and, therefore, the union's chief negotiator has little input into the selection process. If discretion is allowed, the chief negotiator would probably not appoint a political rival or member of an opposing faction to the negotiating team.

Proposal Determination and Assessment

Management relies on several sources to determine what the union will seek in collective bargaining. A review of recent settlements negotiated by the company's competitors and by other local firms may suggest issues that will be raised by the union. The company and union may have negotiated settlements at other facilities that might also be used as a starting point in the current negotiations. Some management officials obtain bargaining insights by reviewing the proceedings of the national union's convention.

Much attention should be given to the previous negotiation, particularly to those issues that the union actively sought and reluctantly dropped. Compromise settlements on previous issues also generate valuable clues because compromise does not mean permanent resolution of the issue.

An analysis of previous grievances at the facility can also identify certain trouble spots. GM, for example, uses a computerized analysis of number, type, and resolution status of grievances in their negotiations preparations. However, caution has to be taken not to overemphasize these grievances. Unions often step up grievance activity just before negotiations to dramatize widespread concern over certain bargaining issues—concerns perhaps more tactical than real.

Formulating Proposals and the Bargaining Range Many management negotiators, unlike their union counterparts, do not formulate bargaining proposals to discuss with the union. Managers might be reluctant to formulate proposals because that will "tip their hand" to the union, revealing management's weaknesses. A recession, however, might prod management to formulate proposals and bargain accordingly.

Managers who do formulate proposals often perform a close analysis of the labor agreement to determine desirable changes in contract language that will reduce labor costs and give management more discretion in operations. Assume, for example, that the current provision restricts supervisors entirely from performing any bargaining-unit work. Management would probably seek to change this language to allow supervisors to perform bargaining-unit work under at least three conditions: (1) when training new employees, (2) in emergency situations (usually interpreted to mean when employees' lives or production equipment are jeopardized), and (3) when experimental production efforts are involved.

Both management and union officials are concerned about the legal implications of current contractual language, particularly in terms of recent decisions by the NLRB and the courts. Management and union officials would also like to nullify the impact of adverse arbitration decisions. This can be accomplished by inserting contract language contradictory to the arbitrator's decision into the subsequent labor agreement. For example, an arbitrator's decision that the company will pay for an employee's safety shoes could be nullified by a provision in the labor agreement that reads, "The Company will provide the employees with safety shoes, and deduct the cost of these shoes from the employee's paycheck."

Both parties would also be interested in knowing if various administrators of the labor agreement (union stewards and first-line supervisors) have difficulties in implementing certain labor agreement provisions on the shop floor. Management should contact first-line supervisors before and during the negotiation process because these individuals know the existence and magnitude of employee workplace concerns and must administer the negotiated provisions.

Efforts will also be made to research data from government reports, especially from the Departments of Commerce and Labor, and from various labor relations services such as the Bureau of National Affairs, Commerce Clearing House, and

Prentice-Hall. Data from these and other sources give both parties substantial information with which to prepare for negotiations.

Union leaders must consider members' expectations, which, if unsolicited or not included in the proposed settlement, can result in rejection of the labor agreement and not supporting an officer's reelection bid. (See "Labor Relations in Action" for an example of a union not considering its members' expectations.)

The Bargaining Range Union and management officials both enter collective bargaining with their own ideas of an acceptable settlement, although both parties know the other will not agree entirely with their position. Therefore, both parties usually enter negotiations with a variety of acceptable positions, which gives them some room for maneuvering.

These positions can be given priorities and grouped into two **bargaining ranges,** one for management, the other for the union. Exhibit 6.2 illustrates bargaining ranges for a few issues; however, it is common for the parties to negotiate a hundred or more bargaining issues. (See Exhibit 6.3 for a general list of issues that may be included in the bargaining range.)

Both management and union representatives have upper and lower limits on their respective ranges. Management's upper limit is usually determined by its objectives, such as profitability and growth. A settlement above this perceived upper limit would be incompatible with the company's objectives. For example, management would close, move its operations, or bring new employees into its existing facility rather than agree to a settlement that would make operating unprofitable. On the other hand, management would not like to be known as the cheapest employer in the area, nor would it want to be unable to recruit, retain, and reward its employees. These concerns help place a lower limit on management's bargaining range—a minimum offer management feels is necessary to maintain employee morale and output.

The union's upper limit is usually shaped by two factors: (1) employment levels and (2) ability to promote and sustain a strike. The union realizes that there can be a tradeoff between a high economic settlement and total number of jobs at a facility—employers might offset their newly negotiated labor costs by laying off some employees. To some extent, the union's upper limit is governed by its desire to maintain the existing labor force or dues-paying membership. Also, a strike cannot be initiated, let alone continued, if union leaders called a strike over a $5-an-hour increase if they and their members recognize that management could realistically only afford a raise of $.80 an hour.

On the other hand, union leaders realize that there is a lower limit on the bargaining range and that a settlement below this limit would result in membership dissatisfaction. Because union leaders are strongly influenced by their desire to assure the survival of the union and their continued roles as union officers, they would seldom accept a settlement below this minimum, except in extreme cases. Members might angrily "accept" such a settlement but subsequently express their dissatisfaction by (1) voting in new union officers, (2) withdrawing their membership from the union, (3) reducing their support for the current officers through wildcat strikes or the formation of uncontrollable factions, or (4) voting out the existing union (decertification).

LABOR RELATIONS IN ACTION

Negotiations in Professional Basketball: Too Many Participants

Most collective bargaining occurs between union and management negotiators. Union members then vote to accept or reject the proposed labor agreement or to authorize a strike. Professional basketball's recent labor negotiations differed from this pattern because the federal government, players' agents, union members, and a subgroup of basketball superstars became directly involved in the process.

When the National Basketball Players Association (NBPA) labor agreement expired in June 1994, no bargaining progress occurred for the next nine months. Charles Grantham, executive director of the NBPA, resigned April 14, 1995, after he was pressured by the union's executive board for neither reaching an agreement nor receiving a strike authorization vote from the membership. The owners threatened to lock out players at the completion of the National Basketball Association (NBA) finals unless a collective bargaining agreement was reached, but NBA Commissioner David Stern lifted this threat because of extensive negotiations conducted from June 12 through June 14, the day before the last championship game was played.

Meanwhile, agents representing more than 50 percent of the NBA players were concerned that the negotiations did not include input from the 324 NBPA members. They labeled Simon Gourdine's (Grantham's successor as executive director) bargaining behavior and strategy as "outrageous" and requested that detailed outlines of both sides' bargaining positions and regional briefing sessions with the players be provided before a scheduled meeting with player representatives on June 23.

Gourdine did not comply with the request and indicated that negotiations were at a "delicate" stage, and any release of information at this time would be premature. Agents then stated that several star players such as Michael Jordon, Patrick Ewing, Reggie Miller, Scottie Pippen, Horace Grant, Moses Malone, and Alonzo Mourning had signed a "Renunciation of Collective Bargaining Rights," indicating that they no longer wished to be represented by the NBPA.

On June 21, union and management officials announced a proposed six-year labor agreement that would increase the minimum salary from $160,000 to $225,000, the average salary from $1.3 million to $3 million, the salary cap for each team from $16 million to $24 million, players' licensing fees from $500,000 to $25 million a year, revenue sharing percentage from 53 percent to 57 percent, and new inclusion of revenue from other sources (such as luxury suites and international television). On June 22, the NBPA overnighted copies of the tentative labor agreement to the 324 players.

Agents and union member dissidents were concerned about the proposed agreement's economic restrictions placed on rookies and a "luxury tax" that could limit free agents' potential salaries.[a] They now had to energize their decertification initiative because a labor agreement ratified by union members would defer this effort for the length of the contract or three years, whichever was shorter ("contract bar doctrine," Chapter 5). Two days before the scheduled contract ratification, a lawyer representing the dissident players submitted a list of names to the NLRB, allegedly sufficient in quantity to initiate decertification proceedings.

Owners unanimously approved the labor agreement on June 23, 1995. About 40 players had a 4½-hour meeting later in the day with some contending that player-members were solidified and "the threat of decertification is null and void." Alonzo Mourning, one of the many players who had signed the decertification agreement, said, "It's definitely dead right now." However, union officials canceled a scheduled labor agreement ratification vote and indicated they would return to the bargaining table to "refashion" some items, particularly the luxury tax.

Agents and player dissidents continued decertification efforts. Lawyer Jerry Kessler, Michael Jordan, Patrick Ewing, and five other players filed a class action antitrust suit against the NBA to be heard by Judge Doty on September 6. Jordan indicated he was not fighting the union and hoped members would join him to eliminate an owner lockout, thereby ensuring continued games and fan support in the 1995–1996 season. Jordan thought the players would receive a better labor agreement in court, and Kessler contended that the suit, if awarded in the players' favor, would award triple damages to those incurring financial damages in a lockout situation.

Union and management negotiators met on June 28, eight days after both groups thought they had an agreement. This action prompted the players who were petitioning the NLRB for decertification to file an unfair labor practice complaint against the NBA.

The owners announced a lockout of players beginning at 12:01 A.M. on July 1, the first such labor action in NBA history. This decision, while not yet directly affecting the games played in the 1995–1996 season, forestalls benefits, summer tryouts, signing of free agents, and trades at this time. Gourdine and Stern blamed this situation on agents' power plays and incorrect legal advice given to the players. Buck Williams, president of the NBPA and a player for the Portland Trail Blazers, who helped Gourdine negotiate the tentative agreement, felt betrayed and confused because he'd never heard of agents attempting to overthrow the union and wondered why dissident players such as Jordan and Ewing had not expressed their concerns directly with him.

Speculation then turned to management and the union's ability to negotiate a labor agreement that would be ratified before a decertification election (thereby precluding decertification), and the contents of this possible labor agreement. On July 25, 1995, a month after the first tentative agreement, management and

(continued)

Negotiations in Professional Basketball: Too Many Participants—cont'd

union officials returned to the bargaining table. Related negotiations had to be influenced by the NLRB's decision a day later to conduct a decertification election that would involve some 400 eligible players casting a ballot at NLRB regional offices on August 30 and September 7. The union indicated that it would join the dissident members and seek decertification if no agreement was reached by midnight, August 8. No formal negotiations took place between August 3 and August 7, although the NBA filed an unfair labor practice complaint against 14 players' agents during this period, charging they improperly interfered in labor negotiations.

The parties did meet hours before the union's self-imposed deadline and reached a second tentative collective bargaining agreement. Management eliminated its previous "luxury tax" provision and agreed to three items union leaders stressed members wanted, although salary restrictions for rookie players basically remained the same. David Stern explained management's capitulation, "I didn't want to face the risk of what decertification would bring. What we need to be, players and owners, is successful. This is not about who's either stronger or more right."[b]

For the union members, a "no" vote on decertification would be regarded as a functional "yes" vote on the tentative labor agreement. Gourdine realized his previous mistake of scheduling a player representatives' ratification meeting less than 48 hours after the first tentative agreement was reached—many players had refused to vote on the agreement, contending they did not have time to study it.

He now regarded the union's next action as a "political effort … You have to get the message out, keep it there, and get the players to support it."[c] Buck Williams agreed that the union must now educate and inform the players of the benefits of the proposed labor agreement.

Few players had publicly disagreed with Jordan when the first tentative agreement was reached. One exception was Charles Barkley, who contended that decertification was bad because it would disrupt the start of the season. Moreover, he said,

> I don't know why we're turning our backs on each other.… Everyone's being selfish instead of looking at the big picture and trying to do what's best for the game. Forget about the owners. Forget about the union. Forget about the agents. This is a time for the players to get ourselves together and not splinter off.[d]

Agent Leonard Armato, who represents Shaquille O'Neal and Hakeem

Olajuwon, was not in favor of the first agreement, but he publicly endorsed the second one. Vern Fleming, Indiana Pacers player representative, indicated that seven out of nine of his teammates would now reverse their previous decertification votes. David Stern attempted to add to the pro-contract ratification momentum by stressing that the union's decertification would eliminate subsequent collective bargaining and the 1995–1996 season, which was scheduled to start on November 6. Stern also indicated that management had gone the "last mile" in negotiations with the union and would not bargain with the dissident group.

Both players' groups (union advocates and dissidents) engaged in get-out-the-vote campaigns. They sent videocassettes to players, outlining their respective positions. Union officials also conducted 17 informational meetings in 12 days that drew 99 players. The Jordan group held three informational meetings that averaged about 25 players. However, neither group could predict the vote outcome with any certainty because many members were geographically scattered and likely apathetic, possibly to the point of not voting either way in the decertification election.

Eighty-six percent of the 421 eligible players eventually voted, with the union and labor agreement receiving 226 votes and the dissidents receiving 134 votes. On September 13, 1995, NBPA union representatives voted to ratify the agreement, and two days later the owners approved the agreement by a 24–5 margin. The 1995–1996 season began with no further involvement by the NLRB, courts, or players' factions. Simon Gourdine was removed from union office after the contract ratification. Buck Williams, NBPA president, promised a restructuring of the union, contending, "This was a serious wake up call. . . . I hope apathy doesn't set in again."

[a]Murray Chass, "Deal or Not, Players Get Ready to Dunk Union," *The New York Times,* June 21, 1995, B-7.

[b]Murray Chass, "NBA Owners Settled Rather Than Risk More Damage," *The New York Times,* August 10, 1995, p. B-6. For additional details regarding differences between the two labor agreements, see Lacy J. Banks, "Dissident Players Try to Rally Troops," *Chicago Sun-Times,* August 16, 1995, p. 120.

[c]Roscoe Nance, "NBA Union Leaders Launch Campaign," *USA Today,* August 10, 1995, p. 1-C.

[d]Bryan Burwell, "Barkley: The Game, Not Players, Is Priority No. 1," *USA Today,* August 4, 1995, p. 3-C.

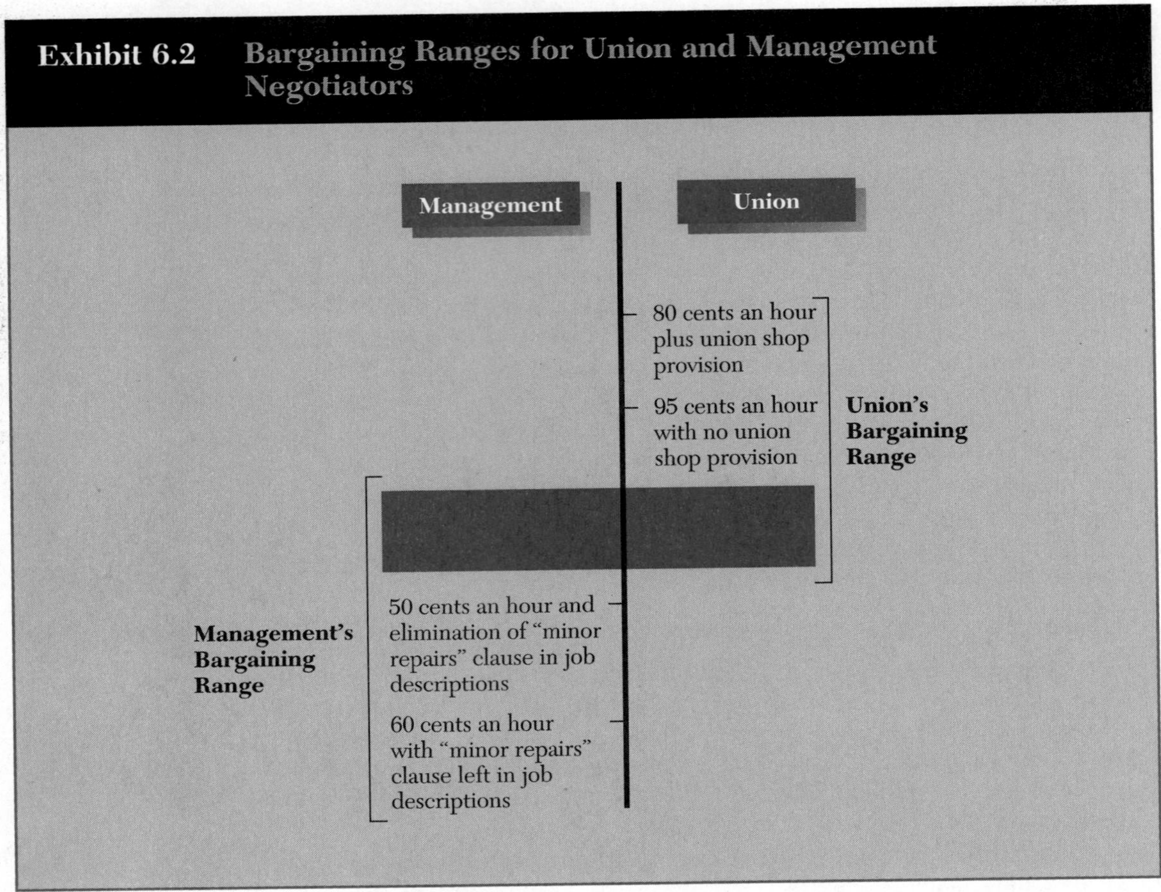

The bargaining ranges, while bounded by upper and lower limits, represent a multitude of issues. Assigning priorities to these issues and their possible combinations produces bargaining ranges of an almost infinite number of possibilities. Bargaining ranges can also change over time (see "Package Discussion of Proposals" in this chapter), usually becoming finalized as the contract expiration date approaches. During the course of negotiations, management and union officials may receive additional information that causes them to alter their upper and lower limits.

Costing Proposals Management has an overriding concern in the eventual cost of a labor agreement. Related calculations occur before and during negotiations, but these calculations rarely include the advice of financial specialists (who are seldom on the negotiating committee) and the impact on operating costs and profits of the agreement. However, management negotiators often use two general costing approaches in negotiations: *preparation of employee background data* and *calculation of a cent-per-hour wage increase.*

Exhibit 6.3 Representative Issues That Might Appear in a Collective Bargaining Agreement and/or Bargaining Range

Ability, Definition of

Absence
Reporting of
With Leave
Without Leave

Arbitration

Bargaining Unit
Definition of

Benefits, Employee
Funeral Pay
Glove, Hat, and Shoe Allowance
Jury Duty
Layoff Allowance
Pension and Insurance
Vacation

Bidding

Call-out
Definition of
Holiday
Regular
Seventh Consecutive Day, in P/R
Sixth Day Worked in Holiday Week

Change of Rate
Permanent
Temporary

Company Service Credit

Contract
Duration
Purpose of Termination

Disability Pay Plans
Nonoccupational
Occupational

Discipline
Discharge
Unsatisfactory Attendance

Dues Deduction
Authorization Form
Duration
Withdrawal, Method and/or Date of

Grievance Procedure

Handicapped Employees

Health and Safety

Holidays and Holiday Pay

Hospitalization Agreement

Hours of Work

Insurance Plan

Interchange of Work

Job Classifications and Rate Schedule

Job Rate Establishment

Job Sequence Charts

Jury Duty Allowance

Layoff
Allowance Plan
Procedure
Recall after
Seniority Rights During
Temporary

Leave-of-Absence
General
Military
Seniority, Accumulation of
Service Credit, Accumulation of
Union Business

Lunch, Overtime

Maintenance of Union Membership

Management Rights

Master Overtime Agreement

Overtime
Daily
Distribution of
Lunch
Pyramiding of
Weekly

Pay
Call-out
For Grievance Meetings
Hiring Rate
Holiday
Overtime
Progression
Rate Schedule
Report-in
Seventh Consecutive Day in Workweek
Shift Differential
Sixth Consecutive Day in Workweek
Sunday Premium

Pension Plan

Probationary Period

Recall

Rehire and Reinstatement
Company Service Credit
Rate of Pay
Seniority Rights
Vacation Eligibility

Seniority
Application of
Definition of
Loss of
Types of Veterans

Stewards

Strikes and Lockouts
General Provisions

Suspension

Temporary Change of Rate

Termination of Contract

Time and One-Half Pay

Transfers (Vacancies)
Out of Bargaining Unit
Pay Changes Because of
Temporary
Within Bargaining Unit

Transportation

Union
Bulletin Boards
Officials, Leave-of-Absence
Plant Visit of Business Representatives
Recognition
Security

Vacancies
Permanent
Temporary

Voting Time

Work
Conditions
Day, Basic
Supervisors
Week, Basic

SOURCE: Union contract.

Management usually obtains statistical summaries of employees cross-tabulated by several variables (age, sex, marital status, seniority, job classification). These summaries provide immediate information necessary to cost out a variety of union negotiation proposals such as vacations, funeral pay, and pensions.

A most significant calculation is the cost of a cent-per-hour wage increase. Since wages are inevitably discussed in negotiations, a cost figure is needed to formulate management's bargaining range and to determine whether a union's wage proposal is excessive. An illustrative calculation of a cent-per-hour wage increase for a bargaining unit of 1,000 employees follows:

$20,800	Straight time pay (1,000 employees × 40 hours a week × 52 weeks × $.01).
900	Premium pay related to wages (1,000 employees × estimated 60-hours-per-year overtime, holiday, and call-out premium worked × $.015).
5,200	"Roll up," or benefits directly affected by the wage increase (profit sharing, pensions, life insurance, employer contributions to social security, shift differential if paid on a percentage basis, unemployment insurance, workers' compensation, and so on), estimated for illustrative purposes at 25 percent of the straight time wage rate.
$26,900	Cost of a cent-per-hour wage increase.

The wage total calculated in this example does not take into account opportunity costs or the spillover effect on wages of nonunion company employees, who will probably receive the negotiated wage increase as a minimum in their subsequent salary increases. For example, GM gave its salaried, nonunion employees a $1,600 lump-sum payment and an average 5 percent salary increase. This action was announced when the UAW announced that its membership had ratified a new labor agreement.[7]

Additionally, many cost categories, such as overtime and holidays worked, have to be estimated from past payroll records and future production and staffing requirements.

Unions often pursue two general negotiating strategies to counter management's costing activities. Union officials often submit proposals that are difficult to cost, thereby weakening management's related statistical objections during negotiations. Assume, for example, a current contract provision provides a Sunday work premium of 75¢ an hour if the employees have no absences during their regularly scheduled work week. The union proposes that employees working on Sunday receive this premium regardless of their attendance record during the week. Management can examine past payroll records to estimate the added cost of this proposal, a difficult task if there are thousands of employees involved, and an uncertain indicator of extra absences that might occur if this proposal is accepted. Other proposals, such as extending a previous labor agreement's three-day paid leave for the death of an immediate family member to include first cousins, are nearly impossible to cost because there is no way to gather accurate data.

Union negotiators also formulate proposals that benefit members while saving management money, a difficult task requiring much ingenuity; examples include:

- Allowing police to keep a squad car for personal use, thereby reducing crime statistics and related expenses.
- Allowing sabbaticals where professors receive one-half their salaries for nine months and management keeps the funded surplus if replacements teach the professors' classes.

Collective Bargaining Behavior

Bargaining Situations

While each bargaining situation is unique and depends on the negotiators' personalities and the issues involved, collective bargaining behavior generally falls into four categories: *distributive, integrative, intra-organizational bargaining,* and *attitudinal structuring.*[8]

Distributive bargaining occurs when the two parties' goals conflict. Certain issues, particularly wages, heighten conflict because resources are limited and one party tends to gain at the other party's expense. Each negotiator tries to discover and modify the opponent's position and values assigned to these issues. This approach encourages threats, bluffs, and secrecy as each party tries to keep the upper hand. **Integrative bargaining** occurs when both parties attempt to resolve such common concerns as training to meet foreign competition or technological change and employee alcohol treatment programs. This approach encourages trust, an understanding of the other negotiator's real needs and objectives, and emphasis on commonalities between the parties instead of differences.[9] **Attitudinal structuring** refers to activities aimed at attaining a desired relationship between the parties. This process does not pertain to particular issues; instead, each party attempts to change the opponent's attitudes and the relationships that affect the negotiation process and subsequent administration of the labor agreement. These activities may be based on the assumption that a good relationship influences cooperation and may even lead to concessions. Related to this are behaving in accordance with the other's values (for example, not swearing or being loud), encouraging the other to "role reverse," thereby assuming your point of view, and conducting business in pleasant places.[10]

Attitudinal structuring can also be negative. During one contract negotiation involving a steel manufacturer, management officials emphasized declining economic conditions to the union negotiators by calling in laid-off employees to empty their lockers. The local union president and prominent bargaining team member noted, "That scares the hell out of them. These [management officials] have no finesse."[11] Management by these actions has communicated to the union bargaining team that labor agreement negotiations are occurring in an atmosphere of economic doom, which may convince them that their initial bargaining expectations were unrealistic. Attitudinal structuring can be used to accomplish either integrative (problem-solving) or distributive (competitive) bargaining, and can contribute to intra-organizational bargaining.

Intra-organizational bargaining occurs when management and union negotiators attempt to achieve consensus within their respective organizations. However, bargaining teams are seldom successfully unified by means of this approach; in fact, union and management negotiators often have more difficulty with members of their respective negotiating teams than with each other.

Management's chief negotiator sometimes takes a back seat to other management officials, particularly lawyers, at the bargaining table. When a settlement is reached, it is also subject to second-guessing by other officials, who usually contend that management negotiators could have obtained a better deal. The union is not exempt from internal disputes either, particularly because its chief negotiator is seldom given a free hand in selecting the negotiating committee. In many cases, at least one member of the union's negotiating team is a political rival of the chief negotiator. More prevalent are factions that attempt to obtain various bargaining demands regardless of the chief negotiator's preferences.

Management and union negotiators spend much time resolving differences within their respective organizations. One observer of labor-management negotiations noted the following:

> [A] large share of collective bargaining is not conflict but a process by which the main terms of the agreement, already understood by the negotiators, are made acceptable, not to those in charge of the bargaining but to those who will have to live with its results.[12]

Bargaining Approaches and Negotiation Communication Style

Union and management negotiators devise various approaches to bargaining situations. Four such approaches, described in Roger Fisher and William Ury's influential book, *Getting to Yes,*[13] are paraphrased below:

1. *Understand the other side's participants* because bargaining differences occur between your thinking and theirs. Bargaining conflict lies in people's heads and not in objective reality. Therefore, the negotiator needs to see the situation from the other side's perspective. This includes several specific tactics such as making bargaining proposals consistent with opponents' values. This tactic enhances "face-saving," or a person's need to reconcile a negotiation stand or settlement with his or her past words and deeds.
2. *Focus on concerns and interests rather than on positions.* A negotiator's ego is often identified with convincing the other negotiator that her or his position is correct, which makes agreement less likely. "Any agreement

reached may reflect a mechanical splitting of the difference between final positions rather than a solution carefully crafted to meet the legitimate interests of the parties."

3. *Invent and broaden bargaining options for mutual gains,* which includes considering and implementing "brainstorming" techniques.
4. *Use objective criteria.* Standards of fairness, efficiency, and scientific merit applied to a negotiation problem will increase the likelihood of a settlement that both parties can live with. Similarly, the more both sides refer to precedent and community practice, the greater the chance of benefiting from past experience.

These and other bargaining approaches are reflected through messages transmitted between union and management negotiators. Most of this communication is channeled into three general directions: language analysis, package discussion of proposals, and argumentation.

Language Analysis In many cases union and management negotiators have to convey their preferences and positions to each other while giving their fellow bargaining team members a slightly different impression. This requires skill at **language analysis** on the part of the listener. For instance, consider the following situation. The chief union negotiator discusses the company's latest negotiation proposal with the union members, who in turn feel that the negotiator should go back to the table and press management for a more favorable settlement. Believing that the company's proposal was reasonable, the union negotiator must communicate this preference (to accept the proposal) to management and at the same time convince the bargaining committee that he or she fought for their rights. Confronted with this difficult situation, the union negotiator might open the next bargaining session with, "The membership disagreed [with the company's economic proposal]. The present contract will not extend beyond 12 o'clock tonight."

At first glance, the union negotiator's statement seems strong and unyielding. However, a skilled management negotiator would analyze it through three dimensions:[14]

1. How final is the statement?
2. How specific is the statement?
3. What are the consequences associated with the statement?

At second glance, the statement appears neither final nor specific. In fact, management could interpret it to mean the union negotiator is relatively satisfied with the proposal, particularly if no specific recommendations for improvement follow. Finally, the union negotiator, by stating "the present contract will not extend," does not give a clear indication that a strike will occur if the offer is not changed.

All three dimensions need to be considered when evaluating negotiators' remarks, as they can maintain their flexibility by being inconclusive or silent on one or two dimensions. For example, Caterpillar's CEO commented before the strike that management's offer was "F-i-n-a-l, Last. That's It." The union's top negotiator responded, "We're not going to accept their final offer today, next month, or next year . . . Global competitiveness is a code word for bottom-line greed."[15] While appearing firm and unyielding, both negotiators by being nonspecific and silent on possible consequences at least enabled future bargaining possibilities.

Package Discussion of Proposals Since maintaining communication between parties during negotiations is essential to the bargaining process, negotiating several issues (a *package*) at the same time is preferable to the item-by-item, or "yes-no," approach. The item-by-item negotiations technique does not allow the parties to communicate their preferences realistically and at the same time maintain flexibility in their decision making.

In the package approach, each party combines several bargaining issues for discussion purposes. For example, the union might propose dropping issues 2 (union shop), 7 (birthday off), and 9 (voluntary overtime) from its bargaining list if management would agree to issues 3 (eliminating subcontracting) and 10 (optional retirement after 30 years). Management might then present the following counterproposal: agree to issues 3 and 10 if the union drops issues 2, 7, 9, and 11 (free dental care). This process would be repeated until the parties resolved the issues. (See Exhibit 6.4 for another example of this approach.)

The advantage of the package discussion approach is that both parties indicate which issues they are willing to concede; and, if agreement is not reached, these issues are still considered negotiable. Moreover, both parties keep track of these proposals because they offer insights into their opponent's bargaining preferences.

Argumentation In essence there are three bargaining positions: "yes," "maybe—keep on talking," or "no." When one negotiator has adopted a "maybe" or "no" position, the other negotiator has to use arguments or justifications for his or her bargaining positions. Effective arguments depend on avoiding some interpersonal strategies while achieving others (see Exhibit 6.5).

Resolution Framework: The Bargaining Power Model

Applications of the Bargaining Power Model

Thus far, bargaining situations and behaviors have been described. A framework is needed to place these behaviors in perspective. One such framework suggests that both parties arrange their strategies and tactics in a manner that will enhance their **bargaining power** and eventual settlement. One of the better-known models based on this framework was suggested by Chamberlain and Kuhn,[16] a model expressed in two equations presented in Exhibit 6.6. These equations can apply to individual issues or to the eventual package settlement. Although the bargaining power model is presented as an equation, it is an imprecise formula based on two major assumptions:

Exhibit 6.4 Package Discussion Approach in Collective Bargaining

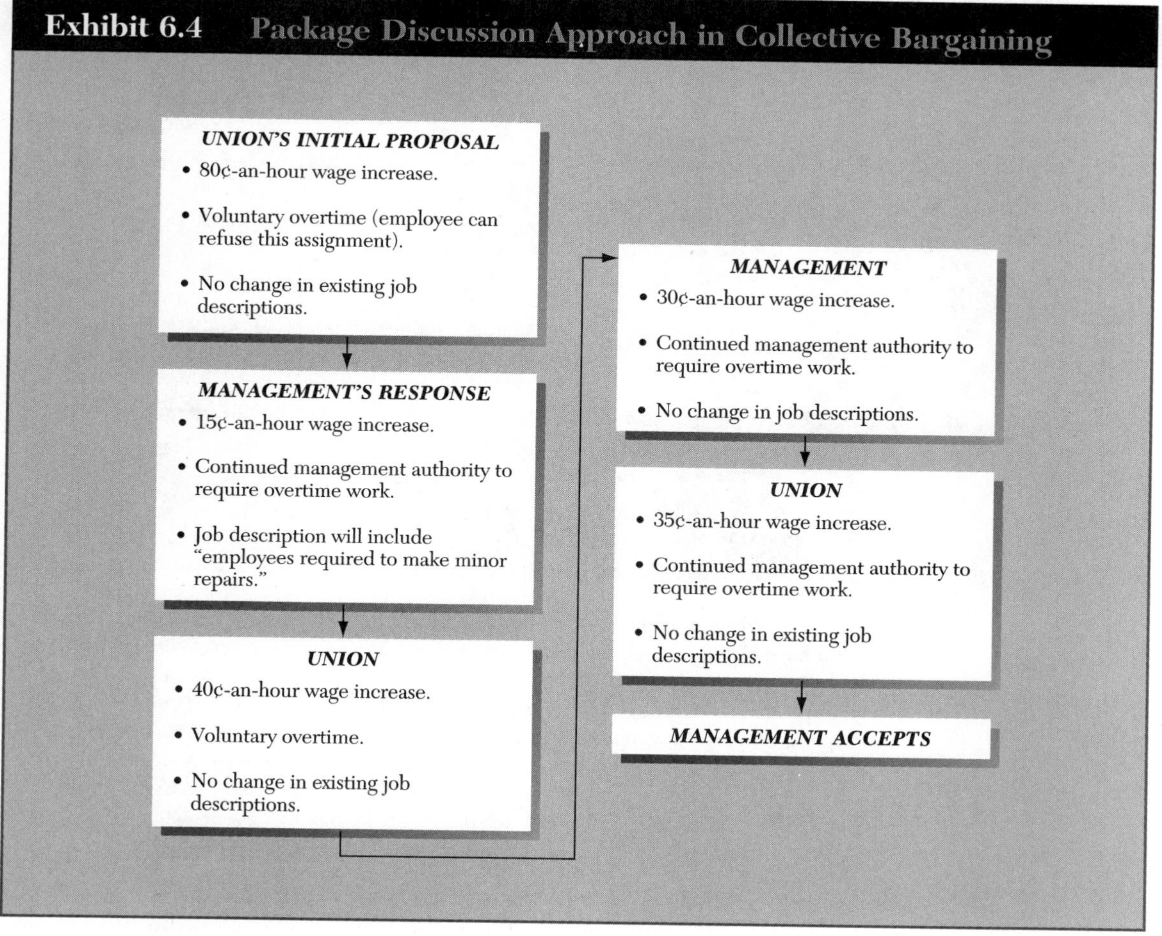

UNION'S INITIAL PROPOSAL
• 80¢-an-hour wage increase.
• Voluntary overtime (employee can refuse this assignment).
• No change in existing job descriptions.
MANAGEMENT'S RESPONSE
• 15¢-an-hour wage increase.
• Continued management authority to require overtime work.
• Job description will include "employees required to make minor repairs."
UNION
• 40¢-an-hour wage increase.
• Voluntary overtime.
• No change in existing job descriptions.
MANAGEMENT
• 30¢-an-hour wage increase.
• Continued management authority to require overtime work.
• No change in job descriptions.
UNION
• 35¢-an-hour wage increase.
• Continued management authority to require overtime work.
• No change in existing job descriptions.
MANAGEMENT ACCEPTS

1. Union and management negotiators cost issues in a similar manner and are rational individuals.
2. If it costs more for a party to disagree than to agree with the other, then the party will agree to the other's position.

Therefore, each side can increase its bargaining power by *increasing the other's disagreement costs* or *reducing the other's agreement costs.*

To illustrate this strategic framework, consider a union bargaining proposal for a ten-minute cleanup time before the end of the work shift. Management would probably refuse this item unless the union presented arguments relating to the bargaining power model. First, the union could reduce management's cost of agreeing with the cleanup time proposal by eliminating some of its other bargaining proposals in exchange. The union negotiator might also reduce management's agreement costs with an argument along the following lines:

Exhibit 6.5 Checklist of Interpersonal Strategies for Effective Arguments

AVOID	PRACTICE
Interrupting	Listening
Point-scoring	Questioning for clarification
Attacking	Summarizing issues neutrally
Blaming	Challenging opponent to justify his or her case on an item-by-item basis (watch for signals)
Being "too clever"	Being noncommittal about opponent's proposals and his explanations
Talking too much	Testing opponent's commitment to positions (looking for clues about priorities)
Shouting your opponent down	Seeking and giving information (be careful about unintended signals)
Sarcasm	
Threats	

SOURCE: Gavin Kennedy, John Benson, and John McMillan, *Managing Negotiations* (Englewood Cliffs, N.J.: Prentice-Hall, 1982), pp. 46–47.

> There are currently many different cleanup practices at our facility. Some departments do not have cleanup time, whereas other departments let their employees stop work a half-hour early to clean up. If you calculated the total cleanup time in the plant, it would probably amount to 15 miutes per employee. Worse yet, you cannot currently discipline employees who are abusing cleanup time since there are so many different practices in the plant. This contract provision would enable management to wipe the past practice slate clean. Management could instruct the supervisors to rigidly enforce this provision, which could actually save the company money.

If management does not accept this argument, the union could follow the second strategic approach—increasing management's cost of disagreeing with the union. The ultimate argument would be to threaten a strike unless the cleanup time provision was granted. This threat might carry some weight if management knew there was widespread dissatisfaction over this issue. Otherwise, chances are that management would view this as an idle threat and would not believe its disagreement cost had increased.

Another threat, however, could raise management's cost of disagreeing with the union over this issue. The union could make arguments regarding safety hazards at the facility and suggest two alternatives: management can allow cleanup time before the end of the shift or the union can lodge a safety complaint with OSHA. Management negotiators would prefer the first alternative because they know it would not cost the union anything to file the complaint, and an OSHA investigation might uncover other safety problems whose correction would be more expensive.

Some factors can affect both union and management costs and bargaining power equations. Others might pertain to either the union or the management negotiators.

Exhibit 6.6 Bargaining Power Equations for Union and Management

$$\text{Union's Bargaining Power} = \frac{\text{Management's Cost of Disagreeing with the Union}}{\text{Management's Cost of Agreeing with the Union}}$$

$$\text{Management's Bargaining Power} = \frac{\text{Union's Cost of Disagreeing with Management}}{\text{Union's Cost of Agreeing with Management}}$$

SOURCE: Equations are modified slightly from Allan M. Cartter and F. Ray Marshall, *Labor Economics*, rev. ed. (Homewood, Ill.: Richard D. Irwin, 1972), p. 283. © 1972 by Richard D. Irwin, Inc. Used by permission.

Factors Potentially Affecting Both Bargaining Power Equations Some factors that may affect union and management bargaining power are unemployment, goodwill, public image, and government intervention.

Unemployment This factor can affect both bargaining power equations presented in Exhibit 6.6. High unemployment in the area increases the union's cost of disagreeing with management because strikers would find it difficult to find employment at other firms. It reduces management's disagreement costs because high unemployment tends to make it easier to find striker replacements.

Goodwill, public image, and government intervention One factor that can influence the decision to strike or not, especially in small plants, is goodwill, which pertains mostly to internal relationships. Management and union negotiations do not want antagonistic attitudes that develop during negotiations or a strike to linger when operations are resumed. They also do not want their activities labeled irresponsible or heedless of the public interest. Possible government intervention for vital industries must also be considered, especially if management or the union believes government intervention will weaken its bargaining position.

Factors Affecting the Union's Disagreement and Agreement Costs Financial supplements given to union members can lower both the union's disagreement costs and management's bargaining power. Employees might be able to supplement their incomes during a strike through their spouses becoming employed, strike benefits, and public aid.

The strike benefits received by many union members, usually $50 or less per week, often determine whether union members will vote to strike as well as how long they will strike. Although the amount that each union member receives during a strike is minimal, the total amount of annual strike payments can be large. For example, the Amalgamated Transit Union paid $250,000 to $300,000 a week to strikers for six months in its dispute with Greyhound.[17] Most unions pay strike benefits when funds are available and the strike has been sanctioned by the national union leadership, but there are often additional stipulations: that the member be in good standing, complete a waiting period, and establish a need for the payments.

When the strike is settled, the strike benefits usually end. Sometimes the benefits stop or the payments are reduced before the strike is over. Some unions set a minimum for their strike fund balance, and payments cease when the minimum is reached. Other unions will either terminate or reduce the benefits for individual members who work for other employers or do not perform their strike duties.

Public aid (welfare and unemployment compensation, for example) can also reduce union members' disagreement costs by supplementing their incomes when they go on strike. These assistance programs might exist at the federal or state level and are subject to various qualifications such as a waiting period for striking employees to qualify for unemployment compensation.

Many arguments can be made for and against public aid being given to union members on strike. Proponents of public aid might claim

- Strikers are taxpayers when they work, so when they do not work, they should receive aid.
- Tax dollars are used to feed hungry people in other countries and prisoners in this country. Strikers who are needy should receive the same consideration.
- Even though some persons may be against public aid for strikers, they should not be against public aid for the families who are directly affected.
- Eligibility for public support should be based on need as determined by law, not on whether a person is on strike.

Opponents of public support to strikers also make several arguments:

- Legislators never intended to provide public aid to strikers, particularly since strikers have refused bona fide employment by refusing to go back to work.
- Giving public aid to strikers violates a traditional policy of government neutrality in labor-management relations.

Factors Affecting Management's Agreement and Disagreement Costs The individual company's characteristics have considerable effect on the bargaining power equation of Exhibit 6.6. Management's agreement costs (and bargaining power) can be reduced if it can pass on the cost of a negotiated settlement to customers. Electrical utilities may represent examples of this situation. Management's disagreement costs (and union bargaining power) can be increased if any of the following factors occur: low inventories combined with high customer demand, fear of permanent loss of customers during a strike, and fixed costs such as rent, interest on loans, payments for equipment, and salaries of nonunion personnel being incurred without goods or services being produced.

Complexities Associated with the Bargaining Power Model

Bargaining power "costs" are often imprecise figures associated with *calculation difficulties, large and sudden change,* and other complexities. Some issues, such as inserting the job requirement "perform minor repairs" into employees' job descriptions, will undoubtedly save the company money as non-craft employees will perform these duties less expensively than maintenance employees, particularly those working at overtime or other premium wage rates. However, management cannot calculate the precise dollar cost savings associated with this provision, particularly if the union negotiator fears that agreeing with a "minor repairs" clause would incur imprecise yet large political costs such as members rejecting the proposed labor contract or his or her reelection bid.

The bargaining power model and related costs are also subject to large and sudden change. The government may suddenly announce wage-price controls or guidelines, forcing unions to agree to wage settlements comparable to the limits set by the government. Or, management could receive a sudden influx of rush orders from a major customer near the contract expiration date. Management's disagreement costs are then sharply increased, particularly if the customer indicates he or she will take unfinished orders to a competitor.

Four additional bargaining power model complexities derived from actual negotiation situations are discussed in "Labor Relations in Action."

The limitations of the bargaining power model do not eliminate its usefulness. Union and management officials do assign costs, however crudely, and direct their strategies toward increasing the other party's disagreement costs relative to agreement costs.

Ethical Considerations in Collective Bargaining Behavior

Union and management negotiators' bargaining behavior often involves at least two general ethical dimensions that were first mentioned in Chapter 5. The first ethical dimension, *moral or ideal behavior,* is subject to varying definitions instead of an either/or distinction. However, negotiator behaviors such as bribing the opponent to reach a settlement, stealing an opponent's confidential information, publicly demeaning or humiliating an opponent, or using electronic surveillance to "bug" an opponent's meeting areas are clearly at the unethical end of the continuum.

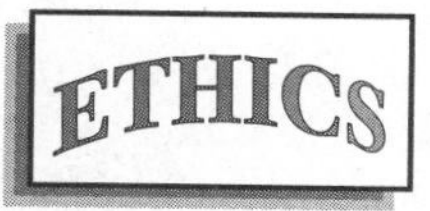

Some bargaining behaviors have more general and longer range ethical implications. Consider, for example, the reflections of Lee Iacocca, the prominent automobile industry executive:

> As long as Detroit was making money, it was always easy for us to accept union demands and recoup them later in the form of price increases. The alternative was to take a strike and risk ruining the company.

LABOR RELATIONS IN ACTION

Bargaining Cost Complexities from Five Negotiation Situations

1. A symbolic action or a principle, while very difficult to measure, can nonetheless significantly affect a negotiator's agreement or disagreement costs.

A bargaining impasse between flight attendants and American Airlines was settled after a five-day strike when President Clinton spoke separately to Mr. Crandall, the airline's chairman, and Denise Hedges, the head of the flight attendants' union, and noted afterward that both sides had agreed to binding arbitration. Mr. Crandall professed disapproval of Mr. Clinton's symbolic gesture; however, he acknowledged its potential influence, "In view of his national responsibilities, we think his requests are entitled to great deference.[a]

Yet, at least some Clinton administration officials indicated that this gesture was influential because it reduced management's agreement costs. Labor Secretary Robert Reich stressed that no pressure was put on Mr. Crandall. A senior administration official indicated that Mr. Crandall realized his airline lost large revenues (later calculated at $38 million a day)[b] due to the strike and called the White House to suggest arbitration, and then Mr. Clinton called Mr. Crandall to confirm the plan.[c]

Professional baseball players' recent strike occurred in large part over principle—insuring that future players would continue to have job rights that former striking players obtained for them. Many players also struck to maintain their "self-respect," particularly since they thought management treated them like a "commodity."

2. Management and union negotiators/members might incur future costs stemming from a current impasse.

Caterpillar's 14,000 employees ended their 5½-month strike against the company but restruck about two years later because they did not have a labor agreement and contended management was engaging in unfair labor practices. Many of the employees on the second strike (which commenced June 21, 1994, and was over by the end of 1995) might never realize future employment with the company because their jobs have been performed by office, temporary, and newly hired employees, retirees, and some 4,100 UAW members who crossed the picket lines. This employment separation might also reduce, even eliminate, pension plan payouts. Moreover, the UAW might lose its employee representative rights if a decertification election were held involving those currently working at Caterpillar. The company also has incurred significant future costs (lawyers' fees and possible settlement) associated with more than 134 unfair labor practice complaints filed by the NLRB against Caterpillar.[d]

One of the more dramatic and personal costs incurred by a manager in a negotiation involved Frank Lorenzo, who was identified as a "union buster" in negotiations with Eastern Airlines. Several years after acrimonious bargaining,

Lorenzo applied for Department of Transportation permission to operate an initially small airline (four planes)—unions mobilized 57 members of Congress against him, and his application was denied.[e]

3. A union negotiator's estimated bargaining power costs can be unexpectedly increased by members and rival leadership.

This situation occurred to Teamster President Ron Carey in a three-week strike when members rejected an increase in union dues to replenish a necessary strike fund that would pay strikers for only one week. Carey then had to search for loans and give serious consideration to cutting the strike short. Carey also faced uncertain political damage when his chief rival for the presidency, R.V. Durham, reflected on the negotiated settlement, "It appears that Carey caved in on the gut issues that the members struck to protect.... Carey should have stayed at the bargaining table and fought for a contract that protects the members' job security."[f]

4. Each side can reduce its disagreement costs in a manner unanticipated by the other side.

American Airlines flight attendants promised that their strike would last only 11 days. That meant they would return to work just before replacement flight attendants completed training. The union did not want other American Airlines unions to become directly involved in the strike (by honoring the picket line, for example), although they did receive help from a business competitor, Northwest Airlines, who flew American Airlines attendants at a special 90 percent discount to their various picket-line destinations.[g]

[a]Gwin Ifill, "Airline Strike Ends as Clinton Steps In," *The Wall Street Journal,* November 23, 1993, p. A-1.

[b]Adam Bryant, "AMR, Citing Strike, Posts $253 Million Loss," *The New York Times,* January 20, 1994, p. C-4.

[c]Peter T. Kilborn, "Strike Is Called Victory for Women, Not Unions," *The New York Times,* November 24, 1993, p. A-16.

[d]"Caterpillar Boasts Record Profits Despite UAW's Seven-Month Strike," Bureau of National Affairs, Inc., *Daily Labor Report,* no. 13 (January 20, 1995), pp. A-6–A-7; "Much Ado About Pettiness," *Business Week,* July 4, 1994, pp. 34, 36; and Robert L. Rose, "*Plowing Ahead:* UAW's Long Strike Fails to Crimp Output at Caterpillar's Plants," *The Wall Street Journal,* October 4, 1994, pp. A-1, A-9.

[e]Bridget O'Brian, "Still Grounded: For Lorenzo, Getting a New Airline Aloft Is Proving Treacherous," *The Wall Street Journal,* January 25, 1994, pp. A-1, A-6.

[f]Kevin G. Salwen and Daniel Machalaba, "Trucking Firms Agree to Settlement," *The Wall Street Journal,* April 29, 1994, p. A-3; and "Teamsters' Strike Shuts Down Trucking Firms," *The Wall Street Journal,* April 7, 1994, p. A-3.

[g]Julie Schmit, "Airline Feud Hits Employee Perks," *USA Today,* November 19, 1993, p. 5-B.

> The executives at GM, Ford, and Chrysler have never been overly interested in long-range planning. They've been too concerned about expediency, improving the profits for the next quarter—and earning a good bonus.
>
> They? I should be saying "we." After all, I was one of the boys. I was part of that system. Gradually, little by little, we gave in to virtually every union demand. We were making so much money that we didn't think twice. We were rarely willing to take a strike, and so we never stood on principle.
>
> I sat there in the midst of it all and I said: "Discretion is the better part of valor. Give them what they want. Because if they strike, we'll lose hundreds of millions of dollars, we'll lose our bonuses, and I'll personally lose half a million dollars in cash."
>
> Our motivation was greed. The instinct was always to settle quickly, to go for the bottom line. In this regard, our critics were right—we were always thinking of the next quarter.
>
> "What's another dollar an hour?" we reasoned. "Let future generations worry about it. We won't be around then."
>
> But the future has arrived, and some of us are still around. Today we're all paying the price for our complacency.[18]

ETHICS

The second ethical dimension, *conforming to professional standards,* is more complicated when applied to negotiators' behaviors. Top union and management bargaining team officials would likely agree on at least three professional commitments in their bargaining behaviors:

- To obtain a settlement as close to the optimal bargaining range as possible (upper range for the union negotiator and lower range for the management negotiator).
- To convince their respective bargaining team members and other constituents that they are effective negotiators.
- To communicate with the other negotiating team in an honest, respectful fashion to enhance the continuing labor relations relationship after the collective bargaining agreement is reached.

All three of these standards are attainable, although maximizing the first two may strain and alter the third. In other words, it is difficult to convince your bargaining constituents that you obtained the best settlement possible if you reveal the complete truth to your negotiating opponent. For example, one account of an inexperienced management negotiator noted,

> Imbued with idealism, he wanted to end the bickering he had seen take place during past negotiations with labor. To do this, he was ready to give the workers as much as his company could afford. Consequently he asked some members of his staff to study his firm's own wage structure and decide how it compared with other companies, as well as a host of other related matters. He approached the collective bargaining table with a halo of goodness surrounding him. Asking for the floor, he proceeded to describe what he had done and with a big smile on his face made the offer.
>
> Throughout his entire presentation, the union officials stared at him in amazement. He had offered more than they had expected to secure. But no matter, as soon as he finished, they proceeded to lambaste him, denouncing him for trying to destroy col-

> lective bargaining and for attempting to buy off labor. They announced that they would not stand for any such unethical maneuvering, and immediately asked for . . . more than the idealistic executive had offered.[19]

Thus, a completely honest and open negotiator may be exploited by his or her opponent, commit to a position that allows no further concessions, or sacrifice what might have been successfully gained through less-candid approaches. Most successful negotiations have featured ritualistic elements such as describing elaborate but irrelevant statistics, using histrionics, or staging false fights or temper tantrums. One management negotiator, for example, noted that his union counterpart approaches him at the start of negotiations and whispers, "We'll get together privately and talk about what we are really going to do to make a deal as soon as this show is over."[20]

ETHICS

Successful negotiators realize that credibility is a necessary personal attribute, and lying or uttering a deliberate falsehood can destroy credibility and ruin a negotiator's effectiveness. However, a fine line exists between lying and withholding the truth. Negotiators are not going to volunteer items that could damage their bargaining positions. They might also exaggerate and bluff on occasion. Successful negotiators are also skilled in asking the correct questions and interpreting the meaning of omissions from the other party's remarks.

> The principled negotiator doesn't resort to trickery, but that doesn't mean he naively gives away his position. He doesn't have to reveal what his final best offer will be. Not all principled negotiators agree on just how principled you have to be. It's OK to mislead the other side as to your intentions, [one principled negotiator] argues. You can say I'm not going to give in, and then give in five minutes later. But never give the other side misinformation about the facts.[21]

Parties can therefore communicate in a flexible manner while still maintaining their integrity and ethical responsibilities.

The Good Faith Bargaining Requirement

Union and management officials are not completely free to shape or ignore ethical considerations in collective bargaining. The government, through the National Labor Relations Act, has indicated that both union and management organizations must negotiate in good faith—they must demonstrate a sincere and honest intent to consummate a labor agreement and be reasonable in their bargaining positions, tactics, and activities.

However, *good faith* represents a state of mind difficult to define precisely. For example, this obligation does not specifically require that a party must agree to the other's proposal or make a concession to the other party. Violations of good faith bargaining can come from four sources: the nature of the bargaining issues, specific bargaining actions (called *per se violations*), totality of conduct, and successor employer bargaining obligations.

Nature of Bargaining Issues Over the years, the NLRB and the courts have categorized bargaining issues as illegal, mandatory, or voluntary. **Illegal bargaining**

issues are not bargainable, and it is illegal for the parties to insert them into the labor contract even if they are in agreement over the issue. Related examples include a closed shop, a "whites only" employment clause, mandatory retirement at 62, and compensation arrangements that violate the provisions of the Fair Labor Standards Act (for example, not paying bargaining-unit employees overtime for work in excess of 40 hours per week).

Mandatory bargaining issues are related to wages, hours, and other conditions of employment. Examples of mandatory subjects are wage systems, bonus plans, pensions, profit sharing, vacations, holidays, plant rules, grievance procedures, and management rights. These subjects must be bargained, and the party advancing these subjects may insist on their inclusion to a point of impasse. However, failure to reach agreement does not automatically constitute a bargaining violation. After an impasse is established, management is free to unilaterally implement its bargaining terms (as in the previous example involving Caterpillar and the UAW).

Union and management officials can also negotiatiate **voluntary issues** (also called **permissive** or **nonmandatory**) such as industry promotion plans, strike insurance, an interest arbitration clause, and benefits for retired employees. Unlike mandatory issues, these do not require either party to bargain. In fact, insisting on their bargaining and inclusion in the labor agreement to a point of impasse (and subsequent union strike or management lockout) would be an unfair labor practice. For example, in a case involving DuPont's management asking employees to participate in a videotape, the NLRB determined this action was a voluntary bargaining issue not to be discussed with the union because it was not part of the employees' day-to-day responsibilities, employees were not compelled to participate, and the taping could not have been a matter of deep concern to the employees.[22]

Specific Bargaining Actions In some cases a specific, single action by an employer constitutes an unfair labor practice in bargaining. For example, management commits a *per se* violation whenever it

- Refuses to meet with the union to negotiate its proposals.
- Insists to a point of impasse on a provision requiring that a secret ballot election be held before a strike can be called.
- Refuses to supply cost and other data relating to a group insurance plan when the union requests this information and management claims inability to pay.
- Announces a wage change without consulting the union.

A union commits a *per se* violation when it

- Insists on a closed shop or discriminatory hiring.
- Refuses to meet with a legal representative of the employer about negotiations.
- Refuses to negotiate a management proposal involving a mandatory subject.

Totality of Conduct Sometimes the NLRB and the courts have determined that one activity alone does not constitute a bargaining violation; however, a combination of activities, *totality of conduct,* might. A prominent and controversial example of this legal consideration involved a General Electric bargaining approach called **Boulwarism** after the late vice president of General Electric, Lemuel Boulware.

General Electric contended that it simply approached bargaining in a manner similar to its product marketing—by finding out what the employees desired and on the basis of employee survey results, formulating a bargaining proposal. General Electric contended that this approach was not capricious, but "fair and firm," as management's bargaining position was based on a careful examination of the "facts" and was capable of being altered if the union presented new and significant information at the bargaining table. This approach, the company maintained, represented a sincere bargaining effort, one that was not aimed at destroying the union, but rather at eliminating a time-consuming and unnecessary ritual from collective bargaining (such as initial unrealistic offers that both parties know will not be accepted).

However, General Electric's totality of conduct was found violative of good faith bargaining primarily because it went directly to the employees rather than working through the employees' exclusive bargaining agent (the union). The NLRB found several bargaining activities that contributed to General Electric's "take it or leave it" bargaining approach. These activities included refusal to supply cost information on an insurance program, vague responses to the union's detailed proposals, a prepared lecture series instead of counteroffers, and a "stiff and unbending patriarchal posture" even after it was apparent that the union would have to concede to the employer's terms.[23] This decision suggests that presenting and holding to your "best bargaining offer," while it appears to be ethically correct, is legally wrong. (It should be noted that, if its behavior is otherwise legal, management can legally communicate to the employees its reasons against the union's bargaining proposal and urge the employees to accept its final proposal presented to the union.[24])

Other rulings involving employer or union conduct have provided indicators of good- and bad-faith bargaining. The following factors, while they probably would not individually constitute bad-faith bargaining, might be considered so if many of them were committed together.

- *Surface bargaining:* The party is willing to meet at length and confer but merely goes through the motions of bargaining. Surface bargaining includes making proposals that cannot be accepted, taking an inflexible attitude on major issues, and offering no alternative proposals.
- *Concessions:* Although the making of concessions is not legally required, the term *good faith* certainly suggests a willingness to compromise and make a reasonable effort to settle differences.
- *Proposals and demands:* Advancing proposals that open the doors for future discussions indicates good faith, whereas proposals that foreclose future negotiations and are patently unreasonable reflect bad faith.

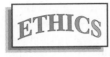

- *Dilatory tactics:* Unreasonable procrastination in executing the agreement, delay in scheduling meetings, willful avoidance of meetings, evasive tactics, delay in providing data for bargaining, and similar tactics are evidence of bad faith.

ETHICS

- *Imposing conditions:* Attempts to specify conditions on bargaining or the administration of the agreement will be scrutinized closely to determine whether such conditions are onerous or unreasonable (for example, insisting that all grievances be resolved before collective bargaining can start). In addition, the requirement of agreement on a specific item as a prerequisite to negotiating other issues reflects bad-faith bargaining.
- *Unilateral changes in conditions:* Such actions as changing the compensation or fringe-benefits plan unilaterally during bargaining is a strong indicator of bad-faith bargaining. Unilateral changes *per se* may not be illegal, but justification must be reasonable and accurate.
- *Bypassing the representative:* Since the collective bargaining agreement supersedes the individual employee contract, the employer must not refuse to negotiate over mandatory issues. The duty to bargain is essentially equivalent to the duty to recognize the exclusive bargaining representative of the employees. Attempts to bypass this representative are evidence of bad faith.
- *Commission of unfair labor practices:* Committing unfair labor practices (such as promoting withdrawal from the union, reducing work hours, and engaging in discriminatory layoffs) during negotations is indicative of bad faith.

In addition, the NLRB and court rulings have consistently decided that unions should have sufficient information to understand and intelligently discuss the issues raised in collective bargaining and in subsequent contract administration; an employer who does not supply appropriate information could be found guilty of an unfair labor practice. Such information may include wage increases given to nonunit employees, work contracted to another employer, wage and employment data, seniority lists, and the names and addresses of unit employees, including striker replacements, unless there is a clear and present danger of violence against employees in this latter category.

In some cases when an employer claims inability to meet a union's financial proposal, production and sales data and other financial information must be given to the union. This obligation is subject to sometimes complicated distinctions.[25] For example, management would not have to supply this information if it says it *will* not financially meet the union's bargaining requests; but it would have to supply the information if it said it *could* not financially meet the union's bargaining requests. In a recent case the NLRB refused the union's request for information because the employer's stated desire to bring its labor costs in line with its competitors, who might be nonunion, was a legitimate bargaining goal.[26] Any information requested by the union when management claims inability to pay is subject to the following prerequisites:

1. The union must make a good-faith demand or request for the information.
2. The information sought must be relevant to the bargaining relationship.
3. The information must be supplied to the union promptly and in a form reasonably useful for negotiation purposes.

Successor Employer Bargaining Obligations Employer successorship tests and corresponding bargaining obligations have been formulated through several NLRB decisions and subsequent Supreme Court interpretations. The successor employer will probably have to continue a bargaining relationship with the former employer's union if[27]

- There is substantial business operations continuity between the former and present employers. This occurs when the new employer acquires a substantial amount of its predecessor's real property, equipment, and inventory; employs workers to do essentially the same jobs that they performed for the predecessor under the same working conditions; and continues its predecessor's product lines.
- The bargaining unit remains appropriate after the change of employers.
- The predecessor employed a majority of the new employer's employees.

Legal Remedies Associated with Violations of Good-Faith Bargaining In 1994, 45 percent (10,736 of 26,058) of NLRB cases alleging employer violations involved employer refusal to bargain in good faith, and 1.9 percent (168 of 8674) of NLRB cases alleging union violations involved similar activities on the part of the union.[28] Although there are many cases to be handled, the NLRB is limited in its remedial powers. Once a violation is found, the board orders the violator to cease and desist bad-faith bargaining and to take affirmative action. This action includes bargaining upon request, posting notices pledging to bargain in good faith, and notifying offices of the NLRB of steps being taken to comply with the order.

Union officials have contended that the lack of significant remedies makes correction of bad-faith bargaining violations a farce. Since NLRB decisions can be appealed to the courts, it might take three or more years for a final determination. If the final decision finds the company guilty, affected employees are not entitled to any remedies.

Collective Bargaining under Bankrupty Proceedings: The *Bildisco* Decision

What happens to the existing bargaining agreement if management files for bankruptcy and contends that it can no longer honor the labor agreement? This question was approached in the Supreme Court's 1984 *Bildisco* decision, which involved a building supply distributor who filed a petition for reorganization under Chapter 11 of the bankruptcy code. After this filing, the company failed to make the wage increases scheduled in the collective bargaining agreement and also failed to give collected union dues to the union. The company also moved to reject the collective bargaining agreement entirely.

The NLRB agreed with the union that this unilateral action violated the good-faith bargaining provision in the National Labor Relations Act. However, the Supreme Court disagreed with the NLRB and determined that management's behavior in this situation did not violate the good-faith provision.

Bildisco has given management more discretion in its collective bargaining efforts with the union. Yet management cannot simply eliminate the existing labor agreement when it files for bankruptcy. Courts have denied some employers who attempted to eliminate the collective bargaining agreement under this procedure. For example, one apparel manufacturer was denied this option because it had assets twice its liabilities and no pervasive evidence of financial trouble. Further, an employer must show that removal of labor agreement provisions is "necessary" to aid the reorganization and "fair and equitable." Congress passed amendments to the federal bankruptcy code (P.L. 98-353) in June 1984 that made it more difficult for employers to abdicate labor agreement prescriptions by establishing several requirements that must be met after the employer files for bankruptcy but before petitioning for rejection of a collective bargaining agreement:[29]

1. The debtor in possession must make a proposal to the union to modify the collective bargaining agreement based on the most complete and reliable information available at the time.
2. The proposed modifications must be necessary to permit the reorganization and must ensure that all the creditors, the debtor, and all of the affected parties are treated fairly and equitably.
3. The debtor must provide the union with the information it needs to evaluate the proposal. (The union cannot demand information simply for the purpose of making a counterproposal.)
4. The debtor must meet at reasonable times with the union and confer in good faith in attempting to reach mutually satisfactory modifications to the collective bargaining agreement.
5. The union must have refused to accept the proposal without good cause.
6. The balance of equities must clearly favor rejection of the collective bargaining agreement.

Summary

Collective bargaining occurs when union and management attempt to resolve conflicting interests by exchanging commitments. Sometimes this activity is centralized and more than one appropriate bargaining unit is included in the negotiation unit (the employees and employers who are subject to the provisions of the labor agreement).

Management and union negotiators are involved in three general prenegotiation activities: selecting the negotiating team, formulating proposals and the bargaining range, and costing these proposals. Bargaining behavior during collective negotiations is extremely varied but can be classified into four bargaining situations:

distributive bargaining, integrative bargaining, attitudinal structuring, and intraorganizational bargaining. Bargaining approaches are found in each of these situations and are communicated to the opposing side through language analysis, package discussion of proposals, and argumentation.

A resolution framework, the bargaining power model, serves to place the varied collective bargaining behaviors into perspective. In essence, union and management negotiators try to manipulate each other's agreement and disagreement costs on the assumption that if it costs more to disagree than to agree, then agreement will be reached. Bargaining costs are calculated in negotiations, albeit imprecisely. Collective bargaining is shaped by ethical and legal considerations, the latter pertaining to good-faith bargaining, successor employer bargaining obligations, and bargaining under bankruptcy proceeding.

Key Terms

collective bargaining
pattern bargaining
negotiating unit
centralized bargaining
bargaining ranges
distributive bargaining
integrative bargaining
attitudinal structuring
intra-organizational bargaining
language analysis
bargaining power
illegal bargaining issues
mandatory bargaining issues
voluntary/nonmandatory issues
Boulwarism

Discussion Questions

1. What are some situations in which management or the union would prefer centralized bargaining? In what situations might both prefer centralized bargaining? Discussion should take into account specific legal considerations affecting centralized bargaining.
2. Our discussion of bargaining power touched on only three variables: timing of negotiations, unemployment, and company characteristics. Relate three other variables (from either Exhibit 1.2 in Chapter 1 or your own experience) to the bargaining power model, indicating how they could affect the equations.
3. Assume that you are a management negotiator and the union presents the following proposal: Any overtime assignment will be guaranteed a minimum of two hours at time-and-a-half the base hourly rate for the classification. Previously, employees working overtime received time-and-a-half pay for the hours they worked but no two-hour guarantee. Indicate in some detail how you would cost out this proposal. Also discuss some arguments the union might use to make it easier to accept this proposal (to reduce your agreement costs).

4. Good- and bad-faith regulations might be easier to define than implement. Discuss problems management and unions believe they face in attempting to bargain in good faith (Boulwarism, *Bildisco,* and legal remedies, for example, are considered problems by management or unions). What recommendations would you suggest for improving these situations?
5. Fully assess the following statement, qualifying it as appropriate: "Communication plays a very small role in labor-management negotiations because this activity is largely determined by established rituals."
6. Explain how attitudinal structuring can relate to the three other collective bargaining strategies discussed in the text.

References

1. For a much more detailed conceptualization of various behavioral and situational aspects of negotiation behavior and a thorough bibliography, see James A. Wall and Michael W. Blum, "Negotiations," *Journal of Management* 17, 3 (June 1991), pp. 273–303.

2. Ira B. Lobel, "Realities of Interest Based (Win-Win) Bargaining," *Labor Law Journal* 45 (December, 1994), p. 771.

3. For related considerations, see Kathryn J. Ready, "Is Pattern Bargaining Dead?" *Industrial and Labor Relations Review* 43, no. 2 (January 1990), pp. 272–279; discussions of Ready's article by Peter Cappelli, Daniel J. B. Mitchell, and Kathryn J. Ready, *Industrial and Labor Relations Review* 44, no. 1 (October 1990), pp. 152–165; John W. Budd, "The Determinants and Extent of Pattern Bargaining," *Industrial and Labor Relations Review* 45, no. 3 (April 1992), pp. 523–539; and John W. Budd, "The Intrepid Union Political Imperative for UAW Pattern Bargaining," *Journal of Labor Research* 26 (Winter 1995), pp. 43–57.

4. For a discussion of several possible factors associated with centralized bargaining in the United States and other countries, see Harry C. Katz, "The Decentralization of Collective Bargaining: A Literature Review and Comparative Analysis," *Industrial and Labor Relations Review* 47 (October 1993), pp. 3–22.

5. Douglas L. Leslie, "Labor Bargaining Units," *Virginia Law Review* 70 (April 1984), p. 414.

6. Douglas L. Leslie, "Multiemployer Bargaining Rules," *Virginia Law Review* 75 (1989), pp. 241–278.

7. For more details, see Doran P. Levin, "GM Gives Its Salaried Staff Raises," *The New York Times,* November 13, 1995, p. C-3. Ford had a similar spillover cost at this time.

8. Richard E. Walton and Robert B. McKersie, *A Behavioral Theory of Labor Negotiations* (New York: McGraw-Hill, 1965), pp. 4–6.

9. Roy J. Lewicki and Joseph A. Litterer, *Negotiation* (Homewood, Ill.: Richard D. Irwin, 1985), p. 108.

10. Dean G. Pruitt, *Negotiation Behavior* (New York: Academic Press, 1981), p. 813.

11. John P. Hoerr, *And the Wolf Finally Came* (Pittsburgh: University of Pittsburgh Press, 1988), p. 10.

12. Albert Blum, "Collective Bargaining: Ritual or Reality?" *Harvard Business Review* 39 (November-December 1961), p. 65.

13. Roger Fisher and William Ury, *Getting to Yes* (Boston: Houghton Mifflin, 1981). For a more current extension of this approach see William Ury, *Getting Past No: Negotiating with Difficult People* (New York: Bantam Books, 1991).

14. Walton and McKersie, *Behavioral Theory,* p. 96.

15. Robert L. Rose, "Caterpillar Inc. Pledges It Won't Yield in UAW Strike; Union Vows to Fight On," *The Wall Street Journal,* March 30, 1992, p. A5A.

16. Neil W. Chamberlain and James W. Kuhn, *Collective Bargaining,* 2nd ed. (New York: McGraw-Hill, 1965), pp. 162–190.

17. "Transit Union Announces Cutoff of Benefits to Greyhound Strikers," Bureau of National Affairs Inc., *Daily Labor Report,* no. 172 (September 5, 1990), pp. A-12, A-13.

18. Lee Iacocca, *Iacocca: An Autobiography* (New York: Bantam Books, 1984), p. 304.

19. Blum, "Collective Bargaining," p. 64.

20. Meyer S. Ryder, Charles M. Rehmus, and Sanford Cohen, *Management Preparation for Collective Bargaining* (Homewood, Ill.: Dow Jones-Irwin, 1966), p. 61.

21. Jeremy Main, "How to Be a Better Negotiator," *Fortune* 108 (September 19, 1983), p. 143; and Roy J. Lewicki and Joseph A. Litterer, *Negotiation* (Homewood, Ill.: Richard D. Irwin, 1985), p. 8.

22. "DuPont Need Not Bargain about Videotape, NLRB Says," Bureau of National Affairs Inc., *Daily Labor Report,* no. 20 (January 30, 1992), p. 2.

23. *NLRB* v. *General Electric,* 72 LRRM 2530 (1969); *General Electric* v. *NLRB* 397 U.S. 965 (1970). See also Thomas P. Brown IV, "Hard Bargaining: The Board Says No, the Courts Say Yes," *Employee Relations Law Journal* 8, no. 1 (Summer, 1982), pp. 37–51. For management's position in General Electric's bargaining, see Virgil B. Day, "Bad Faith Bargaining?" *Contemporary Labor Issues,* ed. Walter Fogel and Archie Kleingartner (Belmont, Calif.: Wadsworth Publishing, 1968), pp. 388–392; and Lemuel R. Boulware, *The Truth about Boulwarism* (Washington, D.C.: Bureau of National Affairs, Inc., 1969).

24. Francisco Hernandez-Senter, Jr., "Closing the Communication Gap in Collective Bargaining," *Labor Law Journal* (July 1990), pp. 438–444.

25. See, for example, Katrina L. Abel, "Current Developments in Labor-Management Relations," *Employee Relations Law Journal* 15, no. 2 (Autumn 1989), pp. 281–289; and "Union Attorney Sees NLRB as More Willing to Inquire Whether Bargaining Is Serious," Bureau of National Affairs Inc., *Daily Labor Report* no. 24 (February 5, 1991), pp. A-6, A-7.

26. "NLRB Rejects Need for Look at Books," Bureau of National Affairs, Inc., *Daily Labor Report,* no. 24 (February 5, 1991), pp. A-6, A-7. See also "Firm Needn't Open Books to Union, Circuit Court Says," Bureau of National Affairs, Inc., *Daily Labor Report,* no. 209 (October 28, 1992), p. 2.

27. Clyde Scott, Trevor Bain, and John Robb, "The Successorship Doctrine: Fall River Dyeing and Beyond," *Labor Law Journal* 45 (April 1994), pp. 230–239.

28. National Labor Relations Board, *Fifty-Ninth Annual Report* (Washington, D.C.: U.S. Government Printing Office, 1995), pp. 6, 92.

29. John Wren and Kent Murrmann, "Chapter 11 and Collective Bargaining Agreements," *Employee Relations Law Journal* 16, no. 1 (Summer 1990), pp. 17–27.

7 Resolving Negotiation Impasses and Developing Cooperation

Labor-management negotiations do not lead to strikes very often. In fact, only about 1 of every 5,000 working hours (0.0002 of every hour or 28.8 seconds per week per employee) is lost due to strikes each year.[1] *Media coverage of the small number of strikes overemphasizes labor-management conflicts and may lead one to believe that strikes are "business as usual." However, it is the exceptional case when labor-management negotiations lead to a strike.*

This chapter begins with a discussion of the ratification of the negotiated labor agreement and explains the impasse resolution procedures involving third parties, such as mediation, varieties of contract arbitration, and fact-finding. It then examines strikes, pickets, and boycotts in terms of their administrative and legal considerations. A concluding section illustrates the potential of various cooperative efforts aimed at avoiding union-management conflicts.

Contract Ratification

Negotiators, after resolving their differences and agreeing on tentative contract language, submit the proposed agreement to the union members for ratification, which usually requires a favorable majority vote. Although a vote by the members is not legally necessary, some affirmation via referendum or delegated authority is normally used in the ratification process. For example, the Steelworkers, Auto Workers, and United Mine Workers have a direct referendum. In recent years, union members have shown increasing interest in greater participation, and more ratification elections have been held.

The ratification process determines whether members can live with the proposed agreement, even though they may not be completely satisfied with all of its provisions. Acceptance by the membership gives management some assurance that the employees will comply with the letter and spirit of the agreement. A vote to accept, therefore, is considered a commitment or willingness to be bound by the agreement.[2] When and if union members find the agreement unacceptable, they may vote to reject it, which they do about 10 percent of the time.[3]

Explanation of Voting Behavior

It is overly simplistic to say that union members vote for the contract when they like it and against it when they don't like it. Researchers have attempted to explain why and when union members will vote to accept or reject the tentative agreements. When employees are vulnerable to layoff, the members tend to vote to accept the agreement, especially if they believe ratification will help to save their jobs. In addition, individual employees may have personal reasons for voting for contract acceptance. For example, when employees with the most seniority are to become eligible for a guaranteed income security plan, those employees could be counted on to favor ratification.

A "no" vote in a ratification election confronts employees with potential costs of a loss of income and the uncertainty of when they will begin work again. While the potential for contract rejection may create incentives for the union negotiators to try to get a little extra for the members, such extras come with increased anxiety as the strike deadline approaches.[4]

Reasons for Rejection of Tentative Agreements

The most frequent reason found for rejection of tentative agreements was that employees felt they were shortchanged in comparison with other agreements in their vicinity. Another major cause of rejection is union members' economic concerns—rejection percentages generally correspond to a downturn in economic activity. Internal union politics is another reason mentioned for contract rejection. Sometimes union leaders are elected by slight majorities, and their rivals will campaign against any labor agreement negotiated by the incumbent leaders.

Other factors contributing to contract rejections include feelings of inequity and lack of upward communication with the union itself. For example, in industrial unions, skilled employees usually represent a minority of the membership, and they might vote to reject the contract when their wages do not compare favorably with those of skilled tradespeople in the building and construction industry.

Other groups (women, racial minorities, and younger employees) may claim intraplant inequities. Although equal employment opportunity laws have been passed, wage differentials continue to exist for racial minorities and women. Moreover, young employees with low seniority view pensions and layoffs, which are usually based on seniority or retirement age, differently from the older employees, causing additional internal friction. Unless people in these subgroups feel that the agreement reflects their own personal needs, they will vote to reject it.[5]

High employee expectations coupled with reasons for union members to question the employer's wage offer has led to rejection of the tentative agreement. To confirm their conclusions, the researchers followed up on the agreements that were ultimately accepted and found that 65 percent included an increase in the final wage package above that of the initial tentative settlement.[6]

It may be that the definition of contract rejection in some studies is too broad and overestimates the number of contract rejections and overemphasizes their problematic nature. For example, considerably lower rejection rates are found when the term *contract rejection* is redefined. Less than 3 percent of the tentative agreements were rejected when a majority of the bargaining committee recommended acceptance.[7]

Impasse Resolution Procedures Involving a Third-Party Neutral

Usually both parties attempt to resolve impasses, which can occur either before or after the contract's expiration date. In some cases, union and management officials need third parties either to facilitate the negotiation process or to resolve the bargaining difference with finality. There are five impasse-resolution procedures involving third parties: **mediation, traditional contract arbitration, final-offer selection arbitration, mediation-arbitration (med-arb),** and **fact-finding.**

Mediation

Many union-management impasses are resolved privately or with help from neutral third-party mediators, obtained either from the Federal Mediation and Conciliation Service (FMCS) or from state agencies. Mediators perform a number of functions: they assist in scheduling meetings, keeping the parties talking, carrying messages back and forth, and making suggestions. The mediator has no authority to make binding decisions and must rely on persuasion and recommendations; the negotiators make the final decisions.[8] The mediator is the "invited guest" who can be asked to leave. However, acceptance of mediators is an indicator of the effort of one or both of the parties to bargain in good faith. The FMCS was involved in 22,184 mediation cases in fiscal year 1994.[9] Added to this number should be the activities of separate mediation agencies in some 18 states and Puerto Rico that assist parties in their own jurisdictions.

The **mediation** process is much more an art than a science. Mediation has been described as a process that "has been helpful in a haphazard way largely because of the talents of certain individuals who themselves would find it difficult to say why they had been successful."[10]

Several characteristics and practices of labor mediators have been associated with mediator effectiveness. Effective mediators have tenacity—they do not give up without exhausting themselves, the parties, and all reasonable avenues of settlement. A second characteristic is experience, which simply means that the more times a mediator is involved in mediating labor disputes, the more effective he or she is likely to be in settling one. Finally, mediators who are active, who pressure the parties to reach a settlement, who generate their own settlement terms, and who play an independent role in the mediation process are more likely to be effective mediators.[11] In "Labor Relations in Action," a judge experienced as a mediator explains the role of the mediator, how mediators do their job, and what it takes to be a good mediator.

Carl Stevens's study of mediation focusing on the mediator's functions and tactics has identified several causal factors that lead to negotiated settlements—the bottom-line criterion of successful mediation. Timing of the mediator's involvement was identified as one of the most important considerations. The mediator should enter before the parties become too fixed in their positions but not so early as to upset the power balance between the parties, causing them to harden their bargaining positions.

In some instances, the mere entrance of the mediator may be sufficient for dispute settlement. For example, assume that one of the chief negotiators leaves an active negotiation in a temper tantrum, vowing never again to return to the bargaining table. Upon subsequent reflection, the negotiator realizes a mistake was made but feels that calling the opposing negotiator would be embarrassing and perhaps indicate weakness. A common tactic used in such situations would be to call the mediator, who could schedule another meeting. Thus, mediation in this sense represents a very potent face-saving device.[12] In other cases, the parties do not desire any specific help from the mediator, but the availability of that mediator and the very existence of the mediation forum facilitates the bargaining process.[13]

Mediators vary in their roles, behaviors, and styles. Some have been characterized as "deal-makers;" they enter the negotiations at an early stage and attempt to manipulate the content of the negotiations. Others seem to serve as "orchestrators" of the process; they try to improve the structure of the negotiations, facilitate communication between the parties, and gain a deeper understanding of the issues. The role assumed by the mediator frequently depends on the intensity of the dispute; where a strike or lockout is pending, the mediator may become very active.[14]

A successful mediator is frequently an interpreter, who clarifies perceptions of the bargaining climate and possible costs of impasse. For instance, if the parties disagree on data about the cost of living, comparative wage rates, and productivity, the mediator could assist in reaching agreement on the use of statistical data. If a negotiator underestimates the cost of a strike or lockout or overestimates the cost of an agreement, the mediator may be able to provide insights enabling the negotiator to evaluate his or her positions more realistically. Frequently a mediator will hold separate meetings with each group before calling for a joint meeting.

Helping each party to understand the tactics or intentions of the other can also aid the bargaining process. If management bluffs about its willingness to accept a strike or to allow an ongoing strike to continue indefinitely, the mediator may attempt to diagnose management's true intentions and then advise the union. On the other hand, if the union threatens a strike to obtain an excessive bargaining demand, the mediator could attempt to diagnose what the union is "really trying to say" and so inform the company negotiator. It is understood that the mediator can be believed as to the real meaning of the words of each party. By holding private caucuses with each, the mediator is privy to much confidential information. While no mediator would reveal this information to the other party, he or she can determine the

LABOR RELATIONS IN ACTION

What Is the Role of the Mediator?

The role of the mediator is to get the parties to do what they say they don't want to do; what, indeed, they may even believe they can't do, but what deep down in their hearts they really need to do; and in the end, with rare exceptions, what they should and must do.

What Mediators Do As we were taught as children when first crossing the street, mediators should "stop, look, and listen."

Stop means, "Do nothing until you have learned." Don't rush in, sure that you know the answers better than the parties; you'll just prove to them what they may suspect anyway, that you're an idiot.

Look means, "Identify the parties and the problems" in hope of understanding how they can be dealt with.

Listen, which is probably the most important of all, means simply what it says, "Listen to what the parties tell you." Equally important, listen to what they don't tell you, because, as you know, there are many messages that are given to you in nonverbal terms, and they often are the keys that open the locked doors of the impasse.

How They Do It

1. You don't allow the parties to bargain over positions.
2. You separate the people from the problem.
3. You focus on interests, not positions.
4. You invent options for mutual gain.
5. You seek, find, and insist upon the use of objective criteria, just another way of saying get the facts—the real facts of the case.
6. You try to make the process nonadversarial—no losers, everybody wins. That's not easy. We're all geared to looking at everything in terms of winning or losing.

What Does It Take to Be a Good Mediator?

1. The wisdom of Ulysses.
2. The courage of Achilles.
3. The strength of Hercules.

magnitude of the real differences and encourage the parties that a settlement may be near if they continue bargaining.

The mediator also may facilitate the bargaining process by proposing solutions to the parties. Little effective bargaining occurs without an overlap of at least some of the issues. Therefore, the mediator must create and propose alternate solutions, compromise settlements, and definitions of the respective bargaining positions.[15]

Mediators attempt to build the parties' trust and confidence by clarifying their role, establishing ground rules for the negotiations, demonstrating competence and understanding, and showing that they are neutral. They also try to reduce interpersonal conflict and avoid unrealistic expectations on the part of the negotiators. Mediators apply

4. The agility of an acrobat.
5. The foresight of an ancient Hebrew prophet.

Advice for Mediators

1. Never say never.
2. Never stop listening.
3. Never stop learning.
4. Never do anything to affect your credibility.
5. Never close a door completely.
6. Never allow anyone to lose face (even when you are alone together).
7. Never back anyone into a corner unless you have arranged for an exit in case it's needed.
8. Never lose control of your own emotions, unless contrived for a purpose, and then only with extreme care, as if you're a Laurence Olivier or a Sarah Bernhardt.
9. Never lose your objectivity.
10. Never lose your sense of humor; it may be the only thing that will keep you sane.
11. Never promise what you cannot deliver. ("Have it in your pocket before you offer it" is the jargon of the trade, as you know.)
12. Never forget that when it's over—win or lose—you go home, but the parties must, as a rule, continue to deal with each other one way or another, and make the best of a bad job.
13. Never forget Murphy's first law: "If anything can go wrong it will;" and, of course, Callahan's corollary, "Murphy was an optimist."
14. Never, never give up even when you know it's impossible.

SOURCE: Address by Alan B. Gold, Chief Justice of the Superior Court of Quebec, Canada, before the National Academy of Arbitrators at its Annual Meeting, 1988, *Arbitration 1988;* adapted from Roger Fisher and William Ury, *Getting to Yes* (Boston, Mass.: Houghton Mifflin Company, 1981).

pressure for settlement by using delays and deadlines, placing responsibility for settlement on the parties, engaging in marathon bargaining, reviewing the costs of a strike or lockout, and making recommendations in a joint conference.[16]

The parties, however, play the dominant role in shaping the mediation process. For example, in cases where experienced negotiators have a clear understanding of their bargaining objectives and strategies, the mediator is primarily the servant of the parties. But where less sophisticated negotiators have not clearly defined their bargaining objectives, the personal qualities and actions of the mediator have their greatest impact. Here, an aggressive mediator may be able to gain the trust of the parties and create the type of negotiating atmosphere that achieves a settlement.[17]

Agreements are more likely to be reached when the disputing parties have had previous bargaining experience. Also, the parties are more likely to reach an agreement when a contract expiration is approaching. In this case, the parties have to consider the possibility of a job action such as a strike or lockout occurring, which may affect hundreds of people.[18]

Because there is no widely adopted code of professional conduct for mediators, and because potentially great danger exists from inept and unscrupulous practitioners, national organizations led by the Society of Professionals in Dispute Resolution (SPIDR) are developing a code of professional conduct to promote ethical behaviors by mediators. This code will articulate qualifications for mediators, standards of practice, and ethical behavior. It will proscribe impermissible actions of mediators, such as holding meetings with one of the parties without prior consent of the other party and revealing to one party what would be considered an acceptable settlement to the other. The code will be patterned after the widely accepted Code of Professional Responsibility for Arbitrators of Labor-Management Disputes, adopted by the National Academy of Arbitrators, American Arbitration Association, and Federal Mediation and Conciliation Service, which has existed since 1951 (revised most recently in 1995).[19]

Traditional Interest (or Contract) Arbitration

Traditional interest (or contract) arbitration involves the selection of a neutral person or panel to hear the bargaining positions of the parties and make a final and binding decision on what should be included in the negotiated agreement. This process differs from grievance arbitration (see Chapter 9), which is concerned mostly with interpreting and applying the terms of the existing labor agreement.

Interest arbitration in the United States dates back to the eighteenth century in the copper mines of Connecticut. It has not been used very frequently in the private sector (approximately 2 percent of negotiations), with a number of notable exceptions: the Amalgamated Transit Union has arbitrated over 700 cases; the law requires that impasses in the postal service are to be resolved by arbitration.[20]

Management and unions in the private sector prefer the arbitrator's decision when it reflects their own final position and avoids a strike. On the other hand, both parties have concerns about the delay created by scheduling an arbitrator and the extra cost involved. In addition, management becomes particularly concerned if the arbitrator fails to take into account the economic effect of the decision or if the award is above the norm for the industry.

Interest arbitration has been criticized because arbitrators may tend to "split the difference," thereby causing the parties to take more extreme positions. Yet research reveals that extreme positions may not be significant. Final offers of the two parties do not appear to play the major role in the arbitrator's decision process. Rather, the employees' present wage rates seem to be the most important consideration. Since neutrals may vary in the norms of their decision making, the parties should define the criteria to be used by arbitrators.[21] (A more thorough discussion of interest arbitration in the public sector appears in Chapter 14.)

Final-Offer Selection Arbitration

Final-offer selection (FOS) arbitration is a form of interest arbitration that gives the arbitrator the authority to select one of the proposals made by the parties. In other words, "splitting the difference" is not an alternative to the arbitrator. Procedurally, union and management present their separate final proposals to the arbitrator, who selects only one proposal, making no change in any of the provisions. Since the parties know in advance that the arbitrator cannot make a compromise decision, they will try to present to the arbitrator an acceptable proposal. Theoretically, if both parties genuinely attempt to present acceptable proposals to the arbitrator, their positions will converge, and they may settle their differences without third-party intervention.

In a study of final-offer arbitration of baseball salaries, researchers found that most arbitrators' salary awards differed significantly from those negotiated by the parties and tended to lie outside the range of negotiated settlements. Thus, instead of converging toward a settlement, the parties maintain their relative positions, one of which the arbitrator must choose.[22] (Variations and results of FOS arbitration in the public sector will be discussed in Chapter 14.)

FOS arbitration has some shortcomings, particularly if standards for arbitration decisions are not supplied. More importantly, the labor negotiations usually involve several issues, making FOS arbitration a very complex process. If the parties do not change or compromise their initial positions on some or all of these issues, the offers will not converge. The arbitrator must then select one of the extreme proposals, possibly heightening union-management tensions during the life of the contract and causing future difficulties in negotiating subsequent contracts.[23]

Mediation-Arbitration (Med-Arb)

Mediation-arbitration, or **med-arb,** occurs when the parties agree in advance that contract language, whether reached by mediation or arbitration, will be final and binding. Usually no decision on the contract language will be sent back to the parties—either the board of directors or the union membership—for ratification. Once the parties agree to med-arb, those issues that cannot be resolved by mediation will be resolved by arbitration. The neutral party will wear the mediator's hat at first, but if no agreement is reached by a predetermined date, he or she will become the arbitrator and decide the remaining unresolved issues. Under this procedure, most issues will be resolved by the parties because, in addition to the traditional pressures, there will be the pressure of knowing that the mediator-arbitrator will make a final and binding decision if the parties do not.

Fact-Finding

Somewhere between the extremes of mediation and interest arbitration lies **fact-finding.** This is a semijudicial process in which the major focus is placed on gathering the facts and using some of the principles of mediation and arbitration. The fact-finder's purpose is to assess the facts and to organize and display them publicly in the hopes that the parties will feel an obligation to settle their differences.

Fact-finding may be used in major disputes under the National Labor Relations Act (NLRA) and Railway Labor Act and under the 1974 health-care amendments of the NLRA. In major disputes, fact-finding reports are useful to presidents in determining what actions to take in national emergencies, such as when to seek an injunction or recommend legislation. Because of its lack of finality, this process does not have a good record in resolving disputes.

In the public sector, the primary role of the fact-finder is educational: to inform union members, legislators, and the electorate of the facts in the case so that they will support the neutral fact-finder's decision. While fact-finding may be considered purely a judicial or semijudicial process, in reality fact-finding has proven also to be political. This is because the neutral fact-finder helps to fashion a settlement that will be acceptable to the different constituent groups.[24]

Combination of Impasse-Resolution Procedures

On some occasions a combination of impasse-resolution procedures is used to settle a labor dispute. For example, in 1995, the two major postal unions, the American Postal Workers Union and the National Association of Letter Carriers, and the U.S. Postal Service attempted mediation to reach a settlement on their respective labor agreements. When the unions and postal service could not achieve an agreement in negotiations, the parties opted to present the unresolved issues to a panel of arbitrators. The postal service selected an arbitrator, the union selected an arbitrator, and a neutral arbitrator was selected by the parties. Hearings were held so that both sides could present evidence to support their bargaining positions. After the hearings, the arbitrators studied the evidence presented at the hearings and made binding decisions on the unresolved issues to be included in the new four-year agreements. Prior to arbitration, the parties agreed that they would be bound by the decisions of the arbitration panel.

The Strike and Related Activities between Union and Management

Work stoppages include both strikes and lockouts that cause a business to stop production, distribution, and sales of its goods or any organization to cease its operations. Generally a **strike** is a temporary stoppage of work by a group of employees for the purpose of expressing a grievance or enforcing a demand. Usually accompanying a strike are boycotts and pickets. The counterpart to a job action by the union is the **lockout,** which is an act by an employer of withholding or denying employment during a labor dispute in order to enforce terms of employment on a group of employees. During a strike or lockout, the employer may choose to continue to maintain operations, possibly by hiring temporary or permanent replacements.

Within this general framework there are a number of different types of strikes, boycotts, or pickets that are designed to increase management's costs of disagreement and to achieve the union's bargaining goals:

- *Economic strikes* are work stoppages during the negotiation of a contract to gain economic goals such as higher wages, improved pensions, and longer vacations.
- *Wildcat strikes* are strikes that occur in violation of the labor agreement and usually without approval from higher-level union officials.
- *Unfair labor practice strikes* are work stoppages that occur as a reaction to an employer's unfair labor practice. Examples include strikes in response to an employer's refusal to bargain or its discharge of a union member for engaging in union activities. The determination of whether a strike is an unfair labor practice is made by the NLRB.
- *Secondary strikes* are work stoppages by employees who have no dispute with their own employer but are striking to support another union.

Picketing refers to the outside patrolling of the employer's premises, usually using placards and handbills to achieve a specific objective. Generally, employees have the legal right to refuse to cross picket lines at the site of employers involved in a work stoppage. This right is considered to be a protected activity under Section 7 of the NLRA. However, employees who honor the picket lines may be placing their own employment in jeopardy because employers are legally able to treat them the same as economic strikers by replacing them, temporarily or permanently. Therefore, although employees who legally honor a picket line may not be discharged for such activity, they may be replaced temporarily or permanently.[25] **Recognitional picketing** is used to gain recognition of the union as the employees' bargaining representative. Recognitional picketing is limited by law to 30 days, at which time the union must petition for an election. Also, recognitional picketing is illegal where a certified union exists or where an election has been held within the last 12 months. **Informational picketing** occurs when the union attempts to inform the public that a labor dispute exists between the workers and their employer. **Product or consumer picketing** attempts to persuade customers to refuse to purchase products from the employer with whom the union has a labor dispute. Often the employees and their supporters also **boycott** the employer's product by refusing to purchase or handle products made by the employer with whom they have the dispute. See Exhibit 7.1 for an example of a boycott announcement.

Reasons for Strikes

Work stoppages from 1947 to 1995, in terms of numbers of strikes and of employees involved and days idled, were among the lowest on record (see Exhibit 7.2). Strike and lockout activity hit a record low in 1993. Work stoppages increased in 1994, but did not return to the levels of the 1980s. Exhibits 7.3 and 7.4 reveal more dramatic trends toward decreased work stoppages over time.

Exhibit 7.1 Example of a Boycott Announcement

SEPTEMBER / OCTOBER 1995

APPAREL & ACCESSORIES

ACME BOOT COMPANY
Western-style boots: Acme, Dan Post, Dingo brands ▶ *Steelworkers*

DECKERS CORPORATION
Sandals: Deckers, Sensi, and Teva brands ▶ *Machinists*

F. L. THORPE & CO.
"Original Black Hills Gold Jewelry" ▶ *Steelworkers*

HOWE K. SIPES CO.
Athletic apparel (chiefly baseball and softball uniforms, satin and wool jackets). Label: Howe Athletic Apparel ▶ *Electronic Workers*

BUILDING MATERIALS & TOOLS

ACE DRILL CORP.
Wire, jobber & letter drills, routers and steel bars ▶ *Auto Workers*

BROWN & SHARPE MFG. CO.
Measuring, cutting and machine tools and pumps ▶ *Machinists*

LOUISIANA-PACIFIC CORP.
Brand name wood products: L-P Wolmanized, Cedartone, Waferwood, Fiberpine, Oro-Bond, Redex, Sidex, Ketchikan, Pabco, Xonolite ▶ *Carpenters and Woodworkers (IAM)*

ROME CABLE CORP.
Cables used in construction and mining ▶ *Machinists*

SOUTHWIRE CO.
Commercial and industrial wire and cable; Do-it-yourself brand Homewire ▶ *Electrical Workers*

APPLIANCES & FURNITURE

LAKEWOOD ENGINEERING & MFG.
Electric fans and heaters for homes ▶ *Teamsters*

SILO, INC.
Retailers of appliances and electronics ▶ *Teamsters*

TELESCOPE CASUAL FURNITURE CO.
Lawn, patio, other casual furniture. Brand name: Telescope ▶ *Electronic Workers*

FOOD & BEVERAGES

BRUCE CHURCH, INC.
Iceberg lettuce: Red Coach, Friendly, Green Valley Farms, and Lucky labels ▶ *Farm Workers*

CALIFORNIA TABLE GRAPES
Table grapes that do not bear the UFW label on their carton or crate ▶ *Farm Workers*

COOK FAMILY FOODS, LTD.
Hams and ham steaks: Cook's, Blue Bird, Fire Side, Lancaster, Nottingham, Shaws, Sherwood, Super Tru, TV's labels ▶ *Firemen & Oilers*

DIAMOND WALNUT CO.
Diamond brand canned and bagged walnuts and walnut pieces ▶ *Teamsters*

MOHAWK LIQUEUR CORP.
Mohawk label gin, rum, peppermint schnapps, and cordials ▶ *Distillery, Wine & Allied Workers*

TYSON/HOLLY FARMS CHICKEN
Chicken and processed poultry products ▶ *Teamsters*

TRANSPORTATION & TRAVEL

ALITALIA AIRLINES
Air transport for passengers and freight ▶ *Machinists*

BRIDGESTONE/FIRESTONE, INC.
Tires. Brands include: Bridgestone, Firestone, Dayton, Triumph, Road King, Roadhandler ▶ *Steelworkers*

GO-MART GAS
Gasoline sold at Go-Mart convenience stores and truck stops ▶ *Oil, Chemical & Atomic Workers*

KAWASAKI ROLLING STOCK, U.S.A.
Railroad cars ▶ *Transport Workers*

MICHELIN
Michelin brand tires ▶ *Steelworkers*

RON JAWORSKI'S STADIUM HOLIDAY INN
Hotel in Philadelphia ▶ *Hotel Employees and Restaurant Employees*

MISCELLANEOUS

BELL ATLANTIC/NYNEX MOBILE SYSTEMS
▶ *Communications Workers and Electrical Workers*

BLACK ENTERTAINMENT TELEVISION
BET cable television, Action pay-per-view, Bet on Jazz ▶ *Electrical Workers*

R. J. REYNOLDS TOBACCO CO.
Cigarettes: Camel Winston, Salem, Doral, Vantage, More, Now, Real, Bright, Century, Sterling, YSL/Ritz; Tobacco: Prince Albert, George Washington, Carter Hall, Apple, Madeira Mixture, Royal Comfort; Little Cigars: Winchester ▶ *Bakery, Confectionery & Tobacco Workers*

UNION LABEL AND SERVICE TRADES DEPARTMENT, AFL-CIO

PAGE TWO UAW WASHINGTON REPORT

SOURCE: Courtesy of *UAW Washington Report,* September 22, 1995, p. 3.

Exhibit 7.2 Work Stoppages Involving 1,000 or More Employees in the United States, 1947 to 1995

		EMPLOYEES INVOLVED	DAYS IDLED	
YEARS	NUMBER/ YEAR	NUMBER (THOUSANDS)	NUMBER OF DAYS	PERCENTAGE OF WORKING TIME
1947–1950	300.3	1824.8	31,414	.29
1951–1960	331.5	1508.2	24,902	.19
1961–1970	298.8	1390.9	22,833	.14
1971–1980	269.4	1320.5	22,818	.11
1981	143	729	16,908	.07
1982	96	656	9,061	.04
1983	81	909	17,461	.04
1984	62	376	8,499	.08
1985	54	324	7,079	.03
1986	69	533	11,861	.05
1987	46	174	4,481	.02
1988	40	118	4,381	.02
1989	51	452	16,996	.07
1990	44	185	5,926	.02
1991	40	392	4,584	.02
1992	35	388	3,987	.01
1993	36	18	3,981	.01
1994	45	322	5,020	.02
1995	31	192	5,771	.02

SOURCE: *Major Work Stoppages, 1995,* Bureau of Labor Statistics, U.S. Department of Labor, February 21,1996.

Despite a few well-publicized strikes, such as in mining, United Parcel Service, Caterpillar, and American Airlines, strikes in the United States during the 1990s have been fewer than at any other period of time since the 1930s. The incidence of work stoppages, the numbers involved, and the percentage of working time lost due to strikes have declined, perhaps because the strike has lost much of its effectiveness as an economic weapon for unions. While many explanations have been advanced, an analysis of strikes from 1935 to 1990 has revealed that the supply of potential striker replacements has increased, which has caused unions to forego strikes as an economic weapon. Consequently, strike costs for employers have lessened because the costs of hiring replacements and avoiding settlements demanded by the unions have been offset by employers resisting union demands and not having to agree to expensive labor agreements.[26]

Work stoppages are not caused by one factor alone. Even so, there can be little argument that the main issue is wages, followed by plant administrative issues, such as safety, promotion policies, and job assignments. The decision to strike depends on the total environment in which bargaining takes place. Interrelated influences include the economic positions of the union and company, characteristics of the production process, the market structure, location of the plants, and occupational and demographic characteristics of the work force.[27]

Researchers have shown that prior to 1980 strikes and economic activity were highly correlated; however, since 1980, strikes have shown a dramatic decline (see Exhibit 7.3) even though the United States experienced eight straight years of economic expansion after 1982. After 1982, strike activity was concentrated in a relatively few industries. Between 1982 and 1990, employees involved in work stoppages in communications, government, transportation equipment, transportation, and construction made up 63 percent of all employees involved in work stoppages.[28] Researchers have developed several conclusions about the causes of work stoppages, which are included in Exhibit 7.5

At a single location, strikes may occur not only to enforce a demand but because of the parties' misconceptions about collective bargaining and their *lack of in-*

Exhibit 7.3 **Number of Strikes Per Year, 1947 to 1994**

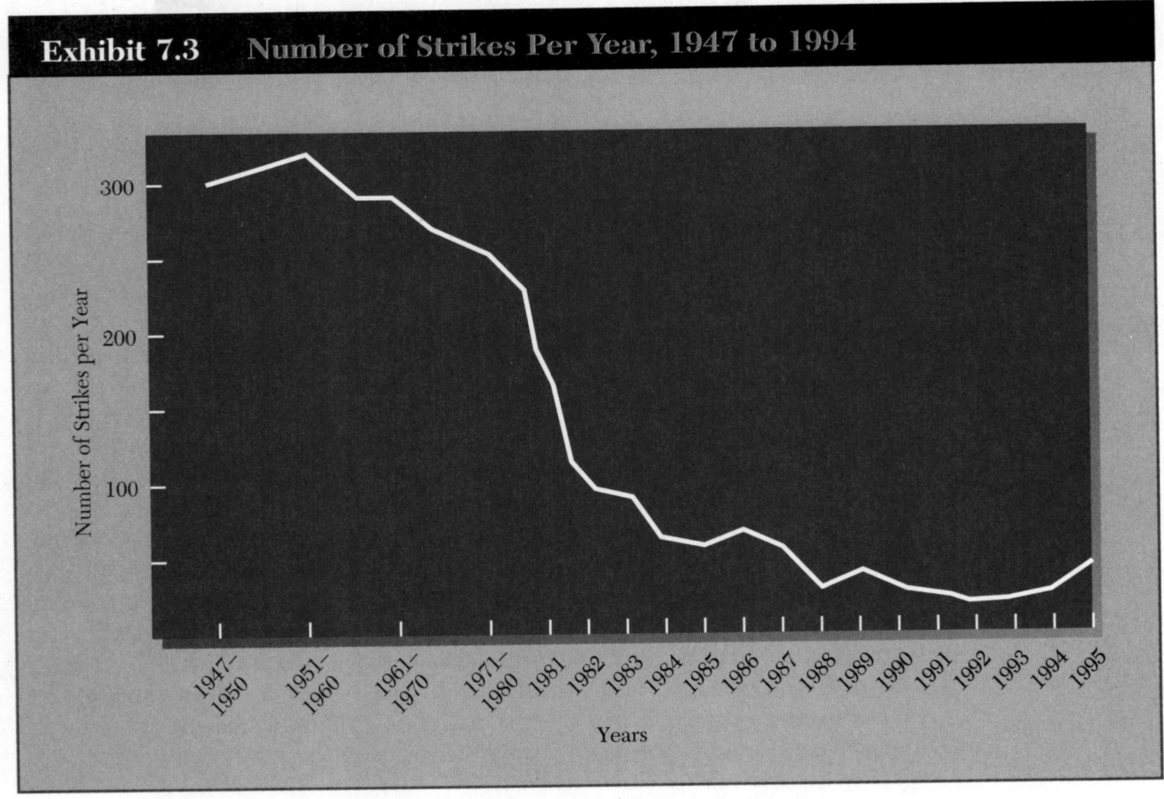

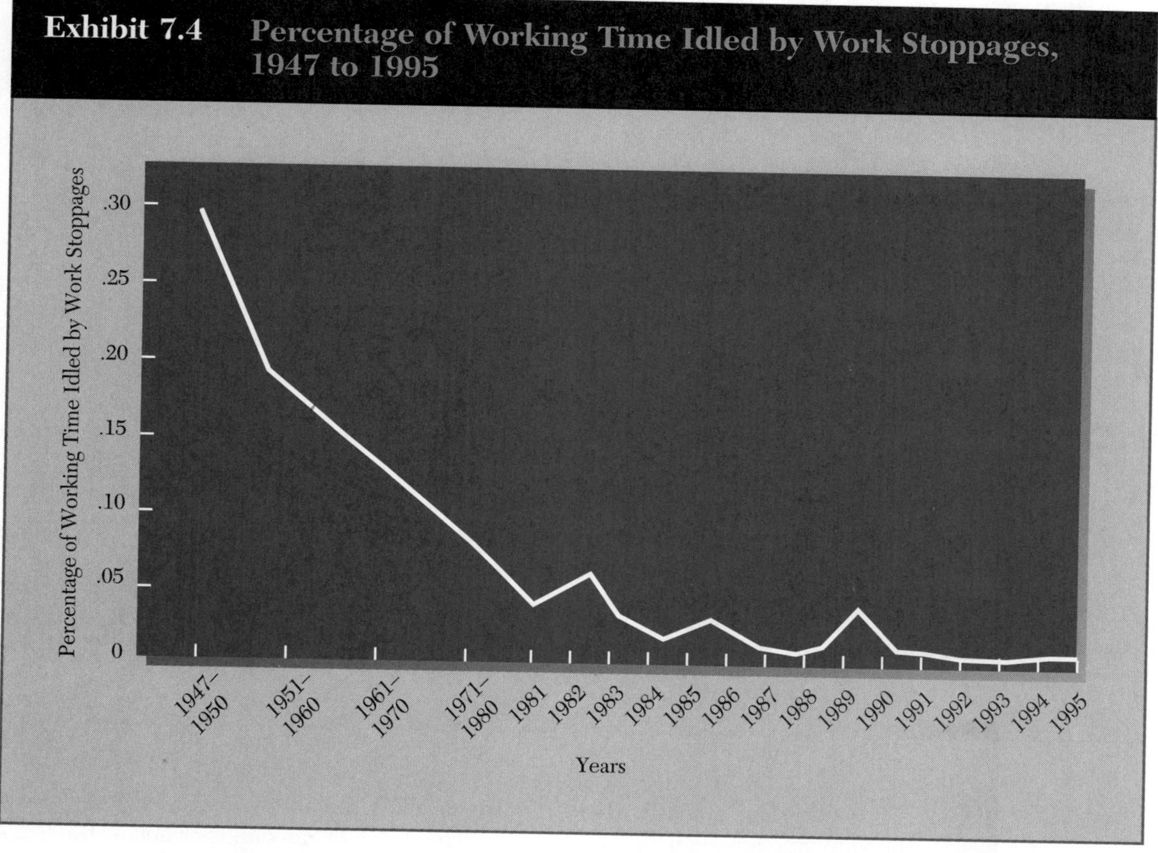

formation about the positions of their bargaining counterparts. The nature of the bargaining process causes each party to hold back on its *"real" position.* Thus, strikes frequently occur when one party misperceives the other's position or thinks the other party will change its offer. Then, when the strike occurs, both parties learn more about what the other party considers unacceptable. Thus, strikes often improve the information exchange between the parties.[29] For example, if the union is asking for a 10 percent increase in wages and the company negotiators believe that the union will accept an 8 percent increase, the union may have to strike in order to show the company that it was serious in its demand of 10 percent.

Although strikes have traditionally been viewed as economic or legal conflicts, the psychological aspects are important. Psychologically, strikes can be categorized as a protest or as a group process for organizational change. Protest strikes include actions by the membership such as walking off their jobs without the approval of their leadership (wildcat strikes). These spontaneous protests may be in reaction to a unilateral change by management, such as introducing production quotas or working conditions or even in lowering thermostats in winter months.

Exhibit 7.5 Conclusions from Research on Work Stoppages Regarding the Likelihood of a Strike

Strikes are more likely when:

- the duration of the preceding contract is longer.
- negotiations serve as a pattern setter for other firms/union pairs.
- the bargaining units are larger.
- there is a large variance (sharp drops and increases in earnings) in the firm's financial performance.
- firms and industries have risk of injury or fatalities.
- firms can inventory or stockpile goods.

Strikes are less likely when:

- fewer issues are being negotiated (such as in a contract reopener over wages).
- firms and industries employ a large proportion of women.
- firms and industries pay a higher wage rate than other firms or industries.

SOURCE: Bruce E. Kaufman, "Research on Strike Models and Outcomes in the 1980s. Accomplishments and Shortcomings," in *Research Frontiers in Industrial and Human Resources*, eds. David Lewin, Olivia S. Mitchell, and Peter D. Sherer (Madison, Wis.: Industrial Relations Research Association, 1992), pp. 110–111.

As a group process, strikes require an issue, the ability to mobilize the membership, and adequate strike resources. The union leadership is critical—the leaders must instill unity among the membership, control courses of action, respond to the feelings of the group, and maintain communication with management.

A strike can be a process for change for the individual as well as the working environment. An individual union member's participation in union actions is determined by perceived costs and benefits. If the perceived benefits are small and the costs are high, willingness to participate will be low. However, if the benefits are perceived to be high and the costs are low, willingness to participate will be high.[30] Employees who feel that their pay is inequitable are not very willing to strike for a small wage increase. On the other hand, they may be willing to strike to support the union for a large increase. Thus, it appears that employees use a calculative strategy to help them determine whether and how long they can afford to strike for specific wage increases. Thus, the union must put forth efforts to reduce hardship (by providing strike benefits, for example) in order to gain support for the strike.[31] Wage increases remain at the center of the dispute; however, other elements may enter the bargaining process.

Strikes can have traumatic effects on the parties' attitudes; they can temper the militants with realism and radicalize the conservatives. Strikes may cause the members to question the credibility of their leaders or management. Furthermore, once a strike is over, much rebuilding must occur.[32]

Strategic Purposes of a Strike

While the main purpose of the strike is to secure a contract, it also serves other purposes. For example, it may be part of an overall union strategy to help resolve internal problems. It may have a cathartic effect on the union members, removing accumulated tensions and releasing frustrations resulting from monotonous jobs. In fact, strikes under these conditions might improve productivity when the strikers return to work. A strike might also help to unify members—rallying the diverse prestrike membership factions to work toward a common goal.

In some cases, the union calls a strike just to show management it can unify the membership over a collective bargaining issue. Over a period of time, threats of a strike lose their effectiveness. If such threats are not carried out, management views the union leader as "the boy who cried wolf." Therefore, union leaders are sometimes forced to carry out a bluff or threat in order to substantiate future threats.

Union leaders might also believe that their members would be more willing to accept a slightly modified offer if they have not received wages during a brief strike. In this sense, strikes are used to "roll the steam" out of employees and their initially unrealistic expectations.[33]

Unions also have to consider the effects of a strike on their institutional security. During the strike, some union members might accept jobs elsewhere and decide not to return after the strike. Sometimes employers hire permanent replacements for union strikers, and the negotiations are never consummated. Possibly rival unions are waiting on the sideline for the legally recognized union to falter. With these considerations, the union must be aware that a decision to strike may be a risk to its own survival.

Some companies include the hiring of striker replacements in their bargaining strategy and begin advertising for permanent replacements before their contracts expire. At the International Paper plant in Jay, Maine, the company started accepting applications at the plant two weeks before the contract expired and while the present employees were working. Applicants formed long lines outside of the paper mill in view of the employees inside.[34]

Unions try to deter strike-breaking by including in their constitutions provisions to levy fines on union members who return to work during an authorized strike. In fact, many of these provisions prohibit a union member from resigning from the union during the strike. However, the Supreme Court restricted the union's ability to deter resignations and ruled that union members enjoyed an absolute right to resign from membership, regardless of union rules and regulations to the contrary, during a strike or when a strike is imminent. If the union imposes a fine on union members who submit their resignation from the union and then cross the union picket line, it violates the Taft-Hartley Act.[35] Later, the NLRB ruled that employees who resign from *full* union membership during a strike to become *financial core* members only (members who pay union fees and dues but who are not subject to any other obligations of union membership) cannot be fined by the union for crossing a picket line.[36]

A strike may serve a strategic purpose for management as well. While management cannot call a strike, it can take actions that it knows are likely to result in a strike. For example, management can demand that the union collect dues rather than have management deduct them from employee paychecks (a procedure called *checkoff*). Unions view this demand as a threat to their security and will often strike in response to it. Management's demand to subcontract at will or to change the wage system will almost certainly lead to a strike. Thus, management may attempt to cause a strike when a strike is to its advantage, such as when inventories are high and customer demand is low. If nonunion employees can produce at a sufficient level to maintain acceptable production, if the union is weak, or if management knows that all employees will not support the strike, it may force an impasse in order to secure a more favorable contract.

Strike Experiences and Preparation

Strikes can range from very peaceful conflicts of short duration to outrageous, unlawful conflicts of months, even years. They have no uniform sequence, although strikers are usually most enthusiastic during the early days of the strike. Indeed, the first few days on a picket line often draw a large portion of union members in an almost carnival-like atmosphere. After several weeks, it may be difficult to recruit members to walk the picket line.

Frustrations, antagonisms, and anxieties usually increase as the strike continues, with increased membership pressure being placed on union leaders to resolve the impasse.[37] The relative peacefulness of a strike is influenced by the attitudes of community citizens, particularly merchants and creditors, toward the dispute. The striker's spouse is perhaps the most influential individual in shaping the striker's behavior and attitudes. It is of course much easier for a striker to sustain a long strike if her or his spouse lends moral and financial support to the cause. On the other hand, tensions created by the strike can create permanent divisions among family members, friends, and other groups in the community as the strike endures and as individuals are asked for their support.[38] Tensions can be especially heightened if the company continues to operate the business with either supervisory employees or striker replacements.

Both parties must prepare for a possible strike before the contract expiration date, whether a strike is called or a settlement is reached. Union leaders must be certain of the extent to which members will actively participate during a strike and present a unified front against the employer. Division within the ranks causes much difficulty and dilutes the union's bargaining strength. Usually, the strike vote taken before the contract deadline will indicate the strength of the membership's willingness to strike.

As the strike date approaches, union officers must schedule pickets, assure appropriate support for those on the line, and properly prepare the pickets for various situations, such as what to do when striker replacements cross the picket line. The union also has to determine qualified recipients of strike benefits as well as any available public aid. Communication channels (telephone hotlines) must be established to inform members of the negotiations' progress.

Management often spends much time in its strike preparations, particularly if it is essential that the employer continue to operate during a strike, as public utilities must do. Management in manufacturing facilities must determine the feasibility of building inventories in advance of the possible strike and its strategy of hiring striker replacements if the strike occurs.

Many organizations have emergency strike manuals that provide specific and detailed plans in the event of a strike. The manual typically has two major components: (1) specific job assignments for nonstriking employees, professional employees, and managers, and (2) checklists of appropriate strike activities, such as notifying customers and suppliers, contacting law enforcement officials, and providing food and housing for those staying on the job. In cases where the work is highly automated, such as in the telephone industry, employees' strikes were much less potent, and companies found it easier to continue to operate, at least during short strikes. Management might also seek professional assistance from employer colleagues, such as members of the Society of Human Resource Management, which has published a *Strike Preparation Manual.*[39]

Although union and management officials carefully consider the advantages and disadvantages of strikes, lockouts, and pickets, they are not entirely free to implement these activities as they please. Various legal considerations can raise additional problems and prospects.

Legality of Strikes and Related Activities

The Right to Strike The right to strike has long been subject to philosophical debate. Opponents of the right to strike usually cite examples of violence and civil disobedience that have occurred in strike activities. Other say strikes are, however, basic to the industrial relations system—inseparable from collective bargaining because they cannot be severed without hurting both.[40]

Legal guidelines have been formulated that attempt to balance employee and employer rights during a strike. The *Commonwealth* v. *Hunt* decision in 1842 (discussed in Chapter 3) was the first judicial decision that recognized employees' right to participate in concerted activities for their own economic welfare. Section 7 of the NLRA guarantees employee rights to engage in "concerted activities for the purpose of collective bargaining or other mutual aid or protection." Section 13 also states: "Nothing in this Act, except as specifically provided for herein, shall be construed so as to interfere with or impede or diminish in any way the right to strike or to affect the limitations or qualifications on that right."

The right to strike is not absolute; there are restrictions on national emergency strikes, secondary strikes, jurisdictional strikes, and recognition strikes. Yet current legislation implicitly assumes that most strikes occur only after intensive negotiations under the rules established by the NLRB and the courts. While both parties are required by law to negotiate in good faith, they do not always reach agreement

LABOR RELATIONS IN ACTION

Unfavorable Rulings Concerning Strikers*

***NLRB* v. *Mackay Radio & Telegraph Co.*, 304 US 333 (1938)** The Supreme Court ruled that Mackay had the right to continue to operate its business during a work stoppage and to hire permanent striker replacements. Also, the employer was not required to discharge these striker replacements to make vacancies for returning economic strikers.

***NLRB* v. *Granite State Joint Board, Textile Workers Union of America, Local 1029, AFL-CIO*, 409 US 213 (1972)** The Supreme Court ruled that the union violated the National Labor Relations Act if it fined union members who resigned their union membership and then returned to work during a strike.

***Belknap, Inc.,* v. *Hale*, 463 US 491 (1983)** The Supreme Court upheld rights of employees who had been hired as permanent striker replacements to sue (in state court) an employer for misrepresentation and breach of contract if they lost their jobs after the strike was over.

***Pattern Makers League* v. *NLRB*, 473 US 95 (1985)** The Supreme Court ruled that a union has no right to restrict its members from resigning from the union at any time, which includes during a strike or lockout. The only statutory requirement for union membership is to pay nondiscriminatory union dues and initiation fees. Having met this requirement, employees may return to work.

***TWA* v. *Flight Attendants*, 109 S. Ct. 1225 (1989)** The Supreme Court upheld the employer's right to follow through with promises to employees who quit a strike and return to work that they will be given work assignment preferences and job protection at the end of the strike.

*These decisions do not apply to unfair labor practice strikers.
SOURCES: John G. Kilgour, "Can Unions Strike Anymore? The Impact of Recent Supreme Court Decisions," *Labor Law Journal* 41 (May 1990), pp. 259–269; Robert W. Schupp, "Legal Status of Incentives for Replacement and Striking Workers," *Labor Law Journal* 41 (May 1990), pp. 311–318; Samuel Estreicher, "Strikers and Replacements," *Labor Law Journal* (May 1987), pp. 287–296.

and strikes do occur, but usually only after authorization from the national union office and a strike vote by the membership.[41]

In addition to the law itself, the Supreme Court has rendered several unfavorable decisions for unions concerning striker rights. The "Labor Relations in Action" highlights several of the rulings.

Many legal questions concerning strikes, pickets, and boycotts involving the employee's immediate, or *primary*, employer have been resolved over the years by statute or judicial decisions. Other activities concerning employers not directly involved in the labor dispute (*secondary* employers) are usually subject to much more complex legal interpretation. While secondary activities often have narrow applications, their significance is especially pertinent to those unions and employers that frequently face these issues.

Strikes and Related Activities Involving the Primary Employer When the union and management fail to reach an agreement on the expiration of their labor agreement, the union normally calls an economic strike accompanied by picket lines and a boycott of the product. If only the immediate employer and the union are involved, the strike, picket, and boycott are considered primary. The overwhelming majority of strikes, pickets, and boycotts that occur in the United States in any given year are of this type.

Hiring striker replacements Management has the right to continue to operate by hiring temporary or permanent replacements during an economic strike. The threat of hiring permanent striker replacements is a powerful weapon in the hands of management during a work stoppage. As noted in Chapter 1, after 12,600 Auto Workers had been on strike for months at Caterpillar in 1991 to 1992, the company set a date for workers to return to work or risk being permanently replaced. With such high risks, the UAW capitulated and returned to work.[42]

The U.S. General Accounting Office (GAO) has reported more common use of striker replacements. GAO found that employers announced that they would hire permanent replacements in about one-third of the strikes, and estimated that employers actually hired permanent replacements in 17 percent of all strikes. Moreover, GAO estimated that 4 percent of all striking employees were permanently replaced. It has been widely believed, without supporting data, that employers have hired permanent striker replacements more frequently since President Reagan fired and permanently replaced about 12,000 air traffic controllers in 1981.[43] There is a belief that his actions set the tone for labor relations in the 1980s and 1990s.

Hiring striker replacements places both the employer and striker at risk. If replacement workers are hired temporarily during a strike, strikers go back to work after a settlement is reached, and the replacements are usually dismissed. If the replacements are hired as "permanent" employees, however, and are dismissed after a settlement is reached, they may file a civil suit against the company for misrepresentation and breach of contract. Thus, economically distressed firms may continue to use replacement workers and declare them as "permanent." However, healthier firms will consider the potential costs of court suits and tend not to hire permanent replacements during strikes.[44]

Other practical considerations can also prevent the employer from exercising the legal right to replace strikers. It is usually not easy to replace all of the striking employees, especially if the operations are complicated and employees cannot be trained in a short period of time. Finally, extreme tensions can occur between strikers and striker replacements at the picket line, possibly resulting in violence and community disorder.

Employees on strike may forfeit the right to reinstatement if they commit acts sufficiently harmful to render them unfit for further employment with the employer. Also, if employers discipline a striker for engaging in a protected activity, such as an economic strike, the employee has the right to be reinstated.

In 1993 and 1994, and again in 1996, Congress considered the Workplace Fairness Act, which would have placed restrictions on employers' right to hire permanent striker replacements as well as provided an incentive for unions to engage in mediation or accept a fact-finding panel's recommendations.

The proposed legislation would:

1. Allow a non-binding mediation board to investigate the dispute and issue its recommendations; and
2. Let the parties decide whether they want mediation:
   - The union members decide whether they want to be protected from being permanently replaced.
   - The employer decides whether it wants the power to hire permanent replacements.
3. Penalize unions for striking by permanently replacing employees if they do not seek mediation through the fact-finding panel or they do not accept the fact-finding panel's recommended settlement.

William B. Gould IV, chairman of the NLRB, has been unequivocal in his support for prohibiting employers from hiring permanent striker replacements. In a speech before the San Francisco Bar Association, he explained:

> I start with the proposition that the right to strike is fundamental to a free, democratic society, a policy reflected in the language of Sections 7 and 13 of the National Labor Relations Act of 1935 and in the Norris-LaGuardia Act which preceded it in 1932. The statute promotes the right of employees to band together for the purpose of protecting or improving their working conditions, to join unions, to engage in collective bargaining, and to be free from various forms of discrimination.
>
> The Supreme Court's 1938 decision in *Mackay* permitting employers to permanently replace economic strikers runs counter to this policy and therefore should be overruled by Congress. This pernicious notion that employees lose their right to reinstatement because they engage in protected activity confounds the statutory scheme and the promotion of freedom of association and collective bargaining, which the preamble of the Act reminds us is still a basic purpose of the statute. . . .
>
> President Clinton recently took note of this limitation in the law in a statement criticizing the Bridgestone/Firestone Company's use of permanent striker replacements. He said such tactics show the need to enact legislation prohibiting such a denial of the fundamental right to strike. A similar view supporting the right to strike was taken by President Lincoln in the spring of 1860, when he spoke out in support of a strike conducted by the boot and shoe workers in New England. . . .
>
> Aside from the right of workers to strike, the public interest is served by allowing the strike or possibility of a strike to perform its essential function in collective bargaining—bringing the parties' positions closer together so that an agreement may be reached. The growing use of permanent striker replacements is impairing the ability of strikes to perform their function in collective bargaining and tipping the balance of bargaining power toward employers.[45]

Employers have argued that a legislative ban against hiring permanent striker replacements will drastically shift the relative bargaining power to unions and would therefore result in higher wages. However, in a study conducted in Canada, where hiring of permanent striker replacements is banned by provincial law, no evidence supported the contention that striker replacement legislation will distort the existing balance of power between management and labor.[46]

Researchers have found an association between length of strikes and employers' strategies to hire permanent striker replacements; that is, where employers' strategies are to hire permanent striker replacements, the strikes are longer. A logical explanation is that the announcement of this strategy hardens the positions of the union as well as those of the employer. Therefore, the parties find it more difficult to reach a mutually satisfactory agreement.[47]

Some scholars have argued that the employer's strategy to hire permanent striker replacements is an attempt to break the union. Research has shown that in situations where permanent replacements were hired, unions failed to survive in 40 percent of the cases. On the other hand, companies that hired permanent replacements, such as Eastern Airlines, Continental Airlines, Greyhound, Daily News, and Pittston Coal, either did not survive, were forced into bankruptcy, or were required to restructure after the strike. In other words, there have been few success stories where hiring permanent striker replacements has been the employer's strategy.[48]

The Workplace Fairness Act was a high priority of organized labor. Despite support from President Clinton and a national poll of 1,000 Americans that showed that 65 percent of the respondents believed that companies should not be allowed to permanently replace striking workers, Congress refused to pass the legislation, primarily because the majority of Congress who supported the legislation could not obtain the 60 votes needed to end a Republican filibuster.[49] The United States and South Africa remain the only industrialized countries in the world where the practice of hiring permanent striker replacements is permitted.[50]

President Clinton's executive order on striker replacement After the failure of passage of the Workplace Fairness Act in 1995, President Clinton issued an Executive Order (see "Labor Relations in Action") that would make employers who hire permanent striker replacements ineligible for federal contracts. In the "Information Sheet" provided by the Labor Department, more detailed reasons for Clinton's Executive Order are provided and the companies potentially affected are covered. Although the Executive Order was challenged by Republican senators who attempted to pass legislation to overturn it, this challenge failed. Then, in February, 1996, a U.S. appeals court struck down the Executive Order. President Clinton instructed the Justice Department to attempt to reverse the court's ruling.

Unfair labor practice strikes If the strike is determined by the NLRB to be taken against an employer who committed an unfair labor practice, such as refusal to bargain in good faith with the union, striking workers are entitled to reinstatement. However, they must first make an unconditional offer to return to

LABOR RELATIONS IN ACTION

President Clinton's Executive Order Sanctioning Federal Contractors That Hire Permanent Striker Replacements

Executive Order Ensuring the Economical and Efficient Administration and Completion of Federal Government Contracts Efficient economic performance and productivity are directly related to the existence of cooperative working relationships between employers and employees. When Federal contractors become involved in prolonged labor disputes with their employees, the Federal Government's economy, efficiency, and cost of operations are adversely affected. In order to operate as effectively as possible, by receiving timely goods and quality services, the Federal Government must assist the entities with which it has contractual relations to develop stable relationships with their employees.

An important aspect of a stable collective bargaining relationship is the balance between allowing businesses to operate during a strike and preserving worker rights. This balance is disrupted when permanent replacement employees are hired. It has been found that strikes involving permanent replacement workers are longer in duration than other strikes. In addition, the use of permanent replacements can change a limited dispute into a broader, more contentious struggle, thereby exacerbating the problems that initially led to the strike. By permanently replacing its workers, an employer loses the accumulated knowledge, experience, skill, and expertise of its incumbent employees. These circumstances then adversely affect the business and entities, such as the Federal Government, which rely on that employer to provide high quality and reliable goods or services.

NOW, THEREFORE, to ensure the economical and efficient administration and completion of Federal Government contracts, and by the authority vested in me as President by the Constitution and the laws of the United States of America, including 40 U.S.C. 486(a) and 3 U.S.C. 301, it is hereby ordered as follows:

Section 1. It is the policy of the executive branch in procuring goods and services that, to ensure the economical and efficient administration and completion of Federal Government contracts, contracting agencies shall not contract with employers that permanently replace lawfully striking employees. All discretion under this Executive Order shall be exercised consistent with this policy. . . .

(b) The head of the contracting department or agency may object to the termination for convenience of a contract or contracts of a contractor determined to have permanently replaced legally striking employees. If the head of the agency so objects, he or she shall set forth the reasons for not terminating the contract or contracts in a response in writing to the Secretary.

Labor Department Information Sheet on Clinton Executive Order

QUESTIONS AND ANSWERS ON THE EXECUTIVE ORDER REGARDING FEDERAL CONTRACTORS THAT PERMANENTLY REPLACE STRIKING EMPLOYEES

Why is this Executive Order necessary?

- As the federal government's chief executive officer, the President has the responsibility by law to assure that the taxpayers get the quality goods and services they deserve in a timely way from reliable federal contractors. Federal contractors must have stable and productive labor-management relationships if they are going to produce the best quality goods in a timely and reliable way.
- The executive order advances cooperative and stable labor-management relations, a central component of this Administration's workplace agenda. The use or the threat to use permanent replacement workers destroys opportunities for cooperative and stable labor-management relations.
- The firing of the PATCO strikers in 1981 set off a series of destructive strikes and permanent replacement of strikers at Greyhound, International Paper, Continental Airlines, and other companies, and it killed Eastern Airlines after a long, bitter strike.
- Since the economical and efficient administration and completion of federal government contracts requires a stable and productive labor-management environment, the federal government has a strong interest in its role as a purchaser of goods and services in prohibiting the use of permanent replacements. The use of replacement workers affects efficiency and economical production in several ways:

  — Research has found that strikes involving permanent replacements last *seven times longer* than strikes that don't involve permanent replacements.

  — Strikes involving permanent replacement tend to be much more contentious, often changing a limited dispute into a broader, more contentious struggle.

  —Permanently replacing strikers means trading in experienced, skilled employees for inexperienced employees. Inexperienced replacement workers start at the bottom of the learning curve. We don't want rookies and minor leaguers making tires for Desert Storm.

How many companies would be affected?

- 16% of non-agricultural workers are

(continued)

LABOR RELATIONS IN ACTION

President Clinton's Executive Order Sanctioning Federal Contractors That Hire Permanent Striker Replacements —cont'd

union members. Only a very small number of collective bargaining relationships between union and employers produce strikes and less than one-fifth of those strikes involve replacement workers.

- The Bureau of National Affairs reports that there were fewer than thirty strikes in 1994 in which replacement workers were used, and not all of those instances involved *permanent* replacement.
- Studies by the Bureau of National Affairs and the General Accounting Office of strike activity in the late 1980s and early 1990s indicate that employers resort to permanent replacements in only 14% to 19% of strikes.

SOURCE: "President Clinton's Executive Order Sanctioning Federal Contractors That Hire Permanent Striker Replacements and Labor Department Information Sheet on Clinton Executive Order," *Daily Labor Report* (March 9, 1995), pp. E-1–E-4.

work; then they must be rehired even if doing so displaces the striker replacements.[51] Any employees unfairly discharged for union activities must be returned to their former positions with back pay. However, if strikers participate in activities classified as unacceptable striker conduct, they lose their reinstatement rights. Such misconduct includes preventing entry to the plant, jumping in front of moving cars, following nonstrikers by car as they leave work, and throwing rocks, eggs, and tomatoes while on the picket line.[52] All strike misconduct is examined in light of the surrounding circumstances, and conduct that may reasonably tend to coerce or intimidate nonstrikers in the exercise of their rights is unprotected.

Wildcat strikes **Wildcat strikes** include work stoppages that involve the primary employer-employee relationship and that are neither sanctioned nor stimulated by the union, although union officials might be aware of them. They can vary in length and number of affected departments in the facility. They may also take the form of heavy absenteeism for several days, especially under no-strike pledges in contracts.[53]

Wildcat strikes are affected by factors external to the relationship between the parties, such as national economic and political trends. But, in essence, they appear to be the culmination of factors indicative of a poor relationship between employees and management, such as increased production demands and poor safety conditions. When this relationship is poor, employees will use any and all means at their disposal to protest their problems. Thus, to prevent wildcat strikes, labor and management officials should work on the qualitative aspects of the total relationship.[54]

Because most labor agreements provide for arbitration as the final step in the grievance procedure, and such agreements to arbitrate are usually accompanied by a no-strike clause, a wildcat strike represents a violation of the labor agreement. Employers can respond to a wildcat strike in several ways: (1) by requesting informally and formally that strikers return to work, (2) by contending that employees have voided their labor agreement, (3) by disciplining or discharging the strikers, and (4) by bringing suit against the union for damages suffered.

Some strikes that have resulted from extremely dangerous and unsafe working conditions, although commonly thought of as wildcat strikes, do not fit the definition, because arbitrators exempt such behavior from the no-strike clause, and Section 502 of the NLRA allows such actions as a protected concerted activity.[55]

Lockouts Lockouts are related to work stoppages involving the primary employer. The right of single employers to lock out employees is considered the analogue of employees' right to strike. Lockouts can be used legally by employers (1) after an impasse has been reached over a mandatory bargaining issue, (2) to prevent seizure of a plant by a sit-down, (3) to forestall repetitive disruption in plant operations by "quickie strikers," (4) to avoid spoilage of perishable materials, and (5) to preserve unity in a multi-employer bargaining arrangement. Yet the right to lock out employees is qualified, particularly because the NLRB maintains that the employer already has the power to counterbalance the strike by permanently replacing the strikers, stockpiling, subcontracting, maintaining operations with nonstrikers, and unilaterally instituting working conditions once the contract has expired.[56]

The NLRB and courts have been more lenient with employers in situations in which the union attempts to "whipsaw" by striking individual employers in a multi-employer bargaining association one at a time to force a more favorable agreement by putting pressure on the struck firm while the others operate. The NLRB and the courts have allowed temporary lockouts to preserve the association's unity. In addition, nonstruck firms in a multi-employer bargaining association have been allowed to hire temporary replacements during the lockout to preserve the bargaining unit structure and to maintain operations. Because the struck firm can hire permanent replacements in order to continue operations, the courts have reasoned that it would be unfair to require that the nonstruck firms be shut down completely while the struck firm operates. Because employers may hire temporary replacements during legitimate lockouts, companies have been aggressively taking advantage of lockouts,[57] and the balance in most labor disputes has shifted to the management side.

Strikes and Related Activities Involving Secondary Employers Secondary parties are those who are not directly bound by the terms of the labor agreement in dispute. They are not at the bargaining table; however, they become affected by the labor dispute when the union attempts to persuade them to influence the primary employer to agree with the union's proposals.

It is not always easy to distinguish between a primary and a secondary party to a negotiations impasse, as will be illustrated by the following discussion of activities involving product boycotts and picketing, common situs picketing, the ally doctrine, and hot-cargo agreements.

Product (consumer) boycotts and picketing Activities such as handbilling, carrying placards, and urging customers to refuse to purchase products from a particular retail or wholesale business are involved in boycotts and picketing. As an example of how the primary and secondary roles can be blurred in these activities, consider that the striking employees of a clothing manufacturer might legally boycott and picket a nearby retail clothing store owned by the manufacturer, say, the factory outlet. But if these employees travel a considerable distance to picket a retail clothing store that sells many items, only one of which is bought from the manufacturer, the legal issue becomes more complex.[58] Picketing in front of a retail clothing store in another city (a secondary employer) violates the NLRA if, but only if, the picketers attempt to convince customers to refuse to shop at the store. If instead the pickets make an appeal to the customers to refuse to buy only the struck product (clothing items produced by the primary employer), the picket is legal.

The presence of shopping malls that include a multitude of separate employers has given rise to interesting questions about legalities of union activities. While the Taft-Hartley Act made secondary boycotts illegal, prohibition against certain acts such as picketing and handbilling may be inconsistent with First Amendment rights.

Exhibit 7.6 Handbill Used at Shopping Mall to Influence Shoppers

PLEASE DON'T SHOP AT EAST LAKE SQUARE.

THE FLORIDA GULF COAST BUILDING TRADES COUNCIL, AFL-CIO is requesting that you do not shop at the stores in the East Lake Square Mall because of the Mall ownership's contribution to substandard wages.

The Wilson's Department Store under construction on these premises is being built by contractors who pay substandard wages and fringe benefits. In the past, the Mall's owner, The Edward J. DeBartolo Corporation, has supported labor and our local economy by insuring that the Mall and its stores be built by contractors who pay fair wages and fringe benefits. Now, however, and for no apparent reason, the Mall owners have taken a giant step backwards by permitting our standards to be torn down. The payment of substandard wages not only diminishes the working person's ability to purchase with earned, rather than borrowed, dollars, but it also undercuts the wage standard of the entire company. Since low construction wages at this time of inflation means decreased purchasing power, do the owners of East Lake Mall intend to compensate for the decreased purchasing power of workers of the community by encouraging the stores in East Lake Mall to cut their prices and lower their profits?
CUT-RATE WAGES ARE NOT FAIR UNLESS MERCHANDISE PRICES ARE ALSO CUT-RATE.

We ask your support in our protest against substandard wages. Please do not patronize the stores in East Lake Square Mall until the Mall's owner publicly promises that all construction at the Mall will be done using contractors who pay their employees fair wages and fringe benefits.

IF YOU MUST ENTER THE MALL TO DO BUSINESS, please express to the store managers your concern over substandard wage and your support of our efforts. We are appealing only to the public—the consumer. We are not seeking to induce any person to cease work or to refuse to make deliveries.

SOURCE: Supreme Court decision in *Debartolo* v. *Florida Gulf Coast Building & Construction Trades Council*, 485 U.S. 568 (1988).

The Supreme Court has upheld the right of unions to peacefully distribute handbills urging customers not to shop at stores located in a mall (the handbill used is shown in Exhibit 7.6) until all construction conducted in the mall was performed by contractors paying "fair" wages. Justice White stated:

> The handbills involved here truthfully revealed the existence of a labor dispute and urged potential customers of the mall to follow a wholly legal course of action, namely, not to patronize the retailers doing business in the mall. The handbilling was peaceful. No picketing or patrolling was involved. On its face, this was expressive activity arguing that substandard wages should be opposed by abstaining from shopping in a mall where such wages were paid.[59]

However, in 1995, the NLRB dealt organized labor a blow when it extended the *Lechmere* decision (see Chapter 5), which had been applied to organizational picketing, to consumer and product picketing. It ruled that employers can bar nonemployee union representatives from engaging in picketing on private property. In other words, the employer can ban nonemployee union representatives from picketing at store entrances and exits urging customers to stay away from the store (because they are trespassing on private property) *unless* the union can show that it has no reasonable alternative means of communicating with the store's customers.[60]

Common situs picketing Common situs picketing involves both the primary and neutral secondary employers who share the same physical work location, as in the case at construction sites and shipping docks. The problem arises when the union that is picketing the primary employer also adversely affects the work or business of the neutral employer located at the same site. The union has the right to picket the primary employer with whom it has a labor dispute. Yet the neutral, or secondary, employers have a right to be free from economic pressure from unions with whom they have no bargaining relationship.[61]

Unions argue that the employers who occupy the same work site *(common situs)* are so intertwined that a labor dispute with one employer is a labor dispute with all; therefore, unions allege that there are no neutral employers on the site. Employers argue they are independent operators and should be legally protected from picketing. The Supreme Court ruled on a case involving a general contractor on a construction project who subcontracted some electrical work to a nonunion subcontractor who paid less than the union scale.[62] When the nonunion employees arrived at work, the union set up pickets on the entire work site, and other union employees honored the picket line and refused to work. The Court ruled that general contractors and subcontractors on a building site were separate business entities and should be treated separately with respect to each other's labor controversies. Therefore, unions in a labor dispute with their employer cannot picket neutral employers on the common site.

Unions have been limited in their flexibility in applying economic pressure via picketing at work sites by another case in which the company, General Electric, used independent contractors to construct a new building, rearrange operations for a new product, and perform general repair work. In order to minimize contact between General Electric employees and employees of the contractors, a separate gate *(reserve gate)* was set aside for employees of the contractor. The union, which had a labor dispute with General Electric, called a strike and picketed all gates, including the separate gate, and most of the employees of the contractor honored the picket line. The NLRB found that picketing at the separate gate was designed to enmesh employees of a neutral employer in the labor dispute and was therefore illegal. The Supreme Court agreed to sustain the NLRB order unless the NLRB found through further investigation that the separate gate was established for the purpose of entry by employees who performed work that was necessary for the normal operations of the plant—work normally performed by General Electric employees who were on strike. Once the neutrality of the reserve gate has been breached, such as if the reserve gate is used by the contractor's employees to perform work normally done by employees on strike, the gate loses its neutrality and the union can lawfully picket the gate.

Alliance between employers (Business Ally Doctrine) If a secondary employer is closely associated with the primary employer and its labor dispute with the union, neutrality is lost and the secondary employer should be treated as a primary party to the labor dispute. For example, a secondary employer would lose its neutrality by accepting a subcontract to do work that would normally be done by workers on strike.

This work performed by the employees of the secondary employer can be classified as *struck work,* which includes "work that but for the strike would be performed by the employees of the primary employer." Another situation occurs in cases where the business relationship of the primary and secondary employer is so intertwined as to almost create a co-employer relationship.[63] Close business relationships can easily be so intertwined within conglomerated manufacturing or insurance companies that picketing the secondary employer is permissible.

Yet the courts have determined that single employers can be protected when distance between facilities is great and the operations are autonomous. For example, when union members having a labor dispute with the *Miami Herald* went to Detroit to picket the *Detroit Free Press* (both owned by Knight-Ridder), the NLRB found the common ownership alone did not in and of itself create an allied relationship. In fact, more recently the NLRB has concluded that separate divisions of the same corporation may also be able to claim protection from secondary picketing if the dispute exists at only one division.[64]

Hot-cargo agreements Designed to promote union-made products and support union members on strike, hot-cargo agreements were negotiated in labor agreements to specify that employees may refuse to use or handle products of certain employers, such as nonunion companies and companies experiencing strikes. Before the enactment of the Landrum-Griffin Act in 1959, these clauses were not illegal and were considered loopholes in the provisions of the Labor Management Relations Act, which dealt with secondary boycotts. While hot-cargo agreements had the same effect as secondary boycotts, they adversely affected neutral employers. In 1959 they were designated as unfair labor practices,[65] by the

1959 Landrum-Griffin amendments; however, a special exception was provided for the apparel, clothing, and construction industries. In addition, in the construction industry the union is permitted to strike in order to obtain a hot-cargo clause.[66]

Resolution procedures for national emergency disputes When labor disputes develop to a stage where they are regarded as having an adverse effect on the national interest, they assume a special significance. Certain legal procedures apply to these occasions. Strikes that have an adverse impact on national economic or defense interests are classified as *national emergency strikes,* and the federal government has used three methods in dealing with them: (1) presidential seizure or other intervention, (2) procedures under the Railway Labor Act, and (3) procedures under the Labor Management Relations Act.

Presidential seizures or attempts at seizure occurred 71 times under four presidents—Lincoln, Wilson, Franklin D. Roosevelt, and Truman—in the interests of maintaining production when actual strikes or threatened strikes caused national emergencies, mostly during wars.

The *Railway Labor Act* provides a procedure for resolving national emergency work stoppages in the railroads and airlines that includes the following:

- The National Mediation Board (NMB) attempts to mediate the dispute, and if unsuccessful, recommends voluntary interest arbitration.
- If arbitration is rejected, a 30-day time period is established during which wage rates, working rules, working conditions, and so forth remain the same.
- If the dispute threatens to substantially interrupt interstate commerce in any section of the country and deprive it of an essential transportation service, the president is notified, and an emergency board is appointed.
- The emergency board investigates the dispute and reports, with recommendations, within 30 days. During this time, the status quo is maintained.

Since the act's passage in 1926, its emergency provisions have been invoked about 200 times, an average rate of four times per year, and work stoppages have occurred at the end of the 60-day period at a rate of one per year since 1947.

However, government interventions in railroad disputes have averaged about one per year since 1980 and have virtually disappeared (only one time since 1980) in the airline industry. Sixteen federal laws have been passed to deal with specific railroad labor disputes, usually by extending the strike date and involving a third-party mediator or arbitrator. The last time a federal law was passed to intervene was 1992, when Congress stopped a national rail strike and mandated mediation and arbitration of the disputes (discussed earlier in this chapter).

The National Labor Relations Act amendment in 1947 authorized the president to invoke its national emergency provisions. These provisions include a step-by-step procedure to halt the strike for 80 days and provide the parties assistance in resolving their disputes. Exhibit 7.7 displays the steps in the national emergency procedure of the National Labor Relations Act. It includes the requirements specified for all parties: the 60-day notice to the other party that a change in the present

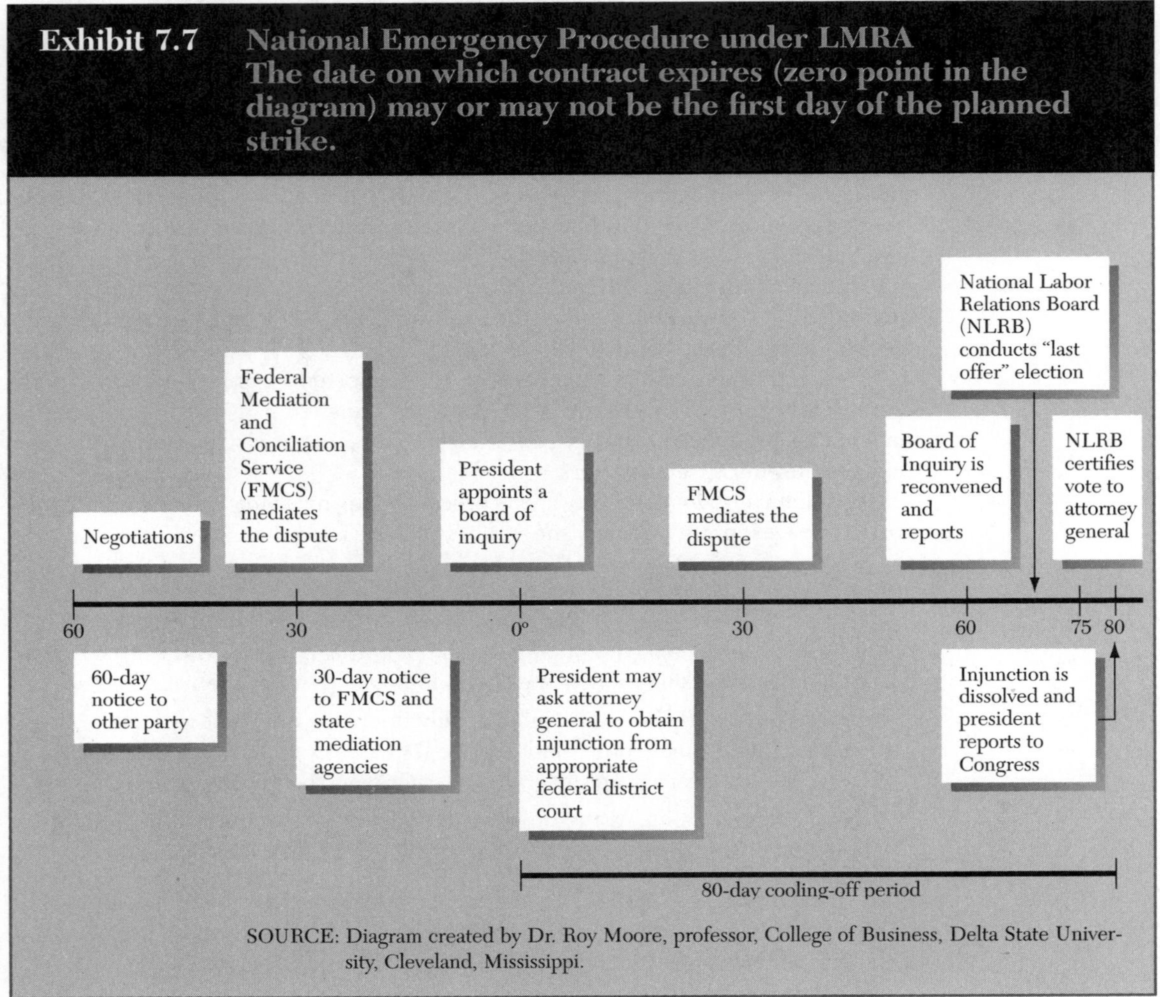

SOURCE: Diagram created by Dr. Roy Moore, professor, College of Business, Delta State University, Cleveland, Mississippi.

agreement is desired and the 30-day notice to the Federal Mediation and Conciliation Service (FMCS) and state agencies that the negotiations are in process and a settlement has not been reached.

The first step for the president is the appointment of a board of inquiry when the strike or the threat of a strike is believed to be of sufficient severity to imperil the national health or safety. Because of the urgency of the matter, the board will investigate the issues in dispute, gather relevant facts, and make a report to the president in a very short time—usually in about one day.

After the president receives and studies the report, he or she may direct the attorney general to secure an 80-day injunction from an appropriate federal district court to prevent or end the strike. Once the injunction is issued, the board is reconvened, and after the first 60 days of the injunction period, it will be asked to report to the president on the employer's last offer and any other relevant factors. During the interim period, the FMCS continues to assist the parties in reaching a settlement. After the board reports the final employer offer, the NLRB will conduct and certify a secret ballot election (between the 60th and 80th days of the injunction period) to determine whether the employees will accept this offer. If they refuse, the attorney general must ask the federal district court to dissolve the injunction at the end of 80 days, and the union may legally strike. The last step involves a full and comprehensive report by the president to Congress, accompanied by any recommendations that he or she may have.

In the first 22 years following the enactment of this NLRA procedure, it was used 29 times. However, since 1960, it has been used only 6 times (5 times in 1971 with stevedoring and grain elevator operations). Since then, government intervention has occurred only once, in 1977 to 1978 during a coal strike in which a federal judge refused to grant the Taft-Hartley injunction requested by President Carter because the federal government could not show that the work stoppage could do "irreparable harm to the national health and safety."

Several reasons have been identified for the decline in the need to invoke these national emergency procedures. They include the internationalization of some product markets, breakup of many centralized, industry-wide bargaining arrangements, decline in the percentage of the work force represented by unions, increase in nonunion operations, increase in tendency of employers to break strikes by hiring replacement employees, and employer willingness to operate during a work stoppage.[67]

Critics have believed the procedures do not adequately resolve national emergency strikes due to the rigidity and predictability of the procedures. When each step is predictable, either party may include the issuance of the injunction as part of its bargaining strategy. Also, the secret-ballot election on the employer's last offer often solidifies the union position rather than facilitating the bargaining process toward settlement. Lastly, because the presidential boards of inquiry are prohibited from proposing settlements, their effectiveness in securing the necessary public support and pressure to move the parties toward settlement is limited.

Cooperation between Union and Management to Reduce Conflicts

Preceding sections of this chapter have emphasized impasse-resolution procedures and conflict. However, there is growing support for greater union-management cooperation to avoid the necessity for such resolution procedures. The following sections include selected examples of union-management cooperative efforts.

Total Quality Management (TQM)

With many companies in the United States having difficulties competing in a global economy and with continuing criticism of lack of high-quality products, American industry has sought ways to improve its competitive status and upgrade the quality of its product. One approach that has been adopted by many American organizations is **Total Quality Management (TQM),** which is a continuous process to improve products and meet the needs of customers. Each organization that decides to adopt this concept adapts several primary elements that are unique to its culture: (1) focus on the customer, (2) continuous improvement based on measurements, (3) prevention of errors rather than detection of them, (4) commitment and involvement of top management, (5) a strategic focus on quality, and (6) employee involvement through problem-solving teams. It is the last element, employee involvement, that requires union cooperation in those organizations adopting and implementing the TQM concept.

While there have been several well-publicized success stories, the general reaction by unions has been mixed. Several concerns explain unions' mixed reactions. The first concern of the union is for its members' job security, and TQM's objective of improved production leads to fewer employees/union members being needed. In those organizations where there has been successful labor-management cooperation, management has made a commitment to minimize the use of layoffs as a means of reducing the number of excess employees and to make creative use of attrition, early retirement, and retraining programs.

Another union concern is its important role of representing employees through the grievance procedure and collective bargaining. While experience has shown that TQM helps to reduce the number of grievances, the union stewards actually spend their time with a broader number of employees. As one union official stated, "[We used to] spend 90 percent of our time on 10 percent of the membership. Now we spend 90 percent of our time with 90 percent of the members." Typically, adversarial interactions are limited to collective bargaining over wages, hours, employment policies, and working conditions; the work teams can then focus on problem solving.

Because the employees may file a grievance for contract violations, the work team members will feel more secure about expressing their views without fear of any reprisals. As well, unions may be able to use the content of the problem-solving sessions to obtain information about employee concerns. The identification of these concerns could be useful to the union in subsequent negotiations and represents a positive way for the union to respond to employee needs.

The final concern of unions is an institutional reaction to a threat to the union's existence. In fact, the National Association of Manufacturers (NAM) has strongly endorsed the employee involvement component of TQM without any mention of the union's role in this endeavor. Thus, when organizations establish an employee involvement program as a substitute for a union or as a mechanism to circumvent the union by dealing directly with employees, a realistic reaction by the union is to have serious mistrust of management's efforts. For this reason, one of the prerequisites for a successful employee involvement program is management's recognition and acceptance of the union as a partner in the TQM process.[68]

FMCS's RBO Program

The FMCS has a program, Relations by Objectives (RBO), that is designed to eliminate factors that cause breakdowns in negotiations and prolong strikes. RBO focuses on intergroup team building, intragroup image clarification and diagnosis, confrontation meetings, coaching, and other developmental approaches. The program consists of four phases:

1. Problem solving and goal setting.
2. Action planning and programming.
3. Implementation of plans and programs.
4. Periodic review and evaluation of progress toward goal accomplishment.

Phases 1 and 4 take place at a neutral, off-site location for three intensive days. Ten to fifteen members of the union and management attend sessions with federal mediators. Separate and joint sessions are held until neutral problem and goal statements are clarified, covering such subjects as communication, grievance handling, supervisor and steward training, and attitudes and positions of both the union and management.[69] Since its inception, the RBO program has had positive results, including improved stability in the parties' relationships, less grievance activity, improved production and plant morale, and smoother contract negotiations after the program.

Joint Labor-Management Committees

Hundreds of joint labor-management committees have been established on the parties' own initiative. These committees provide labor and management with an opportunity to discuss problems without the pressures of the bargaining table. Sixty percent of the labor agreements include union-management cooperation pledges.[70]

Joint committees attempt to resolve problems between contract negotiations and through cooperative efforts develop trust and a spirit that carries over to the bargaining table. Examples of neutral problem solving in the retail food industry include a study of working conditions, such as exposure to hazardous materials, use of protective gloves and aprons, and using knives and other cutting equipment.[71] In the health-care industry, joint committees have explored the alternatives to strikes for achieving peaceful settlements, treatment of registered nurses by physicians and hospital administrators, use of temporary employment agencies, work shifts, quality of care, and staffing.[72]

A follow-up study by the FMCS reported that 84 percent of the parties believed that their relationships with the other side had improved as a result of the work of the labor-management committees. These improved relationships were also reflected in better working conditions, reduced grievances, and improved bargaining relationships.[73]

Fremont, California—United Auto Workers, General Motors, and Toyota One example of joint cooperation is the venture incorporated as New

LABOR RELATIONS IN ACTION

The NUMMI-UAW Experience in Labor-Management Cooperation

Before NUMMI In 1982 before the venture began, work at the Fremont, California, plant was monotonous and required little skill; employee training was nonexistent; and 81 job classifications performing routine functions and 14 skilled classifications existed. The plant was referred to as "the battleship" because employees were constantly at war with management: over a thousand grievances were pending, absenteeism exceeded 20 percent frequently, drugs moved freely around the plant, beer bottles littered the parking lots, and productivity and quality were inferior.

Agreement between NUMMI and the UAW The company and the union negotiated an arrangement for a priority hiring of laid-off employees and, as a result, 85 percent of the new hires at NUMMI were former GM employees. There is only one job classification for unskilled employees and only three for skilled employees. The company and the union committed to the following:

1. To work together as a team (in Japanese philosophy, "wa" means harmony between the company, process, and employees).
2. To build the highest quality automobile in the world at the lowest possible cost.
3. To provide employees with a voice in decisions that affect their lives.
4. To constantly seek improvement in quality, efficiency, and the work environment (in Japanese philosophy, "kaizen" means continuous improvement in oneself, the work team, the company, and the community; "jidoka" means pursuit of superior quality, striving always to perform as well as possible).
5. To maintain a prosperous business operation to provide fair wages and benefits, job security, and opportunity for advancement.

Changes under the New Agreement

- The 2,400 hourly employees are organized into teams of 5 to 10 members who rotate among as many as 15 jobs.
- Each team has a leader selected with input from the union.
- There are only four supervisory levels, whereas there are six or seven at other U.S. plants.
- All employees share restrooms, parking spaces, and two excellent cafeterias.
- Most employees wear the blue outfits provided by the company.

United Motor Manufacturing Inc. (NUMMI) established by General Motors and Toyota. The venture, with agreement from the UAW, has provided about 2,700 jobs in the Fremont, California, plant.[74] The success at NUMMI laid the groundwork for General Motors' Saturn experiment. In fact, a former GM chairman has stated that if NUMMI had not been successful, GM would not have gone for-

- Each day starts with a voluntary exercise program.
- There is continuous learning through training to allow employees to think creatively and solve problems.
- Veteran team members have access to training opportunities to learn new methods and technologies; employees are encouraged to study on their own, visit other manufacturing facilities, attend trade shows, and take college courses.
- Employees are encouraged to submit at least one suggestion per year (a typical employee submits three or four per year); the company adopts over half of them; employees are awarded points that later lead to extra pay for their suggestions.

Results of Working under the NUMMI-UAW Agreement

- Quality of the product is consistently near the top in the United States.
- The work force remains highly motivated.
- Labor-management relations are excellent.
- Grievances have fallen to 50 to 60 per year.
- The absenteeism rate is about 3 percent per year.
- A recent survey shows that 90 percent of the employees are satisfied with their jobs.
- Profits have been inconsistent: there was a loss in 1985 and $20 million in profit each year in 1986, 1987, and 1989. In 1988, there was a $80 to $100 million loss due to start-up costs for a new model and slow sales of the Chevy Nova.
- A third production line, a Toyota compact pickup truck, was added, and 600 new hourly and 200 new salaried employees were hired in 1991.

SOURCE: Paul D. Staudohar, "Labor-Management Cooperation at NUMMI," *Labor Law Journal* 42 (January 1991), pp. 57–63; Douglas Henne, Marvin Levine, W.J. Usery, Jr., and Herbert Fishgold, "A Case Study in Cross-Cultural Mediation: The General Motors—Toyota Joint Venture," *The Arbitration Journal* 41 (September 1986), pp. 14–15.

ward with the Saturn project.[75] The "Labor Relations in Action" highlights the conditions before NUMMI, the agreement between NUMMI and the UAW, and the results.

Xerox and the Clothing Workers Xerox's primary manufacturing complex in Rochester, New York, faced a major competitive shock in the early 1980s when management discovered that Xerox's share of the worldwide revenues from copiers had dropped from 82 percent to 41 percent. With the cooperation of the Amalgamated Clothing and Textile Workers Union, joint efforts were initiated. These included joint union-management study teams to investigate outsourcing of work, establishment of a no-layoff policy, involvement of the union in strategic human resource planning, redesign of the plant, multiple forms of employee participation, autonomous work groups, and the initiation of a top-down total quality program entitled "Leadership Through Quality."

Several economic performance measures were improved through these joint union-management efforts. These included fewer monthly hours lost to scrap and more timely deliveries. In comparison, the more traditional, adversarial labor-management relationships were associated with higher cost levels, more employee hours lost, a higher monthly level of defects per employee, greater delivery variance, and a lower net return from the hours worked.[76]

When the company announced that it would close its wire harness facility, which would eliminate 240 jobs, and buy copier parts from a plant in Mexico, the union formed a cooperative team to identify ways to lower costs and to make a competitive bid. The goal was to identify $3.2 million in savings; the team found $3.5 million in savings, which preserved the union members' jobs.

By 1993 the company was winning back its market share, and its manufacturing jobs increased from 2,600 in the early 1980s to 4,100 in 1993.[77]

Saturn Agreement—UAW and General Motors General Motors and the UAW negotiated the Saturn agreement to cover GM's plant in Spring Hill, Tennessee, that employs nearly 10,000. The agreement, which was negotiated and agreed on before the plant was opened, included the following key features:

1. *Job security*—Permanent job security to all UAW-GM members hired into the Saturn plant; new employees will gain permanent job security based on seniority; 80 percent of the work force will have permanent job security at all times.
2. *Decision making*—Full participation of the workers and their union, free flow of information, and consensus decision making at all levels of the organization.
3. *Elimination of artificial distinctions between workers and management* in methods of pay, options to buy GM products, separate cafeterias, reserved parking spaces, separate entrances, and so on.
4. *Employee identification*—All production and skilled tradesmen will be designated as "Saturn" members.
5. *Compensation*—5 percent of pay is tied to training, product quality, and production goals. Each year this percentage will be increased by 5 percent until 20 percent is reached in 1995.
6. *Job classifications*—There is one production classification and three to five skilled classifications.

Because Saturn has been successful in producing a high-quality automobile that is in high demand, the company hired an additional 1,800 employees in 1992 and increased the work week to 50 hours. The company and union negotiated an agreement to hire the additional employees from those laid off at other General Motors plants. These employees came to Saturn after having gone through traumatic experiences from previous plant closings and had more distrust of management than the first 3,200 employees, who had been volunteers from General Motors facilities throughout the company. Moreover, because of the time pressures to place the new hires on the job to meet the production demand for additional cars and to reach the goal of breaking even in 1993 (the plant lost $700,000 in 1992 due mostly to high start-up costs), the new hires' training was reduced from 700 hours to 175 hours. Instead of having training on conflict management and learning Saturn's ethic of employee self-management, their training was more job specific in such subjects as power-tool operations.

Then in January 1993, the UAW held a referendum vote of the union members to determine whether to retain the current labor-management partnership or to shift back to a more traditional, arms-length labor relationship. Undercurrent issues included the belief by dissident employees that union leaders in the plant were becoming "too cozy with management." Dissident union members contended that shop-floor union leaders who acted as middle managers sometimes ignored members' gripes and focused on what was best for the company. Also, the dissident members wanted to elect the shop-floor leaders directly, instead of having them appointed by union and management officials. When the votes were counted, 29 percent had cast ballots in favor of return to traditional labor relations. While 71 percent chose to retain the labor-management partnership, the question of whether this model of progressive labor-management relations will last and remain successful will be determined only in time.[78] In 1994 and 1995, Saturn turned a profit and generated average bonuses of $3,245 and $10,000 per employee respectively for the 8,000 employees, whereas only an average of $587 and $800 was paid to employees at other General Motors vehicle divisions in North America during the same years.[79]

Characteristics of Successful Labor-Management Cooperative Efforts

The NUMMI, Xerox, and Saturn agreements incorporate several of the important characteristics of successful labor-management cooperative efforts in other places, which include

- Involvement of the organization's CEO, the union as an institution, and supervisory management.
- Mutual trust between the parties.
- Joint problem solving, which in turn relies on the formulation of clear objectives.
- Willingness to experiment and innovate.

- Constant communication between the parties.
- Self-reliance.

The "Labor Relations in Action" displays these characteristics in actual experiences.

Cautions about Union-Management Cooperative Efforts

While most academicians and practitioners almost unanimously paint a bright picture on employee involvement and labor-management cooperative programs, actual success of the efforts is determined by the circumstances at each site. For example, at each setting there is a bargaining relationship that has developed over time. If the experience of the parties has been destructive, conflictive, and hostile, the union will not be an eager supporter of or participant in the program until the relationship between the parties improves.

Sharing Power A study of 303 local unions in the paper industry revealed that the company gains the union's commitment by first taking steps to improve production. Further, the company must be willing to put sufficient effort into the program for it to be successful, and management must be willing to share power with the union. Withholding effort and power, will, in all likelihood, provoke animosity and undermine the goal of creating a cooperative bargaining environment.[80]

Unions have been concerned that participative and cooperative programs may pose a threat to the institutional integrity of the union and the rights of employees represented by the union. To avoid harmful effects, the union needs to exercise some control over the program by being involved extensively in the process of participation. If the union is not involved, success in the program is made difficult.[81] While there are well-publicized success stories of labor-management cooperation, such as already noted with Xerox and the Clothing Workers, Saturn and UAW, and AT&T and Bell South with the Communications Workers of America, there is evidence that even those managers who believe their companies have a cooperative relationship with their unions do not believe that unions should have input into decisions within their companies.[82]

Union Member Resistance Within the UAW, a group of dissident members under the label of "New Directions" has challenged the union leadership's "cozy" relationships with management. The dissidents' leaders contend that by participating in joint cooperation programs the union is betraying the interests of the union members and contradicting the unions' traditional role as an adversary to management. The Mike Parker book *Choosing Sides: Unions and the Team Concept* alleges that cooperative teamwork is nothing more than a "union-busting" device designed by companies to do away with unions.

Legal Considerations Several important legal issues must also be addressed. When union-management cooperation programs thrust employees into higher-level decision making, their involvement and influence may be sufficient to classify them as "managerial employees,"[83] which might exclude them from coverage under the

LABOR RELATIONS IN ACTION

Characteristics and Examples of Labor-Management Cooperation

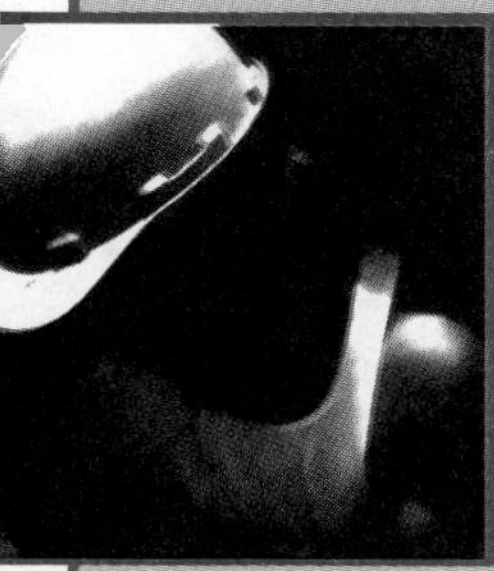

1. Mutual Trust between Employer and Union: Bell South and the Communications Workers of America (CWA) The parties established 416 joint quality-of-work-life (QWL) committees throughout the company. One QWL committee in Florida developed a new work process that eliminated eight jobs—their own. The committee members had enough trust in the system to make the recommendation because they knew that they would be prepared for comparable or better jobs in the organization.

2. Problem-Solving Approach to Bargaining: General Motors and UAW The company and union at the Doraville, Georgia, plant adopted a spirit of cooperation to work together to resolve mutual problems. Outsourcing of work, a problem for the union because it meant job losses for members, had been a focal point of potential strikes. To overcome the negative impact of outsourcing, a joint union-management team was formed to study the feasibility of keeping the work within the company. The team studied the possibility of building seat cushions for midsized models and discovered a way to produce the seat cushions within the plant for slightly less than the outside contractors. The company allowed the team to bid on the work and it won the contract, and seat cushions are now built in-house. Also, bids are now accepted from in-house teams not only to counter new outsourcing but to insource (bring back work that has been outsourced) as well.

3. A Willingness to Experiment and Innovate with Joint Activities to Meet Mutual Needs: Pacific Maritime Association and International Longshoremen's and Warehousemen's Union (ILWU) The companies and union committed to joint problem solving to adjust to technological changes that increase productivity while preserving work opportunities for ILWU members. The result was the Mechanization and Modernization Agreement, which dealt with problems of displacement caused by improvements in technology. Economic security of the existing work force was maintained and no layoffs resulted from lack of work. However, employers were able to reap net gains in productivity due to mechanization.

4. Constant Communication between Parties: General Electric and International Union of Electronic, Electrical, Technical, Salaried, and Machine Workers of America (IUE) The company concluded that it would no longer enter negotiations with its own conclusions about what is good for employees, asking the union to tell them what is wrong with the company's approach. Instead, the company encourages sharing of information, explanation of issues, and participative development of solutions. In negotiations, the company typically provides the union with an idea of the overall size of

(continued)

LABOR RELATIONS IN ACTION

Characteristics and Examples of Labor-Management Cooperation—cont'd

the negotiated package and then the parties jointly shape the individual items in the package. Throughout the years of the agreement, the parties continuously communicate with each other. For example, if an issue arises that may have legal implications for their relationship, they will discuss it before any action is taken. Neither party wants to be surprised, so the key officials talk to each other several times a week.

5. Self-Reliance: General Electric and the International Union of Electrical Workers (IUE), Bell South, and the Communications Workers of America The parties rely on themselves, rather than legal counsel or outside consultants, to manage their relationship. General Electric and the International Union of Electrical Workers (IUE) have not used any third party in their contract negotiations since 1970 because they believe they can and must jointly find a better way to resolve their differences. Bell South and the Communications Workers of America use grievance mediation with the assistance of a third-party mediator; however, 86 percent of the grievances that would have otherwise gone to arbitration are being settled by the parties themselves.

SOURCES: Donald P. Crane and Michael Jay Jedel, "Mature Collective Bargaining Relationships," in Gladys W. Guenberg, ed. *Arbitration 1988: Emerging Issues for the 1990s* (Washington, D.C.: Bureau of National Affairs Inc., 1989), pp. 346–364; Donald P. Crane, "Patterns of Labor-Management: Cooperation," *Employee Responsibilities and Rights Journal* 5 (December 1992), pp. 357–367.

National Labor Relations Act. In addition, Section 9(a) of the NLRA requires a union certified by the NLRB to be the exclusive representative of all the employees in the bargaining unit for purposes of collective bargaining in respect to rates of pay, wages, hours, and other conditions of employment. This "exclusivity" doctrine prohibits employers from bargaining with a union other than the one certified, if one exists, and it prohibits employees from bargaining collectively through any other labor organization. Employers who choose to negotiate with representatives other than the certified union will be circumventing the collective bargaining agent or will be committing an unfair labor practice [Section 8(a)(5)]. If a case arose in which the union challenged an employee committee operating outside union control and directly with the employer, the NLRB and courts would probably rule that the committee violated the union's exclusivity jurisdiction and that the employer was committing an unfair labor practice.[84]

Section 8(a)(2) of the NLRA prohibits an employer from dominating or interfering with the formation or administration of any labor organization or from contributing financial or other support to it. In the past the NLRB has construed Section 8(a)(2) very narrowly so as to preclude many forms of employee interaction with management.[85] In the well-publicized *Electromation* decision in December 1992, the NLRB developed tests to determine the legality of union-management joint efforts. Electromation, a nonunion manufacturer of electrical components, set up "action committees" of employees in response to a unionization campaign. These committees were established to discuss (1) absenteeism/infractions, (2) no smoking policy, (3) communication network, (4) pay progression for premium positions, and (5) attendance bonuses during working hours. The union afterwards requested recognition, contended that the action committees were labor organizations, and filed an unfair labor practice charge, which alleged that the company had violated Section 8(a)(2) of the NLRA by its domination of the committees and assistance given to these committees. The NLRB ruled that the action committees were dominated by the company. As a result of the unfair labor practice, the company was directed to disband the action committees. The tests developed by the NLRB address the topics discussed, the representational nature of the group, and the authority of the group. See Exhibit 7.8 for these tests.

In nonunion settings, the NLRB and courts have ruled that employee participation programs will probably be found permissible under the NLRA if the following factors are present: (1) employee terms on the participation committees are rotated frequently and employees are elected by their co-workers, (2) no evidence exists of anti-union bias or employee dissatisfaction with the program, (3) there are no union organizing activities at the time the program is established, (4) participation is voluntary, (5) employees are permitted to join a union, (6) the committee is delegated final and binding decision-making authority, and (7) the subjects are restricted to those not considered bargainable in the collective bargaining arena.[86]

Among its many recommendations to improve labor-management relations in the United States, the Commission on the Future of Worker-Management Relations recommended changing Section 8(a)(2) of the NLRA to give companies greater latitude in the operation of employee participation programs. Strongly endorsed by the business community, the commission stated that it was in the national interest to promote expansion of such programs provided that they do not impede employee choice of whether or not to be represented by an independent labor organization. The commission urged that the growth of employee involvement programs be facilitated in nonunion settings and that discussions of terms and conditions of employee compensation be allowed where such discussions are incidental to the broad purposes of the programs.[87]

The Republican majority in the Senate and House of Representatives leaped on this recommendation with proposed legislation entitled Teamwork for Employees and Managers Act, commonly referred to as the "Team Act"[88] (see Exhibit 7.9). The Team Act is strongly opposed by organized labor and President Clinton has threatened a veto if the legislation is passed.

Exhibit 7.8 Post-Electromation: Tests to Determine Whether Work Teams and Their Activities Are in Violation of 8(a)(2) of NLRA

1. Is the work team discussing Section 2(5) topics, such as grievances, labor disputes, wages, rates of pay, benefits, hours of employment, safety, or working conditions? If so, the chances are increased that the company is violating Section 8(a)(2) of the National Labor Relations Act.
2. Are work team members acting in an individual or representative capacity? If the team members are addressing issues that affect nonteam employees or are addressing issues on behalf of other employees, the chances are increased that the company is violating Section 8(a)(2) of the National Labor Relations Act. In considering the question of representation, the following factors will be investigated:
   - *Function of the work team:* Presenting employee views, making recommendations to management, and presenting other employees' grievances are indicators of representation.
   - *Form of the plan under which work team exists:* Consider the number of team members, how they were selected, and the formal organization of the team: the more formal a team's organization, the more a representative purpose is inferred. Consider collection of dues, defined electoral grouping, existence of a governing written instrument.
   - *Employer's intent in forming the work team:* Was the work team formed in response to an attempted union organizing drive? Is the team a substitute for a legitimate and independent representational union?
   - *Employee's perception of the work team:* Do the employees consider the committee to resemble a labor organization or to represent anyone?
3. Is the authority of the work team limited to making recommendations to management, or does the team have delegated management authority to make decisions? If the work team only has power to make recommendations, this is an indicator of "labor organization" status; however, if the work team has the power to make decisions, the presence of managerial decision-making authority is an indicator that the work team is *not* a labor organization.
4. Does the employer retain veto power over any action of the work team and who will serve on each team? Does the employer have power to abolish the team at will? Retention of discretionary veto power and power to abolish the team at will is an indication of management's unlawful domination.
5. Did the company create the work team or decide what it would do and how it would function? In other words, does the company dominate the work team? If the company establishes the work team, then selects the members, supports the work team financially, gives direction and assigns projects to the team, and so on, the chances are increased that a legal violation has occurred.

SOURCES: Michael S. Beaver, "Are Worker Participation Plans 'Labor Organizations' within the Meaning of Section 2(5)? A Proposed Framework of Analysis," *Labor Law Journal* 36 (August 1985), pp. 226–237; Aaron Bernstein, "Making Teamwork Work—Appeasing Uncle Sam," *Business Week*, January 25, 1993, p. 101, *Electromation, Inc. and International Brotherhood of Teamsters, Local Union No. 1049,* 309 NLRB No. 163, December 16, 1992; *E.I. DuPont de Nemours SG,* 311 NLRB No. 88, May 28, 1993 in *Daily Labor Report,* June 8, 1993, pp. AA-1–AA-2, and D-1–D-10; Raymond L. Hogler, "Employee Involvement and Electromation, Inc.: An Analysis and a Proposal for Statutory Change," *Labor Law Journal* 44 (May 1993), pp. 261–274.

Exhibit 7.9 Excerpts from the Proposed Team Act

SECTION 1. SHORT TITLE.

This Act may be cited as the "Teamwork for Employees and Managers Act of 1995."

SEC. 3. EMPLOYER EXCEPTION.

Section 8(a)(2) of the National Labor Relations Act is amended by striking the semicolon and inserting the following: ": *Provided further,* That it shall not constitute or be evidence of an unfair labor practice under this paragraph for an employer to establish, assist, maintain, or participate in any organization or entity of any kind, in which employees participate, to address matters of mutual interest, including, but not limited to, issues of quality, productivity, efficiency, and safety and health, and which does not have, claim, or seek authority to be the exclusive bargaining representative of the employees or to negotiate or enter into collective bargaining agreements with the employer or to amend existing collective bargaining agreements between the employer and any labor organization."

SEC. 4. LIMITATION ON EFFECT OF ACT.

Nothing in this Act shall affect employee rights and responsibilities contained in provisions other than section 8(a)(2) of the National Labor Relations Act, as amended.

SOURCE: *Daily Labor Report,* January 31, 1995, p. E-33.

William Gould IV, chairman of the NLRB, has opposed this legislation because

> There is no assurance in the proposed amendment that employee free choice will be honored. The amendment simply limits lawful forms of participation to those which do not have or seek the authority to negotiate collective bargaining agreements with the employer or to amend existing collective bargaining agreements.[89]

Summary

Early research led to the conclusion that contract rejection is relatively high; however, more recent research finds a lower rate when contract rejection is redefined as rejection of the bargaining committee's recommended labor agreement.

Third-party procedures to assist the parties in resolving negotiation impasses range from mediation (where the third party attempts to facilitate resolution by keeping the parties bargaining, acting as a go-between, and offering alternatives) to arbitration, a quasi-judicial procedure in which the bargaining positions are presented to the arbitrator, who makes a final and binding decision. Within the range are the med-arb procedure (which attempts mediation first and then arbitration if mediation fails) and fact-finding (in which the parties present their positions to the fact-finder, other facts are collected, and a report, which includes a recommended resolution of the impasse, is written and presented).

Not all bargaining issues are resolved through negotiations: strikes, boycotts, pickets, lockouts, and related activities do occur. However, both parties have to seriously consider their positions and the consequences of their actions before taking any actions. Each hurts the costs, profits, and production of the companies and the income and public image of the union. While both parties may prepare for work stoppages, a high percentage of strikes, boycotts, pickets, and lockouts have taken their toll in terms of costs to both parties.

The right to concerted actions by employees is an intrinsic part of the labor relations process and is guaranteed by law. On the other hand, possession of a right to strike does not mean that it should be exercised frequently. The data show that strikes occur very infrequently, but those that do occur can be damaging economically and are well publicized by the media.

Most strikes and related activities involve primary employers, but often secondary employers (not directly involved in the employer-employee relationship) are affected. A complex body of law and judicial decisions covers such activities as consumer and product boycotts and picketing, common situs picketing, employer ally relationships, and hot-cargo agreements.

Strikes and related activities that have an adverse effect on the national interest may be declared national emergency strikes. Procedures are available in the Railway Labor Act and the Labor Management Relations Act to facilitate their resolutions. While such impasses occur infrequently, they are significant when they do.

Efforts by unions and management to organize and develop cooperative efforts to reduce the possibility of conflict are still relatively infrequent. However, several unions and companies have spent much time, money, and effort to minimize conflicts. A number of successful labor-management cooperation programs have received national attention.

The final section addresses the controversial Team Act, which would amend Section 8(a)(2) of the National Labor Relations Act.

Key Terms

mediation
traditional interest (or contract) arbitration
final-offer selection (FOS) arbitration
mediation-arbitration or med-arb
fact-finding
strike
lockout
recognitional picketing
informational picketing
boycott
product or consumer picketing
wildcat strike
Total Quality Management (TQM)

Discussion Questions

1. What are the chief reasons union members reject tentative agreements?
2. What problems may result from contract rejection?
3. Define the major types of third-party interventions. How do they differ, and how do they appear similar?

4. What specific qualities should a mediator possess? Why do these qualities facilitate impasse resolution?
5. Why is interest arbitration used so infrequently in the private sector?
6. Discuss the following statement: "Strikes are an intrinsic and essential element of the collective bargaining process."
7. Discuss the following: "It appears that the balance in labor-management relations during the labor disputes has shifted to management."
8. Define and discuss the various types of secondary activities of unions that may occur during impasses.
9. List the arguments for and against President Clinton's Executive Order, which prohibits federal government contractors from hiring permanent striker replacements.
10. List the issues in which management and the union can cooperate to their mutual advantage. Do you know of other cooperative efforts by union and management to reduce conflict? List the strong and weak points of these efforts.
11. What are the arguments for and against the Team Act? Compare the elements to the Employee Representation Plans on page 54.

References

1. "Major Work Stoppage: 1994" *News* (Washington, D.C.: Bureau of Labor Statistics, U.S. Department of Labor), pp. 1–4.

2. Clyde W. Summers, "Ratification of Agreements," in *Frontiers of Collective Bargaining,* ed. J. T. Dunlop and N. W. Chamberlain (New York: Harper & Row, 1967), pp. 82–83.

3. Federal Mediation and Conciliation Service. *Thirty-Fourth Annual Report* (Washington, D.C.: Government Printing Office, 1982), p. 21. (FMCS does not collect those data at this time.)

4. Peter Cappelli and W. P. Sterling, "Union Bargaining Decisions and Contract Ratifications: The 1982 and 1984 Auto Agreements," *Industrial and Labor Relations Review* 41 (January 1988), p. 195.

5. William E. Simkin, "Refusal to Ratify Contracts," *Industrial and Labor Relations Review* 21 (July 1968), pp. 528–529.

6. Charles Odewahn and Joseph Krislov, "Contract Rejections: Testing the Explanatory Hypothesis," *Industrial Relations* 12 (October 1973), pp. 289–296.

7. D. R. Burke and Lester Rubin, "Is Contract Rejection a Major Collective Bargaining Problem?" *Industrial and Labor Relations Review* 26 (January 1973), pp. 832–833.

8. William E. Simkin, *Mediation and the Dynamics of Collective Bargaining* (Washington, D.C.: Bureau of National Affairs, Inc, 1971), pp. 25–28.

9. Federal Mediation and Conciliation Service, *Forty-Sixth and Forty-Seventh Annual Report* (Washington, D,C.: FMCS, 1995), p. 22.

10. Carl Stevens, "Mediation and the Role of the Neutral," in Dunlop and Chamberlain, *Frontiers of Collective Bargaining,* p. 271.

11. Steven Briggs and Daniel J. Koys, "What Makes Labor Mediators Effective?" *Labor Law Journal* 40 (August 1988), pp. 517–520.

12. Stevens, "Mediation and the Role of the Neutral," pp. 280–284.
13. Joseph Krislov and Amira Ealin, "Comparative Analysis of Attitudes Towards Mediation," *Labor Law Journal* 30 (March 1979), p. 173.
14. Richard B. Peterson and Mark R. Peterson, "Toward A Systematic Understanding of the Labor Mediation Process," in *Advances in Industrial and Labor Relations,* vol. 4, eds. David Lewin, David B. Kipsky, and Donna Sockell (Greenwich, Conn.: JAI Press, Inc., 1987), p. 145.
15. Stevens, "Mediation and the Role of the Neutral," pp. 280–284.
16. Richard B. Peterson and Mark R. Peterson, "Toward a Systematic Understanding," pp. 152–153.
17. Thomas A. Kochan and Todd Jick, "The Public Sector Mediation Process," *Journal of Conflict Resolution* 22 (June 1978), p. 236.
18. Homer C. LaRue, "An Historic Overview of Interest Arbitration in the United States," *The Arbitration Journal* 42 (December 1987), pp. 13–17.
19. Robert A. Baruch Bush, "Efficiency and Protection or Empowerment and Recognition?: The Mediator's Role and Ethical Standards in Mediation," *Florida Law Review* 41 (Spring 1989), pp. 253–286.
20. William H. Ross, Jr. "Situational Factors and Alternative Dispute Resolution," *The Journal of Applied Behavioral Science* 24, no. 3 (1988), pp. 251–260.
21. Max H. Bazerman, "Norms of Distributive Justice in Interest Arbitration," *Industrial and Labor Relations* 38 (July 1985), pp. 568–570.
22. Paul L. Burgess and Daniel R. Marburger, "Do Negotiated and Arbitrated Salaries Differ Under Final-Offer Arbitration?" *Industrial and Labor Relations Review* 46 (April 1993), pp. 557–558.
23. David E. Feller, "The Impetus to Contract Arbitration in the Private Area," *Twenty-fourth Annual NYU Conference on Labor* (New York: Matthew Bender, 1972), pp. 95–98.
24. Michael Marmo, "The Role of Fact Finding and Interest Arbitration in 'Selling' a Settlement," *Journal of Collective Negotiation in the Public Sector* 24, no. 1 (1995), pp. 78–82.
25. Neal Orkin and Michael Halvorsen, "There Is No Honor in Honoring a Picket Line," *Labor Law Journal* 44 (October 1993), p. 639.
26. Michael H. LeRoy, "The Changing Character of Strikes Involving Permanent Striker Replacements, 1935–1990," *Journal of Labor Research* 16 (Fall 1995), p. 437.
27. Bruce E. Kaufman, "The Determinants of Strikes Over Time and Across Industries," *Journal of Labor Research* 4 (Spring 1983), pp. 173–174.
28. Bruce E. Kaufman, "Research on Strike Models and Outcomes in the 1980s: Accomplishments and Shortcomings," in *Research Frontiers In Industrial and Human Resources,* eds. David Lewin, Olivia S. Mitchell, and Peter D. Sherer (Madison, Wis.: Industrial Relations Research Association, 1992), pp. 78–79.
29. Martin J. Mauro, "Strikes as a Result of Imperfect Information," *Industrial and Labor Relations Review* 35 (July 1982), pp. 536–538.
30. Bert Klandermans, "Perceived Costs and Benefits of Participation in Union Action," *Personnel Psychology* 39 (Summer 1986), pp. 380–381.
31. James E. Martin, "Predictors of Individual Propensity to Strike," *Industrial and Labor Relations Review* 39 (January 1986), pp. 224–225.
32. N. Nicholson and J. Kelly, "The Psychology of Strikes," *Journal of Occupational Behavior* (October 1981), pp. 275–284.
33. William Serrin, *The Company and the Union* (New York: Knopf, 1973), p. 4.
34. "Testimony of Senator George Mitchel before the Subcommittee on

Labor-Management Relations of the Committee on Education and Labor, U.S. House of Representatives, March 30, 1988," *Daily Labor Report,* March 31, 1989, pp. F-1–F-3.
35. "Supreme Court Endorses Board Holding That Union Members Can Resign During Strike," *Daily Labor Report,* June 28, 1986, p. AA-1.
36. "NLRB Holds 'Financial Core' Members May Not Be Fired for Crossing Picket Line," *Daily Labor Report,* December 12, 1985, p. A-3.
37. George Getschow, "Strike Woes Pile Up for Leader of Local That Started It All," *The Wall Street Journal,* August 8, 1977, pp. 1, 17.
38. John R. Emshwiller, "Strike is Traumatic for a Quiet Village in Michigan Woods," *The Wall Street Journal,* July 30, 1977, pp. 1, 24.
39. American Society for Personnel Administration, *Strike Preparation Manual* (Berea, Ohio: American Society for Personnel Administration, 1974). Also see L. C. Scott, "Running a Struck Plant: Some Do's and Don't's," *SAM Advanced Management Journal* 38 (October 1973), pp. 58–62; and John G. Hutchinson, *Management under Strike Conditions* (New York: Holt, Rinehart and Winston, 1966).
40. Theodore W. Kheel, "Is the Strike Outmoded?" *Monthly Labor Review* 96 (September 1973), pp. 35–37.
41. Kheel, "Is the Strike Outmoded?" pp. 35–37.
42. Gregory A. Patterson and Robert L. Rose, "Labor Makes a Stand in Fight for Its Future at Caterpillar, Inc.," *The Wall Street Journal,* April 7, 1992, p. A-1.
43. "Statements of Franklin Frazier, Director of Education and Employment Issues, General Accounting Office," *Hearing Before the Subcommittee on Labor-Management Relations of the Committee on Education and Labor, House of Representatives* (Washington, D.C.: Government Printing Office, June 13, 1990), p. 202.
44. David B. Stephen and John P. Kohl, "The Replacement Worker Phenomenon in the Southwest: Two years after *Belknap, Inc.* v. *Hale," Labor Law Journal* 37 (January 1986), pp. 48–49.
45. William B. Gould IV, "The Right to Strike in a Democratic Society," *News Release from the National Labor Relations Board,* February 24, 1995.
46. John W. Budd and Wendell E. Pritchett, "Does the Banning of Permanent Strike Replacements Affect Bargaining Power?" *Proceedings of the 46th Annual Meeting of the Industrial Relations Research Association* (Madison, Wis.: IRRA, 1994), pp. 370–376.
47. John F. Schnell and Cynthia L. Gramm, "The Empirical Relations Between Employers' Striker Replacement Strategies and Strike Duration," *Industrial and Labor Relations Review* 47 (January 1994), p. 203.
48. George S. Roukis and Mamdouh I. Farid, "An Alternative Approach to the Permanent Striker Replacement Strategy," *Labor Law Journal* 44 (February 1993), pp. 86–88.
49. "Poll Shows Two-Thirds of Americans Oppose Replacing Workers Who Strike," *Daily Labor Report,* June 15, 1994, p. AA-1.
50. Roukis and Farid, "An Alternative Approach to the Permanent Striker Replacement Strategy," pp. 81–88.
51. Roukis and Farid, "An Alternative Approach to the Permanent Striker Replacement Strategy," pp. 81–82.
52. John R. Erickson, "Forfeiture of Reinstatement Rights through Strike Misconduct," *Labor Law Journal* 31 (October 1980), pp. 602–616.
53. K. C. Miller and W. H. Form, *Industrial Sociology,* 2nd ed. (New York: Harper & Row, 1964), pp. 385–388.
54. Dennis M. Byrne and Randall H. King, "Wildcat Strikes in U.S. Manufacturing, 1960–1977," *Journal of Labor Research* 7 (Fall 1986), p. 400.

55. B. A. Brotman, "A Comparative Analysis of Arbitration and National Labor Relations Board Decisions Involving Wildcat Strikes," *Labor Law Journal* 36 (July 1985), p. 440.

56. Walter E. Oberer and Kurt. L. Hanslowe, *Labor Law* (St. Paul, Minn.: West Publishing, 1972), pp. 482–483. See *Buffalo Linen Supply Company,* 353 U.S. 85 (1956); and *Brown Food Store, et al.,* 380 U.S. 278 (1965).

57. Thomas P. Murphy, "Lockouts and Replacements: The NLRB Gives Teeth to an Old Weapon," *Employee Relations Law Journal* 14 (Autumn 1988), pp. 253–261.

58. Ralph M. Dereshinsky, Alan D. Berkowitz, and Philip A. Miscimarra, *The NLRB and Secondary Boycotts,* rev. ed. (Philadelphia: Industrial Research Unit, University of Pennsylvania Press, 1981), pp. 191–195.

59. "Supreme Court Endorses Union Right to Handbill in Support of Consumer Boycott of Shopping Mall," *Daily Labor Report,* April 21, 1989, pp. A-5–A-6.

60. "Divided Board Extends *Lechmere* to Area Standard Picketing," *Daily Labor Report,* January 21, 1995, p. AA-1.

61. Dereshinsky et al., *The NLRB and Secondary Boycotts,* pp. 9–11.

62. *NLRB* v. *Denver Building Trades Council,* 341 U.S. 675 (1951).

63. Dereshinksy et al., *The NLRB and Secondary Boycotts,* p. 128.

64. Robert J. Denney, "Secondary Boycotts," in *Strikes, Stoppages, and Boycotts, 1978,* ed. Walter B. Connolly, Jr. (New York: Practicing Law Institute, 1978), pp. 128–135.

65. Dereshinksy et al., *The NLRB and Secondary Boycotts,* pp. 237–239.

66. Joshua L. Schwarz and Taryn Shawstad, "Establishing Stability in Labor Law: A Lesson from the Landrum-Griffin Act's Provisions for the Construction Industry," *Labor Law Journal* 38 (December 1987), p. 767.

67. Charles M. Rehmus, "Emergency Strikes Revisited," *Industrial and Labor Relations Review* 43 (January 1990), pp. 176–180.

68. Marvin J. Levine, "Labor and Management Response to Total Quality Management," *Labor Law Journal* 43 (February 1992), pp. 107–112.

69. David A. Gray, Anthony V. Sinicropi, and Paula Ann Hughes, "From Conflict to Cooperation: A Joint Union-Management Goal-Setting and Problem-Solving Program," in *Proceedings of the Thirty-Third Annual Meeting: Industrial Relations Research Association,* ed. B. D. Dennis (Madison, Wis.: Industrial Relations Research Association, 1982), pp. 26–28.

70. *Basic Patterns in Union Contracts,* 14th ed. (Washington, D.C.: Bureau of National Affairs, Inc., 1995), p. 83.

71. Philip E. Ray, "The Retail Food Industry," in *Proceedings of the Thirty-Fourth Annual Meeting: Industrial Relations Research Association,* ed. B. D. Dennis (Madison, Wis.: Industrial Relations Research Association, 1982), pp. 146–149.

72. Laurence P. Corbett, "The Health Care Experience," in *Proceedings of the Thirty-Fourth Annual Meeting: Industrial Relations Research Association,* ed. B. D. Dennis (Madison, Wis.: Industrial Relations Research Association, 1982), pp. 156–157.

73. Internal study by the Federal Mediation and Conciliation Service, June 1, 1987.

74. Douglas Henne, Marvin J. Levine, W. J. Ussery, Jr., and Herbert Fishgold, "A Case Study in Cross-Cultural Mediation: The General Motors–Toyota Joint Venture," *The Arbitration Journal* 41 (September 1986), pp. 14–15.

75. W. J. Ussery, Jr., "New Industrial Relations and Industrial Justice," *Arbitration 1991: The Changing Face of Arbitration in Theory and Practice,* ed. Gladys W. Gruenberg (Washington, D.C.: Bureau of National Affairs, Inc., 1992), p. 174.

76. Joel Cuther-Gershenfield, "The Impact of Economic Performance of a Transformation in Workplace Relations,"

Industrial and Labor Relations Review 44 (January 1991), pp. 241–260.

77. Patty de Llosa and Richardo Sookedo, "Look What the Unions Want Now," *Fortune*, February 8, 1993, p. 132.

78. David Woodruff, "Saturn: Labor's Love Lost?" *Business Week*, February 8, 1993, pp. 122–124.

79. "Auto Workers Complain about Disparity in Size of Their Profit Sharing Checks," *The Wall Street Journal*, February 1, 1996, p. A6.

80. Jill Kriesky and Edwin L. Brown, "Implementing Employee Involvement: How Paper Companies Gain Local Union Support," *Employee Responsibilities and Rights Journal* 5 (June 1992), pp. 125–126.

81. Adrienne E. Eaton, "The Extent and Determinants of Local Union Control of Participative Programs," *Industrial and Labor Relations Review* 43 (July 1990), pp. 618–619.

82. Martin M. Perline and Edwin A. Sexton, "Managerial Perceptions of Labor-Management Cooperation," *Industrial Relations* 33 (July 1994), p. 385.

83. Kenneth O. Alexander, "Worker Participation and the Law: Two Views and Comment," *Labor Law Journal* 36 (July 1985), p. 433.

84. Donna Sockell, "The Legality of Employee-Participation Programs in Unionized Firms," *Industrial and Labor Relations Review* 37 (July 1984), pp. 541–556.

85. Raymond Hogler, "Employee Involvement Programs and *NLRB v. Scott Fitzer Co.:* The Developing Interpretation of Section 8(a)(2)," *Labor Law Journal* 35 (January 1984), pp. 21–27.

86. Barbara A. Lee, "Collective Bargaining and Employee Participation: An Anomalous Interpretation of the National Labor Relations Act," *Labor Law Journal* 38 (April 1987), pp. 206–219.

87. "Dunlop Panel Urges Clarification of Section 8(a)(2)," *Daily Labor Report*, January 10, 1995, p. AA-1.

88. "House Panel Approves Team Act, Restricts EI Committee Activities in Union Settings," *Daily Labor Report*, June 23, 1995, p. AA-1.

89. Speech by William B. Gould IV, "Cooperation or Conflict: Problems and Potential in the National Labor Relations Act," New York University's 48th National Conference on Labor, May 31, 1995.

8 CONTRACT ADMINISTRATION

Labor agreement negotiation is usually the most publicized and dramatic aspect of labor relations. Strike deadlines, negotiators in shirtsleeves working around the clock to avert a possible strike, and the economic settlement of the labor agreement receive attention from the news media. The day-to-day administration of the labor agreement, on the other hand, receives little, if any, recognition beyond that given by the involved parties. Contract administration, however, involves more labor and management officials than does collective bargaining, and it applies meaning and common law principles to negotiated labor provisions. In contract negotiations the union is typically the initiator, but in contract administration management assumes this role. Management makes many decisions such as who to promote, who to lay off, whether just cause exists for discipline, and so on. The union monitors these decisions and may file a grievance when they appear inconsistent with the provisions of the labor agreement.

This chapter first defines employee grievances, then explores their sources and significance. The next section examines the grievance procedure: its typical steps, the relationships among grievance participants, and theoretical as well as practical concerns involved in contract administration. Then the union's fair representation obligation is discussed.

GRIEVANCES: DEFINITION, SOURCES, AND SIGNIFICANCE

An employee **grievance** represents the core of contract administration and is defined as any employee's concern over a perceived violation of the labor agreement that is submitted to the grievance procedure for resolution. A grievance is therefore distinguished from an employee's concern that is unrelated to labor agreement provisions and is not submitted to the grievance procedure. Most grievances are written out (see Exhibit 8.1), which has several advantages for management and union officials:

Exhibit 8.1 Examples of Incorrect and Correct Grievance Forms

THE WRONG WAY

FILL OUT IN TRIPLICATE

GRIEVANCE REPORT

USA Local Union No.

Location

Name Union Ledger No. Age

Address

Department Operation Check No.

Service

Nature of Grievance

The foreman is against me. He always has it in for me. Lots of times he gives me dirty jobs. Now he refuses to give me holiday pay when I ought to get it. It s

WHEN? Be specific, give dates.

WHY? What section or sections of the contract are involved?

GET WHAT? Describe the adjustment sought.

SPELL IT OUT! Is this another grievance? What do these statements have to do with the Holiday Pay issue?

COPY FOR LOCAL UNION

THE RIGHT WAY

FILL OUT IN TRIPLICATE

GRIEVANCE REPORT

USA Local Union No.

Location

Name Union Ledger No. Age

Address

Department Operation Check No.

Service

Nature of Grievance

I, the undersigned, a laborer in the Melt Department, claim that the Company violated Section 10 — Holidays, of the Basic Agreement when it failed to pay me for the July 4th unworked holiday even though I had satisfied the eligibility requirements. I request that the Company compensate me for 8 hours pay on July 4th as

COPY FOR LOCAL UNION

SOURCE: Reprinted with permission from United Steelworkers of America, *The Grievance Man's Handbook,* (n.p., n.d.)

1. Both union and management representatives need a written record of their daily problem resolutions. This record generates precedents that can guide future actions and save time in deciding similar grievances.
2. Written grievances tend to reduce the emotionalism present in many employee concerns. Verbal confrontation on an emotional issue can produce exaggerated accusations that may irreparably harm the relationship between the parties. Consequently, writing the grievance may be necessary for its rational discussion.

3. A written concern allows management representatives to focus on the employee's original grievance. As will be discussed further, a grievance can proceed through several steps that involve many more individuals than the aggrieved employee. Union officials may alter an employee's initial concern into a broader philosophical issue. (For example, a complaint over the company's unilateral increase in prices of candy bars for the vending machine could conceivably be magnified in subsequent steps to protest the company's arbitrary and capricious actions in other working conditions.) Management always has the option of returning to the concern(s) expressed in the original grievance because it is in written form.
4. Written grievances can benefit management in cases where the employee is apprehensive about signing a written protest. One research effort found that supervisors react negatively in subsequent performance ratings of employees who file grievances against them that are decided in the employees' favor.[1] Even though most labor agreements permit a union officer to file a grievance on behalf of the grievant, requiring grievances to be written probably reduces the total number that management representatives must administer.

Our definition of a grievance is extremely broad and hinges on the employee's perception that he or she has a grievance. Assume, for example, that Employee A protests Employee B's "immoral" behavior. This protest could be an oral complaint without reference to the grievance procedure, or the employee could insist the complaint represents a violation of the terms of the labor agreement. The supervisor can attempt to convince the employee that the complaint is unrelated to the terms of the labor agreement.

Yet what happens if the employee insists that the concern is a grievance and should be processed as such? Further, suppose the employee cites a contractual provision in the argument, such as an article stressing the "company's obligation to maintain a work environment in as safe a condition as possible." After unsuccessfully discussing the issue with Employee A, the supervisor has two options: (1) to refuse to accept the employee's grievance or (2) to accept the employee's grievance and deny it in the written grievance answer on the basis that there is no contractual violation. Not wishing to risk a time-consuming unfair labor practice charge, the supervisor will probably take the second alternative.

The broad definition of a grievance realizes, then, that there is a difference between accepting an employee's grievance and deciding the merits of an employee's grievance. The broader definition safeguards against unfair labor practice charges and at the same time preserves management's right to deny the grievance in its written answer.

Reasons for Employee Grievances

Some research has focused on differences between employees who do not file grievances and employees who do. One such study found that employees who file grievances are younger, more active in their unions, and less satisfied with their job, supervisor, and union.[2]

In order to better understand the reasons behind employee grievances, the following example is given. A first-line supervisor administers a labor agreement that has the following provisions pertaining to management's right and the scheduling of work to be performed on a holiday:

Article III: Management Rights
Section 1. The Company's right to hire, fire, and direct the working force, transfer or promote is unqualified as long as this right is not used in any conflict with any provision of this contract.

Article IX: Holiday Scheduling
Section 1. When less than a normal crew is required to work on a holiday, the following procedure will apply:
(a) The senior employee working in the classification desired will be given the opportunity to work.
(b) Employees assigned holiday work will be paid a minimum of 8 hours at time and one-half the contract rate of pay.
(c) If an employee works out of classification on the holiday, the senior employee in the appropriate classification will also be paid a minimum of 8 hours at time and one-half his or her contract rate of pay.

With these provisions in mind, consider the following chain of events. A crane operator is needed to work the July 4th holiday. The senior employee in this classification starts work on his shift; however, after he has worked 1/2 hour, the crane breaks down and can no longer be operated. Management believes the maintenance department will be able to repair the crane within three hours. All job classifications typically perform some minor housekeeping and cleanup work, such as dusting and picking up debris around the work station; however, there is also a janitor's classification in the labor agreement.

The first-line supervisor has three options. He can send the employee home, although Section 1(b) of the labor agreement compels management to pay that employee 8 hours at one and one-half times the employee's hourly pay rate and the same amount to another employee who is called to work once the crane is repaired. Consequently, the first option is not attractive to management.

The second option would have the employee remain at work and do nothing until the crane is repaired. Since management is already obligated to pay the employee for the entire shift, it does not cost any additional money to have the employee sit in the work shed until crane operations can be renewed. The first-line supervisor is not likely to take this option, particularly if higher-level management officials and other hourly employees see this individual being paid while not performing work.

The third option, having the crane operator perform minor housekeeping chores until the crane is repaired, appears most beneficial to management. Yet there is a good possibility that this action will result in a grievance from the senior employee in the janitorial classification, asking payment for 8 hours at time and one half since Section 1(c) would apparently have been violated. The aggrieved employee could file this grievance for one or more of the following reasons.

1. To Protest a Contractual Violation When labor and management officials negotiate a labor agreement, they are mainly concerned with agreement over the major issues. The negotiators are not concerned with determining the precise meaning of every word in the labor agreement, particularly if few or no previous problems have arisen from the contract language. Similarly, these officials cannot possibly anticipate all of the unique situations that could potentially destroy or add to the negotiated terms of the labor agreement. Consequently, union and management negotiators often gloss over the "unimportant" provisions, leaving potential interpretational problems to those who must live with and administer the labor agreement on a daily basis.

In the crane operator example, local union officials could contend that the crane operator did "work out of classification"—a clear violation of Section 1(c). Management, on the other hand, could contend that the needed holiday work was within the scope of a crane operator's job and point out the impracticality of paying an employee an amount equal to 12 hours pay simply to dust or straighten up the workplace. Another management contention could be that minor housekeeping chores are performed by all employees; therefore, the crane operator did not work out of classification on the day in question. Hence, Article III, "Management Rights," would prevail in this situation.

2. To Draw Attention to a Problem in the Plant Some grievances do not protest violation of the labor agreement; instead, they stress that management has obligations beyond the scope of the labor agreement. Most grievances over alleged safety hazards fall into this category because few labor agreements specify management's obligation in this area. The employee might realize that there is no contractual violation but still file the grievance to communicate concern to management over a safety issue. In our example, the grievance over holiday scheduling might have been filed, not over receiving payment for the senior janitor in the classification, but in order to give union officers the forum in which to stress the inadequate number of maintenance employees for equipment repair.

Unions quite often draw attention to a problem in the hopes of setting the stage for future labor agreement negotiations. A common union tactic is to file several grievances over a particular issue to buttress and document union demands during negotiation of the subsequent labor agreement.

For example, labor unions adhering to a job-protection philosophy do not want supervisory personnel performing their members' work since these activities could reduce overtime opportunities or even result in employees being laid off. In the course of the workday, supervisors may perform several chores that could be classified as bargaining-unit work. A union wishing to obtain a contractual restriction against supervisors performing bargaining-unit work might encourage employees to file a grievance whenever the supervisor engages in this practice no matter how minor that physical activity may be (for example, changing a light bulb). Armed with several grievances, in formal contract negotiations the union can dramatize its concern that (1) supervisors performing bargaining-unit work is a widespread problem and (2) a contractual provision restricting supervisors from performing bargaining-unit work would save the company time and money by eliminating related grievances.

3. To Make the Grievant and Union Feel Important In nonunion settings, the authority of managerial policies and actions often goes unchallenged. However, the grievance procedure permits and encourages an employee to protest an alleged wrong committed by management officials. Some employees raise their perceived organizational status by calling their organizational superiors on the carpet to explain their actions. Such grievances are often filed against a supervisor who flaunts authority unnecessarily, to protest the supervisor's personality as well as actions.

Similarly, some union officials wish to emphasize their importance through grievance involvement. Those falling into this category use grievances and contract administration problems to advance to high political office in the union. One research study found a positive relationship between encouragement of grievances and union rivalry as measured by closeness of vote in the most recent union election. "As incumbent union leaders contend with challengers for member support, they may seek to use the grievance process to extend support for themselves."[3] Grievances in these cases provide a forum where the union steward can demonstrate his or her verbal and intellectual capabilities to other management and union officials. Other union officials might wish to strengthen the union as an institution through the grievance procedure. Here, the importance of the union (not of the union official) is stressed—the union is safeguarding its members from management's arbitrary and capricious actions.

4. To Get Something for Nothing Some managers believe that a few employees file grievances to receive pay related to their skill in formulating and writing grievances instead of their work efforts. The janitor in our crane operator example might not have been inclined to file a grievance at the time the work was denied. Indeed, he may have had previously scheduled holiday plans and refused to work if management had made the initial offer. However, assuming the janitor's classification paid $6 an hour, the janitor might have felt that time and one-half for eight hours ($72) was worth the effort to file a grievance. The payment could be particularly attractive to an individual who did not have to alter holiday plans to obtain it.

Employees filing grievances for this reason find opportunities in the area of overtime administration. A common labor agreement provision requires management to equalize overtime opportunity among qualified bargaining-unit employees desiring overtime. Additionally, management is often contractually required to pay the employee for the overtime worked by another employee if an administrative error was made. For example, assume the following list represents the names of employees in the electrician's classification who signed the daily overtime list, thereby volunteering to work overtime if the assignment occurs after the completion of their normal work shift.

Name of Employee	Number of Overtime Hours Worked and/or Refused Since January 1
A. Jones	89 hours
T. Grant	76 hours
B. Simms	43 hours

The figure to the right of the employee's name represents the number of overtime hours worked by the employee to date and also includes any overtime assignments refused by the employee—if Jones refused to work an eight-hour overtime assignment eventually worked by Grant, both employees are charged the eight hours. If an overtime assignment for electricians is needed on the day in question, the supervisor checks the overtime list and determines that Simms is lowest in overtime hours. Consequently, the supervisor would give Simms the first opportunity to accept or refuse the overtime assignment.

Suppose, however, that Simms desires to receive the overtime payment without having to work the overtime assignment. Simms could accomplish this by actively avoiding or hiding from the supervisor at the end of his or her shift when overtime assignments are determined. Confronted with an overtime emergency, the supervisor has to offer the assignment to Grant, the employee next lowest in overtime. The next day, Simms could file a grievance on the "administrative error" and be paid the equivalent of Grant's overtime assignment for no corresponding work effort. Needless to say, this reason for filing a grievance draws management's ire, particularly since some employees appear to make a contest out of acquiring grievance "freebies," or payment for time not worked.

There are other reasons employees file grievances. Motives are as varied and complex as the employees' personalities and life experiences. For example, an argument with the employee's family, friends, or work associates might provoke a grievance. Other motives, such as poor employee/job match or a generally poor managerial climate, are perhaps more easily rectified by managerial action. Uncovering the motive behind a grievance may be helpful to management. However, it must be stressed that management must process the grievance even if it feels the employee's motives are illegitimate or improper.

Significance of Employee Grievances

Unresolved employee grievances or concerns can significantly affect both nonunion and union firms. In some cases, unsettled employee grievances or concerns have prompted successful union-organizing drives. Managers in nonunion firms might adopt some sort of grievance procedure to minimize discrimination suits, enhance employee input into organizational decision making, and minimize or eliminate the employee's desire to join a union. However, most nonunion grievance procedures do not enable the employee to have representation or to have his or her grievance decided by a third-party neutral, elements which are found in most grievance procedures in unionized firms.[4]

In unionized firms, employees often have unique concerns that are neither addressed in collective bargaining nor explicitly covered in the labor agreement. Union officials therefore demonstrate their intent to represent members' particular job interests against perceived arbitrary managerial actions through the use of the grievance procedures. A union not demonstrating its interest in union members through an effective grievance procedure runs the risk of lawsuits (discussed later in this chapter under "fair representation") or membership dissatisfaction with union leaders, which, in turn, can result in members voting leaders out of office or decertifying the union.

Employee grievances and the grievance procedure can offer an organization two advantages, namely, *conflict institutionalization* and *open upward communication.* Employees who attempt to resolve grievances at an organization having no grievance procedure might participate in various job actions such as sabotage, wildcat strikes, and job slowdowns to solve the problem; or they might quit their jobs. Indeed, one study of New York state public school teachers under the age of 55 found that individuals with strong grievance procedures[5] in their labor agreements were less likely to quit than those working under weaker grievance procedures. All of these outcomes are costly to management, particularly when recruiting and training costs of employee replacements are considered.[6]

A grievance procedure, however, institutionalizes conflict. It recognizes that disagreements between employees, management, and the union are inevitable and provides an orderly, consistent approach for resolving differences. Grievances and related procedures represent a major upward communication forum for **employee voice** whereby an individual has an opportunity to offer input into management's decision making and to discuss, even appeal, adverse employment actions.

Some think that grievances might assume even more significance because other employee-voice mechanisms are eroding as management, facing increased foreign and domestic competition, has become preoccupied with plant closings and large layoffs. Furthermore, many employees, while theoretically able to do so, are unwilling to pursue adverse job actions in a variety of court venues because of excessive costs and time delays.[7]

Grievances have also assumed research significance. Many studies have examined how grievances relate to organizational characteristics and to outcomes.[8]

Steps in the Grievance Procedure

The process for resolving employee grievances is specified in approximately 99 percent of existing labor agreements. However, the procedures are as varied as the labor agreements themselves. Some consist of only one step, whereas others contain as many as nine. While no one grievance procedure is applicable to all labor-management relationships (21 percent of surveyed grievance procedures have two steps, for example), the four-step procedure illustrated in Exhibit 8.2 and discussed here is fairly representative (48 percent of these procedures, according to one survey).

First Step of Grievance Procedure

The first step of the typical grievance procedure consists of two phases. First, the employee (with or without the union steward) discusses the alleged grievance with his or her first-line supervisor. Actually, the employee can file a grievance without any union endorsement. If agreement is not reached, then a written grievance is filed by the grievant or the union steward acting on the grievant's behalf. The supervisor then answers the employee's grievance in writing. Time limits for filing a grievance and managerial response exist in 66 percent and 53 percent, respectively, of the grievance procedures. If management or the union does not follow the time limits, the grievance might be challenged by either party as not meeting the procedural requirements in the labor agreement.

The purpose of the discussion is to resolve the grievance as early and as informally as possible. The union does not want to delay any remedy (particularly back pay) owed its members, and management does not wish to incur any unnecessary continuing liability if back pay is owed an employee who is suspended or discharged and remains unemployed until the grievance is eventually resolved.

However, in some cases, the oral discussion is *pro forma*—the employee initiates this step with a written grievance on the assumption that no amount of discussion will change his or her mind. As is true with the next two steps of the grievance procedure, if the employee accepts management's answer to the written grievance, then the grievance is considered resolved and subsequent steps are unnecessary.

Second Step of Grievance Procedure

In addition to the individuals in the first-step grievance meeting, the union grievance committeeperson and management's labor relations representative are brought in to discuss the supervisor's first-step grievance answer. Both of these individuals are aware of administrative precedent throughout the entire facility; their main role is to determine whether the grievance should be resolved at this stage on the basis of this precedent.

For example, Employee A files a grievance protesting management's unilateral action in reducing wash-up time in her work area. The grievance committeeperson might be aware, however, that (1) the contract does not have a provision pertaining to wash-up time, and (2) employees in other departments do not receive any time before the end of the shift to clean their hands. Therefore, he or she would probably encourage the grievant to accept the reduction in wash-up time rather than risk losing the privilege entirely in subsequent steps of the grievance procedure.

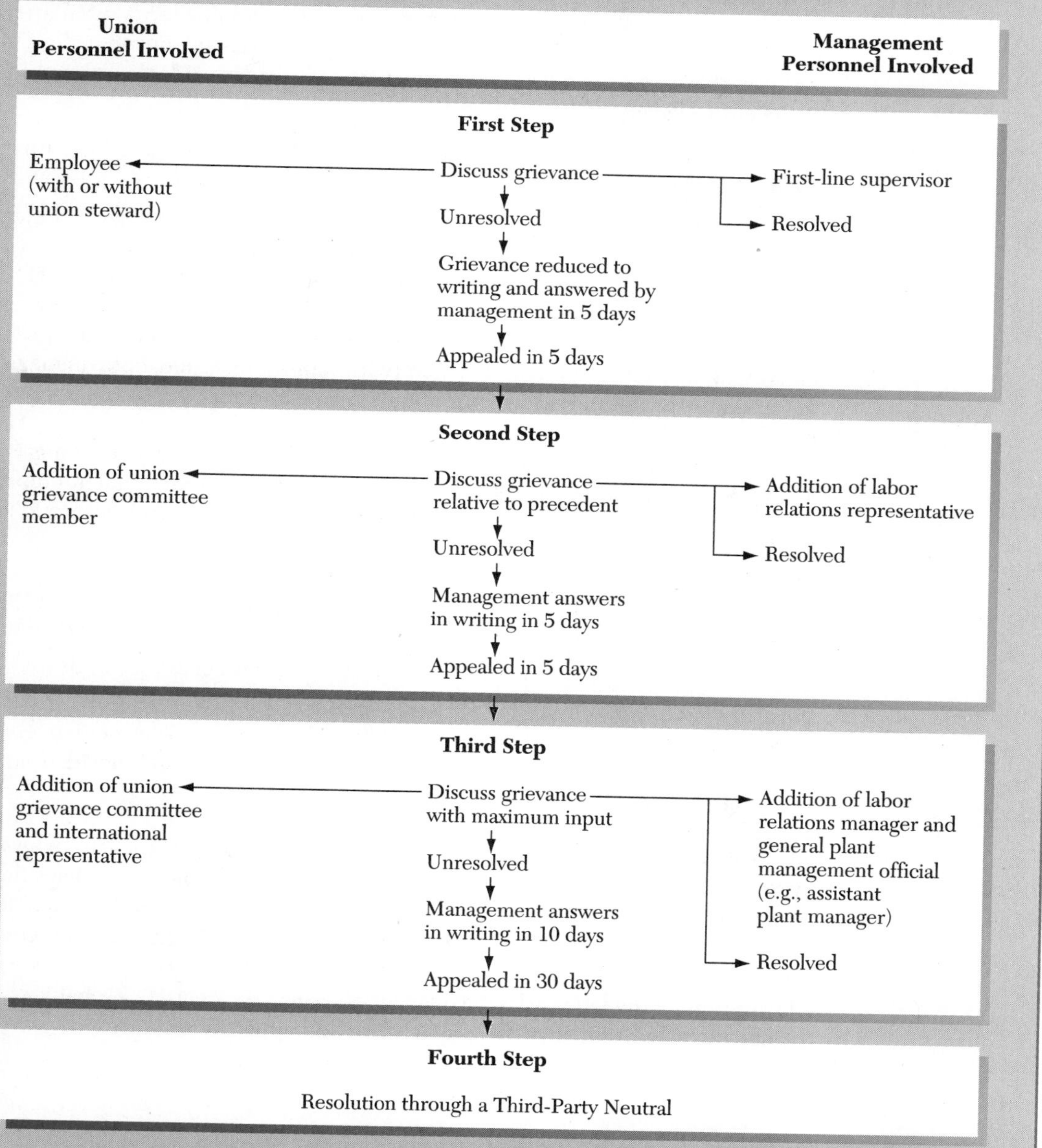
Exhibit 8.2 Example of a Typical Grievance Procedure
Union Personnel Involved
Management Personnel Involved
First Step
Employee (with or without union steward)
Discuss grievance
First-line supervisor
Unresolved
Resolved
Grievance reduced to writing and answered by management in 5 days
Appealed in 5 days
Second Step
Addition of union grievance committee member
Discuss grievance relative to precedent
Addition of labor relations representative
Unresolved
Resolved
Management answers in writing in 5 days
Appealed in 5 days
Third Step
Addition of union grievance committee and international representative
Discuss grievance with maximum input
Addition of labor relations manager and general plant management official (e.g., assistant plant manager)
Unresolved
Management answers in writing in 10 days
Resolved
Appealed in 30 days
Fourth Step
Resolution through a Third-Party Neutral

On another issue—for example, an employee working out of his or her normal work classification and demanding an upgrade in pay for the time worked—the labor-relations representative might reverse the supervisor's first-step answer to avoid sending the grievance to the third step, where it might affect employees with similar work experiences in other departments. The second-step written grievance answer is furnished by the labor-relations representative, and any precedent resulting from this answer usually applies only to the particular work department instead of the entire facility.

Third Step of Grievance Procedure

The third-step meeting involves the same individuals as the second step but also includes the labor-relations manager and another management official (such as a general foreman, superintendent, or assistant plant manager), members of the union's grievance committee (see Chapter 4), and the union's international representative. These individuals are added because the grievance answer at this level could affect plantwide operations, and both management and union representatives wish to obtain as much input as possible before making the decision.

One study found that during the third step the union discusses the grievance and its related rationale and management mostly listens and does not attempt to resolve the grievance in this meeting.[9] This step offers union officials several advantages:

- It provides new union stewards who sit in on the meeting with free training—many labor agreements require paid time off for grievance meetings.
- It impresses the grievant that many union officials back his or her interests.
- It may serve as a buck-passing device for the union representative who claims that the union grievance committee, not he or she, decided not to pursue the grievance.

This step can also serve a therapeutic function for the grievant, who simply wishes to express concern to many levels of management officials. Perhaps the most important function of the third-step meeting is the inclusion of additional union and management officials who are not personally involved in the grievance outcome and can assess its merits with relative objectivity. The third-step grievance answer is usually written by the labor-relations manager because the decision probably will have plantwide, even companywide, implications and applications.

Fourth Step of Grievance Procedure

In the fourth step, a third-party neutral may furnish either a final, binding **arbitration** decision or help the parties to resolve the issue themselves through **mediation.** (Both possibilities are discussed in more detail in Chapter 9).

LABOR RELATIONS IN ACTION

Tough Contract Administration Questions

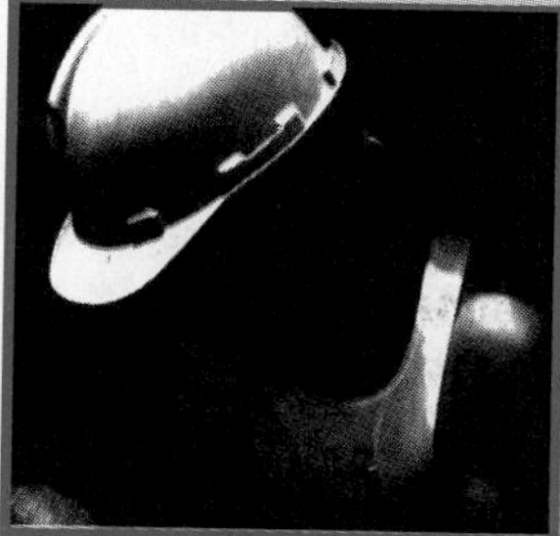

The grievance procedure involves more than a number of steps and related participants and time limits for filing, answering, and appealing grievances. Union and management officials, and sometimes arbitrators, often have to resolve complex administrative issues during the process; these are reflected in the following questions:

1. Can management interrupt and order back to work employees who are also union officials investigating a grievance?
2. Does an employer have the right to charge the union a fee for processing requested information pertaining to a grievance?
3. Can employees be discharged for secretly taping a grievance meeting?
4. Do outside union representatives have the right to visit the facility to investigate a grievance?
5. Is a grievance "legitimate" if it is filed or appealed by someone not affected by the grievance? by a group of employees? by a union official over the original grievant's objections? by someone who states the grievance orally but not in writing?
6. Do clear time limits between grievance steps mean that a grievance cannot be processed if the union exceeds these limits? Must the employer agree to the grievance if it exceeds these limits?
7. Does the initial time limit in which a grievance may be filed start from the day of the incident or the date of the grievant's knowledge/discovery?
8. Does management have to pay union officials for all of the time spent investigating and processing grievances during company work hours?
9. Can the effective date of management's grievance adjustment (paying for an overtime administrative error, for example) precede the date the grievance was filed?
10. Can an employer file a grievance against the union even if the labor agreement does not specifically refer to this action?

The answer to all of these questions is "it depends." A specific "yes" or "no" answer at a particular facility depends on the formal (labor agreement language and/or memorandums or understanding) and informal (past practices) arrangements between union and management officials.

All grievance procedures, even though they may vary in terms of steps, time limits for the processing of each step, and participants, represent a progression of the initial grievance to higher-level management and union officials for consideration. These procedures can raise several administrative complexities (see "Labor Relations in Action") and often appear inflexible. However, they also serve as the arena for the dynamic social relationships and interactions among management and union officials.

Grievance Resolution: Relationships and Flexibility

A wide variety of activities, tactics, and relationships occur between the most frequently involved union and management participants: the union steward and the first-line supervisor.[10]

Codified Relationships

Codified relationships stress the rights and privileges of union stewards and first-line supervisors established through the labor agreement and various union and management publications. These publications urge the steward and first-line supervisor to treat each other as "organizational equals" in grievance resolution, and to realize that both benefit from resolving grievances at their level instead of involving higher-level and possibly disinterested officials.

Foremen and union stewards may be aware of normative philosophies and codes, but often do not take them into account when interacting. For example, the *AFL-CIO Manual for Shop Stewards* strongly urges union stewards to present their grievances directly to the first-line supervisor in the first step of the grievance procedure.

> It is important to observe the steps in the grievance procedure even if the foreman has limited authority. Leapfrogging to a higher step may have undesirable effects. The lower level of management will resent this and will be more difficult to deal with the next time, or the company may seek to get the grievance thrown out because the proper steps were not followed.[11]

Yet many first-line supervisors maintain that they are often completely bypassed by the union steward in the grievance process. Indeed, the steward can also bypass the employee involved by filing a grievance in the name of the union. This "bypass capability" given to the union steward is not given to management or to the employee.[12]

Many first-line supervisors do not implement another codified relationship aspect: treating the union stewards as "organizational equals" in the grievance process. It is often difficult for a first-line supervisor, accustomed to giving daily work orders to the union steward, to turn around in a grievance meeting and consider the union steward as a peer. Some first-line supervisors can accept this situation; others have problems:

> This guy, Walker (union steward) here, doesn't realize that the gang is kidding him. They haven't got anything to kick about. All the stuff he is bringing up is old stuff. We've gone over it before with the other representatives. The other representative was sick of the job and gave it up. So the gang decided to elect this squirt because nobody else wanted the job. This fellow doesn't know anything about the department. He's only been there three months. He's only a kid and doesn't know what it's all about. I haven't got time to rehash this all over again. . . . He's not qualified to talk about anything that happens in my department, and I haven't got time to waste with him. He brings up all this stuff and nonsense just so he can be a big shot.[13]

Codified relationships also suggest that first-line supervisors should have authority for resolving grievances at the first step of the procedure in order to give the employee a prompt response. Resolution of grievance at the first step can also help prevent the plantwide precedents that are established in the third step. However, other management officials, who prefer to be kept informed on employee grievances, often instruct the supervisors to inform the labor-relations representative of the situation before taking any action. Indeed, one study found that 27 percent of 800 first-line supervisors believed that higher-level managers sharply limited their authority to settle grievances informally or at the first step.[14]

Power Relationships

Conflicting **power relationships** develop in situations where the foremen and union stewards pursue differing interests or goals. This situation has recently characterized shop-floor relationships in the steel industry:

> The local unions became highly politicized; any leader who made peaceful overtures to the company was promptly denounced as a "sell-out artist." Union officials and supervisors conducted daily warfare over such matters as discipline, job assignment, and the handling of worker grievances. It was as though each side had to prove itself, day after day, that it had the capacity to hurt the other.[15]

Power relationships typically begin when both steward and supervisor are encouraged by their superiors to be attentive to problems in the department. The supervisor is encouraged to discover problems before they become grievances, whereas the steward is encouraged to talk to the potential grievant before that employee talks to the foreman. Competition for the employee's attention might become particularly intense, as one research study found that stewards and supervisors are equally successful in communicating with employees.[16]

Another type of power relationship results from the union steward's knowing the labor agreement better than the foreman does. Union stewards can concentrate on particular provisions of the labor agreement and their application to the shop. The foreman, on the other hand, has major responsibilities for production scheduling, meeting departmental quality and quantity standards, participating in cost-reduction programs, and so on, which reduce the amount of time available for grievance and labor agreement analyses.

Intimidation is another power relationship strategy that can be employed by both the union steward and the supervisor. In some situations the union steward anticipates that the supervisor is vulnerable when he or she receives an excessive number of grievances—the supervisor will be concerned with how management officials will react to this apparent inability to resolve labor relations problems. Even though the grievances might not be valid, some management officials might hold the following opinion:

> A supervisor who is the subject of grievances creates red flags for us. We expect supervisors to be able to handle most employee relations issues, and if they can't then we

> question whether or not they have a future with us. I know that grievances are sometimes filed with no justification whatsoever, but on the whole a supervisor who avoids formal grievances looks a lot better to management than a supervisor who's tying up his and our time in grievance hearings.[17]

Consequently, a union steward can use the threat of additional grievances (bogus or real) to persuade the foreman to concede to the grievance in question or to alter the foreman's overall approach to labor relations. The practice is explained by a union official:

> A short time ago we had a lot of trouble with a certain foreman. . . . He was making them toe the line . . . no quitting early, work from whistle to whistle, no sitting down, no horseplay, this and that. I told the committeeman there, "You do the same thing. Every time he does any work, even if he picks up a box, write a grievance. . . ." The first thing you know grievances started mounting—finally had a pile like that.
>
> Things got so bad . . . this foreman was removed from the department. He was moved to our department and it's his last chance. If he doesn't do good in this department, out he goes. So I went to the guy and told him, "It's your last chance here and you know it. You cooperate with us and we'll cooperate with you. If you don't we'll put the screws on you and out you go." Things are working out pretty good so far.[18]

Intimidation tactics are not always one-sided; a clever foreman can make industrial life very difficult for the union steward, probably without incurring an unfair labor practice charge. For example, many job classifications have a wide variety of work assignments, with some of these assignments being less desirable than others. A foreman could assign undesirable work assignments to the union steward, who would have little recourse as long as they were within his or her job classification. The foreman could also undermine the steward's formal position in the union by (1) restricting the amount of freedom and time for the steward to investigate the grievance and (2) refusing to resolve any grievance in the first step when the union steward is present with the grievant. These tactics are usually successful only if the union steward is inexperienced.

Regardless of the "success" of such actions, a grievance relationship governed by power and intimidation tactics distorts the primary purpose of contract administration: rational decision making.

Sympathetic Relationships

Sympathetic relationships occur between individuals when each is aware of the other's situation and is guided by an understanding appreciation. An example of this appreciation comes from a union steward's comment:

> You can't have industrial relations without giving and taking on both sides. You'll always win more cases by getting along with supervision than by being tough. You've got to swap and make trades. . . . Sometimes I have to talk like hell to explain some of the deals I make with them and sometimes I keep what I'm doing to myself if I see a chance to get something good later on. The thing some grievers never get through their heads is that a lot of bosses are on the spot themselves. If you go a little easy on them when they're on the pan, by God—you make friends—they'll stand by you

> sometime when you're back of the eight ball. Sometimes when I have a rotten grievance, I'll take the case up to the supe [superintendent] and let him know I won't push it hard.[19]

Sympathetic relationships are aided when the first-line supervisor and the union steward realize that they both occupy marginal positions within their own organizations. For example, one study found that first-line supervisors can have a rather loose identification with upper management. This might be due to several factors, including transient upper and middle management and reconsideration of the supervisor's original decision by other management officials.[20]

Union stewards have also experienced this situation in contract administration. On one hand, constituents expect their union steward to actively press every grievance because they think that the union should be attentive to their needs. Consequently, it is difficult for the steward to accept the foreman's first-step rejection of the grievance, even if he or she feels the foreman is correct. On the other hand, union officials receiving the grievance in subsequent steps of the grievance procedure may tend to view the union steward as either ignorant of the labor agreement or gutless.

Flexible Consideration of Employee Grievances

The preceding varieties of interpersonal relationships reveal how individual objectives, strategies, and personalities force the contractual procedure to be more flexible in practice. This real-world consideration negates the theoretical principle that each grievance be considered on its individual merits. The grievant wishes to receive an answer uncolored by any political or tactical concerns, but the union must consider political influence and overall strategy in its determination of which grievances will be filed and pursued. Not all grievances are clear-cut issues; in fact, many involve confusing or opposing interpretations of the labor agreement. In these cases, management has two options—decide the grievance in the employee's favor or appeal the grievance to arbitration. The latter alternative is not always attractive, particularly if management realizes there is little contractual guidance in the issue (as in the example of the holiday scheduling of a crane operator) and insufficient past practice or precedent to support the decision. Contract administration has many gray areas that are open to interpretation. This uncertainty is compounded when the parties solicit a neutral party to resolve the issue in binding arbitration. Also, the arbitrator's decision might refute management's action in terms that further erode management's discretion in future matters. Unions also tend to use arbitration only as a last resort because such cases can drain the union's treasury.

In these instances, flexibility may be possible with the addition of an informal **third-and-one-half step** in the grievance procedure. This may not be specified in the labor agreement but occurs after management's "final" third-step decision and before the third-party neutral hears the grievance. During the third-and-one-half step meetings, management and union representatives meet to discuss and trade grievances, dispatching several cases originally scheduled for arbitration. For example, they might trade a grievance requesting one-day pay upgrades for five employees who allegedly worked in a higher job classification for a grievance on management performing bargaining-unit work filed against a very unpopular first-line supervisor, which would give one union member a two-hour overtime payment as a remedy. Usually the grievances involved in the negotiated package are settled "without prejudice" to either party's position in future related issues. This statement preserves management's discretion on these issues and the union's right to file future related grievances.

Opponents of this practice contend that valid employee grievances are bargained away for an expedient settlement. Grievance trading in the third-and-one-half step can also discourage first-line supervisors from actively trying to resolve grievances if they believe their efforts will be overturned in a mass grievance settlement. For example, the following remarks were made by a foreman who had sent an employee home for repeated tardiness. The employee filed a grievance with the foreman's supervisor, who sent the employee back on the job.

> I went over to O'Brien's [the superintendent's office] to find out why he had overruled me. He handed me a line of salve about "having to do it." Said, "It was a small item after all" and that he "might want a big favor from the union sometime in the future." He said, "We have to trade back and forth. Sometimes we give in; sometimes they give in. That's why we never have any big trouble!" Then he said he might have to reverse some of my decisions again sometime, but if he did, not to get sore about it, because he wouldn't mean no offense by it. Well damn that noise! If O'Brien wants to make me look like a fool every time I make a decision, why by God, he can make all the decisions. You know two can play that game. I can give the boys [workers] every damn thing he can give them. Then when they come up with a big one that I know well he can't give them, I'll tell 'em to take it up to him.[21]

As a result of management using the third-and-one-half step in the grievance procedure, unions might be encouraged to file more grievances in the belief that they can obtain more from a trade involving 50 fabricated grievances than they can from five legitimate ones. Furthermore, those settlements "without prejudice" can result in more grievances of the same sort because the issues are not considered jointly resolved by management or union officials.

Advocates state that this process merely represents another legitimate cooperative effort between labor and management officials in efficiently dealing with day-to-day administrative problems. These individuals indicate that the union's and management's organizational self-interests require considerations and possible use of the third-and-one-half step grievance trading session. Opponents state that the third-and-one-half step hinders the union's fair representation obligation discussed in the next section.

The Legal "Fair Representation" Obligation in the Grievance Procedure

Thus far grievance procedures have been discussed from the perspectives of the union, management, and employee participants. As is true with most labor relations activities, grievance resolution can be strongly influenced by the fourth participant, the government. As noted in Chapter 5, the union has the right to be the exclusive bargaining agent for all employees in the appropriate bargaining unit. This right has a corresponding *fair representation* legal obligation to represent all of the bargaining-unit employees, union members and nonunion members alike, in both contract negotiation and administration. This section focuses on the extent of the union's obligation, particularly when some of the bargaining-unit employees believe the union has acted in an unsatisfactory manner.[22]

The fair representation issue is very difficult to resolve. On the one hand, some individual freedom must be sacrificed if the union wishes to effectively represent its members. However, the individual member's right to dissent must also be protected, and all employees represented must be safe from negligent or corrupt representatives. The NLRA adds to this issue's complexity, since it does not contain any explicit provisions obligating the union to represent fairly all bargaining-unit employees. Therefore, jurisdictional disputes over the fair representation issue have occurred among the governmental participants, more specifically the NLRB and the courts.

The NLRB had for many years claimed that it alone had jurisdiction to determine fair representation issues because related unfair labor practices came under its statutory jurisdiction. However, the Supreme Court countered the NLRB in a 1987 decision (*Breininger* v. *Sheet Metal Workers Local 6*) and indicated that district courts do have jurisdiction over such claims because the fair representation obligation is a fundamental part of federal labor relations policy and precedes the NLRB's statutory role in such cases.[23] A subsequent Supreme Court decision indicated that employees claiming breach of fair representation are also entitled to a jury trial.[24]

Related court decisions have addressed the following question: How far must the union go in representing employees whose interests or claims could potentially disrupt union goals and policies? The importance of this question is magnified when we consider that many decisions help some members while hurting others. However, if unions were required to process contradictory claims, nothing would be accomplished.

One such double-edged issue is seniority. Union actions pertaining to this issue (such as merging seniority rosters and calculating seniority credits for employees returning from the armed services) will hurt some bargaining-unit members while helping others. Not surprisingly, two Supreme Court cases involving fair representation concerned the seniority issue.[25] These decisions indicated that the union satisfies its fair representation obligation in collective bargaining and grievance processing if it *considers the interests of all members* and *takes its ultimate position honestly, in good faith,* and *without hostility or arbitrary discrimination.*[26]

These rather broad guidelines were also applied in another landmark Supreme Court decision, *Vaca* v. *Sipes,* which considered the union's fair representation obligation in the grievance procedure. A bargaining-unit employee claimed that the union "arbitrarily, capriciously, and without just or reasonable reason or cause" refused to take his grievance to arbitration. The employee, a long-term high blood-pressure patient, returned to work after a sick leave and was judged by the company's doctor as being unfit for reemployment. The employee's personal physician as well as a second doctor indicated that the employee was fit for work; therefore, the employee asked the union to seek his reinstatement through the grievance procedure. The grievance was processed; however, the union, in attempting to strengthen its case before going to arbitration, sent the employee to a third doctor. The third doctor did not support the employee's position; therefore, the union refused to take the employee's case to arbitration.

The Supreme Court decided that the union, in this case, acted in good faith and was neither arbitrary nor discriminatory. It also indicated (in this and in another case) the following:[27]

- The employee has the burden of proof in establishing that the union breached its fair representation obligation.
- Fair representation does not require the union to take every grievance to arbitration because this would create an intolerable expense for the union and management and would destroy the effectiveness of the lower steps in the grievance procedure.
- Courts should only examine the union's fair representation obligation, not the merits of the case.

A more recent Supreme Court decision indicated that any judicial examination of a union's performance must be "highly deferential," giving "wide latitude" to union officials in the performance of their duties. A breach of fair representation has to be so far outside a "wide range of reasonableness" that it is wholly "irrational" or "arbitrary." Moreover, a union's decision is not irrational simply because it turns out in retrospect to have been a bad settlement.[28]

Currently, fair representation poses two difficult questions to the union and the employer. First, what specific types of conduct constitute violation of the fair representation duty? As previously noted, the Supreme Court has given only broad guidelines ("arbitrary," "bad faith," "dishonest," and so on). Sometimes these guidelines can be rather easily applied; for example, a union refusing to process grievances of any black, female, or nonunion employees is clearly guilty of violation.[29] Other cases can become more complicated. The union, while not needing to take every grievance to arbitration, has an obligation to consider the merits of the grievance and effectively use the grievance procedure. In some cases the courts have determined that union *"perfunctory conduct"* (simply going through the motions) makes the union liable for breach of fair representation. Related actions include:

- Providing inadequate defense of the grievant at an arbitration hearing.
- Delaying grievance processing until the time limits in the grievance procedure have expired.
- Failing to inform the grievant that the union accepted a different remedy than that asked for by the grievant.

- Failing to keep members informed about an arbitration award that affects members' seniority rights.[30]

Yet some courts have suggested that negligence or "honest mistakes" alone will not constitute a fair representation violation because union members always have the option of voting in new officers or even a new union to better represent them.

A second question concerns employer and union liability if the union fails to fairly represent a bargaining-unit employee. Employees currently can sue the union and the employer for breach of the labor agreement including fair representation under Section 301 of the NLRA.

Assume, for example, that an employee is discharged, then later establishes that the union breached its duty of fair representation. Both organizations can be liable according to the Supreme Court in its *Bowen* v. *United States Postal Service* decision. Bowen, an employee for the Postal Service, was discharged for an altercation with another employee. Bowen sued both the union and the employer in the district court. His evidence at trial indicated that the responsible union officer, at each step of the grievance procedure, had recommended pursuing the grievance but that the national office, for no apparent reason, had refused to take the matter to arbitration. The jury found that the company had discharged Bowen wrongfully and that the union had breached its fair representation obligation.

The Supreme Court eventually found that both the employer and the union contributed to this wrongful discharge. The employer, of course, made the initially wrong termination decision and therefore owed Bowen reinstatement with some of his back wages. However, the court also agreed that the union also owed Bowen a portion of his lost wages because he could not have proceeded independently of the union—if the union had arbitrated his grievance, he would have been reinstated. Thus, the employer was responsible for the back wages from the termination to the approximate date of his reinstatement if the case had been submitted to an arbitrator; the union was responsible for losses beyond that date. It also contended that joint employer-union liability might be in the interest of national labor relations policy.

> In the absence of damages apportionment where the fault of both parties contributes to the employee's injury, incentives to comply with the grievance procedure will be diminished. Indeed, imposing total liability solely on the employer could well affect the willingness of employers to agree to arbitration clauses as they are customarily written.[31]

Bowen has controversial implications for the labor-management relationship. Managers believe that they should not be held accountable for the union's errors, particularly since management is legally prohibited from dealing in the internal affairs of the union. However, it can easily be argued that the union would not have violated the law in the first place if the company had not wrongly discharged the employee. There is also the possibility that this decision would encourage the union to take many marginal grievances to arbitration to avoid any possible breach of fair representation and related financial liability. Research has yet to verify that this situation could be detrimental to the labor-management relationship.

Summary

Employee grievances and grievance administration extend collective bargaining by giving dynamic meaning to the negotiated terms of the labor agreement. A grievance is broadly defined as any employee's concern over a perceived violation of the labor agreement that is submitted to the grievance procedure for resolution.

An employee might file a grievance for any of various reasons, such as to protest a contract violation, to draw attention to a problem in the plant, to get something for nothing, or to feel more important. Regardless of motives for filing grievances, management must process them through the grievance procedure specified in the labor agreement.

Although no one grievance procedure applies to all labor-management relationships, two important aspects of a typical grievance procedure are inclusion of higher-level management and union personnel and, particularly in the private sector, binding arbitration by a third-party neutral. Grievance procedures typically offer an organization two major advantages: conflict institutionalization and open upward communication. However, the grievance procedure as actually carried out involves a variety of behavioral dimensions, including social relationships (codified, power, and sympathetic) enacted among the grievance participants in resolving the grievance according to appropriate contractual provisions. The variety of personalities and motives of the participants suggests a flexible approach in grievance resolution instead of considering each grievance on its individual merits.

Unions have a legal obligation to fairly represent their members in the grievance procedure. While unions do not have to take each grievance to arbitration, they must consider and process grievances in an effective, good-faith manner. Legal complications can arise when the courts determine whether the union has violated its fair representation obligation and whether the employer should be financially liable for this activity.

Key Terms

grievance
arbitration
mediation
codified relationships
fair representation obligation
power relationships
sympathetic relationships
third-and-one-half step

Discussion Questions

1. A thin line differentiates employee grievances and employee complaints. Discuss the problems involved in defining a grievance, indicating why a broad definition of employee grievances is both confusing and necessary.
2. Discuss two reasons grievances might be filed, furnishing examples of these reasons other than those found in the text.
3. Why does a typical grievance procedure have so many steps when the employee is either right or wrong and a one- or two-step procedure would save time and money? In your answer, discuss the various functions, opportunities, and problems each of the grievance steps can offer.

4. Why is it difficult for union and management officials to resolve each grievance on its own merits?
5. Briefly discuss the broad judicial guidelines concerning unions' fair representation obligations to members. Also discuss the reasoning behind these obligations, furnishing some appropriate examples.

References

1. Brian S. Klass and Angelo S. DeNisi, "Management Reactions to Employee Dissent: The Impact of Grievance Activity on Performance Ratings," *Academy of Management Journal* 32, no. 4 (1989), pp. 705–717.

2. Robert E. Allen and Timothy J. Keaveny, "Factors Differentiating Grievants and Nongrievants," *Human Relations* 38 (November 1985), p. 529.

3. Chalmer E. Labig, Jr., and I. B. Helburn, "Union and Management Policy Influences in Grievance Initiation," *Journal of Labor Research* (Summer 1986), pp. 269–284.

4. Douglas M. McCabe, "Corporate Nonunion Grievance Procedures: Open Door Policies—A Procedural Analysis," *Labor Law Journal* 41 (August 1990), pp. 551–557. See also Mark J. Keppler, "Nonunion Grievance Procedures: Union Avoidance Technique or Union Organizing Opportunity?" *Labor Law Journal* 41 (August 1990), pp. 557–563; George W. Bohlander and Ken Behringer, "Public Sector Nonunion Complaint Procedures: Current Research," *Labor Law Journal* 41 (August 1990), pp. 563–568; Richard B. Peterson and David Lewin, "The Nonunion Grievance Procedure: A Viable System of Due Process," *Employee Responsibilities and Rights Journal* 3, no. 1 (1990), pp. 1–18; and Richard B. Peterson and Douglas M. McCabe, "The Nonunion Grievance System in High Performing Firms," *Labor Law Journal* 45 (August 1994), pp. 529–534.

5. "Strong grievance procedures" define a grievance as a dispute over any condition of employment that affects employee welfare and ends in arbitration no matter what the subject of the grievance. Daniel I. Reese, "Grievance Procedure Strength and Teacher Quits," *Industrial and Labor Relations Review* 45 (October 1991), p. 35.

6. Richard B. Freeman and James L. Medoff, *What Do Unions Do?* (New York: Basic Books, 1984), p. 10.

7. Richard B. Peterson, "Organizational Governance and the Grievance Process: In Need of a New Model for Resolving Workplace Issues," *Employee Responsibilities and Rights Journal* 7 (March 1994), p. 13.

8. For a fine research framework for grievances, see Michael E. Gordon and Sandra J. Miller, "Grievances: A Review of Research and Practice," *Personnel Psychology* 37 (Spring 1984), pp. 117–146. See also David Lewin, "Empirical Measures of Grievance Procedure Effectiveness," *Labor Law Journal* 35 (September 1984), pp. 491–496; Thomas R. Knight, "Feedback and Grievance Resolution," *The Industrial and Labor Relations Review* 39 (July 1986), pp. 487–501; Casey Ichiowski, "The Effects of Grievance Activity on Productivity," *Industrial and Labor Relations Review* 39 (October 1986), pp. 75–89; Thomas R. Knight, "Correlates of Informal Grievance Resolution Among First-Line Supervisors," *Relations Industriel* 41, no. 2 (1986), pp. 281–291; Brian Bemmels, Yonatan Reshef, and Kay Stratton-Devine, "The Roles of Supervisors, Employees and Stewards in Grievance Initiation," *Industrial and Labor Relations Review* 45 (October 1991), pp. 15–30; Jeanette A. Davy, Greg Steward, and Joe Anderson, "Formalization of Grievance Procedures: A Multi-Firm and Industry Study," *Journal of Labor Research* 13 (Summer 1992), pp. 307–316; Richard P. Chaykowski, George A. Slotsve, J. S. Butler, "Simultaneous Analysis of Grievance Activity and Outcome Decisions," *Industrial and Labor Relations Review* 45 (July 1992), pp. 724–737; Peter Capelli and Keith Chauvin, "A Test of an Efficiency Model of Grievance Activity," *Industrial and Labor Relations Review* 45 (October 1991), pp. 3–14; and Morris M. Kleiner, Gerald Nickelsburg, and Adam Pilarski, "Monitoring, Grievances, and Plant Performance," *Industrial Relations* 34 (April 1995), pp. 169–190.

9. Judith L. Catlett and Edwin L. Brown, "Union Leaders' Perceptions of the Grievance Process," *Labor Studies Journal* 15 (Spring 1990), p. 61.

10. See, for example, Ralph Arthur Johnson, "Grievance Negotiation: An Analysis of Factors Popularly Associated with Success," *Labor Studies Journal* 9 (Winter 1985), pp. 271–279.

11. *AFL-CIO Manual for Shop Stewards* (n.p., n.d.), p. 37.

12. William D. Todor and Dan R. Dalton, "Union Steward: A Little Known Actor with a Very Big Part," *Industrial Management* 25 (September-October 1983), pp. 7–11.

13. Paul Pigors, "The Old Line Foreman," in Austin Grimshaw and John Hennessey, Jr., eds., *Organizational Behavior* (New York: McGraw-Hill, 1960), p. 98.

14. Michael E. Gordon and Roger L. Bowlby, "Propositions about Grievance Settlements: Finally, Consultation with Grievants," *Personnel Psychology* 41 (Spring 1988), p. 120. Another study also found that a high proportion of local union leaders believe that first-line supervisors have no authority to resolve grievances. See Catlett and Brown, p. 59.

15. John P. Hoerr, *And the Wolf Finally Came* (Pittsburgh: The University of Pittsburgh Press, 1988), p. 22.

16. P. Christopher Earley, "Supervisors and Stewards and Sources of Contextual Information in Goal Setting: A Comparison of the United States with England," *Journal of Applied Psychology* 71 (February 1986), pp. 111–117. See also Mick Marchington and Roger Armstrong, "Typologies of Union Stewards," *Industrial Relations Journal* (Autumn 1983), p. 44.

17. David Lewin and Richard B. Peterson, *The Modern Grievance Procedure in the Unites States* (New York: Quorum Books, 1988), p. 195.

18. Delbert C. Miller and William Forum, *Industrial Sociology,* 2nd ed. (New York: Harper & Row, 1964), pp. 401–402.

19. Melville Dalton, "Unofficial Union-Management Relations," *American Sociological Review* 15 (October 1950), p. 613.

20. Marc G. Singer and Peter A. Veglahn, "Correlates of Supervisor-Steward Relations," *Labor Studies Journal* 10 (Spring 1985), pp. 46–55. For a study and related methodology revealing a sympathetic relationship, see Brian Bemmels, "The Determinants of Grievance Initiation," *Industrial and Labor Relations Review* 47 (January 1994), pp. 293, 300.

21. Melville Dalton, "The Role of Supervision," in Arthur Kornhauser, Robert Dubin, and Arthur Ross, eds., *Industrial Conflict* (New York: McGraw-Hill, 1958), pp. 183–184.

22. For related legal violations (unfair labor practices), see Paul A. Brinker, "Labor Union Coercion: The Misuse of the Grievance Procedure," *Journal of Labor Research* 5 (Winter 1984), pp. 93–102.

23. Arthur Hamilton and Peter A. Veglahn, "Jurisdiction in Duty of Fair Representation Cases," *Labor Law Journal* 41 (September 1990), p. 668. See also Martin H. Malin, "The Supreme Court and the Duty of Fair Representation," *Harvard Civil Rights—Civil Liberties Law Review* 27.

24. "Decision of Supreme Court in *Teamsters Local 391* v. *Terry,*" Bureau of National Affairs Inc., *Daily Labor Report,* no. 55 (March 21, 1990), pp. D-1–D-11. An appeals court decision interpreting a subsequent Supreme Court decision indicates the employee has a six-month time period to sue starting from when he should have reasonably known about the union's alleged breach of duty. "Court Affirms That Fair Representation Claim Over Abandoned Grievance Was Untimely Filed," Bureau of National Affairs Inc., *Daily Labor Report,* no. 151 (August 6, 1990), p. A-1.

25. *Ford Motor Co.* v. *Huffman et al.,* 345 U.S. 320 (1953); and *Humphrey* v. *Moore,* 375 U.S. 335 (1964).

26. For examples of judicial decisions that have upheld and rejected unions' fair representation actions along these lines, see "Court Immunizes Union Failure to Pursue Grievance," Bureau of National Affairs Inc., *Daily Labor Report,* no. 48 (March 9, 1994), p. A-1; and "Court Finds UFCW Breached Duty, but Vacates Fee Award," Bureau of National Affairs Inc., *Daily Labor Report,* no. 101 (May 27, 1993), p. A-4.

27. *Vaca Sipes,* 386 U.S. 191 (1967); and *Amalgamated Association of Street, Electric, Railway and Motor Coach Employees of America* v. *Wilson P. Lockridge,* 403 U.S. 294 (1971).

28. *"Air Line Pilots Association, International* v. *Joseph E. O'Neill et al.,"* Bureau of National Affairs Inc., *The United States Law Week,* March 19, 1991, pp. 4175–4180.

29. For an example of a relatively straightforward breach of fair representation, see *Hines* v. *Anchor Motor Freight Inc.,* 424 U.S. 554 (1976).

30. "Union Failure to Publicize Award Held Fair Representation Breach," Bureau of National Affairs Inc., *Daily Labor Report,* no. 112 (August 13, 1984), p. 1.

31. *Daily Labor Report,* June 11, 1983, p. D-5. See also T. Charles McKinney, "Fair Representation of Employees in Unionized Firms: A Newer Directive from the Supreme Court," *Labor Law Journal* (November 1984), pp. 693–700.

9 Labor Arbitration: A System of Industrial Jurisprudence

This chapter discusses grievance or rights arbitration over the existing terms of the labor agreement, which is used far more than interest arbitration over unresolved bargaining issues (discussed in Chapters 7 and 14). Arbitration is first discussed from a historical perspective, then elements of a typical arbitration proceeding and arbitrator's decision are described. Current jurisdictional issues involving the arbitrator and various government agencies are also discussed, and, finally, the process is appraised.

Development of Labor Arbitration

1865 through World War II

Arbitration first occurred in the United States in 1865, but it was used rarely before World War II, when it was used by the War Labor Board. In many cases employee grievances were resolved through sheer economic strength. For instance, a union desiring resolution of a particular grievance often needed to mobilize the entire work force in a strike against the employer—a difficult task—before the company would attempt to resolve the grievance. Union and management officials were legally free to ignore the arbitrator's decision if they did not agree with it.

Other factors limiting the early growth of arbitration were the relatively few unionized facilities and the vague language found in labor agreements, which gave little contractual guidance for the arbitrator's decision. Consequently, the early arbitration process combined elements of mediation and humanitarianism in an effort to reach a *consensus decision,* one that would be accepted by both parties to a grievance. The arbitrator under these circumstances had to draw on diplomatic and persuasive abilities to convince the parties the decision should be accepted.

Arbitration's popularity increased during World War II, when President Franklin Roosevelt's Executive Order 9017 provided for final resolution of disputes interrupting work that contributed to the war effort. Essential features of this order included a no-strike, no-lockout agreement and a **National War Labor Board** (NWLB) composed of four management representatives, four union representatives, and four representatives of the public—all presidential appointees. The board was to encourage collective bargaining and, if necessary, resolve disputes over the terms of the agreements.

The advent of World War II encouraged the role of arbitration in several ways. Many union and management officials realized that uninterrupted wartime production was essential and that grievance resolution was more effectively accomplished through arbitration than through strikes.

The NWLB urged labor and management officials to resolve their own disputes and encouraged the parties to carefully define the arbitrator's jurisdiction in the labor agreements. Thus, the board gave any negotiated restrictions full force when deciding cases and denied arbitration where it was reasonably clear that the arbitration clauses meant to exclude a subject from arbitral review. It further defined grievance arbitration as a quasi-judicial process, thereby limiting a decision solely to the evidence presented at the hearing.

Results of the NWLB's activities further popularized and enriched the arbitration process, as the board resolved some 20,000 disputes during its tenure. Additionally, these efforts served as a training ground for many arbitrators who were able to apply their newly acquired skills to the arbitration process after the war.

The Postwar Years and the Steelworkers' Trilogy

Although the use of arbitration increased during World War II, the role and authority of arbitrators were far from resolved.[1] Both parties in a labor dispute still remained legally free to ignore the arbitrator's award. In 1957, however, the Supreme Court declared in its *Lincoln Mills* decision that an aggrieved party could legally bring suit against a party that refused to arbitrate a labor dispute for violation of the labor agreement, under Section 301 of the Taft-Hartley Amendments. Thus, grievance procedures including arbitration could be subjected to judicial review, although much confusion remained over the court's role in these activities.

Either party could refuse to submit the grievance to arbitration if the labor agreement did not cover the issue in question. Some state statutes that made the agreement to arbitrate enforceable resulted in attempts to persuade the court to compel arbitration of various issues. Many courts then became involved in assessing the merits of a particular grievance and whether it should be arbitrated. These actions, of course, contradicted arbitral belief that arbitrators alone should rule on the merits of the grievance. Confusion resulted when labor and management representatives played the courts against the arbitrators in their attempts to obtain favorable decisions.

In 1960 the Supreme Court clarified and strengthened the arbitrator's role with three decisions commonly referred to as the **Steelworkers' Trilogy.** These decisions can be summarized as follows:

- Unless certain subjects are restricted from arbitration, the arbitrator, not the courts, determines whether the grievance is arbitrable. Therefore, the courts have no business weighing the merits of the grievance.[2]

- Arbitrators have far more expertise than judges in interpreting the *common law of the shop* (experiences and precedents at a particular facility), which is fundamental to resolving existing grievances in a manner consistent with the continuing labor-management relationship.[3]
- Arbitrators have no obligation to the court to give their reasons for an award. Therefore, they have great latitude in fashioning a decision and its remedy.[4]

In summary, the Steelworkers' Trilogy greatly enhanced the authority and prestige of the arbitrator in interpreting the terms of the labor agreement and deciding the merits of a particular grievance. It also endorsed the arbitrator as most qualified to fashion a resolution of a grievance if it is based on the essence of the labor agreement. However, the Supreme Court has reaffirmed that the courts should determine whether a grievance should be submitted to arbitration when one party refuses, on the basis of its contention that the labor agreement excludes this particular subject from the arbitration procedure.[5] Other related decisions are presented in the next section.

Legal Obligations to Arbitrate and Enforce Arbitration Decisions

The Supreme Court has determined that the obligation to arbitrate a grievance cannot be nullified by a successor employer[6] or by the termination of a labor agreement. Management representatives in this latter situation argued that arbitration is a feature of the contract that ceases to exist when a contract terminates; therefore, a grievance cannot be processed to arbitration if the labor agreement is no longer in effect. Consequently, management representatives felt that the issue of severance pay was not subject to arbitration since the labor agreement had expired and management had decided to permanently close its operations. However, the Supreme Court indicated that arbitration was still appropriate because the labor agreement furnishes continuing rights and the parties continued to express confidence in the arbitrator's expertise and in arbitration as a prompt, inexpensive alternative to lawsuits.[7] A recent Supreme Court decision indicated that management's obligation to honor a union's request for arbitration after the labor contract has expired occurs only if the dispute either arose before the contract expired or concerned "a right that accrued or vested under the agreement."[8]

Another issue resolved by the Supreme Court in recent years concerns how far the courts are willing to go in enforcing the role of the arbitrator. More specifically, what happens when one party is willing to arbitrate a grievance while the other party prefers to use the strike or lockout in order to resolve a dispute? As previously mentioned, a strike was a plausible alternative in resolving a grievance in the early years of arbitration. Also, the Trilogy did not specifically consider this alternative in its conclusions.

The award enforceability issue was brought before the courts in 1969 when a union protested a work assignment given to nonbargaining-unit personnel. The union expressed its concern by striking even though the labor agreement contained a provision for arbitrating disputes over the terms of the agreement. In federal district court, management officials stressed that the union should use the contractually specified arbitration procedure and be enjoined or prevented from striking the employer. The Supreme Court agreed in its *Boys Market* decision.[9]

Employer Promulgated Arbitration

Recently, employers have initiated and used **employer promulgated arbitration** in situations such as the following:

- Employment discrimination claims in union and or nonunion firms (instead of using the courts).
- Employee grievances in nonunion firms (instead of using unilateral management decision making).

See "Labor Relations in Action" for a summary of how employer promulgated arbitration differs from arbitration found in labor agreements.

The use of arbitration to resolve employment discrimination suits was enhanced by the Supreme Court in *Gilmer* v. *Interstate Johnson Lane Corp.* A securities representative signed an employment application (Form U-4, which is common in the securities industry) in part agreeing to arbitrate any dispute, claim, or controversy with his employer that was required to be arbitrated under the employer's rules. After being terminated at age 62, Gilmer filed an age discrimination complaint with the Equal Employment Opportunity Commission (EEOC) and subsequently in federal court. The Supreme Court agreed with Gilmer's employer that arbitration, not the courts, was both the agreed upon and proper dispute resolution forum that did not counter the legislative history of the Age Discrimination in Employment Act.[10] A subsequent Supreme Court decision seemed to recognize arbitration as a proper resolution of other employment discrimination claims in the securities industry and possibly other industries as well.[11]

Elements of a Typical Arbitration Proceeding

Selection and Characteristics of Arbitrators

During a dispute or grievance process, management or union representatives may request a list of possible arbitrators from the Federal Mediation and Conciliation Service (FMCS). The FMCS compiles and statistically summarizes the subsequent arbitration decisions; these are presumed to be somewhat representative of the overall arbitration experience in the United States. As expected, nearly all the requests for arbitration pertain to existing contract provisions (rights or grievance arbitration) as opposed to proposed employment conditions in collective bargaining (interest arbitration). While arbitration has occurred over a wide variety of work

How Employer Promulgated Arbitration Differs from Arbitration Found in Labor Agreements

1. What are the conditions under which the arbitration system is devised?

If the arbitration system is established to avoid a union, then many acceptable, well-qualified arbitrators will refuse to serve. If the employer designs a system for the purpose of providing a mechanism for employees to resolve their grievance by an independent neutral party, qualified arbitrators will be willing to serve. Under a collective bargaining agreement, the union and company have negotiated and designed the arbitration procedure that best fits their purposes. In other words, the parties design a system of self-governance for resolving conflicts.

2. What subjects will be covered under the employer promulgated system, and will employees be required to waive their statutory rights, such as employment discrimination on the basis of race, gender, age, national origin, disability, and so on?

If the employees are required to waive their statutory rights as a condition of employment, the arbitration decision may not stand a court review. Under a collective bargaining agreement, arbitration involves contract interpretation and application of provisions negotiated and agreed to by the parties. Various federal agencies have different policies regarding deferral to arbitration.

3. How are the arbitrators selected? How long are they retained?

If the arbitrators are selected only by the employer and serve at the pleasure of the employer, then a perception may persist that the arbitrator is loyal to the employer and can be terminated if a decision unfavorable toward the employer is rendered. Under a collective bargaining agreement, the arbitrators are selected and retained by a procedure negotiated and agreed on by the union and company. To avoid problems and misperceptions, selections may be made through independent agencies such as the American Arbitration Association and the Federal Mediation and Conciliation Service.

4. What are the employee's due process rights, if any?

Employer promulgated arbitration systems contain no guarantees of due process; however, under collective bargaining agreements, arbitrators recognize these important employee rights that include:

- Right to counsel by a union representative.
- Right to face one's accusers.
- Right to information in order to prepare for the arbitration hearing.
- Right to notice of hearing.
- Right to copy of written charges against employee.

5. Who pays the arbitrator?

Under employer promulgated arbitration procedures, the employer typically pays the arbitrator. The concern is that the arbitrator might show loyalty to the party who pays the fee. Under most collective bargaining agreements, the union and the company jointly decide the method by which the arbitrator will be paid. Usually, the two parties share the costs; however, on a few occasions, the union and company negotiate the method whereby the loser pays. To avoid the perception of bias toward the payer of the fee, one organization designed a system whereby each employee pays a monthly fee to support an arbitration system; the arbitrator, then, is paid jointly by the employer and from employee fees.

6. How final is the arbitrator's decision?

Under employer promulgated arbitration, the arbitrator's decision is final if the employer wants the decision to be final. While overturning the arbitrator's decision would be bad policy unless fully justified, no legal basis exists for prohibiting the employer from taking such action. Under collective bargaining agreements, the arbitrator's decision will stand in nearly all cases, except in those limited cases where the arbitrator's decision is inconsistent with public policy, the arbitrator is incompetent, or the arbitrator has personal ties with one of the parties.

7. How are employees who file grievances protected?

Under the employer promulgated arbitration system, employee protection survives as long as the employer allows the system to survive. Under the collective bargaining agreement, employees who file grievances are protected under the grievance and arbitration procedure, which lasts as long as the collective bargaining agreement lasts.

8. What issues are arbitrated under the arbitration systems?

Under the employer promulgated arbitration system, the employer decides the issues that may be grieved and arbitrated. Under the collective bargaining agreement, the union and company jointly decide; this usually includes conflicts over interpretation and application of provisions of the collective bargaining agreement.

9. What authority do arbitrators have to grant remedies?

Under employer promulgated arbitration, the employer determines the extent of the arbitrator's authority. However, when there are statutory issues involved, such as gender discrimination, sexual harassment charges, and so on, remedial authority may include awarding attorney fees, punitive and compensatory damages, interest on back pay, and so on—in other words, issues normally decided by a jury. Under a collective bargaining agreement, back pay, reinstatement, and "make whole" remedies are common. Interest may be paid where the parties have agreed to such payments. In the federal sector, arbitrators have authority to award attorney fees and interest on back pay awards.

rules, nearly half the arbitration cases pertain to employee discipline. In fiscal year 1994 there were 2,286 discipline cases out of the 4,859 rights grievances filed with the FMCS.[12]

The Supreme Court has encouraged the use of arbitration, contending that this essentially private, self-governing process is best suited to labor relations issues and to the unique needs of the parties at a particular facility. This means the particular arbitration procedures are essentially determined by the parties themselves and there are no universally applicable rules concerning arbitration hearings. For example, the number of participants (even arbitrators) can vary; also, the location of the hearing might be at the plant conference room, a hotel room, or a courtroom. There are, however, some considerations and procedures that are acceptable for most, if not all, arbitration hearings. According to one study, 16 percent of the grievances filed in the first step of the grievance procedure are eventually resolved in the arbitration hearing.[13]

First, the number of arbitrators needed to resolve a grievance must be determined. The most common method (approximately 75 percent of related provisions), however, is for the impartial arbitrator selected by management and union officials to be solely responsible for the decision, with no help from other individuals in formulating the written decision. Sometimes (in about 15 percent of the related labor agreement provisions) the labor agreement specifies a three-member arbitration board or panel, with management and the union each selecting a member and these two individuals selecting the third member. Most decisions are made by this impartial arbitrator because the other two members of the panel are influenced by their respective management and union constituents, although the impartial arbitrator does consult with the other members. In either case, the arbitrator's decision is final and binding unless, in extremely rare circumstances, both management and the union agree to disregard or set aside the arbitrator's award.

About 5 percent of the labor agreements in the United States provide for a **permanent arbitrator** or umpire to resolve all disputes during the life of the labor agreement.[14] Usually, this provision applies to large companies or industries in which a large number of arbitration hearings are anticipated. Presumably, the permanent arbitrator can better allocate and schedule time to meet the grievance load of the union and employer so that settlements can be reached more promptly. This type of selection arrangement also allows the permanent arbitrator to become more knowledgeable of the complex and unique terms of the parties' labor agreement and industrial operation.

Assume, for example, that an arbitrator is hearing a grievance in the railroad industry for the first time. How long would it take for the arbitrator to accurately interpret the meaning of the following witness's testimony?

> At 3 P.M. Mott Haven Yard was a busy place. A crew of gandy dancers tamped methodically on a frong near the switching lead. L.S. 3 was all made up and ready to be doubled over. She had forty-six hog racks on the head end and sixty-five empty reefers on the hind end. Her crew were all new men on the run. Mike Madigan, the hog head, had just been set up. Bill Blanchard, the fire-boy, was a boomer who had recently hired out. Jack Lewis, the brains of the outfit, had been a no bill since he was fired out of the

> Snakes for violating Rule "G." Brady Holms, the flagman, used to work the high iron in a monkey suit, and J.B. Wells was a "stu" brakeman, right off the street. Over the hump lead, the yard rats were riding 'em in the clear and typing 'em down. The east side switcher was kicking loaded hoppers around, despite the violent washouts of the yardmixer who had discovered a hot box. Two Malleys were on the plug and three more were at the coal pocket. Our train, Number B.D. 5, was all ready to pull out.[15]

A permanent arbitrator saves time and expense because the parties do not have to repeatedly explain the meaning of these terms in the arbitration hearing or show the work location. Greater consistency can be attained where one individual applies the same decision-making criteria to all of the arbitrated grievances. Consistent decisions aid union and management officials in the day-to-day administration of the labor agreement. They also should enable the parties to better predict the arbitrator's subsequent decisions on similar issues, perhaps decreasing the number of frivolous grievances referred to arbitration as the parties become more certain of the arbitrator's reasoning. On the other hand, a retainer paid to the permanent arbitrator might encourage the parties to increase the grievance case load so that they can "get their money's worth."

Most labor agreements specify an **ad hoc arbitrator,** meaning that the arbitrator will be selected on an *ad hoc,* or case-by-case, basis; union and management representatives choose an arbitrator for a specific grievance, then select other arbitrators for subsequent grievances arising during the life of the labor agreement. Particularly in the case of an established collective bargaining relationship, management and the union often reach an informal agreement regarding the appropriate arbitrator for a particular grievance. However, if they cannot agree, they usually obtain a list of arbitrators' names from either the FMCS or the American Arbitration Association. In some cases when the parties cannot agree on an arbitrator from the list provided, they might request that these organizations select an arbitrator.

Clearly, for unions and companies having few arbitration hearings, *ad hoc* arbitrators are less expensive than permanent arbitrators. Regardless of the grievance load, *ad hoc* arbitration offers the advantage of flexibility. Permanent arbitrators usually are appointed by the parties for a specified period of time; neither side can discontinue the appointment alone if it views the permanent arbitrator's decisions with disfavor. There is no obligation to retain the *ad hoc* arbitrator in future grievances if one or both sides are displeased with the award.

Since some *ad hoc* arbitrators specialize in particular categories of grievances, such as job classification or wage incentives, they should be better informed than the permanent arbitrator on such issues. Permanent arbitrators may be more familiar with the parties, but may have seldom encountered a particular issue in their arbitration experience. Because both types of arbitrators have comparative advantages and disadvantages, management and union officials should carefully assess their particular situation before agreeing to either selection method.

According to one survey, arbitrators are likely to be males over 50 years of age with more than 14 years of experience in arbitration and a law degree or a graduate degree in another discipline.[16] Arbitrators' characteristics can be significant for at least two reasons. First, union and management officials select an arbitrator possessing certain characteristics that might, according to one study, include name recognition, reputation for integrity, and a specific geographic location. Other studies found that employers tend to prefer arbitrators with training in economics, while union and management officials who have law degrees prefer arbitrators who also have law degrees.[17]

Second, there is at least the possibility that certain background characteristics might influence arbitrator's decisions. However, research studies have not established a strong relationship between arbitrators' age, experience, and education and decision outcomes[18] (upholding or denying the grievance, for example).

Prehearing Briefs

Prehearing briefs, which highlight the issues and positions of the parties, can be filed by management and union representatives before the arbitrator arrives at the hearing. The briefs alert the arbitrator to the matters he or she will face at the hearing. These optional briefs, which are uncommon, vary in length from a one-page letter to an extensively footnoted document. Most of the time, the parties prefer to introduce the matter of arbitration at the beginning of the hearing.

The prehearing brief might backfire for the presenting party, who is subject to challenges on the assumed facts and inconsistencies that may surface in the witnesses' testimonies. On the other hand, prehearing briefs can be viewed as keeping the parties honest—they tend to approach their contentions thoroughly and are forced to adhere to them during the arbitration proceedings.

Perhaps more arbitrators would agree to the value of *prehearing stipulations*—joint union-management statements as to the issues involved and certain applicable grievance "facts." They save time in the arbitration hearing, for neither party feels obligated to repeat what the other has either previously said or agreed to in principle. Additionally, through the process of working together to stipulate the issues and facts, the parties may be able to resolve the disputes without arbitration. If briefs or stipulations are not agreed to prior to the hearing, the parties will have to educate the arbitrator on the background of the case.

The Arbitration Hearing

Held on a date convenient to the arbitrator and parties, the **arbitration hearing** varies in length from half an hour to several days. Union and management officials from the grievance site (the local union president and the labor relations manager, for example) will likely be at the hearing, and might present their versions of the arbitration case. However, either party might defer to another presenter, such as an international union representative or corporate manager of labor relations, at the hearing. Sometimes one or both parties employ an attorney; according to recent research, attorneys generally discourage pre-arbitration settlements between union and management and increase the use of pre- and post-hearing briefs.[19]

Variations also occur in the extent to which courtroom procedures and behaviors are used or required during the hearing. Usually the *grievance issue* to be resolved by the arbitrator is first presented in the hearing. The issue can become very complex, although it may be stated with deceptive simplicity. It is usually a one-sentence question to be answered by the arbitrator's award. Typical examples include the following:

- Did the company violate Section VI, Part 3, of the labor agreement when it transferred Sally Smith from the position of leadman to Welder III?
- Was Betty Brooks discharged for just cause? If not, what shall be the remedy?
- Did the duties of Machinist A's job undergo a significant change, thereby allowing the company to change the wage scale?
- Did Joe Jones's off-the-job activities have a sufficiently adverse effect on the company to justify dismissal?

Unfortunately, the issue is not always agreed on by union and management representatives, and the arbitrator has to frame the issue after hearing the case. The holiday scheduling grievance example in Chapter 8 illustrates the problems surrounding issue information. Assume, for example, that the labor agreement has *two* provisions pertaining to arbitration:

Article XX:	Arbitration Procedures
Section 1.	The arbitrator's authority is solely derived from the clear and unequivocal terms of the labor agreement.
Section 2.	The arbitrator may not add to, subtract from, or otherwise modify the express terms of the labor agreement.

In this situation, the union would claim that the issue pertains to the senior janitor's entitlement to holiday pay for the time involved due to the violation of Section 1 on the day in question. Management would contend that the issue of arbitrability is at stake, questioning whether the arbitrator has the authority to hear the case.[20] The determination of the specific grievance issue could take a lot of time, but it is important, for the nature of the issue often determines whether the grievance is upheld or denied.

The major part of the hearing is devoted to the presentation of (1) union exhibits, management exhibits, and jointly agreed upon exhibits (such as the collective bargaining agreement and the employee's written grievance); (2) the opening statements in which each party's spokesperson states what he or she plans to prove and highlights the major issues and background of the case; (3) union and management witnesses for testimony and cross-examination and related evidence to support union and management contentions (such as pictures of a job site, warning letters, performance ratings, and so on); and (4) summaries and closing statements by the union and management representatives or submission of post-hearing briefs that stress why their respective positions should be accepted by the arbitrator.

One or both parties can file a written *post-hearing brief* after the arbitration proceedings have ended. This device can be helpful when the arbitration case is very technical or complicated or includes statistical data that are difficult to explain in an oral argument.[21] In many cases, however, a post-hearing brief is unnecessary if the parties have prepared and presented their cases well during the hearing.

This summary of arbitration proceedings does not do justice to the considerable effort and drama shown in preparing and presenting an arbitration case. "Labor Relations in Action" gives some techniques for preparing for an arbitration hearing.

Mental effort, skill, and tensions are not eliminated once the hearing begins. Assume, for example, that you are a labor relations manager charged with proving an employee deserved discharge for smoking marijuana on company premises. Consider the following:

- How do you prove the employee actually smoked the marijuana when the evidence was destroyed and it is the employee's word against supervisory observations?
- Can the supervisor convince the arbitrator that he or she had sufficient training to recognize the shape and smell of the object in a dimly lit location?
- Will the grievant's testimony be strengthened or broken under cross-examination?
- How long can the supervisor remain calm under cross-examination without becoming upset?
- What if the arbitrator gives little weight to the circumstantial evidence presented by the company and a great deal of weight to the grievant's previous long and exemplary work record with the company?
- Will the union introduce a surprise contention or witness not previously discussed in the grievance proceedings (for example, that the grievant's discharge was due to the racial bias of the supervisor or because of a long-running dispute between the employee and supervisor)?

Management and union officials often enter arbitration hearings emotionally charged and uncertain. They are usually skillful in establishing their respective positions to the arbitrator's satisfaction and damaging their opponents' case by exploiting the opponents' weaknesses and uncertainties. The arbitrator must also display many skills in keeping an orderly hearing while at the same time objectively understanding and recording all of the facts presented.

One arbitrator has noted the following paradox: the union and management officials own the arbitration hearing, but the arbitrator is in charge of it. Union and management officials wrote the labor agreement and hired the aribitrator. Therefore, arbitrators should not treat the process as theirs, act like judges, be arrogant, or talk too much.

> Let the parties do the talking, work out the problems. You will be surprised how many knotty issues will be resolved during the hearing if you just ask the other side to re-

LABOR RELATIONS IN ACTION

Preparation Techniques for the Arbitration Hearing

1. Study the original statement of the grievance, and review its history through every step of the grievance machinery.
2. Review the collective bargaining agreement. Often, clauses that at first glance seem to be unrelated to the grievance will be found to have some bearing.
3. Assemble all documents and papers you will need at the hearing. Make copies for the arbitrator and for the other party. If some of the documents you need are in the possession of the other party, ask that they be brought to the arbitration. The arbitrator [might have] authority to subpoena documents and witnesses if they cannot be made available in any other way.
4. Interview all of your witnesses. Make certain they understand the theory of your case, as well as the importance of their own testimony. Run through the testimony several times. Rehearse the probable cross-examination.
5. Make a written summary of the testimony of each witness. This can be useful as a checklist at the hearing to ensure that nothing is overlooked.
6. Study the case from the other side's point of view. Be prepared to deal with opposing evidence and arguments.
7. Discuss your outline of the case with others in your organization. A fresh viewpoint will often disclose weak spots that you may have overlooked.
8. Read published awards on the issues that seem to be involved in your case. While awards by other arbitrators on cases between other parties are not decisive as to your own case, they may be persuasive. The American Arbitration Association has published summaries of thousands of labor arbitration awards in its monthly publications. Use these summaries and their cumulative indexes as a research tool.

SOURCE: Robert Coulson, *Labor Arbitration—What You Need to Know*, 3rd ed. (New York: American Arbitration Association, 1981), pp. 51, 52.

spond, and then ask the original side to add something, and so on. By the time they have killed off each other's contrariness, the problem has disappeared.

Do not try to take their procedure away from them. Give it back whenever they try to abdicate or place the burden of procedure on you. For example, it is an old ploy for one party or the other to say, Mr. or Ms. Arbitrator, do you want us to put in some evidence on this subject? This can put you into a trap. If your answer is no, then it is your fault when they lose the case because you excluded crucial evidence. If you say yes, then you are implying that the subject is important. Tell them it is up to them. Remind them that this is an adversary proceeding to elicit information and that it is their obligation to select whatever information they think is important.[22]

For example, many arbitrators have suggested that eliminating post-hearing briefs represents a major way to reduce arbitration costs.[23] Yet, they also indicate that post-hearing briefs are significant in analyzing the case or writing the decision, and it is up to the union and management officials to determine if and when they are used.

Comparison of Arbitration and Judicial Proceedings

The arbitration proceedings share some similarities with judicial proceedings, but their differences are profound. Many arbitration hearings differ from courtroom proceedings in that testimony of witnesses is not always taken under oath and transcripts of the proceedings are not always taken. Arbitrators may subpoena witnesses at the request of one of the parties. This is particularly true if management requests the subpoena to protect bargaining-unit employee witnesses whose testimony is used to support management's position. This way other employees realize the employee had to testify because he or she was under subpoena. However, arbitrators have the legal authority to subpoena witnesses in only a few states.

Common Law of the Shop

The most significant difference between arbitration and judicial proceedings is the arbitrator's reliance on **common law of the shop** principles in the resolution of disputes. Arbitrators, unlike judges, are selected by the parties to the dispute, and they are responsible for interpreting contract provisions that were negotiated and written by the parties to cover the specific location. Each of the over 150,000 separate labor agreements is different even though the subjects are similar. Judges are responsible for interpreting laws that are enacted by state and federal legislatures.

Thus, the arbitrator's major responsibility is to resolve a dispute in a manner that the parties can live with. Unlike judicial decisions in lower courts, the arbitrator's decision is usually final and not subject to further appeals. Consequently, arbitrators must be concerned with the subsequent effects of their decisions on union-management relationships. A judge has no such allegiance to the particular parties, the major responsibility being adhering to the statute in question, to established courtroom and legal procedures, and to precedent resulting from other applicable cases.

The common law of the shop often narrows the scope of arbitral decision making to the labor agreement language, intent of the parties, and past practices of the union and management officials at a particular industrial facility. The arbitrator uses these elements to convey to the union and management participants that their grievance is being resolved in terms of shop floor realities.

The distinction between judicial reasoning and common law of the shop principles can be shown through the following example. Assume that an employee has been discharged at Company A for drinking alcohol on the job. After an arbitral decision upholding the discharge has been reached, an employee at Company B is also discharged for drinking alcohol on the job. Strict adherence to judicial principles would uphold the second employee's discharge for drinking on the job. More specifically, the judicial principle of *stare decisis* (letting the decision at Company A stand in Company B's situation) would probably disregard the differences in work environments of the two companies.

However, the common law of the shop principles governing arbitration could lead the arbitrator to render an opposite decision at Company B than that reached at Company A. For example, supervisors at Company B may have been condoning this behavior, and other employees at this company may have been caught drinking on the job without being discharged for the infraction. Consequently, the arbitrator recognizes the two companies are independent with potentially unique circumstances and therefore deserve mutually exclusive decisions.

Evidence in Arbitration versus in Judicial Proceedings

It is also important to note that arbitrators are much more liberal than the courts in the types of evidence permitted at the hearing. For example, lie detector tests (polygraphs) have been allowed by some arbitrators under certain conditions (having the administrator of the polygraph present for cross-examination), although their use and weight in the arbitrator's decision remains controversial.[24] Usually, arbitrators give this evidence little weight unless the obtained information is corroborated by supporting evidence. The rationale for liberal admission of evidence is that the parties are seeking a solution to their perceived unique problem. In addition, some arbitrators maintain that arbitration performs a therapeutic function, that the parties are entitled to air their grievances regardless of the eventual decision. Arbitrators may allow aggrieved employees to digress from the pertinent subject or "tell it like it is" in front of higher-level union and management officials in order to serve this function.

Occasionally, new evidence is introduced by one or both parties in the arbitration hearing. The arbitrator may accept or reject this new evidence, depending upon the weight attached to the following sometimes conflicting considerations: (1) the arbitrator's desire to learn all of the pertinent facts surrounding the grievance, (2) the need to protect the integrity of the pre-arbitral grievance machinery, and (3) general concepts of fairness.[25] Because union and management officials and their designated arbitration panels are entitled to receive all evidence presented at the hearing, the arbitrator will offer the opposing party additional time to review and respond to new evidence.

Offers of compromise settlements before the hearing are given no weight by the arbitrator. For example, management officials with no major weakness in their original position might compromise their third-step discharge decision before arbitration by offering the grievant reinstatement with no back pay. A union could potentially use this evidence to indicate to the arbitrator that management admitted being wrong by revising its original decision. However, arbitrators maintain that the parties should make every effort to resolve their disputes internally instead of going to arbitration. Thus, a compromise settlement between the parties is viewed by the arbitrator as a genuine attempt to accommodate differences and save costs of going to arbitration, not an admission of guilt.

Other types of evidence are subject to varying arbitral consideration. Hearsay (second-hand) testimony might be allowed;[26] however, it is typically given little or no weight, particularly if it is not corroborated by other testimony and/or it is deduced that the witness has self-serving motives for testifying.

Arbitrators also vary in the weight they give to medical evidence presented in a grievance. Consider, for example, an employee who has her doctor testify that her previous back injury does not disqualify her from her present job. Management uses its doctor to counter the testimony, and the arbitrator now has to decide which doctor's testimony, if either, should be given the most weight. Exhibit 9.1 provides the results of two studies of arbitrators' use of medical evidence. Arbitrators are now more likely to rely on specialists' opinions, possibly because of the increase in the number of specialists over the past 20 years. However, these and other statistical changes might be more attributable to the arbitrators who answered the survey and the unique cases they were considering. Arbitrators' considerations of conflicting medical opinions can be further complicated by offsetting response categories. For example, how would an arbitrator who responded positively to the first two situations in Exhibit 9.1 handle the testimony of a nonspecialist who gave the most extensive examination?

The Arbitrator's Decision

Characteristics and Scope

The *arbitrator's decision* is a written document submitted to the management and union officials. Its components are as follows:

Exhibit 9.1 Survey of Arbitrators' Consideration of Conflicting Medical Opinions

	1975 STUDY	1987 STUDY
1. Use specialist over non-specialist	0	77 (26%)
2. Use report that indicates most intensive examination.	90 (51%)	133 (45%)
3. Use report that indicates most intimate knowledge of work performed.	34 (19%)	79 (27%)
4. No response.	53 (30%)	7 (2%)

SOURCE: Daniel F. Jennings and A. Dale Allen, Jr., "Arbitrators and Medical Evidence: A Longitudinal Analysis," *Labor Law Journal* (June 1994), p. 382.

1. A statement of the issue(s).
2. A statement of the facts surrounding the grievance.
3. Names of union and management representatives involved in the case, along with others who gave testimony (employees or expert witnesses, for example).
4. Pertinent provisions of the labor agreement.
5. A summary of the union and management contentions.
6. A discussion and opinion of the validity and relative weight of the facts and contentions.
7. The arbitrator's award (grievance upheld, grievance denied, or a compromise between union and management contentions).

Few prospective guidelines govern the form and content of the arbitrator's decision. However, the arbitrator should demonstrate through the decision a thorough understanding of all the facts and contentions raised in the arbitration hearing. While arbitrators should address each argument and the evidence presented by both parties, some arbitrators address their decisions to the losing party because the winners do not have to be convinced they are right.

The necessity of the arbitrator's opinion has been the subject of considerable controversy. Some union and management officials basically look only at the arbitrator's award to see who "won" or "lost." Others read the decision to obtain principles and guidelines for future labor-management relationships and to assess the arbitrator's interpretative abilities.

Controversy notwithstanding, the decision should tell the parties how the dispute was resolved and why. "Ideally, an opinion convinces the losing party that its arguments were heard, that the system used to decide the case is a fair one, and that the result makes sense."[27] An arbitrator's decision should explain the relative weight given to the parties' evidence and contentions and should indicate in clear language the benefits to which the parties are entitled and the obligations that are imposed on them. Thus, the arbitrator's decision should *educate* the parties (including other union and management officials, who often select an arbitrator after researching his or her published decisions) within the context of the common law of the shop and established arbitration principles.

In some cases, the arbitrator's opinion can be even more important than the award. Assume, for example, the union grieves management's assignment of work normally performed in Job Classification A, loading trucks on Saturday, to an employee in Job Classification B, a laborer. Further, the union seeks a remedy of eight hours at overtime rate of pay for the appropriate employee in Job Classification A, the senior employee in the shipping department, on the reasoning that the company's violation of the contract had deprived a Classification A employee of the overtime opportunity. However, the arbitrator denies the grievance and stresses the following in his opinion: "The various job classifications are for pay purposes only and do not restrict management's prerogative to assign work across different job classifications." This statement significantly harms the union in related matters, particularly if the language was not expressly stated in the labor agreement. Now the union will have a difficult time in grieving any work assignment controversy, even though the above decision pertained to one specific situation.

In other situations the arbitrator's gratuitous advice in the opinion may harm one or both of the parties. There is often a thin line between advising management and union practitioners on more effective and humane ways to run the operation and arbitrating the grievance solely on the merits of the case. The latter approach does not advise but merely determines whether management's action was justified under the terms of the labor agreement and applicable *past practice* (which will be discussed later in this chapter).

Decision-Making Criteria Used by Arbitrators

Few consensually defined principles are applicable to arbitrators' decisions because arbitrators do not follow precise or identical methods in making decisions. However, one study indicated that individual arbitrators have been consistent in the importance they assign to various decision-making criteria over the years.[28] The following generally accepted guidelines have been developed and serve as focal points subject to interpretation, consideration, and application by arbitrators in resolving grievances.

Burden of Proof, Witness Credibility, and Cross-Examination The union files a grievance claiming that management violated the spirit or letter of the labor agreement. In such cases the union is the charging party and has the burden of proof in convincing the arbitrator that management acted incorrectly. A major exception occurs in employee discipline cases, where management is the charging party and has the burden of proof in establishing that its actions were correct.

The burden of proof is typically approached through evidence (discussed earlier in this chapter) and testimony from credible witnesses. Witness credibility is often assessed through rather subjective behaviors such as talking softly or hesitantly, looking downward, or giving long, evasive answers to questions. The testimony is also subjected to cross-examination by the other party, who attempts to establish that the witness is inconsistent or unfamiliar with the facts or has bias or some other self-serving motive behind his or her testimony. A cross-examiner must avoid a major potential problem; namely, reinforcing the witness's testimony. This avoidance is easier said than done, as evidenced in Exhibit 9.2, which illustrates incorrect cross-examination after two direct questions.

As noted earlier, participants' general characteristic categories (age and gender of the grievant or arbitrator, for example) do not have a strong correlation to the arbitrator's decision. Arbitrators are, however, influenced by witnesses' credibility, which includes perceived mental attitudes of the grievance participants. A rambling, disjointed presentation by a witness, a union or management representative, or a grievant who comes across as insolent or sneaky will likely receive a strong, negative arbitral evaluation that might not be offset by other decision-making criteria.[29]

Exhibit 9.2 Transcript from an Arbitration Hearing Reflecting Poor Cross-Examination

(Direct questions of employee witness by a union spokesperson)

Q: How did your supervisor sexually harass you?

A: He mooned me.

Q: Describe the circumstances to the Arbitrator.

A: I was working overtime and as far as I knew we were the only ones left in the laundry. As I was counting the inventory, the door to a broom closet opened and there was this man's bare butt sticking out at me with his pants down around his ankles.

(Subsequent cross-examination of employee witness by a management spokesperson)

Q: Was the area near the broom closet well lighted?

A: No, it was rather dim.

Q: Was the broom closet well lit?

A: No, the light in the closet wasn't even lit.

Q: Was there a mirror that you could clearly see the face of the man?

A: No, I never saw his face when it happened. He stepped back into the closet and I went and punched out right away.

Q: (Triumphantly) How then can you be sure that the bare fanny belonged to your supervisor?

A: Because of the tattoo.

Q: I've come this far so I might as well ask what is the significance of the tattoo.

A: Well he was always bragging to us women about his tattoo, describing it and offering to show it to us. Of course, none of us ever took him up on it but there it was—just as he had pictured it. (Whereupon the grievant proceeded to describe in some scatological detail the tattoo which had been so prominently displayed.)

SOURCE: John J. Flagler, "A Few Modest Proposals for Improving Conduct of the Hearing," in Gladys W. Gruenberg, ed., *Arbitration 1990: New Perspectives on Old Issues*, Proceedings of the Forty-third Annual Meeting, National Academy of Arbitrators (Washington, D.C.: Bureau of National Affairs Inc., 1991), p. 55.

Provisions of the Labor Agreement Obviously, an important decision-making criterion will be the provisions of the labor agreement, which reflect the collectively bargained rights of union and management officials. Adherence to common law of the shop principles stresses that the major function of the arbitrator is the interpretation of the labor agreement's provisions. Indeed, many arbitrators adhere at least in part to the **parole evidence rule,** which in its classic form holds that evidence, oral or otherwise, cannot be admitted for the purpose of varying or contradicting written language recorded in the labor agreement. Consider, for example, the following labor agreement provision: "Notice of a promotional opening shall be posted for five working days." Even though "five working days" is clearer than "five days," a dispute could arise if the contract specified "working days" and the Saturday in question was a regularly unscheduled day on which certain employees were called in for emergency overtime. One of the parties might successfully argue before the arbitrator that the term "working day" is clear and applies to days on which work is performed and that this precludes any evidence that Saturday was unscheduled and never contemplated as a working day. Rationale for this rule is that the parties have spent many hours in negotiating standardized employment conditions; thus, disregarding negotiated terms would damage stable labor-management relationships and communicate to the parties that there is little or no point in reducing contract terms to writing.

A problem remains when the labor agreement language is ambiguous, since it normally cannot prescribe all essential rules or guidelines for day-to-day administration of labor relations. Also, many labor agreement terms, such as "reasonable," "make every effort," "minor repairs," and "maintain the work environment as safely as possible" might have resolved negotiation impasses but still pose interpretive problems for the arbitrator.

Some contract provisions that appear clear on the surface can cause differences of opinion among union and management officials as well as arbitrators. Consider the following three examples and related questions.[30]

Example 1: "The company will provide required safety clothing." Does the company have to pay for safety clothing or merely make it available for employees to purchase?

Example 2: "An employee must work on the scheduled day before and after the holiday in order to receive holiday pay." What happens when the employee works three hours the day before the holiday, goes home because of sickness, and works the full eight hours the day after the holiday?

Example 3: "Management will distribute overtime as equally as possible." Does a supervisor making overtime request calls to employees' homes stop making such calls until contact is made with an employee whose telephone is busy or goes unanswered? Has the company met its obligation if the supervisor calls, leaves a message on the senior employee's answering machine, then offers overtime to the next senior employee?

Arbitrators prefer to approach the ambiguity problem initially in terms of the labor agreement and to construe ambiguous language or provisions of the labor agreement so as to be compatible with the language in other provisions of the agreement. Thus, the contract should be viewed as a whole, not in isolated parts, and any interpretation that would nullify another provision of the contract should be avoided. When ambiguity remains, the arbitrator must seek guidance from sources outside the labor agreement.

Intent of the Parties Another guideline, the **intent of the parties,** refers to what union and management officials had in mind when they (1) negotiated the labor agreement or (2) engaged in an action that resulted in a particular grievance. Intent is entirely subjective; however, arbitrators consider observable behavioral manifestations of the intent to determine what a reasonable person would conclude from that behavior. For an example of labor agreement intent, consider the previously cited holiday pay situation. To demonstrate that it intended for holiday pay to be given only to those individuals who worked a full eight hours the day before and the day after the holiday, management might supply the arbitrator with notes on various proposals and counterproposals made during labor agreement negotiations to prove what they intended the contract language to mean. Arbitrators are strongly influenced by this evidence of intent because they are reluctant to give in an award what could not be obtained at the bargaining table.

An example of an action's intent considered in a grievance might occur when a supervisor believes an employee has stolen some company property. The supervisor approaches the employee stating the following:

> You and I both know you were caught stealing. Therefore, you have two options. You can file a grievance which will be denied in arbitration and the discharge on your record will make it difficult for you to find a job elsewhere. Or you can sign this resignation slip, quit, and we won't tell any other companies about the stealing incident.

The employee hastily signs the slip and leaves the company premises. However, the next day she returns, informing management that she wants to work because she never really quit. If the company refuses the employee's request and a grievance is filed, the arbitrator would have to determine the grievant's and management's intent. Observable behaviors of an employee intending to quit are cleaning out the locker, saying good-bye to colleagues, and asking management for the wages earned for that week. An employee usually resigns only after giving the decision careful thought and consideration. Since none of these behaviors were operative in this case, the arbitrator might attempt to determine management's intent in this action. Possibly, the supervisor was simply trying to do the employee a favor by letting her off the hook. However, management may have given the employee the alternative of quitting to avoid subsequent arbitration of the discharge and the risk of the discharge decision being overturned. The latter intent is viewed by arbitrators as being *constructive discharge.*

Under this principle, the arbitrator would view the termination of employment as being subject to the employee discipline provisions of the labor agreement. These provisions usually call for union representation and written explanation at the time of the employee's discharge. Because these procedures were not followed, many arbitrators would reinstate the grievant with full back pay. Sometimes, union and management officials attempt to convince the arbitrator of their specific intent by producing written notes of previous discussions so that there will be documentation of their related past behaviors.

Past Practice The principle of **past practice** refers to a specific and identical action that has been continually employed over a number of years to the recognition and satisfaction of both parties.[31] This decision-making criterion demonstrates to the arbitrator how the parties have carried out the labor agreement and has been used by both management and the union. Management is usually more concerned about past practice because it administers the labor agreement through various supervisory directives to the hourly employees. Since established contractual provisions place restrictions on managerial discretion, management attempts to avoid further reductions on supervisory decision making by pressing for a past-practices clause to be included in the labor agreement, similar to the following:

> Article XXVIII: Other Agreements
> Section 2. The parties do hereby terminate all prior agreements heretofore entered into between representatives of the company and the unions (including all past understandings, practices, and arbitration rulings) pertaining to rates of pay, hours of work, and conditions of employment other than those stipulated in this agreement between the parties.[32]

However, this clause does not guarantee that management does not add to its contractual restrictions by repeatedly handling a situation in a similar manner. Thus, a continued managerial practice of unilaterally giving employees a Thanksgiving turkey might become a binding, implied term of the labor agreement. Further, management will likely have to negotiate a labor agreement provision to the contrary (even if the current labor agreement is silent on the subject) if it wishes to discontinue the gift in subsequent years.

In addition to interpreting ambiguous language or resolving problems not covered in the agreement, past practices may even alter clear and convincing contractual provisions. At one company, it had been a practice for many years to require clerks to perform cleanup operations at the end of their work day and to pay them no money for up to 10 minutes' work, 15 minutes straight time for 11 to 15 minutes' work, and time and one-half for work of more than 15 minutes in duration. There was clear contractual language specifying that work in excess of eight hours per day would be computed at time and one-half overtime premium. The union eventually filed a grievance stating that clear contractual language compelled overtime payment for any amount of daily work exceeding eight hours. However, the arbitrator maintained that past practice was more significant than the express terms of the labor agreement in this case.

> The written contract is, of course, the strongest kind of evidence of what the parties willed, intended or agreed upon. An arbitrator will not ordinarily look beyond its *unambiguous* language. Where, *however,* as here, the parties have unmistakably demonstrated *how they themselves* have read and regarded the meaning and force of the language, and *where the meaning varies* from its normal intendment, the arbitrator *should not,* indeed, *cannot* close his eyes to this demonstration.[33]

Past practice, while influential, is not interpreted the same by arbitrators. For example, it is very difficult to determine in a consistent fashion how long or how frequently an action must be continued before it becomes a binding past practice.

Sometimes the nature of the issue further complicates the past practice criterion. Consider a situation where management wants to unilaterally change a "clear" past practice of employee smoking at work. Some arbitrators indicated that management could not unilaterally change this past practice, particularly if no specified evidence was presented to show that smoking adversely affected efficiency or productivity. However, some arbitrators have let management establish a no-smoking rule, thereby disregarding past practice, for the following reasons:[34]

- Past practice pertains to employee benefits, not management's direction of the work force, and smoking is not an employee benefit.
- The past practice of permitting employee smoking can be broken because this activity has now proven to be detrimental to employees' health.

Previous Arbitration Awards Also used as a guideline are previous arbitration awards when they could bolster either party's position in the arbitration case. Similarly, the arbitrator may cite these awards to refute the parties' contentions or to illustrate the arbitral opinion. Arbitrators accord some weight to prior arbitration awards issued at the same facility, particularly if the situation and contractual language are similar. Of course, few prior arbitration awards meet these requirements because the parties would be extremely reluctant to arbitrate the same issue a second time, given the first arbitrator's decision.

Arbitrators are far less likely to be influenced by awards concerning different labor agreements at other facilities, as arbitrators recognize the common law uniqueness and autonomy of a particular operation. In fact, arbitrators might negatively regard the introduction of prior arbitration awards into a current arbitration hearing.

> Unwillingness to present a case solely on its own merits may come to be interpreted as a sign of weakness. Also it may be considered that citation of prior arbitration awards indicates either a lack of confidence in the judgment of an arbitrator or a belief that he may be swayed by irrelevant considerations. An attempt to induce an arbitrator to follow some alleged precedent may come to be recognized as at least bad etiquette.[35]

Current Issues Affecting Arbitration

Legal Jurisdiction

As previously noted, the Steelworkers' Trilogy and other judicial decisions clarified and enhanced arbitrators' roles in resolving employee grievances. Yet, arbitration decisions can sometimes involve various government agencies and the courts, which might be concerned with specific aspects of a grievance. Consider, for example, a case in which a black union steward is discharged for insubordination. A grievance is filed and proceeds to arbitration under the terms of the labor agreement.

However, the employee claims that the discharge was prompted by racial bias and the fact that he was a union steward as well. Conceivably, the discharge grievance could claim the attention of a number of persons—the arbitrator and officials from the EEOC and the NLRB. The problem involves untangling the various jurisdictional squabbles that could arise over this one grievance.

Arbitration and the Equal Employment Opportunity Commission The passage of the 1964 Civil Rights Act (amended by the Equal Employment Opportunity Act of 1972), subsequent judicial decisions, and the passage of the 1991 Civil Rights Act have emphasized that management's well-meant intentions are not sufficient to preclude a charge of racial discrimination. Indeed, in administering this aspect of public law, the EEOC holds that employers must actively devise and implement employment procedures that remove present as well as possible residual effects of past discrimination. Hiring, promotion, and discipline procedures may be carefully scrutinized by the EEOC to protect employees from arbitrary and discriminatory practices. In a unionized facility, arbitrators also often assume a related decision-making role, particularly in grievances protesting discipline of an employee. This situation poses at least two questions:

1. Should management, the union, and the employee turn to the arbitrator, the EEOC, or both in resolving a minority employee's grievance?
2. How do the courts and the EEOC view the arbitrator's decision in terms of Title VII of the 1964 Civil Rights Act?

The first question was answered by the Supreme Court in its 1974 *Alexander* v. *Gardner-Denver Company* decision. The Court contended that the arbitrator's expertise pertains to labor agreement interpretation and not to resolving federal civil rights laws. Moreover,

> The factfinding process in arbitration usually is not equivalent to judicial fact-finding. The record of the arbitration proceedings is not as complete; the usual rules of evidence do not apply; and rights and procedures common to civil trials, such as discovery, compulsory process, cross-examination, and testimony under oath, are often severely limited or unavailable.[36]

Consequently, a minority employee is almost encouraged to pursue both the arbitration process and appropriate judicial procedures.

Some predicted that the *Gardner-Denver* decision would create havoc as every discrimination grievance lost in arbitration would be overturned by the appropriate government agency or the courts. Yet research does not support this prediction. One study found that a grievance reviewed by the EEOC or related agencies only stood a 1-in-6 chance of being reversed. Also, the chances of a trial court overturning a discrimination grievance heard by an arbitrator are slim, 6.8 percent according to one study and 10 percent according to another.[37] Apparently, the courts believe that arbitrators are adequately covering the legal considerations of discrimination in their decisions.

The Supreme Court's *Gilmer* decision, discused earlier in this chapter, might enable arbitrators instead of the EEOC and the courts to resolve a discrimination grievance filed under the terms of the collective bargaining agreement. However, this has not yet happened. The EEOC, while encouraging use of alternative dispute resolution techniques, including arbitration, to resolve discrimination claims,[38] has not yet waived its involvement on the issue. Moreover, Congress, in the passage of the 1991 Civil Rights Act, reinforced *Gardner-Denver's* rationale for judicial oversight in unionized settings.[39]

Arbitration and the National Labor Relations Board Perhaps the most frequent supplements to arbitral decisions have come from the NLRB because the grievant could have been discharged for reasons pertaining to provisions of the labor agreement that are similar to laws, such as engaging in union activities on the job or acting overly aggressive in the capacity of a union official. Section 10(a) of the National Labor Relations Act provides that the NLRB "is empowered . . . to prevent any person from engaging in any unfair labor practice (listed in Section 8) affecting commerce. This power shall not be affected by any other means of adjustment or prevention that has been or may be established by agreement, law, or otherwise."

Although it has the power, the NLRB does not ignore arbitration awards covering unfair labor practice issues. In fact, it often withholds its jurisdictional determination and investigation pending the arbitrator's decision. In 1955 the NLRB's deferral to arbitration policy was formulated in the *Spielberg Manufacturing Company* case. In that case, the board honored an arbitration award that denied reinstatement to certain employees guilty of strike misconduct. Resulting deferral guidelines stressed that the arbitration proceedings must be fair and regular, there must be adequate notice and representation, the arbitrator must address the issue of the alleged unfair labor practice, and all parties must agree to be bound by the arbitration awards.[40] However, the board will disregard the arbitrator's award if it is ambiguous or if the board obtains pertinent evidence not presented in the arbitration proceeding.

The NLRB's deferral to arbitration policy was enhanced in the *Collyer* case, in which the NLRB administrative law judge had found that the company had committed an unfair labor practice when it made certain unilateral changes in wages and working conditions.[41] The company maintained that the issues should be resolved through existing arbitration proceedings instead of the NLRB. The board in essence agreed with the company's position. While reserving the right to investigate the merits of the issue, the board maintained that

1. Related disputes can be better resolved through the special skills and experiences of the arbitrators.
2. The objectives of the National Labor Relations Act, industrial peace and stability, can be significantly realized through adherence to arbitration procedures established in the labor agreement.

Under *Collyer*, the employee was obligated to use the arbitration procedure before the NLRB would review the merits of the case.[42]

The NLRB's subsequent *Olin Corporation* and *United Technologies* decisions established new guidelines that make it even more likely that the NLRB will defer to arbitration decisions. Under *Olin*, the unfair labor practice does not have to be considered in the arbitration hearing. The NLRB will still defer to an arbitrator's award "if the contractual and unfair labor practice issues were factually parallel and the facts relevant to resolving the unfair labor practice were presented generally to the arbitrator."[43]

Yet, one research effort found only about half of the arbitrators cited related external law in their decisions when at least one of the parties had filed an unfair labor practice charge with the NLRB. It also found that most of these arbitrators engaged in only cursory or conclusory consideration of relevant external law. The study urged that, at a minimum, arbitrators and union and management officials should be aware that they may provide the grievant his or her only opportunity to litigate a statutory claim; therefore, an explicit, informed choice should be made on "whether to vote, argue, discuss, and explore statutory issues in the arbitration forum, or to reject the discussion of such issues as inappropriate to the arbitration process."[44]

In summary, the Supreme Court has recognized the ability of arbitrators to interpret the labor agreement provisions and has even encouraged parties to arbitrate the issue before proceeding to the NLRB. However, this encouragement is not given to the same extent in Title VII Civil Rights Act disputes.

Arbitration, the Courts, and Public Policy: The *Misco* Decision Federal courts can occasionally become involved when union or management officials request consideration of arbitration matters, particularly where a case heard by an arbitrator involves public-policy considerations. The Supreme Court approached this situation in its recent *Misco* decision. Misco fired an employee who operated a "slitter-rewinder," which cuts rolling coils of paper, for allegedly smoking marijuana on company property. The grievant was arrested in his car in the company's parking lot. Police found a lit marijuana cigarette in the front ashtray of the car, and a subsequent police search of the car revealed a marijuana residue.

The arbitrator reinstated the grievant because the evidence did not establish that the grievant smoked or even possessed marijuana on the company's premises. He noted the grievant had been in the back seat of the car. The arbitrator also refused to consider the police report as evidence and ruled that the case must be limited to what the employer knew at the time of the firing. Management appealed the arbitrator's decision to the courts, claiming that bringing the employee back would violate public policy—operating dangerous equipment under the influence of drugs.

In *Misco* the Court restated a principle established in an earlier decision *(W.R. Grace)*. It said that a "court may not enforce a collective bargaining agreement that is contrary to public policy." However, the Court noted that the public policy must be *"explicit," "well defined* and *dominant,"* and *"ascertained by reference to the laws and legal precedents and not from general considerations of supposed public inter-*

ests." The Supreme Court upheld the arbitrator because none of these prerequisites were examined by the lower courts and would unlikely be found in this situation.[45]

Misco, therefore, reinforces the wide latitude given to arbitrators' decision-making authority by the Trilogy. It will probably reduce the number of instances in which the courts "second-guess" the arbitrator's award on public-policy grounds. However, the public-policy exception, while made narrow by *Misco,* still exists. An employer does not have to honor an arbitration award that would require a violation of law (reinstating a bus driver who lacks a driver's license, for example).[46]

Sexual harassment (discussed further in Chapter 11) represents a controversial public policy issue that has been subsequently interpreted by arbitrators and judicial officials. The courts can have very different interpretations of this situation. For example, one federal district court vacated an arbitrator's award that reinstated an employee who allegedly harassed a female customer. The judge found that the arbitrator's decision contained some "disturbing comments" that evidenced bias in favor of the employee and insensitivity toward the customer-accuser. For example, the arbitrator noted that the employee was married and had children, whereas the customer weighed 225 pounds, "was unattractive and frustrated," and possibly fabricated the incident to attract her mother's caring attention. The judge ordered the case to be heard by a new arbitrator.[47]

However, another federal court refused to set aside an arbitration award reinstating an employee who, during a phone conversation, put down the receiver, approached the co-worker from behind, and grabbed her breasts. He then picked up the phone and said, "Yup, they're real." The court commented, "While we do not condone (the employee's) behavior, it was within the purview of the collective bargaining agreement and public policy for the arbitrator to order his reinstatement."[48]

Similar judicial rationale was used in the case of a trading-room secretary at a California brokerage firm. The secretary's boss admitted to calling her a "hooker" and a "bitch" and placing at least one condom on her desk. She filed a sexual harassment suit and was then told to submit her charge to an arbitration panel, which was mandated by the industry. The panel dismissed her charge agreeing with the defendant that "[i]t's just the way that it is in every trading room."[49]

Appraising Labor Arbitration's Effectiveness

Although the courts have praised the effectiveness of arbitration, some critical assessments have come from participants—union and management officials and even some arbitrators (see "Labor Relations in Action" for some related insights).

Arbitrators seldom, if ever, know why they were not chosen for a subsequent grievance. Little information is available concerning why the parties continually return to some arbitrators but not to others. Exhibit 9.3 approaches this void by grouping criticisms that several union and management practitioners have leveled at arbitrators. These criticisms apply to two general areas: arbitrators' capabilities and ethics and the potential procedural problems in the arbitration process.

Arbitrators' Capabilities and Ethics Some contend arbitrators might compromise their decisions to minimize or avoid displeasure from one or both of the

LABOR RELATIONS IN ACTION

Things They Never Told Me Before I Became an Arbitrator

- The difficulty of setting up a hearing date when union and company representatives have such busy schedules.
- The ease of reading finished cases and the difficulty of writing one from scratch.
- The need to know about admission of evidence and reasons for sustaining and overruling objections at a hearing and making quick decisions about them.
- How physically tiring it is to fly or drive to some of the hearing sites.
- How unglamorous travel and hotels can be when all airports look alike and you are not even sure where you are.
- How mature and conscientious some parties can be in trying to do "what is right," while some parties enter the hearing armed for combat and confrontation.
- How much money, time, and effort could be saved if the parties prepared better and attempted to resolve their differences before arbitration.
- The role of the cancellation fee in making sure the parties are going forth to arbitration. (If there is no cost of canceling, one of the parties can abuse the arbitration process by canceling at a late date.)
- How one party will hold out for a compromise settlement until right before the hearing. When no settlement is forthcoming and their case is weak, the party will drop the grievance.
- How important the fee is to the parties—it cannot be too low because the parties think you are not good enough; it cannot be too high because you price yourself out of a job.

SOURCE: From an experienced, somewhat weary arbitrator who enjoys relaxing in anonymity.

parties or even to ensure re-employment in future arbitration cases. The following are examples of compromise decisions that might be used to appease both sides.[50]

- Reinstating a discharged grievant without any back pay awarded.
- Changing the 50–50 outcome assessment of one case to 51–49 in favor of the party who had lost the other three cases heard at the hearing.

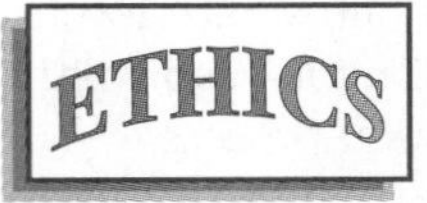

In some instances, union and management representatives believe that the arbitrator "owes them one" due to their support (financial and otherwise). One arbitrator, who expressed surprise to officials at being selected to replace another prominent arbitrator, was given the following reason why the previous arbitrator was fired:

> I'll tell you why we fired him. The last case he had ended here at about 4:00. Mr. ______ expressed considerable concern since he had to make a plane for New York

Exhibit 9.3 Summary of Criticisms Union and Management Practitioners Have toward Arbitrators

1. Fails to treat all parties with respect (for example, has offensive personal traits; tends to apply his or her feelings of "fairness" or "justice" as opposed to applying the parties' intent; regularly exceeds his or her authority).
2. Cannot control the hearing properly (for example, cannot rule on objections, is too legalistic or not legalistic enough, cannot stop gratuitous hostile exchanges or rambling or redundant testimony).
3. Awards are either too brief or too long, unclear, take a long time, emphasize compromise, evidence poor reasoning or writing skills, or fail to give parties direction on language issues.
4. Either too much experience with management or the union or insufficient experience with labor relations as a neutral or with the jobs and industry in question.
5. Decides cases on grounds other than those argued (for example, fails to consider precedents; is too academic; fails to pay sufficient attention at hearing; reviews evidence not presented in hearing; discusses cases with uninvolved parties prior to decision being issued; does not address all facts or issues).
6. Too expensive (for example, generally unavailable in a reasonable time frame thereby increasing potential back-pay liability; cancellation policy is unreasonable).

SOURCE: Adapted from Thomas L. Watkins, "Assessing Arbitrator Competence: A Preliminary Regional Survey," *Arbitration Journal* 47 (June 1992), p. 45.

> and was running late. I assured him that he would have no problem. I carried his bags to his car, drove in excess of all the speed limits, went through back roads, even proceeded through changing traffic lights. After a hectic ride and at considerable risk, I got him to the airport just in time to make the plane. I parked my car in a no parking zone. I even carried his bags to the gate. After all this, you know, that [deleted] ruled against me.[51]

Yet other participants or students of arbitration maintain that the arbitrator's indebtedness to the parties is a necessary ingredient of dispute resolution. They maintain that the arbitrator owes allegiance to both union and management, thereby providing a well-formulated decision. The ethics issue has been directly approached by three organizations: the National Academy of Arbitrators, the Federal Mediation and Conciliation Service, and the American Arbitration Association. These organizations have come up with the following guidelines:

- An arbitrator, deciding that he or she does not have the technical competence to deal with the issue under consideration, is expected to withdraw from the case. Issues commonly included in this category are incentive systems, job evaluation plans, and pension and insurance programs.
- An arbitrator is not to make an award public without the consent of the parties.

- Prior to an arbitrator's appointment the parties should be made aware of the arbitrator's fees for the hearing, study time, travel time, postponement or cancellation, office overhead expenses, and any work of paid assistants.
- If either party requests the arbitrator to visit the workplace, the arbitrator should comply.
- An arbitrator should not consider a post-hearing brief that has not been given to the other party.
- If the arbitrator knows any of the parties or has any private issue in the organization, he or she must make disclosure of any potential conflict of interest before the hearing.

Other criticisms of arbitration have focused on the quality of the arbitrator's decision. The arbitrator's written opinion and award dissatisfy the parties if they do not reflect the original expectations and understandings of one or both regarding the nature or scope of the grievance. But some arbitral decisions reflect legal considerations as much or more than union and management concerns expressed at the hearing. This potential "over lawyering" problem of arbitration decisions might be due to the large amount of legislation at the local, state, and federal levels that might pertain to the grievance or the preferences of union and management officials and possibly the arbitrator[52] to minimize subsequent judicial reviews by considering related laws at the hearing and in the decision.

Management and union representatives might also obtain poor arbitration awards under the *garbage in, garbage out* theory. Because the arbitrator's decision is based on the merits of the grievance, a sloppy grievance formulation and presentation might result in a relatively lackluster arbitral decision. Sometimes union and management officials present an arbitrator with poorly conceived grievances that should have been resolved before going to arbitration. Such grievances are often prompted by political considerations—the union or management officials take the grievance to arbitration to show support for their union stewards or first-line supervisors even though they know them to be wrong. Arbitration in this sense serves as a buck-passing device; the errant union steward or supervisor is apparently given support but in reality is provided an education through the arbitrator's decision.

One almost inescapable concern arises from the finality of the arbitrator's award. While the Supreme Court has encouraged single-person resolution of an industrial dispute, opponents of this practice suggest that an arbitrator has more authority than a judge, whose decisions may be overturned through judicial appeal. Unfortunately, many problems would result if arbitration awards were subjected to an appeals procedure. Any such procedure would be time consuming and expensive. If the arbitrator's award were reversed by a second arbitrator in the appeals procedure it would be impossible to determine which arbitrator wrote the "correct" decision. Also, the "arbitrator as judge of last resort" situation might beneficially place pressure on the arbitrator to produce high-quality opinions.

Procedural Problems The two general categories of procedural problems are time lag and expense of the arbitration proceedings. The FMCS reports that the average length of time between the filing of a grievance and an arbitrator's award was 326 days.[53] Clearly, this delay affects employees who rightfully maintain that their complaint should be resolved promptly and efficiently. Similarly, management equates the arbitral decision-making delay in many grievance issues, such as discipline and job reclassification, with unnecessary expense, because adverse awards can also include remedies for back pay retroactive to the date of management's original action.

Many times this delay is due to a limited supply of experienced arbitrators who handle a large proportion of the cases. Also, many union and management officials candidly admit that they will wait months for an experienced arbitrator who has previously shown excellent hearing direction and decision-making skills. In some cases experienced arbitrators have assumed responsibility for training new arbitrators. In this situation, often called *internship,* the intern progresses from merely observing hearings and discussing cases to drafting awards for the arbitrator's use and sitting as a hearing officer.

Time delay is only one of several expenses associated with arbitration. The FMCS reports that arbitrators' average per diem rate of $540, when applied to the arbitrator's average hearing time (1.13 days), travel time (.40 days), and study time (2.33 days), plus average travel expenses ($247), resulted in an average charge of about $2,352 for an arbitrated grievance.[54] While most labor agreements provide for the sharing of arbitration expenses between union and management organizations, each party can incur additional expenses such as the fees for the parties' attorneys, which usually exceed the arbitrator's fee; wage payments to plant personnel who take part in the proceedings; and stenographic transcription costs, if a record of the hearing is desired.

Arbitral fees have increased over the years, which is understandable in view of inflation. In many cases, however, management and union officials bring added expenses upon themselves when they insist that the arbitrator review unnecessary materials, such as transcripts, prior arbitration awards, superfluous witnesses, and prehearing and post-hearing briefs. They may also insist on expensive frills, such as renting a hotel suite for a neutral arbitration site, that do not materially affect the quality of a decision.

Grievance Mediation and Other Alternatives to the Arbitration Procedure

Some union and management officials have reduced expenses by expediting the arbitration procedures before, during, or after arbitration hearings. Prehearing suggestions include (1) appointing a panel of arbitrators for the length of the contract rather than working through a new list of arbitrators each time an arbitration is scheduled, and (2) appointing a permanent umpire for a specific amount of time (one year or the life of the agreement, for example). Hearings may be expedited by substituting tape recordings for transcripts. Post-hearing expedition includes (1) setting a deadline for the award to be returned to the parties, (2) reducing or eliminating the number of citings for the arbitrator to research, and (3) setting a maximum on the length of the award statement or establishing the maximum amount to be paid for the decision ahead of time.[55]

Other possibilities also exist for streamlining the arbitration process. For example, some grievances solely concern interpretations of the labor agreement. Unlike discipline cases, these grievances do not personally involve employee grievants and thus do not entail related therapeutic or political considerations. Perhaps these grievances could be argued on paper without the necessity of a hearing and related expenses.[56]

The use of expedited or experimental approaches illustrates two fundamental issues concerning arbitration:

1. This process, while not perfect, appears to offer great advantages over alternative methods of grievance resolution, such as sudden strike activity.
2. Union and management officials created the arbitration process and are charged with controlling it in accordance with their jointly determined needs. They must monitor the process as well as their related actions and attitudes to ensure a relatively inexpensive, efficient, and objective means of dispute resolution.

The Grievance Mediation Alternative Currently, some union and management practitioners are considering or implementing **grievance mediation** before using arbitration.[57] This alternative, while subject to many variations, typically occurs in the step before arbitration and involves a third-party neutral who hears unresolved grievances involving application of labor agreement language and attempts to help the parties resolve the grievance themselves. If a joint resolution is not forthcoming, the mediator, after meeting with the parties jointly and possibly separately, issues a nonbinding opinion on how the dispute would likely be resolved in arbitration and why. Union and management officials are then free to submit the issue to an arbitrator, usually another individual, although none of the comments and offers of compromise submitted by the parties to the mediator or the mediator's opinion can be submitted at the arbitration hearing.

Grievance mediation is not new. It was used in the 1930s and 1940s and received a great deal of publicity in the 1980s when it was used in the bituminous coal industry. Eighty-nine percent of grievances submitted to this process were resolved without the necessity of arbitration. A not-for-profit program, the Mediation Research and Education Project, was formed, and representatives of this venture have claimed that 85 percent of some 2,000 mediated grievances have been resolved without arbitration.[58] A pilot program at AT&T resulted in 49 out of 50 grievances being resolved in mediation, a success that prompted AT&T and the Communications Workers of America to have the first nationwide grievance mediation clause inserted in their labor agreement.[59]

While less than 4 percent of labor agreements recognize grievance mediation, this alternative offers some major short-term and long-term advantages for union and management officials. Its apparent major advantage, high resolution rate, is derived from other possible advantages of the process: namely, a high degree of informality in which the parties are encouraged to engage in open communication aimed at problem solving instead of focusing on winning their positions through mountains of evidence and cross-examination. Labor and management officials might further find it easy to "swallow their pride" because a mediated grievance settlement has no precedent implications for future related grievances. The mediator, who usually has had extensive arbitration experience, is often able through separate meetings with the parties to obtain sensitive information that might not otherwise be obtained in a public setting. This individual can therefore play a significant role in providing new ideas for a settlement, convincing one or both parties that a portion of their position lacks merit, and bringing out the underlying causes of a problem.

The high resolution rate and attendant advantages have generated much satisfaction among all participant categories, including grievants, who often maintain that they had an opportunity to participate in the meeting and to help bring out all of the relevant information concerning the grievance. This process is also much quicker and cheaper than arbitration, according to one study,[60] because the mediator can usually hear more grievances in a day and does not have to charge for subsequent research and study days in formulating an opinion because it is given at the end of the hearing.

Grievance mediation's advantages could very well extend beyond the immediate grievance to the overall improvement of labor-management relationships at a particular location. Authors of one related investigation suggested,

> Inevitably, grievance mediation serves as a mechanism to enable discussion of fundamental relationships, even heretofore "unspoken" issues that lie at the root of the grievance dispute in question. Thus, the problem-solving nature of mediation may facilitate the resolution of a number of grievances or related issues at one time and illuminate hidden causes of dissatisfaction that, if left to fester, could provide the spawning ground not only for new grievances but also for deterioration in the parties' basic relationship.[61]

Given grievance mediation's purported advantages, why have relatively few labor and management officials adopted it? One likely answer is that its resurgence is limited to less than ten years. Many union and management officials would like to see more enduring success stories of grievance mediation, particularly if they regard their existing grievance procedures as time-tested and effective. For example, few, if any, court cases have indicated whether this practice assists, neutralizes, or hinders the union's fair representation obligation and possible management liabilities if this obligation is breached.

There are also at least three other reasons for a cautious approach in accepting grievance mediation. First, this practice's heavily publicized success in the bituminous coal industry was in large part due to the very hostile relationships that existed before its introduction. In short, the parties may have embraced grievance mediation because it had to be better than previous dispute resolution techniques such as wildcat strikes.

Some wonder whether the addition of mediation to existing grievance procedures will add to rather than reduce expenses. Projected savings when grievances are resolved in mediation are based on the assumption that most of these unresolved grievances would have proceeded to arbitration. Yet, most grievances are not taken to arbitration; therefore, a contention could be made that grievance mediation requires more time and dollars than would be spent in the typical last step (the third or third and one-half step) before arbitration in the grievance procedure. Grievance mediation could further increase uncertainty, time, and expense if unresolved grievances are subsequently submitted to arbitration.

Some fear that the union might view grievance mediation as a "new toy" to which all grievances must be submitted.[62] Finally, there is little reason to think that grievance mediation could engender union-management cooperation if the parties were not open to this situation. Its success and use depends more on the participants' problem-solving skills and attitudes than on any intrinsic features of the process, including the mediator's advisory decision.[63]

Summary

The arbitration process was little used during the period from 1865 to World War II; however, during World War II, the National War Labor Board encouraged its widespread use. While the increased reliance upon arbitration continued after World War II, a major problem of enforcing the arbitrator's decision remained. Either party could refuse to abide by the arbitrator's decision, with uncertain consequences from the courts. This problem was initially approached in the *Lincoln Mills* decision, which provided a judicial avenue for enforcement, and the Steelworkers' Trilogy, three cases that established the superiority of the arbitration process over the courts in resolving industrial grievances. Subsequent Supreme Court decisions have indicated that termination of the labor agreement does not eliminate the possibility of arbitration, and injunctive relief might be granted when one party refuses to arbitrate according to grievance procedures established in the labor agreement.

Before the arbitration hearing, arbitrators must be selected on either an *ad hoc* or permanent basis. Each of these selection techniques has unique advantages depending on the particular circumstances. The same can be said of prehearing and post-hearing briefs. Other elements of an arbitration hearing include the grievance issue, presentation of witnesses for testimony and cross-examination, and presentation of separate and joint exhibits.

The hearing scene is a dramatic one; union and management officials display their skills in attempting to convince the arbitrator that their positions are correct. The arbitration hearing shares many similarities with a judicial trial but differs in several ways. Perhaps the most significant difference is the arbitrator's reliance on the common law of the shop.

In determining the common law of the shop, the arbitrators give particular weight to the provisions of the labor agreement, the intent of the parties, past practice, and, to a much lesser extent, prior arbitration awards in arriving at their decisions. Since arbitration procedures differ in some respects from those used in a courtroom, various jurisdictional disputes can occur regarding interpretations of contract provisions by arbitrators and the legal interpretation of federal policy. For example, a discharge case decided by the arbitrator could be subsequently considered by the Equal Employment Opportunity Commission or the National Labor Relations Board.

Some criticisms directed toward arbitration pertain to the arbitrator's capability and ethics and potential procedural problems in the arbitration process. Certain arbitral problems, such as expense, time lag, and excessive formality, may be due to labor and management preferences rather than any characteristics inherent in the arbitration process. Management and union officials have reduced some of these problems by using expedited arbitration, new arbitrators, and grievance mediation.

Key Terms

National War Labor Board
Steelworkers' Trilogy
employer promulgated arbitration
permanent arbitrator
ad hoc arbitrator
arbitration hearing
common law of the shop
parole evidence rule
intent of the parties
past practice
grievance meditation

Discussion Questions

1. How did World War II and the National War Labor Board greatly expand the use of arbitration?
2. "The Steelworkers' Trilogy greatly enhanced the arbitrator's authority when compared to previous years, yet did not give the arbitrator final jurisdiction over certain issues." Thoroughly discuss the preceding statement in terms of the specific features of these judicial decisions; also consider current jurisdictional issues arbitrators face in terms of government agencies.
3. Discuss the similarities and differences between arbitration and judicial hearings with particular emphasis on the common law of the shop, admission of evidence, and the role of the arbitrator versus that of the judge.
4. Why are arbitrators' decisions usually lengthy when one sentence could indicate who was right and wrong? Your discussion of this question should include the purposes of arbitration and advantages as well as disadvantages of an extensive arbitral decision.
5. Discuss two decision-making criteria used by arbitrators, furnishing specific examples (not mentioned in the text) of how these criteria can come into play.
6. Cite and defend three specific methods you would use to make the typical arbitration procedure more effective. Also indicate the advantages and disadvantages of your suggestions.
7. Discuss the following: "The refusal to use grievance mediation as a step in the grievance procedure illustrates the stubbornness of many union and management officials."

REFERENCES

1. For a detailed historical perspective of labor arbitration, see Dennis R. Nolan and Roger I. Abrams, "American Labor Arbitration: The Early Years," *University of Florida Law Review* (Summer 1983), pp. 373–421.

2. *United Steelworkers of America* v. *American Manufacturing Company;* 363 U.S. 566–567 (1960).

3. *United Steelworkers of America* v. *Warrior and Gulf Navigation Company,* 363 U.S. 582 (1960).

4. *United Steelworkers of America* v. *Enterprise Wheel and Car Corporation,* 363 U.S. 598 (1960).

5. "AT&T Technologies Inc. v. Communications Workers of America," *The United States Law Week,* April 8, 1986, p. 4341.

6. The case is *John Wiley and Sons* v. *Livingston* (1964), discussed in Ralph S. Berger, "The Collective Bargaining Agreement in Bankruptcy: Does the Duty to Arbitrate Survive?" *Labor Law Journal* 35 (November 1984), pp. 385–393.

7. *Nolde Brothers Inc.* v. *Local No. 358, Bakery and Confectionary Workers Union AFL-CIO,* 430 U.S. 254 (1977). See also Irving M. Geslewitz, "Case Law Development Since Nolde Brothers: When Must Post-Contract Disputes Be Arbitrated?" *Labor Law Journal* 35 (April 1984), pp. 225–238.

8. Paul F. Hodapp, "The U.S. Supreme Court Rules on Duty to Arbitrate Post-Contract Grievances," *Labor Law Journal* 42 (December 1991), pp. 827–829.

9. *The Boys Market Inc.* v. *Retail Clerk's Union, Local 770,* 398 U.S. 249, 250, 252–253 (1970). It should be noted that injunctive relief applies only when one party refuses to arbitrate issues that are subject to grievance procedures specified in the labor agreement. For additional details, see *Buffalo Forge Company* v. *United Steelworkers of America,* 428 U.S. 397 (1970).

10. Thomas J. Piskorski and David B. Ross, "Private Arbitration as the Exclusive Means of Resolving Employment-Related Disputes," *Employee Relations Law Journal* 19 (Autumn 1993), p. 206; and Loren K. Allison and Eric H. J. Stahlhut, "Arbitration and the ADA: A Budding Partnership," *Arbitration Journal* (September 1993), pp. 53–60.

11. Helen LeVan, "Decisional Model for Predicting Outcomes of Arbitrated Sexual Harassment Disputes," *Labor Law Journal* (April 1993), p. 231. See also Robert A. Shearer, "The Impact of Employment Arbitration Agreements in Sex Discrimination Claims: The Trend Toward Nonjudicial Resolution," *Employee Relations Law Journal* 18 (Winter 1992–1993), pp. 479–488; Stuart L. Bass, "Recent Court Decisions Expand Role of Arbitration in Harassment and Other Title VII Cases," *Labor Law Journal* (January 1995), pp. 39–47; Arthur Eliot Berkeley and E. Patrick McDermott, "The Second Golden Age of Employment Arbitration," *Labor Law Journal* (December 1992), pp. 772–779; Stuart H. Bompey and Michael P. Pappas, "Is There a Better Way? Compulsory Arbitration of Employment Discrimination Claims After Gilmer," *Employee Relations Law Journal* 19 (Winter 1993–1994), pp. 197–216; and Evan J. Spelfogel, "New Trends in the Arbitration of Employment Disputes," *Arbitration Journal* 48 (March 1993), pp. 6–15.

12. Jewell L. Myers, "Arbitration Update, Memorandum," April 28, 1995.

13. Jeanette A. Davy and George W. Bohlander, "Recent Findings and Practices in Grievance Arbitration Procedures," *Labor Law Journal* 43 (March 1992), p. 187.

14. Bureau of National Affairs Inc., *Basic Patterns in Union Contracts* (Washington, D.C.: Bureau of National Affairs Inc., 1992), p. 38.

15. Delbert C. Miller and William Form, *Industrial Sociology,* 2d ed. (New York: Harper & Row, 1964), p. 264.

16. Daniel F. Jennings and A. Dale Allen, Jr., "Labor Arbitration Costs and Case Loads: A Longitudinal Analysis," *Labor Law Journal* (February 1990), pp. 80–88.

17. David E. Bloom and Christopher L. Cavanagh, "An Analysis of the Selection of Arbitrators," *American Economic Review*

(June 1986), pp. 408–422; and Arthur Eliot Berkeley and Susan Rawson Zacur, "So You Want to Be an Arbitrator: Update of a Guide to the Perplexed," *Labor Law Journal* 41 (March 1990), pp. 170–174. For a thorough analysis of arbitrator's backgrounds, experiences, and preferences, see Mario F. Bognanno and Charles J. Coleman, *Labor Arbitration in America* (New York: Praeger, 1992).

18. Clarence R. Deitsch and David A. Dilts, "An Analysis of Arbitrator Characteristics and Their Effects on Decision Making in Discharge Cases," *Labor Law Journal* 40 (February 1989), pp. 112–116; Brian Bemmels, "Gender Effects in Grievance Arbitration," *Industrial Relations* 29 (Fall 1990), pp. 513–525; Stephen M. Crow and James W. Logan, "Arbitrators' Characteristics and Decision-Making Records, Gender of Arbitrators and Grievants, and the Presence of Legal Counsel as Predictors of Arbitral Outcomes," *Employee Responsibilities and Rights Journal* 7 (1994), pp. 169–185; and Kenneth W. Thornicroft, "Gender Effects in Grievance Arbitration . . . Revisited," *Labor Studies Journal* 19 (Winter 1995), pp. 35–44.

19. Clarence R. Deitsch and David A. Dilts, "Factors Affecting Pre-Arbitral Settlement of Rights Disputes: Predicting the Method of Rights Dispute Resolution," *Journal of Labor Research* 12 (Winter 1986), p. 76.

20. For a fine conceptionalization of arbitrability's dimensions and implications, see Mark M. Grossman, *The Question of Arbitrability* (Ithaca, New York: ILR Press, 1984).

21. For guidelines pertaining to an effective management or union post-hearing brief, see Douglas E. Ray, "On Writing the Post-Hearing Arbitration Brief," *Arbitration Journal* (December 1992), pp. 58–60.

22. Ronald W. Haughton, "Running the Hearing," in Arnold M. Zack, ed., *Arbitration in Practice* (Ithaca, New York: ILR Press, 1984), p. 37.

23. Jennings and Allen, "Labor Arbitration Costs."

24. See, for example, James B. Dworkin and Michael M. Harris, "Polygraph Tests: What Labor Arbitrators Need to Know," *Arbitration Journal* 41 (March 1986), pp. 23–33; Kimberly Janisch-Ramsey, "Polygraphs: The Search for Truth in Arbitration Proceedings," *Arbitration Journal* 41 (March 1986), pp. 34–41; Herman A. Theeke and Tina M. Theeke, "The Truth About Arbitrators' Treatment of Polygraph Tests," *Arbitration Journal* 42 (December 1987), pp. 23–32; and Marvin F. Hill, Jr. and Anthony Sinicropi, *Evidence in Arbitration,* 2d ed. (Washington, D.C.: Bureau of National Affairs Inc., 1987).

25. Frank Elkouri and Edna Asper Elkouri, *How Arbitration Works,* 4th ed. (Washington, D.C.: Bureau of National Affairs Inc., 1985), p. 302.

26. See, for example, Cynthia L. Gramm and Patricia A. Greenfield, "Arbitral Standards in Medical Screening Grievances," *Employee Responsibilities and Rights Journal* 3, no. 3 (1990), pp. 169–184.

27. Steven Starck, "Arbitration Decision Writing: Why Arbitrators Err," *Arbitration Journal* 38 (June 1983), pp. 30–33. See also David Elliot, "When the Hearing is Over: Writing Arbitral Awards in Plain Language," *Arbitration Journal* 46 (December 1991), p. 53.

28. Daniel F. Jennings and A. Dale Allen, Jr., "How Arbitrators View the Process of Labor Arbitration: A Longitudinal Analysis;" *Labor Law Journal* (Winter 1993), p. 44.

29. Stephen M. Crow and James Logan, "A Tentative Decision-Making Model of the Strong and Weak Forces at Labor Arbitration," *Journal of Collective Negotiations in the Public Sector* 24, no. 2 (1995), pp. 111–120.

30. The first two examples are from Allan J. Harrison, *Preparing and Presenting Your Arbitration Case: A Manual for Union and Management Representatives* (Washington, D.C.: Bureau of National Affairs Inc., 1979), pp. 23–24. The third example is suggested by Thomas R. Knight, "Arbitration and Contract Interpretation: Common

Law v. Strict Construction," *Labor Law Journal* 34 (November 1983), pp. 714–726.

31. For arbitration examples of these dimensions of past practice, see Arthur Dobbelaere, Williams H. Leahy, and Jack Reardon, "The Effect of Past Practice on the Arbitration of Labor Disputes," *Arbitration Journal* 40 (December 1985), pp. 27–43.

32. This provision on past practice was taken from Walter E. Baer, *Practice and Precedent in Labor Relations* (Lexington, Mass.: Lexington Books, 1972), p. 8.

33. Ibid, p. 38.

34. Donald J. Petersen, "No Smoking! The Arbitration of Smoking Restricting Policies," *Dispute Resolution Journal* (January 1995), pp. 45–50.

35. William H. McPherson, "Should Labor Arbitrators Play Follow the Leader?" *Arbitration Journal* 4 (1949), p. 170.

36. *Harrell Alexander, Sr* v. *Gardner-Denver Company,* 415 U.S. 60 (1974).

37. Michelle Hoyman and Lamont E. Stallworth, "The Arbitration of Discrimination Grievances in the Aftermath of Gardner-Denver," *Arbitration Journal* 39 (September 1984), p. 55; Karen Elwell and Peter Feuille, "Arbitration Awards and Gardner-Denver Lawsuits: One Bite or Two?" *Industrial Relations* 23 (Spring 1984), p. 295; Aubrey R. Fowler, Jr., "Arbitration, the Trilogy, and Industrial Rights: Developments Since *Alexander* v. *Gardner-Denver,*" *Labor Law Journal* 36 (March 1985), pp. 173–182. See also Elaine Gale Wrong, "Arbitrators' Awards in Cases Involving Discrimination," *Labor Law Journal* 39 (July 1988), pp. 411–417.

38. Equal Employment Opportunity Commission, "Notice," no. 915.002 (July 17, 1995).

39. Stephen L. Hayford, "The Coming Third Era of Labor Arbitration," *Arbitration Journal* 48 (September 1993), p. 17. See also Martha S. Weisel, "The Tension Between Statutory Rights and Binding Arbitration," *Labor Law Journal* 42 (July 1991), pp. 766–772.

40. *Spielberg Manufacturing Company,* 112 NLRB 1080 (1955).

41. *Collyer Insulated Wire and Local Union 1098, International Brotherhood of Electrical Workers,* 192 NLRB 150 (August 20, 1977).

42. Curtis L. Mack and Ira P. Bernstein, "NLRB Deferral to the Arbitration Process: The Arbitrator's Demanding Role," *Arbitration Journal* 40 (September 1985), pp. 33–43. For a related research effort, see Benjamin W. Wolkinson, "The Impact of the Collyer Policy on Deferral: An Empirical Study," *Industrial and Labor Relations Review* 38 (April 1985), pp. 377–391.

43. Pat Greenfield, "The NLRB's Deferral to Arbitration Before and After Olin: An Empirical Analysis," *Industrial and Labor Relations Review* 42, no. 1 (1988), pp. 34–49. See also "Remarks of NLRB Chairman Gould on Deferral to Arbitration," Bureau of National Affairs Inc., *Daily Labor Report,* no. 114 (June 16, 1994), pp. E-1–E-3.

44. Patricia A. Greenfield, "How Do Arbitrators Treat External Law?" *Industrial and Labor Relations Review* 45 (July 1992), p. 695.

45. "Decision of Supreme Court in *Paperworkers* v. *Misco, Inc.,*" Bureau of National Affairs Inc., *Daily Labor Report,* no. 230 (December 1, 1987), pp. D-1–D-5. See also Bernard F. Ashe, "Arbitration Finality and the Public-Policy Exception," *Dispute Resolution Journal* (September 1994), pp. 22–28, 87–89.

46. "Practitioners Assess Impact of Court Decisions Bolstering Finality of Labor Arbitration Awards," Bureau of National Affairs Inc., *Daily Labor Report,* no. 238 (December 14, 1987), p. A-1. For additional consideration of public policy intertwined with arbitration decisions in drug testing, see Lorynn A. Cone, "Public Policies Against Drug Use: *Paperworkers* v. *Misco Inc.*" *Labor Law Journal* 40 (April 1989), pp. 243–247. See also Bernard D. Meltzer, "After the Labor Arbitration Award: The Public Policy Defense" *Industrial Relations Law Journal* 10, no. 2

(1988), pp. 241–251; Robert F. Wayland, Elvis C. Stephens, and Geralyn McClure, "*Misco:* Its Impact on Arbitration Awards," *Labor Law Journal* (December 1988), pp. 813–819; and Arthur Hamilton and Peter A. Veglahn, "Public Policy Exceptions to Arbitration Awards," *Labor Law Journal* 42 (June 1991), pp. 366–370.

47. "Court Vacates Reinstatement of Employee Charged with Sexual Abuse of Customer," Bureau of National Affairs Inc., *Daily Labor Report,* no. 61 (March 29, 1991), pp. A-4–A-5. See also "Reinstatement of Sexual Harasser Overturned as Public Policy Violation," Bureau of National Affairs, Inc., *Daily Labor Report,* no. 204 (October 22, 1990), pp. A-8–A-9.

48. "Accused Sex Harasser Gains Reinstatement," Bureau of National Affairs Inc., *Daily Labor Report,* no. 70 (April 10, 1992), pp. A-1, A-2. See also Thomas J. Piskorski, "Reinstatement of the Sexual Harasser: The Conflict Between Federal Labor Law and Title VII," *Employee Relations Law Journal* 18 (Spring 1993), pp. 617–623; and Christie L. Roszkowski and Robert F. Wayland, "Arbitration Review: Is the Public Policy Against Sexual Harassment Sufficient Cause for Vacating an Arbitration Award?" *Labor Law Journal* 44 (November 1993), pp. 707–717.

49. Margaret A. Jacobs, "Men's Club: Riding Crop and Slurs: How Wall Street Dealt with a Sex Bias Case," *The Wall Street Journal,* June 9, 1994, pp. A-4, A-6; Barbara Presley Noble, "Attacking Compulsory Arbitration," *New York Times,* January 15, 1995, p. F-21; and "Reinstatement of Alleged Sexual Harassers Does Not Violate Public Policy, Forum Told," Bureau of National Affairs Inc., *Daily Labor Report,* no. 6 (January 10, 1994), pp. A-10, A-11.

50. Richard Mittenthal, "Self-Interest: Arbitration's 'Unmentionable' Consideration," *Dispute Resolution Journal* (March 1994), pp. 70–72.

51. Harry J. Dworkin, "How Arbitrators Decide Cases," *Labor Law Journal* 25 (April 1974) p. 203.

52. "Arbitrator Traces Growing Legalism as Proceedings are Modeled on Courts," Bureau of National Affairs, Inc., *Daily Labor Report,* no. 106 (June 3, 1991), p. A-6; and James Oldham, "Arbitration and Relentless Legalization in the Workplace," in Gladys W. Gruenberg, ed., *Arbitration 1990: New Perspectives on Old Issues* (Proceedings at the Forty-Third Annual Meeting, National Academy of Arbitrators) (Washington, D.C.: Bureau of National Affairs Inc., 1991), pp. 23–40.

53. Myers, "Arbitration Update."

54. Ibid.

55. Nancy Kauffman, "The Idea of Expedited Arbitration Two Decades Later," *Arbitration Journal* (September 1991), p. 35.

56. Dennis R. Nolan and Roger I. Abrams, "The Future of Labor Arbitration," *Labor Law Journal* 37 (July 1986), pp. 441–442.

57. For insights into related procedures, see Nels E. Nelson and A. N. M. Meshquat Uddin, "Arbitrators as Mediators," *Labor Law Journal* 46 (April 1995), pp. 205–213; and Sylvia Skratek, "Grievance Mediation: The Preferred Route for Resolution of Contractual Disputes" (n.p. 1988).

58. "Employees Resolve Worker Complaints Through Alternatives to Litigation," Bureau of National Affairs Inc., *Daily Labor Report,* no. 1 (January 2, 1992), pp. A-5, A-6.

59. "Experimental Grievance Mediation Clause Is Included in Labor Contracts at AT&T," Bureau of National Affairs Inc., *Daily Labor Report,* no. 119 (June 22, 1989), pp. A-1, A-2.

60. Stephen B. Goldberg and Jeanne M. Brett, "Disputants' Perspectives on the Differences Between Mediation and Arbitration," *Negotiation Journal* 6 (July 1990), p. 253.

61. Thomas J. Quinn, Mark Rosenbaum, and Donald S. McPherson, "Grievance Mediation and Grievance Negotiation Skills: Building Collaborative Relationships," *Labor Law Journal* 41 (November 1990), p. 763.

62. Sylvia Skratek, "Grievance Mediation:

How to Make the Process Work for You," *Labor Law Journal* 44 (August 1993), p. 510.

63. Peter Feuille and Deborah M. Kolb, "Waiting in the Wings: Mediation's Role in Grievance Resolution," *Negotiation Journal* 10 (July 1994), p. 256. See also Peter Feuille, "Why Does Grievance Mediation Resolve Grievances?" *Negotiation Journal* 8 (April 1992), p. 140; and Matthew T. Roberts, Roger S. Wolters, William H. Holley, Jr., and Hubert S. Feild, "Grievance Mediation: A Management Perspective," *Arbitration Journal* 45 (September 1990), p. 22.

CASES FOR PART TWO

Case 2.1 *Toll Bell Company* v. *Workers of America:* Protected Rights and Company Interference

On August 6, 1985, the collective bargaining agreement between the company and the union expired. Two days later, the union called a strike at the company's facilities, including those at 3303 Weslaylan, St. Louis, Missouri. The strike ended on August 28 with the signing of a new three-year agreement. The following day, employees began returning to work. During the strike, a substantial number of bargaining-unit employees at 3303 Weslaylan continued to work at the company's facility behind the union's picket line.

On September 2, the union distributed materials to its stewards for posting on its bulletin boards at the company's facilities, including the following commentary by Jack London:

Definition of a Scab

> After God had finished the rattlesnake, the toad, and the vampire, he had some awful substance left with which he made a SCAB. A SCAB is a two-legged animal with a corkscrew soul, a water-logged brain, and a combination backbone of jelly and glue. Where others have hearts, he carries a tumor of rotten principles.
>
> When a SCAB comes down the street men turn their backs and angels weep in Heaven, and the devil shuts the gates of Hell to keep him out. No man has the right to SCAB, so long as there is a pool of water deep enough to drown his body in or a rope long enough to hang his carcass with. Judas Iscariot was a gentleman . . . compared with a SCAB; for betraying his master, he had the character to hang himself—a SCAB hasn't. Esau sold his birthright for a mess of pottage. Judas Iscariot sold his Savior for thirty pieces of silver. Benedict Arnold sold his country for a promise of a commission in the British Army. The modern strikebreaker sells his birthright, his country, his wife, his children, and his fellow man for an unfulfilled promise from his employer, trust or corporation.
>
> Esau was a traitor to himself. Judas Iscariot was a traitor to his God. Benedict Arnold was a traitor to his country. A strikebreaker is a traitor to himself, a traitor to his God, a traitor to his country, a traitor to his family, and a traitor to his class.
>
> THERE
IS
NOTHING
LOWER
THAN
A
SCAB . . .

Union steward Cora Able immediately posted "Definition of a Scab" along with another article, entitled "From Bessie's Desk," praising the strikers and criticizing those who remained on the job, on a union bulletin board in the computer terminal room, adjacent to Room 1002 at the company's 3303 Weslaylan facility. A chief steward, employee Anita Cain, had left the articles for Able with a note requesting that she post them.

Able has been responsible for posting material on the union bulletin board in the computer terminal room since she became the union job steward in 1982. Able had previously posted campaign literature of candidates for union office, notices of union meetings, and articles from union newsletters on this bulletin board. She had also removed comic strips from the bulletin board. Prior to September 2, no company supervisor had ever told Able what she could or could not post on the union's bulletin board. Nor had any company supervisor ever removed anything from this board prior to September 2.

The company had no rules concerning the posting of literature on the union's bulletin boards on the company's premises. The company's supervisors reflected the absence of any such rules. The collective bargaining agreements in effect since 1980, covering the company's employees, contain no provisions regarding the union's bulletin boards at the company's facilities.

During the afternoon of September 2, company supervisor Joe Bay saw several employees near the bulletin board, apparently reading the posted articles. He removed the "Definition of a Scab" and deposited it in a garbage can. Able noticed the article had been removed and asked Bay where it was. Bay told her he had removed it, balled it up, and thrown it into the garbage can.

Able took the sheet from the can, then got another copy from her desk and hung it on the board. Bay promptly snatched this copy down, telling Able, "This mess [isn't] going to hang up here." He then specifically prohibited her from posting another copy and warned her of disciplinary action if she did so. Able called chief steward Miller, who spoke to Bay and requested that he leave the literature on the bulletin board. Bay told Miller that the "Definition of a Scab" had no business on the board and was causing animosity among the clerks.

A half hour later, supervisor Linda Trevino informed Able that a second-line supervisor, Ralph Coe, wanted to see her. Coe had a copy of "Definition of a Scab" in his hand as he told Able, "We're not going to have this mess hanging in this office." In the presence of Trevino and Bay, Coe also warned Able that Bay could discipline her "for insubordination." Able asked to be excused and upon returning to her desk called Miller again.

Fifteen minutes later, Trevino told Able, "We would like to see you for five minutes." Able told Trevino that she did not want to go back to Coe's office. However, she complied upon Trevino's assurance that the return to Coe's office would take only five minutes, long enough to receive an apology. Coe then asked Able to tell her side of the incident. Coe apologized, as did Bay, for the way Bay had treated Able in front of the employees. Coe did not retract his support for Bay's action in removing the article and preventing its reposting.

On September 1, union job steward Milton Musk posted a copy of "Definition of a Scab" on a union bulletin board located in a break room next to Rooms 208 and 209, the Switching Control Center, at the company's 3303 Weslaylan facility. Musk had been responsible for posting material on this bulletin board from 1980 through November 1983. As a matter of practice, Musk had posted on the board notice of union meetings, listings of job vacancies provided to the union, lists of union officers' names, announcements for an employee charitable organization, and the campaign material of candidates for union office. Occasionally, Musk removed from the board cartoons that had been posted by employees. Prior to September 1, no supervisor had ever told Musk what he could or could not post on the union bulletin board.

"Definition of a Scab" remained on the union bulletin board in the Switching Control Center break room until about 4 P.M., September 1. About that time, company supervisor Wesley Vie directed Musk to remove "Definition of a Scab." Musk said he did not wish to do so. Vie removed it as Musk watched.

The following day, before 7 A.M., "Definition of a Scab" again appeared on the bulletin board. Company supervisor Tom Davis summoned Musk to his office at approximately 8 A.M. and told him to take down the "Definition of a Scab" from the union's bulletin board. Musk protested that he did not put it up and he should not have to take it down. Davis then warned that he would suspend Musk if he persisted in his refusal. Davis asked for Musk's building pass and key, whereupon Musk requested permission to make a telephone call. After consulting a union district steward, Musk removed the "Definition of a Scab." Musk again told Davis it was unfair that he had to remove the article when he had not posted it. Davis told Musk that he "didn't want trash like that posted."

The union contended that the company violated Section 8(a)(1) of the NLRA by removing "Definition of a Scab" from union bulletin boards and by threatening employees with punishment if they posted or reposted London's commentary to those bulletin boards. The company denied that it violated the NLRA on the ground that the posting of Jack London's pejorative appraisal of nonstriking employees had disrupted the discipline of its employees and thus was beyond the protection of Sections 7 and 8(a)(1) of the act.[1]

Questions

1. How does a union gain the right to the use of a bulletin board on company premises?
2. Why was the union so insistent on having the "Definition of a Scab" posted on the bulletin board?
3. Since the union already exists and already has an agreement, how does Section (8)(a)(1) apply to this case?
4. Could this case go to arbitration? Why? Why not?
5. You be the NLRB administrative law judge. How would you rule? Why?

References

Container Corporation of America, 244 NLRB 318 (1979).

Nugent Service, Inc., 207 NLRB 158 (1973).

Southwestern Bell Telephone Co., 200 NLRB 667 (1972).

Republic Aviation Corp. v. *NLRB*, 324 US 793 (1945).

Old Dominion Branch No. 496 National Association of Letter Carriers v. *Austin*, 418 US 264 (1974).

Cambria Clay Products Co., 106 NLRB 267 (1953).

[1]Section 7 of the NLRA provides in part, "Employees shall have the right to self-organization, to form, join, or assist labor organizations, to bargain collectively through representatives of their own choosing, and to engage in other concerted activities for the purpose of collective bargaining or other mutual aid or protection."

Section 8(a)(1) of the NLRA provides in pertinent part, "It shall be an unfair labor practice for an employer . . . to interfere with, restrain, or coerce employees in the exercise of the rights guaranteed in Section 7."

Case 2.2 Reason for Discharge: Work Incidents or a Protected Concerted Activity?

Retiree Care operates a nursing home in Urbana, Arizona, where it employed Julia Gold, Cynthia Cord, and Ruby Weld as licensed practical nurses (LPNs).

Jay Mills, the human resource manager, visited the Urbana facility on three different occasions in response to the three nurses' concerns about tension and unrest at the facility. On January 16, 1989, he met with the department heads in a group discussion. At this meeting he asked each person to write the names of anyone associated with the tension and unrest at the facility. He explained that he had recently become aware of this situation through his talks with Jane Stable and regional manager Sue Neverall. Mills found that Cord's and Weld's names appeared on every slip and Gold's name appeared on many. A few other employees were named, but not as often as any of these three.

Two days later, Mills met with the employees in each department. He listened to their complaints and concerns. Mills determined that the concerns raised by the three nurses were shared by many others, and that some of their complaints were valid. Mills cautioned, however, that the employees were supposed to support decisions made by management, and he felt that all the nurses agreed with him on this point.

On March 2, Mills traveled to the Urbana facility for the final time to meet with all the nurses to inform them of the results of his investigation. He met privately with Gold, Cord, and Weld before the general meeting to tell them of his decisions. During the meeting with all the nurses, there was some "heated conversation" among the nurses about the appropriateness of the policies at the facility and about how things should be done. Mills observed "resistive behavior" on the part of Gold, Cord, and Weld to his comments. In particular, he observed that they rolled their eyes and sat with their arms crossed. Mills believed that the three nurses demonstrated an unwillingness to change their mode of operation and attitude for the cooperative good of the facility. Based on his observations and perceptions of the three nurses at the meeting, Mills made the decision to terminate them. He consulted with Neverall and two others, who agreed with him that the discharges were appropriate. On March 14, Stable told Cord and Weld that either they had to resign or they would be fired. Both refused to resign and were fired. On March 16, Gold was given the same option. Gold resigned. All three were told that the "resign-or-be-fired" ultimatum was because of their "attitude" and their opinions toward management.

Afterwards, the three nurses filed unfair labor practice charges with the NLRB, and the NLRB conducted an investigation. Additional information was discovered.

1. By February 27, 1989, Cord had received three written warnings and Weld had received four. Another nurse, Connie Thatch, had received two written warnings on February 23, 1989, and four written warnings on March 10, 1989.
2. Nurses Cord and Thatch had received a notice of "verbal warning" for mistakes made in their January 1989 treatment records. Weld had received a more serious "written warning" for the same offense. All the warnings were dated February 15, 1989.
3. The employer previously had employed a patient-assessment nurse who had corrected errors in the nurses' treatment

records. On February 1, 1989, the employer was notified by the State of Arizona that its records for the months of November, December, and January were to be audited the next day. Members of management attempted to review the records and make the necessary corrections. They corrected the A wing records but did not have time to correct the B wing records. They found numerous errors committed by many nurses in the A wing, but only nurses Cord, Thatch, and Weld were disciplined.

4. The company conducts training services for its nurses called "in-services." For some in-services, attendance is mandatory. On February 16, 1989, the employer conducted a mandatory in-service on documentation. Although many nurses missed the meeting, only Cord and Weld received written disciplinary notices for missing the meeting.
5. On March 9, 1989, the employer's director of nursing instituted a new system for the assignment of aides. Thatch had some difficulty that night in following the new instructions, and it led to some problems among her aides the next day. On March 10, 1989, Thatch received one of her warnings.
6. The employer maintained a policy that two absences in one month or six absences in one year are excessive and will result in progressive discipline. The policy had been routinely ignored, but sometime in late 1988 or early 1989 the policy was reimposed. To arrive at the number of absences necessary to discipline Cord, management included an absence for funeral leave, a specified employee benefit. Weld was issued two warnings, both of which included the same absence. Weld had volunteered to work on Friday, February 3, 1989, which was not her regular work day. Administrator Stable was to inform her in advance who she was replacing. Stable did not do so, nor did the February schedule contain Weld's name for that Friday. Weld left Stable a note that morning confirming that she assumed she was not to work because she had not heard back from Stable and her name was not on the schedule. Stable proceeded to brand Weld a "no call/no show" and disciplined her for an unexcused absence as well as for two occurrences in a month.

The approach taken by the NLRB in deciding this case was covered in the *Wright Line* decision, 251 NLRB 1083 (1980), enfd. 662 F.2d 899 (1st Cir. 1981), cert. denied 455 U.S. 989 (1982). The NLRB set forth its causation test for cases alleging violations of the act that turn on employer motivation. The General Counsel must submit evidence sufficient to support the inference that protected conduct was a "motivating factor" in the employer's decision. In rebutting the General Counsel's case, the employer cannot simply present a legitimate reason for its action but must also persuade by a preponderance of the evidence that the same action would have taken place even in the absence of the protected conduct.

Questions

1. Evaluate the fairness of the NLRB procedures as outlined in the *Wright Line* decision.
2. What action, if any, taken by the nurses is a protected concerted activity?
3. Separate from the alleged protected concerted activity, does the employer have sufficient grounds for terminating the three nurses?
4. You be the judge. How do you rule? Give your reasoning.

Case 2.3 In-Plant Work Stoppage: Protected Activity

After clocking into work on February 13, 1989, a group of employees at MoJo Motors Corporation assembled in the employee break room located just off the production floor and refused to work until MoJo management agreed to a wage increase. This work stoppage lasted until management seriously pledged to consider the employees' demand and to get back to them in short order. Management did so a few days later in a letter distributed and read to all MoJo employees explaining that foreign competition and rising costs prevented it from granting a pay raise at that time.

Dissatisfied with this response, 22 production employees engaged in another work stoppage on February 20, 1989, clocking in at 6:00 A.M. and again assembling in the employee break room. This time the standstill lasted several hours, during which the employees repeated their demand for higher wages while management repeated its position that costs and competition prevented any increase. This went on for over five hours until Donald Bodine, the director of manufacturing, told the employees at 11:10 A.M., "either you go to work or you will be terminated."

When that admonition failed, 20 minutes later Bodine gave the employees one last warning: "This is my final request. If you do not go back to work, you will be terminated for refusing to work. If you don't go back to work or don't leave, I will call the police." The employees refused to budge so Bodine called the police, who arrived a few minutes later and informed the employees that they were subject to arrest for trespassing. This did the trick and the employees left without incident. A few days later, several of them asked for their jobs back, but management declined their request.

The employees filed a charge against MoJo alleging that it had committed an unfair labor practice under Section 8 of the National Labor Relations Act by discharging workers for engaging in concerted activity protected under Section 7 of the act. The employer argued that at some point, it is entitled to assert its private rights and demand its premises back. Both parties acknowledged that the line between a protected work stoppage and an illegal trespass is not clear-cut.

The union stated that all employees were peaceful, did not interfere with other employees' use of the break room, entered the plant when their shift began, and left before it ended. MoJo argued that it did not engage in an unfair labor practice that triggered the work stoppage, did not act precipitously in firing the workers, and that the employees adamantly refused to leave the plant even after five hours of negotiations. MoJo argued that the work stoppage may have been a protected concerted activity at its inception, but the employees' insistence on remaining in the plant for such an extended period of time transformed it into an illegal trespass. The employees had no compelling reason to continue protesting in the plant, rather than outside the plant where economic strikes traditionally occur.

The union argued that the employees were engaged in protected concerted activity and questioned as an initial matter MoJo's proffered motivation (trespass) for firing the employees. The union claimed that the protected activity was a "motivating factor" in the employer's decision to discharge the employees. There is no evidence that it would have taken the same action in the absence of the prohibited motivation.

The NLRB must now address whether MoJo fired the striking employees for refusing to take the strike outside the plant or for refusing to work.

Questions

1. What are examples of protected concerted activities under Section 7 of the NLRA? Are there legal limits to these activities?
2. Is this a case in which the NLRB applies the *Wright Line*, 251 NLRB 1083 (1980), 105 LRRM 1169 (1980) principle? See Case 2.2.
3. Were the employees engaged in a protected concerted activity?
4. Was there sufficient evidence for MoJo to terminate these employees?
5. How would you rule? Give your reasoning.

Case 2.4 Bargaining in Good Faith and Employer Lockouts

Issue

Is the company bargaining in good faith or committing an unfair labor practice by locking out employees?

Moline is a wholly owned subsidiary of Onra. Moline's production and maintenance employees have been represented by the union for over 20 years. During this period the parties have entered into eight collective bargaining agreements. During these past eight labor negotiations, the union has not called a strike, and the company has not implemented a lockout. The last collective bargaining agreement between the parties was signed on January 31, 1990, and was due to expire on October 28, 1993.

The parties began negotiations for a new agreement on June 17, 1993. Fernando Espinosa, Moline's director of human resources, was the spokesperson for the company. Ray Godbout, Onra's vice-president of human resources, and Fred Lange, Moline's general manager, appeared and spoke at various meetings. Human Resources Manager Elba Delgado drafted the minutes for most meetings. Arturo Figueroa was the spokesperson for the union. Twenty-two sessions were scheduled from June 17, 1993, to October 27, 1993. Four were canceled. The parties had 18 labor negotiations sessions.

At the first meeting, Fred Lange explained the changes that had occurred in the corporate structure of Moline. Lange informed the union that Moline had become part of more than 60 companies that belong to what is known as Onra Grain Processing Company. Lange informed the union that henceforth Moline was going to be evaluated in a different way than how it had been in the past; it was going to be compared against the other 60 Onra companies and not against other unrelated companies. Lange spoke about the need for Moline to become competitive and how it was essential for the union to understand this. Lange added that Moline had to make significant changes to be successful in the future. He told the union representatives that if Moline did not take immediate measures, the company might cease to exist. Lange informed the union that Moline's business was at a critical point and that it was losing sales and market share. To substantiate his position, Lange presented a graph showing that Moline had lost 20 percent of its market share in the flour business and had recently lost its largest customer and its largest distributor. Lange further suggested that Moline was considering shipping the flour directly from other plants, rather than milling there. Regarding the animal feed business, Lange explained that it also had lost considerable market share and sales volume in the recent months. Lange went on to present a competitive analysis of several local companies.

After that part of the presentation, Lange explained the negative effects on Moline of other matters. He spoke about potential changes to the federal tax exemptions under Section 936 of the Internal Revenue Code and their potential negative impact on the company. He also spoke about the effects of NAFTA on Moline's business and about how state taxes might adversely affect the business. Lange finished his presentation by telling the union that Moline could not continue in business if it was not competitive, and that companies that are not competitive cannot survive.

At the end of this first meeting, Espinosa stated the following: "Faced with our company's difficult situation, we are going to present our proposal." Moline then gave the union its complete proposal for a new collective bargaining agreement. The proposal called for a reduction of wages and benefits from an hourly average of $17.84 to $11.11.

At the second meeting, on June 22, 1993, the union reacted to Moline's first proposal by stating that it believed Moline was bargaining in bad faith by presenting a regressive proposal that was considered disrespectful and below that of its competitors. The union contended, for example, that Moline's proposal included a provision that the Christmas bonus be reduced from 8.5 percent to 2 percent. The union then handed its proposal to Moline. Moline's management reiterated that its proposal reflected the need to become competitive and stated that if the company is not competitive, it could not survive. The union replied that if Moline insisted on such a radical proposal, it would take it to the employees. Moline insisted on the need to become competitive; Moline's spokesperson responded:

> The situation is a serious one and fragile. Because of that we wanted to emphasize more volume and sales losses. The company is affected in the measure of a loss in sales volume and increases in our costs. If you do not fill expectations, since you are a very, very small part of Onra's operations, why should Onra care about the operation? If it does not matter to the membership that a lock be placed on it. . . . We are trying to make the organization competitive so that it can survive with that competition that operates with a lot less employees and low operational costs.

The parties then began discussing those sections of Moline's proposal about which they agreed.

At the third meeting, on June 24, 1993, the parties continued discussing Moline's proposal; the union agreed on some provisions but disagreed on most. At the twelfth meeting, on August 24, 1993, Moline negotiators discussed, among other matters, a management proposal to eliminate providing employees with a bar of soap. Union committee members laughed; Espinosa stated, "Things like this are what make us not be competitive and can make us have to close shop because we cannot compete."

The fourteenth meeting was canceled; at the fifteenth meeting, on September 14, 1993, the parties bargained over economic matters. Moline submitted a graph comparing hourly costs of Moline to other companies (this was the same graph that Lange had originally presented at the first meeting)—the graph showed an asserted competitive weakness. Moline negotiators read aloud each economic section from the proposed agreement, all calling for decreases, but the union would not agree to any of them. Espinosa once again spoke of competitiveness and the need to reach a level of $10 per hour in labor costs. He asked the union for suggestions on how to reach such a figure. The union reiterated that there was no possibility of reaching a level of $10 or $11 an hour in labor costs. Espinosa stated that the union's proposal would add costs rather than decrease them—the union's proposal increased the labor costs from the present $17.84 hourly rate to $20. He added that the union's proposal would be considered only if it helped reach Moline's goals of decreasing costs and becoming more competitive.

The union requested Moline's financial statements for the past five years. Espinosa stated that Moline's proposal was based on competitiveness and its financial situation. He requested that the union make its financial disclosure demand in writing, including the reasons for its request. The union stated that it wanted the audited financial statements and a list of Moline's clients. Figueroa asked three times whether Moline was not alleging inability to pay. Espinosa evaded the question by not providing a straight yes or no answer but responded that the issue was not inability to pay but rather competitiveness in the market. The union formally requested the financial statement in a letter dated September 20, 1993.

At the sixteenth meeting, on September 21, 1993, Moline distributed a document entitled "Company's Last Position with Respect to Noneconomic Issues as of September 21, 1993."

Espinosa stated that this document included some changes from its previous position, such as leaving the grievance and arbitration procedure as it was in the previous contract (not accepting the union's proposed modification), changing the duration of the contract from five to four years, and modifying the union's proposal for Article X, Section 5 (temporary employees). Espinosa claimed that Moline could not accept the union's economic proposals because of their increased costs. Moline representatives then submitted a new economic proposal, the only modification from the original proposal. In its original proposal, Moline had proposed only 3 job classifications—skilled, semiskilled, and unskilled—while in this new proposal it proposed 5 by adding "specialized" and "semi-specialized." The existing collective bargaining agreement had 55 classifications. Additionally, Moline offered to pay a lump sum of $1,000 per employee at the end of the first six months of the new contract. The union stated it disagreed with Moline's proposal and that it would make a counteroffer at the next meeting to Moline's economic and noneconomic proposals.

Moline answered the union's written request for financial data in a letter dated September 20, 1993. Moline refused to provide the requested data and advised the union to specify reasons for requesting the information and its relevancy to the negotiations. Moline further stated that while the union was depicting Moline's posture as inability to pay, Moline was still claiming competitiveness and a need to reduce labor costs.

At the seventeenth meeting, on September 28, 1993, the parties discussed the issue of subcontracting work. The union then complained that Moline was posting armed personnel at the plant. Figueroa complained that Moline had offered a final proposal on September 21, 1993, very early in the negotiations and said that the union could have done the same, yet it did not. He said the company was preparing for a strike and that the union could be. However, Figueroa mentioned that, if there is a strike, everyone would lose—the employees and the company.

Espinosa responded that Moline did not want a strike. He stated that they only wanted to "close the agreement on October 28, 1993," and that even though their intention was not to provoke a strike, they had to be prepared for the possibility. The union then submitted its counteroffer. Espinosa requested more time to analyze the union's proposal.

At the eighteenth meeting, on October 5, 1993, Espinosa stated that the union's proposal had been considered, but it did not take into account Moline's competitiveness. Instead, it increased rather than decreased costs. Management distributed its counterproposal to union representatives and maintained its previous position regarding all issues, except the medical plan. The union rejected Moline's health proposal. Espinosa countered that the company would not move further from its proposal because the union was not giving consideration to Moline's competitiveness. Figueroa stated that the union was not willing to accept a decrease in wages and benefits. Espinosa stated that the parties were miles apart and proposed engaging a mediator. Figueroa responded that it was too soon to get a mediator because the parties were still too far apart.

Management restated that to be competitive it had to lower labor costs. The union renewed its request for the audited financial statements for the past five years. Moline replied that it was considering furnishing the information but was waiting for the union's written reasons for its requests. Both parties requested counteroffers.

At the nineteenth meeting, October 12, 1993, Figueroa stated that the union was waiting for a response to its last offer; Espinosa responded that Moline had previously presented its last offer and maintained its previous position.

At the twentieth meeting, on October 19, 1993, the union presented a new counteroffer, which Moline rejected, claiming that it still called for increased costs and ignored Moline's competitive objective. Management reiterated that it maintained its position from its last offer, and made no new offer. The union announced that it would make yet another counteroffer. Moline stated that it would not make any more counteroffers to the union's demands unless they reduced costs. The union stated it would not make further movements from its last offer, but asked Moline to make counteroffers. The union again requested Moline to furnish the financial information it had petitioned for and asked for sales information, contracts, and information regarding the salaries and benefits of supervisors, managers, and salespeople. The union explained that, once Moline furnished the requested financial information, the union would be able to consider a reduction in salaries and benefits. Espinosa told the union that the company was not claiming inability to pay but was rather claiming competitive disadvantages. Espinosa stated that management was waiting for the union's letter explaining why this information was relevant. The union requested that Moline reply to its last two proposals.

On October 21, 1993, the union once again requested financial information in a letter addressed to Lange. The company answered by letter dated October 25, 1993. In the letter the company formally refused to provide the data because the union had failed to provide reasons for requesting the information and because Moline was not claiming inability to pay.

At the twenty-first meeting, on October 26, 1993, Godbout spoke for Moline. He stated that Moline had prospered and done very well, but that the company had realized that its labor costs were far above the competition. He stated that Moline was losing money in its food business, but, as a company it was still making money. Furthermore, he contended that Moline's future was at risk because it had the highest production costs in the area, and that Moline had to reduce the number of employees in order to remain competitive. Godbout stated that the issue was not the amount of profits made but the concern of Moline to remain competitive. He stated that a reduction in volume of business had been noticed and it was attributed to aggressive competition. Consequently, sales had decreased.

The union then requested all sales information for the past three years. The union asked Godbout whether he or another company official had studied the present and projected contracts of its competitors. Godbout admitted he had not studied them but had only looked at the differences in labor costs. The union stated it believed Moline could continue being competitive, and that it would like to continue negotiating. Godbout stated he would speak to those at the corporate level, including General Manager Lange, to see if Moline would reevaluate its position and to see how far it could go. The union informed Moline that, if the parties did not reach an agreement the following day at their scheduled meeting, the union would go to a federal mediator to intervene in the negotiation.

On October 27, 1993, the union's committee arrived at Moline's offices at 6:00 P.M. While they waited for Moline's committee, a maintenance employee announced a bomb threat. The union's committee left the building and waited outside. Upon observing that Moline's committee had not abandoned the building, they returned. They met with Espinosa, Godbout, and Delgado, the human resources manager. Espinosa handed the union committee a document and stated that it was Moline's final offer and that nothing else was left to negotiate. This proposal was identical to what Moline had offered on October 5, 1993. He also delivered to the union committee a letter stating that he believed the parties had reached an impasse, and negotiations were not progressing because the union continued to insist on wage and benefit increases. The letter gave notice to the union that Moline would close down operations that evening, October 27, 1993, but employees would be paid as if they had worked their regular schedules. The letter stated that Moline would then continue operating under the previous collective bargaining agreement on the first shift on the following Monday, November 1, 1993, at which time it would implement its final offer. Finally, the letter stated that employees should show up for their regular schedules on

November 1, 1993. Espinosa said the discussion was over, and the company committee left.

On October 28, 1993, Figueroa wrote to Espinosa requesting further bargaining negotiations, pleading to Moline not to implement unilateral changes and suggesting that they meet on November 1, 1993. Espinosa responded by letter dated October 28, 1993. He stated: "The time for negotiating is over," and declined the union's invitation to meet. On October 29, 1993, the union submitted a new proposal by letter making a substantial cutback from its previous demands and further stating that they "had even more flexibility in their proposals." Moline did not reply to this new proposal until November 23, 1993, at a bargaining meeting between the parties, where it once again stated that Moline was willing only to bargain down from the terms of the collective bargaining agreement.

On October 29, 1993, Espinosa had written to Figueroa stating that Moline would reduce its labor force, and that it would do so on November 1, 1993, by laying off 40 employees. At a subsequent meeting, on November 23, 1993, Godbout informed the union that regardless of when the collective bargaining agreement would be signed, Moline had already decided to reduce the work force to 85 employees. On November 1, 1993, when the morning-shift employees showed up to work, Delgado delivered to employees a memorandum signed by Espinosa stating that Moline had determined not to authorize employees to work until an agreement was signed by the parties.

During the week of October 27, 1993, management had called Moline's corporate offices in Nebraska and asked that employees from other Onra facilities in the state be sent to work at the Moline facility to replace locked out employees. These employees began to arrive on October 30 and 31, 1993. After November 1, 1993, Moline continued its operations with the replacement employees. Moline paid replacement employees from other Onra facilities wages and benefits *above* those offered in the negotiations as of October 27, 1993, and over and above the wage scales under the collective bargaining agreement. Immediately after November 1, 1993, Moline started hiring replacements from the local area by offering them wages and benefits *lower* than what it had offered the union as of October 27, 1993. Moline continued its operations with these replacements.

After November 1, 1993, mediator Elizabeth Guzman called the parties to coordinate a joint meeting. On November 12, 1993, Moline agreed to meet with the mediator and the union on November 23, 1993. On November 23, 1993, the mediator held separate meetings with the union and with Moline. At the later meeting, Godbout, the spokesperson for Moline, informed the mediator that the company had locked out the employees because of alleged security reasons and to apply pressure on the union to accept its final proposal. Moline did not come up with new offers and reiterated that it maintained its last offer. She informed Moline that the union was still requesting the financial and sales information that had been requested prior to the lockout. Godbout replied that all the financial information that Moline was going to provide to the union had been orally given by Lange at the first meeting.

By letter dated November 24, 1993, Moline announced to all unit employees that they would no longer be covered by the medical plan. In a letter dated November 24, 1993, the union requested the company's comparative studies of wages and benefits, financial statements, contracts with competitors, wage surveys at competitors, sales to competitors for the last five years, projected sales, margin of profits of other Onra Group companies, operational costs and comparison with competitors, information on the pension plan, all collective bargaining agreements of Onra, and copies of payrolls for employees working at Moline.

Moline replied by letter dated December 29, 1993. It once again refused to provide the requested financial information. The company asserted that it had never alleged inability to pay, that the union had no right to that information, and that it had no contracts with its competitors to supply to its clients. However, it did provide the wage surveys it had on its competitors and sales information for the past three years (it requested that the union explain why it needed sales information for an additional two years). Moline refused to provide information for other companies in the Onra Group, but provided a copy of their pension plans and a list of respective wages and job classifications of temporary replacement employees presently working at Moline but refused to provide the names of the temporary replacement employees.

On December 16, the union reiterated its request that the parties continue negotiations. Moline responded by letter to the mediator that the parties continued to be at an impasse and that it should be informed if any "significant change" occurred in the position of the union. The union in turn responded by letter dated December 29, 1993, that there had never been an impasse and that Moline had created a fictitious impasse in order to refuse to bargain. The union continued to request the information previously sought.

The union then filed an unfair labor practice charge with the National Labor Relations Board.

Questions

1. What are the legal considerations in this case?
2. Evaluate the company's request on October 5, 1993, to bring in a mediator.
3. Distinguish between the company's contention that it was not claiming inability to pay but was claiming competitive disadvantages. Why is this distinction important?
4. What are the rules governing the union's right to information in a bargaining setting?
5. On what legal basis can the company implement its final offer?
6. What are the consequences to the company if it is determined that the company had refused to bargain in good faith and had illegally locked out its employees?
7. Evaluate the action of the company on November 1, 1993. Was its action legal? Explain.

Case 2.5 Unilateral Action: Refusal to Bargain

On April 1, 1987, WXYZ, Inc., a television station, declared an impasse in its negotiations with the union and unilaterally implemented its last offer. On April 9, 1987, WXYZ provided the union with the new terms and conditions of employment it had put into effect. One of those terms, the mileage reimbursement rate paid to employees who use their own automobiles, had been 20 cents per mile under the most recent contract with the union, which ran from June 25, 1983, through June 24, 1986.

On January 1, 1987, however, the company had unilaterally increased the rate to 21 cents per mile. In October 1987, WXYZ further increased the rate to 22.5 cents per mile. On December 8, 1988, WXYZ notified its employees that, effective January 1, 1989, the rate would increase to 24 cents per mile. The company did not notify the union of any of these changes. The union was unaware that the company had made these changes until shortly before Christmas of 1988, when union representative O'Mara, by chance, noticed an interoffice memorandum to employees. The memorandum stated that as of January 1, 1989, the reimbursement rate would change from 22.5 cents per mile to 24 cents per mile.

On learning of this change, the union did not request to bargain with the company over this issue. O'Mara stated that there were several reasons he did not contact any WXYZ officials. First, the company was not honoring the grievance-arbitration procedure provided for in the previous contract. Second, O'Mara was recently told by WXYZ officials that it was going to do what it wanted and that "no union was going to tell them what to do." Third, he had attempted unsuccessfully to meet with WXYZ's general manager in later November or early December to discuss other issues. O'Mara said that this attempt involved a call to the general manager's office in which he was "rebuffed" by a secretary. Further, the general manager never returned his call. O'Mara also noted that in December 1988 relations between the union and the company were in limbo and there were no negotiations going on, as the parties were awaiting the NLRB's decision in a previous case. Finally, O'Mara said that it was close to the holidays and he was in guild training when he learned of this change. He therefore decided to wait until after the holidays before investigating the matter and consulting with the union's attorneys and other union officials.

The union claimed that the increase in the mileage reimbursement rate constituted a unilateral change in a material term and condition of employment. The union had not waived its right to bargain over this issue. The union concluded that the company violated Section 8(a)(5) and (1) of the NLRA by unilaterally changing the mileage reimbursement rate.

WXYZ responded that the record fails to establish that a request to bargain would have been futile. The reasons O'Mara gave are not sufficient to excuse the union from its obligation to request bargaining over the change. O'Mara's first reason, that the company was refusing to honor the grievance-arbitration procedure, does not preclude the union from making a request to bargain nor does it indicate whether the company would agree or refuse to bargain over this issue. The company's adherence to the grievance-arbitration procedure was not necessary to set the mileage reimbursement rate. This issue concerns establishing a term and condition of employment, not interpreting a contract.

O'Mara's second reason was that WXYZ's officials told him that they would do what they wanted and that "no union was going to tell them what to do." The company noted that O'Mara had stated these were simply comments made in general conversations. Thus, these statements were not made in response to specific requests for bargaining nor did O'Mara attribute them to a specific individual or to a specific time or place. Under these circumstances, these statements are not tantamount to a refusal to bargain. At most, these statements indicate an unwillingness to allow the union to run WXYZ's business. They do not compel the conclusion that the company would refuse to discuss the mileage reimbursement issue with the union.

The company also responded that O'Mara's fourth reason, that relations with WXYZ were in limbo pending the outcome of the NLRB's decision in the previous case, does not excuse the union from its obligation to request bargaining. The company had not withdrawn recognition of the union, and its actions in the case did not justify the union in assuming that it would refuse to bargain over future issues such as the mileage reimbursement rate.

O'Mara's last reason for not requesting bargaining was that he was in guild training and it was close to the holidays. The company responded that this has no bearing on the company's willingness to bargain. The union cannot excuse itself from its duties merely because they occur at an inconvenient time.

Questions

1. Is it legal for the company to implement its last offer unilaterally after the contract has expired and the negotiations have reached an impasse? Give your reasoning.
2. By the time O'Mara discovered the change in the mileage reimbursement rate, was it reasonable for him to assume that the change was final, not subject to negotiation?
3. If the NLRB were to decide that the company violated the NLRA, what would be an appropriate remedy, now that employees are already receiving the higher mileage rate?
4. Why would the union want to bargain over an issue, such as an increase in the mileage rate, that is an obvious benefit to all bargaining-unit employees?
5. Now, you decide the case. Give your reasoning.

PART THREE

Part 3 examines the variety of work rules that represent the outcomes of the labor relations process. Employee discipline is a significant factor establishing work rules as well as the basis for much arbitration. Next, institutional issues pertaining to the rights and responsibilities of unions and management, including their responsibilities to minorities and women, are explored. A discussion of many administrative and economic issues that are resolved through collective bargaining concludes this part.

THE OUTCOMES OF THE LABOR RELATIONS PROCESS: COLLECTIVE BARGAINING ISSUES

EMPLOYEE DISCIPLINE 10

We devote an entire chapter to employee discipline, an important union-management issue, because

- *It is the most frequently heard grievance in arbitration—it comprises approximately 50 percent of the decided cases.*
- *It is approached consistently by arbitrators, who typically rely on established principles to make their determinations.*[1]
- *It is the most likely to involve readers of this book, who are likely to discipline employees in their careers in unionized or nonunionized settings and have that action challenged by the union, government agencies such as the EEOC, and/or the courts.*

Employee discipline is approached in this chapter by discussing its changing significance over time and its various elements, thereby enabling the reader to apply considerations discussed in Chapter 9 to this issue.

THE CHANGING SIGNIFICANCE OF INDUSTRIAL DISCIPLINE

Employee discipline represents both organizational conditions and actions. Organizational conditions can lead employees to form a disciplined work group that is largely self-regulated and willingly accepts management's directions and behavioral standards. Managerial actions are taken against an employee who has violated organizational rules.[2] This dimension has changed over time.

Historical Overview of Employer Disciplinary Policies

During the eighteenth and nineteenth centuries, the employer exercised "uncontrolled discretion" in directing the work crew. Discipline during this time was sometimes harsh. Employees who were verbally insolent to employers could have their tongues burned with a hot iron or be subjected to public humiliation (a public whipping in the town square, for example).

By 1935, management's total discretion to discipline employees was challenged on pragmatic and legal grounds. Frederick Taylor's theory of *scientific management*, popular by 1920, stressed the financial waste that occurred when employees were discharged in an arbitrary or capricious manner. According to Taylor, management had an obligation to determine and obtain desired employee work behavior and to correct, rather than discharge, the employee who deviated from managerial standards.

The Wagner Act of 1935 legally shaped management's disciplinary policies. A primary feature of this legislation was the prohibition of discriminatory discipline of employees because of their union activities or membership. An independent agency, the National Labor Relations Board (NLRB), was created, in part, for enforcement purposes. Management often had to defend disciplinary actions against charges filed with this agency, with a potential remedy being reinstatement with back pay. This was the first time that management could be legally held accountable for employee discipline, a situation that encouraged further development of corrective disciplinary principles and policies.[3] The NLRB also affected organizational discipline procedure indirectly when it ruled that discipline and grievance procedures were mandatory issues subject to collective bargaining. As a result of this NLRB decision, nearly all existing collective bargaining agreements now have both a provision regulating discipline and a grievance procedure that makes possible the submission of discipline issues to arbitration.

From the 1940s to the present, managerial policies regarding employee discipline were greatly influenced by the growth and development of labor arbitration. Currently, arbitrators have three broad powers regarding discipline:

1. To determine what constitutes "just cause" for discipline.
2. To establish "standards of proof and evidence."
3. To review and modify or eliminate the penalty imposed by management when warranted.

The Wrongful Discharge Consideration in Nonunion Firms

A **wrongful discharge** claim might be filed by an employee who is terminated by management even if a union or grievance procedure is not available. This challenge might be based on an alleged violation of federal laws (see Exhibit 10.1 for examples) or under the following rationales:[4]

- *Implied contract* (applicable in courts in 34 states) relies on oral or written evidence (statements made in employment interviews, employee handbooks, and so forth) indicating that the company will make every effort to develop the employee and treat the individual fairly in personnel decisions.
- *Public policy* (applicable in courts in 39 states) prohibits management from discharging an employee who refused to commit perjury on the employer's

Exhibit 10.1 Impact of Federal Legislation on Employee Discipline

LEGISLATION	DISCIPLINARY INFLUENCE
Railway Labor Act (1926)	Protection from discharge for union-related activities.
National Labor Relations Act (1935)	Negotiated agreements providing for arbitration on unjust discharge disputes.
Title VII of the Civil Rights Act (1964, 1972, 1978, 1991)	Protection from unjust discharge based on race, color, religion, sex, or national origin.
Civil Service Reform Act (1978)	Just cause protection from discharge, grievance procedures, and appeal processes.
Fair Labor Standards Act (1938)	Prohibits discharge for filing a complaint under the statute.
Age Discrimination in Employment Act (1967, 1987)	Prohibits age-based discharge of persons over 40 years old.
Rehabilitation Act (1973)	Prohibits federal contractors of federally supported programs from discriminating against persons with disabilities.
Vietnam Era Veterans Readjustment Assistance Act (1979, 1982)	Provides veterans with protection from discharge from civilian service.
Occupational Safety and Health Act (1970)	Prohibits discharge of employees in reprisal for exercising their rights under these acts.
Energy Reorganization Act (1974) Clean Air Act (1981) Federal Water Pollution Control Act (1978)	Protect employees from discharge for instituting or testifying at proceedings against an employer in relation to these acts.
Employee Retirement Income Security Act (1974)	Prohibits discharge of employees to avoid the attainment of vested pension rights.
Consumer Credit Protection Act (1982)	Prohibits discharge of employees for garnishment of wages for an indebtedness.
Judiciary and Judicial Procedure Act (1982)	Prohibits discharge of employees who serve on juries in federal court.

SOURCE: Robert J. Paul and James B. Townsend, "Wrongful Termination: Balancing Employer and Employee Rights—A Summary with Recommendations," *Employee Responsibilities and Rights Journal* 6 (March 1993), p. 71.

behalf, reported illegal company activities, filed a legal worker's compensation claim, and so forth.

A RAND Corp. study has found that employers overestimate potential costs of a wrongful discharge suit and incur indirect costs that are 100 times higher when they attempt to avoid these suits. These indirect costs occur when employers do not terminate employees who perform poorly, establish complex and more costly hiring and decision-making processes, or use severance payments to deter wrongful termination claims.[5] Employers could both prevent successful wrongful discharge suits and minimize related indirect costs by employing disciplinary considerations found in unionized firms and related labor agreements.

Present-Day Significance of Discipline

Management and union officials as well as employees at unionized firms are strongly affected by disciplinary actions and arbitrators' decisions concerning disciplinary actions. (See the "Labor Relations in Action" for potential disciplinary situations that have occurred on an automobile assembly line.) An arbitrator has two typical options in cases involving a discharged employee. The arbitrator can (1) uphold management's discharge decisions or (2) reinstate the employee with some or all back pay for wages lost due to the employee's forced absence.

Management loses more discipline cases than it wins, as arbitrators follow the second alternative in a majority of their decisions.[6] This loss is advertised when the reinstated employee is brought back to the shop floor. Reinstatement of the employee with back pay represents a financial loss to management, and supervisory authority may also be lost, for it is a rare supervisor who, upon experiencing the return of one disciplined employee to his work group with a large back-pay check, will pursue subsequent disciplinary action with as much vigor and initiative.[7]

There is also no guarantee that the reinstated employee will perform well when returned to the job. Two studies have found that 51 to 62 percent of the reinstated employees performed their work in a "below average" capacity, with a large majority having subsequent disciplinary problems.[8] Moreover, the seniority of the discharged employee (often considered an influential mitigating circumstance by arbitrators) was insignificant in predicting the employee's performance after reinstatement.[9]

Arbitral reversal of management decisions can also create tensions between different levels of management officials. As noted in Chapter 1, management participants in the labor relations process do not constitute a unified group. The first-line supervisor is often most involved in employee discipline: he or she has typically trained the employee, created past practices in the department that might influence the arbitrator's decision, and witnessed, reported, and in some cases participated in the events resulting in discipline. The supervisor also directly administers discipline to employees.

Other management officials, such as labor relations representatives, monitor these activities to make sure that supervisory actions are consistent with company policy, reversing them if they are not to avoid adverse arbitration. This reversal can cause tensions, as indicated in the following remarks of a first-line supervisor:

> I had this one troublemaker. He was a solid goldbricker. He couldn't cut the buck on any job. I tried everything, but he was lazy and he was a loudmouth. I caught him in the toilet after being away from his machine for over an hour. I told him he was through and to go upstairs and pick up his check. And [deleted]. Do you know what those college boys in personnel did? He gives them some bull about being sick and weakly and the next day he is sitting on a bench in the department next to mine. He

Disciplinary Possibilities on the Assembly Line

The following excerpts are taken from *Rivethead* (New York: Warner Books, 1992), written by Ben Hamper concerning his work experiences on an automobile manufacturing line. These situations reflect vivid, real-world employees' behaviors that management attempts to correct through disciplinary actions. Unions could claim management's response to each of these actions was inappropriate by filing a grievance that might, in time, be resolved by an arbitrator. The first five considerations involve employees Hamper knew on the line; the remainder of the events were perpetrated by Hamper and co-workers.

- Roy captured a tiny mouse at work and built a home for the rodent. He took care of the mouse until one lunch break when he claimed it was mocking his job performance. He then grabbed the mouse by the tail, took a brazing torch, and "incinerated his little buddy at arm's length."
- Lightnin' had no known job assignment but would spend each work day in the men's washroom leaning up against the last urinal wall, asleep.
- Jack hated the company and thought management was out to get him. One night he claimed that the company purposefully robbed him by not returning cigarettes for cash he placed into a vending machine. He then took a sledgehammer (which he labeled "the Better Business Bureau") and beat the vending machine to a glass and metallic pulp.
- Franklin was a man who took real pleasure in beating up other employees. He snuck up on one employee who refused to give him an extra pair of safety gloves and "smashed him over the head with a door latch." The employee received a dozen stitches in his head, and Franklin received a 30-day suspension.
- Louie peddled half pints of Canadian Club and Black Velvet at the work place, delivering the alcohol to the customer's work station.

Mr. Hamper also admitted to drinking rather substantially at work. His regular intake included "a forty ouncer at first break, another one at lunch, then . . . a pint or two of whiskey for the last part of the shift."

He and another employee also doubled up on the job, where one employee would perform both jobs, allowing the other employee to sleep in a hiding place. This practice basically gave each employee a four-hour nap during the work shift.

> says to me, "Well wise guy you don't count for nothin' around here. Every time I see you, I'm going to call you 'Mr. Nothin'."[10]

What management loses in arbitration hearings appears to be the union's gain. Most if not all union members believe the union should be responsive to problems arising from their day-to-day working conditions that remain after the formal labor agreement has been negotiated. There is no more dramatic example of union concern for its members than "saving" an employee's job. Almost every union newspaper contains at least one article per issue that describes (along with appropriate pictures of union representatives, the grievant, and the back-pay check) how the union successfully defended an employee against an unjust act of management. A representative article from one union newspaper proclaimed in bold headlines, "Worker Wins $5,895 in Back Pay When Fired for Opening Beer Can."[11]

Perhaps a disciplinary action carries the most significance for the affected employee. Discharge, the ultimate disciplinary act, has been viewed by many arbitrators as *economic capital punishment,* for it deprives the employee of currently earning a livelihood and at the same time (with the discharge on his or her work record) makes it difficult to find future employment elsewhere. Any form of discipline represents an embarrassment to individuals who do not like being told they are wrong and, in some instances, have to explain their unpaid removal from work to their friends and family.

Principles and Elements of Discipline

Discipline for Just Cause and Discipline's Legitimate Purpose

Arbitrators and government agencies such as the EEOC and the NLRB indicate that employee discipline must be for **just cause,** which must meet all of the following criteria:[12]

1. There is clear and convincing evidence that a disciplinary offense was committed by the grievant.
2. The disciplinary action taken by management was appropriate for the offense committed.
3. The discipline cannot be arbitrary or discriminatory; instead, it must be applied equally to employees given similar circumstances.

Arbitrators have long held that management has the right to direct the work force and manage its operations efficiently. Indeed, inefficient operations harm both the employer and employees since subsequent reduced profits can result in employee layoffs. Discipline can improve efficiency by accomplishing the following interrelated purposes:

- *To set an example of appropriate behavior.* For example, management impresses upon its employees the seriousness of being tardy by giving one tardy employee a five-day suspension.

- *To transmit rules of the organization.* As illustrated in the preceding purpose, management has transmitted a rule of the organization—lateness will not be accepted.
- *To promote efficient production.* Discipline those employees who either cannot or will not meet production standards.
- *To maintain respect for the supervisor.* In a sense, discipline shows the employee who is the boss. A supervisor who does not discipline poor employees weakens managerial authority.
- *To correct an employee's behavior.* Indicate what is expected, how the employee can improve, and what negative consequences might result in the future if the behavior does not change. The assumption here is that most employees have good intentions and will improve if management will simply show them the error of their ways.

Discipline can accomplish all these purposes, but arbitrators must be convinced that management based its action on "correction," which is discipline's only legitimate purpose. Because discharge is a remedial and not a corrective action, this type of discipline is appropriate only when all other attempts at correction have failed or the nature of the offense is so heinous as to make lesser forms of discipline inappropriate. Correction permeates the elements of discipline as shown in Exhibit 10.2,[13] which is a guide for management in employee disciplinary cases.

Degree of Proof in Disciplinary Cases: Nature of the Evidence and Witness Credibility

An overriding consideration in discipline cases is management's burden of proof to establish that the employee committed an infraction. Such proof is easier to establish in situations having objectively measured indicators (for example, absenteeism and related attendance records) than those that do not (for example, insubordination).[14]

Subjective standards can also apply to other employee infractions. For example, one arbitrator contends that a major difference exists between "nodding off" (eyes closed, head nodding lower and lower, jerking up, and then nodding again) and "sleeping on the job," because the former condition, if successfully fought by the person, "would lead to completely restored wakefulness."[15]

Arbitrators use two levels of proof. The first is **preponderance of evidence.** The testimony and evidence must be adequate to overcome opposing presumptions and evidence; the grievance decision is influenced by who presents the best case instead of by an absolute standard. The second level of proof, **beyond a reasonable doubt,** represents a higher degree of proof, which some arbitrators use in "criminal" cases (for example, fighting or stealing) that can more adversely affect the grievant's chances of finding subsequent employment. Some believe that this level of proof is extraordinarily high and should not be used in arbitration because the level of proof used in NLRB and unemployment insurance cases do not require this level in theft cases.[16]

Exhibit 10.2 Schematic Diagram Indicating Elements of Discipline

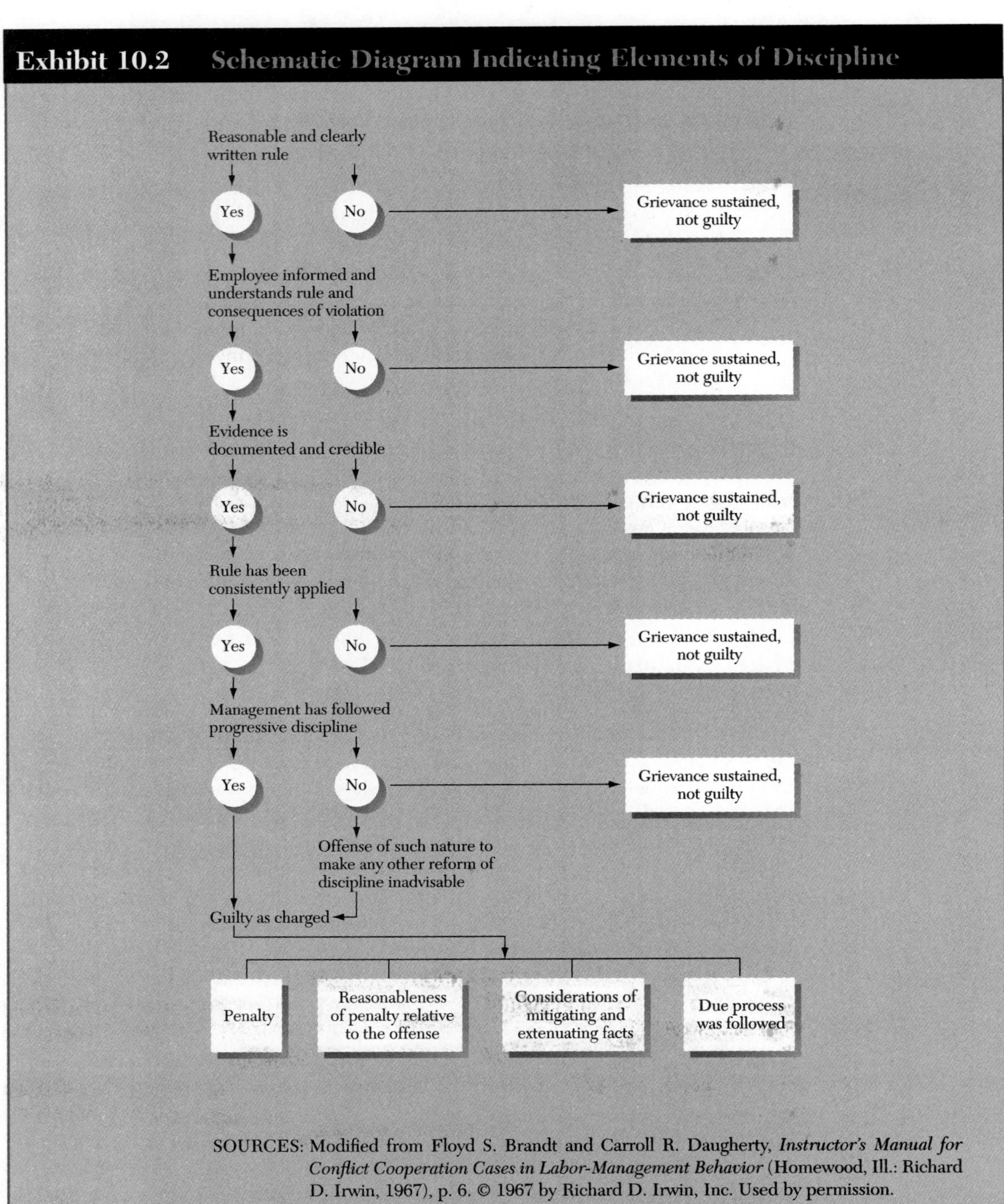

SOURCES: Modified from Floyd S. Brandt and Carroll R. Daugherty, *Instructor's Manual for Conflict Cooperation Cases in Labor-Management Behavior* (Homewood, Ill.: Richard D. Irwin, 1967), p. 6. © 1967 by Richard D. Irwin, Inc. Used by permission.

Another problem can occur when management uncovers the evidence while using search-and-seizure techniques. Few arbitrators deny the employer's right to impose, as a condition of employment, an inspection of the employee's clothes and packages on entering and leaving the plant; however, a problem arises when company officials search an employee's locker or, in some cases, home, with or without the employee's permission. Many arbitrators (and the Supreme Court in *Dennis M. O'Conner* v. *Mango Ortega*) permit evidence obtained without the employee's knowledge if it is from company property, even if the property (such as a locker or tool chest) is momentarily under the control of the employee. On the other hand, few, if any, arbitrators believe evidence should be accepted if management obtained the evidence by forcibly breaking into the employee's personal property, even if the property is located on company premises.

Arbitrators often have to assess witnesses' testimony in a discipline case. These individuals are deemed "credible" if they had neither motive for an incorrect version (for example, personal bias against the grievant) nor physical infirmity (for example, poor hearing).[17] Yet, one arbitrator notes,

> It is simply impossible to tell by observation if someone is lying under oath. You cannot tell by looking at and listening to the person. A trial judge in Chicago once compiled a list of tests to see if a witness is telling the truth: does he perspire; lick his lips; fidget in his seat; is he shifty-eyed? From my experience as an arbitrator, I can tell you that shifty-eyed people often tell the truth, while most honest-looking people will lead you by the nose right down the primrose path.[18]

Documented and credible evidence is a necessary but not sufficient disciplinary element, but other elements (as shown in Exhibit 10.2) have to be established to the arbitrator's satisfaction.

Effect of Work Rules on Discipline

Management's right to establish (even without initially advising the union) and administer work rules is generally acknowledged as fundamental to efficient plant operations. Yet managerial administration of work rules also assumes some fundamental responsibilities and obligations that, if not followed, may affect management's disciplinary efforts.

A first question that arises is, what happens if management has no rule governing the alleged offense committed by the employee? Such an event is not uncommon because employers cannot possibly anticipate the endless variety of employee misbehaviors. Arbitrators, for example, have upheld the discharges of employees who

- Watched a fire develop and destroy a portion of a company over a lengthy period of time without notifying the company.[19]
- Called management officials in the early morning hours to belch over the telephone.[20]
- Urinated on the floor of a delivery truck even though there were restroom facilities nearby.
- "Streaked" (ran naked) through a portion of an airport.[21]

Needless to say, management had no previously established work rules covering these behaviors. Arbitrators have also upheld management's right to discipline employees for those offenses that are commonly regarded as unwritten laws—prohibitions against stealing or striking a supervisor, for example.

However, in most disciplinary situations, particularly those cases that are somewhat common in industry (poor performance, absenteeism, insubordination, and so forth), management is on weak ground with the arbitrator when it does not have established work rules. Further, written work rules must be *reasonable, clear,* and *state the consequences of their violation.* Reasonable rules are related to the orderly, efficient, and safe operation of the employer's business, and the performance that the employer might properly expect of the employee. Unions will contend a rule is unreasonable if it is unrelated to business operations or outweighed by the employee's personal rights on and off the job.

Determining rule reasonableness can be complicated. For example, some arbitrators view a unilateral rule prohibiting smoking as "reasonable," particularly if management presents evidence that nonsmoking employees can be harmed by being exposed to secondhand smoke. However, other arbitrators regard a no-smoking rule to be unreasonable, particularly if there has been a clear past practice permitting this activity.[22] The reasonableness of an industrial work rule can vary according to industrial or company differences. A unilateral ban on moonlighting (working a second shift with another employer) is regarded as reasonable in the utility industry, which often needs emergency work performed during off shifts. Other industries not having emergency-related concerns might have a difficult time establishing the appropriateness of this rule.[23] Rule reasonableness can also vary within an industrial production facility. For example, an employer might reasonably require a longhaired employee working in the cafeteria to wear a hair net (for sanitary reasons); it would be unreasonable to request the same compliance if the employee worked in the shipping department. Further complications regarding rule reasonableness can occur when an employee is disciplined for off-the-job conduct. At first glance, this infraction would not appear to be job related; however, discipline would be appropriate if management establishes that it adversely affected the employer (for example, damaged its reputation or standing in the community).[24]

The clarity of a work rule is also an important issue in corrective discipline because employees cannot adequately perform or correct behavior if they do not know what is expected. Management officials can create a problem when they discipline employees for infractions of a vague or confusing work rule, such as discharge for "gambling on company premises," or "falsifying an employment application." These rules may, at first glance, appear clear and conclusive; however, their vagueness becomes apparent to the first-time supervisor who tries to enforce them. "Gambling" poses a managerial problem, particularly if employees are disciplined for participating in a card game on company premises while a management representative is sponsoring a World Series pool with hourly employee participants. Also, does gambling occur when employees are playing cards during their lunch break for matches or a numerical score that management (perhaps correctly) assumes will be converted into cash payments once the employees are off the company premises?

In another example of a vague work rule, does omitting application information constitute "falsification?" Some arbitrators would say yes, particularly if the omissions are numerous and job related. Other arbitrators maintain that "falsification" involves a definite response and might not accept discharge, much less discipline, of the employee if management did not promptly seek an explanation for any blank application items.[25]

The existence of work rules carries the implicit if not explicit obligation for management to inform its employees of the rules as well as the consequences of their violation. Sometimes an employee disciplined for violating a rule contends that he or she was unaware of the directive. Management then usually has the difficult task of proving otherwise. Some arbitrators have even suggested that a card signed by an employee indicating he or she had read the rules is insufficient because it is signed in haste as part of the employee's orientation, and the signed card does not indicate that management has explained each rule to the employee, allowing time for questions. Many times management indicates in rules or warnings that an employee's continued misconduct could be "subject to dismissal." However, arbitrators regard this term as carrying the potential for lesser penalties such as written warnings or suspensions.

Finally, management must administer the rules consistently for those employees violating the rules under similar circumstances. Management will likely have its disciplinary action reduced or eliminated by the arbitrator if the union establishes that the employer was inconsistent or lax in enforcing the rule for the same misconduct on previous occasions or gave different penalties to employees who were involved in the misconduct.[26] Problems can also occur if management did not take different circumstances into account. In one case management stressed its consistent anti-horseplay approach by indicating that it had discharged not only the grievant in the current situation but also another employee who engaged in horseplay in the past. The arbitrator overturned management's action, however, noting that the horseplay committed in this case was far less serious than in the previous situation, where another employee placed razor blades in a doughnut.[27]

In assessing the degree of consistency, arbitrators place particular emphasis on past practice, which refers to the customary way similar disciplinary offenses are handled and penalized. Some organizations seek to impose consistent discipline by including a price list in the labor agreement; it cites specific rules and furnishes uniform penalties for single or repeated violations (see Exhibit 10.3). This form of rule making has advantages: (1) the employee is clearly informed of the specific rules and consequences of violations, (2) the standardized penalties suggest consistent disciplinary action is implemented, and (3) if agreed to by the union, the price list assumes more legitimacy than a unilateral work rule posted by management. However, some individuals contend that the price list represents a mechanical imposition of discipline that runs counter to the corrective philosophy because it does not consider each case on its own. Say, for example, management finds two employees fighting—one a short-term employee, the other a long-term employee with a fine work record. According to the price-list approach, management is obligated to discharge both employees; yet it is likely that the arbitrator will reinstate the senior

Exhibit 10.3 Example of a Disciplinary Price List

TYPE OF OFFENSE	FIRST OFFENSE	SECOND OFFENSE	THIRD OFFENSE	FOURTH OFFENSE	FIFTH OFFENSE
1. Abusive language toward a supervisor	3-day suspension	Discharge			
2. Failure to punch in and out on time clock	Oral warning	Written suspension	3-day suspension	5-day suspension	Discharge
3. Failure to report an absence	Oral warning	Written suspension	3-day suspension	5-day suspension	Discharge
4. Stealing company property	Discharge				
5. Sleeping on the job	Written warning	3-day suspension	5-day suspension	Discharge	
6. Damage of company equipment	Written warning	3-day suspension	5-day suspension	Discharge	
7. Gambling or engaging in a lottery on company premises	5-day suspension	Discharge			
8. Striking a supervisor	Discharge				

employee, who, because of his past record, will typically respond to corrective measures in order to retain job seniority investments.

Progressive Discipline

Progressive discipline refers to increasingly severe penalties corresponding to repeated identical offenses committed by an employee. It relates to correction in at least two ways: (1) by impressing upon the employee the seriousness of repeated rule infractions and (2) by furnishing the employee additional chances to correct his or her behavior before applying the ultimate penalty of discharge. Management might have to give an oral warning, a written warning, and at least one suspension before it can discharge an employee for repeatedly committing a similar offense, such as failure to wear safety equipment, poor attendance, or ineffective performance.

An **oral warning** represents an informal effort to correct and improve the employee's work performance. The informality of this reprimand is for corrective training purposes; however, the oral warning can be prejudicial to the employee if it is entered as evidence in arbitration hearings. This disciplinary action, however, is subject to the following employee defenses: (1) the employee might have thought the supervisor's remarks were instructional and been unaware of the disciplinary aspects or consequences of the warning, and (2) an oral warning given in private can lead to conflicting testimony—the employee can state that the supervisor never gave an oral warning. However, because of its relative harmlessness, the union seldom contests this form of discipline.

A **written warning** is a much more serious matter because it summarizes previous oral attempts to correct the employee's behavior and is entered in the employee's work record file. More official than an oral reprimand, it brings disciplinary actions into focus by warning the employee of future consequences of rule violation.

A **suspension** is a disciplinary layoff without pay given by management to impress upon the employee the seriousness of the offense. Oral and written reprimands might also achieve this purpose, but they do not involve a financial sacrifice by the employee. A suspension serves as an example of the economic consequences associated with discharge and at the same time indicates that management is willing to retain the employee if he or she will comply with directives and change errant ways. Management initially imposes a mild suspension (one to three days) and will seldom impose a suspension greater than ten days for a repeated offense. Under these circumstances, arbitrators are reluctant to reduce the suspensions unless it can be shown that other employees were given lesser penalties for identical offenses under similar circumstances.

Discharge, unlike suspension or warnings, is not a corrective measure because it means the employee is permanently released from the company. As mentioned earlier, arbitrators have attached tremendous significance to the effects of discharge upon the employee, regarding it as a last resort to be used when all other corrective attempts have failed and the employee totally lacks usefulness to the firm. An exception to this procedure occurs when the nature of the offense is so heinous (stealing, striking a supervisor, setting fire to company property) as to make other forms of corrective discipline inappropriate.

Progressive discipline also implies a *statute of limitations.* For example, it would be difficult to discharge an employee who has previously received two suspensions for failing to report an absence to management if the worker has worked for a fairly long period of time (say, three to five years) before committing a similar present offense. Management is usually not obligated to return to the first step, that is, an oral warning; however, discharge is not warranted—the employee's offense-free period indicates that corrective measures did have some effect and should be tried again before separating the employee from the firm.

A discipline price list does not take the statute of limitations into account—its penalties are for repeated infractions regardless of the intervening time period. In these circumstances, should management negate its own price list by returning to a suspension even though discharge is the next step in the procedure? Or should it proceed with the discharge, knowing that many arbitrators, employing a statute of limitations, would reinstate the employee because of the period of time between his or her previous and recent offenses? Both courses of action have risks: In the first case, management might establish precedent that can adversely affect other cases; in the second, management might appear arbitrary in its discipline administration.

Disciplinary Penalty and Mitigating Circumstances

Arbitrators will determine whether management was correct in assigning a particular disciplinary penalty for an employee found guilty of an infraction. (See "Labor Relations in Action" for a discussion concerning employee theft.) They often consider **mitigating circumstances,** which might reduce management's assigned penalty (for example, from a discharge to a suspension), based on one of three assumptions:

1. Management contributed to a problem and must therefore assume part of the responsibility for the wrongdoing.
2. The circumstances of the case were so unusual as to give great doubt that it will occur again, particularly if management uses corrective techniques instead of discharge.
3. Personal factors (such as marital, financial, or substance abuse problems) caused a stressed or troubled employee to perform the disciplinary incident (absenteeism, poor work performance, or insubordination, for example). Therefore, the employee will not continue these infractions once his or her personal problems are identified and resolved.

An example of mitigating circumstances under the first arbitral assumption occurs when management has provided the employee with faulty tools and equipment and subsequently disciplines the employee for low production output. A more common example of mitigating circumstances occurs when a management representative provokes the employee into committing physical or verbal abuse. In a representative discharge grievance an arbitrator reinstated an employee who was discharged for striking his supervisor after he found out that the supervisor was asking other employees questions regarding his wife's fidelity.[28]

Management might also contribute to a disciplinary infraction by condoning, either openly or tacitly, offenses committed in the shop. Related examples include supervisors observing employees engaged in horseplay without attempting to stop the situation and subsequently disciplining employees for the action, and supervisors encouraging employees to violate quality standards in the name of production efficiency.

A thorough discussion of the numerous mitigating circumstances suggested by the second arbitral assumption regarding unusual circumstances is beyond the scope of this chapter, but the following example is illustrative: An employee has been repeatedly warned and suspended for failure to report his absence to management when he is unable to work a production shift; at the last suspension the grievant was informed that another infraction would result in discharge. One month after suspension the employee again failed to report his absence to management and was discharged when he reported to work the following morning. The employee contended (and added evidence in the form of a doctor's slip) that his wife became suddenly and seriously ill and that his concern for his wife, coupled with no telephone in the apartment, resulted in his failure to report his absence to management. Here, management has followed all the principles of progressive discipline;

LABOR RELATIONS IN ACTION

Arbitrators and Employee Theft: Proof and Penalty

Theft of company property or products represents a rather frequent, always serious management allegation that the arbitrator must resolve. A review of some 30 related grievances protesting the employer's discharge decision reflects various complexities arbitrators face when considering two aspects of the case: proof that the theft occurred and whether the discharge penalty fit the offense.

Problems of Proof In some cases the evidence clearly indicates that the employee committed the act, but the union and the arbitrator maintain that the act is not "theft." This situation might occur when the grievant does not remove the property from the company premises or places items in his or her car in the company parking lot.[a] One employee admitted taking a can of tea; however, the arbitrator noted that payment for the product is required only when a customer reaches the check-out counter and fails to pay, situations that were not given a chance to occur.[b] In other cases employees were considered not to have committed theft when they "hoarded" new tools in a locker,[c] returned another employee's tools that were hidden in a locker,[d] and "picked a lock" on a company tool chest to get a bulb for a flashlight so that they could resume work.[e]

The employee's intent (subjectively assessed state of mind based on observable behaviors) to steal might also be determined by the arbitrator. One employee was discharged for taking a battery clamp home without seeking required permission. The grievant contended he belatedly realized his action and put the clamp on the front seat of his car so that it could be returned to work the following day. He further noted that the cable slipped between the seats of his car, causing him to forget to seek permission the following morning when he was eventually confronted by management. The arbitrator did not hold the grievant blameless for this infraction. But he did reduce the grievant's discharge to a 30-day suspension because the following behaviors suggested the grievant did not intend to steal the item.

> When (A) found the clamp in his pocket, he did not install it on his car. Instead, he put the clamp on the front seat of his car and took it to work with him the next day. (A) readily confirmed that he had the clamp and he just as readily went to his car, got it, brought it in, and handed it to (Superintendent). He had no reason to bring the clamp back to the plant unless he intended to show it to a supervisor and get permission to take it home.[f]

Credibility becomes significant when the grievant denies the theft allegation. Sometimes lack of credibility is easy to determine. In one case, for example, the grievant claimed that a box of master locks found at his house was there because he had accidentally and unknowingly knocked the box into his laundry bag at work. He also contended that he intended to return the locks to work;

(continued)

LABOR RELATIONS IN ACTION

Arbitrators and Employee Theft: Proof and Penalty—Cont'd

however, they were in his possession for one and one-half years.[g] An employee might also damage credibility if he does not testify on his own behalf.[h]

Arbitrators assess the witnesses who testify against the grievant and will find them credible if they have nothing to gain by lying; they will also assess witnesses' ability and opportunity to know, remember, and relate the facts; their manner and appearance; their sincerity or lack thereof; the reasonableness or unreasonableness of their testimony in light of the presented evidence; and any inconsistency of their testimony.[i]

Lie detectors have been deemed permissible considerations in some cases. However, one arbitrator indicated they were only of some use in corroborating a participant's version of the events but of no weight when an employer relies solely on their results.[j] Another arbitrator concluded that the company was not obligated to accede to the grievant's request for a polygraph test during investigation of his alleged theft because results are unreliable.[k]

Penalty The relationship between the penalty and the offense, assuming the grievant to be guilty in theft, is perhaps the most controversial arbitration dimension. Arbitrators have upheld the discharge for theft of a relatively inexpensive item. One arbitrator upheld the discharge of a grievant who stole seven gallons of gas because "[t]he company is not required to have a standard that says, in effect, employees shall be approximately honest and approximately trustworthy."[l]

Another arbitrator upheld an employee's discharge for taking an allegedly bruised tomato that fell from a produce box because, "It cannot be left to an employee's own determination as to when a company product is no longer of worth."[m] However, this rationale was directly contradicted in two other cases where employees took fixtures and six-foot copper cables. The arbitrators maintained that the employees reasonably assumed that the materials had no value to the company and that the company would have given permission if asked.[n]

however, the employee's discharge might be set aside if the arbitrator concludes that the circumstances were so unusual as to give management no reason to think it will happen again in the future.

Arbitrators often consider the mitigating effects of the grievant's role as a union officer. Compared with other employees, union officials usually have special rights and privileges, particularly when conducting union business. Many arbitrators regard the union steward and foreman as organizational equals in discussion of union matters. Arbitrators therefore give the union steward leeway if harsh words are exchanged in these meetings, whereas other employees might be successfully charged with insubordination for identical actions.

Union officers can also have greater responsibilities that correspond to their rights. For example, arbitrators and the NLRB have upheld more serious discipli-

At least one arbitrator interpreted the penalty for theft of "up to and including discharge" to mean that a lesser penalty could be given for this serious offense if mitigating circumstances were present.[o] A lengthy good-work record may be considered a mitigating circumstance, but this consideration is very controversial—some arbitrators ignore it completely,[p] whereas others use it to reduce management's original discharge decision.[q]

The following arbitration decision citations refer to Bureau of National Affairs Inc., *Labor Arbitration Awards.* For example, 80 LA 19 would be found in volume 80 of this series, starting on page 19. A different abbreviation ("88-1 Arb. 8164") indicates the case came from Commerce Clearing House, *Labor Arbitration Reports.*

[a]88-1 Arb. 8164. Frost.
[b]98 LA 664. Miller.
[c]98 LA 941. Nicholas, Jr.
[d]85 LA 1001. Jones, Jr.
[e]98 LA 982. Seinsheimer.
[f]84-2 Arb. 8499. Duda.
[g]99 LA 1137. McKay.
[h]83-2 Arb. 8466. Sass.
[i]94 LA 621, Berquist; 90-1 Arb. 8732, Stephens; 83-2 Arb. 8349, Duff; 84-2 Arb. 8453, Shearer; and 93 LA 1113. Yarowsky.
[j]85 LA 435. Alsher.
[k]94 LA 621. Berquist.
[l]79 LA 79. Eisle.
[m]83-1 Arb. 8060. Dallas.
[n]92 LA 813. Seidman; and 94 LA 667. Shearer.
[o]98 LA. Seinsheimer.
[p]83-1 Arb. 8060, Dallas, and 98 LA 355. Stutz.
[q]71 LA 989. Heinsz; and 97 LA 377. Duff. See also, Ken Jennings, Dilip D. Kare, and Amit Goela, "An Analysis of Arbitration Decisions in Employee Theft Cases," *Labor Law Journal* 42 (March 1991), p. 161.

nary action for union officers who failed to prevent a wildcat strike than for employees who actually participated in the strike. This differential penalty implies that union stewards should be more knowledgeable about contractual prohibition against a wildcat strike and thus should uphold their contractual obligation to maintain uninterrupted production during the term of the labor agreement.

Perhaps the most commonly considered mitigating circumstance in discharge cases is the employee's work record. An arbitrator will likely consider reinstating a discharged employee who violated a work rule (one that prohibits insubordination, for example) if that employee has a long and good work record with the company. The arbitrator in this situation realizes the potential of the employee returning to previous work habits, so he or she might reinstate the employee with no back pay, which would represent a suspension. One study has shown that discharges of grievants with little seniority (less than two years' service with the organization) are more likely to be upheld than discharges of grievants having more than eleven years of service.[29]

The most complicated and controversial mitigating circumstances are found in the troubled employee assumption. Many management officials contend that arbitrators exceed their authority to interpret the labor agreement in these discipline cases, and instead assume the roles of clergymen, psychiatrists, and medical doctors in indicating that management has an obligation to nurture these employees even though this is not required by the contract language. One arbitrator acknowledged that he and some of his peers have addressed one troubled employee issue, alcohol abuse, with little medical or scientific foundation:

> Curiously, published arbitral decisions involving alcohol abuse rarely distinguish between social drinking, heavy drinking, and alcoholism—distinctions that are crucial in the mental health field. Moreover, although hundreds of arbitration decisions have adopted the popular view that alcoholism is a "disease" that involves "loss of control" over drinking, I am unaware of any decisions (including my own) that express an understanding of what arbitrators actually mean when they call alcoholism a "disease." Even in the literature of arbitration, there is little recognition of whether alcoholism is a medical disease, a social disorder, or some complex combination, and whether it has a natural progression and a unitary etiology.[30]

Due Process and the *Weingarten* Decision

Due process has both substantive and procedural aspects. Substantive due process focuses on the purpose or rationale of the work rules to ensure that an employee has not been arbitrarily disciplined or discharged. This aspect is reflected in the previously discussed purposes and elements of discipline. Procedural aspects of due process are usually covered in labor agreements and include the following:

1. The discipline process will follow certain time limits specified in the labor agreement.
2. The employee will be entitled to union representation when discipline is being administered and be given an opportunity to respond (defend himself or herself).
3. The employee will be notified of the specific offense in writing.

The due process procedure of union representation has been influenced by NLRB decisions and by the Supreme Court in its *Weingarten* decision. This decision will be discussed in detail because it illustrates the model of the labor relations process presented in Chapter 1 (Exhibit 1.2), and because it illustrates the impact of the fourth participant, the government, on labor-management relations.

The *Weingarten* decision pertained to an employee who was believed to have paid only a fraction of the price of food she took out of the store. During the interview with management representatives she repeatedly asked for a union representative to be present but was denied. Management subsequently found her version of the incident to be supported, but in her emotional state she admitted that over a period of time she had taken free lunches (totaling approximately $160) from the store, something a management official and other employees had also done. She was not disciplined for her actions; however, she informed her union representatives of the events and an unfair labor practice was filed. The NLRB decided that management did commit an unfair labor practice, violating Section 8(a)(1) of the National Labor Relations Act (mentioned in Chapter 3), by denying the employee union representation.

Union representation must be given to the employee at the employee's request when the employee reasonably believes an investigation will result in disciplinary action. Employees, however, have no legal requirement to bargain with any union representative who attends the interview.

The NLRB's *Weingarten* decision was appealed through the courts, and eventually upheld by the Supreme Court. Rationale for this decision was in part based on the union official's potential contribution to the disciplinary investigation:

> A single employee confronted by an employer investigating whether certain conduct deserves discipline may be too fearful or inarticulate to relate accurately the incident being investigated, or too ignorant to raise extenuating factors. A knowledgeable union representative could assist the employer by eliciting favorable facts, and save the employer production time by getting to the bottom of the incident occasioning the interview. Certainly [the union representative's] presence need not transform the interview into an adversary contest.[31]

This decision also refuted the company's contention that union representation is necessary only after the company has made its discipline decision. The Supreme Court contended that this practice would diminish the value of union representation, thereby making it increasingly difficult for the employee to vindicate himself or herself in the subsequent grievance proceedings. The NLRB has unanimously agreed, however, that *Weingarten* does not extend to employees who are not represented by a union.[32]

The written notice element of due process has caused some problems for management and is a major reason for the involvement of labor relations representatives in the discipline process. For example, an employee gets into a heated argument with a supervisor, refuses to work an assignment, and shouts an obscenity at the supervisor. The foreman could discipline the employee for "directing obscene and profane language toward a management representative." Once the charges are in writing, management must convince the arbitrator that this charge warrants discipline, a task that is not easy given the usual arbitral recognition that obscene language is regarded as common shop talk in an industrial facility. In this instance, management would have been wiser to have disciplined the employee for a more serious offense: "Insubordination: refusal to follow supervisory orders." However, management can seldom change the offense once it is in writing and handed to the grievant. Consequently, a member of the industrial relations department is usually present for consultation or direction before the charges are reduced to writing.

Another related element of due process is *double jeopardy*—assigning an employee a more severe penalty than the one originally given. The rationale against double jeopardy is that management is held to any decision that purports to be final; therefore, it is important that it act only after ascertaining all relevant facts and determining the magnitude of the offense. Management can avoid the problem of double jeopardy if it makes clear to the grievant that the action taken in the first instance is tentative, pending further investigation by higher company officials. Usually, this takes the form of an indefinite suspension that, pending a subsequent investigation, can be converted to discharge without arbitral disapproval. A final element of due process is the keeping of secret records on the employee, which most arbitrators maintain is worse than keeping no records at all.

One arbitrator notes three alternative positions that the arbitrator can take regarding procedural or due process irregularities:

> (1) [T]hat unless there is strict compliance with the procedural requirements, the whole action will be nullified; (2) that the requirements are of significance only where the employee can show that he has been prejudiced by failure to comply therewith; or (3) that the requirements are important, and that any failure to comply will be penalized, but that the action taken is not thereby rendered null and void.[33]

Arbitrators tend to favor the third alternative, reasoning that management should suffer the consequences of its errors, but not to the point of exonerating an employee who is guilty of a serious offense (particularly if it has not prejudiced the employee's case).

Currently, NLRB cases indicate that an employee who is discharged for cause will not be reinstated solely because the employer violated his or her *Weingarten* rights.[34] This means that if the employer has obtained evidence from sources other than from the illegal interview, the employee's discharge will stand.

Summary

In many respects, employee discipline represents the most significant day-to-day issue in administering the labor agreement. For the union and management organizations, administration of discipline is a key factor related to control and production; the supervisor and the affected employee are even more directly and personally affected.

Management had a unilateral right to discharge or discipline employees until the 1930s, although psychological reform and efficiency movements in the early 1900s urged management to critically examine its disciplinary policies. Some managers realized that an employee represented an investment that could be unnecessarily lost due to whimsical disciplinary actions. These individuals realized that they had an obligation to provide employees with clear work rules and proper training that would minimize the number of discipline problems and lead to increased productivity. The establishment of the NLRB further refined employers' disciplinary policies, as employees discharged for their union activities could be reinstated to their jobs with back pay.

Discipline in unionized settings must be for just cause, a concept consisting of several dimensions. Management has the burden of proof to establish that an employee committed an infraction. While discipline can accomplish several purposes for the organization, management may have to prove that its actions were taken to correct an employee's behavior. Correction suggests that an employee must be aware of work rules that are clear in their content as well as consequences for their infraction. The work rules must also be reasonable—that is, related to the job—and consistently applied to all employees under similar circumstances.

Discipline's corrective emphasis also suggests progressive or more serious penalties be given to an employee for repeating a similar offense. Progressive discipline impresses upon the employee the seriousness of repeated rule infractions while giving the employee additional chances to correct work behavior. Usually, management has to give an employee an oral warning for the first offense, then a written warning and suspension for subsequent, similar offenses. Discharge is a last resort, used only when all other attempts at correction have failed or the nature of the offense is so unacceptable as to make corrective efforts inappropriate.

Management must also establish that the penalty fits the crime and that it considered all possible mitigating circumstances before imposing discipline.

Management must also provide the employee with due process in the disciplinary procedure; that is, it must ensure that the appropriate contractual provisions are upheld. The employee usually has the right to union representation and the right to be notified of the offense in writing.

Key Terms

- wrongful discharge
- just cause
- price list
- progressive discipline
- oral warning
- written warning
- suspension
- mitigating circumstances
- due process

Discussion Questions

1. Why is discipline the most significant issue for the union and management organizations? Describe how this significance has shifted over time.
2. One union newspaper indicated how it saved an employee's job. The employee was in the mechanic's classification and was discharged for refusing to comply with management's sudden, unilateral rule that mechanics must perform janitorial duties. Given this sketchy situation, discuss the many possible reasons for the disciplinary action, indicating why the arbitrator might not have been convinced that management's discipline was for a legitimate purpose. (You are free to make and state assumptions in your answer.)
3. Explain in some detail the difficulties management would have in administering the following work rule in accordance with the disciplinary principles established in the chapter: "Any employee reporting to work under the influence of alcohol will be subject to discharge."

4. Indicate the comparative advantages and disadvantages of a disciplinary price list (Exhibit 10.3) of disciplinary prerogatives in the labor agreement and a one-sentence contractual provision indicating "management has the right to discipline or discharge an employee for cause."
5. While not subject to judicial scrutiny, evidence in an arbitration hearing still has its complexities. Discuss related considerations that could be involved in an arbitration hearing involving an employee who was discharged for smoking marijuana on the job.
6. Assume you are in charge of establishing a training program for supervisors in administering discipline. Based on the supervisor's potential role in the disciplinary process, formulate and discuss three major principles you would stress in this session.

References

1. Ahmad R. Karim, "Why Arbitrators Sustain Discharge Penalties," *Labor Law Journal* 45 (June 1994), pp. 374–378; and Stephen M. Crow, Elvis C. Stephens, and Walton H. Sharp, "A New Approach to Decision-Making Research in Labor Arbitration Using Alcohol and Drug Disciplinary Cases," *Labor Studies Journal* 17 (Fall 1992), pp. 3–18.
2. For consideration of other, more informal disciplinary actions taken by management, see Bruce Fortado, "Informal Supervisory Social Control Strategies," *Journal of Management Studies* 31 (March 1994), pp. 251–275.
3. For an example of how the NLRB can alter an organization's decision policies, see Marcia A. Graham, "Obscenity and Profanity at Work," *Employee Relations Law Journal* 11 (Spring 1986), pp. 662–677.
4. Milo Geyelin, "Fired Managers Winning More Lawsuits," *The Wall Street Journal*, September 7, 1989, B-1. See also William H. Holley, Jr. and Roger S. Wolters, "An Employment-at-Will Vulnerability Audit," *Personnel Journal* 66 (April 1987), pp. 130–138; and William H. Holley, Jr. and Roger S. Wolters, *Labor Relations: An Experiential and Case Approach* (Hinsdale, Ill.: The Dryden Press, 1988), pp. 33–35. See also Giles Trudeau, "Is Reinstatement a Remedy Suitable to At-Will Employees?" *Industrial Relations* 30, no. 2 (Spring 1991), pp. 302–315; P. S. Partee, "Reversing the Presumption of Employment-at-Will," *Vanderbilt Law Review* 44, no. 3 (April 1991), pp. 698–712; Jay E. Grenig, "Dismissal of Employees in the United States," *International Labor Review* 130, no. 5–6 (1991), pp. 569–581; Marcia P. Miceli, Janet P. Near, and Charles R. Schwenk, "Who Blows the Whistle and Why?," *Industrial and Labor Relations Review* 45 (October 1991), pp. 113–130; Jeffrey M. Hahn and Kevin M. Smith, "Wrongful Discharge: The Search for a Legislative Compromise," *Employee Relations Law Journal* 15 (Spring 1990), pp. 515–539; "Employer Opportunism and the Need for a Just Cause Standard," *Howard Law Review* 103, pp. 510–529; A. D. Hill, *"Wrongful Discharge" and the Derogation of the At-Will Employment Doctrine* (Philadelphia: The Wharton School, 1987); Alan B. Drueger, "The Evolution of Unjust-Dismissal Legislation in the United States," *Industrial and Labor Relations Review* 44 (July 1991), pp. 644–660; Roger L. Anderson and James W. Robinson, "Is Arbitration the Answer in Wrongful Termination Cases?" *Labor Law Journal* 42 (February 1991), pp. 121–124; Daniel P. Westman,

Whistleblowing: The Law of Retaliatory Discharge, (Washington, D.C.: Bureau of National Affairs, Inc., 1991); Paul F. Gerhart and Donald P. Crane, "Wrongful Dismissal: Arbitration and the Law," *Arbitration Journal* 48 (June 1993), pp. 56–70; Lisa B. Bingham, "Employee Free Speech and Wrongful Discharge," *Labor Law Journal* 45 (July 1994), pp. 387–400; and Melissa S. Baucus and Terry Morehead Dworkin, "Wrongful Firing in Violation of Public Policy: Who Gets Fired and Why," *Employee Responsibilities and Rights Journal* 7, no. 3 (1994), pp. 191–206.

5. "RAND Corp. Study Links Job Losses to States' Wrongful Termination Rules," Bureau of National Affairs Inc., *Daily Labor Report,* no. 142 (July 23, 1992), p. A-2. For somewhat similar conclusions reached by another survey, see "Wrongful-Discharge Claims Increasing, Management Association Survey Finds," Bureau of National Affairs Inc., *Daily Labor Report* no. 25 (February 6, 1990), pp. A-8, A-9.

6. See Kenneth M. Jennings, Barbara Sheffield, and Roger S. Wolters, "The Arbitration of Discharge Cases: A Forty Year Perspective," *Labor Law Journal* 38 (January 1987), p. 35. See also Ahmad Karim and Thomas H. Stone, "An Empirical Examination of Arbitrator Decisions in Reversal and Reduction Discharge Hearings," *Labor Studies Journal* 13, no. 2 (Spring 1988), p. 47.

7. See, for example, Thomas R. Knight, "The Impact of Arbitration on the Administration of Disciplinary Policies," *Arbitration Journal* 39 (March 1984), pp. 43–56.

8. Arthur Anthony Malinowski, "An Empirical Analysis of Discharge Cases and the Work History of Employees Reinstated by Labor Arbitrators," *Arbitration Journal* 36 (March 1981), p. 39; and William E. Simkin, "Some Results of Reinstatement by Arbitration," *Arbitration Journal* 41 (September 1986), p. 56.

9. Chalmer E. Labig, Jr., I. B. Helburn, and Robert C. Rodgers, "Discipline, History, Seniority, and Reason for Discharge as Predictors of Post-Reinstatement Job Performance," *The Arbitration Journal* 40 (September 1985), p. 49. For additional considerations of this relationship, see Robert C. Rodgers, I. B. Helburn, and John E. Hunter, "The Relationship of Seniority to Job Performance Following Reinstatement," *Academy of Management Journal* 29 (March 1986), pp. 101–114; and I. B. Helburn, "Seniority and Postreinstatement Performance," in *Proceedings of the Forty-Third Annual Meeting, National Academy of Arbitrators,* Gladys W. Gruenberg, ed. (Washington, D.C.: Bureau of National Affairs Inc., 1991), pp. 141–149.

10. D. C. Miller, "Supervisor: Evolution of a Forgotten Role," in *Supervisory Leadership and Productivity,* eds. Floyd Mann, George Homans, and Delbert Miller (San Francisco: Chandler, 1965), p. 113.

11. "Oil, Chemical, and Atomic," *Union News,* July 1970, p. 9.

12. *Hoosier Panel Co., Inc.,* 61 LA 983 (M. Volz, 1973). Marvin Hill, Jr. and Diana Beck, "Some Thoughts on Just Cause and Group Discipline," *Arbitration Journal* 41 (June 1986), pp. 60–62.

13. For more thorough explanations of this exhibit, see Donald S. McPherson, "The Evolving Concept of Just Cause: Carroll R. Daugherty and the Requirement of Disciplinary Due Process," *Labor Law Journal* (July 1987), pp. 387–403; and Adolph M. Koven and Susan L. Smith, *Just Cause: The Seven Tests* (San Francisco: Kendall/Hurst, 1985).

14. David A. Dilts, Ahmad Karim, and Mashalah Kahnama Moghadam, "The Arbitration of Disciplinary Matters: Do Objective Standards Make a Difference in Proof?" *Labor Law Journal* 42 (October 1991), pp. 708–712.

15. Arthur Eliot Berkeley, "Asleep at the Wheel: How Arbitrators View Sleeping on the Job," *Arbitration Journal* 46 (June 1991), p. 48.

16. Randall M. Kelly, "The Burden of Proof in Criminal Offenses of 'Moral

Turpitude' Cases," *Arbitration Journal* 46 (December 1991), pp. 45–48.
17. Laura Davis, "Discipline and Decisions: A Study of Arbitration Cases Dealing with Employee Discourtesy," *Labor Law Journal* 46 (February 1995), p. 84.
18. Edgar A. Jones, Jr., "Selected Problems of Procedure and Evidence," in *Arbitration in Practice,* ed. Arnold M. Zack (Ithaca, N.Y.: ILR Press, 1984), p. 62.
19. *Buick Youngstown Company,* 41 LA 570–753 (H. Dworkin, 1963).
20. *A. B. Chance Company,* 57 LA 725–731 (P. Florey, 1971).
21. Terry L. Leap and Michael D. Crino, "How to Deal with Bizarre Behavior," *Harvard Business Review* (May–June 1986), pp. 18–25. This article also furnishes eight criteria for management in determining whether discharge for previously unconsidered disciplinary infractions is justified.
22. Donald J. Petersen, "No Smoking!" *Dispute Resolution Journal* 50 (January 1995), p. 48.
23. For additional consideration of the "moonlighting" employee, see Muhammad Jamal, "Moonlighting Myths," *The Personnel Journal* 67 (May 1988), pp. 48–53.
24. Robert A. Kearney, "Arbitral Practice and Purpose in Employee Off-Duty Misconduct Cases," *Notre Dame Law Review* 69, no. 1 (1993), pp. 135–156; and Janie L. Miller, David B. Balkin, and Robert Allen, "Employer Restrictions on Employees' Legal Off-Duty Conduct," *Labor Law Journal* 44 (April 1993), pp. 209–219.
25. Donald J. Petersen, "Trends in Arbitrating Falsification of Employment Application Forms," *Arbitration Journal* 47 (September 1992), pp. 32–33.
26. Gregory G. Dell'Omo and James E. Jones, Jr., "Disparate Treatment in Labor Arbitration: An Empirical Analysis," *Labor Law Journal* 41 (November 1990), pp. 739–750.
27. Lisa Davis and Ken Jennings, "Employee Horseplay and Likely Managerial Overreaction," *Labor Law Journal* 40 (April 1989), pp. 248–256.
28. *Gindy Manufacturing Company,* 58 LA 1038–1040 (M. Handsaker, 1972).
29. Jennings, Sheffield, and Wolters, "The Arbitration of Discharge Cases," p. 43.
30. Tim Bornstein, "Getting to the Bottom of the Issue: How Arbitrators View Alcohol Abuse," *Arbitration Journal* 44 (December 1989), p. 47.
31. *NLRB* v. *J. Weingarten, Inc.,* 420 U.S. 262, 1974. See also M. J. Fox, Louis V. Baldovin, Jr., and Thomas R. Fox, "The *Weingarten* Doctrine," *The Arbitration Journal* 40 (June 1985), pp. 45–54. The *Weingarten* decision has also been held by an appeals court to be applicable in at least some federal sector situations. See "Court Permits Union Representation at Meetings with DOD Investigators," Bureau of National Affairs Inc., *Daily Labor Report,* no. 173 (September 7, 1988), A-1.
32. "NLRB Limits *Weingarten* Rights to Union-Represented Employees," Bureau of National Affairs Inc., *Daily Labor Report,* no. 132 (July 11, 1988), p. 2. See also Neil N. Bernstein, "*Weingarten:* Time for Reconsideration?," *Labor Lawyer* 6 (Fall 1990), pp. 1005–1027.
33. R. W. Fleming, *The Labor Arbitration Process* (Champaign: University of Illinois Press, 1965), p. 139.
34. Raymond L. Hogler, "Taracorp and Remedies for *Weingarten* Violations: The Evolution of Industrial Due Process," *Labor Law Journal* 37 (July 1986).

11 Institutional Issues: Managerial Rights, Union Security, and the Rights of Minority and Female Employees

A major collective bargaining issue pertains to the rights and obligations of labor and management organizations. Management's major institutional issue concerns its rights to manage. The union has a corresponding institutional concern of union security, or its ability to preserve its organization—mainly by enrolling and retaining employee members. These two concerns are discussed in this chapter, as is the relationship between organized labor and minority and female employees.

Managerial Rights

Background and Extent of Managerial Rights

Before the passage of the National Labor Relations Act in 1935, management rights and discretion in operating facilities were seldom questioned, and managers were virtually free to run their operations as they saw fit. In many cases unions were considered intruders into managerial prerogatives, since there were few laws regulating managers' actions toward employees. Consider, for example, the following management quotation, which could have been widely applicable in the early 1900s but is out of date today due to employment laws:

> Who but a miserable, craven-hearted man would permit himself to be subjected to such rules, extending even to the number of apprentices he may employ, and the manner in which they shall be bound to him; to the kind of work which will be performed in his own office, at particular hours of the day, and to the sex of the persons employed. . . For ourselves, we never employed a female as compositor, and have no great opinion of apprentices; but sooner than be restricted on these points, or any other, by a self-constituted tribunal outside of the office, we would go to the employment of our boyhood and dig potatoes. . . . It is marvelous to us how any employer having a soul of a man within him can submit to such degradation.[1]

Although unions have become more accepted today, managers remain concerned over the gradual erosion of their rights in the labor relations process. Two related questions are:

1. Does management have inherent rights regarding its employees?
2. To what extent does the union desire to assume managerial discretion?

Under common law, management officials were relatively free to manage their businesses and their employees. In unilaterally running the operation, the employer drew from the concepts of property rights and the laws of agency as well as the legal and social acceptance of "private enterprise," "ingenuity," and the "profit motive." Hence, management assumed the right to manage derived from the property rights of the owners or stockholders. The authority of these owners is delegated to management, which in turn directs the employees in achieving the goals of the company. Following this line of reasoning, management contends it cannot share its prerogatives with employees or any other group, as that would represent a dereliction of legal responsibility to the stockholders.

There is no question that management can organize, arrange, and direct the machinery, materials, and money of the enterprise; however, at least one author contends that managers have no comparable right to direct the employees. Property rights carry no duty on the part of others to be managed—they can quit or be discharged without regard to the employer's property rights. Thus, management's property rights have never extended over the employees. "What has happened is that, through the union, the employee has acquired sufficient power to exercise the legal right that he has always possessed."[2]

Most unions in the United States, unlike their European counterparts (see Chapter 15), are typically reluctant to become "partners with management"—directly involved in managerial rights pertaining to layout of equipment, financial policies, sources of materials, and so forth. Union officers realize that many union members second-guess or challenge management decisions instead of supporting or echoing them.

Yet the unions' desire to avoid the management rights issue is not absolute. Management rights are implemented to achieve significant managerial goals of organizational flexibility and efficiency. These goals are often challenged and limited by a union organization that is concerned about arbitrary or inconsistent managerial actions and job security protections for its members.[3] Some research has found that craft and industrial unions have become more interested in joint determination of traditional management issues (products to be manufactured, services to be performed, and customer relations, for example) over the past 20 years. This new emphasis is largely attributed to competitive pressures, which have influenced union officials to evaluate a broader range of managerial decisions that could reduce union members' job opportunities.[4]

Reserved Rights and the Collective Bargaining Agreement

Management does not have any inherent rights over employees, and employees can sometimes alter working conditions through collective bargaining and the negotiated labor agreement. Yet problems sometimes occur when management claims it has full discretion to administer issues that are not covered in the labor agreement. There is a **reserved rights doctrine** that indicates management has full authority and discretion regarding all matters that are not covered in the labor agreement. For example, if the labor agreement is silent on overtime administration, then under the reserved rights doctrine, management can assign overtime to whomever it sees fit. Yet the reserved right doctrine is qualified by the following three factors:[5]

- *Legal obligations* placed on management to negotiate "mandatory" collective bargaining issues with the union.
- *Arbitrator's decisions,* which often interpret labor agreement provisions differently from management (consider the implications of "just cause" for discharge in Chapter 10, for example). Arbitrators also consider past practices, which can add to the terms of the labor agreement (see Chapter 9).
- *Attitudes and related actions of some arbitrators, management, and union officials* that the labor agreement is a "living document" reflecting the dynamics of labor-management relationships. Managers do not reflect a homogeneous group; some enhance or increase management rights, even those that are restricted by labor agreement language, while others "give away" contractually specified rights in their daily administration of the labor agreement.[6]

Thus, management cannot rely too strongly on the reserved rights doctrine. In fact, management officials usually negotiate either a long- or short-form *management prerogatives* or *management rights* provision in the labor agreement. The following management rights provision illustrates the short form:

> Employer retains all rights to manage, direct, and control its business in all particulars, except as such rights are expressly and specifically modified by the terms of this agreement or any subsequent agreement.

Some managers prefer this all-encompassing provision on the assumption that it guarantees management complete discretion in those matters not cited in the labor agreement. Originally, managers felt this provision could justify their refusal to go to arbitration over an issue not specifically stated in the labor agreement. However, as discussed in Chapter 9, the Supreme Court, in *United Steelworkers* v. *Warrior and Gulf Navigation Company,* stated that the arbitrator should determine whether an issue is a managerial prerogative if it is not specifically included in the labor agreement.

Many management officials responded to this decision by adopting the long form of the management rights provision—indicating several specific areas where management rights are unqualified (see Exhibit 11.1). Presumably, arbitrators, upon seeing these prerogatives clearly stated in the labor agreement, would rule in management's favor on whether the grievance is subject to arbitration. However, the long-form management rights clause has its problems:

1. It is difficult to list items that clearly specify management's unilateral discretion.
2. Management rights are a mandatory subject for negotiation. For management to obtain a strong management rights provision, it may have to

Exhibit 11.1 Example of a Long-Form Management Rights Clause

ARTICLE 2
MANAGEMENT RIGHTS

The Company has, retains and shall possess and exercise all management functions, rights, powers, privileges and authority inherent in the Company as owner and operator of the business, excepting only such rights that are specifically and expressly relinquished or restricted by a specific Article or Section of this Agreement.

The Company shall have the exclusive right to manage facilities; to direct the working forces; to fix or change the number, hours, and duration of work shifts; to establish or alter work schedules or standards; to control the use of scheduling of operations; to allocate and assign work to employees; to schedule overtime; to hire, classify, train, promote, transfer, suspend, demote, discipline; to discharge employees for just cause, . . . and to discipline or discharge employees for violation of such rules and regulations; to determine safety, health and property protection measures for any and all employees, operations, and facilities; to select and to change tools, equipment, machinery, material, layout, and facilities with which it shall carry on its operations; to determine the products to be manufactured or sold or the services to be rendered; to determine at all times the number and composition of the work force as a whole or of any unit, shift, job classification, or work within such job classification; to create new organization groups deemed appropriate by the Company and to determine the organization and structure of each; to determine, implement, modify, or eliminate techniques, methods, processes, means of manufacture, maintenance, and distribution, schedules, crew, or production team sizes, and line speeds; to control raw material; to shift types of work and production or maintenance in and out of any facility; to place production, service, maintenance, or distribution work with outside contractors or subcontractors; to use labor-saving devices; to determine and implement actions necessary to operate as economically and efficiently as possible when and where the company deems the same necessary or desirable, including layoff of employees; to determine the qualifications and duties of employees; to establish or modify reasonable quality and quantity standards; to judge the quantity and quality of workmanship required and discipline or discharge employees whose work does not meet such standards; to establish or revise pay grades for jobs; to change the method of compensation of employees, to establish or modify job classifications and related rates of pay, or revise or eliminate existing jobs; to transfer and assign work and duties to job classifications when the Company deems the same necessary or desirable; to select, demote, promote, or transfer bargaining unit employees from one unit, section, department, division, plant, or other unit to another; to transfer work from one job to another; to determine the location of the business, including the establishment of new plants, departments, divisions, or subdivisions and the relocation, closing, selling, merging, or liquidating of any plant, department, division, or subdivisions thereof either permanently or temporarily; to determine financial policy, including accounting procedures, prices of goods or services rendered or supplied, and customer relations; to determine the size and character of inventories; to determine the policy affecting the selection and training of new employees; to determine the amount of supervision necessary; and generally to control and direct the Company in all of its affairs and operations.

SOURCE: Excerpted from a labor agreement.

trade elsewhere; for example, it may have to allow the union a strong union security clause such as a "dues checkoff" or "union shop" clause, discussed later in this chapter.

3. Management may overlook an item and fail to include it in the labor agreement. Arbitrators view a detailed management rights provision as

> expressing managerial intent to define all its prerogatives. Although it is impossible for management to express all of its assumed prerogatives, most arbitrators would conclude that management should not view an omitted issue as being within its exclusive domain.

Both long and short forms of management rights clauses can cause additional problems. Most of the items cited in these provisions are subject to union involvement. Items in the short form are usually qualified by the terms of the agreement, whereas items in the long form can eventually become collective bargaining topics. By insisting on including the management rights clause in the labor agreement, management runs the risk of stirring up ideological differences with the union. The items in the management rights provision might also influence the unions' bargaining goals in subsequent negotiations.

Management apparently believes the advantages of the management rights clause offset potential risks. Approximately 80 percent of labor agreements contain management rights clauses that help remind arbitrators, union officials, and other managers (particularly first-line supervisors) that management never gives up its administrative initiative to establish the status quo.[7] The union likewise seeks contractual language to strengthen its security. This issue is discussed in the following section.

Union Security

A **union security clause** in the labor agreement makes it easier for the union to enroll and retain members. Unions are essentially guaranteed only a one-year existence upon NLRB union certification under the National Labor Relations Act. They therefore can be challenged by a rival union or by a decertification election after 12 months or at the end of the negotiated labor agreement (not to exceed three years' duration). A union security provision does not eliminate this possibility but can make it easier for the current union to enroll members, which is an initial step in winning their loyalty.

Union security provisions also tend to strengthen the union's financial resources by increasing the number of dues-paying members. Unions would like to recoup their initial time and money investments spent on organizing employees at an industrial facility by subsequently obtaining dues from the eligible members. Union leaders also feel they are morally justified in asking employees to pay for services provided by the union, because it is legally obligated to represent all bargaining-unit employees regardless of their union membership.

Union security provisions are therefore sought to strengthen the union, which can offer benefits to the employer as well as the union. Many might contend that employers prefer dealing with a weak instead of a strong union. Weak unions might aid the employer who wishes to terminate the union-management relationship, but they frustrate an employer who earnestly tries to resolve working condition disputes through an established union-management relationship. It is commonly the union, not the employer, who sells the collective bargaining agreement to the membership. A union has difficulty in accomplishing this objective when there are nonunion member factions that vocalize their dissent.

Union officials contend that union security provisions also offer other advantages to the employer. They contend that less time will be spent in recruiting new members and collecting dues of existing members during the work day. However, management officials counter that this time saving will not result in more production, because union officials might use the extra time to police the labor agreement and formulate additional grievances. Unions also maintain that morale would be improved if all employees were union members. Tensions arise when some people do not pay for the services shared by all. However, a counterargument could be made that tensions are not reduced by union security, merely redirected. The possible anger of union members working with nonunion employees is replaced by the anger of forced members who feel they have to pay for unwanted services.

Union Security Provisions

In view of their potential advantages and disadvantages, union security provisions have taken one or more of the following forms.

Closed Shop In order for an employee to obtain a job in a **closed shop,** the employee must first become a member of a union. The closed shop was made unlawful by the Taft-Hartley Act of 1947.

Union Hiring Hall According to the **union hiring hall** provision, employers hire employees referred by the union if the union can supply a sufficient number of qualified applicants. This provision in about 21 percent of the labor agreements is usually found in the construction trades, where a union provides the employer with qualified employees for a relatively short-term project. This provision has been supported by the Supreme Court, with the provision that the union hiring hall does not discriminate between union and nonunion applicants.

Union Shop Under a **union shop** contract provision provided in about 64 percent of the labor agreements, the employee does not have to be a union member in order to be hired by the company. However, the employee must become a union member after a probationary period of not less than 30 days in order to remain employed by the company. Under a union shop provision, the company does not always have to discharge an employee who is not a union member if (1) the employer believes union membership was not offered to the employee on the same terms as other employees or (2) membership was denied for reasons other than the failure to tender dues.[8] The union shop provision does not give the union the right to reject certain employees for membership and then seek their discharge for not being union members.

Agency Shop An employee is not required to join the union by an **agency shop** provision (in about 10 percent of the labor agreements); however, in order to remain employed by the company, the employee must pay to the union a sum equal to membership dues. This provision assumes that employees should not be forced to join a union but nonetheless should help defray the bargaining and grievance costs. The Supreme Court has upheld the validity of the agency shop in both the private and public sectors.[9]

The Supreme Court (*Communications Workers* v. *Beck*) has limited the amount of fees that a union can use under an agency shop arrangement. Unions cannot exact fees beyond those necessary to finance collective bargaining (contract negotiation and grievance handling) whenever a nonmember objects to the use of his or her dues payments for political or other purposes. Agency fee payers must notify the union of their objections to this use of the funds. However, the union must set up accounting practices to anticipate agency fee payers who raise this objection. The impact of *Beck* on the number of employee charges to seek dues returns is uncertain, although one observer anticipates that many agency shop members will raise objections to get some of their dues payments back.[10] Employer application of the *Beck* decision could reduce union dues by $2.4 billion a year.[11]

The Supreme Court in another decision also applied *Beck* guidelines to similar expenses paid by public sector employees' union dues. It stated that public employees did not have to pay the portion of union dues that paid for any union activities that were not oriented toward the ratification or implementation of the dissenters' collective bargaining agreement. This decision was not clear cut, however, as it indicated, for example, that dues payments can properly go toward a teacher union's strike preparation tactics even if a strike is illegal under state law. In essence, the Supreme Court agreed with the union that a strike threat represented a reasonable, albeit illegal, bargaining tactic.[12]

Maintenance of Membership This provision (found in about 4 percent of the labor agreements) does not require all employees to become members of a union as a condition of employment. However, an employee who joins the union must remain a member for a specified period of time, such as the duration of the labor agreement. Maintenance-of-membership provisions also contain an escape period (usually 15 days) after the subsequent labor agreement becomes effective. Employees who do not leave the union during the escape period must remain members until the next escape period.

Quasi-Union Shop It is illegal to require the union shop provision in right-to-work states (where union membership cannot be a condition of employment). However, these legal restrictions are sometimes avoided through **quasi-union shop** provisions in the labor agreement. Usually, the first page of the agreement states that employees will have to join the union as a condition of employment—a union shop provision. The union steward shows the new employee this provision, which usually results in that employee joining the union. A second provision, usually buried in a footnote elsewhere in the labor agreement, states, "Any provision found in this agreement that conflicts with local, state, or federal law is considered null and void." These provisions have the same effect as a union shop (because the new employee will seldom research the labor agreement when confronted by the union steward) and at the same time comply with anti-union shop legislation.

Contingency Union Shop Some labor agreements in right-to-work states have a **contingency union shop** provision stating that the union security provision currently in force will automatically convert to a union shop provision if the state's right-to-work laws are eliminated. This clause, unlike the quasi-union shop, does not try to dupe new employees into joining the union; instead, it mandates a labor agreement clause change if state legislation permits.

Preferential Treatment Clause A negotiated labor agreement provision that indicates union members will be given employment preference over nonunion members when a new facility is opened is called the **preferential treatment clause.** This arrangement was negotiated between the United Auto Workers and General Motors for the new Saturn manufacturing plant located in Spring Hill, Tennessee, and was upheld by the NLRB.

Dues Checkoff A provision that can be used in connection with any of the previously cited union security provisions or can stand alone in the labor agreement is the **dues checkoff** clause. It is not a union security clause in the strict sense of the word because it does not guarantee that some or all employees will become union members. However, dues checkoff allows the union members to have their dues automatically taken out of their paychecks (as for any other payroll deduction) and transferred to the union. This provision is most important to the union; indeed, most unions, given an either/or choice, would prefer dues checkoff over any other union security provision because it assures the union of an uninterrupted flow of income. Without a systematic dues deduction, union officers would have to spend a great deal of time with recalcitrant members who kept delaying their dues payments. In many cases, the employer automatically agrees to this provision in the first contract negotiation on the assumption that every other labor agreement contains it. Often an administrative fee is charged the union for the collection of dues and other paperwork. In negotiations, astute management officials usually bargain for something in return for this provision, such as flexibility in making work assignments, subcontracting, and writing job descriptions.

Union security provisions were found in 98 percent of the labor agreements reviewed in a recent survey. Union shop provisions were by far the most common (64 percent of the surveyed agreements) followed by union hiring hall (21 percent), agency shop (10 percent), and maintenance of membership provisions (4 percent). Likewise, over 98 percent of the agreements provided for checkoff procedures for dues, assessments, and initiation fees.[13] In many cases, however, the parties are not free to negotiate a particular union security provision. Right-to-work laws that restrict this discretion are discussed in the next two sections.

Right-to-Work Laws: Controversy and Effects

Employers, some employees, and the courts have long been concerned with union security provisions.[14] The Taft-Hartley Act in 1947 gave federal permission to states to enact right-to-work laws. More specifically, Section 14(b) of the act remains in force today and states:

> Nothing in this Act shall be construed as authorizing the execution or application of agreements requiring membership in a labor organization as a condition of employment in any State or Territory in which such execution of application is prohibited by State or Territorial law.

Under this provision, states may initiate legislation prohibiting union membership as a condition of employment. However, continuing lobbying efforts must be made by individuals or organizations to pass such a state law, a difficult task because there are corresponding attempts by others to oppose right-to-work legislation. Current efforts are mainly conducted by the National Right to Work Committee, founded in 1955, whose stated purpose is to protect the employee's right to determine whether to join a union. The committee does not regard itself as being against unions, merely against union security provisions that compel employees to become members. However, it has been alleged that the committee's "pro-union, anti-union security" stance has been modified to a flat "anti-union" approach in recent years. A related but separate organization, the National Right to Work Legal Defense Foundation, provides legal representation in right-to-work cases.

Exhibit 11.2 shows the votes in 40 years of elections concerning the right-to-work issue in various states. In terms of vote totals in these elections, more voters in various state elections have voted against right-to-work laws. The South is the only geographic region in the United States where voters have clearly and repeatedly supported right-to-work laws. Controversy occurs over right-to-work laws' meaning, morality, and impact on the union organization.

Meaning and Morality of Right to Work Supporters of **right-to-work laws** contend the underlying definition affirms the right of every U.S. citizen to work for

Exhibit 11.2 Aggregate Totals in Right-to-Work Elections, 1944–1966

REGION	YES	NO	PERCENTAGE RATIO
East	566,060	1,416,595	29/71
South	1,484,753	1,129,302	57/43
Midwest	2,598,680	3,492,567	43/57
West	4,708,018	7,000,251	40/60
National Totals	9,354,511	13,038,715	42/58

SOURCE: Gilbert J. Gall. "Right-to-Work Referendum Voting: Observations on the Aggregate Historical Statistics," *Labor Law Journal* 39 (December 1988), p. 810.

a living, whether or not he or she belongs to a union. In their view, compulsory unionism in any form (union shop, agency shop) contradicts a fundamental human right—freedom to join or not to join a union. Even Samuel Gompers, at least on occasion, stressed the necessity for "voluntarism" in labor unions:

> The workers of America adhere to voluntary institutions in preference to compulsory systems which are held to be not only impractical but a menace to their rights, welfare, and their liberty.[15]

Supporters further contend that nobody should be required to join a private organization, particularly if that organization uses the individual's dues to support causes that the individual believes are morally unjust or contrary to his or her religious beliefs. This attitude has been reinforced by an amendment to the National Labor Relations Act and actions by the Supreme Court that have, in effect, stated that employees may refuse to pay union dues because of religious objections.[16]

Opponents of right-to-work laws contend the term *right-to-work* represents a gimmicky public relations slogan designed to restrict union security and related bargaining power. They argue that unions do not deny anyone the fundamental freedom to seek work. Union security represents one of many negotiated working conditions such as work schedules, type of work performed, or wages. If an employee does not like a particular working condition, that employee is free to seek employment elsewhere. This argument can also be supported by a quotation from Samuel Gompers:

> [T]he union shop, in agreement with employers, mutually entered into for the advantage of both employees and unions and the maintenance of industrial peace . . . is to the economic, social, and moral advancement of all our people.[17]

Opponents further believe that union security provisions requiring some union attachment are moral because a person is a member of society with responsibility for contributing to the common good. Industrial society's common good might demand that individuals conform to norms (for example, a union security provision) for the good of all.

Impact of Right-to-Work Laws on the Union Organization and Employees

Currently, 21 states have right-to-work laws. These laws have an uncertain impact on union activities and bargaining results.[18] One research effort suggested that these laws might have little influence on employees' decisions to join or stay in a union because many are misinformed about related legal rights. Only 46 percent of respondents in right-to-work states knew that the following survey question was false: "[In your right-to-work state] if the company and union agree, they can require all employees to join the union and/or pay dues." The researcher maintained that misinformation about right-to-work laws occurred because there is no objective forum for related discussions. Unions are not going to explain employee rights in this situation, nor are nonunion employers. Managers in unionized firms might not educate their employees regarding these laws for fear of incurring the unions' wrath and a legal challenge that they violated the National Labor Relations Act.[19] Yet, another research effort found that in the first ten years after passage of right-to-work laws, union organizing was reduced 32 to 38 percent.[20]

The right-to-work laws' impact on employees' economic and democratic welfare is subject to controversial speculation. Advocates of right-to-work laws contend employees benefit economically in states where these laws are established. They contend that right-to-work states attract new firms and jobs. However, opponents of right-to-work laws counter that firms relocated because of the low wages found in right-to-work states. Exhibit 11.3 shows the median household income by state in 1993 and reveals that income in right-to-work states is more likely to be below the U.S. median household income (81 percent versus 34 percent for states not having right-to-work laws).

Right-to-work advocates also claim that voluntary union membership increases union democracy by making leaders more responsive to members. With

Exhibit 11.3 Median Household Income by State and Right-to-Work Status, 1993

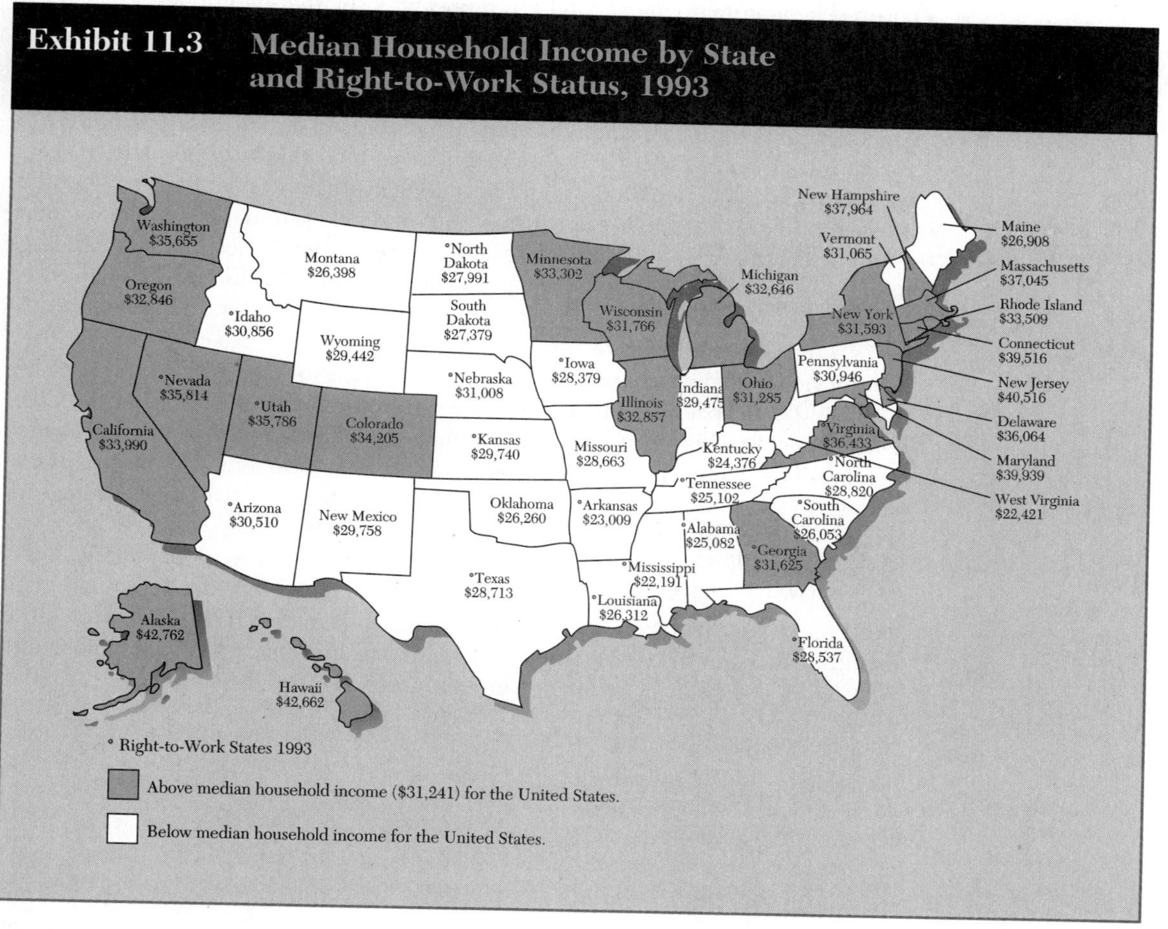

compulsory union membership, the members cannot express their dissent by withdrawing from the union. They must remain "captive passengers" of the union if they wish to keep their jobs. Union leaders can become indifferent or even corrupt because members have no economic way of voicing their displeasure. Union leaders should have to earn their dues through their responsive, diligent actions. "Good unions don't need compulsory unionism—and bad unions don't deserve it."[21]

Opponents stress that under the National Labor Relations Act unions are responsible for representing all bargaining-unit employees. Also, unions may be sued for lack of fair representation by bargaining-unit employees who are nonmembers. Those individuals who do not join the union are regarded by union members as being free riders—they never go near the kitchen but always show up for dinner. Unions believe that all employees represented should pay their fair share, just as citizens pay taxes for public services.

Some 2 million employees are currently in appropriate bargaining units covered by labor agreements and are represented by the union but are not union members.[22] Thus, right-to-work laws at a minimum permit reduced union membership in bargaining units,[23] which in turn influences the union membership's composition and related attitudes and behaviors.

One research effort examined union members at a police organization in a right-to-work state. Dues-paying members were more likely to be male, married with more financial dependents, and have longer organizational tenure.[24] Another study also found that females as a group were more likely to not be union members, a finding possibly due to their lower wages, concentration in occupations with large proportions of nonunion members (professional specialties, for example), and less employment in job categories having large proportions of union members (precision production, craft, and repair, for example).[25]

Sociodemographic characteristics are sometimes associated with attitudes toward unions and participation in union activities.[26] At least some unions, including the Communications Workers of America and the United Steelworkers of America, have urged their locals to identify and enroll individuals who are in sociodemographic groups that tend not to join unions. Such organizing efforts within the workplace are advantageous because these employees are easy to contact and their recruiting would not be particularly opposed by employers because the bargaining unit is already unionized.

Thus far we have discussed institutional issues that affect the union and management organizations in their relationships with each other. However, intra-institutional issues also exist, such as the relationship between labor unions and black and female employees, which are discussed in the next section.

Unions and Minority Groups

Unions and African American Employees

Historical Overview Trade union policies regarding black employees have varied greatly, from full acceptance with all membership privileges to systematic discrimination, which could mean exclusion through constitutional provisions, initiation rituals, segregation in separate locals, or separate job classifications. The Knights of Labor (KOL) actively recruited black members, consistent with their galitarian social-reform philosophy discussed in Chapter 2. The KOL also wanted to stop employers' efforts to use nonunion African Americans as strikebreakers, a widespread practice in the late 1800s and early 1900s.[27]

The American Federation of Labor (AFL) also proclaimed a firm antidiscrimination policy regarding black employees. Samuel Gompers, president of the AFL, at first refused to grant an AFL charter to national unions that practiced racial discrimination, including the Order of Sleeping Car Conductors, which prohibited black members through its constitution: "The applicant for membership shall be a white male, sober and industrious and must join of his own free will. He must be sound in mind and body."[28]

He soon realized that compromises regarding black membership were needed because member unions were ignoring the AFL's objectives. He admitted unions that did not specifically exclude African Americans in their constitutions but excluded them for initiation rituals and membership rosters.[29] Indeed, 11 unions affiliated with the AFL had formal race bars as late as the 1930s. A 1902 study found this practice yielded only 40,000 black members, with half of these belonging to one union, the United Mine Workers.[30]

Gompers rationalized accepting unions that discriminated against black employees on the basis that the AFL would have no power to effect change if the unions were outside its jurisdiction. Presumably, once in the AFL, national union leaders would see the error of their ways and accept minority members. His rationalization for continued racial inequality within the labor movement may have been based on an attitudinal bias against African Americans, perhaps caused in part by their previous strikebreaking activities. One historian claimed that Gompers also took delight in publicly labeling African Americans with racist stereotypes.[31]

Gompers, whatever his motive, indicated that African Americans would have to earn their way into AFL membership by obtaining necessary job skills. His attitude was reinforced by his successor, William Green, and two other AFL officials, who claimed discrimination existed before the AFL was born, and minorities should be grateful for what the organization had accomplished.[32]

At least two forces have influenced a more progressive union stance for black employees: a prominent black labor leader, A. Philip Randolph, and the emergence of the Congress of Industrial Organizations (CIO). Randolph, president of the Brotherhood of Sleeping Car Porters, became involved in the AFL's racial betterment activities when his union received a national charter from the federation in 1936; his 35,000 members made up one-half of the total black AFL membership at the time. In 1941 his threat to lead 50,000 African Americans in a Washington, D.C., protest march resulted in President Roosevelt's executive order that created the first federal Fair Employment Practices Committee.[33] He also clashed with AFL leadership on civil rights issues, which continually ensured that the AFL's leadership could not forget the black employee.[34]

The independent CIO also pressured the rival AFL to enroll black employees because, unlike the AFL craft unions, the CIO's unions had no control over employment. Therefore, they had to organize *all* existing employees, black and white, at a facility if they were to be successful.[35] The CIO also needed broad-based support in pressing its legislative goals of minimum wages, unemployment insurance, and social security. The AFL, on the other hand, usually having higher-wage earners as members, could not see similarities between their craft jobs and lower wage classifications that were populated largely by black employees.

Current Relationships between Unions and African American Employees Many union leaders at the local, state, and federation levels maintain that their organizations' democratic characteristics hinder racial integration. Leaders feel obliged to respond to white majority members who often feel economically threatened by black employees, with whom they compete for jobs, promotions, and job security. Some white members' concerns might also be attributed to racism.[36]

Union leaders therefore tend to stress racial equality solutions that are outside their organizations' activities and accountabilities. For example, employers, not unions, are responsible for hiring employees/union members. Union leaders thus contend that a predominantly white workforce is the employer's fault. Related efforts to solve the problem[37] seek equal employment opportunity legislation, other government policies that create more jobs for all employees, and employer fair employment practices in employee recruiting, training, and promotion. Today, black employees are more unionized than the workforce as a whole.[38]

In some cases, all-black organizations have been formed within the local or national union to monitor or change the union's policies toward minority members. Coordinated efforts across national unions have been made through the Coalition of Black Trade Unionists (CBTU), which was formed in 1972 and insists "that black union officials become full partners in the leadership." CBTU consists of 20,000 members who also belong to unions affiliated with the AFL-CIO. The CBTU did not endorse either Thomas Donahue or John Sweeney for president of the AFL-CIO; however, it presented both candidates with formal demands that sought the following:[39]

- Alteration of the federation's executive council to include more minority participants. This was successful in 1996.
- Inclusion of more minorities and women in union delegations sent to AFL-CIO conventions.
- Commitment by the federation to hire more African Americans for staff jobs as department heads.
- Participation of African American leaders "in the drafting of strategies for organizing industries and plants that employ a higher number of minorities."

In 1989, two African Americans were elected to the 35-member AFL-CIO executive council. Four current examples of African American leadership in national unions include John N. Sturdivant, president of the 156,000-member American Federation of Government Employees; William Burris, executive vice president of the American Postal Workers Union; Gene Upshaw, president of the National Football League Players' Association; and William Lucy, the secretary-treasurer of the 1 million-member American Federation of State, County, and Municipal Employees.

Recently, African American union members' influence has been complemented by government agencies and the courts. In Chapter 9 we noted that under the *Gardner-Denver* decision minority employees can file a grievance over alleged discriminatory action while also filing charges with the EEOC. Unions can also be legally liable for discrimination if their officials do not fairly represent minority and female employees (discussed in Chapter 8), or if they actively discriminate (or cause employers to discriminate) against an employee.[40]

Minority employees can also seek legal recourse if they believe that a union seeking and winning the representation election discriminates racially. A 1973 court of appeals decision *(NLRB* v. *Mansion House Center)* upheld the National Labor Relations Board's contention that unions engaging in racial discrimination or sexism should be denied initial certification and that employers could invoke the discriminatory practices of a union as a reason for refusing to bargain with that union.

However, minorities cannot protest alleged racial discrimination by using "self-help" techniques. A related Supreme Court decision *(Emporium Capwell)* concerned several black employees who believed the grievance procedure in the labor agreement was an inadequate forum to resolve racial discrimination issues. Over the objections of their union officers, these employees picketed the allegedly discriminatory employer instead of processing a grievance and were eventually discharged for their picketing activities. The Supreme Court addressed itself to the following question: Are such attempts to engage in separate bargaining protected by the National Labor Relations Act? The Supreme Court concluded that the employees' actions were not protected by the act; employees can be discharged for engaging in these unprotected activities. The Court further reasoned as follows:

> The potential for conflict between the minority and other employees in this situation is manifest. With each group able to enforce its conflicting demands—the incumbent employees by resort to contractual processes and the minority employees by economic coercion—the possibility of strife and deadlock is high; the likelihood of making headway against discriminatory practices would be minimized.[41]

Minority employees' rights in promotion and layoffs have also occupied the time of union and management officials and the courts. These issues are discussed in Chapter 12 because they are typically intertwined with seniority systems.

Unions and Female Employees

Many of the issues confronting female employees are similar to those black employees face. This is especially true of legal remedies, because both groups are covered by the Equal Employment Opportunity Act. Yet some differences in relationships of women and unions emerge when the history of female union employees is considered.

Historical Overview One difference is that female employees, unlike their African American counterparts, were involved in collective action including strike activities in the early 1800s. The first major strike conducted by females occurred in 1828. The dispute was not over wages; rather it protested paternalistic work rules prohibiting gambling, drinking, or other "debaucheries" and requiring church attendance.[42] A woman who became known as Mother Jones was one of the more fiery and energetic figures of the U.S. labor movement from the 1880s through the 1920s. Her role in mine workers' strikes and in helping to form the IWW reached legendary proportions. However, female unions during the 1800s were usually short-lived—the organizations were formed prior to a strike and lasted only for its duration.

From its formation until World War I, the AFL felt that a woman's place was in the home—allowing women to work would be contrary to its public principles supporting motherhood and the family. In addition to the lack of support from the AFL, union leaders faced many difficulties in organizing female employees into permanent union organizations, such as

- Low wages of female employees, making it difficult for them to pay union dues.
- Many female employees' belief that they would be working for only a short period of time.
- Strong employer opposition to unions.
- Lack of female union organizers.

The AFL increased its attention toward female employees when it appeared likely that the United States would enter World War I. Gompers was initially concerned about women's ability to do work traditionally performed by men. However, he was also concerned that women who might be employed during the war could pose a threat to the unionized male employees returning from the war. Trained, experienced female employees who would work for lower wages could place higher-salaried male union members at a competitive disadvantage. Hence, the AFL—perhaps out of organizational necessity rather than ideological commitment—became interested in the prospects of enrolling female union members.

The AFL's encouragement of female unionization continued through World War II, although some maintained the AFL was long on words and short on action. The number of female union members increased from 800,000 at the time of Pearl Harbor to 3,000,000 in 1945; however, only one out of five working women belonged to a union. Many male union leaders and members contended that female union members were basically unenthusiastic, even hostile to union principles and efforts following World War II. Some of this hostility was due to the fact that many women working in the factories during the war were summarily sent home at the end of the war.[43]

Current Relationships between Organized Labor and Female Employees Union growth now may well depend on the ability to organize female employees.

During the past 20 years the rate of female participation in the labor force has nearly doubled to almost 50 million employees, a figure that represents 44 percent of the labor force.

By the year 2000, it is estimated that 80 percent of the U.S. workforce will be employed in service positions, and that 90 percent of the new entrants will be females, minorities, and immigrants. This likely increase in female workforce participation might further expand the increase in female participation in unions over the years (from 18.4 percent in 1956 to 34.1 percent in 1987),[44] particularly because one study found that nonunion women in private-sector white-collar positions were more likely than their male counterparts to express interest in joining unions and were more likely than men to believe that a union would raise wages and enable employees to participate more in decisions.[45] A recent report published by the AFL-CIO indicates that unions have a 57 percent win rate in representation elections when women make up more than 75 percent of the appropriate bargaining unit.[46] While many statistics suggest an inevitable increase in female union members, a challenge remains for unions to convert these prospects into reality because only 12.3 percent of female employees are union members.

Some unions, such as the Service Employees International Union (SEIU), have converted these statistics and attitudes into a high percentage of representation election victories involving clerical workers. Unions will represent larger groups of female employees if they address the following issues:[47]

- *Child care,* a popular issue because nearly 48 percent of women with children under one year old are in the workforce today. This issue includes facilities or subsidies for child care, parental leave, extended pregnancy disability benefits, and flexible or reduced work hours and shifts.
- *Safety problems* such as chronic back or eye problems and potential reproductive difficulties associated with computers. Other safety problems particularly affecting female employees arise from jobs having repetitive motion and a variety of chemicals used in copying machines.
- *Career development* with specific job progressions for many entry-level positions.
- *Elimination or modification of electronic monitoring of work* (a situation discussed in Chapters 1 and 12).

Two other significant issues affecting nonunion and union women are *pay equity* and *sexual harassment.* A recent survey, *Working Women Count! A Report to the Nation,* involved the responses of nearly 200,000 women. Some 55 percent of the respondents earning less than $25,000 a year did not think they were getting paid what they are worth. Many respondents also felt that they were still not being paid the same wages as men who do the same jobs. They recognized that men and women do not have the same kinds of jobs, with many women being in low-wage and minimum-wage positions where their skills are not well compensated.[48] One union, AFSCME, has been particularly successful in obtaining pay adjustments for female-dominated job classifications (such as secretaries and nurses) under the "comparable worth" rationale (discussed more in Chapter 13).

Sexual harassment, discussed in Chapter 9, also affects many female employees. This issue can pose many challenges for both union[49] and management organizations as illustrated in "Labor Relations in Action."

Another indicator of female potential in the labor movement is the degree of influence that women can exert in labor organizations. Recently, female leadership has greatly increased at the local and regional levels. For example, one AFSCME publication indicated that about half of its officers in 3,000 local unions across the country were female.[50]

However, equal representation for women at the national level is far from a reality. One survey of 13 national unions[51] found that the percentage of female officers at the national level is far lower than the percentage of female union members. Several possible reasons[52] for this discrepancy are as follows:

- Women have family demands and have interrupted their careers to bring up children.
- Women are less likely than men to be in the high-status, visible positions from which union officers are generally selected.
- Women have difficulty developing necessary political coalitions and grassroots support.

Women may also encounter restrictive, sexist attitudes from the other participants in the labor relations process. For example, former New York City Mayor Ed Koch commented to the press that Sandra Feldman, president of the United Federation of Teachers, had "nice legs," and reporters besieged her for pictures.[53]

Some progress occurred in 1980 when the AFL-CIO executive council elected Joyce Miller, vice president of Amalgamated Clothing and Textile Workers Union, as its first woman member.[54] Miller did resign in 1993 to head the Labor Department's Glass Ceiling Commission. However, the executive council now has three female members: Linda Chavez-Thompson, Executive Vice President, Leonore Miller, president of the Retail, Wholesale and Department Store Union; and Denise Hedges, president of the Association of Professional Flight Attendants. Another female union leader, and the first black president of the National Education Association, Elizabeth Duncan Koontz, died in 1989. Exhibit 11.4 reflects the AFL-CIO's desire and strategy to recruit female and minority organizers and subsequent female and minority members.

Influence of female union members can also cut across local and national unions. For example, the Coalition of Labor Union Women (CLUW), formed in 1974, is largely staffed by female officers from AFL-CIO affiliated unions. The CLUW works with other women's organizations in carrying out its four major goals: seeking affirmative action in the workplace, strengthening the role and participation of women in their unions, encouraging legislative and political activity among union women, and organizing unorganized women.

LABOR RELATIONS IN ACTION

Sexual Harassment and Labor Unions

During the last decade, federal agency guidelines and court rulings involving sexual harassment have had a dramatic impact on business and industry. As charges of sexual harassment increase, unions have incorporated this issue into their organizing, collective bargaining, and contract administration efforts.

In *Sexual Harassment in Employment Law,* Barbara Lindemann and David D. Kadue cite the following major problems related to sexual harassment.

1. Sexual harassment has been pointed out as the most increasing, widespread problem faced by women in the work force.
2. Sexual harassment may occur in various forms, including "rape, pressure for sexual favors, sexual touching, suggestive looks or gestures, sexual joking or teasing, and the display of unwanted sexual materials."
3. Men tend to be the harassers and women the victims in the severest situations of sexual harassment.
4. Men and women may differ in determining acceptability of sexually related conduct. What some men may consider to be normal conduct may be highly offensive to some women. [See *Ellison* v. *Brady* 924 F.2d 872, 54 FEP Cases 1346 (9th Cir. 1991).] Moreover, women often remain silent when confronted with sexual harassment.

Title VII of the Civil Rights Act of 1964 (amended by the Civil Rights Act of 1991) prohibits discrimination in employment because of an individual's gender. The 1976 decision in *Williams* v. *Saxbe* was the first to recognize sexual harassment as a form of sex discrimination [413 F.Supp 654, 12 FEP Cases 1093 (D.D.C. 1976)]. In 1980, the Equal Employment Opportunity Commission issued *Guidelines on Sexual Harassment,* in which it defined sexual harassment as "unwelcome sexual advances, requests for sexual favors, and other verbal or physical conduct of a sexual nature," such as intentional patting, pinching, leering, or obscene gesture. The *Guidelines* indicate that sexual harassment occurs when submission to such conduct is made either explicitly or implicitly a term or condition of an individual's employment; is used as the basis for employment decisions; or unreasonably interferes with an individual's work performance or creates an intimidating, hostile, or offensive working environment.

Two types of sexual harassment are recognized by the EEOC guidelines and the courts. *Quid pro quo* harassment occurs when an employee rejects a superior's sexual demands and as a result loses an economic benefit, such as a promotion, increase in salary, or employment. In *Meritor* v. *Vinson,* the U.S. Supreme Court held that Title VII forbids sexual harassment even when no economic loss is suffered by an employee. The court defined hostile environment sexual harassment as a form of sexual discrimination and stated that the

(continued)

SEXUAL HARASSMENT AND LABOR UNIONS—CONT'D

harassment must be severe enough to change the victim's employment conditions and create an abusive work environment. [*Meritor Savings Bank* v. *Vinson*, 40 FEP Cases 1822, 477 U.S. 57 (1986). See also 29 FEP Cases 787, and 44 FEP Cases 332.]

Since the issuance of the *Guidelines*, the EEOC has noted a significant increase in reported charges of sexual harassment. Before the *Guidelines* in 1980, the EEOC received about 1,000 sexual harassment charges per year. The Commission received 3,453 charges in 1981 and over 5,300 in fiscal year 1990. Sexual harassment complaints increased at an even greater rate after the Anita Hill–Clarence Thomas hearings in 1991.

Unions have also shown an increased interest in sexual harassment issues over this time period. Joyce Miller of the Coalition of Labor Union Women maintains that the nonunion woman remains relatively powerless in defending herself against sexual harassment, whereas the union "gives power to the powerless" through its educational efforts and grievance procedure.

Education of employees regarding sexual harassment can occur during union organizing drives or with existing members. Publications such as the AFL-CIO's *Working in the USA*, the UAW's *When I Say No, I Mean No*, and *Stopping Sexual Harassment: An AFSCME Guide* indicate several measures the local union can take to combat sexual harassment. Delegates at a recent American Nurses' Association convention stressed that hospital employers should sponsor educational programs on the subject (such as teaching skills nurses *can use* to deter sexual harassment).

Unions have also been successful in negotiating collective bargaining provisions on sexual harassment. AFSCME has a somewhat standard clause that indicates that "sexual harassment includes any sexual attention that is unwanted;" urges employees to file grievances on this issue, which will be processed in an expedited manner; and provides for an employee's transfer at the same salary or grade if he or she feels unable to return to the same job after sexual harassment has occurred.

The union, which is bound by the duty of fair representation, may be faced with a problem when a grievance is directed at another bargaining unit employee. When a case is brought by a female member of the bargaining unit against a male who is also a member of the unit, the union faces a dilemma of loyalties.

Arbitrators have reinstated some male employees in this situation (see 80 LA 19[a] and 85 LA 11 for example) because of lack of evidence or the arbitrator's perception that the male and female employee had already resolved the problem.

There are cases in which arbitrators have reduced a penalty of discharge because they decided the penalty was too severe. The arbitrator may consider factors such as seniority, a good work record, evidence that the behavior was an isolated incident, the quality of proof of the employee's guilt, and management's failure to address the problem with a sexual harassment policy or with disciplinary procedures (see 73 LA 520, 86 LA 1017).

Arbitrators have also upheld an employer's decision to discharge an employee when it was shown that the employee's behavior created an offensive work environment that interfered with job performance. (See 89 LA 41 and 90 LA 1230. For other cases in which an arbitrator upheld an employer's decision to discharge an employee charged with sexual harassment, see 82 LA 921, 84 LA 915, 87 LA 406, 78 LA 690, 88 LA 75, and 75 LA 592.)

Arbitrators have supported management's decision to discipline employees for sexual harassment in cases of vulgar conduct, unwelcome amorous advances, and the sexual harassment of customers or clients. Cases of vulgar conduct have included, according to Lindeman, "sexual or crude language directed at a co-worker, obscene sexual gestures, exposing self to female co-worker, intentionally entering a women's restroom with a female co-worker present, and spreading stories about the sexual activities of a co-worker." Arbitrators have handled cases requiring a distinction between harmless romantic conduct and obsessive and compulsive behavior that may indicate psychological problems. Under the law of the shop, employees are expected to refrain from harassing customers, clients, and other nonemployees with whom they deal in their employment.

In some cases, Title VII guidelines have been incorporated into collective bargaining agreements; therefore, arbitrators adhere to these guidelines in making decisions (see 78 LA 417, 78, LA 690, and 82 LA 921). Arbitrators will also consider these guidelines if they are not in the labor agreement because they reflect public policy.

As noted in Chapter 9, the Supreme Court in its *Misco* decision indicated that the courts could overturn an arbitrator's decision if it violated sharply defined public policy. The circuit courts have been divided over whether and when arbitrators' decisions should be overturned because they violate public policy prohibiting sexual harassment. Recently the Supreme Court *(Teamsters Local 776* v. *Stoehmann Bakeries)* gave some direct guidance when it refused to hear an appeal of a Third Circuit decision that indicated an arbitrator could not reinstate an employee discharged for alleged sexual harassment without considering whether the employee actually committed the action as charged. The arbitrator's decision was based solely on procedural irregularities—management did not ask the grievant for his version before discharging him. Thus, the Supreme Court in future decisions will likely view sexual harassment as a violation of clear public policy and therefore subject to judicial reversal of arbitrators' decisions.

SOURCE: We are grateful to Sarah Philips, who researched and wrote most of this material.

[a]All arbitration decision citations refer to Bureau of National Affairs Inc., *Labor Arbitration Awards.* For example, 80 LA 19 would be found in volume 80 of this series, starting on page 19.

Exhibit 11.4 AFL-CIO Recruiting Brochure for Minority/Female Organizers

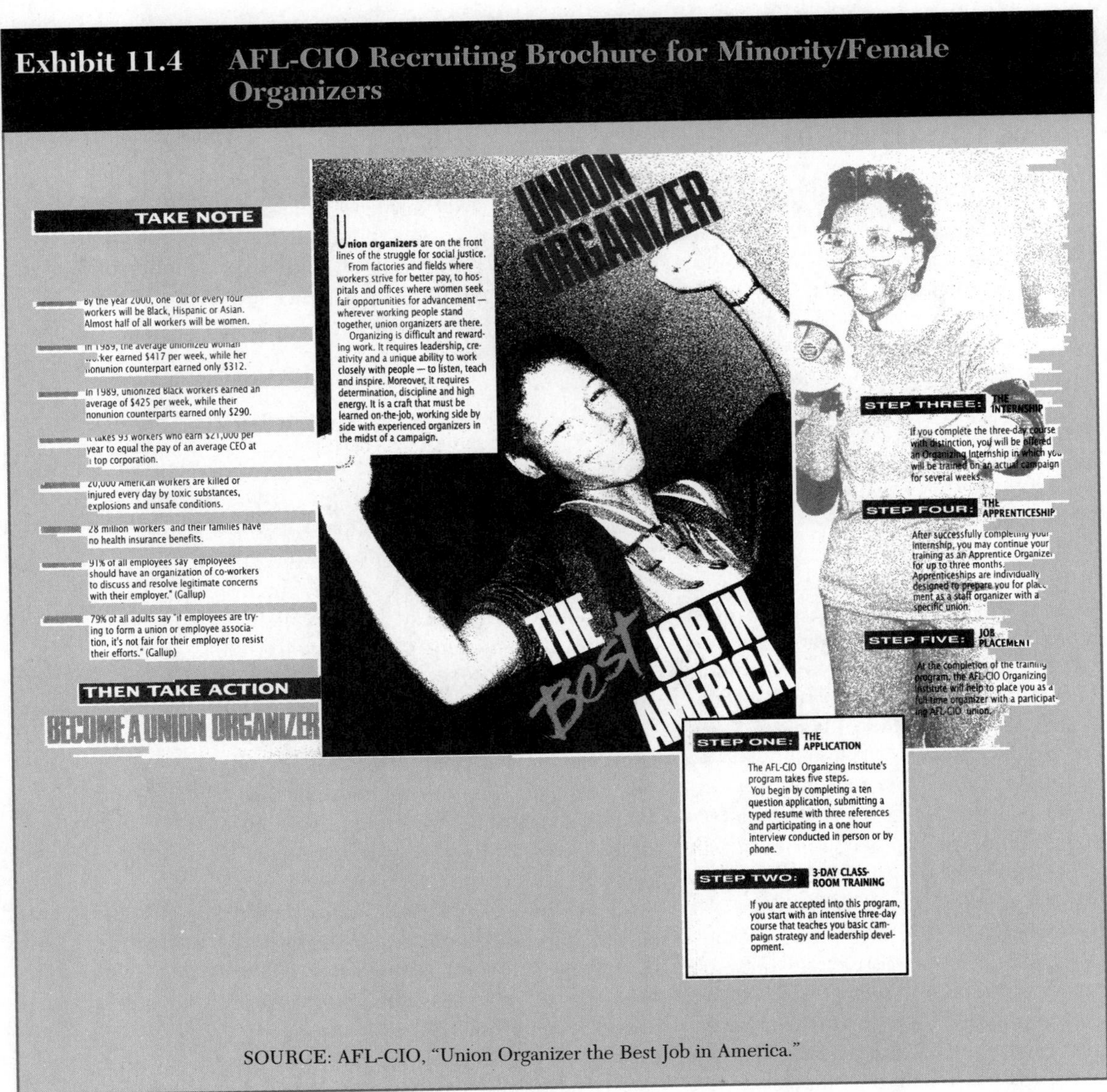

SOURCE: AFL-CIO, "Union Organizer the Best Job in America."

Unions and Hispanic Employees

The racial/ethnic shift in the U.S. population increased more in the past decade (1980 to 1990) than at any other time in the twentieth century. Much of this change was attributed to an increase in the number of people of Hispanic ancestry—some 7.7 million people, or 56 percent over 1980.[55]

This increase poses prospects and challenges for the union movement because many Hispanics have moved out of the agricultural sector, where they have been concentrated in the past, into a wide range of industries such as railroads (an estimated 22 percent of the workforce), garment and needle trades in New York City, light manufacturing in Chicago, and service in California and the Southwest. A recent survey by the Labor Council for Latin American Advancement (LCLAA) indicated that 1.4 million Hispanics pay dues to unions affiliated with the AFL-CIO.

Jack Otero, president of the LCLAA and an international vice president of the Transportation Communications Union, contends Hispanic membership in the LCLAA increased 30 to 40 percent over the past 10 years because of Hispanics' former jobs and cultural emphasis on family ties.

> They occupy some of the dirtiest, lowest-paid, and most dangerous jobs . . . [and] find that unions give them the representation that they need. . . . They know that if they stick together they can get ahead, and that's what unions are about.[56]

One study found that Hispanic unionization increased by 16 percent in the 1980s and will likely increase even more if labor organizations target Hispanic employees[57] as did the SEIU with its "Justice for Janitors" organizing campaign.

SUMMARY

Management and union officials want to maintain and strengthen their respective organizations through the collective bargaining process. Management has been long concerned about maintaining its rights to run the organization. While union officials do not appear to be particularly concerned about management's property rights pertaining to the machinery, materials, and money of the enterprise, management's prerogatives regarding its employees have been weakened or eroded through decisions by arbitrators, the NLRB, and the courts, as well as collective bargaining. Management rights are usually specified in the labor agreement in either the long or short form.

Unions are also concerned about their organizations when they attempt to negotiate a union security provision (such as union shop, union hiring hall, or agency shop) into the labor agreement. However, certain union security provisions cannot be negotiated in states having right-to-work laws, permitted under Section 14(b) of the Labor-Management Relations Act. Controversy occurs over right-to-work laws' meaning, morality, and impact on the union organization.

A variety of relationships occur between unions and minority employees. Although there have been exceptions, historically African Americans have not been well received by organized labor. At least three forces have influenced a more progressive union stance for black employees: a prominent labor leader, the emergence of the CIO, and civil rights legislation. Although female employees became active in labor relations earlier than African Americans, women have not been as well integrated into the labor-management relationship in terms of the percentage of unionized female employees. Unions have recently attempted to correct this situation by addressing relevant issues, organizing occupations that are dominated by women, and developing female organizations within the AFL-CIO. Hispanics also represent growth potential for unions as their presence in the work force increases.

Key Terms

reserved rights doctrine
union security clause
closed shop
union hiring hall
union shop
agency shop
quasi-union shop
contingency union shop
preferential treatment clause
dues checkoff
right-to-work laws

Discussion Questions

1. What are the comparative advantages of the long and short forms of management rights clauses?
2. Discuss how management rights can be eroded even though most unions have no desire to "run the business."
3. Formulate a one- or two-sentence argument for or against the right-to-work philosophy. Fully defend your statement from arguments that could be made against your position.
4. Discuss the similarities and differences between black and female employees' experiences with unions.

References

1. George A. Stevens, *New York Typographical Union No. 6, Annual Report of the Bureau of Labor Statistics* (New York: State Department of Labor, 1911), part 1, pp. 240–241, cited in Neil W. Chamberlain, "The Union Challenge to Management Control," *Industrial and Labor Relations Review* 16 (January 1963), pp. 185–186.

2. Stanley Young, "The Question of Managerial Prerogatives," *Industrial and Labor Relations Review* 16 (January 1963), p. 243.

3. Marvin Hill, Jr. and Anthony V. Sinicropi, *Management Rights* (Washington, D.C.: Bureau of National Affairs Inc., 1986), p. 6.

4. Martin M. Perline and David J. Poynter, "Union Orientation and the Perception of Managerial Prerogatives," *Labor Law Journal* 40 (December 1989), pp. 781–788.

5. We are grateful to Paul Gerhart for suggestions in formulating these factors.

6. Bruce Fortado, "Management Rights: A Topological Survey of the Terrain," *Employee Responsibilities and Rights Journal* 4, no. 4 (1991), pp. 293–308; and Bruce Fortado, "Exercising Managerial Prerogatives: The Findings of Four Field Studies," *City and Society* 5 (June 1991), pp. 76–96.

7. Bureau of National Affairs, Inc., *Basic Patterns in Union Contracts* (Washington, D.C.: Bureau of National Affairs Inc., 1995), p. 79.

8. Billie Ann Brotman and Thomas J. McDonagh, "Union Security Clauses as Viewed by the National Labor Relations

Board," *Labor Law Journal* 37 (February 1986), pp. 104–115.

9. *Retail Clerks International Association Local 1625 AFL-CIO* v. *Schermerhorn et al.*, 373 U.S. 746 (1963); and *D. Louis Abood et al* v. *Detroit Board of Education*, 431 U.S. 209 (1977).

10. Bureau of National Affairs Inc., *Daily Labor Report*, no. 131 (July 8, 1988), pp. A-1–A-2. For subsequent NLRB administrative implications and interpretation of this decision, see Bureau of National Affairs Inc., *Daily Labor Report*, no. 255 (November 22, 1988), p. D–1. See also Jan W. Henkel and Norman J. Wood, "Limitations on the Uses of Union Shop Funds After Ellis: What Activities Are Germane to Collective Bargaining?" *La-bor Law Journal* 35 (December 1984), pp. 736–746; "Supreme Court Sets Standards for Collection of Agency Fees," *Daily Labor Report*, March 5, 1986, p. AA–1; "Board Holds Hearing on Beck Dues Rulemaking," Bureau of National Affairs Inc., *Daily Labor Report*, no. 216 (November 6, 1992), pp. 1, 2; Peter Florey, "Fair Share Proceedings: A Case for Common Sense," *Arbitration Journal* 44 (March 1989), pp. 35–44; and David A. Lebowitz, "Limits on the Use of Agency Fees: The Revival of *Communications Workers of America* v. *Beck*," *Employee Relations Law Journal* 18 (Winter 1992–1993), pp. 437–461.

11. Robert Pear, "Bush Sets Attack on How Unions Use Nonmembers' Fees," *The New York Times*, April 12, 1992, pp. 1, 15.

12. "Supreme Court Trims Use of Agency Fees," Bureau of National Affairs Inc., *Daily Labor Report*, no. 105 (May 31, 1991), p. 1.

13. Bureau of National Affairs Inc., *Basic Patterns*, pp. 97–99.

14. For further historical insights into the right-to-work issue, see Gilbert J. Gall, *The Politics of Right to Work* (New York: Greenwood Press, 1988); and William Canak and Berkeley Miller, "Gumbo Politics: Unions, Business, and Louisiana Right-to-Work Legislation," *Industrial and Labor Relations Review* 43 (January 1990), pp. 258–271. For a classification system of right-to-work laws' various dimensions and related bibliography, see Thomas R. Haggard, "Union Security and the Right to Work: A Comprehensive Bibliography," *Journal of Labor Research* 11 (Winter 1990), pp. 81–106.

15. "The Voluntarism of Samuel Gompers," National Right to Work Committee (Fairfax, Va.: n.d.), p. 1.

16. See, for example, "Supreme Court Reviews Objection to Agency Fee," Bureau of National Affairs Inc., *Daily Labor Report*, May 3, 1982, pp. 2, 3. Amendments to the NLRA put restrictions on religious reasons and can require a donation to a charity (other than the religion) equivalent to a fair share of union costs.

17. *The Truth About "Right-to-Work" Laws* (Washington, D.C.: American Federation of Labor and Congress of Industrial Organizations, January 1977), p. i.

18. For related complexities, see William J. Moore and Robert J. Newman, "The Effects of Right-to-Work Laws: A Review of the Literature," *Industrial and Labor Relations Review* 38 (July 1985), pp. 571–575; and Joe C. Davis and John H. Huston, "Right-to-Work Laws and Union Density: New Evidence from Micro Data," *Journal of Labor Research* 16 (Spring 1995), pp. 223–230.

19. Marc G. Singer, "Comprehensive of Right-to-Work Laws among Residents of the Right-to-Work States," *Journal of Collective Negotiations in the Public Sector* 16 (1987), pp. 311–326. See also Marc G. Singer and K. Shannon Davis, "Comparison of Right-to-Work Law Knowledge Between Business Students in Maryland and Virginia," *Journal of Collective Negotiations in the Public Sector* 23 (Summer 1994), pp. 225–237.

20. David T. Ellwood and Glenn Fine, "The Impact of Right-to-Work Laws on Union Organizing," *Journal of Political Economy* 95 (April 1987), pp. 250–274.

21. Reed E. Larson, "Are Right-to-Work

Laws Desirable? Yes," in *Contemporary Labor Issues,* ed. Walter Fogel and Archie Kleingartner (Belmont, Calif.: Wadsworth Publishing, 1968), p. 272.

22. "Union Members in 1995," *U.S. Department of Labor News,* February 12, 1996.

23. Casey Ichniowski and Jeffrey S. Zay, "Right-to-Work Laws, Free Riders, and Unionization in the Local Public Sector," *Journal of Labor Economics* 9, no. 31 (1991), pp. 255–271.

24. John M. Jermier, Cynthia Fryer Cohen, Kathleen J. Powers, and Jeannie Gaines, "Paying Dues: Police Unionism in a Right-to-Work Environment," *Industrial Relations* 25 (Fall 1986), pp. 265–276.

25. Gary N. Chaison and Dileep G. Dhavale, "The Choice between Union Membership and Free-Rider Status," *Journal of Labor Research* 13 (Fall 1992), pp. 355–369.

26. See, for example, Michele M. Hoyman and Lamont Stallworth, "Participation in Local Unions: A Comparison of Black and White Members," *Industrial and Labor Relations Review* 40 (April 1987), pp. 323–335; and Jack Fioritio and Charles R. Greer, "Gender Differences in Union Membership Preferences, and Beliefs," *Journal of Labor Research* 7 (Spring 1986), pp. 114–148.

27. Herbert G. Gutman, "The Negro and the United Mine Workers of America," in *The Negro and the American Labor Movement,* ed. Julius Jacobson (Garden City, N.Y.: Doubleday, 1968), p. 99.

28. Herbert Hill, *Black Labor and the American Legal System,* vol. 1 (Washington, D.C.: Bureau of National Affairs Inc., 1977), p. 20.

29. Marc Karson and Ronald Radosh, "The American Federation of Labor and the Negro Worker: 1894–1949," in *The Negro and the American Labor Movement,* ed. Julius Jacobson (Garden City, NY: Doubleday, 1968), pp. 155–156; Ray Marshall, *The Negro and Organized Labor* (New York: John Wiley, 1965), p. 16; and Derek C. Bok and John Dunlop, *Labor and the American Community* (New York: Simon and Schuster, 1970), p. 119.

30. Karson and Radosh, "The American Federation of Labor and the Negro Worker," p. 156. For more details of the role of blacks in the United Mine Workers, see Herbert Gutman, *Work, Culture, and Society in Industrializing America* (New York: Alfred A. Knopf, 1976), pp. 121–208.

31. Philip S. Foner, *History of the Labor Movement in the United States,* vol. II (New York, 1955), pp. 359–60, cited in Karson and Radosh, "The American Federation of Labor and the Negro Worker," p. 159; and Samuel Gompers, "Talks on Labor," *American Federationist* 12 (September 1905), p. 636. For a more detailed account of this shift in philosophy, see Bernard Mandel, "Samuel Gompers and the Negro Workers: 1866–1914," *Journal of Negro History* 40 (January 1955), pp. 34–60. See also Michael Flug, "Organized Labor and the Civil Rights Movement of the 1960s: The Case of the Maryland Freedom Union," *Labor History* 31 (Summer 1990), pp. 322–346.

32. Herbert R. Northrup, *Organized Labor and the Negro* (New York: Harper & Bros., 1944), p. 13.

33. For more details concerning this march, see Herbert Garfinkel, *When Negroes March* (New York: Atheneum, 1959).

34. Herbert Hill, "The Racial Practices of Organized Labor: The Contemporary Record," in *The Negro and the American Labor Movement,* ed. Julius Jacobson (Garden City, N.Y.: Doubleday, 1968), p. 288. For additional details concerning Mr. Randolph and his union, see William H. Harris, *The Harder We Run: Black Workers Since the Civil War* (New York: Oxford University Press, 1982), pp. 77–94.

35. Summer M. Rosen, "The C.I.O. Era: 1935–1955," in *The Negro and the American Labor Movement,* ed. Julius Jacobson (Garden City, N.Y.: Doubleday, 1968), p. 202. For additional insights into the relationship between unions and African

Americans in the steel and automobile industries, see Horace R. Cayton and Kevin Boyle, "There Are No Union Sorrows That the Union Can't Heal: The Struggle for Racial Equality in the United Automobile Workers," *Labor History* 36 (Winter 1995), pp. 5–24. For a provocative, well-researched discussion of the negative impact of the AFL-CIO merger on black employees, see Herbert Hill, "The AFL-CIO and the Black Worker: Twenty-Five Years after the Merger," *The Journal of Intergroup Relations* X (Spring 1982), pp. 1–78. See also Alan Draper, *Conflict of Interests: Organized Labor and the Civil Rights Movement in the South, 1954–1968* (Ithaca, N.Y.: ILR Press Cornell), 1994; and Louis Uchitelle, "Union Goal of Equality Fails the Test of Time," *The New York Times,* July 9, 1995, p. A-1, which also updates the Philadelphia Plan, a nearly 30-year program involving construction unions and minority employees.

36. For an example of racist attitudes of some union members, see Scott Greer, *Last Man In: Racial Access to Union Power* (Glencoe, Ill.: The Free Press, 1959), pp. 149–150.

37. See, for example, "Activists Gather in Washington Seeking Jobs, Justice, and Peace," Bureau of National Affairs Inc., *Daily Labor Report,* no. 167 (August 31, 1993), pp. A-4, A-5; and "Testimony of John J. Sweeney, International President, Service Employees International Union, AFL-CIO, CLC on Affirmative Action in the Workplace Before the Subcommittee on Employer/Employee Relations, U.S. House of Representatives, May 2, 1995," Bureau of National Affairs Inc., *Daily Labor Report,* no. 85 (May 3, 1995), pp. E-1–E-13.

38. Normal Hill, "Forging a Partnership Between Blacks and Unions," *Monthly Labor Review* (August 1987), p. 38.

39. Louis Uchitelle, "Blacks See Opening in AFL-CIO Leadership Fight," *The New York Times,* July 15, 1995, p. 6.

40. See Russell K. Schutt, "Craft Unions and Minorities: Determinants of Change in Admission Practice," *Social Problems* 14 (October 1987), pp. 388–401; and "Court Holds Union Liable for Failure to Combat Racism," Bureau of National Affairs Inc., *Daily Labor Report,* no. 46 (March 8, 1991), pp. A-7–A-9.

41. *Emporium Capwell Co.* v. *Western Addison Community Org.* 420 U.S. 68–69 (1975).

42. John B. Andrews and W. D. P. Bliss, *History of Women in Trade Unions* (New York: Arno Press, 1974), p. 24; and Ruth Milkman, ed., *Women, Work, and Protest* (Boston: Routledge and Kegan Paul, 1985). For an analysis of the impact of World War II on employment increase and career considerations of women, see Claudia D. Goldin, "The Role of World War II in the Rise of Women's Employment," *American Economic Review* 81 (September 1991), pp. 741–756. For a historical overview of women in unions and related bibliography, see Marion Crain, "Feminizing Unions: Challenging the Gendered Structured of Wage Labor," *Michigan Law Review* (1990), pp. 1155–1221.

43. For additional insights into the relationship between females and unions during this time period, see Jim Rose, "The Problem Every Supervisor Dreads: Women Workers at the U.S. Steel Works During World War II," *Labor History* 36 (Winter 1995), pp. 24–52; and Nancy F. Gabin, *Feminism in the Labor Movement: Women and the United Auto Workers, 1935–1975* (Ithaca, N.Y.: Cornell University Press, 1990), pp. 47–111.

44. Esta R. Bigler, "The Changing Workforce and Its Effect on Unions," in Bruno Stein, ed., *Proceedings of New York University 43rd Annual National Conference on Labor* (Boston: Little, Brown and Company, 1990), p. 391.

45. Lisa S. Schur and Douglas L. Druse, "Gender Differences in Attitudes Toward Unions," *Industrial and Labor Relations Review* 46 (October 1992), p. 100.

46. *Statistical Abstract of the United States* (Washington, D.C.: U.S. Department of Commerce, 1989), p. 416.

47. For several examples of how these issues can be incorporated into the labor agreement, see *Bargaining on Women's Issues and Family Concerns, Clauses from ACTWU Contracts,* 2nd ed. (New York: Amalgamated Clothing and Textile Workers Unions, n.d.).

48. "Clinton Directs Labor Department to Seek Initiatives in Response to Women's Concerns," Bureau of National Affairs Inc., *Daily Labor Report,* no. 198 (October 17, 1994), pp. AA-1–AA-2.

49. For situations in which the alleged harasser is a member of the same union as the alleged harassee, thereby posing difficulties for union leaders, see Ken Jennings and Melissa Clapp, "A Managerial Tightrope: Balancing Harassed and Harassing Employees' Rights in Sexual Discrimination Cases," *Labor Law Journal* 40 (December 1989), pp. 756–765; and David S. Hames, "Disciplining Sexual Harassers: What's Fair?" *Employee Responsibilities and Rights Journal* 7, no. 3 (1994), pp. 207–217.

50. "AFSCME on the Job for Working Women" (Washington, D.C., n.d.), p. 9.

51. Naomi Baden, "Developing an Agenda: Expanding the Role of Women in Unions," *Labor Studies Journal* 10 (Winter 1986), p. 238.

52. Daniel J. Brass, "Men's and Women's Networks: A Study of Interaction Patterns and Influence in an Organization," *Academy of Management Journal* 28 (June 1985), pp. 327–343; and Dale Melcher, Jennifer L. Eichstedt, Shelly Eriksen, and Dan Clawson, "Women's Participation in Local Union Leadership," *Industrial and Labor Relations Review* 45 (January 1992), p. 276.

53. Lois S. Gray, "The Route to the Top: Female Union Leaders and Union Policy," in Dorothy Sue Cobble, ed., *Women and Unions* (Ithaca, N.Y.: ILR Press, 1993), p. 385.

54. Miller did resign her position in 1993 to head the Labor Department's Glass Ceiling Commission. At this time, five women were members of the 30-member Industrial Union Department.

55. Felicity Barringer, "Census Shows Profound Change in Racial Makeup of the Nation," *The New York Times,* March 11, 1991, pp. 1, 12.

56. Labor Union Focus on Hispanics as Source of Membership Growth," Bureau of National Affairs Inc., *Daily Labor Report,* no. 31 (February 14, 1990), pp. C-1–C-3. Mr. Otero resigned his international union position in 1993 to become deputy undersecretary of labor for international affairs.

57. Gregory Defreitas, "Unionization Among Racial and Ethnic Minorities," *Industrial and Labor Relations Review* 46 (January 1993), p. 298; Greg Goldin, "The New Surge in Latino Union Organizing," *Service Employees Union,* 3 (June–July 1989), pp. 25–28; and David Gonzalez, "Unions Open Drive to Recruit Immigrants," *The New York Times,* September 5, 1995, p. A-14. For a somewhat less optimistic assessment of Hispanic union membership and influence, see Ronnie Silverblatt and Robert A. Amann, "Race, Ethnicity, and Voting Predilections," *Industrial Relations* 30 (Spring 1991), pp. 277–283.

12 ADMINISTRATIVE ISSUES

Several important administrative issues can cost as much as or more than negotiated wage increases. This chapter focuses on six broad administrative issues: (1) technological change and its impact on labor relations; (2) job security and personnel changes; (3) employee training; (4) work restructuring; (5) safety and health; and (6) accommodating employees with disabilities.

Management wishes to have complete discretion in arranging work content and schedules in order to maximize efficiency. Unions seek to protect employees' jobs and job rights in cases of new job assignments. The attempts of management and labor to achieve their respective priorities are discussed throughout this chapter.

TECHNOLOGICAL CHANGE AND JOB PROTECTION

Technological change refers to changes in the production processes that result from the introduction of labor-saving machinery and changes in material handling and work flow. **Automation,** a type of technological change, goes one step farther in that machines perform tasks formerly performed by humans, and the human operator is replaced by automatic controls.[1]

Use of new and sophisticated technology is now the arena of international competition, and countries that are able to make the most effective use of new technologies will hold the advantage. Thus far, Japan and Germany hold the upper hand because their highly skilled and well-educated employees are focused on effective use and implementation of new technologies and are adopting new products invented in the United States. The United States remains focused on inventing new products, an activity to which U.S. firms are well suited. American universities are excellent, and college graduates do most of the research and development work. As example, the video camera and recorder, robotics, and the fax machine were invented in the United States; however, Japan dominates the world markets for these products.[2] Unlike Japan, the United States has not capitalized on the best available technologies; furthermore, the number of low-wage jobs in the United States is increasing, the real income of employees is stagnant, and more employees are earning poverty-level wages than in 1979. While America excels in robot science, Japan leads in the "nuts and bolts" of robotics. Japan's engineering workforce had already installed 220,000 robots by 1994, compared with only 37,000 in the United States. This has resulted in economies of scale for Japan, funding for future research and development, and a broad base of suppliers for manufacturers. The Ministry of International Trade and Industry alone has invested $100 million over the last eight years to develop robot prototypes.[3]

Technological change generally occurs in three phases: (1) the development phase, in which key choices about the design and configuration of the new technology are made; (2) the resource allocation phase, in which claims for resources by different organizational units are presented and evaluated against performance criteria; and (3) the implementation phase, in which the new technology is constructed, put into service, and modified if necessary. The third phase, implementation, is typically where the union enters the picture because implementation of new technologies affects the work structure and consequently the employees performing the job tasks. The consequences of the implementation of new technologies naturally are the concern of the employees as well as the union that represents their job-related interests.[4]

Unions and management have a long history of bargaining over the effects of technological change. In fact, 26 percent of agreements now have provisions that address the introduction of new technology. Only 17 percent provide for discussion with or notification to the union prior to the introduction of new technology, and only 8 percent require retraining of workers.[5] There are, however, important agreements containing these requirements covering large numbers of employees.

Some companies will involve employees and union representatives in the early stages of selecting new technology. Employees and union representatives accompany engineers on trips to vendors, assess the new technology, and render opinions on what types of equipment to purchase. They are consulted on how to operate the equipment and how to organize the work after the new technology is introduced. This approach has shown that when the union is consulted early in the technological development process, it is more likely to become an advocate for the new technology and is more able to assure its members that the technology will secure more jobs than it threatens.

The General Motors–United Auto Workers agreement provides for advance notice, special committees to deal with technology-related layoffs, and guaranteed employment with full pay as long as the displaced employee is willing to be retrained.[6] The recent negotiations of AT&T and its unions, the Communications Workers of America and the International Brotherhood of Electrical Workers, focused on competitiveness and job security issues. During the previous three years, AT&T had reduced its workforce by 36,000 and planned additional cutbacks in 1992 to 1995. Entering the negotiations, the unions wanted job guarantees; AT&T wanted flexibility. Their negotiations concluded with a program under which surplus employees may receive termination pay plus all wages and benefits for up to two years while having access to transfers to new permanent or temporary jobs.[7]

Southern Bell and the Communications Workers of America have included a "responsible union-company relationship" clause in their labor agreement and have set up joint committees to help introduce new equipment. (See the "Labor Relations in Action.") General Electric and Westinghouse negotiated provisions with the International Brotherhood of Electrical Workers that require advance notification of technology, committees, retraining, and safety measures for people who work with robots.[8]

Ford Motors has agreed to a lifetime pay guarantee program covering employees with 15 years or more service. If these employees are laid off, they will continue to receive pay until they reach retirement age or 62 years of age. With such guarantees of employment or income, employees will more likely accept technological change, and employers will be motivated to make training available so that employees can adjust to new technology.

While more manufacturing companies are adopting some or all of these elements, many firms have not. Many times, the union and management must address mistrust before adopting new technology. This may require continuous joint problem-solving sessions and labor-management committees to deal with quality of work life or workplace safety. The need for consultation with the workforce may be viewed as a loss of authority by supervisors and middle managers, who may resist transferring their power to employees. Upper management and union leaders will have to communicate their commitment to cooperation so that innovative work practices can be effective.[9]

Unions are often portrayed as being obstacles to technological change in the workplace because many Americans remember the controversy of the railroad firemen who wanted to remain on diesel engines, the reluctance of plumbers to adapt to plastic pipes, or the resistance of typographers to computerized typesetting in the newspaper industry. They envision unions negotiating a complex web of rules that restrict management's ability to manage the workplace and management's right to introduce technological advancements. Job protective provisions include

- seniority rules
- advance notice to union
- layoff prohibitions
- joint committees
- income guarantees
- "bumping" clauses
- layoff-recall rights
- severance pay
- preferential hiring
- other job guarantees

On the contrary, many experts and government panels have concluded that unions have participated constructively in the introduction of new technology. While unions are concerned about the job security of their members, they have not impeded efficiency. In fact, unions have generally accepted the doctrine of "high wages, high productivity, and low labor costs" as the best approach to maintaining income growth and employment stability.[10]

In general, technological progress in the United States has resulted in higher productivity, the elimination of many menial and dangerous jobs, higher wages, shorter hours, and a higher standard of living.[11] Technological advances have

LABOR RELATIONS IN ACTION

Responsible Union-Company Relationships

The company and the union recognize that it is in the best interests of both parties, employees, and the public that all dealings with them continue to be characterized by mutual responsibility and respect. To ensure that this relationship continues and improves, the company and the union and their respective representatives at all levels will apply the terms of this contract fairly in accord with its intent and meaning and consistent with the union's status as exclusive bargaining representative of all employees in the unit.

Each party shall bring to the attention of all employees in the unit, including new hires, their purpose to conduct themselves in a spirit of responsibility and respect and of the measures they have agreed upon to ensure adherence to this purpose.

Joint committees the parties have organized include the following:

- The *Joint Technological Study Committee* functions to keep everyone informed of technological change and how it will impact employees.
- *Joint Steering Committees* operate in each state to administer joint programs. They provide overall guidance for the Quality of Work Life effort.
- *Quality of Work Life (QWL) Committees* operate in each state and at lower levels throughout the Company to explore and recommend improvements in technology and work methods, cost savings ideas, and so on. Members of these committees define their own issues and perform substantial research and analysis in preparing their recommendations.
- The *Common Interest Forum*, comprising of top people from both union and management, meets on a regular basis to discuss future common interest plans.

SOURCE: Donald P. Crane and Michael J. Jedel, *Patterns of Industrial Peace* (Atlanta, Ga.: College of Business, Georgia State University Business Press, 1990).

brought about numerous positive effects: more wealth is produced with less effort; machinery that performs tasks that humans cannot or performs with more reliability and efficiency has lowered the costs of production and allowed products to be sold at lower prices; better working conditions prevail; back-breaking work assignments are minimized; and skill levels of workers have increased, with consequent increases in pay.

After an exhaustive study of the role of unions in technological change, researcher Jeffrey Keefe came to the following conclusions:

- Unions have no effect on a firm's use of advanced manufacturing and microelectronic technology.
- Unionized establishments are more likely than nonunion ones to be using advanced technology, primarily because they are larger, more likely to be part of multiplant enterprises, and operate in shifts.
- In most cases, unions welcome technological modernization; sometimes encouraging it, most often accepting it, infrequently opposing it, but usually seeking to protect their members.
- Both labor law and arbitration allow American businesses broad discretion over the introduction of new technology in unionized settings.
- The current legal and managerial framework confines unions to a reactive role in technological and organizational changes. This may impede employee participation and prevent the full use of new manufacturing technologies.[12]

Electronic Monitoring

While technological advancement has brought about much positive change for the employee, it has also increased the sophistication of methods of monitoring employees at the workplace. The Office of Technology Assessment has estimated that 6 million employees are monitored electronically. As many as 66 percent of all computer operators are monitored. This percentage will increase because it is estimated that almost 50 million employees will use computers at work by the year 2000.[13]

This monitoring includes supervisors listening to telephone conversations, computerized tracking systems of phone use, and computer monitoring in which video display terminals (VDTs) keep track of employee productivity and activity including counting keystrokes, error rates, time taken to complete tasks, and time away from the terminal. Printouts are provided to supervisors, who may use the data to determine production standards and pay rates, monitor speed and accuracy, evaluate performance, and discipline for failure to perform in a satisfactory manner.[14]

ETHICS

While employers argue that electronic monitoring of employees is a useful way to evaluate their employees' performance, increase productivity, and plan for future business needs, union officials respond that it is a source of stress on employees, robs them of dignity, and invades employees' privacy. Some employees have reported that electronic monitoring has caused nausea, severe sleep disturbances, and weakened eyesight. In the early 1990s, three states—Massachusetts, New Jersey, and New York—and the U.S. Congress had legislation introduced to restrict electronic monitoring. These bills would require advance notice of monitoring, prohibit collection of personal information, and prohibit disclosure of personal information without prior approval. As well, AT&T and the Communications Workers of America negotiated an agreement that required advanced notice on monitoring of employees' performance.[15]

Union officials are concerned that electronic/computerized monitoring invades employees' privacy, a situation that erodes their sense of dignity and increases high levels of workplace stress and related problems such as heart disease, high blood pressure, and digestive ailments.[16] They seek elimination of these actions, or at least the implementation of one or more of the following restrictions.[17]

- Notifying employees that their performance is subject to electronic monitoring.
- Imposing "beep" provisions requiring employers to use lights or tones to inform employees when they are being monitored.
- Prohibiting management from collecting information not directly related to an employee's work performance.
- Prohibiting disclosure of this information to other people or companies without prior employee approval or in connection with a criminal investigation.

Job Security and Personnel Changes

As mass manufacturing dominated industry from the 1900s to the 1970s, mass customization will dominate manufacturing after the year 2000. For example, by 2010 acquiring a custom-made suit for an overseas business trip will be simple. A few days before the trip, the individual will go the mall, step into a kiosk, and be optically scanned for sizing information, and record the choice of style and fabric. This information will be automatically relayed to the plant, where lasers will cut the cloth precisely to size. A few days later the suit will be sent to the purchaser, ready for the trip. This possible scenario will have dramatic effects on jobs and employees. It is expected that factories will be smaller, with fewer machines that have greater capabilities. There will be growth in jobs for software designers, technical writers, those in robotics, and those who provide services to emerging manufacturers, and unions and employees will continue to be interested in job protection.[18]

A primary concern of unions is ensuring that members' jobs are protected from elimination due to technological change or managerial decision making. Unions have been able to protect jobs by negotiating clauses about job security, subcontracting, outsourcing, work assignments and jurisdiction, work scheduling, and use of seniority in personnel changes. Despite surging corporate profits in 1995, the number of jobs cut approached those of the 1990 to 1991 recession. Corporate profits rose 11 percent in 1994 while 516,069 jobs were being cut.[19]

Job-Security Work Rules

Job-security work rules are provisions that attempt to make jobs more secure, such as spreading the workload by placing limits on the load that can be carried, restricting the duties of employees, limiting the number of machines one operator can tend, prohibiting modern tools or equipment, and requiring standby crews.[20] Such practices carried to an extreme are known as **featherbedding,** which exhibits "unreasonable limits to the amount of work employees may do in a given period, . . . payment for unneeded employees, unnecessary tasks, work not performed, or jobs duplicating those already done."[21] This practice is viewed negatively by the public as a waste of resources.

Workload restrictions lie at the foundation of many labor relations conflicts. From an overall (macro) viewpoint, union leaders agree that change is necessary for economic progress, but from an individual (micro) view, where significant adjustment would be necessary, change is resisted.[22] Congress attempted to help reduce featherbedding practices when it amended the National Labor Relations Act in 1947 and included Section 8(b)(6), which prohibits a labor union from causing or "attempting to cause an employer to pay or deliver or agree to pay or deliver any money or other thing of value, in the nature of an exaction, for services which are not performed or not to be performed."

After two Supreme Court decisions involving newspapers, Section 8(b)(6) lost much of its potential for restricting featherbedding practices. In one case, the Supreme Court agreed with the NLRB that some of the work practices at issue were wasteful, but that the work was actually performed and that employees had been hired by the employer to perform this work although some of it was not necessary.[23] Thus, the courts have given fairly specific direction to unions and management to resolve these featherbedding practices in collective bargaining. Recognizing that there may be some value to this approach rather than a purely legalistic one, the NLRB and the courts have set ground rules for these issues. The same means by which unions seek to improve wages, hours, and working conditions are available to maintain or establish job security provisions. Employers can resist these union demands, but they may also have to give up or trade something in return.

This tradeoff is the essence of collective bargaining. Resolving such employment security issues through collective bargaining enables the parties themselves to deal with the problem in a manner suited to their specific needs and situation (see Chapter 13 on productivity bargaining). Such issues include the following:

- *Job assignment:* Reducing crew size, adding duties, or eliminating unneeded jobs.
- *Job content:* Combining jobs such as millwright, welder, rigger, and boilermaker, allowing journeymen to perform helpers' tasks.
- *Hours:* Providing no relief or wash-up time, more flexibility in schedules, or more working hours for the same pay.
- *Seniority:* Restricting the use of seniority in filling vacancies, bumping, and scheduling shifts.
- *Wages:* Permitting pay for knowledge, not function.[24]

Work rules negotiated between the longshoremen and shipping companies that prevent truckers and warehousemen from unloading cargo from containers within 50 miles of the pier were upheld by the Supreme Court. These work rules were designed to preserve a portion of the traditional longshore work that is dwindling because of use of containers.[25]

International Harvester and the UAW negotiated a Job Content Preservation Program aimed to protect jobs from company decisions to outsource, use overtime, and introduce technological change. The agreement commits the company to a minimum guarantee of straight-time hours.

The commitment to employment security has several advantages: it induces employees to support change, encourages employers to invest in training employees, helps all employees to concentrate on a common goal, reduces costs associated with turnover, retains skills, avoids costs and turmoil associated with "bumping," and maintains employee morale.

Recently, unions have shown their willingness to assist management in remaining competitive by adjusting long-standing work rules. General Motors placed a high priority on work rule concessions in its last negotiations. In fact, it reported that changes in the following work rules had the potential of increasing productivity by as much as 25 percent:

- Reduction of relief time (46 minutes).
- Alteration or elimination of production quotas in nonassembly plants.
- Broadening job classifications so that employees perform a wider variety of tasks.
- Penalizing employees whose "controllable absences" exceed 20 percent of the available work hours during a 6-month period by reducing their vacation pay and supplemental unemployment benefits.

Plant Closures, Downsizing, and WARN

After 7,800 employers either shut down or initiated layoffs affecting over 1 million employees, and more than 50 percent of these employers gave less than 14 days notice or no notice at all in 1983 to 1984, Congress passed the **Worker Adjustment and Retraining Notification Act (WARN)** in 1988. This law requires employers with 100 or more employees to give 60-day advance notice to employees (excluding those employed less than 20 hours per week), unions, and state and local governments of a plant closing or major layoff. WARN also allows negotiation of a clause requiring more than 60 days advance notice. In 1995 only 23 percent of agreements had plant shutdown or relocation provisions. Less than half of these provided transfer rights for displaced employees and only 23 percent required the company to pay relocation expenses. Just under 70 percent of the agreements required advance notice to the union or discussion with the union prior to closing or relocating a plant.[26]

WARN requires employers found liable for violation to provide affected employees up to 60 days' back pay and benefits. The only means of pursuing such remedies, however, is through suits in federal district court. Because no federal agency is responsible for enforcing the law, employees have to take the expensive step of hiring an attorney to sue the employer who they believe has violated the law.

One study "suggests that *at most* there was only a slight increase in the length of notice specifically provided for under the Act." Explanations for this apparent disregard of the act include employer ignorance of the act's requirements, evasion of the law on the part of employers, and a strategic decision on the part of employers to keep the number of employees in their establishment under 100 or layoffs under one-third, thereby avoiding coverage under the act.[27] Analysis of advance notices in the two years immediately following passage of the WARN Act revealed that the act had virtually no effect on the length of advance notice given to employees. In fact, the incidence of written notices provided less than one month before separation appears to have increased after WARN.[28]

Since the passage of WARN, only one decision has been appealed to the U.S. Supreme Court. Since Congress did not specify a statute of limitations on filing claims under WARN, management groups requested a uniform six-month limit be established, as is the case in the National Labor Relations Act. The court rejected this request to impose a six-month limit without a congressional mandate.[29]

On occasion, the rules under the WARN Act and the National Labor Relations Act are intertwined. In 1991, the Dallas *Times Herald,* which had a longstanding bargaining relationship with the Dallas Typographical Union and Mailers Local, actively misled the unions about rumors of a closing during their negotiations of a new contract. On the date the sale was finalized, the business was then closed. *The Times Herald* then informed employees and the union. The NLRB ruled that remedies (back pay) to employees under the National Labor Relations Act are separate from payments under the WARN Act. Therefore, an employer may be obligated to make payments to employees when they violate both the WARN Act and the National Labor Relations Act.[30]

Subcontracting, Outsourcing, and Work Transfer

Subcontracting (also called "contracting work out") usually occurs when a firm determines that it cannot perform all the tasks that are necessary to operate its business successfully or that another firm can perform the needed tasks (janitorial and cafeteria services, equipment repair, parts production, and so on) better and/or at a lower cost. **Outsourcing,** a similar process, is a cost-cutting strategy of shifting work away from one's own plant to lower-cost producers—sometimes nonunion producers—and purchasing parts needed in production from these producers. For example, Ford Motor gets 58 percent of its parts from outside its company. In either case, the firm may contract with others to assume responsibility for certain work requirements.

The practice of outsourcing continues to cause conflict between the United Auto Workers and the Big Three automobile manufacturers. For example, 3,000 employees walked out of two General Motors brake plants in Dayton, Ohio, in 1996, when a 26-hour negotiation session failed to resolve a local issue over outsourcing. The UAW contended that 500 employees could have lost their jobs if parts produced in Dayton were purchased from outside suppliers. General Motors argued that it needed to reduce costs and purchase more parts from outside suppliers whose labor costs were half those at the Dayton plant.[31]

A strike by machinists at Boeing in 1995, the first since 1989, was caused in large part by outsourcing. Between 1989 and 1995, Boeing's worldwide workforce had shrunk by 62,000, and forecasts for plane production were the lowest in 11 years. To help win orders in Asia, the aircraft industry's fastest growing market, Boeing agreed to farm out parts production to manufacturers in those countries. As an example, Shanghai Aviation in China, with 2,000 employees who earn $120 per month compared with $3,530 per month for Boeing employees in Seattle, are producing 1,500 tail assemblies for Boeing. Although Boeing's aircraft are still assembled in Seattle, much of their fuselages and components, such as landing gear, are produced in and imported from Asia.[32]

In some cases, the parties attempt to reverse the outsourcing activities. For example, at the General Motors plant in Doraville, Georgia, the UAW and GM organized a joint union-management team to study the feasibility of keeping outsourced work. The committee found a way to produce seat cushions for one of GM's midsized models in-plant for less than the vendor charged. The team bid on the work and won the contract; now the cushions are produced at the Doraville plant. Since that time, the corporate office has decided to assign the assembly of GM-10 cars to that plant rather than shutting it down.[33]

The subcontracting process, seemingly a normal economic practice, is a volatile and complicated collective bargaining issue. From management's view, subcontracting raises issues of managerial flexibility, the firm's ability to progress economically, and its right to pursue its economic goals free from union interference. From the union's perspective, subcontracting raises problems of job security, challenges from competing groups of workers, and undermining of contract standards.[34]

Unions have increasingly attempted to influence management's decisions to subcontract. These decisions usually are motivated by the company's need to reduce production costs. Unions generally try to limit management's freedom to subcontract in order to protect and maximize work and economic opportunities for their members and to protect the members' jobs against competition from nonunion firms. The example of a subcontracting clause in Exhibit 12.1 shows how employers' actions can be limited.

Subcontracting clauses may vary across industries because unions in the construction and apparel industries do not attempt to limit subcontracting as such. Instead, they attempt to extend the provisions of the collective bargaining agreement to the subcontractors that are commonly used in those industries. Subcontracting is generally considered a mandatory issue of collective bargaining; however, the company is not required to bargain if all of the following conditions are met: (1) subcontracting is motivated solely by economic conditions, (2) subcontracting is the usual method of doing business, (3) the case at issue does not vary much from the kind of subcontracting done by the company as an established practice, (4) there is no adverse impact on employees in the bargaining unit, and (5) the union was provided an opportunity to bargain over changes in the subcontracting practices in negotiations.[35]

Exhibit 12.1 Example of Subcontracting Clause

The Company agrees that it will not contract normal routine maintenance work, excluding dryer, coagulation, recovery unit cleaning and the cleaning of any other equipment which has normally been contracted or requires special cleaning equipment, so long as it has the necessary manpower and equipment to timely and properly perform such work. On occasions when it is necessary to contract such work, such contracting shall not result in the displacement of bargaining unit employees. Before such work is contracted, the Union will be given advance notice. Such contract is to be for specific work of a definite duration and shall not be for the purpose of performing any such work on a full-time basis for the sole purpose of eliminating work from the bargaining unit. If it should become necessary to contract such work under this condition, the Company will determine whether such a job will be contracted to an outside contractor, to the Company's Roving Crew, or through another source and the Union will be so notified. (Phillips Chemical Company and Oil Workers)

SOURCE: *Collective Bargaining Negotiations and Contracts* (Washington, D.C.: Bureau of National Affairs Inc., 1982), p. 65:183.

Unions have made significant inroads on this issue in collective bargaining. Subcontracting is now limited or prohibited in 55 percent of the labor agreements, and inclusion of these clauses has not changed significantly in the last 10 years. Labor agreements seldom strictly prohibit subcontracting but often limit it in one or more of the following ways: they require advance consultation with the union, prohibit subcontracting if layoffs would result, allow subcontracting only if the necessary skills and equipment are not available, or require use of skilled workers for maintenance and construction jobs within the bargaining unit.[36] AT&T Information Systems, for example, employs 50,000 people who are represented by the Communications Workers of America and has agreed to make monthly disclosures of the amount of subcontracting being done and quarterly projections of future subcontracting as well.

Arbitration likewise has played an increasingly important role in the subcontracting issue. This role has usually involved such aspects as determining whether subcontracting is an arbitrable issue without explicit contractual language on the subject. Arbitrators are commonly asked to interpret the recognition clause and any accompanying bargaining-unit work and appraise commonly specified criteria, such as "good faith," proof of "sound business practices," and "no harm to members of the bargaining unit."[37]

The arbitrator will rule in favor of the union's position if management violates the agreement. The union's position is likely to be upheld where management's action "appears to deprive employees of overtime work, or where the act is seen as an attempt to nullify the contract or appears to have the effect of reducing the work of employees covered by the contract."[38] Typically, the company will prevail if the action taken by management was "not unreasonable, arbitrary, discriminatory, nor intended to harm, prejudice, or undermine the union."

Work transfer is similar to subcontracting and outsourcing. An employer who unilaterally transfers work from a union subsidiary to another subsidiary during the life of a labor agreement in order to cut labor costs violates the National Labor Relations Act when the labor agreement contains a work preservation clause. However, the NLRB has ruled that an employer is free to transfer bargaining-unit work during the life of the labor agreement after bargaining to an impasse with the union when there is no work preservation clause in the agreement.[39]

The Supreme Court has ruled that an employer has the duty to bargain over the *effects* of a business decision (such as severance pay, extension of health benefits, and so on), but not the decision itself. Thus, a company has no bargaining requirements if it plans to completely abandon a particular product line or service or to close a business. The NLRB's position is that an employer has the duty to bargain with the union over a decision to relocate an operation where there is no basic change in the nature of its operation. For example, the NLRB ruled that a company violated its duty to bargain when it shut down its hog operations at one location without bargaining with the union and moved them to another location when there was no basic change in the nature of its operation and labor costs were a motivating factor in its decision to relocate the work.[40]

Arbitrators as well have limited work relocation when they conclude that the parties have already placed limits on work relocation by including in their labor agreements the following standard contract provisions: (1) a recognition clause that acknowledged the union's status as representative of employees and established the scope of the bargaining unit, (2) clauses that established job classifications and wage rates, (3) seniority clauses that included layoff and recall procedures, and (4) job security clauses that limited circumstances in which employees could be terminated or jobs eliminated.[41] Practically speaking, there is usually good reason for the company to bargain about this decision as well as its effects. The union may offer helpful suggestions or offer concessions that make the relocation less practical. More importantly, if the company acts unilaterally and its acts are later determined to be unlawful, it risks large back-pay awards and in isolated cases a costly order to reopen a closed operation.[42] A recent legal analysis of this issue provided the following discouraging conclusion:

> The lesson to be learned is simple—the duty to bargain upon midterm transfer of bargaining-unit work must be analyzed on a case-by-case basis, and even then a high degree of uncertainty regarding the duty to bargain will remain.[43]

Work Assignments and Jurisdiction

In an organizational setting, management can assign individual duties and tasks to employees on the job more easily than it can assign employees to particular jobs that have permanent job classifications. Yet these assignments often give rise to union-management confrontations, especially where changes in operations, job descriptions, and technology occur and where more than one union represents employees.

While the National Labor Relations Act prohibits unions from engaging in or inducing strike action to force an employer to assign work to a particular union or craft, disputes do occur. Such disputes occur usually under three types of circumstances:

1. When two or more unions claim jurisdiction over specific work assignments.
2. When bargaining-unit employees believe their work is being assigned to other employees outside the bargaining unit, such as supervisors.
3. When disagreement occurs within a union over particular work assignments.

These disputes over work assignments are called *jurisdictional disputes* (see Exhibit 12.2 for an example of a work jurisdiction clause in a labor agreement), and they are costly and frustrating to employers if not settled rapidly. Under the Taft-Hartley Act, there is a special NLRB procedure for deciding these cases within ten days of filing an unfair labor practice charge. Factors considered by the NLRB in resolving these types of disputes are skills and work involved, the union certifications already awarded by the NLRB, industry and local practice, awards of arbitrators, the employer's desires, and economy and efficiency of operations.[44] The

Exhibit 12.2 Example of a Work Jurisdiction Clause

It is the intent of the parties to this Agreement to protect the work performed by employees in the bargaining unit.

The Employer recognizes that it is important and desirable to utilize its own equipment and drivers to the greatest extent possible prior to using sub-haulers and/or non-Company trucks.

The Union recognizes that under certain conditions, such as those dictated by customer demands, equipment requirements, daily dispatch determinations, materials to be hauled and similar factors, that sub-haulers and/or non-Company trucks are necessary and have been so utilized throughout the industry for many years.

The Employer, in accordance with the above, must however, determine the number, type and location of its working equipment in conformity with its business requirements. The Employer further must be able to determine, in keeping with sound business practices, the extent to which it will replace equipment which is too costly to operate, obsolete or damaged.

Under these conditions, the Employer agrees the sub-haulers and/or non-Company trucks will not be utilized as a subterfuge to defeat the protection of the bargaining unit work.

In keeping with the above, the Union recognizes that the Employer will utilize such sub-haulers and/or non-Company trucks as required by location and classification only after all the available Company trucks at such locations and in similar classifications have been initially dispatched.

Building and Construction Trades Department and several national contractors' associations have attempted to avoid the NLRB by establishing a national joint board to consider and decide cases of jurisdictional disputes in the building and construction industry.[45]

Some labor agreements require that bargaining-unit work be performed only by bargaining-unit employees except in instructional, experimental, or emergency situations. In instructional situations, there must be a clear, direct, and immediate connection between work done by members of management and instructions given to bargaining-unit employees. Experimental work includes the introduction of a new technique, method, or procedure, and emergency conditions occur as the result of unforeseen circumstances, such as a tornado, fire, or power outage, that call for immediate action.[46] However, it is generally recognized that bargaining-unit work may be performed by supervisors in situations requiring only a few minutes of time. Even though this subject may not be addressed in the labor agreement, several interesting issues regarding this matter must be addressed:

- Is a clear division between hourly employees and management in the best interest of effective labor relations?
- With more college graduates becoming first-line supervisors, how can they realistically get a feel for their subordinates' jobs if they are precluded from working on these jobs?
- If challenged over a production standard or promotion, how can management prove that the jobs can be done a certain way and within a certain time?

Intra-union work assignment problems, although not as critical and dramatic as other issues, often are very sensitive matters for local union leaders. Conflicts between members of the same union over work assignments can cause problems, especially in industrial unions having both craft and semiskilled employees as members. Whenever production processes are automated, reassignment of work from skilled employees to semiskilled production employees causes emotional conflicts within the union. For example, having pipefitters do welding tasks when welding is not included in their job description gives rise to disputes.

To resolve these conflicts, unions favor specific, written job descriptions and would like to refuse to perform work outside their jurisdictions. However, companies prefer general job descriptions that include phrases such as "perform related duties" and "make minor repairs" in order to provide flexibility in making work assignments.[47] Whether detailed or vague, the particular duties included in a job description often result in disagreements between management and union officials.

Work Scheduling

Collective bargaining agreements frequently deal with **work scheduling,** such as regulating shifts and fixing the workday or work week. Management also has the right to schedule work unless restricted by the agreement. For example, it usually has the right to suspend operations temporarily, reduce the number of shifts, and change the number of days to be worked. Moreover, it can usually make unscheduled emergency changes in the work schedule if such changes are made in good faith and for reasonable cause, such as extreme weather conditions, bomb threats, and civil disturbances. Unions and management continue to negotiate the workday and work week issues. While the five-day, 40-hour work week has been standard since 1938, when the Fair Labor Standards Act was passed, unions have continued their attempts to reduce the hours of work. Individual unions continue to attempt to adjust the work week.

Unions in the United States and elsewhere have shown increasing interest in *flextime programs,* which allow an employee to start and finish work at his or her discretion, as long as the specified total number of hours per week or per day are worked and the employee is present at work during the core-hour period (for example, 9:00 A.M. to 11:00 A.M. and 1:30 to 3:30 P.M.). These programs are designed to fit together job requirements and personal needs for individual employees. While flextime has much potential for meeting employee needs, some operations require all workers to be on the job at the same time, and in these cases work schedules cannot be altered unless the entire group accepts the alternative schedule.[48]

The Role of Seniority in Personnel Changes

Employers usually have a free hand in selecting employees who best fit the needs of their organizations and who best meet the prescribed job requirements. However, once any employee has been selected and placed on a job within the bargaining unit, the employer must abide by provisions of the labor agreement regarding personnel decisions such as promotions, transfers, and layoffs. This section highlights issues involving administrative determination and presents the concept of **seniority,** which is usually measured by the length of an employee's continuous service.

> [Seniority is] an integral part of the institutionalized web of rules that affect the administration of human resources in the internal labor market. Specifically, seniority has come to represent an enforceable priority under a collective bargaining agreement which qualifies an employee for benefits from the employer and provides a common basis for employees to estimate their relative status in terms of job security and opportunities for advancement.[49]

Seniority has played a key role in labor relations since the 1920s, when foremen's discretion (often abused) in personnel decisions was replaced by seniority-based decisions such as compensation or reward structures and promotion, transfer, layoff, and recall systems.[50]

Seniority can be divided into two categories of employee rights:

1. *Job rights* (also called *competitive rights*) apply in decisions on promotion, layoff and recall, transfers, work assignments, shift preference, selection of days off, overtime, and vacation date selection. The most senior employee usually will be given preferential treatment—will be laid off last, recalled first, and offered a shift preference and overtime first.

2. *Benefits rights* concern eligibility for certain employee benefits, such as vacations, pensions, severance pay, sick leave, and insurance. These rights are not competitive with those of other employees and begin to accumulate immediately upon employment with the organization.

Seniority provisions, found in 91 percent of all labor agreements,[51] show how seniority accrues over an employee's continuous service and, in some cases, how it can be lost for a variety of reasons (layoff, failure to respond to recall, unauthorized absences, or taking a job elsewhere during leave of absence).

Job seniority may be measured in a number of ways: total length of time with an employer (employment, mill, or plant seniority), length of service in a line of progression (progression line seniority), and length of service in a job classification (job seniority). While the particulars of the seniority system may vary greatly, some type of preference is usually accorded the more senior employees.

Seniority is considered "sacred" by most union members, yet it is doubtful that any other concept of labor relations has been as troublesome in collective bargaining. Management seldom objects to providing some sense of security to long-service employees, and unions and management generally agree that senior employees should be entitled to greater security and superior benefits as a matter of equity and fairness. However, for other reasons, seniority has played an increasingly important role in the labor relations environment. For example, it serves as an important objective measure for making personnel decisions—the concept dictates that length of service, not managerial discretion, determines who will be promoted or laid off. In addition, the number and types of employee benefits tied to seniority have increased dramatically.[52]

Seniority can be very costly to the company as well as to union members. It is difficult to compute the specific costs of problems caused by seniority systems, such as an aging work force, the possibility of lessening ambition and motivation in younger employees, and the loss of key personnel low in seniority.

Union and management representatives carefully negotiate the seniority provisions of their agreements in anticipation of future negotiation issues and in accordance with rules of clarity, equity, and simplicity. Seniority provisions usually include such items as the *seniority unit* (company, plant, department, job), *how it is used* (promotion, transfer, layoff, and recall), and *how it accumulates* (effects of interruptions of service such as military leave or layoff); *rules on loss of seniority* (voluntary quit, discharge for cause, failure to report from layoff, unexcused absence, and misuse of leave of absence); *administration of the seniority list* (posting requirements, supplying lists to the union, and keeping lists up to date); *special arrangements* (mergers, acquisition of firms, and succession); and *special exemption of certain employees.* In some cases, unions and management include a seniority provision called *superseniority,* which provides that highly skilled technical employees and union officials will be the last ones laid off. This provision allows the company to retain essential skills and at the same time promote stable labor relations.

Promotions and Transfers Personnel changes within an organization that advance the employee to a position of more responsibility, usually accompanied by a wage increase, are **promotions.** Appearing in 67 percent of collective bargaining agreements, promotion provisions usually state that seniority and ability are the deciding factors. While seniority can be easily measured, determination of ability is more complex. **Transfer** provisions, appearing in 57 percent of agreements, cover personnel changes from one position to another with relatively equal authority, responsibility, and compensation. Seniority and ability are also usually the determining factors used in making the transfer decision.

Four basic types of seniority clauses are used in promotion and transfer decisions:

1. Seniority is the sole factor (5 percent).
2. Seniority is the determining factor among qualified employees (49 percent).
3. Seniority is used only when other factors are equal (40 percent).
4. Seniority is given equal consideration with ability (2 percent).[53]

Straight seniority is the easiest to administer for determining eligibility for promotions and transfers. However, there is a possibility that the eligible senior employee is unfamiliar with the new job and will need extensive training.

Seniority with minimum ability simply means that the more senior employee gets the job if minimum qualifications can be demonstrated. Such a provision requires that the employer promote or transfer not the most competent candidate but the most senior employee among the qualified candidates.

When seniority and ability are given equal weight as determining factors, arbitrators have concluded that when seniority is relatively close, it is reasonable to use relative ability. But when seniority differs extensively, ability must be substantially greater to justify equal consideration.[54]

Ability, the measure usually accompanying seniority, includes skill, knowledge, attitudes, behavior, performance, pace, and production. While the employer has the right to establish any valid criteria for assessing ability, it must comply with the standards negotiated and written in the collective bargaining agreement. The employer may be required to meet the "Uniform Guidelines on Employment Selection Procedures" covering race, sex, national origin, and religious discrimination. These guidelines, used by the EEOC, Office of Personnel Management, and Departments of Labor and Justice, specify requirements covering employment defined broadly as tests and other selection procedures that serve as a basis for any employment decision including hiring, promotion, demotion, selection for training, or transfer. Moreover, the provisions of the labor agreement itself must not be discriminatory or perpetuate past discriminatory practices.

Even though promotion and transfer procedures differ, job vacancies must be posted for a specified period of time in 67 percent of contracts. Then, these jobs are bid for by employees interested in being considered. Usually, employees are given only a specific period of time to complete the bidding process.[55]

A study of 276 managerial decision-making processes on promotion decisions revealed that seniority is a major consideration in promotion in both union and nonunion settings. When jobs are posted, the more senior employees have the first opportunity to apply. If they do apply, managers usually favor them over more junior employees. Some managers believe that because seniority is objective, it is the fairest basis for advancement.[56]

Employers may design selection techniques to determine employees' qualifications for promotions and transfers. Techniques most commonly used are tests, experience, education, production records, performance ratings, personality traits, and absence, tardiness, and discipline records.[57] Because each of these criteria may be limited in its specific relationship to the needs of particular jobs, the determination of employee qualifications is usually based on several criteria. Where superior qualifications are identified, the determination may be clear-cut. However, where the criteria produce conflicting results, the burden is on the employer to assure accurate determination.

Transfer procedures are basically the same as those for promotion, except that employee requests are used more frequently. An employee dissatisfied in his or her present job and requesting transfer to more pleasant working conditions or a preferred work group, or to a more favorable line of progression, is generally granted the transfer if the employee qualifies and a vacancy occurs.

Other related labor agreement provisions are included to prevent possible administrative problems. For example, agreements should prescribe whether an employee carries his or her seniority to a new position or whether seniority will be retained only after a predetermined period of time. Other provisions should specify whether an employee who transfers out of the bargaining unit or is promoted to supervision will be allowed to retain seniority or will lose it.

Layoffs and Recall Layoff provisions are included in 94 percent of the contracts, and nearly half consider seniority first in retaining employees during layoffs. Increasingly, seniority has become the sole factor in layoff determination; however, some contracts still consider seniority as the determining factor only if employees are qualified for available jobs. In others, seniority is given consideration only when ability is equal.

Of course, there are exceptions to these general rules. For example, union stewards and local union officers may have *superseniority* and will be the last ones laid off in their respective departments. Unions sometimes desire this provision to encourage members to run for the many positions available in the union. In some cases, superseniority can be a strong incentive, if not the only one, to become a union steward. To protect the organization from having unqualified employees, some contracts stipulate that the union representatives must be qualified for the jobs available if they are to be exempt from layoff.

Advance notice of impending layoffs to the employees and the union is required in 49 percent of agreements, such as one to four days' notice. Frequently, employees scheduled for layoffs are permitted to displace or "bump" less senior employees, although they usually must qualify for the jobs in order to do so. While companywide or plantwide bumping is allowed in some agreements, it is confined to the employee's own classification or work group in a majority of cases. Most agreements provide for recall of employees after layoff. These provisions usually specify that employees be rehired in reverse order of layoff, but only if they are qualified for the open position.[58]

Over 80 percent of the senior employees in private, nonconstruction jobs enjoy substantial protection against losing their jobs. These employees are covered by plans that specify that no senior employee will be involuntarily terminated before a junior employee. Only about 40 percent of employees in nonunion firms are equally protected. Research on the effect of unions on layoff decisions has shown that unionized firms have layoff rates only slightly higher than their nonunion counterparts in both manufacturing and nonmanufacturing.[59]

Alternatives to layoffs include pay freezes, pay cuts, productivity improvement through changed work rules, new products, attrition and hiring freezes, voluntary leave, early retirement, buffer production demands, hours reduction, rotating layoffs, moving work, and work sharing. Unions at some U.S. companies such as Xerox, Mazda Motor, New United Motor, and National Steel have been successful in negotiating "no-layoff" provisions in their labor agreements.

Work sharing is provided for in 17 percent of agreements. These labor provisions specify that work sharing will be implemented for a limited time or that the company must consult with the union before work sharing may be implemented. Work sharing enables the employer to retain the skill mix of a full work force and consequently to retain its investment in employee training, keeps the employer's unemployment compensation tax contribution rates from increasing, and is considered by many employers as more equitable than retaining some employees and laying off others. Unions have shown a preference for the use of seniority in layoffs, rather than work sharing. Moreover, employers have no right to institute work sharing arrangements without first bargaining to an impasse unless such action is permitted in the labor agreement, such as in the management rights clause.[60]

Legal Issues Involving Seniority in Administrative Determinations Job rights guaranteed by the labor agreement may conflict with employees' legal rights. Use of seniority in administrative determinations such as promotions and layoffs has been the focus of much legal attention. In some cases it has been shown that minorities have been locked in departments or jobs with unfavorable lines of progression, and these practices tend to perpetuate past employment discrimination.

The Supreme Court has encouraged unions and management to engage in voluntary affirmative action programs for the hiring and promotion of minorities to rectify past discrimination. In some cases adjustments might need to be made for those minorities who were improperly denied previous employment opportunities.

While the Supreme Court encourages voluntary affirmative action plans, the high court upheld the right of white employees to challenge promotions made under a court-approved affirmative action plan when the white employees did not participate in the negotiation of the plan. The white employees sued their employer, claiming racial discrimination, and alleged that they had been denied promotions under the affirmative action plan that had been given to less-qualified black employees.[61] Two years before, the Supreme Court had upheld an employer's promotion of a female who had received two points less on an interview score than a male in order to rectify employment disparities between males and females as long as rights of other workers are not "unnecessarily untrammeled."

Another Supreme Court decision involved a white male employee who was denied entrance into an apprenticeship program even though he had more seniority (days employed with the organization) than some minority employees who were accepted into the program. This affirmative action arrangement between the employer and the union was found to be appropriate as the plan was temporary (limited to a short time) and did not greatly harm the interests of nonminority employees. Thus, a certain number of promotions in various job classifications can be reserved for minority employees even though these individuals have less seniority than qualified nonminority employees and have not been specifically identified as being victims of past discrimination.[62]

The Supreme Court has tended to view affirmative action in employee layoffs in a different perspective, contending that layoffs represent a potentially permanent loss of income, thereby placing great harm on employees. Also, layoffs represent the loss of something one already has, whereas promotions represent something one wants. In one decision the Supreme Court indicated that a court cannot award "competitive" seniority to black employees (more days of service than they have actually worked) if black employees who are given this extra credit were not specifically identified victims of past discrimination.[63]

The Supreme Court has also limited layoff procedures favoring minority employees even if the procedures are specified in the labor agreement. One such situation occurred between a board of education and a teacher's union. The labor agreement provided that in the event of a layoff, those with the most seniority would be retained, except that at no time would there be a greater percentage of minority personnel laid off than the current percentage of minority personnel employed at the time of the layoff. During layoffs, nonminority teachers were laid off while minority teachers with less seniority were retained. The court recognized that the labor agreement provision represented an affirmative action attempt. However, it stated that this provision could not be implemented because[64]

- Affirmative action for racial classifications must be justified by a compelling stated purpose. The rationale that minority teachers needed to be retained to provide "role models" for minority students was not found to be compelling.
- Societal discrimination alone is not sufficient to justify racial classifications in layoff situations. There must also be convincing evidence that remedial action is needed in the specific workplace.

Employers as well as unions face difficult dilemmas. Assuming that employers have been hiring minorities recently at a greater rate than in the past, the company seniority list would consist of white males toward the top and minorities toward the bottom. At times when product demand is low the employer may face the probability of laying off the newly hired minority employees in accordance with the last-hired, first-fired provision in the labor agreement.[65] In those cases where plant, department, or job seniority is used, the layoffs would erase much of the employer's progress in its affirmative action plan and affect minority employment disproportionately.

The Supreme Court has recognized that the Civil Rights Act affords broad immunity and latitude to seniority systems, particularly those that are *bona fide:* established before 1964, adopted in a good faith (nondiscriminatory) fashion, and do not exhibit any intent to discriminate in the layoff activity. Indeed, the Supreme Court has stated that layoffs based on this type of seniority will be upheld even if a disproportionate number of minorities are adversely affected.

Employee Training and Work Restructuring

Apprenticeship and Training Programs

America's continued well-being depends on how well our human resources are managed. Changing demographics and increasing complexity of work have made employee training and retraining a critical issue. In the past decade, the number of employees receiving training in registered apprenticeship programs has declined.

Apprenticeship training in the United States is not as widely used as it is elsewhere, particularly in Europe. Only 300,000 U.S. workers (less than three-tenths of 1 percent of the workforce) are currently enrolled in apprenticeship training programs—most of these are in the unionized construction industry. In fact, the United States ranks fourteenth out of 16 developed Western nations in the share of the workforce enrolled in apprenticeship training programs. For example, the total number of apprentices in the United States is smaller than in Great Britain, even though the American labor force is five times the size of the labor force in Great Britain.[66] In the United States, employer investment in formal training averages about $385 per employee per year, whereas German firms spend an average of $633, nearly twice the U.S. average. A more striking difference is the German investment of $4,447 per apprentice per year as compared with $263 per employee per year in the United States.[67]

Unions are involved in **apprenticeship programs** that usually consist of structured, long-term (three to four years) on-the-job training combined with related theoretical instruction that leads to certification as a journeyman in a skilled trade. In the United States, about two-thirds of the apprentices work in 20 occupations, mainly in construction and metal trades.

In contracts covering apprenticeship training the three most common types of outside education required are vocational schools, correspondence courses, and classroom instruction. Labor agreements calling for outside education usually specify a required number of hours of instruction, and employees are frequently paid for their time if attendance occurs during normal working hours. Often, the company agrees to pay a certain amount, such as 25 cents per employee hour, into an apprenticeship training fund to finance the apprenticeship training. In the construction trades, the unions usually operate the programs, whereas in manufacturing plants, the companies operate the programs within the guidelines established by the collective bargaining agreements.[68]

U.S. corporations now recognize that they are facing a training dilemma because advances in technology and global competition require a skilled workforce. Until recently, U.S. firms have devoted few resources to training their line employees. With the exception of the building trade unions, U.S. unions have traditionally left training activities to management. Recently, unions have begun a more active role.[69]

In 1995, despite a growing economy, job-security issues remained a concern to union negotiators, particularly due to layoffs occurring as a result of automation, competition, downsizing, and restructuring. Employee training has been elevated to a primary component of contract negotiations, particularly for employees whose skills are being rendered obsolete by advances in technology and shifting requirements for skills. Training programs that provide opportunities for employees to learn new skills required by present employers or to help them find new jobs have become part of a job-security package.[70]

Unions and companies have recognized the need for employee training and the need for skill upgrading. For example, Ford Motors has reported that one-third of its production-line employees will need some training beyond high school. In anticipation of future needs, the UAW has joined Ford, General Motors, and Chrysler in developing an impressive set of programs for employees to upgrade their skills and further their education in personal and work-related matters. One program is the Paid Education Leave Program, which provides leadership training to both production and managerial employees to equip them to take an active role in the economic transformation occurring in the automobile industry.[71]

Another effort to connect training with labor-management cooperation is the Bell South–Communications Workers of America PARTNERSHIP program. In 1984, Bell South made a strategic corporate decision to cooperate with the CWA in order to have a more competitive and flexible workforce. It was determined that employees would need to take responsibility for developing and maintaining their skills to keep pace with changing job requirements, and they would have to master new jobs if their former jobs were eliminated. Today, the mission of the PARTNERSHIP program is to prepare employees to take responsibility for their own career development and to provide them with the essential tools to accomplish their goals. Bell South's $25 million commitment to this program is highlighted in the "Labor Relations in Action."[72]

Four unions, United Auto Workers, United Steelworkers of America, Communications Workers of America, and U.N.I.T.E., in conjunction with the AFL-CIO's George Meany Center for Labor Studies and the U.S. Department of Labor, have organized the Labor Leadership Institute designed to develop skills for co-management within these respective industries. In San Francisco, the Hotel Employees and Restaurant Employees Union negotiated an agreement with 12 hotels

LABOR RELATIONS IN ACTION

Bell South–Communications Workers of America PARTNERSHIP

Phase 1: Exploration

- Identify learning areas, both personal and job-related, that employees want to pursue.
- Attend an orientation on company time to receive an overview of changes in the telecommunications industry, how those changes affect jobs, and how employees can respond.
- Participate in a career/life planning workshop to analyze their own values, career preferences, and personal options and to recognize their underused abilities and interests.
- Consult with a professional career counselor to evaluate current skills, identify skill gaps, and devise a career action plan.
- Attend special workshops, such as test orientation, job search skills, and "learning today for tomorrow," to meet common needs.

Phase 2: Skill Building

- Specific training and education courses are offered through a network of 150 community colleges close to employees' homes or work sites (with tuition reimbursement).
- Employees may take a single specific course or pursue a college degree program.
- Correspondence courses are offered in basic math and language skills as well as advanced technical subjects.
- Training is offered in general skills, clerical and computer subjects, electronics, and telephone principles.
- Upon completion of a course, the employee is paid a bonus of $50 to help defray expenses such as meals, child care, parking, and books.

Phase 3: Practical Application

- Employees apply the knowledge and capabilities acquired in the exploration and skill-building phase.
- Employees have access to a data bank that lists job vacancies and the skills required for company positions.
- The company targets jobs that are identified as surplus and gives priority to employees in these jobs for career assessment counseling and placement into new jobs for which they are qualified.
- For employees who have to leave the company because of job loss, company-paid training for up to two years is made available.

SOURCE: Dennis K. Allen, "Bell South–CWA Partnership: Teaming Up to Meet the Challenges of a Changing Industry," *Employee Relations Today* (Summer 1994), pp. 163–168.

to create a $3 million training program directed toward employee empowerment, consensus decision making, and skill development in new technologies.[73]

Work Restructuring

Unions and companies are changing the nature of the work performed by employees. While these work restructuring programs come under many different labels, such as employee involvement, worker participation, labor-management jointness, or self-managed work teams, they all involve major departures from the traditional way of assigning specific tasks to each employee. For example, a work team may include 5 to 12 multi-skilled workers who rotate jobs and produce an entire product with a minimal amount of supervision. The team approach wipes out tiers of managers and tears down bureaucratic barriers between departments. It requires employees to improve their technical and behavioral skills. Some work teams not only gain a more direct voice in shop-floor operations, but also take over some managerial duties, such as scheduling work and vacations, hiring new members, and ordering materials. These programs have unleashed enormous energy and creativity in employees and increased their feelings of dignity and self-worth, and have enjoyed successes in such companies as General Electric, General Motors, Champion International, and Ford. A newly created subsidiary of AT&T Credit Corp. reported productivity increases of 100 percent after restructuring employees' jobs and organizing the team concept.

A study by the U.S. Department of Labor and Ernst & Young found that American companies have discovered that investing in employees and innovative workplace strategies pays off in profits. Such practices include integrating business process and technology improvements with high-performance work practices, such as just-in-time (JIT) inventory management and Total Quality Management (TQM). These practices are most effective when implemented with employee training and empowerment programs. Those companies that adopted aggressive employee development and involvement practices, such as skill training and team-based management, made significantly larger productivity gains than those that did not.[74]

One of the major efforts in work restructuring, particularly in the metals industry, has been the development of cell manufacturing. The need to improve product quality has driven companies to realize that traditional functional layouts of similar machinery for batch manufacturing is costly and obsolete. Cell manufacturing involves placing groups of dissimilar machinery in a small, cell-like configuration dedicated to machining a particular part or family of parts. Cell manufacturing requires highly skilled employees who are generally more satisfied with their jobs because their tasks are varied and their authority is enhanced. Cell manufacturing is usually introduced with just-in-time inventory and employee involvement programs. In cell manufacturing, employees are trained to perform new tasks, assume more responsibility, relinquish old habits and ideas, and become more involved in decision making through participation in work teams. Cell manufacturing is not an anti-union device, and unions around the United States are actively involved in these innovative efforts to make their companies more competitive. A union's involvement and cooperation in these efforts actually reduce the resistance to changing to cell manufacturing. Though some contend that cell manufacturing may lead to mistreatment of employees, the union remains the representative of the employees to protect their job security and seniority rights, improve their wages, and so on. Unions can provide a meaningful presence in helping cell manufacturing work to its capacity when they are involved.[75]

Safety and Health: The Occupational Safety and Health Act

Occupational safety and health clauses are found in 89 percent of labor agreements. The topics covered range from a general statement of responsibility for the safety and health of employees (62 percent) to details about such issues as safety equipment (43 percent), first aid (22 percent), physical examinations (33 percent), investigation of accidents (21 percent), employee obligations (69 percent), hazardous work (27 percent), and joint union-management safety committees (53 percent).[76] Many of these provisions have resulted from legislation, namely the Occupational Safety and Health Act passed in 1970 in an attempt to improve industrial safety statistics.

The employer's overriding duty under the Occupational Safety and Health Act is to furnish each employee with conditions free from recognized hazards that may cause illness, injury, or death and to comply with all occupational safety and health standards adopted by the Department of Labor. Employers must permit inspectors to enter their establishments and conduct inspections, and must post notices, provide equipment, and maintain records.

Since 1970 there have been more than a million Occupational Safety and Health Administration (OSHA) inspections and thousands more by state inspectors. The percentage of collective bargaining agreements that include a safety and health clause has increased from about 70 percent in 1957 through 1971 to over 90 percent in 1995. During the same period, labor agreements establishing joint safety and health committees in manufacturing have increased from 38 to 67 percent. However, despite the investment of enormous resources, injury rates appear to be unaffected. The percentage of manufacturing workers losing work days due to injuries actually increased from 4.0 in 1972 to 5.8 in 1988 through 1991. As well, the yearly number of lost work days per hundred manufacturing employees rose from 73 days in 1975 to 121 in 1991.[77] OSHA inspects only 2 percent of workplaces each year; therefore, the threat of inspections does not appear to be an effective deterrent to safety and health violations or an incentive to voluntarily comply with the act.[78] On the other hand, OSHA investigations in response to employee complaints yield more effective enforcement.[79]

In 1994, Labor Secretary Robert Reich announced that he intended to step up enforcement of workplace safety laws after 12 years of unaggressive enforcement under the Reagan and Bush administrations. Secretary Reich supported proposed legislation to require all companies with 11 or more full-time employees to set up safety and health committees, to increase criminal penalties to those whose "willful violations" of the law caused a death, and to direct OSHA to revise rules on exposure to toxic substances every three years. However, by 1995 this legislation did not receive enough support in Congress for enactment.[80]

A recent study by the congressional Office of Technology Assessment (OTA) revealed that OSHA has generally performed its regulatory tasks with "workable accuracy." However, OSHA has long been derided by employers and industry groups during its 25-year history. Nevertheless, OTA concluded that not only did employers use innovative measures to protect employees, but compliance with OSHA standards proved to be considerably less costly than OSHA's estimates. One reason for the lower than expected costs was employers' retooling and modernization efforts to meet OSHA standards. OTA reported, for example, that the costs of complying with OSHA's vinyl chloride standards were 25 percent less than estimated, and compliance with the cotton dust standard was 33 percent less than OSHA's estimate.[81]

Unions might also become directly involved in five controversial safety issues: *employees who walk off the job; the union's right to receive safety information; women working on jobs that could be harmful to unborn children; safety problems from video display terminals;* and *no-smoking rules.*

Employees who walk off their jobs in an expression of concern over unsafe working conditions are protected by the National Labor Relations Act. Under the NLRA, when employees act as a group, they are protected for their concerted activities if they believe in good faith that they are exposed to a safety risk. In such cases, they may protest exposure to the dangerous condition without being subjected to subsequent discipline or discrimination by the employer.[82]

A second issue is the OSHA rule that allows employees, their designated representatives, and OSHA inspectors the right to examine on-the-job medical records as well as company records of exposure to hazardous conditions. Employers are not required to measure exposure to toxic substances or to conduct medical surveillance of employees. However, if an employer does conduct these activities and records the results, this information must be accessible to employees, their representatives, and OSHA inspectors. Refusal by the employer or occupational physician to provide such information is allowed only when the information would be detrimental to the employee's mental health, such as information about the employee's psychiatric state or a diagnosis of terminal illness.[83] The union, as the employees' representative, as well as the NLRB may become involved in obtaining information. Recently, a federal appeals court upheld an NLRB order that a company honor a union's request for information about industrial chemicals and medical conditions of employees exposed to potentially hazardous substances.[84]

Another controversial safety- and health-related issue was decided by the Supreme Court when it ruled that companies could not bar women from jobs that may be hazardous to unborn children. The court explained that decisions about the welfare of future children must be left to the parents. Unions and women's groups had challenged the policy of Johnson Controls, Inc., an automobile battery manufacturer, which banned women who could not prove they were infertile from working in areas of the plant where they were exposed to lead, the principal material used in making batteries. The challengers successfully argued that the company policy discriminated against female employees because they were blocked from higher-paying jobs. To reduce the possibility of potential employer liability, employers were advised to fully inform employees of the risk involved.[85]

Repetitive motion injuries, called cumulative trauma disorder or carpal tunnel syndrome by doctors and "the VDT (Video Display Terminal) disease" by employees, have become the fastest-growing occupational injury in the United States. The National Institute for Occupational Safety and Health estimates that 5 million people, or 4 percent of the workforce, are affected. These injuries result from frequent bending of the wrist, which causes tendons and tissues to swell in the tunnel formed by the carpal bones and ligaments, pinching and incapacitating the median nerve, which gives feeling to the hand. Meat cutters, food processors, assembly employees, office employees who work at VDTs, and others are likely to be affected.[86] These injuries account for more than 60 percent of all illnesses reported to OSHA. To mitigate these injuries, employers have developed ergonomic programs that include analyzing the work site to identify ergonomic hazards and symptoms; adopting preventative measures such as providing protective equipment and redesigning work stations; allowing administrative measures, such as frequent breaks, job rotation, and medical monitoring; and flexible return-to-work policies. Ford Motor Company agreed to implement ergonomic programs at most of its plants and paid a $1.2 million fine stemming from one plant inspection. Pepperidge Farm was fined $638,500, and Wickes Manufacturing was fined $243,000 for ergonomic violations.[87]

Since the U.S. Surgeon General's report on smoking's health consequences, the issue has gradually moved to the labor relations area. In 1986, the Surgeon General's Report on the Health Consequences of Involuntary Smoking disclosed that secondhand smoke may expose the involuntary smoker to greater amounts of carcinogens than those to which the smoker is exposed, which raised the level of concern at the workplace. As a result, employers began considering no-smoking rules, smoke free workplaces, and designated places for smoking. Emerging issues will be the rule-making procedures (unilateral and negotiated) and union action to protect bargaining-unit employees who may be disciplined for rule violation.[88]

Even though courts have been reluctant to find a legal duty to provide a healthy workplace by restricting smoking at work, arbitrators have embraced the concept wholeheartedly. They have concluded that companies have a reasonable basis for unilaterally imposing smoking restriction policies. The most successful programs have been those that have a lengthy phase-in period of up to six months. During this time classes are provided to help employees quit smoking, and some smoking areas, possibly outside the facility, are identified.[89]

Americans with Disabilities Act

The Americans with Disabilities Act of 1990 (ADA), which covers an estimated 43 million Americans, went into effect in January 1992. Considered a "Bill of Rights" for Americans with a wide variety of disabilities, the act applies to employment, public accommodations, transportation, and telecommunications.

In the United States, 17 percent of the population has a disability. Two-thirds of people with disabilities between the ages of 16 and 64 were unemployed in 1990 even though 66 percent indicated they would prefer to be employed. The EEOC has estimated that the annual productivity gains from passage of ADA could be $164 million plus reduced government support payments and increased tax revenues of $222 million.[90]

Passage of the Americans with Disabilities Act has made job restructuring to meet the "reasonable accommodation" requirements a challenge to companies as well as to the unions. A **person with disabilities** is broadly defined as (1) a person with a physical or mental impairment that substantially limits that person in some major life activity, (2) a person with a record of such a physical or mental impairment, or (3) a person who is regarded as having such an impairment. While individuals who are currently using illegal drugs are excluded, the following individuals are protected under the act: (1) a person who has successfully completed a drug rehabilitation program and is no longer illegally using drugs, (2) a person who has otherwise been rehabilitated and is no longer illegally using drugs, (3) a person who is participating in a rehabilitation program and is no longer illegally using drugs, and (4) a person who is erroneously regarded as illegally using drugs.[91] (See "Labor Relations in Action" for a look at dilemmas faced by employers, unions, and employees under ADA.) The enforcement agency for ADA is the EEOC. During the first year after enactment, 15,274 charges of disability discrimination were filed with the EEOC and accounted for 17.4 percent of the total charges filed. These disability charges caused the total intake of cases to increase by 22 percent.[92]

Because most labor agreements do not include provisions on the initial selection of employees, the hiring requirements are essentially the employer's obligation. However, employment decisions after the initial hiring, such as promotions, transfers, layoffs, and recalls, are addressed in most labor agreements and come under the employment provisions of ADA. In those cases, conflict is possible between an individual's rights under ADA and an employee's seniority rights under the labor agreement. In addition, as employees in the bargaining unit grow older, impairments such as cancer, diabetes, back problems, heart and circulatory disease, repetitive motion injuries, and hearing problems occur. The union will have a direct interest in helping the employer abide by the law by reasonably accommodating those affected employees and by representing the interests of all bargaining-unit employees.

Under ADA provisions, the employer must make **reasonable accommodation** for a person with a disability if that accommodation will allow the person to perform the "essential functions of the job." Thus, if the employer can make a modification in a job's requirements or structure that will not cause the employer "undue hardship" and that will allow the disabled employee to do the job, then that modification or change in the job must be made. In cases where jobs have been defined and wage structures have been negotiated for inclusion in a labor agreement, the union will have a role to play in the modifications.[93]

SITUATIONAL DILEMMAS UNDER THE AMERICANS WITH DISABILITIES ACT

For each of these yet unresolved dilemmas, take the employee's side, the union's side, or the employer's side. View the following situations as an arbitrator or an employee of the federal enforcement agency (EEOC) and give a decision:

Situation one: An employee who suffers from anxiety disorder brought about from service in the Vietnam War requests to transfer to a grocery store (multi-store operations under one labor agreement) closer to his home. The company refuses on the grounds that more senior employees have preferable bidding rights to the vacant jobs at that store under the agreement.

Situation two: An employee in a shipping department operates a labeling machine and loads trucks as the major tasks in his job. He requests that this job be limited to operating the labeling machine because he has problems with a bad back. The company concludes that if he cannot load trucks, he does not continue to meet the qualifications necessary for the job. He files a grievance and a complaint with the EEOC.

Situation three: A ten-year machinist who is being treated for a psychological disorder has been absent an average of 6.6 percent in 1993. This rate compares with the company average of 3.0 percent and a plant average of 1.6 percent. He has already received an oral and a written warning and has been suspended. The company determines his absence rate to be excessive and terminates him.

Situation four; A job is posted for a typing job and two individuals apply. An applicant has a disability and types 50 words per minute; a current employee has no disability and types 75 words per minute. The employer hires the applicant in order to make a reasonable accommodation for his disability. The second employee files a grievance.

Situation five: Warehouse employees are allowed rest breaks only between 10:00 A.M. and 10:15 A.M. and between 2:15 P.M. and 2:30 P.M. If they take breaks at other times or leave the work area without permission, they are subject to disciplinary action. The supervisor allows a new employee with a disability to take rest breaks and use the restroom at his discretion. Other employees request similar treatment, but the supervisor refuses. The warehouse employees file a grievance that alleges unequal treatment.

SOURCES: Adapted from examples in Stephen M. Crow, "Excessive Absenteeism and the Disabilities Act." *The Arbitration Journal* 48 (March 1993), pp. 65–70; Andria S. Knapp, "The Law and Arbitration," *National Academy of Arbitrators—The Chronicle* (April 1993), p. 6; and Eric J. Stahlhut, "Playing the Trump Card: May an Employer Refuse to Reasonably Accommodate under the ADA by Claiming a Collective Bargaining Obligation?" *The Labor Lawyer* 9 (Winter 1993), pp. 71–96.

Job performance and other disciplinary problems relating to employee alcoholism or substance abuse are treated in a straightforward manner under ADA, that is, employers are not required to tolerate performance and disciplinary problems. An employer's responsibility toward employees impaired by alcohol and/or drugs primarily extends to accommodating treatment and recovery and not to accommodating diminished job performance and employee misconduct. Furthermore, the initiative for accommodation must come from the employee, not the employer. The employer's obligation in a unionized setting is significantly greater than in a nonunionized setting as a result of an established body of arbitration decisions going back many years. Not only must the employer comply with ADA, but labor arbitrators will consider mitigating circumstances in the case of long-term employees or when performance and disciplinary problems may have been caused by alcoholism or drug addiction.[94]

Although ADA encourages the use of alternative dispute resolution procedures such as mediation and arbitration to resolve ADA claims without resort to court actions, employees covered under both ADA and a collective bargaining agreement containing a broad nondiscrimination clause may have the opportunity to file a grievance under the agreement as well as pursuing a discrimination claim under ADA. As explained in Chapter 11, the Supreme Court has ruled that any denial of an employee's grievance claim under the collective bargaining agreement does not preclude the employee from subsequently pursuing a similar discrimination claim under ADA.[95]

Summary

The six general categories of administrative issues—technological changes, job security and personnel changes, employee training, work restructuring, safety and health, and accommodating employees with disabilities—have many important facets that may be negotiated and become part of labor agreements.

Technological change, an essential ingredient of a dynamic economic system, is broadly defined to include such activities as introduction of labor-saving machines, power-driven tools, and automatic loading equipment. While unions generally accept these changes as inevitable, they attempt to negotiate provisions in labor agreements to protect members' present jobs and establish the means for assuring future protection. Collective bargaining has provided avenues for working together to resolve complicated problems emanating from technological changes; significant examples have occurred in the auto, communication, and meat-packing industries.

Two interrelated issues, job security and personnel changes, raise questions about employee protection. Often, unions will seek to protect their members by negotiating work-load restrictions, limiting management's rights to subcontract, demanding specific work assignments and jurisdiction, and structuring jobs and scheduling work to the advantage of the employees. When personnel changes are made, seniority becomes a key issue. Likewise, where firms are growing and opportunities for advancement are present, seniority and merit are key considerations. Employers and unions must consider EEOC regulations and court rulings in addition to labor agreement factors in deciding courses of action on personnel adjustment.

Employee training emphasizes apprenticeship and work restructuring programs. Unions and employers alike expend much effort in apprenticeship programs. Work restructuring efforts are often initiated by management, but union cooperation is essential to the complete success of such programs. While some unions are reluctant to become involved with them, major breakthroughs have been identified in selected unions, such as the United Auto Workers.

Safety and health issues have become important since the passage of the Occupational Safety and Health Act of 1970. Criticism of the act's administration has led to reevaluation and a focus on major problems. Some progress has been made in its administration, but controversial issues remain. These include rights to walk off the jobs, rights to receive safety information, women performing jobs that may be harmful to unborn children, safety and health problems while operating video display terminals, and smoking.

The chapter concludes with a section on accommodating the Americans with Disabilities Act. The significance of the problems faced by disabled Americans and the potential benefits of addressing their problems by making reasonable work accommodations are addressed.

Key Terms

technological change
automation
job-security work rules
featherbedding
Worker Adjustment and Retraining Notification Act (WARN)
subcontracting
outsourcing
work scheduling
seniority
promotions
transfer
ability
apprenticeship programs
person with disabilities
reasonable accommodation

Discussion Questions

1. Why do unions' reactions to technological change vary in accordance with their industry affiliation?
2. Think of an industry or company with which you are familiar, and assume that you are the local union president. What types of clauses regarding technological issues would you attempt to negotiate with your employer?
3. Explain why unions place priority on seniority in personnel decisions, while employers seek to identify other determining factors.
4. Assess the Supreme Court decisions discussed in this chapter in terms of their fairness to minority groups.
5. Compare the legal restrictions that apply in selecting applicants for apprenticeship programs and promoting employees in the bargaining unit.

6. Why are many unions critical of OSHA, whose purpose is to protect the physical well-being of their members?
7. Evaluate potential reactions of employees exposed to the AIDS (acquired immune deficiency syndrome) virus, VDTs, smoking on the job, and substance abuse by other employees.
8. Consider an organization with which you are familiar. What actions could you take on various jobs to reasonably accommodate an employee with a disability without undue hardship to the employer?

References

1. Julius Rezler, *Automation and Industrial Labor* (New York: Random House, 1969), pp. 5–6.
2. "Faulty Approach to New Technologies Costing U.S. High-Wage Jobs, Economist Says," *Daily Labor Report,* May 29, 1992, pp. A-21–A-22 (a speech by Lester Thurow of Massachusetts Institute of Technology before the National Press Club).
3. Neil Gross, "Why They Call Japan 'Robot' Paradise," *Business Week,* August 20, 1995, p. 93.
4. Robert J. Thomas, "Technological Choice and Union-Management Cooperation," *Industrial Relations* 30 (Spring 1991), pp. 189–190.
5. Editors of Collective Bargaining Negotiations and Contracts, *Basic Patterns in Union Contracts,* 14th ed. (Washington, D.C.: Bureau of National Affairs Inc., 1995), p. 81.
6. John Lund, "Computerized Work Performance Monitoring and Production Standards: A Review of Labor Law Issues," *Labor Law Journal* (April 1991), pp. 195–203.
7. "Industry, Labor Clash over Proposed Curbs on Electronic Monitoring," *Daily Labor Report,* no. 199 (October 15, 1990), p. C-1.
8. Richard M. Cyert and David C, Mowery, eds., *Technology and Employment: Innovations and Growth in the U.S. Economy* (Washington, D.C.: National Academy Press, 1987), pp. 129–133.
9. Michael H. Cimini, Susan L. Behrmann, and Eric M. Johnson, "Labor Management Bargaining in 1992," *Monthly Labor Review* 116 (January 1993), p. 24.
10. *Collective Bargaining Negotiations and Contracts* (Washington, D.C.: Bureau of National Affairs Inc., 1992), p. 65:3.
11. Richard M. Cyert and David C. Mowery, eds., *Technology and Employment: Innovation and Growth in the U.S. Economy* (Washington, D.C.: National Academy Press, 1987), p. 133.
12. Jeffrey H. Keefe, "Do Unions Hinder Technological Change?" in *Unions and Economic Competitiveness,* eds. Lawrence Mishel and Paula B. Voos (Armonk, N.Y.: M. E. Shapre, Inc., 1992), pp. 109–110.
13. Richard W. Riche, "Impact of New Electronic Technology," *Monthly Labor Review* 105 (March 1982), p. 37.
14. Keefe, "Do Unions Hinder Technological Change?" pp. 109–111.
15. "Need for Legislation on Electronic Monitoring Debated by Labor, Industry at House Hearing," *Daily Labor Report,* June 12, 1991, pp. 1–12.
16. Marcia L. Greenbaum, "Employee Privacy, Monitoring, and New Technology," in *Arbitration 1988: Emerging Issues for the 1990s,* ed. Gladys W. Greunberg (Washington, D.C.: Bureau of National Affairs Inc., 1989), pp. 163–166.
17. "Industry, Labor Clash over Proposed Curbs on Electronic Monitoring," *Daily Labor Report,* no. 199 (October 15, 1990), p. C–1.
18. "Technology and Manufacturing, 21st Century Capitalism," *Business Week,* No-

vember 18, 1994, pp. 144–150; Otis Port, "Custom-Made Direct from the Plant," *Business Week,* November 18, 1994, p. 158; Stephen Baker and James B. Treece, "New U.S. Factory Jobs Aren't in the Factory.," *Business Week,* November 18, 1994, p. 160.

19. Matt Murray, "Amid Record Profits, Companies Continue to Lay Off Employees," *The Wall Street Journal,* May 4, 1995, p. A1.

20. Sumner H. Slichter, James J. Healy, and E. Robert Livernash, *The Impact of Collective Bargaining on Management* (Washington, D.C.: Brookings Institute, 1960), pp. 317–335.

21. Robert D. Leiter, *Featherbedding and Job Security* (New York: Twayne Publishers, 1964), pp. 32–33.

22. William Gomberg, "The Work Rules and Work Practices," *Labor Law Journal* 12 (July 1961), pp. 643–653.

23. Benjamin Aaron, "Government Restraint on Featherbedding," *Stanford Law Review* 5 (July 1953), pp. 687–721.

24. "A Work Resolution in U.S. Industry," *Business Week,* May 16, 1983, pp. 100–103.

25. "Supreme Court Upholds Container Rules on Lawful Work Preservation Measures," *Daily Labor Report,* June 28, 1985, p. A–12.

26. William D. Torrence, "Plant Closing and Advance Notice: Another Look at the Numbers," *Labor Law Journal* (August 1985), pp. 463–465; Editors of Collective Bargaining Negotiations and Contracts, *Basic Patterns in Union Contracts,* 14th ed. (Washington, D.C.: Bureau of National Affairs Inc., 1995), p. 81.

27. John T. Addison and McKinley L. Blackburn, "The Worker Adjustment and Retraining Notification Act: Effects on Notice Provision," *Industrial and Labor Relations Review* 47 (July 1994), pp. 650–661.

28. John T. Addison and McKinley L. Blackburn, "Has WARN Warned? The Impact of Advance-Notice Legislation on the Receipt of Advance Notice," *Journal of Labor Research* 15 (Winter 1994), pp. 83–89.

29. "WARN Act: Supreme Court Rejects Six-Month Limit for Suits Filed Under Plant Closing Law," *Daily Labor Report,* May 31, 1995, p. AA–1.

30. "NLRB Holds Payments Under WARN Are Not to Be Offset from Unfair Practices Remedy," *Daily Labor Report,* January 6, 1995, pp. A-4–A-5.

31. Douglas Lavin, "Two GM Facilities Are Struck by UAW Over Outsourcing," *The Wall Street Journal,* March 15, 1994, p. A8.

32. "Widgetless in Wichita," *The Economist,* October 14, 1995, p. 77.

33. Donald P. Crane and Michael Jay Jedel, "Mature Collective Bargaining Relationships," in *Arbitration 1988: Emerging Issues for the 1990s,* ed. Gladys W. Gruenberg (Washington, D.C.: Bureau of National Affairs Inc., 1989), p. 358.

34. Slichter, Healy, and Livernash, *Collective Bargaining,* pp. 280–285.

35. Marvin J. Levine, "Subcontracting and 'Privatization' of Work: Private and Public Sector Developments," *Journal of Collective Negotiations in the Public Sector* 19, no. 4 (1990), pp. 275–277.

36. Editors of Collective Bargaining Negotiations and Contracts, *Basic Patterns in Union Contracts,* pp. 65:1–3.

37. Slichter, Healy, and Livernash, *Collective Bargaining,* pp. 309–312.

38. Marlise McCammon and John L. Cotton, "Arbitration Decisions in Subcontracting Disputes," *Industrial Relations* 29 (Winter 1990), p. 142.

39. "Board Holds Mid-Term Transfer of Bargaining-Unit Work Unlawful," *Daily Labor Report,* March 18, 1986, p. A–4; *Milwaukee Spring II,* 115 LRRM 1065 (1984).

40. Roger S. Wolters and Stewart D. Langdon, "The Duty to Bargain over Business Decisions," *Labor Law Journal* 43 (September 1992), pp. 583–587.

41. Kenneth A. Jenero and Patrick W. Kocian, "The Relocation of Work Between Plants: A Planning Checklist of Statutory and Contractual Obligations," *Employee*

Relations Law Journal 20 (Spring 1995), p. 622.

42. Leonard E. Cohen, "The Duty to Bargain Over Plant Relocations and Other Corporate Changes: *Otis Elevator* v. *NLRB*," *The Labor Lawyer* 1 (Summer 1985), pp. 525–532.

43. Louis P. DiLorenzo and Peter A. Jones, "Mid-Term Bargaining Over Unit Work Transfers," *Labor Law Journal* 45 (July 1994), p. 446.

44. James K. McCollum and Edward A. Schoreder IV, "NLRB Decisions in Jurisdictional Disputes: The Success of the 10(k) Process," *Employee Relations Law Journal* 13 (Spring 1988), pp. 649–652.

45. NLRB, *42nd Annual Report,* p. 113. This board uses two procedural rules that are worthy of note: (1) A request for a decision in a specific case does not have to wait until the dispute occurs. Once the contractor makes the initial work assignments, a request for a decision can be made. Thus, time is saved by facilitating the dispute resolution process. (2) Decisions of the board are not precedent setting. This does not mean that similar decisions within an area are not based on patterns; it means that conditions vary from region to region, union to union, even agreement to agreement. Therefore, the board is not bound completely by precedent, but past practice is also a factor. Custom in the industry and skills, training, and job content are important elements that are considered.

46. Elvis C. Stephens, "A Supervisor Performs Bargaining-Unit Work: Is the Contract Violated?" *Labor Law Journal* 31 (November 1980), pp. 683–688.

47. Slichter, Healy, and Livernash, *Collective Bargaining,* pp. 266–276.

48. Jeffrey M. Miller, *Innovations in Working Patterns* (Washington, D.C.: Communications Workers of America and German Marshall Fund of the United States, 1978); and W. H. Holley, A. A. Armenakis, and H. S. Feild, "Employee Reactions to a Flexitime Program: A Longitudinal Study," *Human Resource Management* 15 (Winter 1976), pp. 21–23.

49. James A. Craft, "Equal Opportunity and Seniority: Trends and Manpower Implications," *Labor Law Journal* 26 (December 1975), p. 750.

50. Jeffrey M. Miller, *Innovations in Working Patterns* (Washington, D.C.: Communications Workers of America and German Marshall Fund of the United States, 1978); and W. H. Holley, A. A. Armenakis, and H. S. Feild, "Employee Reactions to a Flexitime Program: A Longitudinal Study," *Human Resource Management* 15 (Winter 1976), pp. 21–23.

51. Editors of Collective Bargaining Negotiations and Contracts, *Basic Patterns in Union Contracts,* p. 85.

52. Slichter, Healy, and Livernash, *Collective Bargaining,* pp. 104–105.

53. Editors of Collective Bargaining Negotiations and Contracts, *Basic Patterns in Union Contracts,* pp. 85–87.

54. Roger I. Abrams and Dennis R. Nolan, "Seniority Rights Under the Collective Agreement," *The Labor Lawyer* 2 (Winter 1986), pp. 99–110.

55. Editors of Collective Bargaining Negotiations and Contracts, *Basic Patterns in Unions Contracts,* p. 80.

56. D. Quinn Mills, "Seniority versus Ability in Promotion Decisions," *Industrial and Labor Relations Review* 38 (April 1985), pp. 424–425.

57. William H. Holley, Jr., "Performance Ratings in Arbitration," *Arbitration Journal* 32 (March 1977), pp. 8–25.

58. Editors of Collective Bargaining Negotiations and Contracts *Basic Patterns in Union Contracts,* pp. 67–70.

59. Mark Montgomery, "New Evidence on Unions and Layoff Rates," *Industrial and Labor Relations Review* 44 (July 1991), pp. 708–712.

60. Steven Briggs, "Allocating Available Work in a Union Environment: Layoffs vs. Work Sharing," *Labor Law Journal* 38 (October 1987), pp. 650–657.

61. "*Martin* v. *Wilks*," *Daily Labor Report*, June 13, 1989, D-1–D-11.
62. "Decision of Supreme Court in *Firefighters Local 93* v. *City of Cleveland*," *Daily Labor Report*, July 3, 1986, p. E–2.
63. "Decision of Supreme Court in *Fire Fighters Local 1784* v. *Stotts*," *Daily Labor Report*, June 13, 1984, p. D–1.
64. "*Wendy Wygant* v. *Jackson Board of Education*," *Supreme Court Reporter* 106 (June 1986), pp. 1842–1843.
65. William H. Holley, Jr., and Hubert S. Feild, "Equal Employment Opportunity and Its Implications for Personnel Practices," *Labor Law Journal* 27 (May 1976), p. 285.
66. Robert J. Gitter, "Apprenticeship-trained Workers: United States and Great Britain," *Monthly Labor Report* 117 (April 1994), p. 38.
67. Samuel Estreicher, "Laws Promoting Worker Training, Productivity and Quality," *Labor Law Journal* 44 (February 1993), pp. 110–112.
68. "Training and Apprenticeship," *Collective Bargaining Negotiations and Contracts* (Washington, D.C.: Bureau of National Affairs Inc., 1995), p. 80:351.
69. John Hoerr, "What Should Unions Do?" *Harvard Business Review* 69 (May–June 1991), p. 42.
70. Fehmida Sleemi, "Collective Bargaining Outlook for 1995," *Monthly Labor Report* 118 (January 1995), p. 4.
71. Henry P. Guzda, "Unions Active in Joint Training Programs," *American Workplace* (January 1995), pp. 1–4.
72. Dennis K. Allen, "Bell South–CWA Partnership: Teaming Up to Meet the Challenges of a Changing Industry," *Employee Relations Today* (Summer 1994), p. 163.
73. Henry P. Guzda, "Unions Active in Joint Training Programs," *American Workplace*, January 1995, pp. 1–4.
74. "News Release: U.S. Department of Labor and Ernst & Young LLP Study Finds Competitive Gains from Innovative Workplace Practices," May 31, 1995 (Study conducted by Sarah C. Mavrinac, Neil R. Jones, and Marshall W. Mayer.)
75. Noel Harvey, "How Unions Should Respond to Cells," *Labor Studies Journal* 18 (Winter 1994), pp. 21–31.
76. Editors of Collective Bargaining Negotiations and Contracts, *Basic Patterns in Union Contracts*, pp. 123–128.
77. Robert S. Smith, "Have OSHA and Workers' Compensation Made the Workplace Safer?" in *Research Frontiers in Industrial and Human Resources*, eds. David Lewin, Olivia S. Mitchell, and Peter D. Sherer (Madison, Wis.: Industrial Relations Research Association, 1992), pp. 557–558.
78. Wallace N. Davidson III, Dan Worrel, and Louis T. W. Cheng, "The Effectiveness of OSHA Penalties: A Stockmarket-Based Test," *Industrial Relations* 33 (July 1994), pp. 283–294.
79. Robert E. Scherer and Crystal L. Owen, "OSHA Inspections: Process and Outcomes in Programmed Inspections Versus Complaint–Investigated Inspections," *Employee Responsibilities and Rights Journal* 8 (September 1995), p. 252.
80. Barbara Presley Noble, "Breathing New Life into OSHA," *The New York Times*, January 23, 1994, p. F25.
81. "OSHA Rulemaking Process Credible but May Overstate Costs, OTA Says," *Daily Labor Report*, October 25, 1995, p. A–9.
82. "Taft-Hartley Act Held to Protect Workers Who Protest Unsafe Conditions," *Daily Labor Report*, November 26, 1982, pp. A-5–A-6.
83. Mary Hayes, "OSHA Final Rule Gives Employees the Right to See Their Exposure and Medical Records," *Personnel Administrator* 27 (March 1982), pp. 71–75.
84. "Court Upholds NLRB Ruling on Disclosure of Safety and Health Data to Unions," *Daily Labor Report*, July 5, 1983, p. A–6.
85. "Supreme Court Invalidates Fetal Protection Policy," *Daily Labor Report*, March 21, 1991, p. A–1; "Employers Rescind Fetal Protection Policies Following

Johnson Controls, but Fear Liability," *Daily Labor Report,* April 1, 1991, p. A–2.

86. "An Invisible Workplace Hazard Gets Harder to Ignore," *Business Week,* January 30, 1989, p. 92.

87. Martin W. Aaron and Richard M. DeAgazio, "The Four-Headed Monster: ADA, FMA, OSHA, and Workers' Compensation," *Labor Law Journal* 46 (January 1995), pp. 48–58.

88. Elizabeth M. Crocker, "Controlling Smoking in the Workplace," *Labor Law Journal* 38 (December 1987), pp. 739–746.

89. Mollie H. Bowers, "What Labor and Management Need to Know about Workplace Smoking Cases," *Labor Law Journal* 43 (January 1992), pp. 48–49.

90. Gary F. Coulton and Roger Wolters, "Employee and Management Rights and Responsibilities under the Americans with Disabilities Act (ADA): An Overview," *Employee Responsibilities and Rights Journal* 6 (March 1993), pp. 55–56.

91. Jeffrey A. Mello, "Employing and Accommodating Workers with Disabilities: Mandates and Guidelines for Labor Relations," *Labor Law Journal* 44 (March 1993), pp. 162–170.

92. "Charges of Disability Discrimination Boost EEOC Intake by 22% in Fiscal '93," *Daily Labor Report,* January 13, 1994, p. AA–1.

93. Stephen M. Crow, "Anti-Drug Programs Under the ADA: Business as Usual or Harassment of a Protected Class?" *Labor Law Journal* 43 (February 1992), pp. 117–124; James G. Frierson, "On Accommodations and Confidentiality," *Labor Law Journal* 43 (May 1992), pp. 308–312.

94. James W. Bucking, "Beyond the ADA: Protection of Employees with Drug and Alcohol Problems in Arbitration," *The Labor Lawyer* 11 (Winter-Spring, 1995), pp. 1–5.

95. Coulton and Wolters, "Employee and Management Rights and Responsibilities," pp. 58–59.

Economic Issues

13

In the mid-1990s, the U.S. economy appeared to be among the best in the world; it experienced strong growth, low inflation, and a steady flow of new jobs. However, these prosperous times were marked by a stagnation in real wages (adjusted by inflation rate) for employees. Only 67 percent of corporate revenue was being paid in wages and salaries, the lowest since the 1960s, as downsizing, job cuts, and wage restraints dominated business strategies. In the 1960s, real wages per hour rose at an average rate of 2.1 percent; during 1993 to 1994, the real wage rate fell by 0.3 percent and then rose slightly in 1995. The Department of Labor reported that from March 1994 to March 1995 real wages fell by 2.3 percent while productivity gained by 2.1 percent. Moreover, since 1973, real wages have risen only 5 percent. For example, General Motors spent about 26 percent of its revenue on wages, salaries, and benefits in 1989; by 1993 the percentage was down to 22 percent. Some economists say that profits have increased, leading to billions of dollars in investments in new equipment, a productivity growth rate of 3 percent (the highest in 20 years), and a growth in jobs; however, others have expressed their concern about low real wages and the lack of consumer demand, especially since consumer spending makes up about two-thirds of the gross national product.[1]

Wages and other economic benefits represent income to the employee, cost to the organization, and a basis for taxes to the government. In addition, wages serve as a factor in the allocation of resources; they influence the individual's selection of an occupation and movement from one firm, industry, or location to another; they influence decisions on plant location and investments in machinery and capital equipment; and they affect employment and unemployment. More importantly, if wages become excessive, employees may be priced out of particular labor markets. Thus, wages are both economic indicators and determinants.

Unions and management are required by the NLRA to bargain in good faith with respect to wages. As a result of NLRB and court decisions, wage-related topics, such as pensions, overtime, shift differentials, job evaluation, and incentive systems must be bargained over if either party presents such topics during negotiations.

Union and management negotiators spend many hours annually bargaining over wages and wage-related issues. This chapter focuses on the methods of wage determination and factors used by negotiators in determining the wage package—wages and other economic benefits.

• • •

Wage Determination

Union and management officials have to agree on what the term *wages* means before they can successfully bargain over this issue. For instance, wages may mean the basic wage rate, average gross hourly earnings, average weekly earnings, or incentive pay (payment per product completed). Basic wage rates for each job class are usually listed in the labor agreement; however, other wage payments (overtime, incentive pay, shift differentials, and other compensation earned in the regular work week) may have to be computed in accordance with provisions in the labor agreement.[2]

After agreeing on the language for the basis of wage negotiations, the parties determine those wage rates and related items of employment.[3] In this process, the parties will consider various factors and will determine numerous wage rates, job classes, and wage ranges. As you may have already experienced, jobs with varying duties and responsibilities are assigned different wage rates. Besides these occupational differentials within a firm, there are regional, industry, and shift differences that cause an employer to pay different combinations of wage rates. Textile employees in the South generally earn less than those in the North; electricians and laborers in the building trades generally have higher wage rates than electricians and laborers in factories.

Wage differentials among individuals, jobs, industries, or regions can be explained in a variety of ways. However, any explanation must consider the interrelationships between labor and capital as factors of production and as contributors to productivity. An example follows:

> It is sometimes said that if productivity rises by "x" percent and the workers receive an "x" percent increase in compensation, then the workers are getting all of the productivity increase, leaving nothing for others. This is incorrect. If productivity rises, say 10 percent, and output increases commensurately, then each factor of production—labor, management, capital—can receive a 10 percent increase. If output does not rise commensurately . . . then total compensation of input factors and rates of return to those factors will depend on the difference between the output increase and the productivity increase, the size of the hourly compensation increase, and the cost of new capital investment.[4]

Industrial Wage Differentials

Industrial wage differentials may be explained in terms of three interrelated factors: (1) the degree of competition or monopoly in the product market, (2) the value added by workers in a particular industry, and (3) the percentage of total costs that labor costs represent.

Competition in the Product Market First, if a firm has a monopoly or near monopoly (the product is essential, with no available substitute), then increased labor cost can easily be passed on to the consumer. In such cases, the employer will resist higher wages less rigidly in negotiation. For example, if a private or public utility agrees to a 12 percent increase with cost-of-living adjustments, it then can add the increased cost to its customers' bills (unless the utility is heavily regulated). Consumers in this situation frequently have little choice but to pay the higher prices. Thus, in those industries where the firm controls the pricing without competitive threats, wages tend to be proportionately higher.

Value Added by Employees The term *value added* refers to the contribution of factors of production to the value of the final product. Comparing labor's contribution for different industries helps to explain industrial wage differentials. For example, the value added by labor in sawmills, cotton weaving, clothes manufacturing, and the mobile home industry is significantly lower than corresponding figures in the steel, petrochemical, and paper industries. However, because employees must use machines, which represent capital investments, and because such a close interrelationship exists between labor and capital investments in machinery and equipment, exact determination of labor's contributions has become a complicated process. In unionized settings, negotiations between union and management representatives determine labor's share in the amount of value added.

Labor Costs as Percentage of Total Costs The relationship between labor costs and total costs must also be considered in determining the industrial wage rate. Highly interdependent with capital investment per employee and the product market, this relationship is important in wage negotiations. For example, labor-intensive organizations, such as health care facilities, textile firms, and government, have high labor costs in relation to total costs. On the other hand, petroleum and chemical firms and electricity-generating plants have relatively low labor costs as a percentage of total costs.

Usually, firms with a high ratio of labor costs to total costs are more likely to resist wage increases. For example, if a hospital where labor costs are 60 percent of total costs grants a 10 percent wage increase, it must raise prices about 6 percent. A petroleum-processing plant where labor cost is 5 percent of total cost would have to raise its price about 0.5 percent to cover a 10 percent increase in wages. We would therefore expect to find employees in the same job classifications receiving higher wages in chemical and petroleum companies than in hospitals or textile firms. Of course, there are many qualifications to this conclusion in specific incidences—for example, consumers may not accept a higher price and a company may choose to cover the wage increase out of its profits. Nonetheless, the relation of labor cost to total cost can be an important factor in industrial wage differentials.

Occupational Wage Differentials and the Role of Job Evaluation and Wage Surveys

Within a company or industry, maintaining proper and rational wage relationships among various jobs is important. The relationships are often maintained under job evaluation programs but in other cases are determined by individual or collective bargaining.[5] The process of determining the relative importance of each job to the organization helps in understanding occupational wage differentials; therefore, the following steps in a job evaluation program are presented.[6]

Evaluating Jobs within the Organization Before conducting a **job evaluation** program, an organizational analysis[7] that appraises and examines the organization's objectives, structure, and authority and responsibility relationships is done. The findings from this analysis help ensure that the job content is up to date.

Then the organization selects and measures the job factors that are found at least to some extent in all of the organization's job classifications. Job factors vary substantially depending on the organization, but skill (education and training), effort, responsibility (for people and equipment), and working conditions (hazards, surroundings) are typically selected. Management must consider the minimum amount of each job factor or qualification necessary to adequately perform the particular job. For example, it may be nice to employ a typist who can edit, interpret, and make complex economic subjects understandable, but few organizations can find or are willing to pay wages needed to attract such a qualified person.

Next, an appropriate job evaluation system for appraising jobs according to the established job factors is selected from four job evaluation methods: ranking, classification, factor comparison, and point system. The *ranking* and *factor-comparison* methods compare jobs nonquantitatively in terms of one or more job factors; the *classification* and *point-system* methods compare jobs to predetermined numerical rating scales designed to measure one or more job factors about each job. Firms' job evaluation systems may use 10 to 15 different job factors, with these factors often divided into subfactors. For example, effort may be divided into physical and mental effort.[8]

The foundation of job evaluation is *job analysis,* which is a process of systematically securing information and facts about the jobs to be evaluated. Throughout the job evaluation process, it is the jobs, not employees in the job classifications, that are being analyzed. The job classifications resulting from job analysis will receive the same rating whether the employee holding the job has a master's degree or high school diploma, is lazy or ambitious, or is a high or low performer.

Job analysts use observation, interviews, and questionnaires to gather data about the jobs that are used to formulate *job descriptions* and *job specifications.* Job descriptions include written summations of the duties and responsibilities; job specifications include the personal characteristics an employee must possess to qualify for the job. Both are used in the job evaluation process. As firms try to relate wages to various degrees of duties and responsibilities, they must also pay more to employ employees who have high qualifications in education, training, and skills.

Management often prefers to conduct its job evaluation independently of the union. Management may prefer not to share its weightings of the job factors, particularly when it believes certain factors (such as training, skill, and responsibility for equipment) should receive more compensation than others. By withholding the weightings, management may avoid confrontations with the union, but the union will probably not accept being totally excluded from the job evaluation process.

Union leaders generally view job evaluation with disfavor because it tends to limit bargaining and freeze the wage structure.[9] Surveys of union officials revealed that unions prefer to establish wage scales through collective bargaining, although their resistance to job evaluation has declined. While unions reserve the right to file grievances to resist or express dissatisfaction with job evaluation, they seldom show strong opposition unless firms attempt to use job evaluation as the sole criterion for wage determination or try to substitute it for collective bargaining.[10] In fact, some unions regard job evaluation techniques not only as useful guides in negotiating wages but as a means by which they can more effectively explain the negotiated wage settlements to their members.[11]

Regardless of the job evaluation method, the objective is to develop a wage structure that prices jobs with less skill, effort, and responsibility at lower wage rates and jobs with greater skill, effort, and responsibility at higher wage rates. Exhibit 13.1 presents an example of a wage structure for a firm that includes job titles, labor grades, point ranges, and starting wage rates for each labor grade. Since a

Exhibit 13.1 Typical Wage Structure for a Manufacturing Firm

JOB TITLES	LABOR GRADE	POINTS	STARTING HOURLY WAGE RATE
Janitor	I	200–249	$6.55
Material Handler	II	250–299	8.30
Shipper	III	300–349	9.45
Tool Room Keeper	IV	350–399	10.20
Machinist B	V	400–449	10.50
Maintenance Worker	VI	450–499	11.80
Mechanic	VII	500–549	12.00
Painter	VIII	550–599	13.30
Carpenter	IX	600–649	14.10
Truck Driver	X	650–699	14.68
Electrician	XI	700–749	17.19
Tool and Die Maker	XII	750–799	17.42
Machinist A	XIII	800–849	18.49

SOURCE: Adapted from *Collective Bargaining Negotiations and Contracts* (Washington, D.C.: Bureau of National Affairs Inc., 1992), p. 18:331.

numerical score should indicate the relative value of the job, the greater the score, the higher the labor grade and the hourly wage rate.

Surveys to Compare Firms' Wage Structures *Wage surveys* are conducted to assure that external labor market considerations, such as comparable wages, are included in the wage structure. While firms attempt to rationalize their wage structure internally through job evaluation, they must also maintain competitive wages externally to ensure that the firm can recruit qualified employees and retain productive ones. Usually a wage analyst either visits, sends questionnaires to, or conducts telephone interviews with the wage analysts of similar organizations or comparable firms. The one conducting the survey provides the responding firms with titles, descriptions, and specifications of the jobs in the wage survey. Participating firms will supply the starting wage rate and the economic benefits paid individuals in these job classifications (see Exhibit 13.2). After the wage survey is complete, the firm must determine how the data will be used. For example, does it want to lead the industry, compete with Firm C, or pay the industry average?

These wage surveys may be conducted by the firm or the union or be obtained from trade groups, employer associations, or the Bureau of Labor Statistics, which periodically publishes industry, area, occupational, and national wage survey data.[12] From such abundant data, union and management officials sometimes have difficulty determining which are most appropriate for their particular situation. (This problem is further discussed in the section on wage comparability.)

The wage plan concludes with a certain number of job classes, wages for each job class, wage ranges (from starting to top wages) for each class, policies and procedures for wage adjustments (seniority, merit, and so on), procedures for job changes to a different class, including temporary job changes, procedures for dealing with jobs that pay above or below their wage range, and policy on union involvement.

After the wage plan and policies are established, individual wage adjustments are made on the basis of merit and seniority. A study of 400 labor agreements by the

Exhibit 13.2 Typical Results from a Wage Survey

	FIRMS						
JOB TITLE	A	B	C	D	E	F	AVERAGE WAGE
Janitor	$6.00	$6.25	$6.75	$6.80	$7.00	$6.20	$6.50
Assembler	10.00	10.60	10.30	10.70	9.90	10.30	10.30
Shop Clerk	11.00	10.00	10.75	10.25	10.40	10.60	10.50
Welder	12.60	12.30	12.00	12.00	12.30	12.60	12.30
Electrician	16.50	17.00	17.50	17.00	16.75	17.25	17.00
Tool and Die Maker	18.00	17.00	17.75	17.25	17.50	17.50	17.50
Machinist	19.00	18.50	18.00	18.75	18.25	18.50	18.50

Bureau of National Affairs revealed that 89 percent provided for wage increases during the life of the labor agreement.[13]

Production Standards and Wage Incentives

Unions and management sometimes negotiate provisions in the labor agreement that cover wage-related issues such as production standards, time studies, and wage-incentive payments. Production standards refer to the expected employee output that is consistent with workmanship quality, operational efficiency, and reasonable working capacities of normal operators. These standards are often determined by time studies that involve analyses of time and motions of workers on the job, and the resulting standards are used to assess performance and determine the wage incentives for individual employees or groups of employees.

Where incentive plans are negotiated, the structure and design are included in the contract, although specific details may not be included. The role of the union in setting and protesting production standards and rate changes and its right to be consulted on related issues are also usually included. Some contracts include provisions about time studies and the involvement of unions. A small number permit a union observer during the time study, and a few go as far as to provide special training for the union time study representative. Other provisions include procedures used for timing an employee, specification of the meaning of normal employee, advance notice to the employee holding the job being studied, and specification for fatigue and personal allowances in setting production standards.[14]

While **wage-incentive plans** vary in structure and specific content, their goals are essentially the same: (1) to increase employee productivity, (2) to attract prospective employees to the company, and (3) to reward employees monetarily for their increased productivity. A typical individual wage-incentive plan is one in which employees are paid for the number of pieces or jobs completed. Others pay bonuses or premiums to employees for production above the standard. Many varieties of incentive plans exist, but all are similar in concept.

Many companies and unions have begun to investigate incentive plans as a way to stimulate employee productivity. In fact, the great majority of production employees continue to be paid time rates. The major reasons for time-based compensation plans are that plant jobs are usually machine-paced, so employees have little control over their pace of work. In only six industries—men's and children's hosiery, women's hosiery, leather footwear, men's and boy's suits and coats, men's and boys' shirts, and basic steel and iron—are a majority of the employees paid by incentive plans. In these six industries, machines are controlled by the operators, employees exercise considerable discretion over the pace of work, and output is identifiable and measurable.[15] Increased interest in incentive plans has resulted from intense competition, foreign and domestic, increased interest in labor-management cooperation, and employee efforts to obtain wage concessions from unions.

Profit-sharing plans have increased 537 percent over the last 40 years. The percentage of employees participating in profit-sharing plans has stablized at about

16 to 18 percent. Most of these plans are designed for deferred benefits upon retirement.[16]

Union experience with incentive programs dates back to the nineteenth century. In fact, the AFL, the CIO, and the AFL-CIO have never opposed profit-sharing and other incentive systems, and only a few individual unions have ever taken a position opposing these plans.[17]

Profit-sharing plans that provided for cash bonuses based on the company's profit to partially or totally take the place of wage increases have been negotiated with several major companies, including Ford, General Motors, Pan Am, Uniroyal, and International Harvester. So that executives would not receive bonuses when employees do not, the agreement negotiated between Chrysler and the UAW prevents top company executives from receiving cash and stock bonuses during years when there is no profit sharing for the UAW-represented hourly workers.[18]

In 1995, Ford employees received profit-sharing checks that averaged about $1,700; this payment was $2,300 less than that received in 1994. Chrysler employees received $3,200 in 1995; however, they received $8,000 in 1994. While General Motors paid its employees only $800 in profit-sharing checks in 1995, Saturn Corporation, a GM subsidiary, paid $10,000, up from $3,245, to each of its 8,540 employees for attaining production and profitability goals.[19]

The concept of profit sharing was introduced 35 years ago by Walter Reuther, then president of the UAW, but the auto industry denounced it as "socialistic." Although interest in profit sharing may last only as long as a recession, experts have concluded that for profit sharing to work, employees, their unions, and management must develop a "common fate" or "we are all in this together for good or for ill" attitude, and management must be willing to provide job security, job training, and a structure for genuine worker participation.[20]

Profit-sharing has been criticized in several ways. First, some are concerned that unions will wind up having a key voice in major management decisions other than wages. Second, it is feared that a costly profit-sharing plan will drain company funds that would otherwise be used for capital improvements and research and development. Third, others are concerned that the union will use the profit sharing to "beef up" benefits in subsequent negotiations.[21]

In *group incentive plans,* gain-sharing companies make monetary payments to a specific group or groups of employees for producing more than expected. Incentives include group bonuses, group piece rates, profit sharing, production sharing, and cost-reduction sharing. In some cases, the plans are limited to a few employees, to specific departments, or to other organizational divisions; in others, the entire company workforce is covered. While group incentives aim to increase production and reduce costs, they are also designed to increase teamwork, provide greater job security, and achieve greater acceptance of new technology.

There are a variety of group incentive plans. One of the most popular is the *Scanlon Plan,* a group plan for sharing labor cost savings that was developed by former union leader Joseph Scanlon in the late 1930s. It provides bonus payments based on a computed ratio of total labor costs (TLC) to total production values (TPV), which typically equal monthly sales, plus or minus inventory adjustments. A reduction in the ratio would be a labor cost savings. For example, if the employees were to reduce costs by working harder, producing more efficiently, and saving on wastes and the TLC/TPV ratio declined from 50 to 40 percent, the 10 percent labor-cost savings would be shared with the employees in relation to their basic wages.[22]

The *Rucker Plan* is based on a change in the ratio between dollar payroll and dollar value added. The value added equals sales less purchased materials. Under this plan, if employees lower the ratio between payroll costs and dollar value added, the productivity gains are shared.

The term *improshare* is derived from "improved productivity through sharing." Improshare productivity measurements use traditional work measurement standards for a selected base period. Productivity gains are divided evenly between employees and company. A study of improshare programs in 34 unionized companies showed an average productivity gain of 26.9 percent after the first year, whereas the average gain for 38 nonunion plants was 21.5 percent.[23] Another study of 112 firms that had introduced improshare found that the median increase in productivity in the first year was 8 percent and the cumulative productivity gains had risen to 17.5 percent by the third year, after which they leveled off.[24]

A study of 269 firms with gainsharing programs wherein employees shared the returns from increased production in the United States and Canada reported the importance of the cooperative role of unions in the success of these programs. While unionization appears to have a generally negative relationship to gainsharing performance (productivity up by 4.61 percent and production costs down by 2.81 percent), union participation in and support for gainsharing positively affected gainsharing effectiveness. In fact, unionized firms with jointly administered employee-participation programs achieved greater performance improvements than those programs administered solely by management. These findings suggest that union participation and support provide an important mechanism for using the full potential of employees' collective input into the gainsharing programs. On the other hand, union opposition to the program reduces employees' efforts and commitment to the program and probably leads to the program's failure. The practical implication for both union leaders and management is that it is wise for management to solicit union support instead of attempting to isolate the union in operating the program. More importantly, it would be a poor decision for management to use the program as a device to weaken the union because such a tactic could lead to the program's failure and cause a great waste in financial and human resources. Furthermore, it would be wise for union leaders to become involved in administering the program, sharing the gains for employees, and obtaining credit for its achievement. Active participation is the most effective way to represent union members' concerns about gainsharing, and it provides an important opportunity for the union to develop an equal partnership in the workplace. Thus, gainsharing is not just an incentive program; it brings about a fundamental change in the traditional adversarial bargaining relationship between management and labor.[25]

Group incentive programs are based on the assumption that by linking earnings to performance, employees will adjust their efforts to optimize income, and, because bonuses are tied to group effort, employees have the incentive to work cooperatively. Considerable evidence suggests that the *combination* of employee participation programs and group incentive programs could exceed gains made by either one alone. Employees have little incentive to share their performance-enhancing ideas with management without respondent rewards. In addition, employees with no participation in decisions cannot respond effectively to such incentive programs. The union can provide more direct and open channels of communication for a collective voice and enhance employee input; however, contract language with fixed wage classifications and confrontational negotiations could inhibit cooperation and employee response to the incentives. Thus, in general, unionized companies may have an environment more conducive to employee participation due to their role in collective bargaining, and nonunion companies an environment more conducive to group incentive programs.[26]

Arguments Used by Management and Union Officials in Wage Determination

Unions and management have recognized that no single causal influence affects wage determination; however, both parties will use any identifiable influence to support their arguments for or against wage increases. Related influences include differential features of the work (usually determined by job evaluation), wage comparability, ability to pay (financial condition of the organization), productivity, cost of living, and legal requirements.[27] Union and management officials do not always accept the same criteria. Moreover, each might emphasize different criteria at different times. During prosperous times unions tend to emphasize the ability to pay; during recessions management presents its poor financial position. Similarly, during periods of rapid inflation, unions emphasize cost-of-living adjustments; when prices are stable, management places much weight on the lack of necessity for cost-of-living adjustments.

Pressure from domestic and international competition has resulted in management's inability to pass increased labor costs to the customer and caused businesses to emphasize efficiency, cost-cutting measures, and productivity. During this period of relatively high unemployment, the unions' ability to affect wage levels within their industries has declined, and companies have become less influenced by industry patterns. Instead, companies emphasize their individual labor costs, expected profits, and local wage rates over those prevailing in the industry. Productivity or labor cost trends have replaced industry patterns as the most important factor used in setting company wage objectives.[28]

Arguments used by management and unions over wages cannot be entered into a computer to yield a precise solution to the wage determination, but they do provide a framework within which the parties attempt to resolve their differences over wage issues through collective bargaining.[29]

Differential Features of the Work: Job Evaluation and the Wage Spread

The job evaluation process described in the preceding section can influence the wages assigned to various job classifications in an organization. The relative influence of job evaluation can be seen in the wage spread, which represents the internal distribution of the proposed or negotiated wage increase to the bargaining-unit employees (see Exhibit 13.3).

At first glance, the wage spread appears to be a formality, determined after the average hourly rate increase per employee is resolved. Yet the particular wage spread can determine whether the parties ever reach an agreement. For example, the union might refuse the first and second wage spreads and accept the third wage with no spread as seen in Exhibit 13.3, even though the total wage costs of the three spreads are nearly identical.

The six employee job classifications in Exhibit 13.3 range in skill and pay from Classification A (highest) to Classification F (lowest), which conform to management's job evaluation procedure. Consequently, management prefers the second wage spread, since it gives more highly skilled employees higher wages that could maintain or increase their wage differential over unskilled employees. This wage differential is important to management for two reasons:

1. It ensures that current skilled employees do not leave because of higher wages offered by other firms.
2. It offers some motivation to employees in lower-paid classifications to train for higher-level classifications in the company.

Exhibit 13.3 Three Examples of Internal Wage Spreads

EXAMPLE	NUMBER OF EMPLOYEES	EMPLOYEE CLASSIFICATION	PERCENTAGE OF PLANT'S TOTAL EMPLOYEES	INCREASE IN CENTS PER HOUR
1	184	A	16%	57.0
	197	B	18	50.0
	165	C	15	48.0
	237	D	21	46.0
	149	E	13	44.0
	193	F	17	42.0
	1,125			
2	381	A&B	34	60.0
	402	C&D	36	44.0
	342	E&F	30	34.0
	1,125			
3	1,125	A,B,C,D,E,&F	100	47.2

Unions are not always concerned with job evaluation as a wage determination factor. The union officers' main concern is to ensure that the negotiated wage spread will result in sufficient votes to ratify the agreement. Satisfied union members will also be likely to vote for reelection of union officers. Assume, for example, that Classification C represents a politically influential group of employees. The union officers would not prefer the second wage spread (44.0 cents per hour increase for Classification C employees). Instead, they would prefer the first (48.0 cents per hour increase) or third (47.2 cents per hour increase) wage spread shown in the exhibit. The union might even propose a different wage spread that would give the employees in Classification C a much higher wage increase.

Management is also concerned that employees ratify the agreement. Consequently, it might agree to an across-the-board increase to all employees regardless of their job classifications. This wage spread might generate enough votes to ratify the collective bargaining agreement, but it will narrow the wage differential between skilled and unskilled employees. Over a longer period of time, management cannot continually grant this type of increase if it wishes to attract and retain skilled employees.

One of the principal goals of unions has been to reduce dispersion of wages. Their goals are to obtain "equal pay for equal work" across establishments and to reduce differentials based on personal characteristics rather than specific job tasks. Unions seek this goal by negotiating a single rate of pay for each occupational group and a seniority-based progression of rates up to a maximum level. Single rates (one pay level for all employees in a given category) eliminate wage dispersion and seniority plans control overall wage rates by requiring similar treatment to workers who have the same seniority. Because of the "spillover" effect of union wage practices, even nonunion companies experience less wage dispersion than one might expect.[30]

Wage provisions that specify that newly hired employees will be paid less than other employees are referred to as **two-tier pay plans.** They may be permanent or temporary. The permanent ones pay new hires at a lower rate for the life of the agreement; temporary ones permit new employees to progress from the lower entry-level rates to the rates received by other employees over a specified period of time. In 1991, only 4 percent of agreements had two-tier wage structures. These wage programs were concentrated in the airline, electric machinery, transportation equipment, and wholesale and retail industries.[31] For reasons for the rise and fall of two-tier pay plans, see "Labor Relations in Action." For an example of a two-tier pay schedule, see Exhibit 13.4.

Because the union may negotiate a wage differential based on skill, type of work, and seniority, it appears to have ample latitude to negotiate two-tier wage levels if they have a purpose in "good faith and honesty." However, a subsequent cost may be incurred in terms of labor solidarity with potential friction between the newly hired employees and the more senior employees.[32] Or, if the low-tier employees view the pay situation as inequitable, they may vote to remove the union leaders or support union decertification. Likewise, they may feel less commitment to their employer, be less productive, and cause higher relative labor costs to the company.[33]

LABOR RELATIONS IN ACTION

The Rise and Fall of Two-Tier Wage Plans

Two-tier wage plans were highly touted in the early 1980s as a solution to the dilemma of reducing labor costs without losing or angering senior, experienced employees. These plans were negotiated in 5 percent of the labor agreements in 1983, 8 percent in 1984, and 11 percent in 1985. Then there was a gradual decline: 10 percent in 1986, 9 percent in 1987, and 5 percent in 1988. Although scholars differ in their predictions about the future of these plans, there are trends toward "hidden" two-tier plans via low-cost subcontracting, temporary employees, part-time workers, leased employees, home-work employment, and so on.

Some reasons for the rise and decline of two-tier wage plans follow.

Reasons for the Rise in Two-Tier Wage Plans

- They deal with high labor costs, especially during recessionary times.
- They retain experienced employees without lowering their wage scales.
- They increase wage differentials between new employees and longer-service employees, reducing the wage compression problem.
- They increase the percentage of employees in the lower wage class in those companies having high turnover.

Reasons for the Decline in Two-Tier Wage Plans

- They cause dissatisfaction within the union among new employees, which creates an interest in decertifying the union (often a hidden agenda).
- They cause conflict between the longer-service employees and the new employees and consequently reduce union solidarity.
- They result in lower morale and frequently cause poor workmanship or reduced customer service.
- They raise a question of whether the union is fairly representing the new employees or subject the union and company to employment discrimination claims if minorities are disproportionately among the lower-tiered.
- They cause high turnover among the lower-tiered and reduce the ability of the company to recruit qualified employees.
- They violate the principle of "equal pay for equal work" when the lower-tiered employees perform the same job as the upper-tiered ones but receive less pay.

SOURCES: Ken Jennings and Earle Traynham, "The Wages of Two-Tiered Plans," *Personnel Journal* 67 (March 1988), pp. 56–63; Marvin J. Levine, The Evolution of Two-Tiered Wage Agreements: Bane or Panacea in Labor-Intensive Industries," *Labor Law Journal* 40 (January 1989), pp. 12–20; Mollie Bowers and Roger Roderick, "Two-Tier Pay Systems: The Good, the Bad, and the Debatable," *Personnel Administrator* 32 (June 1987), pp. 102–106; and James E. Martin and Melanie M. Peterson, "Two-Tiered Wage Structures: Implications for Equity Theory," *Academy of Management Journal* 30 (June 1987), pp. 297–315.

Exhibit 13.4 Examples of Two-Tier Pay Scales

JOB CLASSES AND HOURLY RATES FOR EMPLOYEES ON PAYROLL PRIOR TO MARCH 1, 1996

JOB CLASSES	WAGE RATE
0	$9.40
1	9.60
2	9.80
3	10.00
4	10.20
5	10.40
6	10.60
7	10.80

All Employees hired after March 1, 1996 shall be considered new hires and . . . shall be paid according to the [following] bracket rate:

JOB CLASSES AND HOURLY RATES FOR EMPLOYEES HIRED AFTER MARCH 1, 1996

BRACKET	WAGE RATE
0	$6.00
1	6.10
2	6.20
3	6.40
4	6.60
5	6.80
6	7.00
7	7.20

The following quote may explain new employees' view of two-tier wage plans because they are pleased at the beginning to obtain a job, after which the reality of the daily comparisons of "equal work for unequal pay" with the upper-tiered employees sets in: "When you're starving, you eat anything you can, human nature being what it is. But when you're not starving any more, you start looking around at what other people are eating."[34]

Wage Comparability

A common argument in wage negotiations is that wage rates in one bargaining unit should be equal or related to the wage rates in comparable bargaining units.[35] Wage comparisons are given considerable weight in wage determination, although these comparisons can become quite complicated. Wage surveys can be helpful, but they do not measure how the job content, method of payment, regularity of employment, supplemental unemployment benefits, vacations, pensions, and holidays vary from company to company. Fundamental considerations such as the size of the appropriate labor market and occupational and geographic differentials must be recognized. At first glance, it appears that bus drivers in Miami would have duties identical to those of bus drivers in Chicago. However, many differences in these similar jobs can exist: weather conditions, number of scheduled stops, location of scheduled stops, number of passengers, and so on. Further, a major difference could arise in situations where the bus drivers are required to make change for passengers. In such cases, the union would claim that this job responsibility creates a safety hazard by increasing the likelihood of robberies and would seek adequate compensation for this additional risk.

The relative importance of wages to total costs is also an important factor in wage comparability. For example, if a modern, highly automated textile mill pays wages that account for 30 percent of total costs, a 10 percent increase in wages would equal a 3 percent change in the sales price. But in an old textile mill with out-of-date machinery, where wages account for 65 percent of total costs, a 10 percent increase in wages would equal a 6.5 percent change in sales price. Even though wage data are often largely fragmented or deficient,[36] negotiators still have to rely on wage comparability in arguing for or against certain levels of wages. Therefore, both parties continue to look for commonalities with other companies, local firms, or similar jobs that can provide a base from which to present their proposals.

Ability to Pay

The ability to pay, or the financial condition of the organization, is a commonly used standard for wage determination. Given much weight by unions during periods of high profitability, it is advanced more frequently by management as the "inability to pay."[37]

Ability to pay has limited usefulness in the wage determination process for a number of reasons:

1. Wages based solely on ability to pay would create a chaotic wage structure and would cause a change in the wage-costs-price-profit relationships that have evolved over time.
2. Unions would not want to apply this criterion uniformly and consistently. To be applicable, it must work both ways, leading to wage reductions when profits are nonexistent or inadequate. Such an approach would be generally unacceptable to unions.
3. It is extremely difficult to determine what part of profits should be used for wage increases. If the profit is distributed to employees in terms of higher wages and none of the profit is shared with stockholders, there will be no incentive for investment, and growth and expansion will be limited.
4. Wages supposedly are paid to employees in accordance with their relative value to the firm, their contribution to its goals, and the relative importance of their services. If ability to pay is the major factor, the relationships between actual pay and actual value could become disproportionate.

5. Wages are negotiated for future application, and there is no necessary relationship between profits of the past and ability to pay in the future. Profits are the result after past costs have been deducted from past sales; they fluctuate greatly in both good and bad times. If wages are dependent upon profits, they, too, will fluctuate erratically.[38]

Poor economic conditions may cause companies to claim an inability to pay, and unions have agreed to wage concessions or "give-backs" in order to preserve employment. When the overall economic situation improves, unions use ability to pay as their argument.

Productivity

While no argument has been advanced with more conviction or sophistication than that wages should vary with changes in productivity, the principle has grave difficulties when applied to specific negotiations. For example, the rate of change in productivity varies widely from industry to industry, firm to firm, even plant to plant. Not only is productivity itself difficult to measure accurately, but any change in productivity (usually measured in output per employee-hour) results from many causes, only one of which is labor.[39]

Those who study productivity have generally agreed that new capital investment and mechanization have been the primary causes for greater productivity, but there are still important issues to reconcile. Who shall share the results from increased productivity? The employees, stockholders, consumers? What are the relative advantages of higher wages, increased dividends, and lower prices? What is the proper balance among the contributing factors of production—labor and capital investments? Any use of the productivity criterion must be handled carefully because the available data are only approximate. Output per employee-hour often overstates gains attributed to labor, and hourly earnings data fail to account for the relative contributions of advanced technology, improved methods, better machines, and so on.

To be competitive, companies and employees must be more productive. Greater productivity may allow higher wages, but it usually results in a smaller workforce. Back in 1960, the Longshoremen's Union allowed mechanization of the waterfronts, increasing productivity by 140 percent. Annual wages for top-rated longshoremen rose over $50,000 plus benefits, but the number of jobs declined from 16,400 to 9,600. The same principle applies to other industries; high productivity is the only way to warrant high wages. However, as witnessed in the steel, auto, and other industries, greater productivity and higher wages do not lead to more jobs.[40]

Productivity Sharing Some union and management officials have undertaken cooperative efforts to bring productivity issues directly into collective bargaining. Labeled as *productivity sharing,* this endeavor is meant to enable greater productivity while providing employees a comparable share of the resulting savings in the form of higher wages. Traditionally, labor agreements have provided protection to workers who are subject to loss of employment (in such forms as advance notice, use of attrition in staff reduction, early retirement, guaranteed wages, and severance pay), and unions have often resisted speed-up efforts of productivity improvement campaigns.

The General Accounting Office identified about 1,000 productivity sharing programs. Its researchers obtained financial data from 24 firms and found that plans over five years old experienced a 29 percent labor savings in the last five-year period and plans less than five years old averaged savings of 8.5 percent. Nonmonetary benefits were also reported: 80.6 percent reported improved labor-management relations; 47.2 percent, fewer grievances; 36.1 percent, less absenteeism; and 36.1 percent, reduced turnover.[41]

Productivity has become a national concern. Although the United States still leads the industrial world in productivity in absolute numbers, it now lags behind all other industrialized countries in productivity growth. Congress has indicated its concern about low productivity in the United States, and a White House Conference on productivity designed to bring together individuals who are experts on productivity, labor relations, and management has been held.

Problems with Productivity Sharing Although productivity sharing offers an innovative approach for mutual gainsharing and cooperative activity, it, too, has its problems. Foremost is the measurement of productivity, because many possible measures exist. Some jobs do not lend themselves to precise measurement of output. It is much easier to measure bricks laid than letters taken by dictation and typed because letters vary in complexity and length. In jobs that are not routine or repetitious, exact measures are impossible.

Another problem is locating and organizing productivity data in such a manner that it may be useful to a firm. Serious arguments over the contribution of specific factors to increased productivity can inhibit the success of any productivity bargaining. What is the chief contributor to productivity gains? Is it the skill, efforts, or attitudes of the employees? Or is it the advanced technology of the machinery and equipment, efficiency of the operations, or scale of operations? Or is it the interaction between these sets of factors?[42] Because productivity gains will be shared under the productivity bargaining concept, they will certainly give rise to rigorous and complicated negotiations, particularly when bargaining-unit employees are accustomed to receiving comparable wages.

Examples of bargaining for productivity improvement have occurred in the construction industry. Negotiations there have resulted in agreements to reduce work stoppages, and provisions covering jurisdictional disputes, inefficient work rules, illegal featherbedding, and nonworking stewards have also been negotiated. Interestingly, the stimulus for productivity bargaining in the construction industry was the loss of work that increasingly went to nonunion and open-shop contractors, along with the desire of union members to protect or expand their employment opportunities, particularly during unfavorable economic conditions.[43]

Joint advisory committees in the steel industry have been formed in plants to deal with productivity problems. The retail food industry has established a joint labor-management committee that aids collective bargaining settlements and technological change. The shipping industry has been involved in joint programs to promote productivity in exchange for improving wages and benefits for longshoremen and their unions. These agreements basically have involved the buy-out of restrictive provisions and practices, which allowed a reduction in the "work gang" size and increased flexibility in manpower use. To obtain these agreements, attractive early retirement provisions and guaranteed work have been included in the labor agreements.[44]

Effect of Unions on Productivity and Efficiency Recently, there has been considerable debate and research about the effect of unions on productivity and efficiency. William Winpisinger, former president of the International Association of Machinists, has identified several ways that collective bargaining has contributed to greater productivity and efficiency:

1. Unions' continuing pressure for higher wages and benefits makes unionized employees expensive, so management must seek better methods, such as technological improvements, to maintain lower unit labor costs.
2. Unions' success in reducing the average number of hours worked per week has actually increased employee productivity because the effort is greater in the fewer hours.
3. An orderly and equitable procedure for settling grievances helps resolve employee problems and therefore improves productivity.
4. Collective bargaining involves negotiating subjects related to industrial accidents and diseases. Accident prevention saves time and consequently increases productivity.
5. Union apprenticeship programs help train employees in critical skills and allow them to produce more.[45]

The presence of unions also can promote efficiency when employees, through their union power, ensure that managers treat them fairly and when unions give them a voice to influence decision making that leads to higher morale and greater productivity. Also, unionized workplaces attract and retain more highly skilled and experienced employees due to higher wages, the opportunity to be heard, and the assurance of fair treatment, which also leads to greater loyalty to the firm.[46]

On the other hand, it may be argued that unions decrease productivity by reducing managerial flexibility, limiting the use of merit-based compensation,[47] imposing work rule restrictions such as limits on work loads, restrictions on tasks performed, and requirements for unneeded standby crews or crews of excessive size, and interfering with the introduction of technological change.[48]

In some settings, unions have resulted in higher productivity because of greater capital intensity, higher labor quality, and the presence of institutional grievance procedures. This is most likely to occur where management uses the collective bargaining process to learn about ways to improve the operations of the workplace and the production processes. However, if management reacts negatively to collective bargaining, or if unions try to prevent the reorganization of the workplace, the effect of unions on organizational performance will be negative.[49]

Critics of unions' effect on productivity claim that unions are not the reason that productivity in unionized plants is higher. In fact, these critics contend that higher wages in unionized plants encourage managers to substitute capital (technology) for labor, and it is this technology advancement that increases employee productivity, not the union. Also, higher wages in unionized plants motivate the employers to seek out the "better quality" employees; likewise, the "better quality" employees of nonunion plants tend to look for work in the higher-paying unionized plants. In other words, productivity in unionized plants may be higher; however, this higher productivity may not be caused by unions but by several other factors.[50] One analysis of unions' effects on productivity follows.

> [O]ne cannot conclude from the evidence (far less than theory) that unions are good for productivity. Moreover, productivity as measured is not the same as efficiency. We do not observe unit cost reductions in unionized settings.[51]

In fact, one study revealed that the presence of the United Auto Workers resulted in a 33 percent increase in compensation with no offsetting productivity increase.[52]

Cost of Living

During periods of rising prices, unions support their wage demands by referring to the cost of living. Union negotiators advance the argument that a rise in the cost of living without a commensurate wage increase is equivalent to a cut in real wages or a drop in purchasing power. Thus, the proposition that wages be raised at least in proportion to the rise in living costs seems quite fair and reasonable. But the complete reliance on this criterion needs careful appraisal.

Unions and management must come to an agreement on the meaning of cost of living. Cost of living usually refers to the Consumer Price Index (CPI) as determined by the U.S. Labor Department's Bureau of Labor Statistics; its computation includes such items as housing, food, and automobiles, which may not be purchased regularly by employees in a specific plant or community. The parties must also negotiate the base period, the starting date, and the CPI most appropriate for use (the Bureau of Labor Statistics publishes an all-cities CPI plus CPIs for most major cities).

Automatic increases in general wages present problems in their effect on the cost-price-profit mechanism. In other words, costs of labor that are automatically increased throughout the economy can increase total costs and sales prices unless there is a commensurate productivity increase. The increases in wages are passed on to the consumer; large firms, having some monopolistic control, simply raise their prices. Thus, the market economy is restricted and does not function effectively as a determiner of prices and an allocator of resources—two of its most important functions.

The cost of living standard, also called the "standard of living," is difficult to apply because of a lack of data from specific geographic areas on the cost of living. The Consumer Price Index is an average consumer price index for the United States, but substantial differences may exist across geographic areas. A source of controversy is whether national data should be applied to specific areas where conditions may not match the average. This is particularly controversial in industry-wide negotiations, such as in the automobile industry, where there are plants throughout the country, and in nationwide negotiations, such as in the postal service. No doubt, the cost of living in New York City or Los Angeles is greater than in other cities, suburbs, and small towns around the nation.[53]

Perhaps management's greatest concern over cost of living is that it receives nothing in return for this wage increase, granted on the basis of factors over which it has no control. The cost-of-living argument seldom, if ever, considers employees' productivity at a particular facility. Additional considerations of cost of living are discussed in the section on wage adjustments.

Comparable Worth

With female employees' wages at about 80 percent of male employees' (up from 60 percent during the 1960s and 1970s), the comparable worth issue may emerge in wage considerations. As pointed out in Chapter 3, the Equal Pay Act, Civil Rights Act, and Age Discrimination in Employment Act protect against wage discrimination. These laws prohibit paying male employees more than female employees unless the wage difference is justified on the basis of skill, effort, responsibility, working conditions, seniority, or performance.

Proponents of the comparable worth issue state that women earn less pay because they are disproportionately represented in lower-evaluated and, therefore, lower-paying jobs and that the value placed on these jobs has been arbitrarily established by companies and negotiated with the unions.

Unions have become involved in the comparable worth issue in cases where operators, traffic, billing, and office employees in telephone companies are mostly female, while line and installation work is performed primarily by higher-paid males.[54]

Some unions, such as the International Union of Electrical Workers (IUE), have sued employers, in this case, Westinghouse. The company had properly evaluated the jobs of men and women; however, the pay for women's jobs thereafter was less than men's of equal value in the job-evaluation plan. This resulted in most women being placed three to four pay grades below the janitors and other unskilled common laborers.

In San Jose, the American Federation of State, County, and Municipal Employees (AFSCME) and the city engaged in a joint job-evaluation study that showed that salaries of jobs held predominantly by women were an average of 15 percent less than salaries of jobs held by men, although the value by points was the same. This caused the study team to ask the following questions:

1. Why do librarians receive less pay than men with jobs requiring less than an eighth-grade education?
2. Why do female M.A.s and Ph.D.s who supervise as many as 25 people earn less than street sweepers and gardeners?
3. Why do nurses earn less than tree trimmers, painters, and parking lot attendants?

4. Why do male toll collectors earn more than medical stenographers?

The city and the union met for over a year and were not able to resolve their differences. A nine-day strike—supported by both male and female employees—occurred before a settlement was reached.[55]

Wage Adjustments During the Life of the Labor Agreement

In addition to wage determination during negotiations, labor and management will likely agree to provisions that will allow adjustment of wages during the life of the contract—usually **cost-of-living adjustments** (or **COLA,** also called *escalator clauses*), deferred wage increases (also called *annual improvement adjustments*), and **wage reopeners** that allow for wages to be negotiated at a predetermined date. Annual wage improvements are specified in 88 percent of contracts, COLA provisions are included in 34 percent, and reopener clauses are written in 8 percent.[56]

COLA, or escalator, clauses first appeared after World War I in the printing and clothing industries, but they were eliminated during the late 1920s. Immediately after World War II they were renewed, as unions tried to negotiate to keep up with rapid inflation in their labor agreement.[57] These clauses imposed "a contractual obligation upon an employer to change rates of pay in accordance with a collectively bargained formula."[58] About 22 percent of employees are covered by these clauses, as shown in Exhibit 13.5.

COLA clauses are designed for protection against inflation. With the economy experiencing low inflation, the length of labor contracts has increased to an average of 35.8 months—the highest since 1972, when the length was 26 months and when the Department of Labor began tabulating these data. For example, contract length in the steel industry is six years (wage reopener after three years), five years in the coal mining industry, ten years between Southwest Airlines and its pilots, and eleven years at Cummins Engine Co. Most of these long-term agreements include provisions for job protection and, in some cases, profit sharing. The company is guaranteed a steady workforce, but it locks the parties to wages and employment terms that may be appropriate in stable economic times but inappropriate during unstable times. On the other hand, lengthy labor contracts allow the parties to spend more time on other activities, such as the union attempting to organize nonunion plants and the company management devoting more time to improving its managerial practices.[59]

When negotiating COLA provisions, union and management representatives usually consider the following matters:

1. Selection of the particular price index and base point. In 92 percent of the agreements, the all-cities CPI (Consumer Price Index) is selected and the beginning date of the contract is specified.

Exhibit 13.5 Proportion of Employees Covered by COLAs in Labor Agreements

YEAR	PROPORTION OF EMPLOYEES COVERED BY COLAs
1971	28%
1972	41
1973	39
1974	39
1975	51
1976	59
1977	61
1978	60
1979	59
1980	58
1981	58
1982	57
1983	60
1984	57
1985	56
1986	48
1987	40
1988	38
1989	40
1990	39
1991	39
1992	32
1993	24
1994	24
1995	22

SOURCE: COLA coverage is reported in *Monthly Labor Review.*

2. Frequency and timing of the wage adjustment. Sixty-eight percent of the agreements in manufacturing call for adjustments every quarter; but 64 percent in nonmanufacturing businesses call for annual adjustments.
3. Formula for adjustment. The most common is a cents-per-hour increase for each point increase in the CPI; the remainder require a percentage change in wages in accordance with a percentage change in the CPI. The most common arrangement is to have wages adjusted 1¢ for each 0.3-point rise in the CPI.[60] (See Exhibit 13.6 for a cost-of-living schedule.)

Exhibit 13.6 Cost of Living Adjustment in General Motors and Auto Workers Labor Agreement

(101)(h) The amount of the Cost of Living Allowance shall be five cents (5¢) per hour effective with the effective date of this Agreement and ending December 5, 1993. Effective December 6, 1993 and for any period thereafter as provided in Paragraphs (101)(d) and (101)(g) the Cost of Living Allowance shall be in accordance with the following table:

THREE-MONTH AVERAGE CONSUMER PRICE INDEX	COST OF LIVING ALLOWANCE
422.1–422.2	2¢ per hour
422.3–422.5	3¢ per hour
422.6–422.8	4¢ per hour
422.9–423.0	5¢ per hour
423.1–423.3	6¢ per hour
423.4–423.5	7¢ per hour
423.6–423.8	8¢ per hour
423.9–424.1	9¢ per hour

And so forth with 1¢ adjustment for each 0.26 change in the Average Index and will be calculated in accordance with the Letter of Understanding signed by the parties.

For each adjustment during the two three-month periods beginning on December 6, 1993, and March 7, 1994, in which an increase in the Cost of Living Allowance shall be required according to the above table, the amount of increase so required each three-month period shall be reduced by four cents (4¢), or by the amount of the increase, whichever is less. For each adjustment during the seven three-month periods beginning on June 6, 1994, and ending on March 3, 1996, in which an increase in the Cost of Living Allowance shall be required according to the above table, the amount of the increase so required each three-month period shall be reduced by two cents (2¢), or by the amount of the increase, whichever is less. However, there shall be no reduction as provided herein in any three-month period in which the Cost of Living Allowance required by the table is equal to or less than the amount of the Cost of Living Allowance provided by the table in the preceding three-month period. For each adjustment during the two three-month periods beginning on March 4, 1996, and June 3, 1996, in which an increase in the Cost of Living Allowance shall be required according to the above table, the amount of increase so required each three-month period will not be reduced. Following the adjustment for the three-month period beginning June 3, 1996, the sum reduced during the eleven periods shall be subtracted from the Cost of Living Allowance table and the table shall be adjusted so that the actual Three-Month Average Consumer Price Index equates to the allowance payable during the period beginning June 3, 1996.

[See Par. (101)(e)]
[See Doc. 87]

(101)(i) The amount of any Cost of Living Allowance in effect at the time shall be included in computing overtime premium, night shift premium, vacation payments, Independence Week Shutdown pay, holiday payments, call-in pay, bereavement pay, jury duty pay, and short-term military duty pay.

(continued)

Continued **Cost of Living Adjustment in General Motors and Auto Workers Labor Agreement**

(101)(j) In the event the Bureau of Labor Statistics does not issue the appropriate Consumer Price Index on or before the beginning of one of the pay periods referred to in Paragraph (101)(g) any adjustments in the Cost of Living Allowance required by such appropriate Index shall be effective at the beginning of the first pay period after receipt of the Index.

(101)(k) No adjustments, retroactive or otherwise, shall be made due to any revision which may later be made in the published figures used in the calculation of the Consumer Price Index for any month or months specified in Paragraph (101)(g).

(101)(l) The parties to this Agreement agree that the continuance of the Cost of Living Allowance is dependent upon the availability of the monthly Consumer Price Index published by the Bureau of Labor Statistics in its present form and calculated on the same basis as the Index for July, 1993, unless otherwise agreed upon by the parties. If the Bureau of Labor Statistics changes the form or the basis of calculating the Consumer Price Index, the parties agree to request such agency to make available, for the life of this Agreement, a monthly Consumer Price Index in its present form and calculated on the same basis as the Index for July, 1993.

Source: *Collective Bargaining Negotiations and Contracts* (Washington, D.C.: Bureau of National Affairs, Inc., 1994), p. 21:37.

4. Effect of COLA on other elements of the compensation package. Little uniformity is found in this matter. Some agreements adjust the gross hourly earnings after incentives; others adjust only the base wage rate. Still other payments, such as overtime, call-in pay, night work, and differentials, must be considered.
5. Limitations on the adjustment. About one-fourth have formulas with caps (limits on the amounts that may be received from cost-of-living provisions within a given period). On the other hand, some agreements specify that wages will not be reduced in the event of a CPI decline.

COLA provisions are becoming more common not only in labor agreements but also outside the collective bargaining arena. For example, social security recipients and military and civil service retirees are covered. It has been estimated that over 50 million U.S. citizens now have their incomes adjusted by some automatic cost-of-living adjustment.[61]

Wage reopener clauses are usually written in such a way that wages may be renegotiated at a specified time during the length of the agreement or when the CPI has risen by a specified amount. Some of the agreements allow only wages to be renegotiated, whereas others allow nonwage items or do not specify the items.

Deferred wage increases, annual improvement factors, and productivity increases have a broad acceptance in most contracts, and many of these are included with cost-of-living adjustments as well as contract reopeners.

Yet cost-of-living adjustments and wage reopeners have their problems. Cost-of-living adjustments are very difficult to negotiate out of a contract because union officers and members assume the COLA will continue in subsequent contracts. This situation makes it difficult for either union or management to receive credit for the COLA. Assume, for example, that management anticipates that COLA will cost 60¢ per employee per hour. If the negotiated wage settlement costs 70¢ per employee, then employees will receive only a 10¢-an-hour increase plus continuation of the COLA. The union officer will have a difficult time selling the labor agreement to the members, because they probably take the established COLA clause for granted. It might be easier to sell the labor agreement if there were not any COLA and the wage package were publicized as an annual increase of 70¢ an hour.

Wage reopeners are subject to problems when the union wishes to extend negotiated items to noneconomic items. While this is not allowable in theory, the distinction between economic and noneconomic discussion becomes blurred in practice. Some practitioners have suggested that a wage reopener is similar to an entirely new contract negotiation as the parties bring noneconomic items into the discussion.

Lump-Sum Pay Adjustment Bonuses

Lump-sum pay adjustments appeared in 19 percent of agreements in 1994, up from 13 percent in 1993 and 12 percent in 1992, but down from 36 percent in 1988. The most common payment was a flat amount—an average of $860 in the first year, $770 in the second, and $778 in the third year of the agreement.[62] These adjustments are popular with management because they do not apply to employee benefits and do not change the permanent wage structure. Therefore, they appear to be more than an equal wage increase. For example, a $1,000 lump-sum payment to a $20,000-per-year employee is much less than a 5 percent increase, because his or her wage the following year remains $20,000 and the base of that employee's benefits has not been increased. With the employee benefits approaching 40 percent of payroll costs, this is an enormous savings to the company.

A three-year agreement containing a 3 percent annual wage improvement each year produces a wage rate 9 percent above the initial base in the third year, but a lump-sum payment each year does not raise the base rate at all. Also, new employees hired after the settlement do not receive this payment. Therefore, tension caused by the two-tier pay scale is created.

Employers benefit from lump-sum payments because all new employees will begin employment at the existing wage rates, and the employer does not have to include lump-sum payments in the overtime calculations (unless the parties include such language in their collective bargaining agreement).

Employee Benefits

In 1993 U.S. employers paid an average of $14,807 ($7.16 an hour) per employee in benefits, or 41.3 percent of payroll costs, up from 19.2 percent in 1953. These benefits include insurance costs, pension payments, payments for time not worked (such as vacations, sick leave, and holidays), legally required payments for unemployment and workers' compensation, paid rest and lunch breaks, and profit-sharing and bonuses. Medically related benefits and payments for time not worked are the highest cost, both at 11.1 percent of payroll costs. Next are legally mandated payments including social security, unemployment compensation, and worker compensation at 8.7 percent of payroll costs.[63] The following sections present major areas of employee benefits, relying largely on an analysis of 400 collective bargaining agreements by the Bureau of National Affairs.[64]

Insurance

Insurance provisions have been substantially expanded: 99 percent of the contracts provide life insurance, and 30 percent include coverage for basic hospitalization benefits, major medical expenses (24 percent), surgery (30 percent), maternity benefits (27 percent), doctor's visits, accidental death and dismemberment (75 percent), and dental insurance (85 percent). Most contracts continue coverage to employees after retirement but reduce the amount of coverage. Hospitalization and surgical insurance for dependents of employees are covered in nearly all of the contracts, and premiums are paid by the company in the majority of cases. There are also increasing numbers of medically related plans covering new areas: prescription drugs (43 percent), optical care (43 percent), supplements to Medicare (56 percent), and alcohol and drug abuse (68 percent) treatment. Growth in these areas of coverage is expected to continue.

Health Care Cost Containment

Health care costs have risen dramatically over the last few years. The costs are over $900 billion, up from $250 billion in 1980. More striking is the estimate that by the year 2000, the United States will be spending 18 percent of its gross national product on health care. For comparison, auto companies report that over $1,000 of the cost of manufacturing a single automobile goes for health care expenditures. Because many countries have national health care programs paid for by taxes, American auto makers who pay for their employees' health care benefits are at a distinct disadvantage in competing internationally.[65]

Employers have attempted either to reduce the costs of health care coverage or to shift pay of the cost to employees. At the same time, unions and employees are more inclined than ever to protect their health care benefits. As a result, widespread work stoppages by the Communications Workers of America and International Brotherhood of Electrical Workers have occurred over these conflicting interests with Bell Atlantic, NYNEX, and Pacific Telesis.

Unions and companies have negotiated contract provisions to lower health care costs. Such provisions appeared in 83 percent of the agreements in 1995, a steep climb from 55 percent in 1986. Health care cost containment clauses included surgical fees for procedures performed on an outpatient basis in 69 percent of the agreements; a second surgical opinion was required in 68 percent. The length of hospital stays was reduced by covering home health care in 69 percent of the agreements, and 57 percent of the agreements required non-emergency tests be performed on an outpatient basis before hospital admission. In addition, there has been an increase from 19 percent in 1986 to 52 percent in 1995 in provisions requiring employees to share in premium costs for comprehensive medical coverage.

Income Maintenance

Income-maintenance provisions that provide income protection for employees are now found in 53 percent of labor agreements. Such provisions usually involve work or pay guarantees, severance pay (separation or termination pay), and supplemental unemployment benefit (SUB) plans. Thirteen percent of the agreements contain work or pay guarantees, with the majority of those providing a weekly guarantee of 40 hours of work.

Severance-pay plans providing for lump-sum payments upon termination are included in 39 percent of the agreements. In most cases, severance pay is extended only to employees whose jobs have been terminated as a result of permanent shutdown, to those whose layoffs continue beyond a minimum length of time, or to those who have no prospect for recall. The amount of severance pay varies with the length of service—each year of service allows for increased benefits. Severance payments are usually restricted to a particular time period (up to one year) or until the employee is reemployed.

Supplemental unemployment benefit plans (SUB), included in 13 percent of the agreements, are usually classified as pooled fund systems (benefits are allowed only in the event of lack of work). A few SUB plans provide individual accounts in which the employee has a vested right and from which he or she may withdraw money for reasons other than lack of work. The most common method provides payment of an amount equal to a percentage of the employee's take-home pay with unemployment compensation deducted. Plans involving the United Auto Workers are the most lucrative for the workers, with SUB payments and unemployment compensation equaling 95 percent of take-home pay minus $12.50 in work-related expenses. Other plans range from $10 per week minimum to 90 percent of take-home pay. Other considerations, such as duration of benefits, length of service requirements, and employer financial requirements, must also be included in the composition of the plan.

Premium Pay—Overtime and Other Supplements

Most labor agreements specify daily or weekly work schedules, and 86 percent provide premium pay for hours worked beyond the normal hours. Most agreements call for an 8-hour day and work weeks of 40 hours—Monday through Friday.

Overtime premiums are usually paid for work over 8 hours per day at a time-and-a-half rate, which is more beneficial to the worker than the Fair Labor Standards Act requirement of time-and-a-half payments for work in excess of 40 hours in a week. (Employees on a 4-day, 40-hour work week would receive 8 hours of overtime pay.) A few agreements provide sixth-day and seventh-day premiums, but the majority of agreements prohibit pyramiding of overtime (combining a number of different premium payments, allowing overtime duplication).

Many labor agreements also contain provisions for overtime administration. For example, overtime assignments may be restricted to employees within a job classification or a given department, to a particular shift, to qualified employees, and so on. In some cases, where management has had difficulty getting employees to work overtime, provisions that make overtime mandatory have been negotiated.

Some agreements that provide for equalization of overtime hours count the hours offered when an employee is offered overtime and refuses to accept it. For example, if an employee is offered 4 hours of Saturday morning overtime and he or she turns it down, those 4 hours of overtime offered are the same as 4 hours of overtime worked in the equalization of overtime process. Likewise, unions have sought provisions in the labor agreement that would enable their members to better plan their off-the-job activities: advance notice, relief from mandatory overtime if not notified by a certain time, and others.

Various forms of premium pay are included in most contracts. For instance, shift differentials (premium payments for working the night shift, for example) are provided in most of the agreements. Other forms, such as reporting pay (pay for employees who report for scheduled work but find no work) and call-back pay (pay for employees who are called back to work at hours other than normal) are also usually included. Reporting pay guarantees pay for from 1 to 8 hours, except with some maritime firms that provide one full week. Call-back or call-in pay guarantees are most frequently for 4 hours. Other supplements include pay for temporary transfer, hazardous work, travel, work clothes, tools, and bonuses other than production.

Payments for Nonwork—Holidays, Vacations, and Rest Periods

While many agreements provide pay for such nonwork activities as rest periods, cleanup time, time lost to job-related injury, waiting time, standby time, travel time, and voting time, the payments for nonwork involving the most money are holidays and vacations. The median number of holidays provided is 11; the range is from 5 to 19. Nearly all agreements provide holidays for Labor Day, Independence Day, Thanksgiving, Christmas, New Year's Day, and Memorial Day. Good Friday, Christmas Eve, and the day after Thanksgiving appear in over half of the agreements. Martin Luther King, Jr.'s birthday as a holiday appears in 14 percent of the agreements, which is 5 percent more than in 1986. Most agreements have eligibility requirements, for example, specified length of service (usually four weeks) before being given a paid holiday, or working the day before and after the holiday. More complicated provisions involve issues such as holidays falling on Saturday, Sunday, or a day off or during vacation, and premium pay for work on holidays.

Nearly all agreements provide for vacations for covered employees; there have been sharp increases in agreements allowing five- and six-week vacations in the last 20 years and slight reductions in amount of service to qualify for nearly all types of vacations. Somewhat surprisingly, vacations for one week only are now less frequent than two-, three-, and four-week vacations for those who qualify because the amount of vacation is linked to length of service. For example, to qualify for a five-week vacation, an employee must have 25 years of service.

Nearly all agreements have provisions that pertain to the administration of vacations. The majority contain specific work requirements, such as a minimum number of hours, days, weeks, or years necessary to qualify for various lengths of vacation. Vacation scheduling provisions appear in 92 percent of all agreements; they cover such items as annual plant shutdowns and consideration of employee seniority and employee preference. These provisions are essential in organizations employing large numbers, not only to reduce friction between employees but to allow management to properly plan its production schedules.

Pensions

Unions greatly increase pension coverage and alter the provisions of pension plans in ways that benefit the senior employees and equalize pensions among employees.[66] Union members receive larger benefits than nonunion employees at the time they retire and also receive larger increases in their benefits in the years following their retirement. They retire at an earlier age than nonunion employees, too. The overall wealth of the pension funds to union member beneficiaries is 50 to 109 percent greater than that of nonunion employees.[67]

Nearly all labor agreements make some reference to pension plans, whether in the form of a general statement mentioning the plan or a fully detailed provision. Items usually mentioned include age for retirement (normal and early), disability retirement, benefits available and requirements for qualifying, vesting provisions, administration procedures, and financial arrangements.

In 1987, the Age Discrimination in Employment Act was amended to outlaw any mandatory retirement; prior to that amendment, the allowable mandatory retirement age was 70. Although this amendment helped the senior employee, the Supreme Court's controversial *Betts* decision in 1989 did not. The Court ruled that virtually all employee benefit programs are exempt from challenge under the Age Discrimination in Employment Act *unless* the employee can prove "intentional discrimination" on the part of the employer.[68]

There are many horror stories about long-term employees retiring without pensions or less-than-anticipated pension payoffs. For example, Continental Can was found guilty of using a sophisticated computer system called the Bell System (reverse acronym for "Lowest Level of Employee Benefits") to keep track of employees and fire them before they became eligible for pension benefits. Employees at 46 plants where the union had negotiated pension benefits were involved. A federal judge found Continental Can guilty of violating the Employment Retirement and Security Act, and the company's financial obligations amounted to as much as $500 million.[69]

Fifty percent of the plans guarantee the retired employee a flat monthly dollar amount for each year of service ($21.75 is the median; the amounts range from $4.00 to $55.00) or a percentage of earnings times years of service. Disability pension benefits are provided for employees who are forced to retire due to total or permanent disability in 89 percent of the agreements. Most of these agreements specify a service requirement. For example, 57 percent require 10 years of service. In addition, voluntary early retirement is allowed in 95 percent of the plans.

Frequently, early retirement plans offer several options to the employee. For example, agreements provide such options as retirement at age 60 after 10 years of service; retirement at age 55 but only when the combined age and service years equal 85; and retirement after 30 years of service, without regard to age. The financial arrangements in 93 percent of the agreements show that the employer finances the pension plan entirely (that is, it is noncontributory); where plans are contributory, labor agreements include very specific provisions about the amounts that the employer and the employees contribute.

Although nearly all of the contracts contain **vesting** provisions stating that an employee whose service is terminated continues to be entitled to earned benefits, the Employer Retirement Income Security Act of 1974 (also known as ERISA or the Pension Reform Act) has very specific regulations governing vesting requirements of pension plans. Although management and labor may negotiate provisions covering pensions that are more favorable than the law requires, most agreements for the time being will no doubt closely correspond to the legal minimum. Under any of these options, an employee must be at least 50 percent vested after 10 years of service and 100 percent vested after 15 years of service, regardless of age.

A major concern in recent years has been the underfunding of employee pension plans. The Pension Benefit Guaranty Corp., the agency that ensures pensioners receive benefits if their employer goes bankrupt, has reported 16,000 underfunded corporate plans. Among the companies with underfunded plans are General Motors, Warner-Lambert, Northwest Airlines, and Woolworth. Ravenswood Aluminum tops the list of underfunded plans with $30 million in pension assets and $137 million in liabilities. The consequence may be increased premiums paid by companies to guarantee employees' pensions when they retire; however, such action would likely increase employee contributions to their pension plans.[70]

Prepaid Legal Services

Twenty years ago, prepaid legal services did not exist. In fact, any attorney who contracted with a group to provide legal services for a predetermined fee would have been disbarred.[71] Now legal assistance is available to organized group members who have pooled prepaid amounts. Prepaid legal service plans include about a million employees under the UAW-General Motors agreement, 400,000 under the UAW-Ford agreement, and 200,000 under the UAW-Chrysler agreement as well as

300,000 members of the New York City Municipal Employees Union.[72] By 1995, 7.6 million employees were covered, up from 1.5 million in 1978. These legal service plans operate in a manner similar to health maintenance organizations (HMOs). In exchange for a monthly premium (ranging from $80 to $200 per year), subscribers are entitled to free legal advice, representation, and document reviews from a network of approved attorneys who provide the service for a fixed fee paid by the plan's provider.[73]

These plans vary in terms of whether the parties will set up open panels (the client chooses the attorney) or closed panels (legal services are provided by a law firm retained under the plan or by an attorney staff). Some plans offer a full array of services, ranging from counsel for criminal offenses to routine matters such as wills, divorces, house closings, and landlord-tenant problems. Most believe prepaid legal services will become more common; these projections are supported by an American Bar Association study that predicted that prepaid legal service plans would become as common as medical insurance is today.[74]

Family and Child Care Benefits

After an eight-year effort in the U.S. Congress, the Family and Medical Leave Act (FMLA) of 1993 was passed. This act requires private employers of 50 or more employees to provide eligible employees up to 12 weeks of unpaid leave for their own serious illness, the birth or adoption of a child, or care of a seriously ill child, spouse, or parent. For eligibility, an employee must have been employed for at least one year and worked at least 1,250 hours within the previous 12 months. The Department of Labor is assigned administrative responsibility for the act, and civil suits by employees are allowed.[75] (See Exhibit 13.7.)

A year after the FMLA took effect, the Department of Labor received and investigated 965 complaints. Labor Secretary Robert Reich reported that roughly 90 percent of the complaints were settled in favor of the employee, often with a phone call to the employer from an employee of the Department of Labor who explained the requirements under the FMLA.[76]

To date, 35 states have passed some form of family leave legislation that requires unpaid family and medical leave for employees. Most of the laws cover public employees only, and some provide for maternity and adoption leave. The laws in 11 states and the District of Columbia guarantee private sector employees either unpaid family and medical leave, family leave only, or just parental leave. Those that provide family and medical leave usually guarantee time off for both men and women to care for a new child or seriously ill family member.[77] By 1994, family leave provisions had been negotiated and included in 36 percent of labor agreements. Maternity leave, parental leave, and paternity leave were the most common. Sixteen percent of the agreements specifically mentioned the FMLA and the parties' agreement to comply.[78]

Unions are now in a position to negotiate family and medical benefits into the collective bargaining agreements that are greater than those guaranteed by the FMLA. However, bargaining-unit employees will apply pressure to grant these

Exhibit 13.7 Basic Fact Sheet on the Family and Medical Leave Act

The Family and Medical Leave Act (FMLA) requires covered employers to provide up to 12 weeks of unpaid, job-protected leave to "eligible" employees for certain family and medical reasons. Employees are eligible if they have worked for a covered employer for at least one year, and for 1,250 hours over the previous 12 months, and if there are at least 50 employees within 75 miles.

Reasons for Taking Leave:

Unpaid leave must be granted for *any* of the following reasons:

- to care for the employee's child after birth, or placement for adoption or foster care;
- to care for the employee's spouse, son or daughter, or parent, who has a serious health condition; or
- for a serious health condition that makes the employee unable to perform the employee's job.

At the employee's or employer's option, certain kinds of *paid* leave may be substituted for unpaid leave.

Advance Notice and Medical Certification:

The employee may be required to provide advance leave notice and medical certification. Taking of leave may be denied if requirements are not met.

- The employee ordinarily must provide 30 days advance notice when the leave is "foreseeable."
- An employer may require medical certification to support a request for leave because of a serious health condition, and may require second or third opinions (at the employer's expense) and a fitness for duty report to return to work.

Job Benefits and Protection:

- For the duration of the FMLA leave, the employer must maintain the employee's health coverage under any "group health plan."
- Upon return from FMLA leave, most employees must be restored to their original or equivalent positions with equivalent pay, benefits, and other employment terms.
- The use of FMLA leave cannot result in the loss of any employment benefit that accrued prior to the start of the employee's leave.

Unlawful Acts by Employers:

FMLA makes it unlawful for any employer to:

- interfere with, restrain, or deny the exercise of any right provided under FMLA;
- discharge or discriminate against any person for opposing any practice made unlawful by FMLA or for involvement in any proceeding under or relating to FMLA.

Enforcement:

- The U.S. Department of Labor is authorized to investigate and resolve complaints of violations.
- Any eligible employee may bring a civil action against an employer for violations.

FMLA does not affect any federal or state law prohibiting discrimination, or supersede any state or local law or collective bargaining agreement that provides greater family or medical leave rights.

SOURCE: Department of Labor

additional benefits if the only benefits received are those obtained through legislation. The FMLA includes a section that states that the law will not be interpreted to diminish any employer obligation to comply with provisions in collective bargaining agreements that provide benefits greater than the FMLA (nor may the collective bargaining agreements diminish benefits under the FMLA). Because family and medical leave is a mandatory subject of collective bargaining, the employer is legally obligated to bargain with the union over these subjects. In fact, the employer would be committing an unfair labor practice by refusing to bargain over family and medical leave issues, even though FMLA has certain legal minimum requirements.[79]

Union Effects on Wages and Benefits

The degree to which unions influence wage and benefit levels is a frequently debated subject among labor economists. In a 1963 classic book, *Unionism and Relative Wages in the United States,*[80] Greg Lewis concluded that union wages ranged between 10 and 15 percent higher than nonunion wages. Further analysis reveals a greater impact on wages of blue-collar employees, younger employees, and less-educated employees. The data in Exhibit 13.8 show that union employees earn $155 more per week than nonunion employees. A difference is present in every occupation and industry listed except mining.

Most research studies have concluded that comparison of wages across industries, areas, or companies shows a positive relationship between the degree and extent of union coverage and wages of union members. For example, the degree of union organization of supermarket employees within a city has a large influence on union wages. In fact, a 10 percent increase in union organization within the supermarket labor force in an urban area would result in an increase of over 2 percent in individuals' wages.

Where bargaining takes place on a national basis, consumers are more likely and able to substitute goods produced outside the area for local union products. For example, in the aerospace industry, unionization of employees has a small and statistically nonsignificant effect on individuals' wages. On the other hand, in the supermarket industry, if there is a strong union presence in the local area, few consumers are willing to commute very far to substitute products.[81]

The union-nonunion wage gap appears to vary by industry, demographics, and time periods. The wage gap differential between union and nonunion employees is greater for black and Hispanic employees than white, nonmanufacturing than manufacturing, blue-collar than white-collar, the South than the Northeast, small cities than large, private than government, and hazardous than nonhazardous labor.

Labor productivity appears to be higher in unionized settings, particularly in manufacturing and construction, where the average differential has been determined to be as high as 20 percent. Explanations vary, but they seem to be concentrated in the following reasons: (1) improved morale due to higher wages, (2) lower quit rates due to higher wages, (3) higher levels of firm-specific skills, (4) enhanced voice in operating the organization. These explanations are not generally accepted

Exhibit 13.8 Median Weekly Earnings of Full-Time Wage and Salary Employees: Union, Nonunion, and Difference, 1992

	PERCENT OF EMPLOYEES REPRESENTED BY UNIONS
Total (16 years and older)	16.7
Sex	
Men	18.8
Women	14.3
Race	
White	15.9
Black	22.3
Hispanic	14.8
Occupation	
Technical sales and administrative support	11.5
Service	15.1
Precision production, craft, and repair	24.8
Operators, fabricators, and laborers	24.4
Farming, forestry, and fishing	5.6
Industry	
Agricultural wage and salary workers	2.7
Private nonagricultural wage and salary workers	11.4
Mining	14.4
Construction	18.8
Manufacturing	18.7
Transportation and public utilities	29.1
Wholesale and retail trade	6.7
Finance, insurance, and real estate	2.6
Services	6.9
Government workers	43.5

by management, however, because most employers oppose recognition of unions, and most employer associations oppose any proposed legislation that might aid unions in organizing and representing employees. One reason for the employers' position is that the increased productivity combined with the higher wages actually produces a small gain in unit labor costs, and consequently, profits in unionized settings might be lower.[82]

Unions have an even greater effect on employee benefits. Blue-collar employees covered by labor agreements receive employee benefits that average 28 to 36

EMPLOYEES REPRESENTED BY UNION	EMPLOYEES NOT REPRESENTED BY UNION	DIFFERENCE IN WAGES UNION OVER NONUNION
$602	$447	+ $155
638	507	+ 131
523	386	+ 137
616	466	+ 150
500	348	+ 152
493	311	+ 182
516	414	+ 102
477	275	+ 202
684	478	+ 206
519	338	+ 181
404	280	+ 124
NA	289	—
567	443	+ 124
682	663	+ 19
730	442	+ 288
544	479	+ 65
673	545	+ 128
454	363	+ 91
490	502	− 12
491	440	+ 51
633	500	+ 133

SOURCE: "Union Membership Declines in 1995" (Washington, D.C.: Bureau of National Affairs, Inc., March 12, 1996), pp. D-1 to D-5.

percent higher than those of blue-collar employees in nonunion settings. The union presence positively influences the likelihood that a pension plan will be offered, although unions apparently do not raise employer expenditures for pensions once the plans are established.[83]

Unions also contribute to wage equalization by decreasing the differential between unionized blue-collar employees and nonunion white-collar employees, as well as reducing wage dispersion (covered earlier in this chapter). This union contribution frequently results in less turnover because seniority-based wage increases, promotion possibilities, and other benefits cause employees to stay with their employers longer.[84]

Some studies have shown that the wage differences between union and nonunion employees are the products of other interrelated influences, such as higher occupational skills, fewer females, lower quit rates, larger organizations, and greater capital intensity of production in unionized industries.[85] Other studies have even contended the union-nonunion wage differential is an illusion, because the higher-paid employees tend to unionize in order to obtain union services.[86] In other words, employees who share a beneficial wage and benefit differential will form unions to protect their advantageous positions.

Unions also have an effect on wages and benefits in nonunion companies. Union wage and benefit changes "spill over" into nonunion companies because nonunion employers who want to maintain their nonunion status will respond to union wage increases by raising wages of their employees. Such increases are provided not only to reduce the threat of unions, but to provide equity and maintain morale and productivity.[87]

Although in some cases unions have responded to nonunion wages in order to remain competitive, craft unions, which have recently been heavily damaged by job losses, have not reduced their wage premium over the nonunion craft employers. Thus far, these unions have apparently been willing to tolerate even higher unemployment to avoid lowering their wage demands.[88]

Employee Stock Ownership Plans

An **employee stock ownership plan (ESOP)** provides employees an opportunity to become shareholders in the company that employs them. Of course, employees can always buy stock in the stock market; but ESOPs create additional incentives by providing discount prices on shares or by matching employees' payments for stock. These plans provide a method, not necessarily related to profits, for employee participation in ownership. ESOPs have been hailed by their supporters as a means for eliminating labor-management conflicts, improving productivity and competitiveness, and increasing employees' motivation and commitment to the firm.

Organized labor, however, has been cautious about ESOPs and in some cases even hostile toward ESOPs because they could (1) eliminate important employee benefit plans and increase the financial risk to employees, (2) result in employees identifying more closely with the firm's interests and undermine the union's bargaining role, (3) allow owners to unload financially and operationally weak firms on employees who wish to save their jobs, and (4) subvert the collective bargaining process and lead to conflicts of interest between unions and employee-owners.[89]

About 10,000 companies employing about 10 million employees offer ESOPs. In approximately 1,500 ESOPs, employees own the majority of the stock.[90] Examples of companies having ESOPs are listed in Exhibit 13.9.

Concession bargaining of trading stock for wages in companies employing more than 1,000 employees has been common in the airline, steel, and trucking industries. Airlines now account for over 11 percent of employee ownership in large firms; in steel, it is estimated that 25 percent of employees were involved in concession-bargaining-based employee ownership in 1985; in trucking, over 20 firms have either used concession-bargaining-based employee ownership or organized their firms with substantial amounts of employee ownership. In many firms in these industries, ESOPs played a major role in preventing disaster until the firms could get their businesses under control.[91]

While often called "tax dodges," "socialistic schemes," and "people's capitalism," ESOPs offer several advantages:

1. Tax breaks that include interest payments on the debt, dividend paid on the ESOP shares, and principal on the debt.
2. Defense against corporate raiders and help in leveraged buyouts.
3. Reduction in pension payments because stock is contributed.
4. Productivity increases and better quality due to higher morale and employee effort.

On the other hand, ESOPs do contain some uncertainties. For example, productivity gains are not likely unless management is willing to give employees a

Exhibit 13.9 Companies Having Major ESOPs

Anheuser-Busch
Avis
Avondale
Epic Healthcare
Healthtrust
J.C. Penney
Lockheed
Parsons
Polaroid
Procter & Gamble
Ralston Purina
Texaco
United Airlines
U.S. West
Whitman

SOURCES: *Business Week* and *Forbes*.

strong and genuine voice in the operations. In fact, managers who alienate the employee-owners may be voted out of their jobs in favor of a corporate raider. Likewise, the government, a key participant in these programs, provides some uncertainty. The U.S. Department of Labor closely monitors the ESOPs for abuses in the administration of the programs, and Congress may change the rules of the game at any time. Perhaps the biggest uncertainty to the employee-owner is that each employee stakes his or her future retirement income on the value of the company's stock.[92]

Companies with ESOPs face continual challenges just like other companies. Even though the employees may be the majority stockholders, they face the same business decisions other companies do.[93] Also, all ESOPs have not been successful. In fact, employees at Dan River, Inc., gave up their pension plan in return for 70 percent of company stock in order to fend off corporate raider Carl Icahn. They have no voice in the management of the company, and employees complain that the management gets "colder and more distant." The company has operated at a loss and the value of the employees' stock has declined, thereby causing the employees' retirement benefits to shrink by 29 percent.

On the other hand, the value of the shares owned by Dan River's management has soared. They had purchased a separate class of stock for a 30 percent interest in the company, and this class of stock has doubled in value. These differences have created much resentment among employees, and some employees have expressed interest in having Icahn return.[94] United Airlines' ESOP is discussed in the "Labor Relations in Action."

Although research on the effects of ESOPs on labor-management relations is tentative at this time because of the lack of widespread or long-term experience, a few preliminary conclusions may be reported:

1. Labor-management cooperation does not emerge automatically when publicly traded companies move into employee ownership.
2. Employee ownership leads to greater identification of the employees with the company and employees receive more information about the company, supervisor-employee relations become more cooperative, and employees and managers express positive attitudes about employee ownership and the organizational climate.
3. No evidence supports the concern that employees want to take over companies with ESOPs and run them democratically from top to bottom.
4. Employee ownership does not have an automatic effect on employees' motivation, work effort, absenteeism, or job satisfaction. However, greater integration of the employee into the organization and participation in decisions have positive results.
5. Generally, the role of the union does not change except in cases where the union made an early and ongoing effort to become involved in the whole process in detail, and unions initiate little change in labor-management relations.

United Airlines' ESOP

Faced with high wages, restrictive work rules, excessive costs, and no profits in four previous years, stockholders of UAL Corporation, United Airlines' parent company, approved on July 12, 1994, an employee buyout of America's second largest airline after five attempts since 1987. The final buyout agreement provided approximately 65,000 employees with 55 percent equity stake in United Airlines in exchange for $4.9 billion in wage and work-rule concessions over the next six years. The 31,000 members of the Airline Pilots Association would own 25.4 percent of the company's stock; 17,000 members of the International Association of Machinists would own 20.5 percent; and 17,000 nonunion employees would own 9.1 percent. This 55 percent was to increase up to 63 percent if the average market value of United Airlines' common stock reached $136 per share after the first year under the plan. In October 1995, the value of United's shares had increased to $172, up from $79 in July 1994.

The agreement called for wage cuts over the next six years, and three employees were to be chosen for membership on the board of directors. Gerald Greenwald, a former deputy of Lee Iacocca's at Chrysler, was named chairman and chief executive officer. The buyout agreement contained restrictions on United's plan to develop a new low-cost "airline within an airline," such as the United Shuttle, to compete on short-distance domestic routes.

The Association of Flight Attendants (AFA) initially participated in the union bargaining coalition, but the 17,000 employees represented by the AFA were not included in the final employee ownership plan. When United announced that it was opening foreign bases for flight attendants in Hong Kong to add to the one currently in Taiwan, the AFA stopped its participation. In response, the company announced that it had postponed indefinitely plans for the Hong Kong base, and talks with the AFA resumed. However, negotiations ceased when the AFA concluded that its members were not receiving sufficient value for their proposed concessions.

Since approval of the plan, United's successes have included the "Shuttle by United," a profitable low-cost operation on the West Coast that competes with no-frills Southwest Airlines and Reno; innovations such as booking reservations through the Internet; and ticketless flying.

Among the controversies of United's ESOP are pay cuts to employees while former United executives received significant economic packages from company stock and options. Reportedly, Stephen Wolf, former UAL chairman and CEO, was to receive up to $28.9 million; after the ESOP agreement was reached, he became a consultant to the investment firm he had hired to advise the UAL board on the ESOP. John C. Pope, UAL's former president and chief operating officer, was to receive $16.3 million for his stock and options. At the same time, pilots took a 15.7 percent pay cut, and the machinists took a 9.7 percent cut.

SOURCE: Michael H. Cimini and Charles J. Muhl, "Labor-Management Bargaining in 1994," *Monthly Labor Review* 118 (January 1995), p. 31.

6. Companies with an active employee ownership philosophy that try to translate it into concrete cooperative efforts have the strongest effect on positive employee attitudes.
7. The presence of an ESOP does not make a firm more productive, efficient, or profitable; however, most studies show that employee-owned firms performed successfully on a number of financial variables, such as profits, stock appreciation, sales, and employment growth. One study showed that where all employees could participate in an ESOP, their firm performed less favorably than the non-ESOP companies on all the measures,[95] although isolating single causes for performance is extremely difficult.

SUMMARY

Economic issues include wages and the variety of economic benefits that make up what is commonly called the wage package. Wage differentials result from several industrial, occupational, and regional factors. Job evaluation begins with an organizational analysis and concludes with a wage structure that includes job classes, wage rates, and wage ranges.

In addition to the basic wage structure, some firms provide either individual or group wage incentives. Negotiators use certain wage-determining criteria in arriving at an acceptable wage structure; commonly accepted criteria include differential features of jobs, comparable wages, ability to pay, productivity, and cost of living.

Since labor agreements usually are negotiated for periods greater than 1 year, provisions are commonly negotiated to adjust wages during the life of the contract. A common form of wage adjustment is the cost-of-living adjustment (COLA), or escalator clause, which adjusts wages in accordance with the Consumer Price Index. Another form of wage adjustment less frequently included in agreements is the wage reopener clause, providing that wages be renegotiated at a predetermined time during the life of the agreement.

Employee benefits have now increased to consume 39.2 percent of the company's total payroll. Numerous types of benefits exist. The major ones include insurance, income maintenance, premium pay, payment for nonwork, and pensions. New benefits, prepaid legal and child care services and family leave, have recently come into existence and are likely to increase in popularity.

The chapter concludes with a discussion of employee stock ownership plans (ESOPs) and the roles that unions have played in these plans. Numerous examples were presented, and the advantages and disadvantages of the various plans were discussed. While there are numerous successful plans, other plans were identified as failures for employees.

Key Terms

job evaluation
profit-sharing plans
cost-of-living adjustments (COLA)
wage reopeners
lump-sum pay adjustments
two-tier pay plans
supplemental unemployment benefit plans (SUB)
vesting
employee stock ownership plan (ESOP)
wage incentive plans

Discussion Questions

1. List the main factors that may help explain the wage differentials for five jobs in an organization with which you are familiar.
2. Explain why job evaluation plans must take into consideration external as well as internal factors if they are to be successful.
3. Assume that labor and management are negotiating a labor agreement and the wage spread becomes an issue of disagreement—management wants a wider wage spread, and the union wants a smaller wage spread. Why should management be cautious about the union's proposal, even though the total costs may be the same?
4. For each of the wage criteria given in the chapter, state the union's expected arguments and management's expected counterarguments, given the following conditions:
   a. High profits, a growing firm, a healthy economy, and the cost of living rising at 8 percent per year.
   b. Low profit, no anticipation of growth, questionable economic conditions, and the cost of living rising but by wide variations each month.
5. Assuming that a firm's costs for employee benefits are 39.0 percent of payroll, why doesn't the firm just let the union determine the manner in which the amounts are apportioned to the variety of benefits, such as insurance, holidays, and vacations, without negotiating each specific clause, especially because the overall costs probably would be the same?
6. Evaluate child care benefits and family leave as union organizing instruments.
7. What must be included in the composition of an ESOP for you as an employee to participate?

References

1. Michael J. Mandel, "Plumper Profits, Skimpier Paychecks," *Business Week*, January 30, 1995, pp. 86–87; "First Among Equals," *The Economist*, January 15, 1994, p. 73; and Keith Bradsher, "Productivity Is A1, but It Doesn't Pay Well," *The New York Times*, June 25, 1995, p. E4.

2. Jules Bachman, *Wage Determination: An Analysis of Wage Criteria* (Princeton, N.J.: D. Van Nostrand, 1959), pp. 1–21.

3. George W. Taylor, "Wage Determination Process," in *New Concepts in Wage Determination*, eds. George W. Taylor and Frank C. Person (New York: McGraw-Hill, 1957), p. 84.
4. Leon Greenberg, "Definitions and Concepts," in *Collective Bargaining and Productivity*, ed. Gerald Somers (Madison, Wis.: Industrial Relations Research Association, 1975), p. 12.
5. Bachman, *Wage Determination*, p. 58.
6. For further reference, see David W. Belcher, *Compensation Administration* (Englewood Cliffs, N.J.: Prentice-Hall, 1974); and J. D. Dunn and F. M. Rachel, *Wage and Salary Administration: Total Compensation Systems* (New York: McGraw-Hill, 1971).
7. Approach developed and advocated by L. T. Hawley and H. D. Janes.
8. David W. Belcher, "Wage and Salary Administration," in *Motivation and Commitment*, eds. Dale Yoder and H. G. Heneman, Jr. (Washington, D.C.: Bureau of National Affairs, Inc., 1975), pp. 6–95.
9. Harold D. Janes, "Issues in Job Evaluation: The Union View," *Personnel Journal* 51 (September 1972), p. 675; see also Research Department, International Association of Machinists, *What's Wrong with Job Evaluation?* (Washington, D.C.: International Association of Machinists, 1954).
10. Harold D. Janes, "Comparative Issues in Job Evaluation: The Union View, 1971–1978," *Personnel Journal* 58 (February 1979), pp. 80–85.
11. Sibson, *Compensation*, p. 120.
12. Belcher, *Compensation Administration*, pp. 6-98–6-103.
13. Editors of Collective Bargaining Negotiations and Contracts, *Basic Patterns* (Washington, D.C.: Bureau of National Affairs Inc., 1992), p. 93:2.
14. Herbert G. Zollitsch, "Productivity, Time Studies and Incentive-Pay Plans," in *Motivation and Commitment*, eds. Dale Yoder and H. G. Heneman, Jr. (Washington, D.C.: Bureau of National Affairs Inc., 1975), pp. 6–61.
15. Norma W. Carlson, "Time Rates Tighten Their Grip on Manufacturing Industries," *Monthly Labor Review* 105 (May 1982), pp. 15–16.
16. Edward M. Coates III, "Profit Sharing Today: Plans and Provisions," *Monthly Labor Review* 114 (April 1991), pp. 19–25.
17. John Zalusky, "Labor's Collective Bargaining Experience with Gainsharing and Profit-Sharing," *Proceedings of the 39th Annual Meeting of the Industrial Relations Research Association* (Madison, Wis.: Industrial Relations Research Association, 1987), pp. 177–178.
18. "Chrysler, UAW Reach Tentative Settlement Barring Executives Bonuses Unless Workers Share," *Daily Labor Report*, May 6, 1988, p. A–8.
19. Angelo Henderson and Nichole M. Christian, "Auto Workers Complain About Disparity," *The Wall Street Journal*, February 1, 1996, p. A6.
20. John Hoerr, "Why Labor and Management Are Both Buying Profit Sharing," *Business Week*, January 13, 1983, p. 84.
21. "Potential Dangers in Expansion of Current Auto Profit-Sharing Plans Cited by Attorney," *Daily Labor Report*, March 24, 1982, p. C–1.
22. Zollitsch, "Productivity," pp. 6–66. Also see J. Kenneth White, "The Scanlon Plan: Causes and Correlates of Success," *Academy of Management Journal* 22 (June 1979), pp. 292–312.
23. Mitchell Fein, "Improved Productivity Through Workers' Involvement," *Hearings before the Subcommittee on General Oversight of the Committee on Small Business* (Washington, D.C.: U.S. Government Printing Office, 1982), pp. 118–123.
24. Robert T. Kaufman, "The Effects of IMPROSHARE on Productivity," *Industrial and Labor Relations Review* 45 (January 1992), pp. 311–315.
25. Dong-One Kim, "Determinants of Effectiveness in Gainsharing Programs: Findings and Implications," *Proceedings of the 46th Annual Meeting of the IRRA* (Madi-

son, Wis.: Industrial Relations Research Association, 1994), pp. 279–287.

26. William N. Cooke, "Employee Participation Programs, Group-Based Incentives, and Company Performance: A Union-Nonunion Comparison," *Industrial and Labor Relations Review* 47 (July 1994), pp. 594–608.

27. Irving Bernstein, *Arbitration of Wages* (Berkeley: University of California, 1954), pp. 26–27; Craig Overton, "Criteria in Grievance and Interest Arbitration in the Public Sector," *Arbitration Journal* 28 (1973), pp. 159–166; Howard S. Block, "Criteria in Public Sector Interest Disputes," in *Arbitration and the Public Interest,* eds. G. G. Somers and B. D. Dennis (Washington, D.C.: Bureau of National Affairs Inc., 1971), pp. 161–193.

28. Audrey Freedman, *The New Look in Wage Policy and Employee Relations* (New York: Conference Board, 1985), pp. 1–10.

29. Bachman, *Wage Determination,* pp. 14–15.

30. Richard B. Freeman, "Union Wage Practices and Wage Dispersions Within Establishments," *Industrial and Labor Relations Review* 36 (October 1982), pp. 3–21.

31. "Two-Tier Wage Plans—1992," *Collective Bargaining Negotiations and Contracts* (Washington, D.C.: Bureau of National Affairs Inc., 1993), p. 18:461.

32. "IRRA Panelists Address the Two-Tier Implications for Fair Representation and Equal Opportunity," *Daily Labor Report,* January 10, 1985, pp. A-5–A-7.

33. James E. Martin and Melanie M. Peterson, "Two-Tier Wage Structures and Attitude Differences" in *Proceedings of the Thirty-eighth Annual Meeting: Industrial Relations Research Association,* ed. B. D. Dennis (Madison, Wis.: Industrial Relations Research Association, 1986), pp. 78–79.

34. "Two-Tier Wage Plans," *Collective Bargaining Negotiations and Contracts,* p. 16:993.

35. John Dunlop, "The Economics of Wage-Dispute Settlements," *Law and Contemporary Problems* 12 (Spring 1947), p. 282; and Bernstein, *Arbitration of Wages,* pp. 26–27.

36. J. Fred Holly and Gary A. Hall, "Dispelling the Myths of Wage Arbitration," *Labor Law Journal* 28 (June 1977), p. 346.

37. Sumner Slichter, *Basic Criteria Used in Wage Negotiation* (Chicago: Chicago Association of Commerce and Industry, January 30, 1947), p. 25.

38. Bachman, *Wage Determination,* pp. 251–258.

39. Dunlop, "The Economics of Wage-Dispute Settlements," pp. 286–289.

40. Aaron Bernstein, "Productivity—Not Pay Cuts—Will Keep Union Members Working," *Business Week,* August 25, 1986, p. 32.

41. General Accounting Office, *Productivity Sharing Programs: Can They Contribute to Productivity Improvement?* (Washington, D.C.: U.S. Government Printing Office, 1981).

42. Jerome Rosow, "Productivity and the Blue-Collar Blues," *Personnel* 48 (March–April 1971), pp. 8–10.

43. William F. Maloney, "Productivity Bargaining in Contract Construction," *Proceedings of the 1977 Annual Spring Meeting: Industrial Relations Research Association* (Madison, Wis.: Industrial Relations Research Association, 1977), pp. 533–534.

44. Joseph P. Goldberg, "Bargaining and Productivity in the Private Sector" in *Collective Bargaining and Productivity,* ed. Gerald Somers et al. (Madison, Wis.: Industrial Relations Research Association, 1975), pp. 28–42.

45. William W. Winpisinger, "Output: Collective Bargaining and Productivity," in F. J. Havelich, ed., *Collective Bargaining: New Dimensions in Labor Relations* (Boulder, Colo.: Westview Press, 1979), pp. 25–28.

46. Maryellen R. Kelley and Bennett Harrison, "Unions, Technology and Labor-Management Cooperation," in *Unions and*

Economic Competitiveness, eds. Lawrence Mishel and Paula B. Voos (Armonk, N.Y.: M. E. Sharp, Inc., 1992), pp. 247–250.

47. Ronald S. Warren, Jr., "The Effect of Unionization on Labor Productivity: Some Time-Series Evidence," *Journal of Labor Research* 6 (Spring 1985), p. 199.

48. Charles Brown and James Medoff, "Trade Unions in the Production Process," *Journal of Political Economy* 86 (June 1980), pp. 355–359.

49. Richard B. Freeman and James L. Medoff, "The Two Faces of Unionism," *Public Interest* 57 (Fall 1979), pp. 69–93.

50. J. T. Addison and A. H. Barnett, "The Impact of Unions on Productivity," *British Journal of Industrial Relations* 20 (July 1982), pp. 145–149.

51. John T. Addison, "Are Unions Good for Productivity?" *Journal of Labor Research* 3 (Spring 1982), p. 137.

52. Robert S. Kaufman and Roger T. Kaufman, "Union Effects on Productivity, Personnel Practices, and Survival in the Automotive Parts Industry," *Journal of Labor Research* 8 (Fall 1987), pp. 332–349.

53. David A. Dilts, "The Consumer Price Index as a Standard in Negotiations and Arbitration," *Journal of Collective Negotiations in the Public Sector* 23, no. 4 (1994), pp. 279–285.

54. Alice H. Cook, "Comparable Worth, Background and Current Issues," *Reports* (Honolulu: University of Hawaii, Industrial Relations Center, 1982), pp. 5–6. For an examination of the chairman of the EEOC's view of the comparable worth issue, see Clarence Thomas, "Pay Equity and Comparable Worth," *Labor Law Journal* 34 (January 1983), pp. 3–12.

55. Winn Newman, "Pay Equity: An Emerging Labor Issue," in *Proceedings of the Thirty-fourth Annual Meeting: Industrial Relations Research Association,* eds. James L. Stern and B. D. Dennis (Madison, Wis.: Industrial Relations Research Association, 1982), pp. 167–170.

56. Editors of Collective Bargaining Negotiations and Contracts, *Basic Patterns in Union Contracts,* 14th ed. (Washington, D.C.: Bureau of National Affairs Inc., 1995), p. 111.

57. John Zalusky, "Cost of Living Clauses: Inflation Fighters," *American Federationist* 83 (March 1976), p. 1.

58. H. L. Douty, "Escalator Clauses and Inflation," *Collective Bargaining Negotiations and Contracts* (Washington, D.C.: Bureau of National Affairs Inc., December 1975), p. 16:1.

59. Robert L. Rose, "Companies, Unions Lengthen Contracts, Encouraged by Stable, Low Inflation," *The Wall Street Journal,* February 8, 1994, pp. A2, A6.

60. Editors of Collective Bargaining Negotiations and Contracts, *Basic Patterns in Union Contracts,* pp. 111–113.

61. Robert J. Thornton, "A Problem with the COLA Craze," *Compensation Review* 9 (second quarter 1977), pp. 42–44.

62. "Lump Sum Pay Provisions: 1994" *Daily Labor Report,* March 8, 1995, p. D–1.

63. "Chamber of Commerce Report on Benefit Cost," *Collective Bargaining Negotiations and Contracts* (Washington, D.C.: Bureau of National Affairs Inc., 1995), pp. 10:501–502.

64. Editors of Collective Bargaining Negotiations and Contracts, *Basic Patterns in Union Contracts,* pp. 13–22.

65. Christopher Farrell, "Health Care Costs: Don't Be Too Quick with the Scalpel," *Business Week,* March 15, 1993, p. 80.

66. Richard B. Freeman, "Unions, Pensions, and Union Pension Funds," *Working Paper Series* (Cambridge, Mass.: National Bureau of Economic Research Inc., 1983), p. 50.

67. Steven G. Allen and Robert L. Clark, "Unions: Pension Wealth and Age-Compensation Profits," *Working Paper Series* (Cambridge, Mass.: National Bureau of Economic Research Inc., 1985), pp. 33–35.

68. "Supreme Court's *Betts* Ruling Expected to Have Major Impact on EEOC," *Daily Labor Report,* July 10, 1989, p. C–1.
69. "Continental Can Held Liable for Scheme to Defeat Vesting," *Daily Labor Report,* May 15, 1989, p. A–1.
70. Christine Del Valle, "Harsh Medicine for Ailing Pension Plans," *Business Week,* September 19, 1994, pp. 91–94.
71. Sandy DeMent, "A New Bargaining Focus on Legal Services," *American Federationist* 85 (May 1978), pp. 7–10.
72. "Legal Service Plans," *Collective Bargaining Negotiations and Contracts* (Washington, D.C.: Bureau of National Affairs Inc., 1986), p. 16:945.
73. Andrea Gerlin, "Companies See Legal Plans as Cheap Perks," *The Wall Street Journal,* March 14, 1995, p. B1.
74. Peter Waldman, "Pre-paid Legal Plans Offer Consultations, Follow-up Calls and Referrals at Low Cost," *The Wall Street Journal,* February 24, 1986, p. 37.
75. "Eight-Year Effort to Pass Federal Leave Had Roots in Pregnancy Discrimination Act," *Daily Labor Report,* February 8, 1993, p. S–4.
76. Barbara Presley Noble, "Making Family Leave a Reality," *The New York Times,* July 31, 1994, p. F–19.
77. "39 States Have Enacted Varying Forms of Family Leave, But Only 11, D.C. Closely Resemble New Federal Mandate," *Daily Labor Report,* February 8, 1993, p. S–8.
78. Editors of Collective Bargaining Negotiations and Contracts, *Basic Patterns in Union Contracts,* pp. 73–74.
79. Frederick L. Douglas, "Collective Bargaining Under the Family and Medical Leave Act," *Labor Law Journal* 45 (February 1994), pp. 102–105.
80. Greg Lewis, *"Unionism and Relative Wages in the United States* (Chicago: University of Chicago Press, 1963); Richard B. Freeman and James L. Medoff, "The Impact of Collective Bargaining: Illusion or Reality," in *U.S. Industrial Relations 1950–1980: A Critical Assessment,"* ed. Jack Stieber et al. (Madison, Wis.: Industrial Relations Research Association, 1981), pp. 53–54.
81. Dale L. Belman and Paula B. Voos, "Wage Effects of Increased Union Coverage: Methodological Considerations and New Evidence," *Industrial and Labor Relations Review* 46 (January 1993), pp. 368–376.
82. Robert J. Flanagan, "The Economics of Unions and Collective Bargaining," *Industrial Relations* 29 (Spring 1990), pp. 300–304.
83. Augustin K. Fosu, "Impact of Unionism on Pension Fringes," *Industrial Relations* 22 (Fall 1983), p. 419.
84. Jacob Mincer, "Union Effects: Wages, Turnover, and Job Training," *Working Paper Series* (Cambridge, Mass.: National Bureau of Economic Research Inc., 1985), p. 42.
85. Daniel J. B. Mitchell, "Collective Bargaining and the Economy," in *U.S. Industrial Relations 1950–1980: A Critical Assessment,* ed. Jack Stieber et al. (Madison, Wis.: Industrial Relations Research Association, 1981), pp. 1–44.
86. Robert J. Flanagan and Daniel J. B. Mitchell, "Wage Determination and Public Policy," in *Industrial Relations Research in the 1970s: A Review and Appraisal,* ed. T. A. Kochan et al. (Madison, Wis.: Industrial Relations Research Association, 1982), p. 74.
87. Susan Vroman, "The Direction of Wage Spillovers in Manufacturing," *Industrial and Labor Relations Review* 36 (October 1982), pp. 102–103.
88. George Ruben, "Collective Bargaining in 1982: Results Dictated by Economy," *Monthly Labor Review* 106 (January 1983), pp. 28–37.
89. Roger G. McElrath and Richard L. Rowan, "The American Labor Movement and Employee Ownership: Objections to and Uses of Employee Stock Ownership Plans," *Journal of Labor Research* 13 (Winter 1992), pp. 99–103.

90. "ESOPs: Are They Good for You?" *Business Week,* May 15, 1989, p. 116.
91. Joseph R. Blasi, *Employee Ownership Through ESOPs: Implication for the Public Corporation* (New York: Pergamon Press, 1987), pp. 29–30.
92. "ESOPs: Are They Good for You?" *Business Week,* May 15, 1989, p. 116.
93. "Has Weirton's ESOP Worked Too Well," *Business Week,* January 23, 1989, p. 66.
94. "How Dan River's ESOP Missed the Boat," *Business Week,* October 26, 1987, p. 34.
95. Joseph R. Blasi, *Employee Ownership Through ESOPs: Implication for the Public Corporation* (New York: Permagon Press, 1987), pp. 40–44.

CASES FOR PART THREE

Case 3.1 Playboy Club of Central City

Subject: Discharge for theft.

Issue

1. Was Laura Kuller (called Bunny Mary) discharged for just cause?
2. If not, what should the remedy be?

The grievant, Laura Kuller, was employed under the name of Bunny Mary at the Central City Playboy Club for four years. No disciplinary action had been taken against her prior to her discharge on August 2, 1987. Then she was terminated for allegedly changing the server's name on a customer's check on July 19, 1987, so that she could obtain the $7.64 tip rather than the employee who provided the service. The following paragraphs present the key events that transpired on that evening.

On July 19, 1987, the grievant was one of four Bunnies working the evening shift in the Living Room section of the Central City Playboy Club. Her station was located in the club's disco dancing area. At approximately 10:00 P.M., one of the Bunnies, Terri James, who was working in the same room away from the dance floor, wanted to leave early for the night, a practice allowed when business was slow. She obtained permission from management to leave after her customers moved forward to tables closer to the disco dancing area, which left her without anyone to serve. Among the customers moving on the night in question was a party of three women who moved to a table in the grievant's area.

Customers at the Central City Playboy Club are charged a 17.5 percent serving charge. This money is given to the Bunny whose name appears on the check, and it is her primary source of earnings. When the party in question moved forward, Ms. James closed out the check with her name on it (included on the check were the cover charge and the cost of dinner and a round of drinks prior to and after dinner). It was undisputed she had served these items, for which her tip was $7.64. She then opened a new check with the grievant's name on it, got the guests another round of drinks, and left. A second cover charge was not imposed, and the grievant continued to serve drinks to the party as requested between 10:00 and 12:00; her total service charge was $2.27.

Feeling that Ms. James had "skimmed the cream" by serving the customers dinner and

This case has been adapted with the permission of the Bureau of National Affairs from its publication *Labor Arbitration Reports*, 70 LA 304 (Stuart P. Herman), 1977. The names of the people involved have been changed. The name of the particular Playboy Club has also been changed.

including the cover charge on her bill, the grievant expressed unhappiness with her leaving early, causing the grievant to have to provide the customers the less lucrative part of their service. There was no dispute that the grievant informed the other Bunnies and the assistant Bunny trainer of the actual facts and what she intended to do. It was not disputed that before closing that night she retrieved the first check with Ms. James's name on it and crossed it out, inserting her own name. The grievant made no attempt to hide what she had done, made the changes in front of other employees, and told several other Bunnies what she had done. While the grievant never informed Ms. James about what she did, the other Bunnies did tell her. Although there was disagreement as to whether any conversation took place between the grievant and Ms. James later that night or within a few days thereafter, there was agreement that Ms. James was informed within a week of the incident. She chose not to discuss it with the grievant but instead reported it to the union shop steward, who informed management of the situation.

No written policy was presented by the employer concerning the changing of a server's name on checks or the signing of someone else's name on them, but shortly after the termination of the grievant, the employer posted a written memo informing the Bunnies such practices were prohibited.

On August 2, 1987, the club supervisor, Janet Thomas, upon being informed of the incident of July 19, 1987, called a meeting with the grievant and her union representative. At that meeting, the grievant admitted changing the check to get the tip for herself and that she had never subsequently discussed the matter with Ms. James. Upon conclusion of the meeting, the decision was made to terminate the grievant.

Pertinent Contract Provisions

Article VII (q)(1):
No Bunny will be discharged, suspended, or otherwise disciplined without just cause.

Article VII(x):
Pertaining to Bunnies: Except as limited and restricted by this Agreement, PCI has and shall retain the right of management and the direction of the Clubs, as it pertains to Bunnies. Such rights of management include, among other things, but are not limited to: the right of PCI to plan, direct, control, increase, decrease or diminish operations in whole or in part; to remove any Club or any portion thereof to another location; to hire, suspend, discharge or discipline employees for just cause or lack of Bunny image, subject to grievance arbitration procedures as herein provided; and to determine the number of employees that it shall employ at any time and the qualifications necessary to any of the jobs, provided it is not inconsistent with this Agreement; to adopt and from time to time modify, rescind or change reasonable safety and work rules and regulations so long as such rules are not inconsistent with a provision of this Agreement and to enforce such rules; and to select and assign such work and duties not covered by this Agreement as it deems appropriate to supervisory and other categories of employees excluded from this Agreement, as specified in this Agreement.

Article IX(g):
The arbitrator shall have no authority to alter or amend the terms of this Agreement.

Positions of the Parties

The Company

The employer argued that it is undisputed that the grievant altered a check in order to get a tip belonging rightfully to another Bunny. The employer further contended that it was undisputed that the policy among the Bunnies, through custom and practice, if not formally reduced to specific writing, that checks should not be altered without the knowledge and consent of another Bunny entitled to receive a tip based on a portion of that check.

Based on the above, the employer contended in its presentation that what the grievant did actually constituted theft from another employee. It presented supporting cases that theft was an adequate ground for discharge, regardless of the value of the item or the employee's work record. (S.A. Shenk, 26 LA 395; Franz Food Products, 28 LA 543; Plough, Inc., 57 LA 369; Borg-Warner, 47 LA 903; United Hosiery Mills, 22 LA 573; Hawaiian Telephone Co., 43 LA 1218.) Therefore, the employer contended that the discharge of Laura Kuller (Bunny Mary) was with just cause pursuant to the provisions of the current collective bargaining agreement.

The Union

It was the position of the union that the conduct of Laura Kuller (Bunny Mary) did not constitute just cause for discharge within the meaning of Article VII(q)(1) of the current collective bargaining agreement, and that she should be reinstated to her former position with full back pay. The union further argued that the supporting cases named by the employer were unlike the present case in both facts and issues.

Questions

1. Assume you are the union representative. Formulate the best, most thorough case that you could present before the arbitrator. Repeat the process, assuming that you are a management representative. On the basis of both sets of formulated contentions, how would you decide the issue as an arbitrator? Why?
2. Who has the burden of proof in this case?
3. To what extent should the arbitrator consider and use the supporting cases referenced by the employer in making the decision?
4. Should the grievant, Laura Kuller, be reinstated? If so, what should be the remedy? What is your reasoning?
5. Where did the employer fail in its managerial practices in this case?

Case 3.2 Contract Interpretation: Demotion and Discrimination Based on Disability and/or Union Membership

Issue

Was grievant Thomas Hart the object of harassment by the company because of his union activities and status? Further, did the company improperly demote the grievant from his position of millwright down to the job of utility helper? If so, what is the appropriate remedy?

Statement of Grievance

Violation Article XII, section 2, discrimination and harassment due to union activities. Violation Article XII, section 5. The union wants Thomas Hart's Millwright pay for the time he worked at the Utility Helper rate.

SOURCE: The authors express their appreciation to Dr. A. Dale Allen, Baylor University, for making this arbitration decision available for use in this book.

Provisions of the Labor Agreement
Article II—Management's Rights

Section 1. Except as explicitly limited by a specific provision of this agreement, the Company shall continue to have the exclusive right to take any action it deems appropriate in the management of this operation and the direction of the workforce in accordance with its judgment. All inherent and common law management functions and prerogatives which the Company has not expressly modified or restricted by a specific provision of this agreement are retained and vested exclusively in the Company and are not subject to arbitration under this agreement.

Section 2. The Company specifically reserves the exclusive right to, in accordance with its judgment, reprimand, suspend, discharge, or otherwise discipline employees for proper cause; hire, promote, retire, demote, transfer, layoff and recall employees to work; determine employees' competency and qualifications, maintain the efficiency of employees; . . .

Article XII—Intimidation, Coercion and Discrimination

Section 2. The Company recognizes and will not interfere with the rights of the employees for whom the Union is the bargaining agent hereunder to become members of the Union and to engage in Union activities. There shall be no discrimination, interference, restraint or coercion by the Company against any employee because of membership in the Union.

Position of the Company

The grievant, Thomas Hart, was initially employed by Prestine Paper Company on March 16, 1981. He was employed with corrected visual acuity of 20/20 in his right eye and less than 20/400 in his left eye. On June 8, 1981, he became a millwright trainee. On November 21, 1983, Hart completed his millwright training and became a millwright in the company sawmill department. From April 6, 1982, through May 23, 1990, eight personnel performance reports were completed by different supervisors who rated Hart's performance. Under item no. 9, Quantity of Work, most of the supervisors checked the box "inclined to be slow."

On April 26, 1990, Hart repaired the broken drive chain on the Chip-n-Saw. Sawmill supervisor Harold Patt asked Hart why the repair took the amount of time it did. Patt alleged that Hart responded he only had one good eye and that he was afraid if he worked any faster he might get hurt. Soon thereafter, on May 23, 1990, Patt completed a personnel performance report on Hart. Under item no. 9, Quantity of Work, Patt checked the box for "inclined to be slow" and followed with the statement, "Every time this is mentioned to Hart, he says he takes his time because he can't see too good." This personnel performance report was reviewed by the sawmill department superintendent, Dee Clark, and by personnel manager Tom Wright, who is responsible for the safety functions at the Prestine mill.

Thereafter, Wright discussed Patt's remarks about Hart's performance with supervisor Patt. Wright was concerned that Hart might have a problem with depth perception and be a risk to himself or to his fellow employees. Wright noted an instance from September 1988 when an employee with only one eye lost a finger in an industrial accident, most likely due to a lack of depth perception.

Based on the accumulated factors, Wright decided to have Hart examined by an ophthalmologist, and an appointment was made with Dr. H. Lewis Pope, at Clarksdale, Mississippi, on July 27, 1990. On that date, personnel manager Wright drove Hart to Clarksdale for his eye examination. Dr. Pope brought Wright into the examination room and demonstrated to him Hart's lack of depth perception via a "butterfly" experiment. Dr. Pope told Wright and Hart that Hart does not have any depth perception with his left eye and that he should not work on moving equipment or work around operating saws or chippers. He said if Hart were to operate a crane, he might not be a danger to himself, but would pose a hazard to others. Dr. Pope followed up his verbal report with a written report in which he stated,

> On his activity, I notice that Hart works around chippers, saws, and cranes. He tells me that they are always turned off when he works on them. As long as they are turned off, I don't see a problem with that; however, he does not have any depth of field with his left eye. That can be dangerous to his hands. I don't think it is a good idea for him to be working around a moving saw. The crane,

> where he would be moving large motors, may not be dangerous to him; however, if there is somebody around the motor when he moves it, it could be a danger to them since he does not have depth of field. I'll leave the work arrangements up to you.

After returning from the doctor's office, Wright told Hart he had decided to remove him from the millwright position for safety reasons. Thereafter, on August 2, Wright met with Hart and union official Charles Watson and told them Hart would be demoted to utility labor. The next day, Watson filed a grievance on behalf of Hart.

Regarding the union harassment charge, the company pointed out that Hart had not joined the union until July 27, 1990. In fact, Wright did not receive Hart's union authorization card until August 13, 1990. Hence, the company's actions had no relationship to Hart's alleged "union activity."

The company scheduled another eye examination for Hart with Dr. David Carey in Memphis, Tennessee. Wright prepared a brief job description of a millwright's duties and gave it to Dr. Carey when he drove Hart to Memphis for his eye examination on November 7, 1990. Dr. Carey followed his examination of Hart with a report on November 8, 1990. In the last paragraph, Dr. Carey stated, "I also believe he should avoid tasks that would require good depth perception which would be hazardous to himself and others. Moving belts, gears, and chippers fall into this category and should be avoided, as should fork lifts and cranes." Thus, Dr. Carey echoed Dr. Pope's opinion.

The company claimed that the union did not offer any proof that the company had discriminated against Hart when it demoted him from millwright to utility labor based upon expert medical advice. Under the EEOC guidelines for the Americans with Disabilities Act, a legitimate defense for removal from a position exists when a significant risk exists of substantial harm to the safety or health of the individual or others. Both eye specialists who examined Hart placed limitations on the work he could do, which prevented him from performing as a millwright.

The company stated it has the legal, ethical, and financial responsibility for the safety of Thomas Hart and of all his co-workers. Hart's concern about safety, while commendable, does not necessarily indicate he is a safe worker. His record of injury for the period of February 28, 1989, through July 9, 1990, indicates a total of 10 reportable first-aid and doctor injuries for less than an 18-month period. While not the worst injury record at the company's sawmill, it was well above average. One might conclude, from the "inclined to be slow" box being checked by his supervisors on his performance reports from 1982 through 1990, that Hart worked slowly to avoid injury because of his lack of depth perception. His injury record contradicts the union's position that he is a safe worker. By definition, a safe employee is one who both works safely and, as a result, is not injured.

The company concluded that it did not discriminate against Thomas Hart either for union activity or because of his handicap. The company acted in good faith when it demoted Hart, because it did so out of concern for Hart's safety and that of his co-workers. The demotion action was based on the recommendation of two ophthalmologists. The agreement states that the company has the right to demote an employee, except as expressly modified or restricted by a provision of the agreement. The union attempted to show that this right was restricted by a violation of Article XII, Section 2. However, the union failed in this attempt. Therefore, the grievance should be denied.

Position of the Union

The union pointed out that Thomas Hart suffered a loss of vision in his left eye at the age of 6 years. He was hired by the company on March 16, 1981 and worked in a utility labor classification until June 8, 1981, when he was promoted to millwright trainee. The company was aware of Hart's loss of vision at the time he was hired and still promoted him to millwright trainee.

Hart progressed through the company's millwright trainee program and advanced to trained millwright on November 21, 1983. Hart received good ratings on all his training progress reports and was advanced to millwright shortly after completing his training in the latter part of 1983. He worked as millwright until August 2, 1990, when he was notified he was being demoted to utility labor effective August 6, 1990.

The company had presented a list of Hart's accidents in 1989 and 1990, which was above average for the plant. However, other employees had had more accidents than Hart. If one examines this list of accidents, one cannot come to a reasonable conclusion that Hart's poor depth perception was the cause of these accidents because most of the incidents were strains. Moreover, Hart's yearly performance reports indicate that he performed his job safely. Indeed, there is not one negative comment in the record with regard to being an unsafe employee during this nine years with the company.

In April of 1990, supervisor Patt questioned Hart about the length of time it took him to repair a broken chain on the Chip-n-Saw outfeed. Although questioned, Hart was not formally counseled. In May 1990, supervisor Patt did make the following comment on Hart's performance report: "Every time this is mentioned to Thomas he says he takes his time because he can't see too good." Hart refused to sign the report because he did not agree with the comment. Hart stated he explained to Patt the reasons for the repair time. Moreover, his inability to see well on the day in question had nothing to do with his eyesight, instead, it was due to poor lighting. Billy Ruth, a co-employee, supported Hart and said there is no lighting under the outfeed chains and it was dark under the chains. Ruth stated that while making the repair by oneself as Hart did, no one was able to hold the flashlight. Therefore, you have to make the repair without a light. Under these circumstances, 15 minutes downtime was not excessive.

The union claimed that in July 1990 Hart was assigned to assist the timber stacker, a production job, along with performing his regular maintenance duties. Union official Charles Watson had filed a grievance alleging violation of Article XII, Section 5 because it was not fair to use the millwrights for production work when the other crafts are not used. After the grievance was filed, supervisor Patt would stand and watch Hart work at the timber stacker. Hart was supervised more closely than other employees. This was verified by fellow employee Richard Burt. Shortly thereafter, Hart was notified by Tom Wright that he had made an appointment for Hart to see Dr. Pope on July 27, 1990. Hart and Wright agreed that this was the first time anyone from the company had mentioned anything to Hart about his vision or seeing a doctor. The union contended that Wright had made the decision to send Hart to the doctor and made the appointment after the production grievance involving Hart was filed, a union activity.

Dr. Pope's report did not uncover anything new about Hart's vision. The company knew when they hired Hart that he had only one good eye. He didn't have depth of field when he was hired in 1981, and it has not gotten worse since 1981.

As to Hart's work activities, Dr. Pope stated he did not see any problem with Hart working on chipper saws as long as they are turned off. It is a strict safety rule of the company that all equipment must be locked out (shut down) during repairs. In fact, anyone found working on a machine without it being locked out should have disciplinary action taken against him. Therefore, according to Dr. Pope's report, Hart can safely perform millwright duties.

Although Hart has operated the crane safely many times in the past, there are normally at least two millwrights present when the crane is needed. It would be easy for the other millwright to operate the crane. Hart said he was never required to learn how to operate the crane, but did so on his own because he wanted to learn how to operate it. The union therefore contends that Hart can safely perform millwright duties, and nothing in Dr. Pope's report indicates anything to the contrary.

The union claimed that the evidence clearly shows nothing changed or occurred to justify the company's demoting Hart from a millwright to utility labor, a $2.43 an hour reduction in pay. Hart was hired and promoted to millwright with excellent vision in only one eye. At the time of his demotion, he still had 20/20 vision in this eye. His duties as millwright have not changed. Hart has not sustained an injury that disabled or prevented him from performing millwright work. In fact, he performed millwright work for some nine years with a fine work record and good marks on safety. The only real change that took place was the fact that on July 10, 1990, a grievance was filed protesting millwrights having to do production work when Hart was assigned to assist the timber stacker. Afterwards, Hart was notified to see Dr. Pope. This occurred shortly after a second step grievance meeting.

The union contended that the company failed to prove it had just cause to demote the grievant Thomas Hart. For the reasons given, the union requested that the grievance be sustained in its entirety, that Mr. Hart be paid for all loss of wages, and that Mr. Hart be returned to the position of millwright with all job seniority restored.

Questions

1. What are the rules concerning the company's responsibilities under the Americans with Disabilities Act? Do they apply here?
2. Is the grievance procedure with arbitration the appropriate forum for resolving charges of discrimination, harassment, and demotion? Are there others? Evaluate the alternatives.
3. Can "demotion" be considered discipline? If so, what are some implications?
4. What are the advantages and disadvantages to the parties for advancing a case like this one to arbitration?
5. Evaluate the evidence and interpret the agreement, then you be the arbitrator.

Case 3.3 Upgrading, Training, Sexual Harassment, and Disqualification

Basic Facts

ABC Can Company manufactures approximately three million aluminum beverage cans each day with two production lines and two 12-hour shifts per day. The cans are manufactured by way of production lines, high-speed machinery, and equipment that form, trim, wash, coat, and decorate the cans according to customer specifications. Line technicians, or line techs, are skilled mechanics who set up, evaluate, adjust, maintain, and repair this machinery to keep it running and meeting specifications. The line techs are bargaining-unit employees who are represented by the ABC Workers International Union.

Most of the facts are not in dispute; however, the reasons for Linda Williams' disqualification and her performance in the training program are as follows. The company's training program provides employees who meet certain criteria an opportunity to qualify and train for the line tech classification. The parties have agreed to certain terms and conditions that are applicable to this program. These terms and conditions include a trial period at the beginning of the qualifying training period during which a trainee may be removed from the program at the company's sole discretion. The company's removal or "disqualification" of the grievant, Linda Williams, is the subject of this arbitration.

Williams has worked for the company as a can plant equipment tender (CPET) for most of her employment since August 17, 1979, except for a period of line tech training. The CPET classification is very broad and actually composed of a number of different and specific job assignments. As a CPET, Williams usually works on the can washers, where she checks the mix of chemicals and assures the temperatures are correct on that machine. She has cross-trained on other jobs because the company has a program to provide CPETs on-the-job familiarization with the several job assignments within the CPET classification.

On October 27, 1989, Williams requested or "bid" for qualifying training in the line tech classification. She discussed her plans with Pat Walker, production supervisor for D-Crew in the D&I (Drawing and Ironing) Department. Williams told Walker that, since the company had consolidated the operator and line tech classifications, she was afraid that the company might do the same thing with the CPETs, and that if she did not bid up to line tech, she might somehow end up losing her job. Walker told her that he did not think this would happen or that her bidding for line tech training was necessary for her to keep her job. Nevertheless, he encouraged her to do so. Although he did not know about her technical skills or mechanical abilities, he told her that he thought she should go ahead with the bid since she had nothing to lose.

The labor agreement provides for two general phases of training for the line tech classification: (1) preparatory training and (2) qualifying period training. The preparatory training phase involves self-study and testing related to certain plant engineering courses, which include basic blueprints, schematics and symbols, shop math, measurements, and metal materials. After completion, the employee's name is placed on a departmental list of those eligible to move to the second phase, the qualifying period training, if and when the company determines that there is a vacancy in the line tech classification. If more than one employee is eligible, the most senior employee will be "awarded the vacancy" and move to the qualifying period training.

On May 13, 1992, Williams successfully completed preparatory training. She was awarded a vacancy and began her qualifying period training. Williams began with on-the-job practical training on actual plant equipment and machinery by working with and learning from other line techs by observing, assisting, and actually performing on-the-job requirements.

The qualifying period training is further broken down into four periods, each consisting of 1,040 actual hours of work. Although working time in this phase is devoted solely to on-the-job training, the employee is also required to complete certain additional plant engineering courses during that particular period. Williams satisfactorily completed two courses, nonmetal materials and hand tools, which corresponded with her period of qualifying training.

Employees are also subject to a trial period of actual work at the beginning of the qualifying training during which they may be removed at the sole discretion of the company. This trial period usually consists of 520 actual hours of work that correspond to the first half of the first qualifying period, but the labor agreement specifically provides that employees may be removed at any time during their trial period. Also, line tech trainees may be disqualified after the end of the trial period. To ensure properly qualified employees required to keep the plant operating with high standards of workmanship, the company monitors the progress of all trainees both during the trial period and throughout all qualifying periods.

It was during the initial trial period that the company determined Williams should be removed from the training. Williams requested and began her training on D-crew. She explained that she had a good rapport with the other employees on D-crew. Walker, who had encouraged her to bid for the training, was her first supervisor. Although Walker noticed early on that Williams lacked a certain mechanical aptitude and basic mechanical skills, he continued to encourage Williams during her first three evaluation report periods. He made a point to note on her first report that her "lack of experience both technically and as an operator" would make the program very tough for her, but that she had "a very enthusiastic attitude." By the second report, he distinguished between her operating and technical abilities. He wrote that he felt "she would make a very good D&I operator," but that "job does not exist anymore and her ability to become an effective line tech was impossible to determine at this point."

During the first two report periods, Williams received the rating of "2" (marginal or below average) for her ability to learn the job. On the third report, she received a rating of "3" (average). Walker explained that it was not necessarily reflective of her abilities to perform the technical aspects of the job as much as it was reflective of the operational aspects.

At the time of the fourth evaluation report, dated August 1, 1992, and after personal observation of Williams' technical abilities, Walker determined that Williams "lacked the mechanical aptitude to really do the job." On her evaluation report he rated her a "2" in ability to learn the job, initiative, quality of work, and quantity of work. He concluded that Williams had not made sufficient progress to advance to the next step and remarked that she was "lacking somewhat in her technical ability and should be further along at this point." He also wrote that he "thinks the world of Linda" and "felt she would be a good operator." However, Walker indicated that Williams lacked the mechanical aptitude for the line tech job. As examples, he wrote that Williams would make several trips to the tool box to find the right tool and would tend to use tools that were not as good or efficient for the particular task. She was slow in actually accomplishing her work, and she needed more help more often from the other line techs than the typical trainee would need. She would fail to check the condition of cans before and after she worked on a piece of equipment. On one particular occasion, she tried to loosen a bolt by turning it clockwise when it should have been loosened counterclockwise.

After Walker's August 1 evaluation report, Glenn Hooper, the D&I Department head, became personally involved in observing and evaluating Williams. Williams asked Hooper what she needed to do to pass her probation period. Because she had disagreed with her evaluation by Walker and because Hooper was responsible for monitoring the evaluation and progress of trainees, he decided to observe her work firsthand. On August 6, 1992, he gave her an opportunity to demonstrate her technical skills and recorded his observations in a memorandum to John Cook, training coordinator for the line tech training program. Hooper noted not only several specific examples of unsatisfactory work, but several examples when Williams insisted that she knew something when she was later proven to be wrong. Williams noticed that the input shaft to the transfer drive was loose and asked Hooper what to do about it. He recommended that she first tighten the bolts and ascertain whether any bearings were bad. She told him that the coupling was bad and the whole unit needed to be pulled out and replaced. He suggested that she just tighten it up first, and they could determine whether any other components were bad. Afterwards, she had considerable difficulty selecting and using basic tools for tightening the bolts. After she selected the appropriate tool, she tried to tighten up the coupling without putting another wrench on the nut. Hooper told her that it was worn out and needed to be changed. He explained that she needed to put something on the nut to be able to tighten the bolt. She had difficulty using the tools she had selected to tighten the bolts. Once they were tightened, the coupling she had said was "worn out" was fine. Williams explained that she did not know there was a nut on the back because it was hidden under a guard.

Hooper decided to remove Williams from the program. T. P. Meggison, the union representative, suggested that if she would go to a technical school and get some outside training, perhaps she could stay in the program. Hooper did not know whether the company could do that or not. Eventually, by union and company agreement, Williams' trial period was extended for an additional 260 hours. Williams continued to train under Walker's supervision. He was in favor of her extension because he "wanted Linda to have every advantage." However, she continued to have difficulties. On her next evaluation, she requested an opportunity to train with some other line techs. She personally suggested a transfer to B-Crew, and the company granted her request. Kenneth Wiggin, production supervisor for B-Crew, completed her next evaluation report. He rated her only a "2" in the category of ability to learn and rated her a "3" on quality and quantity of work. He noted she had only been on B-Crew for a short time, and during this time, they "really hadn't had any major things happen that required any type of mechanical, as opposed to operational, skills to perform other than changing dies and punches."

Because of her extension, her time would be up while Wiggin was on vacation. In order to supply Hooper with accurate and fair information on Williams' progress, Wiggin "decided that we needed to let her try to perform some typical line tech duties to see how she could do." Wiggin explained that he did not necessarily expect Williams to perform these duties on her own, but that he intended to see how much assistance she needed, if any. He gave her specific instructions on how to do the job, on having her tools ready before stopping the machines, and on checking both her trimmed and untrimmed cans before and after performing each job. She told him she understood these instructions and received several reminders; however, she failed to follow the instructions three times in a row. Wiggin concluded that Williams had not demonstrated the mechanical aptitude necessary for the line tech job.

Wiggin wrote a memorandum to Hooper about these occurrences. On October 9, 1992, Hooper removed Williams from the program. His decision was based on her consistently low ratings in the technical areas of her evaluations, his own personal observations both during her initial trial period and her extended trial period, no dramatic improvement during the granted trial period extension, and Wiggin's assessments contained in his memorandum to Hooper.

Hooper discussed his decision with Williams and union steward Tony Adams. Williams said she just needed more training on the machinery. Hooper explained his decision was not based on her lack of knowledge of specific machinery, but on her failure to perform basic skills. Williams stated, "It isn't fair . . . you are just doing this because I am a female." Hooper responded that being a woman had nothing to do with his decision and that "her physical strength may in fact be superior to some of the men working on the platform." They discussed another instance where Hooper had observed Williams turning a bolt the wrong way. She had attempted to remove a pillow block from the washer oven, but was tightening the set screw on the locking collar rather than loosening it. He noted that two or three times he passed by the oven and saw another line tech to whom he had assigned a different job actually doing the job that he had assigned to Williams.

Williams and Adams suggested that she be allowed to go to technical school and remain in the company training program. Hooper responded that the labor agreement contained no provisions for that and that he had to base his decision on what had occurred during the trial period.

Williams then indicated for the first time that her training and evaluations had been affected by Don Carter, an hourly line tech on her first crew. She said she had learned things on her new crew, B-crew, that Carter had never shown her. Adams stated that he thought there was a "little back stabbing going on or happening on that crew." Hooper explained that the decision was not based on any input from other hourly employees, and that Carter never said or made one derogatory remark about her.

Adams and Williams expressed their interest in filing a grievance based on Williams' willingness to go to school and desire to be a technician. Hooper asked Adams to make sure Graham, the union representative on the Training Advisory Committee, was aware of this decision. Williams was then returned to her previous job as CPET.

On October 14, 1992, the union filed the following grievance on behalf of Williams:

> Date of the event giving rise to the grievance: October 9, 1992.
>
> *What happened (give dates, times, names and the circumstances)?* Linda was told that she was taken out of the line tech training program after she had completed all of her books and passed the tests. Training provisions used to disqualify Linda Williams were unequal treatment and provided no opportunity for past practice of 14 years.
>
> *What do you want the company to do (relief requested)?* Reinstate and give her equal treatment in the line tech training program.

On October 21, 1992, T. P. Meggison, local union president, amended the grievance to:

> As to relief requested: She be paid back pay plus overtime and any other benefits to which she would be entitled.

Ms. Williams revealed a series of sexual harassment incidents involving another employee, Don Carter. On the same day, Trish Bowman, human resources manager, wrote a letter to Meggison, which stated:

> The company is willing to place Linda back in the line technician training program if she enrolls in and successfully completes on her own time a mechanical training program at an appropriate training institution under the provisions of the tuition reimbursement program.

Also, on the same day, Bowman wrote the following letter to Williams:

> Linda, this will confirm our conversation on Friday, December 4, where you charged Don Carter with sexual harassment. As noted in our conversation, the company has a commitment to affirmative action. We will continue to strive to take positive measures to assure equal opportunity in all areas. In addition, provocative remarks directed toward an individual's race, color, religion, national origin, sex, or age are not appropriate. In the event any further situations or difficulties of this type arise, please make me aware of them as soon as possible.
>
> Thanks for your cooperation.

The union appealed the grievance to the fourth step, and R. J. Mitchell, industrial relations director, denied the grievance in his letter, which stated:

> The grievant was disqualified from the line technician program. Additional time was given to the employee during her trial period. In the company's step 3 answer to the grievance, the company offered to put the grievant back in the training program if she successfully completed an outside mechanical training program at an accredited institution. The employee and union refused.
>
> Based on the above, I feel the disqualification was proper. The grievance is denied.

Williams filed a charge with the EEOC and claimed that the company's decision to remove her from the training was based on sex discrimination. The EEOC issued a no-cause determination and dismissed the charge on September 30, 1993, primarily because at least one other woman had gone through the training and had become a line tech, and at least one man had been disqualified. Cindy Rumley, the woman who worked her way up from CPET to operator to line tech, was acknowledged by everyone at the company to be a very good line tech.

Williams also filed a charge with the EEOC claiming that she had been sexually harassed by Carter. She claimed that she had been sexually harassed by him prior to being removed from the program and felt that Carter had affected her evaluation. The company indicated that it first found out about Williams' sexual harassment allegations *after* her removal from training. Carter had previously gone to Hooper and alleged harassment by Williams against him based on her threats to call his wife and tell her that Carter was making sexual advances to her. Hooper issued a disciplinary warning to Williams based on her threats, but the discipline was removed after the company heard the whole story. In the company's step 3 answer in order to settle the matter, the company offered to put Williams back in the program if she would successfully complete an outside mechanical training program. Her costs for the program would be reimbursed under the company's tuition reimbursement program. This was the union's original proposal, but the union refused the offer and appealed the grievance to arbitration.

Issue

Did the company violate the agreement when it removed Linda Williams from the qualifying training for the line tech classification during her trial period? If so, what is the appropriate remedy?

Relevant Provisions of the Agreement

Article V

Nondiscrimination

The Company and the Union agree not to discriminate against any employee because of race, color, creed, national origin, sex, Vietnam era service, handicapped persons, or Union activity in any matters pertaining to hiring, wages, hours, or working conditions. The Company also agrees to comply with all applicable laws and regulations which prohibit discrimination because of age.

Article XVIII

Departments—Training Provisions for Line Technician Classification and Lines of Progression

Section 1. Departments already established for seniority purposes or that may be established in the future under the terms of this Agreement shall be considered a part of this Agreement.

Section 2. There is attached hereto and made a part hereof Rules and Procedures governing Training Provisions for the Line Technician classification. The Lines of Progression already established or which may later become necessary to establish shall be considered a part of this Agreement. The Lines of Progression shall be subject to mutual review and necessary changes at any time during the life of this Agreement by plant management and the Union.

Positions of the Parties

The Company

The company first argued that an important issue to the company is at stake, that is, whether its good-faith determination that Williams lacked the basic mechanical aptitude to learn and satisfactorily perform the line tech job is to be accorded controlling weight in light of the company's contractual right to make this determination. Under the labor agreement, the company not only has the right to ensure the properly qualified employees required to keep the plant operating with high standards of workmanship, but to make sure by way of the trial period that trainees have the necessary aptitude and abilities to learn and satisfactorily perform the job in the normal amount of time.

The company claimed that the evidence fully supports the company's determination that Williams did not have the necessary aptitude and abilities. The evidence does not support the union's claim that management discriminated against Williams on the basis of her gender or on the basis of anything other than her failure to demonstrate within her trial period that she possessed the necessary skills and abilities. The company provided Williams not only with an equal opportunity to train and demonstrate her abilities, but it may have provided her with special accommodations because her treatment may have moved beyond "equal" to preferential.

The company stated that its decision to remove Williams during her trial period did not violate the agreement because the language in the agreement provided that it is the company's discretion under the agreement. The trial period provision is clear and unambiguous. The agreement provides that "Promotions and filling of permanent vacancies shall be made on the basis of departmental seniority provided the employee has the ability and physical fitness to perform the required work." If this provision were applicable, the union might have an argument that the burden is on the company to show that Williams does not have "sufficient ability" to perform the line tech job. Even though the evidence would fully support the determination that Williams does not have the requisite abilities, the company does not have this burden.

The company addressed the intent of the parties with respect to the trial period, which is very clearly expressed in the agreement, that is,

> Employees who are selected to enter the qualifying wage rate progression of the Line Technician job classification shall be subject to a trial period of 520 actual hours of work at the beginning of their qualifying period training and may be removed from the progression at any time during this trial period at the sole discretion of the Company.

The company stated that to the extent that any conflict arises between these two provisions, the second provision, which is specifically applicable to the line tech training program, is controlling. Under a controlling contract interpretation principle, where conflict arises between specific language and general language in an agreement, the specific language will govern.

The company claimed that the "sole discretion" language is not the only important expression of the parties' intent in this provision. The trial period during which the company judges the trainee's performance does not fall at the end of the training after the person is fully trained. Rather, it is at the beginning of the training. This distinguishes this training provision from any other that may have been arbitrated and determined to require full or "adequate" training before the employee's ability to perform the job is determined.

The company addressed the union's contention that it takes a long time to train someone to be a line tech. That is the reason the trial period is at the beginning of the training so it can be determined early on whether the employee has the basic abilities required to learn the job in a reasonable amount of time with the normal amount of training. The company does not expect the trainee to be a "full-fledged technician," but it does expect the employee to demonstrate the ability to learn the job within the time period agreed to as reasonable by the parties when they signed the agreement.

The company noted that the agreement provided that employees who stay in the program past the initial trial period may be disqualified for failure or undue delay in advancing from one qualifying period to the next. The company has the right to hire qualified employees directly into the line tech classification from outside the company. If the company is short of line techs, it not only has a legitimate business interest in making sure it has "properly qualified employees required to keep the plant operating with high standards of workmanship," but also that the employees in the training program have the necessary aptitude to train for the job in the normal time.

The company stated that it is appropriate to compare new trainees with other trainees who have been through the program. This indicates whether the trainee has the ability to learn the job under the normal training conditions and in a reasonable amount of time. Even without the comparisons, if an employee does not demonstrate a basic mechanical aptitude for learning or performing the job of a line tech, the employee could be removed from the program.

The company claimed that the agreement provides that, because of the degree of competition in the industry, the employees and the union agree to cooperate fully and in good faith with the company's efforts to achieve the most efficient and economical operation of the plant through the best utilization of human resources and equipment. In keeping with this agreement, the company returned Williams to her CPET job at which she is a good employee and which management believes best utilizes her skills and talents.

The company argued that its decision was not unreasonable, arbitrary, capricious, or discriminatory. Williams was disqualified because she lacked the aptitude for the job, not because she is a woman. The relevant job is line tech, not "operator" and not line technician trainee. The purpose of her trial period was to give her an opportunity to demonstrate the skills and abilities necessary for the job of line tech, for which she was bidding. The company made this decision based on what had been demonstrated during her trial period at the beginning of her training and based on a reasonable determination of her abilities to learn and perform the job in the normal time.

The company explained that it no longer has a separate operator classification. The line tech must be able to perform both the operation and maintenance of the machinery. The company's consolidation of these jobs is not an issue. The company combined these classifications three years before to improve the efficiency of its operations by having the same employees maintain and operate the equipment. The single issue here is whether the company fairly determined that Williams did not have the necessary mechanical aptitude for the line tech job.

Williams has already worked for the company as a CPET and has cross-trained in the various specific assignments within this classification. This means she has been exposed to different specific jobs and machines at the plant, but was never before expected to bring "troubleshooting" skills or technical or mechanical skills or abilities to any of these jobs. CPET jobs are unskilled assignments that can be easily taught; however, the line tech job is different. It requires basic mechanical skills and mechanical aptitude, that is, a fitness or "aptitude for using machines or tools." Since line techs are responsible for maintaining, repairing, and setting up the machinery required to make cans to customer specifications, this is an important job to the company.

The company argued that it had not unfairly deprived Williams of the opportunity to become an operator first and then train for the line tech job. However, she had never bid for the operator job as Rumley had done. The evidence did not prove the union's claim that Williams would have qualified for the line tech job if she had first been an operator. At most, the evidence would support that she might have been able to qualify as an operator if that separate classification still existed. Still, she would have been disqualified from the line tech training due to her lack of basic mechanical skills and aptitude to learn and perform this job.

Walker distinguished between Williams' operator and technician skills in his second evaluation. He noted that she might be good at one but not the other. He fairly and reasonably took into account her lack of previous operator experience when he was evaluating her progress. He ended up concluding that she lacked the basic technical skills and abilities for the job, the line tech job, for which she had bid.

The company argued that, if Williams was ever prejudiced by her lack of previous operator experience, the company "cured" this prejudice by agreeing to an extension of her original trial period. Thereby, it made up for any delay in her progress due to her lack of previous experience. The company agreed to all her other special requests, her crew requests, and her request for outside training, even though it had never been done with anyone else before.

The real reason she failed to qualify for the line tech job was not her lack of operator experience or her gender, but her lack of technical abilities. Hooper explained that Williams tried to turn a bolt both ways until she got it right, but her problems with bolts caused her to assess and evaluate machinery in the course of her work improperly. She insisted that a coupling was "worn out" when all that needed to be done was to tighten the bolts. Her unsatisfactory performance included her failure to follow specific and important instructions.

The company claimed that difficulties were not due to inadequate training or opportunity. Williams' training was fair and fully adequate; it was not adversely affected by Carter. When asked who had trained her, she responded that she had good response from anyone asked. She confirmed that her supervisors and all of the line techs on both D-Crew and B-Crew, other than Carter, were helpful to her, and she had trained on each crew at her own request.

When asked specifically about working with Carter, she responded that she worked with others more than him. Therefore, even though she claimed he affected her evaluations, she readily admitted that she had received good training from all the other line techs and both supervisors. This is objectively supported by the list of jobs she performed or was trained on during her trial period.

Williams claimed that Carter had affected her evaluations by speaking badly about her. While she no doubt believed this to be the case, Carter did not say one derogatory remark to management about her. Walker spoke to all the line techs on his crew when he completed evaluations, including Carter, but Walker's evaluations and opinions were fully supported by independent personal observations about her work and her abilities. The record shows that Walker liked and still likes Williams very much and gave her every benefit of every doubt. The evidence does not support the union's contention that Carter unfairly affected Williams' evaluations. In addition, supervisory opinion regarding Williams' lack of basic mechanical aptitude was unanimous and fully supported by factual events and observations.

The fact that Wiggin's first evaluation of Williams was actually better than his subsequent evaluation of her after sufficient personal observations and her failure to follow specific instructions is not consistent with any personal bias against her or women in general. Rather, it is reflective of having based his conclusions on her performance alone. The union's evidence, the opinion of one line tech who was not even on Williams' crew, is not enough to overcome management's unanimous opinion of her lack of mechanical aptitude based on numerous examples. The results of Williams' self-study and testing does not prove that the company was wrong about her practical mechanical skills. Under the agreement, trainees must be able to do both satisfactorily (1) the more theoretical, math, and map-related engineering courses and (2) the actual work on the job. No one contested that Williams was sufficiently successful at the first; she failed the second. It was Williams' lack of mechanical aptitude that was the primary factor in her failure, not the training itself.

The union did not prove its claim that Hooper based his decisions on Williams' gender. Hooper recorded his observations of Williams' work. He became involved in her evaluations only after she went to him and after she disagreed with Walker's evaluations, not because he had singled her out. His observations fully supported his conclusions about her lack of mechanical aptitude and skills necessary for the line tech job. Thus, the union did not show any of these observations to have been inaccurate.

The company argued that the union has attempted to prove that Hooper based his decision on Williams' gender, not her performance and abilities, by way of an incident that was told to management *after* her removal from the training program. The first time Williams told management about her alleged sexual harassment by Carter was after her disqualification. She had spoken of the incident as having occurred since her return to the CPET job and having occurred in retaliation for her initial EEOC charge related to the disqualification. Her subsequent claim that Carter harassed her all along is inconsistent with her sworn affidavit to the EEOC wherein she alleged that the harassment was in retaliation for her having filed the EEOC charge. It is also inconsistent with what she said and did not say when she and Adams met with Hooper at the time of her removal from the program. At that time, she said Carter spoke unfairly about her and did not help to train her.

The company argued that Hooper's initial reaction to Carter's harassment claim does not prove that Hooper was biased against Williams because she is a woman. The first Hooper heard about any harassment occurred when Carter came to him claiming harassment by Williams. Hooper did not know at that time that Williams had blamed Carter for her having been disqualified. Carter claimed that Williams was threatening and harassing him in retaliation for her having been disqualified. When Williams was questioned about the incident, she was obviously upset and believed that she was in the right to threaten to call Carter's wife. While Carter denied that he had harassed Williams, Williams readily admitted that she had threatened him and was still threatening to call Carter's wife. This is why the company issued a warning to her initially, that is, for admitting to making and continuing to make these threats against Carter.

After the whole story came out, the company confirmed its policy against sexual harassment and removed the warning against Williams. Then, based in part on these new allegations of sexual harassment, the company offered to provide Williams with the outside training that she and the union had originally requested.

The company claimed that it acted where necessary to provide equal opportunity to Williams. Article V of the labor agreement provides that the company will not discriminate on the basis of race, color, religion, national origin, or sex, and the company will affirmatively act where necessary to provide equal opportunity in training. The company has provided Williams with so many accommodations and special treatment that it is arguably subject to being challenged for reverse discrimination for having acted beyond what is necessary to provide equal opportunity. In fact, the company agreed to every single accommodation with respect to her training that Williams requested, up to and including her request for outside mechanical training that was never contemplated in the agreement.

Williams was selected and given an opportunity for preparatory training even though she did not have significant or any maintenance repair or shop experience or training in her work history. The agreement provides that before an employee will be considered for preparatory training, the employee must meet certain minimum requirements, which include a consideration of the employee's work history including related maintenance repair or shop experience or training, attendance record, general plant conduct, and so on. Although Williams had a good work history with respect to her limited duties as a CPET, she most definitely did not have the sort of work history or experience that would make her stand out as a candidate for the line tech job. Rather than screen her out of this basic training, the company affirmatively acted to provide her with an opportunity to train and qualify. Williams was accommodated with respect to her choice of initial crew, the extension of her initial trial period, and her subsequent request that she train on a different crew. The extension of the trial period had never been done before. Thus, the company had most definitely and affirmatively acted to provide her with this additional opportunity.

When Williams requested that she be allowed to switch crews, she had not told the company anything at all about any problems with Carter. The company granted her request, an example of affirmative, as opposed to corrective, action. She did not mention any problem with Carter until she was being removed from the program for the last time. Even then, she did not mention anything about sexual harassment. She mentioned only that she thought he had adversely affected her evaluations and training. She claimed that he had not taught her well, although she readily agreed that everyone else had and that maybe he had spoken badly about her and her abilities.

Since Carter had not in fact said anything derogatory about Williams to management, Williams had received additional training on another crew, and her evaluations had been independently verified through personal observations of both supervisors and Hooper. Hooper reasonably concluded that what caused her disqualification was her lack of abilities, not any incorrect evaluation or influence due to Carter. The company still stands by its determination of her abilities and firmly believes that she has had more than an equal opportunity to train and qualify for the job. At the time of her removal, nothing in what she said about Carter would have alerted management to any possible or alleged sexual harassment. Management cannot be expected to act on sexual harassment claims or factor them into its determination until it knows or should have known about them.

The company did not initially agree to the outside training because this would have been another accommodation that had never been made before. The company had already made a good-faith determination of Williams' abilities, and Williams had already been granted several accommodations. After her allegations of sexual harassment, her EEOC claims, and several grievance meetings, the company decided to go beyond what is required by the agreement and agreed to provide her with additional training. Although the company's offer was made very shortly after the grievance was filed and the company learned of Williams' claims, the union rejected the company's offer of outside training.

The company argued that its offer was not made because management doubted its determination of her abilities—the company firmly stands by this determination. This offer also was not made because the union convinced the company that Williams was not treated equally or did not have equal opportunity to train and qualify for the job because the company had already acted beyond what was necessary to provide Williams with equal opportunity. Nevertheless, the offer was made in an effort to go the extra step and settle the matter.

The company argued that if the arbitrator sustains the grievance, it would not be appropriate to award Williams back pay. The union steward specifically stated that the union would be filing a grievance based on Williams' willingness to go to an outside training school and her desire to be a technician. Hooper responded that there were no provisions in the labor agreement for this, and that he had to base his decision on what had occurred in the trial period. This initial response was very reasonable since it is entirely true. Hooper based his decision on Williams' performance, and he reasonably determined that she lacked the basic skills to become proficient in the line tech job. She had already been accommodated with respect to two requests to train on particular crews and with respect to an extension of her trial period. Furthermore, the agreement most definitely does not contemplate the provision of outside training to make up for an employee's lack of basic mechanical skills and aptitude. Nevertheless, when the company learned that Williams claimed to have been sexually harassed and prejudiced by Carter and, in an effort to be more than fair in providing opportunity as well as to simply settle the matter, the company offered in the step 3 answer to do just what the union had requested, that is, put her back in the program if she successfully completed an outside mechanical training program for which the company would pay. This offer was made very shortly after the grievance was filed, and the company learned of her claims on December 4, 1992.

The union and Williams refused the company's offer apparently because it was inconsistent with the union's new position that she did not need this training, but that she had simply been discriminated against on the basis of gender. The union has failed to act where necessary to provide Williams with equal opportunity in training to the extent it has discouraged her from accepting the offer. It would not be appropriate for the company to have to pay damages when management already offered to do the very thing the union originally requested very shortly after the time of this request.

The company concluded:

> The Union is accusing the Company of treating Ms. Williams unfairly on the bases of her gender

and her having no previous Operator experience. However, due to these issues and concerns, the Company has in fact gone out of its way to accommodate Ms. Williams and make sure that she has had more than an equal opportunity to demonstrate her abilities for the job. If she were not a woman and were not the first person to go through the training program without prior Operator experience, she would probably not have been given these special accommodations.

It is the Company's responsibility under the Agreement to "ensure the properly qualified employees required to keep the plant operating with high standards of workmanship." It is also the Company's responsibility to operate the plant efficiently and prudently in order to realize profits and provide continued employment. Furthermore, the Union and the Employees have specifically agreed to cooperate with "the Company's efforts to achieve the most efficient and economical operation of the plant through the best utilization of manpower and equipment."

This whole matter began when Ms. Williams was worried about losing her CPET job. The Company is happy with her current performance in this job, and she can rest assured in this. However, if she were to be artificially put back in a job for which she is ill-suited, this could not only harm the Company, but could also harm her own employment, since she would likely make mistakes and put everyone's safety and job security at risk.

The Company has not violated any provision of the Agreement. Not only did Management have the sole discretion to determine whether Ms. Williams should be disqualified, but it also exercised this discretion in a fair and reasonable manner. Management also affirmatively acted where necessary to provide Ms. Williams with more than equal opportunity in training and qualifying for the job.

The Company requests that the Arbitrator should deny this grievance.

The Union

The union explained that prior to the time the company outlined the operator and line tech classification, there was a line of progression wherein the employee could advance from the lowest paying job classification, CPET, to the top paying job classification, line tech. An employee could start out in the CPET classification, advance to the operator classification, then to the line tech classification. The operator and line tech worked on the platform together. The operator operated the equipment. The line tech set up the equipment for the operator, repaired the equipment when it broke down, and did preventive maintenance. The operator assisted the line tech in repairing the equipment, was totally familiar with the equipment, and knew generally how to troubleshoot the equipment. The operator had the basic skills for repairing the equipment. When an operator advanced to line tech, the employee had to go through the line tech training program in accordance with the training provisions in the agreement. When the two jobs were combined three years before, all the operators were supposed to have proceeded through the training program and passed all the tests, but the evidence shows that some operators never did. However, they were still classified as line techs. When the operator and line tech jobs were combined, the line of progression was broken. The CPET now goes directly to the training period. The CPET does not work on the platform or directly on or around the equipment that produces the can. Thus, the CPET does not acquire nearly as much knowledge of repairing the equipment as the operator who worked on the equipment every day.

Williams has worked in the CPET classification the entire time of her employment with the company. She was the first employee to go directly from the CPET classification into the line tech training program. She did not have the advantage of working several years as an operator and acquiring the knowledge as had previous trainees. She could not have been expected to advance as quickly as she would have if she had experience as an operator. If she had been given the time required to train to be an operator as extra time in the line tech trial period, she would have been a whiz of a line tech when she finished the trial program.

The union contended that, in light of the fact that Williams had to start from scratch, she did an excellent job of learning and performing the job in the period of time she was allowed on the job. The company's own records filled out by her supervisor show that she was average or above in their overall evaluations of her performance. According to Hooper, in five of the most important components of the evaluation of her last evaluation on September 20, 1992, she was rated "4" in desire to learn; in capacity to learn she was rated "2;" in quality she was rated "3;" in quantity she was rated "3;" and in safety she was rated "3;" for an average of "3," which is average job performance for a typical apprentice/trainee with the same training time. Her overall evaluation in all the components in all her evaluations was "3.3," which is slightly above average, and her last evaluation averaged "3.2," slightly above average.

In her final evaluation, her supervisor made the following comments: "Linda continues to work hard and is showing some improvement. She does a good job as an operator, but needs to continue to work on her technical skills." He wrote: "Ms. Williams had been on the job only three months. She was doing a good job as an operator." The union claimed that, if she had learned to be a good operator at that time, there is no doubt that she had the ability to become a good full-fledged line tech.

In his last evaluation of the five most important aspects of the job, supervisor Wiggin made the following comments:

> Desire to learn—Linda is definitely eager to learn.
>
> Capacity to learn—there is a lot to learn on the D&I platform about the operations of the D&I's, trimmer, magnesium elevators, and so on, Linda still has a long way to go in learning all that is needed to know to be a full-fledged Line Tech.
>
> Quality—Linda does a good job checking specs. And recording them on the check sheets and graphs. It seems to take her a little longer than the other Techs, but I feel that she should get faster with these checks as she gets more accustomed to doing them.
>
> Quantity of work—Here again, Linda is slower than the other Techs when it comes to clearing a jam on one of the D&I's or trimmers. This, too, should improve as she gets more accustomed to doing them.
>
> Safety—Linda seems to take time to make sure she knows that everything is clear before starting or restarting a piece of equipment. She also does a good job of keeping cans picked up and the machines washed off.

Wiggin indicated that he had no comment in the space asking whether she had made sufficient progress in her on-the-job training to advance to the next step. He wrote: "Linda had only been on this crew since 9-8-92. So it is too early to evaluate how far advanced she is in her training." In her probationary period, personnel evaluations, Wiggin stated: "I feel that Linda tries as hard as any employee that has ever gone through the training program. She gets along well with her fellow employees and also does a good job on safety and housekeeping, but I feel that she has a long way to go on being a full-fledged line tech."

The union contended that it appears that her supervisors were comparing Williams to the line techs who had been line techs for years. In fact, they had her working as a line tech in the crew because each shift has four line techs, and two work together as a team. She did not work as an extra or a helper, watching others, or working as instructed; she filled a vacancy, the same as the other line techs. The program requires 4,160 hours to become a full-fledged line tech; Williams had only worked a few hours over 500 at that time. Therefore, it seems that the company has forgotten that she had not worked as an operator.

A union witness, a senior line tech, testified that he had worked with Williams on several days and her work was "real good." The union claimed that Williams was doing extremely well in the situation she was in and that she was not afforded the opportunity to work as an operator before going into the line tech training program.

The union argued that Williams was doing a good job and would be a "great line-tech." She had been trained and actually performed just about all the jobs required of a full-fledged line tech. If she had and could perform these jobs, then she would be a full-fledged line tech long before completing the 4,000 hours required by the program.

The Union questioned why she was removed from the program. The union contended that she was removed from the line tech training program because she was a woman. Carter, the hourly line tech, had openly expressed his opinion that he did not believe a woman should be working in the plant, much less with the men in the line tech classification. A union witness heard Carter say many times that the line tech job was "no job for a woman." Williams testified that frequently throughout her training period Carter continuously "pinched her on her rear end and told her she charged his batteries." Carter bothered her so much that it affected her work. She was embarrassed to go to Management. She finally told him to stop this behavior and then told him if he didn't stop she would call his wife. Carter immediately then went to Hooper, the department head, and reported to him that Williams had threatened him. Instead of investigating the situation, Hooper issued Williams an official "Final Warning Before Termination" for threatening a co-employee.

The union claimed that Williams was forced to go the EEOC for relief. Although one of the incidents happened after Williams had been removed from the line tech program, she claimed she had been sexually harassed by Carter frequently while in the program. The union argued that Carter and Hooper both turned in bad reports on Williams and it was Hooper who made the decision to remove her from the line tech program. Carter had apparently discussed Williams while she was still in the program. Why else would Carter go straight to Hooper, the department head, to report the incident, instead of going through his supervisor and general foreman? The union claimed that it is clear that Carter knew exactly where to go to get the results he wanted. In addition, the union found it unusual that Carter was not called as a witness to refute Williams' claims; therefore, the arbitrator should accept her version of the sexual harassment incidents.

The union noted that the language in paragraph 3, "A. Preparatory Training" of the labor agreement states:

> Selection and training shall be without discrimination because of race, color, religion, national origin, or sex. It is agreed that affirmative action will be taken where necessary to provide equal opportunity in training. When affirmative action is taken, it shall not be considered a violation of the training provisions or the Labor Agreement. In referring to employees, the masculine gender is used for convenience only and shall refer to both males and females.

This language gives the company any latitude needed to have allowed Williams extra time to train if she had needed it. The union firmly believes that, if Williams had been a male, she would be a line tech today. The union concluded:

> For all of the above, the Union requests that you allow the grievance and order the Company to reinstate the Grievant to the Line Technician Training Program and pay her all wages and benefits lost and that you retain jurisdiction for ninety days to decide any question that might arise involving the implementations of your award.

Questions

1. Evaluate the company's argument that it has the sole discretion to determine whether or not to allow a trainee to continue in the line tech training program.
2. Explain why Williams might have waited until after the grievance was filed to tell management about the sexual harassment charges. Is the company responsible for actions not known to management?
3. Assess the comparative advantages of taking this case through the grievance procedure and to arbitration instead of to the EEOC.
4. Assess the company's action when Carter told management that Williams had threatened him.

5. Would this type of case be appropriate for grievance mediation? You may wish to try it for resolving the differences.
6. Evaluate the company's argument that it could be charged with reverse discrimination and that it should not be held liable for any back pay.
7. Suspiciously, Carter did not testify at the arbitration hearing. By his absence, what conclusion should be drawn by the arbitrator?
8. Remembering that the arbitrator's job is to consider the evidence and to interpret the provisions of the labor agreement, how should the arbitrator rule?

Case 3.4 Racing Cars on Leave of Absence

Background

The Electronic Workers Union (EWU) is the bargaining representative for the production and maintenance employees of Hooper, Inc. in Beauregard, Alabama. During the term of their collective bargaining agreement dated May 5, 1989, the parties were unable to resolve a grievance involving the termination of Bubba Jones, a member of the bargaining unit. Under the provisions of the agreement's grievance procedure, the matter was appealed to arbitration.

The grievance was filed by Bubba Jones and his union representative, Jimmy Short, on August 15, 1990. It states:

> I, Bubba Jones, was terminated on August 5, 1990 from Hooper for engaging in employment while on a leave of absence. I race stock cars Class C at Beauregard Motor Speedway in my spare time for a hobby. I was hurt pretty bad in a car wreck one weekend racing. I then had to go on a leave of absence. While on leave of absence, my name was put in the newspaper for taking a first one time, first and second the second time weeks later. The Company then found out about the articles and terminated me for engaging in employment while on a leave of absence. Now none of these races pays any money at all, just trophies. Also, most of the time I have had someone in my pit crew driving the car for me till I had recovered from injuries back on June 22, 1990. Larry Tate, Jim Grimes, and Billy Jack Jones have alternated driving the car most of the time. If this is employment, where is my paycheck? I wish to be reinstated with all seniority, back pay, and all benefits.

SOURCE: The authors express their appreciation to Dr. Paul Gerhart, Case Western Reserve University, for providing this case.

The parties stipulated that Bubba Jones's winnings while he was on leave totaled $65, including $10 won on July 2, $40 on July 9, $5 on July 16, and $10 on July 23. They agreed that he was on a leave of absence at the time he received these prizes and that the injury sustained by the grievant in his June 22 accident was a lumbar strain—injuries to his neck and back.

Bubba Jones testified that he was 29 years old, and had been hired by Hooper in June 1978. His last day of work was June 21, 1990. He reported off on personal leave on June 22. That night he was injured in a car wreck at the Beauregard Motor Speedway when he was hit from behind and his car went into the wall. He sustained injuries to his neck and back. He reported off on sick leave for 6 or 7 days and then applied for a leave of absence. It was approved. His doctor indicated he would be able to return to work on September 12. During the period following his injury he went to a physician for treatment three or four times per week.

Mr. Jones testified that at no time during his leave did anyone from the company contact him to tell him he should return to work because he was driving a race car. He said he was not employed by anyone at any time during his leave of absence. He denied receiving any compensation for working while on leave.

Mr. Jones stated that 1990 was his first year of racing. Prior to his injury he had won some prize money but had not won any races. He said there were three classes of racing at the Speedway. Class A is professional or semiprofessional and the drivers receive compensation but he was not aware whether the Speedway owners paid them. They receive prize money for all races. Class B is one step up from amateur and they also receive prize money for all races. Class C is amateur, and only the "feature race" in Class C pays prize money; $50 for first, $40 for second, $30 for third, and $20 for fourth and fifth place. In the feature race, anyone who starts and finishes get $10; anyone who starts and does not finish gets $5. In addition to the feature race, there are three other Class C races for which only trophies are awarded to winners.

Bubba Jones stated that the owner of the Speedway is Bill Gates. Gates paid him nothing other than the prize money for driving in the races. The grievant's brother introduced him to racing, but before the five weeks prior to his accident, he had never raced. He never considered racing as a possible occupation, but only as a hobby.

Mr. Jones stated that while he was on leave, he received sick leave pay of $198 per week. He said he was injured on a Wednesday. He did not race until about 2 weeks after that. At that time, since his car had been demolished in his accident, he drove one of his brother's cars. He said there are four or five people in the pit crew, who receive no compensation.

After August 5, the date of his termination, Mr. Jones said he continued to race and won additional prize money. He said that all the prize money he received was given to his brother to pay for repairs to the car he drove. Mr. Jones did not pay his brother anything in addition to that. His brother did not pay him and Mr. Gates did not consider Bubba Jones to be his brother's employee. Mr. Jones said he finished out the summer and fall races using his brother's car. He said he has not been employed by his brother at any time after his termination.

After his termination, Mr. Jones got a job at Briarwood in landscaping. After he was laid off from Briarwood at the end of the season, he received unemployment compensation and has been unemployed since then.

Mr. Jones said he was never told by anyone at the Hooper Company that racing his car violated the agreement. No one from the company ever called him to say that what he was doing was wrong and that he should stop. He said there was no withholding for taxes or social security from his winnings. His understanding with his brother was that he could keep the trophies, but his brother got the prize money.

Mr. Jones explained that the newspaper articles upon which the company based its decision to fire him reported only "trophy" races in which he had won no money. He explained that that was the reason why his grievance stated there was no money associated with his racing. He said his name was not listed in any newspaper reports of feature races in which he actually did win money, although there was one "championship" race at the end of the year that paid more than $50 in Class C.

Mr. Jones said that when he wrote his grievance he had the newspaper articles about his races and knew they referred only to the trophy races he had won. When he filed the grievance he based what he said on what he knew was in the news articles. No one specifically had told him the company had terminated him for the articles in the newspaper; he figured that was the reason.

Mr. Jones testified that there was a mid-season race in addition to the championship race at the end of the season that paid more than $50 for first place. He did not win that race, but did win $50 in it. That was on June 18, before his injury.

Billy Jack Jones, brother of the grievant, testified that he was employed by Faust Auto Parts, Inc., as a mechanic and that he races stock cars as a hobby in Class C. He also testified that his brother had raced one of his cars in 1990. He said he had not paid his brother anything for driving the car and that he did not consider him his employee. They did have an understanding that any winnings would be put back into the car to keep it going. His brother was entitled to keep any trophies he won. Billy Jack testified that his pit crew members were also not paid; they performed their service as a hobby.

Jim Grimes, president and business manager for the local union, testified he had held that position since 1981 and prior to that had been chief steward. He said in his experience, he was unaware that the company had any practice of monitoring amateur sports activities of employees who were on leave. He stated that there had never been a company directive that employees could not receive prize money while competing in amateur sports. It was the union's understanding that amateur sport activities are not considered employment. If the company had any question about an employee's ability to perform his or her job based on outside activities, the company would have the right to cancel the employee's leave of absence and tell him or her to report to work.

Mr. Grimes recalled only one employee who was terminated for working while on leave of absence. That employee owned a body shop and was receiving direct compensation for working on cars while on leave. He was self-employed.

The Issues

Did Bubba Jones violate Section XII, Leave of Absence, (G) Working While on Leave of Absence. If not, what is the appropriate remedy?

Relevant contractual provisions are as follows:

Section XII
Leave of Absence
(G) Working While on Leave of Absence

No employee may engage in other employment while on an approved leave of absence unless he first secures written permission from the Manager of Labor Relations. Failure to obtain such permission will result in termination.

Position of the Company

In 1983, the company stated that it had terminated under the same language an employee on a medical leave of absence who worked for himself at a body shop and garage during the time he was on leave. This grievant had no intention of deceiving the company and was in fact ignorant of the provisions of the agreement. The provisions of the agreement were clear and unambiguous and the parties have agreed on the penalty for engaging in employment while on leave—termination.

In that case as in this, the grievant was earning money from an activity that he had engaged in before his leave of absence and continued to be engaged in during the leave. In both cases, the grievant did not ask permission from the company to continue to engage in such employment.

The company argued that the applicable language in the case mandates that all other employment must cease while on a medical leave of absence, regardless of whether carried on before the leave, unless written permission is obtained from the company. This mandate is particularly significant where the grievant is unable to perform his duties at the company, but continues to engage in the same activity for profit that he was engaged in when he suffered his injury, thereby depriving the employer of his services.

The company contended that the fact that the grievant earned only $65 while on leave is not at all relevant to this case. If he had advanced to Class A or B, he might have earned as much as a fully employed person in many industries. It is also irrelevant that the grievant gave his brother his earnings. Once the grievant won the prizes, he could do whatever he wished with his prize money. The principle is not the amount earned or the time during which he was employed as a race driver. The principle is that the grievant violated the contractual rule; the penalty is termination.

The company responded to the union contention that this is a recreation or hobby, not employment, by asking, what is the result of that argument had the grievant been so proficient as a driver that during the period of his leave he had raced at tracks all around the Southeast? The point is that he was engaged in this employment for profit while on medical leave without asking permission and that it was the same employment in which he initially injured himself.

The company pointed out that the *American Heritage Dictionary* defines *employment* as follows:

> 1.a. The act of employing. b. The state of being employed. 2. The work in which one is engaged; business. 3. An activity to which one devotes time.

Under these definitions, the grievant was clearly engaged in an activity to which he devoted time, and moreover, from which he received financial remuneration, irrespective of the amount.

The company claimed that if the arbitrator were to allow this grievance, it would be a change in the words of provisions of the agreement, an action prohibited by the agreement.

Position of the Union

The union stated that Bubba Jones's activity was not employment. The majority of cases in which an employer attempts to enforce a provision similar to the one in the instant case involves an employee who is "moonlighting" by holding a second job during off hours. It is usually clear in these cases that the employee has engaged in other employment. Arbitrator Volz, in *Alcan Aluminum Corp*, 90 L.A. 16 (1987), held that the company must meet its burden of proof by showing that the grievant engaged in other employment within the meaning of the applicable provision. He cited *Ballentine's Law Dictionary:*

> Work. Noun: Employment. Any form of physical or mental exertion, or both combined, for the attainment of some object other than recreation or amusement. . . . Physical or mental exertion, whether burdensome or not, controlled or required by an employer.

In *Standard Brands, Inc.*, 52 L.A. 918, 919 (1969), the grievant, while on a leave, frequently waited on customers and closed a friend's tavern at night, but was not paid. Arbitrator Trotta determined that this was not employment.

The company discharged Jones for engaging in employment while on leave of absence. Clearly amateur stock car racing does not fall under the definition of the word "work." Jones raced stock cars purely for recreational purposes. He did not consider himself an employee and no taxes were withheld from his prize money, which he gave to his brother for maintenance of his brother's car. Therefore, Jones was not self-employed, nor did he work for another employer. Jones himself stated this best in his grievance, "If this is employment, where is my paycheck?" The fact that Jones won a little money and two trophies does not turn a recreation into a job or employment.

The union claimed that the company had not published a rule that certain recreation would be considered employment. For discharge to be just, the employee must reasonably know his actions might lead to discharge. An employee could not have known stock car racing would result in discharge. To give such an interpretation to Section XII (G) would be unfair to Jones. While stock car racing may not have been the wisest thing to do while on leave of absence, it certainly is not employment and no different from any other form of recreation.

Jones considered a later job to be employment. After his separation and after he was released for work in September, Jones worked for a landscaping business. This was a job: it was work considered by him to be employment.

The previous arbitration's matter is distinguishable. The employee had established an auto repair and body shop business in 1976. While on a leave in 1982, he was working in his repair shop.

The company discharged him for working while on leave. The arbitrator upheld the discharge because he concluded the employee was engaged in self-employment that was supported by a stipulation of the parties that he was "working" during his leave. Unlike that case, Jones was not working while on a leave of absence but was only engaged in recreation.

The union concluded that the company has failed to meet its burden of proof by showing that Jones was engaged in other employment within the meaning of the provision. Therefore, the grievance of Bubba Jones should be sustained and he should be reinstated to his employment with full back pay and without loss of seniority and benefits, less any interim earnings from employment.

Questions

1. Evaluate the use of dictionary definitions in terms of their value in the arbitration proceedings.
2. Of what value is the use of previous arbitration cases and decisions of other arbitrators?
3. Does the arbitrator have any leeway in making a decision based on the language of Section XII?
4. After reviewing the elements of employee discipline, did the company violate the agreement? Explain. If so, what should be the remedy?

PART FOUR

Part Four presents the opportunity to apply the previous chapters' discussions of the labor relations process to various labor relations situations. Collective bargaining in the public sector at all government levels is discussed, and a discussion of foreign labor relations processes is presented for comparative purposes. A concluding chapter draws upon the previous ones, suggesting some implications reflecting the book's contents.

APPLYING THE LABOR RELATIONS PROCESS TO DIFFERENT WORK ARRANGEMENTS

Chapter 14 Labor Relations in the Public Sector

Chapter 15 Labor Relations in Multinational Corporations and in Other Countries

Chapter 16 The Labor Relations Process—Synthesis and Possibilities

LABOR RELATIONS IN THE PUBLIC SECTOR 14

The public sector has to become an important factor in the U.S. labor scene. As the number of public employees has increased, so has the number of these employees joining unions. This chapter presents an overview of labor relations in the public sector and provides a brief summary of the similarities and differences in public- and private-sector labor relations. It also examines public-sector bargaining at the local, state, and federal levels and concludes with a discussion of several affected groups.

SIGNIFICANCE OF PUBLIC-SECTOR LABOR RELATIONS

The field of public-sector labor relations has developed from a time when public employees were required to lobby their respective legislators for favorable employment terms to one in which bona fide collective bargaining occurs. It has moved from a generation characterized by rapid union growth, management's inability to react to collective bargaining, and a fear of strikes to a generation characterized by slow union growth, few states passing enabling public-sector legislation, and a willingness to take strikes.[1] With many state legislatures and the U.S. Congress interested in legislation to cut taxes, many public employees have become more concerned about their job security and welfare. Therefore, union leaders are showing increased attention to public-sector employees, hoping that gains in membership in this area will offset the lack of membership gains in the private sector. Unions represented 8,195,000 government employees, or 44.7 percent of all government employees, in 1994.[2] The percentage of union representation was higher at the local level than at the state and county levels. In terms of government function, unions represented a majority of teachers, firefighters, and police.[3] Government employment is 18.3 million, 210,000 less than in 1991, and most of the employment is at the state and local levels.[4]

The AFL-CIO has recognized the importance of the public sector as a vibrant component of its membership by creating the Public Employee Department to focus attention on issues facing public employees. Public employees account for about one-fourth of the AFL-CIO membership, up from 15 percent in 1976. During the last 15 years, the United Steelworkers, United Mine Workers, and United Auto Workers have lost over 30 percent of their members; however, during this same period the American Federation of State, County, and Municipal Employees (AFSCME) has nearly doubled its membership, up to 1.1 million members (see Exhibit 14.1).[5]

In the federal sector, the American Federation of Government Employees (AFGE) represents 665,328 federal employees (see Exhibit 14.2); however, only 149,000 pay dues. This gap between the "free riders" and dues-paying members represents about 77 percent of federal government employment. In the public sector, like the private sector, unions are required by law to represent all bargaining-unit employees in negotiations, contract administration, and grievance arbitration even though they are not dues paying members (as discussed in Chapter 11). Furthermore, the free riders may sue the union if it fails to meet its legal obligation of fair representation. In other words, about 23 percent of federal government employees are paying dues to support the representational activities of all who are represented.[6]

Under the Civil Service Reform Act (CSRA) of 1978 and the Postal Reorganization Act, union security clauses, such as union shops and agency shops, are pro-

Exhibit 14.1 State and Local Union Membership

UNION	NUMBER OF MEMBERS
National Education Association (NEA)	2,000,000
American Federation of State, County, and Municipal Employees (AFSCME)	1,167,000
American Federation of Teachers (AFT)	574,000
Service Employees' International Union (SEIU)	919,000
Fraternal Order of Police (FOP)	170,000
International Association of Fire Fighters (IAFF)	151,000
Teamsters*	150,000
Laborers' International Union of North America*	85,000
Communications Workers of America (CWA)*	85,000
American Association of University Professors (AAUP)	45,000
American Nurses Association	25,000

*Public sector only

SOURCES: Courtney D. Gifford, *Directory of U.S. Labor Organizations,* 1994–1995 Edition (Washington, D.C.: Bureau of National Affairs Inc., 1994), pp. 67–68; Sar A. Levitan and Frank Gallo, "Can Employee Associations Negotiate New Growth?" *Monthly Labor Review* 112 (July 1989), pp. 59–61; John Burton, Jr. and Terry Thomason, "The Extent of Collective Bargaining in the Public Sector," *Public-Sector Bargaining,* 2nd ed., eds. Benjamin Aaron, Joyce M. Najita, and James L. Stern (Washington, D.C.: Bureau of National Affairs Inc., 1988), p. 54.

Exhibit 14.2 Exclusive Recognition by National Unions 1994

FEDERAL EMPLOYEE UNIONS	EMPLOYEES REPRESENTED
American Federation of Government Employees (AFGE)	665,328
American Postal Workers Union	249,000
National Association of Letter Carriers	210,000
National Federation of Federal Employees (NFEE)	146,767
National Treasury Employees Union (NTEU)	148,882
National Association of Government Employees (NAGE)	66,302
Metal Trades Council (MTC)	57,227
International Association of Machinists and Aerospace Workers (IAM) (federal employees only)	28,869

SOURCE: *The Federal Labor-Management and Employee Relations Consultant* (Washington, D.C.: U.S. Office of Personnel Management, January 21, 1994), p. 3; Courtney D. Gifford, *Directory of U.S. Labor Organizations*, 1994–95 Edition (Washington, D.C.: Bureau of National Affairs, Inc., 1995), pp. 67–68.

hibited. Therefore, unions are required to represent all employees in recognized bargaining units but receive no fees or dues from those who choose not to be union members. Because the so-called free riders receive benefits at no cost to them, there is not a significant incentive to join and pay dues. The AFGE suffers the most financial strain because it negotiates 342 agreements per year and is required to represent 665,328 employees, but has only 149,000 dues-paying members. In other words, 665,328 federal government employees enjoy representational rights in negotiation, grievance administration, and arbitration that are paid for by the 149,000 dues-paying members.[7]

More than two-thirds of federal government employees, including 1.2 million nonpostal employees and over 700,000 (or 86.0 percent) postal employees, are represented by labor organizations. In the federal sector, three sets of labor relations policies and programs have emerged. One set applies to the executive branch; another to the postal service; and the third to 19 other organizations such as the Tennessee Valley Authority, whose policies have evolved over a long period of time.[8]

Patterns of union membership in the public sector closely resemble those of the private sector. While nonwhite and male employees are more likely to be union members than are white and female employees, the differential is relatively small. Right-to-work laws and part-time employment are negatively associated with the number of union members. Positive influences are mandatory bargaining provisions, strong union security provisions, compulsory agency shop, compulsory checkoff, compulsory arbitration, and the right to strike.[9]

Favorable public-sector laws appear to be a sufficient condition for union growth in public sector labor relations. Favorable legislation increases the probability that a municipal department will be governed by a collective bargaining agreement, and the presence of a comprehensive labor law sharply increases the percentage of departments that bargain with unions within a state.[10] In 25 states having comprehensive collective-bargaining laws, 71 percent of the public employees are represented for bargaining purposes. On the other side, in states without such laws, only 14 percent of the public employees are represented by unions.[11] (See Exhibit 14.3.)

Labor Legislation in the Public Sector

In the public sector, labor relations at the state, county, and municipal levels are governed by policies, statutes, executive orders, and ordinances. At the federal level, most labor relations activities are governed by the Civil Service Reform Act, and postal labor relations are governed by the Postal Reorganization Act of 1970.

An analysis of the existing laws and policies suggests that favorable legislation is concentrated in the states located in the Northwest, North, Midwest, West Coast, Alaska, and Hawaii. The so-called sun-belt states, located on the lower Atlantic Coast, Southeast (except the state of Florida), Southwest and lower Rocky Mountains, generally do not have labor relations legislation that comprehensively covers the public sector, that is, covering administrative agency, bargaining rights, scope of bargaining, impasse provisions, unfair labor practices, and strike provisions.[12] (See Exhibit 14.3.)

Exhibit 14.3 States Having Comprehensive Laws Covering Most State and Local Employees (Duty to Bargain, Unfair Labor Practices, Administrative Agencies, and Impasse Procedures)

Alaska
California
Connecticut
Delaware*
Florida
Hawaii
Illinois
Iowa
Maine
Maryland
Massachusetts
Michigan
Minnesota
Montana
New Hampshire
New Jersey
New York
Ohio
Oregon
Pennsylvania
Rhode Island
South Dakota
Vermont
Washington
Wisconsin

Note: District of Columbia has comprehensive legislation.
*No unfair labor practices listed.
SOURCE: Karl O. Magnusen and Patricia A. Renovitch, "Dispute Resolution in Florida's Public Sector: Insight into Impasse," *Journal of Collective Negotiations in the Public Sector* 18, no. 3 (1989), p. 241.

Forty states and the District of Columbia have statutes or executive orders that provide for collective bargaining for at least one group of employees. However, de facto bargaining occurs in other states or cities.[13] Most states prescribe bargaining over wages, hours, terms of employment, and working conditions for some or all public employees. However, a majority of the states have statutory limitations on the scope of collective bargaining, such as limitations guaranteeing management rights.

Another important element of labor legislation is unfair labor practices. Although these vary somewhat from state to state, most states have legislation defining unfair labor practices for some or all public employees. The existing legislation typically prohibits strikes. Exceptions to outright prohibition are twofold: either they are not mentioned in the statute, or the states allow strikes only under specific circumstances.

In eight states, Delaware, Georgia, Indiana, Maryland, Minnesota, New York, Oklahoma, and Virginia, mandatory penalties are levied against striking government employees.[14] For example, New York's Taylor Law prohibits work stoppages and provides penalties against both the strikers—loss of two days pay for each day on strike, loss of tenure, and job security protections—and the union—suspension of dues checkoff.[15]

Many states have sanctions varying from injunctions to dismissals, jail sentences, substantial fines, and loss of union recognition when a strike occurs. An investigation of teacher strikes revealed that increasing the level of sanctions against strikers reduces strike activity up to a point, but beyond that point, more strikes, not fewer, occur. The reason for this occurrence seems to be that severe sanctions are seldom enforced, but more moderate ones are. Thus, it seems that strikes can be reduced if moderate, enforceable sanctions are provided.[16]

Thirteen states have affirmatively sanctioned public-sector strikes by some groups of public employees. Nine have done so by statute (Alaska, Hawaii, Illinois, Minnesota, Ohio, Oregon, Pennsylvania, Vermont, and Wisconsin). In three states (California, Idaho, and Michigan), either courts or administrative agencies have interpreted pertinent legislation to confer a limited right to strike to certain public employees. In California, a state court upheld public employees' right to strike without enabling legislation.[17] Thirty-eight states have laws that prohibit strikes by all or some employees in the public sector. Twenty-two states have litigated the strike issues and the courts have found that no right to strike exists unless legislation permits such a right.[18]

In states allowing a limited right to strike, certain employees, such as police, fire fighters, hospital employees, and correctional employees, are usually named as not being allowed to strike under any circumstances. Services of these employees are deemed to be critical to the health and safety of the citizens. Therefore, a ban of the right to strike is considered justified. Some states prohibit a strike during the negotiations period and some permit a strike only after efforts at mediation and fact-finding have been exhausted and a cooling-off period has elapsed.[19]

Municipal and county policies tend to have similar provisions and coverage. The bargaining obligation is enforced by an administrative agency and includes the duty either to bargain or to meet and confer over such topics as wages, hours, and terms of employment. Strikes are usually prohibited, and procedures have been established in the event that an impasse occurs.

Without legislation enabling collective bargaining, unions have difficulty maintaining their membership, collecting dues, and entering into agreements with public officials. Some unions have survived adverse court decisions and the lack of favorable enabling legislation by representing their members in grievance procedures and becoming involved in political activities.[20] The absence of a clear, easily applied recognition procedure frequently leads to much unproductive and unnecessary bickering among the parties. Unfortunately, this bickering spills over into other areas, such as high absenteeism and distrust between parties when bargaining finally occurs.[21]

Provisions in Collective Bargaining Agreements—State, County, and Municipal Employees

Unions representing state, county, and municipal employees generally negotiate collective bargaining agreements similar to those negotiated in the private sector. These agreements in the public sector fall into two categories: (1) contractual agreements and (2) memoranda of understanding. A Census Bureau study reported nearly 30,000 agreements in effect between state and local governments and their respective employee organizations and over 7,000 memoranda of understanding. Although specific bargaining items, such as merit system subjects, are often excluded by statute, most issues are quite similar to those negotiated in the private sector.[22]

Many bargaining issues cut across public employee job classifications. Wages, for example, are a concern of state, local, and county employees regardless of their particular job duties. However, as indicated in Chapter 1, the technological features of the work place can generate certain unique work rules and concerns. For example, firefighters and police are often more concerned than other public employees about safety provisions. Labor and management officials have explored safety-related issues (improved fire hose nozzles, fire coats, chemicals, and so on); however, many of these improvements require rather large expenditures. For example, one company has introduced "Rapid Water," a chemical additive that reduces friction in the fire hoses, resulting in 50 percent more flow with the same pump pressure. Yet only a few of the nation's approximately 25,000 fire departments spent funds to obtain this system.[23]

Police are also concerned about safety problems. A recent demand by a Washington, D.C., police officers' union sought two related proposals: (1) better marksmanship training and (2) deadlier, "all-lead semi-wadcutter" bullets, which are used in other cities. In some cases, safety issues can involve broader issues of management's right to schedule and direct the work force. One of the more emotional issues in police negotiations concerns one-person versus two-person squad cars. Management wants the freedom to assign one-person cars on the basis of crime data reported for various areas and shifts. The unions want two-person cars to maximize patrol officer safety under unsafe street conditions.[24] Police are also concerned about other job-related issues, for example, the benefit of "false-arrest" insurance.

Another major concern of public-sector unions is the direction of privatization. See "Labor Relations in Action."

Federal-Sector Labor Relations Legislation

Federal-sector labor relations are governed by the Civil Service Reform Act (CSRA), which was passed in 1978. While the CSRA retained many provisions of previous executive orders, the following discussion centers on the provisions of the CSRA as they currently exist. The act's ramifications extend beyond the labor relations function—it deals with other functions, such as merit system principles, civil service functions, performance appraisal, adverse actions, staffing, merit pay, and senior executive service. Its Title VII, "Federal Service Labor-Management Relations," is the primary focus here.

The CSRA establishes the **Federal Labor Relations Authority (FLRA),** an independent, neutral agency that administers the federal labor relations program and investigates unfair labor practices. The FLRA oversees the creation of bargaining units, supervises elections, and assists federal agencies in dealing with labor relations issues. It is headed by a chairperson and two members, appointed on a bipartisan basis for five-year terms. Its structure provides for a General Counsel that prosecutes unfair labor practices and incorporates the existing **Federal Service Impasse Panel (FSIP),** which provides assistance in resolving negotiation impasses.

The FLRA's leadership responsibilities include determining appropriate bargaining units, supervising and conducting elections, prescribing criteria for determining national consultation rights, conducting hearings and resolving complaints on unfair labor practices, and resolving exceptions to arbitrator awards. The General Counsel investigates any alleged unfair labor practices, prosecutes complaints under the act, and exercises such powers as the FLRA may prescribe.[25]

The role of the FSIP is to resolve bargaining impasses between federal agencies and unions in the federal government that arise over negotiations of terms and conditions of employment. The FSIP is composed of a chairperson and at least six other members who are appointed by the president for five-year terms; these individuals are familiar with federal government operations and knowledgeable in labor-management relations. The FSIP has jurisdiction over 71 federal departments and agencies representing 1.3 million federal employees. It appoints an executive director who is responsible for the day-to-day operations.[26]

Although the Federal Mediation and Conciliation Service (FMCS), the federal agency established in 1947 by the Taft-Hartley Act, is required to assist the parties in resolving negotiation impasses, either party may request that the FSIP consider the matter or pursue binding arbitration. The panel must investigate the impasse and recommend a procedure for resolution or assist the parties through whatever means are necessary, including fact-finding and recommendations. If these actions fail, it may conduct a formal hearing and take whatever action is necessary and legal to settle the dispute.

LABOR RELATIONS IN ACTION

Privatization of the Public Sector

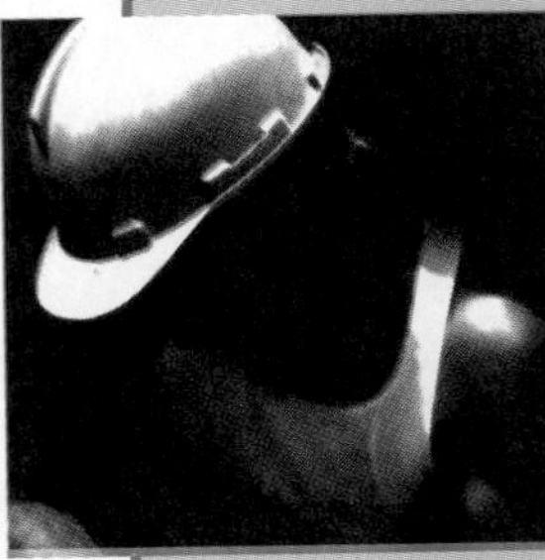

Privatization of public-sector services or transfer of governmental services to the private sector has received much attention over the last two decades. This is due largely to cost differences between public- and private-sector service delivery. However, an important consideration is the role of public employee unions in the privatization process as an interest group and as political actors in blocking the privatization efforts. Some governmental services are technically and politically easier to contract out to the private sector because they can be more easily monitored; they handle a tangible product, and quantity is more important than quality. These services include trash collection, custodial services, food services, recycling services, public works, and landscape maintenance. Less applicable for privatization are governmental functions that deal with people and are characterized by highly normative service delivery debates, such as law enforcement and criminal justice functions, education, and health care.[a]

One consideration in the decision whether or not to privatize is the differing labor laws that cover private- and public-sector employees. Employees in the private sector are covered primarily under the National Labor Relations Act; employees of interstate carriers in the railroad and airline industries are covered under 35 various state laws; and federal government employees are covered under the Civil Service Reform Act. Thus, when government services are contracted to private firms, employees are covered under different statutes. This means that in some states where there are no laws protecting public employees' right to bargain, employees of the private contractor will be covered. Also, in some states where there is a public-sector labor law providing bargaining rights to public employees, the employees of firms contracting government services will now have to seek union representation through the procedures of the National Labor Relations Act or the Railway Labor Act, whichever is applicable.

Another issue in privatization is that a different employer takes over the responsibilities for the contracted public service, and this employer is responsible to the contracting agency for the performance of the public service, not directly

Appropriate Bargaining Units and Union Recognition in the Federal Sector The appropriate bargaining units for exclusive recognition may be established on an agency, plant, installation, function, or other basis in order to assure a clear and identifiable community of interests among employees and to promote effective dealings with efficiency of the agency operations. The criteria used for determining community of interests are similar to those that have been used by the NLRB in the private sector. These include common duties and skills, similar working conditions,

to the citizens. The private employer takes over the publicly owned buildings and equipment either by renting or purchasing them or, in regard to small contracts, provides equipment and building space already owned but charges overhead costs to the public employer.[b]

While no difference exists between nonunion cities and unionized cities as to whether they privatize public services, the type of relationship between the union and city management is a significant factor. If the union-management relationship is very cooperative, the probability of the city contracting out services performed by employees who are members of unions is lower than in nonunion cities. On the other hand, the probability of a city considering privatizing when the relationship is very adversarial is higher than in nonunion cities.[c]

Rights of public employees are protected by the U.S. Constitution. These rights include due process rights and equal protection under the 14th Amendment. If the services of public employees are contracted to a private firm, the rights of employees in the private firm will be the same as those in the private sector, which includes employment-at-will in those states that still adopt the employment-at-will doctrine (see Chapter 10).

Another interesting dilemma is the difference in employees' rights to strike. In most public-sector jurisdictions, the right to strike has been eliminated or limited. If the services of public employees are contracted to a private employer covered by the National Labor Relations Act or the Railway Labor Act, employees are granted the right to strike under those statutes. While strikes do occur in the public sector, employees in the private sector have protected legal rights to strike.[d]

[a]Timothy D. Chandler and Peter Feuille, "Cities, Unions, and the Privatization of Sanitation Services," *Journal of Labor Research* XV (Winter 1994), pp. 53–67.
[b]David A. Dilts, "Privatization of the Public Sector: *De Facto* Standardization of Labor Law," *Journal of Collective Negotiations in the Public Sector* 24, no. 1 (1995), pp. 37–47.
[c]Chandler and Feuille, "Cities, Unions, and the Privatization of Sanitation Services."
[d]R. Hebdon, "Contracting Out in New York State: The Story the Lauder Report Chose Not to Tell!" *Labor Studies Journal* 20 (Spring 1995), pp. 3–10.

and common supervision and work site. Similarly, certain positions are generally excluded from the bargaining unit, such as confidential employees, management and supervisory personnel, personnel employees, and professionals unless they vote in favor of inclusion.

About 60 percent of all eligible employees are represented by various labor organizations in 2,589 bargaining units, and 87 percent are covered by labor agreements.[27] A federal agency accords **exclusive recognition** to a labor union if the union has been selected as the employee representative in a secret-ballot election by a majority of the employees in the appropriate unit who cast valid ballots. As noted above, there may be a gap between actual members and those represented.

Negotiable Subjects in the Federal Sector As in the private sector, the federal agency and the exclusively recognized union must meet at reasonable times and confer in good faith with respect to *mandatory* subjects of collective bargaining, such as certain personnel policies and practices and working conditions, to the extent that appropriate laws and regulations allow such negotiations. The parties are allowed to bargain over subjects that are *permissible,* but the CSRA does not require negotiation over permissible subjects—one party can legally refuse to negotiate these issues. Permissible subjects include numbers, types, and grades of positions assigned to any organizational unit, work project, or tour of duty; technology of the workplace; and methods and means of performing the work. Subjects *prohibited* from negotiations include wages and the following management rights:

- To determine the mission, budget, organization, number of employees, and internal security practices.
- To hire, assign, direct, lay off, and retain employees in accordance with applicable law.
- To suspend, remove, reduce in grade or pay, or take other disciplinary action.
- To assign work, subcontract, and select employees for promotion from properly ranked and certified candidates and other appropriate sources.
- To take whatever actions may be necessary to carry out the agency mission during emergencies.

Although the CSRA limits the negotiable subjects, the parties have ample opportunity to negotiate many issues, as illustrated in Exhibit 14.4. However, federal unions and management representatives do not have a totally free hand in negotiating these items, and either party may run the risk of committing an unfair labor practice by refusing to negotiate its mutual working conditions concerns in good faith. The fact that management and the union are required to bargain in good faith means that the parties must intend to reach an agreement.

Unfair Labor Practices in the Federal Sector The Civil Service Reform Act specified unfair labor practices in order to protect the rights of individual employees, labor organizations, and federal agencies. The General Counsel investigates charges of unfair labor practices and prosecutes them before the three-member FLRA. Employee grievances over matters concerning adverse action, position classification, and equal employment opportunity are issues covered by other laws, statutes, or agency rules, and cannot be raised in the forum of an unfair labor practice hearing.

Unfair labor practices under the act are very similar to those covered under previous executive orders, the National Labor Relations Act, and the Labor Man-

Exhibit 14.4 Potential Negotiation Issues in the Federal Sector

Procedures and standards to determine which employee(s) from a group of employees will be selected to perform work.
Merit promotion procedures and union participation on promotional panels.
Reduction-in-force procedures and management's obligation to notify employees and the union.
Procedures on job assignments.
Dues withholding.
Union rights regarding office services and space.
Safety considerations, including inspection, equipment, clothing, and union representation.
Discipline procedures.
Union participation in wage surveys.
Overtime distribution.
Meal and rest periods.
Excused time, including training and sick leave.
Travel time and transportation.

SOURCE: A survey of 2,418 labor agreements by the Office of Personnel Management, published in *The Federal Labor-Management Consultant* (Washington D.C.: Office of Personnel Management, July 31, 1981), p. 3. For analysis of FLRA cases, see H. H. Robinson, *Negotiability in the Federal Sector* (Ithaca, N.Y.: Cornell University, 1982); and Douglas McCabe, "Labor Relations, Collective Bargaining, and Performance Appraisal in the Federal Government Under the Civil Service Reform Act of 1978," *Public Personnel Management Journal* 13 (Summer 1984), pp. 133–135.

agement Relations Act. For example, prohibited management activities include restraining and coercing employees in the exercise of their rights; encouraging or discouraging union membership; sponsoring, controlling, or assisting the labor organization; disciplining union members who file complaints; and refusing to recognize or negotiate with a designated labor organization. The labor organization is prohibited from interfering with, restraining, or coercing employees in the exercise of their rights; attempting to induce agency management to coerce employees; impending or hindering an employee's work performance; calling for or engaging in job action; and discriminating against employees or refusing to consult, confer, or negotiate with the appropriate federal agency. In such cases, the FLRA can issue cease and desist orders and/or require reinstatement with back pay.

The CSRA makes it an unfair labor practice to refuse or fail to cooperate in impasse procedures and decisions. Moreover, an agency cannot enforce regulations that conflict with a negotiated agreement, and the union cannot picket if it interferes with the agency's operation. The FLRA has authority to revoke recognition of a union that commits an unfair labor practice or encourages a strike or slowdown and can also require the parties to renegotiate a labor agreement in accordance with an FLRA decision and seek temporary restraining orders in unfair labor practice cases.

The CSRA requires that all negotiated agreements in the federal sector include a grievance procedure with binding arbitration as its final step. A grievance is broadly defined to include any complaint by an employee or labor organization relating to employment with an agency and any claimed violation, misinterpretation, or misapplication of any law, rule, or regulation affecting conditions of employment. Certain issues are exempt from the grievance procedure, such as employee appointment, certification, job classification, removal for national security reasons or political activities, issues concerning retirement, and life and health insurance. However, the scope of grievance procedure coverage has been extended considerably. In fact, all matters within the allowable limits of the CSRA are within the scope of any grievance procedure negotiated by the parties, unless the parties have specifically agreed to exclude certain matters from coverage. Thus, in departing from previous practices and private-sector practices, the parties will not be negotiating matters into coverage; they will, however, be negotiating them out of coverage.

Negotiated grievance procedures now serve as the exclusive forum for bargaining-unit employees in most cases; however, in cases of adverse action and removals and demotions for poor performance, the employee may choose either the negotiated procedure or the statutory procedure, but not both. Moreover, in discrimination cases, the grievant may proceed to arbitration and then appeal to the EEOC or the Merit System Protection Board, an independent agency established to hear federal employee grievances under CSRA.

In 1993, President Clinton directed Vice-President Gore to conduct a six-month National Performance Review of the federal government. Vice-President Gore reported a "hostile and demoralized labor relations program." In 1993, President Clinton issued Executive Order 12871, which established the National Partnership Council (NPC) composed of federal agency and union officials with the purpose of recommending reforms to empower federal employees and promote labor-management cooperation. Executive Order 12871 also expanded the scope of bargaining by making some "permissive" items "mandatory." This meant that matters such as numbers, types, and grades of employees or positions assigned to any organizational units must be negotiated if one of the parties proposes the subject in negotiations. In addition, negotiators should be guided by a legislatively mandated "good government" standard, the pursuit of increased quality and productivity, customer service, employee empowerment, mission accomplishment, efficiency, organizational performance, and, in the case of the Department of Defense, military readiness. In regard to union security, the NPC recommended two options: (1) in units where voluntary union membership exceeds 60 percent of the represented employees, all nonmembers are required to either join the union or pay a fair-share service in lieu of dues, or (2) the parties will be allowed to negotiate a fair-share fee or a fee for individualized service, such as representation in grievance administration regardless of union density within the unit.[28]

Postal Reorganization Act of 1970

The Postal Reorganization Act (PRA) signed by President Nixon on August 12, 1970, fulfilled the desires of the postal unions to have their labor-management relations programs established by statute. Under Kennedy's executive orders, the Post Office Department never fully accepted collective bargaining, even though it was the largest single employer in the United States and had the largest proportion of employees belonging to unions.

The act created the U.S. Postal Service (USPS) as an independent establishment within the executive branch of the federal government. The office of postmaster general, previously a position in the cabinet, was made independent of Congress and the president. The postmaster general was to be selected by an 11-member board of governors.

Under the PRA, the national labor rules that have evolved over the years under the National Labor Relations Act apply to the USPS. Wages, hours, benefits, and terms and conditions of employment are to be determined through collective bargaining. Grievance, adverse action, and arbitration procedures are subject to negotiation. The NLRB supervises representation elections and prosecutes unfair labor practices. Although the right to strike was prohibited, a fact-finding and arbitration procedure was made available if a bargaining impasse persisted longer than 180 days after bargaining began. Since the PRA was passed, contracts have been negotiated without major disruptions of postal services.

Over the 25 years since the passage of the Postal Reorganization Act, there have been four occasions when the agreements were reached via arbitration. In 1978, the parties relied on med-arb for a settlement. Then in 1984, the agreement was decided by an arbitration panel. The panel agreed with the management position that wages were higher than comparable private jobs but decided that this discrepancy should be corrected over time rather than all at once.

The 1987 negotiations were not as dramatic as previous ones. The issue of greatest disagreement was management's proposal to create a new category of part-time employees and to increase the use of "casuals" (employees who do essentially the same job and receive $5.25 per hour with no health, leave, or retirement benefits). Jurisdiction problems over the introduction of new technology and assignment of new jobs emerged as issues of disagreement that caused difficulties.[29]

The 1991 negotiations ended in a dispute over wages, cost-of-living allowances, health insurance, safety and health, subcontracting, and automation. The unresolved issues from all four negotiations were submitted to interest arbitration; however, the Mail Handlers broke ranks, resumed negotiations, and signed a three-year agreement in February 1991. The agreement included provisions for lump-sum payments in lieu of wage increases, cost-of-living adjustments, and a two-tiered wage schedule with new hires being paid at 20 percent less than regular employees for their first 96 weeks of employment.

A five-member arbitration panel issued its award for a four-year contract covering the Postal Workers and Letter Carriers. This award included wage increases for each year of the contract, a lump-sum payment, cost-of-living adjustments, a new starting rate for new hires, an increase in the number of part-time employees, and provisions involving the transition to automation. Ten days later, the Postal Service and the Rural Letter Carriers reached an agreement that included similar economic provisions but included eligibility for cash bonuses based on customer satisfaction and financial performance of the Postal Service.[30]

In the fall of 1995, arbitration panels between the U.S. Postal Service and two of its unions, the American Postal Workers Union, covering 350,000 postal employees, and the National Association of Letter Carriers, covering 240,000 city letter carriers, rendered a decision for a four-year agreement that provided a pay increase of just over 5 percent, a one-time cash payment of $400, and cost-of-living adjustments beginning with the second year.[31]

Differences between Private-Sector and Public-Sector Bargaining

Nature of the Public Sector

One difference between the public and private sectors can be explained in terms of the economic system and the market economy. Unlike the private sector, many of the services in the public sector (such as public education and police and fire protection) are supplied to the citizens at little or no additional cost (beyond taxes). The market economy therefore does not operate in the public sector and cannot act as a constraint on the labor union and management negotiators.

Moreover, monopolistic conditions often exist in the public sector, and public organizations often control the services rendered or the products offered. For example, the police and fire departments are the primary organizations that provide certain types of security protection. Public education has very little real competition from the private sector, and even that is usually among only the more affluent families. Thus, products and services provided by the government cannot be readily substituted if they become more costly.

The lack of substitute goods or services distinguishes public-sector collective bargaining from related activities in the private sector and adds to the critical nature of public services. For example, citizens usually take garbage-collection services for granted; yet a strike by city garbage collectors would be regarded by the public as a crisis, because there is no immediate alternative means for garbage disposal. The lack of substitute services also eliminates one of management's strike costs: loss of business to a competitor. In fact, some union leaders contend that municipal leaders use a strike to their advantage—the payroll savings during a strike are transferred to other government budgetary accounts.

Finally, the relatively vague aspects of the particular public service institutions make productivity bargaining difficult. Clear and precise productivity measures are a necessary first step in productivity bargaining (although many private-sector companies have these figures and do not engage in productivity bargaining). Most public-sector bargaining parties do not have specific productivity measures at their disposal and could not engage in productivity bargaining even if they desired this approach. Many public services are provided regardless of customer use. Police officers and bus drivers can legitimately contend that they should not be financially punished for nonuse of their services; their salaries should not be a direct function of the number of crimes detected or riders served, respectively, if the service is available for all. Hence, much of the public-sector wage determination process is based on comparison with similar jobs in the public and private sectors rather than on employee performance records.[32] Because the market does not act as a moderator in the public sector, budgetary limitations, public attitudes, and administrative discretion must operate to successfully maintain order, equity, and balance in collective bargaining relationships.[33]

Relationship between the Budget and Public-Sector Bargaining Processes

The budget usually tends to have a more conspicuous role in public-sector collective bargaining than in private-sector bargaining. Most municipal budgets are posted in advance before public hearings and subsequent adoption. Although many citizens ignore public hearings, key taxpayers such as local companies give close attention to the budget in terms of its implication for increased property taxes. The anticipated salaries for public employees are recorded as separate line items on the budget, something not done in the private sector. Thus, the opportunity exists for concerned taxpayers to pressure city officials in the hopes of keeping the budget and subsequent taxes at a minimum.

The specific influence of the budget on the public-sector bargaining process remains uncertain. Some suggest that there is a great deal of flexibility in the budget-bargaining relationship in terms of budget padding, transfer of funds among line items, and supplemental or amended budgets that can often be filed after the final approval date.[34] In these cases, the government officer in charge of labor relations may have little concern with the agency's financial activities. The following related comments were expressed by a former director of the budget for New York City:

> The director of the budget is less a part of a unified management team than a part of the problem, an adversary not unlike the union leaders themselves. . . . Underlying the situation is the belief held by most labor negotiators that they know "what it takes" to effect a settlement and that, in the large complex public body, alleged or actual limits on available resources have no effect upon the ultimate settlement. And they are, in fact, largely correct.[35]

Similarly, as illustrated by one union official's comment, public-sector unions seldom allow the budget to influence their collective bargaining strategies and settlements:

> The budget does not mean too much to me—if we based our bargaining demands on the budget, we would never get any money. The union is never cognizant as to the amount [in the budget] because there never is enough money. We are aware of the dire need for money and campaign politically [to obtain additional funds], but when we go into negotiations we don't discuss the budgetary problems.[36]

Their major concern pertains to securing benefits for their members; it is up to management to find sufficient funds for an equitably negotiated settlement. Thus, there is little union-management agreement over the budget's significance in contract negotiations; few if any public-sector collective bargaining agreements have provisions specifying the role the budget will assume in the collective bargaining process.

The amount of funds available certainly is an important consideration. That is why the North America Free-Trade Agreement (NAFTA) bears close scrutiny. If NAFTA has an adverse effect on the tax base for public-sector revenues or on wage rates in the private sector, there will be a spill-over effect on public-sector unions. For example, two of the wage standards commonly used in negotiations of wages and in arbitrator decisions are (1) comparable wages and (2) ability to pay. If tax revenues are less or if wage rates in the private sector are lower, management negotiators will certainly use these arguments to defend their wage proposals in negotiating with public-sector unions.[37]

Collective Bargaining Structures and Decision-Making Processes

The bargaining structure within municipal governments is very decentralized, and, with few exceptions, negotiations are conducted on a single-employer basis. The bargaining-unit coverage extends only as far as the municipal jurisdiction, and municipal officials are reluctant to relinquish their political autonomy and decision-making authority. The chief administrative officer of the municipality will most frequently serve as chief negotiator, followed by the personnel director or an attorney retained by the city. An increased level of political activity by public employees, increased level of strike activity, and occurrence of prior job actions by organized public employees will increase the likelihood that a labor relations specialist will be included on the negotiations team. However, if the negotiations activities become complex, the city is more likely to employ a labor relations professional as the chief negotiator.[38]

It is more difficult to define the appropriate bargaining unit in the public sector than in the private sector.[39] Private-sector legislation and related administrative enforcement agencies provide direction for determining the appropriate bargaining unit. For example, plant guards in the private sector are required to be in separate bargaining units, and supervisors are not eligible for membership in the bargaining unit. The public sector, especially at the state and local levels, experiences many different combinations of appropriate bargaining units. Depending on the particular applicable state law or administrative determination, public-sector supervisors can be prohibited from joining unions, they can be in the same bargaining units as other employees, or they can join unions in separate bargaining units.[40]

In Louisiana, no employee is excluded from appropriate bargaining units. However, managerial employees and confidential employees are excluded in 20 other states, elected and appointed officials in 11 states, and supervisory employees in 9 states. Supervisors are included in the same unit as others in 3 states, but in 10 states, separate units are established for supervisory employees.[41]

Another organizational difference applies to the chief negotiator in the public sector, who often lacks authority to reach a final and binding agreement with the union on behalf of the public organization. The *sovereignty doctrine* makes it difficult to delegate decision-making authority to specific administrative officials. Many elected officials still refuse to give up their legislative authority to make final decisions on matters that they believe are important to effective government operations, because they feel responsible directly to the electorate. They do not want appointed negotiators to bind them to wage settlements and other provisions of collective bargaining agreements that they believe are unworkable.[42] For example, unionized schoolteachers might encounter a variety of managers in collective negotiations—the school principal, the superintendent of schools, the school board, and possibly state education officials. The problem of determining "who is management?" can negatively affect the negotiations process in two ways:

1. Management can pass the buck to other management officials in the bargaining process. Union officers are often shuffled off to a variety of government officials in collective bargaining on the premise that another individual has specific authority for a particular issue or a portion of available funds. Often, political rivalries prompt certain government officials to either intervene or pass the buck in the hopes of looking good at another official's expense. This situation can result in a more confusing collective bargaining relationship than is typically found in the private sector. In some cases, it can almost entirely prevent serious collective bargaining efforts between management and the union.
2. The unwillingness of some government agencies to delegate sufficient authority to a labor relations representative can result in a lack of labor relations understanding on management's side of the negotiation table. In some cases, taxpayers are affected if unions take advantage of the inexperienced management negotiators. Perhaps in other cases a public strike could have been avoided if the parties had had a more realistic understanding of the collective bargaining process.[43]

Negotiable Issues and Bargaining Tactics

Exemption by statute of many of the traditional collective bargaining subjects from negotiations is another difference between private- and public-sector labor relations. Under the Civil Service Reform Act of 1978, wages and position classifications of federal employees cannot be negotiated. (The postal service is covered under another law.) In many states operating under merit system rules and regulations, related subjects such as promotion, pension plans, and layoff procedures cannot be negotiated.[44]

A problem arises if public-sector negotiation topics are restricted to those already found in the labor agreement. One study found that some public-sector labor agreement provisions are not actually negotiated between the parties, while other decisions are jointly determined but not included in the formal labor agreement.[45] Thus, relatively few generalizations can be made regarding collectively bargained items in the public sector.

Sometimes the public-sector bargaining tactics differ from those in the private sector. Certain bargaining practices allowed in the public sector would probably be considered unfair labor practices in the private sector. When maneuvers such as not making genuine proposals are employed, they usually intensify hostilities and create barriers to future negotiations. On the other hand, a union frustrated by management's intransigence at the bargaining table may believe that there is no alternative available.[46]

Negotiations in the private sector stem from a bilateral relationship—management and union representatives negotiate the terms of the labor agreement with little involvement from outside groups. Public-sector bargaining, particularly at the state and local levels, is multilateral, involving various groups of community citizens and government officials as well as the formally designated negotiators. Thus, it often becomes an exercise in politics—who one knows and what one can do to help or hurt a government official's political career can play a decisive role. Public-sector unions therefore often have opportunities to engage in **end-run bargaining** before, during, or after negotiations; that is, they make a direct appeal to the legislative body that will make final decisions on the agreement. For example, one mayor made concessions to the police association in return for its endorsement in the gubernatorial primary. He changed the regular police work schedule from 5 days on and 2 off to 4 days on and 2 off (increasing the annual days off by 17), guaranteed two patrol officers in all cars, and agreed that 50 percent plus one of the patrol cars in each police district would be on the street during night hours. Because public labor unions in many settings are politically potent, elected officials are generally more receptive to this end-run process than a corporation president, members of the board of directors, or majority stockholders of a corporation would ever be in the private sector. In fact, such attempts by the union to bypass the management negotiators of a private-sector organization would probably result in an NLRB determination of refusal to bargain in good faith.[47]

Occasionally, the media aid the end-run tactic—management and the union present their positions to the press rather than to the other party at the bargaining table. Public-sector bargaining is usually given more press coverage than similar activities in the private sector because more related information is typically furnished to the press and the eventual settlement will have a more direct impact on the government's constituents. The end-run to the news media can harm the collective bargaining approach, as evidenced by a union leader's account of one contract negotiation between New York City and the uniformed forces:

> All of this [bargaining issues] should have been brought to the bargaining table. It would have given both labor and management a chance to work out of these very difficult trouble spots. . . . But, almost nothing was done at the table; instead both sides took to the television, advertising, and the loud and dramatic press releases. . . .
>
> Experts . . . know the best way to insure trouble is to bring collective bargaining into the public arena. Instead of labor and management representatives talking to each other, they will talk to the public and to their principals only. Invariably, the wrong things will be said.

> Management will talk of the "irresponsibly high demands" of the workers, and about how services will have to be cut back or taxes raised. . . .
>
> The labor leader now has to talk tough. The strike threat becomes almost obligatory, because he is now put in an impossible squeeze. When the union leader goes public he first must talk to the people he represents, and retain their confidence. Understandably, the public responds not to the facts of the situation but to the militant rhetoric. Everybody loses in the process, a process that has little or nothing to do with collective bargaining.[48]

The media play an important role in determining the priority issues, in providing information about the issues, and in helping the public formulate its attitudes toward the parties in negotiations. The local press is highly influential because many times it is the only channel of information for the general public. Since voters cannot directly observe union and management interactions, they rely on the media, which itself has biases. These biases include personal beliefs, ideologies and prejudices, budgetary and technological constraints, and dealing with problems stereotypically.

During negotiations both parties try to manipulate the media, because frequently the negotiations are dependent more on the people's perceptions than on the soundness of the position. In fact, sometimes the parties jointly manipulate the media to their own advantage. The union blames the city official for its members receiving less than the wage increase they demanded; the city official blames the union for a tax increase needed to pay for the wage increase that was given.[49]

Accompanying the upsurge of collective bargaining in the public sector have been efforts to open negotiations to citizen observation and participation through the **sunshine laws.** The rationale for this approach is that citizens can provide more input into how tax dollars are spent by their involvement, and openness reduces public distrust. While every state has some form of sunshine law, 25 states require labor negotiations to be conducted in the open, and 12 states even require that the strategy sessions in preparation for labor negotiations be open.[50]

The open approach to public-sector bargaining differs widely from the private sector, as a private enterprise's owners (stockholders) are excluded from collective bargaining sessions. Also, flexibility and honesty are necessary prerequisites of successful labor-management relationships, and these qualities are often lost if union and management negotiations have to posture their efforts before a public audience.

Grievance Administration

The public sector has widely accepted the grievance procedure with binding arbitration as the mechanism for resolving conflicts over interpretation and application of the collective bargaining agreement. While most grievance procedures are multistep, unlike in the private sector, most grievances are not settled at the first step. Instead, they tend to be settled at the second or third step. Some evidence indicates that where there are fewer steps in the grievance procedure, grievances are resolved more quickly. In fact, a positive relationship exists between the number of steps in the grievance procedure and the number of cases taken to arbitration. Once the demand for arbitration is made, the parties make a significant effort to resolve their grievances prior to the formal arbitration hearing. Then, when the parties proceed to arbitration, labor officials and managers, instead of outside attorneys, are most likely to present their cases in arbitration.[51]

The Right-to-Strike Controversy

The right to strike, considered by many a vital instrument for successful collective bargaining, is usually prohibited by statute in the public sector. The federal government and most state governments prohibit strikes by public employees. Despite the fact that strikes are illegal in most states, researchers have not been able to find any consistent and significant relationship between actual strikes and laws prohibiting strikes.[52]

The basic argument given for legislative prohibition of strikes is that the services provided by public organizations are essential to the general welfare of the citizens, and work stoppages or refusals to work would adversely affect the delivery of these vital services and create disorder in the community. As is true with many industrial relations concepts, the words "essential services" are subject to many diverse interpretations. Some maintain that all public services are essential, while others suggest that many public employee classifications (such as clerks, mechanics, and motor pool personnel) are no more essential than their counterparts in private labor. Police and firefighters are almost always viewed as crucial for public safety; however, at least one police strike saw no increase in the area's crime rate. One police official, believing that criminals fear irate citizens more than they fear the police, commented, "Hoods have no rights without police protection. Shop owners will use their shotguns."[53]

The right to strike in the public sector has other debatable dimensions. Some would prohibit public-sector strikes because they would place too much power in the hands of the union relative to the taxpayers. Also, unions would unnecessarily benefit at the expense of other groups that are dependent on government revenues but that do not strike or participate in power ploys with public officials.[54]

One research project found that successful bargaining gains in the public sector occur when unions either use the threat of a strike despite its illegality or intertwine themselves closely with their employers by exchanging patronage for political support. If this assessment is correct, prohibiting strikes leads to changes in patterns of political decision making that subvert the "normal" political processes.[55]

Some contend that prohibiting public-sector strikes distorts the collective bargaining process. Yet others believe that the right to strike in the public sector is not essential to collective bargaining, because public-sector unions are already influential interest groups and effectively use their lobbying and political support techniques to obtain collective bargaining goals. Regardless of the arguments for or against the right to strike or statutory penalties assigned to strikers, significant strikes have occurred in the public sector. The largest number of strikes occurred in education; and seven states, California, Illinois, Michigan, New Jersey, New York, Ohio, and Pennsylvania, accounted for 90 percent of the idle days.[56] Moreover, strikes are often prolonged until all strikers or discharged employees have been granted amnesty or reinstatement to former positions.

Thus, laws have not prevented strikes; they have not been invoked against all employees who have participated in strikes, and, when invoked, the law has not been applied with like effect to all strikers. Some believe that laws prohibiting strikes may have deterred some strikes and injunctions may have had a sobering effect on some strikers, but prohibiting strikes by passing a law has not realized a great degree of success. Some statistics suggest that such laws make no difference at all. Strikes have occurred in strike-permissive Oregon, Ohio, and Illinois, and they have occurred in New Jersey where strikes are prohibited.[57] However, well-enforced penalties against illegal strikes and threats of firing have reduced strikes in the public sector. Poorly enforced prohibitions and legalization of strikes have increased the frequency of strikes.[58]

Employee Rights and Obligations

Another way that public employment differs from private employment is that public employees have some legal rights and obligations that private employees do not. Numerous laws and executive orders pertain only to public employees. Political activities, personal appearance, place of residence, and off-the-job behavior have been regulated more closely. For example, public employees in particularly sensitive jobs and those whose misdeeds are most susceptible to adverse publicity, such as teachers, police officers, and firefighters, are held to higher standards than most other employees.[59] Because citizens pay the taxes that pay public employees' salaries, employers have to be careful of the image employees project.

While freedom of speech and association are constitutional rights, there are limits to their exercise by public employees. The Supreme Court has identified several reasons for which these rights may be limited, including the need to maintain discipline and harmony in the workforce, the need for confidentiality, and the need to ensure that the proper performance of duties is not impeded.[60] However, in 1987, the Court ruled that public employers cannot give priority to efficient work operation over an employee's First Amendment right to expression about a matter of public concern.

Generally, the courts have not attempted to substitute their judgment for that of executive branch officials on whether an individual public employee should be dismissed. Rather, they have sought to establish guidelines for the constitutional treatment of public employees in adverse action cases such as a discharge. Procedural due process requires the right of notice of the proposed government action, the reasons for the action, the opportunity to respond, the right to a hearing before an impartial official, and the rights to counsel, to confront accusers, and to cross-examine and subpoena witnesses.

In *Board of Regents* v. *Roth,* the Supreme Court delineated the following grounds upon which a public employee whose employment has been terminated could assert the right to procedural **due process:**

- Where an employee had a property right to the job.
- Where the termination harmed the individual's reputation and/or adversely affected his or her future employability.
- Where termination was in retaliation for an exercise of a protected constitutional activity, such as the freedom of speech or freedom of assembly.

The legislature can confer a property interest upon public employees by statutorily limiting the grounds for the employee's removal. Then the procedure by which dismissals can take place is controlled by the Constitution.

In the case of *Cleveland Board of Education* v. *Loudermill,* the Supreme Court has held that before tenured public employees can be fired, they must be informed of the charges against them and given an opportunity to respond. Their due process rights under the U.S. Constitution include written or oral notice of the charges against them, an explanation of the employer's evidence, and an opportunity to rebut the evidence.[61]

Differences in Approaches to Labor Relations

Public-sector unions have had an effect in ways that range beyond collective bargaining, such as through lobbying and political campaigning that influence the citizen's view of public service. Because public managers are beholden to an electorate that includes public sector employees and politically active unions, they tend to take a less adversarial approach to labor relations than do private employers, who are responsible to stockholders. Labor unions represent twice the proportion of public employees as private sector employees. In the public sector, public unions can be an important ally in convincing the electorate, the legislature, and other government bodies of the need for an increased budget. Another reason for the less conflict-ridden atmosphere is that the right to strike has been limited and has been replaced by other impasse resolution procedures such as arbitration.[62]

Similarities between Private-Sector and Public-Sector Bargaining

While there are differences between private- and public-sector labor relations, there are also similarities. First, *many of the participants in public-sector bargaining are trained and gain their experience in the private sector.* They tend to mold the emerging institutions in the public sector in a familiar image, using NLRB criteria for appropriate bargaining units, subjects for collective bargaining, use of labor injunctions, and standards for arbitration. Also, some of the unions, such as the Service Employees International Union and the Teamsters, have much experience in the private sector. Other unions, such as the National Education Association, the American Federation of Teachers, AFSCME, and civil service employee groups, hired their professional staffs from the private sector.[63]

A second similarity is the *reasons why employees form and join unions.* Public employees, like their private-sector counterparts, form and join unions when they are dissatisfied with their monetary compensation and their conditions of employment, which include their work, supervision, and promotional opportunities; have favorable attitudes toward unions as institutions; and believe that unionization will be instrumental in yielding positive outcomes.[64]

A third similarity is that *the collective bargaining settlement will often be influenced by the personalities of the negotiators and their abilities to increase their bargaining power relative to the other party (the bargaining power model has been discussed in Chapter 6).* To reiterate briefly, each party increases bargaining power over the opponent by either increasing the cost to the opponent of disagreeing or reducing the cost to the opponent of agreeing. Public opinion represents a most significant cost item in public-sector labor relations—both union and government officials often structure their tactics in a manner that gains public support for their position, which places pressure on their opponents to concede negotiation items.

However, public opinion and political support can be a double-edged sword in the bargaining power model. Public unions can use at least three general strategies to increase management's cost of disagreeing with the union's position.[65] The first technique is a union threat to "blow the whistle" on a questionable practice unless the government agency agrees with the desired settlement. Examples include threatening to release information on the unpublicized practice of dumping raw sewage in a river or on the dollar amount of government officials' liquor bills, which are paid by the taxpayers. Of course, the union is hoping that government officials will capitulate rather than risk vote loss in subsequent elections due to the public revelation of an incident. Management's cost of disagreeing can be more directly increased by the union's threat of withdrawing political support.[66] The success of this tactic depends on the number of union members and the ability of the union to mobilize a cohesive voting bloc.

The union can also use various job action techniques to raise management's cost of disagreeing. Strikes by public employees have occurred frequently in spite of legal sanctions. Perhaps these actions are taken under the assumption that most public-sector strikes have eventually been resolved without fines or other sanctions, even though they are illegal. Some other job actions that have been used are also outside the law or proscribed by the job requirements (for example, government employees in New York raising the toll bridges at rush hour when walking off the job), while others are marginally outside the law or job requirements (for example, all public employees calling in to say they are too sick to work).[67]

From the union standpoint, a most promising job action is working within the law while placing pressure on management to resolve the dispute. Job slowdowns fall marginally into this category because most public-sector labor agreements give management the right to discipline employees for poor production performance. Yet there is a thin line between a job slowdown and malicious obedience (also called *work-to-rule*), by which the employees follow the agency's rules to the letter. For example, a fingerprint technician is charged with verifying an individual's address during his criminal booking. This can be done by simply telephoning the individual's purported residence. However, fingerprint technicians desiring to follow the malicious-obedience technique might personally visit the individual's residence for a more accurate verification. Needless to say, this approach creates an assignment backlog. Other public employees can also use bureaucratic rules to their advantage. For example, toll booth employees could check paper currency serial numbers against a list of counterfeited bills, and postal workers could check each item to ensure a proper ZIP code. Malicious obedience has the tactical advantage of cutting back services. More importantly, employees continue to receive wages under this tactic while being relatively immune from disciplinary actions.

The variety of job action techniques depends on the creativity and resourcefulness of the union leaders. New York City's police and firefighters announced that off-duty employees would distribute a pamphlet at the city's airports, railroad stations, bus terminals, and hotels. The cover of the pamphlet featured a human skull in a shroud with the caption, "WELCOME TO FEAR CITY." Union officials contended that this pamphlet represented an educational "survival guide" for tourists, because the city was contemplating police and firefighter layoffs. Included in the pamphlet were the following helpful hints:

- Avoid public transportation.
- Do not walk.
- Beware of fire hazards.

Job actions of this nature, although not initially illegal, run the risk of an eventual restraining order. This occurred in the New York City pamphlet example when the New York Supreme Court at least in part accepted the city's contention that such conduct endangers the citizens' lives and threatens the economic well-being of the city.

Public-sector unions can also reduce management's cost of agreeing with the union by campaigning for referendums to fund the negotiated labor settlement or eliminating some of their initial proposals. They can also push for certain issues that contribute significantly to their economic well-being at little cost to the political incumbents. Employee pensions usually fall into this category since they can be increased without immediate cost implications; the bulk of pension costs will be incurred by some unhappy politician in the distant future.

Management can reduce its political cost of agreeing on wages by publicizing a rather low across-the-board settlement along with general improvements in the pay step plan. This plan usually gives progressive salary increases to each job classification. For example, an employee in a particular classification might receive a 5 percent wage increase after three years' service in that classification. Management can improve the employee's situation by either raising the percentage increase or reducing the number of service years needed for a step wage increase. However, it is difficult to determine and report the precise cost of these changes. Most news media presentations are limited to specific reports on the average wage gain of public employees and ignore the more detailed cost implications of the modified pay plan.

Another similar issue is the continuing controversy over nonunion employees' obligation to pay for their representational rights. Public-sector employees not joining unions are required to pay for representational services provided by the union (collective bargaining, grievance handling, arbitration, and so on), but not for non-collective bargaining activities (such as political action committees, lobbying, or public relations activities).[68] Under agency shop agreements authorized by state statute, similar rules (discussed in Chapter 11) apply to private employees.

In summary, public-sector collective bargaining is generally similar to that found in the private sector. In both situations, the parties are trying to increase their bargaining power relative to their opponent's by increasing the cost to the opponent of disagreeing with the party's position or by reducing the cost to the opponent of agreeing with the party's position. There are several differences between public- and private-sector bargaining processes; however, once these differences are acknowledged and understood, one can better appreciate the public sector as it fits into the overall framework of labor-management relations in the United States. Moreover, skills learned in private-sector labor relations are easily transferred to the public sector.

Impasse Resolution Procedures in the Public Sector

Because legislation usually prohibits public employees from striking or requires participation in impasse resolution procedures before striking, these procedures play an important role in labor relations in the public sector. Also, because the laws establish many different impasse resolution procedures, much experimentation is occurring in the public sector. These procedures normally involve a third party, who assists the parties in reaching an agreement without interrupting services or endangering the public interest.

Public-sector impasse resolution procedures are controversial and have received considerable attention; they have been instituted in 38 states. Impasse resolution procedures may combine mediation, fact-finding, and arbitration (available in 20 states).[69] Fact-finding is a legislatively mandated mechanism in public-sector bargaining in 31 states, second only to mediation, which is required in 35 states.[70]

These impasse resolution techniques are covered in Chapter 7; therefore, they will only be briefly discussed here. Similarities between public- and private-sector impasse procedures and unique public-sector implications will be mentioned.

Mediation Mediation involves a third-party neutral who has no binding authority but assists the parties in reaching an agreement. Of the impasse resolution procedures used in the public sector, mediation is the least intrusive and is little more than an adjunct to the negotiations process.[71] Mediators often have to rely on their intense mediation behavior when disputes are difficult.[72] The key ingredient for mediator effectiveness is experience, with related mediator training and knowledge. Effective mediators need tenacity—for example, not taking "no" for an answer—and they need to take an active role in the process by such actions as pressuring the parties with successive proposals for compromise, rather than simply relaying messages back and forth to the parties.[73]

Mediation tends to be more successful when the parties are unsure of themselves or have personality conflicts. It is less effective when it is followed by another impasse resolution procedure, although mediation works better when it is followed by arbitration instead of fact-finding.[74]

Fact-Finding and Arbitration Fact-finding and arbitration are separate impasse resolution procedures; however, they are discussed and assessed jointly because of their many similarities. Both involve a third-party neutral who, through a quasi-judicial hearing, assesses union's and management's collective bargaining positions. Those neutrals who are generally accepted to serve as fact-finders or arbitrators are likely to have much experience, as evidenced by their membership in the National Academy of Arbitrators, and are more likely than not to be attorneys trained in the evidentiary process.[75]

Fact-finders have multiple roles in the impasse resolution process. They interpret data and information that have been presented to them (rather than gathering facts themselves) and recommend settlement positions to the parties.[76] However, this recommendation is not binding. The final decision is generally left to the elected legislative body.

Arbitration entails a binding decision by a third-party neutral that settles the negotiation impasse. A variation of this technique is final offer selection (FOS) arbitration, where the arbitrator either selects the best package settlement presented by the union or management or resolves the impasse on an issue-by-issue basis. In both cases, the arbitrator can select only one party's final offer; there is no compromise or splitting the difference.[77]

Fact-finding and arbitration can be successful in resolving impasses because these techniques provide deadlines for the parties to resolve their differences, fresh knowledgeable perspectives, and political advantages because negotiators can blame the neutral for the eventual settlement. Also, the mere possibility of these procedures might pressure the negotiators to resolve their differences for fear that the neutral would not understand their positions.

These techniques can also carry some disadvantages. For example, the fact-finder's recommendation and arbitrator's decision might not resolve genuine union-management differences. Moreover, these techniques might cause the negotiators to cement their respective positions because the parties believe they can get a better deal from the arbitrator or more favorable recommendations from the fact-finder. Instead of earnestly attempting to resolve their differences in the final negotiations, the representatives focus their time and thoughts on preparing for the fact-finder or arbitrator. Also, politicians tend to challenge these individuals as "outsiders" or "limousine liberals" who have no accountability—they make the decisions and then leave town.

Variation in Procedures In the public sector few jurisdictions have the same arbitration scheme. Within the FOS approach there are several variations. In some cases, the parties are permitted to submit several final offers. Another variation specifies the number of steps that may be used. For example, the state of Iowa mandates the intermediary step of fact-finding between mediation and FOS arbitration. Where mediation and fact-finding fail, the dispute proceeds to FOS arbitration at either party's request. Further, the FOS arbitrator may select the fact-finder's recommendation or one of the final offers from union or management. Other variations include use of a single arbitrator or a panel, selection on an ad hoc or permanent basis, different criteria to be used by arbitrators and fact-finders, and the range of issues subject to arbitration.

Effectiveness of Fact-Finding and Arbitration Many variables influence the bargaining process and outcomes. One general measure of effectiveness is the "cost to at least one of the parties of continuing to disagree while lowering the cost to the other party of agreeing voluntarily."[78] Union and management officials are likely to push disputes to the last step of an impasse resolution procedure when one or both parties

- Are uncertain of future costs or continued collective bargaining (a situation that particularly applies to inexperienced negotiators).[79]
- Expect to receive a better settlement through the impasse procedure.
- Need to pass the blame for an "unfavorable" settlement to a third-party neutral instead of accepting personal responsibility for the results.[80]

Assessing fact-finding is particularly difficult. Its effectiveness does not hinge on the fact-finder's ability; this individual is presented facts by the parties in hopes that he or she will agree with their respective positions. The success of such a procedure is based on the assumption that the fact-finder's report will structure public opinion, which will in turn place pressure on the parties to resolve their differences in accord with published recommendations. Thus far, there is no concrete evidence to show that public pressure has noticeably affected public sector management and union officials. (See "Labor Relations in Action.")

Overall, interest arbitration in the public sector seems to have passed the test, at least in the short run; most of the participants as well as the analysts have been satisfied with the process. Its availability has not substantially lessened serious negotiations. Also, the number of strikes has been reduced substantially in cases where employees have been covered by compulsory arbitration legislation. Even though some management officials feared arbitration, arbitrators have not stripped them of their rights and authority. The settlements have not been significantly greater than the parties would have reached themselves in similar circumstances, and the public in general has not openly indicated displeasure with the process. Most significantly, arbitration has been increasingly adopted as an impasse-resolution procedure in the public sector, and the parties have expressed satisfaction with their experience.[81]

LABOR RELATIONS IN ACTION

The Facts about Fact-Finding

There is virtually no consensus about fact-finding. How it is spelled is not even clear. "Fact-finding," "factfinding," or "fact finding" have all found their way into statute or state agency documents. Most dictionaries spell it with the hyphen.

Just what facts is a fact-finder to find? Naturally the parties have their preferences, and *most* of the time they are at odds. In one notable case involving the firefighters of Iowa City, perhaps the clearest analogy ever of the fact-finder's role was presented. There were five hours of testimony with respect to the city's ability to pay. The city, of course, noted how various budget lines had been reduced for lack of funds. The firefighters followed, pointing out the growth of other lines, some of which were labeled "miscellaneous" and all of which, the firefighters asserted, were the new "hiding places" for money in the city's "overflowing coffers."

Finally, the time for closing arguments came. The firefighter spokesman reached under the table for a used brown lunch bag and hauled out three walnut shells and a pea. After refreshing the fact-finder's memory about "the old shell game," he proceeded to demonstrate how, at least in an *honest* shell game, the pea was always present. It was only a matter of finding it. The fact-finder was left with the clear inference that unless he could find a "pea" in Iowa City of sufficient size to fund the firefighters' request, the "game" could not possibly be honest. In the spokesman's opinion, the "facts" the fact-finder was supposed to find were green, but they weren't peas!

Another unsettled question about fact-finding is exactly what role fact-finding should play. One pundit even raised the question, "Should a fact-finder be concerned with whether his report will be rejected?" Given that fact-finding is part of a dispute resolution process, it seems obvious to most of us that he should. In one well-known teacher dispute, the fact-finder was convinced that the teachers' position was correct and, moreover, he was told by the board's negotiator that the superintendent "wants a strike." Foolishly, he recommended the full 8 percent increase sought by the teachers even

One of the biggest concerns about public-sector interest arbitration is its so called **chilling effect** on the parties' incentives to reach an agreement. If either believed that it could get a better settlement from an arbitrator than from negotiation, there would be an incentive to maintain excessive demands in hopes that the arbitrator would **"split the difference"** and make a favorable award. When one side acts in such a manner, the other side has no realistic choice but to respond similarly, widening the gap between the parties.[82]

Research into this aspect of arbitration has produced mixed results. Analysis of arbitral decisions regarding police impasses revealed that some management offi-

though he believed the teachers would settle for less. The strike lasted ten weeks.

Most state statutes contain a list of criteria fact-finders shall consider in making their recommendations. Among them is always one that opens Pandora's box, for example, ". . . and such other factors that are customarily considered in making recommendations in labor disputes." One of the "facts" must be what recommendation will most likely be accepted by the parties. Especially when fact-finding is followed by the right to strike, a failure to recognize the relative power of parties is foolhardy.

Some might argue that the role of the fact-finder is to persuade the union membership and public body's constituency of the rightousness of the fact-finder's recommendations. But most fact-finders are not even second-rate prophets, let alone God (though some pretense along these lines does appear to be a prerequisite for the profession). Their recommendations are no closer to what is "right" than are the positions of either party. Besides, it is doubtful whether a union member or voter ever read a fact-finding report. The bottom line *recommendation* is what gets read, and if it is close enough to what constituents will tolerate, it will be accepted.

A better analogy for a fact-finder is a general, all-purpose maintenance worker with a big, old, rusty station wagon filled with tools and spare parts. No two calls are alike—the parties, the issues, the propensity to want a settlement, and many other factors all differ. Moreover, the fact-finder won't know what is needed until after the process is well along. Even then it is often difficult to diagnose. With experience and good fortune, maybe the "maintenance worker" will keep things running smoothly. If the maintenance worker guesses wrong, the boiler may blow up. But the question of who was "right" is irrelevant!

SOURCE: A neutral who wishes to remain anonymous.

cials are reluctant to reveal their final offer prior to arbitration because the arbitrators will use management's final offer as a starting point in their decisions.[83] Yet this concern is somewhat dampened by a study of several arbitration awards in firefighters interest disputes, which revealed that a large majority of the arbitrators took an intermediate or compromise stance on a few negotiation issues, such as wages and clothing allowances, but did not compromise the other issues; they supported either management's or the union's final position. It seems that there is no guarantee that arbitrators will compromise on any or all of the issues presented for their decisions.[84]

Another concern about public-sector interest arbitration is that the mere existence of impasse resolution procedures could create a so-called **narcotic effect.** That is, once the parties start using the procedures, they become increasingly reliant on them in subsequent negotiations. However, this frequently expressed concern is not warranted.[85]

In a study of impasse resolution procedures in Minnesota, researchers found evidence that the types of employees may make a difference in the degree to which a chilling effect occurs on the negotiations. When the employees are "essential" and therefore not allowed to strike, and unresolved issues are decided in arbitration, 30 percent of the cases end up in arbitration. This is in sharp contrast to the cases involving "nonessential" employees who are allowed to strike, where only 9 percent go to arbitration. Thus, the strike possibility appears to present a greater incentive to reach an agreement in negotiations.[86]

In Florida, impasse resolution procedures include voluntary mediation, voluntary interest arbitration (a form of fact-finding with recommendations), and resolution of unsettled issues by an appropriate legislative body, such as the state legislature, school board, city commission, and so on. About 55 percent of all individual recommendations made by special masters have been jointly accepted by the parties. The most effective tactics of the special masters (neutral third parties who render advisory decisions) were focusing on managing the format of negotiations, facilitating the exploration of possible solutions, and emphasizing the costs of continued disagreement. The least effective tactics included face-saving, improving objectivity, and enhancing each side's understanding of the issues.[87]

Strike-potential bargainers spend more time in negotiations, while bargainers in cases resolved in arbitration spend more time in strictly procedural delay. Thus, it seems clear that the greater threat associated with the strike encourages hard bargaining, and the use of arbitration reduces the incentive for hard bargaining and therefore has a chilling effect on negotiations.[88]

Final-offer selection arbitration has been used in several states (Iowa, Massachusetts, Minnesota, and Wisconsin) and has been found to perform a reasonably good job of protecting the parties' incentives to negotiate[89] when the arbitrators do not "flip-flop" their awards (awarding the decision to one party the first time and to the other party the next time) so they will be rehired in the future. Other studies found that final-offer selection arbitration could be more effective if it did not follow fact-finding in the impasse procedure and gave the arbitrator more flexibility to determine the particular issues to be decided in this fashion. Flexibility, however, is relative as some arbitrators believe that there should be some guidelines for wage determination. Some issues, such as the type of union security clause, do not lend themselves to final-offer selection arbitration.[90]

Arbitrators in interest disputes tend to rely, at least initially, on internal wage comparisons and to consider the unique and historical circumstances of the particular community and the desirability of maintaining such circumstances. The criterion of ability to pay plays a secondary role behind comparable wages and cost of living unless well-supported arguments against this are presented. In addition, interest arbitrators view their role in the arbitral process as continuing the existing nature of the parties' relationship that has stemmed from the bilateral process of negotiations. Arbitrators believe that any major deviations from this relationship must come from the parties, not the arbitrator.[91]

In wage disputes using final offer selection arbitration, evidence suggests that arbitrators are heavily influenced by wage settlements in comparable units of government. As a result, union bargaining associations discourage their locals from settling for a wage less than a statewide target.[92]

Referendum

Another impasse resolution procedure places the unresolved issues on a taxpayer referendum or vote. The following item, for example, might be placed on a ballot: "Do you approve of granting a wage increase of X cents per hour to our police officers at an estimated additional annual cost of property taxpayers of Y million dollars?"[93]

This procedure would avoid the problems of an outsider (fact-finder or arbitrator) determining the cost of a negotiated settlement. Citizens could not complain if the union's settlement was achieved in a democratic manner. Similarly, the union's integrity would be at stake if it refused to abide by the "will of the public." Yet, this procedure could turn collective bargaining into a public relations campaign directed at a body of individuals (citizens) largely unfamiliar with labor relations' complexities. Further, the procedure has no precedent in private-sector labor relations because no company submits labor agreement proposals to stockholders or consumers.

Referenda, or direct submission to the electorate for final and binding settlement of labor-related issues, have been used in several Texas cities. Employees have won over two-thirds of the elections involving civil service and bonus issues, but lost 56.6 percent where the issue was pay parity.[94]

Use of the referendum has two potential advantages:[95]

1. It ensures that the negotiations will be conducted in a pragmatic, realistic environment where the parties have an incentive to reach an agreement and costs are too high to fail to reach an agreement.
2. It motivates citizens to take an active interest in the matter of public employment.

However, in cities where this method has been used, assessment of this approach has not been favorable. First, the electorate has little understanding of the law and the issues, and it is highly susceptible to propaganda campaigns by both parties. Second, the referendum appears to help make the strong stronger and the weak weaker without regard for what is equitable or reasonable for all the parties involved.[96]

There are many varieties and combinations of public impasse resolution procedures, yet the objectives remain the same: to avoid strikes, to minimize dependence on outsiders, to maximize good-faith bargaining between parties, to protect the public interest, and to build a commitment to accountability and mutual problem solving.

Labor Relations Activities among Various Groups in the Public Sector

The following section highlights labor relations in some of the major employee groups in the public sector. Included are elementary and secondary teachers, college professors, police, and firefighters.

Elementary and Secondary Teachers

More than 80 percent of public elementary and secondary teachers belong to the American Federation of Teachers (AFT) or the National Education Association (NEA), and more than 60 percent are covered under formal collective bargaining agreements. Teacher unions have successfully used a dual strategy of collective bargaining and political action that has significantly improved their salaries and working conditions.

A majority of teacher bargaining units have negotiated contract provisions that regulate the school day, allow teacher response to administrator evaluations of teaching performance, permit teachers to exclude disruptive students from their classrooms, and provide a detailed procedure for reducing the size of the teacher force. However, less than a third have attained contract provisions that limit class size, curb requirements of teaching outside of one's field, or establish an instructional policy at each school.[97]

Where elementary and secondary teachers have chosen to be represented by unions, they have made significant inroads into educational issues, including curriculum, student placement, teacher placement, grading policies, transfer rights, class size, school calendar, length of school day and year, textbook use, promotion and tenure, and use of substitutes.[98]

Higher Education

In higher education, 226,875 faculty members are represented by unions on 1,027 campuses; 96 percent of the faculty represented are employed by public institutions.[99] Non-faculty collective bargaining agreements exist within 360 institutions having 775 campuses.[100]

Thirty states have passed laws enabling faculty to unionize if they chose. However, the U.S. Supreme Court limited the right of faculty members employed by private universities to unionize when it decided that faculty at Yeshiva University were "managerial employees" and therefore had no statutory rights to bargain under the protection of the National Labor Relations Act. This dilemma has caused one recognized authority to ask: "If *Yeshiva* is good law, why has it not been applied in the public sector?"[101]

Separate bargaining units of graduate teaching assistants or fellows are included on the campuses of the University of Michigan, University of Oregon, University of Massachusetts, University of Wisconsin,[102] University of Florida System, and State University of New York. When graduate student teaching and research assistants at the University of California at Berkeley sought union representation by the United

Auto Workers, the California Public Employment Relations Board ruled that these assistants were not university employees and denied their request. Later, the courts upheld this decision. In response, the graduate students struck, causing 60 percent of the classes to be canceled and 16 percent to be less than half filled.[103] In 1996, over 200 Yale teaching assistants (TAs) withheld grades for the fall semester to pressure Yale administration to recognize their union. Yale issued an ultimatum to the protesting TAs to submit their grades or lose their teaching assignments. On the day before the deadline, the grades were turned in and no union was recognized.

Over one-third of professors on approximately 1,000 campuses are represented by certified bargaining agents. Seventy-five private institutions of higher education have refused to bargain with faculty unions or have cited the Supreme Court's *Yeshiva* decision in order to avoid bargaining. As a result, private-sector faculty union organizing remains at a standstill.

Interestingly, faculty senates are institutionalized and have traditionally been the mechanism for collegial decision making, peer review, and shared governance. On unionized campuses, faculty senates address education and other academic matters, whereas faculty unions negotiate terms and conditions of employment. An interesting question is whether faculty senates fall within the Section 2 (5) definition of a labor organization under the National Labor Relations Act (see Chapter 7). For example, if faculty members must participate in faculty senate activities, if the purpose of the faculty senate is to "deal" with the employer, or if the issues between the employer and the faculty senates involve terms and conditions of employment, it can be argued that the faculty senate is a labor organization. In addition, if faculty senates are provided free office space, material support, released time for participation, clerical assistance, or other benefits from the university administration, the argument that the faculty senate is a labor organization is strengthened.[104]

Initially, faculty unions considered monetary compensation the primary reason for unionization and unions proved to have a positive effect on faculty salaries. In the mid-1970s, the emphasis shifted to issues involving personnel matters such as job security, tenure, faculty appointment, dismissal, seniority, promotion, and grievance administration, and the faculty's role in setting institutional policy. Faculty members wanted to strengthen their job security and gain greater access to policy-making power and autonomy. In recent years, faculty unions have made inroads into academic areas related to class size, the academic calendar, work load, and class scheduling.[105]

While work stoppages by faculty members are infrequent, they receive much publicity. When they do occur, they are quite bitter, and classes are usually disrupted. In the last few years, work stoppages have occurred at the University of Bridgeport, Temple University, and Wayne State University, primarily over salary disputes.[106]

Police

By the 1970s police officers had become one of the most highly unionized segments of the public sector. Twenty-five states and the District of Columbia now have duty-to-bargain laws, and three states have meet-and-confer laws. The scope of bargaining varies greatly, but most agreements focus on salary and fringe benefits, pay supplements, equity, union security, working conditions, and individual security. Police unions have successfully pushed salary levels above those prevailing in nonunion locations (however, this differential is smaller than the 10 to 30 percent reported in the private sector), and the favorable bargaining climate created in 16 states having compulsory arbitration of unresolved disputes has increased police salaries even more.

No state allows police the right to strike, but strikes do occur, usually in the form of the "blue flu" (police calling in sick on the same day). Collective bargaining is extremely decentralized, and membership in a police union is almost always limited to police department personnel. It is extremely rare for employees in different cities to join together for bargaining purposes. While there is no single dominant police union, the largest is the Fraternal Order of Police with about 170,000 members. A local union may be affiliated with a national organization, but the focus of police bargaining remains primarily local with no intervention from the national union.

Police unionism has increased the costs of delivering police services; however, it has also given police officers considerable protection from arbitrary, inconsistent, and inequitable managerial actions. Unionized police officers are not required to work extra hours for no pay, they have due process in internal investigations, and their agreements have a grievance procedure for appealing managerial decisions that are perceived as unfair.[107]

Firefighters

The International Association of Fire Fighters had its origin in the nineteenth century as a fraternal organization that addressed work-related problems encountered by firemen. The American Federation of Labor recognized the IAFF as a trade union in 1901, and the union has grown to a membership of 157,000 with 1,658 local unions throughout the United States. Unions represent 66.5 percent of state and local employees in fire protection.[108]

Summary

Public employee unions have struggled against unfavorable public opinion and publicity and adverse state legislation, but with permissive legislation, favorable judicial interpretations of constitutional rights, and an increasing interest among public employees, many public employees have joined unions. Union efforts culminated in organizational representation for a majority of employees in education, police protection, and fire protection in state and local governments.

Permissive state labor relations legislation or policy generally developed according to geography. Alaska and Hawaii passed favorable legislation, as did states located on the West Coast and in the Northeast, North, and Midwest. Most of the lower Atlantic Coast, Southeast (except Florida), Southwest, and lower

Rocky Mountain states have no comprehensive legislation. In states having laws, the legislation typically specifies the administrative set-up, bargaining rights, impasse procedures, unfair labor practices, and strike provisions. Within this framework, the parties attempt to negotiate labor agreements covering permissible subjects.

In the federal sector, legislation and executive permission to allow federal employee unions was absent for many years. However, unions still developed, even under adverse conditions. Executive Order 10988 did not offer many substantive benefits to federal employee unions but provided the framework for a labor relations system in the federal government and gave tremendous impetus to union organization and growth. Each subsequent executive order added new features, and federal employees were eventually given many rights similar to those of employees under many state statutes and the National Labor Relations Act.

The administrative agencies under the Civil Service Reform Act (CSRA) of 1978 include the Federal Labor Relations Authority, the General Counsel, and the Federal Service Impasse Panel. Also available for assistance are the Federal Mediation and Conciliation Service, labor arbitrators, and fact-finders, who provide important services for the negotiating parties. The direction and interpretations of the CSRA in various types of cases are not yet fully manifest.

Public- and private-sector labor relations differ in several ways: (1) in its very nature, public service differs from private-sector services economically and in its demand characteristics; (2) the effect of the budget on bargaining processes differs; (3) the bargaining structure differs, affecting decision-making processes; (4) negotiable issues and bargaining tactics may be less predictable; (5) the right to strike is usually prohibited by law; and (6) effects on and approaches to labor relations differ.

Public- and private-sector similarities include the role of personalities and skills of negotiators and the interplay of bargaining power model variables such as public opinion, political support, and various forms of job actions. The impasse resolution procedures often established to substitute for the strike alternative include mediation, fact-finding, arbitration, and various combinations of these; the latter seem to be most popular. Such terms as *splitting the difference, chilling effect,* and *narcotic effect* have become common in assessing the effectiveness of these procedures. Definitive conclusions about impasse procedures have not been made, and further research into their effectiveness is needed. However, some promising results, such as serious negotiations and low incidence of strikes, have been identified in many states. In some states, chilling effects and narcotic effects have been identified.

The chapter concluded with highlights of labor relations in several public employee groups that include elementary and secondary teachers, college professors, police, and firefighters.

Key Terms

Federal Labor Relations Authority (FLRA)
Federal Service Impasse Panel (FSIP)
exclusive recognition
end-run bargaining
sunshine laws
due process
chilling effect
"split the difference"
narcotic effect

Discussion Questions

1. Think of a public organization with which you are familiar. Explain how it differs from a private company in terms of the following:
   a. nature of its service
   b. relationship between its budget and collective bargaining processes
   c. bargaining structure and decision-making processes
   d. negotiable issues and bargaining tactics
   e. its right to strike
2. Using the same public organization as in Question 1, discuss the similarities between collective bargaining in this organization and a typical negotiation between a private company and its union.
3. Give reasons why unions developed later in the public sector than in the private sector.
4. Public-sector labor relations legislation differs on a geographic basis. Explain why this might have occurred.
5. Describe the different types of impasse resolution procedures used in the public sector, and discuss the relative effectiveness of each.
6. Compare the chilling effect and the narcotic effect as they pertain to negotiations and impasse resolution procedures in the public sector.
7. Considering the multitude of subjects that are bargainable in the federal sector, list some of the more important ones that are not.
8. Compare and contrast the negotiated grievance procedures under the CSRA with those found in the private sector.

References

1. David Lewin, Peter Feuille, and Thomas Kochan, *Public Sector Labor Relations: An Analysis and Readings*, 2d ed. (Glen Ridge, N.J.: Thomas Horton & Daughters, 1988), pp. 1–5.
2. Bureau of Labor Statistics, "Union Members in 1995" (Washington, D.C., February 8, 1995), p. 4.
3. "AFL-CIO Membership Reflects Growth Among Government, Service Unions," *Daily Labor Report*, November 12, 1991, pp. D-1–D-3.
4. Bureau of Labor Statistics, "Union Members in 1995."
5. Mark de Bernando, "Public Sector Sees Organized Labor Boom," *The Wall Street Journal*, December 18, 1986, p. 26.
6. Marick F. Masters and Robert S. Atkin, "Reforming Federal Sector Labor Relations: Recommendations of President

Clinton's National Partnership Council," *Labor Law Journal* 45 (June 1994), pp. 353–354; updated by Courtney D. Gifford, *Directory of U.S. Labor Organizations, 1994–1995 Edition* (Washington, D.C.: Bureau of National Affairs Inc., 1994), pp. 67–68.

7. Marick Masters and Robert S. Atkin, "Public Policy, Bargaining Structure, and Free-Riding in the Federal Sector," *Journal of Collective Negotiations in the Public Sector* 19 (November 2, 1990), pp. 97–109.

8. Charles J. Coleman, "Federal Sector Labor Relations: A Reevaluation of the Policies," *Journal of Collective Negotiations in the Public Sector* 16, no. 1 (1989), pp. 37–40; updated from *The Federal Labor-Management and Employee Relations Consultant* (Washington, D.C.: U.S. Office of Personnel Management, March 15, 1991), p. 3.

9. Greg Hundley, "Who Joins Unions in the Public Sector? The Effect of Individual Characteristics and the Law," *Journal of Labor Research* 9 (Fall 1988), pp. 301–306.

10. Richard B. Freeman and Casey Ichniowski, "Introduction: The Public Sector Look of American Unionism," in *When Public Sector Workers Unionize,* eds. Richard B. Freeman and Casey Ichniowski (Chicago: The University of Chicago Press, 1988), p. 3.

11. "40 percent of State and Local Employees Have No Bargaining Rights, AFL-CIO Finds," *Daily Labor Report,* March 30, 1987, p. A–2.

12. Raymond L. Hogler, *Public Sector Strikes: Employee Rights, Union Responsibilities, and Employer Prerogatives* (Alexandria, Va.: International Personnel Management Association, 1988).

13. Roger E. Dahl, "Public Sector Bargaining Issues in the 1980's: A Management View," *Proceedings of New York University Thirty-Third Annual National Conference on Labor* (New York: Matthew Bender, 1981), p. 288; updated from "BNA's Digest of State Public Employee Bargaining Statutes," *Government Employee Relations Report* (1993), p. 51:101.

14. Michael Grace, "The Chaos in Public-Sector Bargaining," *AFL-CIO American Federationist* 88 (July 1981), pp. 9–12; updated from "BNA's Digest of State Public Employee Bargaining Statutes," *Government Employee Relations Report* (1993), p. 51:101.

15. Joel M. Douglas, "Injunctions under New York's Taylor Law: An Occupational Analysis," *Journal of Collective Negotiations in the Public Sector* 10, no. 3 (1981), p. 249.

16. Alan Balfour and Alexander B. Holmes, "The Effectiveness of No Strike Laws for Public School Teachers," *Journal of Collective Negotiations in the Public Sector* 10, no. 2 (1981), pp. 133–143.

17. Raymond L. Hogler, *Public Sector Strikes: Employee Rights, Union Responsibilities, and Employer Prerogatives* (Alexandria, Va.: International Personnel Management Association, 1988), pp. 5–6.

18. B. V. H. Schneider, "Conferring Strike Rights by Statute: Experience Outside California," *Government Union Review* 9 (Fall 1988), pp. 40–46.

19. Powers McGuire, "A Comparison of the Right of Public Employees to Strike in the United States and Canada," *Labor Law Journal* 38 (June 1989), pp. 304–309.

20. James K. McCollum, "Decertification of the Northern Virginia Public Sector Local Unions: A Study of Its Effect," *Journal of Collective Negotiations in the Public Sector* 10, no. 4 (1981), pp. 345–353; James K. McCollum, "Politics and Labor Relations in Virginia: The Defeat of Public Sector Unionism," *Employee Relations Law Journal* 7, no. 3 (1981), pp. 414–431.

21. Alan Balfour and Sandra Jennings, "Chaos in Union Recognition Procedures: A Case History of Oklahoma's School Teacher Bargaining Law," *Journal of Collective Negotiations in the Public Sector* 11, no. 1 (1982), pp. 82–83.

22. U.S. Department of Commerce, Bureau of the Census, *Labor-Management*

Relations (Washington, D.C.: Government Printing Office, 1983), p. vi.

23. Jeffrey A. Tannenbaum, "Frustrated Firemen: Fire Fighting Gear Improves, but Cities Can't Afford to Buy It," *The Wall Street Journal,* January 30, 1975, pp. 1, 21.

24. Hervey A. Juris and Peter Feuille, *Police Unionism* (Lexington, Mass.: Lexington Books, 1973).

25. Murray Nesbitt, *Labor Relations in Federal Government Service* (Washington, D.C.: Bureau of National Affairs Inc., 1976), pp. 6–17.

26. George W. Bohlander, "The Federal Service Impasse Panel: A Ten-Year Review and Analysis," *Journal of Collective Negotiations in the Public Sector* 24, no. 3 (1995), pp. 194–195.

27. Bohlander, "The Federal Service Impasse Panel: A Ten-Year Review and Analysis."

28. Marick F. Masters and Robert S. Atkin, "Reforming Federal Sector Labor Relations: Recommendations of President Clinton's National Partnership Council," *Labor Law Journal* 45 (June 1994), pp. 353–354.

29. Gregory Giebel, "Recent Developments in Federal/Postal Service: Collective Bargaining 1987," *Labor Law Journal* 38 (August 1988), p. 510.

30. Michael H. Cimini and Susan L. Behrmann, "Collective Bargaining, 1991: Recession Colors Talks," *Monthly Labor Review* 115 (January 1992), pp. 26–27.

31. "Arbitration Panel Awards Postal Union Four-Year Contract with Raises, COLAS," *Daily Labor Report,* October 3, 1995, pp. A-1–A-2.

32. Walter Fogel and David Lewin, "Wage Determination in the Public Sector," *Industrial and Labor Relations Review* 27 (April 1974), pp. 410–431; Paul D. Staudohar, "An Experiment in Increasing Productivity of Police Service Employees," *Public Administration Review* 35 (September–October 1975), pp. 518–522.

33. Michael Moskow, J. J. Loewenberg, and E. C. Koziara, *Collective Bargaining in Public Employment* (New York: Random House, 1970), pp. 14–18; and H. H. Wellington and R. K. Winter, Jr., "Structuring Collective Bargaining in Public Employment," *Yale Law Journal* 79 (April 1970), pp. 806–822.

34. Milton Derber et al., "Bargaining and Budget-Making in Illinois Public Institutions," *Industrial and Labor Relations Review* 27 (October 1973), pp. 49–62; and Kenneth M. Jennings, J. A. Smith, and Earle C. Traynham, Jr., "Budgetary Influences on Bargaining in Mass Transit," *Journal of Collective Negotiations in the Public Sector* 6, no. 4 (1977), pp. 333–339.

35. Frederick O'R. Hayes, "Collective Bargaining and the Budget Director," in *Public Workers and Public Unions,* ed. Sam Zagoria (Englewood Cliffs, N.J.: Prentice-Hall, 1972), p. 91.

36. Derber et al., "Bargaining and Budget-Making," p. 58.

37. David D. Dilts, William H. Walker, and Constanza Hagman, "The Impact of the North America Free Trade Agreement on Public Sector Collective Bargaining," *Journal of Collective Negotiations in the Public Sector* 23, no. 1 (1994), pp. 92–94.

38. Rafael Gely and Timothy D. Chandler, "Determinants of Management's Organizational Structure in the Public Sector," *Journal of Labor Research,* pp. 381–395.

39. William H. Holley, Jr., "Unique Complexities of Public Sector Labor Relations," *Personnel Journal* 55 (February 1976), p. 75.

40. Stephen L. Hayford, "An Empirical Investigation of the Public Sector Supervisory Bargaining Rights Issue," *Labor Law Journal* 26 (October 1975), pp. 641–652; Alan Balfour, "Rights of Collective Representation for Public Sector Supervisors," *Journal of Collective Negotiations in the Public Sector* 4, no. 3 (1975), pp. 257–265; and William H. Holley, Jr., J. Boyd Scebra, and William Rector, "Perceptions of the Role of the Principal in Professional Negotiations," *Journal of Collective Negotiations* *in the Public Sector* 5, no. 4 (1976), pp. 361–369.

41. Helen S. Tanimoto and Gail F. Inaba, "State Employee Bargaining: Policy and Organization," *Monthly Labor Review* 108 (April 1985), pp. 51–55.

42. Louis V. Imundo, Jr., "The Federal Government Sovereignty and Its Effect on Labor-Management Relations," *Labor Law Journal* 26 (March 1975), pp. 145–152.

43. Milton Derber, "Management Organization for Collective Bargaining in the Public Sector," in Aaron, Grodin, and Stern, *Public Sector Bargaining,* pp. 80–117.

44. I. B. Helburn and N. B. Bennett, "Public Employee Bargaining and the Merit Principle," *Labor Law Journal* 23 (October 1972), p. 619; and I. B. Helburn, "The Scope of Bargaining in Public Sector Negotiations: Sovereignty Reviewed," *Journal of Collective Negotiations in the Public Sector* 3 (Spring 1974), pp. 147–166.

45. Paul F. Gerhart, "The Scope of Bargaining in Local Government Negotiations," *Labor Law Journal* 20 (August 1969), pp. 545–552.

46. W. Gary Vause, "Impasse Resolution in the Public Sector—Observations on the First Decade of Law and Practice Under the Florida PERA," *University of Florida Law Review* 37 (1985), pp. 105–188.

47. Peter Feuille, "Police Labor Relations and Multilateralism," *Journal of Collective Negotiations in the Public Sector* 3 (Summer 1974), p. 216.

48. Victor Gotbaum, "Collective Bargaining and the Union Leader," in Zagoria, *Public Workers,* pp. 83–84.

49. Michael Marmo, "Public Employee Collective Bargaining: A Mass-Mediated Process," *Journal of Collective Negotiations in the Public Sector* 13, no. 4 (1984), pp. 291–307.

50. "Characteristics of 'Sunshine' Laws in the 50 States," *The Chronicle of Higher Education,* October 10, 1984, p. 18.

51. George W. Bohlander, "Public Sector Grievance Arbitration: Structure and Administration," *Journal of Collective Negotiations in the Public Sector* 21, no. 4 (1992), pp. 282–283; Greg Stewart and Jeanette A. Davy, "An Empirical Examination of Grievance Resolution and Filing Rates in the Public and Private Sectors," *Journal of Collective Negotiations in the Public Sector* 21, no. 4 (1992), pp. 331–334.

52. Dane M. Partridge, "The Effect of Public Policy on Strike Activity in the Public Sector," *Journal of Collective Negotiations in the Public Sector* 19, no. 2 (1990), pp. 87–94.

53. "Crime Rate Is Same Despite Police Strike," *Miami Herald,* July 20, 1975, p. 15–A.

54. Paul D. Staudohar, "Reappraisal of the Right to Strike in California," *Journal of Collective Negotiations in the Public Sector* 15, no. 2 (1986), p. 91.

55. Theodore Kheel, "Resolving Deadlocks without Banning Strikes," *Monthly Labor Review* 91 (July 1969), pp. 62–63.

56. "Work Stoppages in Government," *Government Employee Relations Report,* 1986, p. 29.

57. Robert E. Doherty, "Trends in Strikes and Interest Arbitration in the Public Sector," *Labor Law Journal* 37 (August 1986), pp. 473–475.

58. Craig Olson, "Strikes, Strike Penalties, and Arbitration in Six States," *Industrial and Labor Relations Review* 39 (July 1986), p. 539.

59. Michael Marmo, "Public Employees: On-the-Job Discipline for Off-the-Job Behavior," *The Arbitration Journal* 40 (June 1985), p. 23; Marvin Hill, Jr., and Donald Dawson, "Discharge for Off-Duty Misconduct in the Private and Public Sectors," *Arbitration Journal* 40 (June 1985), pp. 24–33.

60. David H. Rosenbloom, "Public Personnel Administration and the Constitution: An Emergent Approach," *Public Administration Review* 35 (February 1975), pp. 52–59.

61. "Public Employees Entitled to

Respond to Dismissals," *Monthly Labor Review* 108 (May 1985), p. 46.

62. Richard B. Freeman and Casey Ichniowski, "Introduction: The Public Sector Look of American Unionism," *When Public Sector Workers Unionize,* eds. Richard B. Freeman and Casey Ichniowski (Chicago: The University of Chicago Press, 1988), pp. 1–13.

63. Tim Bornstein, "Legacies of Local Government Collective Bargaining in the 1970s," *Labor Law Journal* 31 (March 1980).

64. Lee A. Graf, Masoud Hemmasi, Kenneth E. Newgreen, and Warren R. Nielsen, "Profiles of Those Who Support Collective Bargaining in Institutions of Higher Learning and Why: An Empirical Examination," *Journal of Collective Negotiations in the Public Sector* 23, no. 2 (1994), p. 155; Kate Bronfenbenner and Tom Juravich, *Union Organizing in the Public Sector* (Ithaca, N.Y.: Cornell University Press, 1995).

65. These techniques were formulated in various discussions with Paul Gerhart of Case Western Reserve University.

66. Michael Marmo, "Public Employee Unions: The Political Imperative," *Journal of Collective Negotiations in the Public Sector* 4, no. 4 (1975), p. 371.

67. Paul D. Staudohar, "Quasi-Strikes by Public Employees," *Journal of Collective Negotiations in the Public Sector* 3 (Fall 1974), pp. 363–371.

68. "Justices Agree to Review Teachers Union's Widespread Use of Non-members' Agency Fees," *Daily Labor Report,* June 12, 1990, p. A–9.

69. U.S. Department of Labor, Labor-Management Services Administration, *Summary of Public Sector Labor Relations Policies, 1976* (Washington, D.C.: Government Printing Office, 1976), pp. 1–126. Totals are greater than 38 because some states have different impasse procedures for different types of employees; for example, Connecticut has mediation, fact-finding, and arbitration for state employees; fact-finding and arbitration for municipal employees; and mediation and fact-finding for teachers.

70. Mark D. Karper, "Fact Finding in Public Employment: Promise or Illusion, Revisited," *Journal of Collective Negotiations in the Public Sector* 23, no. 4 (1994), pp. 288–296.

71. David A. Dilts, Ahmad Karm, and Ali Rassuli, "Mediation in the Public Sector: Toward a Paradigm of Negotiations and Dispute Resolution," *Journal of Collective Negotiations in the Public Sector* 19, no. 1 (1990), pp. 49–50.

72. Paul F. Gerhart and John E. Drotning, "Dispute Settlement and the Intensity of Mediation," *Industrial Relations* 19 (Fall 1980), pp. 352–358.

73. Steven Briggs and Daniel J. Koys, "An Empirical Investigation of Public Sector Mediator Effectiveness," *The Journal of Collective Negotiations in the Public Sector* 19, no. 2 (1990), pp. 121–126.

74. Thomas P. Gilroy and Anthony Sinicropi, "Impasse Resolution in Public Employment: A Current Assessment," *Industrial and Labor Relations Review* 25 (July 1972), pp. 500–501.

75. Stanley W. Elsea, David Dilts, and Lawrence J. Haber, "Factfinders and Arbitrators in Iowa: Are They the Same Neutrals?" *Journal of Collective Negotiations in the Public Sector* 19, no. 1 (1990), pp. 61–81.

76. Kenneth M. Jennings, Steve K. Paulson, and Steven A. Williamson, "Fact-finding in Perspective," *Government Union Review* 8 (Summer 1987), pp. 54–70; Nels Nelson, "Fact-finders View the Factfinding Process," *The Journal of Collective Negotiations in the Public Sector* 19, no. 2 (1990), pp. 141–149.

77. For an excellent review of the distinctive nature of arbitration in the public sector, see Helen LaVan, "Arbitration in the Public Sector: A Current Perspective," *Journal of Collective Negotiations in the Public Sector* 19, no. 2 (1990), pp. 153–163.

78. Paul F. Gerhart and John E. Drotning, "Do Uncertain Cost/Benefit Estimates Prolong Public-Sector Disputes?" *Monthly Labor Review* 103 (Sept. 1980), pp. 26–30.

79. David E. Bloom, "Is Arbitration *Really* Compatible with Bargaining?" *Industrial Relations* 20 (Fall 1980), pp. 233–244.

80. Henry S. Farber, "Role of Arbitration in Dispute Settlement," *Monthly Labor Review* 104 (May 1981), p. 34.

81. Karl O. Magnusen and Patricia A. Renovitch, "Dispute Resolution in Florida's Public Sector: Insight into Impasse," *Journal of Collective Negotiations in the Public Sector* 18, no. 3 (1989), pp. 241–252; J. Joseph Loewenberg, "Compulsory Arbitration in the United States," in *Compulsary Arbitration,* ed. J. J. Loewenberg et al. (Lexington, Mass.: D.C. Heath, 1976), p. 166; Hoyt N. Wheeler, "An Analysis of Fire Fighter Strikes," *Labor Law Journal* 26 (January 1975), pp. 17–20; and Charles M. Rehmus, "Legislated Interest Arbitration," *Proceedings of the Annual Meeting: Industrial Relations Research Association, 1974* (Madison, Wis.: Industrial Relations Research Association, 1975), pp. 307–312.

82. Lewin, Feuille, and Kochan, *Public Sector Labor Relations,* p. 229; and Charles M. Rehmus, "Public Employees: A Survey of Some Critical Problems on the Frontier of Collective Bargaining," *Labor Law Journal* 27 (September 1976), pp. 588–599.

83. Craig E. Overton and Max S. Wortman, "Compulsory Arbitration: A Strike Alternative for Police?" *Arbitration Journal* 28 (March 1974), p. 40.

84. Hoyt N. Wheeler, "Is Compromise the Rule in Fire Fighter Arbitration?" *Arbitration Journal* 29 (September 1974), pp. 176–185.

85. Marian M. Extejt and James R. Chelius, "The Behavioral Impact of Impasse Resolution Procedures," *Review of Public Personnel Administration* 5 (Spring 1985), pp. 46–47.

86. Frederic Champlin and Mario F. Bognanno, "'Chilling' Under Arbitration and Mixed Strike-Arbitration Regimes," *Journal of Labor Research* 6 (Fall 1985), pp. 375–386.

87. Karl O. Magnusen and Rodney G. Lim, "Special Master Mediation in Impasse Resolution: The Florida Experience," *Journal of Collective Negotiations in the Public Sector* 23, no. 4 (1994), pp. 348–356.

88. Frederic C. Champlin and Mario F. Bognanno, "Time Spent Processing Interest Arbitration Cases: The Minnesota Experience," *Journal of Collective Negotiations in the Public Sector* 14, no. 1 (1985), pp. 53–64.

89. Peter Feuille, "Final-Offer Arbitration and Negotiating Incentives," *Arbitration Journal* 32 (September 1977), pp. 203, 220.

90. Daniel Gallagher and M. D. Chaubey, "Impasse Behavior and Tri-Offer Arbitration in Iowa," *Industrial Relations* 21 (Spring 1982), p. 146; see also Daniel Gallagher and Richard Pegnetter, "Impasse Resolution Procedure under the Iowa Multistep Procedure," *Industrial and Labor Relations Review* 32 (April 1979), pp. 327–328.

91. Gregory G. Dell'omo, "Wage Disputes in Interest Arbitration: Arbitrators Weigh the Criteria," *The Arbitration Journal* 44 (June 1989), pp. 4–8.

92. Craig A. Olson and Paul Jarley, "Arbitration Decisions in Wisconsin Teacher Wage Disputes," *Industrial and Labor Relations Review* 44 (April 1991), p. 546.

93. J. H. Foegen, "Public Sector Strike-Prevention: Let the Taxpayer Decide," *Journal of Collective Negotiations in the Public Sector* 3 (Summer 1974), p. 223.

94. I. B. Helburn and J. L. Matthews, "The Referendum as an Alternative to Bargaining," *Journal of Collective Negotiations in the Public Sector* 9, no. 2 (1980), pp. 93–105.

95. Raymond L. Hogler and Curt Kriksciun, "Impasse Resolution in Public Sector Collective Negotiations: A Proposed Procedure," *Industrial Relations Law Journal* 6, no. 4 (1984), pp. 481–510.

96. Donald T. Barnum and I. B. Helburn, "Influence the Electorate Experience with Referenda on Public Employee Bargaining," *Industrial and Labor Relations Review* 35 (April 1982), pp. 330–342.
97. Steven M. Goldschmidt and Leland E. Stuart, "The Extent and Impact of Educational Policy Bargaining," *Industrial and Labor Relations Review* 39 (April 1986), pp. 350–356; Timothy Loney, "Public Sector Labor Relations Research: The First Generation," *Public Personnel Management* 18 (Summer 1989), pp. 162–175.
98. Lorraine M. McDonnell and Anthony Pascal, *Teacher Unions and Educational Reform* (Santa Monica, Calif.: RAND, 1988), pp. 1–3.
99. Joel M. Douglas, "The Impact of *NLRB* v. *Yeshiva University* on Faculty Unionism at Public Colleges and Universities," *Journal of College Negotiations in the Public Sector* 19, no. 1 (1990), p. 4.
100. Debra E. Blum, "Colleges' Financial Straits Could Improve Relations Between Officials and Faculty Unions, Some Say," *The Chronicle of Higher Education,* March 27, 1991, p. A18.
101. Douglas, "The Impact of *NLRB* v. *Yeshiva University* on Faculty Unionism," p. 4.
102. "Faculty and Campuses Represented by Certified Bargaining Agents," *Chronicle of Higher Education,* July 12, 1989, p. A16.
103. "Strike Continues as Graduate Assistants at UC Berkeley Reject University Offer," *Government Employee Relations Report,* December 7, 1992, p. 1,614.
104. Joel M. Douglas, "Faculty Senates as Labor Organizations: An Investigation of Governance Structures in Higher Education," *Labor Law Journal* 46 (February 1995), pp. 118–120.
105. Gwen B. Williams and Perry A. Zirkel, "Shift in Collective Bargaining Issues in Higher Education: A Review of the Literature," *Journal of Collective Negotiations in the Public Sector* 18, no. 1 (1989), pp. 73–86; Daniel J. Julius and Margaret K. Chandler, "Academic Bargaining Agents in Higher Education: Do Their Achievements Differ?" *Journal of Collective Negotiations in the Public Sector* 18, no. 1 (1989), pp. 9–58.
106. Debra E. Blum, "Walkout by Professors Is Settled at Wayne State, but Strikes Continue at Temple and Bridgeport," *The Chronicle of Higher Education,* September 19, 1990, p. A23.
107. John T. Delaney and Peter Feuille, "Police," in *Collective Bargaining in American Industry,* eds. David B. Lipsky and Clifford B. Donn (Lexington, Mass.: Lexington Books, 1987), pp. 263–303.
108. Gary Fink, ed., *Labor Unions* (Westport, Conn.: Greenwood Press, 1977), p. 103; Leo Troy, "The Proposed Fire Fighters' Labor Act of 1987: An Analysis and Critique," *Government Union Review* 8 (Summer 1987), pp. 4–6.
109. *Federal Labor Relations: A Program in Need of Reform* (Washington, D.C.: General Accounting Office, 1991), pp. 2–3; Barry E. Spapiro, "The Future of Labor Relations in the Federal Sector," *Labor Law Journal* 43 (August 1992), p. 510.

Labor Relations in Multinational Corporations and in Other Countries

15

With the development of a global economy, movement in Eastern Europe toward greater political democracy and market-oriented economies, and the elimination of trade and travel restrictions within the western European countries, the study of labor relations within multinational corporations (MNCs) and foreign countries becomes imperative to today's student. This chapter begins with a general discussion of the operations of multinational corporations in a global economy and unions' approaches and problems in dealing with MNCs. Then, principal characteristics of the labor relations systems of the major trading partners of the United States are presented.

Multinational Corporations and Transnational Collective Bargaining

The growing interdependency among nations and the activities of **multinational corporations (MNCs)** have become important facets of economic life. Although multinational corporations have existed for more than 150 years, their numbers and share of world output have expanded their importance and visibility in recent years.

To appreciate the enormity of the MNCs, note that the Conference Board has reported that of the 100 top economic units in the world, 47 are multinational corporations. For example, General Motors is not only the world's largest corporation, but it is also the twentieth largest economic unit. Its sales of $126.9 billion are greater than the gross national products (GNPs) of Finland and Denmark combined. Ford's sales of $96.9 billion are greater than the GNPs of Norway, Saudi Arabia, and Indonesia. U.S. corporations in the top 100 economic units include IBM, General Electric, DuPont, Philip Morris, and Procter & Gamble.[1]

MNCs are now producing as well as marketing their products in several countries, instead of producing only at the home base and selling abroad, and they are doing so with increasing impact. Many of the largest MNCs have been labeled "stateless corporations" because a high percentage of their sales and a high percentage of their assets are outside their home country. Well-known U.S. firms with over 50 percent of their sales outside the United States include Gillette, Colgate, IBM, NCR, Coca Cola, Dow Chemical, Xerox, and Caterpillar. Those having more than 50 percent of their assets in other countries include Gillette and Xerox.[2] U.S. MNCs had worldwide assets of $8.8 trillion, sales of $6.3 trillion, and total employment of 29.7 million employees. The largest employment is in the United Kingdom with 917,000, followed by Canada with 873,000, and Mexico with 661,000.[3]

Foreign direct investments in the United States reached $47.2 billion in 1994, an 80 percent increase, which followed an increase of 71 percent in 1993. Investments from the United Kingdom accounted for $19.0 billion, half of the total. Japanese investments in the United States fell for the fourth year in a row to one-tenth of the total. U.S. direct foreign investments reached $57.8 billion, for a total of $785.0 billion.[4]

Foreign-owned companies accounted for only 4 percent of the total employment in the United States (7 percent of manufacturing) with over one-fourth of the employment by foreign-owned firms being located in California, New York, and Texas. Typically, these firms are concentrated in capital-intensive industries such as manufacturing, employ a higher-skilled labor force, and pay higher wages (a payroll-per-employee average 29 percent higher than U.S.-owned firms).[5]

Exchange rates have a great deal to do with the trade between countries and production within a specific country. The importance of fluctuating exchange rates is reflected in Exhibit 15.1, which shows the indexes of hourly compensation costs for production workers in manufacturing for 30 countries during four time periods from 1975 to 1994. In 1994, hourly compensation costs for manufacturing production workers in Austria, Belgium, Germany, Japan, Denmark, Finland, Netherlands, Norway, Sweden, and Switzerland were 10 to 60 percent higher than those in the United States. Compensation costs were 80 percent of the U.S. figure in the United Kingdom, 80 percent in Australia, 67 percent in Spain, 28 to 37 percent in Hong Kong, Korea, and Taiwan, and 15 percent in Mexico (the peso declined 55 percent in 1995).

Because the U.S. dollar has fallen in value in relation to the currencies of most other countries, the relative hourly compensation costs of these countries have increased. For example, in 1985 Japan's hourly cost was 50 percent of that of the United States; however, it had increased to 125 percent by 1994. In Germany, in 1985 the cost was 74 percent of that of the United States; it had risen to 160 percent by 1994[6] (see Exhibit 15.1 for comparisons).

Operating in different countries creates opportunities for MNCs to bypass protective tariffs by making parts in one country and assembling the final product in another. For example, the European Community accused Ricoh, a maker of photocopiers, of making 90 percent of its parts in Japan, doing the assembly work in the United States, and shipping products from the United States as U.S. exports. Such situations create other possibilities in the auto industry because England limits the

Exhibit 15.1 Indexes of Hourly Compensation Costs for Production Workers in Manufacturing for 30 Countries or Areas, 1975 to 1994

COUNTRY OR AREA	PERCENTAGE OF WORKFORCE IN UNIONS	INDEX (UNITED STATES = 100) 1975	1980	1985	1990	1992	1994	COMPENSATION COSTS IN 1994 DOLLARS
United States	16.8%	100	100	100	100	100	100	$17.10
Canada	29.2	92	86	84	107	105	92	15.23
Brazil	22.0	14	14	9	17	—	—	—
Mexico	27.4	31	30	16	12	15	15	2.57
Australia	39.6	84	82	61	88	80	80	13.68
Hong Kong	18.0	12	15	14	22	24	28	4.79
Israel	56.0	35	39	31	57	56	53	9.06
Japan	24.1	48	57	50	87	101	125	21.38
Korea	10.3	5	10	10	28	30	37	6.33
New Zealand	34.3	50	54	34	56	49	52	8.90
Singapore	14.5	13	15	19	22	31	37	6.33
Sri Lanka	30.0	4	2	2	2	2	—	—
Taiwan	34.9	6	10	11	27	32	32	5.47
Austria	53.0	68	87	56	114	122	127	21.72
Belgium	76.6	101	134	69	127	133	134	22.91
Denmark	80.0	99	111	63	126	124	120	20.52
Finland	81.0	72	84	62	139	166	110	18.81
France	10.0	71	91	58	103	104	100	17.10
Germany	37.2	100	125	74	144	160	160	27.36
Greece	30.0	27	38	28	45	46	—	—
Ireland	55.0	47	60	45	79	83	—	—
Italy	15.0	73	81	57	119	121	95	16.26
Luxembourg		100	122	59	110	116	—	—
Netherlands	24.0	103	123	67	125	128	122	20.86
Norway	65.8	107	119	82	147	143	122	20.86
Portugal	42.0	25	21	12	24	31	27	4.62
Spain	11.0	41	61	37	78	83	67	11.46
Sweden	84.0	113	127	75	141	150	110	18.81
Switzerland	32.4	96	113	75	139	144	145	24.80
United Kingdom	36.0	52	76	48	84	91	80	13.68

Note: Dash indicates data not available.

SOURCE: Janet Kmitch, Pedro Laboy, and Sandra Van Damme, "International Comparisons in Manufacturing Compensation," *Monthly Labor Review* 118 (October 1995), p. 6; *Foreign Labor Trends* (Washington, D.C.: U.S. Department of Labor, Bureau of International Labor Affairs, 1994–1995).

LABOR RELATIONS IN ACTION

Dealing with an MNC—A Scenario

When the 500 employees of a forklift factory in Irvine, Scotland, reported to work, they were instructed to attend a plant meeting in the company cafeteria. At 9:00 A.M. the plant manager and senior staff announced that the company was willing to invest $60 million in the present plant, close two production lines at its Dutch factory, and increase employment at the Irvine plant by 1,000. In return, the company wanted the employees to take a 14 percent pay cut; and they had 48 hours to decide whether or not to accept this proposal.

The next day each employee received a letter from the company president, who was located in Portland, Oregon, stating that he did not know whether Irvine was the best alternative. He indicated that he was trying to make up his mind whether the Irvine plant should be the lead plant in Europe. At the bottom of the letter, each employee could vote "yes" or "no."

Only 11 employees voted no. The plant industrial relations manager stated that if the employees had refused the proposal, the work would have been done elsewhere. The union president made no bones about his bitterness; he called it "industrial rape—do it or else." Thus, while the employees in Irvine considered their destiny, at corporate headquarters the staff calculated the alternatives in the far corners of the world through the screen of a desktop personal computer.

The corporate management could have taken the following approach: The Irvine employees could have been told that the work was going to the Dutch plant if the 14 percent pay cut was not approved. Then the Dutch employees could have been told that the Irvine employees were willing to go as far as a 14 percent cut and could have been asked for a proposal. Next the Portland employees could have been told that the

Japanese share of its auto market to 11 percent, France to 3 percent, and Italy allows only 3,300 cars per year. With Japanese automakers locating in the United States, such issues will provide challenges in trade between countries.[7]

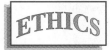

MNCs have the capacity to force concessions from unions by threatening to shift production to another country and essentially pit one group of employees against another. One automaker that operates a plant in Ohio sought to introduce new technology; the union resisted because the membership would lose jobs. The company then took a number of the union leaders to a new plant in Juarez, Mexico—just across the border from El Paso—showed them the technologies used in the plant, and said: "It is your choice. Either you concede what we are asking in terms of bargaining or the work that you do in Ohio will be transferred to Juarez. If you think this is an idle threat, this is the plant. This is the production process."[8] See "Labor Relations in Action" for an explanation of how MNCs may deal with employees in different countries to achieve their goals. Although such practices are not illegal, one could easily argue that the practices are not ethical.

European employees were more cooperative and that unless there were fewer grievances, arbitrations, and conflicts, work would be transferred from Portland for economic reasons.

Because employees and their unions do not have a systematic communication mechanism, rarely exchange vital information, and do in fact compete with each other for jobs, MNCs have the opportunity to take advantage of the situation in the manner just described.

In this case, two days after the employees voted "yes" or "no," the votes were tallied, the pay cut was accepted, and the company president telexed the Dutch plant manager and told him that the work normally done in Holland would be moving to Scotland. The end result was the termination of a number of Dutch employees and the early retirement of the plant manager.

Because Dutch law requires advance consultation about plant closures, the union took the company to court. The judge ordered the company to discuss its strategy with members of the factory work councils and reveal the corporate plan. The union did not like the plan and went to court again.

After a long legal battle, the company struck a deal—the employees would drop the suit, and the company would not transfer production for three years. As a result, the Scottish employees were held in limbo during the interim period.

During all this time, the director of European operations continued his concern about increasing shares of the market gained by Japanese producers.

SOURCE: Barry Newman, "Single-Country Unions of Europe Try to Cope with Multinationals," *The Wall Street Journal,* November 30, 1983, pp. 1, 24.

Organized labor has been critical of the effect of U.S. MNCs on employment and labor relations for the following reasons:

- U.S. MNCs' foreign investments deplete capital resources needed for domestic investment and undermine economic growth and new job creation at home.
- U.S. MNCs export U.S. technology to exploit low-cost foreign labor, depriving American employees of their rightful share of the rewards of technology.
- U.S. MNCs substitute imports from their affiliates in low-wage countries for American-made goods, thereby undermining the American wage standard, depressing economic conditions at home, and decreasing employment and payrolls.
- U.S. MNCs displace U.S. exports with foreign-produced goods from their foreign affiliates, thereby adversely affecting our trade balance.[9]

Foreign MNCs have grown rapidly and installed facilities in the United States. Unions have often viewed these MNCs with suspicion, but the management and employment practices tend to be more similar to those of home-based firms than dissimilar. The labor relations activities and decisions tend to be locally determined and highly decentralized. American unions have found that organizing foreign-based MNCs has been just as difficult as organizing a home-based company. In addition, the management of the various plants of foreign-based MNCs uses essentially the same tactics to keep unions out of the plant. These tactics include use of lawyers and management consultants, positive human resources management, consultation with employees on decisions, delays allowed under National Labor Relations Board procedures, and local politicians making statements to support the company. Unions essentially use the same organizing tactics, with the addition of negative publicity directed toward the foreign owners and appeals to American patriotism. With these counteractive tactics, the results of elections have not been significantly different—fewer than 50 percent wins for the unions. Whenever American unions have contact with foreign-based unions, these contacts are generally of the information-sharing nature.[10]

In some cases, MNCs transplant their management practices into their foreign affiliates. In recent years, Japanese MNCs have been successful in making this transfer in unionized plants. In Fremont, California, New United Motor Manufacturing, Inc., the joint venture between General Motors and Toyota, was successful; successes have also been noted by the Japanese-owned MNC Sumitomo Rubber, which purchased the Dunlop tire plant in Birmingham, England. The Fremont plant had one of the worst labor relations records in the United States in 1982, but its performance became one of the best in the industry by 1992.

Japanese practices that have been introduced include elimination of executive perks, such as reserved parking places and separate cafeterias, work teams of six to eight members who rotate jobs, emphasis placed on trust between managers and employees, managers spending more time on the shop floor with the employees, regular meetings to inform employees about production and financial results of the company, wearing of "team" jackets by managers and employees, flexibility in job assignments, and holding each employee responsible for the quality of products produced.

Not all results of management transfer are positive, however, especially when sales decline, the foreign manager does not speak the local language, or employees resist imposition of a new way of doing things. In Forrest City, Arkansas, for example, the Sanyo Company, maker of televisions and microwave ovens, had only one Japanese manager who spoke English, so that every meeting required an interpreter. In 1985, when sales lagged, the company demanded medical insurance cuts, changes in the seniority system, and the right to shift employees from job to job. The union reacted by striking for three weeks, and there were incidents of stone-throwing, tire-slashing, and charges of an attempted fire-bombing, resulting in 39 persons arrested.[11] The plant has since closed.

Unions particularly have difficulty dealing with MNCs for the following reasons:

1. *If a strike occurs* in the parent company country, the union does not shut down the flow of financial resources to the corporation. Operations in other countries continue to function and generate profits, which may relieve management of much pressure in negotiations and reduce the costs of the strike.
2. *MNCs have an internal source of products* from facilities in several countries and use this position as leverage to bargain down wages, benefits, and other conditions of employment (called **whipsawing** the union). If a strike occurs at one facility, the MNCs increase production at other units, destroying the potency of the strike.[12] Many specific examples of whipsawing can be identified. General Motors was able to expand the work week from 37.5 hours to 40 hours by convincing the union in Germany that it must increase hours to retain competitiveness. General Motors has considered increasing its auto production in Brazil and Mexico as part of its wage concession demands, and when Canadian unions resisted wage concessions, GM considered shifting production back to the United States.[13] While there are specific examples of using production shifts in bargaining, it does not appear that firms locate production facilities overseas for the primary purpose of discouraging strikes in their home country.[14]
3. *MNCs with complex tiers of management* do not delegate authority to local management to make labor relations decisions, thereby complicating the negotiation process because unions do not know who is in charge.[15] Empirical evidence indicates that most unions have not encountered different behavior between domestic and foreign-owned MNCs, but there seems to be a wider variation in behavior among the MNCs than among single-nation corporations in terms of grievance settlement prior to arbitration, amount of local autonomy in negotiations, and difficulty in negotiating the first agreement.[16] However, because budget and investment decisions are made at the home office, local negotiations are certainly affected.
4. *MNCs shift profits to different facilities,* manipulate prices on internal transactions, and change marketing emphasis, confusing the unions in negotiations when they seek the facts necessary to address and resolve collective bargaining issues.

Because U.S. unions are accustomed to bargaining on ability to pay and are entitled to wage and financial information that allows them to conduct informed negotiations, they are frustrated when MNCs furnish only information that is required by law. Such information about MNCs' locating plants in foreign facilities and operating data on these plants may be refused by the MNCs with the approval of the NLRB.[17]

Union Approaches to Multinational Bargaining and Employer Reactions

A primary motivator for American and foreign-based unions to seek transnational bargaining and to standardize labor conditions among the MNCs is to lessen competition from lower-wage areas and to protect their own standards—in other words, to take wages out of competition. To combat the power of the MNCs and to seek objectives that are mutually beneficial to the unions and their members, union leaders have tried two main approaches: (a) collective bargaining and (2) legislative enactment. Through collective bargaining, unions have either attempted to bargain directly with the MNCs or coordinate their bargaining activities with unions in other countries by sharing information and supporting one another's activities.

The unions have become frustrated with attempts to achieve any degree of transnational bargaining, so they have concentrated on the adoption of codes of conduct to regulate MNC behavior. The International Labor Organization, a tripartite organization with governments, employers, and unions from 150 countries represented, established labor codes that state the MNCs should give priority to human rights, employment, safety, occupational development, social justice, and promotion and advancement of local nationals and should provide stable employment and pay comparable wages.

The Organization for Economic Cooperation and Development, an international organization headquartered in Paris, has also established "Guidelines for MNCs" concerning conduct in labor-management relations. These guidelines include certain rights: the rights to organize and bargain collectively, to have access to data for negotiations, to be trained as a member of the workforce, and to be given advance notice of changes in operations. Further, subsidiaries of MNCs are expected to observe employment standards comparable to those in the host countries; MNCs are expected not to threaten to shift production to other countries to influence negotiations or to prevent unionization, and local management representatives should be authorized to negotiate on behalf of the MNCs.[18]

Unions, as well as some governments, have asserted that collective bargaining on a national basis has considerable limitations in facing MNCs. This assertion is based on the belief that MNCs have adopted global strategies, so a union acting alone within one nation cannot effectively respond. Likewise, some governments are uneasy about the fact that MNCs cannot easily be made accountable to any one country's economic and social policies. Moreover, there has been persistent fear that if a union or government in one country acted without the support of unions or governments in other countries, it would risk transfer of operations by the MNC to a more hospitable nation.[19]

The creation of the European Community has led to a resurgence of interests in prospects of transnational collective bargaining. However, recent initiatives have taken the form of joint consultation at a transnational level rather than true collective bargaining.

There have been several cases of multinational consultation in Europe. For example, Thomson-Grand Public established European Work Councils with the European Metalworkers Federation, which included employees from France, Germany, Italy, Spain, and the United Kingdom. Volkswagen established European-level work councils with representatives from VW, Audi, and Seat (Spain) in 1990. However, none of the arrangements envisioned any transnational collective bargaining—the arrangements are limited to information exchange and consultation.[20]

The reality is that transnational collective bargaining remains a distant possibility, at least until a European monetary system is established.[21] With the uncertainty of the Maastricht treaty, which would create a unitary currency system in the European Community, the development of a single currency is still in its future.[22]

Although some form of transnational labor relations seems to be inevitable, most MNCs generally consider it a distant prospect and one that will not be lightly entertained by management. Part of management's opposition stems from the unions' potential for shutting down production internationally. Further, transnational bargaining would introduce a tri-level structure of bargaining that would include multinational negotiations, followed by national ones, then local. This additional level would increase the complexity of negotiations as well as companies' vulnerability to strikes at the international level without a comparable reduction in vulnerability at the national and local levels.

In some cases, countries themselves are not encouraging investments by MNCs; taxation policies, building limitations, requirements for local partners, the possibility of nationalization and expropriation of facilities, and the risks of political uncertainties are factors deterring MNC investment. Less-developed countries seek additional investments by MNCs for economic stimulus to the countries' development, income, employment programs, and so on, and MNCs find these countries attractive because of the low wage structure, tax incentives, and political guarantees. Such advantages are particularly appealing to the MNC that must operate in a very competitive product market. But when unions press via transnational bargaining for improved wages, benefits, and working conditions—all socially desirable goals for the populace—they become a force running counter to the short-run national economic goals of the country. The economic boost MNCs can give a developing nation will not occur if firms fail to locate there; MNCs might well decide to avoid countries with the high wages and benefits that transnational bargaining has instituted.

Obstacles for Unions in Bargaining with Multinational Corporations

American and foreign unions face formidable tasks in their efforts to arrange transnational bargaining because they must be successful in mediating and balancing the conflicting interests of different groups encompassed by the MNCs' employees, labor leaders, companies, and governments.[23] In fact, unions themselves provide some of the more important obstacles to transnational bargaining; however, these obstacles are not insurmountable. Only when these obstacles are overcome can attention be turned to external factors.

Differences in Labor Relations Laws Legal systems for labor relations vary widely among countries. There are different methods for determining union representation, different union jurisdictions and structure, and differences in the scope of bargaining.[24]

Absence of a Central Authority Unions lack strong, centralized decision-making authority regarding transnational affairs, and most national union leaders are reluctant to allow an international body to make decisions that affect their unions and members.

Cultural Differences Among complicating factors are the differences in ideological and religious beliefs among, for example, free trade unions and socialist- or communist-linked unions. Such differences have made joint undertakings between unions in the free world and elsewhere almost impossible.

Lack of Coordination of Activities Unions have not been very successful in coordinating their international bargaining, boycott, and strike activities. An excellent example occurred in the last major rubber strike of Goodyear, Uniroyal, B.F. Goodrich, and Firestone. Each had extensive overseas operations. Support for the U.S. strikes came from the International Federation of Chemical, Energy, and General Workers Unions (ICEF), which has affiliates in Europe, North America, and Japan. The ICEF Rubber Division approved a ban on overtime by employees of nonstruck companies and a system of monitoring and preventing shipments to the United States. At the end of the strike—the longest rubber strike in U.S. history—the ICEF claimed that its efforts had had a significant effect on the bargaining outcome; however, the facts seemed to contradict this claim. A study by Northrup and Rowan of the U.S. rubber workers' strike did not reveal a single instance of interference with tire shipments from Europe, Japan, or North America; in fact, they found that imports jumped substantially in anticipation of the strike and never fell below the pre-strike level. Furthermore, even Canadian imports were significantly increased during the strike, reversing what had occurred several years before, when U.S. rubber workers refused to support a strike by Canadian rubber workers.[25]

Differing National Priorities The economic, social, legal, and political differences among countries serve as yet another obstacle to transnational bargaining. Few if any countries would subvert their national needs in the interest of developing an international system of labor relations.

Employer Resistance Employer resistance is less obvious than other obstacles at this time, mostly because of the inability of the unions to overcome the other hurdles that they face. Once the initial hurdles are overcome, employers' opinions and attitudes concerning transnational collective bargaining will no doubt emerge, but in the meantime, MNCs may sit idly by until the unions get their own houses in order.

Activities of Multinational Unions

Although much of what unions have accomplished in achieving international cooperation and coordination is considered by some a "public relations coup," there have been some tangible activities among unions. The International Confederation of Free Trade Unions and International Trade Secretariats have proposed that the United Nations adopt charters for MNCs, specifying their obligation to recognize trade unions, observe fair labor standards, observe prevailing wage rates, attempt betterment of social conditions, reinvest profits made from less-developed countries in those countries, establish works councils worldwide, and use labor-intensive technology when possible. In Western Europe, unions have backed the European Community statutes that require employee participation and works councils' agreement on such issues as rules for recruitment, career advancement, dismissal, training, health and safety, welfare and social programs, pay methods, and holidays. In addition, four multinational labor organizations have been quite active in international activities: ICEF, International Metalworkers Federation (IMF), International Federation of Petroleum and Chemical Workers (IFPCW), and International Federation of Air Line Pilots Associations (IFALPA). Their activities thus far have essentially included gathering information about MNCs, providing education programs, and coordinating collective bargaining activities (although the federations themselves do no actual collective bargaining).[26] Each of these organizations believes that it must establish a firm foundation upon which to develop more penetrating actions in the future.

Effects of Unions on Multinational Corporations

Research conducted mostly in European countries has indicated that unions have had little direct effect on investment and production allocation policies of MNCs. However, they have had considerable indirect effect because union relations with employers help shape the investment climate of a country.

Thus far, MNCs rarely have been able to afford to switch production to other countries as a bargaining or union intimidation tactic because of the costs involved. They no doubt would shift production to another country in cases where a labor dispute stops production and the move is economically and practically possible. However, such decisions are considerably limited because companies must have the necessary excess production capacity available and management must expect the labor dispute to last sufficiently long to justify any shift in production before it would be feasible.

Overall, little evidence exists of substantial negative effects of MNCs on labor relations in countries in which they operate. They usually offer prevailing or superior wage standards and provide comparable working conditions for several reasons. The strengths of unions in the respective countries, the highly integrated and institutionalized nature of labor relations systems, and the socioeconomic and political climates of the countries have clearly constrained the potential for direct adverse effect.[27]

Conclusions and Predictions on Transnational Bargaining

Systematic investigations of transnational collective bargaining reveal that it does not yet exist in any realistic form and is not likely to occur in the near future. MNCs are generally opposed to it, and trade unions are not of a single mind regarding its desirability. While there have been several cases of information exchange between multinational unions and MNCs and a few instances of union-management consultation, only one trade union secretariat—the International Transport Workers Federation (ITF)—has actually negotiated an agreement (with shipping companies). Further, only in the unique U.S.-Canadian environment does much transnational bargaining occur.

There has been no identifiable trend toward transnational collective bargaining by companies and unions in the United States, Europe, or Japan. Some believe that no effective transnational collective bargaining will occur in the near future. However, others believe that such collective bargaining is inevitable. It will probably develop first in either the European Community, North America, or Central America and deal initially with general topics, such as employment protection, investment policies, and codes of fair practices, before broadening into other bargaining topics.

Unions in Other Countries

With the growing interdependency among nations, major improvements in communication and travel between countries, and the increasing role of multinational corporations (MNCs), there is an imperative need to learn more about labor relations systems in other parts of the world. Books have been written about many of the specific topics in this chapter, and no attempt will be made to present detailed descriptions or analyses of labor relations systems in the countries mentioned. This section presents unique and interesting features of a variety of countries with the hope of encouraging readers to pursue more thorough investigations. Its coverage ranges from the developing countries of Latin and South America to the countries nearest our borders—Mexico and Canada—to the major trading partners of the United States such as Japan and the Western European countries. The extent of discussion of each country's labor relations system is determined by its proximity to the United States; its trade, economic, and political relationships with the United States; and its uniqueness among the world's labor relations systems. From these discussions, specific attention is directed toward multinational corporations and transnational collective bargaining.

Many U.S. residents tend to view the rest of the world in terms of their own patterns of living. The fact is that virtually no country has a labor relations system like ours. One example of the differences between countries is the degree of employee protection against termination without cause. In the United States, only 20 percent of employees have such protection. In other words, the vast majority of American employees can be terminated from their employment without any justification unless termination is a violation of a contractual agreement, such as a collective bargaining agreement, or a law. As shown in Exhibit 15.2, 50 percent of Canadian employees are protected, and 90 percent in Australia and the United Kingdom are protected. In Belgium, France, Germany, Italy, and Spain, 100 percent of em-

Exhibit 15.2 Percentage of the Labor Force That is Protected against Termination without Cause

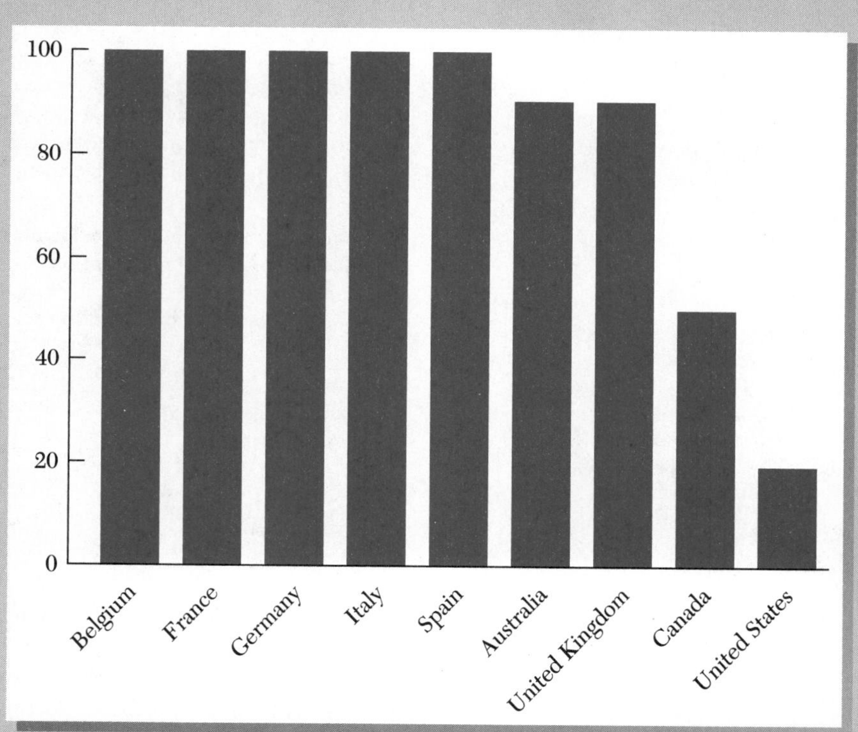

SOURCE: Hoyt N. Wheeler and Jaques Rojot, "General Comments," *Workplace Justice: Employment Obligation in International Perspective* (Columbia, S.C.: University of South Carolina Press, 1992), pp. 368–369.

ployees are protected against termination without cause. As discussed in Chapter 10, there are basic principles for terminating employees for cause.[28]

Canada has several major departures from typical U.S. labor relations practices. Unions of Europe have much closer ties to political parties; Japanese unions are organized on the enterprise level; Latin American unions are split along ideological lines. By contrast, the U.S. labor relations system is based on majority rule, exclusive representation for bargaining agents, and political independence. Exhibit 15.3 presents an overview of distinguishing features of foreign labor relations systems; the following discussion briefly explains these systems.

Exhibit 15.3 Overview of Distinguishing Features of U.S. and Foreign Labor Relations Systems

United States
Exclusive bargaining representation
Majority rule
Political independence

Canada
Influence by unions and companies from U.S.
Two major linguistic and cultural groups
Decentralized and fragmented collective bargaining
Legal influence within provinces

Central and South America
Wide variation in the degree of sophistication in labor relations systems
Close connection between trade unions and political parties
Voluminous labor codes and government regulations that cover wages and terms of employment
Predominantly negotiations at plant level only

Western Europe
Exclusive bargaining representation nonexistent
Much negotiation between employer association and union confederation with individual bargaining under the resulting agreement
Many fringe benefits established by law
Worker participation mandated in many countries

Japan
Labor-management consultation/Teamwork
Lifetime employment in large firms
Enterprise unions
Wage system with much weight on seniority

Australia
Decentralized bargaining
Nonunion bargaining
Unfair dismissal law

Eastern Europe
Little collective bargaining
No labor agreements

Another distinguishing feature between labor relations in the United States and that of other countries of the world is the percentage of employees who are union members. Exhibit 15.4 shows that the United States is classified among the least unionized countries such as Columbia, Egypt, France, Mexico, Portugal, and Spain. Denmark, Finland, and Sweden are the most unionized countries, with 80 percent or more of the workforce being unionized.

Canada

Canada's labor relations system is affected by a number of variables: foreign influences, climate, natural resources, and two major linguistic and cultural groups. Its economy is subject to cyclical fluctuations resulting from harsh winters, seasonality of its industries, and foreign influences (mostly the United States). In addition, Canada's geographical spread and regional concentration of resources and production have led to decentralized and fragmented collective bargaining. The penetration of U.S. corporations into Canada has had a significant effect on Canadian labor relations due to the fact that many major decisions still are made in the United States. The French- and English-speaking division of Canada has produced two distinct labor movements; further, relationships between management, which is primarily unilingually English-speaking, and the predominantly French-speaking workforce have not been ideal.[29] In 1995, the citizens of Quebec, Canada's

Exhibit 15.4 **Comparison of Worldwide Union Density: 1994**

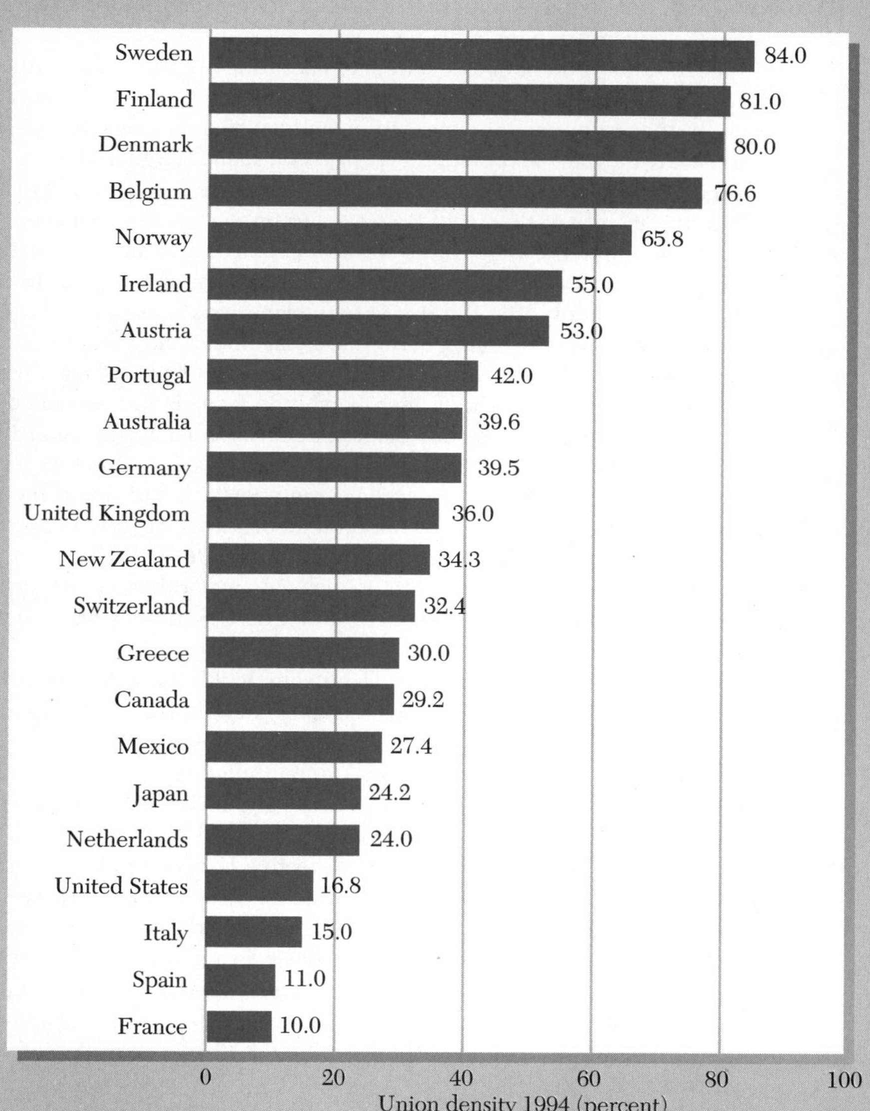

SOURCE: *Foreign Labor Trends* (Washington, D.C.: U.S. Department of Labor, Bureau of International Affairs, 1994–1995).

predominantly French-speaking province, voted by a slight margin to remain in Canada. Of the four largest labor unions in Canada, three are in the public sector. Half of the largest 16 unions have their headquarters in the United States. The Canadian Autoworkers and the Canadian Paperworkers are two of the largest unions and were formerly affiliated with U.S.-based unions.

Forty-four percent of assets in manufacturing are foreign controlled; so is 48.1 percent of the revenue and 47.2 percent of the profits. On the union side, 50.4 percent of the union membership in manufacturing belongs to the international unions, down from 89.6 percent in 1972. With such foreign influence, the effects of international unions in Canada have been questioned. Researchers have found no difference in either the incidence or duration of strikes between domestically owned and foreign-owned firms or between national and international unions. Thus, researchers concluded that the presence of multinational institutions, coupled with the complexities they bring to the labor relations process, does not appear to increase the overall conflict between management and labor in Canada.

In 1956, union membership in Canada and the United States was about one-third of the labor force. Union membership in Canada has remained at about the same strength, while there has been serious membership erosion in the United States. Since 1980, unions in the United States have been unable to recruit sufficient members to offset job losses and membership, and union membership has fallen to less than 16 percent of the total labor force. At the same time, Canadian unions have gained 700,000 members, an increase of 20 percent.[30] Unions in Canada have used their strength to achieve major bargaining gains and have wielded significant political influence, while the U.S. unions have been placed in a defensive bargaining and political position.

Collective bargaining in Canada remains highly localized, with the predominant bargaining unit being the single-establishment union. This bargaining arrangement prevails in over 60 percent of the contracts covering 500 employees or more, and covers over 50 percent of Canada's union members. Corporatewide bargaining occurs in railways, communications, airlines, and broadcasting due to the highly integrated technology in these industries.[31]

In terms of public policy toward collective bargaining, Canada differs significantly from the United States. The distinction between mandatory and voluntary subjects for collective bargaining has never been adopted in Canada. There is no such thing as a right-to-work law in Canada; in fact, the provinces of Quebec, Manitoba, and British Columbia impose the agency shop as a minimum requirement. British Columbia and Manitoba require the collective bargaining agreements to include "just cause" provisions, although Manitoba excludes probationary employees from coverage.[32]

Unlike the United States, Canadian law does not allow employers to conduct lengthy election campaigns against unions. Every Canadian province, except Alberta and Nova Scotia, allows unions to be certified without any secret ballot election. The union certification process in Canada is faster, campaigns are less protracted, and fewer employer unfair labor practices occur, mostly because the labor boards have greater remedial powers, such as automatic certification if the true wishes of employees cannot be determined.[33]Unions are required only to obtain 60 percent of the employees' signatures on authorization cards before the union will be certified. In addition, several of the Canadian provinces—British Columbia, Quebec, Manitoba, and Ontario—have assisted new unions in obtaining the first contract with an employer by requiring interest arbitration when negotiations and mediation efforts fail.[34]

During strikes, employers in the provinces of British Columbia, Ontario, and Quebec are prohibited from hiring striker replacements (temporary or permanent),[35] which has not led to a greater number of strikes or longer strikes.[36] In Ontario and Manitoba, firms that provide strike-breaking services are outlawed. Canadian legislation is more favorable to public-sector bargaining; the federal government and all of the provinces have extended the right to bargain to the vast majority of public employees. In addition, fewer restrictions are placed on negotiable issues in Canada, and bargaining is practiced more extensively in Canada than in the U.S. public sector.[37]

Business groups were vociferously outraged at the passage of these laws, and they contended that the bargaining power between the parties leaned heavily toward unions. However, research on the effect of striker replacement legislation on wage settlements in Canadian manufacturing between 1966 and 1985 found no support for a distortion of the balance of bargaining power between the parties.[38]

In 1991, the Supreme Court of Canada rendered a ruling opposite to the *Beck* decision in the United States (see Chapter 11). Unions can use membership dues for activities not directly related to collective bargaining, including political contributions. If the decision had gone the other way, unions would have seen their political activities thwarted by lack of funds and a restriction on their support for the New Democratic Party (NDP).[39]

Trade with other countries represents 30 percent of Canada's gross national product, and over 70 percent of this trade is with the United States. As a result, Canada's Free Trade Agreement (FTA) with the United States (not to be confused with NAFTA) has had greater significance in Canada and is a greater public-policy issue than in the United States. Canadian unions have long been critical of the FTA and have concluded that Canada has not prospered under the agreement. Since the agreement, the unemployment rate has risen to over 10 percent, the economy has stagnated, plant closures have accelerated, and Prime Minister Mulroney's popularity declined to a record low, after which he resigned from office.[40]

The two major federations, the Canadian Labour Council (CLC) and the Canadian Federation of Labor (CFL), continue their long-standing opposition to NAFTA. They maintain that Canada has been ill served by the U.S.-Canada FTA and that expanding free trade to Mexico would cause numerous manufacturing jobs to be lost to Mexico without improving conditions for the Mexican workers.[41]

Mexico, Central and South America

Collective bargaining in Central and South America is far less extensive and sophisticated than corresponding activities in the United States; however, the number of agreements has been increasing. About one-fourth of the employees are covered by labor agreements in Mexico, Venezuela, and Argentina, much more than in the

United States. This amount reflects more of a government extension of contract terms than actual industrywide bargaining patterns. The extent of development of collective bargaining may be illustrated in three categories:

1. The advanced group, as exemplified in parts of Mexico and Argentina.
2. A much larger middle group in which bargaining ranges from advanced collective bargaining with larger firms to very simple or no bargaining in smaller firms, as in Chile and Brazil.
3. A large third group in which collective bargaining is not widespread, as in Costa Rica, Ecuador, and Nicaragua.

Mexico is highly unionized with nearly 30 percent of the workforce in unions. Since only 40 percent of the workforce is employed in the formal sector (those covered under social security and related programs), the percentage of eligible employees who are union members is much higher. Mexico's largest labor organization is the Confederation of Mexican Workers (CTM) with about 5.5 million members. Fedel Velazquez, aged 95, has led the CTM since the 1940s. Although the unions have achieved many of their objectives through their close affiliation with political parties, they now believe that with an economy becoming more decentralized and privatized, union gains will be achieved through collective bargaining, not legislation.

Because Mexican employees played such a critical role in the Mexican revolution, collective bargaining and certain employee rights were written into the Mexican constitution. Furthermore, Mexico has comprehensive, progressive labor legislation, which provides extensive rights and protections for labor and the unions. Under Mexican laws, employees have the right to form and join unions of their own choosing, the right to bargain collectively, and the right to strike. However, strike notice is required 6 to 10 days prior to the strike, and during this time, government mediation is attempted and employees must remain at work.[42] Unions are troubled by the lack of enforcement of the laws. As a result, incidents of labor racketeering, sweetheart deals with employers, and undemocratic practices within labor unions are widespread. Under the labor side agreements of NAFTA, it is expected that these problems will be reduced at the insistence of the United States and Canada.

Unions in Mexico are not certified, unlike in the United States and Canada. Any 20 Mexican employees who wish to register as an independent union can do so, and the employer is legally obligated to negotiate a contract. However, in practice, the employer will often sign a deal with a union that it prefers and contend that any other group does not truly represent a majority of the employees.

Although the average minimum wage in Mexico is about $5.00 per day in U.S. dollars, wages make up less than 30 percent of the labor costs, unlike in the U.S., where wages make up about 70 percent. In Mexico, employees receive six days of paid vacation during the first year, benefits of 25 percent, 15 days of paid leave for Christmas holiday, automatic double time for overtime work, and a share in the mandated 10 percent of the company's pretax profits (about one month's wages).[43]

Mexico mandates seven holidays, and a minimum wage is established regionally by a tripartite minimum-wage commission. In 1995, the daily minimum wage for Mexico City and Acapulco was 16.34 pesos (U.S. $2.72); in Guadalajara and Monterrey, the minimum wage was 15.18 pesos (U.S. $2.53). However, industrial employees are said to average three to four times the minimum wage in the advanced and prosperous enterprises. This is not the case for the 614,000 employees in the 2,100 employer *maquiladora* operations just south of the U.S. border. Companies have been able to operate assembly operations primarily and are charged tariffs by the United States on the value added to the product, which was based on an average wage rate of $2.50 per hour in 1994. But, after the peso devaluation, the wage rate was reduced to $1.80.

Employees are entitled to severance pay when termination is without just cause (just cause includes dishonesty, violence, immorality, alcoholism, and drug addiction); however, the general practice is for employers to pay any way rather than have to prove just cause to the labor board. This legal provision creates an interesting situation when an employee is terminated for union activity—the employer simply pays the employee severance pay. By the acceptance of severance pay, the employee agrees to forgo claims to reinstatement.

Most employers are required to pay 10 percent of their pretax profits into a profit-sharing plan whereby employees share an amount based on the number of days worked during the year and their base earnings.

In October 1995, the Mexican government and labor and business leaders reached a pact on wages and prices in an attempt to calm nervous foreign investors. With an anticipated inflation rate of 20 percent, it was determined that the minimum wage should be increased 10 percent in December, 1995, and 10 percent in April, 1996, to minimize social unrest, another fear of financial investors.

The opening of the Mexican markets to NAFTA and international trade, the devaluation of the peso, plant closing, and corporate downsizing to become more competitive has created an economic challenge to the entire country. Free collective bargaining in the last few years has been limited voluntarily and replaced by annual national pacts negotiated by the government, the major trade unions, and employers with the major goal of controlling inflation. Many efforts have been made by employers, unions, and the government to create greater flexibility and labor-management cooperation to improve productivity, quality, and employee remuneration.[44]

In Central and South America, negotiations between unions and employers take place primarily at the plant level. Only Argentina, Venezuela, and Mexico have widespread industrywide bargaining. The principal reason for this arrangement is that legislation in the various countries typically does not require employers to bargain except at the plant level.

An interesting departure from most of the rest of the world is the important role of collective bargaining between employers and nonunion employees. In fact, over 25 percent of the labor agreements in Columbia and Venezuela are negotiated without trade unions. Obviously, the unions look with disfavor on this arrangement because employers use the nonunion groups as a means to bypass trade unions.

In the more industrialized countries of the world, people interpret labor-management relations to mean the wide range of relationships between employers and employees. However, people of Latin American countries tend to define labor relations in terms of the voluminous labor codes and government regulations.

Labor relations vary widely among the countries in Latin America, but they have one common feature: a close connection between trade unions and political parties. For example, in Mexico, unions constitute a large section of the ruling political party and therefore are assigned a quota of candidates on the party's ticket for office. Thus, unions have some assurance of having a voice in the party's program and on its council. Some unions have been very effective in gaining relatively high wages for members. For example, the electrical workers in Mexico earn two to three times more than the urban working class.[45] Likewise, unions have been criticized because they have made gains for their own members while neglecting the interests of the great mass of people, including the peasants, who are terribly poor.

Labor agreements vary in content both within countries and among countries. In Argentina, labor agreements include provisions that set forth in some detail the employment conditions and establish a highly developed shop steward system to administer grievances and assure that employers abide by the agreements. In Chile, labor agreements are more general, but they do establish certain minimum rules and include a grievance mechanism to enforce the agreement. In Brazil, where unions have struggled since 1945 to have a greater say in determining employment rules and conditions for their members, they have achieved more through labor legislation than by engaging in collective bargaining.

In Latin American countries, political parties maintain close ties with unions for their support, votes, and influence. Likewise, trade unions depend on the politicians for laws to protect their members, to legalize their organizations, and to regulate their relations with employers. On the other hand, political parties have appealed to organized labor to favor their own policies, and in some cases, they have accommodated organized labor in hopes that it will remain satisfied and continue to support the existing economic and political system.[46]

Western Europe

Unionization in Western Europe is significantly greater than in the United States, with the exception of France and Spain. Of the largest countries, the range is from 36 percent in the United Kingdom to over 80 percent in Finland and Sweden. Unions have been able to use this membership strength to accumulate political influence at the national level. Further, they have been able to coordinate their efforts with large, well-established labor parties in government to achieve their goals.

As in the United States, union membership in Western Europe is declining. Nationwide and industrywide bargaining is less frequent, and employers are winning more concessions for efficient work rules and wages. Also, as in the United States, unions are trying to sign up new members in growing industries, such as leisure and finance, where technological change has fueled worries about job security.[47] Unions have achieved significantly greater worker participation in the operation of the firm—many times through legislative mandate, and sometimes through management reaction to wildcat strikes and worker dissatisfaction. In addition, public opinion in these countries strongly supports the idea that worker participation enhances production, fosters harmony, and enriches the workers personally.

The labor relations system in Western Europe can be contrasted with that of the United States in a number of ways.[48]

1. In the United States, unions are selected by the majority of the appropriate bargaining unit, whereas in Western Europe, exclusive representation is not a common concept.
2. In the United States, the exclusive bargaining representative has a monopoly over all employee bargaining, and the employer is required to bargain only with the legally certified union. In Western Europe, the employer often bargains with a number of unions in addition to councils elected by the employees.
3. In Western Europe, negotiations take place between representatives of employer associations and those representing a confederation of unions; in the United States, this bargaining arrangement is adopted only in a few industries, primarily construction.
4. In North America, the focus of union-management interaction is the shop floor, whereas in Europe, national levels are more important to the unions.[49]
5. The number of fringe benefits established by law is greater in Europe; therefore, trade unions have found that they can obtain benefits more quickly through the political arena and have tied themselves more closely to political parties.
6. Western European countries have a greater commitment to employee training. For example, German firms spend twice as much on this activity as U.S. firms, or nearly 17 times as much per apprentice. About 65 percent of each class of middle school graduates in Germany enter apprenticeship training. In contrast, 57 percent of high school graduates in the United States enroll in postsecondary education, and the majority drop out before graduation.

One major reason for the disparity in support for employee training between Germany and the United States is the role of unions and employer associations. German companies band together in employer associations to negotiate with unions over wages and other personnel matters, such as training. Because unions represent about 40 percent of the labor force and unions are stronger in Germany, the labor agreements require investments in training, and collective bargaining provides the mechanism for collecting fees. This approach is similar to the high-quality apprenticeship programs financed by contracts between craft unions and trade associations in the U.S. construction industry.[50]

European Community (EC)

By 1992 the economies of 12 countries in Western Europe were joined together as the European Community (EC) (see Exhibit 15.5). The EC consists of 12 nations

Exhibit 15.5 The European Community

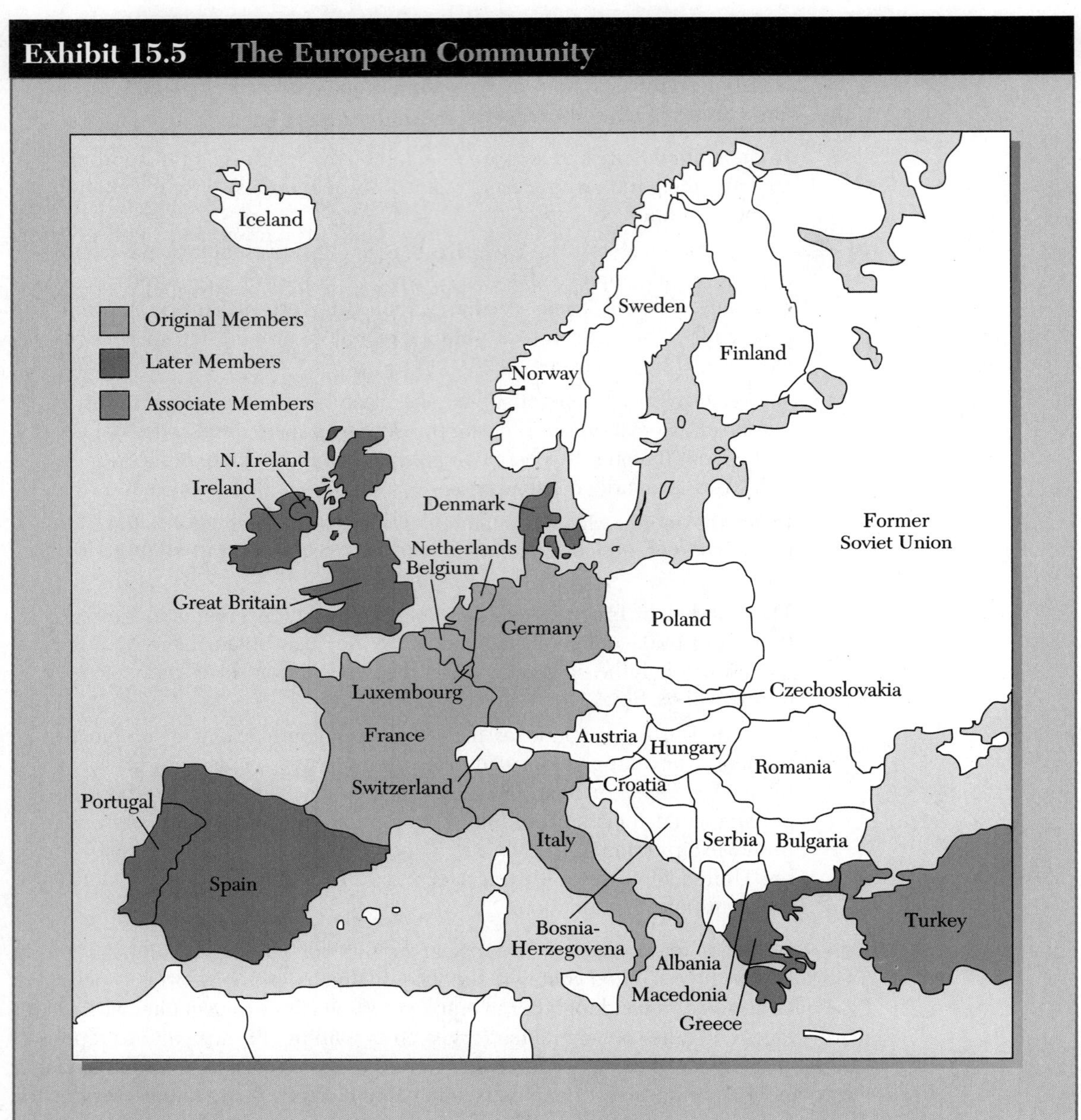

in Western Europe: Belgium, Denmark, Germany, Greece, France, Ireland, Italy, Luxembourg, the Netherlands, Portugal, Spain, and the United Kingdom. The EC's goal is to gradually eliminate economic barriers among member countries. The target date of December 31, 1992, called for the elimination of restrictions on the movement of goods, capital, and labor across national borders. While this target was not completely met, much progress was made toward it.[51]

The Charter of Fundamental Social Rights (called the "Social Charter") was approved by all EC countries except Great Britain. This arrangement establishes certain standards for working conditions throughout the EC so that some countries cannot attract industry merely because their pay and working conditions are below those of other countries. The charter stipulates statements of principles on fundamental rights that include freedom of movement, working conditions, and association and encourages collective bargaining, vocational training, equal treatment for men and women, health and safety, child protection, and rights of information, consultation, and participation for workers.[52]

Critics of the Social Charter have argued that the EC has returned Western Europe to a re-regulation phase that will raise labor costs, inhibit employment growth, and disproportionately affect the poorer employees. They contend the end result of mandated benefits in the Social Charter will lead to higher costs and an erosion of their external competitive position.[53]

Companies are already considering the effects of the EC. Tentatively, they believe there will be increased mobility of employees between operations in the various countries, more recruiting from overseas, more active monitoring of pay and benefits developments in other countries, and increased language training, as well as a premium placed on language skills. These areas and others will provide much opportunity for trade unions to be involved at the bargaining table.

Great Britain

The traditional system in Great Britain is characterized by voluntary collective bargaining, implemented without legal compulsion through unenforceable labor agreements that have been negotiated by a large number of multi-union–multi-employer negotiating committees. The United Kingdom has nearly 600 labor unions, over three times the number in the United States, and a manufacturing firm typically negotiates with about seven unions. Over the years little labor relations law has evolved; thus, a wide diversity in the collective bargaining arrangements developed. One of the most important negotiations involved the Engineering Employers' Federation, representing 5,000 companies, and the Confederation of Shipbuilding and Engineering Unions, representing 34 unions and over 2 million employees. This agreement sets forth general guidelines that establish the floor for additional bargaining at the plants. Labor agreements are administered at the plant level; however, they are not enforceable by law, and grievances are not subject to private arbitration.

Shop stewards are volunteers serving without pay. Unlike their U.S. counterparts, they cannot be removed by union executives. Often they accumulate much authority and influence at the plant and have more control over local union affairs than any national union official. Steward councils composed of union stewards from various unions and work councils representing members of the various departments are important in the labor relations system.

Labor agreements at the plant level are often negotiated by representatives of the national union, steward councils, and work councils. These agreements usually have no fixed term and include letters of understanding, minutes of meetings, and oral understandings. While there is no legal obligation to negotiate, unions have gained extensive power and control over jobs, refusing to work with any employer whom they find in bad standing and maintaining strict membership discipline.

British unions tend to be closely integrated with the Labor Party. They support state pensions and nationalized health service. Consequently, fringe benefits have not been a major bargaining topic. The law plays a minor part in Great Britain's labor relations system because laws historically have worked against unions, causing much distrust.

Unlike the United States, where strikes result primarily from bargaining disputes, wildcat strikes during the contract term are predominant in Great Britain. Grievance arbitration has basically been rejected as a method for resolving disputes during the terms of contracts.[54]

Although union membership was below 40 percent of the labor force in 1994, union membership is down significantly from the 53 percent of 1978. This reduction is blamed on causes similar to those forwarded in the United States: a hostile federal government; unfavorable legislation, such as that abolishing the closed shop and requiring secret ballot election before striking; uncooperative employers, especially in growth industries such as electronics and finance; widespread plant closing in industries in which unions have been strong; and persistent high unemployment due to an economic recession.[55]

Codetermination Policies (Germany)

Unlike the collective bargaining-oriented system of labor relations in the United States, the German system features two distinct levels and mechanisms for employee representation, one of which is directly concerned with collective bargaining. The 16 major unions reach highly general bargaining agreements with employer associations, usually annually. These agreements provide a general framework for implementation at the local levels with emphasis on the specific circumstances of the company and the work councils at the work site.

Employees are guaranteed rights, through the National Works Constitution Act, to **codetermination** via representation on supervisory boards of large companies. The work councils cover more than two-thirds of all German employees and represent blue- and white-collar employees proportionately. Their rights include the right to information, consultation, and codetermination over a variety of workplace issues. Their strongest rights are in the area of basic personnel decisions, such as hiring, firing, overtime, and transfers. Their rights to consultation and information include changes in the economic situation of the firm and in production and work organization, such as the kind of changes occasioned by new technology.

The work councils are formally separate from the union; however, most councilors are active members of the union. Therefore, the unions in many ways shape the strategies and actions of the work councils. Research has revealed that managers and employer association representatives believe that work councils are positive productive factors associated with industrial peace and employee acceptance of technological and other organizational change. Because collective bargaining occurs at the industry level through employer associations, individual employers need not worry about certain costs that are thereby taken out of competition between companies. Individual employers can focus on the potential gains to be achieved through cooperation with work councils around issues not directly regulated by collective bargaining. As a result, this cooperation by companies with the work councils enhances productivity, quality, and, ultimately, profits.[56]

In Germany the most important formal focus of wage bargaining is at the regional industry level, followed by the company or plant level. Since unions in Germany are organized on an industry basis, they generally do not have to compete for members. The largest union is the engineering union, I.G. Metall, which covers about 35 percent of employees. The I.G. Metall's main objective is to increase employment in engineering industries, such as autos and steel. Therefore, I. G. Metall needs to ensure that wage developments do not erode the competitiveness of engineering in the world economy. Much time in negotiations is spent discussing world engineering prices, export prospects, evolution of world prices and costs, prospective growth in labor productivity, and exchange rates.[57]

Sixteen industrial unions reach general bargaining agreements with employer associations, usually on an annual basis. These broad agreements are then tailored to specific circumstances within each company and operate within the work council system. Thus, bargaining between the industrial unions and the employer associations covers issues such as the costs of labor and human resource management practices, taking them out of competition among the individual firms.[58]

In 1994, Gesamtmetal, an employer association, and I. G. Metall, representing three million members, reached an agreement on an across-the-board wage increase of 3.5 percent and reduction in the work week from 36 hours to 35. This agreement continued wage levels that were the highest in the world and established the pattern for negotiations in 1995. With vacations averaging 30 days and 10 days of holidays, it is inevitable that labor costs will continue upward. Many of the member-employers had anticipated no wage increase for the next two years and vowed that they would leave the association. Gesamtmetal's executive director was forced out, and many employers took advantage of provisions in the agreement that allow individual employers to negotiate special deals with employees directly when jobs are threatened. Daimler-Benz, which employs 148,900 in Germany and 50,100 abroad, agreed to build cars in Germany only after employees accepted wage increases below the negotiated level; however, plans proceeded to build plants in the United States, China, and Mexico, where wages were comparatively lower than in Germany. Pirelli stated it would make no additional investments in Germany unless production was increased. Kathrein-Werk KG, an antenna maker with 1,600 employees, opened a factory in Rumania, where wages were 20 percent of the wages of German employees. Employer Robert Bosch GMBH, a diversified company, obtained concessions from its employees after it showed them plans for building a plant in Scotland.[59]

Unification in Germany was made particularly difficult because of the disparity in wage systems between East and West Germany. East German workers were earning about 30 percent of the wages of West German workers prior to unification.[60] No democratic unions have existed in the eastern part of Germany since 1933, except for a brief time after 1945. Prior to unification, the sole responsibility of trade unions in East Germany was to transmit the communist party's policies to the employees on the shop floor.[61]

Eastern Europe—Former Soviet Bloc Countries

Trade unions represent workers all over the region; however, their major role in many countries has been to exert political pressure. For instance, Solidarity in Poland, the original independent union in Eastern Europe, has 2.5 million members and played a major role in the breakup of the Soviet bloc. Trade unions in Czechoslovakia led the revolution and then members voted out the old leadership and democratized the union movement; however, the unions wanted the country to be divided along Czech and Slovak ethnic lines. In the former Soviet Union, the trade union movement has been in a state of rapid flux; however, coal miners have maintained their relative strength throughout the developments.[62]

Some countries in the former Soviet bloc are enjoying success in attracting new industries. Offering lower wages and lower manufacturing costs, businesses primarily from western Europe are investing in central Europe particularly. For example, $15 billion alone had been invested in Hungary, Poland, and the Czech Republic (Slovakia and Slovenia) by the end of 1994. Audi has built a $195 million engine plant in Hungary and has plans for an additional $280 million expansion. GM Europe built a $300 million plant in Hungary that now supplies six plants in Europe. Fiat bought a Polish auto maker for $640 million and plans a $450 million expansion. Volkswagen paid $322 million for a 25 percent share of a Czech auto maker.[63]

The transition to a market economy in Russia has been slow and judged not successful thus far. With 60 million workers, many have not been paid on time or are paid in rubles, which have continually lost their value. In 1993, 264 strikes occurred, increasing to 288 from January to April in 1994. Factories do not have the funds to upgrade their plants, buy products from one another, or make payrolls. Faced with massive restructuring and operational inefficiencies that have been allowed to develop over the years, it is predicted that unemployment could increase up to 20 percent.[64]

In the new Russia, employee shareholders appear to have little formal power, and trade unions also seem to lack power. Under communist control, trade unions were state organizations that were appendages to state-owned firms. Trade unions mainly served as social service organizations that helped to distribute social benefits. In other words, trade unions were company unions and had little independent power.[65]

The transformation of the labor relations system in Russia is proceeding slowly. Both unions and employers are basically independent of the state. At the national level, unions are independent of employers. At the enterprise level, collective bargaining is not being implemented.[66] Unions are only just beginning to learn the fundamentals of confronting management, negotiating contracts, and mapping out effective strike strategies.

Four countries—Poland, Hungary, Slovenia, and Slovakia—have requested membership in the European Community by 2000. If they are admitted, these countries will be required to abide by the EC's Social Charter. Currently being debated is whether these countries will be able to meet these requirements by 2000. The wage rates in these countries are so low in comparison with those of countries in the EC that EC governments are worried about competition from them as low-cost producers of textiles, footwear, coal, and steel.[67] The direction of labor relations activities is still uncertain and impossible to predict.

Japan

Japan's labor relations system has four distinguishing characteristics: labor-management consultation and teamwork, lifetime employment, a wage system based on seniority, and the enterprise or company union. Management and employees communicate considerably more in Japan than in most other countries. Ninety percent of all Japanese companies have some sort of labor-management consultation. The flow of information is extensive. As examples, management reports to employees on the company's financial status, its problems, and its expectations and plans, and on contemplated technological innovations before they occur. All aspects of employment, training, discipline, working conditions, and employee benefits are open for examination. Joint consultation includes subjects that the U.S. manager would classify as management prerogatives.[68]

Research has shown that when Japanese firms increase their information sharing with employee unions the negotiations are shorter and easier, unions tend to demand and accept lower wage increases,[69] and profitability and productivity are improved.[70]

Teamwork and consensus building are a cultural heritage in Japan. Japanese employees feel comfortable with this approach and both sides stress sharing of goals, responsibilities, and rewards. The communication links are through the normal channels at work, such as meetings, newsletters and bulletins, labor unions, and labor-management councils.[71]

Lifetime employment, a standard in Japan since the 1950s when employers agreed to this arrangement to quell labor unrest, has been applied to regular employees of large employers (500 or more employees), which make up about one-third of the nonagricultural workforce. These "regular employees" are hired after completing high school or college, with the expectation that they will be retained by the company until they reach the mandatory retirement age of 60. Legal, written contracts are nonexistent; however, unacceptable behavior may lead to a suggested voluntary resignation or a "hidden discharge." The result of this lifetime employment has been eagerness of employers to invest in training these long-term employees, and responsiveness of employees not only to participate in training but to willingly accept innovation and technological advancement, knowing that they will not be adversely affected by a layoff.[72]

By 1995, unemployment in Japan had reached 3.2 percent (U.S. unemployment was about 5.5 percent) and the Japanese yen had increased in value against the U.S. dollar by 15 percent, thereby causing Japanese products to be priced higher in international markets. More and more Japanese manufacturers were moving jobs and facilities to low-wage Southeast Asia and Mexico. As a result, some well-known companies, such as Nissan and Nippon Steel, announced that lifetime employment was a concept of the past.[73]

The **wage system** in Japan has several distinguishing characteristics:

1. Salaries are paid monthly, even if the employee has been absent (with justification) from work.
2. Wage differentials are small between regular line employees and staff personnel, all of whom are members of the same union.
3. Wage distinctions exist between amounts earned for one's work (for example, efficiency output) and amounts earned for just being an employee (such as allowances for housing, transportation, and dependents).
4. Wages are accepted as permanent and lasting for the employee's entire career, including a minimum annual increase and a lump sum at retirement.[74]

Length of service and age are more highly correlated with wages in Japan than in other industrially developed countries. For example, between the ages of 40 and 50 the Japanese workers' wages are 67 percent greater than those of 21- to 24-year-old employees, whereas in the United States, the older employees' wages average only 23 percent more than those of younger workers. Peak earnings in Japan are 243 percent greater than entry-level earnings; in the United States the differential is 110 percent.[75]

The **enterprise union** is composed of employees working for a single employer at a single location. These unions comprise nearly 90 percent of all union organizations in Japan and include all categories of skills among employees of a company. The development of the enterprise union has been aided substantially by the system of lifetime employment and a heavy reliance on seniority. Thus, the individual employee identifies more closely with the company than does the typical employee in many Western countries.

The enterprise unions are affiliated at the national level and have national organizations in the textile, electricity, shipbuilding, automobile, steel, appliance, and chemical industries. They hold conferences to discuss industrial policies; however, they do not discuss such topics as wages, working conditions, and other employment policies. These topics are discussed within the enterprise union. At the national level, industrial problems are discussed in a more general context, and issues such as economic growth, employment forecasts, retirement ages, and improved communications are addressed.[76]

Unions in Japan represent about one-fourth of the labor force, 8 percent more than in the United States. They have received low wage increases in the last several years and are becoming more adversarial. While the work days lost due to strikes in

Japan average less than in Canada, Australia, and the United States, work day losses are greater than those of Sweden, Norway, Germany, Austria, and the Netherlands, where work council systems prevail.

In Japan, the spring of each year brings on the annual labor offensive, or *shunto.* The unions participate in nationwide demonstrations, singing labor songs, wearing red armbands, and refusing to work for short periods. While these demonstrations may be mistaken by an outsider as an indication of deteriorating labor-management relations, it actually is a time for labor to voice its views and to allow employees to let off steam.

With Japan's strong trade balance (exports exceeding imports) and the subsequent appreciation of the yen, products made in Japan and shipped elsewhere have become more expensive, and pressures have mounted to reduce production and labor costs or to shift more production to countries where wages are lower, such as Korea, Taiwan, Singapore, or Hong Kong.

In the final analysis, Japanese employers and unions eventually will have to face a number of critical issues that may cause a break with the traditional system: early retirement, higher unemployment, elimination of automatic pay increases and promotions, introduction of labor-saving devices, union emphasis on job security rather than wage hikes, decline of employee loyalty to the firm, and declining competitiveness with rapidly developing countries such as Brazil, China, South Korea, Singapore, and Taiwan.[77]

South Korea

Labor relations in South Korea[78] dramatically changed in 1987 with the election of President Roh Tae Woo. During the previous four decades of autocratic and suppressive government, the institution of collective bargaining and the right to strike existed only on paper. Collective bargaining was never open to employees as a viable mechanism to address industrial justice, distribution of income, or oppressive working conditions. Consequently, in the late 1980s when collective bargaining was allowed, the parties lacked basic expertise in bilateral decision making. Then, in 1987, there were 3,749 work stoppages, more than ten times as many as in the previous year. Since 1987, work stoppages have declined each year, and in 1992, there were only 235, but 36 percent were illegal. Researchers who examined strike data from 1988 to 1990 found that intra-union rivalries were strongly associated with strike activity. In addition, the presence of more experienced and skillful union negotiators reduced the likelihood of a strike.[79]

South Korea has been considered a developing country for the past several decades; however, this characterization is not proper given the rapid economic development over the past few years. During the 1980s, South Korea experienced double-digit growth in gross national product; however, the last two years' growth has been 6.8 percent and 9.3 percent. The average personal disposable income after taxes has risen to $4,787 in 1991, which is 15.9 percent more than in 1990.

There are 7,656 labor unions in South Korea with some 1.81 million members. This comprises 12 percent of the total workforce, several percentage points less than the United States. There are 20 industrial federations, and each federation is the exclusive, industrywide union to represent workers within the industrial jurisdiction specified by the federation's charter. Most of the 20 federations and national unions are affiliated with the Federation of Korean Trade Unions. This organization has been criticized for its close ties with the national government. The Trade Union Law, the major piece of legislation governing labor relations, allows organizing and negotiating rights for unions, provides for third-party impasse resolution procedures, and has a defined procedure for unions to follow prior to strikes. The law allows local unions to entrust their negotiations to the industrial federations, and the trend is in this direction.

The South Korean workforce can be characterized as young, well-educated, and highly motivated. The average monthly wage (regular salary, step increases, overtime, and bonuses and allowances) is only $1,029 in U.S. dollars. Korean employees work 54 hours per week, more hours than any other country reported by the Industrial Labor Organization. Working conditions are frequently unfavorable; many employees work in small, cramped, and often dangerous sweatshops.

Substantial employment discrimination exists against women. Women account for 40.7 percent of the workforce, but their average wage is only 53 percent that of men. Even recent female university graduates have found that their starting salary is 40 percent less than that of their male counterparts. In spite of the 1988 Equal Rights Law, women do not enjoy equal rights at work. In addition, the Labor Standards Law prohibits employment of children under 13 years of age; however, children under 18 may obtain work if they have written permission from their parents or guardian. Women and children are the majority workforce in textile, apparel, footwear, and electronics factories.[80]

Australia

Australian unions are organized more on a craft or occupational basis than on an industrial or enterprise basis. The Australian labor force is 40 percent unionized. The majority of union members in Australia are white-collar or service employees. Over half of the employees in government, finance and insurance, transport and storage, and metal products are union members.[81]

In 1983, when the Labor Party became the majority party in Australia, the government and the Australian Council of Trade Unions negotiated an annual social contract known as "the Accord," which is a form of centralized pay bargaining. In 1991, the Industrial Relations Commission (IRC) decided that direct collective bargaining should be permitted between companies and their employees; however, any enterprise productivity agreements had to be ratified by the IRC to ensure that they complied with IRC rules.[82]

In 1994, Prime Minister Paul Keating of the Labor Party led the effort to pass the Industrial Relations Reform Act to overhaul an old practice of centrally fixed wage agreements and to encourage a more flexible system of bargaining between employers and unions. This new system is designed to moderate wage claims and to encourage the merger of national unions. By 1995, the number of unions had been reduced from over 200 to 48, of which 20 are large, industry-wide unions (called super unions or mega unions). While the business community generally supports the decentralization of the labor relations system, the new labor law contains a stringent provision that forbids the "unfair dismissal" of employees, thereby making it more difficult for employers to terminate employees.[83]

With the decentralization of enterprise bargaining, unions turned their attention toward pattern bargaining in an attempt to negotiate and standardize wage rates within an industry. While unions had planned to press for national wage rates, which existed previously, Prime Minister Keating has noted that employers have achieved their goals of decentralized enterprise bargaining and now it is up to them to resist high wage demands of unions.[84]

Under the Industrial Relations Reform Act, unions are allowed to conduct legal strikes for the first time in Australian history. Ironically, during the 1993 to 1994 period, strikes were at a historically low level. This new right to strike has restrictions, however. For example, employees may be classified as being employed in "essential services" and they have strike restrictions when strikes are inconsistent with the public interest, safety, and health. In addition, a provision in the act allows the Industrial Relations Commission to halt a strike that causes significant damage to the Australian economy or an important part of it.

An unusual part of the act is the nonunion bargaining provision, which allows companies to negotiate agreements with their nonunion employees without the union. Although unions vehemently oppose this provision and practice, by 1995, 11 nonunion agreements had been negotiated, only one of which covered a large number of employees. Unions fought against the inclusion of this provision in the act because they believed that it would lead to deunionization, reduced wages, and poorer working conditions.

Summary

Multinational corporations and transnational collective bargaining are becoming increasingly important topics of labor relations. While multinational corporations continue to grow in sales volume, capital investments, and economic influence, they have also aroused trade unions in various countries to combine their energies, skills, and power in an effort to negotiate on an equal footing. Thus far, little success has been achieved because of legal, political, social, economic, and organizational obstacles. However, it is obvious that transnational collective bargaining could have a tremendous impact on the world's economy if the obstacles can be eliminated. Time will tell whether unions will be able to overcome the obstacles.

With the growing interdependency among nations, it is imperative that students who study labor relations learn more about labor relations systems throughout the world. This chapter highlights the major features of the major trading partners of the United States.

The labor relations system of Canada has expressed concern over the United States' economically dominant role in North America and its influence in the internal affairs of that country. Its system features two major linguistic and cultural groups and highly decentralized collective bargaining activities that are governed by provincial law. Labor relations vary widely among the countries in Latin and South America, but they have one common feature: a close connection between trade unions and political parties.

Unionization in most of western Europe is significantly greater than in the United States, and there is wide implementation of codetermination and employee participation policies. In 1992, 12 countries in western Europe joined together to form the European Community, which provided for greater deregulation and a decrease in trade and travel barriers between member countries. The formation of the EC increased the need to learn more about the labor relations system in each of these countries and will probably bring these countries closer together. In the past, the labor movements in many eastern European countries were dominated by the Soviet Union. *Perestroika* and *glasnot,* introduced to enhance individual freedom and economic development, helped lead to the dissolution of the Soviet Union. The countries of the former Soviet bloc are now trying to adjust to a market economy. Four of these countries have requested membership in the European Community by 2000.

Unique features of the Japanese system include labor-management consultations, teamwork, a lifetime employment policy, a unique wage system, and the enterprise union. However, international money exchange rate fluctuations and recession could quickly alter these special union-management relationships of the Japanese system.

South Korean labor relations have developed rapidly from a strike-ridden system in 1987 to more successful collective bargaining. With high growth rates, South Korea still has problems of discrimination against women and employment of child labor. The Australian system involves the right to strike, decentralized bargaining, nonunion bargaining, and an unfair dismissal law.

Key Terms

multinational corporation (MNC)
whipsawing
codetermination
wage system
enterprise union

Discussion Questions

1. While we share a common border with Canada, its labor relations system is affected by a number of variables that do not greatly affect the United States. Enumerate and explain these variables.
2. Explain why labor unions in many Latin American countries have developed more slowly than those in the United States.
3. Western Europe seems to be uniquely involved with various forms of worker participation. What are some reasons that these worker participation systems have developed so fully there instead of elsewhere?
4. What are the four special features of the Japanese system? Why haven't they been adopted in the United States?

5. While multinational corporations seem to be growing in size and influence, what must occur before transnational collective bargaining can be effectively carried out?
6. Which features of Canada's labor relations system would you transfer to the United States?

References

1. Ronald E. Yates, "47 Giant Corporations Rank Among World's 100 Biggest Economies," *Atlanta Constitution,* December 14, 1991, p. D-3.
2. William J. Holstein, "The Stateless Corporation," *Business Week,* May 14, 1990, pp. 98–105.
3. Raymond J. Mataloni, Jr., "U.S. Multinational Companies: Operations in 1993," *Survey of Current Business* 75 (June 1995), p. 32; Raymond J. Matloni, Jr., "A Guide to BEA Statistics on U.S. Multinational Companies," *Survey of Current Business* 75 (March 1995), p. 46.
4. Mahnaz Fahim-Nader and William J. Zeile, "Foreign Direct Investment in the United States," *Survey of Business* 75 (May 1995), pp. 57–59.
5. Ned G. Howenstine and William J. Zeile, "Foreign Direct Investment in the United States: Establishment Data for 1987," *Survey of Current Business* 72 (October 1992), pp. 44–47.
6. Janet Kmitch, Pedro Labuym, and Sandra Van Damme, "International Comparisons of Compensation Costs," *Monthly Labor Review* 114 (October 1995), p. 6.
7. Thane Peterson, "Is Japan Using the U.S. as a Back Door to Europe?" *Business Week,* November 14, 1988, p. 57.
8. Harley Shaiken, "Globalization and the Worldwide Division of Labor," *Monthly Labor Review* 110 (August 1987), p. 47.
9. Marvin J. Levine, "Labor Movements and the Multinational Corporation: A Future for Collective Bargaining?" *Employee Relations Law Journal* 13 (Winter 1987–88), pp. 382–398.
10. Rajib N. Sanyal, "Unionizing Foreign-Owned Firms: Perceptions of American Union Officials," *Labor Studies Journal* 14 (Winter 1989), p. 66.
11. "Hands Across the Workplace," *Time,* December 26, 1988, pp. 15–18; "Working for the Japanese," *Time,* September 14, 1987; Paul Hemp, "Britain's 'Intransigent' Rubber Workers Bow to Japanese Management Practices," *The Wall Street Journal,* March 29, 1988, p. 26.
12. "Canada's UAW Thumbs Its Nose at Concessions," *Business Week,* July 26, 1982, p. 23.
13. Charles R. Greer and John Shearer, "Do Foreign-owned U.S. Firms Practice Unconventional Labor Relations?" *Monthly Labor Review* 104 (January 1981), pp. 45–47.
14. Duane Kujawa, "Collective Bargaining and Labor Relations in Multinational Enterprise: A U.S. Public Policy Perspective," in *Research in International Business and Finance,* ed. Robert G. Hawkins (Greenwich, Conn.: JAI Press, Inc., 1979), p. 37.
15. Greer and Shearer, "Do Foreign-owned U.S. Firms Practice Unconventional Labor Relations?" p. 47.
16. Kujawa, "Collective Bargaining and Labor Relations," pp. 37–38.
17. Robert F. Banks and Jack Stieber, "Introduction," in *Multinationals, Unions, and Labor Relations in Industrial Countries* (Ithaca, N.Y.: New York State School of Industrial and Labor Relations, 1977), p. 1.
18. See Richard L. Rowan, Herbert R. Northrup, and Rae Ann O'Brien, *Multinational Union Organizations in the Manufacturing Industries* (Philadelphia, Penn.: University of Pennsylvania, 1980).
19. Geoffrey W. Latta and Janice R.

Bellace, "Making the Corporation Transparent: Prelude to Multinational Bargaining," *Columbia Journal of World Business* 18 (Summer 1983), p. 73.

20. *World Labour Report 1992* (Geneva: International Labour Office, 1992), p. 57.

21. Paul Marginson, "European Integration and Transnational Management—Union Relations in the Enterprise," *British Journal of Industrial Relations* 30 (December 1992), p. 529; Stephen J. Silva, "The Social Charter of the European Community: A Defeat for European Labor," *Industrial and Labor Relations Review* 44 (July 1991), pp. 626–643.

22. "The Maastricht Mire," *The Economist,* March 13, 1993, p. 20.

23. Banks and Stieber, *Multinationals, Unions, and Labor Relations,* pp. 11–12.

24. Levine, "Labor Movements and the Multinational Corporation," pp. 392–398.

25. G. B. J. Bomers, *Multinational Corporations and Industrial Relations* (Amsterdam, The Netherlands: Van Gorcum, Assen, 1976).

26. Banks and Stieber, *Multinationals, Unions, and Labor Relations,* pp. 15–16; and Bomers, *Multinational Corporations and Industrial Relations,* pp. 179–185.

27. Herbert R. Northrup, "Why Multinationals Bargaining Neither Exists Nor is Desirable," *Labor Law Journal* 29 (June 1978), pp. 330–331.

28. Hoyt N. Wheeler and Jaques Rojot, "General Comments," in *Workplace Justice: Employment Obligations in International Perspective* (Columbia, S.C.: University of South Carolina Press, 1992), pp. 368–369.

29. Joseph B. Rose and Gary N. Chaison, "Union Density and Union Effectiveness: The North American Experience," *Proceedings of the 9th World Congress of the International Industrial Relations Association* (Sydney, Australia: International Industrial Relations Association, 1992), p. 528.

30. Joseph B. Rose and Gary N. Chaison, "Canadian Labor Policy as a Model for Legislative Reform in the United States," *Labor Law Journal* 46 (May 1995), p. 259.

31. Mark Thompson, "Canada," in *International Handbook of Industrial Relations,* ed. Albert A. Blum (Westport, Conn.: Greenwood Press, 1980), p. 86.

32. Thomas R. Knight and Donna Sockell, "Public Policy and the Scope of Collective Bargaining in Canada and the United States," in *Proceedings of the 41st Annual Meeting of the Industrial Relations Research Association,* ed. Barbara D. Dennis (Madison, Wis.: Industrial Relations Research Association, 1989), pp. 283–286.

33. Rose and Chaison, "Canadian Labor Policy as a Model for Legislative Reform in the United States," p. 262.

34. Richard S. Belous, "The Impact of the U.S.–Canadian Free Trade Agreement on Labor-Management Relations: Facing New Pressures," unpublished paper presented at the University of Lavel, September 20, 1988, pp. 1–6.

35. Rose and Chaison, "Canadian Labor Policy as a Model for Legislative Reform in the United States," p. 266.

36. John W. Budd, "Canadian Strike Replacement Legislation and Collective Bargaining: Lessons for the United States," *Industrial Relations,* forthcoming.

37. Roy J. Adams, "North American Industrial Relations: Divergent Trends in Canada and the United States," *Industrial Labour Review* 128, no. 1 (1989), p. 59.

38. John W. Budd and Wendel E. Pritchett, "Does the Banning of Permanent Strike Replacements Affect Bargaining Power?" *Proceedings of the 46th Annual Meeting of the Industrial Relations Research Association,* ed. Paula B. Voos (Madison, Wis.: Industrial Relations Research Association, 1994), pp. 370–378; John W. Budd, "The Effect of Multinational Institutions on Strike Activity in Canada," *Industrial and Labor Relations Review* 47 (April 1994), pp. 401–415.

39. *Canada* (Washington, D.C.: U.S. Department of Labor, Bureau of International Labor Affairs, 1992), pp. 5–11.

40. Gerald P. Glyde, "Canadian Labor and the Free Trade Agreement," *Labor Studies Journal* 17 (Winter 1993), pp. 5–23.
41. *Canada,* pp. 5–6.
42. *Foreign Labor Trends: Mexico* (Washington, D.C.: U.S. Department of Labor, 1993), pp. 4–12.
43. Pamela M. Prah, "Mexico May Have Lower Wages but Benefits Boost Costs, Attorney Says," *Daily Labor Report,* October 12, 1995, p. A-5.
44. Craig Torres, "Mexico Reaches Wage and Price Accord," *The Wall Street Journal,* October 30, 1995, p. A14.
45. Everett M. Kassalow, *Trade Unions and Industrial Relations: An International Comparison* (New York: Random House, 1969), pp. 302–303.
46. "Europe's Unions Are Losing Their Grip," *Business Week,* November 26, 1986, pp. 80–84.
47. Everett M. Kassalow, "Conflict and Cooperation in Europe's Industrial Relations," *Industrial Relations* 13 (May 1974), pp. 156–163.
48. "Eleven European Leaders Endorse EC Worker Rights Code, Thatcher Objects," *Daily Labor Report,* December 12, 1989, p. A-3; "Social Charter: Action Programme Released," *European Industrial Relations Report* no. 112 (January 1990), pp. 11–14.
49. Roy J. Adams, "Industrial Relations in Europe and North America: Some Contemporary Themes," *European Journal of Industrial Relations* 1, no. 1 (1995), p. 50.
50. Margaret Hilton, "Shared Training: Learning from Germany," *Monthly Labor Review* 114 (March 1991), pp. 33–35.
51. Robert J. Gitter, "Job Training in Europe: Lessons from Abroad," *Monthly Labor Review* 115 (April 1992), pp. 25–27.
52. "Introduction—Special Report," *Daily Labor Report,* June 22, 1990, p. 3.
53. John T. Addison and W. Stanley Siebert, "The Social Charter of the European Community: Evolution and Controversies," *Industrial and Labor Relations Review* 44 (July 1991), pp. 597–623.
54. Brian Towers, "Running the Gauntlet: British Trade Unions Under Thatcher, 1979–1988," *Industrial and Labor Relations Review* 42 (January 1989), pp. 163–186.
55. Bob Mason and Peter Bain, "The Determinants of Trade Union Membership in Britain: A Survey of the Literature," *Industrial and Labor Relations Review* 46 (January 1993), pp. 332–333.
56. Kirsten S. Wever, "Learning from Work Councils: Five Unspectacular Cases from Germany," *Industrial Relations* 33 (October 1994), pp. 467–481.
57. David Soskice, "The German Wage Bargaining System," *Proceedings of the 46th Annual Meeting of the Industrial Relations Research Association,* ed. Paula B. Voos (Madison, Wis.: Industrial Relations Research Association, 1994), p. 350.
58. Kirsten S. Wever, "German Employers' View of Labor Representation," *Proceedings of the 45th Annual Meeting of the Industrial Relations Research Association* (Madison, Wis.: Industrial Relations Research Association, 1992), pp. 109–110.
59. Greg Stainmetz, "German Firms Sour on System That Keeps Peace with Workers," *The Wall Street Journal,* October 17, 1995, p. A1; Aubrey Choi, "For Mercedes, Going Global Means Being Less German," *The Wall Street Journal,* April 27, 1995, p. B4; Ferdinand Protzman, "Rewriting the Contract for Germany's Vaunted Workers," *The New York Times,* February 13, 1994, p. F5.
60. Gerhard Bosch, "Collective Bargaining in the Unified Germany," *Proceedings of the 45th Annual Meeting of the Industrial Relations Research Association* (Madison, Wis.: Industrial Relations Research Association, 1993), pp. 123–126.
61. Michael Fichter, "A House Divided: German Unification and Organized Labor," *Proceedings of the 45th Annual Meeting of the Industrial Relations Research Association* (Madison, Wis.: Industrial Relations Research Association, 1993), p. 115.

62. *World Labor Report 1992* (Geneva: International Labour Office, 1992), p. 57.
63. Karen Lowry, Bill Javetski, Peggy Simpson, and Tim Smart, "Europe: The Push East," *Business Week,* November 7, 1994, pp. 48–49.
64. Peter Galuszka, "Toss Another Match into the Russian Tinderbox: Labor," *Business Week,* June 6, 1994, p. 51.
65. Joseph R. Blasi, "Russian Labor-Management Relations: Some Preliminary Lessons from Newly Privatized Enterprises," *Proceedings of the 47th Annual Meeting of the Industrial Relations Research Association,* ed. Paula B. Voos (Madison, Wis.: Industrial Relations Research Association, 1995), p. 230.
66. Michael Ballot, "Labor Relations in Russia and Eastern Europe," *Labor Law Journal* 46 (March 1995), p. 170.
67. "Eastern Europe," *The Economist,* March 13, 1993, p. 3.
68. Joseph Krislov, "How Does the Japanese Industrial Relations System Differ?" *Labor Law Journal* 40 (June 1989), pp. 338–344.
69. Motohiro Morishima, "Information Sharing and Collective Bargaining in Japan: Effects of Wage Negotiations," *Industrial and Labor Relations Review* 44 (April 1991), pp. 469–482.
70. Motohiro Morishima, "Information Sharing and Firm Performance in Japan," *Industrial Relations* 30 (Winter 1991), pp. 37–57.
71. Kiyoshi Kawahito, "Labor Relations in the Japanese Automobile and Steel Industries," *Journal of Labor Research* 11 (Summer 1990), pp. 232–237.
72. Katsumi Yakabe, *Labor Relations in Japan* (Tokyo: International Society for Educational Information, 1974), pp. 1–14; Hisashi Kawada and Ryuji Komatsu, "Post-War Labor Movements in Japan," in *The International Labor Movement in Transition,* eds. Adolph Strumthal and James G. Scoville (Urbana: University of Illinois Press, 1973), pp. 122–148; and Tadashi A. Hanami, "The Multinational Corporation and Japanese Industrial Relations," in *International Labor and Multinational Enterprise,* ed. Duane Kujawa (New York: Praeger Publishers, 1975), pp. 183–185.
73. "Management in Japan," *The Economist,* September 16, 1995, p. 79; Andrew Pollack, "Japan Finds Ways to Save Tradition of Lifetime Jobs," *The New York Times,* November 28, 1993, pp. 1, 9; Eamonn Finleton, "Jobs for Life: Why Japan Won't Give Them Up," *Fortune,* March 20, 1995, pp. 119–125.
74. Krislov, "How Does the Japanese System Differ?" p. 340.
75. Koji Taira and Solomon B. Levine, "Japan's Industrial Relations: A Social Compact Emerges," in *Industrial Relations in a Decade of Economic Change,* pp. 283–286.
76. Glenn Halm and Clinton R. Shiels, "Damage Control: Yen Appreciation and the Japanese Labor Market," *Monthly Labor Review* 111 (November 1988), pp. 3–5.
77. "An Aging Workforce Strains Japan's Traditions," *Business Week,* April 20, 1981, pp. 72–85.
78. Drawn primarily from Mario F. Bognanno, *Korea's Industrial Relations at the Turning Point* (Seoul: Korea Development Institute, 1988), pp. 4–90.
79. Mario F. Bognanno, John W. Budd, and Young-Myon Lee, "Institutional Turmoil and Strike Activity in Korea," *Journal of Industrial Relations* 36 (September 1994), pp. 360–367.
80. *Korea* (Washington, D.C.: U.S. Department of Labor, Bureau of International Labor Affairs, 1992), pp. 6–8.
81. George Strauss, "Australian Labor Relations through American Eyes," *Industrial Relations* 27 (Spring 1988), pp. 131–147.
82. "Australia," *International Labour Review* 132, no. 2 (1993), p. 143.
83. "The Neighbors Stay Home," *The Economist,* April 12, 1995, p. 36.
84. Diana Kelly, "Trade Unionism in 1994," *Journal of Industrial Relations* 37 (March 1995), pp. 132–139.

THE LABOR RELATIONS PROCESS—SYNTHESIS AND POSSIBILITIES

16

Previous chapters have explained the labor relations process enumerated in Chapter 1. This concluding chapter serves as a transition, generalizing how the labor relations participants are interacting and being affected by various influences at this time. These chapter sections should recast Exhibit 1.2 on page 11, which should reveal additional insights in assessing this subject as well as the cases for Part Four.

PARTICIPANTS IN THE LABOR RELATIONS PROCESS

As noted in Chapter 2, many union members indirectly helped President Clinton win the 1992 election by diverting their votes from President Bush to Ross Perot. Also noted was President Clinton's lack of promises to labor unions; indeed, he had a very active role in the passage of the North American Free Trade Agreement over organized labor's strenuous opposition.

However, organized labor has benefited from three executive orders signed by Clinton that accomplished the following:

- Reversed President Bush's requirement that government contractors tell their employees that they may refuse to pay the part of their union dues used for political purposes.
- Permitted government contractors to restrict subcontracting to unionized companies.

President Clinton also signed the family leave bill into law and indicated that he would sign legislation that would prohibit the hiring of permanent strike replacements.

Robert Reich, Clinton's secretary of labor, indicated that unions need to be restored to a level playing field in the United States because in the last 10 years employees have been penalized for "even trying to create unions." Reich labeled the labor movement "the most articulate, indeed, the only voice of the front-line worker in America." He also informed a reporter that he "absolutely" believed employees should join unions. Reich had indicated that a major Department of Labor (DOL) priority is improving employees' quality of work life. However, according to one study (which Reich did not contradict), various quality-of-work-life efforts such as job enrichment, employee involvement programs, and employee performance feedback are more likely to be found in nonunion firms.[1]

Some have contended that the DOL has given somewhat superficial attention to the specific problems and issues confronting organized labor. For example, Reich has seemingly backed off from a previous urging that the minimum wage be increased; however, one analyst noted that a one-day conference on one of his major interests, job training, cost taxpayers $250,000 with few, if any, tangible results.[2] Similar concerns have been raised about another event during the Clinton administration: namely, the Commission on the Future of Worker-Management Relations, also known as the Dunlop Commission. The commission conducted 21 public hearings involving 411 witnesses and nearly 5,000 pages of transcript.[3] Its findings were criticized by both organized labor and business. The AFL-CIO thought that insufficient protections were recommended for those belonging to or seeking to join a union. The U.S. Chamber of Commerce expressed bitter disappointment that the commission report was "out of step with the real world of today's global marketplace."[4] One observer labeled the Dunlop Commission "a clearly intended time filler,"[5] while Douglas Fraser, former United Auto Workers president and a commission member, expressed doubt over the implementation of the commission's findings and recommendations: "I've given up trying to change the attitude of employers in America. . . . I want to change their behavior, and the only way to do that is to change the law to give the courts and the board the tools they need."[6] Fraser maintained that the 1994 election results represented the worst electoral defeat for organized labor that he had ever seen, and that thinking any legislation favorable to unions would occur is just "daydreaming."

Many more nonunion employees have turned to the courts in recent years for redress of problems relating to job security and employment discrimination. Indeed, one observer predicts that the courts will be an alternative to, rather than a supporter of, labor unions in the 1990s.[7]

Union and management participants in the labor relations process will continue to experience varied relationships in the 1990s and beyond. The likelihood of mutual gains at a particular location will be affected by the extent that the participants agree that a business's survival is necessary for revenues, returns to shareholders, and employees' jobs. Management and union officials must clearly recognize a payoff for cooperation. Union leaders and members will not likely urge a cooperative approach if previous, related efforts result in higher productivity and fewer jobs. For example, Lynn Williams, president of the United Steelworkers of America, maintains that employee input programs can be justified because

- People who have invested their lives in a company should by rights have an understanding of what the company is doing.

- Collective bargaining works well if both sides of the table know everything there is to know about the enterprise.[8]

Yet, Williams also notes that job security is a necessary prerequisite:

> Because of the traditional worry in the United States: if you give the company all your good ideas, you're going to work yourself out of a job, they'll use your good ideas to get rid of you. There needs to be an understanding that the purpose of having the enterprise work more efficiently is not to get rid of workers but to enhance their jobs and provide a higher level of employment security.[9]

Adequate mechanisms, such as two-way communication, for mutual gains need to be established so that employees can voice opinions without fear of managerial retaliation and union officials do not have to worry about their organization and positions being subverted by the process. Problem solving also relies on the sharing of sufficient information, such as financial and production data, sales data, and revenue projections, between management and unions so that both may be informed participants. Morton Bahr, president of the Communications Workers of America, indicated how this mechanism influenced recent negotiations that were regarded as successful by both union and management officials at AT&T:

> In the years before 1992, the union was in a reactive mode. . . . We had no role in the decision-making process. Everything that was negotiated took place essentially after decisions were made. This contract guarantees us, in writing, to be involved in the information-sharing process that's so necessary before decisions are made.[10]

Sound interpersonal relationships are another prerequisite for attaining mutual gains for union and management participants. Some research has indicated that this will be more important than economic pressures in implementing successful cooperative programs. Union and management officials will need to trust each other, and cooperation will be more likely to occur in situations where at least some management officials have also experienced the hardship of layoffs and reduced wages and benefits.[11]

In some situations, unions will have difficulty trusting management because of management's previous behavior. For example, at one rubber plant, the union accepted wage and work-rule concessions as a cooperative effort to help the company cut its costs and be competitive. Later, during a representation election at a nonunion plant, company officials told employees that the union had "sold out its members by taking concessions." The plant has remained nonunion. Likewise, employees find it difficult to accept management's requests to control wage demands or accept wage reductions when they read about executive pay levels and raises. One union official, for example, reported that executive pay rates had more than tripled between 1980 and 1988, whereas factory employee wages rose only 44 percent. Moreover, by 1990, salaries of chief executive officers were 95 times the wage of the average factory employee, compared with 45 times in 1960.[12]

Adversarial relationships will not end in the 1990s. One leader of a national union suggested that noncooperative relationships will remain, at least at some locations, because American managers "can't clobber us with [their] right hand and try to shake hands with [their] left."[13] For example, Caterpillar and E.E. Staley Manufacturing are two companies that unilaterally imposed working conditions after an acrimonious collective bargaining impasse was declared. In retaliation, employees at these facilities have lowered productivity by following to the letter inefficient company work rules such as installing a large hose before installing a small hose behind it and driving a delivery truck on company property at the posted 15-mile-an-hour speed limit instead of the previous, informal 25 mile-an-hour speed limit.[14]

Success of union representatives' efforts will depend on various characteristics and predispositions of employee participants. According to one survey, 32 percent of nonunionized employees would vote to join a union if an election were held at their workplace.[15] Unions will be successful to the extent that they can convert these statistics into union membership. For example,

> [First] . . . as women become increasingly committed to the labor force they may become less and less satisfied with their traditional jobs, and so more prone to the argument of comparable worth and to unionism. This may be the case especially in white-collar factories, such as banks and insurance companies, where heavy layoffs occurred in the recent recession. Second, as the South becomes increasingly industrialized, both racial tensions and anti-union sentiments may decline. Third, unions may win converts among college-trained members of the "baby boom generation." Only a fraction of this group can be accommodated in professional and managerial jobs, tremendous frustrations may develop as their occupational aspirations become thwarted. Conceivably, unions could take advantage of these frustrations, although doing so may require substantial changes in organizing strategies and bargaining goals.[16]

Union growth might also be offset by management's human resource strategies, such as hiring temporary employees and increasing overtime for current employees. In 1992, employers filled an estimated 50 percent of their job vacancies with part-time or temporary employees, who receive few, if any, benefits. These employers attempt to remain competitive by retaining a core of valued managers and other employees while employing part-time workers and laying off many employees as business spurts and slumps. In 1993, with the economy showing signs of improvement, many employers chose to increase employee overtime rather than add new employees. This situation, in the short run, will likely discourage union growth, particularly if existing employees fear replacement by job applicants who will work for less or that the employer might cease operations or relocate to a foreign country. However, as noted in Chapter 5, employees' "scarcity consciousness" might result in union membership gains in the long run.

Unions also have to satisfy employee concerns if they are to be successful in the remaining two steps of the labor relations process: negotiating and administering the labor agreement. Many of these concerns can be grouped into two general employee preference categories: (1) short-run, measurable, and material improvements in workforce conditions and (2) long-run, broad improvements affecting employees' off-job life.

Some maintain that unions will self-destruct in the 1990s because they will continue to focus on the first employee preference category to the exclusion of the second. One labor relations observer contends,

> Unions are dead in the water. . . . They're victims of a completely inefficient and bureaucratic leadership that has pursued narrow self-interest, and bought into the corporatist system, instead of building a strong labor movement to oppose it. The labor movement in the United States is not a labor movement at all, but a collection of insurance companies parading as unions.[17]

The day after John Sweeney was elected to the AFL-CIO presidency in 1995, he led a march to New York City's garment district, symbolically demonstrating the organizing tactics he had used to obtain significant membership gains when he was president of the Service Employees International Union. Sweeney's aggressive attempts to restore organized labor's waning significance is further revealed in Exhibit 16.1.

Yet union organizing gains can be thwarted by *lack of union member interest and solidarity* and *employers' use of various human resource strategies to remain competitive.* Stephen Yokich, the new president of the UAW, indicated after Sweeney's election that, "This is the first time in 20 years there's excitement." Perhaps this is the case, although one report suggests that a large segment of the labor community in the Midwest expressed minimal interest in Sweeney's election.[18] Moreover, some evidence suggests that currently more antagonism and feuding exist between various national unions over securing membership status for both unorganized and organized employees.[19] This contention might be supported by no less than the founder of the AFL, Samuel Gompers. His classic "more" speech has been assumed by many to pertain exclusively to the first employee preference category, yet Gompers's following statement where "more" was uttered covered elements of social reform as well.

Exhibit 16.1 Selected Campaign Proposals of AFL-CIO President John Sweeney

- **Organizing:** Create a separate AFL-CIO organizing department.
- **Politics:** Create a training center to develop campaign organizers, campaign managers, and candidates. Create a policy to develop new approaches to economic and public policy.
- **Corporate campaigns:** Create a Strategic Campaign Fund that could provide grants to unions "in important and difficult fights."
- **Strikes:** Create a support team to help in long-running strikes.
- **Pensions:** Create a clearinghouse to manage a database of union pension-fund investments to support unions in corporate-governance campaigns.
- **Other:** Expand AFL-CIO Executive Council from 33 to 45 vice-presidents and bar individuals over 70 from running for top AFL-CIO offices.

SOURCE: Robert L. Rose and G. Pascal Zachary, "New Labor Chief's Top Job: Resuscitation," *The Wall Street Journal*, October 23, 1995, p. B-1.

> We want more school houses and less jails, more books and less arsenals; . . .
>
> More learning and less vice, more constant work and less crime, more leisure and less greed, more justice and less revenge.
>
> In fact, more of the opportunities to cultivate our better natures, to make manhood more noble, womanhood more beautiful, and childhood more happy and bright.[20]

Proscriptions made by academics and labor union officials, while provocative, are not decisive. The AFL-CIO's Executive Council has noted, ". . . the labor movement exists to advance the interests of workers as workers see their interests."[21] Employees will continue to assess their union's success on the first preference dimension, not the second. Unions, in attempting to achieve this success, will likely experience more intraorganizational bargaining during this period.

Influences on the Participants and Related Work Rules

Public opinion generated through the media will continue to influence employee attitudes toward unions and their subsequent decisions to unionize or to participate in collective bargaining activities such as strikes. A shift in media portrayal of unions and collective bargaining appears to be taking place during the 1990s. The unions involved in the Eastern Airlines, Pittston (coal), and Bridgestone-Firestone strikes were portrayed as "underdogs" fighting for a principle against financially questionable managerial practices. The three-year labor dispute between management and several unions at the *New York Daily News* (Case 4.2) was not given an anti-union treatment by the media, and baseball owners were portrayed by many reporters as being the instigators and sustainers of the 1994 players' strike. On the other hand, violence that occurred during the Pittston, Greyhound, and *Daily News* strikes, as well as allegations of corruption within the Teamsters and subsequent intervention by the Justice Department, did nothing to endear the unions to the public.

The public has become increasingly interested in foreign-made products, which may contribute to a situation not conducive to union growth. Exhibit 16.2 indicates those industries where U.S. employers have maintained or lost their competitive advantage against **international forces.** In some cases companies will attempt to regain or maintain their competitive advantage by extending their **product market** to include purchase of parts made by foreign operations. This situation prompted a strike of 32,500 members of the International Association of Machinists and Aerospace Workers at the Boeing company. The union contended that most components could be made better and cheaper domestically; however, management countered that some use of foreign subcontractors is necessary, if only to win sales in an increasingly global marketplace.[22]

Employers' 1996 bargaining objectives indicated in a survey conducted by the Bureau of National Affairs might shape related work rules/labor agreement provisions for the rest of this century.[23]

Exhibit 16.2 Examples of U.S. Manufacturers' Competitive Edge

INDUSTRIES IN WHICH THE UNITED STATES HAS LOST ITS COMPETITIVE EDGE	INDUSTRIES IN WHICH THE UNITED STATES HAS RETAINED ITS COMPETITIVE EDGE
General industrial machinery	Drugs
Household appliances	Bakery products
Leather tanning and finishing	Dairy products
Toys and sporting goods	Pulp and paperboard mills
Knitting mills	Metal cans and shipping containers
Women's and misses' outerwear	Aircraft bodies and parts
	Household audio and video equipment
	Communication equipment

SOURCE: "U.S. Manufacturers Advised to Boost Competitiveness through Better Technology," *Daily Labor Report,* March 12, 1990, p. A-1.

- Lump-sum benefits in lieu of wage increases are increasingly popular (26 percent of 228 responding employers in 1995 versus 21 percent in 1994).
- Employers will retain a two-tier wage system (86 percent of the respondents) if they already have one in force (applicable to 41 percent of the respondents). However, only 9 percent of the employers not having this mechanism would seek to establish such a plan.
- Management strongly prefers (82 percent) to keep average annual pay increases below 4 percent.
- A majority of employers will seek insurance cost containment measures at the bargaining table in 1996, even if employee contributions (paying deductibles, for example) are already in effect.
- Fifty percent of employers indicated they would consider increasing pension benefits in 1996, and 23 percent of the management respondents indicated they would consider negotiating early retirement incentives.
- More than half (57 percent) of the existing labor agreements contain sexual harassment provisions; only 4 percent of management officials seek to establish such policies in 1996.
- Labor-management cooperation programs existed in a minority (41 percent) of the surveyed organizations' 1995 labor agreements; only 7 percent of management representatives seek to establish this arrangement in future negotiations.
- About 99 percent of the surveyed employers said they would not consider bargaining over increased vacation days, holidays, or personal leave time.

Unions will focus on the impact of external influences on job security. Labor agreement provisions for employment guarantees, advance notice of layoffs and technological change, restrictions on subcontracting, and job retraining and relocation services will all be important issues. Unions will also attempt to increase compensation for learned skills commensurate with technological innovations. However, union leaders will likely not employ the strike tactic to obtain these bargaining gains.

The number of strike days lost in the 1990s will remain as low or lower than in the 1980s. Eighty-two percent of recently surveyed employers indicated they would consider replacing employees if they went out on strike.[24] As indicated by strikes at AT&T, NYNEX, Eastern Airlines, Greyhound, and Bridgestone-Firestone, management can continue operations during a strike through technological features in the workplace or by hiring strike replacements of even skilled employees.

Some companies will also consider tactics used by International Paper and Greyhound to increase pressure on the unions and their members prior to negotiations. International Paper advertised for replacement employees and had the new applicants line up outside the employment office within viewing distance of the mill workforce so that present employees would be aware of its intentions in the case of a strike. Greyhound started hiring and training replacement drivers in anticipation of a strike by the union.

In response to these "hard-ball" tactics, unions will increasingly resort to "corporate campaigns" (see Case 4.1) as an alternative to strikes. Unions will wage these campaigns on many fronts, making it difficult for management to plan a response as is possible when anticipating a strike. Corporate campaign tactics will include adverse publicity about the employer, consumer boycotts, targeting financial institutions that do business with the employer, political lobbying, and putting pressure on shareholders.[25] Unions will also increase their use of informational picketing and telepicketing (calling potential customers by phone) to advise shoppers to avoid patronizing nonunion retail establishments.

In the next decade, unions will play an ever-increasing role in the financial arena. In Chapter 4, we mentioned that unions are learning to use their financial clout by purchasing stock or participating in corporate takeovers. In Chapter 13, we discussed union participation in employee stock option plans. The AFL-CIO has established the Employee Partnership Fund (EPF), for which it hopes to raise $200 million for small and medium-size financial deals. The EPF will be used for investments and will sell shares to employees or the public.[26] Lynn Williams maintains that the **financial influence** has resulted in his union's reorganizing and bargaining over "corporate issues":

> We want to ensure that the parent corporation accepts responsibility for whatever its subsidiaries or joint ventures may be doing. For example, we want to make sure that when a piece of a corporation is sold off, pension obligations aren't passed onto a new subsidiary where we could lose track of them.
>
> Another objective is to obtain the right of first refusal when a piece of a corporation is sold off so that we can consider turning it into an employee-owned venture. We have

not accomplished the objective of gaining the right of first refusal, though we do have a number of employee-owned ventures and several contracts in which we're entitled to information or the right to make a bid.[27]

You should be able to apply much of what you have learned in this book regardless of the direction of the labor relations process in the United States. Some topics, such as negotiations, bargaining power, and employee discipline, should apply to your career and personal situations beyond the field of labor relations. The book's emphasis on interpersonal relationships, resolving conflict, and cooperation through attitudes (such as respect) and activities (such as face saving) should have general applicability as well. Above all, remember that the best answer to a labor relations question, such as "When will a particular strike be over?" is a thoroughly qualified, "It depends."

References

1. U.S. Department of Labor, Bureau of Labor-Management Relations and Cooperative Programs, *Human Resource Policies and Practices in American Firms* (Washington, D.C.: Bureau of Labor Management, 1988), pp. 33–40.

2. Byron York, "Reich's Opulent Photo-Op," *The Wall Street Journal,* May 31, 1994, p. A-16.

3. Commission on the Future of Worker-Management Relations, *Report and Recommendations* (Washington, D.C.: Department of Labor, December 1994).

4. "Union Leaders Unhappy with Report on Labor Issues," *USA Today,* January 10, 1995, p. 1-B.

5. Howard Banks, "Clinton's Pro-Labor Agenda Emerges," *Forbes,* March 29, 1993, p. 37.

6. "Fraser Calls for Changing Employers' Behavior," Bureau of National Affairs Inc., *Daily Labor Report* no. 94 (May 16, 1995), p. A-16.

7. Daniel J. B. Mitchell, "Will Collective Bargaining Outcomes in the 1990s Look Like Those of the 1980s?" *Labor Law Journal* 40 (August 1989), p. 425.

8. Barbara Noble, "Reinventing Labor: An Interview with Union President Lynn Williams," *Harvard Business Review* 71 (July–August 1993), p. 120.

9. Ibid., p. 20. For additional considerations the Dunlop Commission found regarding employee involvement programs, see Commission on the Future of Worker-Management Relations, *Report and Recommendations,* pp. 8–13.

10. Barbara Presley Noble, "More Than Labor Amity at AT&T," *The New York Times,* March 14, 1993, p. 25.

11. Gary N. Chaison and Mark S. Polvnick, "Is There a New Collective Bargaining?" *California Management Review* 28 (Summer 1986), p. 59.

12. "High Executive Pay Is Not Product of Market Forces, Union Official Says," *Daily Labor Report,* March 7, 1990, p. A-12; and Robert Reich, "Executive Paychecks," *The Miami Herald,* March 15, 1992.

13. "Future of Labor Unions Focus of Debate at Management Conclave at Wharton School," Bureau of National Affairs Inc., *Daily Labor Report* no. 189 (October 2, 1989), p. A-5.

14. Louis Uchitelle, "Labor Draws the Line in Decatur," *The New York Times,* June 13, 1993, Sec. 3, pp. 1, 6.

15. Commission on the Future of Worker-Management Relations, *Report and Recommendations,* p. 17.

16. George Strauss, "Industrial Relations: Time of Change," *Industrial Relations* 23 (Winter 1984), pp. 12–13.

17. Karen J. Winkler, "Precipitous Decline of American Unions Fuels Growing Interest Among Scholars," *Chronicle of*

Higher Education, November 12, 1986, p. 16.

18. Peter Kilborn, "AFL-CIO Picks Militant as President," *The New York Times,* October 26, 1995, p. A-16. See also "Midwestern Unionists Show Little Interest in AFL-CIO Contest," Bureau of National Affairs Inc., *Daily Labor Report* no. 200 (October 17, 1995), p. C-1.

19. Asra Q. Nomani, "Shaken Solidarity: Struggling to Survive, Unions Battle Unions to Build Memberships," *The Wall Street Journal,* October 25, 1995, p. A-1.

20. "Statements on Collective Bargaining during the Next 50 Years," Bureau of National Affairs Inc., *Daily Labor Report* no. 134 (July 7, 1985), p. D-1.

21. *The Changing Situation of Workers and Their Unions* (AFL-CIO, 1985), p. 17.

22. Lawrence M. Fisher, "Union Rejects Boeing Offer; Goes on Strike in Three States," *The New York Times,* October 7, 1995, p. 8.

23. "Employer Bargaining Objectives, 1996" Bureau of National Affairs Inc., *Daily Labor Report,* special supplement (September 28, 1995), pp. 1–8.

24. Ibid., p. 1.

25. "Lawyers Predict Corporate Campaigns Will Remain Popular as Strike Alternatives," *Daily Labor Report,* March 7, 1990, p. A-11. See also "Steelworkers' President Urges Unions to Target Employers' Pressure Points," Bureau of National Affairs Inc., *Daily Labor Report* no. 107 (June 4, 1991), pp. A-3–A-4.

26. Aaron Bernstein, "Soon, LBOs May be Union-Made," *Business Week,* February 26, 1990, p. 91.

27. Noble, "Reinventing Labor," p. 122.

CASES FOR PART FOUR

Case 4.1 UFCW's Campaign against Food Lion: A Split Strategic Outcome

Unions have initiated corporate campaigns designed to generate public concern over management practices, embarrass executives, and limit the ability of the targeted nonunion organization for at least two reasons:

- The action might make the company or other nonunion companies witnessing the campaign more passive, even receptive, to a union-organizing drive.
- Union members at other facilities might have increased job security if the targeted company/competitor has higher labor costs after the campaign.

The United Food and Commercial Workers (UFCW) campaign against Food Lion had two immediate objectives: protesting illegal employment practices committed by the company and focusing public attention on unsanitary food-handling practices. In the fall of 1991 the union attempted to become the exclusive bargaining representative for Food Lion employees, in part by representing 183 former and current employees allegedly exposed to illegal employment practices (such as working "off the clock" and not receiving compensation). By January 1993, 846 employees were involved in related litigation.

Source: Adapted from Ronald J. Adams, Kenneth M. Jennings, and Dilip D. Kare, "An Analysis of the UFCW's Corporate Campaign Against Food Lion," *Labor Law Journal*, September 1994, pp. 555–560.

Eight months of related negotiations between Food Lion and the Department of Labor produced a record settlement of $16.2 million paid to former and current employees. The company was also required to implement several steps to ensure compliance with the Fair Labor Standards Act, such as continue operating an "800" telephone number through which employees could anonymously report violations.

On November 5, 1992, ABC's *Prime Time Live* reported with videotaped "evidence" that Food Lion repackaged meat, dairy, and deli products with extended "sell by" dates; doctored rotted food items with lemon juice, baking soda, and chlorine bleach solutions to remove the odors; and used unsanitary equipment in handling and preparing fresh meats. The specific role of the union in this telecast was unclear. No union officials were interviewed in the segment, and several former employees indicated that they were not interested in the union and were currently working for other nonunion companies.

However, a UFCW spokesperson acknowledged that the union supplied names of some current and former employees to ABC while the *Washington Times* contended that the union had helped an assistant producer at ABC become employed at Food Lion so she could use a hidden camera to record operations. The union also referred to the segment in a subsequent commercial, indicating that Food Lion's health infractions could never occur at a unionized food store.

The corporate campaign seriously and adversely impacted Food Lion. The company's earnings were down 55 percent in the fourth quarter of 1992. Moreover, the company's first-quarter earnings for 1993 showed a 56 percent decrease when compared with first-quarter 1992 figures, even though sales had increased 4 percent when the two time periods were compared. Sales and net income for the second quarter of 1993 posted increases (5.6 percent and 40 percent, respectively) when compared with first-quarter 1993 figures; however, the company reported a net income decrease of 41.6 percent for the second quarter of 1993 compared with the second quarter of 1992.

Food Lion paid the DOL settlement in the third quarter of 1993. Some of the settlement funds came from previously established reserves; however, some of it affected third-quarter net income ($6.2 million, or $0.0128 per share). The company reported a sales increase of 7.1 percent and a net income decrease of 49.1 percent for the third quarter of 1993 compared with the third quarter of 1992.

These figures precipitated a reduction in the price of Food Lion stock. Two days before the *Prime Time Live* telecast aired, Food Lion's Class A and Class B stock was $11 1/2 and $10 1/2, respectively. Both stocks dropped sharply after the report and remained at low levels throughout the spring, summer, and fall of 1993 (for example, Class A was $6 per share and Class B was $6 1/4 a share on October 8, 1993).

Yet, these effects have not been completely realized and/or linked to the corporate campaign's intended consequences: raising Food Lion's operating costs to ensure a level playing field with food chains having unionized employees and acceptance of the UFCW by Food Lion and/or other nonunion food chains. Moreover, unintended results from a corporate campaign could conceivably retard or worsen the union's financial and/or membership status.

There have been few, if any, publicized accounts of an increase in UFCW membership figures, either at Food Lion or at other neighboring food stores for November 1992 to November 1993. Indeed, an unintended consequence of the UFCW's corporate campaign might make it more difficult for the union to organize food store employees in the future. There is a strong possibility that other nonunion food store chains, such as Winn Dixie, have regarded Food Lion's settlement with the DOL as a wake-up call and taken additional steps to avoid violations of the Fair Labor Standards Act. This situation may narrow the gap between nonunion and union labor costs; but employees at these organizations might view these efforts in a positive sense, making it more difficult for the union to organize them.

The success of these effects on intended union consequences should address the following considerations: How much revenue is needed to achieve these intended consequences? How should these consequences be measured? These considerations, in turn, must be qualified by the appropriate measurement time periods and potential unanticipated consequences of the campaign. A corporate campaign can inflict dramatic and significant impact on a nonunion employer; however, a union cannot automatically expect or even measure the campaign's success until the preceding considerations are first realized and determined.

Questions

1. Evaluate the pros and cons of the UFCW's corporate strategy.
2. What other alternatives are available?

Case 4.2 Peripheral Bargaining at the *New York Daily News*

The 1990 to 1993 strike and collective bargaining experience at the *New York Daily News* was punctuated by beatings, stabbings, and fire-bombed vehicles and buildings. This experience, while dramatic and compelling (it sometimes jostled with Operation Desert Storm for top news coverage, particularly in New York City), carries a potential for deeper changes in the second phase of the labor relations process, negotiation of the labor agreement.

The first part of this case conceptualizes *peripheral bargaining,* an alternative to the traditional collective bargaining discussed in this book. Then discussed are influences affecting the 1990 *Daily News* negotiations and collective bargaining at the newspaper around contract expiration time. The fourth section describes the antecedents and aftermath of the strike/lockout incident, "Battle of Wounded Knee," followed by the strike-related activities of the next 100 days. Finally, two subsequent purchases of the *News* and their implications for labor-management relationships are considered.

Peripheral Bargaining Compared with Traditional Bargaining

Richard Walton and Robert McKersie's classic book, *A Behavioral Theory of Labor Negotiations,* maintained that traditional bargaining activities represent "the deliberate interaction of two or more complex social units which are attempting to define or redefine the terms of their interdependence." Moreover, the relationship between the parties to labor negotiations is usually unique, continuing, and long-term.

Source: Adapted from Kenneth M. Jennings, *Labor Relations at the New York Daily News: Peripheral Bargaining in the 1990 Strike* (New York: Praeger, 1993).

Hence, traditional bargaining focuses on the output of labor-management relationships and work rules, and usually features the following:

- Intensive bargaining efforts by labor and management officials, who have a joint goal of reaching agreement;
- A sense of mutual respect and trust between union and management negotiators;
- The realization that both parties have to live with each other after the labor agreement is obtained; and
- A nonreliance on or avoidance of external bargaining tactics (such as appeals to public opinion) and outside organizations (such as the press, courts, or government agencies).

Peripheral bargaining has none of the aforementioned features of traditional bargaining. There is also very little focus on measurable bargaining issues such as wages or containment of health costs. Instead, vague considerations such as personalities and principle are stressed by one or both parties. Thus, the parties are likely to spend little time in formulating, costing, and anticipating proposals in the prenegotiations stage. Any previous issues that were amicably resolved between the parties are also ignored, while hostile negotiations or issues are emphasized.

One or both of the parties in peripheral bargaining might engage in dilatory maneuvers, surface bargaining, and other tactics that would violate their good faith bargaining obligation under the National Labor Relations Act. Yet this alternative bargaining approach does not have to include these tactics and includes broader dimensions such as efforts to weaken solidarity between or within unions, possibly through back-to-work movements or hiring striker replacements. One or both parties might rely more on external agencies and individuals (such as courts, the National Labor Relations Board, elected government officials, public hearings, and the media) because the need for persuasion increases as negotiations proceed with few tangible bargaining results. Management and union negotiators rely on press clippings and other external measures of bargaining success and attempt to save face without having to justify the lack of bargaining results to their bargaining constituents (stockholders and union members).

A bargaining impasse is almost inevitable in peripheral bargaining, therefore, as union leaders do not have measurable accomplishments to show members to justify a ratified labor agreement. Each party then focuses on blaming the other for this situation instead of looking for superordinate goals and other factors that could end the dispute.

Influences Affecting the 1990 *Daily News* Negotiations

The 1990 *Daily News* negotiations were influenced by three previous collective bargaining negotiations, one in 1985 involving the *Chicago Tribune,* which, like the *Daily News,* was owned by the Chicago Tribune Company, and the 1982 and 1987 labor agreements reached at the *New York Daily News.* Charles Brumback was the *Chicago Tribune* executive most identified with the organization's collective bargaining stance in 1985. He had 26 years of experience with newspaper operations before becoming president and chief executive officer (CEO) at the *Chicago Tribune.* On August 1, 1990, he became CEO of the Chicago Tribune Co., which owned several newspapers, including the *Chicago Tribune* and the *Daily News,* and was a major influence in the 1990s *News* negotiations. Brumback's education and experience were in accounting and finance. He enjoyed a fine reputation among financial analysts. However, some maintained that he had little, if any, notion of how the contents of the newspaper should be obtained and delivered.

Brumback was directly involved in the 1985 negotiations between the *Chicago Tribune* and three of its unions representing the printers, mailers, and pressmen, which initiated a strike on July 18th. He also departed from previous management bargaining strategy when he hired the Nashville law firm of King, Ballow and Little, known by many labor leaders as "the biggest union-busting law firm in America."

The *Chicago Tribune* strike's first year was marked by bickering between the unions, union rallies, an unsuccessful boycott, union attempts to bring politicians into the situation, management's hiring of striker replacements, and no progress at the bargaining table. Management benefited from this action because it also eliminated some 400 jobs, more than 25 percent of the workforce, and reduced the number of unionized pressmen from 375 in 1985 to 27 in 1990. Moreover, striker replacements were paid much less than the strikers. The printers reached an agreement with the *Chicago Tribune* in 1989; however, the pressmen and mailers filed unfair labor practices with the National Labor Relations Board (NLRB) over their members' job losses. These charges were unresolved as negotiations were occurring at the *Daily News* in 1990.

The 1990 *News* negotiations were also influenced by previous negotiations in 1982 and 1987 involving the *News* and the Allied Printing Trades Council (APTC), an umbrella organization of 10 newspaper unions in New York City that represented *News* employees (see Exhibit C4.1).

Both negotiations followed the traditional bargaining approach with the unions agreeing to job reductions. In 1987, unions and management at the *News* agreed on a Mutual Investment Plan (MIP) that called for $60 million to be invested in the newspaper and up to $50 million in buyouts and severance pay in return for $30 million in contract concessions from the unions. This agreement contained rather complex and sometimes vague language to protect both union and management interests. For example, the agreement outlined what an investment could represent but

Exhibit C4.1 Summary of Ten *News* Unions Represented by the Allied Printing Trades Council

UNION	MEMBERSHIP	FUNCTION	PRESIDENT
International Brotherhood and Electrical Workers, Local 3	43	electrical maintenance	Dennis McSpedon
International Typographical Union, Local 6	199	typesetters and composing room employees	James Grottola
Machinists Local 434	32	maintain presses and other equipment	Joseph Armao
Newspaper Guild of New York	786	newsroom and advertising employees	Barry Lipton
Newspaper and Mail Deliverers Union of New York and Vicinity	743	drivers	Michael Alvino
Newspaper Printing Pressmen's Union No. 2	410	operate the presses	Jack Kennedy
New York Mailers, Union Local 6	116	bundle and prepare newspapers for delivery	George McDonald
Paperhandlers Union	79	load and unload paper rolls onto printing presses	Pat Flannery
Photoengravers Union Local 1P	16	take pictures of completed pages	Stan Aslanian
Stereotypers Union Local 1	37	use film to make plates for presses	Jack Kennedy (not same as Pressmen's president)

SOURCE: Harry Berkowitz, "Unions Vow to Bring *News* To Its Knees, Guild Members Join Strike Upon Word of Mass Firings," *Newsday,* October 27, 1990.

gave management discretion in where to invest. Possibilities included color printing equipment, a new inking system, and front-end systems for various departments. The MIP did include a $20 million cap on how much of the $60 million could be used for buying land for a new plant site.

The MIP also gave the unions extra severance if the *News* folded or was sold before the full $60 million was invested. Unions would receive half the investment shortfall; for example, $15 million would be added to severance payments if the *News* invested $30 million during the life of the labor agreement. A representative for the *News* reported "no major stumbling blocks" in reaching the agreement and further stressed that the agreement "demonstrates that both the company and unions are deadly serious about turning this newspaper around."[1]

Thus, 1990 negotiations at the *News* were subjected to opposing influences: the 1985 strike at the *Tribune* and two traditional "win-win" bargaining experiences at the *News.* Brumback appeared so intent on replicating his 1985 *Chicago Tribune* bargaining "success" at the *News* that some of his colleagues labeled the 1990 labor-management confrontation, "Charlie II." Yet, many thought he could not achieve a similar situation in a "union town" like New York City.

Some union leaders and newspaper executives strongly maintained that nonunion newspaper delivery during a strike could not take place in New York City, particularly if it occurred without police protection, a prediction supported by past experience. Previous newspaper strikes in New York City during the 1960s had hastened the demise of the *Herald Tribune,* the *Mirror,* the *Journal American,* and the *World-Telegram and Sun.* The *News* had also experienced a strike in 1978 during which delivery was impeded by rock throwing, firebombed trucks, and numerous arrests. When *News* reporters went on strike, the newspaper continued to hit the stands for only two days until the drivers joined the strike and brought circulation to a halt. After this strike, some 12 percent of the paper's circulation never returned.

Collective Bargaining Considerations and Activities around the Contract Expiration Date

The *News* had not experienced financial success in 1988 and 1989. Operating profit for 1988 was approximately 4 percent of revenues, compared with the average return of metropolitan papers of 18 to 20 percent. The *Daily News* had revenues of $420 million in 1989 and still lost several million dollars. Estimates from 1990 projected that the *News* would lose $20 million on revenues close to $400 million. From 1980 through 1989, the paper had lost $134 million on $4 billion in revenues. Average daily paid circulation had fallen by 400,000 copies since 1979; the paper's circulation was 1.2 million on September 30, 1989, which was down 7 percent from 1988.

A portion of the dire financial conditions influencing the bargaining was due to extraneous factors. For example, there had been a nationwide trend of reduced newspaper reading. Only 66 percent of Americans now read a newspaper on an average day, compared with 75 percent 20 years ago.

Management and union officials approached the 1990 negotiations blaming each other for the *News*'s financial troubles. The unions thought management in general, and publisher James Hoge in particular, were responsible for the newspaper's difficult situation. As George McDonald, president of the Mailers' union and the APTC noted, "The *News* has bum management," and James Hoge is "a sociable guy, but as publisher he's a 4 on a scale of 1 to 10."[2] Jack Kennedy, president of the New York Printing Pressmen's Local, maintained that the *News*'s biggest problem was that it was "the most mismanaged paper in America."

Ever since *Esquire* had featured Hoge along with Hollywood personalities such as John Travolta and George Hamilton in a 1979 piece called "The Dangers of Being Too Good Looking," Hoge has had to contend with a public image that tends to focus on his physical appearance and elegant lifestyle.[3] Union leaders equated Hoge's public image with management's insincere, superficial bargaining and regarded Hoge as a "patrician errand boy for the Tribune Tower in Chicago." They also associated Hoge's hiring and first contract negotiations with "double crosses" in which management did not make investment in the *News* corresponding to the 1982 and 1987 labor agreement settlements, MIP promises, and union concessions.

Hoge, on the other hand, claimed that archaic work rules and high wages put the newspaper in a "financial straitjacket" because the newspaper's labor costs (48 percent of annual revenues) were much higher than those experienced by competitors (25 to 30 percent of annual revenues). Management wanted real flexibility to direct its workforce and proposed that the following 200-word management rights clause be included in the ten labor agreements:

> The sole and exclusive rights of management shall include but not be limited to the right to: hire, assign, schedule, lay off, recall, transfer, suspend, discharge, or otherwise discipline employees; determine, establish and implement terms and conditions of employment; establish or con-

tinue policies, practices, and procedures for the conduct of the business and, from time to time, to change or abolish such policies, practices, or procedures in order to prevent any redundancy or duplication of work or for any other reason; determine and select the equipment to be used in the Publisher's operations and, from time to time, to change or to discontinue the use of any equipment and to select new equipment for its operations, including equipment for new operations.[4]

Theodore W. Kheel, who had mediated most of the newspaper strikes in New York since the 1950s and served as an unpaid advisor to labor in the 1990 negotiations, admitted that the Tribune Company's aggressive bargaining stance at this time was due to the organization's being in a very good position, which Kheel, McDonald, and Kennedy attributed to the Tribune Company not desiring to remain in New York. McDonald suggested that these conditions forced unions to recognize and counter management's "win-win" situation. The *News* could beat up or even break the union with wage concessions or a smaller nonunion payroll, situations that would make the paper attractive to a potential buyer. Or management could blame the union for costly work rules and/or a strike and close operations with relatively low shutdown costs.

Union officials thought that management could obtain at least one major advantage through its hardline bargaining approach and goals of selling or closing the newspaper, namely, avoiding $150 million in employee severance payments and unfunded pensions. Kheel admitted that unions would contest this loss if the facility were sold or shut down, even through a strike; yet he felt that the risk of losing the severance payments through litigation was less than that of continuing to run the paper.

There were few common bargaining goals between management and the unions in the 1990 negotiations, and both sought to convince the public that their position was just. Management ordered 5,000 copies of a *Vanity Fair* issue that portrayed it a victim of union featherbedding abuses and sent the magazines to advertisers and those considered to be influential New Yorkers. It also stressed to New York's minority community that increased flexibility would enable the newspaper to ignore union hiring lists that contained only the names of white males and hire more minorities.

The union hired a public relations organization, the Kamber Group. Included in its initial work was the following press release from Jack Kennedy on January 25, 1990:

In yet another attempt to deceive the people of New York and divert attention from their dismal failures as managers, the *Daily News* yesterday planted an erroneous and misleading film clip with "Eyewitness News." . . . James Hoge sent a video crew into the *News* Brooklyn plant in November to allegedly film footage of a running press, for internal purposes. The crew told my members who were working at the time to please step aside for a few moments so they could get a clean shot of a press in action. My members agreed, not realizing that this was just another in a long line of carefully orchestrated dirty tricks planned by Hoge to deceive and distort the truth.

The Kamber Group also transmitted general themes, such as that unions and management had both agreed to various "costly and outmoded" work practices in the 1960s and that it was unreasonable to expect the union to give these practices up in one sitting, particularly to a management that could not be trusted to keep its commitments to the union. Union officials also wanted the public to know that they strongly preferred to save the newspaper at the bargaining table, whereas *News* management wanted a show of force. They pointed to the *News*'s hiring of Robert Ballow as management's chief negotiator and overt, dramatic strike preparations as evidence of management's hard-line position. One member of the Newspaper Guild's bargaining committee described his reactions to Ballow's behavior at the first session:

He came on cocky, all Southern drawl and home-turf confidence, like some cracker sheriff who

> had just caught a New York driver doing five miles over the speed limit through some jerkwater town. Ballow plopped his contract proposal on the table and invited us to sign it right then and spare ourselves the pain he implied would certainly ensue if we tried to get around him.[5]

Ballow's hiring, coupled with turnover of previous management bargaining representatives, meant that no traditional relationships could be relied on by either party.

The following strike preparation tactics were used by management, which generated union hostility:

- Stationed armed guards in brown uniforms at four of its printing plants.
- Made sure there were trained and available striker replacements.
- Introduced these individuals to an alternative publishing site such as a Sears warehouse in North Bergen, New Jersey.

Throughout the winter and spring of 1990, management kept a "preparedness pool" in which editors would form car pools complete with "captains," who were assigned to pick up members along designated routes should the need arise.

No bargaining progress occurred during the first three months of 1990, although the head of the Typographer's union said that he would advise his members not to strike to protect lifetime employment guarantees given the printers in 1974 in exchange for allowing *News* management to introduce automated typesetting equipment. Further tensions occurred both between Allied unions when management seemed interested in only three unions (electricians, machinists, and the Newspaper Guild) and within unions like the Newspaper Guild where some members, particularly reporters, doubted they would support a strike when the labor agreements expired on March 31.

The lack of bargaining progress continued through the summer. On July 24, labor leaders announced an "all-fronts boycott" against the *News,* which would be coordinated by hired specialist Samuel McKnight. George McDonald stressed that this action was necessary because the *Daily News* and the Tribune Co. represented the "enemy." The announcement came less than a week after unions had begun mailing thousands of "informational" letters to advertisers that suggested a boycott possibility: "Because you support the *Daily News* with your advertising, you are directly involved in the bitter labor dispute that now exists at the paper."[6] However, no specific details regarding how or when the boycott would emerge were given in this announcement.

The Strike/Lockout Incident: "Battle of Wounded Knee"

The previously discussed nonproductive bargaining and tensions between union and management were crystallized at 2:00 A.M. Thursday, October 25, 1990, when a supervisor at a printing plant ordered an employee to stand as he was working at a machine that bundled newspapers. The employee had been given this "light work" assignment because of a work injury, torn knee ligaments, and he informed the supervisor that this work could be performed while sitting down. The supervisor said that the machine was jammed and that the employee was insubordinate when he refused to stand up and fix it.

The suspended employee then talked to a nonemployee union official and both were ordered out of the facility. About 230 members of the drivers' union followed them out of the facility. Management then asked a business agent whether he could provide replacements. When he responded "No," a bus carrying 14 striker replacements arrived at the facility within the hour. Some union officials contended that the drivers' union made two mistakes: walking out of the facility instead of filing a grievance and not indicating that they could find substitute employees.

However, the suddenness of the replacements' arrival led many unionized employees to believe that management provoked the incident to achieve its long-denied goal of publishing with a nonunion work force. One union official commented that, "If I had a topless dancer, I couldn't get twenty guys together in 20 minutes."[7] Angry drivers threw rocks at the bus, which broke the windshield. They also smashed the side-view mirrors and dented the bus's sides and doors with trashcans and baseball bats. The bus did not get through. Management made videotapes of some of the violence, which included the firebombing of four delivery trucks and slashed tires and/or punctured radiators on 40 more vehicles. Police surrounded the plant by 5:00 A.M. so that a second bus carrying replacements could enter the facility by 7:30 A.M., and the first truckloads of papers could leave with a police escort an hour later.

About 10 hours after the strike/lockout incident, management informed the union participants that 60 employees had been offered and had accepted permanent replacement jobs. These individuals would replace the 60 drivers with the lowest seniority. Moreover, 200 of the drivers who walked out could return to work their Friday night shift, although the other 60 would not be reinstated.

McDonald likened this action to a declaration of war because no union leader could in good conscience endorse this arrangement. Michael Alvino, president of the drivers' union, announced nearly 20 hours after the "Wounded Knee" incident that his union was forced by management to conduct an unfair labor practice strike. Seven more Allied unions joined the strike by Thursday night. A day later the Newspaper Guild voted to join the strike after members found that card keys they had used to enter their offices were no longer valid, and replacement editorial employees with the correct card keys were already performing assignments in the city room. However the Guild's strike decision was far from unanimous, as many members were confused, even angry, about being on strike because a production employee would not stand up. The typographers' union returned to work and was removed from the Allied.

Management's Distribution Problems Immediately After Wounded Knee

Management attempted to publish its Friday newspaper using replacements, some of whom drove trucks containing newspapers out of two facilities at 1:15 A.M. Saturday. The trucks were escorted by a dozen automobiles and were pursued by striking employees.

Arrests of strikers were recorded for reckless endangerment and criminal possession of either instruments (rocks, baseball bats, and bottles, for example) or explosive devices such as M80 firecrackers. Other strikers threw rocks and eggs at buses transporting strike replacements, shouted, "Your wife should get cancer," at replacements, sat down in the middle of a busy thoroughfare, and stole copies of newspapers. *News* management claimed that it printed 611,000 copies of a 48-page newspaper (half the normal size) and delivered 500,000 of them. The union contended only 200,000 were delivered. Management admitted that delivery of its Saturday newspaper was 200,000 copies less than normal, a situation attributed to union violence.

On Saturday, a bus taking seven strike replacements from a printing plant was attacked while stopped at a traffic light. A van and a jeep pulled alongside the bus; one man jumped from the jeep and fired two shots in the air while seven men wearing ski masks jumped out of the van and started banging on the bus with baseball bats. Another incident concerned a substitute driver who was attacked and beaten with a baseball bat when his truck was waylaid near an exit of the Brooklyn-Queens Expressway. Management maintained that since the strike had begun, eight delivery trucks, each worth about $35,000, had been destroyed by firebombs, and 60 others had been damaged by slashed tires, punctured radiators, and smashed windows and windshields.

Many of the *News*'s delivery problems were caused by the new drivers not knowing all of the stops. Many vendors complained that they received too many or too few newspapers, or none at all. Some of these individuals were also intimidated, a situation that further curtailed newspaper sales. For example, one vendor in Brooklyn noted that club-wielding men had seized all 300 copies of the Sunday *News* and scattered them in the gutter. At about the same time, a convenience store employee noted that windows at his workplace had been smashed after the strike began and that three individuals with masks warned him in the middle of the night that if *News* copies were again sold, his store would be burned down.

The *News*'s competitors attempted to take quick advantage of this situation. The *New York Times* was reportedly distributing more of its newspapers to newsstands; *Newsday* delivered an additional 100,000 copies of its *New York Newsday* each day. The *New York Post* increased its daily distribution by 200,000 copies and indicated that it was considering the start-up of a Sunday edition to be published during the strike.

On October 31, strikers distributed "Boycott the Daily News" leaflets outside and encouraged the public (1) not to buy the *News,* (2) to urge news dealers not to sell the *News,* (3) to report any dealer who did sell the newspaper to a telephone hotline; and (4) to refuse to shop in stores having items advertised in the *News.* They were also encouraged to ask their congressional representative to support any bill that banned striker replacements and to make a $5 contribution to help support strikers and their families via a "900" telephone number. The October 31 issue contained 29 pages of advertisements and four pages of classified advertisements, compared with a typical 41 pages and 8 pages, respectively, before the strike began. One advertising agency executive indicated that none of his clients' advertisements would be run in the *News* until the strike was over because he could not rely on the *News*'s circulation.

The Strike's Next Four Months

Some 200 bargaining sessions had occurred from January 1990 to December 1990, but only a dozen since the strike began on October 25. On December 2, the Newspaper and Mail Deliverers' union participated in their second negotiation since the strike began. Management's attitude regarding its 200-word management rights provision appeared to be a major stumbling block for all unions in seeking a negotiated settlement. Wayne Mitchell of the mailers' union indicated that management appeared unwilling to take the prerequisite action of putting its machismo aside. Michael Alvino, the drivers' union president, indicated that whenever he asked Robert Ballow what management specifically wanted in negotiations, Ballow would always respond, "Give us management rights and we'll tell you."

Management and the unions continued to rely on outside sources and actions instead of bargaining table behaviors in November. James Willse, editor of the *News,* sought mailing lists of minority reporters from three related organizations: the Asian-American Journalists Association, the National Association of Hispanic Journalists, and the National Association of Black Journalists.[8] He noted that striker replacements featuring minorities would give the *News* a rare and quick opportunity to build an editorial staff that mirrored the community. However, these organizations refused Willse's request.

Unions conducted at least six rallies in November 1990 with audiences of some 10,000 to 15,000. Jesse Jackson appeared at the second rally and was scolded by Hoge for endorsing six "lily-white" craft unions; however, Jackson retorted "There are racial sins on both sides."[9] At the rally, Jackson said that the *News* was using the race issue as bait, a technique that must be rejected. "When they lock you out, close the doors, and pull the blinds, you can't use color for a crutch."[10] Jackson also reminded replacement employees that if they took a $10 job, an $8 crowd would wait the next day.

The APTC also appealed to other labor organizations for support in November. It published one million copies of the *Real News,* an eight-page graphic twin of the *Daily News,* which, along with traditional news features and subjects, included information on the "what and why" of the labor-management dispute. These newspapers were given to many city unions representing teachers, Teamsters, hospital workers, and firefighters to distribute free of charge.

The APTC also announced the formation of a \$2 million strike fund for a media campaign run by the Kamber Group public relations firm to spread the strikers' message. Half of the fund represented a loan guarantee from local units of the Transport Workers Union, Local 1199; the Teamsters; the United Federation of Teachers; the Communications Workers of America; the United Automobile Workers; and the Retail, Wholesale, and Department Store Workers Union (RWDSU). The remainder was to come from weekly collections of \$1.00 per member from those belonging to the New York City Central Labor Council and the New York State AFL-CIO. The November 14 rally generated additional funds of nearly \$300,000.

Several unions offered more than financial support to the striking unions during November. For example, some 200 members representing 23 unions canvassed neighborhoods in Queens to ask subscribers of the *News* to cancel home delivery. The RWDSU provided sandwiches and drinks daily at all picket locations, and the Service Employees International Union reported that volunteers had made a computerized list of names and addresses of some 8,800 outlets where the *News* was being sold. There had been some 25,000 outlets selling the *News* before the strike.

The Transport Workers Union (TWU) also provided nonfinancial support to the Allied Printing Trades Council when TWU president Sonny Hall said the newspaper would be banned from the subways, as any sellers of the *News* in this area would have "their ass belong to us." This bold statement later proved incorrect as a judge allowed *News* hawkers in the subways.

In December, January, and February, the AFL-CIO maintained this strike had national implications concerning a win or loss for organized labor when management employed a "union-busting" approach including the hiring of striker replacements. Its assistance to the striking unions included the full-time support of three staff members, outside legal and public relations help, and \$300,000 to underwrite strike activities. The organization even paid strike benefits to drivers, whose union was not an AFL-CIO member, which enabled all *News* strikers to receive some form of benefits. AFL-CIO affiliate unions also picketed other Tribune Co. newspaper properties along with the homes of Charles Brumback and the publisher of the *Chicago Tribune*.

George McDonald indicated the nine striking unions were "100 percent united together" as the strike approached three months. Nevertheless, tensions between and within unions occurred during the latter months of the strike. Other unions in the APTC were no doubt concerned about the back-to-back negotiation sessions held with the drivers' union in February 1991, while the Newspaper Guild experienced a substantial number of its own members crossing over the picket lines and returning to work.

Sam McKnight indicated, however, that another APTC peripheral bargaining tactic, the advertising and consumer boycott, met with success in November as the *News* had lost all but 40 of its 615 prestrike advertisers. By November 13, 1991, the *News* had become almost completely devoid of advertising. Its Veteran's Day issue had only four full-page ads for a new brand of cigarettes, an airline, the city's foster care program, and the *News* seeking newspaper vendors. These results were in spite of reported rebates of more than 80 percent made by the company. Adding insult to injury, *New York Newsday* published a 176-page newspaper on November 9, a near record for a weekday, filled with many advertisements traditionally placed in the *News*. Advertising losses were reinforced by declining circulation figures; management acknowledged that some two weeks into the strike, deliveries were being made to only 2,000 of the *News*'s more than 12,000 outlets.

Management's Strike Miscalculations

The *News*'s management had made at least five miscalculations that turned its win-win situation at the strike's start into a no-win "dance of death." It first underestimated union solidarity found in the Allied Printing Trades Council and in New York City that reinforced the strikers' resolve. Second, management erroneously assumed that *News* advertisers would continue to advertise because of an ideological identification with management in this dispute. One advertising agency representative suggested that decisions to advertise in the *News* were based on business considerations of where to spend "precious money" instead of on a desire to support the *News*'s quest to receive more managerial discretion over its employees. This situation was intensified by a factor also not anticipated in management's strike preparations—the skidding local economy, which made *Daily News* advertisers especially nervous.

Management's third miscalculation pertained to the sales outlets, particularly newsstands. One executive, who was involved in strike preparations, likened the dispute to a "war" and assumed that the dealers "would be on our side and wouldn't be intimidated." Yet, another *News* spokesperson acknowledged that management failed to consider the ethnic composition of current newsstand dealers, whom he labeled as "easily intimidated" immigrants who were unlike the "old-timers," who would have told the unions to "shove it" and continued to sell papers.

Management in its strike preparations also had a narrow focus on not repeating its failure during the 1978 strike to load trucks with newspapers. This focus gravely obscured or discounted other considerations, such as the fact that other members of the drivers' union visited almost all the sales outlets every day to deliver the *New York Times,* the *New York Post,* and magazines. At a minimum, these nonstriking drivers reminded dealers what could happen if they sold the *News.*

Perhaps management made its biggest miscalculation when it recruited homeless people to sell the newspaper. Jerry Nachman, editor of the *New York Post,* expressed amazement at this recruiting development, "The homeless are so repulsive to New Yorkers . . . that in many minds, the *Daily News* has replaced the empty, stretched-out hand as an object of aversion."[11] Many angry verbal exchanges took place between the homeless hawkers and New York City residents, particularly those who were union members. George McDonald of the APTC commented,

> Hoge wants New Yorkers to think he is a humanitarian, but the truth is that in desperation to get his scab paper out, he is using the most desperate group of people in our city to do his dirty work for him. . . . As soon as Hoge gets what he wants, he'll discard the poor homeless just as he ruthlessly discarded 2,600 of his loyal long-time employees last month. People mean nothing to him.
>
> The next thing you know, Hoge will be using poor children to peddle his scab rag. Obviously, his greed knows no bounds, and human life is cheap to him.[12]

Some newsstand dealers also thought that homeless hawkers were "bad news," because the dealers received only 7 cents for each *News* sold while the homeless hawkers could keep all the proceeds. Several hawkers reported they made beteen $10 and $150 a day and experienced some verbal but no physical harassment.

Little evidence exists, however, to suggest that employing 800 homeless hawkers, although it increased circulation (according to a management representative, to 150,000 copies a day), resulted in any significant advertising or newspaper revenues for the *News.* Indeed, this action likely galvanized union solidarity and public support, which ignored or condoned strike-related violence in the city.

Management indicated that the *News*'s circulation on December 1 was a "stone cold" 525,000 copies, a figure unions suggested was some 400,000 copies too high. This major disagreement notwithstanding, the circulation of the *News*'s competitors, *New York Post* and *Newsday,* increased dramatically. James Hoge announced on January 16, 1991, the eighty-third day of the strike, that investment banker Lazard Freres had been retained to put the newspaper up for sale because its losses of more than $200 million over the past decade, coupled with continued workplace inefficiencies and the strike's violence against vendors and operations, made long-term operations impossible. He further noted, "In the little time left, we will take every effort to reach cost-efficient contract settlements and to achieve the other business conditions necessary for the *Daily News* to continue to serve New York."[13]

A second alternative was closing the operation if a potential purchaser could not be found. Hoge indicated that current employees and strikers at the *News* would be informed that the paper might close down in 60 days as required under the federal Worker Adjustment and Retraining Notification Act. Theodore Kheel said the provisions of this act (WARN), including a 14-day extension of the statutory 60-day WARN period, suggested April 3, 1991, as the likely date by which the newspaper would sell or close. No potential purchaser appeared at this time, and there was some resumption of bargaining during January, prompted by management's sale announcement.

Strike Violence

Police had recorded about 180 strike-related incidents and made at least 89 arrests by November 18. Management had indicated that 130 arrests had occurred by November 30 and that a total of 722 serious incidents had impeded or obstructed the distribution and publication of the newspaper. They further contended that 51 people had been injured (10 of them hospitalized) and 112 *Daily News* trucks and buses had been damaged. Most of these incidents occurred in the first two weeks of the strike. For example, management reported that 655 serious incidents had occurred by November 8.

Violence continued to be directed toward outlets that sold the *News* and those who delivered the *News*. Yet other conditions also prompted newsstand operations not to sell the newspaper. Dealers had "no brand loyalty," particularly if they could obtain the same revenue selling another newspaper along with related items such as tobacco, candy, and so forth.

Yet James Hoge continued to file civil suits against strikers associated with violence, a situation that was punctuated in early December when a *Daily News* driver, Carlos Chacon, and his helper were attacked by 12 to 15 men who beat them with baseball bats and bottles. Chacon was also stabbed with a knife three times (twice in the abdomen and once in the buttocks). According to the victims, one assailant said, "These people that work for the *Daily News* are taking my job. I'm going to kill you."[14] Chacon was left bleeding on the street while the truck was stolen and subsequently abandoned by the assailants.

The *News* continued its concerns with violence through early 1991 with big headlines such as "Bodega Bombed in News War," "It's Organized Terror: Hoge"; and "They Live in Fear of Violence." Hoge was dismayed that the *Post* and *Newsday* had not recognized and promulgated these messages of union-inspired violence; however, a *Newsday* representative countered that his newspaper's inactions did not represent a media conspiracy against the *News* because dozens of bombs exploded in New York City every day, and his newspaper would never report each event. A *New York Post* representative contended that Hoge's accusations represented "tragic" grandstanding because he blamed the competing press along with the unions, the governor, the mayor, the police department, and the Cardinal.

James Hoge was outraged that Mayor Dinkins, the police department, and the public did not condemn the violent acts. He charged the labor unions with criminal conspiracy in two forums: civil suits against individuals involved in strike-related incidents and a New York state legislative hearing November 26. Neither forum offered immediate vindication of Hoge's concerns.

George McDonald sent a telegram to Mayor Dinkins and the New York City Police Commissioner to counter Hoge's allegations that indicated *News* management released a private army of "combat ready troops" and "terrorists" with ski masks and martial arts sticks along with other "illegal and life threatening weapons" to be used on strikers and the general public as well.

Unions also criticized the police for providing too much protection for delivery operations at taxpayers' expense. The bill for the police overtime from the date the strike began until November 18 was $3.2 million, an average of $145,000 a day, although police had also stopped the practice of escorting delivery trucks during this time period.

The Maxwell Factor

Peripheral bargaining continued into February 1991 with one rather novel event. The strikers returned hundreds of copies of the *Daily News* to the newspaper's headquarters on East 42nd Street. This effort symbolized the presumed attitude of some newsstand dealers, who refused to sell the *News* and authorized the strikers to return the unsold bundles to management. Some 500 newsstand dealers signed letters that informed management that they were receiving poor service from replacement employees and did not want to be included in "fabricated circulation figures" released to the media, advertisers, and the general public. Another group of local merchants, florists, also agreed not to advertise in the *News* in the days just before Valentine's Day, traditionally their biggest week of the year.

Violence had not been eliminated by February, although an analysis of related incidents (2,072 strike-related incidents tallied by the *News* security staff or 586 confirmed by police and 153 arrests of strikers through February 21) reflected the following trends:

- a sharp decrease in the number and seriousness of the incidents after the first six weeks of the strike;
- an overall less violent strike situation at the *News* compared with recent labor-management confrontations at Pittston Coal Group (more than 3,000 incidents in Virginia alone) and Greyhound Bus Lines (where there had been 52 sniper attacks on buses carrying passengers); and
- a shift in the nature of the violence from ambushes and assaults on trucks and drivers (only four after January 1) to vandalism against vendors and advertisers.

Mediation was considered on February 11; however, subsequent meetings proved unsuccessful. James Hoge indicated that the newspaper would cease publication on March 15, 1991, unless a binding agreement to sell the newspaper was reached by that date.

Robert Maxwell, a British publishing tycoon with a "wheeler-dealer" reputation, expressed purchase interest, and the unions shifted their attention to bargaining with him. In England, union employees cursed Maxwell as "Captain Bob" for his autocratic approach toward labor relations and the hypocrisy they perceived when the billionaire called himself a socialist. However, they and other union officials acknowledged that Maxwell was quite adept at wringing concessions out of unions through his conflicting interpersonal skills of charm (even pampering union leaders with food and other perks), intimidation, and persistence (seven bargaining sessions in a week, each longer than 18 hours, for example).

Maxwell's first bargaining session with the unions was March 7, wherein he imposed a firm March 11 deadline for settlements or else he would walk away from the newspaper purchase. He later had to extend this deadline and indicated that he would leave the country if deals with all unions weren't reached. The drivers' union was the last to reach a tentative bargaining settlement about an hour after that deadline, around 4:00 P.M. on March 12.

The three-year labor agreements resulted in some $70 million in concessions and the elimination of some 800 jobs, or about one-third of the prestrike unionized work force at the *News*. Replacement employees would be terminated and rehired only when all union members were employed; however, crossovers, unions members who had crossed picket lines to return to work during the strike, would continue to be employed and would retain all their seniority except that obtained during the strike. The settlement also indicated that the unions would drop all charges filed against management with the National Labor Relations Board and give up five days of vacation or personal leave. Maxwell also obtained another union concession: a longer work week (37 1/2 hours, versus the previous 34 1/2 hours), which had been sought unsuccessfully by the Tribune Co. Employees would receive three more hours of straight-time pay per week; however, the paper would likely reap a large net gain through decreased overtime expenses.

Employees in most of the unions could receive severance pay of two weeks of pay per year of service or a $40,000 buy-out, whichever was greater. Members of the Printers, stereotypers, and Photoengraver's unions would be eligible for a $50,000 buy-out alternative plus medical benefits through age 65 because of lifetime guarantees in previous labor agreements.

Perhaps the only point of agreement between James Hoge and union leaders was the pivotal role played by Robert Maxwell in the bargaining sessions (Hoge remained with Maxwell for about 3 1/2 months after the purchase of the *News* and received a separation settlement of some $2 million). Theodore Kheel also praised Maxwell's collective bargaining involvement: "It was a performance to end all performances. . . . He was in everything. He dominated. He cajoled. He met with the full committees and he met with the small committees. He got involved in the minutia." Kheel also took a last shot at Robert Ballow, the *News* negotiator, who, unlike Maxwell, was "the world's greatest deal-breaker," and who had established himself as "the Saddam Hussein of collective bargaining."[15]

Some union members and financial analysts were surprised that the Tribune Co. blundered in its "sale" of the *News* to Maxwell. The organization could have received $150 million in union concessions a year before this figure was included in Maxwell's settlement. One observer figured that the organization's strike-related costs were $75 million a year for two years and that this amount plus indirect costs (hiring and training replacement workers, resolving unfair labor practice charges, and so forth) of $50 million should be added to the $60 million paid to Maxwell to take the newspaper off its hands to arrive at the true cost of transferring ownership of the newspaper. He further maintained that the Tribune Company's decision to throw this money "down a sewer . . . in a fit of pique" was not business. "That's just nuts."[16]

Developments after the Sale of the *Daily News* to Maxwell

Maxwell's flamboyant approach to labor relations and publishing continued after his "purchase" of the *Daily News* for about eight months until his mysterious death in November 1991 off the Canary Islands. His son, Kevin, became publisher of the *Daily News* the day of Robert Maxwell's death. Union leaders were impressed with Kevin Maxwell's commitment to the newspaper and his involvement of the unions in the newspaper's organizational and financial aspects. Despite this hope, Kevin Maxwell resigned his *News* position a month later (December 3, 1991) when financial investigations suggested Robert Maxwell's empire was crumbling and Kevin Maxwell was facing personal bankruptcy.

Management at the *Daily News* indicated that it had filed for Chapter 11 bankruptcy protection on December 5. Under this arrangement, the *News* would continue its operations while a creditors' committee was formed to develop a reorganization plan. The announcement indicated that the *News* was ahead of its 1991 business goals but nonetheless required a continuing short-term investment of funds to maintain operations and achieve consistent profitability. Unions were involved in this financial development when representatives of the drivers, pressmen, mailers, and Newspaper Guild were named to four of the 13 positions on the creditors' committee established in the bankruptcy proceedings. Barry Lipton, president of the Newspaper Guild, maintained that the *News* situation as it entered 1992 was "secure for the moment" with no "anticipated crisis."

Labor-Management Negotiations under Bankruptcy Proceedings

Lipton's perspective regarding labor-management tranquility soon had to change as collective bargaining over the next 13 months became shaped by bankruptcy proceedings and concerns and potential outside purchasers.

George McDonald maintained a coordinated posture among the nine *News* unions in the Allied Printing Trades Council, which now excluded the Typographers: all had to accept a potential purchaser's bargaining proposal or there would be no agreement involving any of the unions. Yet this solidarity was undermined by the union officials, who realized that a holdout under bankruptcy proceedings might result in the loss of their labor agreements, members, and organizations.

Conrad Black, a Canadian publisher, emerged as the first candidate to purchase the *News,* although another potential purchaser, Mortimer Zuckerman, owner of real estate holdings as well as the *Atlantic* and *U.S. News and World Report,* also held early discussions with the unions.

Black sought the elimination of 600 union members' jobs with a proposed 49 percent or more reduction coming from the pressmen, mailers, paperhandlers, plate engravers, stereotypers, and the International Typographical Union. Zuckerman proposed smaller reductions for pressmen and drivers; however, he sought a free hand to dismiss any reporter-member of the Newspaper Guild without subsequent arbitration.

Neither Black nor Zuckerman made any substantial progress with the unions through July 1992, a situation that concerned U.S. Bankruptcy Court Judge Tina Brozman. The Newspaper Guild favored Black's proposal, while the drivers and the pressmen preferred Zuckerman's. The other nine unions apparently could vote for either purchaser.

Perhaps the most significant bargaining development as of August 17, 1992, occurred among the unions in the APTC. George McDonald apparently reversed his previous position that all unions must receive acceptable labor agreements, although the president of the drivers' union indicated that he would not leave the Newspaper Guild "in the street."

On September 10, 1992, Conrad Black rather abruptly withdrew from negotiations with the unions. He would not match Zuckerman's offers made to the drivers and pressmen because these offers would forego any management progress with work rule changes and return the *News* to pre-Maxwell managerial limitations that he thought would destroy the newspaper. Black maintained that his "radical" bargaining proposals needed to be stressed up front because the previous *News* strike revealed that local politicians, John Cardinal O'Connor, and even the police department would side with the unions if a long peripheral bargaining session or impasse occurred.

Black contended that Zuckerman's offer represented "very little money for a property that is worth very little" and that Zuckerman's negotiations with the unions concerning future *News* operations would be difficult and long. "[Zuckerman is] going to have to either go for increased cost savings, negotiating with unions whose sense of avarice and inflexibility have been whetted and confirmed by this experience, or he's going to preside over an inexorable, continued decline of that franchise."[17]

Negotiations between the Guild and Zuckerman continued through September 16. The Newspaper Guild indicated it would consider giving Zuckerman more discretion over future Guild members hired after the labor agreement was settled. The new employees would likely be subject to dismissal without arbitration for a probationary period of one year instead of the previously agreed-upon 90 days. Lipton indicated that many items were still subject to negotiation, particularly the number of staff reductions, but he also expressed optimism that an agreement could be reached.

Zuckerman called for the reduction of 200 jobs from a base of 1,400 through buy-outs in the Newspaper Guild and layoffs in the craft unions. The remaining employees would have their job security guaranteed through their labor agreements running through the year 2005. A 3-percent wage increase would be applied after the first year, followed by annual wage increases of no more than 3 percent. Zuckerman stated that these increases would amount to half of the year's rise in the consumer price index, with half of that amount to be funded with cash and the other half contingent on productivity improvements. The proposed 13-year labor agreements also included no-strike provisions.

Seven of the nine unions in the APTC had ratified the labor agreements as Zuckerman's October 22 purchase approval date approached, with the eighth union, the Photoengravers, expected to ratify its agreement shortly thereafter. Two unions, however, the typographers and the Newspaper Guild, posed purchase obstacles. Both reflected peripheral bargaining considerations: the typographers became entangled with external judicial activities and the Newspaper Guild posed a bargaining issue derived from principle.

Zuckerman offered the typographers a number of jobs, but indicated that he would not honor their lifetime guarantees and would walk away from the sale if the courts ordered him to do so. Judge Brozman agreed with Zuckerman that the typographers' contract provision did not have to be honored, a position subsequently affirmed by the U.S. Court of Appeals.

Judge Cardamone, while throwing out the typographers' lifetime employment guarantees, indicated that this December 22, 1992, decision was conditioned on Zuckerman leaving his previously described final offer on the table. This offer, including buy-outs of 50 jobs, would cost Zuckerman $30 million over the proposed 13-year labor agreement, or 90 percent of the typographers' last offer, and the union indicated it would not appeal Judge Cardamone's decision. A *News* attorney maintained the decision cleared the last major obstacle to closing the deal.

Zuckerman's negotiations with the remaining holdout union, the Newspaper Guild, focused on a principle; namely, management retaining editorial control over the product. McDonald reaffirmed the APTC's support of the Guild but gave no indication of what form this support would take if the Newspaper Guild did not reach an agreement, stating, "There's been no betrayal of the Guild, no more than the Guild betrayed the other unions when they said they were opposed to going ahead with the sale. There are two sides to the coin."[18] Zuckerman claimed that the other APTC unions agreed not to honor the Newspaper Guild's picket line should a strike occur over the bargaining impasse. Zuckerman then announced that Guild members would have to reapply for their jobs if a collective bargaining agreement were not reached by December 6. When an agreement was not reached by this date, Guild members complied with his request "under protest."

Zuckerman assumed ownership of the *News* January 7, 1993. George McDonald commented on this situation:

> Over the last several years our membership has endured a devastating strike, bankruptcy, and almost daily uncertainty about their futures at the newspaper. We now look forward to a long, prosperous and stable future under Mort and Fred's leadership at the *New York Daily News.*[19]

About a week later management effected two implications of the Guild's lack of a labor agreement. It stopped deducting members' dues from their paychecks and dismissed 200 members of the Newspaper Guild (100 reporters and editors and another 100 employees in circulation and advertising) without regard to layoff or disciplinary provisions. The union reinstated a boycott against the newspaper, but the APTC and the state AFL-CIO did not support this action.

Assignment

Assume that you are management's chief negotiator in another organization, negotiating your second labor agreement with the union. Formulate and explain four implications/lessons from the *Daily News* case that might help your efforts.

References

1. Andrew Radolf, "*New York Daily News* Talks Make Progress," *Editor and Publisher,* July 4, 1987, p. 38.

2. Patrick M. Reilly, "At *New York News,* Threat of Strike Is Looming Larger," *The Wall Street Journal,* April 2, 1990, pp. B, 7-G.

3. Thomas B. Rosenstiel, "A Giant of Journalism Faces Its Most Critical Decline," *Los Angeles Times,* March 27, 1990, p. D-1.

4. David E. Pitt, "200 Contract Words Stall *News* Talk," *New York Times,* December 4, 1990, p. B-6.

5. Don Singleton, "New York Forum about the *News*—II. The Strikers Won Weeks Ago," *Newsday,* March 15, 1991. Dialog File 638, item 060787228.

6. David E. Pitt, "Unions Prepare Boycott Against the *Daily News,*" *New York Times,* July 25, 1990, p. B-2.

7. William Bunch, "This Time the Buses Did Come: After Months of Anxiety, the Explosion," *Newsday,* October 28, 1990. Dialog File 638, item 05807406.

8. David E. Pitt, "*News* Hopes to Lure Minority Journalists," *New York Times,* November 6, 1990, p. B-4. The AAJA had 1,000 members, the NAHA had 900 members, and the NABJ had 2,000 members.

9. "It's Organized Terror: Hoge," *New York Daily News,* November 3, 1990 (located in News Bank), *Media and Communications* 52, p. A-4.

10. George Garneau, "*Daily News* Shifts Strategy," *Editor and Publisher,* November 10, 1990, p. 25.

11. James Warren, "*Odd Couple:* The *News* Strike is Not Without Its Domicile for *Post* Editor Nachman," *Chicago Tribune,* December 16, 1990, sec. 5, p. 2.

12. "McDonald Blasts Hoge for Exploitation of Homeless," *PR Newswire,* November 10, 1990. Dialog File 613, item 0320581-NYSA002. For a detailed account of the hawkers' experiences and attitudes similar to McDonald's, see Keith M. Brown, "New York Forum about Labor: I Sold My Body to the *News,*" *Newsday,* December 11, 1990. Dialog File 638, item 05852061.

13. "*Daily News* Announces Tentative Decision to Close or Sell: Prospect for Material Charged Against Earnings," *PR Newswire,* January 16, 1991. Dialog File 613, item 0336130-NY006B.

14. Guy Sterling, "Two *Daily News* Workers Injured in Mob Attack on Irvington Street," *Newark* (New Jersey) *Star-Ledger,* December 7, 1990 (located in News Bank), *Media and Communications* 56, p. F-6.

15. Alan Finder, "Unions in Accord Allowing a Sale of *New York News,*" *New York Times,* March 13, 1991, pp. 1, C-9.

16. Alan Sloan, "Tribune's Expensive Fit of Pique," *Newsday,* March 17, 1991. Dialog File 638, item 06079344.

17. Tim W. Ferguson, "Press Lords Haven't Put *Daily News* to Bed," *The Wall Street Journal,* October 6, 1992, p. A-19.

18. "Judge Approves *Daily News* Sale to *U.S. News* Owner Zuckerman," Bureau of National Affairs Inc., *Daily Labor Report,* no. 208 (October 27, 1992), p. A-11.

19. Elizabeth Sanger, "Union to *Daily News* Buyer: Bargain or Face Boycott," *Newsday,* January 6, 1993. Dialog File 638, item 07006077.

Case 4.3 When the Rubber Hits the Road: Implications of the URW Strike at Bridgestone/Firestone

Events Leading Up to the Strike

A tentative three-year labor agreement was reached between Goodyear Tire and Rubber Company and the United Rubber Workers (URW) union on April 24, 1994. The contract maintained an annual COLA of 0.26 percent (which was estimated to boost wages $1.75–$2.00 per hour over the life of the agreement); gave each employee a lump-sum signing bonus of $500; improved the pension plan, insurance, and health care benefits; and established a first-time profit-sharing plan that could provide each employee $1,500 per year.

Nearly 22,000 of the URW's 100,000 members are covered by the "Big Three" master contracts with Goodyear, Uniroyal Goodrich, and Bridgestone/Firestone, and they earn an average hourly rate of $17.00. Kenneth L. Coss, president of the URW, hoped to continue the established pattern bargaining arrangement by presenting the agreement reached at Goodyear to the two other companies. However, a major ownership change at Bridgestone/Firestone occurred some six years prior to the Goodyear settlement that made Bridgestone/Firestone's acceptance of the pattern settlement unpredictable.

Three months of subsequent bargaining produced Bridgestone/Firestone's "final" offer, which fell far short of the Goodyear agreement and seemed to be made to be refused. It proposed:[1]

- $5 per hour wage cut for some job classifications, and a new-hire wage that would be 30 percent lower than the current rate but gradually increased to the full rate over three years.
- Continuous operation with 12-hour shifts, seven days a week, with no premium overtime pay, as employees would work three 12-hour shifts one week and four 12-hour shifts the next week.
- Double-time pay for those working holidays instead of the former triple-time pay.
- Discontinuation of supplemental employment benefits for laid-off employees and those injured on the job.
- Requirement that employees having more than three weeks vacation must take pay instead of time off for two weeks of vacation.
- Termination of COLA; instead, wage increases would be tied directly to company-set productivity levels. The company said the productivity increases would approximate the salary increase at Goodyear, while the union contended that productivity increases could not continue forever and were influenced by things beyond the employees' control.
- Reduced health-care coverage in which employees would make a 10 percent copayment and pay a $68 monthly premium for family coverage ($25 a month for a single person).

A Five-State Strike against the Company

Some 4,000 unionized employees at four tire manufacturing facilities in Oklahoma City, Oklahoma, Des Moines, Iowa, Decatur, Illinois, and Akron, Ohio, plus a shock absorber facility in Noblesville, Indiana, struck the company on July 12, 1994. However, this geographically diverse job action affected only about 10 percent of the company's workforce. A management representative said that minimal, if any, disruption of meeting customer needs would occur because the company had four other tire plants in the United States, two in Mexico, and one in Canada that were not covered by the disputed labor agreement.

Management contended that acceptance of its last proposal was necessary so that the company could remain competitive. However, many strikers blamed management's last offer on Japanese ownership. For example, the president of URW Local 138 at Noblesville maintained:

> I just feel like they're trying to make it like it is in Japan. . . . We're not Japanese workers, we're proud American workers. . . . We may work for them, but we don't have to beg.[2]

Another local union president in Des Moines thought that a management strike tactic also originated in Japan. Company-hired security guards wore black T-shirts that read on the front, "Tough times don't last, tough people do." The back of the T-shirts read, "Asset Protection Team" and "Vance International's Tactical Response Force." The union official retorted,

> The message is coming from Tokyo: They are going to make every attempt to beat us into submission. . . . Ownership has to realize that we are an American work force and we will be treated with respect.[3]

Labor-management tensions escalated when the URW filed unfair labor practice charges against the company on August 24, 1994, in Indianapolis, and management announced that it would hire new employees on August 25. This latter situation would occur at the high-volume tire manufacturing facilities in Oklahoma City, Decatur, Illinois, and Des Moines, Iowa, which were being operated by supervisors at 20–30 percent capacity. The company indicated that it could maintain operations with temporary and supervisory employees at the Akron and Noblesville plants. More than 4,000 applicants responded to company advertisements for the 110 positions (50 in Oklahoma City and 30 each in Decatur and Des Moines).

The Strike at Three Months

The last negotiation session between labor and management officials occurred July 10, two days before the strike, and management turned to external sources for assistance. It ran full-page newspaper advertisements in Des Moines and Oklahoma City, accusing the URW of "stirring up fear and prejudice based on race and national origin while obscuring real issues." The president of URW Local 998 in Oklahoma City responded that his organization could not afford to counter the company's public relations campaign because of members' medical coverage and bills. Some 90 of the 1,100 strikers returned to the Oklahoma facility at this time.

A district judge indicated that strikers at the Des Moines facility had to stand in restricted places at plant gates so that vehicles would have access into and out of the facility. The union responded by conducting informational picketing at Sears and other retail stores, urging potential customers not to purchase Bridgestone/Firestone and Pirelli-Armstrong tires.

In early November, 20 newly hired employees were given a police escort and were met with strikers' jeers as they crossed the picket line at the Noblesville plant. A management representative claimed the replacements were necessary to complete current customer orders and would augment the workforce once the strike ended. Before the bus arrived, strikers burned a Japanese flag to demonstrate their sentiment about foreign ownership.

Nearly $12 million in strike funds had been given to members who had been on strike against various tire manufacturers. For example, the nearly 1,300 striking members in Des Moines received $100 a week. However, a spokesperson for the international URW said these funds were evaporating, and there was no assurance of how long this remuneration would continue. The URW set up a special convention on January 24 to determine how to bolster its strike fund, which was down to $500,000 on January 4, 1995, from a peak of $13 million before the union received a $3 million cash infusion from the AFL-CIO in December.

The union also approved an amendment to its constitution at the convention that would rebuild the strike fund. Beginning March 1, membership dues earmarked for the fund were either doubled, or in some cases tripled, for the period March 1, 1995, to October 31, 1996.

These monies would be used to increase the strike fund for possible job actions taken by other URW locals and to repay the AFL-CIO loan. Bridgestone/Firestone strikers would not benefit from these funds.

Kenneth Coss, URW international president, acknowledged in mid-November that each side had demonstrated that it could hit the other pretty hard and still stand up after being punched; however, he also thought that union and management officials should return to the bargaining table while there was still something to be salvaged. A company spokesperson retorted that management had always been willing to negotiate when the URW had something positive to discuss, a situation he contended had not yet occurred.

Bargaining did not resume, and members of Local 310 in Des Moines engaged in two additional job actions on November 17 and December 8. The first event involved a massive traffic jam involving many of the 1,200 strikers in cars that were stalled with "mechanical problems" at the time of the shift change, when the newly hired employees were coming off their work shifts. This union solidarity demonstration was reinforced by a rally attended by Senator Tom Harkin and by Jesse Jackson, Jr. However, the crowd of 1,000 strikers and sympathizers advanced on the plant at shift change, hurling snowballs and epithets at the facility's employees. A district judge found the local in contempt of court for both events, limited the number of pickets at each plant gate to six (20 if the police department were given advance notice), and permanently enjoined the union from impeding access to the plant. The National Labor Relations Board (NLRB) also accused the Local 310 of unfair labor practices arising from these and other alleged incidents of violence at Des Moines, Decatur, Noblesville, and Oklahoma City, discharging 36 strikers, including several union leaders, about two weeks before Christmas.

A New Year and New Bargaining Developments

On January 4, 1995, Bridgestone/Firestone announced that it had permanently replaced approximately 2,000 of the strikers at its plants in Oklahoma, Iowa, Illinois, and Indiana. Many employees received letters indicating that even though they had been permanently replaced, they had an opportunity to return to work if they crossed picket lines and if their old job or an equivalent job was available. If such a position did not exist, the employees could ask to be placed on a preferential hiring list to be drawn from when openings occurred. The letter also indicated that some 600 strikers had already crossed the picket line and returned to work. A company spokesperson said that customer demand mandated a seven-days-a-week, continuous operation schedule that could not be accomplished with its previous skeletal staff.

Senator Tom Harkin labeled the company's action an outrage that would be considered illegal in Japan. Moreover, the company's unionized employees in Japan received an average annual income of $52,000 compared with $37,045 for its U.S. employees. Yet, he said, the company is telling "our workers they have to take less money." However, Harkin's colleagues preferred a wait-and-see attitude as U.S. senators voted 56–23 on January 6 to table a resolution that urged Bridgestone/Firestone to reconsider its practice of hiring permanent replacements.

In early January, many rank-and-file members were running out of patience with their own negotiators. Some of them, as well as other observers of the situation, contended that the union should have been able to predict that Bridgestone/Firestone could not match Goodyear's labor agreement because the company had incurred $1.5 billion in losses over six years and invested

$1.5 billion in plant improvements and $2 billion in 1988 to purchase the predecessor organization. Bridgestone/Firestone escalated union members' tensions when it reduced health benefits for thousands of URW retirees, who, in turn, angrily sought explanations from the union leadership. The URW international president responded that the company was treating the employees as "chattel" and suggested that URW members experiencing this situation would understand why union officers could neither trust nor work cooperatively with the company in the future.

Union solidarity was mixed on January 12, the strike's six-month anniversary. Hundreds of striking tire workers marched to the Iowa capitol to protest their situation. However, leaders of URW Local 7 in Akron told their 150 members to return to work, breaking ranks with four other striking locals. They were not threatened with permanent replacements but were nonetheless concerned that the product manufactured at the Akron plant (race tires) could easily be taken elsewhere. A management official indicated that the employees could report to work; however, 50 members were not part of the initial call-back. Moreover, the company did not bring back members on the basis of seniority, but on the basis of how early they quit the strike. The local union president was not allowed to return to work because his job had been eliminated.

By mid-January, the company had hired about 2,300 replacements to join some 800 strikers who had crossed the line to work under the previously described final company offer. The company stated that the Oklahoma City plant was back to pre-strike production levels and that full production would resume at the Decatur and Des Moines facilities in a couple of days. U.S. government officials used a meeting between President Clinton and Japanese Prime Minister Tomiichi Murayama at this time to suggest that the Bridgestone/Firestone top executive, Masatoshi Ono, discuss the situation with Secretary of Labor Robert Reich. According to one Labor Department official, Reich became upset when he was offered to meet only with the company's chief negotiator, Charles Ramsey, instead of with Ono:

> With all due respect, Ramsey is not the head of the corporation; Ono is. . . . Reich wants to bring both sides together and point out that what the company is trying to do here—replace workers—is illegal in Japan.[4]

The company responded that Ono was busy traveling and that he did not speak English well. President Clinton, aware that no American chief executive or labor leader involved in a strike had refused a meeting invitation from Reich, noted:

> By bringing in permanent replacements for their workers who are on strike, while refusing to come to the bargaining table, the management of Bridgestone/Firestone is flagrantly turning its back on our tradition of peaceful collective bargaining to solve labor disputes.[5]

The URW had been meeting with federal mediators infrequently during the strike to no avail regarding management's return to the bargaining table. This situation did change, however, on January 18, when management, the URW, and federal mediators met for more than two hours to go over a union proposal aimed at restarting negotiations. Management said that it would study the union's proposal, although no details were released about its reaction for some three months.

At least two negotiating sessions were conducted with management, labor officials, and federal mediators in March, although the details of these sessions and management's response were never made public. A virtual bargaining standstill remained in force through the first week in May.

Strike Termination and Related Uncertainties

On May 8, URW Local 713 in Decatur voted by a 2-to-1 ratio to end the strike on management's terms so that the members could vote in any possible decertification election to retain the union and ". . . live to fight another day." Management welcomed the union's initiative but also stressed that it planned to "protect the rights of the replacement workers." Out of 1,252 employees who initially struck the Decatur facility, only 714 strikers remained. About 300 URW members of this local crossed the picket line to return to work, and the remainder had retired prior to the strike termination vote.

Two weeks later, URW locals at the remaining locations (Des Moines, Noblesville, and Oklahoma City) unconditionally ended their 10-month job actions against the company. However, as of June 1, only 153 positions were offered to employees who had remained on strike (117 positions in Decatur and 9, 11, and 16 positions in Des Moines, Noblesville, and Oklahoma City, respectively). A management spokesperson said it was impossible to indicate how many employees were without jobs at this time because he did not know how many had obtained alternative employment during the strike:

> Originally 4,000 went on strike. . . . Since that time 1,300 returned to work and 400 retired so, theoretically, 2,300 could still be without jobs but we just do not know until we offer a position.[6]

Management clearly "won" this particular bargaining dispute, as employees essentially accepted management's previously described proposal that increased managerial discretion and reduced labor costs. Moreover, a large majority of the active URW strikers was precluded from immediate, if not permanent, re-employment. A possibility remains, however, that Bridgestone/Firestone's victory is ephemeral, particularly if the URW can survive and successfully challenge the company's bargaining tactics along two legal fronts.

National leaders of the United Rubber Workers (98,000 members) and the United Steelworkers of America (565,000 members) agreed to merge, an arrangement whereby the Steelworkers' $160 million strike fund could help replenish the URW's strike funds. George Becker, president of the United Steelworkers, also suggested that the merger could give the URW more bargaining power in the subsequent negotiations with Bridgestone/Firestone and other companies:

> Together we are stronger than steel. . . . Workers need stronger democratic unions in an increasingly hostile and competitive world dominated by more powerful multinational corporations.[7]

In late March 1995, the URW filed suit in U.S. District Court in Nashville, Tennessee, on behalf of some 20,000 retirees whose health benefits were reduced. The union sought unspecified damages because the company reduced retirees' prescription drug benefits and froze some Medicare reimbursements, and URW international president Kenneth Coss contended that the retirees' benefits were lifetime, covered by a legally negotiated labor agreement.

The union also awaits final disposition of its unfair labor practice charge filed with the NLRB contending that the company bargained in bad faith. If the NLRB and subsequent judicial courts, possibly extending to the U.S. Supreme Court, agree, then the union's job action could be labeled an unfair labor practice strike with participants likely to be returned to their former positions with back pay. However, final legal resolution of this issue will likely be lengthy.

In addition to the union's legal challenges, President Clinton issued an executive order on March 8, 1995, that could affect Bridgestone/Firestone and other companies that hired permanent strike replacements. He contended that this management bargaining tactic adversely affects necessary stable labor-management relationships and can change a limited dispute into a "broader, more contentious struggle, thereby exacerbating the problems that initially led to the strike. . . ." This situation could in turn jeopardize the government's ability to receive timely, high-quality goods and services. White House Press Secretary, Michael McCurry, applied this concern to Bridgestone/Firestone when he commented that the government would not like to have "minor leaguers and rookies making the tires for the next Desert Storm." The executive order would enable the Secretary of Labor to seek disbarment of any federal contractor that has hired permanent striker replacements, a situation predictably challenged by a spokesperson for Bridgestone/Firestone:

> As far as this company is concerned, the quality of our products and the service to our customers is the same high standard as it was before the United Rubber Workers' strike and before we replaced striking employees. . . . We are also disappointed the President would apparently attempt to penalize a company with considerable investment in the United States and which employs over 40,000 in North America, particularly when the action we took was completely in accordance with U.S. law and was for the purpose of improving our competitive position.[8]

Clinton's executive order was overturned by a Federal Court of Appeals (see Chapter Seven for more details concerning the order and related court citation). The effects of the URW's pursuit of legal redress and President Clinton's executive order on Bridgestone/Firestone remain to be seen. However, it is possible that the company, while winning the battle, might be adversely affected in the subsequent aftermath.

Questions

1. Formulate and explain three differences and two similarities of this collective bargaining situation with that of the *Daily News*.
2. Relate this case to the bargaining power model discussed in Chapter Six.

References

1. "Firestone Strike Issues," *The Des Moines Register*, October 3, 1994, p. 9.

2. "Firestone Strikers Express Anti-Japanese Sentiment," *The Indianapolis Star*, July 15, 1994, p. B-2.

3. "Firestone Guards to Change Message," *The Des Moines Register*, July 21, 1994, p. 8.

4. "Weakened Union Scrambles to Save Bridgestone/Firestone Jobs," *Akron Beacon Journal*, January 13, 1995.

5. Peter T. Kilborn, "Japanese Tire Maker Clashes with Labor Chief Over Strike," *New York Times*, January 14, 1995, p. 11. Mr. Ono apparently met with Labor Secretary Reich on January 20, 1995; however, details of this occasion were not made public.

6. "Bridgestone/Firestone Recalls Striking Employees" (June 1, 1995), *Business Wire* [online]. Dialog File 610.

7. Michael Arndt, "Rubber, Steel Unions' Leaders Agree to a Merger," *Chicago Tribune*, May 13, 1995, Business, p. 1. Since 1980, the URW membership has shrunk by almost half, from 180,000 members in 1980, and the Steelworkers union membership has been reduced from roughly 1 million to 565,000.

8. "Bridgestone/Firestone Responds to Executive Order" (March 8, 1995), *Business Wire* [CD-ROM]. Business Newsbank Plus.

Appendix A
Collective Bargaining Negotiations Exercise: QFM Company and IWU

Learning Objectives

1. To gain an understanding of negotiation preparations, actual negotiations, and assessment of negotiations' outcomes.
2. To develop an appreciation for the psychological interactions and the realism of contract negotiations.
3. To learn the mechanics of give-and-take, compromise, and trading issues and to practice the art of negotiation.
4. To familiarize the participants with the issues in collective bargaining and the difficulty of writing provisions to the satisfaction of both parties.
5. To realize the importance of and problems associated with teamwork within a bargaining situation.
6. To gain an appreciation for the application of bargaining theories to negotiations.

Rules of the Negotiations Exercise

1. Participants must not discuss the exercise with anyone except their assigned team members.
2. Each participant will be assigned a role (organization position) by the instructor.
3. The negotiations must take place within the framework of the present company and union at the St. Louis plant. Creativity is encouraged, but a realistic and pragmatic approach is recommended.
4. Data, materials, and information used for each position or argument on behalf of a proposal should not be falsified.

5. Each team may have as many meetings *outside* class as are needed and desirable.
6. Team members must follow the instructions of their respective team leaders.
7. All activities of team members should be directed toward negotiating an agreement that is mutually acceptable and that the parties can live with, survive on, and prosper under.

Instructions to the Participant

1. Each participant will be assigned to either the management or the union team. An organization position will be assigned to each person.
2. The team leaders—the president of the Industrial Workers United (IWU) and the labor relations director of Quality Furniture Manufacturing Company (QFM)—will call separate meetings to discuss and prepare for the upcoming negotiations and anticipate each other's proposals. Within your team, you should observe intraorganizational bargaining. Major issues for negotiations should include:
   a. Union security, dues checkoff, union shop
   b. Wages, job classes, premiums
   c. Management's rights
   d. Promotions and layoffs (use of seniority)
   e. Grievance procedure and arbitration
   f. Affirmative action plans
   g. Pension plans
   h. Supplemental unemployment benefits
   i. Vacations
   j. Holidays
   k. Sick leave
   l. Other issues allowed by instructor
3. In the preparatory meeting, each team will study the present agreement, identify its problems and items needing change, and gather materials, data, and information to justify the team's proposals and positions.
4. Based on study and analysis, each team must determine its strategy and goals.
5. Each team must complete the first four columns of Form 1 and give it to the instructor. (The form is not to be shown to anyone else.)
6. The union president and the industrial relations director and their respective teams will meet at a time specified by the instructor for the purpose of negotiating a new agreement.

Form 1

BARGAINING PRIORITY (1=MOST IMPORTANT, 2=SECOND MOST IMPORTANT, AND SO ON)	SUBJECT AREA FOR NEGOTIATIONS (BRIEF DESCRIPTION)	PROPOSALS TO OTHER PARTY (FIRST DAY)	REALISTIC OBJECTIVE FOR NEGOTIATIONS	ACTUAL ACCOMPLISHMENT (TO BE COMPLETED AFTER NEGOTIATIONS)

7. At the first meeting, the union will present its proposals and explain the need for each proposal. Then management will present its proposals and/or counterproposals and justify each proposal.
8. Actual negotiations will begin after the proposals are exchanged and will continue until a new agreement is negotiated and signed or the present contract expires. (The instructor will specify time periods.)
9. Upon completion of the negotiations, each team will project the total annual costs of the new agreement. If assigned by instructor, the teams will submit a written agreement.
10. Additional instructions may be given the participants by the instructor.

Sources of Materials for Preparation

Government publications: U.S. Department of Labor, Bureau of Labor Statistics, *Area Wage Surveys, Employment and Earnings, Handbook of Labor Statistics, Monthly Labor Review, Characteristics of Major Collective Bargaining Agreements.* U.S. Department of Commerce, *U.S. Industrial Outlook* (published every year).

Binder services of Bureau of National Affairs Inc. (BNA) and Commerce Clearing House. Especially helpful is the BNA *Collective Bargaining Negotiations and Contracts.*

Business publications: *Business Week* and *The Wall Street Journal.*

Professional labor relations journals: *Arbitration Journal, Employee Relations Law Journal, Industrial and Labor Relations Review, Industrial Relations, Industrial Relations Law Journal, Journal of Collective Negotiations in the Public Sector, Labor Law Journal,* and *Monthly Labor Review.*

Proceedings: Industrial Relations Research Association, Labor Law Developments, National Academy of Arbitrators, and NYU Conference on Labor.

Labor agreements between companies and labor unions (as available).

The Furniture Manufacturing Industry

The furniture industry can be characterized as a "highly competitive, nonintegrative industry composed largely of small and medium-sized family-controlled businesses."[1] Although the industry consists of about 1,200 companies, only 50 are publicly held, and most of the others are family operated. The latter show little inclination to adopt efficiencies already common in other manufacturing industries. Most furniture manufacturers still operate only one shift and remain highly labor-intensive. High-quality workmanship and craftsmanship have been their goals, and much of the work is still done by hand to give the products their distinctiveness.[2]

While plants are scattered throughout the United States, two-thirds are located in the Southeast, the Middle Atlantic, and the Great Lakes regions. Because the Pacific Coast has an ample supply of softwood and hardwood, more plants are currently locating there. Manufacturers using plastics and metals rather than wood in their furniture are able to locate closer to their markets and have therefore spread throughout the country.

Products are distributed over fairly wide geographic areas, and 70 percent of the output is sold directly to retailers. Brand names and product line identity are important to some of the larger manufacturers, but there are problems of design copying and enormous pressures for frequent restyling.[3] The demand for high-quality furniture, such as the "Eagle" brand for Quality Furniture Manufacturing Company, is basically recession-proof.

Household durable goods, which include household furniture, have generally rebounded during the recent economic recovery. With lower interest rates, more homes are being built; and consequently, the need for household goods has increased. Optimism was enhanced by international demand resulting from a decreased value of the U.S. dollar and favorable exchange rates for exporting American products. With the approval of the North American Free Trade Agreement (NAFTA), trade with Mexico should be increased. Currently, Canada and Mexico account for 50 percent of U.S. exports of consumer durables and exceed $7 billion.

The demand for household furniture is related to a number of factors: residential construction, sales of homes, interest rates, consumer confidence, and disposable personal income. Into 1996, each of these factors was positive for increased purchases of household furniture. It was anticipated that shipments of U.S. household furniture would exceed $22.0 billion in 1995 and that exports should increase $1.2 billion, an annual rate of about 5 percent through 1996. Total employment in the household furniture manufacturing industry was approximately 250,000 in 1994; however, with an economic recovery and potential for increased demand, employment should reflect an increase in sales.[4]

The QFM Company and the Union

QFM Company began in 1820 in Laconia, New Hampshire, as a family-owned and operated furniture manufacturer. It was headed by Herman Sweeny, one of the early settlers in Laconia. The company grew to 30 employees by 1920, but at that time Ben Franklin Sweeny, Herman's son, decided to move the firm to St. Louis, Missouri—a location more central to the firm's market. Barely surviving the 1930s depression, QFM was one of the first companies to convert its manufacturing processes to the production of war materials. The company prospered during the war, and afterward Sweeny decided to expand, sell stock publicly, and focus on producing metal and plastic-laminated furniture. With the production experience it had gained during the war and with its location some distance from the predominantly wood-furniture manufacturers, QFM Company launched a new era for itself in 1946.

By 1970 the St. Louis plant of Quality Furniture Manufacturing Company had 1,300 employees and was producing 450 dinette sets, 200 sets of lawn tables and chairs, and 300 bar stools and miscellaneous furniture daily. Then came the 1971 to 1973 furniture boom, with its expectations of continuous growth. QFM's new president, Gerald Brooks, decided that a new, modern plant and more diversity in the product line were necessary to meet the expected demand. Taking into consideration location, material supply, transportation, markets, labor situations, and other factors, Brooks decided to build the new plant in Dallas, Texas. This plant was to specialize in the new product lines, and the St. Louis plant was to concentrate only on dinette sets. In 1972, 200 employees were transferred from St. Louis, and another 200 were hired from the Dallas–Fort Worth area. The Dallas plant started with no union and 400 employees. In 1993 the founder's granddaughter, Bethany Sweeny, became plant manager, and the plant size had grown to a 900-employee work force, still with no union. It pays its Dallas employees at least $1 less per hour than it pays the St. Louis employees in comparable jobs. The St. Louis plant continues to produce 450 dinette sets per day, mostly for chain retailers, and employs about 1,000 employees. No new product lines have been added at the St. Louis plant, and its employment level is the same as in the pre-1970 days. The Dallas plant has started producing a new product line—dinette sets under the Eagle brand name. Consumer response has been positive, and the Dallas plant's future looks very promising.

Throughout its history, QFM Company has prided itself on being a progressive employer; however, recent events—building the Dallas plant, increasing employment in Dallas while lowering it in St. Louis, paying QFM employees in St. Louis less than comparable area wages—resulted in an NLRB representation election for the Industrial Workers United Union in St. Louis in 1975. After a heated campaign by both management and the union, NLRB investigations of unfair labor practices, and challenged ballots, the union lost the election by a vote of 497 to 481. Two years later, the union returned and won the election by a vote of 611 to 375. The election campaign was bitter, and the negotiations that followed were even more bitter. After a six-week strike, a labor agreement was signed. There have been seven negotiations since 1977, and no strikes have occurred. However, the current agreement is close to expiration. Although the company officials now express a commitment to return to the era when management and labor trusted each other, worked cooperatively, and shared mutual goals and benefits, the union leaders are reacting by waiting to see their deeds. The upcoming negotiations will determine the company's commitment. The union believes it is strong, with 80 percent of the bargaining unit now union members.

References

1. Wickham Skinner and David C. D. Rogers, *Manufacturing Policy in the Furniture Industry,* 3d ed. (Homewood, Ill.: Richard D. Irwin, 1968), p. 1.

2. "Why Furniture Makers Feel So Comfortable," *Business Week,* July 30, 1979, p. 76.

3. Skinner and Rogers, *Manufacturing Policy,* pp. 2–12.

4. John Harris, "Household Consumer Durables," *U.S. Industrial Outlook, 1994* (Washington, D.C.: Government Printing Office, 1994), pp. 36-1–36-9.

Exhibit 1 QFM Company Balance Sheet, 1996

Assets	
Current Assets:	
Cash	$ 2,200,599
Notes and Accounts Receivable	50,884,385
Inventories	64,291,324
Prepaid Expenses	842,853
Total Current Assets	$118,219,162
Fixed Assets	
Land	$ 10,248,700
Buildings	25,621,750
Machinery and Equipment	20,127,626
Total Fixed Assets	55,998,076
Total Assets	$174,217,238
Liabilities and Stockholders' Investment	
Current Liabilities	
Notes and Accounts Payable	$ 16,919,372
Accrued Payroll	6,764,142
Taxes (local, state, federal)	54,318,110
Total Current Liabilities	$ 78,001,624
Stockholders' Investment	
Common Stock (common @ $20 per share)	$ 40,995,533
Earned Surplus	55,220,081
Total Stockholders' Investment and Earned Surplus	96,215,614
Total Liabilities and Stockholders' Investment	$174,217,238

Exhibit 2 QFM Company Income Statement

	1995	1996
Net Sales	$196,789,296	$216,468,428
Costs of Goods Sold		
Production (labor, materials, overtime)	$158,650,125	$165,740,468
Administrative	13,447,503	14,369,497
Sales	6,559,168	8,608,908
Other	1,664,824	1,888,631
Total Cost of Goods Sold	180,321,620	190,607,504
Income before Taxes	16,467,677	25,860,924
Taxes (local, state, federal)	4,784,094	6,377,800
Net Income	$ 11,683,583	$ 19,483,124

Exhibit 3 QFM Company Net Sales and Income

	NET SALES	NET INCOME
1995	$196,778,296	$11,683,583
1996	216,468,428	19,483,124
1997 (estimated)	231,660,000	23,770,000

Exhibit 4 Number of QFM Production and Maintenance Employees by Seniority in St. Louis and Dallas Plants

YEARS	ST. LOUIS	DALLAS
0–1	5	100
1–2	15	150
2–3	40	160
3–4	45	150
4–5	45	158
5–10	205	115
10–15	200	25
15–20	105	20
20–25	120	10
25–30	152	10
30 or more	78	2
	1,010	900[a]

[a]Includes those transferring from St. Louis.

Exhibit 5 Number of QFM Employees in Each Job Title, by Wage Grade

WAGE GRADE	JOB TITLE	ST. LOUIS	DALLAS
1	Janitor	10	9
2	General Laborer	30	32
3	Materials Handler	45	48
4	Packer	36	35
	Machine Operator B	120	120
	Utility Worker	38	20
	Interplant Truck Driver	16	18
	Sander	40	40
	Assembler	295	319
5	Welder	16	10
	Machine Operator A	120	62
	Electrician B	5	7
	Maintenance Worker B	11	12
	Gluer	56	40
6	Mechanic	10	8
	Spray Painter	43	35
	Cutoff Saw Operator	25	18
7	Electrician A	15	8
	Maintenance Worker A	11	8
	Inspector	26	18
8	Tool Grinder A	5	5
9	Tool and Die Maker A	12	8
10	Leadman	25	20
		1,010	900

Exhibit 6 Average Hourly Earnings, Excluding Overtime, for All Manufacturing Employees

	JULY 1993	JULY 1994
Total Manufacturing	$11.76	$12.06
Durable Goods	12.34	12.67
Lumber and Wood Products	9.61	9.83
Furniture and Fixtures	9.27	9.55
Stone, Clay, and Glass Products	11.85	12.11
Primary Metal Industries	14.00	14.31
Fabricated Metal Products	11.69	11.93
Industrial Machinery and Equipment	12.73	12.98
Electric and Electronic Equipment	11.24	11.51
Transportation Equipment	15.84	16.49
Instruments and Related Products	12.25	12.47
Miscellaneous Manufacturing Industries	9.37	9.65
Nondurable Goods	11.00	11.25
Food and Kindred Products	10.43	10.67
Tobacco Products	11.04	18.76
Textile Mill Products	8.89	9.14
Apparel and Other Textile Products	7.10	7.33
Paper and Allied Products	13.42	13.76
Printing and Publishing	11.94	12.13
Chemicals and Allied Products	14.84	15.18
Petroleum and Coal Products	18.55	17.11
Rubber and Miscellaneous Plastic Products	10.60	10.70
Leather and Leather Products	7.62	7.97

SOURCE: *Collective Bargaining: Negotiations and Contracts,* May 11, 1995, p. 18:371.

Exhibit 7 Mean Hourly Earnings of Manufacturing Plant Employees in Dallas and St. Louis

JOB TITLES	DALLAS	ST. LOUIS
Carpenter	$14.11	$16.16
Electrician	16.81	19.84
Painter	10.97	16.92
Machinist	14.58	19.81
Mechanic	16.92	15.22
General Maintenance	7.91	10.95
Tool and Die Maker	18.05	17.17
Truck Driver	13.09	15.47
Shipper	9.58	10.41
Receiver	8.24	11.59
Warehouse Worker	9.89	11.09
Order Filler	6.33	10.57
Packer	5.82	11.21
Material Handler	8.74	15.28
Forklift Operator	9.90	13.47
Janitor	5.85	11.73

SOURCE: U.S. Department of Labor, Bureau of Labor Statistics, *Area Wage Survey: Dallas–Ft. Worth, Texas Metropolitan Area, November 1993* (Washington, D.C.: U.S. Government Printing Office, 1995), pp. 4–5; U.S. Department of Labor, Bureau of Labor Statistics, *Area Wage Survey: St. Louis, Missouri–Illinois Metropolitan Area, March 1995* (Washington, D.C.: U.S. Government Printing Office, 1994), pp. 15–18.

Exhibit 8 Consumer Price Index for Urban Wage Earners and Clerical Workers and Percent Changes, 1995

YEAR	INDEX	PERCENT CHANGE
1967	100	—
1968	104.2	4.2
1969	109.8	5.4
1970	116.3	5.9
1971	121.3	4.3
1972	125.3	3.3
1973	133.1	6.2
1974	147.7	11.0
1975	161.2	9.1
1976	170.5	5.8
1977	181.5	6.5
1978	195.3	7.6
1979	217.7	11.5
1980	247.0	13.5
1981	272.3	10.2
1982	288.6	6.0
1983	297.4	3.0
1984	307.6	3.4
1985	318.5	3.5
1986	323.4	1.5
1987	340.4	5.3
1988	354.3	4.1
1989	371.3	6.6
1990	391.4	5.4
1991	408.0	4.2
1992	420.3	3.0
1993	432.7	2.7
1994	444.0	2.6
1995 (Sept.)	459.0	3.3

SOURCE: Updated by U.S. Department of Labor, Bureau of Labor Statistics, *Monthly Labor Review* 11 (November 1995), p. 126.

Exhibit 9 Average Gross Hours and Earnings of Manufacturing Production Workers and Furniture Production Workers, 1978–1995

	Manufacturing			Household Furniture		
	WEEKLY EARNINGS	WEEKLY HOURS	HOURLY EARNINGS	WEEKLY EARNINGS	WEEKLY HOURS	HOURLY EARNINGS
1978	$249.27	40.4	$ 5.91	$167.91	38.7	$4.35
1980 (Dec.)	315.70	41.5	7.40	268.77	39.7	6.77
1982 (Nov.)	337.90	39.5	8.62	246.77	38.2	6.46
1985 (Aug.)	384.35	40.5	9.49	253.99	38.6	7.20
1986 (Aug.)	391.15	40.2	9.73	255.98	37.7	7.44
1987 (Aug.)	403.27	40.7	10.39	311.92	40.3	7.74
1988 (July)	413.92	40.7	10.13	310.81	38.9	8.25
1989 (July)	424.44	40.5	10.48	318.45	38.6	7.99
1991 (Aug.)	453.29	40.9	11.17	348.00	39.5	8.81
1992 (Aug.)	470.65	41.1	11.45	364.11	40.1	9.08
1993 (June)	486.86	41.40	11.76	343.17	39.4	8.71
1994 (June)	506.52	42.0	12.06	356.29	39.5	9.02

SOURCE: *Collective Bargaining: Negotiations and Contracts,* June 8, 1995, p. 18:352.

Exhibit 10 Average Hourly and Weekly Earnings for All Private Workers and for Manufacturing Workers

	AUGUST 1993	AUGUST 1994
Hourly Earnings		
Total Private	$10.83	$11.12
Manufacturing	11.17	11.45
Average Weekly Earnings		
Total Private	$373.64	$384.75
Manufacturing	486.86	506.52

SOURCE: *Collective Bargaining: Negotiations and Contracts,* May 11, 1995, p. 18:371.

The Labor Agreement between Quality Furniture Manufacturing Company (QFM) and Industrial Workers United (IWU), AFL-CIO

This agreement is entered into on ____________ by the Quality Furniture Manufacturing Company (QFM), located in St. Louis, Missouri, and Industrial Workers United (IWU). This agreement covers employees at the St. Louis plant only.

Article 1

Recognition The company recognizes the IWU as the sole and exclusive collective bargaining agent in all matters pertaining to rates of pay, wages, hours of employment, and other conditions of employment for all production and maintenance employees, excluding professional employees, storeroom employees, office clerical employees, guards, and supervisors, as defined in the National Labor Relations Act.

Article II

Union Security The company agrees not to interfere with the right of employees to join the Union and will not discriminate against employees who are Union members. Employees in the bargaining unit are completely free to participate in the affairs of the Union, provided that such activities do not interfere with their work duties and responsibilities.

While no employee will be required to join the Union as a condition of employment, union dues will be deducted from any bargaining unit employee's pay check, provided proper written notification is given to the Company. At the end of each pay period, the Company will forward the collected dues, minus a 5 percent administrative fee, to the Union.

Article III

Management Rights All management functions of the enterprise that are not specifically limited by the express language of this agreement are retained by the Company. The functions and rights listed here are examples of the exclusive responsibilities retained by the Company and are not intended as an all-inclusive list: to manage the manufacturing operations and methods of production; to direct the work force; to decide what work shall be performed in the plant by subcontractors or by employees; to schedule working hours (including overtime work); to hire, promote, demote, and transfer; to suspend, discipline, and discharge for cause; to relieve employees due to lack of work or for other legitimate reasons; to create and enforce reasonable shop rules and regulations; to establish production standards and rates for new or changed jobs; to introduce new and improved methods, materials, equipment, and facilities; to change or eliminate existing methods, materials, equipment, and facilities.

Article IV

No Strike and No Lockout The company agrees that during the life of this agreement there shall be no lockout of bargaining unit employees. The Union agrees that during the life of this agreement there shall be no strike, work stoppage, slowdown, work refusal, delay of work, refusal to report for work, or boycott.

Article V

Hours of Work The normal workweek shall consist of eight (8) hours per day, forty (40) hours per week, for a five (5) day week, from Monday to Friday. The starting time shall be made by the Company, and it can be changed by the Company to suit varying conditions of the business. Such changes in working schedules shall be made known to the Union representative in the plant as far in advance as possible. Employees shall be notified by a written bulletin or other communications medium.

Article VI

Grievances and Arbitration Procedures Grievances arising out of the operation and interpretation of this agreement shall be handled and settled in the following manner:

- *Step 1.* The aggrieved employee and/or shop steward shall discuss the grievance with his or her supervisor.
- *Step 2.* Should the answer provided by the supervisor not produce a satisfactory solution to the grievance, the grievance shall be reduced to writing and shall state the provision of the agreement which has been violated. The department head shall arrange for a meeting of the aggrieved employee, the shop steward, the supervisor, the employee relations supervisor, and himself or herself for the purpose of discussing the grievance. The department head shall provide a written answer to the grievance after the close of the meeting.
- *Step 3.* If a satisfactory conclusion is not reached, the grievance can be referred to the plant manager by the Union. The plant manager shall schedule a meeting to discuss the grievance with the Union. The local Union can bring in a representative of the International Union at this step, and the plant manager can bring in anyone who he or she feels may aid in the resolution of the grievance.
- *Step 4.* If a grievance is appealed to arbitration, the Company and the Union shall attempt to select an arbitrator. If this attempt fails, the Company and/or Union shall ask the Federal Mediation and Conciliation Service to submit a list of seven (7) arbitrators. Each party shall eliminate

three (3) names from the list by alternatively striking one name at a time, and the person whose name remains shall serve as the arbitrator.

The arbitrator shall render a decision in writing that shall be final and binding upon the parties. The arbitrator to whom any grievance is submitted shall have the authority to interpret and apply the provisions of this agreement, and the arbitrator's decision must be in accordance with and based upon the terms of this agreement or of any written amendment thereto. But the arbitrator shall have no jurisdiction or authority to add to, subtract from, or modify any of the terms of this agreement.

The Company and local Union shall each pay its own expenses incurred in connection with the arbitration and one-half of the expenses and fees of the arbitrator and the facilities used in the arbitration hearing.

Article VII

Seniority "Seniority" as used in this agreement shall be the period of continuous service in the job or plant from the date of the employee's appointment.

"Probationary employment" consists of a period of one hundred twenty (120) days of employment.

Layoffs shall be made in the following order:

a. Probationary employees
b. Other employees in order of job seniority

Recall shall be made in the following order:

a. Employees in order of job seniority, given equal job ability
b. Probationary employees

Promotions shall be made on the basis of qualifications, merit, and seniority. Promotions out of the bargaining unit remain management's prerogative.

An employee who quits or is discharged for cause shall lose all seniority rights.

If the Company decides to terminate any operation or job and the employees remain on layoff for a period of twelve (12) months, the employees shall be considered to have been terminated for cause at the expiration of said twelve (12) month period.

Article VIII

Wages and Classifications Job classifications and a wage schedule setting forth the rates of pay of the various job classifications are included in Schedule A and are hereby made part of this agreement.

If and when the Company creates a new job classification or modifies, alters, amends, or combines existing jobs, or revises the skills and responsibilities of a job, job descriptions will be drawn and a wage rate assigned. The Union shall have a maximum of five (5) working days to examine the job description to determine whether it accurately describes the principal functions and whether the pay range is consistent with established job classification pay ranges.

If the Union takes exception, it can review both factors with the Company. If the issue cannot be resolved, the Union can take the issue through the grievance procedure.

Job classifications are for pay purposes only and do not pertain to whoever might perform the work in that classification—unless modified by the terms of the agreement.

Article IX

Insurance An employee who has completed ninety (90) days of employment is eligible for enrollment in the company group insurance programs on the monthly premium date for each particular insurance coverage that next follows the completion of ninety (90) days of employment.

1. Group Life Insurance $20,000 — Accidental Death and Dismemberment $20,000
2. *Accident and Health Insurance.* One-half of the employee's weekly pay up to a maximum of $150. It is understood and agreed that the cost of the hospitalization, medical and health insurance, major medical insurance, accident and health and life insurance will be borne 50 percent (50%) by the Company and 50 percent (50%) by the employee, when subscribed to by the employee. It is understood and agreed that in the event that the Company wishes to change carriers, there is no obligation to negotiate with the Union prior to instituting the change.

Employees on medical leave for a period in excess of ninety (90) consecutive days may continue to be covered under the group insurance program after the first ninety (90) days, providing the employee pays the total insurance premium.

Article X

Pension Plan A pension plan for bargaining unit employees of the Company is hereby incorporated as a part of this agreement.

As of October 6, 1977, the normal retirement benefit for all years of service continues to be $20 per month per year of service.

Article XI

Holidays All employees, after completing six (6) months of service with the Company, shall be paid seven (7) hours' pay for the following holidays:

- New Year's Day
- Independence Day

- Labor Day
- Thanksgiving Day
- Day after Thanksgiving Day
- Christmas Eve Day
- Christmas Day

To be eligible for holiday pay, the employee must have worked the days immediately preceding and following the holiday. Legitimate excuses for absences will be considered.

Article XII

Vacation Employees shall qualify for vacation with pay in accordance with the following (determined June 1 of each year):

Continuous Service	Vacation with Pay
More than 1 but less than 5 years	1 week
More than 5 but less than 10 years	2 weeks
More than 10 but less than 20 years	3 weeks
More than 20 years	4 weeks

Vacation pay shall be computed on the basis of each employee's average weekly earnings from June to June. Payment will be made on the work day prior to the vacation period.

Article XIII

Sick Leave A full-time employee is eligible for sick leave after completing six (6) months' service with the Company. An eligible employee will accumulate sick leave at the rate of one-half day per month of service from date of hire. Sick leave will not be carried over from one year (January 1 to December 31) to the next, and it can be used only for personal illness not covered by workers' compensation. The Company retains the right to require a doctor's certificate as proof that absence was due to a legitimate injury or illness.

Article XIV

Duration of Agreement This agreement shall become effective as of ________, and shall continue in effect until 11:59 P.M., __________. Thereafter, it shall renew itself for yearly periods unless written notice of termination is given by one party to the other not less than sixty (60) nor more than ninety (90) days prior to the expiration of this agreement.

Schedule A Wages and Classifications

WAGE GRADE	JOB TITLE	WAGE RATE
1	Janitor	$9.24
2	General Laborer	10.29
3	Materials Handler	10.40
4	Packer	12.32
	Machine Operator B	12.32
	Utility Worker	12.32
	Interplant Truck Driver	12.32
	Sander	12.32
	Assembler	12.32
5	Welder	13.31
	Machine Operator A	13.31
	Electrician B	13.31
	Maintenance Worker B	13.31
	Gluer	13.31
6	Mechanic	14.41
	Spray Painter	14.41
	Cutoff Saw Operator	14.41
7	Electrician A	15.40
	Maintenance Worker A	15.40
	Inspector	15.40
8	Tool Grinder A	16.39
9	Tool and Die Maker A	17.38
10	Leadperson	18.37

mean pay: 13.56

Total: 311.97

Appendix B
Internet Possibilities for the Labor Relations Process*

The Internet is a worldwide network of networks that holds vast potential for meeting information and research needs in labor relations. Your university, college, or employer may pay a fee to a commercial Internet provider and make available to you a browser or search software such as Netscape, Mosaic, MacWeb, or Lynx, that will enable you to access the World Wide Web, Gopher sites, and newsgroups for free. Check with your library or computer center in your institution for directions in gaining access. Many Internet surfers subscribe to CompuServe, Prodigy, America Online, or a local provider to have access at home. Regardless of how you get to the Internet, the result in information retrieval should be the same.

Be aware that you cannot obtain, through this montrous network, all information necessary for complete and thorough research on a subject. You will still have to consult books, indexes to periodical literature, library catalogs, and other more traditional methods of information retrieval to round out your research. The Internet usually does not provide, for free, full-text articles that you will find in established scholarly journals. Some sites provide this service to paying users who have an account with them, or your school or college may provide you with access to a collection of the increasing number of periodicals being marketed via the Internet.

The Internet *does* provide very current information not available in print sources, particularly statistics and current news items. Communication with and access to individuals, organizations, and groups has become more efficient and faster than ever before. The World Wide Web is full of home pages devoted to almost anything and can be developed by anyone who has access to it and knows how to write HTML code. Unless you know a specific address or become proficient in searching with various search engines, you can spend a tremendous amount of time "wandering around" without good results.

Know the source of your information if you plan to cite an Internet source in a paper or research project. Investigate the credentials or affiliation of the publisher

*Written by Sarah Philips, Head of Reference, Thomas G. Carpenter Library, University of North Florida, Jacksonville, Florida, email sphilips@unf.edu.

of the home page, and check for currency if you are using statistics or information in which timeliness is important. If you reach a page that does not provide you with information on the publisher or developer of the page or does not provide a way back to a home page that will allow you to contact the developer, you probably should not use the information to support a paper or project. Jim Alderman, library research skills instructor from the University of North Florida, says it well when he writes, "Don't let the bells and whistles fool you into thinking you've hit a gold mine when, instead, you've hit a land mine that will destroy the accuracy of your own research."

Glossary of Internet Terms

Definitions derived from Ed Krol, *The Whole Internet* (Sebastopol, Calif.: O'Reilley & Associates, 1994); and Richard J. Smith, *Navigating the Internet* (Indianapolis: Sams.net Publishing, 1995).

bookmark—Browser feature that places selected URLs in a file for quick access.

FTP (file transfer protocol)—Tool for transferring files between computers on the Internet. Often used to transfer large files of statistics, scientific experiments, and full-text articles.

Gopher—Text-based Internet search engine developed by the University of Minnesota providing subject access to files on the Internet through menus.

home page—The first hypertext document displayed on a Web server. A home page is often a menu page with information on the developer and links to other sites.

HTML (Hypertext Markup Language)—Code in which World Wide Web documents are written and presented.

HTTP (Hypertext Transfer Protocol)—Protocol used by the Web to transfer hypertext documents.

hypertext—Documents that contain links to other documents, allowing the user to jump from one document to another.

URL (Uniform Resource Locator)—Web address that gives the exact location of an Internet resource.

Usenet—Group of systems that enable users to exchange discussion on specific topics through "newsgroups."

World Wide Web—A hypertext-based system for finding and accessing Internet resources.

How Do You Begin?

Learning how to use a few tools will make your research easier and the vast network of networks more controllable and less overwhelming. The home page of an Internet site, sometimes set up as a menu, is the first page of a site linked to other sites by hypertext, which lets you jump from place to place in a document or in another related document in a totally different site. Each site has an address, which is referred to as a URL, or Uniform Resource Locator. Using a URL is a fast way to get to a site. Setting a bookmark makes getting to a useful site at a later time even faster. If you do not know a specific URL, you can use any of various search engines to conduct a search.

Because the Internet is a constantly changing network of networks, no subject list is ever complete. Addresses change, new sites are added, and old sites disappear without warning every day. The following list is an attempt to provide you with sites and corresponding URLs that are most likely reliable and that you can depend on for accuracy, currency, and relative permanence.

URLs for Labor Relations Sites

Following are addresses for major pages providing links to numerous other sites related to labor relations.

Cornell University's Industrial and Labor Relations Virtual Library

http://www.ilr.cornell.edu/vlib/

Subject index includes links to sites on compensation, government and labor, union benefit plans, news on current collective bargaining negotiation, labor statistics, labor union activities and membership, human resource management, international relations, labor-management relations, legislation, litigation, occupations, safety, and other labor-related topics.

LaborNet

http://www.labornet.org/labornet/

Sponsored and developed by the Institute for Global Communications, includes links to unions and labor organizations, a labor events calendar, publications, news services, print materials, and labor conferences (requires credit card to access). LaborNet is "a community of labor unions, activists, and organizations using computer networks for information-sharing and collaboration with the intent of increasing the human rights and economic justice of workers." LaborNet's list of unions and organizations includes more than 250 participants from around the world and provides links to those who are developing home pages.

United States Government Sites

Bureau of Labor Statistics

http://www.bls.gov

A wealth of economic surveys and data related to employment trends. The Most Requested Series includes Labor Force Statistics from the Current Population Survey.

Census Bureau

http://www.census.gov

Includes numerous tables from the many statistical areas that the Bureau is responsible for collecting. The Employment link from the home page goes to statistics on agriculture, manufacturing, construction, international trade, retail, wholesale, services, and governments.

Department of Labor Gopher

gopher://marvel.loc.gov:70/11/federal/fedinfo/byagency/executive/labor

Davis-Bacon Act through FedWorld, Bureau of Labor Statistics databases, Consumer Price Index, employment statistics, *Occupational Outlook Handbook*, Producer Price Index, OSHA gopher, and U.S. Department of Labor Federal Glass Ceiling Commission Report.

House of Representatives Internet Law Library

http://law.house.gov/100.htm

Sites related to employment, labor, and pension law worldwide with links to education law, taxation, U.S. federal laws, U.S. state and territorial laws, laws of other nations, treaties, law school library catalogs, attorney and legal profession directories, and review of law books.

National Labor Relations Board

http://www.doc.gov/nlrb

Includes an Information Locator that provides links to weekly summaries of NLRB cases, decisions and orders of the NLRB, the annual report of the Board, the NLRB Election Report, speeches and press releases, and the NLRB Privacy Act Notices of Systems of Records, a directory of NLRB offices, as well as links to other sites related to employment, labor and pension law, state statutes, and international law.

Occupational Safety and Health Administration

http://www.osha.gov

Menu includes links to an OSHA office directory, media releases, publications, programs and services, compliance assistance, OSHA software, statistics and data, standards, technical information, and other U.S. government sites.

White House

http://www.whitehouse.gov

Briefing Room provides "hot topics, today's releases, and latest Federal statistics." The Virtual Library contains documents, speeches, and photos.

Unions and Related Organizations

AFL-CIO's LaborWeb

http://www.aflcio.org

Policy statements, press releases, issue papers, strike news, boycott list, links to other sites, Union Summer Program for workers and students who want to become involved in union organization campaigns and political initiatives.

AFSCME

http://www.afscme.org

Workplace issues, bargaining table, politics, policy and legislation, AFSCME news, and articles from *Collective Bargaining Reporter.*

British Columbia Teachers' Federation

http://www.bctf.bc.ca/bctf/

Union of professionals representing 40,000 public school teachers in the province of British Columbia, Canada. The site "provides information about hot topics in education, professional development events and services, as well as the full text of BCTF publications."

Communications Workers of America

http://www.cwa-union.org

Includes pages on organizing the workplace; news items, for example, "The Bell Atlantic Crisis" and "The USAir Situation"; and "hot links" to government information, corporation and economic research, and union and labor information.

International Brotherhood of Teamsters

http://www.teamsters.org

Articles from *Teamster Magazine,* news on political action, contract campaigns, job rights, and other Teamster activities.

United Auto Workers

http://www.uaw.org

Menu items include UAW releases and worker news, UAW magazines online (*UAW Solidarity* and *AMMO*), Frequently Asked Questions (FAQs) on the union, fun and useful information for workers, consumer products by UAW members, UAW regions and local unions, and a guide to interesting Web Sites.

Other Sites of Interest

Bureau of National Affairs

http://www.bna.com/hub/bna/labrel/

Provides information on products available for sale through BNA, including *Daily Labor Report, Labor Relations Reporter, Labor Relations Week, Union Labor Report, Collective Bargaining Negotiations and Contracts, Construction Labor Report,* and *Government Employee Relations Report.*

CNN Interactive

http://www.cnn.com

Very current news items by topic. Keyword searchable.

Employment Relations Web Picks

http://www.webcom.com/garnet/labor

Service of NYPER Publications and written and maintained by Garnet Net Events, Inc. Rated by Lycos as one of the "top 20 business information pages in the world" in quality of content. Includes links to employment law, affirmative action, labor relations, personnel management, collective bargaining, Americans with Disabilities Act, and other topics.

Industrial and Labor Relations Review

http://www.ilr.cornell.edu/depts/ilrrev/

Tables of contents and article abstracts beginning with 1994.

Martin P. Catherwood Library

http://www.cornell.edu:3002/library/irllib.html

The industrial and Labor Relations Library at Cornell University "maintains an extensive collection of industrial and labor relations materials used by many visiting scholars as well as faculty members and students."

Wire Service Guild

http://www.users.interport.net/~wsg/222.html

Local 222, The Newspaper Guild/Communications Workers of America, AFL-CIO. Represents workers at the Associated Press and the United Press International. Provides CWA and AFL-CIO sites, Detroit newspaper strike links, LaborNet, BLS.

An Eclectic List of Events in U.S. Labor History

http://www.nitehawk.com/alleycat/labor.html

Compiled by Allen Lutins, who provides a good annotated list of major events in labor from April 17, 1825 through 1989.

Search Engines

If you don't know a URL for a site, you can perform a keyword search, usually with Boolean operators, by using the name of a developer or by subject, through various search engines. As with everything connected with the Internet, these search tools are changed daily, and new ones are added. Following is a sampling of often-used search tools.

Alta Vista

http://altavista.digital.com

Digital Equipment Corporation claims to provide access to the largest Web index. Use quotation marks to search for words in a phrase. A capital letter requests the engine to search for a capital letter, while a lowercase search will return either capital or lowercase. Example: *Detroit newspaper strike* retrieves 168 pages of related documents.

Deja News

http://www.dejanews.com

Searches Usenet newsgroups. Most search engines search for newsgroups, but since Deja News searches *only* for newsgroups, the coverage may be more comprehensive than that provided by other search engines. A Power Search submitted on *United Auto Workers* retrieves, among others, a list of discussion sessions from the newsgroup alt.society.labor-Unions.

InfoSeek

http://guide.infoseek.com

Allows phrase searching through World Wide Web, Categories of Sites, Usenet groups, and Reuters News. Sorts by score. Use capital letters for proper names. A search specifying Reuters News Service using *baseball strike* returns 1,160 pages sorted "by relevance," plus links to related topics.

Lycos

http://www.lycos.com

Searches for any word, not all words, in a search. This engine can turn up a lot of pages to wade through. Provides two additional search forms for more specific searching. The Lycos Catalog contains thousands of occurrences of the word *labor,* while a Point Reviews search returns only 91.

Open Text Index

http://www.opentext.com

Searches every word of every Web page the company has indexed and claims to be one of the largest indexes available. Provides a form that allows searching anywhere in the document or in the summary, title, heading, or URL. A search for the phrase *collective bargaining* in titles results in seven pages of documents.

Yahoo!

http://www.yahoo.com

Stands for "Yet Another Hierarchical Officious Oracle." A good catalog of links to other sites for any subject. Because Yahoo! was one of the first guides to the Internet and one of the first to begin "cataloging" pages, the search engine has had time to become well developed. A search under *labor* returns a menu with links to sites related to education, employment, employment law, institutes, labor interest groups, occupational safety and health, state governments, and Usenet newsgroups.

How to Cite Internet Sites

If you plan to use information that you have culled from the Internet in a research paper or homework assignment, you need to know how to cite the information correctly. Although formats are still being developed for the various types of electronic documents, new editions of most of the accepted style manuals have a section on citing electronic resources, including the Internet.

The University of Michigan's Internet Public Library has a list with links to recommended electronic information citation guides. The address is: http://www.ipl.org/classroom/userdocs/internet/citing.html. Another site that is highly useful offers citation formats based on the forthcoming book by Li & Crane, *Electronic Styles: An Expanded Guide to Citing Information,* according to the American Psychological Association and the Modern Language Association styles. The address is http://www.uvm.edu/~xli/reference/estyles.html.

Glossary

ability. A measure usually accompanying seniority; includes some combination of skill, knowledge, attitude, behavior, performance, production, and talent.

absorption. The merger of two unions in which the larger union takes over the smaller union.

ad hoc arbitrator. An individual hired by union and management officials to resolve a labor dispute on a case-by-case basis.

administrative law judge. Person employed by the National Labor Relations Board to conduct hearings involving unfair labor practices and render decisions to the NLRB in Washington, D.C.

AFL-CIO. American Federation of Labor and Congress of Industrial Organizations, formed by a merger in 1955.

Age Discrimination in Employment Act. Federal act that prohibits employment discrimination against those over 40, permits compulsory retirement for certain executives, and authorizes jury trials in covered cases.

agency shop. Place of employment having a provision that requires employees to pay the union a sum equal to membership dues to defray bargaining and grievance expenses although it does not require employees to join the union.

alienation theory. A theory that employees might form a union as a relief for their mental sense of estrangement from work, in which they cannot derive meaning from the work tasks or products.

ally doctrine. A doctrine used by the National Labor Relations Board to determine how closely allied an apparent secondary employer is to a primary labor dispute.

amalgamation. The merger of two or more unions into one.

American Federation of Labor (AFL). A labor organization formed in 1886 by Samuel Gompers and others to improve the short-range, material, and decentralized goals of union members; a forerunner of the AFL-CIO.

American Plan. A movement by employees in the 1920s and 1930s that stressed the principles of "rugged individualism" and the right of employees not to join unions.

apprenticeship programs. Formal, supervised programs of training and experience gaining, often supplemented by off-the-job instruction.

appropriate affirmative action. An NLRB order to an employer or union requring certain actions and/or the granting of relief to a person whose Section 7 rights have been violated.

appropriate bargaining unit. The minimal collective bargaining unit recognized by the National Labor Relations Board; a grouping of jobs in which employees share common employment interests and conditions such that the NLRB designates employees in those jobs as qualified to vote in union representation elections.

arbitration. The terminal step in most grievance procedures, in which the arbitrator resolves a labor dispute by making a binding decision.

arbitration hearing. A meeting with the grievance participants and the arbitrator wherein evidence, exhibits, and testimony are presented that will provide the basis for the arbitrator's decision.

arbitrator. A third-party neutral employed by union and management officials to make a binding decision on an employee's grievance.

associate membership program. An AFL-CIO program offered to nonunion employees with certain benefits to encourage the employees' connection with the AFL-CIO and its affiliated international unions.

attitudinal structuring. A process that involves activities aimed at attaining a desired relationship between the parties that will, in turn, affect the negotiation process and subsequent administration of the labor agreement.

attrition. A reduction in employment involving no layoffs; the reduction is usually accomplished by not replacing those who retire or leave voluntarily.

automation. Technological change in which machines perform tasks formerly performed by humans and in which human operators are replaced by automatic controls.

bargaining power. A desirable bargaining position that is increased when a union or management negotiator increases the other party's disagreement costs or reduces the other party's agreement costs.

bargaining ranges. A multitude of negotiation issue priorities for union and management officials that is bounded by upper and lower bargaining limits.

beyond a reasonable doubt. Level of proof in arbitrating employee discipline cases, required by some arbitrators when dealing with "criminal" (e.g., theft) disciplinary cases. Requiring proof beyond a reasonable doubt is usually considered work against the employee's favor.

blacklist. A list of union activists maintained by employers and exchanged with other employers; declared to be an unfair labor practice in 1935.

bona-fide occupation qualification. A legitimate qualification necessary in order to perform a job task.

Boulwarism. A collective bargaining approach once used at General Electric and found violative of good faith bargaining because it focused on the employees instead of on the union.

boycott. The refusal to purchase or to handle products from companies involved in a labor dispute.

bumping. The practice of replacing a less senior or less-skilled employee with a more senior or more highly skilled employee. The "bumped" employee is either laid off or "bumps" another employee.

business agent. A full-time union administrator, usually of a craft union, who is responsible for the union hiring hall, serves as the "watchdog" over the local labor agreement, and leads the local negotiations.

captive audience. Employees who have been required to attend a meeting to hear a presentation by their employer during a pre-election campaign.

case law (common law). Court decisions that are made in the absence of statutory laws and that stand until either overturned by a higher court or changed by legislation.

cease and desist order. An order to stop certain activities by the National Labor Relations Board directed toward violators of the National Labor Relations Act.

centralized bargaining. Collective bargaining covering more than one appropriate bargaining unit, such as single employer-multi-plant bargaining or multi-employer bargaining.

chilling effect. The result of a belief that one or both parties may get a better settlement in arbitration than in negotiation, leading to a lack of effort at reaching an agreement during negotiation.

clinical approach. A desirable but not always attainable grievance resolution method to try and uncover all causes of an employee's grievance and have those causes influence the remedy.

closed shop. A labor agreement provision requiring that an employee be a union member before obtaining a job. Closed shops are currently illegal.

codetermination. A concept put to use in several European countries in which unions and employers codetermine designated policies and procedures.

codified relationships. Relationships that occur in contract administration when first-line supervisors and union stewards behave according to some established norm or code, such as the labor agreement.

COLA. See cost-of-living adjustments.

collective bargaining. An activity whereby union and management officials attempt to resolve conflicting interests in a manner that wil sustain and possibly enrich their continuing relationships.

collective bargaining structure. Employee/employer groupings that can affect the collective bargaining outcome and/or be subject to the provisions of the negotiated labor agreement.

common law. See case law.

common law of the shop. A major influence on the arbitrator's decision that refers to the labor agreement language, intent, and past practices of the union and management officials at a particular industrial facility.

common situs picketing. Picketing by several unions of an entire work site even though the labor dispute might have involved only one union and one employer working at that site.

company union. Illegal union that receives financial help from the company.

Comprehensive Organizing Strategies and Tactics (COST). Office opened by the AFL-CIO to train union leaders in conducting corporate campaigns and battling employers' resistance to union organization.

concession bargaining. Occurs when management obtains from unions reduced wage levels and/or modification or elimination of work rules (combining job classifications, for example) to increase managerial discretion.

conference boards. Organizations within national unions that discuss issues pertaining to the union and a particular company.

constitution. Governing document of a national union; authorizes major national union functions and protects individual rights and the rights of local unions in relation to the national union.

consumer picketing. See product (consumer) picketing.

contingency union shop. Place of employment in a right-to-work state where a labor agreement provision indicates that the union shop provision will apply if and when the state's right-to-work laws are repealed.

contract arbitration. See traditional interest (contract) abritration.

contract bar doctrine. NLRB rule specifying that a valid, signed agreement for a fixed period of three years will bar any representation election for the life of the agreement.

convention. Supreme governing body of a national union, held annually or biennially.

cost-of-living adjustments (COLA). Improvement of wages during the life of the contract to compansate for the effect of inflation on real wages.

craft union. A union composed of members whohave been organized in accordance with their craft or skill, such as bricklayers and electricians.

de facto bargaining. Bargaining that occurs in the public sector but that is not authorized by legislation.

decertification. A National Labor Relations Board procedure available for employees when they believe, usually as the result of an election, that the union no longer represents the interests of the majority of the bargaining unit.

deferred wage increase. Wage increase put off to a later date or to the occurrence of some specific event, such as the company's becoming profitable.

distributive bargaining. Bargaining that occurs over some issues (wages, for example) in which one party's goals conflict with those of the other party, so that each party tries to keep the "upper hand."

due process. The procedural aspect of disciplinary cases, such as following time limits prescribed in the labor agreement, providing union representation, and notifying an employee of a specific offense in writing.

dues checkoff. Not a union security provision in the strictest sense, but a feature that allows union members to have their dues automatically deducted from their payroll checks (as for any other payroll deduction) and transferred to the union.

economy. The system of production, distribution, and consumption of goods and services.

Employee Representation Plans. Company-established unions in the 1920s and 1930s that were instituted as an alternative to the more autonomous, independent labor organizations.

employee stock ownership plan (ESOP). A plan giving employees an opportunity to become shareholders in a company by providing discount prices on shares or by matching employees' payment for stock.

employee voice. The opportunity for an individual employee to offer input into management's decision making and to discuss or appeal adverse employment actions.

employer promulgated arbitration. Unilateral arbitration procedure taken by nonunion employers to handle issues pertaining to its employees.

employment at will. A legal doctrine meaning that an employee can quit his or her job for any reason at any time and the employer can discharge the employee for any reason at any time.

end-run bargaining. An attempt on the part of a union to bypass an employer's negotiators and bargain directly with the decision makers.

enterprise union. A union within one company or enterprise.

Ethical Practices Committee. AFL-CIO committee established to control corrupt practices and racketeering in its member unions.

exclusive recognition. A designation of labor unions by the federal government indicating that a union has been selected by employee secret ballot to be the exclusive representative of a group of employees.

exclusivity doctrine. Legal doctrine meaning that one and only one union exclusively represents a group of employees and that the employer may bargain with only this union (certified by the National Labor Relations Board as the exclusive bargaining representative).

Executive Order. An order given by the chief of the executive branch of a government, e.g., the President of the United States, the governor of a state, or the mayor of a city.

fact-finding. The type of third-party involvement in which a neutral party gathers facts, organizes them, and presents related recommendations either privately or publicly.

fair representation. A union's legal obligation to evenhandedly represent all bargaining-unit employees, both union members and nonmembers alike.

featherbedding. Receiving payment for work that is not needed; employees' working at reduced speed; or employees' duplicating the work of others.

Federal Labor Relations Authority (FLRA). An independent, neutral federal agency that administers the federal labor relations program.

Federal Service Impasse Panel (FSIP). Committee within the Federal Labor Relations Authority that investigates any negotiation impasse presented to it and takes any action it considers necessary to settle the dispute.

final-offer selection (FOS) arbitration. The type of interest arbitration that gives the arbitrator the authority to select one of the proposals presented by the parties with no compromised settlement allowed between proposals.

financial market. The arena in which employers and unions seek to borrow funds to develop their investment strategies.

good faith bargaining. Negotiators' obligation under the National Labor Relations Act to demonstrate a sincere and honest intent to consummate labor agreements and to exhibit reasonableness in their bargaining positions, tactics, and activities.

grievance. Any employee's concern over a perceived violation of the labor agreement that is submitted to the grievance procedure for eventual resolution.

grievance mediation. A grievance resolution alternative in which a third-party neutral attempts to informally resolve the grievance between the parties before arbitration.

Haymarket Riot. A protest over the eight-hour work day on May 4, 1886, that resulted in the deaths of several participants and turned public opinion against labor as well as the Knights of Labor.

Homestead Incident. A sharp wage cut coupled with replacement employees at the Carnegie Steel Works in 1894 that resulted in prolonged union violence and elicited somewhat favorable public opinion for organized labor.

hot-cargo agreement. An agreement that union members will not be required to handle goods made by nonunion labor and/or employees at a struck plant.

illegal bargaining issues. Topics, such as hiring no minority members or females in certain job classifications, that are not bargainable and that are illegal if inserted into the labor agreement.

industrial union. A union composed of members who have been organized on an industry basis, such as steelworkers and autoworkers.

Industrial Workers of the World. A loosely knit organization formed in 1905 by Big Bill Baywood and others to "emancipate the working class from the slave bondage of capitalism."

informational picketing. Attempt by a union to inform the public that a labor dispute exists.

injunction. A court order that restricts or requires certain activities.

integrative bargaining. An approach characterized by trust and openness when both parties attempt to resolve a common problem or concern to their mutual benefit.

intent of the parties. The motive that union and management officials had in mind when they negotiated the labor agreement or engaged in an action that resulted in a particular grievance.

interest arbitration. See traditional interest (contract) arbitration.

international forces. Pressures, such as higher quality or lower cost, from other countries on U.S. employers; such forces can adversely affect unions in the United States.

intra-organizational bargaining. Activities employed by management and union negotiators to achieve consensus within their respective organizations or bargaining teams.

job evaluation. Process of determining the relative importance of each job to the organization to help in understanding occupational wage differentials.

job-security work rules. Provisions that attempt to make jobs more secure, such as spreading the workload by placing limits on the load that can be carried, restricting the duties of employees, limiting the number of machines one operator can tend, prohibiting modern tools or equipment, and requiring standby crews.

joint councils. Groupings of local unions that have common goals, employers, and interests.

journeyman. The classification of a highly skilled employee who has normally completed certain training and experiential requirements.

just cause. A reason for discipline by management in which the discipline was logically derived from the nature of the employer-employee relationship, contract provisions, proper rules of conduct, and/or established and accepted practices; in arbitration, management has the burden of proof that the discipline was for "just cause."

Knights of Labor (KOL). The first large labor organization in the United States, formed in 1869 and dedicated to long-range social-reform goals.

labor market. An external influence on the labor relations process that pertains to wage levels, skills, characteristics, and availability of employees in the local community.

labor relations process. Process in which management and the union jointly decide upon and administer terms and conditions of employment.

laboratory conditions. A National Labor Relations Board goal of conducting union election campaigns in conditions as nearly ideal as possible, determining the uninhibited desires of the employees.

Landrum-Griffin Act (Labor-Management Reporting and Disclosure Act). Law passed in 1959 to amend the National Labor Relations Act; this act was intended to promote union democracy and financial integrity and contains several provisions governing union operations and government.

language analysis. A process occurring when union and management negotiators interpret the others' remarks along three dimensions: how specific the statement is, how final the statement is, and the consequences associated with the statement.

leapfrog. Action by a union to use a settlement with one company as a base from which to obtain a better settlement with another company.

lifetime employment. Arrangement in which an employee is guaranteed employment for as long as he or she wants or until he or she retires.

lockout. An act by an employer when it shuts down its operation during or before a labor dispute.

lump-sum pay adjustment. A one-time payment made to adjust wages; the amount is not included in the base pay.

maintenance of membership. Contract requirement that any employee who decides to join a union must remain a union member for a certain period of time.

mandatory bargaining issues. Topics related to wages, hours, and other conditions of employment that must be bargained; however, failure to reach agreement does not automatically constitute a bargaining violation.

master labor agreement. A collective bargaining agreement negotiated at the national level that covers all plants within the bargaining unit. For example, General Motors negotiates a master labor agreement with the UAW. Then, negotiations occur at each plant about local plant issues.

mediation. Process whereby a third-party neutral attempts to help union and management officials resolve a grievance.

mediation-arbitration (med-arb). The type of third-party settlement in which the neutral serves first as the mediator and, if unsuccessful, serves as an arbitrator.

mediator. A third-party neutral, often a federal government employee, who has no binding authority but nonetheless assists union and management officals in reaching a collective bargaining settlement.

Military Selection Act of 1967. Congressional act that requires employers to restore veterans whose military service time does not exceed four years to their former positions or to positions similar in seniority, status, and pay.

mitigating circumstances. Considerations (such as an employee's good work record and/or management's contribution to a problem, for example) that influence an arbitrator to reduce or eliminate mnagement's initial disciplinary action against an employee.

multinational corporation (MNC). A corporation that does business or that has operations in more than one country.

narcotic effect. A dependence on or "addiction" to arbitration, resulting from experience with the consequences of arbitration in bargaining impasses.

national consultation rights. A designation granted by the federal government indicating that a union is the representative of at least 10 percent of the employees and that allows the union to be notified of proposed substantive changes in the conditions of employment.

national emergency dispute. Any strike or lockout that creates a national emergency and that results from a negotiation impasse.

National War Labor Board. A panel of union, management, and public representatives established during World War II that arbitrated some 20,000 disputes and publicized arbitration's potential benefits.

negotiating unit. The employees who will be bound by the negotiated labor agreement that can (1) be identical to the appropriate bargaining unit, (2) include more than one appropriate bargaining unit, or (3) represent a combination of the preceding arrangements depending upon the particular bargaining issue.

nonmandatory issues. See voluntary issues.

oral warning. A rather mild form of discipline representing an informal effort to correct and improve an employee's work performance.

outsourcing. A cost-cutting strategy of shifting work away from a plant to lower-cost producers and purchasing parts needed in production from these producers, often eliminating union jobs.

parole evidence rule. Rule holding that evidence, oral or otherwise, cannot be admitted for the purpose of varying or contradicting written language recorded in the labor agreement.

past practice. A specific and identical action that has been continually employed over a number of years to the recognition and satisfaction of both parties.

pattern bargaining. A collective bargaining settlement at one company or one segment of an industry that strongly influences the bargaining objectives and/or results at another company or segment of an industry.

permanent arbitrator. An individual employed by union and management officials to resolve disputes during the life of the labor agreement.

permissive issues. See voluntary issues.

person with disabilities. (1) A person with a physical or mental empairment that sutstantially limits that person in some major life activity, (2) a person with a record of such impairment, or (3) a person who is regarded as having such an impairment, as broadly defined by the Americans with Disabilities Act.

picketing. Outside patrolling by union members of any employer's premises for the purpose of achieving a specific objective.

power relationships. Relationships that occur in contract administration situations in which the first-line supervisors and union stewards pursue differing interests or goals.

preferential treatment clause. A negotiated labor agreement provision indicating that union members will be given employment preference over nonmembers when a new facility is opened.

premium pay. Pay that is an addition to the base wage rate.

prepaid legal plan. An employee benefit that allows union-member employees to obtain legal counsel from an attorney for a specified period of time.

preponderance of evidence. Level of proof in arbitrating employee discipline cases in which testimony and evidence must be adequate to overcome opposing presumptions and evidence.

prevailing wage. The wage rate most often used within a particular area or labor market.

price list. A list citing specific rules and uniform penalties for single or repeated infractions, covering a number of possible disciplinary offenses.

product (consumer) picketing. Attempt by a union to persuade customers to refuse to purchase products from the employer with which the union has a labor dispute.

product market. An external influence on the labor relations process that indicates where the company either sells its product or purchases key elements for the product's manufacture.

profit-sharing plans. Motivational plans designed to improve performance by allowing employees to share (usually a percentage) in the employer's profits.

progressive discipline. Increasingly severe penalties corresponding to repeated, similar offenses (violations) committed by an employee.

promotions. Position changes within an organization that advance employees to positions of more responsibility, usually accompanied by wage increases.

public opinion. Opinions of influential individuals and organizations within a community and attitudes/traditions held by community residents.

Pullman Strike. A nationwide, unsuccessful strike of the American Railway Union (led by Eugene Debs) against unilateral wage cuts and layoffs at the Pullman Company in 1894.

quasi-union shop. Place of employment that has a union shop provision in the labor agreement even though the shop is in a right-to-work state. The union shop provision, however, is obscurely nullified later in the agreement.

reasonable accommodation. A term used in the Americans with Disabilities Act to require employers to make accommodation for disabled individuals unless doing so would cause an undue hardship. For example, an employer may redesign a job so that a disabled person could qualify for the job.

recognitional picketing. Attempt by a union to gain recognition from employees of the union as their bargaining representative.

red-circled wage rate. A wage rate paid to an employee that is greater than that assigned by the job evaluation plan.

referendum. A direct vote by union members to approve or reject the terms of a newly negotiated labor agreement.

reserve gate picketing. Picketing at a gate designated by the employer as an entry for employees not involved in the labor dispute.

reserved rights doctrine. Doctrine statibg that management's authority is supreme in all matters except those it has expressly conceded in the collective bargaining agreement and/or those restricted by law.

right-to-work laws. Laws found in 21 states that have implemented point 14(b) of the National Labor Relations Act, which prohibits union membership (and related union security clauses) as a condition of employment.

scarcity consciousness. Employees' belief that they are living in a world of limited opportunity and that unions can help them in achieving more job security.

secondary employers. Employers who are not directly involved in a labor dispute with a union or unions.

seniority. Length of an employee's continuous service.

severance pay. Payment made to an employee who severs the relationship with his or her employer by either layoff or retirement (but not by discharge).

shop steward. The elected representative of the employees in a particular unit who represents its members at local union meetings, handles grievances at the first level, and collects dues.

Social Security Act of 1935. Congressional act that, as amended, established two national systems of social security to protect against loss of income due to unemployment, old age, disability, or death.

sovereignty doctrine. Doctrine stating that the legislative body cannot delegate its authority to make decisions.

"split the difference". A hoped-for result in public-sector interest arbitration, achieved by maintaining excessive demands so that the arbitrator will give in to some of them and return a favorable settlement to one of the parties.

state of the economy. An external influence on the labor relations process; broadly defined as an absolute or relative movement among such quantitative indicators as inflation, unemployment, and productivity; more narrowly defined, the same movements, but pertaining to a specific industry or organization within that industry.

statutory law. Law passed by legislative bodies such as Congress or a city council.

Steelworkers' Trilogy. Three Supreme Court decisions in 1960 that gave considerable prestige and discretion to arbitrators in resolving employee grievances.

strike. A temporary stoppage of work by a group of employees for the purposes of expressing a grievance or enforcing a demand.

strike benefits. Payments made to union members on strike, taken from funds sets aside for that purpose by the national union.

strikebreakers. Employees who continue to work during a strike and who are willing to cross the union picket line; also refers to others who are hired for the specific reason of working during a strike.

strike insurance. Payments made to union officials by management to prevent the union's going on strike.

struck work. Work done during a strike that normally would be performed by the employees who are on strike.

subcontracting. An employer arrangement for another firm to perform those tasks the employer cannot perform or those tasks necessary for successful operation of the business. Employers may also subcontract tasks that can be performed elsewhere at lower cost or higher quality.

successor employer. An employer who takes over a facility that has an already-established labor organization; the successor might be obligated to honor any previously negotiated labor agreement.

sunshine laws. Laws that make public many meetings by government officials, such as those held to negotiate with union officials.

superseniority. A privilege granted in a labor agreement that entitles a union officer or highly skilled employee to be the last person laid off should a layoff occur.

supplemental unemployment benefit plan (SUB). Benefits made to supplement payments that are already received, such as unemployment benefits.

suspension. Disciplinary layoff without pay given by management to impress upon the employee the seriousness of the offense.

sweetheart contract. A contract in which the union official settles for less than he or she could have obtained had he or she not "sold out" to management.

sympathetic relationships. Relationships that occur in contract administration between individuals when each is aware of the other's situation and is guided by an understanding and appreciation of that situation.

technological change. Change(s) in a production process that result(s) from the introduction of labor-saving machinery and/or changes in material handling and work flow.

technology. A most significant influence on work rules; it affects the pace and scheduling of work, characteristics of the work environment, tasks to be performed, and information exchange.

tenure. Form of job security that protects faculty rights of expression; means that faculty generally cannot be terminated except for cause.

third-and-one-half step. An informal grievance step in which union and management representatives meet to discuss and trade grievances.

total quality management (TQM). A continuous process to improve products and meet customer needs by focusing on the customer, measures, prevention of errors, inclusion and commitment of top management, quality, and employee involvement.

totality of conduct doctrine. A doctrine guiding National Labor Relations Board interpretations of unfair labor practices in union campaigns; holds that isolated incidents must be considered within the whole of the general circumstances or campaign.

traditional interest (contract) arbitration. A type of arbitration in which the arbitrator makes a final and binding decision on issues that will be included in the labor agreement.

transfer. A personnel change in which an employee switches from one position to another with relatively equal authority, responsibility, and compensation, determined by seniority and ability.

two-tiered pay plans. Pay plans in which employees currently employed will earn more per hour than new employees. All new employees will start at the lower wage rate, and their wages will be increased incrementally over time until they earn the same as those employees who were already employed when the plan went into effect.

union hiring hall. A place that serves as a clearinghouse for the placement of union members, usually in the construction trades.

union instrumentality. Employees' perception of whether the union wil function to attain desired outcomes such as higher wages, improved working conditions, job security, and protection from arbitrary treatment by management.

union shop. A place of employment having a contract requirement that once hired, an employee has a certain amount of time to become a union member in order to keep his or her job.

vesting. An agreement that an employee's pension is guaranteed, regardless of whether that employee remains with his or her present employer.

Vietnam Era Veteran Readjustment Act. Congressional act that requires employers that have government contracts of $10,000 or more to take affirmative action to employ and advance disabled veterans and other qualified veterans of the Vietnam War.

Vocational Rehabilitation Act of 1973. Congressional act that requires employers that have government contracts of $2,500 or more to take affirmative action to employ and advance qualified physically and/or mentally disabled individuals.

voluntary issues (permissive issues, nonmandatory issues). Topics, wuch as benefits for retired employees, that can be bargained only if both parties so desire.

wage-incentive plans. Employer plans designed to increase employee productivity, attract prospective employees to the company, and reward employees monetarily for increased productivity.

wage indexation. Wage adjustments that occur in accordance with the Consumer Price Index.

wage package. The total amount of compensation for an employee, including wages, premium pay, incentives, and so forth.

wage reopener. Clause written in a labor agreement to allow the parties to negotiate wages during the life of an agreement.

wage system. The method generally used in a given country of paying employees, such as the frequency of pay (e.g., weekly, monthly), wage differentials, and so on.

whipsawing. Actions on a union's part to put pressure on employers when it strikes one or more employers of a multi-employer bargaining group in hopes of getting a better settlement from those employers not struck.

wildcat strike. Work stoppage involving the primary employer-employee relationship that is neither sanctioned nor stimulated by the union, although union officials might be aware of it.

work preservation clause. Clause written into a labor agreement to preserve a certain number of hours of work or number of employees to be covered by the labor agreement.

work rules. The focal point of labor relations, work rules can relate to compensation or to employee rights, and they reflect the dynamic and sometimes vague aspects of the labor relations process.

work scheduling. Regulating shifts and fixing the workday or work week.

Worker Adjustment and Retraining Notification Act (WARN). Congressional act requiring employers of 100 or more employees to give 60-days' advance notice to employees, unions, and state and local governments of a plant closing or major layoff.

written warning. Document that summarizes previous oral attempts to correct an employee's behavior and that is entered in the employee's work record file.

wrongful discharge. An employee's claim that his or her discharge resulted from alleged violation of federal laws, implied contract, and/or public policy.

yellow-dog contract. An agreement between an employer and employee stating that the employee will not join a union or assist in organizing a union as a condition of employment.

Name Index

Subject Index

Credits

Exhibit 1.4 reprinted with permission from the New York State Nurses Association.

Exhibit 1.6 reprinted with permission from the American Federation of State and County Municipal Employees.

Photograph, page 42, courtesy of the Library of Congress.

Photograph, page 46, courtesy of the AFL–CIO.